Information Technology Law

FOURTH EDITION

Diane Rowland, Uta Kohl and
Andrew Charlesworth

Routledge
Taylor & Francis Group

LONDON AND NEW YORK

Fourth edition published 2012
by Routledge
2 Park Square, Milton Park, Abingdon, Oxon OX14 4RN

Simultaneously published in the USA and Canada
by Routledge
711 Third Avenue, New York, NY 10017

Routledge is an imprint of the Taylor & Francis Group, an informa business

First edition published by Cavendish Publishing 1997
Third edition published by Cavendish Publishing 2005

British Library Cataloguing in Publication Data
A catalogue record for this book is available from the British Library

Library of Congress Cataloging in Publication Data
Rowland, Diane.
Information technology law / Diane Rowland, Uta Kohl, Andrew
Charlesworth. — 4th ed.
  p. cm.
  Includes bibliographical references and index.
  ISBN 978-0-415-48227-1 (hardback) — ISBN 978-0-415-48237-0 (paperback)
  — ISBN 978-0-203-09369-6 (e-book) 1. Computers—Law and legislation—
  Great Britain. 2. Internet—Law and legislation—Great Britain. 3. Data
  protection—Law and legislation—Great Britain. 4. Electronic commerce—Law
  and legislation—Great Britain. 5. Copyright—Computer programs—Great
  Britain. 6. Computer software—Law and legislation—Great Britain.
  7. Information technology—Great Britain. I. Kohl, Uta. II. Charlesworth,
  Andrew, 1966- III. Title.
  KD667.C65R69 2011
  343.4109'99—dc22

ISBN: 978-0-415-48227-1 (hbk)
ISBN: 978-0-415-48237-0 (pbk)
ISBN: 978-0-203-09369-6 (ebk)

Typeset in Joanna
by RefineCatch Limited, Bungay, Suffolk

MIX
Paper from
responsible sources
FSC
www.fsc.org FSC® C004839

Printed and bound in Great Britain by the MPG Books Group

Contents

Preface

When the original version of this book was first written with my previous co-author, Elizabeth Macdonald, the emerging landscape of information technology (IT) law looked rather different from today. An impetus for that volume had been the difficulty that students encountered in accessing materials from different sources and different jurisdictions. The development of the technology itself has entirely removed that problem; it has become a trivial task to locate a wide range of primary and secondary materials from a range of jurisdictions. The advances in both the technology and its uses have been matched by new legal challenges and consequent responses. All of this indicated that a complete overhaul of both the contents and approach of the earlier editions was not only timely, but also essential. The widespread availability of relevant legal materials has obviated the need for long extracts of text, and has permitted more detailed analysis and commentary. A radical overhaul of the contents has resulted in the reorganisation and revision of the chapters, while still retaining some of the original discussion where relevant. Inevitably in a book covering such a potentially wide topic, it is impossible to be entirely comprehensive and still examine individual areas in sufficient depth and so a choice has to be made as to what to include. Entirely new to this edition are chapters on 'Regulatory Issues', 'National Regulation of Transnational Online Activity', and 'Surveillance, RIPA, and Encryption'. More than ever, the scholar of IT law cannot easily embrace all of the legal disciplines that are represented in this volume, and I am delighted that Uta Kohl and Andrew Charlesworth agreed to share in the production of this new version, each bringing their own valuable expertise. Together, we are extremely grateful for the assistance of Fiona Kinnear at Routledge, whose encouragement and support has been vital in ensuring that this project, which proved rather more daunting than first expected, was completed.

As before, the book is primarily aimed at undergraduate and postgraduate law students. Against that background, it will hopefully provide reassurance that a detailed knowledge of the technology is unnecessary to an understanding of the legal issues. Where some rudimentary understanding is helpful, minimum technical explanations have been included. The book may also prove both useful and of interest to computer scientists, who increasingly have to consider the wider implications for their discipline. Information technology has provided, and continues to provide, exciting challenges and opportunities for the law and lawyers. We hope that we have managed to communicate this to the reader.

Diane Rowland
February 2011

Table of Cases

Table of Statutes

Table of Statutory Instruments

Table of European Legislation

Decisions

Recommendations

Regulations

Treaties and Conventions

Table of Abbreviations

ACLU	American Civil Liberties Union
ACMA	Australian Communications and Media Authority
ACPA	Anticybersquatting-Consumer Protection Act 1999
ACPO	Association of Chief Police Officers
ADR	Alternative Dispute Resolution
AGPL	Affero General Public Licence
AI Lab	Artificial Intelligence Laboratory
ALI	American Law Institute
APIG	All Party Internet Group
ASCII	American Standard Code for Information Interchange
ASP	Application Service Provision
ATCSA	Anti-Terrorism, Crime and Security Act 2001
ATM	Automated Teller Machine
B2B	Business-to-Business
B2C	Business-to-Consumer
BCR	Binding Corporate Rules
BCS	British Computer Society
BERR	Business, Enterprise and Regulatory Reform
BSD	Berkeley Software Distribution
C2C	Consumer-to-Consumer
C & L	Computers and Law
CA	Communications Act 2003
CCRO	Community Charge Registration Officer
CDA	Communications Decency Act 1996 (US)
CDPA	Copyright, Designs and Patents Act 1988
CEO	Chief Executive Officer
CEOP	Child Exploitation and Online Protection Centre
CIPL	Centre for Information Policy Leadership
CL	Computer Law
CL & P	Computer Law and Practice
CLR	Commonwealth Law Reports
CMA	Computer Misuse Act 1990
Comm L	Communications Law
COPA	Child On-line Protection Act 1998 (US)
CPA	Consumer Protection Act 1987
CPS	Crown Prosecution Service
CPU	Central Processing Unit
CRM	Customer Relationship Management
CSA	Common Services Agency
CSP	Certification Services Provider
Cth	Commonwealth of Australia

DDoS	Distributed Denial-of-Service
DEA	Digital Economy Act 2010
DERs	Data Retention (EC Directive) Regulations 2009 (SI 2009/9870)
DMCA	Digital Millennium Copyright Act 1998/2000 (US)
DNS	Domain Name Server
DoS	Denial-of-Service
DPA	Data Protection Act 1984/1998
DPP	Director of Public Prosecutions
DRM	Digital Rights Management
DTI	Department of Trade and Industry
DVR	Digital Video Recorder
EBA	Enlarged Board of Appeal
ECA	Electronic Communications Act 2000
ECHR	European Convention on Human Rights
ECJ	European Court of Justice
ECR	European Court Reports
ECtHR	European Court of Human Rights
EEA	European Economic Area
EIPR	European Intellectual Property Review
EPC	European Patent Convention
EPIC	Electronic Privacy Information Center
EPO	European Patent Office
ERP	Enterprise Resource Planning
EU	European Union
EULA	End-User Licence Agreement
FDL	Free Document Licence
FHA	Fair Housing Act 1968 (US)
FIPR	Foundation for Information Policy Research
FOISA	Fraudulent Online Identity Sanctions Act 2004
F/OSS	Free and Open Source Software Licensing
FSA	Financial Services Authority
FSF	Free Software Foundation
FSFE	Free Software Foundation Europe
FSMA	Financial Services and Markets Act 2000
FSR	Fleet Street Reports
FTC	Federal Trade Commission
FTDA	Federal Trademark Dilution Act 1996
GATT	General Agreement on Tariffs and Trade
GDP	Gross Domestic Product
GMC	General Medical Council
GP	General Practitioner
GPL	General Public Licence
HADOPI	Haute Autorité pour la Diffusion des Oeuvres et la Protection des Droit sur Internet
HLL	High-Level Languages
HMRC	HM Revenue and Customs
HTML	Hypertext mark-up language
IANA	Internet Assigned Numbers Authority
ICANN	Internet Corporation for Assigned Names and Numbers
ICO	Information Commissioner's Office
IDN	Internationalised Domain Names

IDNA	Internationalizing Domain Names in Applications
IEE	Institution of Electrical Engineers
IMEI	International Mobile Equipment Identity
IMSI	International Mobile Subscriber Identity
Int JLIT	International Journal of Information Technology
IOC	Initial Obligations Code
IOC	International Olympic Committee
IOCA	Intercepton of Communications Act 1985
IP	Internet Protocol
ISP	Internet service provider
ISSP	Information society service provider
IT	Information Technology
ITU	International Telecommunication Union
IWF	Internet Watch Foundation
JANET	Joint Academic Network
JBL	Journal of Business Law
JIC	Joint Intelligence Committee
JMRI	Java Model Railroad Interface Project
LBPR	Telecommunications (Lawful Business Practice) (Interception of Communications) Regulations 2000
LGPL	Lesser General Public Licence
LICRA	League against Racism and Ant-Semitism
MDA	Media Development Authority (Singapore)
MDU	Medical Defence Union
MEP	Member of the European Parliament
MIT	Massachusetts Institute of Technology
MP	Member of Parliament
NHTCUS	National Hi-Tech Crime Unit Scotland
NTAC	National Technical Assistance Centre
NTIA	National Telecommunications and Information Administration
OECD	Organisation for Economic Co-operation and Development
OFT	Office of Fair Trading
OSCE	Organization for Security and Co-operation in Europe
OSD	Open Source Definition
OSI	Open Source Initiative
OTC	Over-the-counter
P2P	Peer-To-Peer
PABX	Private Automated Branch Exchange
PACE	Police and Criminal Evidence Act 1984
PCIJ	Permanent Court of International Justice
PCP	Parliamentary Control Panel
PECR	Privacy and Electronic Communications (EC Directive) Regulations 2003
PIA	Privacy impact assessment
PNC	Police National Computer
PROTECT	Prosecutorial Remedies and Tools against the Exploitation of Children Today Act 2003
RIAA	Recording Industry Association of America
RIPA	Regulation of Investigatory Powers Act 2000
RPC	Report of Patent Design and Trademark Cases
RTR	Road Traffic Reports

SaaS	Software as a Service
SCM	Supply Chain Management
SCPA	Semiconductor Chip Protection Act 1984 (US)
SFLC	Software Freedom Law Center
SGA	Sale of Goods Act 1893
SGSA	Supply of Goods and Services Act 1982
SLA	Service Level Agreement
SLD	Second-Level Domain Name
SME	Small-To-Medium-Sized Enterprise
SOCA	Serious Organised Crime Agency
SoGA	Sale of Goods Act 1979
SSGA	Sale and Supply of Goods Act 1994
SSO	Structure, Sequence and Organisation
TBA	Technical Board of Appeal
TDNA	Truth in Domain Names Act 2003
TDRA	Trademark Dilution Revision Act 2006
TFEU	Treaty on the Functioning of the European Union
TLD	Top level domain
TMA	Trademarks Act 1994
TPM	Technological Protection Mechanisms
TRIPS	Trade-Related Aspects of Intellectual Property Rights
TTP	Trusted Third Party
UCC	Uniform Commercial Code (US)
UCE	Unsolicited Commercial Emails
UCITA	Uniform Computer Information Transactions Act (US)
UCTA	Unfair Contract Terms Act 1977
UDRP	Uniform Domain Name Dispute Resolution Policy
UDRP	Uniform Dispute Resolution Policy
UEJF	French Jewish Students Union
UKIPO	UK Intellectual Property Office
UNCITRAL	United Nations Commission on International Trade Law
USC	United States Code
Web JCLI	Web Journal of Current Legal Issues
WHO	World Health Organization
WIPO	World Intellectual Property Organization
WLAN	Wireless Local Area Network
WTO	World Trade Organization

Chapter 1

Regulating Information Technologies

> Laws are generally not understood by three sorts of persons, *viz*, by those who make them, by those who execute them, and by those who suffer if they break them.
>
> (George Savile, Lord Halifax, 1633–95)

Information Technology Law?

Researching and teaching in the area of information technology (IT) law can occasionally lead to charges of dilettantism being levelled at an academic by his or her colleagues. Certainly, to work effectively in the field, one needs to be able to draw upon a range of knowledge and skills from across the legal sphere, whether the criminal law, contract and tort law, intellectual property law, constitutional and administrative law, European Union (EU) law, or public and private international law.

Yet it is that breadth of interaction with other academic legal domains that makes the subject such an involving and vibrant arena in which to participate. It has not been unusual for IT law to be the proving ground for developing jurisprudential thought on issues not yet sufficiently mainstream to merit a place within more established subject areas. Indeed, within university law courses, such issues often migrate between the IT curriculum and more familiar surroundings. For example, in the early to mid-1990s, the question of the admissibility of computer-generated evidence in criminal and civil cases exercised IT lawyers, as the courts struggled to come to terms with the application of the common law (for example, the hearsay rule) and legislation (for example, s 69 of the **Police and Criminal Evidence Act 1984**).[1] By 2000, the issue was largely of historical interest to IT lawyers, as the passage of the **Civil Evidence Act 1995** and repeal of s 69 **PACE** respectively clarified the civil and criminal law perspectives, and computer-generated evidence once again returned to the fold of traditional evidence law courses. A similar trajectory may perhaps be traced in time with issues such as internet jurisdiction and digital copyright.

Equally importantly, the changing nature of the subject means that academic writers constantly enter and leave the field, as their interests intersect with topics in the IT law limelight. For some, their interaction is transitory and fleeting (an article here, a book chapter there); for others, the relationship may develop into a rather longer-lasting one. This access to ideas from other jurisprudential areas, however, is key to the way in which the subject has developed, and is developing, over time. The nature of the subject also invites cross-disciplinary input, both from the information sciences and from the social sciences (notably political science), which provides broader context for consideration of the potential and actual legal responses to developing issues. Finally, the influence of writers from other jurisdictions has been crucial in the process of evaluating and re-evaluating national legal responses to IT developments. This additional cross-fertilisation has been enhanced significantly by the increased access to international materials brought by the internet, and the international legal databases such as Westlaw, HeinOnline, and LEXIS.[2] Each new technological development thus encourages a plethora of perspectives drawing on different jurisprudential, jurisdictional, and cross-disciplinary viewpoints.

This, however, leads to questions about the role of IT law as a legal discipline:[3] is it simply a holding area, or talking shop, for subject matter that does not yet fit comfortably within the

---

1 See, eg, Michael Hirst, 'Computers and the English law of evidence' (1992) 1(3) LC&AI 365; Graham JH Smith 'When is a computer not a computer?' (1994) 10(2) CLSR 84; Amanda Hoey. 'Analysis of the Police and Criminal Evidence Act s 69: Computer-generated evidence' (1996) 1 Web JCLI, available online at http://webjcli.ncl.ac.uk/1996/issue1/hoey1.html

2 This is often regarded by academics and students alike as being both a blessing and a curse: the blessing is that there is so much more material available upon which to draw for ideas and inspiration; the curse is that there is so much more through which to search in order to find relevant material.

3 See, eg, Brian Napier, 'The future of information technology law' (1992) 51(1) CLJ 46; Stephen Saxby, 'A jurisprudence for information technology law' (1994) 2(1) IntJLIT 1; Lawrence Lessig, 'The law of the horse: What cyberlaw might teach' (1999b) 113 Harv L Rev 501; Andres Guadamuz González, 'Attack of the killer acronyms: The future of information technology law' (2004) 18(3) IRLCT 411.

established legal corpus? Or is there a more purposive role that it can play? The answer to these questions depends largely on whether the subject is treated as:

● a set of discrete topics linked solely by virtue of their transient novelty and relationship to information technologies; or
● a set of topics that raises new political, social, and economic issues, and thus requires consideration of appropriate legal and regulatory approaches to tackling them, outside of traditional legal paradigms.

To pose those questions another way: is IT law simply a collection of legal areas that happen to touch upon IT? Or is it greater than the sum of its parts, with some unifying underlying themes allowing for unique insights into law and society? Arguably, during its early years, IT law was probably closer to the former model, being driven as it was primarily by practitioner interests. This pragmatic influence resulted in a discipline concerned with short-term perspectives on legal changes in given areas. The aim was essentially to understand what impact those changes might have on existing practices, rather than why the law was developing in a particular way, and whether there might be longer-term advantages in plotting a different legal/regulatory path to that being taken.

Over the last decade or two, as the discipline has matured, the approach in academia has increasingly shifted towards the latter model. The black-letter, piecemeal perspective remains a significant element, but legal inquiries now also feature broader, more theoretical analyses: for example, about new methods of combining legal and non-legal regulatory techniques to achieve more efficient and effective outcomes.[4] The subject of IT law has been embraced as a worthy independent field of legal inquiry, with courses and books that lend themselves to wider reflections upon the information age, and its threats and opportunities – for lawyers and regulators, as well as society at large. In fact, to the extent that some of the former IT law subject matters are being absorbed by the traditional legal disciplines, IT law – to have legitimacy in itself – has to carve out a new identity that can only come in the form of inquiries into the special features and effects of IT and its interaction with the established legal order.

The Information Age, IT Law, and their Paradoxes

The information age and the regulator's response to it are beyond bare infancy; yet we are still far removed from a time that would allow a detached account of technological and regulatory happenings. Both are peppered with tensions and fractions between multiple interest groups, with starkly contrasting narratives, with paradoxes and curiosities – some of these simply mirror, albeit more sharply, offline society; others are truly peculiar to the technological age; some are to be resolved; and others are likely to remain permanent fixtures. Where the future will lead us remains obscure, not the least because – taking a non-determinist view – it is in our hands: we are the makers of our future; it is our choices that will shape the information age of the future. So how far have we come to date? What are some of the emerging themes, trends, and paradoxes?

Information as a Source of Power

The information age raises as a key issue the use and abuse of information by economic and political actors as a means of control. On the one hand, there is the state seeking to use data, often

---

4 See, eg, Lawrence Lessig, *Code: And Other Laws of Cyberspace*, 1999a, New York: Basic Books; Andrew Murray, *The Regulation of Cyberspace: Control in the Online Environment*, 2007, Abingdon: Glasshouse.

See Chapter
6 →
generated by private communications, as a way in which to enhance law and order – recently under the guise of anti-terrorism measures. The initial helplessness of the state vis-à-vis activities on the internet has given way to the recognition of its unique potential for keeping a tab on the connections, whereabouts, and moves of everyone – on the premise that everyone harbours the risk of delinquencies. On the other hand, there are the large multinational companies scrambling for control over consumers through pinning down their preferences, shopping habits, lifestyle choices, and general web behaviour. The surveillance interests of these commercial actors sometimes overlap with those of consumers, but this is by no means always the case, as is illustrated, for example, by the debate surrounding 'cookies'. The threat and, to some extent, the reality of a surveillance society driven by both private and public actors has prompted a heightened interest by civil society in data protection and privacy. Thus a large chunk of IT law can be understood as the conflict of the legitimate boundaries of surveillance with the legitimate expectation to a private life away from the prying eyes of government or business. How these legal boundaries have been shifting in recent years provides a wider commentary about our society in general. The privacy paradigm is not only in juxtaposition to the surveillance state, but equally to the relatively recent phenomenon of data accessibility. As data protection shields private information from government, the data accessibility movement pushes for greater transparency of public data – thus the information age has led to a sharpening of the private–public divide in terms of data management.

Of interest in this area – from a sociological, as well as a legal, perspective – is also the seeming paradox between the calls for privacy and the widespread bare-all attitudes on social networking sites. How can the very users who happily reveal the most personal information to the world at large still claim certain privacy entitlements in respect of that information? Legally, the solution to this paradox may draw upon notions of property/ownership:[5] personal information is a type of property the use of which is within the individual's control: he or she possesses it, can use and dispose of it as he or she sees fit, can transfer it – with or without payment – and may attach conditions to such transfers. In short, the individual is the ultimate arbitrator of how, when, and why any of information about himself or herself is used. Whether such proprietary notions are appropriate and valid in this personal-information context leaves much room for speculation, as did previous borderline property controversies, such as those concerning the human body: can and should the human body or any of its parts, such as genetic material, be treated in law like commodities?[6] Likewise, can and should we be able to commodify personal information? Interestingly, in the case of genetic material, it is also 'personal' information over which the person claims ownership. These questions go to the heart of foundational concepts such as personhood and property, including intangible property. They also touch upon wider issues about the legal status that should be attached to 'information' in the information age. This latter issue has been at the centre of possibly one of the most visible legal controversies concerning the internet – namely, the role and continued viability

See Chapter
9 →
of copyright law. The pervasiveness of online piracy has forced regulators and commercial actors to re-evaluate accepted wisdoms and strategies regarding to how to protect intangible goods, and ultimately the feasibility and legitimacy of holding onto those goods.

Empowerment through Abundance of Information?

Further trends of the information age with repercussions for IT law arise out of the sheer abundance of information. To start with, the abundance challenges the traditional information establish-

---

5 Other than copyright, because the use of the information by commercial or state actors may not actually entail any copying of the information.

6 Rohan Hardcastle, *Law and the Human Body: Property Rights, Ownership and Control*, 2007, Oxford: Hart Publishing. Traditionally under common law, the human body is not property: *Haynes' case* (1614) 77 ER 1389; *R v Lynn* (1788) 2 TR 733; *R v Price* (1884) 12 QB 247; *Williams v Williams* (1882) 20 ChD 659.

ment and thereby creates challenges for the regulator. Information is no longer channelled through a few bottlenecks, such as the traditional print and broadcasting media companies, but can be produced and accessed by anyone from anywhere. The rise of the man-on-the-street publisher challenges traditional regulatory models, not least because of the internet's global nature. Furthermore, it is no longer only the acquisition of information that is problematic, but also its use after acquisition.

See Chapter ◄ 2

Paradoxically, an abundance of information does not necessarily equal empowerment. The traditional wisdom that 'information is power' is based on an assumption of scarcity of information. When information is no longer scarce, it is those who can most effectively filter, extract, prioritise, and discriminate who have a head start. In the same vein, Barry Schwartz, in *The Paradox of Choice: Why More is Less*,[7] argues that, from a psychological perspective, excessive choice or 'choice overload' does not lead to a happier life, but conversely may lead – in the search for perfection, the best deal, the best answer, etc – to anxiety, stress, dissatisfaction and depression, and (in the long term) the paralysis of decision-making. Then choice – a perceived prerequisite for personal freedom and self-determination – stifles the achievement of the very values that it is designed to underpin. For similar reasons, the abundance of information in the information age is, from a regulatory perspective, not an entirely positive phenomenon. For example, although consumers appear to have a greater online choice of products, as well as access to tools such as price comparison sites, and feedback and review sites, it is questionable whether these actually allow for better, more efficient decision-making and a more responsive, consumer-friendly market. More likely than not, even in the online age, consumer protection regulation is likely to retain its value.

Similarly, the abundance of information to which the regulator has access will not necessarily allow for greater regulatory efficiency. First, the instances in which a huge amount of information has been accidentally lost or made public by public servants show that the informational abundance also significantly multiplies the risk for the management of that data, with breaches of confidentiality and data protection and security threats looming large in the background.[8]

Second, by the same token, the retention of information as part of a regulatory agenda must be coupled with intelligent systems that allow for the efficient use of the information; otherwise, it is worthless. For example, there is evidence that the growing DNA database in the UK has not lived up to expectation in terms of delivering more convictions.[9]

Third, more information in the hands of the regulator may also lead to unexpected forms of overregulation, or what is referred to in medical terms as 'iatrogenic' illness – that is, the exacerbation of a disease or medical condition by the doctor's activity. For example, surveillance powers given initially to certain public authorities to fight terrorism and internet crime[10] have been hijacked by local councils to uncover relatively minor offences, such as dog fouling, fly tipping, smoking in certain places, repairing vehicles in the street, or misrepresenting residence status within a certain school catchment area.[11] Whether such regulatory growth indeed achieves greater compliance or simply generates more and costly enforcement activity is debatable.[12] Certainly, more information may simply slow down regulatory efforts in key areas by creating regulatory activities in the margins.

---

7   2003, New York: Ecco.

8   One of the powerful reasons against a one-stop governmental 'superdatabase': Afua Hirsch, 'Superdatabase tracking all calls and emails legitimate, says DPP' (2009) *The Guardian*, 9 January, available online at www.guardian.co.uk/uk/2009/jan/09/dpp-keir-starmer-superdatabase

9   Home Affairs Committee, *Eighth Report: The National DNA Database* (2010) HC 222-I, Session 2009–10, para 7, available online at www.publications.parliament.uk/pa/cm200910/cmselect/cmhaff/222/22202.htm

10 Regulation of Investigatory Powers Act 2000.

11 Richard Ford, 'Smokers and tramps join 8,000 council surveillance targets' (2010), *Timesonline*, 25 May, available online at www.timesonline.co.uk/tol/news/politics/article7134529.ece

12 That this is part of a more general trend can be seen from the discussion in the context of anti-cartel law enforcement in Christopher Harding, 'The Anti-Cartel Enforcement Industry: Criminological Perspectives on Cartel Criminalisation' in Caron Beaton-Wells and Ariel Ezrachi (eds) *Criminalising Cartels: Critical Studies of an International Regulatory Movement*, 2011, Oxford: Hart Publishing.

The general point of all of the above examples is that it would be foolish to believe that the new abundance of information is delivering us a better regulatory environment. It creates at least as many regulatory problems as it resolves, and further research on this subject matter is long overdue.

Disembodied Information

Another regulatory 'trauma' caused by the information age arises out of the nature of online information and, more specifically, its digital nature: its easy alterability, reproduction, and transport. Information on paper is relatively stable – it can be 'caught', locked up, and relied upon; digital information is slippery and ephemeral – one moment you see it, the next it is gone. Owners of intangible properties – that is, the music, software, and film industries, as well as the media – have felt the blow of this new type of information and are still struggling to imbue digital information with software characteristics that mimic their offline counterparts, or to find alternative avenues to protect their value. Also, both governmental agencies and commercial players have had to find new mechanisms to ensure the authenticity and reliability of digital information – because data may be quickly and, to all intents and purposes, untraceably amended, concepts such as 'original' or 'copy' make no real sense in the digital context.

The Democratisation Effect of the Internet

The information age also challenges many established power parameters, but often in ways that are not immediately obvious and which at times appear counterintuitive. For example, in the mid-90s, there were those who argued that the internet was a democratising force that would spell the end of authoritarian regimes. While it is too early for the final word on those predictions, at least currently many authoritarian regimes have remained perfectly intact despite the internet. In the meantime, the internet has been utilised by terrorist and criminal elements to organise their activities, which has prompted countries with long democratic traditions, such as the UK, to make significant inroads into well entrenched civil liberties, such as privacy or the presumption of innocence, in the name of anti-terrorist measures – thus perhaps weakening, rather than strengthening, democratic traditions. Having said that, it can be argued that the internet is fostering bottom-up democracy on a worldwide level by stimulating vast public debates on political news and often mobilising political activism.

From a commercial perspective, it was initially assumed that the internet would benefit businesses by opening world markets to them, and benefit consumers by giving them access to worldwide businesses. Again, while this expectation may not be entirely unrealised, on some levels, the possible benefits have clearly not been fulfilled. A UK consumer who would have previously bought books or music from a variety of mainly local or national businesses now buys it online, mainly from international powerhouses such as Amazon or iTunes with which few national businesses can effectively compete. So rather than creating a more level playing field, the internet encourages monopolies or, at least, gravitates towards global market leaders. National competition law is hard pressed to rise to the challenge.

IT Law as a Trigger for Regulatory Re-evaluations

Last, but not least, the internet also provokes fundamental questions about regulation: generally, what are the appropriate forms of regulation for online activities, how much regulation is required, and who should regulate? For example, when it comes to the protection of minors from online adult material, the question is whether it is the state or the parent who should assume the protective role. Should the internet herald a new age of governmental paternalism, or a new age of personal responsibility? Should it be the state that protects us from online villains as well as from ourselves (for example, in respect of online gambling) and, if so, how should it go about doing it? These are not issues that can, in any meaningful way, be neatly contained within the world of technology. As IT, with all of its peculiarities, becomes integrated with every facet of our lives, it is no longer simply the traditional law that gets transplanted to the technological world, but it is also the legal parameters that emerge from that world that shape our ordinary law. This means that the information age forces us to fundamentally re-evaluate law and regulation in our society: its function or role, its efficiency, its costs and benefits, and any alternative avenues for shaping behaviour.

Regulatory Theory: Lessig and Beyond

Regulatory theory – in the socio-legal sense of that term, rather than the political economy and economics sense – is a relatively new arrival to IT law, although it has a considerable history in areas such as environment law and utilities law. Regulation is a commonly used term, but one that, as Baldwin and Cave note, may be utilised in several ways. It can refer to a specific set of commands devised for a particular purpose. More broadly, it can cover all government action designed to respond to a particular type of behaviour or activity. Finally, it can refer to any form of influence that affects behaviour, whether or not this emanates from the state or from other sources, such as the market.[13] The last of these definitions is considered here, in the context of the interrelationship of various factors, including the law, which are combined to 'regulate' the uses of IT.

Lessig's Regulatory Model

In his book *Code: And Other Laws of Cyberspace*,[14] Lawrence Lessig talks of the above factors, or 'modalities of regulation', as being law, norms, market, and architecture. His main thesis is simple and applicable beyond the technological realm – which perhaps explains Lessig's popular success. According to Lessig, law – popularly understood as a command coupled with the threat of an *ex post* sanction for a violation – is only one of the ways in which behaviour may be regulated, and not necessarily the most efficient one. He lists other factors or restraints that may have an impact on our behaviour: social norms; markets; and what he refers to as 'architecture'.[15] Social norms will control how we behave in different circumstances and therefore exert a regulatory effect. Prices within a market can, for example, regulate the extent to which people are able to travel and therefore impact on their lifestyle. By 'architecture', Lessig means 'the physical world as we find it', which obviously has consequences for the way in which we are able to behave.

Importantly, the state cannot only use 'law' (direct regulation) to achieve a certain desired result, but can also influence and change the other three factors via regulation. Here, the regulation is indirect and often invisible to the subject, because it is channelled through the non-legal modalities. As an illustration, Lessig uses the example of the regulation of smoking and the consumption of cigarettes: the law may ban smoking (that is, the direct regulation of behaviour); it may tax cigarettes (that is, market regulation); it may provide a public education programme (that is, an attempt to regulate social norms); or it may control the amount of nicotine in cigarettes (that is, changing the 'architecture' of cigarettes). Clearly, all of these may have an effect on the consumption of cigarettes, the benefit of the regulation, but each also has a cost attached. Given the value that society places on autonomy, it may be that the education approach is preferred to the 'architectural' regulation.[16] A common feature of regulation by architecture is that it removes the individual's ability to choose whether or not to comply.

---

13 Robert Baldwin and Martin Cave, *Understanding Regulation: Theory, Strategy and Practice*, 1999, Oxford: Oxford University Press, p 2.
14 1999, New York: Basic Books. The same ideas are more succinctly put in Lessig (1999b), 506ff.
15 Ibid, 507. Lessig also calls architecture 'code'; hence the title of his book (1999a).
16 Lessig (1999b), 512.

Alternatively, 'norms', 'market', and 'architecture' can be left untouched by the regulator, who may leave it to the individuals to protect themselves as well as they can. For example, having reliable locks and security alarms (that is, architecture or code) provides the individual with greater protection against burglary than any offence written in a statute book. In the IT context, code comes to the forefront of the regulatory debate, because the entire regulatory domain is man-made and thus relatively easily manipulated by private or public actors:

> Many believe that cyberspace simply cannot be regulated. Behavior in cyberspace . . . is beyond government's reach. The anonymity and multijurisdictionality of cyberspace makes control by government in cyberspace impossible. The nature of the space makes behavior there *unregulable*. This belief about cyberspace is wrong, but wrong in an interesting way. It assumes either that the nature of cyberspace is fixed – that its architecture, and the control it enables, cannot be changed – or that government cannot take steps to change this architecture. Neither assumption is correct. Cyberspace has no nature; it has no particular architecture that cannot be changed.[17]

Thus influencing the architecture of the internet to achieve a regulatory objective becomes a highly attractive option for the regulator. A classic example would be the creation of a criminal offence prohibiting the circumvention of digital rights management technology (technologically embedded copyright protection) or requiring internet service providers (ISPs) to block illegal sites.

The advantages of regulation by code are numerous. Code (used to implement legal provisions) generally leaves users – other than the technologically savvy – no choice whether to comply with the law or not, because they are physically prevented from non-compliance. Thus the compliance rate of indirect regulation via code is often close to 100 per cent.[18] In addition, code is self-enforcing – thus saving significant costs that would be associated with ordinary law enforcement. Finally, to comply with code, the subject need not have any awareness of it nor of the legal duties that the code implements. In contrast, to ensure compliance with direct regulation (that is, a norm backed by a sanction), it is necessary for the government to raise awareness of the law, because such awareness is a prerequisite for the subject's decision to comply with it.

This then brings us to the disadvantages of code as a regulatory tool. Because code does not need visibility to be effective, the state can easily influence code – and thereby behaviour – without attracting much attention. So regulation through code may therefore lack transparency and proper democratic accountability. Lessig argues that the 'government gets an effect at no political cost. It gets the benefit of what would be an illegal and controversial regulation, that is, without even having to admit any regulation exists'.[19] In other words:

> Indirection misdirects responsibility. When a government uses other structures of constraint to effect a constraint it could impose directly, it muddies the responsibility for that constraint and so undermines political accountability. If transparency is a value in constitutional government, indirection is its enemy.[20]

A second problem of regulation through code is that it removes 'moral agency' or personal autonomy. We do not need to decide whether we want to comply with the 'law' or not, because that

---

17 Ibid, 505 (internal marks omitted).
18 Although, as Lessig notes, the modalities interact with each other, and the use of indirect regulation via code may result in negative social or market responses. For example, regional coding on DVDs – a form of regulation by code imposed by manufacturers – created a thriving industry in mod chips and software hacks: a market-based response.
19 Lessig (1999a), p 98.
20 Ibid, p 96.

decision is forced upon us through the physical restraint. Some may argue that this cannot be a bad thing: the habitual compliers simply do what they would have done anyway and those that might have broken the law are forced to comply with it. The result is an end to freeloading and thus greater fairness all around. However, as Brownsword convincingly argues, liberal society gives people on the whole the freedom to comply or not to comply with the law.[21] This is not simply legal indulgence, but an essential attribute of liberal society in which personal choices (even if they are bad and later penalised) are respected as a requirement of human dignity and being an autonomous actor. In Brownsword's words:

> a fully techno-regulated community is no longer an operative moral community . . . [I]f techno-regulators know how to stop us from being bad only by, at the same time, stopping us from being good . . . [then ordinary law] for all its imperfections, has something going for it.[22]

Beyond these two main reasons, technological solutions to regulatory problems may (depending on their sophistication) also be too effective. Too effective? Legal restrictions in the case of direct regulation are invariably accompanied by defences or exceptions. Yet code tends to be better at implementing the main restriction, without taking into account any of the exceptions. This makes it a 'blunt force tool', inflexible and insensitive to other interests and values. For example, digital rights management technology has frequently been accused of trumping the 'fair dealing' or 'fair use' defence to copyright infringement.

See Chapter 9

Last, but by no means least, code – as employed by private or public actors in cyberspace to protect certain values – often involves the recreation of characteristics from the physical world, given that these characteristics are essential for the proper functioning of the traditional law. For example, in the copyright law context, the perfection of digital copies is problematic because it gives users with access to a copy no incentive to buy the official product – because the official product would in no way be distinguishable from the 3,056th copy of that product. A regulatory solution to this dilemma would be to programme digital data in such a way that their quality degrades with an increasing number of copies:

> With the code changed, when a machine is used to copy a particular CD, a serial number from the CD is recorded in the tape machine's memory. If the users tries to copy that tape more than a limited number of times, the machines adjusts the quality of the copy. As the copies increase, the quality is degraded.[23]

Another example of such technological mirroring of characteristics of the offline world would be the recreation of territorial boundaries in cyberspace. While using technology in such a way as to replicate the 'old world' is understandable in the absence of alternative regulatory solutions, it cannot avoid the accusation of being a rather desperate attempt to reverse technological progress.

See Chapter 2

Developing Lessig's Model

The virtue of Lessig's approach is its simplicity; in an attempt to capture the complexity of the regulatory environment, Scott and Murray have developed these ideas in a more detailed fashion.[24] They propose four top-level categories, which broadly correspond to Lessig's four 'modalities of

---

21 'Code, control, and choice: Why east is east and west is west' (2005) 25 Legal Studies 1.
22 Ibid, 20.
23 Lessig(1999a), p 128.
24 Andrew Murray and Colin Scott, 'Controlling the new media: Hybrid responses to new forms of power' (2002) 65(4) MLR 491.

regulation'. In their terminology, these are 'control systems' (that is, methods of controlling or modifying behaviour):

- hierarchical control (Lessig's 'law');
- competition-based control (Lessig's 'market');
- community-based control (Lessig's 'norms'); and
- design-based control (Lessig's 'architecture').

However, Scott and Murray elaborate on these 'control systems' by identifying three stages in the regulatory process in respect of each of the above four modalities.

(1)   Standard setting (that is, what is the source and content of the restraint?)

(2)   Information gathering (that is, how does the restraint interact with its subject? how is its compliance monitored?)

(3)   Behaviour modification (that is, how is the restraint enforced or made effective vis-à-vis the potential violator/wrongdoer?)

Each of these control systems may operate alone or in conjunction with one or more of the other three to provide a regulatory matrix.[25]

Murray and Scott note that even where there may appear to be a 'pure basis of regulation' (that is, where legal or other hierarchical measures alone appear to be the sole method of regulation), it may still be influenced indirectly by other control systems. It is not uncommon, for example, for legal rules to be influenced by community considerations (for example, those of regulator and regulatees), or by competition or arbitrage between regulators operating in the same regulatory space.[26] An example of the latter point is the relationship between the UK Information Commissioner's Office (ICO) and the Financial Services Authority (FSA). Both have regulatory powers with regard to data privacy: the ICO generally, and the FSA within its financial services remit. In principle, this could lead to regulatory competition. In practice, given the FSA's ability to levy greater fines than the ICO on those financial services companies breaching good practice with regard to customer data, it appears that the ICO has been willing to let the FSA take the lead in such cases.[27] This regulatory relationship may change in due course as the ICO acquires new enforcement powers.

Regulation, then, may occur within a particular regulatory space via the application of different, but interrelated, control systems. To continue the data protection example, we can see clearly the hierarchical control based around the **Data Protection Act (DPA) 1998** and **Privacy and Electronic Communications (EC Directive) Regulations (PECR) 2003**, the operation of which is monitored by the ICO. In parallel, the **Financial Services and Markets Act (FSMA) 2000** provides the FSA with the rule-making powers to create its Principles for Businesses for those organisations within its remit. Principle 3 provides that '[a] firm must take reasonable care to organise and control its affairs responsibly and effectively, with adequate risk management systems', and this includes having adequate systems and controls in place to protect its customers' confidential details from being lost or stolen.

Monitoring within the **DPA 1998** framework is also carried out by individuals in their capacity as data subjects. They can make subject access requests concerning the processing of their personal data, prevent processing of that personal data on various grounds, and require data controllers to

---

25 Ibid, 504.
26 Ibid, 504–5.
27 See, eg, Financial Services Authority, 'HSBC firms fined over £3m for information security failings' (2009) Press release, available online at www.fsa.gov.uk/pages/Library/Communication/PR/2009/099.shtml

rectify, block, erase, or destroy their personal data, where it is being held in reach of their rights under the Act. It is arguable that data controllers, through their (usually contractual) relationship with those processing personal data on their behalf (data processors), are similarly part of the monitoring process established under the Act.

In parallel with this, we can also see the use of community-based controls (that is, social norms). In the UK, we have particular expectations about the privacy of our personal data, premised partly on legal rules (for example, confidentiality, data protection), but also on our normative expectations of how a responsible organisation will treat such data (for example, good business practice, respect for clients). If organisations engage in activities that breach those expectations, various 'mechanisms' may be used to notify other community members. These mechanisms may take many forms, from word-of-mouth, to complaints in the media and negative ratings on opinion websites, blogs, and wikis. The resulting sanction for a commercial organisation is likely to be loss of trust, leading to loss of current and potential future customers. Community-based control may be the focus of third-sector organisations (such as Liberty, Privacy International) or targeted campaigns (such as NO2ID).

It is important to notice the overlaps between the hierarchical control and the community-based control. A subject access request that discovers breach of the **DPA 1998** by a data controller may trigger both a hierarchical control response, such as an audit by the ICO, and a community control response, such as a boycott of the data controller. Additionally, in a business environment, the information about the breach may be seized upon by competitors of the breaching data controller and used by them to create competitive advantage in the marketplace: for example, in terms of attracting customers who would otherwise have gone to the breaching data controller, or in terms of justifying their higher prices by virtue of claiming more effective data privacy practices. Thus competition-based control is also likely to play a role in some circumstances.

Design-based control (that is, code) may operate to protect personal privacy, in the form of privacy-enhancing technologies, such as web browsers that permit individuals to control releases of information when accessing websites, by limiting the information that the website can collect from, or place onto, the individual's computer, or by indicating when a website is insecure or compromised. Equally, however, it may work to undermine privacy controls, such as those social networking sites that encourage individuals to expose their personal data by virtue of having default privacy settings that display private information more widely than necessary. Here, again, there may be interaction with the other control systems: the ICO might put pressure on the social networking site to change the default settings to ones that are more privacy-protective; privacy groups may encourage individuals to check their settings more carefully; or other social networking sites might begin to offer a 'more privacy-friendly' service.

Given the potential complexity of the interaction between the control systems, it is clear that those wishing to regulate a particular sphere of activity need to consider very carefully the context of the regulatory goal that they are seeking to achieve, and seek not only to achieve the best approach available from the combination of the control systems, but also to be careful not to create 'perverse incentives' for those affected by the regulatory approach eventually adopted.

An example of such a 'perverse incentive' would be a scenario in which the regulatory goal was to prevent obscene material being displayed on websites. Obvious chokepoints for such content are the internet intermediaries that host the websites. A regulator seeking to use those chokepoints might thus decide to require those intermediaries to address the issue, by making them legally liable for not ensuring its removal. However, would it not be unfair if an intermediary were to be held responsible in the absence of knowledge about the content? A regulatory solution might be that the liability falls on an intermediary only if it is, or should have been, aware of the obscene material within its control.

What are the implications of this for an intermediary? Does it make it more or less likely that the intermediary will take proactive measures to prevent obscene content being made available,

See Chapter 3 →

through exercising editorial control? As discussed elsewhere in this book, an intermediary that takes proactive measures (rather than simply waiting for someone to complain about the material) is potentially opening itself up to greater liability, because exercising editorial function makes it more likely that it should have known about the material. Setting up an editorial process that then fails in some circumstances is thus more likely to have serious consequences for the intermediary than having no editing process at all. In such circumstances, a pragmatic intermediary might very well decide to do less screening of material on its hosted websites, because it could then more plausibly claim that it was unaware of the unwanted content.[28]

A different solution to the problem might be to grant all intermediaries immunity from liability for the content that they host, in order to encourage them to be more proactive about tackling unwanted content, because they themselves face no consequences if errors are made whilst actively seeking it out. However, providing intermediaries with blanket immunity from content liability for the websites that they host will work only if there is an additional incentive for them to be proactive – after all, if they have immunity from liability for the content that they host, why would they spend their money tackling what is now someone else's problem? Furthermore, if they have blanket immunity from liability for content, they may also neglect to pay attention to complaints about other forms of content liability, such as defamation.[29]

It would appear therefore that the achievement of the regulatory goal of controlling certain forms of internet content will take more than a simple hierarchical control system. In practice, in the UK, regulating obscene internet content has tended to combine:

- legal measures, including criminal provisions, such as the **Obscene Publications Acts**, and some limitation of ISP/II liability, such as the **Electronic Commerce (EC Directive) Regulations 2002** (hierarchical);
- independent action by ISP/IIs, such as editing, filtering, and blocking, or by their sectoral representatives, such as the Internet Watch Foundation (IWF) (community/competition); and
- public action, including the education of users, and citizen reporting (community).

Future regulation may include built-in automated content control, such as filtering based on skin tones for nudity, or by algorithmic 'hash value' under which data comprising known illegal content – for example, an obscene photograph – is used to create an automated search pattern that can be used to identify copies of the same image (design).

Regulatory Strategies

Another way of viewing the types of process outlined above is to think of them in terms of regulatory strategies variously involving legal authority, the deployment of wealth, the use of markets, the provision of information, direct action, or the conferment of rights.[30] These capabilities or resources can be utilised by government to fashion a range of basic strategies. There are many examples of the use of such regulatory strategies in IT law and this section will briefly consider some of the key regulatory strategies. It does not aim either to be an exhaustive overview of possible strategies or to

---

28 See, eg, the US case *Stratton Oakmont, Inc v Prodigy Services Co*, 1995 WL 323710 (NY Sup Ct, 1995); cf *Cubby, Inc v CompuServe Inc*, 776 F Supp 135 (SDNY 1991).

29 See s 230 of the Communications Decency Act, 47 USC § 230, and *Zeran v AOL*, 129 F 3d 327, 330 (4th Cir 1997), cert. denied, 524 US 937 (1998); *Blumenthal v Drudge*, 992 F Supp 44, 49–53 (DDC 1998); *Doe v MySpace*, 528 F 3d 413 (5th Cir 2008); *Barnes v Yahoo!, Inc*, 570 F 3d 1096 (2009).

30 Baldwin and Cave, op cit, 34, citing Christopher C Hood, *The Tools of Government*, 1983, London: Macmillan, p 5; Terence C Daintith, 'The techniques of government', in J Jowell and D Oliver (eds), *The Changing Constitution*, 3rd edn, 1994, Oxford: Oxford University Press.

explore the concepts in great depth, both of which have been done at length elsewhere,[31] but rather to provide the reader with a basic introduction to the area. Examples of the use of different approaches in the regulation of IT are used as illustrations, but the general points raised in the subsequent discussion should be kept in mind when considering any of the topics that are discussed in the rest of the book.

Criminal and Administrative Law: Command and Control

A common regulatory technique is often referred to as 'command and control',[32] defined by Baldwin as 'the exercise of influence by imposing standards backed by criminal sanctions'.[33] In command-and-control regulation, therefore, legal rules are imposed by government and failure to meet the standards imposed in these provisions can result in the imposition of standards – usually criminal, but sometimes also administrative. Command-and-control regulation is very popular with governments, and sometimes also with the public too: '. . . there is a powerful and radical segment of opinion which, seeing a social evil, recommends a law of strict liability as the best legislative panacea.'[34] Such rules can be presented as evidence that action is being taken on issues of concern – that 'something is being done'. This can give the impression of an immediate and bene- ficial effect, even though, as we shall see, there may be adverse effects that only gradually come to light. As well as being popular with some, command-and-control regulation has some other impor- tant advantages: it can be both clear and straightforward both for the regulated and the regulator;[35] and, once formulated, there is usually very little discretion available to either side to deviate from the required standard. However, command-and-control regulation may not be uniformly effective and may be more suitable for use in some circumstances than others. In particular, although it may be fairly easy to enforce against corporations and other large institutions, it is much more difficult to apply to more diffuse and transitory operators, of which there are many examples on the internet. Enforcement of command-and-control regulation can also be problematic because there are consid- erable costs associated with compliance, inspection, detection, and enforcement.[36] Again in terms of activity on the internet, the difficulties in enforcement can be one of the major problems for the effective use of command-and-control regulation.

The **Data Protection Act 1998** provides an example of rules of the command-and-control type. Data controllers are required to undertake particular actions, such as notification, and refrain from other actions, such as processing for the purposes of direct marketing. Further, there are both criminal and administrative sanctions that can be imposed for failure to comply with these requirements.[37] Restrictions are also placed on other third parties in particular circumstances. Adherence to these standards is overseen by a specific regulator: in the UK, this is the Information Commissioner's Office (ICO). Unlike some regulators,[38] this office does not have its own rule-making capacity, but both provides guidance on, and enforces, the regulatory standards set out in the

See Chapter 5

---

31 For example, Baldwin and Cave, op cit; Anthony Ogus, *Regulation: Legal Form and Economic Theory*, 1994, Oxford: Oxford University Press; Robert Baldwin, Colin Scott, and Christopher Hood (eds), *A Reader on Regulation*, 1998, Oxford: Oxford University Press.

32 See, eg, Anthony Ogus, op cit, p 5; Baldwin, Scott, and Hood, op cit, p 24.

33 Robert Baldwin, 'Regulation: After "command and control"', in K Hawkins (ed), *The Human Face of Law*, 1997, Oxford: Clarendon, ch 3, p 65.

34 Charles D Drake and Frank B Wright, *Law of Health and Safety at Work: The New Approach*, 1983, London: Sweet and Maxwell, p 14.

35 Neil A Gunningham and Peter Grabosky, *Smart Regulation: Designing Environmental Policy*, 1998, Oxford: Oxford University Press, p 41.

36 See, eg, ibid, pp 42–5. Interestingly, when discussing firms that are readily identifiable and accessible, the authors cite Robert A Kagan, , 'Regulatory enforcement', in DH Rosenbloom and RD Schwartz (eds), *Handbook of Regulation and Administrative Law*, 1994, New York: Dekker, as referring to 'the difference between regulating "elephants" and "foxes": it is harder for elephants to hide' – a clear foreshadowing of Peter P Swire's later analysis of the Data Protection Directive, 'Of elephants, mice, and privacy: International choice of law and the internet' (1998) 32 International Lawyer 991.

37 For further details, see Chapter 5.

38 For example, the FSA: see Andromachi Georgosouli, 'The nature of the FSA policy of rule use: A critical overview' (2008) 28(1) Legal Studies 119.

legislation. The use of the command-and-control approach in the data protection regulatory regime illustrates a number of the general problems with this type of regulation. In practice, the reliance placed on the ability of data subjects to question data controllers about the use of their personal data is difficult to apply both generally and in relation to use on the internet or in m-commerce. If data subjects see no benefit in engaging with the regulatory process, then the overall effectiveness of the regulatory regime will be significantly reduced. In addition, as the technology develops, the rules may no longer be so easily applicable to the new environment.[39] This is very apparent in data protection legislation: the original rules were developed for large, centralised databanks, and have not proved easy to translate to the amorphous and diffuse use of personal data on the internet.[40]

Two other key problems frequently referred to in the literature are 'legalism' and 'regulatory capture'. Legalism is a blanket heading for a range of connected issues that arise from the difficulty of producing (and maintaining) rules to cover a broad range of circumstances, and which tend to result in the production of inflexible and over-inclusive rules. The reactive nature of command-and-control regulation encourages such highly prescriptive and inflexible rules. It engenders a view that problems will be identified by central government and that rules created will then be dealt with by a suitable regulatory agency. Thus, despite any particular knowledge and expertise that they may possess, the role of the regulated is essentially passive. A possible example of an overbroad provision is that of 'health' within the categories of 'sensitive' personal data in the **Data Protection Directive**. In Case C-101/01 *Bodil Lindqvist*, the European Court of Justice (ECJ) held that basic information posted by a church worker about her fellow church volunteers on a webpage, which included, amongst other things, the information that one volunteer had injured her foot and was working part-time on medical grounds, was sufficient to constitute personal data concerning health within the meaning of the Directive.[41] In the face of the current social networking boom, in which (in principle) each individual networker, blogger, or wiki user could be deemed to be a data controller, this interpretation seems likely to be unenforceable in any meaningful way.

One of the most trenchant criticisms of command-and-control regulation has been in relation to 'regulatory capture', a phrase used to suggest that regulatory agencies are 'captured' by those whom they seek to regulate with a spectrum of outcomes ranging from leniency in enforcement, to actual bribery and corruption. In this process, a regulator may, over time, consciously or unconsciously, come to put the interests of those that it regulates before the public interest goals with which it is tasked.[42] A number of explanations have been advanced as to how 'capture' arises. One, based on the lifecycle theory of regulation developed by Bernstein,[43] suggests that it is an inevitable part of the regulatory aging process, and that altruism and public interest concerns, which initially create enthusiasm and crusading zeal, gradually give way to self-interest on the part of both regulator and regulatee, with a resultant slide into inefficiency and incompetence, and maybe, eventually, corruption, and so promoting capture. A different explanation based on the so-called 'revolving door' theory is that, due to the 'paradoxical nature of the need for specialist regulators',[44] similar

---

39 Andrew Charlesworth, 'The future of UK data protection regulation' (2006) 11(1) Inform Secur Tech Rep 46, 47 and 50, with regard to 'instrument failure', 'information failure', 'implementation failure', and 'motivation failure'; Julia M Black, 'Decentring regulation: Understanding the role of regulation and self regulation in a "post-regulatory" world' (2001) 54 CLP 103.

40 For a consideration of the development of data protection legislation in this context, see Chapter 5.

41 Case C-101/01 *Bodil Lindqvist v Kammaraklagaren* [2003] ECR I-12971, ECJ. See further discussion in Chapter 5.

42 See, eg, Baldwin and Cave, op cit, p 36; Ogus, op cit, pp 57–8 and 94–5; Amitai Etzioni, 'The capture theory of regulations: Revisited' (2009) 46(4) Society 319. This has been an area of great interest to economists: see, eg, Michael E Levine and Jennifer L Forrence, 'Regulatory capture, public interest, and the public agenda: Toward a synthesis' (1990) 6(Special Issue) JL Econ & Org 167. Ogus and other legal commentators are perhaps more sceptical about the practical effects.

43 MH Bernstein, *Regulating Business by Independent Commission*, 1955, Princeton, NJ: Princeton University Press, criticised in LL Jaffe, 'The independent agency: A new scapegoat' (1956) 65 Yale LJ 1068. Michael Moran suggests that few would now support the lifecycle theory on the grounds that it is too simplistic: see 'Understanding the regulatory state' (2002) 32 B J Pol Sci 391, 393.

44 Barry Mitnick, *The Political Economy of Regulation*, 1980, New York: Columbia University Press, p 207; see also Toni Makkai and John Braithwaite, 'In and out of the revolving door: Making sense of regulatory capture' (1992) 12(1) JPP 61.

expertise is a prerequisite for both the regulators and the industry being regulated. Accordingly, there may be a constant and considerable interchange of personnel between the regulatory agency and the industry. This, in turn, engenders a close relationship between the two, with the consequent likelihood that the regulators tend to be overly sympathetic to the needs of the regulated, making capture a possibility or even a probability.

These factors are often found in relation to data privacy regulators, in which instance close contact is common with both public and private sector data controllers, and in which former key personnel – including former commissioners – often join from, and depart to, law firms, lobbying organisations, or similar business-oriented groups.[45] Nevertheless, the evidence for 'regulatory capture' in the data protection sphere is slight, although regulators are clearly aware of the risk.[46] Claims of capture have, however, been made with regard to the UK ICO's relationship to central government,[47] and in relation to the lack of action taken by the ICO with regard to the Phorm 'deep packet inspection' trials run by BT.[48] In practice, the UK ICO's limited enforcement powers, and lack of rule-making powers, has meant that a cooperative, educative, or consultative approach has often been the only one available to it, but it has not shied away from measures that might discomfort significant groups of regulatees[49] or major corporations.[50]

The solution frequently suggested to the possibility of regulatory capture is 'tripartism', under which, put simply, relevant public-interest groups are given a direct involvement in the regulatory process, through access to the same information available to the regulator, involving them in discussions/negotiations between the regulator and regulatees, and standing to take legal action via the same processes as the regulator. Of course, without methods of keeping the public-interest groups accountable, perhaps by competition between such groups, they are no less prone to the risks of capture than a regulator.[51]

In the IT sphere more generally, there is one other potential problem raised in regard to command-and-control strategies – that is, the issue of how to impose strategies predicated on national rules upon international scenarios. Data privacy regulation is clearly affected by such considerations,[52] and so, in principle, are many other IT-related regulatory goals, such as internet content control. So if command-and-control strategies are unsuitable in certain circumstances, then how else might regulatory goals be achieved?

See Chapter 2

Self-regulation

In IT law, the standard answer to the question posed above is 'self-regulation'. The difficulty with that answer lies in determining what exactly 'self-regulation' means. At one level, self-regulation can be used in a literal sense to refer to the individual's ability to control his or her own behaviour.

45 For example, Richard Thomas, the UK's Information Commissioner from November 2002 to June 2009, came to the job from Clifford Chance LLP. On retiring, he joined Hunton & Williams' Centre for Information Policy Leadership (CIPL). The Centre was founded in Washington, DC, in 2001 by Hunton & Williams, a privacy and data protection law firm, in conjunction with a number of global companies.

46 Blair Stewart (Assistant Commissioner, Office of the Privacy Commissioner, New Zealand), 'The economics of data privacy: Should we place a dollar value on personal autonomy and dignity?' (2004) 26th International Conference on Privacy and Personal Data Protection, Worclaw, 14–16 September.

47 Foundation for Information Policy Research (FIPR), *Consultation Response on the Data Sharing Review*, 2008, available online at www.fipr.org/080215datasharing.pdf

48 All Party Parliamentary Communications Group, *Can We Keep Our Hands off the Net? Report of an Inquiry by the All Party Parliamentary Communications Group*, 2009, available online at www.apcomms.org.uk/uploads/apComms_Final_Report.pdf

49 Information Commissioner's Office, 'ICO seizes covert database of construction industry workers' (2009) Press release, 9 March, available online at www.ico.gov.uk/upload/documents/pressreleases/2009/tca_release_060309.pdf

50 Stewart Room, 'Regulators need to build bridges, not burn them' (2009) *The Lawyer*, 30 November.

51 Ian Ayres and John Braithwaite, *Responsive Regulation: Transcending the Deregulation Debate*, 1992, Oxford: Oxford University Press, pp 54–100.

52 Consider the disagreement between the USA and EU regarding cross-border data flows, including air passenger information and financial information carried by SWIFT.

More broadly, it may be used to refer to any regulatory activity that is not initiated by the state, whether originating in individual or collective actions. In the general field of corporate and business regulation, it is frequently used to describe the rules and codes of conduct imposed on their members by trade and professional organisations. Self-regulation is thus a fluid and amorphous concept that it has been suggested has 'no accepted definition'.[53] It is frequently merely one element of an overarching centralised regulatory scheme, but, within that context, can run right across the spectrum from informal, non-binding, and voluntary procedures, to rules that are enforceable through the courts. As this suggests, there is no accepted model of self-regulation: self-regulatory schemes may exhibit varying degrees of formality; and the extent to which third parties participate in rule formulation, enforcement, or supervision may differ, as may whether or not they have any legal effect. In many cases, self-regulation is 'much better seen not as a pervading regulatory approach, but as part of a shifting set of regulatory techniques, the mix depending on external political, economic, and social factors'.[54]

The availability of appropriate sanctions and rewards for good compliance records may also be issues in the comparison between the desirability and efficacy of self-regulation vis-à-vis those available in relation to command-and-control regulation. Violations may be dealt with relatively informally – for example, without necessarily having recourse to external legal procedures. This may be both quicker, less resource-intensive, and more effective, but will also be less publicly visible, raising both problems of perceived leniency and the spectre of lack of accountability. Cynics might also suspect the level of achievement to be significantly lower than that for traditionally enforced command-and-control rules, and this may well be so if there is no motivation towards compliance with self-regulatory standards. On the other hand, it is also possible for the reverse to be the case and for self-regulation to raise standards by inspiring 'ethical standards of conduct which extend beyond the letter of the law'.[55]

One particular reason why self-regulation has the propensity to be effective is that those directly involved with the activity themselves become the repository of the relevant expertise and information. Proponents would further suggest that, in consequence, self-regulators have a special appreciation of what will be seen as reasonable regulatory demands, and that this will, inevitably, lead to higher levels of voluntary compliance and consequent regulatory efficiency. Capture theorists, on the other hand, would say that this is precisely the mechanism that allows the industry to influence the regulatory process in its favour. Certainly, the public perception – and, in many cases, this may be confirmed by the reality – is that self-regulators do not have the commitment to regulate in the public interest unless that interest happens to coincide with their private interests. On occasion, this fear may not be realised if the alternative to administering a self-regulatory scheme is external regulation and state intervention. Although there are some powerful and vocal advocates of self-regulation, there is probably an equal level of scepticism amongst those who doubt that it has any positive attributes, as summed up by the comment that 'self-regulation is a euphemism which means no regulation at all'.[56] This polarisation of views is summed up eloquently by Black:

> . . . self-regulation is such a normatively loaded term. For some it denotes regulation that is responsive, flexible, informed, targeted, and which at once stimulates and draws on the internal morality of the sector or organization being regulated. For others it is self-serving, self-interested, lacking in sanctions, beset with free rider problems and simply a sham. The rhetoric affects policy attitudes and decisions and can result in poor regulatory design.[57]

---

53 Baldwin, Scott, and Hood, op cit, p 27.
54 Tony Prosser, 'Self-regulation, co-regulation and the Audio-visual Media Services Directive' (2008) 31(1) J Consum Pol 99, 100.
55 Neil Gunningham and Joseph Rees, 'Industry self-regulation: An institutional perspective' (1997) 19 Law & Pol 363, 366.
56 Paul Rose, Hansard HC, vol 871, col 1323 (1974).
57 Black, op cit, p 115.

Ogus notes that 'lawyers and economists have been equally scathing in their criticisms of self-regulation',[58] and that these criticisms have been based on the lack of accountability, the potential for abuse, etc. He goes on to point out, however, that a number of traditional criticisms are 'based on a narrow, stereotyped conception of the phenomenon'. Although the criticisms can certainly be justified in some cases, it is possible to conceive of systems that take these drawbacks into account and also benefit from the perceived advantages.

The UK's Internet Watch Foundation (IWF) provides an interesting example of a number of the above issues. The IWF was established in 1996 by a variety of internet companies as a mechanism to allow the public and IT professionals to report criminal online content in a secure and confidential way. Initially envisaged as a means to tackle the dissemination of child sexual abuse images online anywhere in the world, its remit has since expanded to include the reporting of criminally obscene adult content and incitement to racial hatred content hosted in the UK. As such it:

- operates a national hotline to enable the public to report instances of potentially criminal online content;
- operates a 'notice and takedown' service to remove potentially criminal online content at source by alerting hosting companies to illegal content on their servers;
- compiles and maintains a blacklist of between 500 and 800 URLs that link to indecent images of children, or advertise or link to such content, with commercial ISPs using the blacklist to block access to those URLs and filtering in this way the internet access of up to 95 per cent of commercial internet customers in the UK;
- acts as a relevant authority and point of expertise as regards the reporting, handling, assessment, and tracing of content;[59] and
- shares expertise, experience, and intelligence with law enforcement and other relevant organisations.

The IWF is an incorporated charity, limited by guarantee, and declares itself to be:

> ... an independent self-regulatory body, funded by the EU and the wider online industry, including Internet service providers, mobile operators and manufacturers, content service providers, filtering companies, search providers, trade associations, and the financial sector.[60]

It goes on to suggest that the 'establishment of the IWF pre-empted the introduction of formal regulatory action' and that 'self-regulation is the preferred method of regulating content amongst the government and Internet' – although these comments are clearly not an accurate reflection of its approach across all areas of activity on the internet. The IWF also cites the various organisations that, together, nominate over ninety members of the IWF Funding Council that oversees policy development.

So how does the IWF's 'self-regulation' operate in practice? It is not funded by the UK government, although it does receive EU financing. Operationally, it is accountable to its board of trustees, industry members, and stakeholders. Its creation in 1996 (as the 'Safety Net Foundation') came about in response to indications that the police were preparing to bring test cases against ISPs for

---

58 Ogus, op cit, p 108.
59 The IWF is a relevant authority as regards reporting, handling, and combating child sexual abuse images on the internet under a memorandum of understanding between the Crown Prosecution Service (CPS) and the Association of Chief Police Officers (ACPO), linked to s 46 of the Sexual Offences Act 2003. Section 46 creates a defence for service providers to secure and retain, for the purposes of prosecution, potentially criminal child sexual abuse content.
60 IWF, 'About the Internet Watch Foundation (IWF)', available online at www.iwf.org.uk/public/page.103.htm

hosting illegal content and that the government was considering legislation.[61] All of these are, in principle, key indicators of self-regulation.

However, on the other side of the coin, three years after it was established, a review of its operation was instigated jointly by the (then) Department of Trade and Industry (DTI) and the Home Office, which resulted in a number of changes to both the IWF's role and its structure.[62] This suggests the IWF's degree of independence from government is not such that the government has no say in its structure and operations, and there appears to be both formal and informal interaction between the IWF and a number of government departments, Members of Parliament (MPs), peers, and members of the European Parliament (MEPs), as is acknowledged on the IWF website.[63] Additionally, without the panoply of UK illegal content legislation,[64] the IWF would have a much harder time gaining compliance from its full members. Indeed, despite explicit government pressure, some ISPs still resist utilising its blacklist.[65] Further, the 'notice and takedown' process, with provisions in the **Electronic Commerce (EC Directive) Regulations 2002**[66] giving information society service providers (ISSPs) a limited immunity from liability for hosting illegal content in certain situations, provides the IWF with significant additional leverage in its role as a private sector regulator. This would be lacking if ISSPs were to have full immunity from content liability.

Finally, the IWF obtains additional powers through its memorandum of understanding with the Crown Prosecution Service (CPS) and the Association of Chief Police Officers (ACPO), linked to s 46 of the **Sexual Offences Act 2003**, which permits its staff to investigate criminal child sexual abuse content without being prosecuted for looking at/making illegal content in the course of their duties.[67] The IWF provide as their main operating contacts the Child Exploitation and Online Protection Centre (CEOP), the Serious Organised Crime Agency (SOCA), the Metropolitan Police Paedophile Unit, and the National Hi-Tech Crime Unit Scotland (NHTCUS), and note that the police provide input into the law and image assessment element of IWF staff training; the IWF provides technical internet training for police staff on occasions.

Given all the foregoing, it can be seen that the IWF's claim to a self-regulatory role places a particularly broad interpretation upon the term 'self-regulation'. Indeed, critics have suggested that its links to government are such that it might be more reasonably considered a quasi-autonomous non-governmental organisation (quango) than an independent entity. What, then, is the benefit of regulating through an organisation such as the IWF? A number of possibilities suggest themselves:

- the regulatory function is carried out at low, or little, cost to government;
- there is greater technical expertise available to and within the organisation than would be available to a government agency;
- the standard of regulation is at a level that the regulatees accept as attainable;
- the hotline/alerting process will be more effective, because it is closer to those required to act on it; and
- changes can be made to self-regulatory rules more quickly to adapt to changing circumstances and government can steer policy without having to invest legislative or administrative time.

---

61 Julian Petley, 'Web control' (2009) 38 Index on Censorship 78, 82–5. See also Alan Travis, *Bound and Gagged: A Secret History of Obscenity in Britain*, 2000, London: Profile.
62 Petley, op cit, and see Wills, Hansard HC, vol 325, col 207-8W (9 February 1999).
63 IWF, 'Government, Parliamentarians, and UKCCIS', available online at www.iwf.org.uk/government/page.6.htm
64 Including the Obscene Publications Acts 1959 and 1964, Protection of Children Act 1978, Sexual Offences Act 2003, and Public Order Act 1986, discussed further in Chapter 4.
65 Vernon Coaker (Parliamentary Under-Secretary, Home Office), HC Deb, 15 May 2006, c715W; see also HC Deb, 16 June 2008, c683W.
66 Electronic Commerce (EC Directive) Regulations 2002, SI 2002/2013, reg 19.
67 See Chapter 4 for discussion of the 'making' of child pornography.

There are, however, potential downsides, including the following.

● Unless the regulatory process is legally enforceable, potential regulatees will still be able to opt out. As noted above, some ISPs do refuse to use the IWF blacklist.

● The rules applied by the self-regulatory body may be designed more to benefit the regulated than the public interest. The use of the blacklist and 'notice and takedown' is designed to protect the ISPs from liability, and those processes may impact on public interest issues, such as freedom of expression (although there is a right to appeal the blocking process).

● There is no requirement of openness, transparency, accountability, and acceptability to the public generally, or to users of ISP services specifically. Both regulatees and government can thus implement policy goals without direct public scrutiny. In recent years, the IWF has, at various times, blocked user access to the Internet Archive and to Wikipedia. In the case of Wikipedia, this concerned content readily available from internet shopping sites and from physical shops. The staff of the IWF makes determinations about the legality of material without reference to independent scrutiny and the content of the blacklist is also not independently verifiable.

Enforced Self-regulation

The potential downsides to the self regulatory process may be overcome by what is sometimes termed 'enforced self-regulation', or 'regulated self-regulation'.[68] Under such a process, the government might, for example, allow the IWF (or possibly its full members as individual entities) to make its own rules, but require those rules to be approved by a government agency in conjunction with public-interest groups. Conformity with the approved rules would be monitored, via the IWF (or possibly by a company's own internal inspectors), which would then be subject to external scrutiny – again in conjunction with public-interest groups. Breach of the approved rules would result in legal sanction.

An example of a regulatory process similar to this model, developing organically, can be seen in the case of website data privacy protection policies in the USA. In the USA, there is no overarching data privacy regime, as there is in the UK. However, many US websites saw having a privacy policy as a useful mechanism through which to build trust with their customers. Despite having made such commitments to their customers through their privacy policies, some firms then breached, or sought to breach, those promises. At this point, the Federal Trade Commission (FTC) became involved – not in the role of a data privacy regulator, but rather in its role as a consumer protection regulator. The justification for the FTC's involvement was that the breach of privacy policies by companies was a breach of their consumer protection obligations. As a result, the FTC became the de facto regulatory body for website data privacy, by virtue of its ability to enforce what websites had, up to that point, considered to be merely self-regulatory and non-legally binding policies.[69]

Rights and Liabilities

In some circumstances, government may choose not to regulate directly through a command-and-control scheme, but rather to seek to change the behaviour of those whom it wishes to regulate by the granting of rights to other parties.[70] An example of this type of regulatory strategy can be seen

---

68 See, eg, Thorsten Held and Wolfgang Schulz, *Regulated Self-regulation as a Form of Modern Government*, 2004, Eastleigh: University of Luton Press.
69 See Steven A Hetcher, 'The de facto Federal Privacy Commission' (2000) 19 John Marshall J of Comp & Info Law 109.
70 Baldwin and Cave, op cit, pp 51–3.

See Chapter 5 → in the **Data Protection Act 1998**. Under the Act, data subjects are granted rights that are enforceable against data controllers. These include rights to:

- know if the data controller holds personal data on them and to have access to that personal data;
- prevent data processing that is likely to cause damage or distress; and
- prevent data processing for the purposes of direct marketing.

If his or her rights are breached, the data subject may, in certain circumstances, take legal action against the data controller to:

- enforce subject access rights;
- obtain compensation from the data controller for damage or distress caused by reason of any contravention by a data controller of any of the requirements of the Act; and
- obtain rectification, blocking, erasure, and destruction of inaccurate data about them.

Granting these rights to data subjects potentially has a twofold effect, as follows.

- It involves the data subject in the regulatory process, in as much as it gives him or her the power to generate information that both he or she and the ICO can use to ensure that data controllers are in conformity with the law – that is, in principle, it encourages the education of the user with regard to the processing of his or her personal data and increases the oversight capability of the regulator.
- It places an economic deterrent upon the data controller: 'The deterrent effect will be the quantum of expected damages multiplied by the probability of those damages being inflicted.'[71] Thus, if a data controller were to have an insecure computer system that could allow hackers to steal 10,000 data subjects' financial information at an average cost of £100 per subject, then the deterrent effect would be:

$$10{,}000 \times £100 \times \text{Probability of being hacked}$$

The higher the risk, the more likely the data controller is to invest the money to secure the system if it will be cheaper than paying compensation. In this case, because the probability of hacking is 100 per cent (or '1'), the maximum investment would be:

$$10{,}000 \times £100 \times 1 = £1 \text{ million}$$

In practice, as intimated in the earlier discussion, the grant of rights to data subjects under the **DPA 1998** has largely failed to achieve the regulatory goals.

The right of subject access is underutilised, for which there are a variety of possible explanations. It may be that the majority of data subjects have insufficient knowledge to use the process, have insufficient incentive to use what is often perceived as an unnecessarily bureaucratic process, or simply do not believe that the data controller will provide useful information. A data subject is often starting from a position of insufficient information: he or she does not know that a data controller's processing is flawed, because he or she has not made a subject access request – but he or she has no obvious reason to make that request, because he or she has no reason to believe the processing is flawed until something goes wrong. Data controllers may also make the process more difficult through obscure procedures and delaying tactics. Because data subjects do

---

71 Ibid, p 51.

not generally make subject access requests, which would expose data protection failings, the ICO loses a useful potential source of information and data controllers have less incentive to comply with the law.

The right to bring legal action against data controllers for failure to comply with the Act, or for causing damage or distress, is also rarely used. Reasons for this may include the facts that the costs of bringing a legal action are prohibitive in itself or that the costs of losing a case will significantly outweigh the likely gains if the case is won. Often, in cases involving misuse of personal data, it may be hard to prove causation for particular damage or stress, or that the damage or stress was significant to an individual. An aggregate loss of 10,000 data subjects' personal data records may be a major breach of the Act, but each individual loss suffered may still be *de minimis* with regards to grounding a successful legal action. This means that the economic deterrent for a data controller will be very weak.

Co-regulation

The division of regulatory strategy into discrete categories, while useful for theoretical discussion of particular regulatory techniques, is less helpful when engaging in actual regulation. The regulatory problem is not, in practice, a stark choice between the big stick of command-and-control regulation and the vagaries of self-regulation – an argument described by Ayres and Braithwaite as 'a debate between those who favor regulatory shotguns and those who favor no guns at all'.[72] The level of this debate between these two regulatory extremes can, on occasion, foster the presumption that the two regulatory extremes of government regulation and pure self-regulation are mutually exclusive – that is, entirely opposing mechanisms that are impossible to reconcile or amalgamate.[73] The reality is that discussing types of regulatory practice in terms of 'strict' command and control, or 'pure' self-regulation clearly oversimplifies the complex reality of the real world, in which circumstances will often necessitate the use of a mix of regulatory techniques in order to achieve an effective solution. Command-and-control legislation is located at one extreme; at the other is pure self-regulation. In fact, even these extremes are, in practice, often ameliorated by elements drawn from other parts of the spectrum. As Brownsword has commented: 'smart regulators know that traditional command and control interventions, however tempting to politicians, are not always an effective or efficient form of response';[74] instead, a regulatory 'mix' is needed and the task for a regulator becomes one of selecting the appropriate point on the regulatory continuum for the activity in question.[75]

An approach that combines different categories of regulatory practice may be described as 'co-regulation' – although the use of this term, like 'self-regulation' itself, varies between authors. For example, Prosser argues (in the context of the **EU Audio-visual Directive**) that the use of the term 'co-regulation' allows a recognition not only of a continuum of regulatory approaches, but also of a mix of regulatory regimes that can take account of differing contextual factors including, for example, issues of effective enforcement.[76] Consideration of the UK data protection regulatory framework, premised on the **DPA 1998**, shows that although many of its provisions fall within the 'command and control' paradigm, it clearly contains several other regulatory elements, not least an attempt to utilise a rights and liabilities-based approach. The limited powers granted to the ICO have resulted in a very different regulatory stance from that of other EU privacy commissioners,

---

72 Ayres and Braithwaite, op cit, p 157.
73 For further discussion on this point, see, eg, Darren Sinclair, 'Self-regulation versus command and control? Beyond false dichotomies' (1997) 19(4) Law & Policy 529, 530–3.
74 Brownsword, op cit, p 3.
75 See Sinclair, op cit.
76 Prosser, op cit, p 111.

some of whom have significantly greater rule-making, audit, and penalty-imposing powers. The ICO's approach has been characterised by light-touch regulation, heavy emphasis on the education of data controllers, and a focus on cooperative problem-solving with data controllers and data subjects. This has resulted in the development and implementation of proactive data privacy protective processes, such as privacy impact assessments (PIAs) and 'privacy by design' planning, which have been slower to be adopted elsewhere in the European Union. It has also seen a growth in the use of social-based strategies, such as 'name and shame'. To quote Prosser:

> . . . even where regulation ostensibly takes the form of command and control, the reality has been shown to involve extensive negotiation between regulators and those they regulate, either through consultation when rules are made or even more importantly through selective enforcement in which rules are enforced not as binding orders but as the basis for negotiation to achieve reasonable results.[77]

The 'self-regulatory' model of the IWF can also be seen to lean heavily on what appear to be elements of command and control, or shades of enforced self-regulation. Without those elements – that is, if it were a 'pure' self-regulatory regulator – the IWF's regulatory activity would be much less likely to be perceived as a necessary service by its membership. That would significantly diminish its ability, via the provision of that service, to effectively control the availability of illegal content within the UK.

Both the data protection regulatory framework and the IWF 'self-regulatory' model also attempt to involve the public and public-interest groups in the regulatory process, with varying degrees of success. The former's primary process for public involvement, the principle of 'subject access', is an inefficient (and arguably ineffective) means of involving the public in the regulatory process; the latter has yet to overcome effectively the problems of legitimacy in regard to the transparency of its administrative and decision-making functions, and the public scrutiny of its actions. However, regardless of their weakness, they still embody an assumption that public participation is a required element in their particular regulatory strategies.

Looking Forward (and Backward and Sideways)

It is instructive when approaching a new area of law – whether IT law, environmental law, or any of the other numerous subjects available in the modern law school curriculum – to consider not only what the law in that area used to be, and what it is now, but why it has developed in that way. Such an analysis needs to consider not only the context surrounding the subject matter of the law, but also the contemporary regulatory context: the regulatory options available to legislators and regulators.

For example, the UK current data protection law is an artefact not only of the social, political, and technological context in which the **Data Protection Directive** and the resulting **DPA 1998** were forged, but also of historical approaches in the European Union and UK to regulatory strategy. As a result, if we were to seek today to develop a wholly new data protection framework, it would undoubtedly look very different from that which currently exists, even if it were still to reflect the same fair information practice principles that have underpinned data protection laws around the world since the 1970s. Our social attitudes towards privacy may have changed; the political balance between privacy and other interests, such as commerce or openness, may have shifted; the

---

77 Ibid, p 101, citing Keith Hawkins, *Law as Last Resort: Prosecution Decision-making in a Regulatory Agency*, 2002, Oxford: Oxford University Press.

technologies in use have certainly changed: all of these factors would undoubtedly influence the nature of the law. What is also clear, however, is that there is an increasing range of regulatory possibilities available to today's legislators and regulators, and that there is, through practice and research across a range of fields, considerably greater understanding of how such strategies might be combined to produce a more flexible, efficient, and effective regulatory regime.

Regulatory theory and practice has developed apace since the early days of IT law, and innovation is not unique to this area of law. This means that, as we look to develop the IT law of the future, we need not only to consider the historical lessons derived from the successes and failures of past and present IT-related laws, but also to cast our net wider and to consider what lessons can be learned from current regulatory theory, and from current practice in other developing areas of law.

Chapter 2

Regulatory Competence over the Internet

Chapter Contents

Introduction

Before answering the question of how online activity is, or should be, regulated, the first question is *who* – that is, which state – has, or should have, an entitlement to do so?[1] In most other legal contexts, the answer is too obvious to require further thought: where an activity falls within the territory of only one state, it is that state which regulates it. On an international level, states are the main players sharing regulatory space between them and each state has regulatory control over its respective territory. The internet complicates this otherwise simple allocation rule, because online activity seems to occur everywhere and nowhere in particular. The question then is which state has the right to regulate that site or online activity? The underlying generic issue is by no means new: competence over transnational activity to national regulators has been allocated for centuries. In the more recent past, transnational trade by transnational corporations, transnational environmental pollution, international travel, and migration have all had to be accommodated within national legal regimes. Yet the explosion of online activity has added a new level of acuteness to the inherent conflict between transnational activity and national law – and this issue of deciding who has competence over what affects the whole spectrum of online activities and attached legal concerns. The regulatory palette that has triggered primary questions of regulatory entitlement is wide – ranging from criminal or regulatory law on pornographic, gambling, pharmaceutical, banking, and terrorist sites, to civil law disputes concerning online defamation, contracts, and intellectual property rights.

Undisputedly, states have a right to regulate sites hosted on their territory. The controversial issue is to what extent states can regulate foreign sites. States have an interest in doing so, because foreign sites have an effect on their territories, which is often in no way distinguishable from that of local sites. But can they regulate them? Principally, yes – but as the discussion below shows, the precise answers to that question (found in national and international competence rules) vary depending, for example, on the civil or criminal nature of the dispute, or the type of dispute. What also becomes clear is that states across the regulatory board have been determined to accommodate online activity within traditional legal frameworks. They have rejected the early proposition by some academics that the internet should be treated as a space apart and that online activity is beyond their regulatory control.[2] This proposition was made (and persuasively so) because online activity appears to defy the sensible sharing of regulatory space between state regulators. As online activity appears to occur everywhere to the same degree, no one state seems more strongly linked to it than any other state and thus no state can make out a regulatory claim superior to that of any other state. Either it is no state or all states that can regulate any online activity, and this in turn would lead to unacceptable under-regulation or unacceptable over-regulation of the online world. Although states have principally 'voted' for the latter option, the regulatory concurrency to which it gives rise is highly problematic. Can website providers really be expected to comply with hundreds of sets of different laws simultaneously, and what are the means, if any, that states have at their disposal to force foreign content providers to comply with their laws? These are not simply academic questions, but have been serious concerns for governments, online actors, and civil society, as well as academics, across the globe.

If applying traditional location-centric state law to online activity is wrought with difficulties and does not really fit the bill, why have states not simply relinquished control over the internet, as suggested by those early academics? Despite the obvious attractions of the hands-off proposition, surrendering regulatory competence over online activity to a global body or, as some suggested, to

---

1 See generally Uta Kohl, *Jurisdiction and the Internet: Regulatory Competence over Online Activity*, 2007, Cambridge: Cambridge University Press. See also Jonathan L Zittrain, *Jurisdiction*, 2005, New York: Foundation Press.
2 David R Johnson and David Post, 'Law and borders: The rise of law in cyberspace' (1996) 48 Stan L Rev 1367.

the online community itself has been unacceptable to states.[3] The reason for this is that it would significantly undermine their authority within their territory more generally. By not regulating online activity, the regulation of the equivalent offline activity would also be compromised. For example, if a state prohibits the sale of a particular drug because of concerns about its safety, this prohibition is undermined generally if people of that state can freely acquire that forbidden drug from an online store. The prohibition loses its force and credibility. Critics of the current regime may assert that this is often precisely the case today, even though states have not relinquished control over the internet. Suffice to say at this stage, while states have limited success in enforcing their prohibitions against foreign online content providers, it appears that the political costs of not even attempting to do so would be too great.[4] Although the problems of deciding who should regulate what online activity are as alive today as they were in the mid-1990s, there is no doubt today that, for the time being, states and their traditional legal institutions are the main regulators. For the foreseeable future at least, online regulation lies within state law and not beyond it.

Substantive Legal Harmonisation

Related to the above internet debate on uniform non-state rules is the debate on uniform state rules in the form of substantive legal harmonisation. Online publications are not, by default, limited to one state; by default, they are global. Is it not imperative that these global publications are governed by one global set of rules – both for the sake of online publishers and users, as well as that of the national regulators? Currently, the same publications may attract very different legal status in different states – ranging from being perfectly legal, to being subject to civil sanctions or even criminal prosecutions. Like beauty, legality and crime is in the eye of the beholder. What may be criminalised terrorist activity under the laws of one state may, in the eyes of another state, be entirely legal political or religious speech. Conversely, what may in one state be a reasonable exercise of the right to free speech may amount to criminalised seditious or blasphemous speech under the laws of another state.[5] Such legal divergence creates huge theoretical and practical problems for users and regulators.

Of course, strong divergence is not present across the regulatory board. States are broadly in agreement in respect of significant areas of criminal activity aimed at the protection of the person and property. Such relative consensus explains why the European Council **Convention on Cybercrime** (Budapest, 2001) could be agreed upon in record time by international standards.[6] By limiting its ambit to matters such as hacking, viruses, fraud, child pornography, and copyright, the Convention covers relatively 'safe' subject matters – 'safe' in terms of international consensus. Differences of opinion emerge in areas of regulation designed to protect the stability of the government and political order, but regulatory divergence is most pronounced in respect of those rules

---

3 With the possible exception of the Internet Corporation for Assigned Names and Numbers (ICANN), which has the authority to coordinate the internet's global naming system and oversees certain domain name/trade mark disputes globally, and is a private, not-for-profit corporation, although it operates under the authority of a number of 'understandings' with the US Department of Trade.

4 Some research appears to suggest significant popular support for tighter restrictions of the internet. According to *The Independent on Sunday* (Media, 8 June 2008, p 11): '90 per cent of people want tighter regulation on social networking sites, according to research.'

5 The most notorious example is the controversy caused by the cartoon featuring the Prophet Muhammad in a Danish newspaper in 2005 and its subsequent publication on YouTube. Viewed as legitimate political debate on criticism of Islam and self-censorship in Denmark, the cartoon was violently decried in the Muslim world, leading to attacks on Danish embassies and Muslim leaders offering rewards to anyone who killed the cartoonist.

6 Marc D Goodman and Susan W Brenner, 'The emerging consensus on criminal conduct in cybercrime?' (2002) 10 UCLA J L & Tech 139, 177ff. For another area of consensus, see the 2003 World Health Organisation (WHO) Framework Convention on Tobacco Control – esp Art 13(4)(e) on tobacco advertising on different media, including the internet.

that seek to protect the moral fabric of society.[7] Thus, for example, hate speech had to be put into the Additional Protocol to the Convention[8] to pre-empt it from undermining its success as a whole.

The existence and absence of an international legal consensus is crucial for the competence debate. Where states take a relatively harmonised approach to the regulation of a particular online activity (whether this is formally reflected in a treaty or not), the competence question is of much lesser significance.[9] Each state, by regulating activity originating on its territory, effectively also upholds the laws of all other states in so far as that activity may have had an impact on those states.[10] Conversely, where states insist on their different laws, it matters very much how exactly online activity is 'shared out' between states – with each state trying to get as big a slice as possible. Inevitably, the cases that have given rise to competence disputes are those in which the laws of states vary strongly. For the moment, the point to be stressed is that substantive legal harmonisation and effective competence regimes present alternative answers to globalisation generally, and internet transnationality more specifically. Although substantive legal harmonisation appears instinctively the superior and natural option to internet governance, it has its problems. Apart from the practical and political difficulties of achieving it, it comes at a high price: states would have to surrender their distinct legal systems, reflecting distinct cultural, political, and social values, in favour of a one-size-fits-all legal order. And at least for the time being, legal diversity seems a good worthy of retention.

Competence under Public and Private International Law

The rules that allocate regulatory control in the transnational setting are rules of jurisdiction. 'Jurisdiction' (deriving from the Latin *juris dictio*, meaning the 'administration of justice') refers in its broadest sense to a state's right to regulate persons, property, and events. The rules that govern the right to regulate have broadly two provenances. On the one hand, the jurisdictional rules of public international law govern the rights of states to impose criminal or regulatory sanctions on transnational or extraterritorial activity and actors.[11] On the other hand, the rules of private international law or conflicts of law govern private or civil transnational disputes. These latter rules are not international, but ordinary national law, and thus vary from state to state, unless, of course, harmonised in a regional or international treaty. These sets of competence rules for civil matters, on the one hand, and criminal matters, on the other, are contained within separate legal disciplines despite a number of basic commonalities.[12]

The broad agenda underlying both regimes is arguably similar. They lay down rules to determine when a state or legal system is sufficiently *closely linked or connected* to a transnational event, person, or dispute so as to make it fair to give the state regulatory control. More specifically, first, with focus on the interests of states, the rules aim at the *juste partage de souveraineté* (the 'just sharing of control') between states, at the protection of states from interferences by other states, and overall internationally at an orderly and effective regulatory structure.[13]

---

7 Goodman and Brenner, op cit, 177–9.
8 Additional Protocol to the Convention on Cybercrime, concerning the Criminalisation of Acts of a Racist and Xenophobic nature committed through Computer Systems (Strasbourg, 2003).
9 For this reason, crimes covered by the Cybercrime Convention are not further discussed in this chapter. But see discussion in Chapter 4.
10 A residual question may be to what extent each state takes its responsibility of enforcing the harmonised area of law seriously.
11 The assumption is that when activity is purely within the territory of one state, no issue of jurisdiction arises – although implicitly it is the territoriality principle that grants regulatory power in such cases.
12 Only very few writers have examined both sets of rules. See, eg, Michael Akehurst, 'Jurisdiction in international law' (1972–73) 46 British Yearbook of International Law 145 and FA Mann, 'The doctrine of jurisdiction in international law' (1964) 111 Recueil des Cours 1 and 'The doctrine of international jurisdiction revisited after twenty years' (1984) 186 Recueil des Cours 9.
13 For an overview of the law on jurisdiction of states, including its objectives, see Bernard H Oxman, 'Jurisdiction of states', in Rudolf Bernhardt (ed), *Encyclopaedia of Public International Law, Vol 10*, 1987, Amsterdam: North Holland Publishing Co, pp 277–8.

Second, both sets of rules aim at the fair and just treatment of individuals within these orders, protecting individuals from conflicting and compounding obligations. Ultimately both objectives must guide new legal developments in the allocation of regulatory power in either discipline. Importantly, particularly in the internet context, the strength of any link conferring regulatory entitlement must always be judged against potential concurrent links/claims. A link with an event that is so weak that it could also be relied upon by innumerable other states in the same instance is both theoretically and practically dubious. It would give rise to a high level of regulatory concurrency and thereby defeat the abovementioned aims – that is, the notion that regulation is most efficient when *divided or shared* between different regulators; the notion that individuals must be protected from overregulation. Thus the strength of a link is relative; it should be assessed vis-à-vis potentially competing links by other states or legal systems.

On a structural level, there also parallels. Both private and public international law distinguish between three types of regulatory activity requiring different competence rules: adjudicating, legislating, and enforcing – in line with the three arms of government.[14] The first type concerns the question of whether a state court has the right to adjudicate a dispute; in private international law, this is referred to as the 'jurisdictional inquiry' ('jurisdiction' in a more narrow sense than used above). The next question is whether a state has the right to 'legislate' in relation to a transnational event – that is, whether it can prescribe its substantive law to it, referred to in private international law as the 'choice-of-law inquiry'. In the civil context, the court of a state may have 'adjudicative jurisdiction' (that is, it can hear and determine the dispute), but not 'legislative jurisdiction' (that is, it may apply foreign law to it).[15] In contrast, in the criminal context, once a court has decided that it will hear a dispute, it will never apply foreign law to it; so adjudicative and legislative jurisdiction effectively collapse into one inquiry. Finally, the third type of regulatory activity refers to 'executive jurisdiction' – that is, whether the state can enforce the judgment or conviction against the defendant or accused. Unlike the former two inquiries, the rules under this heading grant extraterritorial competence to a state only very exceptionally. A state can never enforce its law on the territory of another state, such as by sending its police officers there, except with the consent of the other state. Enforcement jurisdiction is strictly territorial, or as Lombois put it colourfully: 'The law may very well decide to cast its shadow beyond its borders; the judge may well have a voice so loud that, speaking in his house, his condemnations are heard outside; the reach of the police officer is only as long as his arm . . . he is a constable only at home.'[16]

What gives a law or dispute a criminal rather than a civil character is that the state assumes responsibility over the rule's enforcement. Scarce public resources are diverted to the systematic monitoring and penalisation of certain behaviour by agents of the state, in contrast to the ad hoc enforcement of civil law, which is instigated and financed by the private parties to the dispute. The criminalisation or public regulation of activity reflects a value judgment by the state of the relative importance of the norms in question: the more important is compliance with a norm in question, the more likely it is that criminal sanctions will be preferred over civil ones to encourage such compliance.

Transnational Online Crime

Because the limits of regulatory competence in criminal matters are set by public international, law they are, at least theoretically, the same for all states. However, most rules of customary international

---

14 See Akehurst, op cit; also Luc Reydams, *Universal Jurisdiction: International and Municipal Legal Perspectives*, 2003, Oxford: Oxford University Press, pp 25ff.

15 Having said that, there is a homeward trend in the choice-of-law inquiry – ie courts asserting adjudicative jurisdictions often also assert that local, rather than foreign substantive law, is applicable to the case.

16 Claude Lombois, *Droit Pénal International*, 2nd edn, 1979, Paris: Daloz, p 536, cited in Pierre Trudel, 'Jurisdiction over the internet: A Canadian perspective' (1998) 32 The International Lawyer 1027, 1047.

law have blurry boundaries, and jurisdictional principles should be seen as no more than useful signposts.[17] Thus there is significant room for different interpretations by different states. Also, public international law is not routinely (and indeed rarely) mentioned by national courts as the source of the limits of competence in transnational criminal cases. Instead, courts, for example, in common law jurisdictions, rely – in order to decide on their right to hear a case – on the national legal maxim 'all crime is local' (unless there is specific statutory authority to the contrary) on the presumption against the extraterritorial effect of legislation.[18] But such national legal concepts cannot detract from the fact that they must ultimately be consistent with public international law, which delimits the criminal jurisdiction of states and a breach of which may give rise to a claim against the state by another state.

The jurisdictional rules under public international law specify when links between a person, property, or an event and a state are sufficiently strong to give the state regulatory power over that person, property, or event. In *Lotus*,[19] the seminal case on state jurisdiction, a French and a Turkish steamer collided on the high seas, resulting in the death of eight Turkish sailors and passengers. The issue was whether Turkey could institute criminal proceedings against a French lieutenant for his acts on the French ship, based on the effects of those acts on the Turkish steamer – which, according to international law, is an extension of Turkish territory. The Permanent Court of International Justice (PCIJ) upheld Turkey's right to do so:

> the first and foremost restriction imposed by international law upon a State is that . . . it may not exercise its power in any form in the territory of another State. In this sense jurisdiction is certainly territorial . . . It does not however, follow that international law prohibits a State from exercising jurisdiction in its own territory, in respect of any case which relates to acts which have taken place abroad . . . Such a view would only be tenable if international law contained a general prohibition to States to extend the application of their laws and the jurisdiction of their courts to persons, property and acts outside their territory . . . But this is certainly not the case under international law as it stands at present.[20]

So *Lotus* confirmed that while states are strictly prohibited from enforcing their laws on foreign territory (enforcement jurisdiction), they can attach legal consequences to extraterritorial events at least in principle (adjudicative/legislative jurisdiction). But to do so, they must bring the claim under one of the recognised links, or 'heads of jurisdiction'. How valuable that regulatory freedom over extraterritorial events is, when not coupled with enforcement power, may be questionable, but it certainly exists under customary international law.

So what are these recognised heads of jurisdiction under international law? The main heads are:

- the territoriality principle;
- the nationality principle;
- the protective principle; and
- the universality principle.

The principle most frequently relied upon by states to make regulatory claims over extraterritorial events is, somewhat surprisingly, the territoriality principle. This principle is the primary basis of

---

17 Reydams, op cit, 23ff.
18 Matthew Goode, 'The tortured tale of criminal jurisdiction' (1997) 21 MULR 411.
19 *The Case of the SS Lotus (France v Turkey)* (1927) PCIJ Reports, Series A, No 10.
20 Ibid, 18. In fact, the PCIJ asserts that states can always claim regulatory competence unless there was a restrictive rule to the contrary – a view not commonly accepted today.

state jurisdiction[21] and has, in the internet context, assumed the greatest significance. The territoriality principle – allowing a state to regulate what is or occurs on its territory – has, over the years, been adapted to accommodate the increasing incidence of activity spanning the territories of numerous states. Already, *Lotus* affirmed the legitimacy of the concurrent regulatory claims by the state in which a crime commenced (the subjective territoriality principle), as well as by the state, or *states*, in which it finished (the objective territoriality principle).

The Objective Territoriality Principle: The Destination Approach

The objective territoriality principle allows a state to regulate a foreign actor when the impact of his or her act is felt on the state's territory. As the PCIJ said in *Lotus*:

> it is certain that the courts of many countries, even of countries which have given their criminal legislation a strictly territorial character, interpret criminal law in the sense that offences, the authors of which at the moment of commission are in the territory of another State are nevertheless to be regarded as having been committed in the national territory, if one of the constituent elements of the offence, and more especially its effects, haven taken place there.[22]

This principle has gone through different incarnations under different labels: it underlies the concept of 'result' crime (versus 'conduct' crime) traditionally used by common law courts;[23] it provides the basis of the US 'effects doctrine' in the antitrust context in the 1970s to 1990s;[24] and it is, in the internet context, referred to as the destination or receipt rule (in contrast with the origin rule).[25] Common to all of these concepts or labels is the focus on the impact of a foreign act on the state's territory, which impact provides the basis for subjecting the foreign actor to the law of the land. In *Lotus*, this impact was the physical impact on the Turkish vessel; in the US antitrust cases, it was the intangible economic effect of the foreign cartels on the US market; in the online world, it is the impact of foreign websites accessible from the state. The problem of extending *Lotus* to non-physical effects is that innumerable states may be affected by the same foreign event, thus giving rise to innumerable concurrent regulatory rights by destination states, and this is precisely the competence dilemma caused by websites. The examples below illustrate the objective territoriality principle in the online context, the problems to which it gives rise, and the varying reasons why states have nevertheless relied upon it. Broadly speaking, states are charged with upholding the collective will of its citizens, safeguarding fundamental shared values of the community.[26]

Hate Speech: Upholding National Moral Values

The most well-known illustration of the destination approach is provided by the French case *LICRA & UEJF v Yahoo! Inc & Yahoo France*.[27] In *Yahoo*, two French organisations – the League against Racism and

---

21 It is the primary basis in terms of quantity, but not necessarily being of a higher order – that is, a territorial connection with the to-be-regulated event does not trump a concurrent claim by another state based on the nationality of the offender.

22 SS Lotus, op cit, 23.

23 *DPP v Stonehouse* [1978] AC 55; *R v Treacy* [1971] AC 557; *R v Markus* [1975] 1 ALL ER 958; *Brownlie v State Pollution Control Commission* (1992) 27 NSWLR 78; *R v Toubya* [1993] 1 VR 226; cf *Air India v Wiggins* [1980] 2 All ER 593; discussed in Goode, op cit, 437ff.

24 AV Lowe (ed), *Extraterritorial Jurisdiction*, 1983, Cambridge: Grotius Publications. The difference between the effects doctrine and the objective territoriality principle, if there is one, is that the former appears to have no explicit requirement that the effects on the territory must be a 'constituent element' of the crime in question, although in fact this is invariably established and can be provided for by framing the offence appropriately.

25 Graham Smith (ed), *Internet Law and Regulation*, 4th edn, 2007, London: Sweet and Maxwell, pp 507ff. On German jurisprudence on 'Handlungs- und Erfolgsort' in the online context, see *Arzneimittelwerbung im Internet* (BGH, 30 March 2006, I ZR 24/03), [10].

26 Thomas Schulz, 'Carving up the internet: Jurisdiction, legal orders, and the private/public international law interface' (2008) 19 Eur J Intl L 799, 805.

27 *LICRA v Yahoo! Inc & Yahoo France* (Tribunal de Grande Instance de Paris, 22 May 2000), aff'd in *LICRA & UEJF v Yahoo! Inc & Yahoo France* (Tribunal de Grande Instance de Paris, 20 November 2000), available online at www.foruminternet.org/

Anti-Semitism (LICRA) and the French Jewish Students Union (UEJF) – sued Yahoo! Inc, a US corporation, and its French subsidiary for allowing surfers from France to buy Nazi artefacts from third parties via auction websites and other sites of Yahoo! Inc. While the action was in form a private action similar to a nuisance action,[28] in fact it was based on a 'manifest' violation of the **French Criminal Code** – that is, the prohibition on distributing Nazi memorabilia. Thus the action cannot easily be characterised as either private/civil or public/criminal, and thus whether the jurisdictional limits under public international law apply is debatable.[29]

The problem with the French action concerning the yahoo.com website (as opposed to the yahoo.fr site) was that the site seemed so much more clearly connected with the USA than with France: it was set up and maintained by a US corporation on a server situated in the USA, and it was in English with the vast majority of its users coming from the USA. So should this site not be governed exclusively by US law, where distributing Nazi memorabilia is legal? The Paris court disagreed: it held that because 'harm was suffered on the territory of France' by virtue of the site's accessibility in France, French law was applicable (whatever other law may also govern it). The fact that Yahoo! Inc operated a separate .fr site dedicated to French surfers and complying with French law did not relieve it of any accountability under French law in respect of its .com site. Because that latter site was also accessible in France, it also had to comply with French law.

Once it is decided that the foreign law is applicable to a site, the next question is how the site could comply with it. If Yahoo! Inc were to comply with French law by removing all material offending French law from its site (as it was not required to do, but in fact did), all users worldwide would also be subjected to the legal standards of France. So, for example, all US users of yahoo.com would forgo the benefits of the more lenient US law on hate speech. If the French approach to extending its laws to foreign online material based on the site's accessibility within the state were to be followed by other states (as in fact it is), Yahoo! Inc would also have to remove material offending the laws of Mongolia, China, Saudi Arabia, and so on. Yahoo! Inc could only operate the site legally by removing all material illegal worldwide – that is, by complying with the most restrictive law or the highest common legal denominator.[30] Not surprisingly, regulatory claims by destination states have been criticised for a number of reasons.

(1) They impose a too high and unrealistic regulatory burden on individual and corporate online publishers.
(2) The superimposition of one state's law on all other states amounts to strong censorship and deprives the online community of valuable content (or would do so if it were effective). Bland content would be all that is left.
(3) If all states were entitled to regulate all online activities, regulatory space would no longer be shared between states – a theoretically unsatisfactory outcome because it is contrary to the aims of the competence regime.

Avoiding some of these criticisms, the French court ordered what is in fact the only alternative compliance strategy: it ordered Yahoo! Inc to prevent access to the artefacts and hate speech sites in question from French territory.[31] By avoiding contact with French territory, Yahoo! Inc could not fall foul of French law. While it was initially disputed whether Yahoo! Inc was technically capable of

---

28 Articles 808 and 809 of the New Code of Civil Procedure.
29 As illustrated by the divergent judicial assessments in *Yahoo! Inc v LICRA & UEJF* 433 F 3d 1199 (9th Cir 2006).
30 Conflicts can generally be resolved by the site provider adopting the highest common legal denominator – ie the most restrictive law. Only rarely would it be impossible for a content provider not to comply with two or more sets of laws simultaneously, which would be the case only if one law were to forbid what another law demands.
31 Backed by a penalty of 100,000 francs per day for non-compliance. There were also orders against Yahoo! France to remove 'negationist' index headings and links to 'negationist' sites, as well as to post a warning on fr.yahoo.com to any users that viewing 'negationist' websites is illegal and subject to penalties under French legislation.

identifying and excluding surfers from France,[32] an expert group concluded that it could do so. Even in 2000, website operators could identify the physical whereabouts of 70 per cent of their users and exclude them, and that, in addition to self-identification, was considered sufficient to comply with the French order. Today, geo-identification technology has advanced significantly and is often used for more specific commercial targeting of users from different states.[33] Such technology also enables website operators to seal their sites from being accessed from legally inhospitable states, although very few do so. But this alternative compliance strategy is also not unproblematic. Because it encourages the creation of territorially limited websites, content providers, consumers, and states would forgo all of the economic, social, and political benefits derived from uninhibited open transnational online communications. In the final analysis, *Yahoo* is a reminder that even where states make wide regulatory claims such as those of the French court, generally states cannot enforce these claims (discussed further below): Yahoo! Inc complied with the French order voluntarily without any real threat of French enforcement action.[34]

Yahoo made headlines at the time, but the same approach to competence has been adopted by many states in most criminal/regulatory law contexts. The German High Court, in *R v Töben*,[35] also adjudicated on the issue of online hate speech, also criminalised under German law. Frederick Töben, a German-born Australian citizen, published anti-Semitic material, denying the Holocaust, on his Australian site. While on holiday in Germany, he was arrested and charged with an offence under the **German Criminal Code**, inter alia, in respect of his website. The German Court claimed regulatory competence based on the objective territoriality principle: the offence had been completed in Germany by creating a real possibility of disturbing the public peace through the website's publication in Germany. Unlike the French court, the German Court made some attempt to show why Germany had a stronger claim than other states to apply its criminal laws to the foreign site, thereby avoiding the legal position that all states can regulate all sites. The Court held that, given the historic connection between the subject matter of the site and Germany, Germany was objectively closely linked to the site, and this link also meant that German users were clearly the intended and actual addressees of the site. However, whether this link between Germany and the site was indeed special is less clear when one considers that the site was in English and its subject matter of universal interest. Also it is doubtful whether a site by a self-appointed historian from a dubious Australian institute was indeed capable of having the effect – disturbing the public peace – required for the commission of the offence, in Germany;[36] in fact there was no evidence that anyone, other than the investigating police officer, had accessed the site from Germany. Thus the special link between Germany and the site, relied upon to claim competence, was more imaginary than real. Perhaps, the case, like *Yahoo*, was designed to set the legal record on internet behaviour straight.

Pornography: Protecting the Vulnerable

See Chapter 4 →

The despicability of child pornography is undisputed worldwide[37] and thus, in jurisdictional terms, not controversial. In contrast, 'normal' pornography has not proved

---

32 *LICRA & UEJF v Yahoo! Inc & Yahoo France* (Tribunal de Grande Instance de Paris, 11 August 2000).

33 Dan JB Svantesson, 'Borders on, or border around: The future of the internet' (2006) 16 ALBLJST 343 or 'Geo-location technologies and other means of placing borders on the "borderless" internet' (2004) 23 John Marshall J Comp & Info Law 101.

34 The most likely explanation for Yahoo! Inc's compliance is the bad publicity generated by the French litigation that seems to suggest that it tolerated anti-Semitic attitudes, which is likely to have affected its reputability and respectability.

35 *R v Töben* (BGH, 12 December 2000, 1 StR 184/00, LG Mannheim), (2001) 8 Neue Juristische Wochenschrift 624; discussed in Yulia A Timofeeva, 'Worldwide prescriptive jurisdiction in internet content controversies: A comparative analysis' (2005) 20 Conn J Int'l L 199, 206ff.

36 Irini E Vassilaki, 'Anmerkung' (2001) 4 Computer und Recht 262, 265.

37 See Art 9 of the European Council Convention on Cybercrime (Budapest, 2001), or the Optional Protocol to the Convention on the Rights of the Child on the Sale of Children, Child Prostitution and Child Pornography (2000). A borderline scenario in this area concerns computer-generated child pornography.

susceptible to regulatory agreement. There is room for disagreement: is it harmless entertainment for adults who should enjoy the autonomy and liberty to choose their pastimes without state inter-ference, or is it a practice exploitive of women that degrades and corrupts society, particularly its more vulnerable members? Even liberal societies disagree to what extent the rights of adults ought to be compromised to protect children, which is addressed differently by different states.[38] But again the transnational internet challenges this regulatory diversity: the danger is that either the more liberal regimes undermine the more restrictive ones, or, conversely, that the restrictive regimes set the tone for the rest of the world.

An example of the latter scenario was the German *CompuServe* case, one of the first cases causing an international outcry concerning the clash of state laws online. In 1995, German police raided CompuServe's German offices in an investigation concerning online pornography (some of it was said to contain child pornography). In response, CompuServe temporarily suspended all of its 200-plus newsgroups (hosted in the USA and accessible worldwide) for its 4 million users, because it was technically incapable of blocking only Germans. This caused controversy, because it effec-tively meant that if material could not be viewed in Germany, it could not be viewed anywhere.[39] Five years later, with the benefit of more advanced geo-identification technology, the French court in *Yahoo* was able to order territorially more select blocking and yet even that decision proved controversial.

Focus on the effects of foreign online activity on English soil provided the basis of the prosecu-tion in *R v Perrin*[40] against Perrin, a French director of a US company operating a US-hosted pornog-raphy website. Perrin, resident in the UK, was convicted of the offence of publishing an obscene article contrary to the **Obscene Publications Act 1959** in relation to the freely accessible preview site of his pornography subscription site. He appealed on the basis that the site had been uploaded on a server abroad and that jurisdiction should only lie with the state in which the 'major steps' in relation to the publication were taken.[41] He argued that applying English obscenity standards extra-territorially – that is, to his foreign site – would be inconsistent with his right to freedom of expres-sion under the **European Convention of Human Rights (ECHR)**. The Court of Appeal rejected that sites could only be regulated by the state from which they originated, as this would encourage online publishers to go forum-shopping for the most lenient legal standards. The Court, like those in *Yahoo* and *Töben*, defended the application of English law to the site on the basis that the site was accessible in England – although again there was no evidence as to whether it was actually accessed in England other than by the Metropolitan Police. Because Perrin was resident in England and admitted responsibility for the publication, it might equally have been argued that the offence had commenced in England and that, contrary to Perrin's argument, the 'major steps' towards the publi-cation had in fact been taken in England. Indeed, in the earlier case of *R v Waddon*,[42] the Court of Appeal implicitly foreshadowed that possibility when it stated that a separate 'publication' for the purposes of s 1(3) the **Obscene Publications Act 1959** occurs when a defendant uploads obscene

---

38 Karsten Bremer, *Strafbare Internet-Inhalte in International Hinsicht: Ist der Nationalstaat wirklich überholt?*, 2001, Frankfurt am Main: Peter Lang Verlag, available online at http://ub-dok.uni-trier.de/diss/diss60/20000927/20000927.pdf, pp 134ff, noting the different emphasises placed in different societies on protecting the moral fabric of society, on the one hand, or vulnerable actors or viewers, on the other hand, in the context of obscenity regulation.

39 In 1998, CompuServe's local manager in Germany, Felix Somm, was convicted under German obscenity laws in relation to CompuServe's Usenet newsgroups, hosted in the USA and accessible in Germany, and received a two-year suspended sentence. His conviction was overturned on appeal, because there was no blocking technology available to CompuServe: *R v Somm* (Amtsgericht München, 17 November 1999). See also discussion in Chapter 4.

40 [2002] EWCA Crim 747. Perrin's application to the European Court of Human Rights (ECtHR) – arguing that the UK regulation breached his right to freedom of expression – was rejected: *Perrin v UK* (ECHR 18 October 2005, No 5446/03). Similarly, in *Sheppard and Whittle* [2010] EWCA Crim 65, the Court held that people who use a server in another country to incite racial hatred in England and Wales can be liable under the Public Order Act 1986.

41 It appears that he admitted being a director and majority shareholder of one or more US companies involved in operating the website from the USA.

42 [2000] All ER (D) 502, [1999] Masons CLR 396.

material from England onto a foreign server (in addition to any 'publication' that occurs on downloading that material in England). Clearly, it would make no sense to draw a distinction between taking the 'major steps' towards uploading a publication onto a foreign server and actually uploading the material onto such server. Thus, although Perrin was convicted based on the objective territoriality principle, the conviction could equally have been based on the subjective territoriality principle focusing on the location of the cause – rather than the location of the effect – of the criminal conduct.

Spam: Protecting the Network and its Players

Junk mail or 'spam' – that is, any unsolicited mail – is another area in which states have not been able to reach an international consensus, despite broad agreement on its general undesirability. Unsolicited email, even if not fraudulent, has very few characteristics to recommend itself. While it may provide a cheap avenue for marketing for some businesses, it is in fact the online community and other businesses that foot the bill of slow networks clogged up with junk mail. So many states have responded with anti-spam legislation,[43] but in so far as these legislative responses are substantively different the question is again: what is the territorial scope of each legislative response? Again, the problem is that a more restrictive anti-spam response by one state would be undermined by foreign spam that may be legal in the more lenient state from which it comes. Thus states are naturally inclined to interpret the territorial scope of their regulation widely to include such foreign spam. The same applies to harmonised regions, such as the European Union (EU), which also fear (and rightly so) that their regulation is compromised by illegal material penetrating the region.

In the EU, spam regulation is harmonised through Art 13(1) of the **Directive on Privacy and Electronic Communications 2002**,[44] which simply prohibits unsolicited commercial email –that is, email not previously consented to by the receiver – which is known as the 'opt-in rule'. Although the Directive does not explicitly touch upon the territorial scope of the opt-in rule, according to the European Commission, foreign spam is covered, given that the Directive applies to the processing of personal data in connection with the provision of publicly available electronic communication networks, and this – it is said – 'implies that . . . the provisions regarding unsolicited commercial communications apply to all communications received over public networks within the EU and should also be respected by senders of such messages established outside the EU but addressing recipients within the EU'.[45] This approach presents a U-turn to the one taken in the **Data Protection Directive 1995**, which only applies to data controllers who are either established within the EU or use equipment within the EU to process data[46] – and thus does not apply to any non-EU data

43 OECD Spam Taskforce, *Anti-spam Regulation*, 2005, DSTI/CP/ICCP/SPAM(2005)10/FINAL, available online at www.oecd.org/dataoecd/29/12/35670414.pdf, pp 29ff (on cross-border issues); International Telecommunication Union (ITU), *ITU Survey on Anti-spam Legislation Worldwide*, 2005, CYB/06, available online at www.gov.mu/portal/sites/spamweb/download/ITU%20Survey%20on%20Anti-Spam%20Legislation%20Worldwide.pdf. There are a number of memorandums of understanding and joint statements concerning the regulation of spam and providing for a commitment to cooperation: eg, between Australia and Korea, Thailand, the UK, the USA, and Canada. See also The London Action Plan on International Spam Enforcement Cooperation (February 2005), available online at www.londonactionplan.com/

44 Directive 2002/58/EC on Privacy and Electronic Communications, [2000] OJ L 201/37 implemented in the UK by the Privacy and Electronic Communications (EC Directive) Regulations 2003, SI 2003/2426; see reg 22.

45 European Commission, 'eCommunications: FAQs', available online at http://ec.europa.eu/information_society/policy/ecomm/site_services/faq/index_en.htm; Department for Business, Enterprise and Regulatory Reform (BERR), *Implementation of the Directive on Privacy and Electronic Communications*, March 2003, London: HMSO, available online at www.berr.gov.uk/files/file15097.pdf, p 15: 'Calls from overseas marketers have started to generate complaints; the Directive does not apply outside the EU.' See also Christopher Kuner, *European Data Protection Law: Corporate Compliance and Regulation*, 2nd edn, 2007, Oxford: Oxford University Press, pp 137ff.

46 Article 4 of the Data Protection Directive, 95/46/EC, is an example of the exclusive country of origin approach. To protect the privacy of individuals within the harmonised region effectively, the Directive extends its provisions to transfers of personal data to states outside the harmonised region by allowing such transfers only if the third state has adequate levels of privacy protection (Arts 25 and 26). See also further discussion in Chapter 5.

controller. An explanation for this change in EU policy may lie in the fact that, in 1995, the commercial use of the internet was still in its infancy and thus data protection within the EU was not perceived to be significantly threatened by any non-EU data controllers.

The same expansive territorial approach to spam regulation, in line with the objective territoriality principle, has also been taken elsewhere. Section 16 of the Australian **Spam Act 2003 (Cth)** prohibits unsolicited commercial electronic messages with an Australian link and, according to s 7, that link is established if the message originated or was commissioned in Australia or *originated outside Australia, but was accessed in Australia*. The US **Controlling the Assault of Non-Solicited Pornography and Marketing Act of 2003 (the CAN-SPAM Act)** does not prohibit unsolicited electronic messages per se, but customers must be given an opportunity to opt out of future messages, which is known as the 'opt-out rule'.[47] This applies to all commercial messages sent to a 'protected computer',[48] defined as any computer 'used in interstate or foreign commerce or communication, including a computer located outside the United States that is used in a manner that affects interstate or foreign commerce or communications of the United States'.[49] The overt focus in this instance is on the location of the effects of the message wherever its source; indeed, the USA goes jurisdictionally even further than the EU and Australia by purporting to regulate messages sent *and* received outside the USA, provided that those messages have an effect on US domestic or foreign commerce.

Because, in terms of substance, the European and Australian opt-in rule is more restrictive than the US opt-out rule, US online marketers would have to comply with the EU rules (and cannot take advantage of the more lenient US rule) in order to comply with both EU and US law, at the very least when they send commercial mail to customers in the EU. But can senders of email know where the recipients of their emails are located? While website operators, with the help of geo-identification technology, can identify and exclude surfers from unwanted territories (with relative high certainty) from accessing their sites, this is not the case for senders of email. Even if an email address has a country-specific domain – for example, aber.ac.uk – it cannot guarantee that this domain will correspond to the place where the email is accessed (which, as seen above, triggers the applicability of the law). Thus the only choice for spammers is to comply with all laws by complying with the most restrictive one, or, alternatively, not to comply with any laws – particularly foreign laws that cannot be enforced against them. The latter option would appear to be the rationally more defensible.

Gambling: Protecting National Economic Interests

Another area that has attracted significant regulatory activity after the commercialisation of the internet is online gambling. Again, regulatory responses have varied, ranging from outright prohibitions, to toleration, to positive encouragement. These variations have again created the danger that the toleration or encouragement of online gambling by one state undermines its prohibition in another.

Gambling, more than any other regulatory area of the internet, highlights another reason why states have so readily applied their national laws to foreign sites that affect their territory. On the one hand, gambling can have very positive economic repercussions for the state in which the gambling provider is established – through the creation of employment and through being a source of significant revenue from the profits made by the provider. These benefits are lost if the gambling services are provided by a foreign operator, which may also, to varying extent, undermine the local industry. On the other hand, gambling creates significant social and economic problems flowing from gambling addiction, and these may be exacerbated by foreign providers that are less regulated than

---

47 US CAN-SPAM Act of 2003, s 5(a)(4)(A). See also discussion in Chapter 5.
48 Ibid, s 5(a)(1),(3)(A),(4)(A) and (5); alternatively, see 15 US Code Annotated §7704.
49 18 US Code §1030(e)(2)(b).

local ones. Because foreign providers offer none of the advantages associated with gambling and all of its disadvantages, they have received significant regulatory hostility and aggressive jurisdictional responses by many states, such as the USA, but also Germany, Australia, Italy, the Netherlands, and New Zealand, all of which take a restrictive approach to gambling – with the notable exception of the UK (see below). In respect of the US attitude, one commentator succinctly summarised its background as follows:

> The fairly harsh approach to online gambling is a reversal of both the federal government's . . . receptivity to tribal gaming, and its acceptance of the recent liberalization of gambling laws in most US states. The fierceness . . . in this area is puzzling until one realises the one factor at stake in . . . traditional gambling, but not at stake in Internet gambling: Money. . . . Internet gambling, hosted by foreign operators, not only generates zero governmental revenue and zero jobs, it also threatens traditional gambling.[50]

There are several examples in which states have extended gambling restrictions to foreign online gambling providers, the USA being one of the foremost, as discussed further below. A Dutch court, in *National Sporttotaliser Foundation v Ladbrokes Ltd*,[51] ordered the defendant, Ladbrokes, based in England and Gibraltar, to make its gambling site inaccessible to Dutch residents because it did not comply with Dutch licensing requirements. Similarly, a German court found, in 2004, that an Austrian company breached German penal law by offering online sport-betting services in Germany without a local licence; its licence under Austrian law did not relieve it of any responsibility under German law.[52] Australia prohibits anyone, whether local or foreign,[53] from offering online gambling services to people in Australia by virtue of ss 8 and 15 of the **Interactive Gambling Act 2001 (Cth)**. However, local Australian providers are free to offer their gambling services to punters abroad.[54] Thus Australia seeks to obtain the benefits derived by gambling operators without any of its losses.

The New Zealand **Gambling Act 2003** also prohibits remote interactive gambling,[55] but – in contrast to the above states – that prohibition does not extend to 'gambling by a person in New Zealand conducted by a gambling operator located outside New Zealand'.[56] This creates the very real danger that foreign online providers undermine the prohibition applicable to local businesses. New Zealand addresses this problem by prohibiting local intermediaries (such as ISPs and local sites), but also offline publishers, from advertising foreign gambling services in New Zealand.[57] This approach is smart: instead of seeking to control local gambling through prohibitions on foreign gambling providers that are difficult to enforce, it targets local intermediaries (which may provide knowledge of, and access to, the foreign services) over which full enforcement power is present. Also, if the foreign gambling sites are not known or not easily used, then the likelihood of them being used is relatively small.

The provision of transnational online gambling services has also been at the centre of two free trade disputes: one at EU level and one at the level of the World Trade Organization (WTO). In both cases, the attempt by states to regulate gambling services offered by foreign online providers was

---

50 Christine Hurt, 'Regulating public morals and private markets: Online securities trading, internet gambling and the speculation paradox' (2005) 86 BUL Rev 371, 375ff.
51 (District Court, The Hague, 27 January 2003); see also *Holland Casino v Paramount Holdings et al* (District Court, Utrecht, 27 February 2003).
52 *Unzulässiges Online-Glücksspielangebot* (OLG Hamburg, 19 August 2004, 5 U 32/04), (2004) 12 Computer und Recht 925; following *Schöner Wetten* (BGH, 1 April 2004, I ZR 317/01).
53 Interactive Gambling Act 2001 (Cth), s 14: ' . . . this Act extends to acts, omissions, matters and things outside Australia.'
54 Unless the foreign country has been declared a 'designated country' (ss 15A, 9A, and 9B). As of May 2009, no country had been declared a 'designated country'.
55 Gambling Act 200, ss 9(2)(b) and 19.
56 Ibid, s 4 on the definition of 'remote interactive gambling'.
57 See ibid, s 16.

challenged as being inconsistent with free trade commitments. In the EU, gambling was specifically excluded from the **Electronic Commerce Directive**.[58] EU Member States were not comfortable with extending the Directive's origin rule (that is, that online service providers should only be regulated by their home state) to online gambling services – but then that origin rule exists already, at least to some extent, in the form of free trade commitments. In *Gambelli*,[59] in 2003, the European Court of Justice (ECJ) was presented with a challenge to Italy's attempt to impose criminal sanctions on Italian agencies that, contrary to local licensing requirements, acted as online intermediaries for the UK bookmaker Stanley International Betting Ltd. Effectively, Italy wanted to protect its very lucrative national monopoly in the sports betting and gaming sector. This protectionist policy was challenged as being an unjustified restriction on the freedom of establishment and freedom to provide services of foreign providers, contrary to Arts 49 and 56 of the Treaty on the Functioning of the European Union (TFEU). These freedoms demanded, it was argued, that Member States take a regulatory hands-off approach to gambling providers from other Member States and regulated by those other states. The ECJ held that Italy's criminal sanctions presented a restriction on the two freedoms and that those restrictions would only be justifiable 'for reasons of overriding general interest' – for example, if they were intended to reduce the incidence of gambling. A fear of losing revenue did not justify restrictions on foreign operators. Thus EU free trade commitments do not categorically prevent Member States from seeking to regulate foreign gambling providers. States can extend their laws to online providers from other EU states, but only for legitimate, non-economic reasons, rather than as protectionist policies.

The WTO Appellate Body had to decide similar issues and came to a similar conclusion in *United States: Measures Affecting the Cross-Border Supply of Gambling and Betting Services*.[60] Antigua and Barbuda lodged a complaint against the USA with the WTO in 2003, alleging that the US prohibition on the cross-border supply of gambling and betting services was inconsistent with 'market access' commitments made by the USA under Art 16 of the **General Agreement on Trade in Services (GATS)**. Antigua blamed the increasingly aggressive US strategy (enforced with the help of local US intermediaries) towards the operation of cross-border gaming activities in Antigua for the significant decline of gambling operators in Antigua: ' . . . from a high of up to 119 licensed operators, employing around 3,000 and accounting for around 10 per cent of GDP in 1999, by 2003 the number of operators has declined to 28, employing fewer than 500.'[61] The WTO Appellate Body rejected the US claim that by excluding sporting services from its **GATS** commitments, it had also excluded gambling and betting services, and held that various US Acts were inconsistent with its **GATS** commitments. However, as in *Gambelli*, the Appellate Body held that 'public moral' or 'public order' may exceptionally justify market access barriers, provided that there were no other reasonable alternative measures. However, in this case, the USA could not rely on these exceptions, because it had exempted domestic providers from the very restrictions and prohibitions that it sought to apply to foreign providers. Its fair trade commitments prevented the USA from imposing restrictions on foreign providers solely as a protectionist measure to safeguard the local industry, rather than as a regulation designed to reduce the incidence of gambling. A similar complaint against the USA was

---

58 Recital 16 and Art 1(5)(d) of the Electronic Commerce Directive, 00/31/EC, [2000] OJ L178/1.

59 *Criminal Proceedings against Piergiorgio Gambelli* C-243/01 [2003] ECR I-13031. In *Criminal Proceedings against Massimiliano Placanica and ors* C-338/04, C359/04 and C-360/04 [2007] ECJ ECR I-0000, it was again held that Italy's licensing regime, which excluded companies listed on a stock exchange from tendering for a betting licence, violated the freedom of establishment and the freedom to provide services, because it went beyond what is necessary to achieve the objective of preventing the exploitation of the industry for criminal proposes.

60 *United States: Measures Affecting the Cross-Border Supply of Gambling and Betting Services*, first heard by the WTO Dispute Settlement Panel (WTO Panel, 10 November 2004, WT/DS285/R), and then by the Appellate Body (WTO Appellate Body, 7 April 2005, WT/DS285/AB/R). In 2007, the WTO panel concluded 'that the United States has failed to comply with the recommendations and rulings of the DSB in this dispute' (WTO Panel, 30 March 2007, WT/DS285/RW), which paved the way for a compensation claim and then trade sanction by Antigua. See online at www.wto.org/english/tratop_e/dispu_e/cases_e/ds285_e.htm

61 Ibid (WTO Panel, 10 November 2004, WT/DS285/R), [3.5].

lodged in 2007, by the Remote Gambling Association with the European Commission, which came to a very similar conclusion to the WTO Panel.[62]

Pharmaceutical Sales: National Safety Concerns

In many states, abortions are illegal or restricted. Post-internet, such restrictions matter less: women can go online and, for example, womenonweb.org supplies – after an online medical consultation with a doctor – the pills that allow them to have a relatively safe abortion at home. In 10 per cent of the cases, complications that require surgical procedures develop.[63] Whether you think the wrong lies with the state that prohibits abortions, or the woman who wants an abortion, or the online provider that provides them, for competence purposes, this scenario illustrates another reason why states often seek to apply their regulation to all locally accessible sites, whether originating at home or not. Although, not unlike in gambling, the pharmaceutical industry raises high financial stakes, most states take a keen regulatory interest in the marketing and sale of drugs, and the provision of medical procedures, in order to protect their residents. Of course, at times, as in the case of abortion, regulation is also designed to protect the moral stance of the particular society. In either event, evasion of such legal restrictions through the easy resort to foreign online suppliers makes local law a laughing stock.

Even within the legally relatively homogenous EU, the origin approach to competence as underlying the free-movement-of-goods concept and as introduced by the **Electronic Commerce Directive**[64] specifically for the online context has been challenged in respect of the trans-EU online drug supply. In *Deutscher Apothekerverband eV v 0800 Doc Morris NV*,[65] an injunction against an online Dutch pharmacy in respect of its supply of certain drugs in Germany, contrary to the German legal requirement of presence sales (that is, that certain drugs can only be sold in pharmacies), was challenged as being inconsistent with the internal market rule of free movement of goods. The ECJ held that because the 'presence sales' requirement was only justified for prescription drugs in relation to which confusion over language or labelling could lead to harmful consequences, but not to over-the-counter (OTC) drugs, the online sale of OTC drugs could not be restricted by the destination state. Since then, the **Electronic Commerce Directive** has come into force and, prima facie, the regulation of drugs is not excluded from the scope of the origin rule required by Art 3 (further discussed below).[66] Yet in *Arzneimittelwerbung im Internet*,[67] the question arose whether a Dutch site advertising and selling drugs to Germans had to comply with German licensing requirements even though the drugs were legal in the Netherlands. The German Federal Court held that the origin rule in the Directive was not applicable to national legal requirements concerning the *delivery* of goods,[68] and furthermore could be excluded if it fell within the exception in Art 3(4)(a)(i), the protection of public health.[69] Thus the application of German licensing requirements to the foreign Dutch site was legitimate. The Court further stated that a disclaimer that products will not be

---

62 European Commission, *Report to the Trade Barriers Regulation Committee: Examination Procedure concerning an Obstacle to Trade, within the Meaning of Council Regulation (EC) No 3286/94, consisting of Measures Adopted by the United States of America Affecting Trade in Remote Gambling Services* 10 June 2009, Brussels: EC.

63 CNN, 'Women buy pills online for "home abortions"', 11 July 2008, available online at http://edition.cnn.com/2008/HEALTH/07/11/abortion.pills/index.html?eref=edition_europe

64 Electronic Commerce Directive, 00/31/EC, Art 3(2).

65 *Deutscher Apothekerverband eV v 0800 Doc Morris NV* Case C-322/01 [2003] ECR I-14887.

66 See also Arts 1(5)(d) and 2(h) of the Electronic Commerce Directive, 00/31/EC.

67 *Arzneimittelwerbung im Internet* (BGH, 30 March 2006, I ZR 24/03), [27]–[30].

68 See Electronic Commerce Directive, 00/31/EC, Recital 21 and Art 2(h)(ii).

69 Consistent with the German marketing prohibition in accordance with Art 2(1) of the Advertising of Medicinal Products Directive, 92/28/EC, and Art 87(1) of the Community Code for Medicinal Products for Human Use Directive, 2001/83/EC (prohibition on the marketing of drugs for which there is no authorisation in accordance with Community law). Note, too, that Art 13(7) of the Framework Convention on Tobacco Control (Geneva, 2003) allows states to ban cross-border tobacco advertising (including advertising via the internet).

delivered to certain states would be effective to avert accountability under the laws of the excluded states – provided that the disclaimer was unequivocal and the provider did not act contrary to his stated intentions.

So even within the EU, which seeks to limit the regulatory claims of destination states in order to facilitate a single market, states have resisted or severely circumscribed it in areas such as gambling or pharmaceutical products, either to protect national fiscal interests or national perceptions of health and safety. Although the destination approach that allows states to apply local law to accessible foreign sites does achieve this in principle, in reality states can only enforce their laws against foreign providers with great difficulty. Providers in turn are subjected to so many compounding legal obligations that compliance becomes unrealistic. Realistically, online providers would have to forgo the benefits of foreign markets on the off-chance that their sites might be in conflict with the foreign rules because actually ascertaining the content of all of these rules would be an enormous task. This would not only be a loss for the providers, but also for states and the online community as a whole.

The 'Reasonable' Effects Doctrine: The Moderate Destination Approach

Whether the objective territoriality principle ought to be interpreted as to allow any state to assert regulatory control over foreign conduct based on any effects, however slight, of that conduct on the state's territory is disputable. In Lotus, the effect in question was physical, thus the number of potential regulators was circumscribed. Once intangible effects, such as economic ones, are allowed to justify competence, concurrency of regulation spirals exponentially, defeating in its wake the aims of the competence regimes. Yet this is precisely the dominant online position: on the whole, states assert the right to regulate every accessible site. Online providers are accountable to the wishes of hundreds of concurrent 'kings', ruling one and the same 'empire', but all expressing different wishes. In the end, the 'king' with enforcement power is the only one worth taking seriously.

However, states have not been entirely insensitive to the problem of concurrency. There have, in the past, been attempts to refine the objective territoriality principle – especially in the context of economic effects – in order to reduce the incidence of overlapping regulatory claims and to mitigate interferences by states in each other affairs.[70] A classic example of such attempts is the effects doctrine, as formulated in the US **Restatement (Third) of Foreign Relations Law of 1986** in response to the international disapproval of the wide antitrust claims made by the USA against foreign companies. Paragraph 403 of the Restatement states that 'a state may not exercise jurisdiction . . . with respect to a person or activity having connections with another state when the exercise of such jurisdiction is unreasonable'.[71] Whether such exercise is 'reasonable' is made dependent on a number of factors, such as the extent to which the activity has a substantial, direct, or foreseeable effect upon the territory, the character of the activity, the degree to which the desirability of regulation is generally accepted, the existence of justified expectations, the importance of regulating the activity, the consistency with traditions of the international systems, the interest of other states in regulating the activity, and the likelihood of conflicting regulation. This test is not easily implemented in any given situation, but in substance its aims are beyond reproach: it goes beyond merely seeking to uphold the state's authority over its territory and seeks to protect individuals, the interests of other states, and the coherence of the allocation system as a whole. Despite

---

70 Oxman, op cit, pp 277–8, on the objectives of jurisdictional rules under public international law.

71 See also Reydams, op cit, p 24: ' . . . applications of the principles to a specific problem will require further balancing of interest of the States involved and the requirements of justice. Moreover, in some cases the question will not be posed in terms of whether a State's claim to jurisdiction is illegal per se, but whether it is a proper exercise of jurisdiction, given the conflicting interests of two or more States as well as the consequences for the individual defendant.'

widespread approval of this moderated effects doctrine by states, academics, and judges at the time,[72] the above examples show that moderation, however rational and desirable, has not guided the internet competence debate. If that were the case, the question of whether the 'offending' foreign site is accessible from the would-be regulating state's territory would be replaced by the question of whether the foreign site has a substantial effect on that state's territory and whether that effect was foreseeable, or intended. A moderate effects test or destination rule would allow only those states that are specifically targeted by the foreign conduct to assert regulatory rights, rather than all states mildly affected.

Although the US Supreme Court later backtracked from the moderate or 'reasonable effects' test,[73] US competence jurisprudence is still infused with moderate rhetoric. Part of the reason is that the USA, unlike other states, treats adjudicative and legislative jurisdiction as two distinct inquiries even in criminal cases. Because adjudicative jurisdiction is generally based on the court's personal jurisdiction over the defendant, the 'due process' requirement under the US **Constitution** comes into play (discussed below). This in turn imports the requirement that the defendant must have purposefully (that is, knowingly) availed himself or herself of the privilege of conducting activity within the state, which, in relation to online activity, is established by evidence that the foreign site 'targeted' the state.[74] Thus the expansive objective territoriality principle gives way to a more moderate version that focuses on the substantiality of the effects of the foreign online activity – that is, the site – on the state.

For example, in *People v World Interactive Gaming Corp*,[75] the question was whether the state of New York could prohibit an Antiguan corporation licensed to operate a casino in Antigua from offering its online gambling services to New Yorkers. Because, in this case, the foreign company was in fact the wholly owned subsidiary (and, according to the court, the alter ego) of a local company that had total control over the unauthorised activities, personal jurisdiction by the court over both companies could easily be established based on their 'presence' within the territory.[76] However, the court also examined the nature and quality of the defendants' internet activities and concluded that New York territory had been targeted by their activities; amongst other things, they had 'engaged in an advertising campaign all over the country to induce people to visit their website and gamble. Knowing that these ads were reaching thousands of New Yorkers, respondents made no attempt to exclude identifiable New Yorkers from the propaganda'.[77] This approach is very different from that adopted by other states in criminal cases, in which states have rarely engaged with the *relative* strength of their claim – that is, to what extent their claim to regulate a site is in any way stronger than that of any other state; a specifically targeted state would clearly have a better claim to regulate a site than one that relies upon the site's mere accessibility in the territory. The French court in *Yahoo* never asked whether yahoo.com was specifically targeted at France, which would have been doubtful. Even in US jurisprudence in criminal cases, it is not entirely clear to what extent such targeting would be required, if it was not in fact present.[78] Currently, given the size of the US economy, the USA is a very attractive market for many internet businesses and thus the targeting element can in many suits easily be proven.

---

72 See, eg, Lowe, op cit, pp 207ff.

73 *Hartford Fire Insurance Co v California*, 509 US 764 (1993) confined the moderate approach to situations in which there is a true conflict between domestic and foreign law, which are very rare indeed.

74 The same approach is adopted in civil matters: see below 'US Traditional Rules on Personal Jurisdiction'.

75 714 NYS 2d 844 (1999) [emphasis added]. For other internet gambling cases, see: *US v Cohen* 260 F 3d 68 (2d Cir 2001); *State of Missouri v Coeur D'Alene Tribe* 164 F 3d 1102 (8th Cir. 1999); *State of Missouri v Interactive Gaming & Communications Corp* WL 33545763 (MoCir 1997); *State of Minnesota v Granite Gate Resorts Inc* 568 NW 2d 715 (Minn App 1997). See also American Bar Association, 'Achieving legal and business order in cyberspace: A report on global jurisdiction issues created by the internet' (2000) 55 The Business Lawyer 1801, available online at www.kentlaw.edu/cyberlaw/docs/drafts/draft.rtf, pp 144ff.

76 The parent company was, in fact, incorporated in Delaware, but because it operated its entire business from its corporate headquarters in New York, the court could rely on its actual physical presence to assert personal jurisdiction over it.

77 *People v World Interactive Gaming Corp* 714 NYS 2d 844, 849 (1999).

78 See above, eg, the US position on foreign spam.

Even in the USA, the targeting approach does not feature in respect of subject matter or legislative jurisdiction – that is, when it comes to deciding on the territorial scope of the substantive law – which would be the more important context for moderation as it determines the liability for the activities in question. In *People v World Interactive Gaming Corp*, the court – having to decide on the territorial scope of the New York gambling legislation – clearly endorsed the wide version of the objective territoriality principle: ' . . . under New York Penal Law, if the person engaged in gambling is located in New York, then New York is the location where the gambling occurred.'[79] Although the court relied on actual gambling activity in its territory via the foreign site, rather than the site's mere accessibility there, it did not insist that New Yorkers must have been a particular target of that site. The court stated that not regulating the site 'would immunize from liability anyone who engages in any activity over the Internet which is otherwise illegal in this state. A computer server cannot be permitted to function as a shield against liability, *particularly* in this case where respondents actively targeted New York as the location where they conducted many of their allegedly illegal activities'.[80] The term 'particularly' suggests that the court would have come to the same conclusion even if New York were not to have been targeted.

Finally, the targeting requirement also plays no part in cases in which courts do not rely on personal jurisdiction over the defendant to assert their right to hear the claim. An alternative basis is provided by in rem jurisdiction, whereby a court's adjudicative right is based on the fact that an object connected to the dispute or illegality is within its territory. Thus the formal defendant in the action is the object, not the person.[81] In rem jurisdiction provides a good testing ground for the reality of moderation in the regulatory assertions of the USA, given that, in in rem cases, the state has the actual physical power to enforce the court's judgment by seizing the object in question. Thus it would be all the harder to abstain from hearing a dispute in the name of lofty notions such as 'reasonableness' and 'moderation'. In *US v $734,578.82 in US Currency*,[82] the US government brought a civil in rem forfeiture action against local bank accounts used in the process of allegedly illegal gambling activity by a local corporation on behalf of an English gambling house, fully licensed in England. Most of its betting business, promoted through the internet and carried out via the telephone, derived from North American sports, and most customers came from Canada and the USA. Although this action was formally civil, in jurisdictional terms it would likely be categorised as 'criminal' or 'public', because the plaintiff was the government seeking to enforce indirectly a criminal prohibition on unauthorised gambling. The government asserted the right to seize the funds in these accounts because they were connected with illegal gambling activity – or, more specifically, 'promoting gambling' contrary to New Jersey law. The court accepted this and rejected that the foreign aspect of the case had in fact any bearing upon it:

> We therefore find no merit in Claimants' jurisdictional challenge to this *in rem* proceeding over New Jersey property based upon conduct occurring in New Jersey. It may well be true that British citizens and British companies will be affected by this *in rem* action in New Jersey. This does not mean that the law of New Jersey or the law of the United States is being applied to those citizens or companies.[83]

---

79 *People v World Interactive Gaming Corp*, 850.
80 Ibid [emphasis added].
81 *United States v US Coin and Currency* 401 US 715, 719 (1971): ' . . . the theory has been that if the object is "guilty", it should be held forfeit. In the words of a medieval English writer, "Where a man killeth another with the sword of John at Stile, the sword shall be forfeit as deodand, and yet no default is in the owner".' In *United States v Sandini* 816 F2d 869, 872 (1987): 'Civil forfeiture is an in rem proceeding. The property is the defendant in the case . . . The innocence of the owner is irrelevant – it is enough that the property was involved in a violation to which forfeiture attaches.'
82 286 F 3d 641 (3rd Cir, 2002).
83 Ibid 660.

As these British companies were the holders and beneficiaries of those accounts, it is disingenuous to deny that US law was being applied to them when their funds were seized. This case shows that, in *in rem* actions, there is less need to justify the extraterritorial application of a state's law on foreign conduct given that competence can be based (or can hide behind) the territorial application of the law to the local property that 'has done the wrong'.

The Subjective Territoriality Principle and the Exclusive Origin Approach

The subjective territoriality principle presents the other side of the coin of the territoriality principle. It allows states to assume competence over a crime commenced on their territory even if it takes effect elsewhere: the dead body lies on other shores. In the internet context, this translates into the uncontroversial position that states are entitled to regulate sites that are hosted on their territories (even if they are not accessible there) or sites that, although hosted elsewhere, are created by locals;[84] in either case, the cause or source or origin of the criminalised or regulated activity is within state borders. While the application of the subjective territoriality principle to the internet is undisputed, online providers have persistently argued that the subjective territoriality principle should be the only basis of establishing competence over online activity – to the exclusion of regulatory claims by destination states. Allowing exclusively the country of origin to govern online conduct has significant merits: online providers would only have to comply with one set of familiar laws, rather than innumerable foreign ones, and the origin states could easily enforce their claims, because such enforcement would be directed against local sites or providers.

How the 'origin state' is defined depends on the court or legislation in question; certainly there is no one single formula for the origin approach. It may focus on the location of the actor, the action, or any 'tools' used in the process. Especially in the corporate context, there is also the choice between the seat of the management of the company, the place of incorporation, or the place of the server on which the material is uploaded.[85] For example, under the **Electronic Commerce Directive**, the origin of the online service is determined by reference to where 'a service provider . . . pursues an economic activity using a fixed establishment for an infinite period. The presence and use of the technical means and technologies required . . . do not, in themselves, constitute an establishment of the provider'.[86] While the notion of a fixed establishment of the provider seems straightforward, the wording of the section is the end product of significant litigation before the ECJ.[87] Nevertheless, relatively speaking, definitional problems of the origin rule are minor compared to the uncertainties arising out of the destination rule. Assuming that a definition of 'origin' is agreed upon, the online publisher can order its affairs fairly straightforwardly: it knows where it uploads its data or where it has a fixed establishment, can control those locations, and would not face any unexpected legal exposure.

But the very reasons that have made states so eager to extend their laws to foreign sites are also the reasons that have dictated against the exclusive country-of-origin approach becoming a mainstream solution to competence over internet activity. The exclusive origin approach to competence has the disadvantages that, most importantly, it undermines the law of destination states and requires them to accept this. It also encourages forum-shopping for the state with the most lenient

---

84 See *R v Perrin* [2002] EWCA Crim 747, above, and associated discussion.
85 In *Dow Jones & Co Inc v Gutnick* [2002] HCA 56, concerning the *Wall Street Journal*, additional possible places of 'origins' of the site were the editorial office in New York or the location in which the material was initially composed. The case is discussed in Australian Law Reform Commission, *Choice of Law*, 1992, Report No 58, Canberra: Australian Government, p 57.
86 Electronic Commerce Directive, 2000/31/EC, Art 2(c).
87 Julia Hörnle, 'Country of origin regulation in cross-border media: One step beyond the freedom to provide services?' (2005) 54 ICLQ 89, 113; *Commission v UK* Case C222/94 [1996] ECR I-4025, concerning Art 2(1) of the Television without Frontiers Directive, 89/552/EC (later revised by 97/36/EC).

law by online providers and leads overall to the lowest common denominator setting the legal standards worldwide. Finally, although it reduces the regulatory burden for online content providers, in actual fact this burden of ascertaining foreign legal standards is often shifted to online users. Given these disadvantages, the question is why, in some rare instances, the exclusive origin approach has nonetheless proved acceptable.

The Electronic Commerce Directive

The **Electronic Commerce Directive** is the prime example of the exclusive origin approach in the online context.[88] Article 3(2) provides that Member States 'may not . . . restrict the freedom to provide information society services from another Member State'. This means that they may not impose their regulation on online providers from other Member States. The rule applies to any legal requirements within 'the coordinated field', such as legal prerequisites for carrying out the activity or requirements concerning the content or quality of the service.[89] Despite some uncertainty as to what exactly falls within the 'coordinated field', there is no doubt that the rule has 'a very wide scope as it applies across all sectors [bar a few exceptions including gambling] and not just to the areas harmonized by the Directive'.[90]

The exclusive origin rule in the **Electronic Commerce Directive** falls within the peculiar EU single market context, and its attendant removal of internal economic borders through the grant of freedoms such as the free movements of goods and the freedom to provide services. Thus EU Member States have long been used to restrictions being imposed on their natural inclination to regulate incoming goods and services – for the greater good of an open market. However, the exclusive origin rule in the **Electronic Commerce Directive** goes a step further than the above freedoms in that it prevents destination states from regulating foreign incoming services altogether, and not only when that regulation would be discriminatory or amount to an obstacle.[91] While that extra step has also been taken before – for example, in the EU **Television without Frontiers Directive**[92] – the origin rule was previously restricted to the areas of law harmonised in the Directive,[93] unlike its open-ended application to 'coordinated fields' in the **Electronic Commerce Directive**. Broadly speaking, though, the exclusive origin rule in the **Electronic Commerce Directive** falls within, and is a natural progression of, the EU tradition of mutual recognition and a climate of mutual respect for each other's legal regimes.

What then may be regarded as prerequisites or fertile ground for the acceptability of the exclusive origin rule, as illustrated by the **Electronic Commerce Directive**? First of all, because the exclusive origin rule requires destination states to abstain from regulating foreign conduct that affects them in favour of the regulatory claim by the origin state, it helps if the legal rules of that origin state are broadly in tune with those of the abstaining destination state; then, the destination state need not fear that local rules would be undermined by the foreign conduct. Legal harmonisation – or at least approximisation, such as within the EU – makes the exclusive origin

---

See Chapter 7 ◀

---

88 Hörnle, op cit; Lokke Moerel, 'The country-of-origin principle in the E-Commerce Directive: The expected one-stop shop' (2001) 7 CTLR 184.

89 Electronic Commerce Directive, 2000/31/EC, Art 2(h).

90 Julia Hörnle, 'The UK perspective on the country of origin rule in the E-Commerce Directive: A rule of administrative law applicable to private law disputes?' (2004) 12 IntJLIT 333, 337. There is some uncertainty as to the scope of the Directive: Department for Business, Innovation and Skills (BIS), *A Guide for Business to The Electronic Commerce (EC Directive) Regulations 2002* (SI 2002/2013), 2002, London: HMSO, paras 4.3–4.8; Joakim ST Øren, 'International jurisdiction over consumer contracts in e-Europe' (2003) 52 ICLQ 665, 668.

91 In respect of the freedom of movement of goods, the ECJ held, in *Deutscher Apothekerverband eV v 0800 Doc Morris NV* Case C-322/01 [2003] ECR I-14887, that the requirement under German law that certain drugs must be sold in pharmacies was, in this case, an unjustified restriction on the online activities of the Dutch pharmacy. Such requirement was only justified for prescription drugs. Since then, the Directive has come into force, with the online sale of drugs being within the scope of the 'coordinated fields'.

92 Television without Frontiers Directive, 89/552/EEC (revised by 97/36/EC), Art 2a(1). Other Directives that adopt the origin rule are 89/646/EEC, 93/22/EEC, 92/49/EEC, and 92/96/EEC.

93 Ibid, Art 2(1).

rule less threatening than it would be in respect of widely diverging legal standards. This explains why, in previous Directives, the origin was tied to the harmonised areas covered by the Directive.

Second, reciprocity – as opposed to the unilateral adoption of the origin approach – makes the exclusive origin rule much easier to bear for states. Such reciprocity of regulatory abstinence entails that states can be assured that their forbearance in respect of foreign providers, and any economic or other loss suffered due to such forbearance, is recompensed by local providers gaining un-hindered access to foreign markets. Again, such reciprocity is provided for in the **Electronic Commerce Directive** as states mutually agree to abide by the origin rule amongst each other.

Last but not least, the origin approach in a reciprocal setting must be understood not merely as an agreement *not to regulate* foreign providers or sites, but equally as the responsibility owed to the other states *to regulate* local providers. The deference to the origin state in the EU goes hand in hand with an expectation that the origin state takes its regulatory responsibility in respect of activities originating from its territory seriously. Consistently, Art 3(1) of the **Electronic Commerce Directive** imposes an obligation on origin states to regulate: 'Each Member State shall ensure that the infor-mation services provided by a service provider established on its territory comply with the national provisions in the Member State in question which fall within the coordinated field.' And this duty is coupled with various remedies in the hand of the destination state, should the duty not be fulfilled.[94] Thus, internationally, an exclusive origin rule would rarely be acceptable to states – other than by way of an international agreement covering clearly delineated subject matters amongst relatively homogenous legal systems with mutual respect for, and confidence in, each other.

The UK Gambling Act 2005

One rare example of a unilateral exclusive origin rule is provided by the UK **Gambling Act 2005**. Under the Act, it is an offence to provide facilities for gambling without an operating licence.[95] This obligation does extend to 'remote gambling', which is defined as gambling in which persons participate by the use of remote communication such as the internet, telephone, television, or radio.[96] However, by virtue of s 36, it only applies to locally based gambling operators – that is, 'to the provision of facilities for remote gambling only if at least one piece of remote gambling equip-ment used in the provision of the facilities is situated in Great Britain'.[97] The equipment that trig-gers the licence requirement includes the equipment used to register a punter, to present a person with a game or virtual event for the purpose of gambling, to determine the outcome of the gamble, or to store information relating to the result,[98] but not, importantly, the computer used by the gambler.[99] Thus if all of the equipment of the gambling provider is located abroad, no operating licence is needed, even though the gambling facilities are used by local punters. In terms of compe-tence, it provides a classic instance of the exclusive origin approach: the UK seeks to regulate local providers, but abstains from regulating foreign providers that offer gambling services in the UK. This approach is unusual in its attitude both to gambling and to competence, but whether it is well conceived is open to debate.

What are the reasons behind the UK's adoption of the origin rule in the gambling context? Does it not share the fear of other Western states that foreign gambling operators may undermine

---

94 The destination state can, first of all, request the origin state to fulfil its duty, and then take measures to restrict incoming services, after notifying the Commission and the origin state of its intention under Art 3(4)(b) of the Directive; it can also initiate infringement proceedings under Arts 258 or 259 TFEU.
95 Gambling Act 2005, s 33(1) and (2).
96 Ibid, s 4.
97 Ibid, s 36(3). For a comparable section, see Art 4 of the Data Protection Directive, 95/46/EC, according to which the data protection rules provided for by the Directive are applicable only when the controller is either established within the European Union or whenever the controller uses equipment situated within the Union in order to process data.
98 Gambling Act 2005, s 36(4).
99 Ibid, s 36(5).

local providers? It seems that the UK also hopes for a strong local industry, but hopes to achieve this by outcompeting foreign providers. The regulatory impact assessment to the Bill reasoned:

> There is a potentially vast international market for which gambling operators based in this country will be encouraged to compete and consumers both here and abroad will be able to access a full range of gambling sites licensed and located here, safe in the knowledge that probity and integrity of the gambling operators and products they offer are assured.[100]

The idea behind the origin rule appears to be that by having a strong, regulated local industry, foreign providers become simply uninteresting to local as well as foreign consumers and thus there is no need even to attempt to regulate the latter. Is this reasoning sound? First, while local consumers may well prefer a local to a foreign provider given that legal remedies seem more accessible, such preference would remain largely intact whether or not an attempt is made to regulate foreign providers. Indeed, not regulating foreign providers might make them more attractive to local consumers, because it gives them a competitive advantage by saving them legal compliance cost. For a respectable gambling provider who targets consumers worldwide, it would probably be cheaper to establish itself in some 'regulated' state other than the UK, as UK consumers can be targeted without any extra legal compliance cost.

Second, just because the UK adopts the origin approach in its gambling regulation, it does not at all follow that local gambling providers are not regulated by foreign states. Indeed, they are, and thus foreign consumers are by no means easy targets for local providers. The lack of reciprocity entails that legal abstinence by the UK in respect of foreign providers is not recompensed through abstinence by foreign states in respect of UK providers. Perhaps, the strongest rationale for the adoption of the exclusive origin rule, generally in the online world and specifically in the UK gambling context, is that states are often incapable of enforcing their regulatory attempts over foreign providers (discussed further below), and in that sense the origin rule accords most closely with the legal reality.

The Universality Principle

Quasi-universal Jurisdiction over Online Activity

Because most online activity can easily be *territorially* linked to any states, there has been little need for states to rely on any other head of jurisdiction under public international law. Nevertheless, the universality principle has some bearing on the internet competence debate, if only in so far as it indirectly comments on the current jurisdictional practices of states.

The universality principle is the only head of jurisdiction that dispenses with the need for any link between the state seeking to assert jurisdiction and the act, actor, or victim in question, and in very limited circumstances gives all states competence.[101] Initially, it applied only to piracy on the high seas – thus concerning an area beyond the territorial reach of any particular state, while at the same time attaching to a phenomenon in which all states shared a common or *universal* interest in its suppression: pirates were enemies of mankind. The ambit of the principle later expanded to include the slave trade and, after World War II, war crimes and crimes against humanity, and has since been applied (at least in treaties) to torture, genocide, hijacking, hostage-taking, and terrorist

---

100 Department for Culture, Media and Sport, *Draft Gambling Bill: Regulatory Impact Assessment*, 2003, London: HMSO, para 6.7; House of Lords/House of Commons Joint Committee on the Draft Gambling Bill, *Draft Gambling Bill*, 2004, London: HMSO, para 556: 'The Henley Centre predicts that net revenues for the UK from remote gambling sources would rise to £613 million by 2010 with the changes proposed by the draft Bill [ie the legalisation of running an online gambling business in the UK].'
101 See Reydams, op cit; Kenneth C Randall, 'Universal jurisdiction under international law' (1988) 66 Texas L Rev 785, 991ff.

activity. The assumption underlying all of these instances is that, in relation to particular heinous crimes that are universally condemned, it is in the interest of the international community for any state to have the right, and possibly a duty,[102] to prosecute if the offender is within the state's actual control.[103]

Relevant to the online competence debate is that the application of the universality principle, despite its expansion in the last half-century, still remains strictly delimited. This could not be otherwise, because the principle runs – in its very design – counter to the very purpose of having competence rules and the notion of *sharing* regulatory space: under it, all states have in theory a concurrent regulatory entitlement, which is only in practice resolved by the state that has apprehended the wrongdoer. But this exceptional position seems not so far removed from the normal state practice pertaining to websites. Although states have invariably based their regulatory claims over internet activity on the territorial link between the site and the state (that is, its territorial effect), given that this is generally universally true for all states, the effect of these regulatory claims has been the creation of a de facto type of universal jurisdiction over websites. Yet unlike universal jurisdiction proper, the impact of this quasi-universal jurisdiction is not contained by strict limits on its application, and also unlike universal jurisdiction proper, the subject matters covered are not universally condemned as crimes against mankind – quite the reverse. Finally, the right to regulate the activity in question by the state is not, and could not be, conceived of as a corresponding duty to other states to do so. In short, all of the conditions of the universality principle that legitimise its exceptional existence generally are absent in respect of all those regulatory claims over websites that could be made by all states. Thus their legitimacy is also dubious.

The UK Terrorism Act 2006

Terrorist activities are a criminal area to which the universality principle may apply under customary international law and does apply under treaties.[104] Recently, there has been a flurry of national and international legislative activity dealing with terrorist activities, including those on the internet. So, for example, under s 1 of UK **Terrorism Act 2006**, it is an offence to publish statements, extending to internet publications,[105] which encourage or induce the commission, preparation, or instigation of terrorist acts. The offence is extremely far-reaching; there are simply no limits on its application. Section 17(1) dispenses with the requirement of any territorial connection of such publication with the UK: 'If (a) a person does anything outside the United Kingdom, and (b) his action, if done in a part of the United Kingdom, would constitute an offence …, he shall be guilty in that part of the United Kingdom of the offence.'[106] Section 17(3) then additionally dispenses with a nationality connection: 'Subsection (1) applies irrespective of whether the person is a British citizen, or in the case of a company, a company incorporated in a part of the United Kingdom.' Thus, in a rather convoluted way, the Act asserts competence over terrorist publications by anyone anywhere – a

---

102 Under traditional customary international law, the universality principle was merely permissive, allowing, but not requiring, them to exercise universal jurisdiction in respect of some offences. However, many treaties make such exercise of jurisdiction mandatory where the offender is within the state's custody. This position may now also apply to some very grave offences under customary international law: Robert Kolb, 'The exercise of criminal jurisdiction over international terrorists', in Andrea Bianchi (ed), *Enforcing International Law Norms Against Terrorism*, 2004, Oxford: Hart, pp 227, 250, and 260ff.
103 Arguably, universal jurisdiction may be exercised even in *absentia*: Reydams, op cit, pp 38ff.
104 Randall, op cit, p 790.
105 See also s 2 of the Terrorism Act 2006, which criminalises the dissemination of terrorist publications. Section 3 provides a notice-and-takedown defence to any secondary electronic publisher that would otherwise be caught by the offences under ss 1 and 2.
106 This provision goes much further than the Electronic Commerce Directive (Terrorism Act 2006) Regulations 2007, SI 2007/1550, which, in reg 3(1), provide: 'If (a) in the course of providing information society services, a service provider *established in the United Kingdom* does anything in an EEA state other than the United Kingdom, and (b) his action, if done in a part fo the United Kingdom, would constitute a relevant offence, he shall be guilty in that part of the United Kingdom for the offence.' This provides for variation of the nationality principle given that the offence may be wholly committed elsewhere, but the offender is linked to the UK through a fixed establishment in the UK.

classic example of universal jurisdiction. The Explanatory Memorandum confirms this when it states that '[t]he overall effect of the section is that if, for example, an individual were to commit one of these offences in a foreign country, they would be liable under UK law in the same way as if they had committed the offence in the UK'.[107]

The section seeks to give effect to the Council of Europe **Convention on the Prevention of Terrorism** (Warsaw, 2005) and in particular Art 14 on 'Jurisdiction'. Article 14(1) and (2) provide a fairly long list of specific heads of jurisdiction when states must or may – depending on the circumstances – assume control over the alleged terrorist activity. Broadly, those heads focus on the territorial and nationality connections of the state with the offence, offender, or victim. They are supplemented by a catch-all provision in Art 14(3) that requires states to assume jurisdiction over terrorist offences whenever the alleged offender is within its territory and the state has not extra-dited him or her to a requesting party whose request is based on a valid head of jurisdiction.[108] The idea is that states cannot, wittingly or unwittingly, become safe havens for offenders, whenever they have no jurisdiction under Art 14(1) and (2) and decide to refuse, for whatever reasons, a valid extradition request. Nevertheless, the insistence on the initial list of heads suggests that jurisdiction ought to lie first and foremost with those states that *have* a link to the offence, and only on secondary basis with a 'disconnected' state. In short, the universality principle is – consistent with its original design – a fallback provision. In so far as s 17 of the UK **Terrorism Act 2006** provides for universal jurisdiction, it is formally in line with the Convention; however, in so far as it gives no indication of the exceptional nature of such claims, it is not within its spirit.

Having said that, in respect of foreign online terrorist publications hosted by foreigners, resort to universal jurisdiction under s 17 would rarely – if ever – be necessary as a basis for a prosecution. Such publications are already within the ambit of the territoriality principle (and particularly the objective territoriality principle) if they are accessible in the UK: for example, a person can be said to 'publish' a terrorist statement on UK soil under s 1 of the Act whenever such statement can be read online on UK soil.

Enforcement

Non-intervention and Non-cooperation

The anything-goes, law-defying reality of the internet seems to belie the above proposition that online providers are severely overregulated through the compounding regulatory claims made by states over both home-grown and foreign sites. This contradiction between the legal and the actual reality of the internet is explicable by reference to the tight territorial limits on states' enforcement jurisdiction. A fundamental principle under public international law – designed to protect the independence of states and their orderly coexistence with each other – is the principle of non-intervention: a state may not engage in public acts on the territory of another state.[109] As the PCIJ said in Lotus: '. . . the first and foremost restriction imposed by international law upon a State is that . . . it may not exercise its power in any form in the territory of another State. In this sense jurisdiction is certainly territorial.'[110] While states may attach legal consequences to foreign acts or actors under local law, they can never compel compliance with it by, for example, sending a local police officer or any public official into the territory of another state to affect an arrest or seize property.

---

107 Terrorism Act 2006, Explanatory Notes, para 82.
108 The validity of that assertion is assessed by the standards of the requested state – ie has the requested state a rule of jurisdiction that would have justified the requesting state's claim? (Also known as the double-jurisdiction rule.)
109 Examples of violations of that principle are the kidnapping of Nazi officer Eichmann by Israeli agents in Argentina in 1960, the sinking of the *Rainbow Warrior* by French government agents in New Zealand territorial waters in 1985, and the kidnapping of Alvarez-Machain by US agents in Mexico (US v Alvarez-Machain, 504 US 655 (1992)).
110 *The Case of the* SS Lotus (*France v Turkey*) (1927) PCIJ Reports, Series A, No 10, 18.

Consequently, on many occasions on which foreign websites violate local law, states can do nothing about it.

This lack of enforcement is, in the criminal context, accompanied by a long-standing profound unwillingness of states to cooperate in the enforcement of each others' criminal, revenue, and other public laws.[111] This uncooperative stance finds expression in two ways: on the one hand, states never apply foreign public/criminal law in local prosecutions; and on the other hand, they never enforce foreign public/criminal law judgments against local offenders.[112] A recent and rather revolutionary inroad into this uncooperative stance has been made by an inconspicuous provision in the UK and Australian online gambling legislation, aptly named the 'good neighbour' clause. Section 44 of the UK **Gambling Act 2005** provides: 'A person commits an offence if he does anything in Great Britain, or uses remote gambling equipment situated in Great Britain, for the purpose of inviting or enabling a person in a prohibited territory to participate in remote gambling.' A territory is a prohibited territory once the Secretary of State has made an order to that effect,[113] presumably following a request by a foreign state. The effect of the section is that a local provider may be penalised in the UK for breaching foreign criminal law on online gambling, even though the provision of this online gambling is legal at home. So far, neither the UK nor Australia have made use of the good neighbour clause, despite clear evidence that, for example, neither Scandinavian states nor the USA look kindly upon online gambling. Thus perhaps these revolutionary cooperative provisions are more rhetoric than reality.

The strict territorial limit of enforcement jurisdiction, coupled with the unwillingness by states to cooperate in the enforcement of each other's criminal or public laws, means that states have to find avenues within their borders, however imperfect, to make their expansive regulatory claims over foreign online providers more meaningful.

Symbolic and Educative Prosecutions

One avenue chosen by states to try to induce respect for their laws in foreign providers are symbolic and educative prosecutions. States have prosecuted foreign providers in the rare circumstances in which they could apprehend them as they happen to be on their soil, for example, on a visit. Let it be a warning to others! One such example is the German *Töben* (discussed above), in which Töben, resident in Australia, was arrested while visiting Germany. Similarly, in the USA, foreign online gambling providers have been arrested in connection with their online activities by US border controls while trying to enter the country.[114] Alternatively, as in *US v $734,578.82 in US Currency*[115] (discussed below), the state's access to relevant property (for example, local bank accounts) connected with the foreign illegal activity had been exploited by them as a lever to impose their rule on foreign online activities. While in these cases the state in question was able to penalise the particular offender in respect of his or her particular activities, the broader objective of such actions – as is the case for any criminal prosecution and, to a lesser extent, civil case – cannot but be that of wider deterrence, that is inducing voluntary compliance in others. Of course, it may simply have signalled to, for example, Antiguan gambling providers that they should not book a holiday in

---

111 Limited cooperation exists at the peripheries of criminal regulation, such as under treaties in respect of the investigation of crimes and the production of evidence, or concerning the extradition of offenders. Within the European Union, significant inroads into this non-cooperative stance have been made, such as the European arrest warrant: see Simon Chalton, 'E-commerce and the European arrest warrant' (2003) 8(4) Communications Law 329. In *Yahoo! Inc v LICRA and UEJF*, 433 F 3d 1199 (9th Cir 2006), the US court refused to rule formally on the enforceability of the French judgment in the USA, but a majority of the judges stated obiter that it would not have been enforced if they had to decide the issue.

112 Even in formally civil cases, such as *Yahoo*, a state may refuse to enforce a judgment if it would indirectly enforce a criminal or public law.

113 Gambling Act 2005, s 44(2). The equivalent section in Australia is s 15A of the Interactive Gambling Act 2001 (Cth).

114 Roy Mark, 'Feds arrest offshore gambling CEO' (2006) *Internetnew.com*, 18 July, available online at www.internetnews.com/bus-news/article.php/3620731

115 286 F 3d 641 (3rd Cir, 2002).

the USA. Sometimes, even in the absence of any enforcement power, the highly unfavourable damaging publicity arising from a court hearing and judgment may induce companies to comply with the foreign law voluntarily, as was the case in *Yahoo*.[116] This certainly holds sway for those highly visible companies for which a clean public image and respectability is an important asset.

Last but not least, the occasional prosecution of foreign website operators serves another function – namely, education. To the extent that legal rules can only be complied with if they are actually known, these cases 'inform' the online community that their legal obligations generally do not stop at their home borders and that states will not simply resign to their inability to catch foreign offenders if they can help it.

Parallel Prohibitions on Local Intermediaries, Facilitators, and End-users

Another avenue that states have used to give reality to their regulatory claims over foreign providers is to enforce parallel prohibitions on local intermediaries, facilitators, and end-users. On the secondary liability of third parties see Chapter 3.

See Chapter ◄ 3

With regard to end-users, for example, it is not only an offence under the **French Criminal Code** to sell Nazi memorabilia, as was in issue in *Yahoo*, but it is also an offence to view it. Thus the downloading of Nazi items by an end-user would be equally caught by the criminal prohibition. Similarly, under Italian law, the participation by local consumers in illegal gambling offers constitutes a criminal offence.[117] As a final example, many state regulators have tried to stem the illegal online copying of music and film files by taking highly publicised actions against the 'little' infringer at home, given that the foreign facilitators were beyond their reach.[118] Again, the strategy behind such actions is to set an example, maximising their deterrent effect. While such actions against some of the innumerable individual users cannot but have some impact, they are clearly not as effective and efficient in suppressing the illegal activity as would be dealing with the source of the illegality. The approach against users has other shortcomings. Sometimes such prohibition would simply not meet the regulatory aims: for example, while it might be an offence to offer pornographic material online without any age verification mechanism, it would not be an offence for an adult to access such material; nor would it make sense to prosecute a child who accessed such material, because, under the regulation, the child is the victim and not the wrongdoer. Similarly, the sale of unlicensed pharmaceuticals by a foreign provider could not be 'enforced' by targeting local consumers who unwittingly buy the drugs. Again, they are meant to benefit from the regulation, rather than be burdened by it.

Focusing on local intermediaries and facilitators to tackle foreign illegal sites is the more promising alternative, because they are fewer, often larger, and thus more visible than end-users.[119] Such intermediaries may be ISPs, the financial institutions used in the course of the transaction (such as PayPal or credit card providers), or advertisers (whether local print, broadcast, or sites with hyperlinks), as well as search engines, which often have a presence in the country through a local subsidiary (such as Google or Yahoo). Reliance on these secondary actors by states to enforce regulatory standards is not uncommon. For example, the US attempts to deal with foreign gambling providers have focused on local financial intermediaries, such as banks and credit card providers, making it an offence to transmit funds to online gambling sites.[120] A similar treatment has been

---

116 *Yahoo! Inc v LICRA and UEJF*, 433 F 3d 1199, 1205 (9th Cir. 2006), discussed in Kohl, op cit, 206f.

117 Art 4 of Law No 401 of 13 December 1989; see *Criminal Proceedings against Piergiorgio Gambelli* Case C-243/01, [2003] ECR I-13031, [9].

118 In France, those guilty of internet piracy may be barred from broadband access for up to a year: Charles Bremer, 'Download pirates face being banned from the internet under Sarkozy law' (2008) *The Times*, 19 June, p 39. Of course, the facilitators have also been subjected to prosecutions and private claims when they were present in the state: see, eg, the decision against providers of peer-to-peer file-sharing software used for copyright infringement in *Metro-Goldwyn-Mayer Studios Inc v Grokster Ltd* 545 US 125 (2005). See further discussion in Chapter 9.

119 For an in-depth discussion of third-party liabilities, see Chapter 3.

120 Unlawful Internet Gambling Enforcement Act 2006 (subject to certain exceptions); see also Hurt, op cit, 432ff.

applied to actors that might advertise offshore gambling services.[121] In New Zealand, the strategy to deal with offshore gambling providers centres squarely on the prohibition on local actors to advertise those services in any way.[122] Google has been forced to implement censorship not only in the obvious non-democratic states, such as China,[123] but also in Western democratic states.[124] None of these avenues is entirely foolproof and impervious to circumvention: gambling providers may bill punters through other companies to disguise payments as product purchases; keen punters in New Zealand can no doubt find the sites of foreign providers with some extra effort; and alternative search engines may provide the results that Google has to censor. Nonetheless, these measures create practical hurdles sufficient to deter many would-be activities and transactions. As the Antiguan complaint to the WTO shows, the US strategies made a significant dent in the number of Antiguan gambling providers.

For states, the temptation to make local intermediaries the gatekeepers of foreign content (or content more generally) is great.[125] Yet, there are serious drawbacks. First of all, attaching liability to intermediaries, especially criminal liability, is problematic, because they are often innocent – that is, they have no knowledge of the offending activity, and thus not the requisite *mens rea*. Second, to require them to monitor the content of all activities would be financially prohibitive, as well as unacceptable from a privacy perspective, at least in Western states.[126] It may be comparable to asking telephone companies to monitor all telephone conversations on their networks.

Given these considerations and the will to do whatever is necessary to encourage online activity, both Europe and the US have opted for a prima facie immunity of *some* local intermediaries for the content of others. But in neither case is the immunity absolute. In Europe, under the **Electronic Commerce Directive**, 'intermediary service providers' are given immunity from any possible criminal and civil liability for the content of others depending on their level of control over the site and their knowledge of its illegality.[127] Broadly, a local intermediary can generally avoid liability for illegal material (either local or foreign) that it hosts or caches if it takes it down as soon as it gains knowledge of its illegality.[128] A similar notice-and-takedown approach has also been adopted in respect of terrorist publications under s 3 of the UK **Terrorism Act 2006**.[129] But, this time, the immunity applies to any secondary electronic publishers and the relevant notice must come from a constable who believes the publication to be a terrorist one. In the USA, s 230 of the **Communications Decency Act of 1996** is both narrower and wider: 'No provider or user of an interactive computer service shall be treated as the publisher or speaker of any information provided by another information content provider.' Thus the immunity is not made dependent on any lack of control over the third-party content or ignorance of its illegality,

See Chapter 3 →

---

121 Aiding and abetting violations of the Wire Act; see also ibid, 435ff, and *People v World Interactive Gaming Corp* 714 NYS 2d 844, 851 (1999), relying inter alia on §225–05 of the New York Penal Code, which prohibits the promotion of unlawful gambling activity.

122 Gambling Act 2003, s 16(1).

123 BBC News, 'Google censors itself for China' (2006) 25 January, available online at http://news.bbc.co.uk/1/hi/technology/4645596.stm; Bill Thompson, 'Google censoring web content' (2002) BBC News, 25 October, available online at http://news.bbc.co.uk/2/hi/technology/2360351.stm. Google's shareholders upheld the company's policy on censorship when voting down an anti-censorship proposal in 2007: Erik Larkin, 'Google's shareholders vote against anti-censorship proposal' (2007) PC World, 10 May, available online at www.pcworld.com/article/131745/google_shareholders_vote_against_anticensorship_proposal.html

124 For censorship in Germany and France, see Jonathan Zittrain and Benjamin Edelman, *Localized Google Search Result Exclusions: Statement of Issues and Call for Data*, 2002, Cambridge, MA: Berkman Center for Internet & Society, Harvard Law School, available online at http://cyber.law.harvard.edu/filtering/google/. For Google censorship in the USA, see, eg, Eric Zeman, 'Google caves to Pentagon wishes' (2008) *Information Week*, 7 March.

125 Ronald Deibert, John Palfray, Rafal Rohozinski and Jonathan Zittrain (eds), *Access Denied*, 2008, Cambridge, MA: MIT Press, esp ch 5. They may also be used for surveillance purposes – ie as data collectors: see The Data Retention Directive 2006/24/EC. For further discussion, see Chapter 6.

126 Electronic Commerce Directive 2000/31/EC, Art 15.

127 Ibid, Arts 12–14.

128 Ibid, Arts 13 and 14.

129 See also Electronic Commerce Directive (Terrorism Act 2006) Regulations 2007, SI 2007/1550, regs 5–7.

but does not apply to federal criminal law or intellectual property law[130] – not insignificant inroads into the immunity.

So while local intermediaries and facilitators are relatively easy targets for indirect law enforcement efforts concerning offending foreign sites, financial and legal/human rights costs may, after all, outweigh the benefits of making them gatekeepers of foreign content.

Blocking of Foreign Illegal Content

States may quite effectively guard against foreign illegal online content by blocking access to foreign illegal sites – an avenue for censorship that seems retrograde and inextricably linked to authoritarian regimes such as China, Burma, Cuba, Singapore, or states in the Middle East. And indeed, in these states, whole sections of the internet are regularly blocked via local intermediaries to prevent access to unsuitable/illegal material.[131] In February 2008, the Pakistan Telecommunications Authority required all local ISPs to block access to YouTube because it had included disrespectful cartoons of the Prophet Muhammad that were initially published in Danish newspapers in 2005 and caused protests across the Muslim world.[132] During the 2008 Olympics, China repeatedly defied the International Olympic Committee (IOC) by censoring online material via local ISPs initially even for foreign journalists; in August 2008, it blocked access to iTunes, Apple's online music store, because Olympic athletes had downloaded a pro-Tibet album.[133] Cuba, even more drastically, restricts access to online material by carefully selecting who can have access to the internet in the first place (that is, government personnel, foreigners, and academic researchers), in addition to blocking sites.[134] These are all classic examples of what is normally associated with online blocking and censorship.

However, censorship in the form of blocking is by no means restricted to non-democratic states; it routinely occurs in all Western states, although rarely is it regarded as blocking, as opposed to notice-and-takedown obligations, or self-censorship by publishers or aggregation sites. As discussed above and elsewhere, certain intermediaries in the EU may be exposed to liability under the **Electronic Commerce Directive** if they do not block access to certain illegal cached or hosted material. Similarly, in the UK, any secondary publisher or intermediary (such as search engines, ISPs, or aggregating site) may commit the offence of publishing terrorist statements if it does not block access to such statements after being served with a relevant notice. The same appears to apply in the USA, where the immunity for intermediaries does not extend to federal criminal laws and thus may not prevent their exposure to prosecution for assisting in the commission of criminal activity of those the content of which they transmit to their subscribers. Google's search results are not only censored in China on political issues such as Tibet, but also in Germany and France on political issues such as Nazi propaganda, and in the USA on political issues such as terrorism.[135] Its subsidiary YouTube blocks access inter alia to videos that breach copyright,

See Chapter 3

---

130 47 USC §§ 230(e)(1) and (2).

131 Deibert et al, op cit, pp 41ff; Kristina M Reed, 'From the Great Firewall of China to the Berlin Firewall: The cost of content regulation on internet commerce' (2000) 13 Transnational Lawyer 451; Shanthi Kalathil and Taylor C Boas, 'The internet and state control in authoritarian regimes: China, Cuba and the counterrevolution' (2001) Carnegie Endowment Working Papers, Global Policy Program No 21, available online at www.carnegieendowment.org/files/21KalathilBoas.pdf; Zhen Feng, 'China to introduce new legislation to deal with ISP liability for copyright infringement' (2004) 5 World Internet Law Report 19.

132 Jeremy Page, 'YouTube is cut off over cartoons' (2008) The Times, 25 February, p 30. Note Richard Owen, 'Comedian Sabina Guzzanti "insulted Pope" in "poofter devils" gag' (2008) TimesOnline, 21 September, available online at www.timesonline.co.uk/tol/news/world/europe/article4732048.ece

133 Tania Branigan, 'China relaxes internet censorship for Olympics' (2008) The Guardian, 1 August, available online at www.guardian.co.uk/world/2008/aug/01/china.olympics; Hannah Fletcher, 'China blocks iTunes over all-star Tibet album free download' (2008) TimesOnline, 22 August, available online at http://technology.timesonline.co.uk/tol/news/tech_and_web/article4579783.ece

134 BBC News, 'Web censorship: Correspondent reports' (2006) 29 May, available online at http://news.bbc.co.uk/2/hi/technology/5024874.stm

135 For government censorship of Google results (including by Western states), see BBC News, 'Google releases censorship tools' (2010) 21 September, available online at www.bbc.co.uk/news/technology-11380677

depict pornography, gratuitous violence, or hate speech.[136] YouTube's policy on blocking cannot purely be understood as a voluntary, commercially motivated act, but is at least partly a direct defensive reaction to the laws of various states.

The examples highlight that censorship/blocking is the necessary by-product of any law that in any way restricts communications; such laws would be nugatory if they did not suppress communications in violations of them. Regulators simply seek to extend their traditional approach to the internet, which, as a freer, more egalitarian and control-defying medium, seems 'violated' by these efforts. Yet censorship is commonplace; media actors long before the advent of the internet have been made to suppress defamatory, racist, violence-inciting, or terrorist material. The profound Western disagreement with states such as China, Saudi Arabia, or Pakistan relates to the content of the speech considered 'unworthy' rather than the practice of suppressing 'unworthy' speech per se. Otherwise, the difference in the practice of blocking is one of degree (albeit in parts substantial). Authoritarian states have resorted to blocking entire domains via closely monitored, often licensed ISPs.[137] In the West, blocking is less crude, with a focus on the specific material rather than entire domains found to be illegal, coupled with a rejection of a television-like licensing regime as a suitable regulatory model for the internet content providers and intermediaries. Also, Western states have placed greater reliance on self-censorship by primary and secondary publishers simply to avoid the threat of litigation. Quite how harmless this is is debatable. Sites such as YouTube, eBay, Yahoo, or Amazon may decide that it is cheaper to have a common policy of use across states, put in effect by complying with the highest common legal denominator of major user states. Such policy deprives users of more lenient states of content that would be legal in their home states. If, on the other hand, local ISPs were the censorship points, such 'unnecessary' self-censorship could arguably be avoided.

The Western rhetoric about free online communications – such as that in the Council of Europe's Declaration on Freedom of Communication on the Internet (2003)[138] – needs to be treated with caution. It certainly does not at all entail regulatory abstinence. Principle 1 of that Declaration states: 'Member States should not subject content on the Internet to restrictions which go further than those applied to other means of content delivery.' This means that Member States *are* free to censor or block online content along existing regulatory lines. Principle 3 starts off by saying that '[p]ublic authorities should not, through general blocking or filtering measures, deny access by the public to information and other communication on the Internet, regardless of frontiers', but continues by expressly legitimising blocking: ' . . . measures may be taken to enforce the removal of clearly identifiable Internet content or, alternatively, the blockage of access to it, if the competent national authorities have taken a provisional or final decision on its illegality.'

Transnational Online Civil Disputes

Like in relation to criminal matters, the transnationality of the internet has triggered competence questions in civil disputes, particularly concerning defamation, contracts, and intellectual property rights. Again, like in the criminal context, the competence question running through these disputes

---

136 YouTube, 'YouTube Community Guidelines', available online at www.youtube.com/t/community_guidelines
137 Control over ISPs may be achieved through a licensing regime (as practised in Singapore) or by routing all traffic through a government proxy server (as practised in Saudi Arabia), which makes the state's entire net activities comparable to the intranet of a company: Smith, op cit, p 932; see also Deibert at al, op cit, chs 2 and 3.
138 Adopted by the Committee of Ministers on 28 May 2003; see also Council of Europe, *Declaration on Freedom of Political Debate in the Media* (adopted by the Committee of Ministers on 12 February 2004), and Organization for Security and Co-operation in Europe (OSCE), *Amsterdam Recommendations on Freedom of the Media and the Internet* (2003); Christian Ahlert, 'Technologies of control: How code controls communication', in Christiane Hardy and Christian Möller (eds) *Spreading the Word on the Internet*, 2003, Vienna: OSCE, p 119.

is: when can a state regulate the transnational dispute? In the civil disputes, this general inquiry is divided into two more specific questions: first, when does a national court have the right to adjudicate the dispute (referred to as the issue of 'jurisdiction'); and second, when is local law (or 'forum law') the appropriate substantive law to govern the dispute (known as the issue of 'applicable law' or 'choice of law')? As noted above, in the criminal context, these are not separate questions, because a court that has assumed the right to adjudicate a criminal matter will automatically apply forum law to the prosecution. That, however, is not necessarily the case in transnational civil matters. Despite this structural difference, many of the competence arguments raised in the criminal context find their counterparts in transnational online civil disputes. Again, states have tended to interpret their competence widely so as to regulate disputes arising out of foreign sites accessible on their territory (that is, taking a country of destination/receipt approach) in order to guard against local legal standards and rights being undermined by foreign non-compliant sites. Again, online providers have argued that this approach exposes them to too many compounding (and possibly conflicting) obligations and that they should only be subject to the laws of the state in which they are established (that is, arguing for an exclusive country-of-origin approach).

Unlike in the criminal context, states have been more ready (although not always) to resolve the clash of interests between local regulators and injured parties, on the one hand, and foreign online content providers, on the other, by a compromise in the form of the moderate destination approach (see discussion above), whereby online providers are exposed only to the legal systems of the states that they specifically target with their sites and not that of all of the states in which their sites can be, or have been, accessed. This greater readiness in civil law to tolerate minor infiltrations of offending sites without any legal repercussions can be explained by reference to the nature of civil law. As it serves primarily individual private interests and only in the second instance the public good, those private interests may, at times, legitimately be compromised in the name of protecting online actors from overregulation.

The discussion below illustrates the competence approaches taken in civil law in the context of defamation and intellectual property disputes. Jurisdiction and choice-of-law questions in contractual disputes, including consumer contracts, are examined elsewhere in the book. Finally, as a reminder, competence in transnational civil disputes is governed by national/municipal, rather than international, law, unless – as, for example, in the EU – there are treaties harmonising national legal regimes.[139]

See Chapter 7

Personal Jurisdiction (and Choice of Law)

The first issue in any transnational civil dispute is whether the court in which the claim has been brought has the right to hear the claim and whether it should exercise that right. Courts assert that right if they have jurisdiction over the person of the defendant, or what is known as 'personal jurisdiction', or 'jurisdiction in personam'. In common law legal systems, personal jurisdiction exists if the defendant is 'present' in the territory of the court and can thus be served with the writ.[140] In civil law countries, the defendant's habitual residence creates jurisdiction in the courts of that place. Similarly, in the EU, Art 2(1) of the EC **Regulation on Jurisdiction and the Recognition and Enforcement of Judgments in Civil and Commercial Matters**[141] provides that 'persons domiciled in a Member State shall . . . be sued in the courts of that Member State'. The strengths of this traditional focus on the location of the defendant in the forum are, first, that the defendant can easily be

---

139 For a summary of EU legislation on judicial cooperation in civil matters, see online at http://europa.eu/legislation_summaries/justice_freedom_security/judicial_cooperation_in_civil_matters/index_en.htm
140 The service of the writ creates the jurisdiction of the court: *Colt Industries v Sarlie (No 1)* [1966] 1 WLR 440 (England and Wales); *Pennoyer v Neff* 95 US 714 (1877) (USA).
141 Regulation No 44/2001 on Jurisdiction and the Recognition and Enforcement of Judgments in Civil and Commercial Matters.

put on notice about the action that is brought against him or her (consistent with the idea of natural justice), and second, that any judgment against the defendant can easily be enforced against him or her without involving another state. It also seems fair that the plaintiff has to bring his or her case in the place of the defendant's location, because it is the plaintiff who has the complaint against the potentially innocent defendant.

Despite its advantages, this basic default rule has long been subject to exceptions that allow plaintiffs to bring actions in their home states.[142] These exceptions have expanded with the increase of international trade, travel, and communications that would often make it unfair to require the plaintiff to instigate proceedings in the defendant's location, particularly when the defendant inflicted the injury on the plaintiff in the plaintiff's jurisdiction. The question examined here is to what extent these exceptions cover online disputes, or more specifically in what circumstances online content providers may be hauled into foreign courts in relation to disputes arising out of the access and use of their sites abroad. Conversely, can a victim of a wrong committed by a foreign content provider go to a local court for remedies? Because US jurisprudence on internet jurisdiction is by far the most comprehensive, the discussion starts with this, and is then followed by an examination of the EU and the English common law legal positions.

The second issue in transnational civil disputes is what substantive laws should be applied to online disputes (varyingly referred to as 'choice of law', 'prescriptive jurisdiction', or 'subject matter' jurisdiction). This has attracted much less judicial attention. In the trade mark context, the explanation is that an assertion of adjudicative jurisdiction against a foreign defendant is generally (but not always, as will be seen below) premised on establishing that the infringing conduct occurred within the state's borders – which then also entails that local trade mark law is applicable to the dispute. This goes hand in hand with the nature of trade marks, which are exclusively governed by the statute that created them in the place of their creation: ' . . . the strictly territorial . . . sphere of their operation . . . cuts down the application of intellectual property legislation to controversies in the country the law or legislation of which created the rights in question coupled with its substantive inapplicability elsewhere.'[143] Trade mark rights do not extend beyond the borders of the place of their creation, although they may indirectly apply extraterritorially when foreign activities penetrate the borders within which the trade mark is effective. Indeed, this goes to the heart of the online trade mark/domain name controversy: if Thore of Norway has a website using a name for which he has a registered trade mark at home, he may still potentially tread on the legal toes of Olga of Russia, who has the same trade mark registered in Russia, if his website is accessible in Russia. As it is Olga's trade mark that is under dispute and Russia is the birthplace of that trade mark, a Russian court would be the appropriate court to determine whether it was infringed (adjudicative jurisdiction) and Russian trade mark law would be the only law that could be applied to her trade mark (subject matter jurisdiction). In that sense, competence issues here are comparable to those in public international law in that there is no real choice of law, although there may be – and often are – issues arising regarding the legitimate reach of local law. In the USA, this parallel was made more explicit recently when the traditional approach for the extraterritorial reach of US antitrust law was applied to trade marks, requiring that the extraterritorial activities of the foreigner must have a 'substantial effect' on US commerce.[144]

In online tort cases, such as defamation claims, the issue of applicable law also often plays a subordinate role to the inquiry into adjudicative jurisdiction. The reason is that the question of whether the court is the appropriate forum to hear the claim (forum conveniens) often depends either

142 For example, submission by the defendant to the court's jurisdiction.
143 K Lipstein, 'Intellectual property: Jurisdiction or choice of law' (2002) 61(2) CLJ 294, 297. See also *R J Reuters Co Ltd v Mulhens* [1954] 1 Ch 50; James J Fawcett and Paul Torremans, *Intellectual Property and Private International Law*, 1998, Oxford: Oxford University Press, pp 517–20; Mireille MM van Eechoud, *Choice of Law in Copyright and Related Rights: Alternative to the* Lex Protectionis, 2003, The Hague: Kluwer Law International. See also discussion in Chapter 8.
144 *McBee v Delica Co Ltd* 417 F3d 107 (1st Cir 2005).

expressly or implicitly on where the tort/damage occurred (that is, *lex locus delicti*) and this location is also generally determinative of the applicable law.[145] Thus a finding in favour of the court's exercise of jurisdiction then also automatically entails a finding in favour of applying local law.

Traditional US Rules on Personal Jurisdiction

Modern US jurisprudence on personal jurisdiction started with the Supreme Court decision in *International Shoe Co v Washington*[146] in 1945, when it abandoned the strict interpretation of the requirement that the defendant must be 'present' in the territory of the court and laid down what has become known as the 'minimum contacts' test. The Court held that the constitutional guarantee of due process of law[147] required that 'in order to subject a defendant to a judgment *in personam*, if he be not present within the territory of the forum, he have certain *minimum contacts with it such that the maintenance of suit does not offend traditional notions of fair play and substantial justice*'.[148] The idea was that rather relying on the often arbitrary question of whether or not the defendant was present in the forum, legal accountability should hinge on the defendant's contacts with the forum. The stronger these contacts, the fairer and more just it would be to require him or her to defend proceedings there. This rationale was made more explicit in the ruling of *Hanson v Deckla*,[149] in which the minimum contacts test was reformulated into the 'purposeful availment' test: a defendant may be sued in a state in which he or she has purposefully availed himself or herself of the privilege of conducting activities, thus invoking the benefits and protections of its laws.[150] In other words, if someone gains the commercial benefits of a foreign market and implicitly its legal protection, he or she must also carry the burden of being answerable to the courts in that place.

The much-adjudicated issue has been whether the provider of a website can be said to avail itself of the privilege of conducting activities in *every* state in which its site can be accessed. US courts have rejected that proposition. The mere accessibility of a site in a state does not expose the provider to legal accountability before its courts, essentially for two reasons. Practically, it would mean that 'every . . . court through the world, may assert jurisdiction over all information providers on the global World Wide Web . . . [which] would have a devastating impact on those who use this global service'.[151] Theoretically, it would 'eviscerate the personal jurisdictional requirement':[152] by saying that every online provider is potentially answerable to every court, courts no longer share adjudicative powers based on the relative strength of the connection of the defendant with the

---

145 See, eg, EC Regulation No 864/2007 on the Law Applicable to Non-Contractual Obligations, Art 4 (European Union); *Regie Nationale des Renault Usines SA v Zhang* [2002] HCA 10 (Australia). For a US-focused comparison, see American Bar Association, op cit, pp 83ff.

146 326 US 310, 316 (1945). For a historic overview of the cases with a special focus on online cases, see ibid, pp 39ff. See also Sam Puathasnanon, 'Cyberspace and personal jurisdiction: The problem of using internet contacts to establish minimum contacts' (1998) 31 Loy LA L Rev 691; Allan R Stein, 'The unexceptional problem of jurisdiction in cyberspace' (1998) 32 The International Lawyer 1167.

147 Firth Amendment to the US Constitution (applicable to federal government) and 14th Amendment (applicable to state governments).

148 *International Shoe Co v Washington* 326 US 310 (1945) [emphasis added]. US courts draw a distinction between general and specific personal jurisdiction, of which only the latter has been used in internet-related case. General personal jurisdiction arises where the out-of-state defendant has very strong connections with the forum (ie substantial or continuous and systematic contacts), which means that he or she may be sued in relation to any dispute regardless of whether that the particular dispute arises out of the contacts with the forum state or not. On the other hand, specific personal jurisdiction arises where the contacts with the forum are relatively weak (ie isolated and sporadic contacts) and then there is the additional requirement that the dispute in question must be linked to those contacts.

149 357 US 235 (1958).

150 *Hanson v Deckla* 357 US 235, 253 (1958). In *World-Wide Volkswagen Corp v Woodson* 444 US 286 (1980), the Supreme Court added a second strand to the purposeful availment test: even if minimum contacts were present, the court may decline to exercise personal jurisdiction if to do so would not be reasonable, taking into account the burden on the defendant, the forum state's interest in adjudicating the disputes, the plaintiff's interest in obtaining convenient and effective relief, and the shared interest of states in furthering fundamental subjective social policies.

151 *Playboy Enterprises Inc v Chuckleberry Pub Inc* 939 F Supp 1032, 1039 (SDNY 1996).

152 *McDonough v Fallon McElligott Inc*, 40 USPQ 2d (BNA) 1826, 1829 (SD Cal 1996); see also *GTE New Media Servs Inc v BellSouth Corp*, 199 F 3d 1343, 1350 (DC Cir 2000) and *ALS Scan Inc v Digital Service Consultants Inc* 293 F 3d 707, 712 (4th Cir, 2002).

court's territory. Instead, US courts have taken a moderate destination approach by insisting that legal accountability shall lie only with the court of the state at which the site was specifically targeted. What type of evidence may indicate such 'targeting' varies and is, to some extent, dependent on the nature of the dispute. While in trade mark disputes the commercial activity between the site and residents of the forum state may be indicative of an intention to reach customers in that state, in defamation claims the content of the site may provide clues about its targeted readership. But ultimately courts examine all of the circumstances surrounding a case (including non-internet-related contacts) to determine at which state in particular a site is directed.

US Sliding-scale Interactivity Test in Trade Mark Cases

One well-accepted interpretation of the 'purposeful availment' test in the online context, especially in trade mark disputes, is the Zippo sliding-scale interactivity test developed in *Zippo Manufacturing Co v Zippo Dot Com Inc*.[153] In that case, the world-famous Pennsylvanian producer of Zippo tobacco lighters and holder of the trade mark 'Zippo' brought an action in Pennsylvania for trade mark infringement against Zippo Dot Com Inc, a Californian corporation operating a website and internet news service using the domain names zippo.com, zippo.net, and zipponews.com. The court reasoned:

> . . . our review of the available cases and materials reveals that the likelihood that personal jurisdiction can be constitutionally exercised is directly proportionate to the nature and quality of commercial activity that an entity conducts over the Internet. This sliding scale is consistent with well developed personal jurisdiction principles. At one end of the spectrum are situations where a defendant clearly does business over the Internet. If the defendant enters into contracts with residents of a foreign jurisdiction that involve the knowing and repeated transmission of computer files over the Internet, personal jurisdiction is proper . . . At the opposite end are situations where a defendant has simply posted information on an Internet Web site which is accessible to users in foreign jurisdictions. A passive Web site that does little more than make information available to those who are interested in it is not grounds for the exercise personal jurisdiction . . . The middle ground is occupied by interactive Web sites where a user can exchange information with the host computer. In these cases, the exercise of jurisdiction is determined by examining the level of interactivity and commercial nature of the exchange of information that occurs on the Web site.[154]

The idea behind this test is that an owner of a site that regularly enters into contracts with residents of the forum state and thus has knowing, or intentional, contacts with the forum cannot claim to have had no awareness with whom it is interacting: credit card details, invoice, and delivery addresses allow sellers not only to know the location of their customers, but also give them the opportunity to exclude customers from legally inhospitable states. The reverse applies to freely accessible sites that simply post information online. The unsuspecting owner of such a site has prima facie neither knowledge of the location of those who access its site, nor control in terms of preventing their access, which in turn would make legal accountability in the states of those surfers unpredictable and unfair.[155] In short, knowing business contacts with forum residents via a site evidences that the forum was targeted and thus gives rise to personal jurisdiction, but simply

---

153 *Zippo Manufacturing Co v Zippo Dot Com Inc* 952 F Supp 1119 (WD Pa 1997). See also discussion in Chapter 8.
154 Ibid, 1123ff, relying in particular on *CompuServe Inc v Patterson* 89 F 3d 1257 (6th Cir 1996).
155 This argument is no longer quite as persuasive given the availability of geo-identification software (which allows site owners to establish the whereabouts of surfers as well as restrict the use of the site in certain jurisdictions): see Svantesson, op cit (2004).

posting a passive site (without more) does not. This test has been applied to many interstate US disputes,[156] as well as to transnational disputes.[157]

One such international case is *Euromarket Design Inc v Crate and Barrel Ltd*,[158] in which the well-known US retailer, selling house wares and furniture under the name of 'Crate & Barrel', wanted to sue the small Irish company Crate & Barrel Ltd, selling similar goods, for an infringement of its trade mark in Illinois in the USA. The Irish company, which had a shop in Ireland, also advertised and sold its goods via a website. While it did not deliver goods to Illinois, the company had accepted online orders from Illinois customers (instigated by the plaintiff) with delivery in Ireland. The site, at least initially, stated its prices in US dollars and was formatted to accommodate US addresses for billing. While this may have been enough to show that the site was targeted at the USA, including Illinois, other non-internet contacts strengthened the plaintiff's case in favour of the Illinois court's personal jurisdiction over the Irish defendant: the defendant used Illinois suppliers, attended trade shows in Illinois, and advertised its business in UK and Irish magazines that were also circulated in the USA. Under these circumstances, the Illinois court felt that the defendant 'deliberately developed and maintained not only minimum, but significant, contacts with the forum'[159] and thus that personal jurisdiction was proper. Whether these contacts were indeed 'significant' is questionable.

In *Toys 'R' Us Inc v Step Two*,[160] the US Court of Appeals, Third Circuit reached the opposite conclusion. Here, the US retailer Toys 'R' Us brought a trade mark infringement action against the Spanish company, Step Two, which also sold toys. Both companies had registered in their respective jurisdictions' trade marks relating to the name of 'Imaginarium', as well as domain names for their respective interactive websites – that is, imaginarium.com and imaginarium.es. Although, like in *Euromarket Design*, the Spanish company had accepted two orders from New Jersey residents, which, like in *Euromarket Design*, had been initiated by the plaintiff to prove the willingness of the foreign defendant to accept orders from forum residents, the Court dismissed these sales as orchestrated contacts that Step Two scarcely recognised as sales with US residents (presumably because the site did not require a billing address). Instead, the Court focused on the facts that the Step Two's site was in Spanish, payment in pesetas or euros, merchandise could only be shipped to Spain, and '[m]ost important, none of the portions of Step Two's web sites are designed to accommodate addresses within the United States'.[161] Ultimately, the formatting of the site's address section made the critical difference between *Toys 'R' Us* and *Euromarket Design*, and tipped the balance in either case. Not surprisingly, the site's address section proves least ambiguous in revealing for whom the site was really created.

US Effects Test in Defamation Cases

The sliding-scale interactivity test has proved less useful in some cases, such as defamation claims,[162] when the offending site – for example, an online newspaper – is not interactive (and would be classified as 'passive' under *Zippo*), but serious damage may still be suffered as a result of it. In such cases, an alternative avenue for establishing personal jurisdiction under the 'minimum contacts' test

---

156 *Morantz Inc v Hang & Shine Ultrasonics Inc* 79 F Supp 2d 537 (ED Pa 1999); *ALS Scan v Digital Service Consultants Inc* 293 F 3d 707 (4th Cir 2002).

157 In international disputes, there appear to be minor additions to the general jurisdiction test: in *Asahi Metal Industry Co v Superior Court* 480 US 102, 103 (1987), the Supreme Court noted that the 'procedural and substantive policies of other nations whose interests are affected by the forum State's assertion of jurisdiction over an alien defendant . . . as well as the Federal Government's interest in its foreign relations policies, will always be best served by a careful inquiry into the reasonableness of the particular assertion of jurisdiction'.

158 96 F Supp 2d 824 (ND Ill 2000).

159 Ibid.

160 318 F 3d 446 (3rd Cir 2003).

161 Ibid, 454.

162 Similarly cybersquatting (trade mark) cases cannot be accommodated by the sliding scale test given the often inherent passivity of the site.

is provided by the intentional effects doctrine established in *Calder v Jones*.[163] In that case, the court held that personal jurisdiction over an out-of-state defendant is proper where an intentional tortious action was expressly aimed at the forum state and in fact causes damage there to the plaintiff. While this test is framed differently from that of *Zippo*, ultimately both seek to establish whether the acts by the out-of-state defendant were specifically aimed, directed, or targeted at the forum state; they simply respond to slightly different factual scenarios.

A prime situation for which the *Calder* effects doctrine was virtually designed occurred in *Blumenthal v Drudge*,[164] in which the issue was whether the Californian online publisher of the Drudge Report, which was alleged to be defamatory of Blumenthal, a White House employee, and his wife in Columbia, could be sued in Columbia. The Columbian court focused on the interactivity of the site (like many lower US courts at the time), when in fact 'a one line cite to *Calder* would have sufficed'.[165] Nevertheless, in substance, the court did adopt the *Calder* approach:

> . . . the subject matter of the Drudge Report primarily concerns political gossip and rumor in Washington . . . the subject matter of the Drudge Report is directly related to the political world of the Nation's capital . . . Drudge specifically targets readers in the District of Columbia by virtue of the subjects he covers . . . Drudge knew that *primary and most devastating effects* of the statements he made would be felt in the District of Columbia.[166]

In other words, the subject matter of the report provided clues about the site's territorial target, which in this case was Columbia. *Calder* was expressly relied upon in *Young v New Haven Advocate*[167] concerning two online Connecticut newspapers alleged to have defamed the plaintiff in Virginia. The court noted that the 'application of *Calder* in the Internet context requires proof that the out-of-state defendant's Internet activity is expressly targeted at or directed to the forum state',[168] and reiterated that such targeting is not established simply by posting matters online. Based on this, the Virginian court refused to hear the case, given that the 'newspapers maintain their websites to serve local readers in Connecticut, to expand the reach of their papers within their local markets, and to provide their local markets with a place for classified ads. The websites are not designed to attract or serve a Virginia audience'.[169]

Both the sliding-scale interactivity test and the intentional effects test are examples of the moderate country-of-destination approach, discussed above, according to which only states specifically targeted by a site can regulate them.

Article 5(3) of the EU Jurisdiction Regulation

In the EU, it is the EC **Regulation on Jurisdiction and the Recognition and Enforcement of Judgments in Civil and Commercial Matters**[170] that governs adjudicative jurisdiction in private matters. According to Art 4, the scope of the Regulation is limited to cases in which the defendant is domiciled in a Member State; otherwise, the national law is applicable.[171] Thus, any action brought in the UK against, for example, a US or Australian defendant would be resolved by reference to the traditional English rules of private international law. When the Regulation is applicable, the default

---

163 465 US 783 (1984).
164 992 F Supp 44 (DDC 1998).
165 American Bar Assocation, op cit, 51.
166 *Blumenthal v Drudge* 992 F Supp 44, 57 (1998) (internal marks omitted; emphasis added).
167 315 F3d 256 (4th Cir 2002); rev'd 187 F Supp 2d 498 (WD Vir 2001); following *ALS Scan Inc v Digital Service Consultants Inc* 293 F 3d 707 (4th Cir, 2002).
168 *Young v New Haven Advocate* 315 F3d 256, 262ff (4th Cir 2002).
169 Ibid, 263.
170 EC Regulation No 44/2001 on Jurisdiction and the Recognition and Enforcement of Judgments in Civil and Commercial Matters. [2001] OJ L12/1.
171 With the exception of Arts 22 and 23.

rule – that the defendant must be sued in his or her state of domicile under Art 2(1) – can, in the tort and intellectual property disputes, be overridden by Art 5(3), which provides that a person may also be sued 'in matters relating to tort, delict or quasi-delict, in the courts for the place where the harmful event occurred or may occur'. The question this raises is this: where does the harmful event occur on the internet? Considering a defamatory article, does the harm occur in the location in which the article was uploaded (country of origin), or is it in the location(s) in which it was downloaded and in which the plaintiff suffered the injury (country of destination)?[172]

In the pre-internet case of *Shevill v Press Alliance SA*,[173] the ECJ held that 'the harmful event' is either the place where the publisher is established or the place where the publication was distributed and the plaintiff suffered his or her injury. Thus where a newspaper is distributed in a number of states, a defamed plaintiff can sue in the place of the origin of the damage – that is, where the publisher is based – which comes close to the default rule and is often inconvenient for the plaintiff. The advantage is that the plaintiff can seek compensation for the entire damage suffered (including damage suffered in other states). Alternatively, he or she can sue in the state in which the publication was distributed, but only for the injury that he or she suffered there.

The critical question is whether a website should be considered to be *distributed* in every state in which it can be accessed. According to US jurisprudence, that is not the case: intrinsically, local publications are not transformed into transnational publication simply by being online. The *Shevill* case cannot provide the answer to that in the European context, but it does provide some clues. In *Shevill*, the allegedly defamatory French newspaper was distributed mainly in France (237,000 copies), but had a small circulation in other countries, including 230 copies in England and Wales. But even in relation to that small circulation, there was a knowing act by the defendant to bring about that distribution, which makes accountability before English courts appropriate. Clearly, it would have been impossible for the defendant to have claimed that it had somehow unwittingly distributed the newspapers in England. That would have been the case if the newspaper had been published only in France and a tourist had brought it back to England. In the latter scenario, the 'distribution' of the paper in England would be beyond the control of the French publisher, and thus personal jurisdiction by the English courts would be unfair. Applying this to the internet (and considering the undesirability of holding that accessibility by itself amounts to a distribution of the site – that is, worldwide legal accountability), websites should only be treated as distributed in the places to which they are knowingly directed or targeted. This would satisfy the notion that legal exposure must be both foreseeable and controllable. It would also be consistent with the 'no gain without pain' maxim – that is, if you seek to reap the benefits from foreign customs, you should also expect to carry the burden of being answerable to the laws of those states. While this interpretation of 'harmful event' would be the most rationally defensible and would address valid concerns about the over-regulation of online content providers, the legal position adopted under the Regulation so far remains uncertain. The national approaches taken to transnational online torts or quasi-torts paint a varied picture, generally with more moderation shown in trade mark cases than in defamation cases.

Article 5(3) was considered in *Re the MARITIM Trade Mark*,[174] a trade mark infringement action brought in Hamburg by the owner of a chain of hotels in Germany named 'MARITIM', for which he had an EU and German trade mark. The Danish defendant ran a bed-and-breakfast (B&B) in

---

172 See also *Football Dataco Ltd & Ors v Sportradar GmbH & Anor* [2011] EWCA Civ 330 for the Court of Appeal referral to the ECJ of the issue whether data from a protected database is 'extracted' and/or 'reutilised' under Art 7 of the Database Directive 96/9/EC in the place where it is accessible online or in the place from which it emanates, ie the server.

173 Case C-68/93 [1995] 2 WLR 499, following *Bier v Mines de Potasse d'Alsace SA*, Case 21/76 [1976] ECR 1735, [24]ff, which was decided under the almost identically worded Brussels Convention on Jurisdiction and the Enforcement of Judgments in Civil and Commercial Matters 1968, the predecessor of the Regulation.

174 *Re the MARITIM Trademark*, Hanteatisches Oberlandsgericht Hamburg, Urteil vom 2.5.2002, *Internet-Zeitschrift für Rechtsinformatik and Informationsrecht*, available online at www.jurpc.de/rechtspr/20020317.pdf

Copenhagen under the name 'HOTEL MARITIME' (protected by a Danish trade mark). He advertised his B&B on his website hotel-maritime.dk in several languages, including German, which also allowed for online bookings. The German court took an expansive approach to Art 5(3), saying that any site accessible in Germany would expose its owner to the jurisdiction of German courts, quite regardless of the strength of substantive allegations. But the court then proceeded to find that, on the facts, no trade mark infringement had been committed. It held that that not every name used online should be subjected to German trade mark law; put differently, German trade mark law will not be applicable/infringed simply because a foreign site is accessible in Germany – thus paving the road for the peaceful coexistence of national trade marks on the international online stage. German trade mark law would extend extraterritorially only if the foreign site were directed at Germany. Here, the court found, this requirement was not satisfied, because the site advertised a service to be delivered entirely in Denmark, because the use of foreign languages was normal in this commercial sector and did not mean that the site was directed at consumers in Germany, and because the .dk domain suggested that the Danish market was the focal point of the site. It may be objected that the use of foreign languages was very much designed to attract foreigners, including Germans, to the site, which is not undermined but rather reinforced by the fact that it is standard practice in the tourist industry. Thus Germany, along with many other states, was a target of the site. But regardless, the German court clearly adopted a moderate destination approach at the merit stage rather than at the initial stage of adjudicative jurisdiction. While to some extent it does not matter at which stage this moderate reasoning kicks in (provided that it does at some point), it would only seem fair to filter out unmeritorious cases at the earliest possible opportunity, which is at the point of jurisdiction. This indeed would also be consistent with the wording of Art 5(3), which, by focusing on the 'harm', makes the prima facie merits of the substantive action the trigger for the court's competence.

A more restrictive approach to Art 5(3)[175] was adopted in the Scottish cybersquatting case of *Bonnier Media Ltd v Greg Lloyd Smith and Kestrel Trading Corp*,[176] in which the Greek defendant registered domain names very similar to the trade marks and domain names of the Scottish plaintiff. He then offered to sell them to the plaintiff under the threat of selling them elsewhere. The Scottish court assumed personal jurisdiction over the defendant, but not simply because the sites were accessible in Scotland:

> While a website could be viewed anywhere in the world, it did not follow that, at least for the purposes of trademark infringement or passing off, the provider of a website or the owner of a domain name was liable anywhere in the world where the website might be viewed.[177]

Instead, the court adopted a classic moderate country-of-destination approach, comparable to US jurisprudence on personal jurisdiction over online activity:

> In my opinion a website should not be regard as having delictual consequences in any country where it is unlikely to be of significant interest. That result can readily be achieved by a vigorous application of the maxim *de minimis non curat praetor* [the law is not interested in trivial matters]; if the impact of a website is insignificant, it is appropriate in my opinion to look both at the content of the website itself and at the commercial or other context in which the website operate.[178]

---

175 Again, this case was decided under the predecessor of the Regulation, the Brussels Convention on Jurisdiction and the Enforcement of Judgments in Civil and Commercial Matters 1968.
176 (Court of Sessions, Scotland, 1 July 2002), available online at www.scotcourts.gov.uk/opinions/DRU2606.html. See also discussion in Chapter 8.
177 Ibid, [16].
178 Ibid, [19].

Given that this was a cybersquatting scenario, the defendant's act – that is, the publication of the sites – was clearly aimed at the plaintiff's business in Scotland, and thus not within the *de minimis* maxim – a result entirely consistent with *Calder*.

In the English case of *Euromarket Designs Inc v Peters and Crate & Barrel Ltd*,[179] the US plaintiff alleged that the Irish defendant had infringed its UK and EC registered trade mark 'Crate & Barrell' by advertising its goods in a UK magazine with a UK and Irish circulation, and on a website of the name crateandbarrel-ie.com. In a summary judgment, the court proceeded straight to the substance of the allegation, without considering the issue of jurisdiction under Art 5(3). On substantive grounds, the court found that no trade mark infringement had occurred: the defendant had not used the mark in the course of a UK trade. According to the court, neither the magazine advert nor the site constituted infringing 'use'. In respect of the magazine (but also insightful for the online context), Jacob J held that 'if the trader is merely carrying on business in X, and advertisement of his slips over the border into Y, no businessman would regard that fact as meaning that he was trading in Y. This would especially be so if the advertisement were for a local business such as a shop or a local service rather than for goods'.[180] In the spirit of *Zippo*, he continued that the website in this case merely allowed the surfer to look into the Irish shop, rather provided an active platform for trade itself:

> [In this case] the internet was more like the user focussing a super-telescope into the site concerned . . . you can look into the defendant's shop in Dublin . . . Other cases would be different – a well-known example, for instance, is Amazon.com. Based in the US it has actively gone out to seek world-wide trade, not just by use of the name on the internet but by advertising its business here, and offering and operating a real service of supply of books to this country. These defendants have done none of that.[181]

In coming to this conclusion, Jacob J relied upon his earlier trade mark decision in *1-800 Flowers Inc v Phonenames Ltd*,[182] in which he said that the question of whether a site is or is not 'used in the course of trade' in the place in which it can be accessed depends on the objective intention of the owner in light of all of the circumstances:

> the mere fact that websites can accessed anywhere in the world does not mean, for trade mark purposes, that the law should regard them as being used everywhere in the world. It all depends upon the circumstances, particularly the intention of the website owner and what the reader will understand if he accesses the site.[183]

Currently, and in the absence of an authoritative statement by the ECJ, EU jurisprudence on transnational online trade mark disputes favours the moderate line according to which some, but not all, sites incur legal accountability in the states in which they can be accessed. So far, it remains unclear at which stage such moderation should occur: is it when deciding on the court's jurisdiction under Art 5(3) of the Regulation, or at the later substantive stage? As argued above, the earlier, the better.

What is at the moment undecided is how Art 5(3) should be applied to other delictual disputes – in particular defamation actions. How would the *Shevill* understanding of 'harmful event' be applied to a defamatory online newspaper? While, as argued below, there is, in principle, no reason to treat defamation claims any differently from trade mark claims, in fact, case law across the

---

179 [2000] EWHC Ch 179. See also discussion in Chapter 8.
180 Ibid, [19].
181 Ibid, [24].
182 [2000] ETMR 369.
183 Ibid, [12].

globe testifies to the reluctance of states to extend the moderate country-of-destination approach taken in online trade mark cases to online defamation actions. Some of the latter actions have arisen in England in claims that fell outside the Regulation and thus within the traditional English principles on personal jurisdiction.

The European approach to the 'applicable law' in non-contractual cases avoids the above ambiguities. The general rule in tort cases in Art 4(1) of the EC **Regulation on the Law Applicable to Non-Contractual Obligations**[184] stipulates that the 'law of the country where the damage occurs' shall be the applicable law quite irrespective of where 'the event giving rise to the damage occurred'.

English Common Law: *Forum Conveniens* in Defamation Cases

If the defendant to a civil action is domiciled outside the EU, the jurisdiction of the court is determined by the national law of the Member State rather than the EC **Jurisdiction Regulation**. The bulk of internet actions that have triggered national jurisdiction rules have been transnational defamation claims. In England, these actions have concerned claims against US publishers that, all things being equal, ought to have been brought in the USA and simply migrated to England for tactical reasons; they would have stood little chance of success in the USA given the publisher-friendly interpretation of 'free speech' under the US **Constitution**.

Under English law on personal jurisdiction, a foreign defendant may be sued in England even if he or she is not 'present' in England, where:

(1)   there is a serious issue to be tried that is a substantial question of fact or law;

(2)   the claim, rather than the defendant, is, broadly speaking, connected with England;[185] and

(3)   England is a *forum conveniens*.[186]

The first two hurdles are easily jumped: where the plaintiff claims to have suffered damage in England by virtue of the foreign allegedly defamatory online publication, there would both be a substantial question of fact and law, as well as a sufficient connection with England. By far the most controversial element in the internet context has been the third hurdle – namely, whether England is, in the circumstances, the most suitable forum in which to hear the claim given the interests of the parties and the pursuit of justice.

The leading case on this issue that set the stage for later internet defamation cases is the House of Lords' decision in *Berezovsky v Michaels*[187] concerning a traditional magazine. The plaintiff, a Russian businessman, wanted to sue the US publisher of *Forbes*, an influential American fortnightly magazine, in England on the basis of a few copies that were distributed in England. The distribution in England made up a meagre 0.2 per cent of the total circulation, the bulk of which had occurred in the USA. Despite this tiny distribution, it would, according to the Lords, not be unfair that the foreign publisher should be sued in England, because 'all the constituent elements of the tort occurred in England'.[188] In other words, in legal terms, the alleged wrong was a purely local wrong: there was a 'publication' in England that had damaged the reputation that the plaintiff enjoyed in England – and, prima facie, the natural forum to adjudicate a tort is the place in which it occurred.[189] Thus the competence of the English court was based on compartmentalising transnational activity

---

184 No 864/2007.

185 Pursuant to r 6.36 of the Civil Procedure Rules, and para 3.1(9) of Practice Direction 6b (which supplement Section IV of CPR, Pt 6), the claimant may serve a claim form out of the jurisdiction with the permission of the court where the claim is made in tort: where (a) damage was sustained within the jurisdiction; or (b) the damage sustained resulted from an act committed within the jurisdiction.

186 *Spiliada Maritime Corp v Cansulex Ltd* [1987] AC 460.

187 [2000] 1 WLR 1004.

188 Ibid, 1013.

189 *The Albaforth* [1984] 2 Lloyd's Rep 91, 94.

into a multitude of national activities that, in turn, allowed for the easy application of national procedures and law. Such compartmentalisation seems already strained and distorting reality in the case of traditional newspapers, in relation to which the circulation in different countries at least presupposes a deliberate choice. In respect of online publications, transnationality is so intrinsic to the conduct that a narrow focus on its purely local effects without any regard to the impact of the publication elsewhere seems like an exercise of blind faith in national law orthodoxy. And yet, this is exactly what happened.

One legal avenue that the court in *Berezovsky* and in later internet cases could have used to decline jurisdiction is the *Kroch v Rossell*[190] holding. In that case, the Court of Appeal held that jurisdiction of the local court will lie only if the alleged tort committed in the jurisdiction was a real and substantial one (analogous to the *de minimis* maxim referred to in *Bonnier Media*)[191]: ' . . . it would be ridiculous and fundamentally wrong to have these two cases tried in this country on a very small and technical publication, when the real grievance of the plaintiff is a grievance against the widespread publication of the two papers in the respective countries where they are published.'[192] Ultimately, jurisdiction was declined because there was no evidence that the plaintiff, being a foreigner, enjoyed a reputation locally. It would take but a small step to extend this holding to cases in which the bulk either of the publication or of the damage occurred elsewhere. But this step would, of course, require judges not only to consider the local effects of the conduct, but also to consider those effects in light of the totality of the transnational activity. In *Berezovsky*, Lord Steyn commented that such a 'global theory runs counter to well established principles of libel law'.[193]

Berezovsky was extended to online publications in *Harrods Ltd v Dow Jones Co Inc*[194] concerning Harrods Ltd's defamation claim against Dow Jones, the publisher of the *Wall Street Journal*. The offending article, which appeared only in the US, not the European, edition of the journal, had been sent to ten subscribers in the UK, in contrast to its US circulation of 1.8 million copies. Similarly, its online edition had a very small number of hits from the UK. In line with *Berezovsky*, Harrods Ltd limited its claim to the damage suffered in the UK[195] and thereby achieved that, technically, the only foreign element in the claim was the defendant; the tort itself occurred in England, and the plaintiff lived in England and enjoyed a reputation there. Therefore the court upheld Harrods' right to sue in England, although substantially the case was quite 'foreign' indeed: the publication was produced in the USA, predominantly for a US market; Harrods Ltd, although a UK company, has a worldwide reputation and was ultimately concerned to vindicate its reputation not only in England, but also worldwide.

A year later, in *Lewis & ors v King*,[196] the allegedly defamatory statements had exclusively been distributed via the internet. The statements in question were made by an attorney representing Lennox Lewis in litigation with King in the USA, and published on fightnews.com and boxingtalk. com. These sites, although of US origin, were, unlike in the above cases, also popular elsewhere, including England. But also unlike in the above cases, both the defendant and the plaintiff were US residents.[197] In reaching its conclusion not to interfere with the decision of the first-instance judge

---

190 [1937] 1 All ER 725.
191 See above.
192 *Kroch v Rossell* [1937] 1 All ER 725, 732.
193 *Berezovsky v Michaels* [2000] 1 WLR 1004, 1013. The *de minimis* maxim, as well as the *Kroch v Rossell* holding, were expressly rejected in *Harrods Ltd v Dow Jones Co Inc* [2003] EWHC 1162 (QB), [39] ('there is no *de minimis* principle when it comes to establishing publication'), and [44], distinguishing *Kroch v Rossell* on the facts.
194 [2003] EWHC 1162 (QB). In *Dow Jones & Co v Harrods Ltd* 237 F Supp 2d 394, the New York district court refused to grant to Dow Jones a declaratory judgment and an injunction requiring Harrods Ltd to abstain from pursuing a defamation claim in the UK.
195 *Berezovsky v Michaels* [2000] 1 WLR 1004, 1032, and also consistent with the European approach: see above.
196 [2004] EWCA Civ 1329, affirming *Lewis & ors v King* [2004] EWHC 168 (QB).
197 As was the case in *Chadha v Dow Jones & Co* [1999] EMLR 724, in which both parties were US residents and the UK number of subscribers to the publication, in comparison with the US subscription, was relatively small; the English court declined to hear the case.

to allow the claim to proceed, the Court of Appeal usefully isolated four strands emerging from existing jurisprudence on *forum conveniens* in transnational online defamation claims.[198]

(1)   The court said that there is a presumption that the natural and appropriate place to hear the case is where the tort occurred, as decided in *Berezovsky*. In defamation, this is where the article is published – that is, downloaded – and where the defendant has a reputation to protect.

(2)   The importance of the location of the tort diminishes the more tenuous the claimant's connection with England is and the more substantial the publication abroad.

(3)   The traditional defamation rule that each publication gives rise to a separate cause of action, as enunciated in *Duke of Brunswick v Harmer*,[199] has survived the internet age; it has not been replaced by an assumption that an online publication gives rise only to one cause of action, which would favour a hearing in the court of the foreign publisher where the bulk of the publication took place. The only difference that the internet makes is that it gives rise to a more open-textured exercise of judicial discretion in deciding where the claim ought to be heard.

(4)   In deciding the appropriate forum in internet cases, the notion of 'targeting' makes little sense because, in truth, the defendant targets every jurisdiction where its site can be downloaded; in any event, a focus on the subjective intention of the defendant would give rise to manipulation and uncertainty, which is not in the interest of justice.

Finally, the court stressed that deciding whether a case ought to be heard in England or not was within the realms of the discretion of the judge at first instance and a matter of practical reasoning, rather than legal rules.

Other jurisdictions have taken much the same approach. Most notably, the High Court of Australia, in *Dow Jones & Co Inc v Gutnick*,[200] declined to make any allowances for the intrinsically global nature of the internet and effectively held that the publication of a website was analogous to the worldwide circulation of a newspaper: the publication took place not in the location of the server where the material was uploaded, but where it was downloaded – where it was read and understood – no matter how large or small the readership. *Gutnick* was given the go-ahead to sue Dow Jones, the US publisher of Barrons Online, in Victoria (Australia), despite the fact that the vast majority of subscribers to the site were from the USA and only a tiny percentage from Australia. Relying on *Berezovsky*, the judges pointed to the fact that there was a small, but perfectly formed, defamation in Australia.

In Rem Jurisdiction

An alternative to personal jurisdiction to establish the adjudicative jurisdiction of the court is *in rem* jurisdiction (Latin meaning 'power against a thing'). Here, the court's competence is based upon the presence within the court's territory of an asset under dispute, rather than the defendant's presence.[201] Classically, *in rem* jurisdiction has arisen in admirality law, in which the presence of a ship within the court's jurisdiction provided the basis of the court's competence.[202] The presence of the ship within the court's enforcement power is used both as a lever against the defendant to defend

---

198 *Lewis & ors v King* [2004] EWCA Civ 1329, [24]–[39].

199 (1849) 14 QB 184.

200 [2002] HCA 56, aff'd *Gutnick v Dow Jones & Co Inc* [2001] VSC 305.

201 Contrast *in rem* jurisdiction, in which the action is against a thing, with jurisdiction *in personam*, which may also be based on the location of the subject matter of the dispute (ie movable or immovable property) within the jurisdiction, but in which the action is still against the defendant.

202 See Supreme Court Act 1981, s 21; *Republic of India v Indian Steamship Company Ltd* [1998] AC 878, in which the House of Lords held that the owners of the ship are parties to an action *in rem*.

the dispute (that is, to submit to the court's jurisdiction), as well as an avenue to enforce a judgment against the defendant. Thus in rem jurisdiction does not entail the enforcement difficulties of other judgments against foreign wrongdoers. For this reason, it is surprising that it has not been exploited more frequently in the online context.

In the USA, in rem jurisdiction has proven useful in both online gambling and domain name disputes. The case of US v $734,578.8 in US Currency[203] concerns online gambling, which, as discussed above, is severely restricted in the USA. In this case, the US government brought a civil in rem forfeiture action to enforce criminal restrictions on internet or telephone gambling indirectly. The action was brought against various US bank accounts used in the process of illegal gambling activity of the defendant English company, American Sports Ltd, which operated under a licence in England, solicited punters in the USA via a website, and finally facilitated the gambling via the telephone. Because a New Jersey company had acted as an intermediary for the defendant to organise the financial side of the business, the court treated the case as a purely domestic case, seeing no need at all to engage with the transnationality of the underlying allegedly illegal transactions. All that the US government had to show, to have the funds forfeited, was that there were reasonable grounds to believe that the New Jersey intermediary had violated US gambling prohibitions, which it did. The defendant's argument that the New Jersey intermediary dealt purely with the financial aspects of the gambling and that all actual gambling took place beyond US borders in England, where it was legal, was rejected by the court: ' . . . the legality and/or licensure of the businesses in England is simply irrelevant to the issues raised in the instant forfeiture proceedings.'[204] Equally, even if 'British citizens and British companies will be affected by this in rem action in New Jersey',[205] that had no bearing on the action. The court could take such a disinterested view of the foreign interests involved because it was in no way dependent upon the cooperation of the foreign state for the enforcement of its judgment – the in rem nature of the action guaranteed enforcement power.

In Cable News Network LP v CNNews.com,[206] in rem jurisdiction was successfully relied upon in a trade mark dispute to catch a foreign defendant who would have fallen through the personal jurisdiction net. The dispute arose because a Chinese company registered cnnews.com with Network Solutions in Virginia in the USA; the site provided news in Chinese to the Chinese market. Because '.cn' is the country top-level domain for China and the name 'cnnews' translates literally into 'Chinese news', it would appear to be an appropriate domain name for a Chinese news company. Nevertheless, the well-known US news corporation CNN took objection and alleged that cnnews.com infringed and diluted its CNN trade mark in the USA. CNN would have had difficulties having the case heard in the USA relying on personal jurisdiction, because the Chinese company had virtually no contacts with the USA. So as an alternative, CNN relied upon the **Anticybersquatting Consumer Protection Act of 1999**,[207] which applies to bad-faith domain name registration and allows plaintiffs to recover the name (but no monetary awards). The Act provides for in rem jurisdiction in respect of domain name in the judicial district where its 'registrar, registry, or other domain name authority . . . is located'. Because all .com names (the most popular name worldwide) are under the control of the US company VeriSign,[208] in rem jurisdiction over any dispute involving these names gives US courts wide powers over foreign registrants.[209] Indeed, in CNN, the Virginian District Court held that the

---

203 286 F 3d 641 (NJ, 2002).
204 US v $734,578.82 in US Currency 286 F3d 641, 657 (3rd Cir 2002).
205 Ibid, 660.
206 In respect of the jurisdiction requirements, see Cable News Network LP v CNNews.com 162 F Supp 2d 484 (ED Va 2001). On the substance of the claim, see Cable News Network LP v CNNews.com 177 F Supp 2d 506 (ED Va 2001), aff'd in part and vacated in part on other grounds Cable News Network LP v CNNews.com 56 Fed Appx 599 (4th Cir 2003).
207 Codified in s 43(d) of the Lanham Act. See also discussion in Chapter 8.
208 Until 2012, for the time being: BBC News, 'Deal signed on.com domain future' (2006) 4 December, available online at http://news.bbc.co.uk/2/hi/technology/6199394.stm
209 CaesarsWorld, Inc v Caesars-Palace.com 112 F Supp 2d 502 (ED Va, 2000); Hartog & Co, AS v Swix.com and Swix.net 2001 US Dist Lexis 3568 (ED Va, 2001); GlobalSantafe Corp v GlobalSantafe.com 250 F Supp 2d 610 (ED Va, 2003); America Online, Inc v AOL.org 259 F Supp 2d 449 (ED Va, 2003); NBC Universal, Inc v NBCUniversal.com 378 F Supp 2d 715 (ED Va, 2005).

'.com' was an 'essentially American top-level domain name'.[210] As far as the in rem nature of the jurisdiction was concerned, the Court held that there was no need either for the Chinese company to have had minimum contacts with the USA,[211] nor was a showing of bad faith a jurisdictional requirement.[212] Thus it did not matter that the target audience of ccnews.com was almost exclusively located in China (99.5 per cent of the site's registered users were from China) and that the site did not sell any products or services to anyone outside China. The Court then found that all of the elements for a trade mark infringement claim under the 1999 Act were satisfied.[213] For the substantive claim, the 'bad faith' requirement was held to be satisfied on the basis that the Chinese company had not previously used the name nor a trade mark of that name.[214] It rejected that the application of US trade mark law would be extraterritorial. In its opinion, the dispute was a purely domestic dispute, as the domain name was within the jurisdiction.[215] It then ordered that the domain name of cnnews.com be transferred to CNN.

In both of the above cases, the location of the property (that is, the bank account and the domain name) within the USA provided the basis of the court's right to hear the dispute in line with traditional in rem jurisdiction. Furthermore, on the basis of the location of the property, the courts treated the disputes as purely domestic also in determining the application of the substantive law (even though, for example, the location of a domain name registration is entirely irrelevant to determining whether local trade mark law was applicable or infringed). The effect of treating in rem cases as purely domestic – regardless of the transnationality of the underlying transaction – means that safeguards normally in place to guard against exorbitant jurisdictional assertions are simply not called into play. The results are unfortunate insular decisions.

Enforcement

The issue of enforceability is as prominent in relation to online civil disputes as it is in respect of criminal matters, and, just like in criminal law, the starting point for civil law is the strict territorial limit of enforcement jurisdiction of states. Neither they nor their officials can take any actions outside their own borders to enforce a judgment against a foreign defendant. However, unlike in criminal law, there is some cooperation in the form of the reciprocal enforcement of foreign judgments frequently enshrined in bilateral or multilateral treaties.

In England and Wales, the default position on the enforcement of foreign judgments is provided for under common law, according to which a plaintiff can apply for a summary judgment on the foreign judgment. Because the defendant has few defences to such claims and because the willingness of English courts to enforce foreign judgments is, rather generously, not dependent on reciprocity,[216] they are relatively easily enforceable. The common law position is replaced by statute in respect of foreign states that have entered into enforcement treaties with the UK, bringing either the **Foreign Judgments (Reciprocal Enforcement) Act 1933** or the EC **Regulation on Jurisdiction and the Recognition and Enforcement of Judgments in Civil and Commercial Matters**[217] into play. The Regulation lays down a strong mutual recognition and enforcement regime in which any judgment (and not only money judgments) from another Member State is automatically

---

210 *Cable News Network LP v CNNews.com* 177 F Supp 2d 506, 517 (ED Va 2001).
211 Ibid, 491. In fact, there was no need for the registrant of the domain name to be joined in the action under the ACPA: ibid, 493ff.
212 Ibid, 492ff.
213 Ibid.
214 Ibid, 524.
215 Ibid, 527. This approach also means that the test (concerning the extraterritorial reach of trade mark law) laid down in *McBee v Delica Co Ltd* 417 F3d 107 (1st Cir 2005) requiring that the extraterritorial activities of the foreigner under the offending name must have a substantial effect on US commerce would not be called into play.
216 *Adams v Cape Industries plc* [1990] Ch 433, 552.
217 No 44/2001.

recognised and, following compliance with some formal procedures, enforceable, unless subsequently successfully challenged on one of five narrow grounds.[218]

One basis for challenging the enforceability of a foreign judgment – recognised under English common law and statute, as well as in most other states – is 'public policy' – that is, that the enforcement would be contrary to the 'public policy' of the enforcing state.[219] This exception to enforceability runs parallel to the exclusion of foreign law in locally adjudicated cases in which the enforcement or recognition of such foreign law would be inconsistent with public policy of the enforcing state.[220] The effect of either exclusionary rule varies from state to state, being modestly applied in some and treated as a catch-all escape route in others. In England, public policy has rarely been invoked to refuse enforcement or recognition of a foreign judgment;[221] in Canada, the narrowness of the defence was recently affirmed in *Society of Lloyd's v Meinzer*,[222] limiting it to cases affecting 'essential principles of justice' or 'moral interests' of the enforcing state.

The public policy exception is routinely used in the USA, particularly to invoke US constitutional free speech standards, in order to deny the enforcement of foreign judgments, often concerning defamation claims. This has been the case even when the enforcement of the foreign judgment would take effect solely in the foreign state and not impact at all on any speech in the USA.[223] This unwillingness does not necessarily stop plaintiffs from bringing their actions, as the Australian and English defamation cases, discussed above, show. In *Gutnick*, the Australian High Court specifically acknowledged the likely unenforceability of any final order against the US-based publisher.[224] Especially in defamation actions, it is often more valuable to the plaintiff to have its reputation vindicated than the promise of a monetary award, and thus the unenforceability of the judgment is a secondary concern for these plaintiffs.

A high-profile internet case in which a US court in fact refused to enforce the foreign judgment is the French *Yahoo* case, discussed above. In that case, the Californian Supreme Court held that enforcement of the French order would be inconsistent with the First Amendment, ostensibly because the enforcement of the foreign order would chill protected speech in the USA.[225] This, however, was a result that the French court had been at pains to avoid by ensuring that Yahoo! Inc had the technical means to restrict access to certain sites for French users only, but not others. The Californian Court also asserted that the unenforceability of the French order on the basis of its unconstitutionality would not give the US First Amendment extraterritorial effect, because it applied to Yahoo! Inc's 'actions in the United States, specifically [to] the ways in which it configures and operates its auction and Yahoo.com sites'.[226] The problem with this argument is that the very point of seeking the enforcement of a foreign judgment is to make the defendant do something in the enforcing state; in other words, it is an argument that would require every foreign judgment to be compatible with the US **Constitution** regardless of where the effects of the judgment would be felt. While the Californian judgment was reversed on other grounds on appeal, a majority of the US

---

218 EC Regulation No 44/200 on Jurisdiction and the Recognition and Enforcement of Judgments in Civil and Commercial Matters, Arts 34 and 35; see also Arts 41 and 45. Unlike common law, the Regulation does not allow for the review of the jurisdiction of the foreign court that pronounced the judgment and thus provides a more robust enforcement regime. Under the Regulation, such review is not necessary, because it harmonises jurisdiction rules and thus guards against exorbitant jurisdictional assertion by any Member State.

219 Under Art 34(1), ibid, the judgment must be 'manifestly' contrary to the public policy of the requested state for the exception to apply.

220 Lawrence Collins (ed), *Dicey, Morris & Collins on The Conflict of Laws*, 14th edn, 2006, London: Sweet & Maxwell, 92.

221 Ibid, 629.

222 (2002) 210 DLR (4th) 519 (Ont CA).

223 Kyo Ho Yum, 'The interaction between American and foreign libel law: US courts refuse to enforce English libel judgments' (2000) 49 ICLQ 132; Jeremy Maltby, 'Juggling comity and self-government: The enforcement of foreign libel judgments in US courts' (1994) 94 Colum L Rev 1978.

224 *Dow Jones & Co v Gutnick* [2002] HCA 56, [53].

225 *Yahoo! Inc v LICRA* 169 F Supp 2d 1181, 1192 (ND Cal, 2001).

226 Ibid, 1193.

Court of Appeals agreed in *obiter* with its unenforceability.[227] The judges acknowledged that foreign laws need not be identical to US laws, but must not be repugnant to local laws and policies, or, put more broadly, to fundamental principles of what is 'decent and just'.[228] Unfortunately, most judges decided that the US **Constitution** laid down what is decent and just, and that anything inconsistent with it could not conceivably be so.[229]

---

227 Because the issue of enforceability had not been appealed by LICRA, it was not within the remit of the court to decide it. Yet six out of the eleven judges held that the order would not be enforceable either on public policy grounds, being contrary to the First Amendment, or (in Ferguson J's case) on the ground that the order was an act of state. Only Fletcher J, Schroeder CJ, and Gould J left enforceability open as a possibility; Tashima J and O'Scannlain J expressed no opinion.

228 *Yahoo! Inc v LICRA & UEJF* 379 F 3d 1120, 1215 (9th Cir 2004).

229 Ibid, 1140.

Chapter 3

Content Regulation: Liability of Intermediaries

Introduction

In the 1990s, the early days of the commercial internet, the term 'disintermediation' played a significant part in academic discussions of the online world. The view was that the internet dispensed with the need for many of the traditional middlemen, allowing transactions and exchanges to occur directly between the primary actors. One commentator wrote, for example:

> Because of the capabilities of computer networks, the functions of central repository and archive are highly vulnerable to disintermediation. As applied to libraries, disintermediation means the diversion of information users from centralized physical repositories to alternate sources available directly through computers and computer networks. The Internet offers publishers a new way of reaching customers and offers users a new way of finding sources. Users no longer have to physically go to a library when the library is open. They can connect to the Internet anytime they want.[1]

Similar views were expressed about many other traditional commercial and non-commercial institutions, such as the press, newsagents, book and music shops, television companies, video stores, security brokers, estate and travel agents, and many other bricks-and-mortar retailers. While some of these predictions have materialised – consider, for example, the dwindling number of music and bookshops, or the direct sale of flight tickets by airlines – the claim of disintermediation on the internet has still failed spectacularly. The online era has not only witnessed the replacement of many traditional intermediaries by online intermediaries (such as Virgin Megastores versus Apple iTunes), but also the emergence of new intermediaries that have no obvious bricks-and-mortar equivalent, such as search engines or networking sites. From a regulatory perspective, the continued existence of intermediaries in the online world is significant, because intermediaries are an indispensable regulatory tool and target.

Although the discussion below is framed in terms of immunities rather than liabilities, these immunities are by no means all-embracing – given especially the relentless pressure towards intermediary liability by intellectual property holders. The approach simply reflects a brief historical period of the mid-to-late 1990s when the hands-off approach to the internet, and particularly online intermediaries, was en vogue with Western governments. Now, we seem to have entered what Debora Spar calls the last phase in the four-phase historical pattern, which, she argues, accompanies major technological innovations in communication. The four phases are:

(1)   innovation;
(2)   commercialisation;
(3)   creative anarchy; and
(4)   rules.[2]

Spar explains:

> If we view cyberspace from history . . . we see a more complex vision. Instead of a one-way scramble to a brave new world, it is a journey of twists and turns, a movement along a frontier whose boundaries shift and stumble and collide. It is a view filled with the normal characters of a frontier town: there are still the pirates and the pioneers, the tinkers and the travelling salesmen. Only, in this view, the pirates and the pioneers aren't necessarily

---

1 Robert Gellman, 'Disintermediation and the internet' (1996) 13 Gov Inform Q 1.
2 Debora L Spar, *Ruling the Waves: Cycles of Discovery, Chaos, and Wealth from the Compass to the Internet*, 2001, London: Harcourt.

the winners. Instead, once the technological frontier has moved beyond a certain point, power and profits – seem to shift way from those who break the rules and back to those who make them.[3]

The discussion below bears testimony to Spar's thesis that once new technology has matured and been embraced commercially by pioneers and pirates alike, these entrepreneurs call for the help of government to protect newly established property interests, to coordinate the use of a limited resource, to intervene to limit dominance, and to ensure fair competition – in short, to regulate. And with this new regulatory agenda, intermediaries are now at the sharp edge of online governance, as shines through in one industry response to the government's call for responses to its consultation document on intermediary liability/immunities:

> The factual changes of the circumstances where internet intermediaries offer their services since the adoption of the Electronic Commerce Directive in 2000 in fact justify the reduction of the scope of Articles 12 to 14 [the immunities], rather than its extension . . . The current scope . . . is too wide . . . The limitation of liability for intermediaries was provided . . . because it was felt necessary at the time to facilitate the development of the then nascent market for intermediaries. The position now is very different, with several intermediaries being in a strong economic position, particularly in comparison to individual composers and music publishers who are struggling to protect and enforce their rights in the online environment. In hindsight, it is evident that the limitation of liability provided in Articles 12 to 14 was disproportionate and unduly geared towards the supposed needs of intermediaries.[4]

Although the government did not cave in to the calls for a reduction of the immunities, it equally refused to extend them to other online facilitators. A similar reticence is also apparent in the USA, where, for example, in *Fair Housing Council of San Fernando Valley v Roommates.com*,[5] the majority reasoned:

> The Internet is no longer a fragile new means of communication that could easily be smothered in the cradle by overzealous enforcement of laws and regulations applicable to brick-and-mortar businesses. Rather it has become a dominant – perhaps the preeminent – means through which commerce is conducted. And its vast reach into the lives of millions is exactly why we must be careful not to exceed the scope of the immunity provided by Congress and thus give online businesses an unfair advantage over their real-world counterpart, which must comply with the laws of general applicability.[6]

Online Intermediaries and Legal Concerns

Types of Intermediary

Internet intermediaries come in all shapes and sizes, but may be grouped into different categories depending on the role that they play in the online communication or transaction chain. These varying roles also frequently impact on the level of their involvement in the primary activity – ranging from being entirely passive middlemen, which simply provide the setting for the interactions, to those that take an active facilitatory role – which in turn is likely to have repercussions for liability.

---

3 Ibid, 8.
4 DTI, 'Consultation Document on the Electronic Commerce Directive: The Liability of Hyperlinkers, Location Tool Services and Content Aggregators – Government Response and Summary of Responses', December 2006, 26.
5 521 F3d 1157 (9th Cir 2008).
6 Ibid, 1164.

- *Connectivity* At the most basic level, there are those intermediaries that provide or facilitate access to the internet, both in terms of providing connectivity for users and hosting content. These intermediaries include the backbone telecommunications providers, including mobile telephone companies and cable companies, internet service or access providers (ISPs) (including hosting companies and institutions such as universities), and wi-fi operators, such as cafes, pubs, libraries, and conference centres.

- *Navigation* Another group of online intermediaries are those that facilitate navigation around the web, by indexing online content and making it easily accessible to users, such as search engines, aggregation sites (that is, sites that collect links relevant to a certain topic), and all of those sites that provide hyperlinks to other related sites. Also within this category fall providers of sites implicated in the illegal downloading of music, films, games, and software, such as 'The Pirate Bay', which allows users to search for and download BitTorrent files necessary for peer-to-peer file-sharing. Although peer-to-peer file-sharing is a classic example of disintermediation, it ultimately cannot quite do without any intermediaries.

- *Commercial and social networking* The next group of online intermediaries are providers of online services, the content of which may be generated by users or consists of connecting users with each other, either for commercial or social purposes. In the commercial context, examples are online auction houses, such as eBay, or sites such as Amazon in so far as it connects buyers with marketplace sellers. In the social sphere, users may be connected with each other via social networking sites, such as Facebook, Twitter, Skype, online messengers, dating or gaming sites, or sites the content of which is generated by and for users, such as YouTube, Wikipedia, blogs, and wikis – much of what falls within Web 2.0.

- *Traditional commercial intermediaries and facilitators* Finally, there are also all those intermediaries that may be exactly the same as the traditional commercial intermediaries or their online equivalents, such as retailers (for example, play.com), financial institutions (for example, credit card providers or PayPal), advertisers (for example, Google), and agents of various descriptions (for example, lastminute.com or expedia.com).

The legal discussion on intermediary liability/immunity that initially concerned 'connectivity' intermediaries is now heavily focused on navigation and networking intermediaries. The central legal issue regarding all of them is the extent to which they are, and should be, liable for the illegal activities of others. This chapter examines the secondary or accessory liability of intermediaries both in civil and criminal law, potentially covering a wide range of activities such as child pornography and speech of an obscene, racist, harassing, or terrorist nature, defamatory or privacy-breaching publications, illegal copying, and other activities infringing the intellectual property rights of others. Should intermediaries bear the burden? If so, why and when? What are the pragmatic regulatory reasons and the principled justifications based on fault and fairness for and against intermediary liability?

Intermediary Liability: Attractions and Concerns

The main attraction of intermediaries as targets for regulatory intervention lies in their size. They simply tend to be bigger than the actual wrongdoers, with a number of follow-on effects, as captured by Swire:

> In considering legal regulation of the Internet, there is an important distinction between large players, which one might call 'elephants', and small, mobile actors called 'mice'. The style of regulation against elephants and mice differs substantially. Elephants are large, powerful, and practically impossible to hide. Consider a transnational corporation that has major operations in a country. If that country has strict regulations, the corporation's actions will be highly visible,

and it may become an enforcement target if it flouts the law. At the same time, elephants are enormously strong and have all sorts of effects on the local ecosystem (potentially crushing trees, smaller animals, etc.). If a particular regulation angers an elephant, it may have the ability to change the rule. The situation is quite different for mice, which are small, nimble, and multiply annoyingly quickly . . . Would-be regulators can run around furiously with a broom, but with little chance of getting rid of all the mice.[7]

While not all intermediaries are 'elephants' and not all 'elephants' are intermediaries, the role of intermediation often triggers growth, for example, due to the network effect.[8] Similarly if a business is more sizeable, it often becomes attractive as an intermediary because its size makes it more well known and trustworthy – matters upon which a smaller player can piggyback (for example, market players on Amazon).

Elephant-sized intermediaries are attractive defendants in civil suits because they tend to have deeper pockets than the actual wrongdoers. Also, both in the civil and criminal sphere, they are attractive regulatory targets because they can be more easily identified and, once sued, the effect of any restraining order is more significant in terms of the ripple effects on primary wrongdoers. So, for the music industry, it is more efficient and effective to sue the relatively few big intermediary operators, such as Pirate Bay or YouTube, for facilitating copyright infringement rather than the millions of actual copyright infringers. In addition and interrelatedly, large intermediaries also function as gatekeepers: regulators may rely upon intermediaries' access to legal expertise to sieve out unlawful content – a matter that is often beyond the knowledge and resources of end users. And because the success of these large visible intermediaries, particularly in the online world, often depends on their perceived respectability, which entails not being a lawbreaker (although not always), there are commercial incentives for legal obedience over and above any legal coercion.[9] Last but not least, in respect of criminal law, while the primary wrongdoer may be beyond the regulatory reach, such as the provider of a foreign gambling site, there may be intermediaries within the reach of the regulator, such as financial intermediaries or local ISPs. Even in civil litigation, the enforcement of a judgment against a local intermediary is much easier and much more likely to be successful than one against a foreign wrongdoer.

The above practical reasons for attaching legal obligations and attendant liabilities to intermediaries must be weighed against a number of disincentives. First, especially in criminal law, but also in civil law, liability is on the whole fault-based – that is, based on the guilty mind, or *mens rea*, or, in civil law, intention or negligence, in contrast with strict liability. This reflects the concern that it is unfair to attach liability or the stigma of being a criminal to an 'innocent' person and anyone who could not have prevented the wrongdoing. This is relevant to intermediaries, who often have no, or limited, awareness of the substance of, and control over, the communications or transactions that they are facilitating. In any event, this raises difficult issues as to what level of knowledge and control by the intermediary may be taken as sufficient to implicate it in the primary wrongdoing. Also, as will be shown, the line between primary actor and secondary actor/intermediary is not necessarily clear and bright.

Second, if monitoring, backed by the threat of liability, is required of intermediaries, it will increase their running costs, which increase they may pass on to end users or absorb in smaller profit margins. In either event, the collateral damage of those increased costs may have a chilling effect on activities that governments are otherwise keen to encourage.

---

7 Peter P Swire, 'Of elephants, mice, and privacy: International choice of law and the internet' (1998) 32 International Lawyer 991, 1019ff.
8 The network effect refers to the phenomenon that the value of some facilities goes up with an increasing number of users. So the more that individuals use the telephone, Facebook, or eBay, the more useful they become.
9 Uta Kohl, *Jurisdiction and the Internet*, 2007, Cambridge: Cambridge University Press, 207ff.

Finally, when, through the imposition of secondary liability, intermediaries are forced to act as gatekeepers, sieving out illegal content, they – as private parties – fulfil a function normally discharged by public agencies, such as courts. However, they lack the independence and expertise of the judiciary, and given the threat of sanctions against them, are likely to be overzealous police officers. This may lead to greater censorship than is legally required – at the cost of less material being available for the general public. For this reason, some ISPs have argued that they will not remove any material or block access to it in the absence of a court order to that effect.[10]

The discussion below shows how the law struggles to accommodate these conflicting concerns.

Immunities under the E-Commerce Directive

Relationship with other Immunities

In Europe, Section 4 of the **Electronic Commerce Directive**[11] (Arts 12–15) creates a staggered regime of immunities for 'intermediary service providers' corresponding to their relative involvement in the primary activities of others. The immunities regime is broadly conceived; it is not restricted to particular legal subject matters (also known as its 'horizontal effect') and may thus overlap with existing immunities framed more narrowly in terms of subject matter, but more widely in terms of the type of intermediary.[12] For example, s 1 of the **Defamation Act 1996** creates an 'innocent dissemination' defence for defamation purposes: a person is not liable for a defamatory statement provided that he or she was an intermediary (that is, 'not the author, editor or publisher of the statement'), took reasonable care in relation to its publication, and had no knowledge (or reason to know) of the existence of the defamatory statement (that is, the notice-and-takedown duty, discussed below). While this defence only covers defamation liability, it is not restricted to any particular type of intermediary, unlike those in the Directive being restricted to internet intermediaries. So the relationship of such subject matter immunities and the overarching ones under the Directive is complementary, in that an intermediary can rely on either of them; even if it is outside one of them, it may be able to rely upon the other.[13]

Which Intermediaries?

Who exactly falls within the immunity regime of the Directive? At the time of the adoption of the Directive, the debate on intermediary liability centred mainly on internet service providers – that is, those players that provide connectivity to the internet – and consequently these provide the focus of the immunities. However, as discussed below, the Directive is not confined to these intermediaries. Although s 4 is titled 'Intermediary service providers', they are not as such defined in the Directive. 'Service providers' are defined as 'any natural or legal person providing an information society service' (Art 2(b)), which is 'any service normally provided for remuneration, at a distance, by electronic means and at the individual request of a recipient of services'.[14] Excluded are services not provided 'at distance', such as a consultation of an electronic catalogue on a shop terminal,

---

10 See, eg, Jeremy Kirk, 'Irish ISP: We won't block the Pirate Bay' (2009) PC World, 24 February, available online at www.pcworld. com/article/160114/irish_isp_we_wont_block_the_pirate_bay.html
11 Directive 2000/31/EC, implemented in the UK by the Electronic Commerce (EC Directive) Regulations 2002, SI 2002/2013. See also European Commission, First Report on the Application of Directive 2000/31/EC of the European Parliament and of the Council of 8 June 2000 on Certain Legal Aspects of Information Society Services, in Particular Electronic Commerce, in the Internal Market, 2003, Brussels: European Commission COM(2003)702 final.
12 For example, s 2(5) of the Obscene Publications Act 1959.
13 See Bunt v Tilley [2006] EWHC 407, [58], QB, discussed below.
14 Article 2(a) defining 'information society services' by reference to the definition of 'services' in Art 1(2) of Directive 98/34/EC [1998] OJ L24/37, as amended by Directive 98/48/EC. See also Recitals 17 and 18.

services not 'by electronic means', such as offline services or non-electronic telephony services, and services not supplied 'at the individual request of a recipient', such as radio and television broadcasting services.[15] Included are activities such as the provision of services that are not remunerated by those who receive them (such as many social networking sites), and those that provide tools allowing for search, access, and retrieval of data (such as search engines), as well as services consisting of the transmission of information via a communication network (that is, the work of the telecommunication, cable, and mobile companies).[16] While the Directive takes a very broad approach to 'information society services' and, by implication, to 'service providers',[17] this is misleading, because the functional requirements on intermediaries in Arts 12–14 draws rather narrow boundaries around those entitled to them.

So despite the prima facie wide horizontal effect of the immunities coupled with the wide definition of 'service provider', the effect of the immunities is, as shown below, circumscribed by:

● functional requirements on the intermediaries (that is, restrictions on the qualifying intermediaries);
● the requirement of absence of knowledge (that is, restrictions on the type of actions in relation to which the immunities would be useful); and
● the availability of specific monitoring obligations and injunctions against intermediaries even where the immunities are applicable (that is, restrictions on the remedies falling within the immunities).

Contractual Release from Liability

A final preliminary comment concerns the effectiveness of disclaimers in the terms and conditions of intermediaries, such as the statement on the BBC website that 'the BBC is not responsible for the content of external websites' (www.bbc.co.uk/home/links/). Such contractual disclaimers are of limited effect because they can only bind those who agree to them – that is, users of the site – and thus are of very limited value in non-contractual civil claims (for example, defamation or copyright claims) unless the injured party was also party to the contract;[18] even then, they may not be enforced for a number of reasons. Furthermore, these disclaimers would have little effect on obligations under criminal/regulatory law because private parties cannot contract out of such obligations (at the most, such disclaimers go towards establishing the intermediary's intention or lack thereof in respect of any third-party conduct).

See Chapter 7

Immunities: Connectivity and Navigation

'Mere Conduit' and 'Caching'

The first two immunities under the Directive apply to those providers of 'information society services' that are involved in the business of 'mere conduit' and/or 'caching' of data – parallel to the immunity of traditional common carriers, such as telephone companies or the postal service.[19]

Article 12 deals with 'mere conduits' involved either in the 'transmission . . . of information provided by a recipient of their service' (for example, an email sent by a subscriber) or the

---

15 See Annex of the Directive 98/48/EC and Recital 18 of the Electronic Commerce Directive, as well as Art 1(5), which excludes from its scope taxation, data protection, cartel law, the activities of notaries and legal representation in court proceedings, and gambling activities.
16 Recital 18.
17 *Google AdWords* C-236/08, C-237/08 and C-238/08 Opinion of Advocate General (22 September 2009), [130]–[136]; *Google AdWords* C-236/08, C-237/08 and C-238/08 (23 March 2010) ECJ (Grand Chamber), [110] (discussed below).
18 See, eg, the US case of *Grace v eBay Inc* 16 Cal Rptr 3d 192 (Cal App Ct 2004).
19 For example, s 90 of the Postal Service Act 2000.

'provision of access to a communication network' (that is, internet access). Such conduits are immune from any liability in civil or criminal law for the information transmitted – as long as they neither initiate the transmission nor select the receiver of the transmission, nor select or modify the information contained in the transmission (Art 12(1)). So as long as the conduit does not get involved in the message, either its substance or the communicating parties, other than simply passing it on, the provider incurs no liability for damages. And this is so even if the transmission or the provision of access requires 'the automatic, intermediate and transient storage of the information transmitted' if such storage is solely for the purpose of transmission and not longer than reasonably necessary (Art 12(2)).

Article 13 also deals with the temporary storage by relieving intermediaries from liability for cached data (that is, 'the automatic, intermediate and temporary storage of ... information, performed for the sole purpose of making more efficient the information's onward transmission'), provided that:

(a) the provider does not modify the information (i.e. no editorial input)

(b) the provider complies with conditions on access to the information (e.g. age verification requirements for adult material, or other passwords)

(c) the provider complies with rules regarding the updating of the information, specified in a manner widely recognised and used by industry (i.e. to prevent out-of-date cached information being passed on to end users when the information on the original site has been updated)

(d) the provider does not interfere with the lawful use of technology, widely recognised and used by industry, to obtain data on the use of the information (e.g. data as to the number of hits on a site for determining advertising rates); and

(e) the provider acts expeditiously to remove or to disable access to the information it has stored upon obtaining *actual knowledge* of the fact that the information at the initial source of the transmission has been removed from the network, or access to it has been disabled, or that a court or an administrative authority has ordered such removal or disablement. [Emphasis added]

So an intermediary forgoes its immunity if it either interferes in any way with the cached data (other than what may legitimately occur as part of the process of storing it), or has knowledge of its removal or imminent removal at its source and fails to remove it expeditiously from the cached source. This is slightly different from the notice-and-takedown duty applicable to hosts, further discussed below, because here a notice by the injured party of the allegedly wrongful material per se would not trigger the takedown duty,[20] as the focus is on the ISP's knowledge of the removal of its source.

ISPs

The primary and possibly only target of these two immunities are ISPs – that is, those companies that provide access to the internet, which, in the UK, would include providers such as BT, Orange, Sky, Tiscali, or Virgin Media.

The underlying assumption of the immunities regime is that, but for them, ISPs would be exposed to liability under general law. Otherwise, they would be superfluous, apart, perhaps, from creating certainty in respect of the non-liability. What would be the liability of ISPs for transporting third-party information? While the immunities in Europe have, to a significant extent, pre-empted

---

20 This position is also more generous to ISPs than s 1 of the Defamation Act 1996. On the relationship of that defence with the Directive's immunities, see above.

suits against ISPs, there have been German cases[21] in which the plaintiffs tried to take advantage of the fact that the Directive's immunities only preclude monetary awards, not injunctions. Yet in these cases the courts refused to order ISPs to impose access restrictions on grounds similar to those underlying the immunities in the Directive – namely, the relative innocence and passivity of the ISP. This in turn is also the reason why ISPs would not be liable under substantive law – thus suggesting that the immunities are not as important as one might expect.

Also, in the English case of *Bunt v Tilley*,[22] John Bunt unsuccessfully tried to make three ISPs – AOL UK, Tiscali UK, and BT – responsible for allowing access to allegedly defamatory postings online, in the case of AOL and Tiscali as internet access providers, not hosts of the material:[23]

> More generally, I am also prepared to hold as a matter of law that an ISP which performs no more than a passive role in facilitating postings on the internet cannot be deemed to a be publisher at common law . . . I would not . . . attribute liability at common law to a telephone company or other passive medium of communication, such as an ISP. It is not analogous to someone in the position of a distributor . . . There a defence is needed because the person is regarded as having 'published'. By contrast, persons who truly fulfil no more than the role of a passive medium for communication cannot be characterised as publishers: thus they do not need a defence.[24]

Thus, under defamation law non-hosting ISPs are not even treated as distributors and therefore incur no liability even when on notice of the defamatory content.[25]

The same result was reached in the Australian copyright/piracy case of *Roadshow Films Pty ltd v iiNet Ltd (No 3)*.[26] In this case, the Federal Court of Australia found that iiNet, the third largest ISP in Australia, was not liable for the copyright infringements (peer-to-peer downloading) of its customers.[27] Even though the ISP had knowledge of the infringements and did not act to stop them, it did not thereby authorise them. It merely provided access to the internet and thereby the preconditions for infringement, which, according to the Court, was not the same as providing a 'means of infringement'; those 'means' were the BitTorrent system over which the ISP has no control. (In the UK, a similar distinction between mere facilitation and procurement is drawn: see below.) Following on from this, the ISP could not be treated as having intended for copyright infringements to occur, unlike providers such as Napster or Kazaa or Pirate Bay, in which cases the site or software was deliberately structured to favour infringement.[28] Justice Cowdroy rejected that a scheme for notification followed by suspension and termination of customer accounts were reasonable steps to prevent infringements within Australia copyright legislation, even where the ISP, as in this case, contractually reserved its right to do so.[29] Because the ISP was not providing the means of infringement, it was not incumbent upon it to stop them, particularly considering that suspension would also lead to much non-infringing activity being suspended by the infringer and non-infringer, such as family members. In any event, the judge reasoned that any sanction for copyright infringement:

---

21 See, eg, the German case Haftung des Access-Providers (OLG Frankfurt am Main, 22 January 2008, Az 6 W 10/08) in which it was held that an internet access provider is no way responsible for illegal sites (here, pornography sites without any access restrictions) to which it provides access through its internet access service and then by providing access to google.de and google.com (discussed below under 'Injunctive Relief').

22 [2006] EWHC 407 (QB).

23 Note, BT was treated as a host of the material in question.

24 Ibid, [36] and [37].

25 Contrast *Godfrey v Demon Internet Ltd* [2001] QB 201, in which it was held that the ISP that hosted the news group exchanges, including the defamatory one, was liable in defamation after it received notice of the defamatory content and failed to remove it.

26 [2010] FCA 24.

27 Thom Holwerda, 'Judge: Norwegian ISP does not have to block the Pirate Bay' (2009) *Osnews*, 7 November, available online at www.osnews.com/story/22456

28 *Roadshow Films Pty Ltd v iiNet Ltd (No 3)* [2010] FCA 24, point 14 of the summary. See also discussion below.

29 Ibid, [430]–[442].

is not imposed until after a finding of infringement by a court. Such sanction is not imposed on anyone other than the person who infringed. Such sanction sounds in damages or, if criminal, possible fines and imprisonment, not removal of the provision of the internet.[30]

As discussed below, the UK has introduced a regime that envisages the very duties on ISPs that the Australian judge refused to impose – that is, the duty of notification followed potentially by suspension of the subscriber's account, as well as the duty to block access to identified copyright infringing sites (ss 9, 10, 17,and 18 of the **Digital Economy Act 2010**, respectively).

Wi-fi Operators and other Subscribers to Internet Access?

Another group of potential players in the online connection chain are wi-fi operators, such as cafes, pubs, libraries, hotels, conference centres, or universities, and also ordinary access subscribers who subscribe to internet access for themselves and other members of the household, and who may through WLAN (wireless local area network) unwittingly give strangers access to the internet. Both public wi-fi providers and private internet subscribers would seem to fit the definition of 'mere conduit' in Art 12 in relation to the third-party beneficiaries because they provide an 'information society service . . . that consists of . . . the provision of access to a communication network'. Yet, in both cases, there may be, depending on the facts, questions of whether the service falls within the definition of the Directive, such as 'for remuneration' and 'at a distance'.[31]

But what is the liability of these intermediaries in the first place? One of the most high-profile legal concerns in the online world is the protection of copyright, which can be infringed either by a primary or secondary wrongdoer. The first category was held to be established in respect of an intermediary in *Sony Music Entertainment (UK) Ltd and ors v EasyInternet Cafe Ltd*,[32] in which EasyInternet Cafe supplied customers with access to the internet and, at a cost of £5, made them copies of any recordings downloaded by them. The court rejected the cafe's argument that the illegal copying was involuntary: by copying the customers' files without checking the content, the cafe turned a blind eye to their infringement. Also, because primary copyright infringement is a strict liability tort, there was no need to establish that the cafe knew that the source was copyrighted.[33] Although this case arose before the Directive came into force in Britain, it is unlikely that EasyInternet Cafe would have fallen into the category of 'mere conduit' because it provided far more than access to the internet.

Yet most current wi-fi providers would be right on the other end of the spectrum of culpability: similar to ordinary ISPs, allowing access to the internet used mainly for legal activity, but at times also for illegal copying. They would not even be secondary copyright infringer because this would require the rights holder to show that they had authorised the infringement. Courts have drawn a line between intermediaries that merely *facilitate* infringements (outside 'authorising') and those that *procure* the infringement[34] – as recently extended to search engines in defamation claims (see below). Thus, for most wi-fi providers, the immunities would not be necessary, albeit reassuring.

To what extent a household or landlord internet subscriber would be caught under the 'authorisation' heading would vary from case to case depending on their knowledge of, and implicit

---

30 Ibid, [441].
31 Article 2(a) defining 'information society services' by reference to the definition of 'services' in Art 1(2) of 98/34/EC, as amended by Directive 98/48/EC. See also Recitals 17 and 18 of the Electronic Commerce Directive.
32 [2003] EWHC 62 (Ch).
33 But note, under s 97(1) of the Copyright, Designs and Patents Act 1988, a defendant is not liable to pay *damages* if he or she 'did not know, and had no reason to believe, that copyright subsisted in the work to which the action relates . . .'. See discussion below.
34 *CBS Songs Ltd v Amstrad Consumer Electronics plc* [1988] AC 1013. Note that, under ss 22–26 of the Copyright, Designs and Patents Act 1988, secondary infringement is dependent on the state of mind of the alleged infringer: he or she must know, or have reason to believe, that he or she deals with an infringing copy of the work.

acquiescence to, the infringements of others.[35] According to German jurisprudence, the subscriber to an internet account is liable (injunctive relief and costs to cover any warnings) for the copyright infringements of members of the household or other users of the account.[36]

Under the **Digital Economy Act 2010**[37] (amending the **Communications Act 2003**), copyright enforcement actions – in the form of notification of infringement, with the possibility of suspending internet access if illegal copying continues – may be taken by the ISP at the initiative of the rights holder against the subscriber to internet access, regardless of whether the subscriber was the actual wrongdoer.[38] The rationale is that it is the 'subscriber . . . who has entered into a contract with the ISP and usually one of the conditions of that contract will be that the service should not be used for any unlawful purpose. It is therefore not unreasonable to assume that the subscriber is the person properly responsible for what happens over the internet service'.[39] A subscriber is anyone who subscribes to internet access, other than those who do it as 'communication providers'.[40] Thus anyone who subscribes to internet access only to make it publicly available to others, such as an internet cafe, would not be a subscriber and thus within the notification procedure. This raises one questions of when an 'electronic communication service' is 'public': is it private simply by virtue of restrictions on who can use it, such as clients of the hotels or members of the university, which applies to most wi-fi providers? It appears that many small wi-fi providers would fall within the concept of 'subscriber', which is intended to give them incentives to 'take steps to prevent infringement occurring on their accounts'.[41] Of course, if a wi-fi provider were not a subscriber, it would simply be at the other end of the notification duty as an ISP.

See Chapter ◄ 9

Search Engines and Hyperlinkers?

While the formulation of the above immunities envisages ISPs as their beneficiaries, there are parallels between ISPs and those facilitating navigation on the internet – that is, search engines and hyperlinkers. Like ISPs, they act as a type of public transport provider by helping people, once on the network, to navigate around it and by dropping them off in the right places. Like ISPs, they have no or limited interest in, knowledge of, and control over the actual place where users are being dropped off. Are or should these navigation intermediaries be covered by Arts 12 or 13? And what would be the effect of not doing so, considering how much they contribute to the user-friendliness of the internet?

There appears to be some consensus that neither Arts 12 nor 13 can, as they stand, be applied to search engines or hyperlinkers.[42] Although search engines and hyperlinkers do not 'modify the information contained in the transmission' (in line with Arts 12 and 13),[43] they – contrary to

---

35 Ibid.

36 *Haftung des Anschlusshabers für volljährige Tochter* (LG Düsseldorf, 27 Mai 2009, 12 O 134/09); *Haftung für Ehemann und Kinder* (OLG Köln, 23 December 2009, Az 6 U 1001/09).

37 Which was granted royal assent on 12 April 2010. For a critique of the way in which the legislative process in respect of this Act, see Struant Robertson, 'The legislative farce of the Digital Economy Bill' (2010) Out-law.com, 4 April, available online at http://out-law.com/page-10900

38 Section 124A of the Communications Act 2003, esp s 124A(1)(b). See also Out-law.com, 'Government denies wi-fi operators copyright exemption' (2010) Out-law.com, 1 March, available online at www.out-law.com/page-10798. Note that the highest German court ruled that an injunction, but not damages, may lie against users of WLAN when their connection is insufficiently secure and used by unauthorised third parties for copyright infringement: *Sommer unseres Lebens* (BGH, 12 May 2010, Az I ZR 121/08).

39 Department for Business, Innovation and Skills (BIS), *Digital Economy Bill: Online Infringement of Copyright – Detail Regarding Clauses 4–16*, 2010, London: HMSO.

40 Sections 32, 124N, and 405 of the Communications Act 2003.

41 BIS, op cit, 2.

42 DTI, 'Consultation Document on the Electronic Commerce Directive: The Liability of Hyperlinkers, Location Tool Services and Content Aggregators', June 2005, 10ff, which is based on the assumption that the immunities are not applicable to search engines and hyperlinkers: *Metropolitan International Schools Ltd (t/a Skillstrain and/or Train2game) v Designtechnica Corp (t/a Digital Trends) & ors* [2009] EWHC 1765, [84], [92], [112], QB.

43 But note ibid, [92].

Art 12 – 'select' it, albeit in the case of search engines automatically. Similarly, Art 13 does not fit either search engines or hyperlinkers because the transmitted information is not provided by the recipient of the service, who would be the person using the search engine or clicking the hyperlink. Still some EU Member States (although not the UK) have specifically extended the immunities to them.[44] Also in *Google AdWords* (discussed below), the European Court of Justice (ECJ) held that a search engine – in that case referred to as an 'internet referencing service provider' – may fall into the Art 14 immunity on hosting provided that a national court makes a finding of 'neutrality'.[45] Yet what will become apparent is that the legal position of search engines and hyperlinkers is generally as good as – and at times better than – it would be with the benefit of the immunities.

In terms of liability, hyperlinkers seem marginally more legally vulnerable than search engines (although both may be liable in different situations) – a result that can be justified on the basis that they have more control over to whom they provide links. Although hyperlinks are generally broadly based on relevance, without necessarily endorsing the specific content of the pages to which they link, there is clearly more human intervention and thus knowledge/intentionality than in the case of search engines. Search results are the returns of automated web searches using an algorithmic functionality and automated referencing, following certain ranking and relevancy criteria – without any further human editing.[46] Also, in taking into account sheer quantity, any editing – that is, exercise of control – in the case of search results would be significantly more onerous than in the case of hyperlinks, in relation to which the choice of links provided assumes already a process of editing.

Liability for the Illegal Content of the Linked-to Site: Defamation and Trade Mark Infringement

An early example of hyperlinker liability for the content linked to is the French case of *Yahoo Inc v LICRA & UEJF*,[47] in which the French subsidiary of Yahoo! Inc was found liable in a civil nuisance/public order action for providing a link to the US Yahoo page on which third parties had offered Nazi memorabilia contrary to French criminal law. The French subsidiary's failing consisted simply in linking to a site with illegal content, although in this case the external site was hardly 'external' because it belonged to the same Yahoo empire. Therefore more knowledge and control over the linked page than would normally be present in the case of truly external links could be assumed.

For this reason, *Yahoo* could be reconciled with the Canadian case of *Crookes v Wikimedia Foundation Inc*,[48] in which the court held that a provider of a hyperlink is not liable for the defamatory content of the linked *external* page. According to the court, a hyperlink does not constitute a 'republication' of the defamatory site and is comparable to a footnote:

> A hyperlink is like a footnote or a reference to a website in printed material such as a newsletter. The purpose of a hyperlink is to direct the reader to additional material from a different source. The only difference is the ease with which a hyperlink allows the reader, with a simple click of the mouse, to instantly access the additional material.[49]

44 DTI (2005), op cit, ch 4. Member States have variously extended Arts 12, 13, or 14 to search engines and hyperlinkers.
45 *Google AdWords* C-236/08, C-237/08 and C-238/08 ECJ (Grand Chamber) (23 March 2010), [113], [114], and [119] – but note that this holding is likely to be restricted to Google's AdWords service, as opposed to its 'natural' search facilities, because Art 14 deals with 'information stored at the request of a recipient of the service . . .'. Nevertheless, the ECJ judgment is useful in making clear that the immunities are not restricted to ISPs.
46 DTI (2005), op cit, 17. The selection of ranking and relevance could be considered a form of editing.
47 LICRA & UEJF v Yahoo! Inc & Yahoo France Tribunal de Grande Instance de Paris (22 May 2000), aff'd in LICRA & UEJF v Yahoo! Inc & Yahoo France Tribunal de Grande Instance de Paris (20 November 2000).
48 [2008] BCSC 1424, aff'd in Crookes v Newton [2009] BCCA 392.
49 Ibid, [29], but note [34]: 'It is not my decision that hyperlinking can never make a person liable for the contents of the remote site. For example, if Mr. Newton had written "the truth about Wayne Crookes is found here" and "here" is hyperlinked to the specific defamatory words, this might lead to a different conclusion.'

But is the ease of access not critical to the issue of whether something has been published or not? Also, a hyperlinker may stop being a neutral pointer if the hyperlinker clearly endorses the unlawful material – an issue elaborated on appeal:

> I would not accept the footnote analogy to be a complete answer to the question of whether a hyperlink constitutes publication. More significant factors would include the prominence of the hyperlink, any words of invitation or recommendation to the reader associated with the hyper-link, the nature of the materials which it is suggested may be found at the hyperlink (for example, if the hyperlink obviously refers to a scandalous, or obscene publication), the apparent significance of the hyperlink in relation to the article as a whole, and a host of other factors dependant on the facts of a particular case.[50]

In other words, knowledge of the wrongful act, coupled with any acts of endorsement, may expose the hyperlinker to liability.

In the case of search engines, it would be virtually impossible to find that the search provider endorsed the defamatory content of a linked site, given the automated nature of search results. And indeed search engines have proven to be the darlings of the judiciary for defamation law, where judges seem to have gone at times further than in copyright law (see below) in protecting search engines from liability and blocking obligations. Given the role of search engines in distributing (defamatory) third-party sites, under defamation law they would appear to fit the category of secondary publisher perfectly and thus could avoid liability under the 'innocent dissemination' defence in s 1 of the **Defamation Act 1996** if they were to remove defamatory material once they have notice of it (see above). However, in the English case of *Metropolitan International Schools Ltd v Designtechnica Corp*,[51] the search engine was not even classified as a secondary publisher, but as a mere facilitator, similar to the ISPs in the above Australian copyright and English defamation cases. In this case, an English training business sued Google and the owner of a review website for publishing an allegedly defamatory review of its distance-learning course (calling it, inter alia, 'nothing more than a scam'), which appeared as an excerpt in Google's search results. Because Google Inc was based in California, the initiating process had to be served outside of England, and to do so the plaintiff had to show a 'reasonable prospect of success', which Google argued it had not. Thus Justice Eady had to consider Google's possible liability and concluded that Google was under common law not a publisher, not even a secondary one, as the concept of publication entails an awareness of the words to be published: '. . . it is not enough that a person merely plays a passive instrumental role in the process.'[52] It could not be a publisher, because its entire process was automated and it played no role in formulating the search terms that determine the 'snippets' displayed in response to the search; Google was a pure facilitator.[53] Therefore it could not be liable even after notification of the alleged defamatory publication.[54]

See Chapter 2

In the process of distinguishing *Godfrey v Demon Internet Ltd*,[55] Eady J asserted that search engines should be treated more generously than online hosts:

> A search engine, however, is a different kind of Internet intermediary. It is not possible to draw a complete analogy with a website host. One cannot merely press a button to ensure that the

---

50 Ibid, [60].
51 *Metropolitan International Schools Ltd (t/a Skillstrain and/or Train2game) v Designtechnica Corp (t/a Digital Trends) & ors* [2009] EWHC 1765 (QB); Out-law.com, 'Google is not liable for defamatory snippets in search results, rules High Court' (2009) Out-law.com, 17 July, available online at www.out-law.com/page-10181
52 *Metropolitan International Schools Ltd*, [49], citing *Bunt v Tilley & ors* [2006] EWHC 407 (QB) (discussed above).
53 Ibid, [51].
54 See discussion above.
55 [2001] QB 201.

offending words will never reappear on a Google search snippet: there is no control over the search terms typed in by future users. If the words are thrown up in response to a future search, it would by no means follow that [Google] . . . has authorised or acquiesced in that process.[56]

Although Eady J treated the issue of being a 'publisher' as separate from the notice-and-takedown duty,[57] he concluded that it would be practically impossible and disproportionate to expect Google to block all the offending snippets.[58] Google had, in fact, blocked the specific URLs that it had been given by the plaintiffs on google.co.uk, but not on other Google sites, nor the specific words complained of, which would have resulted in significant overblocking. Google was also found not liable for the defamatory sites linked to in its search results with snippets in the Spanish case of *Paloma v Google Inc*,[59] in the Swiss case of *Subotic v Google Inc*,[60] the French case of *SARL Publison System v SARL Google France*,[61] and the Dutch case of *Jensen v Google Netherlands*[62] – and amongst these states, it is only Spain that has specifically extended the Directive's immunities to search engines.[63] Google's natural search facilities are protected under ordinary substantive law, at least for defamation purposes. Perhaps it is the importance of search engines for the information society that has translated into a general judicial reluctance to tamper with their operations.

A similar spirit shines through the ECJ case of *Google AdWords* – that is, joined ECJ cases[64] *Google France v Louis Vuitton Malletier*,[65] *Google France v Vaiticum Luteciel*,[66] and *Google France v CNRRH, Pierre-Alexis Thonet, Bruno Raboin Tiger*.[67] These cases concerned Google's practice of selling keywords identical to the trade marks of others either to imitators or competitors, and then, if the keyword is searched, displaying the imitators' or competitors' AdWords above or alongside the 'natural' results. The trade mark proprietors tried to attack Google's system and sought to put certain words beyond the realm of public accessibility, which – in the opinion of the Advocate General – would:

See Chapter 8 →

> . . . create serious obstacles to any system for the delivery of information. Anyone creating or managing such a system would have to cripple it from the start in order to eliminate the mere possibility of infringements by third parties . . . How many words would Google have to block from AdWords . . . It is no exaggeration to say that, if Google were to be placed under such an unrestricted obligation, the nature of the internet and search engines as we know it would change.[68]

Also, because these AdWords are a significant source of revenue for Google, restrictions of such severity would have put Google's business model under threat. The ECJ upheld the legality of

---

56 *Metropolitan International Schools Ltd*, [55].
57 This distinction is questionable because the legal status of 'secondary publisher/distributor' translates into the notice-and-takedown duty; it makes no sense to say that a person is under the takedown duty, but not a publisher. Also: what are the consequences of failing to comply with the duty, if not ordinary defamation liability?
58 *Metropolitan International Schools Ltd*, [62]–[63], but at [56] he also mentioned that 'a degree of international recognition that . . . search engines should put in place such a [notice-and-takedown] system (which could obviously either be on a voluntary basis or put upon a statutory footing) to take account of legitimate complaints about legally objectionable material'.
59 (Court of First Instance, Madrid, 13 May 2009).
60 (Court of First Instance, Geneva).
61 (Court of Appeal, Paris, 19 March 2009).
62 (District Court of Amsterdam, 26 April 2007).
63 DTI (2005), op cit, 14ff.
64 *Google AdWords* C-236/08, C-237/08 and C-238/08 ECJ (Grand Chamber) (23 March 2010). For an English case on the same issue, see *Interflora v Marks and Spencer* [2009] EWHC 1095 (Ch), which Arnold J referred to the ECJ for guidance.
65 (Court of Paris, 4 February 2002).
66 (Court of Appeal of Versailles, 10 March 2005).
67 (Court of Appeal of Versailles, 23 March 2006).
68 *Google AdWords* C-236/08, C-237/08 and C-238/08 Opinion of Advocate General (22 September 2009), [121], [122]; for a critique, see Lilian Edwards, 'Stuck in "neutral"? Google, AdWords and the E-Commerce Directive Immunities' (2009–10) 20(5) Society for Computers and Law, available online at www.scl.org/site.aspx?i=ed14010

Google's keyword system. According to the Court, Google had not itself 'used' the signs identical to the trade mark, which is a necessary ingredient to show an infringement:[69] 'A referencing service provider allows its clients to use signs which are identical with, or similar to, trade marks without itself using those signs.'[70] And this conclusion could not be undone by the fact that Google created 'the technical conditions necessary for the use of a sign and being paid for that service'.[71] Having said that, the Court left open the possibility, first, that the actual advertisers may be liable for trade mark infringement over and above any other liability, such as for unfair competition,[72] and second, that Google might be liable as contributory under national law, other than those implementing **Directive 89/104** and **Regulation 40/94**.[73] But even in respect of this latter possibility, the Court concluded that Google might be protected under the Art 14 hosting immunity if a national court were to consider it sufficiently 'neutral'. For reasons discussed below, this holding is unlikely to extend to Google's ordinary search facilities. Interestingly, at the very time that the ECJ passed its judgment, one of the most advanced US cases on keywords/sponsored links was dropped by the plaintiffs.[74]

Liability for the Acts of Users of the Link: Copyright Infringement

While the above cases concern the issue of whether a link to an unlawful third-party site exposes the hyperlinker to liability for that material, an equally prominent issue has been whether hyperlinking and providing search facilities may expose the intermediary to liability as a contributory for allowing those who follow the link to engage in wrongful conduct, such as copyright infringement.[75] Here, the linked-to site is often also infringing, but the primary wrongdoers that may expose intermediaries to liabilities are the users of the link. The consensus appears to be that the hyperlinker or search engine is not liable for secondary copyright infringement in respect of the piracy of those who follow the link[76] – unless the linked-to content is unlawful or triggers unlawful activities and the hyperlinker or search engine is aware of this.

This latter 'exception' has been confirmed by a number of courts that broadly agree that only the failure to prevent the illegality after being on notice about it triggers liability. The sticky issue is what amounts to 'notice'? Typically,[77] a German court held in *Heise*[78] that liability for contributory copyright infringement for a hyperlink in an online newspaper was a justified interference with the freedom of the press where the linked site created a danger of significant infringement by those who followed the link (by providing software to circumvent digital rights) and the hyperlinker was aware of that. The decision is not inconsistent with the earlier judgment of the highest German court in *Schöner Wetten*,[79] in which an online newspaper provided, in the course of reporting, a link to a foreign gambling site not licensed in Germany and therefore illegal. Because the link was provided in the course of an ordinary newspaper story and designed not to advertise or in any way encourage such gambling, but to provide a complete story, the newspaper had not acted anti-competitively as a primary actor. Neither was it culpable as a secondary actor, because the illegality

---

69   Article 5(1)(a) of the Directive 89/104 and, in the case of Community trade marks, Art 9(1) of the Regulation 40/94.
70   *Google AdWords*, [56].
71   Ibid, [57].
72   Ibid, [87]–[90].
73   Ibid, [57]. See also *Google AdWords*, Opinion of Advocate General, [123].
74   *Rescuecom Corp v Google Inc* 562 F3d 123 (2d Cir April 3, 2009); Out-law.com, 'Rescuecom drops AdWords suit' (2010) Out-law.com, 8 March, available online at www.out-law.com/page-10818
75   Alain Strowel (ed), *Peer-to-peer File Sharing and Secondary Liability in Copyright Law*, 2009, Cheltenham: Edward Elgar.
76   DTI (2005), op cit, [5.13], relying on *CBS Songs Ltd v Amstrad Consumer Electronics plc* [1988] AC 1013.
77   See also the US cases of *Intellectual Reserve Inc v Utah Lighthouse Ministry Inc* 75 F Supp 2d 1290 (D Utah, 6 December 1999) and *Universal City Studios Inc v Reimerdes* 111 F Supp 2d 294 (SDNY 2000), aff'd 273 F3d 429 (2d Cir 2001); the Australian case of *Cooper v Universal Music Australia Pty Ltd* [2006] FCAFC 187 (based on 'authorising' the infringement of others).
78   (OLG München, 23 October 2008, Az 29 U 5696/07).
79   (BGH, 1 April 2004, Az I ZR 317/01).

of the linked site was not at all apparent without further investigations, which it was not obliged to conduct in the circumstances. The need and extent for such further investigations depend on all of the facts, including the context and purpose of the link, and the awareness by the provider of possible illegalities or the ease with which he or she could find out about it.[80] According to the court, a takedown duty may arise on notice by a third party – taking into account whether the site is already easily accessible through other sources, as well as the more general public need for hyperlinks as an organisational tool in information wealth of the internet.

A US case dealing with this issue – albeit in the context of search engines that magnify both the effect of hyperlinks and the resultant conflicting interests – is *Perfect 10 Inc v Amazon.com Inc*.[81] In this case, the Ninth Circuit Court held that Google could only be liable for contributory copyright infringement by virtue of indexing and linking to sites if it intentionally encouraged direct infringements by users through a 'knowing failure to prevent infringing actions'.[82] More precisely, Google would be liable if it were to have '*actual* knowledge that *specific* infringing material is available using its system' and could 'take simple measures to prevent further damage',[83] but chose not to do so. So a general awareness that illegal material is available through its search facilities does not trigger the notice-and-takedown duty/liability for search engines; as in the case of hyperlinkers, more specificity is needed. The same outcome would have been achieved under s 512(d) of the US **Digital Millennium Copyright Act of 1998** (discussed below), which creates an immunity in the USA for *unsuspecting* search engines and hyperlinkers, insulating them from contributory copyright liability for linking to unlawful content.

See Chapter 9 →

Liability for Linking

See Chapter 9 →

The starting point here is that those who post information on the internet can be assumed to have consented to being hyperlinked and searched – that is, there is an implied licence to do so, and thus there is no primary liability.[84]

Nevertheless, linking intermediaries have also found themselves accused as primary wrongdoers. One such instance concerns the very common practice of deep-linking – that is, linking to a page other than the front page of a site. Such links were at the heart of the early Scottish case of *Shetland Times Ltd v Jonathan Wills & anor*.[85] In this case, *Shetland Times*, a newspaper with an online version, complained about a competitor newspaper, *Shetland News*, copying the *Times'* headlines onto its site, with deep links to the *Times'* articles bypassing the *Times'* front page and frame, which diminished their value to potential advertisers. The court granted a preliminary injunction on the basis that the articles linked may constitute a 'cable programme' or the headlines a 'literary work' – and thus the copied headlines with the deep links presented a prima facie case of copyright infringement. Under the terms of the eventual settlement, *Shetland News* agreed not to deep-link, to link only to the front page of the *Times*, and to include a prominent reference to the *Shetland Times* on its news website. Quite how unfortunate this decision is is illustrated by the Danish case *Danish Newspaper Publishers Association v Newsbooster*,[86] which went one step further by extending the *Shetland* approach to a news

---

80 Note also the Norwegian case of *Phonefile v Startsiden* (District Court of Oslo, 29 October 2003), in which an internet portal was held not liable for the provision of links to file-sharing programmes on the basis that the sites could be found anyway and that it could be used for non-infringing purposes.

81 487 F3d 701 (9th Cir 2007).

82 Ibid, 728.

83 Ibid, 729 (emphasis added).

84 DTI (2005), op cit, para 5.14. See also *Church of Spiritual Technology v Dataweb* [2000] ECDR 83; *IPPI v Belgacom Skynet NV* [2000] ECDR 239; *Finn Eiendom AS and Finn No As v Notar AS Trondheim* DC (Norway), in which the court held that 'surface hyperlinking is a normal practice on the Internet'. Of course, the licence to link may be expressly revoked or implicitly such as, for example, where the hyperlink would circumvent password or other requirements, as reinforced in the copyright context, by Arts 6 and 7 of the Copyright in an Information Society Directive 2001/29/EC.

85 1997 FSR (Ct Sess OH, 24 October 1996).

86 (Bailiff Court of Copenhagen, 5 July 2002).

search engine — a type of content aggregator that is very useful in making online information manageable. The court enjoined Newsbooster from deep-linking to other news sources — in response to which, it closed down. This approach, if adopted more widely, would have drastic repercussions for the internet because it would make it significantly harder, and often impossible, to find, retrieve, and use the vast wealth of online information. Yet there is also contrary authority: the highest German court in *Verlagsgruppe Handelsblatt v Paperboy*[87] exonerated the news search engine paperboy.de of all liability in respect of deep links to the plaintiff's articles, which deprived the plaintiff of advertising revenue from its front page. The plaintiff had argued that the articles could not, without breaching copyright and competition law, be searched by any but its own search engine or be linked to by outsiders. The court disagreed. It was up to the plaintiff to take up technical measures to prevent deep-linking or to structure its site in such a way that advertising was not limited to the front page. The court was at pains to stress the importance of retaining the efficiency of the internet; in its opinion, the internet is all about finding information quickly and without detours — and search facilities to freely accessible material were at the heart of that.

Immunities: Content Hosts and Web 2.0 Providers

'Hosts'

The third and most controversial of the immunities section under the Directive is Art 14, which deals with hosts of online material. On the primary wrongdoer/intermediary spectrum, this category comes closest to the dividing line between the two, because here the intermediary takes a greater part in the publishing process, which may undermine its status as a neutral, and therefore innocent, immunity-deserving middleman.

Pursuant to Art 14(1), where:

> ... an information society service is provided that consists of the storage of information provided by a recipient of the service [third party], Member States shall ensure that the service provider [the intermediary] is not liable for the information stored at the request of a recipient of the service [third party], on condition that:
>
> (a) the provider does not have actual knowledge of illegal activity or information and, as regards claims for damages, is not aware of facts or circumstances from which the illegal activity or information is apparent; or
>
> (b) the provider, upon obtaining such knowledge or awareness, acts expeditiously to remove or to disable access to the information.

Again, this Article imposes a notice-and-takedown duty[88] that requires that the host acts *expeditiously* upon obtaining the relevant knowledge — a condition that has, in practice, given rise to some uncertainty. How long is 'expeditious'? Does it allow time for investigating the legitimacy of the takedown request? Does it take account of any logistical issues in the particular organisations? Notably, under s 3(2) of the **Terrorism Act 2006**, it is two working days within which an intermediary needs to respond to a notice by a constable about a terrorist-related publication and block it before it is taken to have endorsed the publication.

---

87 (BGH, 17 July 2003) I ZR 259/00, available online at www.jurpc.de/rechtspr/20030274.htm; note that, at [19], the Court stated that it had not been shown that single sentences or phrases could be capable of being copyright-protected works — contrary to *Shetland Times*.

88 Electronic Commerce (EC Directive) Regulations 2002, SI 2002/2013, reg 22, elaborates on the notice requirement for the purposes of actual knowledge.

Level of Knowledge

Article 14 also distinguishes what amounts to notice in respect of criminal and civil claims: the former entailing actual knowledge of the illegal activities; the latter, awareness of facts from which the illegal activity is apparent. Thus, like the previous immunities, it is fault-dependent, focusing on the intermediary's knowledge of the third-party content. Yet what does this actually entail?

How does the criminal law test of 'actual knowledge of illegal activity' differ from the civil law one of an 'awareness of facts from which the illegal activity is apparent'? Although it appears that a higher level of knowledge is required before liability under criminal law is triggered, the difference between actual knowledge and awareness of the relevant activity is a fine one indeed – if there is one at all. In either case, it is unclear whether the intermediary must have knowledge or an awareness of the *illegal nature* of the activity. Also, if under the civil law test the illegality must be apparent, it is unclear to whom it must be apparent: to the actual intermediary, the reasonable intermediary, or the reasonable man? In the UK, it is the actual intermediary to whom it must be apparent by virtue of reg 19(a)(i) of the **Electronic Commerce (EC Directive) Regulations 2002**. And as every lawyer knows, whether something is illegal or not is often not as clear-cut as it may appear at first sight, given, for example, the availability of defences such as truth in defamation.[89] By the same token, it may not be that straightforward for an intermediary to judge whether content hosted includes 'unlawfully terrorism-related information'.[90] For this reason, Spain's insistence on a legal declaration is understandable:

> The service provider shall be deemed to have the actual knowledge . . . when a competent body has declared that the information is unlawful or ordered that it be removed or that access to it be disabled . . .[91]

Such interpretation of 'actual knowledge' makes sense in that, prior to such a declaration by a competent body, there cannot be any certainty that the activity is indeed illegal. It means that intermediaries need not second-guess the illegality or otherwise of the hosted content, and neither do they need to act overcautiously in removing the allegedly illegal content out of fear of future liability. In the UK, for example, intermediaries are forced to play safe and remove any material upon any requests by any allegedly injured parties, legitimate or otherwise – a matter that has been exploited by competitors and weighty commercial players relying on the unlikelihood of litigation to establish the invalidity of their takedown requests.[92] In a study concerning the notice-and-takedown duty under US law (see below), Google stated that 57 per cent of notices sent to it and demanding removal of links in the index were sent by competing businesses.[93] The downside of the Spanish interpretation is that it defeats the point of the notice-and-takedown duty, which is to get quick extrajudicial results and thereby minimise the damage caused. Also the Spanish interpretation makes the condition of knowledge redundant because the intermediary's duty would be triggered by the competent body's order.

Application of Immunities: Strict Liability and Negligence-based Wrongs

The knowledge condition of the host immunity (and to a lesser extent of the other immunities) has repercussions for the immunity's application or ambit. If an intermediary can only rely on the

---

89 See Bunt v Tilley & ors [2006] EWHC 407, [72], QB: 'in order to be able to characterise something as "unlawful" a person would need to know something of the strength or weakness of available defences.'

90 Terrorism Act 2006, s 3(7), and Electronic Commerce Directive (Terrorism Act 2006) Regulations 2007/1550, reg 7.

91 Article 17 of Spanish Law 34/2002; reproduced in DTI (2005), op cit, p 41; discussed in *Metropolitan International Schools Ltd v Designtechnica Corp* [2009] EWHC 1765, [99]–[100], QB.

92 Contrast with s 512(f) of the US Digital Millennium Copyright Act of 1998, which penalises frivolous and illegitimate takedown demands (discussed below).

93 Jennifer M Urban and Laura Quilter, *Efficient Process or 'Chilling Effects'? Takedown Notices under Section 512 of the Digital Millennium Copyright Act: Summary Report*, 2005, Berkeley, CA: University of Southern California/University of California, available online at http://mylaw.usc.edu/documents/512Rep-ExecSum_out.pdf

immunity when it does not know or is unaware of the activity in question, the section creates a mental element and is thereby relevant to strict liability offences/wrongs – that is, those that do not already have a mental element, such as defamation,[94] or contempt of court. It would be superfluous for most criminal offences, because they require a *mens rea*. For example, the offence of inciting religious or homophobic hatred may be committed by an intermediary when it 'publishes or distributes written material which is threatening . . . if [it] *intends* thereby to stir up religious hatred or hatred on the grounds of sexual orientation'.[95] Where the intermediary has the state of mind to satisfy the element of intention, it would also have to have the knowledge to disentitle it from the immunity. Where, on the other hand, the intermediary is unaware of the illegal activity, it could not be liable for the offence and thus would not need the immunities. For this reason, the **Electronic Commerce Directive (Hatred against Persons on Religious Grounds or the Grounds of Sexual Orientation) Regulations 2010**,[96] which reaffirm the immunities of the Directive, would have been unnecessary. The same applies to the exemption in the **Electronic Commerce Directive (Terrorism Act 2006) Regulations 2007**[97] that neutralises ss 1 and 2 of the **Terrorism Act 2006**. Similarly in civil law, given that a defendant cannot be liable for damages for copyright infringement if he or she 'did not know, and had no reason to believe, that copyright subsisted in the work to which the action relate',[98] the immunities would not provide greater protection than is already available under existing law.

Beyond strict liability wrongs, all three immunities also capture negligence-based offences or wrongs, as any notice-and-takedown duty must be read in conjunction with Art 15, which requires Member States to refrain from imposing:

> a general obligation on providers, when providing the services covered by Articles 12, 13 and 14, to monitor the information which they transmit or store, nor a general obligation actively to seek facts or circumstances indicating illegal activity.[99]

Article 15 pre-empts any attempt to read the actual knowledge/awareness requirement in Art 14 as a constructive knowledge requirement – that is, the intermediary knows whatever it could know upon monitoring the hosted material, but negligently failed to do. Therefore any negligence-based offence or wrong based on a reasonable duty to keep an eye on hosted material is defused through the immunities provisions.[100] The fact that the **Electronic Commerce (EC Directive) Regulations 2002** and the **Electronic Commerce Directive (Terrorism Act 2006) Regulations 2007**, which implement the immunities, do not at all deal with monitoring by intermediaries is explicable simply on the basis that Art 15 imposes a negative obligation on Member States – that is, *not* to impose a general monitoring duty.

ISPs and Other 'Neutral' Hosts

As in the case of the 'conduit' and 'caching' immunities, the critical question is who falls within the hosting exemption. Again, the main candidates are ISPs, but the immunity also extends to hosting companies and other institutions, such as universities, as well as providers of 'cloud computing'[101] – all

---

94 But note that many strict liability torts or offences incorporate a mental element in the defence.
95 Section 29C(1) of the Public Order Act 1986, inserted by the Racial and Religious Hatred Act 2006 (emphasis added). Or see also Obscene Publications Act 1959, s 2(5).
96 SI 2010/894.
97 SI 2007/1550.
98 Section 97(1) of the Copyright, Designs and Patents Act 1988.
99 Article 15's emphasis on 'general' means that Member States are free to impose more specific monitoring duties in relation to particular individual cases (see discussion below).
100 For example, s 2(1)(c) of the Terrorism Act 2006 refers to recklessness as the sufficient *mens rea* for terrorist publications.
101 Cloud computing allows users to rely on remote computing resources and storage facilities rather than those on their own PCs.

of which provide space on their servers for third parties to publish (or simply store, in the case of cloud computing) their content and thus provide a service that 'consists of the storage of information provided by a recipient of the service' within Art 14. Article 14 expands on the storage definition only in so far as it excludes the immunity 'when the recipient of the service [the third party] is acting under the authority or the control of the provider [the intermediary]' (Art 14(2)). For example, if the content is created by an employee of the intermediary, as in the case of a university or the BBC website, then the employer would seem to be outside the hosting immunity given its authority and control over the employee. Or to put it differently, in such circumstances, the BBC would no longer be an intermediary, but rather the primary publisher of the material.

'Neutrality'

Some of the uncertainty surrounding the ambit of Art 14 has been alleviated by the ECJ judgment in *Google AdWords*,[102] in which the Court held that Art 14 may extend to online intermediaries, such as search engines.[103] Article 14 is not restricted to ISPs and comparable actors that facilitate the jump from the offline to the online world. According to the Court, taking into account Recital 42 of the Directive, the immunities are available where 'the role played by that service provider is neutral, in the sense that its conduct is merely technical, automatic and passive, pointing to a lack of knowledge or control of the data which it stores',[104] and this was a matter for national courts to decide in each case.[105] The Court then proceeded to note – without further comment – that 'with the help of software . . . Google processes the data entered by advertisers and the resulting display of the ads is made under condition which Google controls'.[106] Of course, intermediaries, by virtue of their mediating role, always have – at least theoretically – some control over the third-party content or the conditions of its transport.

Last but not least, the ECJ added that 'the mere facts that the referencing service is subject to payment, that Google sets the payment terms or that it provides general information to its clients cannot have the effect of depriving Google of the exemptions from liability . . .'.[107] It is unlikely that the ECJ meant that the financial benefit derived from third-party wrongdoing does not matter at all, but only that it is not decisive in every case in deciding on the application of Art 14. The contrary conclusion would be surprising, because, first, such financial benefit impacts on the intermediary's incentive to encourage or suppress the wrongdoing, and second, it seems fair that someone who benefits from an activity should also shoulder some of the responsibility for it[108] – or it is a free lunch. Although the Court's comments related to search engines, they provide useful guidelines for assessing the neutrality of other online hosts such as social networking sites. Google itself is unlikely to benefit from these comments in relation to its 'natural' search facilities because no keywords are stored *at the request* of the site providers in line with Art 14.

Voluntary Monitoring?

Whether the notion of neutrality of the service provider requires that it does not voluntarily monitor the site's content is unclear, although it may be argued that monitoring is a form of exerting control over the site and thus places the provider outside the immunities. This would seem to be consistent with the opinion of the Advocate General in *Google AdWords*:[109]

---

102 *Google AdWords* C-236/08, C-237/08 and C-238/08 ECJ (Grand Chamber) (23 March 2010).
103 This view was supported by the European Commission, at [108] of the judgment. Note that, although the ECJ did not agree with the AG in respect of the applicability of Art 14 to the case, this was not based on any disagreement over Art 15.
104 *Google AdWords*, [114].
105 Ibid, [119].
106 Ibid, [115].
107 Ibid, [116].
108 See s 512(1)(B) of the US Digital Millennium Copyright Act of 1998 (discussed below), according to which a service provider does not qualify for the safe harbour if it receives a financial benefit directly attributable to the infringing activity in a case in which the service provider has the right and ability to control such activity.
109 *Google AdWords* C-236/08, C-237/08 and C-238/08 Opinion of Advocate General (22 September 2009).

I construe Article 15 of that directive not merely as imposing a negative obligation on Member States, but as the very expression of the principle that service providers which seek to benefit from a liability exemption should remain neutral as regards the information they carry or host.[110]

In his opinion, intermediaries that assert control over the third-party content through monitoring can no longer be considered neutral. This approach is problematic in so far as it creates a disincentive for intermediaries to monitor their content, which they might want to do for commercial reasons.

In the USA, s 230 of the **Communications Decency Act of 1996** (discussed below) does not deprive online intermediaries of any immunity from civil liability on the basis of 'any action voluntarily taken in good faith to restrict access to or availability of material that the provider or user considers to be obscene, lewd, lascivious, filthy, excessively violent, harassing, or otherwise objectionable' (s 230(c)(2)). Indeed, the section was designed specifically 'to remove disincentives to self-regulation and encourage service providers to monitor the hosted material without the fear of incurring liability as a result of their trouble'.[111] It came in response to *Stratton Oakmont v Prodigy Services Co*,[112] in which a bulletin-board operator was held liable in defamation as a publisher, and not only a distributor, because it had assumed control over the third-party content through its monitoring efforts and therefore was presumed to know its content. Thus its efforts were penalised through the imposition of liability – a situation that s 230 seeks to reverse, albeit unsuccessfully, as discussed below.

While in Europe the relationship of monitoring and the immunities remains ambiguous, there are some signs, at least in the context of Web 2.0 providers, that national courts are moving towards rewarding, rather than penalising, monitoring efforts with immunities,[113] but whether this approach is feasible within the meaning of Arts 14 and 15 is doubtful (see below).

Web 2.0 Providers: Social and Commercial Networking Sites?

Does the 'hosting' immunity apply to online auctions, such as eBay, to networking sites, such as Facebook, MySpace, Twitter, Friends Reunited, or to YouTube or Wikipedia – that is, the wide range of Web 2.0 applications with user-generated content? In light of the ECJ holding in *Google AdWords* (see above), it is likely that the vast majority of these Web 2.0 providers – all of which in one way or another store information at the request of the recipient of the service – are not in principle excluded from the hosting immunity, but must persuade national courts of their 'neutrality' in relation to their user-generated content. The ECJ decision certainly puts a question mark on some of the recent decisions by national courts concerning Web 2.0 providers, although – as argued below – these may legitimately be treated less generously than navigation tools.

National courts across Europe have disagreed on where portals like eBay, Facebook, or YouTube fall on the liability scale: primary actor – contributory actor – innocent intermediary? This disagreement is unavoidable and reflects different policy considerations, with the overarching question being: which actor should be burdened with the risk of wrongdoing? Sub-issues are: which of the innocent actors – that is, intermediary or injured party – is 'more' innocent and who is in a better position to guard against the loss? Who benefits from the activity and what would be the consequences of imposing liability on the intermediary? These considerations are by no means new or

---

110 Ibid, [143].
111 *Austin v CrystalTech Web Hosting* 125 P3d 389, 393 (Ariz App Div 1, 2005), citing *Zeran v America Online Inc* 129 F3d 327, 331 (4th Cir 1997) (internal marks omitted).
112 1995 WL 323710 (NY Sup Ct 1995).
113 *L'Oreal v eBay* (Tribunal de Grande Instance de Paris, 13 May 2009); *ROLEX v Ricardo* (BGH, 11 March 2004) Az I ZR 304/01; *ROLEX v eBay* (BGH, 19 April 2007) Az I ZR 35/04 (discussed below).

limited to the online world. Previously, one might have asked: who are the primary wrongdoers and who are the mere intermediaries in the distribution chain of a defamatory newspaper article, starting with the journalist and proceeding to the editor, the copy-editor, the newspaper company, the printer, and the newsagent? Even assuming that traditional law has settled this question in relation to traditional media, in the online world, we are left with issues of comparability: is Facebook more comparable to the traditional copy-editor, or the newspaper company, or the newsagent?[114] What is noteworthy about the national court decisions on the liability of Web 2.0 providers is that, despite taking different legal routes, they all impose monitoring obligations on Web 2.0 providers and thereby effectively circumvent – or at least limit the ambit of – Art 15.

Primary Publishers?

In some cases, Web 2.0 providers have been classed as primary wrongdoers rather than as secondary actors. In the French *MySpace* case,[115] the Tribunal de Grande Instance de Paris ruled that MySpace had breached the copyright and personality rights of the French comedian Lafesse (in English, 'the Butt') by allowing users to post unauthorised copies of the comedian's work on its networking site. The Court treated MySpace as the publishers of the offending material because, according to the Court, the information posted by MySpace members was published in a way strictly dictated and confined by MySpace's layout, and was accompanied by MySpace's advertisements. Thus by imposing such a specific, frame-based structure for members to present their personal information and by displaying ads for each and every visit, MySpace acted as a publisher. MySpace's control over the format and financial benefit arising from each page was taken as indicative of MySpace's close association with, and implicit endorsement of, the substance of each page. Certainly, the weight attached to the financial factor is, in light of *Google AdWords* (see above), dubious. By the same token, it is not clear that MySpace exercises more control over the formatting of the third-party content than Google does in relation to its AdWords. And while MySpace, like Google, has control over how the data is processed, the process itself is automated, ostensibly in line with Art 14: the conduct is 'technical, automatic and passive, pointing to a lack of knowledge or control of the data which it stores'.[116] By categorising MySpace as a primary actor and thereby taking it out of the immunities regime, the Court implicitly imposed a monitoring obligation on MySpace and thus a requirement that it exercise more control over the content.

The same approach of treating the online intermediary as a primary wrongdoer and thus outside the host immunity was taken towards eBay in respect of counterfeit products by French courts in *Louis Vuitton Malletier v eBay Inc*,[117] *Hermès International v Mme Cindy F, eBay International*,[118] and *Christian Dior Couture SA v eBay Inc*.[119] Even though the more recent French decision in *L'Oreal v eBay*[120] backtracks from the above position, the court does not let eBay off the hook entirely: eBay escaped liability in recognition of its anti-counterfeiting efforts and both parties were ordered to submit to mediation to come up with a cooperative arrangement in the fight against counterfeits.

Contributory Wrongdoer?

An alternative approach is to treat the intermediary as a contributory actor, which is an approach different in form, but often similar in substance. In these instances, the intermediary is considered

---

114 See also Michael Deturbide, 'Liability of internet service providers for defamation in the US and Britain: Same competing interests, different responses' (2000) 3 JILT, available online at www2.warwick.ac.uk/fac/soc/law/elj/jilt/2000_3/deturbide/
115 *Lafesse v MySpace* (Tribunal de Grande Instance de Paris, 22 June 2007); consistent with *Lucky Comis v Tiscalis*, Cour d'Appel de Paris (7 June 2006).
116 *Google AdWords* C-236/08, C-237/08 and C-238/08 ECJ (Grand Chamber) (23 March 2010), [114].
117 Tribunal de Commerce de Paris (20 June 2008).
118 Tribunal de Grande Instance de Troyes (4 June 2008).
119 Tribunal de Commerce de Paris (30 June 2008).
120 Tribunal de Grande Instance de Paris (13 May 2009).

culpable on the basis of authorising or endorsing the third-party activities by virtue of its 'mediating' acts. As shown above, this position has either been rejected for connectivity and navigation intermediaries, or at least made dependent upon specific knowledge of the wrongdoing. Not so for Web.2.0 providers.

In the French *Dailymotion* case,[121] Dailymotion, a French version of YouTube, was considered a contributor to the infringement of its users. The director and producer of the film *Joyeux Noel* sued Dailymotion for copyright infringement of the film illegally accessible on its site. The court held that Dailymotion had not caused the publication and therefore was not its publisher. Nevertheless, the court held that Dailymotion had forgone the immunities under the Directive, because the success of the website was largely predicated upon copyright infringements (that is, the broadcast of famous works that captured larger audiences and thus ensured greater advertising revenue), and it was thus 'aware of facts or circumstances from which the illegal activity or information is apparent'. The court accommodated the fact that Dailymotion could only have found the specific infringing content through general monitoring of the site by noting that the Art 15 prohibition of a general monitoring duty applied only to intermediaries that did not create or induce the offending activities. So, like in *MySpace*, Dailymotion was too closely associated with the material to be able to absolve it of any blame.

Innocent Intermediary?

As shown above, ISPs, hyperlinkers, and search engines are, in the ordinary course of events, treated as innocent 'facilitators' either not in the line of legal fire at all, or only so where they had specific knowledge of the wrongdoing (rather than a general awareness of some wrongdoing) and failed to do anything about it. As shown from the cases, this position has not been endorsed in relation to Web 2.0 providers.

A court that has flirted with the idea of innocent facilitator, but ultimately did not endorse it, is the Bundesgerichtshof, the highest German court, in two trade mark decisions brought by ROLEX concerning counterfeits on offer on online auctions. In 2004,[122] the court held that, although Ricardo.de, a competitor of eBay, could neither be considered a primary wrongdoer nor a participant of the wrongdoing, it could nevertheless incur an injunction as a *Störer* ('omittor'), because it had knowingly contributed to the infringement of the plaintiff's rights by omission.[123] In respect of this lesser liability redressed via injunctive relief in the form of a takedown duty,[124] the immunity was ineffective because it only affected damages claims (see below) – so the court assumed that, prima facie, the online auction fell within the Directive's protective regime. And this takedown duty extended beyond the particular infringing item of which the auction house was made aware. According to the court, the auction provider must take all reasonably technically feasible measures to ensure that no further infringements occur – or, in short, monitor the site with a view to spotting similar infringements. While the court stressed that the site provider was under no general monitoring duty, as prescribed by Art 15 and as would jeopardise the auctioneer's business model, the actual monitoring obligation that it imposed was hardly far removed from the more general obligation. In 2007, the court reaffirmed this holding in respect of eBay.[125] While the line of reasoning is very different from that in the above French cases, the substantive outcome is, in the final analysis, not so different: both rely on very fine distinctions to avoid the effect of Art 15 that

---

121 (Tribunal de Grande Instance de Paris, 24 October 2007).
122 *ROLEX v Ricardo* (BGH, 11 March 2004, Az I ZR 304/01).
123 Ibid, [27].
124 Ibid, [31].
125 *ROLEX v eBay* (BGH, 19 April 2007, Az I ZR 35/04), [33], [40], and [45], available online at http://medien-internet-und-recht. de/pdf/VT_MIR_2007_246.pdf; see also *Haftung von Rapidshare* (OLG Hamburg, 2 July 2008, Az 5 U 73/07), in which the court held that in cases in which there have been a series of similar infringements, the host is obliged to carry out more proactive, preventive monitoring.

absolves intermediaries of any general monitoring. They do not allow Web 2.0 providers to take the benefit of user-generated content without taking any responsibility for it by hiding behind the 'don't shoot the messenger' shield.

Injunctive Relief

All of the above three immunities under the Directive cater for the possibility – even where the immunities are applicable – that a court or administrative authority may order an intermediary 'to terminate or prevent an infringement' and, in the case of hosting, also to disable access to the hosted content (Arts 12(3), 13(2), and 14(3)). For example, Art 14(3) reads:

> This Article shall not affect the possibility for a court or administrative authority, in accordance with Member States' legal systems, of requiring the service provider to *terminate* or *prevent* an infringement, nor does it affect the possibility for Member States of establishing procedures governing the removal or disabling of access to information. [Emphasis added]

This means that a court could require intermediaries to block access to an identified illegal site[126] or to disconnect any subscribers who are engaged in illegal activities. It ought to be stressed that both powers need to be grounded in legislative or common law provisions/bases of liability: Art 14(3) does not create them, but simply establishes the retention of existing ones.[127] For example, both are now possibilities under the **Digital Economy Act 2010** in the context of online copyright infringements, ss 17 and 18 (blocking sites), and ss 9 and 10 (suspending accounts). With respect to the latter, the Secretary of State may impose technical obligations on ISPs to limit internet access to subscribers who have repeatedly infringed copyright. Such measures may be limiting the speed or capacity of the service, preventing the subscriber from accessing particular material, suspending the service, or limiting it in another way.

The issue is to what extent the right of courts to issue an injunction to *prevent* infringements may intrude on the obligation of Member States not to impose general monitoring obligations on service providers under Art 15. As noted above, the Bundesgerichtshof in the ROLEX judgments[128] held that the injunctive relief ordered extends beyond the specific infringing item complained of, and that the online auction site provider was obliged to take reasonable and technically feasible measures to avoid similar infringements in the future. The reasonableness depends on:

- a clear infringement being present;
- similar infringements being easily detectable; and
- the overall circumstances of each individual case, including the financial benefit received by the intermediary.

While the court was at pains to distinguish its order from a general monitoring obligation, it nevertheless introduced a limited monitoring obligation through the back door. Indeed, the court thereby also introduced possible damage awards, because the intermediary forgoes its immunity upon failure to take the 'preventative' monitoring. Whether the German approach to monitoring is reconcilable with the Directive is questionable, although it may be argued that it rightly seeks to share the burden of infringement between Web 2.0 providers and the intellectual property holders.

---

126 District Court of Frederiksberg, Copenhagen (5 February 2008), aff'd Eastern High Court of Denmark (26 November 2008), requiring one of Denmark's largest ISP to block access to The Pirate Bay.

127 See above.

128 ROLEX v Ricardo (BGH, 11 March 2004, Az I ZR 304/01); ROLEX v eBay (BGH, 19 April 2007, Az I ZR 35/04); see above.

German courts have, however, not extended the ROLEX holdings to mere access providers. In one case,[129] the provider of an online pornography site brought an action against an ISP for allowing its subscribers to access google.com and google.de, which, on searches for pornography, returned results to pornographic sites that operated without the legally required access restrictions in unfair competition with the plaintiff's site. The plaintiff argued that the ISP should block access to those two Google sites as long as they returned search results containing these illegal sites. The court did not oblige. It found that while access to such sites may well create unfair competition, the ISP, as a mere conduit, is not responsible for the content of the site to which its subscribers may have access. The court refused to accept that an ISP is comparable to an online auction provider in terms of creating within its sphere of influence a 'danger zone' in which third parties may engage in wrongful conduct and for which it is responsible. When an ISP allows access to the internet, the content on the internet is not within its sphere of influence. In short, the ISP is one step removed from the danger space within which others may misbehave. In any event, according to the court, it would be disproportionate to expect the ISP to block access to an important search engine, such as Google, just because a small percentage of the subscribers will come across the offending sites. Had the courts granted the blocking order against the ISPs in question, it would have been likely to have been the end of their business because customers would have switched to another ISP. In the other case,[130] the facts were very similar, except that, here, the plaintiff wanted the ISP directly to block access to the pornography sites without age verification. The court came to the same conclusion, but stressed that the ISP, unlike the online auction scenario, stood in no contractual relationship with the offending sites, did not profit from them in any way, and did not increase the danger of the distribution of illegal content on the web by providing access to the web.

US Intermediary Immunities

From the outset, the USA has taken a more generous position towards online intermediaries than courts in Europe, despite the occasional judicial attempt to tighten the net around them.

Like those in Europe, US courts have at times simply found online intermediaries not liable under substantive law provisions regardless of any potential immunity, but unlike in Europe, they have done so with respect to Web 2.0 providers, and not only connectivity and navigation intermediaries. For example, in *Gentry v eBay Inc*[131] concerning fake sports memorabilia sold on eBay, a Californian court concluded that eBay is a mere facilitator and not the 'dealer' of the goods under the **Autographed Sports Memorabilia statute** and thus not responsible for the authenticity of the goods to the buyers.[132] Similarly, in *Tiffany (NJ) Inc v eBay Inc*,[133] eBay was absolved of trade mark infringements in the absence of specific knowledge of the particular counterfeit listing; a general knowledge that certain listings of its site might be infringing is not sufficient for contributory liability under US trade mark law. The distributor of a trade mark infringing good is only liable as a contributory if he or she knows, or has reason to know, about the infringement – a 'reasonable anticipation' of such infringements is not enough.[134] Thus the onus is not on eBay to monitor its site for infringing copies; it is up to the trade mark holder to do so and to put eBay on notice about any specific auction item.

---

129 *Haftung des Access-Providers* (OLG Frankfurt am Main, 22 January 2008, 6 W 10/08).
130 *Haftung des Access-Providers* (LG Düsseldorf, 13 December 2007, 12 O 550/07).
131 99 Cal App 4th 816 (2002).
132 In respect of liability for negligence or breaches of unfair competition law, eBay was protected by the immunity in s 230 of the Communication Decency Act 1996.
133 576 F Supp 2d 463 (SDNY 2008).
134 *Inwood Laboratories Inc v Ives Laboratories Inc* 456 US 844 (1982).

Section 230 of the Communications Decency Act of 1996

A more intermediary friendly position than in Europe is also provided for by the immunity in s 230 of the **Communications Decency Act of 1996**,[135] which, in s 230(c) headed 'Protection for "Good Samaritan" blocking and screening of offensive material', states:

(1)   Treatment of publisher or speaker

No provider or user of an interactive computer service shall be *treated as the publisher or speaker of any information* provided by another information content provider. [Emphasis added]

(2)   Civil liability

No provider or user of an interactive computer service shall be held liable on account of—

(A)   any action voluntarily taken in good faith to restrict access to or availability of material that the provider or user considers to be obscene, lewd, lascivious, filthy, excessively violent, harassing, or otherwise objectionable, whether or not such material is constitutionally protected; or

(B)   any action taken to enable or make available to information content providers or others the technical means to restrict access to material described in paragraph (1).

This immunity from liability (other than liability under federal criminal law and intellectual property law)[136] has been expressly designed to reward self-regulatory efforts by online intermediaries, consistent with the general US regulatory preference for the self-regulation of the internet and minimal government intervention. This broad sweeping section extends immunities for third-party content not only to providers of online services, but also to users of such services.

The ambit of s 230 has seen a number of challenges. The first goes to the heart of the self-regulatory agenda of s 230 – that is, the question of whether s 230 relieves intermediaries of liability only as a publisher, or also of the lesser liability – at least for defamation law – as distributor. Put differently, do intermediaries have to remove objectionable content when put on notice of such content, which is a normal distributor's duty, or are they also exempt from that duty? And going further, should intermediaries that make no monitoring efforts at all also benefit from the exemption? In *Zeran v America Online Inc*,[137] s 230 was interpreted widely: it protects intermediaries in respect of third-party defamatory content from the liability both as a publisher and distributor. The difference between the two is that a publisher is presumed to know what it is publishing and is therefore liable even in the absence of actual knowledge of the objectionable content, while a distributor's liability only arises upon that knowledge – that is, notice. According to the court, everyone in the publishing process is a 'publisher', and this includes distributors; the legal distinction between the two merely 'signifies that different standards of liability may be applied within the larger publishers category'.[138] From a policy perspective, the court reasoned that s 230 immunity should extend to distributor liability because providers that monitor content are likely to be considered distributors and thus the threat of distributor liability might discourage such efforts. But as case law shows, monitoring is more likely to turn intermediaries legally into publishers, not distributors.[139] From a

---

135   Title 47 of the US Code. See also: Brandy Jennifer Glad, 'Determining what constitutes creation or development of content under the Communications Decency Act' (2004) 34 Sw U L Rev 258; Bryan J Davis, 'Untangling the 'publisher' versus 'information content provider' paradox of section 230: Toward a rational application of the Communications Decency Act in defamation suits against internet service providers' (2002) 32 N M L Rev 75.
136   Section 230(e)(1) and (e)(2), respectively.
137   129 F3d 327 (4th Cir 1997).
138   Ibid, 332.
139   See above.

pure legal perspective, the court reasoned that knowledge of the wrongdoing transforms the 'distributor' in law into the 'publisher', which is the very person to whom s 230 refers. Thus excluding distributors from the immunity if they have notice of the wrongdoing would lead to the paradoxical outcome of imposing liability on the intermediary for 'assuming the role for which § 230 specifically proscribes liability – the publisher role'.[140] This, however, is merely an issue of semantics: there is no need to hold that a 'distributor' becomes a 'publisher' upon notice, because one can simply say that a distributor becomes liable upon notice. The effect of Zeran is that the s 230 exemption is not coupled with a notice-and-takedown duty comparable to Art 14. The wider effect is that while monitoring turns the intermediary into an immune 'publisher', taking no action at all even where there is notice of wrongdoing means that the intermediary is an immune 'distributor' – thus self-regulatory monitoring is not encouraged:

> If this reading is sound, then § 230(c) as a whole makes ISPs indifferent to the content of infor-
> mation they host or transmit: whether they do . . . or do not . . . take precautions, there is no
> liability . . . As precautions are costly, not only in direct outlay but also in lost revenue from the
> filtered customers, ISPs may be expected to take the do-nothing option and enjoy immunity . . .
> Yet § 230(c) . . . bears the title 'Protection for "Good Samaritan" blocking and screening of
> offensive material', hardly an apt description if its principal effect is to induce ISPs to do nothing
> about the distribution of indecent and offensive materials via their services. Why should a law
> designed to eliminate ISPs' liability to the creators of offensive material end up defeating
> claims by the victims of tortious or criminal conduct?[141]

For this reason, in *Grace v eBay*,[142] the court refused to follow Zeran given that doing so 'would eliminate potential liability for providers and users even if they made no effort to control objectionable content, and therefore would neither promote the development of technologies to accomplish that task nor remove disincentives to that development as Congress intended'.[143] So eBay was not protected by s 230 in respect of its failure to remove libellous feedback after notice. Ultimately, it avoided liability by virtue of its release of liability clause in its user agreement.[144] However, *Grace* was later 'depublished', and therefore could no longer be considered by later courts.[145] Despite its obvious deficiencies in argument and effect, Zeran has been followed in *Ben Ezra, Weinstein & Co Inc v America Online*,[146] *Green v America Online*,[147] and *Austin v CrystalTech Web Hosting*.[148]

A second challenge to the ambit of s 230 arises from the requirement that the wrongful information must have been provided '*by another* information *content* provider', which is defined as 'any person or entity that is responsible, in whole or part, for the creation or development of information provided through the internet or any other interactive computer service' (s 230(f)(3)). Thus, an intermediary is liable for its own speech[149] (that is, as primary wrongdoer) and for third-party speech to which it made a material contribution (that is, as contributory wrongdoer). For example,

---

140 Zeran, 394.
141 Doe v GTE Corp 347 F3d 655, 660 (2003).
142 16 Cal Rptr 3d 192 (Cal App Ct 2004); see also *Barrett v Rosenthal* 9 Cal Rptr 3d 142 (App 2004).
143 Ibid, [3.c].
144 See also above. Notions of contracts can also work to the disadvantage of intermediaries and override s 230 immunity otherwise available. In *Barnes v Yahoo! Inc* 565 F3d 560 (9th Cir, 7 May 2009), amended by 570 F3d 1096 (9th Cir, 22 June 2009), Yahoo could not rely on the s 230 immunity because one of Yahoo's employees had promised the plaintiff to take down a false website profile and then failed to act upon that promise. Yahoo was thereby estopped from reliance on the immunity.
145 *Austin v CrystalTech Web Hosting* 125 P3d 389, n 5 (2005), in which the court noted that because the Californian Supreme Court had granted review of the case, it was thereby 'depublished', which in turn meant that the decision could not be cited to the court and the court could not consider it.
146 206 F3d 980 (10th Cir 2000).
147 318 F3d 465 (3rd Cir 2003).
148 125 P3d 389 (Arz Crt App, 2005).
149 *Universal Communication System v Lycos* 478 F3d 413 (1st Cir 2007).

the latter was established in *Fair Housing Council of San Fernando Valley v Roommates.Com*,[150] in which the court held that Roommates.com was a contributory content creator – by virtue of the design and question in its questionnaires, which sought, for example, information about the preferred sexual orientation of the prospective roommate – and therefore not immunised under s 230 from liability for a discrimination claim under the **Fair Housing Act of 1968**. Although s 230 recognises the notion of a contributory wrongdoer who falls outside the immunity, similar to that endorsed in Europe, it defines 'contributory' more narrowly. The issue is framed in terms of when an intermediary 'helps to develop the unlawful content'.[151] This does not occur when, for example, a search engine allows a query for a 'white roommate', or when a website operator edits user-generated content by correcting spelling, removing obscenity, or shortening it,[152] but it does occur when an intermediary, such as Roommate.com, provides users with discriminatory choices on drop-down menus and checking-off boxes.[153] So, unlike in Europe, the emphasis is more on the *active* help by intermediaries in the creation of the wrongdoing, as opposed to passively allowing them to happen.[154]

The Digital Millennium Copyright Act of 1998

The blanket immunity created in s 230 does not apply to liability under intellectual property law – which in itself suggests the greater value attached to these property rights. Here, the **Digital Millennium Copyright Act of 1998** creates a much more moderate intermediary immunities regime for copyright infringements that is, in a number of ways, comparable with the immunities regime under the European **Electronic Commerce Directive**:

(a)   it creates a staggered regime that differentiates between data conduits, caching systems providers, hosts, and, unlike the Directive, also information location tools providers;

(b)   it imposes similar conditions for qualifying for each of the above categories;

(c)   it creates a notice-and-takedown duty for the latter three categories; and

(d)   the immunities entail a complete bar on monetary damages and, unlike the Directive, restrict injunctive relief.

Unlike the Directive, the host provision explicitly disentitles any host who has the right and ability to control the infringing activity from the immunity if he or she receives any financial benefit directly attributable to the infringing activity (s 512(c)(1)(B)). The critical question here is when a financial benefit is 'directly attributable' to the infringing activity. The approach taken has, again, been relatively pro-intermediary: the intermediary is only liable if the third-party infringing activity hosted by the intermediary is of such an extent that it 'constitutes a draw for subscribers, not just an added benefit'.[155] In other words, does that intermediary essentially live off the wrongdoing? Thus the court has to look at the scale of wrongdoing carried out via the host.

Finally, unlike the Directive, the Act seeks to address the issue of frivolous or illegitimate take-down demands counteracting the chilling effect of these notices on online communications. Under s 512(f), any person who knowingly materially misrepresents that the material is infringing, or that it was removed or blocked through mistake or misidentification, is liable for any resulting damages incurred by the alleged wrongdoer, the copyright owner or its licensee, or the service provider.

---

150   *Fair Housing Council of San Fernando Val. v Roommates.Com* 521 F3d 1157 (9th Cir 2008); aff'ing *Batzel v Smith* 333 F3d 1018 (9th Cir 2003); see also *Shiamili v Real Estate Group of New York Inc* 892 NYS 2d 52 (NY App Div 2009).

151   Ibid, 1167–70.

152   Ibid, 1169.

153   Ibid, 1180–6.

154   For another US case on the issue of inducement of illegalities, see *Dart v Craigslist Inc* 665 F Supp 2d 961 (ND Ill 2009).

155   For example, *A&M Records Inc v Napster Inc* 239 F3d 1004 (9th Cir 2001). An example of when an intermediary was not held to benefit directly from the infringing activity, see *Ellison v Robertson* 357 F3d 1072 (9th Cir 2004).

Trends in Intermediary Liability

The discussion above shows that the topic of the liability of online intermediaries is not for the fainthearted. There are not only a myriad of different types of online intermediary, but also a rising tide of decisions by different national courts and the ECJ, which, applying different concepts, have handed down different decisions on the culpability of the intermediary in question. These decisions are at times substantively not dissimilar, but by no means always. There is a wide range of outcomes in respect of intermediary liability for third-party wrongdoing: from imposing no legal responsibilities, to imposing notice-and-takedown duties, specific monitoring obligations, and finally general monitoring duties. The overall conclusion to be reached is that this is still an emerging and highly dynamic area of the law in which the last word has not been spoken.

This is not to say that there are not already some emerging trends across the intermediary liability board. In determining the immunity/liability, courts have taken into account – to a greater or lesser extent – the relative involvement of the intermediary in the wrongdoing by reference to factors such as their actual or constructive knowledge, their relative control over the activity, and the financial benefit gained from those activities. In Europe, it is the concept of 'neutrality' that is the emerging cornerstone of the hosting immunity; equally, US courts have excused providers of 'neutral tools' even when they are used to carry out illegal activities.[156] The problem with the concept of neutrality, as well as the abovementioned factors, is that they are highly elastic, allowing for very divergent decisions depending on underlying value judgments. Indeed, a finding of neutrality is by no means the result of a pure objective fact-finding mission upon which the immunity is then based, but rather the conclusion drawn from those facts in conjunction with policy judgments. To say that Google is a neutral intermediary is not to suggest that it is a pure word matchmaker: '. . . the modern Google is more than a match engine: it ranks search results, provides prompts beyond what the user enters, and answers questions.'[157] Neither is it to say that Google does not, or cannot, know about, or have control over, any third-party illegalities. When judges decide that Google is neutral, they simply say that it should not be burdened with knowing and controlling its search results given its crucial role in facilitating navigation around the net and the impact that a contrary finding may have on this. Ultimately, courts always weigh whether it would be more fair and efficient, and in the public interest, to let the loss caused by the third party fall where it falls at the expense of the 'innocent' injured party or to make the 'innocent' intermediary pick up the bill. This still raises the question of why courts have handed down different judgments in this weighing process when presented with similar facts.

Before turning to some of the underlying reasons for the different judicial attitudes to intermediaries, a final word should also be said about the judicial attitudes to the relationship between substantive liability and the immunities. Prima facie, one would expect that the immunities regime presupposes that, but for the immunities, the intermediary would be exposed to liability. However, as shown above, in respect of connectivity and navigation intermediaries, courts have often not relied on the immunities and found the intermediary not liable under substantive law, making the immunity redundant. Conversely, at least in Europe, content hosts have frequently not benefited from the immunity, as judges have been at pains to find ways of avoiding the effect of the host immunity either by constructing the intermediary as a primary or secondary wrongdoer, or by reinventing the host immunity to allow for obligations close to those under substantive law. Again, the immunity becomes effectively redundant. This paradox is captured by the dissenting judges in *Fair Housing Council of San Fernando Valley v Roommates.Com*:[158]

---

156 *Fair Housing Council of San Fernando Valley v Roommates.Com* 521 F3d 1157, 1169 (9th Cir 2008).
157 Ibid, 1183.
158 Ibid, 1182ff. A typical case that conflates the issues of liability and immunities is *Bunt v Tilley & ors* [2006] EWHC 407, QB, in which the judge states (at [380]): 'They [the Regulations] define the circumstances in which Internet intermediaries should be held accountable for material which is hosted, cached, or carried by them but which they did not create.' The immunities do not at all define when there is liability, but rather when there is an immunity – which does not necessarily mean that there is liability.

Whether Roommate is entitled to immunity for publishing and sorting profiles is wholly distinct from whether Roommate may be liable for violations of the FHA [the **Fair Housing Act of 1968**]. Immunity has meaning only when there is something to be immune *from*, whether a disease or the violation of a law. It would be nonsense to claim to be immune only from the innocuous. But the majority's immunity analysis is built on substantive liability: to the majority, CDA immunity depends on whether a webhost materially contributed to the unlawfulness of the information. Whether the information at issue is unlawful and whether the webhost has contributed to its unlawfulness are issues analytically independent of the determination of immunity. Grasping at straws to distinguish Roommate from other interactive websites such as Google and Yahoo!, the majority repeatedly gestures to Roommate's potential substantive liability as sufficient reason to disturb its immunity.

At least in Europe, one must question whether the immunities under the **Electronic Commerce Directive** are, in fact, needed and useful. If ultimately the 'substantive liability' trumps the immunity no matter what, then the answer is negative. This position is not necessarily regressive, because the various substantive laws have, over the years, developed and tested defences that fairly reflect the relative fault or faultlessness, as the case may be, of those who are not the primary source of the wrongdoing. And why should online intermediaries not simply be accommodated within these traditional substantive concepts, just like their offline counterparts? Or put differently, do we need a separate cyberlaw for intermediaries?

Now, let us briefly review the underlying reasons that may help to explain the myriad of judgments and which no doubt deserve closer academic inspection than is possible here. The most obvious trend in intermediary liability in Europe is that Web 2.0 providers are treated more stringently than navigation intermediaries – that is, hyperlinkers and search engines. This difference in judicial attitude may be explicable by reference to their perceived relative usefulness: Web 2.0 providers are considered to be less essential to the use and functioning of the internet than search engines, which judges have described as essential building blocks of the internet. Put simply, would you rather do without Google or without Facebook? Even amongst Web 2.0 providers, despite superficial similarities, there may be a hierarchy in their perceived value or contribution to society that can explain the different judicial attitudes towards them. The question is: are sites such as eBay, Facebook, YouTube, or Wikipedia one of a kind – for all to be subjected to the same liability/ immunities regime? As a commercial facilitator, eBay may be rated more highly than is Facebook as a social networking site, or YouTube, which is mainly used for entertainment – disregarding for the moment the more marginal uses of such sites for more worthy political or social purposes. In contrast again, Wikipedia, being non-profit and educational, is likely to be viewed with more favour by judges than Twitter, or Bebo, or Friends Reunited. Thus, for example, despite the tendency of French courts to find online intermediaries liable, in MB, PT and FD v Wikimedia Foundation Inc,[159] a French judge found that Wikipedia was not liable for defamation and invasion of privacy, basing that finding on Art 14 of the Directive: as an online host, Wikipedia is immune from liability in the absence of actual knowledge of the wrongdoing. But is Wikipedia's involvement with the user-generated content really that different from MySpace's involvement? Although the host immunity in Art 14 does not overtly cater for the value hierarchy of sites, the ECJ's neutrality test, as informed by Recital 42,[160] leaves significant room for manoeuvre through words such as 'passive nature', 'knowledge', and 'control'. In light of such flexibility, the ECJ's Google AdWords judgment and its anticipated ruling on eBay's liability for trade mark infringement (following a referral from the English case of L'Oréal SA v eBay International)[161] will be only to a limited extent transferable to other Web 2.0 providers.

159 (Tribunal de Grande Instance de Paris, 29 October 2007).
160 See above n 104 and accompanying text.
161 [2009] EWHC 1094 (Ch).

A second underlying reason for the difference in judicial attitude towards online intermediaries may be reflective of different national sentiments and regulatory traditions, which make some courts more predisposed towards or against intermediary liability. For examples, from the judgments above – from *Google AdWords* (following the three French cases in which Google was found liable for trade mark infringement), to the French *eBay* judgments, to *MySpace*, to *Dailymotion* – it is noticeable that France favours intermediary liability. In contrast, the USA has shown a clear preference for intermediary-friendly legal provisions – both in terms of the substantive law (for example, its trade mark law according to which 'reasonable anticipation' of infringements is insufficient for secondary liability) and its generous legislative immunities regime. Although the express purpose of the immunities regime is to promote self-regulation, in fact it fails to provide a self-regulatory incentive (as argued above). Perhaps a more plausible explanation for national differences to intermediary liability is economic factors. It is, for example, noteworthy that most, if not all, of the large global online intermediaries such as eBay, Facebook, and Google have their home in the USA and thus it is in the US economic interest not to burden them unduly with heavy regulatory expectations. Equally, the French *eBay* cases or *Google Adwords* cases concerned French brand names as victims of trade mark infringement and thus it would be in France's economic interest to shift the liability onto the intermediary. This is not to say that there is a necessary correlation between economic interests and liability, but simply that economic factors are likely to influence judicial and legislative baseline positions, and not illegitimately so.

Finally, other matters underlying the different conclusions of liability of intermediaries are the subject matter of the complaint and the – often interrelated – scale of the wrongdoing. For example, the very fact that intellectual property rights are taken out of the very generous US immunities regime under s 230 suggests that these rights raise special interests. Similarly, it is clear that judges everywhere are more intermediary-friendly in defamation cases than in intellectual property cases, which may be partly a reflection of the varying scale of the wrongdoing, and its attendant effects on public and private interests. The scale of the wrongdoing figures implicitly in knowledge concepts (that is, was the scale of the wrongdoing such that the intermediary could not not know about it?) and the 'financial benefit' factor (that is, how much did the intermediary benefit from the wrongdoing?).

Chapter 4

Cybercrime

Introduction

August Bequai, writing in the preface to an early Council of Europe Recommendation on Computer-related Crime,[1] suggested that: 'In the information society, power and wealth are increasingly becoming synonymous with control over our data banks . . . The computer revolution has provided tools with which to steal with impunity, control and manipulate the thoughts and movements of millions, and hold an entire society hostage.' In his report for the COMCRIME study in 1998, Sieber referred to international computer networks as 'the nerves of the economy, the public sector and society', such that any attack or intrusion could have a devastating effect on the functioning of the information society.[2] Sieber underlines the potential for a particular type of abuse of computer systems, but there is now a whole spectrum of activity that may be referred to as 'computer crime', 'computer-related crime', or now 'cybercrime',[3] which began to become apparent as the so-called computer or information revolution progressed.[4] This includes a number of 'traditional' crimes that may be facilitated by the use of computer systems, such as: offences of theft, deception, and fraud; offences related to obscenity and indecency; criminal breaches of copyright arising from intentional distribution and commercial exploitation of copyright works; and criminal damage aimed at the computer system itself. The diverse nature of the criminal activities relating to computer use and misuse was later reflected in the Cybercrime Convention, which made provision for acts based on illegal access, illegal interception, data interference, system interference, misuse of devices, computer-related fraud, computer-related forgery, offences related to child pornography, and offences related to copyright and related rights. That these are different in kind, both from each other and from the 'new' offences related to or relying on computer hacking, goes without saying, but together they make up a body that has come to be referred to, however inaccurately, as 'computer crime', and which, in varying degrees, has caused problems for the interpretation and development of the law in this area.

When the last edition of this book was written, it was estimated that cybercrime might be costing as much as US$50 billion per year and that there could be almost 6 million intrusions per annum into computer systems by outside hackers. Precise (or even any) statistics on computer or cybercrime are very difficult to obtain, and once obtained they can be very difficult to interpret,[5] but it seems unlikely that these figures will have declined in the interim. Indeed, it was estimated in 2008 that there were 6,000 cyber attacks per day worldwide,[6] and in 2009 it was suggested that there was more cybercrime than ever before – that the amount of malicious software had increased by as much as 400 per cent annually and that it had 'become a trillion dollar problem'.[7] Although hacking and virus attacks still occur and cause damage, disruption, and financial loss, the range of

---

1 Council of Europe, *Recommendation R(89)9 on Computer-related Crime*, 1990, p 4.

2 U Sieber, *Legal Aspects of Computer-related Crime in the Information Society: Report for the European Commission of the Outcome of the COMCRIME Study 1998*, 1998. This document is no longer available on the Europa website, but a copy is available online at www.edc.uoc.gr/~panas/PATRA/sieber.pdf

3 The use of this term has itself led to some controversy. Tapper, in 'Computer crime: Scotch mist?' [1987] Crim LR 4, describes the phrase as 'ungrammatical and inelegant', although other writers are rather more dismissive of any perceived semantic difficulties: 'Clearly it is easy to argue over a definition of computer crime. Such an argument seems fruitless, and will not be engaged in here' (Saxby (ed), *Encyclopedia of Information Technology Law, Vol II*, 1990, London: Sweet & Maxwell, para 12.03). This writer is clearly of a much more pragmatic persuasion: 'The notion of computer crime is retained here merely because it serves as a useful umbrella under which to address a range of quite new and difficult criminal law problems . . .' The advent of the internet led to the adoption of the word 'cybercrime' and this has now gained widespread currency.

4 For an anecdotal account of some of the early high-profile cases and examples, see B Clough and P Mungo, *Approaching Zero: Data Crime and the Computer Underworld*, 1993, London: Faber & Faber.

5 See, eg, ME Kabay, 'Understanding studies and surveys of computer crime', in S Bosworth, ME Kabay, and E Whyne (eds), *Computer Security Handbook*, 5th edn, 2009, New York: Wiley, ch 10.

6 See World Economic Forum, 'The future of India's cyberculture' (2008) weforum.org, 16 November, available online at www.weforum.org/en/knowledge/Events/2008/index.htm

7 See World Economic Forum, 'Is the internet at risk?' (2009) weforum.org, 31 January, available online at www.weforum.org/en/knowledge/Events/2009/AnnualMeeting/index.htm

subversive activity is far wider than this. Those wishing to cause disruption to computers and computer systems are just as likely to instigate a denial-of-service (DoS) attack or distributed denial-of-service (DDoS) attack, in which the perpetrator sets up a system that will generate a high volume of traffic to the target site, severely impeding normal communications with the site or preventing them altogether. While hacking and virus attacks are unlikely to be confused with legitimate use, the same effects as those produced by DoS attacks can occur quite innocently, making criminalisation more problematic.[8]

In addition, there are other categories of nefarious activity that may be far less evident to the ordinary user and may not even impair the operation of the computer network or individual computers in question. An early example was computer fraud; advances in the technology have provided even more avenues for implementing fraudulent activities. For example, a system of computers can be set up to generate communications with other computers on the internet – each of these is then effectively controlled by a master computer and provides a means of disseminating spam or phishing emails, propagating Trojans and viruses, etc. These networks of 'master' and 'zombie' computers (often ordinary home PCs) are referred to as 'botnets',[9] and pose one of the most significant threats to users of the internet and world wide web. They can be used to initiate DoS attacks,[10] and also for other invidious and invasive activities, including phishing. A typical phishing scam involves setting up a website that has the appearance of a legitimate website, usually a bank or other financial institution. Phishing emails are then sent (often via a botnet) to recipients advising them of some security issue with their account and requiring them to visit the spoof website to confirm their account details, provide passwords, etc. Pharming, on the other hand, redirects users from the legitimate site that they were intending to access to a spoof site, which may appear identical to the intended site.[11] This is often achieved by installing malware on the user's own computer. Anecdotal evidence points to the fact that these activities are rapidly becoming a very common type of cybercrime.[12] The technological response to malware has been to develop anti-virus software, but, in a vicious circle, this also can provide a shield for those with criminal intent. In the early case of R v Pile,[13] a virus was introduced via anti-virus software and, more recently, it is not uncommon to encounter so-called 'scareware', which suggests that a user's computer has been infected with a virus and offers to scan the computer; accepting this offer can potentially have catastrophic results for the user. This provides a graphic demonstration of the insidious nature of the latest generation of computer crime – the fact that much of it can appear entirely legitimate to the innocent and unsuspecting user. There are thus many activities that might be expected to attract the attention of the criminal law and the legal response to such activities is the subject matter of this chapter.

The Nature of Cybercrime and Cybercriminals

Although the original term 'computer crime' has been subject to some discussion in the past about its utility and appropriateness, it is not the purpose of this chapter to examine the accuracy of the

---

8 See, eg, Lilian Edwards, 'Dawn of the death of distributed denial of service: How to kill zombies' (2006) 24 Cardozo Arts & Ent LJ 23, and further discussion at pp 125–127.

9 In 2009, the BBC found itself at the centre of a controversy when it sought to investigate the murky world of computer crime by buying a botnet that provided control of thousands of infected computers around the world. See, eg, Mark Perrow, 'Click's botnet experiment' (2009) BBC News, 13 March, available online at www.bbc.co.uk/blogs/theeditors/2009/03/click_botnet_experiment.html, and Warwick Ashford, 'BBC botnet experiment broke law, says lawyer' (2009) Computer Weekly, 13 March, available online at www.computerweekly.com/Articles/2009/03/13/235257/bbc-botnet-experiment-broke-law-says-lawyer.htm

10 See, eg, the facts of Caffrey, discussed below at p 125.

11 For more information about phishing and pharming, see, eg, Scot M Graydon, 'Phishing and pharming: The new evolution of identity theft' (2006) 60 Consumer Fin LQR 335.

12 See, eg, www.apwg.org/reports/APWG_GlobalPhishingSurvey_1H2009.pdf

13 See the discussion below at p 124.

phrase 'computer crime': whatever the shortcomings of this term, it has become accepted terminology for a particular species of activity with the common ingredient of computer use. Nevertheless, specific and workable definitions of what is meant by 'computer crime' or 'cybercrime' have proved notoriously difficult to draft. Although one school of thought might suggest that it is not necessary to delineate a specific category, as we shall see, cybercrime can display some different characteristics from 'traditional' crime and so attempting to define its scope may not be a completely futile exercise. Categorisations could be made in a number of ways. The US Department of Justice describes computer crime as 'any violations of criminal law that involve a knowledge of computer technology and their perpetration, investigation and prosecution'.[14] It suggests that computer crime can be subdivided into three categories in which the computer is the object of the crime, the subject of the crime, or the instrument of the crime.[15] The first of these refers to the theft of the hardware itself and will not be considered further here. The second category refers to criminal activity directed at the integrity of the computer itself or at a computer network, including the internet, and encompasses a range of behaviour that may have no exact parallel outside the computer context. Examples include: hacking; the introduction of malicious software (so-called malware), such as viruses and other damaging software; DoS attacks; and botnets that facilitate the sending of spam and phishing emails, etc. The third category covers those instances in which the computer is used as a tool to facilitate other crimes, such as fraud, identity theft, and also content-based crimes, such as child pornography. An alternative categorisation, which may be more appropriate for a book of this nature, is to separate those crimes that can be committed both offline and online, those that deal with content rather than the integrity of the computer systems themselves, and those that have no clear parallel in the offline world.[16] This chapter will consider the way in which computer technology has facilitated and even diversified activities that occur offline, using the examples of computer fraud and content-based crimes, such as pornography, together with a consideration of the response of the criminal law to activities that are specific to computers and computer networks.

Whatever method of classification is employed, it certainly appears that criminal activity is in no way diminishing as computer technology and computer networks have continued to develop, and as their use has become ever more ubiquitous. Attacks on computers with a view to mere malicious damage are perhaps less frequent, because criminals realise that there may be more to gain by more subtle means such as introducing malware that does not actually impair the operation of the computer or network, but instead compromises or removes data stored on it. Card fraud and online identity theft are now arguably two of the fastest-growing computer crimes, facilitated by a combination of phishing and malware.[17] Indeed the growth and development of the internet and world wide web has facilitated the transition from computer crime to cybercrime as 'malicious activity has increasingly become Web-based',[18] facilitated also by the growth of peer-to-peer and social networking, organised crime groups on the internet, and new types of 'malware'.[19] Whatever form the activity takes, it can be extremely costly for victims as a result of remedying the disruption caused by damage and loss of data, or because of direct pecuniary loss due to fraud.

---

14 National Institute of Justice, *Computer Crime: Criminal Justice Resource Manual* 2, 1989, Washington, DC: US Department of Justice, and see also M Battle, MW Bailie, E Hagan, and S Eltringham, *Prosecuting Computer Crimes*, 2007, Washington, DC: Office of Legal Education, available online at www.justice.gov/criminal/cybercrime/ccmanual/ccmanual.pdf

15 For an alternative formulation based on the computer as tool, storage device, and victim, see Richard W Downing, 'Shoring up the weakest link: What lawmakers around the world need to consider in developing comprehensive laws to combat cybercrime' (2005) 43 Colum J Transnat'l Law 705.

16 For another approach, see Anne Flanagan, 'The law and computer crime: Reading the script of reform' (2005) 13 IJLIT 98, 100.

17 For a summary of the latest malicious activity, see, eg, Symantec Internet Security, *Threat Report Vol XIV: Trends for 2008*, 2009, available online at www.symantec.com/business/theme.jsp?themeid=threatreport

18 Ibid.

19 See Terence Berg, 'The changing face of cybercrime' (2007) 86 Mich BJ 18.

In parallel with the evolution of the technology, there has been an evolution in the characteristics of the cybercriminal. In the early days, a modicum of technical knowhow was probably a
prerequisite for criminal activity, but as applications software has become more user-friendly, and
more and more people have also become more computer literate, so it has become easier to engage
in criminal activity. Although teenage hackers are by no means a thing of the past, the development
of new web-based tools has meant that activities such as spamming and phishing,[20] which have
risen dramatically in the last few years, are not restricted to the technologically savvy, but can easily
be executed by the averagely competent computer user. In addition, it is as easy to obtain downloads of such software via the web as it is to obtain any other applications software.[21] Organised
crime groups on the internet have apparently created a thriving 'underground economy' with a
turnover of millions of dollars.[22]

The absence of homogeneity of subject matter that this introductory section has outlined has
meant that a coherent legal response to 'computer crime' and 'cybercrime' has proved to be problematic. There is a demonstrable lack of consensus both in the definition of, and in the severity of,
the offences, and also in identifying the jurisdiction in which the offence occurred. Discrepancies
in the type of regulation because of the former, together with the confusion raised by the latter,
may inevitably lead to the likelihood of 'forum shopping' in the hope of a favourable hearing in
situations in which an offence can be deemed to have taken place in one of a number of jurisdictions. An explanation for the continued increase in computer crime is difficult not only because of
the problems in defining appropriate offences, but also because of a lack of homogeneity coupled
with continued transmutation.[23] As early as 1990, Wasik pointed out that such factors made 'any
monolithic explanation of this phenomenon quite implausible'.[24] No significantly different explanations have been advanced subsequently; indeed the current diversification of criminal activities
relating to computers and computer networks suggests that a 'monolithic explanation' may be even
less feasible now than it was then. However, arguably, there has been little attempt to identify or
examine possible explanations, because computer crime appears to be widely underreported and,
in any case, computer crime statistics are rarely separated from other crime statistics. There appears
to have been relatively little discussion amongst criminologists about the nature of any differences
between patterns of offending and the characteristics of offenders on and offline, and commentary
thus far has been inconclusive. There has been rather more discussion about the nature of the
computer hacker than the characteristics of the computer criminal – although 'hacking' might be
equated with illicit behaviour in common parlance, this is neither the sense in which it originated,
nor the way in which it is commonly understood in the computing fraternity.[25] Nonetheless the
characteristics that are popularly supposed to define computer hackers[26] have also been identified
by Rogers as those that most often attach to computer criminals: namely, male, young, and un-
attached.[27] A further study also suggested that introversion might be more common amongst those

---

20 See later discussion at p 109.
21 See, eg, the facts of DPP v Lennon, Wimbledon Youth Court, 2 November 2005, unreported, discussed below at p 109; Byron
    Acohido, 'DIY cybercrime kits power growth in net phishing attacks' (2010) USA Today, 18 January, available online at www.
    usatoday.com/money/industries/technology/2010-01-17-internet-scams-phishing_N.htm
22 Ibid; see also Rob Thomas and Jerry Martin, 'The underground economy: Priceless' (2006), available online at www.
    team-cymru.org/ReadingRoom/Articles/
23 See also Charlotte Decker, 'Cyber Crime 2.0: An argument to update the United States Criminal Code to reflect the changing
    nature of cyber crime' (2008) 81 S Cal L Rev 959.
24 M Wasik, Crime and the Computer, 1990, Oxford: Clarendon, p 33.
25 See, eg, http://encyclopedia2.thefreedictionary.com/Computer+hacking
26 See, eg, Debora Halbert, 'Discourses of danger and the computer hacker' (1997) 13 The Information Society 361, 363.
27 Marcus K Rogers, 'A social learning theory and moral disengagement analysis of criminal computer behavior: An exploratory
    study' (2001) Unpublished PhD Thesis, Winnipeg, MB: University of Manitoba, Table 1, p 86. But see also Tim Jordan and Paul
    Taylor, 'A sociology of hackers' (1998) 46 Sociological Review 758, suggesting that, notwithstanding such characteristics,
    hackers do associate within specific social groups and communities.

engaging in unlawful behaviour on computer networks.[28] The extent to which this assists in the analysis is uncertain since these characteristics are also frequently shared by perpetrators of street crime, but one aspect that differentiates the two, at least anecdotally, is that it appears that, in a number of cases, convicted hackers not only eventually become law-abiding citizens, but also actually use their knowledge and expertise to improve computer security systems or even to assist with law enforcement.[29]

In terms of explanations for criminal behaviour, Capeller, for example, remarks that 'a revision of criminological patterns is necessary as the criminological universe is incapable of explaining the new forms of criminality and deviance which make up cybercrime',[30] whereas Grabosky takes the opposite line and suggests that '[criminological theories] derived initially to explain conventional "street" crime [are] equally applicable to crime in cyberspace'.[31] Capeller's analysis of deviant behaviour made possible on the internet to an extent parallels the analysis above in that she distinguishes between computers as a 'support' for criminal activity – that is, as providing a tool to engage in deviant behaviour – and also as an 'environment' in which criminal activity is increasing. She identifies the evolution, noted above, from 'an occasionally provocative deviance, committed within the electronic computer system, towards a more and more sophisticated virtual criminality',[32] and suggests that this marks a move from behaviour that could be termed merely 'problematic' to that which is genuinely criminal. This parallels the observation that computer crime is no longer the sole prerogative of the lone computer criminal, if indeed it ever was, but that such behaviour is now eclipsed by criminality, whether organised or not, which is motivated by the promise of financial gain. Grabosky agrees that computer crime is proliferating in both variety and extent, but is of the view that the human motivation to criminal activity remains the same and is independent of the technology: '. . . the thrill of deception characterized the insertion of the original Trojan Horse no less than did the creation of its digital descendants.'[33]

Debate and theorising from both a legal and a criminological perspective will clearly continue as to the causes and explanations of computer crime and cybercrime, but in whatever way the debate evolves, it is clear that global computer networks have created an environment that provides fertile ground for criminal behaviour both old and new, and the phenomenon of cybercrime has become a permanent feature of the internet. Whatever the origin and type of behaviour at issue, it is clear that the law has had to respond to these activities, and it has done so with varying degrees of consistency and success. This chapter will consider the response of the law and will draw conclusions as to its effectiveness.

Computer Fraud

The Background

Computers facilitate many types of fraudulent activity, and computer fraud in its many manifestations is one of the most common forms of computer crime. As long ago as 1985, the Audit Commission defined computer fraud as 'Any fraudulent behaviour connected with computerisation by which someone intends to gain dishonest advantage'.[34] All of the evidence points to the fact

---

28 Marcus K Rogers, Kathryn Seigfried, and Kirti Tidkea, 'Self-reported computer criminal behavior: A psychological analysis' (2006) 3S Digital Investigation S 116.
29 Probably the best example in the UK is Robert Schifreen. See the discussion of *R v Gold and Schifreen* [1988] AC 1063; [1988] Crim LR 437 (HL) below, and compare Robert Schifreen, 'The internet: Where did IT all go wrong?' (2008) 5(2) ScriptEd, available online at www.law.ed.ac.uk/ahrc/script-ed/vol5-2/schifreen.asp
30 Wanda Capeller, 'Not such a neat net: Some comments on virtual criminality' (2001) 10 Social and Legal Studies 230.
31 Peter Grabosky, 'Virtual criminality: Old wine in new bottles?' (2001) 10 Social and Legal Studies 243, 248.
32 Capeller, op cit, p 235.
33 Grabosky, op cit, p 248.
34 Audit Commission, *Computer Fraud Survey*, 1985, London: HMSO, p 9.

that fraud in general is on the increase. In the UK, recommendations in the Attorney General's *Fraud Review*[35] culminated in the establishment of a National Fraud Strategic Authority on 1 October 2008, which was followed by publication of the first *National Fraud Strategy*.[36] Although this Strategy does not separate out computer and internet fraud as a specific area of concern, that this technology is a frequent tool in the perpetrating of frauds is implicit in both its reinforcement of the importance of a specialist e-crime unit to improve the approach to online offences, and its acknowledgement of the power of the technology both to exploit large numbers of victims at low cost and to operate within sophisticated global markets that cross national borders.[37]

Fraudulent schemes are intended to create some pecuniary benefit for the perpetrators or to relieve them of a financial burden. Early studies in this area, in common with that of the Audit Commission, identified three species of computer fraud: namely, input fraud, output fraud, and program fraud. Input fraud might include the misuse of cash cards or the creation of accounts for 'ghost employees', whereas theft of pre-signed cheques is an example of an output fraud. Program frauds are necessarily rather more elaborate and include the so-called 'salami' type, in which a program is written that automatically 'slices off' small amounts from a number of accounts and transfers them to another account created for the purpose. A small deficit may not be noticed or reported on one account, but if the process is repeated on a vast number of accounts, a considerable sum can be accrued in the illicit account. Salami and other program frauds can also be activated at a later date, creating consequent problems in detection of both the fraud and the perpetrator. These types of fraud may still exist, but are now very much the tip of the iceberg as they have been over-taken by a whole variety of other ways of defrauding people via the internet. However, the 'salami' approach is still common, whereby the total scale of fraudulent activity may be large, but the loss to each individual is small. This can often mean not only that the fraud is not detected, but also that it may often not even be noticed. Thus if, as a result of computer hacking or the use of malware, such as a botnet, small amounts are extracted from many thousands of individuals, the total can rapidly escalate. If such an incident is reported, it may well not even be investigated due to the fact that the individual amount lost is not deemed sufficiently significant. As has been pointed out, it may be necessary 'to aggregate thousands of individually small crimes to build up a picture of the true scale of criminality'.[38]

Some of the categories of reported fraudulent activity may not strictly be categorised as fraud in the technical sense, but, in terms of popular reporting, many scams that are capable of giving rise to actual or potential monetary loss are often designated as fraudulent. In recent years, in addition to credit card fraud, one of the most commonly reported frauds has been internet auction fraud, but there are a whole host of other scams that are designed to dupe the unwary internet user. Many of these involve email scams that may amount to direct extortion, but also include phishing and pharming for bank account details, and to enable identity theft more generally.[39] Although, as mentioned already, statistics on any type of computer crime are notoriously difficult to collect and interpret, the USA has a national system for reporting frauds and those reported to the Internet Crime Complaint Center showed a total loss of US$559.7 million in 2009.[40]

---

35 Office of the Attorney General, *Fraud Review: Final Report*, 2006, London: HMSO, available online at www.northeastfraudforum.co.uk/government-fraud-review

36 National Fraud Strategic Authority, *The National Fraud Strategy: A New Approach to Combating Fraud*, 2009, London: HMSO, available from www.attorneygeneral.gov.uk/nfa/GuidetoInformation/Documents/National%20Fraud%20Strategy

37 Ibid, p 29.

38 House of Lords Science and Technology Committee, *Fifth Report of Session 2006–07: Personal Internet Security*, 2007, London: HMSO, para 7.19, and see also discussion in the preceding paragraphs in the section entitled 'High-volume, Low-denomination Crime'.

39 For further details, see Internet Crime Complaint Center, *Internet Crime Report*, 2009, available online at www.ic3.gov/media/annualreport/2009_IC3Report.pdf

40 Ibid.

Computers and 'Traditional' Fraud

How has the law responded to the issue of computer fraud? In its first consideration of the problem, the Law Commission concluded that, in general, the existing criminal law was adequate to deal with cases of computer fraud.[41] The exception to this was identified as those offences that had proof of deception as an element and this will be discussed in more detail below. A further complication may be that, although an appropriate offence can be identified, the nature of computer technology may make it more difficult to identify both when and where the offence occurred, both of which factors may have important ramifications for the final outcome of the case.

The potential difficulties that could arise in such situations were illustrated by the facts of R v Thompson.[42] Thompson was a computer programmer, employed by a bank in Kuwait. He identified five accounts that were both substantial and dormant – that is, no transactions had been made into or out of them for a long time. He then opened five accounts in his name at various branches of the bank and transferred money into these accounts from the dormant accounts.

To cover his tracks, the program did not execute until he had left the bank's employment and was returning to the UK. The intention was that the program would erase itself and all records of the transfers after executing. Once in the UK, Thompson opened accounts in UK banks and wrote to the Kuwaiti bank manager, asking him to transfer the money now in the five accounts held in his own name. This led to him being found out, and he was charged and convicted of obtaining property by deception, contrary to what was then s 15 of the **Theft Act 1968**.[43]

The issue in the case itself was not so much a question of whether or not this offence had been committed, but rather when and where, and, in consequence, whether or not the English courts had jurisdiction to hear the case. Section 15(2) of the **Theft Act 1968** defined 'obtaining property', for the purposes of the offence of obtaining by deception in s 15(1), as obtaining ownership, possession, or control. The argument for the Crown was that the offence had occurred in England when the credit balance in the fraudulently created accounts was transferred to the accounts in England, because this was the moment at which Thompson obtained ownership, possession, or control. The defence argued that, on the contrary, control was obtained in Kuwait, at the time when the manipulation of the balances in the respective accounts was made. The Court of Appeal, in an early manifestation of technological neutrality, recognised the points raised, but was anxious not to treat the fraud in any different manner from a similar case of fraud perpetrated by more traditional means. It therefore likened Thompson's actions to those of a traditional book-keeper who entered false amounts in a ledger.[44] Thus, in this case, the decision was arrived at by applying exactly the same principles as would be applied in a more conventional case. Although the use of the computer clearly facilitated the fraud, the law as it then stood, which was based on deception, was still capable of application: a human mind could be identified that had been deceived by the acts of the accused – namely, the bank manager in Kuwait at the time of receiving the letter of instruction from Thompson. Could there have been a conviction if no such person could have been identified? This is perhaps a moot point, but the Scottish Law Commission, in its consideration of the matter, noted that, in this respect, Scots law perhaps provided an advantage over English law because, in that jurisdiction, fraud did not require deception, but rather involved 'a false pretence made dishonestly to bring about some definite result'.[45]

This difference highlights the fact that the applicability of existing legislative provisions to otherwise 'traditional' offences committed with the aid of computers may depend both on the vagaries of language and on the capability of that language of being interpreted in such a way as to

41 Law Commission, *Report on Computer Misuse*, Cm 819, 1989, London: HMSO.
42 [1984] 1 WLR 962.
43 Now repealed by the Fraud Act 2006.
44 [1984] 1 WLR 962, 967, per May LJ.
45 Scottish Law Commission, *Report on Computer Crime*, Cmnd 174, 1987, London: HMSO, para 2.4.

take into account any special features of computer crime. This was particularly the case for those offences in English law that were based on deception. As summarised by Buckley J in *Re London and Globe Finance Corp Ltd*,[46] deception relates to the state of a person's mind and, in cases in which there was no communication or intervention by humans, reliance on a concept of deception in order to utilise certain offences under the **Theft Act 1968** would inevitably, at some point, require wrestling with the thorny question of whether a machine (that is, a computer) could be deceived. In the early reviews of computer crime by the Law Commissions for both Scotland, and England and Wales, it was suggested that such occasions would be rare and generally concluded that most cases of computer fraud could be dealt with adequately by the existing provisions. Although it was recognised that there might be a lacuna in the law,[47] no action was taken at the time and for some years it remained the position that it was not, in law, possible to deceive a machine. It was not until the decision of the House of Lords in *R v Preddy*[48] that relevant amendments were made to the Act. This case arose as a result of false statements made to obtain mortgage advances that were credited electronically, leading to a charge of obtaining property by deception. As the building society representatives could be identified as the target of this deception, the salient issue in the particular case was whether any property as such had been transferred. The House of Lords was of the view that the creation of a new chose in action could not be equated with obtaining property, precipitating swift action by the Law Commission[49] and Parliament to resolve the situation. The result was the **Theft (Amendment) Act 1996**, which introduced new ss 15A and 24A into the **Theft Act 1968**, creating offences of obtaining a money transfer by deception and dishonestly obtaining a wrongful credit. In the haste to respond to the decision in *Preddy*, the opportunity for a more comprehensive overhaul of the legislation, which could have taken into account the difficulties with the concept of deception and computerised accounting methods, was missed. The result was that there still appeared likely to be a range of conduct that could result in an acquittal on a charge based on deception, and which might not fit comfortably into any of the other offences in the **Theft Act 1968**.

As more and more transactions could be, and were being, instigated without human input or intervention, the time was clearly ripe for a change in the law. As Chapman had pointed out: 'If it is essential that criminal offences attach liability to the wrong conduct itself, rather than to some peripheral activity associated with the same, then it is equally important to identify accurately the conduct that attracts moral obloquy.'[50] This was the situation when the Law Commission returned to the issue of computer fraud as part of a more general consideration of the law of fraud at the end of the 1990s.[51] The consequent report[52] summed up the difficulties surrounding the issues related to deceiving a machine, pointing out that, as the use of the internet expanded, the 'gap in the law will be increasingly indefensible'.[53] The report concluded that the problem should be tackled 'head on'[54] and new offences created that did not depend on deception, but instead on dishonesty.[55] This proposal was qualified by two provisos that 'it should not be possible to commit the offence by omission alone'[56] and that 'the offence could be committed only where the dishonesty lies in an intent not to pay for the service'.[57]

---

46 [1903] 1 Ch 728, 732.
47 Law Commission, *Reforming the Present Law: Hacking*, Working Paper No 110, 1988, London: HMSO, paras 2.2–2.7.
48 [1996] AC 815.
49 Law Commission, *Offences of Dishonesty: Money Transfer*, Law Com No 243, 1996, London: HMSO.
50 M Chapman, 'Can a computer be deceived? Dishonesty offences and electronic transfer of funds' (2000) 64 J Crim L 89, 96.
51 Law Commission, *Legislating the Criminal Code: Fraud and Deception*, Consultation Paper No 155, 1999, London: HMSO.
52 Law Commission, *Fraud*, Law Com No 276, Cm 5560, 2002, London: HMSO.
53 Ibid, para 3.35.
54 Ibid, para 8.4.
55 Ibid, para 8.8.
56 Ibid, para 8.11.
57 Ibid, para 8.12.

As a response to the Law Commission's proposals, the Home Office responded by issuing a Consultation Paper seeking views on the proposal to 'create a general offence of fraud with [three] different ways of committing it'.[58] The outcome was the **Fraud Act 2006**, which has made significant changes to this area of the law including repealing the amendments introduced as a result of the decision in Preddy.[59]

Although, for the purposes of this discussion, we shall be concentrating only on those changes in the law that are relevant to computer fraud, the **Fraud Act 2006** has made sweeping changes to the law of fraud in its entirety. It completely repeals the offences based on deception in the **Theft Acts of 1968 and 1978** and replaces them with a single fraud offence that can be committed in three specific ways – namely: fraud by false representation (s 2); fraud by failing to disclose information (s 3); and fraud by abuse of position (s 5). As Ormerod has pointed out, 'it is worth emphasising how dramatic is the shift from a result-based deception to a conduct-based representation offence'.[60]

The 2006 Act was generally very well received; Lord Lloyd described the Bill as 'one of the best Bills to come out of the Home Office for many a long year',[61] and Spencer suggested that it had been 'drafted with admirable clarity'.[62] It is, however, still early days for an accurate assessment of the impact of this statute in cases of computer and internet fraud. Unlike cases based on deception in which a crucial part of the case rested on the state of mind of the victim, fraud under the new s 2 is complete on making the false representation, independently of whether or not anyone is actually taken in by the scam. This section therefore should allow phishers to be prosecuted even if there is no identifiable victim, and it was certainly the intention that s 2 was drafted sufficiently widely to deal with cases of phishing.[63] In the absence of this provision, it is not clear that the mere act of phishing would be caught under existing provisions. The original **Computer Misuse Act 1990 (CMA)** made it an offence to cause an unauthorised modification to computer material[64] – but it is a moot point whether the receipt of a phishing email could be categorised in this way. The High Court in Re Yarimaka was of the view that a 'spoofing' email, which, like a phishing email, purports to come from one source, but actually comes from another, could be a breach of the **CMA** because 'if a computer is caused to record information which shows that it came from one person, when it in fact came from someone else, that manifestly affects its reliability'.[65] However, the Court of Appeal in Lennon was not entirely persuaded that this would always be the case.[66] The new section certainly seems to augment the prosecutor's armoury in relation to phishing, although it remains to be seen how juries will react to prosecutions in which actual victims are not identified, or how this fact might be reflected in sentencing. The law against phishing is also strengthened by s 7 of the Act, which makes it an offence to make, adapt, supply, or offer to supply any article, including software,[67] knowing that it is designed or adapted for use in connection with fraud, or intending for it to be used in this way. In contrast, in the USA, a number of states have passed

58 Home Office, Fraud Law Reform: Consultation on Proposals for Legislation, 2004, London: HMSO. See also discussion in GR Sullivan, 'Fraud: The latest Law Commission proposals' (2003) J Crim L 139.

59 After the Law Commission report, but before legislative action, it was reiterated in Re Holmes [2004] EWHC 2020, [12], in relation to the new s 15A, that it remained the position that it was not possible in law to deceive a machine.

60 David Ormerod, 'The Fraud Act 2006: Criminalising lying' [2007] Crim L Rev 193, 196. This article provides a general assessment of the provisions of the Fraud Act; see also Carol Withey, 'The Fraud Act 2006: Some early observations and comparisons with the former law' (2007) 71 J Crim L 220.

61 Hansard, 22 June 2005, col 1664.

62 JR Spencer, 'The drafting of criminal legislation: Need it be so impenetrable?' (2008) 67 CLJ 585.

63 Fraud Act 2006, Explanatory Notes, para 16, and see discussion in section 2 of Anne Savirimuthu and Joseph Savirimuthu, 'Identity theft and systems theory: The Fraud Act 2006 in perspective' (2007) 4(4) SCRIPTed, available online at www.law.ed. ac.uk/ahrc/script-ed/vol4-4/savirimuthu.asp

64 See discussion below at pp 122–125.

65 [2002] EWHC 589 Admin, [2002] Crim LR 648, [18]. See also discussion in Maureen Johnson and Kevin M Rogers, 'The Fraud Act 2006: The e-crime prosecutor's champion or the creator of a new inchoate offence?' (2007) 21 Int Rev LCT 295.

66 [2006] EWHC 1201 Admin, [12].

67 Fraud Act 2006, s 8.

specific legislation to deal with the problem of phishing,[68] although it is also possible to use the generic offences of wire fraud and mail fraud.[69]

Internet Auction Fraud

Aside from the potential problems with deception, it appeared originally that the existing law was sufficiently adaptable to deal with instances of computer fraud. This certainly seemed to be the case where the methods used for perpetrating the fraud broadly correlated with those that would have been used before the advent of computers. However, we cannot leave this topic without a consideration of another type of 'fraud', incidences of which have apparently become the source of the some of the most frequent complaints of monetary loss via computer networks: the phenomenon of online auction fraud.[70] The online auction phenomenon began in 1995 with the establishment of ebay.com, and has since expanded dramatically to the extent that there may now be approaching 1.5 million transactions a day on internet auction sites.[71] Although eBay is by far the most high-profile internet auction site and, according to its website, the total worth of goods sold on eBay was US$62 billion in 2010,[72] it is not the only such site and the number of providers has proliferated, as a simple web search will confirm.[73] Although there are many satisfied users of internet auction sites, they also provide an environment in which fraudulent activities can flourish. As Gray J remarked in *Anderson and Rice*: 'Internet fraud, and more particularly eBay internet fraud, is relatively easy to commit. It can, and in this case did, affect a large number of individuals.'[74]

Most internet auction sites distance themselves from the actual transaction process and explicitly state that they should not be treated as traditional auctions.[75] The validity of such statements has been doubted by Harvey and Meisel, who suggest that it is at least arguable that they act as auctioneers in some ways if, for example, they charge a fee and/or commission on sales, provide advice to buyers and sellers, and offer dispute resolution procedures, etc.[76] Certainly, to an outsider, a typical internet auction has obvious similarities with a traditional auction, in which the items are offered for sale and potential buyers make bids, the sale being concluded with the person who has offered the highest bid at the predetermined time when bidding is concluded (analogous to the fall of the hammer). The website can therefore be likened to the sale room, but without providing the chance to see or examine the goods; the bidder must act purely in response to the details and description provided on the website. With the exception of the case in which the website operates as a business providing the merchandise, the auction site will facilitate consumer-to-consumer (C2C) transactions so that, when the auction is over and a bid has been accepted, the seller deals directly with the buyer in relation to payment and delivery. Such a system provides much scope for the less-than-honest buyer or seller.[77] There is considerable scope for fraudulent activity, which may include

---

68 See, eg, discussion in Jasmine E McNealy, 'Angling for phishers: Legislative responses to deceptive e-mail' (2008) 13 Comm L & Pol'y 275.
69 These offences are discussed below in connection with internet auction fraud.
70 See successive reports from the Internet Crime Complaint Center, available online at www.ic3.gov/media/annualreports.aspx, also P Selis, A Ramasastry, and A Sato, 'Bidder beware: Towards a fraud-free marketplace – Best practices for the online auction industry', an update of a report originally published in April 2001 and available online at www.atg.wa.gov/InternetSafety/OnlineAuctions.aspx
71 Ibid.
72 www.ebayinc.com/who
73 See, eg, www.auctionlotwatch.co.uk/auction.html
74 *R v Anderson and Rice* [2005] EWCA Crim 3581, [21].
75 eBay's current user agreement, valid from 27 May 2009, contains the following text: 'You acknowledge that we are not a traditional auctioneer. Instead, our sites are a venue to allow anyone to offer, sell, and buy just about anything, at anytime, from anywhere, in a variety of pricing formats and locations, such as stores, shops, fixed price formats and auction-style formats.'.
76 Brian Harvey and Franklin Meisel, *Auctions Law and Practice*, 3rd edn, 2006, Oxford: Oxford University Press, p 17.
77 For a comprehensive summary of the possibilities, see, eg, MR Albert, 'E-buyer beware: Why online auction fraud should be regulated' (2002) 39 Am Bus LJ 575; Dara Chevlin, 'Schemes and scams: Auction fraud and the culpability of host auction web sites' (2005) 18 Loy Consumer L Rev 223; Mary M Calkins, Alexei Nikitov, and Vernon Richardson, 'Mineshafts on Treasure Island: A relief map of the eBay fraud landscape' (2007) 8 U Pitt J Tech L & Pol'y 1.

auctioning of intentionally substandard goods,[78] or even fictitious goods,[79] or operating illicit bidding arrangements.

What is the best method of regulating these activities? Can the existing law be applied satisfactorily? A number of the problem issues are more accurately and appropriately analysed in contractual terms, but the discussion in this chapter will be confined to those areas in which the criminal law does, may have, or perhaps should have, a role to play. Many jurisdictions already have laws that govern the conduct of auctions and/or which create offences in certain situations of fraudulent dealing. Can these be applied directly or by analogy? In a study focused mainly on business auctions online, rather than the consumer interactions that are the subject of this section, Ramberg points out, with some specific examples, that jurisdictional difficulties make the regulation of internet marketplaces by national legislatures problematic, and that this is just as much an issue in relation to illicit and fraudulent behaviour as to more general commercial activities.[80]

See Chapter 7

However, that is not to say that there is no pre-existing law that might be capable of application. Conventional auctions are an old, established method for the sale of goods, and as such are the subject of a well-developed body of law. The first issue to consider is the extent to which this existing law might be applicable and suitable to online and internet auctions. There is no authoritative or comprehensive definition of an 'auction' in English law, but the essential element is generally agreed to be sale to the highest bidder in a public competition.[81] There are a number of different types of auction. Arguably, the most common model is the so-called 'English', or 'ascending bid' auction, but there are a number of other possible variants;[82] the one that most closely represents the online situation is a now-obsolete form in conventional auction houses in which a time limit is placed on the bidding, traditionally by the burning of a candle or the use of another timing device. One notable difference between an internet auction and a traditional auction is the absence of an auctioneer. This is a significant distinguishing feature because, in a conventional auction, the role of the auctioneer is subject to a number of legal controls.[83] The auctioneer is technically an agent of the seller, but will have duties and responsibilities in relation to both parties to the sale; these could provide some form of legal remedy if similar improper actions to those that are possible on online auction sites were to occur in a conventional auction.

The very nature of a sale by auction lends itself to fraudulent activity by rigging the bidding. Sellers can arrange to inflate the bidding artificially by either alone, or in collusion with others, making bids on their own items. This is sometimes referred to, especially in the USA, as 'shill bidding'. Unscrupulous buyers, on the other hand, either alone or in collusion with others, can place multiple bids of differing values for an item, some of which will be high to deter other potential purchasers – a practice sometimes referred to as 'bid shielding'. In the final minutes of the auction, the buyer then removes all of the high bids leaving only their own low bid at which the item must be sold. Engaging in such activities can be much easier on internet auction sites than in a traditional sales room. A detailed consideration of the law relating to bidding is beyond the scope of this chapter, but, in many jurisdictions, criminal sanctions can be invoked in relation to certain illicit bidding arrangements. In commercial terms in the UK, the **Sale of Goods Act 1979**, s 57(4), generally proscribes bidding on behalf of the seller and s 57(5) goes on to provide that any such sale may be treated as fraudulent by the buyer. Further, certain types of collusion between bidders

---

78 See, eg, the facts of *US v Gajdik* 292 F 3d 555 (7th Cir 2002).
79 See, eg, the facts of *R v Anderson and Rice* [2005] EWCA Crim 3581.
80 Christina Ramberg, *Internet Marketplaces: The Law of Auctions and Exchanges Online*, 2002, Oxford: Oxford University Press, p 27.
81 See, eg, Harvey and Meisel, op cit.
82 See, eg, ibid, p 3, and Ramberg, op cit.
83 In the UK, for example, the activities of the auctioneer are governed by the Auctioneers Act 1845, s 7 of which requires that the name and place of residence of the auctioneer should be displayed prominently to all those attending the auction. In some jurisdictions, auctioneers still require a licence to operate, but in the UK, this provision in the 1845 Act was repealed by the Finance Act 1949.

are regulated by the **Auctions (Bidding Agreements) Act 1927**, as amended by the **Auctions (Bidding Agreements) Act 1969**. The 1927 Act, as amended, is generally aimed at dealers who contrive to obtain goods on a low bid by offering a consideration, in some form, to a bidder in return for abstention from bidding. In particular, s1 (1) creates an offence in the case that 'any dealer agrees to give, or gives, or offers any gift or consideration to any other person as an inducement or reward for abstaining, or for having abstained, from bidding at a sale by auction either generally or for any particular lot, or if any person agrees to accept, or accepts, or attempts to obtain from any dealer any such gift or consideration'. As a result of s 2, any resultant sale can be regarded as having been induced by fraud.[84]

There are thus some pre-existing offences related to fraudulent activity in conventional auctions. Can these be applied as they stand to similar activity on online auction sites? Civil remedies are also possible: in a traditional auction, if the auctioneer sells items of which the seller is not the true owner, then a purchaser who was subsequently pursued by the true owner could both seek to recover from the auctioneer and possibly sue the auctioneer personally for his or her part in any fraudulent activity. In an online auction, a purchaser of such goods would not have this option. A crucial issue for application of existing provisions may be the definition of an auction. As noted previously, despite fulfilling the requirements of sale to the highest bidder in a competitive sale, most C2C auction sites are at pains to point out in their conditions of use that they are not true auctions, but merely provide a 'venue' within which the buying and selling of goods to the highest bidder can be facilitated – that is, the better analogy is with a bazaar rather than a conventional auction.[85] The question is then not so much whether the site is an 'auction' as such, but whether it can be held to have played any part in the perpetration of the fraud. This issue has not yet been directly addressed by the courts, but there may be some circumstances in which they could operate in similar ways. In the French case of *Chambre Nationale des Commissaires Priseurs v Nart SAS*,[86] the defendants, who operated an online auction site, argued that sales via its website could not be considered as a public auction and neither could the internet be construed as an auction house in Paris. In addition, it was suggested that 'the sales should not be treated as auctions because they do not create the pressure to bid more provoked by the heat of the auction and the simultaneity of the bidding'.[87] In contrast, the court was of the view that, although it might achieve the end result in a different way from its real-world counterpart, an online auction could present all of the characteristics of a public auction, including the 'same atmosphere and heat in the bidding';[88] the court described the internet as 'a vast auction room extending to infinity and able to change in order to take account of the changes in physical space in which the offers of auctions are distributed'.[89] Although the Tribunale de Grande Instance de Paris found that the French law on auctions could be applied in this case, the internet auction site in question was operated by a conventional auction house. In other words, there was both control and management of the auction process, and it would perhaps be dangerous to extend this view directly to some other forms of online auctions. On the other hand, for all online auctions, it seems clear that the primary characteristics of competitive bidding and sale to the highest bidder are fulfilled, and the points about the need for identification of bidders in ways that are appropriate to the situation are also relevant in making the parallel between the two activities.

---

84 The Auctions (Bidding Agreements) Act 1969, s 3, provides further rights for the seller of goods by auction where an agreement subsists that some person shall abstain from bidding for the goods, but these are basically confined to the provision of contractual remedies and relate to the situation in which one of the parties to the collusion is a dealer, as defined in the 1927 Act. However, this statute has been so rarely used that it has been suggested that its lack of application must be a deliberate policy: see discussion of *R v Jordan* [1981] CLY 131, cited in Harvey and Meisel, op cit, p 209.

85 See, eg, the eBay user agreement, noted above at n. 75.

86 [2001] ECC 24.

87 Ibid, [21].

88 Ibid, [27].

89 Ibid, [25].

An alternative view is that, in considering the volume of transactions on online auction sites, there is more similarity with an ISP for which the liability issues have been well rehearsed by both courts and academics, and have also been the subject of legislative intervention in some jurisdictions. There is an argument that, given that the major role of auction sites is one of facilitation rather than active interaction, there should be no liability, especially in relation to the potential imposition of criminal sanctions, in the absence of actual knowledge of fraudulent activity or collusion in the same.[90]

See Chapter
3

As mentioned above, one scam that is used by the unscrupulous vendor is to instigate fictitious bids in order to artificially inflate the price that the eventual buyer has to pay to secure the desired item. In the old case of *Heatley v Newton*,[91] a property was being sold by auction. The prospective buyer believed that it was about to be sold to a bona fide bidder for £12,950 and so offered £13,000 to clinch the sale. The reality was far different and the nearest bona fide bid was some £5,000 below that. The immediately preceding bids, which led to the offer of £13,000 being made, were made by the vendors or their agents, or were entirely fictitious, because the auctioneer was also a party to the collusion and, in many of the instances in which he intimated that he had received a bid, in fact he had not. Murdoch discusses the view of the Court of Appeal in the action for recovery and goes on to analyse the reasons for the illegality on the basis of the law as it stood at that time.[92] He noted that if offers that constitute misrepresentations are done knowingly, then this activity can be classified as fraud. Even where such bids are below the reserve price, they can still influence the bidding above that figure and, as long as dishonesty can be established, there seems no reason not to regard this as obtaining by deception. In addition, at least, prior to the **Fraud Act 2006**, such collusion might feasibly be sufficient to establish the common law offence of criminal conspiracy. Although the Law Commission report that preceded the Act recommended the abolition of this offence, this did not occur, because consultation showed widespread support for its retention. Although in principle, therefore, prosecution for this offence remains a possibility, the expectation is that it will become less relevant following the implementation of the Act.[93] Similar arguments can be applied to damping the bids for fraudulent reasons. By analogy with the situation above, it might be expected that it would also be a criminal conspiracy for bidders to collude to depress the hammer price – by bid shielding, for example, as referred to above – but it appears that this is not the case.[94]

Harvey and Meisel suggest that there are some policy reasons both for and against regarding the activity of organised collusion in auction rings as unlawful per se.[95] Setting a reserve price allows a seller to ensure that goods are not sold unrealistically cheaply and the mere fact of an auction ring being in operation does not, of itself, mean that a good price is not obtained. Markets involve both elements of expertise, and also elements of luck or good fortune, and finding an unidentified masterpiece is part of the excitement of the process. However, an inevitable corollary is that a private buyer may find goods resold at a vastly inflated price. This may breed mistrust of the auction process and the predatory behaviour of auctions rings may also act as a deterrent to new entrants to the market. It is patently in the auctioneer's interest that this practice is subject to some regulatory oversight.

---

90 Note also that if these websites were auctions as defined in the UK, there would also be criminal liability under the Trade Descriptions Act 1968, s 1, for any false or misleading descriptions of the goods: see, eg, *May v Vincent* (1990) 154 JP 997. It should also be noted that auction sites such as eBay are cognisant of the potential fraud problems and do operate procedures that are intended to minimise any such damage: see http://resolutioncenter.ebay.com/

91 (1881) 19 ChD 326.

92 John Murdoch, *Law of Estate Agency and Auctions*, 4th edn, 2003, London: Estates Gazette, p 187.

93 See Office of the Attorney General, *Guidance on the Use of the Common Law Offence of Conspiracy to Defraud*, 2007, London: HMSO, available online at www.attorneygeneral.gov.uk/Publications/Documents/conspiracy%20to%20defraud%20final.pdf. This document also points out that whether a need for this offence remains will be considered when the Home Office reviews the implementation of the Fraud Act.

94 Ibid, p 196.

95 Harvey and Meisel, op cit, pp 270–1.

The former argument highlights one of the points of distinction between traditional and online auctions – namely, that traditional auctions, although attended by private persons, are dominated by dealers and professional collectors such that the law may then be reluctant to interfere in what has become widely accepted as custom and practice in the trade. In contrast, although dealers may also be active in online auctions, C2C transactions in which neither party is expert or professional are very much more common than in traditional auctions. It may be, therefore, that similar activity in online auctions would not be so acceptable and would correspond far more with the second argument put forward above. However, the issue of criminal liability would still be problematic, especially if it were sought to be imposed on the operator of the auction site.

In the USA, the operation of auctions is governed by the **Uniform Commercial Code (UCC)** §2=N328, and para 4 is a parallel provision to that in the **Sale of Goods Act 1979**, s 57(4), which merely provides contractual remedies. Any criminal activity that may have taken place is left to be dealt with by, for example, generic fraud offences. Because they focus on the communication method by which the fraud is perpetrated, the provisions on 'mail fraud' and 'wire fraud', in 18 **USC** §§ 1341 and 1342, have proved to be easily adaptable to situations of online auction fraud.[96] Both provisions are similar in essence. They require that: there be a scheme or plan for obtaining money or property by the use of false statements that would reasonably influence someone to part with the money or property; the statements were known to be false; and there was an intention to defraud. For mail fraud, the offence is complete when the statements are made via the mail, and for wire fraud by the transmission of wire, radio, etc. Charges under these sections have been used successfully in a number of cases in which the relevant medium was an online auction, and in which the prospective vendors either did not possess, or did not intend to deliver, the items for which bidders had offered payment.[97]

Computer 'Hacking'

Before the Computer Misuse Act 1990

The above discussion has shown that the fact that a 'new' medium is used to perpetrate a fraud, for example, need be no bar to an application of legal provisions that would apply if the fraud were committed offline; so, clearly, some 'traditional' legal offences can still be applied to online activities. However, some other behaviour provided rather greater challenges for the application of existing criminal offences. During the 1980s, a number of cases came to court in a number of jurisdictions that could, perhaps, be regarded purely as examples of antisocial behaviour, but which caused problems for the law in trying to locate the behaviour within existing legal provisions. A number of these were cases of computer hacking and the outcomes were often inconsistent, even in relation to ostensibly similar facts. In some cases, there might be an acquittal because the charge chosen was deemed to be inappropriate or, alternatively, because the law was interpreted in novel ways in order to found a conviction.[98] Prior to the enactment of the **CMA**, one of the most celebrated cases in the UK that illustrated the nature of these challenges was R v Gold and Schifreen.[99]

96　See, eg, Decker, op cit.
97　See, eg, US v Hartman 74 Fed Appx 159 (3rd Cir (Pa) 2003); US v Jackson 61 Fed Appx 851 (4th Cir (Va) 2003); US v Blanchett 41 Fed Appx 181 (10th Cir 2002). More recently, see Dan Goodin, 'eBay scammer gets four years in slammer' (2009) The Register, 28 April, available online at www.theregister.co.uk/2009/04/28/ebay_scammer_sentenced/. Custodial sentences have also been imposed for convictions for, inter alia, mail fraud and wire fraud on a number of defendants in a bidding ring involving shill bidding: see Brian Melley, 'California eBay scam artist sent to federal prison' (2004) USA Today, 27 May, available online at www.usatoday.com/tech/news/2004-05-27-ebay-art-fraud_x.htm
98　Compare, eg, the contested behaviour and the reasoning in R v Gold and Schifreen [1988] AC 1063; [1988] Crim LR 437 (HL), Cox v Riley (1986) 83 Cr App R 54, and R v Whiteley (1991) 93 Cr App R 25, discussed subsequently in this section.
99　[1988] AC 1063; [1988] Crim LR 437 (HL). See also FJ Kwiatkowski, 'Hacking and the criminal law revisited' (1987) 4 CL & P 15.

Gold and Schifreen hacked for a hobby, and had managed to obtain the password for the Prestel System operated by BT, which provided subscribers with both email facilities and access to a number of database services. The password that they obtained was, in fact, that issued to BT engineers, so not only did it not charge them for use, but it also gave widespread access to all parts of the system – and they even left messages in the email inbox of the Duke of Edinburgh! Because of this or their other activities, suspicion was aroused, and they were tracked down by monitoring their telephone usage. The question then arose as to what could be an appropriate charge. A prosecution was brought under s 1 of the **Forgery and Counterfeiting Act 1981**, which provides that:

> A person is guilty of forgery if he makes a false instrument with the intention that he or another shall use it to induce somebody to accept it as genuine and by reason of so accepting it do or not do some act to his own or any other person's prejudice.[100]

Gold and Schifreen were convicted at first instance, but appealed on the basis that no false instrument had been made. 'Instrument' is defined in s 8 of the Act and includes disks, tapes, etc, on which the material is stored by electronic means. The prosecution argument relied on the assertion that the dishonestly obtained password could constitute such an instrument, because it generated and was transmitted in the form of electrical impulses. This contention was rejected for two reasons. First, it was felt that any instrument for the purposes of this Act had to be *ejusdem generis* with the other examples in the statutory definition, which were all physical objects, and because the electrical impulses in question were only transient, this did not correspond well with the idea of the creation of an instrument. In addition to the difficulties with the definition of the instrument, the inapplicability of the charge was held to be due to the nature of the offence of forgery. In this case, the password was not false – it was genuine – but there was no entitlement to use it. As a result, the Court of Appeal was of the view that the use of the statute was inappropriate; it was not intended to apply to this type of activity. Lord Lane summed up these views as follows:

> The Procrustean attempt to force these facts into the language of an Act not designed to fit them produced grave difficulties for both judge and jury which we would not wish to see repeated. The appellants' conduct amounted in essence, as already stated, to dishonestly gaining access to the relevant Prestel data bank by a trick. That is not a criminal offence. If it is thought desirable to make it so, that is a matter for the legislature rather than the courts.

The wholehearted and unanimous endorsement of this approach by the House of Lords shows the disdain with which the attempt to squeeze the activity of computer hacking into the framework of an inappropriate statute was treated. The clear message was that although it might be appropriate in some areas of the law to expand and develop the interpretation of existing legal provisions to take account of advances in technology, such provision had to be consonant with the alleged 'offence', in order not to stretch the law beyond its breaking point.[101]

Other attempts to bring antisocial computer users to book resulted in charges of offences under the **Criminal Damage Act 1971**. The question for the court in *Cox v Riley*[102] was whether the deliberate erasure, by a disgruntled employee, of a computer program from a plastic card controlling a computerised saw, so as to render the saw inoperable, could be construed as criminal damage

---

100 Note that, for offences under this section, the problems identified in relation to the deception of a machine are overcome by express provision in the Act.

101 This should, however, be distinguished from the situation in *R v Governor of Brixton Prison, ex p Levin* [1997] 1 Cr App R 355, in which it was held that the word 'disk' was within the definition of 'instrument' in the Forgery and Counterfeiting Act 1981, s 8(1)(d), and embraced the information stored, as well as the medium on which it was stored. By entering false instructions on the disk, it was, in the court's opinion, falsified, and the applicant had thereby created a false instrument.

102 (1986) 83 Cr App R 54.

for the purposes of s 1(1) of the **Criminal Damage Act 1971**. It was agreed by all parties that the card was 'property' within the meaning of s 10(1) — but had it been damaged? At first instance, damage was found in the fact that the card could no longer be used to operate and control the saw. On appeal, the opposing argument was placed that, in reality, it was not the card that had been damaged, but the program; the physical state of the card was unchanged. Because the program was intangible, it was argued that it could not, of itself, be construed as 'property' within the meaning of s 10(1).

Stephen Brown LJ found, however, that the card was indeed damaged, in that it had been deprived of its usefulness, and it would take both time and money to remedy this situation. In arriving at this conclusion, he relied on dicta of Cantley J in the case of *Henderson and Battley*,[103] which took the definition of 'damage' from the *Concise Oxford Dictionary* as 'injury impairing value or usefulness'. Both Stephen Brown LJ and Cantley J relied also on the much earlier precedent of *Fisher*,[104] concerning a discontented employee who put a steam engine out of action in such a way as not to damage the engine as such, but to ensure that considerable time and effort was needed to make it operative again. The use of this reasoning to reach the decision in *Cox v Riley* was later criticised by the Law Commission on the basis that it was decided under the provisions of the **Malicious Damage Act 1861**,[105] an Act that contained a different concept of damage. However, notwithstanding whether or not either *Henderson and Battley* or the **Malicious Damage Act 1861** is applicable to the situation in *Cox v Riley*, this arguably shows a rather more flexible judicial approach than that shown in *Gold and Schifreen*. The situation that the court had to consider was obviously not one that was originally envisaged by drafters of the statute, but the approach taken to its application to the new technology is inherently pragmatic, as can be seen in the concluding remark that 'it seems to me quite untenable to argue that what this defendant did on this occasion did not amount to causing damage to property'.[106] As subsequently pointed out by the Law Commission, however:

> For the commission of a criminal offence to depend on whether it can be proved that data was damaged or destroyed while it was held on identifiable tangible property not only is unduly technical, but also creates an undesirable degree of uncertainty in the operation of the law.[107]

In addition, as will be appreciated, the reasoning on this point does not really attack the crux of the opposing argument, which is directed at where the damage lies, and it is perhaps more informed by the fact that it was well established that the defendant had the requisite *mens rea*, rather than confirmation that the necessary *actus reus* had been proved. The court did not therefore exhibit the same contempt for the use of the **Criminal Damage Act 1971** as was shown towards the attempted use of the **Forgery and Counterfeiting Act 1981**, but, as emphasised by the Law Commission, the legal reasoning in this case does not really stand up to scrutiny.

A rather different approach was taken to the application of the **Criminal Damage Act 1971** in computer-related cases in *R v Whiteley*,[108] but, on any assessment, this was a radically different type of case. In brief,[109] Whiteley's hobby was hacking into computer networks and a particular target of his was JANET, the Joint Academic Network. Whilst engaged in such activities, he assumed the identity of 'Alan Dolby', the 'Mad Hacker', and deleted and changed data and 'locked out' authorised users by effecting changes of passwords, etc. He was eventually traced, following monitoring of the system at Queen Mary College, one of his prime targets, and charged with criminal damage.

---

103 (1984) unreported, ICA.
104 (1865) LR 1 CCR 7.
105 Law Commission, *Report on Computer Misuse*, Cm 819, 1989, London: HMSO, para 2.30.
106 (1986) 83 Cr App R 54, 58, *per* Stephen Brown LJ.
107 Law Commission, op cit, para 2.29.
108 (1991) 93 Cr App R 25. See also the case comment by D Cowley, 'Criminal damage: Computer disc' (1992) 56 JCL 37.
109 For a more detailed account of events, see Clough and Mungo, op cit, pp 42ff.

Again, the argument was put that the damage was not to the tangible parts of the computer system, but rather to the information contained on the disk. The manner in which such disks store information is in the arrangement of magnetic particles on the surface; if the information is changed (maliciously or otherwise), then this pattern will be altered. The court found that such a change could be classified as damage and could therefore found a charge of criminal damage.[110]

In considering the matter, the court noted that what the Act required was that tangible property had been damaged, not that the damage itself should be tangible. In its view, the particles were clearly part of the disk, so that if they had been altered intentionally and without lawful excuse and, as a result, the value or usefulness of the disk was impaired, then that would be damage within the meaning of s 1. Just because the damage would only be manifest when the computer was operated did not mean that the situation was not covered by the Act. Such reasoning might have provided a suitable avenue for the use of existing legal provisions to deal with cases of computer hacking – particularly of the more antisocial variety, which involve rather more than mere browsing in the contents of files – but, by the time this decision had been reached, the Law Commission's recommendations for reform of the law in this area had resulted in the passing of the **Computer Misuse Act 1990**, which, due to the criticisms of the reasoning in *Cox v Riley*, had effectively removed such cases from the ambit of the **Criminal Damage Act 1971**.

The Legal Response to 'Hacking'

Because of situations such as those that gave rise to the cases above, the Law Commissions for both Scotland, and England and Wales, reviewed the existing criminal law and its relation both to hacking and to computer misuse more generally. The Scottish Law Commission reported first[111] and recommended that the problem could be tackled by the creation of an unauthorised access offence. The Herculean task of drafting such legislation was noted by Tapper, who commented that 'the encapsulation of the burgeoning technology within the strait jacket of the ordinary language and comprehensible structure ideally characterising Acts of Parliament constitutes a formidable task'.[112] He considered the three separate alternative approaches to computer misuse – relying on the judiciary to interpret existing rules; amending existing rules to facilitate judicial interpretation; and enacting new offences – and concluded that there was no clear choice as to which of these was preferable, or likely to be most effective.

Despite some adverse criticisms of the Scottish Law Commission's proposal, it was clearly quite influential when the Law Commission for England and Wales came to consider the problems created by this new species of 'computer crime'. The first exploration of the issues considered whether or not it was in the public interest that the type of activity in question should be regarded as criminal.[113] It concluded that there were the following arguments for the use of criminal offences: the overall importance of computers to society as a whole and a consequent need to maintain their integrity; the need to signal society's disapproval of deliberate hacking, especially as this might cause damage to the computer system itself; and the fact that prohibition of hacking might also reduce other conduct, such as computer fraud etc. On the other hand, it also noted that there were a number of arguments against criminalisation: the fact that although obtaining unauthorised access might breach privacy it was not, of itself, a matter for the criminal law, and that enforcement was likely to cause a number of problems.

---

110 (1991) 93 Cr App R 25, 27.
111 Scottish Law Commission, op cit.
112 Tapper, op cit, 8.
113 Law Commission, *Reforming the Present Law: Hacking*, Working Paper No 110, 1988, London: HMSO, Pt VI.

When the Law Commission finally reported on the matter,[114] it concluded that the existing criminal remedies were inadequate to deal with many instances of computer crime and misuse, although it conceded that a number of charges under the **Theft Act 2006** might be appropriate in cases of computer fraud. Taking all of the issues into account and the outcome of the consultations, two new criminal offences were proposed,[115] and it was noted that 'the main argument . . . does not turn on the protection of information but rather springs from the need to protect the integrity and security of computer systems'. The new offences were to have a broad and a narrow ambit, respectively: the first created an offence for all types of unauthorised access to computer access; and the second imposed more severe penalties on those who obtained unauthorised access to computer systems for the purpose of committing more serious crimes.

Despite the Law Commission's report, the government did not implement the recommendations and, in the end, the **CMA** was the result of a private member's Bill introduced by Michael Colvin. This Bill did, however, follow fairly closely the Law Commission's proposals. In particular, it took a two-tier approach: the first section contains a basic hacking offence; and the second, an ulterior intent offence designed to cover situations in which there is unauthorised access with the intent to commit a further crime. These sections are hierarchical and when charges are bought under s 2, it is still possible to convict under s 1, even where the necessary intent for a s 2 offence is not proved. Certain activities, however, do not fall within the ambit of the statute – in particular, reading of the contents of files non-interactively, for example, unauthorised reading after printing out in cases in which the print operation had been performed by an authorised user, or mere reading of information on a computer screen. Depending on the nature of the material, such acts could fall within the scope of the **Data Protection Act 1998**. Section 3 then went on to create an offence of unauthorised modification of computer material. This was a response to the Law Commission's criticism, referred to above, of the use of the **Criminal Damage Act 1971** in such cases and, to put the matter beyond doubt, s 3(6) excluded the use of the 1971 Act in cases of computer misuse unless the effect of the misuse was to impair the physical condition of the computer, or computer-storage medium.[116] In common with statutes in other jurisdictions, the Act does not define the word 'computer',[117] but a lengthy interpretation section demonstrates the wide-reaching scope of some of the other crucial concepts in the Act.[118]

See Chapter 5 →

The Computer Misuse Act in Operation

The **CMA** does not appear to have had conspicuous success in deterring or apprehending computer criminals and the total number of prosecutions under the Act has been relatively small.[119] In addition, some of the early cases under the relevant provisions sometimes seemed to reveal some misunderstandings of both the provisions themselves and the behaviour that the Act was intended to address.

---

114 Law Commission, 1989, op cit.
115 Whether this outcome is desirable has been questioned: see, eg, M Wasik, 'Misuse of information technology: What should the role of the criminal law be?' (1991) 5 LC & T Yearbook 158.
116 The original s 3 has now been repealed and replaced as a result of the amendments introduced in the Police and Justice Act 2006: see later discussion at pp 125–127.
117 One exception is the legislation in Singapore: see, eg, A Endeshaw, 'Computer misuse law in Singapore' (1999) 8 ICTL 5; I Mahalingham Carr and KS Williams, 'A step too far in controlling computers? The Singapore Computer Misuse (Amendment) Act 1998' (2000) 8 Int JLIT 48.
118 Computer Misuse Act 1990, s 17.
119 See All Party Internet Group (APIG), *Revision of the Computer Misuse Act: Report of an Inquiry by the All Party Internet Group*, 2004, London: HMSO. The APIG was subsumed into the All Party Parliamentary Communications Group (apComms) in 2007 and copies of the report can now be accessed from the latter's website at www.apcomms.org.uk/apig/archive/activities-2004/computer-misuse-inquiry.html

The 'Hacking' Offence

Section 1(1)(a) of the Act provides that:

> a person is guilty of an offence if (a) he causes a computer to perform any function with intent to secure access to any program or data held in any computer; (b) the access he intends to secure is unauthorised; and (c) he knows at the time when he causes the computer to perform the function that that is the case.

As far as access is required, it appears that any sort of activity will suffice other than merely reading a screen and that the Act extends to access to, or modification of, the contents of portable storage devices, such as disks and memory sticks, if this occurs while they are in any computer. The very first case under the Act, R v Cropp,[120] was arguably not actually representative of the popular view of hacking. Cropp had used his knowledge of his ex-employer's computer system to give himself a 70 per cent discount on goods. He was charged with the ulterior intent offence in s 2(1) and a submission of 'no case to answer' was made, on the grounds that, in order to contravene s 1(1) (and, therefore, s 2(1)), it had to be established that the accused had used one computer with intent to secure unauthorised access into another computer. This was not what Cropp had actually done, but correlates with the commonly accepted meaning of 'hacking', which was popularly supposed to be the activity that was proscribed by the legislation. This argument succeeded at trial, but the Court of Appeal gave it short shrift and, referring to the 'plain and natural meaning' of the section, found that there were 'no grounds whatsoever for implying such an interpretation'.[121] The Act had been drafted so as to deal not only with the situation in which indirect access to a computer system is gained by using another computer, but also with the situation in which a person misuses a computer to which he or she has direct (but unauthorised) access. If the Court had not arrived at such an interpretation, the potential usefulness of the **CMA** could have been severely curtailed, resulting in what was described at the time as 'total emasculation'.[122] The dramatic effect that this might have had is particularly apparent with hindsight, as a number of prosecutions have been brought that have far more in common with the situation in Cropp than with hacking.

Another early case, that of Bedworth,[123] achieved a certain amount of notoriety. Bedworth was a teenager whose hacking activities started when he was given a computer for his 14th birthday in 1987. By the time he was arrested in 1991, together with fellow hackers who had all communicated under pseudonyms via an electronic bulletin board, he had hacked into an impressively long list of computer systems, including the Financial Times, a cancer research institute in Brussels, the European Commission offices in Luxembourg, and many others, resulting in significant financial losses being incurred by the institutions involved. At his trial, he made no attempt to deny that he had done the acts of which he was accused. His defence was that he was obsessed: he was subject to compulsive behaviour, so that although he knew that what he was doing was unlawful, his obsession denied him the freedom to stop – in other words, he was addicted to hacking. For addiction to be a sufficient defence to a criminal charge, the individual should be affected to such an extent that the affliction may be viewed as a 'disease of the mind', sufficient to prevent the formation of the requisite mens rea. This would then effectively equate with a defence of insanity. Whether or not there is clinical evidence to support any finding of addiction to computer hacking is not a subject that can be debated here, although supporting evidence was produced during the trial. It is

---

120 (1991) unreported, but see Case note at (1991) 7 CLSR 168.
121 AG's Reference (No 1 of 1991) [1992] WLR 432, 437.
122 EA Dumbill, 'Computer Misuse Act 1990: Recent developments' (1992) 8 CLSR 105.
123 (1993) unreported. See further A Charlesworth, 'Addiction and hacking' (1993a) 143 NLJ 540 and 'Legislating against computer misuse: The trials and tribulations of the UK Computer Misuse Act 1990' (1993b) J L & IS 80; C Christian, 'Down and out in cyberspace' (1993) 90 Law Soc Gazette 2; D Fisch Nigri, 'Computer crime: Why should we still care' (1993) 9 CLSR 274.

certainly the case that, at the trial, Bedworth gave repeated assertions not only that he had committed the acts at issue, but also that he was aware that these acts were wrong and would not be repeated. If he were truly addicted, would he be able to make this latter promise? Charlesworth,[124] citing the case of *Lawrence*,[125] points out that courts are unlikely even to take addiction into account in mitigation. *Lawrence* was, of course, a case in which the offence (of burglary) was committed to feed the addiction rather than being directly related to that addiction. Whilst it can be problematic to draw analogies between such cases and those, such as *Bedworth*, in which the addiction is to the criminal behaviour itself, there is also confirmation for the absence of a general defence of addiction in *Kopsch*:[126] 'The defence of uncontrollable impulse is unknown in English law.' Nevertheless, despite the judge's summing-up, the defence of addiction apparently persuaded the jury and Bedworth was acquitted. At the time, there was concern that this outcome might drive the proverbial 'coach and horses' through the enforcement of the **CMA**. However, notwithstanding the success of Bedworth's defence, there appears to have been no further attempt to plead such a defence despite anecdotal references to addiction to computers; neither was any leniency extended to his co-defendants, Strickland and Woods, who, having pleaded guilty, were sentenced to six months' imprisonment – a recognition, perhaps, of the fact that the behaviour in question resulted in significant financial loss, can cause serious damage to the systems affected, and should be viewed seriously.

Questions of Authorisation

Authorisation, or the lack of it, is of central importance not only to the provisions of the **CMA**, but also to the legal protection offered to computer systems in other jurisdictions.[127] In relation to the **CMA**, it has been described as the 'keystone'.[128] Section 1, quoted above, deals with unauthorised access and the original s 3 concerned the unauthorised modification of computer material. This section has been amended following the All Party Internet Group (APIG) report of 2004 and the subsequent enactment of the **Police and Justice Act 2006**,[129] and now refers to impairment rather than modification, but the requirement that this be unauthorised remains an imperative. The issue of authorisation is less likely to be controversial in relation to a remote hacker with no connection to the hacked site, but has proved to be an issue in cases of 'inside hacking' such as where the alleged unauthorised access occurs in employment. On this specific issue, the Law Commission suggested that:

> . . . an employer should only have the support of the hacking offence if he has clearly defined the limits of authorisation applicable to each employee, and if he is able to prove that the employee had knowingly and recklessly exceeded that level of authority.[130]

It was made clear in *Ellis v DPP*[131] that a person's subjective belief that he or she should have access to a computer network was not sufficient to provide the requisite authorisation. Ellis was an alumnus of a university and had thus previously been authorised to use the university's computer network. Several years after graduating, he continued to use the system via terminals that had been left logged on by a previous user. It was concluded that although he thought that he should have

---

124 A Charlesworth, 'Between flesh and sand: Rethinking the Computer Misuse Act 1990' (1995) 9 LC & T Yearbook 31.
125 [1989] Crim LR 309.
126 (1925) 19 Cr App R 50.
127 See, eg, Peter A Winn, 'The guilty eye: Unauthorized access, trespass and privacy' (2007) 62 Bus Law 1395.
128 Neil MacEwan, 'The Computer Misuse Act 1990: Lessons from its past and predictions for its future' [2008] Crim L Rev 955, 957.
129 See later discussion at p 125.
130 Law Commission, 1989, op cit, para 3.37.
131 [2001] EWHC Admin 362.

such access, he neither had authorisation nor believed that he was so authorised. The question of authorisation was returned to in *DPP v Bignell*,[132] in which no criminal liability was found on the basis of lack of authorisation, even though the consequent access was then exploited in an unauthorised manner. The reasoning in this decision, although not the outcome as such, was subsequently criticised by the House of Lords in *R v Bow Street Magistrates Court and Allison, ex p United States*,[133] because, in attempting to distinguish the control of access from the authority to access, it introduced 'a number of glosses which are not present in the Act'.[134] Lord Hobhouse suggested that the words of s 1 in relation to authorisation were 'clear and unambiguous',[135] but that problems had arisen in the reasoning of the court in *Bignell*, and also in the Court of Appeal in *Allison* itself, because of confusion between s 1 and the definition of authorisation set out in s 17(5):

Access of any kind by any person to any program or data held in the computer is unauthorised if –

(a)   he is not himself entitled to control access of the kind in question to the program or data; and

(b)   he does not have consent to access by him of the kind in question to the program or data from any person who is so entitled.

Lord Hobhouse pointed out that it was, for example, possible for individuals to have authority to view data, but not to do anything further with it, and set out a detailed explanation of how the various issues relating to access and authorisation should work together. In identifying the two ways in which authority could be acquired, the meaning of s 17(5) was clear, but also subsidiary to the requirements of s 1. In particular, he made it clear that 'the authority must relate not simply to the data or programme but also to the actual kind of access secured',[136] and summarised the matter by suggesting: 'These plain words leave no room for any suggestion that the relevant person may say: "Yes, I know that I was not authorised to access that data but I was authorised to access other data of the same kind".'[137]

As mentioned above, s 3 also originally made it an offence to make an unauthorised modification. There was little difficulty in applying this concept to virus attacks,[138] but as the use and functionality of the internet developed, so did other ways of causing problems for users of computer networks.[139] A particular example is provided by the initiation of DoS attacks and DDoS attacks, in which the perpetrator sets up a system that will generate a high volume of traffic to the target site. They also raise both separate and related questions about whether or not there was authorisation to send the traffic to the site. In *Caffrey*, discussed in more detail below, the issue was raised as to whether or not the **CMA**, s 3, covered DoS attacks. In so far as the requirements of s 3 hinge on unauthorised modification, the natural conclusion might be that those attacks that result in data or program modification would fall within the Act, but those that merely clog up the system with excessive traffic would not. The relevant matters were further underlined by the case of *DPP v Lennon*.[140] Lennon had been dismissed from his job and, in retaliation, he sent emails to his former

132   [1998] Crim LR 53, [1998] 1 Cr App R 1.
133   [2000] 2 AC 216.
134   Ibid, 225.
135   Ibid, 226.
136   Ibid, 224.
137   Ibid.
138   See, eg, the discussion of *R v Pile* (1995) unreported and similar cases below at p 124.
139   See, eg, Bill Goodwin, 'The law must be changed to redefine criminal activities' (2002) *Computer Weekly*, 14 March, available online at www.computerweekly.com/Articles/2002/03/14/185735/the-law-must-be-changed-to-redefine-criminal-activities.htm
140   Wimbledon Youth Court, 2 November 2005, unreported. For details, see [2006] EWHC 1201 (Admin).

employer using a 'mail bombing' program that he had downloaded from the internet. The majority of the emails received purported to come from the firm's HR manager. Estimates as to the number of emails sent vary (para 2 of the official transcript of the case suggests 5 million, whereas paras 5 and 9 refer to half a million), but the volume was certainly sufficient to cause significant disruption to the firm's communications. At first instance, the defence pleaded that, because the function of the firm's servers was to receive emails, potential senders were authorised to modify the contents of the server by sending them. This argument succeeded and it was held that there was no case to answer because any modifications could not be shown to be unauthorised.

This decision was compared unfavourably at the time with the case of *Cuthbert*, in which a software tester was convicted of unauthorised access to a charity website.[141] His intention was to donate money to the tsunami appeal, but, when he received no acknowledgement, he became suspicious about a number of factors about the website and concerned that, having given his name address and credit card details, he had been the victim of a phishing scam. Accordingly, he used his technical expertise to test the security settings and was relieved to find there was no problem. However, this attempt was logged by the site as a potential intrusion and he was eventually charged with breach of s 1 of the **CMA**. There were detailed logs of his web activity, which showed that there were no attempted frauds or other illicit activity; in addition, although he had considerable technical expertise that could have caused widespread disruption to computer networks, he clearly had not done so. Nevertheless, he was found guilty of unauthorised access to the website and fined £400. Although the judge apparently reached this outcome 'with some considerable regret',[142] in comparison with other **CMA** cases, this could be viewed as a harsh outcome – the alternative of a conditional discharge would presumably have been a possibility.

However, *Lennon* was subsequently appealed by way of case stated.[143] With regard to authorisation, the Court was of the view that implying authorisation via consent to receive emails could not be without limit and that the behaviour complained of had to be considered as a whole. Whereas consent for the sending of one email might be granted, it was unlikely that permission would be given for the sending of half a million emails. It was therefore held that there was a case to answer, but in the event Lennon pleaded guilty and so there was no further legal discussion of the matter. Although the amendments to s 3 discussed below are intended to make the Act easier to apply to DoS and DDoS attacks, there has been no specific clarification of the meaning of 'unauthorised' and so authorisation arguably remains a slippery concept.

Application of the Computer Misuse Act 1990 to Malware

The term 'malware', an abbreviation of 'malicious software', has been coined to denote any software that is intended to cause damage, disruption, and annoyance to users. It includes viruses, worms, Trojans,[144] keystroke loggers, botnets, and any other programs of a potentially destructive nature. Such software can spread rapidly across networks and may do anything from destroying the

---

141 See Peter Sommer, 'Computer misuse prosecutions' (2006) 16(5) Computers and Law 24.
142 See John Oates, 'Tsunami hacker convicted' (2005) *The Register*, 6 October, available online at www.theregister.co.uk/2005/10/06/tsunami_hacker_convicted/
143 [2006] EWHC 1201 (Admin).
144 These, and similar terms, are sometimes used interchangeably in non-technical parlance and even from a technical perspective the differences between them are now of diminishing importance. A virus is a self-replicating program that may not be immediately apparent on examination of a system, but which copies itself into the computer memory and, from there, to any disks that are subsequently loaded and/or in the memory of other computers attached to the same network as data is exchanged. The type of program commonly referred to as a 'worm' is an example of a program that was developed for exploring the capabilities of computer systems and networks, and may adversely affect systems on which it is unwanted by consuming resources. A 'Trojan' is a program that appears to be a program performing an innocuous function, but which hides the fact that it also has another, usually more sinister, function. For general definitions, see, eg, Joseph Audal, Quincy Lu, and Peter Roman, 'Computer crimes' (2008) 45 Am Crim L Rev 233. The word 'virus' is itself often used as a generic term for many types of malware: for a history of viruses, see, eg, M Klang, 'A critical look at the regulation of computer viruses' (2003) 11 IJLIT 162, 163–7.

contents of a hard disk, to generating facetious messages. The ILOVEYOU virus, which was estimated to have infected some 45 million computers in 2000 and caused billions of dollars worth of damage, has even been described as 'the most devastating crime in history'.[145] More recently, the Conficker worm, which was first reported to Microsoft in November 2008,[146] was reported to have infected more than 15 million computers by the end of January 2009.[147] The activities of botnets and keystroke loggers can be controlled from external sites and be used to steal data – often personal details, and especially bank and credit card details – and can be used to propagate spam, phishing, and pharming emails.[148] The targets of this activity will vary – business and government sites are most likely to be the victims of DoS and DDoS, and well-respected and frequently visited sites also provide fertile ground for harvesting data from visitors to these sites for subsequent targeting. However, domestic users are not immune: they may be less likely to be targeted directly by hackers, but they may be extremely vulnerable to malware, which can be spread by apparently innocuous activities including sending emails or visiting websites.

The first worm to be released onto the embryonic internet was created in 1988 by a Cornell University student, Robert Morris, who was subsequently successfully prosecuted under the US **Computer Fraud and Abuse Act of 1986** (18 **USC** § 1030) on what was basically a hacking charge. This decision was upheld by the US Court of Appeals for the Second Circuit,[149] which found that Morris had both exceeded the authorisation for those computers that he was allowed to access and, because the program was designed to spread to other machines, had also accessed computers that he had no authority to access. A short while later, not long before the **CMA** was passed in the UK, the strange case of Dr Lewis Popp hit the headlines. A large number of people associated with computer use received disks through the post purporting to contain important information about the AIDS virus. If, in fact, the disks were used, although they did reveal information on that subject, they also contained a Trojan horse that was programmed to activate after the computer had been used about a hundred times. Although the contents of the hard disk would have been destroyed, at that time, there would have been little action that could have been taken as a result of this particular activity, unless the courts would have been happy to use the reasoning in *Whiteley* discussed above.[150] This incident was referred to in the parliamentary debates on the Computer Misuse Bill and it was also evident that, at this stage, it was intended that the new legislation would cover such activities: ' . . . circulation of an infected disk, such as this is not an offence. However, the Bill will make it one.'[151]

As a result, the original s 3 of the **CMA** created an offence of doing any act that caused the unauthorised modification of the contents of any computer with the requisite intent and knowledge, as defined by the section. The Law Commission had found no evidence that such activities should not be criminalised and was also of the view that the existing law on criminal damage was unsuitable.[152] Section 3, even as first drafted, appeared to be capable of catching a wide variety of

---

145 NK Katyal, 'Criminal law in cyberspace' (2001) 149 U Pa L Rev 1003; see also, eg, SC Sprinkel, 'Global internet regulation: The residual effects of the "iloveyou" computer virus and the Draft Convention on Cyber-Crime' (2002) 25 Suffolk Transnat'l L Rev 491; K Cesare, 'Prosecuting computer virus authors: The need for an adequate and immediate international solution' (2001) 14 Transnat'l Law 135, 145.

146 See www.microsoft.com/security/worms/conficker.aspx, which also includes an explanation of how the worm works.

147 See World Economic Forum, op cit (2009).

148 For details of the latest such activity, see, eg, Symantec Internet Security, op cit. For further discussion of the legal response to spam, see Chapter 5.

149 *US v Morris* 928 F 2d 504 (2nd Cir 1991).

150 See, eg, Y Akdeniz, 'Section 3 of the Computer Misuse Act 1990: An antidote for computer viruses!' [1996] 3 Web JCLI, available online at http://webjcli.ncl.ac.uk/1996/issue3/akdeniz3.html. In fact, Dr Popp was eventually arrested in Ohio and charged with extorting money with menaces, because those affected were also directed to transfer sums of money to a bank account in Panama. In the event, there was evidence that Popp's mental condition had deteriorated to such an extent that he was pronounced unfit to plead.

151 Michael Colvin, Hansard, vol 166, col 1139, 1990.

152 Law Commission, Cm 819, 1989, paras 2.27–2.29 – note that this was before the judgment in *R v Whiteley* (1991) 93 Cr App R 25, discussed above.

types of activity, including not only the type of modification and erasure seen in *Cox v Riley*,[153] but also the intentional introduction of viruses, worms, Trojan horses, and other programs of a potentially destructive nature. Since the intent did not need to be directed at any particular computer, the liability of the person who originated the virus or worm would be unaffected if, in the event, a virus was introduced to a system by means of an infected disk innocently acquired by a third party. On the other hand, it was clear that anyone knowingly introducing an infected disk had an intent to modify the contents of a computer. Nevertheless, there was some discussion after the statute was enacted as to whether s 3 was suitable for apprehending those who introduced viruses into computer systems,[154] but the fact that s 3 could, in principle, be used in this way was put beyond doubt in the case of *R v Pile*.[155] Pile, who referred to himself as the 'Black Baron', developed two particular viruses – Queeg and Pathogen – and also Smeg, a guide to writing viruses. These viruses were capable of masquerading as other, innocent programs, and he was even successful in incorporating a virus into an anti-virus scan program. This was the first time that a person had appeared in court as a result of intentionally introducing computer viruses to a system and the court had no problems in finding a breach of s 3. In addition, expert opinion was also presented on the likely damage caused by Pile's activities and this resulted in the imposition of a custodial sentence of 18 months.

Since these early days, many virulent virus programs have been unleashed on the world's computer networks causing damage estimated at many billions of dollars. The originators of some of the more high-profile attacks have been detected, although not necessarily apprehended. The creator of the Melissa virus, the major effect of which was to cause infected computers to send emails containing an infected attachment to the first 50 names in the user's computer address book, was prosecuted in the USA under 18 **USC** § 1030 and sentenced to 20 months' imprisonment, together with a fine of US$5,000.[156] On the other hand, although Filipino ex-computer science student Onel de Guzman was identified as the creator of the ILOVEYOU virus referred to at the beginning of this section, there were no appropriate charges that could be brought against him in the Philippines.[157] The writer of the Anna Kournikova virus voluntarily confessed, and was charged and convicted in the Netherlands; two people have appeared in court in connection with the Blaster worm;[158] and in the UK, a man was jailed for two years for releasing viruses onto the internet. In the unsuccessful appeal against sentence in the latter case, Penry-Davey remarked that 'criminal conduct of this kind has the capacity to cause disruption, consternation and even economic loss on an unimagined scale',[159] showing that courts were becoming aware of the potential severity of such activities. It has been suggested that whoever produced the Conficker worm is 'a criminal mastermind worthy of a James Bond thriller'.[160] Microsoft has offered a reward of US$250,000 for information leading to arrest and conviction of anyone responsible for Conficker, but to date no one has been apprehended.[161]

---

153 Discussed above at pp 115–116.
154 See, eg, M Wasik, 'Introduction' (1995) 9 LC & T Yearbook, ix.
155 (1995) unreported. For further details, see, eg, S Jones, 'Computer terrorist or mad boffin?' (1996) 146 NLJ 46; Akdeniz, op cit.
156 *US v Smith* DNJ 2 May 2002; see www.cybercrime.gov/cccases.html
157 New law has since been enacted in the Philippines, but it does not have retrospective effect. For further discussion, see, eg, Sprinkel, op cit; MD Goodman and SW Brenner, 'The emerging consensus on criminal conduct in cyberspace' (2002) UCLA J L & Tech 3, which also contains details of the new law in the Appendix.
158 *US v An Unnamed Juvenile* WD Washington 26/9/2003; *US v Parson* WD Washington 29/8/2003; see www.cybercrime.gov/cccases.html
159 *R v Vallor* [2004] 1 Cr App R (S) 54, [7].
160 Paul Thurrott, 'April Fools: World preps for Conficker attack' (2010) *Paul Thurrott's Supersite for Windows*, 6 October, available online at www.winsupersite.com/article/windows-server/april-fools-world-preps-for-conficker-attack
161 Charles Arthur, 'Microsoft offers $250,000 bounty on Conficker worm author's head' (2009) *GuardianOnline*, 13 February, available online at www.guardian.co.uk/media/2009/feb/13/microsoft-offers-250k-bounty-conficker-worm. For a more detailed consideration of the application of the law to computer viruses, together with some alternative points of view, see, eg, Klang, op cit.

Trojan horses can be installed on a computer without the user's knowledge and provide a common vehicle for the introduction of other types of malware. A range of different actions can then be initiated that may or may not come to the notice of the user. As an example, the Sinowal Trojan was able to install itself on the computers of those who visited infected websites, and was then able to collect personal and financial data undetected by the user. It was estimated that many thousands of bank accounts, credit cards, and debit cards had been compromised in this way.[162] The operation of Trojans was a central feature in three separate cases in the UK: those of *Green* (2002), *Caffrey* (2003), and *Schofield* (2003).[163] The common feature in all of these cases was that the defendant alleged that the acts complained above resulted from the installation of a Trojan on their computers of which they were unaware. Both Green and Schofield were charged with possession of indecent images of children, but succeeded in bringing evidence that the presence of the images on their computers were due to them having been infected with Trojans that then, without their knowledge, downloaded the images whenever the internet was accessed. Caffrey, on the other hand, was a prosecution under **CMA**, s 3, in which Caffrey was acquitted for a DoS attack on the Port of Houston computer network. The result of the attack was to impair the operation of the network to such an extent that necessary navigation data was inaccessible. There was no dispute that Caffrey's computer was not the source of the attack, but the prosecution case was that it was initiated by Caffrey as a misdirected attack on a fellow chatroom user, whereas the defence argument was that the attack was the result of the activity of a Trojan, which had infected Caffrey's machine and over which he had no control. No trace of the Trojan was found, but evidence was accepted that the Trojan had self-deleted after launching the attack, despite the prosecution's view that such technology did not exist. These cases all demonstrate the evidential difficulties for both sides when it is possible that the acts, harm, or damage complained of could have originated from a Trojan. Certainly, a browse through a virus library shows that there are Trojan programs that exhibit some of the properties alleged in the above cases,[164] meaning that the mere facts of the case may not provide any indication of whether or not the act complained of occurred with or without the user's knowledge or consent.

DOS Attacks and the Police and Justice Act 2006

DoS and DDoS attacks created two major issues for application of the original provisions of the **CMA**. The first was the question of authorisation, but as was demonstrated by the reasoning of the appeal court in *Lennon*, this need not be fatal to a charge under s 3. More fatal, however, is the fact that data may not actually be modified. Although the DoS attack initiated by Caffrey's PC may have arisen as the result of infection by a Trojan, which could bring it within the ambit of the original s 3, it is clear that many DoS and DDoS attacks will not modify computer material as such, but instead will merely clog up the victim's computer system and be generally disruptive.[165] Similar effects can be seen when websites crash because of an unusual amount of traffic attempting to access the site;[166] more sophisticated attacks exploit known and/or foreseeable vulnerabilities in the software, and, especially if a DDoS harnesses a network of other computers, the effect of a deliberately targeted attack can be on a radically different scale. Nevertheless, if there is no actual modification of the data, then whether or not the actions of the attacker are deemed to authorised or unauthorised, it is difficult to see

162 See Maggie Shiels, 'Trojan virus steals banking info' (2008) BBC News, 21 October, available online at http://news.bbc.co.uk/1/hi/technology/7701227.stm

163 All unreported, but see discussion in S Hill, 'Driving a Trojan horse and cart through the Computer Misuse Act' (2003) 14(5) C&L 31, and SW Brenner, B Carrier, and J Henninger, 'The Trojan horse defense in cybercrime cases' (2004) 21 CHTLJ 1.

164 Troj/Newsflood, for example, is a Trojan horse that continually posts messages about child pornography to Usenet newsgroups: see www.sophos.com/virusinfo/analyses/

165 It has been suggested that they should therefore be categorised as 'unauthorised disruptions': see Katyal, op cit, 1023–7.

166 At the time of writing, for example, widespread concern about the swine flu pandemic caused a massive number of people to try to access the information and the website crashed almost immediately it went live.

how s 3 can be applied. Neither is it easy for victims to take adequate precautions, as pointed out by Wyatt:

> Providing protection against some types of DOS and especially DDOS attacks can be technically challenging. It is often hard to distinguish legitimate from illegitimate activity, which means that genuine traffic can be discarded through protective measures.[167]

The undesirability of the legality of DoS and DDoS depending of the precise mode of execution was one of the issues discussed by the APIG in its public inquiry into the operation of the **CMA**, noting that 'it is the particular circumstances of each attack that makes it obvious whether the CMA wording applies'.[168] Although it was perhaps more likely that the **CMA** would be applicable to instances of DDoS attacks because software, such as the disputed Trojan in *Caffrey*, would need to be installed, to put the matter beyond doubt, a specific recommendation was made to enact an 'explicit "denial-of service" offence of impairing access to data'.[169] It was intended that this would cover all instances of deliberate DoS whether or not they would currently fall within s 3, and thus remedy both actual and perceived deficiencies in **CMA**, s 3. The EU Council Framework Decision on attacks against information systems of the following year then required Member States to criminalise illegal interference with both systems and data.[170] The **Police and Justice Act 2006**, s 36 of which creates a new s 3 **CMA**, eventually gave effect to both the requirements of this Decision and the recommendation of the APIG report. The new section creates an offence where anyone does an unauthorised act in relation to any computer with the knowledge that the act is unauthorised and the act is done with the intent to impair the computer's operation, to prevent or hinder access to a program or data, to impair the operation of a program or the reliability of data, or to enable any of these things. In addition, s 3(3) now specifically allows that the offence will also be committed if these acts are done recklessly as to whether they will have any of the above effects.

A number of points can be made about the new section. First, it is clear that the scope of the new section is far wider than the old, and the fact that the need for actual modification of computer material has been removed suggests that the section is clearly capable of encompassing both DoS and DDoS attacks. As is frequently the case, however, it may be that the solution to one problem has resulted in the creation of new ones. Most obvious is the replacement of the objective criterion of 'modification' with the more subjective requirement of 'impairment': an act could be done with the requisite intent to impair the operation of the computer, but the actual effect be unnoticed by the user. It is not clear what would be a better word. Fafinski suggests that 'a meaningful legal definition of impairment ... might be "deterioration in performance that is noticeable by the senses"',[171] which has the advantage of excluding technical, but *de minimis* impairment, but it could still be a matter of debate at what point an alleged impairment became noticeable – it seems likely that computer experts would be more likely to notice an impairment before the average user, for example. This issue may, of course, be resolved by the question of when it might be in the public interest to prosecute on occasions on which all of the other elements of the offence appear to be in place. The new section retains the requirement for the act to be unauthorised, and for the perpetrator to have the knowledge that that is the case, so any residual problems with the concept of authorisation have not been resolved. The old s 3(6) required that any modification should not be

---

167 Derek Wyatt, HC Debs, 5 April 2005, col 1294, and APIG, op cit, para 58.
168 APIG, op cit, para 2.
169 Ibid, para 75. Some of the other issues raised in the report are discussed in subsequent sections. A similar gap has been identified in the German legislation relating to unauthorised modification of data: see Julia Hörnle, 'Germany: Denial of service attack – Case review' (2006) 8 EBL 11, 15.
170 Council Framework Decision 2005/222/JHA of 24 February 2005 [2005] OJ L/69, 67.
171 Stefan Fafinski, 'Computer misuse: The implications of the Police and Justice Act 2006' (2008) 72 JCL 53; see also S Fafinski 'Access denied: Computer misuse in an era of technological change' (2006) 70 JCL 424.

regarded as damage for the purpose of the **Criminal Damage Act 1971** unless it resulted in physical damage to the computer or computer system. Because the whole of the original section has been repealed, this could, in theory at least, allow the courts to resurrect the reasoning in *Whiteley*.[172]

Review and Reform

As mentioned above in connection with DoS attacks, prior to 2005, there had been many calls for a review to establish whether the provisions of the Act were still appropriate in the light of new technological advances. The pressure was intensified by observations that the **CMA** had not originally been designed to deal with the internet and that, in that respect, its 'premature birth' had left it 'weak and vulnerable'.[173] The spread of all types of malware can be accomplished far more effectively and efficiently via the internet and world wide web than by any other means, and this accentuated the views of some that the **CMA** was ill-equipped to respond to virus attacks.[174] In addition, the internet also provides access to such software for use by the non-specialist and, whereas it used to be the case that a certain amount of technical knowhow was required to launch a virus attack, for example, this is no longer the case; as already mentioned, it is as easy for the non-specialist to download malware as any other applications software.[175]

Further criticisms related to the apparently small number of prosecutions even though, as discussed at the beginning of this chapter, the apparent incidence of computer misuse is both large and increasing. A major obstacle to a realistic assessment of both the magnitude of the problem and the law's response to it is the difficulty in collecting accurate data. The most recent crime statistics from the Home Office make specific mention of neither computer misuse nor computer crime.[176] As pointed out by the House of Lords Science and Technology Committee,[177] for some offences, it can often be difficult to extricate computer crime from the same crime committed by more traditional methods, but nevertheless the Committee recommended that a more coordinated approach to data collection should be introduced, including a classification scheme for recording the incidence of all forms of e-crime.[178] From the numbers that are available, it certainly appears to be the case that there have been very few prosecutions.[179]

On a first examination, it can appear that the bespoke provisions of the **CMA** had not had any more conspicuous success at deterring or apprehending computer misuse than the hotchpotch of offences in use prior to its enactment. Certainly, significant problems of detection have bedevilled apprehension of computer criminals throughout the history of the enforcement of the **CMA**. Although there have been some high-profile cases, those responsible for the damage caused by many destructive viruses and worms have never been traced and identified, much less prosecuted. This is compounded by jurisdictional problems, because it is frequently the case that the damage is felt in a jurisdiction remote from that of the perpetrator. Although the Filipino ex-computer science student Onel de Guzman was identified as the creator of the highly destructive ILOVEYOU virus, he was effectively immune from prosecution in the Philippines, because there was no Filipino computer crime statute and so he could not be extradited. At the time of writing, Gary McKinnon

---

172 See above p 116 and see also LH Leigh, 'Some observations on the Police and Justice Act 2006' (2007) 171 JPN 28, 31.

173 MacEwan, op cit, 956.

174 See, eg, M Wasik, op cit (1995), ix; cf Michael Colvin, Hansard, vol 166, col 1139 (1990). More recently, see APIG, op cit, para 23.

175 See, eg, the facts of *DPP v Lennon*, Wimbledon Youth Court, 2 November 2005, unreported, above.

176 Home Office, *Crime in England and Wales* 2008/9, Statistical Bulletin 11/09, 2009, London: HMSO, and Home Office, *Crime in England and Wales* 2007/8, Statistical Bulletin 07/08, 2008, London: HMSO, both available online at www.homeoffice.gov.uk/rds/crimeew0809.html

177 House of Lords Science and Technology Committee, op cit, para 2.29.

178 Ibid, para 2.42.

179 See HC Debs, 19 March 2007, col 668W. The Home Office evidence to the APIG Inquiry was that there had been a total of 214 defendants for the period in which the CMA had been in force, of which 161 had been found guilty: see www.apcomms.org.uk/apig/archive/activities-2004/computer-misuse-inquiry/computer-misuse-inquiry-written-evidence.html

– who is accused of hacking into a number of US government computers, including high-level military computers, between February 2001 and March 2002, and then, amongst other things, extracting passwords, installing unauthorised software, and deleting data from 97 computers – is currently fighting extradition from the UK to the USA. He has already been unsuccessful in pleading his case in the House of Lords[180] and the European Court of Human Rights (ECtHR) subsequently rejected his application that his extradition would infringe his rights under the **European Convention on Human Rights (ECHR)**.[181] Because the fact that he suffers from Asperger's syndrome came to light fairly late in the proceedings, he was granted a judicial review of both the Home Secretary's decision to extradite and permission to review the Director of Public Prosecution's refusal to prosecute in the UK, on this basis that has also been unsuccessful.[182] The need for international cooperation in the apprehension and detection of computer criminals was apparently addressed by the **Cybercrime Convention**, and will be discussed further below.

Contemporary reports of the McKinnon case in the British press certainly seem to suggest that many do not perceive his alleged crime as a serious issue, even though the damage was estimated at some US$7 million, and have tended to focus on his alleged vulnerability.[183] On the other hand, the view of the House of Lords was that 'the gravity of the offences alleged against the appellant should not be understated'[184] and the case of Cuthbert does not demonstrate a particularly lenient approach.[185] The APIG review, when it came, therefore focused not only on whether the 1990 Act was broad enough in scope and whether there were loopholes that needed attention, but also on whether revisions were necessary to meet international treaty obligations and whether the Act provided for a sufficient level of penalties.[186]

Interestingly, in the light of all of the criticisms and the perception that the statute had passed its sell-by date, the general impression from the report was one of satisfaction with the way in which the **CMA** was perceived to have stood the test of time and a finding that some of the expressed dissatisfaction with the statute was due to misapprehension about its provisions – a fact described by the report as 'an entirely undesirable state of affairs'.[187] A number of respondents, for example, had asked for the statute to be extended to deal with hacking and viruses, despite the fact that ss 1 and 3 had been used successfully with respect to both activities. The report also concluded that the absence of definitions had not been shown to be an impediment to application of the Act by the courts, because the relevant terms had been understood to 'have the appropriate contemporary meaning'.[188] Given the clear evidence of ignorance about the nature and application of the provisions, there was a need for the Home Office to 'prioritise the provision of website material about the CMA because it is directly relevant to internet users and because it is clearly widely misunderstood'.[189] On more specific issues, the report noted that the revisions suggested by the Law Commission report on Fraud[190] would address the concerns on computer fraud, that expediting the Law Commission work on misuse of trade secrets would allow the 'theft' of data to be

---

180 McKinnon v Government of USA [2008] UKHL 59, [2008] 1 WLR 1739.

181 [2009] EWHC 2021, [16]; see also case comment by Nick W Taylor, 'R (on the application of McKinnon) v DPP' [2010] Crim L Rev 422.

182 Ibid. For a useful timeline of events, see also The Telegraph, 'Gary McKinnon: Timeline of the computer hacker's case' (2009) The Telegraph, 31 July, available online at www.telegraph.co.uk/news/worldnews/northamerica/usa/5945693/Gary-McKinnon-timeline-of-the-computer-hackers-case.html

183 See, eg, Afua Hirsch, 'Computer hacker Gary McKinnon to be extradited to US' (2009) The Guardian, 26 November, available online at www.guardian.co.uk/world/2009/nov/26/computer-hacker-gary-mckinnon-extradition; Azmina Gulamhusein, 'Gary McKinnon case is acid test of coalition government's integrity' (2010) Law Society Gazette, 7 June, available online at www.lawgazette.co.uk/opinion/gary-mckinnon-case-acid-test-coalition-government-s-integrity

184 [2008] 1 WLR 1739, [38].

185 See discussion above at p 122.

186 APIG, op cit, para 2.

187 Ibid, para 23.

188 Ibid, para 17.

189 Ibid, para 25.

190 Discussed above at pp 108–109.

criminalised, and that the problems with the interpretation of unauthorised access had been aired extensively by the House of Lords in *Allison*,[191] suggesting that no further clarification was required.

Substantive changes that did have their origins in the report, in addition to the repeal and replacement of s 3, include a revision of the penalties for the s 1 offence. It was felt that this would allow a more realistic reflection of the damage that might be done, and this change was effected by s 35 of the **Police and Justice Act 2006**, which amended s 1 **CMA** both to make the offence triable either way and to increase the maximum penalties. Whilst this may send out 'a clear message that society now takes hacking offences rather more seriously than in 1990',[192] an important aspect of sentencing is not only the robustness of the penalties and the perceived deterrent effect, but also that they actually fit the crime. For technology-specific crimes such as the basic hacking offence in s 1 **CMA**, penalties are defined in statute, and the 2006 amendments probably address any perceived shortfall. However, for other computer crime – particularly offences involving fraud – the problem of high-volume, low-denomination crime may mean that large scams go unpunished.[193]

Content Crimes

Thus far, the focus of discussion in this chapter has been on crimes related to the use of computers and computer networks, either as the means of the perpetration of criminal acts, such as fraud, or as newly identified criminal acts, such as hacking or other unauthorised access. The **CMA** and similar statutes in other jurisdictions are a particular example of the law's response to some of these activities, which, despite the differences between the jurisdictions, in many respects shows a remarkable consistency of philosophy and approach. This is especially apparent in relation to the almost-universal choice of criminal sanctions as appropriate to penalise such activities.

However, the increase in both the size and the capability of computer networks – and, in particular, the development of the internet and the world wide web – have also raised concerns about the ease of propagation of criminal content. Computer networks facilitate communications between both individuals and groups, as well as provide the means to access and retrieve extensive information from a variety of sources across the globe. Not surprisingly, this not only includes educational and informative material, but also includes information that might, at the least, be undesirable or antisocial, but might also be defamatory, obscene or pornographic, racist, malicious, threatening or abusive, or may constitute undesirable religious or political propaganda. Much of this information might attract the application of the criminal law in a number of jurisdictions. Although there are clearly great benefits to be gained from the use of global computer networks, regulating the type of content available has proved challenging in a number of ways. It may be, for example, that the existing law in a jurisdiction is not tailored appropriately for application to computer networks. In addition, although there is a broad consensus between jurisdictions over the types of computer misuse discussed already in this chapter, there is unlikely to be such consensus over the standard of content that is made available through this medium. Certain governments may be sensitive about the expression of some political or religious views, and it is also evident that acceptable standards and definitions of obscene or pornographic material will vary from place to place. Although, in line with international instruments, many states now guarantee a constitutionally protected right to freedom of expression, there is no consistency about the extent to which content deemed undesirable may fall outside the scope of such a right. Exceptions to the right of freedom of expression are heavily dependent on historical, cultural, and political factors, as well as general social mores within a jurisdiction. Some jurisdictions may concur on one type of speech,

---

191 See above p 121.
192 APIG, op cit, paras 98 and 99.
193 See House of Lords Science and Technology Committee, op cit, para 7.70, and discussion above at p 106.

but have widely divergent views on others. Thus Germany and the USA both protect freedom of expression in their respective constitutions, but, as noted by Delacourt, although they are 'at least on the same page with regard to pornography . . . their treatment of divisive political propaganda differs dramatically'.[194] Given the ease of accessing information that originates in another jurisdiction, is it possible to control the propagation of such material or to enforce national laws on a medium that does not recognise national boundaries? What factors should determine the acceptability of content on global networks? Should the same standards be applied as are applied to publishing of hard copy, or to television and radio broadcasts? The fundamental difference between the internet or world wide web and these other forms of communication is that the global network is capable of fulfilling all of these functions simultaneously; thus, in some circumstances, it may be appropriate to utilise similar rules as are used for traditional publication, but at other times, such an attempt may be felt to be a violation of the right to free speech, or even the right to privacy. This section will consider some of the issues raised by the publication of criminal content, using the legal response to pornographic material as a specific example, although other content will be referred to as appropriate.[195]

The US Communications Decency Act of 1996 and Child Online Protection Act of 1998

In the USA in the 1990s, the use of the internet as a medium for the circulation of various types of pornography, together with the fact that such material could then easily be accessed by minors, caused both concern and controversy amongst both politicians and the public. An examination of the legislative and judicial response to this issue provides a useful illustration of some of the difficulties encountered when attempting to regulate content on the internet. The US **Communications Decency Act (CDA)**, passed in 1996, was aimed at preventing young people from accessing indecent material via computer networks. It made it a criminal offence to engage in communication on computer networks that was either 'indecent' or 'patently offensive' if the contents of that communication could be viewed by a minor. Neglecting the not-inconsiderable difficulty of ascertaining the age of those accessing the material, although the motive behind the legislation was generally recognised as benevolent, the wide scope of the provisions was regarded by many as an unacceptable intrusion into the right to free speech, and consequently a potential breach of the First Amendment. This led to the American Civil Liberties Union (ACLU) immediately challenging the constitutionality of the statute, and beginning what turned out to be lengthy saga of litigation and legislation.

The primary issue was, of course, that some forms of pornography were entirely legal for distribution and consumption by an adult audience. Given the nature of the medium, it was likely that action to prevent viewing by minors would also prevent legitimate viewing by adults. A further feature of the challenge to the **CDA** was the assertion that the provisions were not only unnecessarily broad, but also vague. 'Obscenity' had a well-accepted definition derived from *Miller v California*,[196] which was based on an application of contemporary community standards. The **CDA**, however, referred not to 'obscene', but to 'indecent', material – indecent speech, as well as obscene speech, could permissibly be regulated on broadcast media, but the former had a rather wider scope, merely referring to 'nonconformance with accepted standards of morality'.[197]

194 JT Delacourt, 'The international impact of internet regulation' (1997) 38 Harv Int LJ 207, 214. See also, in this context, JF McGuire, 'When speech is heard around the world: Internet content regulation in the United States and Germany' (1999) 74 NYUL Rev 750, and the *Yahoo! v LICRA* litigation discussed in Chapter 3.
195 For a discussion of other extreme content, see, eg, A Roversi, *Hate on the Net, Extremist Sites, Neo-fascism On-line, Electronic Jihad*, 2008, Farnham: Ashgate.
196 413 US 15 (1973).
197 See discussion in *FCC v Pacifica Foundation* 438 US 726 (1978).

At first instance, the court considered extensively the characteristics of the medium, and the distinctions between it and other methods of mass communication – particularly the broadcast media – and noted that:

> Four related characteristics of Internet communication have a transcendent importance to our shared holding that the CDA is unconstitutional on its face . . . First, the Internet presents very low barriers to entry. Second, these barriers to entry are identical for both speakers and listeners. Third, as a result of these low barriers, astoundingly diverse content is available on the Internet. Fourth, the Internet provides significant access to all who wish to speak in the medium, and even creates a relative parity among speakers . . . [198]

Further the court noted that, unlike broadcast media, which had the potential to be particularly invasive,[199] locating information on the internet required deliberate, affirmative acts. The court found evidence that communication on the internet had more in common with a telephone conversation than with broadcasting and that, based on this reasoning, the government had little pretext for regulating its content. Although it was well established that First Amendment guarantees would be lost in cases of obscenity and child pornography, the court was of the view that the existing law that proscribed this type of content could equally be applied to the internet. But in any case, the target of the **CDA** was not obscene material, but that which was 'indecent' or 'patently offensive'. 'Obscene' might have a recognised meaning, but that was not the case with regard to 'indecent' and neither was it defined by the statute. Given the criminal penalties attached to breach of the Act, and the difficulties in ascertaining what material would be covered and the range of defendants, the court was unanimously of the opinion that the statute was unconstitutional for reasons of vagueness.

This decision was upheld by the Supreme Court, which discussed what it saw as the impossibility of applying the community standards test for obscenity to the propagation of material on the internet, because it would inevitably mean that the standard applied would have to be that of the community most likely to be offended by the material. This would reduce the constitutionally protected material available to adults to 'only what is fit for children'.[200] Justice Stevens drew particular attention to factors already underlined in the lower court, such as the democratising effect on speech, the growth and acceptance of internet communication, and the important issue of proportionality, noting that the **CDA** could not be constitutional if its objectives could be achieved by 'a more carefully drafted statute'.[201]

A further attempt at legislative intervention followed immediately[202] in the form of the **Child Online Protection Act of 1998 (COPA)**, in which Congress intended to rectify the specific concerns raised in the **CDA** litigation. The provisions of **COPA** made it a federal crime to propagate material online that was 'harmful to minors' for 'commercial purposes' (47 **USC** § 231(1)). By virtue of 47 **USC** § 231(e)(2)(A), it would only be inferred that the communication was for commercial purposes if the person were 'engaged in the business of making such communication'. The phrase 'engaged in the business of communication' was defined in 47 **USC** §231(c)(2)(B) and 'harmful to minors' was defined in 47 **USC** §231(e)(6) in terms of obscenity, appearing to or pandering to the prurient interest, as recognised by 'contemporary community standards'. This

---

198 *ACLU v Reno I* 929 F Supp 824, 872 (ED Pa 1996).
199 See *FCC v Pacifica*, above.
200 521 US 844, 888.
201 Ibid, 874.
202 Blanks Hindman reports that this statute passed through Congress quickly with limited debate and that the House of Representatives only devoted about half an hour to its discussion: Elizabeth Blanks Hindman, 'Protection childhood: Rights, social goals and the First Amendment in the context of the Child Online Protection Act (2010) 15 Comm L Pol'y 1.

statute was again challenged by ACLU on the basis that it was invalid, both because it violated the First Amendment rights of both adults and minors (on the grounds that what might be inappropriate for a 6-year-old might be permissible for someone aged 16), and because it was constitutionally vague. The government's view that the statute was aimed purely at commercial pornographers received short shrift from the court, which pointed out that there was nothing in the text that suggested that the statute's provisions were limited in this way. Like its predecessor, the **CDA**, the court was of the view that **COPA** infringed the right of adults to freedom of speech and expression, concluding, albeit somewhat reluctantly, that 'the protection of children from access to harmful to minors materials on the web, the compelling interest sought to be furthered by Congress in COPA, particularly resonates with the court', and that its decision to allow an injunction against enforcement would 'delay once again the careful protection of our children'. However, the court was 'acutely cognizant of its charge under the law of this country not to protect the majoritarian will at the expense of stifling the rights embodied in the Constitution', and so the injunction was granted.

On appeal, the Court of Appeals for the Third Circuit[203] focused specifically on the application of contemporary community standards in cyberspace and came to the conclusion that the overbreadth of the definition 'harmful to minors' consequent on using this standard must lead inexorably to a holding of unconstitutionality of the whole statute. The Court thus arrived at the conclusion that the concept of community standards derived from *Miller* was not applicable in this situation, although it remained a 'useful and viable tool in contexts other than the internet and the Web'[204] and this was the primary basis on which the Court upheld the decision that **COPA** was unconstitutional. The Supreme Court, however, disagreed on this point. It specifically considered the rejection of the *Miller* test, disagreeing with the finding that it was inappropriate for computer networks, and concluded that this of itself did not result in **COPA** being overbroad.[205] Given that the legal argument on appeal had only focused on this one aspect of unconstitutionality, the case was remanded to the Third Circuit for further consideration. On this occasion, the court considered all of the issues relating to whether **COPA** could withstand strict scrutiny, whether the statute served a compelling governmental interest, and whether it was narrowly tailored to achieve that interest and was the least restrictive means of advancing that interest, as well as whether it was overbroad.[206] Although accepting that there was a compelling interest, the court found a number of the provisions not to be narrowly tailored, including the definitions of 'material harmful to minors' and 'commercial purposes'. In addition, in considering less restrictive means of achieving the same objective, there was significant discussion of the use of technological devices in place of legislation to control content. The conclusion was reached that 'the various blocking and filtering techniques . . . may be substantially less restrictive than COPA'.[207] The use of filtering and blocking mechanisms for undesirable content provides a method of self-regulation of content in line with the view that 'at the heart of the First Amendment lies the principle that each person should decide for himself or herself the ideas and beliefs deserving of expression consideration and adherence'.[208] This in turn is also in line with the judgment in *Pacifica*[209] that regulatory intervention could be supported for broadcast media because listeners were not always able to control what they received; this was one of the bases for the distinction made between the internet and broadcast media in *ACLU v Reno I*, discussed earlier.

---

203 *ACLU v Reno II* 217 F 3d 162 (3rd Cir 2000).
204 Ibid, 180.
205 *Ashcroft v ACLU* 535 US 564 (2002) (renamed following a change in Attorney General).
206 322 F 3d 240 (3rd Cir 2003).
207 Ibid, 265.
208 *Turner Broad Sys Inc v FCC* 512 US 622, 641 (1994).
209 *FCC v Pacifica Foundation* 438 US 726 (1978); see also John B Morris Jr and Cynthia M Wong, 'Revisiting user control: The emergence and success of a First Amendment theory for the internet age' (2009) 8 First Amend L Rev 109.

Although the case had still not been subjected to the rigours of a full trial, this decision of the Third Circuit led to the case once more being considered by the Supreme Court.[210] On this occasion, the Supreme Court supported the imposition of the injunction. It noted that 'content-based prohibitions, enforced by severe criminal penalties, have the constant potential to be a repressive force in the lives and thoughts of a free people',[211] and so focused particularly on the use of filtering software as a method of regulating content, which was, in its view, both less restrictive and more effective than **COPA**. As a result, the case was then remanded for full trial to determine whether a permanent injunction should be issued – a decision that led to acid comments from Breyer J, who had given a dissenting judgment: '. . . after eight years of legislative effort, two statutes and three Supreme Court cases the Court sends this case back to the District Court for further proceedings. What proceedings? I have found no offer by either party to present more relevant evidence. What remains to be litigated?'[212] Cognisant, perhaps, of the strong lobbies on both sides of the debate, the Court made it clear that it was not deciding that it was not possible to draft suitable legislation relating to minors' access to the internet, and that its decision did not therefore 'foreclose the District Court from concluding, upon a proper showing by the Government, . . . that COPA is the least restrictive alternative available to accomplish Congress' goal'.[213] However, this was not to be the outcome. In 2008, the Third Circuit Court of Appeals upheld the decision of the District Court[214] to issue a permanent injunction and, by using substantially the same reasoning that had been employed previously, effectively affirmed Breyer J's contention that there was little else to be litigated. The overall conclusion was that **COPA** 'could not withstand strict scrutiny, vagueness or overbreadth analysis and thus is unconstitutional'.[215] Nevertheless the US government remained undeterred and made a further appeal to the Supreme Court, but its refusal to hold a further hearing[216] finally terminated the long cycle of litigation.

This saga of judicial and legislative debate provides a vivid demonstration of the almost-irreconcilable tension between different interests even within one jurisdiction. Notwithstanding the US courts continuing to maintain strong judicial protection for free speech, the persistence of the US government attempts to get **COPA** onto the statute book highlights the strength of the lobby on the other side of the argument, which views the internet as an anarchic mode of communication justifying legislative intervention to regulate content and forming the 'compelling interest' recognised by the courts. As we have seen, the original litigation dates back to 1996, and the **COPA** litigation alone was of ten years' duration as it worked its way 'through three levels of the court system (some of them three times), four attorneys general and through all or part of the terms of three presidents'.[217]

Other Approaches to Content Regulation

If it has proved this difficult to achieve any consensus on either an appropriate standard, or an appropriate regulatory method, then finding a global solution seems extremely remote and the evidence shows that, as might be expected, there is a plethora of approaches to these issues, reflecting a variety of cultural and legal traditions. Reference has already been made, for example, to the difference in approach between Germany and the USA. At the end of 1995, a situation arose in Bavaria

210 *Ashcroft v ACLU* 542 US 656 (2004).
211 Ibid, 660.
212 Ibid, 688
213 Ibid, 673. For discussion of the proposition that a combination of regulatory techniques might be a more viable way forward, see Douglas Husack, 'The criminal law as last resort' [2004] OJLS 207.
214 *ACLU v Gonzales* 478 F Supp 2d 775 (ED Pa 2007).
215 *ACLU v Mukasey* 534 F3d 181, 207 (3rd Cir 2008).
216 129 SCt 1032 (2009).
217 Blanks Hindman, op cit. For discussion of First Amendment philosophies with respect to the protection of children, see also Samuel D Castor, 'Internet Child Protection Registry Acts: Protection children, parents and . . . pornographers? Allowing states to balance the First Amendment with parents' rights to privacy and sovereignty in the home' (2009) 59 Cath U L Rev 231.

that was subsequently to receive worldwide attention when a police search on a court order showed that customers of the ISP, CompuServe Germany, could access certain pornographic sites. This eventually led to the parent company, CompuServe USA, blocking access to sites that the police had designated unsuitable because they contained representations of violent, child, or animal pornography. As a result, for a short period, no customers of CompuServe worldwide could access the sites in question, showing the potential for the actions of only one jurisdiction to have a global effect. Following the global block, general access was restored, but customers in Germany were offered free blocking software. Nonetheless, despite the provision of this software, the offending sites could still be accessed by German customers and, eventually, the local manager of CompuServe Germany, Felix Somm, was charged with assisting in the dissemination of pornographic writings contrary to s 184 of the **German Penal Code**. Despite an exemption for access providers in the German **Telecommunications Service Law**, Somm was initially given a two-year suspended sentence, but was eventually acquitted on appeal,[218] Somm's defence commenting that the case showed that, for effective regulation of the internet, there has to be 'closer international cooperation'.[219]

Many other jurisdictions have also introduced legislation purporting to regulate the content and use of information on the internet, or have applied existing legislation to regulate undesirable content on computer networks. Below is just a sample of that activity, but there are a number of sources that can be accessed for an overview of legislative activity on this topic in many more states.[220] Reaction to the legislative activity in different parts of the world has been mixed, although none seems to have precipitated the volume of litigation that has been seen in the USA. Coroneos points out that there are three forces, the interaction of which feed into the way in which new internet content regulation is likely to be promulgated:[221]

(i)   Cultural values and institutions within a country. Institutions in this sense could include the traditional media;

(ii)   The ease with which political debate can actually be translated into new legislation;

(iii) The existence of constitutional guarantees such as freedom of expression and the extent to which new laws can be enacted which will survive a constitutional challenge.

Applying these criteria to the situation in Australia, Coroneos observed that they created fertile ground for the creation of a strict regime regulating content and access to the internet. The traditional media had been active in pointing out the 'dangers' of the internet and these views then became espoused as a political cause of importance to the public: Bills were able to become law sometimes with 'only perfunctory scrutiny and debate'; and there was no explicit protection for

---

218 For full details, see Lothar Determann, 'Case update: German Compuserve director acquitted on appeal' (1999) 23 Hastings Int'l & Comp L Rev 109. The current situation in Germany is that effective age verification systems must be in place to ensure that only adults can access pornographic sites. This is an onerous requirement and the Bundesgerischtshof has ruled that such systems will not be considered to be effective unless steps have been taken to prevent obvious circumvention methods: see Mark Turner, 'European national news' (2010) 26 CLSR 237, 239.

219 See http://archive.apnic.net/mailing-lists/apple/archive/1999/11/msg00010.html, and also T Palfrey, 'Policing the transmission of pornographic material' (1996) 5 ICTL 197, who suggests international cooperation to combat those who disseminate illegal and harmful material via the internet, along the same model as is currently in use for policing money-laundering activities.

220 For a general consideration of the situation in a number of jurisdictions, see, eg: the OpenNet initiative, http://opennet.net/; Human Rights Watch, *World Report* 2010, 2010, available online at www.hrw.org/world-report-2010; Electronic Frontiers Australia (EFA), 'Internet censorship: Law and policy around the world' (2002) 28 March, available online at www.efa.org.au/Issues/Censor/cens3.html; Reporters without Borders, 'Publication of second annual report on cyberspace: "The internet under surveillance – Obstacles to the free flow of information online"' (2003) 19 June, available online at http://en.rsf.org/publication-of-second-annual-19-06-2003,07280.html; and Reporters without Borders' list of 'Internet enemies' available online at http://en.rsf.org/

221 Peter Coroneos, 'internet content policy and regulation in Australia', in Brian Fitzgerald, Fuping Gao, Damien O'Brien, and Sampsung Xiaoxiang Shi (eds), *Copyright Law, Digital Content and the Internet in the Asia-Pacific*, 2008, Sydney: Sydney University Press, ch 4, p 49.

freedom of expression. The enabling statute in question is the **Broadcasting Services Act 1992**, as amended, which is now administered by the Australian Communications and Media Authority (ACMA).[222] Even prior to action at the federal level, a number of states in Australia had introduced legislation aimed both at restricting access to certain material on the internet and controlling content, but with little opportunity for public debate on the issue.[223] The 1992 Act was subsequently amended by the **Broadcasting Services Amendment (Online Services) Act 1999 (the 'Online Services Act')** in the belief that 'responsible online content regulation will help to create an environment in which the internet's positive opportunities and advantages are able to be nurtured, developed and accessed by a growing number of citizens, while allowing the proper concerns of current and future users to be addressed'.[224] The amendments were aimed at restricting content that 'is likely to cause offence to a reasonable adult' and at protecting children from exposure to 'internet content that is unsuitable for children'.[225] These amendments came into force at the beginning of 2000, and basically apply the same level of censorship to the internet as is applied to films and videos by using the same classification system. In relation to regulation of the internet, ACMA states that it 'works closely with relevant industries to achieve active self-regulation, while ensuring industry compliance with licence conditions, codes and standards', and that it 'monitors the effect of regulations to ensure they are responsive to the community's needs'.[226] However, it appears to operate primarily in a reactive way and action under the statute is mainly initiated as a result of complaints. The rules have had a mixed reception; criticism has been based on a questioning of the underlying rationale,[227] of the difficulties of ensuring compliance,[228] and on wider concerns about restrictions on freedom of expression.[229] On the other hand, some have taken the pragmatic approach that, whatever the imperfections of the new regime, it should be welcomed because 'the internet's power and (potential) persuasiveness make it crucial to immediately begin trying to develop an effective and usable system for extending classification to it. . . . the "Online Services Act" represents a useful first step in that direction'.[230] Further, there has also been the suggestion that although there appear to be more and more restrictions in place, this is a result of the degree of politicisation of the issue and, in reality, 'most Australians can access the same range of content that they always could'.[231] There were also plans to require ISPs to filter prescribed websites;[232] initially, the targets were intended to be sites associated with child pornography and the abuse of children, although the scheme could easily have been extended further. The belief of the government was that filtering at the ISP level would be more effective at achieving the objective of protecting children than filters on individual PCs, and steps had been taken for ISPs to trial the filtering software. However, despite the fact that these proposals were in the Labour Party's election manifesto in 2007, the plans have apparently been shelved and are not likely to be debated until after the next general election.[233]

---

222 www.acma.gov.au/. ACMA was formed in 2005 as a result of the merger of the Australian Broadcasting Authority and the Australian Communications Authority.
223 See, eg, G Greenleaf, 'Law in cyberspace' (1996) 70 Aust LJ 33.
224 J Corker, S Nugent, and J Porter, 'Regulating internet content: A co-regulatory approach' (2000) 23 UNSWLJ 5.
225 Australian Broadcasting Services Act 1992, s 3(1), as amended.
226 ACMA, 'The ACMA overview', available online at www.acma.gov.au/WEB/STANDARD/pc=ACMA_ORG_OVIEW
227 See, eg, P Chen, 'Pornography, protection, prevarication: The politics of internet censorship' (2000) 23 UNSWLJ 4, suggesting that 'from the outset the premise on which the legislation was proposed was highly questionable'; see also K Heitman, 'Vapours and mirrors' (2000) 23 UNSWLJ 10, expressing the view that drawing an analogy with television and film was a tragic fallacy.
228 See, eg, Chen, op cit; N Arasaratnam, 'Brave new (online) world' (2000) 23 UNSWLJ 205; also P Argy, 'Internet content regulation: An Australian Computer Society perspective' (2000) 23 UNSWLJ 126.
229 See, eg, T Voon, 'Online pornography in Australia: Lessons from the First Amendment' (2001) 24 UNSWLJ 141; R Trager and S Turner, 'The internet down under: Can free speech be protected in a democracy without a Bill of Rights?' (2000) 23 U Ark Little Rock L Rev 123.
230 E Handsley and B Biggins, 'The sheriff rides into town: A day of rejoicing for innocent westerners' (2000) 23 UNSWLJ 13.
231 Coroneos, op cit, p 66.
232 For further details, see, eg, Alana Maurashat and Renée Watt, 'Clean feed: Australia's internet filtering proposal' (2009) 12 Internet Law Bulletin; [2009] UNSWLRS 60.
233 Nicola Berkovic, 'Rudd retreats on web filter legislation' (2010) The Australian, 19 April.

In Singapore, the broad definitions of broadcasting, programme, etc, in the **Broadcasting Act 1994** and the **Broadcasting Authority Act 1994**, as amended, which do not refer to a specific medium of communication, have the result that all content, including that on the internet, can be regulated under the umbrella of these statutes. Under these auspices, a licence scheme has been applied to ISPs and content providers since 1996.[234] The scheme is administered by the Singapore Media Development Authority (MDA), which describes itself as adopting a 'balanced and light-touch approach to ensure that minimum standards are set for the responsible use of the internet while giving maximum flexibility to industry players to operate'.[235] All ISPs are subject to a class licence and must, inter alia, block access to any site that is considered against the public interest, public order, or national harmony, offends against public decency, or violates the Singapore Internet Code of Practice.[236] These class licences are automatically applicable, but, in addition, ISPs and certain types of content provider, such as political parties and religious groups, are also required to register with the MDA.

Seng has criticised the regulatory model used in Singapore on the basis that it is predicated on a 1990s' conception of the internet that does not so readily adapt to more recent developments such as Web 2.0 and the growth of user-generated content.[237] He points out that this type of regulation depends on the nature of the communication rather than the type of parties that are communicating. Although private communications are excepted from the regulatory ambit, current technology means that something that may have been initiated as a private communication can readily be transmitted to a much more public forum, thus blurring the edges between what can be regarded as private or public. The MDA itself describes the approach as 'co-regulation' with industry, meaning that the MDA does not actively censor content, but provides guidelines and codes of practice for content providers.[238] In practice, although internet content providers have to exercise their judgment and not place anything on the internet that is prohibited under the code of practice, it is clear from the MDA's Internet Industry Guidelines that the main concerns are with pornography, violence, and incitement of racial or religious hatred.[239] However, there have been reports that censorship also takes the place of sites that are critical of the government.[240]

In a number of other jurisdictions, the regulation of the internet has not only been about the content that might objectively be seen as against a societal interest, such as pornography or hate speech, but has also been focused on the harsh suppression of dissenting political views. In China, in particular, many regulations have been issued that attempt to censor the internet and restrict access only to sites that will assist in the economic development of the country. In the rest of the world, this has often been most apparent when sites from outside China, such as Google, have been blocked, but there are also examples of the strict enforcement of the relevant laws that has been directed at both ISPs and also individual computer users.[241] However, there are also reports that

---

234 Geoffrey Pereira, 'Internet regulation to start on Monday' (1996) *Straits Times*, 13 July. For details of the scheme, see www.mda.gov.sg/Licences/Pages/IntSCPCLicence.aspx
235 www.mda.gov.sg/Policies/PoliciesandContentGuidelines/Internet/Pages/default.aspx
236 www.mda.gov.sg/Documents/PDF/licences/mobj.981.Internet_Code_of_Practice.pdf
237 Daniel Send, 'Regulation of the interactive digital media industry in Singapore', in Brian Fitzgerald, Fuping Gao, Damien O'Brien, and Sampsung Xiaoxiang Shi (eds), *Copyright Law, Digital Content and the Internet in the Asia-Pacific*, 2008, Sydney: Sydney University Press, ch 5, p 67.
238 www.mda.gov.sg/Policies/Pages/CoRegulationwithIndustry.aspx
239 www.mda.gov.sg/Documents/PDF/Policies/PoliciesandContentGuidelines_Internet_InternetIndustryGuidelines.pdf
240 See, eg, Reporters without Borders, 'Singapore' (2007) 1 February, available online at http://en.rsf.org/singapore-01-02-2007,20796.html
241 See, eg, Reporters without Borders, 'A "journey to the heart of internet censorship" on eve of party congress' (2007),10 October, available online at http://en.rsf.org/china-a-journey-to-the-heart-of-internet-10-10-2007,23924.html; Wentao Sha and Difei Yu, 'Internet content provider licences in the People's Republic of China internet industry: A practical perspective', in Brian Fitzgerald, Fuping Gao, Damien O'Brien, and Sampsung Xiaoxiang Shi (eds), *Copyright Law, Digital Content and the Internet in the Asia-Pacific*, 2008, Sydney: Sydney University Press, ch 7, p 143; Justine Nolan, 'The China dilemma: Internet censorship and corporate responsibility' (2009) 4 Asian J Comp Law Article 3; Diane Rowland, 'Virtual worlds, real rights?', in Marco Odello and Sofia Cavandoli (eds), *Emerging Areas of Human Rights in the 21st Century: The Role of the Universal Declaration of Human Rights*, 2011, London: Routledge, ch 1.

there is some small progress with regard to legal reform in this regard and, in addition, a plan to require approved filtering software on all PCs sold in China has been indefinitely delayed.[242]

Content Regulation in the UK

In the UK, there has been debate about the extent to which existing laws were adequate to deal with the distribution of pornography on the internet;[243] this included the extent to which they were capable of dealing with instances in which children are exposed to material intended only for an adult audience, as well as instances in which the internet was used to propagate child pornography. In response to the widespread concern surrounding the perceived proliferation of 'indecent' material available via the internet, a Home Affairs Committee was given a wide brief to examine and assess the extent of the problems caused by the use of information technology (IT) to disseminate such material and the likelihood of additional problems arising as a result of the development of the relevant technologies, and, in particular, to ascertain whether any changes in legislation were required to deal with existing and potential concerns relating to computer pornography.[244] Although the possibility of dedicated legislation at some future date was not ruled out, the Committee decided that it was possible to deal with the matter by amending the existing legislation to make it clear that it applied equally to the dissemination of material via computer networks. Its recommendations were given effect in the **Criminal Justice and Public Order Act 1994**, which amended certain sections of the **Obscene Publications Act 1959** and the **Protection of Children Act 1978**.

Section 1(1) of the **Obscene Publications Act 1959** makes it a criminal offence to publish any obscene article. 'Article' is defined as 'any description containing or embodying matter to be read or looked at or both, any sound record, any film etc'. Unlike the standard in the USA, which allows for different standards in different communities, such matter will be obscene if, taken as a whole, it is such as to 'tend to deprave and corrupt persons likely to read, see or hear matter contained or embodied in it'. To avoid any possibility that 'article' could be construed as not including information on computer, this section was amended by the **Criminal Justice and Public Order Act 1994** to include the transmission of electronically stored data that, on resolution into user-viewable form, is obscene. Because the definition of 'publication' includes distribution, circulation, etc, this could have the effect of making a network provider liable for obscene material, as well as the originator of that information. One issue with general availability on the internet is that it is impossible to predict what section of the public is 'likely' to be exposed to it, but no specific recommendation was made on this point. This point was considered in *R v Perrin* when it was suggested that all that the section requires is that there is a likelihood that vulnerable people may see the material, not that any actually did.[245] Such a condition will easily be met by publication on open-access web pages, which was what was under consideration in the appeal in *Perrin*.[246]

In addition, there may be more specific offences applicable to particular types of material, such as offences under the **Children and Young Persons (Harmful Publications) Act 1955**, which applies to any book, magazine, or other like work that is of a kind likely to fall into the hands of children and young persons. Such publications have to be pictorial in the main to attract the provisions of this Act and include stories portraying 'the commission of crimes, acts of violence or cruelty or incidents of a repulsive or horrible nature in such a way that the work as a whole would

---

242 See Human Rights Watch, op cit, pp 285–8.
243 See, eg, C Manchester, 'Computer pornography' [1995] Crim LR 546; T Gibbons, 'Computer-generated pornography' (1995) 9 LC & T Yearbook 83.
244 Home Affairs Committee, *Computer Pornography*, HC No 126, 1993–94, London: HMSO.
245 [2002] EWCA Crim 747, [22].
246 See also discussion in Jacob Rowbottom, 'Obscenity laws and the internet: Targeting the supply and demand' [2006] Crim L Rev 97, 99.

tend to corrupt a child or young person'. In the absence of specific amendments, the application of this statute will rest on whether an interpretation of 'other like work' includes material available on computer. The **Protection of Children Act 1978** creates offences relating to the display and distribution of indecent photographs of children. These provisions have also been amended by the **Criminal Justice and Public Order Act 1994** to include both photographs and 'pseudo-photographs', the latter referring to computer-generated or partially computer-generated images of children. Data stored on a computer disk or other electronic means that is capable of conversion into a photograph or 'pseudo-photograph' is also included.[247] In addition, there have been other amendments and enhancements of the law relating to child pornography and, more generally, in relation to sexual offences involving children in the **Sexual Offences Act 2003** that will apply to the internet, just as much as they do to other methods of creation and dissemination. As a result of these changes, the upper age limit for a 'child' in the **Protection of Children Act 1978** has been changed from 16 to 18, new offences relating to child pornography have been introduced,[248] and new defences in respect of indecent images have been provided.[249] A further offence introduced by s 15 of the 2003 Act is directed at the conduct known as 'grooming', in which adults gain the confidence of children on prior occasions with the intention of committing a sexual offence at a later date.[250] This preparatory behaviour often takes place in internet chatrooms and so this new provision is expected to close the previous loophole in the law in this respect.[251]

The interpretation of the relevant sections of the **Protection of Children Act 1978** has been discussed in R v Fellows and Arnold,[252] in which the Court of Appeal dismissed an appeal against convictions for possessing indecent photographs of a child, having an obscene article for publication, and distributing indecent photographs, the material in question being available over a computer network. The defendants had contended that such computer data did not constitute a photograph for the purposes of s 1 of the 1978 Act and that the data were not, in any event, distributed or shown merely by reason of being made available for downloading. In contrast, Evans LJ decided that the data 'was a form of copy which made the original photograph, or a copy of it, available for viewing by a person with access to the disk'.[253]

In the case of R v Bowden, the question was whether downloading such images from the internet should be construed as 'making' or 'possessing',[254] both of which are offences under this statute, in contrast to the **Obscene Publications Act 1959**, which has no offence of possession. Further, 'making' a pseudo-photograph is considered a more heinous offence and is subject to a more severe sentence than mere possession. It could be argued that downloading images is more analogous to possession, since, if the material were acquired by traditional means, there would be no suggestion of 'making' of an image.[255] However, because of the nature of the technology and the objective of the statute, the court inclined to the view that downloading and printing of images is more akin to 'making' them. The court agreed that the 'Act is not only concerned with the original creation of images but also their proliferation'. Further, if the images in question were to originate outside of the UK, such activities would have the effect of creating new material that was

---

247 Protection of Children Act 1978, s 7(4)(b). For a comprehensive discussion of issues relating to child pornography on the internet, see, eg, Yaman Akdeniz, *Internet Child Pornography and the Law: National and International Responses*, 2008, London: Ashgate.
248 Sections 48–50.
249 Sections 45 and 46, and see discussion in A Gillespie, 'The Sexual Offences Act 2003: (3) Tinkering with "child pornography"' [2004] Crim LR 361, 363.
250 For a review of this provision, see JR Spencer, 'The Sexual Offences Act 2003: (2) Child and family offences' [2003] Crim LR 347, 351.
251 See, eg, A Gillespie, 'Children, chatrooms and the law' [2001] Crim LR 435.
252 [1997] 2 All ER 548, and see Case note by C Colby (1997) 2 Comm L 30; T Palfrey, 'Pornography and the possible criminal liability of internet service providers under the Obscene Publication(s) and Protection of Children Act' (1997) 6 ICTL 187.
253 [1997] 2 All ER 548, 557.
254 [2000] 2 All ER 418.
255 See also A Gillespie, 'Sentences for offences involving child pornography' [2003] Crim LR 81.

not previously in this jurisdiction:[256] '. . . a person who either downloads images onto a disk or who prints them off is making them.'

Atkins v DPP,[257] an appeal by way of case stated, concerned not only downloading from the internet, but also the question of whether images stored in the computer's cache were either 'made' or 'possessed'. It was submitted in this case that *Bowden* was wrongly decided, but although the divisional court declined to follow this, it did decide that this could not be extended to the inadvertent storing or unintentional making of images in the cache – an issue that had not been raised in *Bowden*; neither could the storage in the cache constitute possession in the absence of the knowledge of the defendant.[258] Whether the defendant had the requisite knowledge will thus be a matter of fact to be decided in every case. Both *Bowden* and *Atkins* were considered in the later joined appeal cases of *Smith* and *Jayson*. This appeal considered two separate cases, both involving the alleged making of indecent pseudo-photographs of a child: one by opening an email attachment; the other by downloading directly from the internet. In each case, temporary copies were also made in the computer cache. The judgment underlined how important the factual matrix is in such cases, since it was shown that the defendant, Smith, had good reason to believe that the attachment in question contained illicit images. However, in the absence of such a belief, it appears that the very fact of opening such an attachment will not inevitably criminalise the unsuspecting and the unwary.[259] In other words, to be guilty of the 'making' offence, there has to be a deliberate and intentional act. This point was returned to in the later case of *R v Harrison*,[260] in which it was decided that the offence would also be made out when illegal material was encountered in unsolicited internet 'pop-ups' that appeared on the user's PC when accessing pornographic, but otherwise legal, sites.

The above cases suggest that downloading of images and copying onto disk or other storage medium will be regarded as the more serious offence of making a pseudo-photograph, notwithstanding analogies that could be made with activities using traditional media.[261] However, the scope of the meaning of 'possession' has also caused some problems in respect of images on computer networks. In *R v Porter*, it was suggested that, to establish possession, 'it may seem superficially attractive to say that all that is required . . . is that, to the knowledge of the defendant, the images were on the defendant's hard disk drive within the computer which was in his custody and control at the material time'.[262] However, in this particular case, the defendant had deleted the images in question and had then emptied the 'recycle bin'. Although he could have recovered the images with forensic software, he neither had such software, nor had he attempted to obtain any, such that, in reality, he could not have retrieved the images. The court therefore reasoned that, 'in the special case of deleted computer images, if a person cannot retrieve or gain access to an image, in our view he no longer has custody or control of it'.[263] In other words, defendants are not automatically in possession of an image merely because they possess the hard disk and the image could be retrieved by forensic techniques, unless they have the wherewithal to do this. Again, this will depend on the particular factual matrix of the case in question.

Notwithstanding the applicability of these offences to material made available over computer networks, a problem may still arise where the source of the material is outside the UK jurisdiction. If the offence is one in which mere possession of the offending material is sufficient, there may be

---

256 [2000] 2 All ER 418, 423.
257 [2000] 1 WLR 1427.
258 See also Criminal Justice Act 1988, s 160(2)(b), and compare also the situation in the Trojan horse cases discussed above at p 125.
259 [2003] 1 Cr App R 13, [19].
260 [2007] EWCA Crim 2976.
261 For further discussion of the meaning of 'possession' in relation to digital images, see, eg, Jonathan Clough, 'Now you see it, now you don't: Digital images and the meaning of possession' (2008) 19 Crim LF 205.
262 [2006] EWCA Crim 560, [16].
263 Ibid, [21].

still a defendant who can be apprehended in the UK courts, but this may not be the case where the offence is one of 'publication'. These factors were significant in more recent changes to the law relating to obscene publications. The issues raised by the availability of pornographic content on the internet, its potential link to violent and abusive behaviour, and the difficulties in controlling material created outside the jurisdiction led to recommendations to establish an offence of possessing 'extreme' pornographic material to parallel the possession offence in relation to child pornography.[264] The proposals for new offences were aimed at specific types of prohibited content rather than the effect that the content might have on the viewer. The latter approach, as embodied in the **Obscene Publications Act 1959**, has proved notoriously difficult to apply, and McGlynn and Rackley have even commented that 'no one really knows what constitutes obscene material'.[265] One possible advantage to the approach under the 1959 Act is that it is able to reflect the fact that what is or is not acceptable is likely to change over time, as evidenced by the fact that material at issue in early successful prosecutions under the Act might legitimately no longer be viewed in the same light. The new offence is contained in the **Criminal Justice and Immigration Act 2008**, s 63, which provides that it is an offence for a person to be in possession of an extreme pornographic image. As Rowbottom remarks, 'for a possession offence, clarity is crucial', and the statute defines the key concepts of 'pornographic' and 'extreme'. However, 'possession' remains undefined and similar problems to those arising in determining possession of images on computer in relation to child pornography[266] may continue to be encountered in the implementation of the new offence.

Cybercrime Convention

A more intransigent problem at the international level is providing suitable procedures for policing global criminal activity and even allowing for a degree of harmonisation of criminal law. Aside from a number of particularly heinous acts over which there is consensus – such as murder and other violent crime, for example – criminal offences are often very particular to a state, and reflect the particular cultures and mores of the society that caused them to be enacted. As we have seen in the discussion so far, certain jurisdictionally based laws have been used, or attempted to be used, to apprehend the perpetrators of what can be termed 'computer crime' or 'cybercrime'. Unlike the scope of the jurisdictionally based laws that are pressed into service, the criminal acts that are committed in or via cyberspace cannot always be confined within convenient jurisdictional boundaries. The territoriality of many criminal provisions, together with the global reach and spread of the technology, provides an almost perfect environment for the perpetrator to be situated in one jurisdiction, but the effect of their acts to be felt in another or others. This can hamper enforcement efforts quite dramatically, since 'while the Internet is borderless for criminals, law enforcement agencies must respect the sovereignty of other nations'.[267] To the extent that cybercrime and cyber-criminals have scant regard for national borders, then, arguably, the appropriate legal response should be one that also transcends these boundaries. Unless there are in place agreements with respect to cooperation, bilateral or multilateral enforcement, and/or extradition, it will be practically difficult, if not impossible, to apprehend those responsible, and many writers have testified, in principle at least, to the desirability of an international regime that could address and hopefully begin to combat cybercrime on a global scale.

The Council of Europe has been active in this area since the second half of the 1980s, and issued recommendations in both 1989 and 1995.[268] This work continued and culminated in the

---

264 Home Office, *On the Possession of Extreme Pornographic Material*, Consultation Paper, 2005, London: HMSO.
265 Clare McGlynn and Erika Rackley, 'Criminalising extreme pornography: A lost opportunity' [2009] Crim L Rev 245, 246.
266 See, eg, R v Porter [2006] EWCA Crim 560, above, and see also the discussion in McGlynn and Rackley, op cit.
267 M Keyser, 'The Council of Europe Convention on Cybercrime' (2003) 12 J Transnat'l L & Pol'y 287, 326.
268 See above n 1 and also Recommendation No R(95)13.

Cybercrime Convention, which was opened for signature on 23 November 2001.[269] Although it has been suggested that 'the inherent difficulties of formulating satisfactory global internet regulation result in model treaties taking years to approve',[270] in fact, the Convention was drafted in a relatively short time in international agreement terms, and was completed in four years and 27 drafts.[271] The Explanatory Report on the Convention refers to this earlier work, but expresses the view that 'only a binding international instrument can ensure the necessary efficiency in the fight against these new phenomena'.[272] The report concludes that the need and rationale for international action to combat cybercrime is due to a number of factors, but that crucial ones are the accessibility and searchability of information, the emergence of new types of crime, as well as the incidence of traditional crime, and that both of these may have consequences that are not easily restricted by national boundaries, and the inability of domestic laws to rise to those challenges.[273]

Participation in this Convention was not confined to the Member States of the Council of Europe itself: the USA, Canada, Japan, and South Africa were also parties to the negotiations. In one sense, the Convention can be viewed as ground-breaking and pioneering, in that it was and remains the only binding international treaty on this subject.[274] The Convention came into force in July 2004 and, at the time of writing, has been ratified by 30 states, including the USA – although, as discussed below, the ratification process itself was not without controversy. Sixteen other states have signed the Convention, but not yet ratified it.[275]

The Convention adopts a three-pronged approach and contains provisions relating to the harmonisation of substantive criminal law,[276] the necessary domestic procedural powers for investigation and prosecution,[277] and also provisions aimed at facilitating international cooperation and mutual assistance.[278] The list of substantive offences is not exhaustive or comprehensive, and follows a fairly conventional classification scheme in being divided into sections relating to: the integrity of computer systems, such as access, interception etc;[279] 'computer-related' crimes, such as computer-related forgery and computer-related fraud;[280] content-related offences (although these relate exclusively to child pornography);[281] and copyright crime subject to the provisions of the **Bern Convention**, the **Trade-related Aspects of Intellectual Property Rights (TRIPS) Agreement**, the **World Intellectual Property Organization (WIPO) Copyright Treaty**, etc.[282] In addition, there are provisions covering aiding and abetting,[283] corporate liability,[284] and sanctions,[285] which should be 'effective, proportionate and dissuasive', and include the possibility of 'deprivation of liberty'. To assist the implementation of the substantive provisions, the procedural provisions include, inter alia, provisions allowing 'expeditious preservation of specified computer data, including traffic data',[286] together with a number of Articles providing powers to require production of such data, and empowerment to search and seize relevant data, to collect data in real

---

269 Convention on Cybercrime, CETS No 185, available online at http://conventions.coe.int/Treaty/en/Treaties/Html/185.htm
270 Sprinkel, op cit, p 509.
271 See further Keyser, op cit, 296.
272 http://conventions.coe.int/Treaty/en/Reports/Html/185.htm
273 Ibid, paras 4–6.
274 www.coe.int/t/dc/files/themes/cybercrime/default_EN.asp
275 For the current state of ratifications, see http://conventions.coe.int/Treaty/Commun/ChercheSig.asp?NT=185&CM=&DF= &CL=ENG
276 Articles 2–13.
277 Articles 14–22.
278 Articles 23–35.
279 Articles 2–6.
280 Articles 7 and 8.
281 Article 9.
282 Article 10.
283 Article 11.
284 Article 12.
285 Article 13.
286 Article 16.

time, and to intercept data.[287] Some of these provisions necessarily require the cooperation and participation of third parties and private organisations, such as ISPs. Significantly for the subsequent discussion, these provisions are expressed to be subject to the provisions of Art 14, detailing the overall scope of the provisions, and Art 15, which, inter alia, requires implementation to recognise general rights under, for example, the **ECHR** and to incorporate the principle of proportionality. The Preamble to the Convention also makes reference to the international human rights instruments referred to in Art 15(1) and in addition reaffirms 'the right of everyone to hold opinions without interference, as well as the right to freedom of expression, including the freedom to seek, receive, and impart information and ideas of all kinds, regardless of frontiers, and the rights concerning the respect for privacy'. Despite the fact that earlier drafts were modified to take into account the concerns of a number of lobby groups,[288] and notwithstanding both the ideals expressed in the Preamble and the content of Art 15 above, much of the early criticism of the Convention centred on the extent to which it preserved an appropriate balance of rights, and was compatible with the general protection of human rights and civil liberties guaranteed by other international treaties or national constitutions.

In particular, major concerns were voiced in the USA in relation to a perceived clash with protected First Amendment rights in that jurisdiction. The apparent problems related both to the substantive provisions on content, the associated procedural provisions, and also to the requirement of cooperation and mutual assistance. Keyser[289] suggested that the criticisms of the Convention could be categorised as follows:

- it curtailed freedom of expression;
- it overextended the powers of the enforcement agencies;
- it required private persons and organisations to provide and retain much further information than previously; and
- it infringed civil liberties.

To what extent are these criticisms legitimate and well founded? It is certainly the case that the First Amendment of the US **Constitution** offers substantial protection to free expression. Indeed, although the USA originally participated in the subsequent Protocol of the **Cybercrime Convention** concerning the criminalisation of acts of a racist and xenophobic nature committed through computer systems,[290] it did not become a party to the final version, believing that it was inconsistent with First Amendment guarantees of free expression. However, it is notable that, despite actions in a number of jurisdictions to address the distribution of pornography on the internet, restrictions on content under the Convention itself are limited to child pornography – presumably because it was not possible to obtain a consensus between negotiating states on other content-based offences. Child pornography was already illegal in the USA by virtue of the provisions of 18 **USC** §§ 2252 and 2252A (the **Protection of Children from Sexual Predators Act of 1998**), but the definitions in Art 9(2) of the **Cybercrime Convention** proscribe not only child pornography as such, but also 'virtual child pornography' – that is, material that has not been created by the use of actual children, but by computer manipulation of images of adult actors, or by altering innocent pictures of children. Earlier attempts in the USA to outlaw such virtual child pornography in the **Child Pornography Protection Act of 1996** were struck down as unconstitutional by the Supreme Court in *Ashcroft v Free Speech Coalition*,[291] which found that law as it stood was unacceptably broad.

---

287 Articles 17–20.
288 See further Sprinkel, op cit, p 510.
289 Keyser, op cit, 324.
290 http://conventions.coe.int/Treaty/en/Treaties/Html/189.htm; see also Yaman Akdeniz, 'Governing racist content on the internet: National and international responses' (2007) 56 UNB LJ 103.
291 535 US 234 (2002).

Virtual child pornography could be distinguished from actual child pornography in that it was not 'intrinsically related to the sexual abuse of children',[292] but this law attempted to outlaw, inter alia, images that were produced without the involvement of actual children, together with images that might pass the community standards test for obscenity. It was in consequence an unacceptable restriction on free expression.

Following this decision, Congress attempted to address the deficiencies in the **Prosecutorial Remedies and Tools against the Exploitation of Children Today (PROTECT) Act of 2003**. This statute outlawed morphed child pornography, provided that it could be proved beyond reasonable doubt that there was an intention to make others believe that the children depicted were genuine. It also contained an amendment introduced by the **Child Obscenity and Pornography Protection Act of 2003** proscribing any solicitation to buy or sell child pornography whatever its origin. The **PROTECT Act** was itself subject to constitutional challenges, but was eventually upheld by the Supreme Court.[293] However, the ability of the US Congress to outlaw virtual child pornography while still satisfying the stringent requirements of First Amendment jurisprudence should not really have any bearing on whether or not to ratify the **Cybercrime Convention**. Although, as shown, the Convention contains provisions dealing with virtual child pornography, Art 9(4) also provides that states can reserve the right not to apply in whole or in part these particular provisions, suggesting that this should, in any case, not be a bar to ratification if there were serious First Amendment concerns.

Another frequent criticism was that the Convention did not satisfactorily provide a balance between the objectives of investigating cybercrime, and the privacy of those who use the internet and world wide web. Such critics highlighted the data preservation requirements in the Convention and their potential to infringe the privacy of innocent internet users, and, in addition, Aldesco suggested that the data preservation requirements could also infringe freedom of expression by exerting a chilling effect on anonymous online speech.[294] Since 11 September 2001 ('9/11'), many countries have passed laws that allow data preservation or data retention in an attempt not to lose data that might be relevant to the investigation of international terrorism. Interestingly, in response to such fears, the USA has favoured data preservation over the mandatory retention of data that has received favour in many European states.[295] Both techniques have the propensity to infringe privacy, but, arguably, expeditious preservation is more likely to meet the proportionality requirement in Art 15(1), to which all of the provisions on expedited preservation of stored computer data are expressly subject, than the data retention regimes being introduced in Europe, including the UK.[296] Arguably, it is difficult in an international convention to be anything other than aspirational, and to rely on the will of the individual participants to translate and implement the provisions appropriately. Nevertheless, Taylor remarked that a 'vague reference to proportionality will not be adequate to ensure that civil liberties are protected'[297] and Jarvie suggested that 'the European Cybercrime Convention is regrettably silent on the appropriate safeguards'.[298]

The final stumbling block for many US civil liberties organisations such as the Electronic Privacy Information Center (EPIC), ACLU, etc, was the provisions requiring mutual assistance and international cooperation. This objection was largely predicated on a distrust of other states to provide a basic level of human rights protection. Thus, although Keyser suggested that 'it seems very

---

292 Ibid, 250.
293 *US v Williams* 553 US 285 (2008).
294 Albert I Aldesco, 'The demise of anonymity: A constitutional challenge to the Convention on Cybercrime' (2002) 23 Loy LA Ent L Rev 81, 110.
295 For further discussion on data retention, see Chapter 6.
296 See, eg, the Anti-terrorism, Crime and Security Act 2001 and the associated Code of Practice on Data Retention 2003.
297 G Taylor, 'The Council of Europe Cybercrime Convention: A civil liberties perspective' (2002), available online at www.crime-research.org/library/CoE_Cybercrime.html
298 N Jarvie, 'Control of cybercrime: Is an end to our privacy on the internet a price worth paying?' (2003) 9 CTLR 110, 115.

important for an international regime to be set up to combat these types of crimes in a growing and integrated global society which is becoming ever more vulnerable to cyber attacks',[299] nevertheless he still espoused the view that 'although it may not be such a big deal to have the United States government wield greater power, the same new powers will also be given to member countries that may not have a strong tradition of checks and balances on police power'.[300] The ACLU was even stronger in its opposition to the mutual assistance provisions, stating that 'ratification of the Council of Europe's Convention on Cybercrime will put the United States in the morally repugnant position of supporting the actions of politically corrupt and evil regimes',[301] and, in its submission to the Senate Foreign Relations Committee considering the ratification, the ACLU suggested that 'the Senate should carefully consider what it means to agree to provide mutual legal assistance to countries whose substantive laws and procedures do not comport with American understandings of justice'.[302]

The original decision of the US government to participate in the drafting of the **Cybercrime Convention** was made in the belief that the USA had 'much to gain from a strong well-crafted multilateral instrument that removes or minimises the many procedural and jurisdictional obstacles that can delay or endanger international investigations and prosecutions of computer-related crimes', and further that 'the central provisions of the Convention on Cybercrime are consistent with the existing framework of US law'.[303] However, although President Bush pressed for its ratification in 2003,[304] the opposition to ratification arising out of the issues outlined above delayed its ratification by Senate until 2006.[305]

In contrast, there was little controversy over the UK's plans for ratification of the **Cybercrime Convention** as indicated in the comment in the APIG report that the inquiry 'received very few comments on the implications of the CMA of ratifying the Convention on Cybercrime, suggesting that this is not widely seen as a contentious issue'.[306] Some of the provisions of the **Cybercrime Convention** may be covered by the existing **CMA**,[307] but, in response to a parliamentary question about ratification of treaties, the Secretary of State reported that new legislation would be required that would delay ratification until late 2004.[308] In the event, despite the matter being apparently uncontroversial, the UK is not yet one of the states that has ratified the Convention. Although there are certainly concerns that could arise if the **Cybercrime Convention** were transposed into the national law of any of the contracting parties without appropriate safeguards for individual rights and liberties, this is not necessarily something that is confined to this international convention.

Concluding Remarks

The discussion in this chapter shows that there are a number of different responses to the phenomenon of so-called 'computer crime'. Aside from the not-insignificant difficulties of detection and

---

299 Keyser, op cit, 296.

300 Ibid, 316.

301 American Civil Liberties Union (ACLU), 'Memo on the Council of Europe Convention on Cybercrime' (2004) 16 June, available online at www.aclu.org/technology-and-liberty/aclu-memo-council-europe-convention-cybercrime

302 American Civil Liberties Union (ACLU), 'Letter to the Senate Foreign Relations Committee on the Council of Europe Convention on Cybercrime' (2004) 16 June, available online at www.aclu.org/technology-and-liberty/aclu-letter-senate-foreign-relations-committee-council-europe-convention-cybe

303 www.usdoj.gov/criminal/cybercrime/COEFAQs.htm

304 Declan McCullagh, 'Bush pushes for cybercrime treaty' (2003) cnet News, 18 November, available online at http://news.cnet.com/Bush-pushes-for-cybercrime-treaty/2100-1028_3-5108854.html?tag=mncol;txt

305 John R Crook, 'Senate approves UK Extradition Treaty and other bilateral and multilateral treaties, attaches reservations and understandings' (2007) 101 Am J Int'l Law 199, 200.

306 APIG, op cit, para 82.

307 Ibid, para 77.

308 Hansard, col 288W, 14 May 2003, available online at www.parliament.the-stationery-office.co.uk/pa/cm200203/cmhansrd/vo030514/text/30514w13.htm

enforcement, for some crimes – notably those based on theft and fraud – it seems that, for the most part, existing law, with some amendment, has been a solution that has been adopted albeit with varying degrees of success. Computer-specific legislation addressed at activities such as hacking and the introduction of viruses has met with a mixed reception, and although there have been some successful cases, it seems likely that the majority of incidents of this type are not redressed. The inherently jurisdictionally based nature of criminal law meets its greatest challenges in relation to content-based offences. There is little prospect of global consensus on a number of relevant concepts and definitions of offending behaviour, and it is significant that, for this type of conduct, the **Cybercrime Convention** contains only provisions relating to child pornography. Further, it is perhaps ironic that, in an area that stands to benefit most from international cooperation, it has been these very provisions that created the greatest stumbling block to ratification.

Chapter 5

Privacy and Data Protection

Chapter Contents

Introduction

Since time immemorial, information has been collected and exchanged about individuals. In the words of Earl Ferrers: 'The collection of personal data is as old as society itself. It may not be the oldest profession but it is one of the oldest habits.'[1] Such activities range from the collection and storage of personal information by government for a multitude of reasons and purposes, to the gossip exchanged at local meeting places. Apart from the fact that increasing computerisation has facilitated the collection and storage of such data, the much-used phrase 'the global village' encompasses the notion that exchange of information can now take place on a worldwide scale. This is converted into practical reality by the growth of the internet, which was recorded as having almost 2 billion users in June 2010, representing a growth of almost 450 per cent since the beginning of the decade.[2] These users come from diverse backgrounds, encompassing domestic, educational, governmental, and commercial sectors. As was pointed out by the UK government prior to the **Data Protection Act 1998**:

> On the one hand modern society increasingly depends on the collection, storage, processing and exchange of information of all kinds, including personal information. On the other hand it is important to ensure that where information about individuals is used their interests, including their privacy, are properly respected.[3]

This chapter is devoted to a consideration of the way in which the law is able to deal with abuses of the global information infrastructure in so far as this relates to information about individuals, whether true or false. This will involve a study of whether, and in what manner, the use of computers and computer networks can compromise an individual's privacy, or facilitate acts that threaten the individual's reputation or integrity, together with an analysis of the legal response to these issues.

Data Protection: The Nature of the Problem

Prior to the so-called 'information revolution', information and data held on individuals would only be kept in traditional filing cabinets or their equivalent. Not only might these be accessed only relatively infrequently, perhaps by the holder of the data, but it would also be difficult for other users of similar information or information about the same individual to gain access. The ease with which even the first generation of computers was able to store and manipulate data caused a dramatic change in this respect, and made it a simple matter for information about particular individuals held in a number of places to be correlated. Indeed, a whole industry arose out of the operation referred to as 'data matching', in which a profile of a particular individual is assembled from data held at a number of sources. Such profiles are now a familiar part of marketing activities: lists of those with similar profiles form a commodity that, itself, can be traded to businesses to enable selective targeting of a particular sector of the market. Neither is this process confined to business use, as pointed out succinctly by Browne-Wilkinson VC:

> If the information obtained by the police, the Inland Revenue, the social security services, the health service and other agencies were to be gathered together in one file, the freedom of the individual would be greatly at risk. The dossier of private information is the badge of the totalitarian State.[4]

---

1 Earl Ferrers, Hansard HL, vol 549, col 37 (11 October 1993).
2 www.internetworldstats.com/stats.htm
3 Home Office, *Data Protection: The Government's Proposals*, Cm 3725, 1997, London: HMSO, para 1.9.
4 *Marcel v Metropolitan Police Comr* [1992] Ch 225, 240.

This highlights the potential dangers of data matching to individual rights and liberties, and is indicative of some of the fears that surround the storage of personal data on computer systems. These fears have been voiced since the advent of widespread computerisation[5] and, even as far back as 1975, a significant amount of information about identifiable individuals was already kept on computer by central government.[6] Such anxieties were exacerbated as industry and commerce also began to rely on the use of computers to such an extent that it is today impossible to imagine business being possible without them; the words of Perri 6, that 'personal information has become the basic fuel on which modern business and government run', remain an accurate description.[7]

In 1972, despite the fact that computerisation was then still at an embryonic stage, the Younger Committee on Privacy identified characteristics that distinguished storage of information on computer from more traditional methods. The Committee noted in particular three specific areas of concern: the use of computers to compile personal profiles; their capacity to correlate information; and the ease with which unauthorised access to data could be obtained, often from remote sites.[8] There was no recommendation for action at that time, because the Committee found insufficient evidence that there had been any abuse of the above capabilities, and so regulatory intervention was, at that time, unwarranted; nevertheless some of these fears had already been recognised as a reality in the USA.[9] Even as such issues were under discussion, the nature of the threat was undergoing a subtle change as the technology continued to progress. In the 1970s and early 1980s, the focus was on the development of large, centralised databases held on mainframe computers. Technological advancement then changed direction and, instead of even larger machines being developed, the advent of the microcomputer resulted in computers rapidly becoming a common tool, both at work and in the home, rather than being confined to large institutions. Further, the creation of computer networks on a global scale moved the emphasis from centralised systems to increasingly decentralised systems, typified by the internet and world wide web.[10] These give rise to qualitatively different problems. In the early days, only large public and private organisations operated computers, giving them the exclusive ability to accumulate and correlate information about individuals from multiple sources. The advent of networked PCs and the later development of Web 2.0, which further blurs the difference between the user and the subject of the personal data, have meant that personal profiling is no longer the exclusive prerogative of the large organisation. As pointed out over ten years ago, when a user surfs the net, transactional data are created, so that 'everywhere we go on the internet, we leave a digital trace. As more and more aspects of our daily activities are conducted on-line, more and more of what we do, our choices, our preferences, will be recorded'.[11] Even in 2000, the US Federal Trade Commission made explicit reference to the potential effect on consumers when it pointed out that 'when the traffic of all sites surveyed is taken

---

5 See, eg, P Ashdown, Hansard, col 86 (30 January 1984); Data Protection Registrar, *Eighth Report of the Data Protection Registrar*, 1992, London: HMSO, Appendix 1, quoting the above comment of Browne-Wilkinson VC.

6 For details, see Secretary of State for the Home Department, *Computers: Safeguards for Privacy*, Cmnd 6354, 1975, London: HMSO, Tables 1 and 2, further updated in Secretary of State for the Home Department, *Report of the Committee on Data Protection*, Cmnd 7341, 1978, London: HMSO, Appendix 6.

7 Perri 6, *The Future of Privacy Volume 1: Private Life and Public Policy*, 1998, London: Demos, p 23.

8 Secretary of State for the Home Department, *Report of the Committee on Privacy*, Cmnd 5012, 1972, London: HMSO, para 581.

9 AR Miller, *The Assault on Privacy: Computers, Databanks and Dossiers*, 1971, Ann Arbor, MI: Michigan University Press, ch 2.

10 Some describe the communication between two computers in the same laboratory in 2 September 2009 as the birth of the internet: see *National Geographic*, 'Internet's 40th "birthday" marked' (2009) 31 August, available online at http://news. nationalgeographic.com/news/2009/08/090831-internet-40th-video-ap.html). Others have pointed out that it is 'impossible to say for certain when the internet began', but nevertheless marked the occasion on 29 October 2009, the apparent anniversary of the first communication between two computers at remote sites: see Oliver Burkeman, 'Forty years of the internet: How the world changed forever' (2009) *The Guardian*, 23 October, available online at www.guardian.co.uk/technology/2009/oct/23/internet-40-history-arpanet). Whenever the internet, as we now know it, was invented, it was not until the mid-1980s that it began to be used on a regular, day-to-day basis outside the research community.

11 Article 29 Data Protection Working Party, *Anonymity on the Internet*, Recommendation 3/97, available online at http://ec.europa.eu/justice/policies/privacy/docs/wpdocs/1997/wp6_en.pdf, p 4. See also Article 29 Data Protection Working Party, *Invisible and Automatic Processing of Personal Data on the Internet Performed by Software and Hardware*, Recommendation 1/99.

into account, there is a 99 percent chance that, during a one month period, a consumer surfing the busiest sites on the web will visit a site that collects personal identifying information'.[12] It is beyond the scope of this chapter to provide details of all of the technological developments since then that may collect and store users' personal data as they use the internet, whether with or without their knowledge. The early reports referred to above noted the use and potential abuse of 'cookies'; cookies remain a significant method by which user activity on the internet is tracked and recorded, but now 'there are many more methods through which users can be tracked, profiled, and monitored in the online world. Cookie technology has matured—cookies are widespread and new uses have been developed. Entirely new technologies have emerged as well, some of which are all but unknown to consumers'.[13] Further, powerful search engines now provide the tools for retrieving all of the available data about a person that might be held on completely unrelated sites and might be no longer either current or accurate. Fears about the power of computer technology to compromise the privacies of its users have not abated and, at the time of writing, have even been voiced by Eric Schmidt, chief executive officer (CEO) of Google, notwithstanding the fact that Google is itself frequently implicated in the creation of privacy-invading applications.[14]

When computers were first brought into use, they were large expensive machines and, in consequence, were only to be found in large organisations, whether private or public. This gave such organisations the ability to accumulate and correlate information about individuals from multiple sources. As computer networks – specifically the internet – developed, the task of aggregating personal data became much more widespread, facilitated by the technology. As a user surfs the net, transactional data are created and, 'with each click in the internet, your browser leaves a piece of information about you behind. As these pieces of information accumulate, a roadmap of personal, private information emerges'.[15] This is by no means a new phenomenon: similar warnings have been made for more than ten years.[16] More recently, the development of Web 2.0,[17] which further blurs the difference between the user and subject of the personal data, has meant that personal profiling is no longer the exclusive prerogative of the large organisation, as illustrated by Zittrain's remark that 'the Net puts private individuals in a position to do more to compromise privacy than the government and commercial institutions traditionally targeted for scrutiny and regulation'.[18] Such developments have resulted in an increased potential for privacy invasion rather than a suggestion that large commercial or government databases are no longer of concern. In respect of the latter, there continue to be examples of organisations both public and private losing or mishandling personal data, often because of poor security and carelessness, rather than any sophisticated technical reason.[19]

Despite the fact that users may recognise, at least in principle, the potential threat to their privacy from these invasive technologies, it clearly does not deter use of the internet; indeed, as

---

12 Federal Trade Commission, *Privacy Online: Fair Information Practices in the Electronic Marketplace*, 2000, available online at www.ftc.gov/reports/privacy2000/privacy2000text.pdf, p 9.

13 Chris Jay Hoofnagle, *Privacy Self Regulation: A Decade of Disappointment – A Report for the Electronic Privacy Information Center*, 2005, available online at http://epic.org/reports/decadedisappoint.html

14 Holman W Jenkins Jr, 'Google and the search for the future' (2010) *Wall Street Journal*, 14 August, available online at http://online.wsj.com/article/SB10001424052748704901104575423294099527212.html

15 Brian Kane and Brett T Delange, 'A tale of two internets: Web 2.0 slices, dices, and is privacy resistant' (2009) 45 Idaho L Rev 317, 318.

16 See, eg, Article 29 Working Party, Recommendation 3/97, op cit; Article 29 Working Party, Recommendation 1/99, op cit; Electronic Privacy Information Center (EPIC), *Surfer Beware III: Privacy Policies without Privacy Protection*, 1999, available online at www.epic.org/reports/surfer-beware3.html; FTC, op cit.

17 So-called Web 2.0 does not reflect any new technical features of the internet, but instead refers to the use of applications that foster and facilitate interactive information-sharing and user-generated content. Well known examples are Wikipedia, social networking sites such as Facebook, and video sharing sites such as YouTube, etc.

18 Jonathan Zittrain, 'Privacy 2.0' (2008) U Chi Legal F 65.

19 See, eg, the Information Commissioner's reports of enforcement action online at www.ico.gov.uk/what_we_cover/data_protection/enforcement.aspx. Many of these relate to the theft of unencrypted laptops or the loss of USB sticks resulting in the loss of personal data. Zittrain refers to similar examples in the USA, including, for example, the loss of 1.2 million Bank of America customer records in 2005: op cit, 70–1.

Kane and Delange have observed, it appears as if the internet 'inspires a trust factor that otherwise does not exist outside of the online world', and although the internet might have originated as 'a one or two-dimensional system of information and transactions', it has subsequently 'morphed into a three dimensional platform through which we participate through online shopping, email and social networking sites . . .'.[20] Unfortunately, this level of trust means that either users do not recognise any potential threat to their privacy, or, if they do, are unconcerned about it,[21] or do not always take appropriate steps to protect their own privacy until they find that privacy unacceptably compromised. Although there have been significant legal initiatives – notably the law on data protection – the rapid development of the internet and Web 2.0 applications in particular has meant that the law has not kept pace; in particular, as we shall see later, the 'European Data Protection directives are intended to deal with the problems of processing as we understood them in 1995',[22] rather than with the current situation.

Data Protection and Privacy

Despite privacy and 'privacy-invading features' being discussed in the context of data protection, the relationship between the terms 'data protection', on the one hand, and 'privacy', on the other, have not always been easy to reconcile. This is not helped by the fact that an agreed definition of privacy remains elusive. Although privacy issues have probably been in existence ever since walls were invented, the legal academic discussion only began in earnest at the end of the nineteenth century, when Warren and Brandeis penned their seminal article in response to developments in a different technology – photography.[23] The analysis of the multifaceted and slippery concept of privacy continues to the present, but with no agreed conclusion or consensus, much less the emergence of any workable legal definition. Westin suggested that 'Privacy is the claim of individuals, groups or institutions to determine for themselves when, how and to what extent information about them is communicated to others', a definition based on the right of self-determination, which may be placed at particular risk by the practice of data matching made so simple by modern information technology (IT).[24] This notion was supported by Miller,[25] in the specific context of this technology, who considered privacy to be 'the individual's ability to control the circulation of information relating to him'. Gavison, on the other hand, is critical of the ability to control personal information as being a determinant of the definition of privacy precisely because a dependence on subjective choice makes both a realisation of the scope of the concept and the provision of legal protection problematic.[26] In a quest for a more neutral approach, she attempts to deconstruct privacy into three components: secrecy; anonymity; and solitude. The definitional difficulties are exacerbated by the fact that whether or not privacy is considered to have been invaded is a very subjective issue, which will depend not only on the view of the person whose privacy is being invaded, but also on who is the invader and what information he or she is uncovering. Even using the apparently neutral approach of Gavison, the question of whether there has, in fact, been an invasion of privacy is likely to remain a subjective one. Perri 6 has submitted that the reason why there is no consensus over definition is that 'as a society we do not and cannot agree on what it is about private life and privacy that we value',[27] while Feldman comments that 'The problem is that

20 Ibid.
21 See, eg, Zittrain, op cit, p 68.
22 Yves Poullet, 'Data protection legislation: What is at stake for our society and our democracy?' (2009) 25 CLSR 211, 216.
23 S Warren and L Brandeis, 'The right to privacy' (1890) 4 Harv L Rev 193.
24 AF Westin, *Privacy and Freedom*, 1967, London: Bodley Head. London; see also Yves Poullet, 'Data protection between property and liberties', in HWK Kaspersen and A Oskamp (eds), *Amongst Friends in Computers and Law*, 1990, The Hague: Kluwer, p 161.
25 Miller, op cit.
26 R Gavison, 'Privacy and the limits of law' (1980) 89 Yale LJ 421.
27 Perri 6, op cit, p 21.

privacy is controversial. The very breadth of the idea and its tendency to merge with the idea of liberty itself produces a lack of definition which weakens its force in moral and political discourse'.[28] More recently, Richards and Solove, having explored the conceptual and doctrinal differences relating to the protection of privacy in both the USA and the UK, conclude that 'privacy cannot be reduced to a single essence; it is a multiplicity of different yet related things'.[29]

Whether or not there is an accepted and acceptable definition of 'privacy', it is usually recognised as a fundamental human right, and accorded specific protection under human rights conventions and national constitutions. In contrast, data protection is often viewed as a technical term relating to specific information management practices – the preferred stance of those who would see data protection primarily as an aspect of business regulation. Even if the precise nature of the relationship between data protection and privacy is elusive, one approach to the undeniable tension between the rights of all those who would seek to exert control over personal information can be found in the terminology of risk and risk assessment, concepts that are, perhaps, more familiar in a business environment. Three risk factors can be identified that could be considered to be elements of privacy.[30] The first of these is the risk of injustice due to significant inaccuracy in personal data, unjust inference, 'function creep' (the gradual use of data for purposes other than those for which it was collected), or reversal of the presumption of innocence, as seen in data matching when correlation of information from disparate sources may produce an impression that is greater than the sum of the parts. The second risk is to one's personal control over the collection of personal information as a result of excessive and unjustified surveillance (which would presumably include monitoring the use of particular websites), collection of data without the data subject's consent, and also the prohibition or active discouragement of the means to remedy these risks, such as the use of encryption and anonymising software. Finally, there is a risk to dignity as a result of exposure or embarrassment due to an absence of transparency in information procedures, physical intrusion into private spaces, unnecessary identification or absence of anonymity, or unnecessary or unjustified disclosure of personal information without consent. Although these have been described in the terminology of privacy, there are echoes of data protection issues and, in the technical sense, data protection measures may be considered as risk management devices that need to balance the risk to the individual from unnecessary invasion of privacy with the measures necessary to control that risk.[31] It may be that such differences in terminology are not so disparate as they might appear at first sight.

The precise relationship between privacy and data protection remains unresolved, and it is possible to continue to find conflicting views. As discussed later in the chapter, Art 1 of the **Data Protection Directive** protects the privacy of an individual with respect to the processing of data; on the other hand, there is no mention of the word 'privacy' in the **Data Protection Act 1998**. In the USA, a tort of privacy has been developed by the courts, but this focuses primarily on physical intrusion and there is no general law on data protection or information privacy – although there are sector-specific rules for data acknowledged to be particularly sensitive, such as that pertaining to medical or health records. How has the unresolved relationship between privacy and data protection affected the development of the legal provisions? As mentioned above, Gavison defines three components of privacy – that is, secrecy, anonymity, and solitude – while Feldman uses the words 'secrecy, dignity, autonomy'. In both of these formulations, the word 'secrecy' is used to encompass the idea of informational privacy, reflecting the desire of individuals to be able to place checks on what is known about them not only in the sense of data released, but also in terms of control over

---

28 D Feldman, 'Secrecy, dignity or autonomy? Views of privacy as a civil liberty' (1994) 10 CL & P 41.

29 Neil M Richards and Daniel J Solove, 'Privacy's other path: Recovering the law of confidentiality' (2007) 96 Geo LJ 123.

30 See Perri 6, op cit, p 40.

31 See also C Raab, 'The governance of data protection', in J Kooiman (ed), *Modern Governance*, 1993, London: Sage, pp 89–103; F Bott, A Coleman, J Eaton, and D Rowland, *Professional Issues in Software Engineering*, 3rd edn, 2000, London: Taylor & Francis, p 323.

its subsequent use and reuse. Does this concept of informational privacy equate with data protection or overlap with it? In 1978, the Lindop Committee was established to look exclusively at the issue of data protection in the UK. The Lindop Report referred to the definitions of both Westin and Miller, quoted above, but was at pains to distinguish 'privacy' and 'data protection'. It noted that the physical aspects of privacy were unrelated to data protection and also that aspects of data protection were not connected with privacy.[32] It conceded, however, that there was an overlap between the two concepts, which could be termed 'informational' or 'data' privacy.[33] But the report also stressed that the subjective nature of privacy meant that there was a wide variation in what might, or might not, be regarded as private, and that 'such variations exist between an individual and another, between different sections of society, between societies in different countries and between different periods of time in the same society'.[34] This also served to indicate that 'privateness' could not be considered to be directly related to the data themselves, nor could it be used as a synonym for secrecy.

Notwithstanding any attempt at semantic differentiation, other sources and commentators have often used the words 'data protection' and 'privacy' interchangeably or appear to assume some link between the two. Gellman, for example, refers to 'the slice of privacy known as "data protection"', and goes on to refer to it as a 'useful European term referring to rules about the collection, use and dissemination of personal information' and an 'important subset of privacy law'. He further suggests that a 'major policy objective of data protection is the application of fair information practices, an organized set of values and standards about personal information defining the rights of record subjects and the responsibilities of record keepers'.[35] It is arguably this entrenchment of good records management practice in law that is the salient characteristic of data protection law. As acknowledged by Gellman, the term 'data protection' originated in Europe, but few would dispute the contention that it has become a globally recognised term. However, it could be argued that the coining of this specific term has itself been the root of the problem – suggesting or being indicative of separate strands of meaning where perhaps none exist. Although recent initiatives seem more likely to stress the link between data protection and privacy, even in 1980, both the Organisation for Economic Co-operation and Development (OECD) and the Council of Europe were in no doubt that data protection was a facet of privacy. In the context of the automatic processing of personal data, the Council of Europe considered that 'it is desirable to extend the safeguards for everyone's rights and fundamental freedoms, and in particular the right to the respect for privacy',[36] while the OECD commented that 'privacy protection laws have been introduced ... to prevent what are considered to be violations of fundamental human rights such as the unlawful storage of personal data or the abuse or unauthorised disclosure of such data'.[37] The now ubiquitous term 'data protection' was reserved for the explanatory memorandum accompanying the Guidelines.

Even in the UK, with its historic reluctance to acknowledge an explicit law of privacy, the link between data protection and privacy has increasingly been recognised. In 1994, the then Data Protection Registrar said, in his Final Report, that 'data protection legislation is about the protection of individuals rather than the regulation of industry. It is civil rights legislation rather than technical business legislation'.[38] Even though the **Data Protection Act 1984** never used the word 'privacy', Lord Hoffman, in R v Brown, remarked: 'English common law does not know a general right of privacy and Parliament has been reluctant to enact one. But there has been some legislation to deal

---

32 Secretary of State for the Home Department, Cmnd 7341, op cit, para 2.03.
33 Ibid, para 2.04.
34 Ibid, para 2.05.
35 Robert Gellman, 'Does privacy law work?', in PE Agre and M Rotenberg (eds), *Technology and Privacy: The New Landscape*, 1998, Cambridge, MA: MIT Press, p 194.
36 Recitals to Council of Europe Convention No 108.
37 Preface to Organisation for Economic Co-operation and Development (OECD), *Guidelines on the Protection of Privacy and Transborder Flows of Personal Data*, available online at www.oecd.org/document/18/0,3343,en_2649_34255_1815186_1_1_1_1,00.html
38 Data Protection Registrar, *Tenth Annual Report of the Data Protection Registrar*, 1994, London: HMSO.

with particular aspects of the problem. The Data Protection Act 1984 . . . is one such statute.'[39] The decision of the then Data Protection Tribunal in *British Gas Trading Ltd v Data Protection Registrar* was more specific, stating that 'an underlying purpose of the data protection principles is to protect privacy with respect to the processing of personal data',[40] a view that looks both back to the Council of Europe Convention and forward to **Directive 95/46/EC**. Following implementation of this Directive, the Deputy Data Protection Registrar asserted that:

> If the 1998 Act satisfies the Directive, then it serves to protect the rights of individuals to privacy, at least in respect of the processing of personal data. If the 1998 Act fails to protect personal privacy in accordance with the Directive, then the UK is in breach of its Community obligations. I do not assert that data protection legislation is comprehensive privacy legislation protecting every aspect of that right, but I do ask how it can be doubted that, as a matter of law, data protection is a form of privacy protection.[41]

Notwithstanding that such comments and pronouncements originate from a variety of sources, the historic lack of legal protection for privacy per se in the UK has meant that there is still resistance, and even suspicion in some quarters, towards any legislation that purports to protect, or that could be regarded as protecting, privacy. Proponents of such views seek to divorce the concepts of data protection and privacy. This has resulted in warnings against data protection law bringing in privacy law surreptitiously by the 'back door'. Those who espouse such views concentrate, instead, on the business regulation aspects of data protection and its role in promoting the free flow of personal data. Thus Viscount Astor stated that 'the Bill which implements the Directive is designed to improve the free movement of personal data throughout the Community . . . we need to protect the rights of individuals but we do not want a back door privacy law'.[42] In the same debate, Lord Wakeham was to suggest that the Data Protection Bill (now the **Data Protection Act 1998**, implementing **Directive 95/46/EC**) was 'an excellent piece of legislation which avoids all the perils of a privacy law. It is entirely in line with the Government's stated commitment to self-regulation and their opposition to a privacy law'.

Both sides of this debate have always recognised that the reliance by business on the increased use of computers and computer networks, both internally and externally to the enterprise, enhances any disparity between business needs and individuals' right of privacy. There is a fundamental conflict at the heart of informational privacy or data protection between the individual whose data is at issue and the person who is collecting or otherwise processing it. Some might suggest that personal information should be under the control of the person to whom it refers. On the other hand, a case can be made out that, in so far as personal data arises from information provided by one person to another that is then recorded or processed in a particular way, the latter should be able to exert at least some rights over its use. This inevitably creates a tension between the two parties. The Lindop Report noted that 'a balance must be found between the interests of the individual and the interests of the rest of society, which include the efficient conduct of industry, commerce and administration'. It also suggested that the balance might need to be 'established differently in different cases. It may also be settled differently in different societies, and may shift within the same society'.[43] Competing interests, although often a reflection of the conflict between the individual and the state, may equally well refer to a balancing of the right of individuals to

---

39 [1996] 1 All ER 545, 555.
40 *British Gas Trading Ltd v Data Protection Registrar* (1998), available online at www.informationtribunal.gov.uk/DBFiles/Decision/i162/ british_gas.pdf, p 11.
41 Francis GB Aldhouse, 'Data protection, privacy and the media' (1999) 4 Comm L 8, 11.
42 Hansard HL, vol 585, col 445 (2 February 1998).
43 Secretary of State for the Home Department, Cmnd 7341, op cit, para 2.09.

privacy and control over the use of their own information with the right of other individuals or organisations to use that same information, which they may have compiled and processed, to the best commercial effect. Whilst, in upholding a general right to privacy, civil libertarians might tip this balance in favour of the right of individuals to control data concerning themselves, this may not be an automatic or obvious result.[44] Whereas it is accepted that civil liberties and human rights cannot be absolute and unfettered, it is clearly difficult to achieve an acceptable balance between the competing rights of those involved. It is the Herculean task of data protection regulation to achieve that balance.

Regulatory Approaches and Initiatives

Recognition of the competing needs raised by the collection and processing, together with consequent pressure from a variety of intergovernmental organisations such as the OECD and the Council of Europe, eventually led to regulation in a number of jurisdictions. However, this has not been accompanied by any global consensus on either the most appropriate way of achieving and maintaining the balance between the competing objectives or the provision of a suitable regulatory framework. If it is accepted that data protection regulation is necessary to respond to the threat to individual privacy from the use of computers and computer networks, it might be supposed that the central issue is merely the problem of reaching agreement on the method of achieving this result. But the counter-argument is that data protection laws impede the free flow of data, stifle rapid innovation and generally restrict the free market. There is also a considerable compliance burden related to the cost of implementation. On this argument, only minimal external regulation is likely to be tolerated and the advantages of market-driven, self-regulatory practices espoused. In other words, strong data protection will, inevitably, hinder commercial activity. Moderating this view, some legal and economic analyses have apparently demonstrated that the reality may not be so simple and that a strong legal infrastructure may actually encourage commerce. Whichever side of the argument is supported, it does seem to be generally recognised that privacy regulation may be more apt and relevant in relation to business-to-consumer (B2C) transactions than for business-to-business (B2B) ones.

If it is taken as a given that some regulation is necessary for the protection of individuals, what is the most suitable method? A clear division in approach is evident between the USA, on the one hand, which favours a sectoral, self-regulatory system, and Europe, on the other, which has a long history of legislative intervention.[45] Indeed, as already pointed out, the very concept of data protection appears to be a European creation. In order to be able to appreciate the nature of the debate that has unfolded surrounding the regulation of data protection in different jurisdictions, especially in the USA and Europe, it is prudent to examine some of the advantages and disadvantages of these apparently opposing philosophies.

See Chapter 1 → As already discussed, 'self-regulation' is arguably a much maligned and frequently misunderstood term. It should not be confused with 'non-regulation',[46] but can reasonably be equated with 'non-governmental regulation', although a number of self-regulatory regimes do, in fact, operate within a statutory framework. At its most reduced form, it suggests the propensity of individuals to provide rules for themselves, although these may include, of course, compliance with external, central regulation. Within the business and commercial sector, the term is usually used to denote a much more formal regulatory framework, which may be established by the industries, trade, and professional associations themselves in response to the need to

---

44 See further Poullet, 1990, op cit, p 174.
45 See also Andrew Charlesworth, 'Clash of the data titans? US and EU data privacy regulation' (2000) 6 EPL 253.
46 See further AC Page, 'Self-regulation: The constitutional dimension' (1986) 49 MLR 141.

be accountable for their members' activities or in response to a statutory framework, imposed for the control of a particular activity, as noted above. This last system is sometimes referred to as 'enforced self-regulation'. Self-regulatory schemes of this nature have become an increasingly familiar aspect of the regulation of commercial activity in many jurisdictions, and it is in reference to such schemes that the majority of academic scrutiny and comment has occurred.[47] Thus, self-regulation provides a particular type of regulatory regime, the flexibility and relative informality of which is often appreciated by the business community. Although frequently the subject of criticism by both lawyers and economists, particularly in relation to apparent inadequacies of enforcement, it nevertheless may be seen as advantageous by businesses. Self-regulatory agencies often have specific technical and sector-specific expertise, the regulatory process is less formal, and there are significant savings that can be made on monitoring activity, updating and revising standards, as well as more general administration of such schemes.[48] In practice, it may be difficult to assess how well the regime has been implemented or performs its functions, but this is a criticism that can also be directed at some statutory regimes. For the purposes of the present discussion, the major question is whether it can be as effective in protecting individual rights as a statutory scheme.

In Europe, there has been little consideration of the use of self-regulatory regimes as the primary method of regulation. In the UK, the origins of data protection legislation can be traced back to the Younger Committee on Privacy,[49] which was established in response to growing concerns during the 1960s about the amount of personal information kept by various organisations to which the individuals concerned had no right of access. Its terms of reference were 'to consider whether legislation is needed to give further protection to the individual citizen and to commercial and industrial interests against intrusion into privacy by private persons and organisations or by companies', suggesting that a statutory framework was what was in contemplation. Although, at this time, the use of computers was still comparatively novel, and was largely confined to big commercial and educational institutions, the potential for the problems identified earlier in the use of computer systems for these purposes had already been identified, and ch 20 of the Younger Report focused specifically on this perceived threat to privacy. Although, as already noted, there was no recommendation to legislate at that time, the Report formulated ten principles of good data management, which were suggested to provide a guide for the use of computers that manipulated personal data.[50] They included: collecting and holding information for a specific purpose and not using it for other purposes; collecting only the minimum information necessary; not holding it longer than was necessary; ensuring its accuracy; informing the subject of the information held on them; and taking appropriate security measures. Similar principles enunciating fair information practices have since formed the backbone of legal instruments for the regulation of data protection, at both the national and international levels. The OECD Guidelines of 1980[51] covered essentially the same ground, referring to its data management principles as covering: collection limitation; data quality; purpose specification; use limitation; security safeguards; openness, individual participation; and accountability. Again, a statutory regime was envisaged, the OECD recommending that these Guidelines be taken into account in the member countries' domestic legislation on privacy. Around the same time, the Council of Europe adopted the **Convention for the Protection of Individuals with regard to Automatic Processing of Personal Data**, based on similar principles.[52] Article 4(1) of this Convention also seemed to envisage an

---

47 See, generally, Robert Baldwin, Martin Cave, and Martin Lodge (eds), *The Oxford Handbook of Regulation*, 2010, Oxford: Oxford University Press; Anthony I Ogus, *Regulation: Legal Form and Economic Theory*, 1994, Oxford: Clarendon.

48 Anthony I Ogus, 'Rethinking self-regulation' (1995) 15 OJLS 97, 98.

49 Secretary of State for the Home Department, Cmnd 5012, op cit.

50 Ibid, paras 592–600.

51 OECD, op cit.

52 Convention for the Protection of Individuals with regard to Automatic Processing of Personal Data, CETS No 108, Ch II (Basic Principles for Data Protection); full text available online at http://conventions.coe.int/Treaty/EN/v3MenuTraites.asp

approach that would be primarily legislative, providing that 'Each Party shall take the necessary measures in its domestic law to give effect to the basic principles for data protection'. It was international activity of this type that was to lead many of the signatories to these agreements to produce legislation for the regulation of this area, recognising that not only did these international instruments provide a benchmark for the appropriate standard, but also that transnational data flows might be compromised without the adoption of a common standard. Amongst such jurisdictions was the UK, the first data protection legislation of which, the **Data Protection Act 1984**, was enacted as a direct result of the perceived need to ratify the Council of Europe Convention.[53]

Both the OECD and Council of Europe documents were thus instrumental in precipitating legislative action in many European states. Indeed, Mayer-Schönberger has commented that, in Europe, 'almost all the national norms enacted after 1981 reflected the spirit if not the text of the OECD Guidelines'. However, notwithstanding the central influence of the various principles of good data management, this has not had the result that the statutory regulatory regimes adopted have had uniformity of provisions. There is clearly room for variation in the scope and emphasis of the protection provided – and neither has the legislative approach remained static. Mayer-Schönberger has further traced this development in terms of a succession of generations of data protection legislation. Of these, he suggests that the first generation represents those laws passed in the early 1970s that reacted to the onset of large databanks and the overall phenomenon of data processing. The second generation, which emerged in the late 1970s, began to focus more explicitly on the individual rights of citizens. This was further developed by the third generation of regulation in the 1980s, which emphasised informational participation and self-determination. The fourth generation, which Mayer-Schönberger suggests focuses more on holistic and sectoral perspectives, is exemplified by **Directive 95/46/EC** and emerged in the 1990s.[54] However, despite the categorisation into generations, not all jurisdictions within Europe necessarily embraced the later generations of norms to the fullest extent. In addition, all of these developments in the regulatory landscape still tended to focus on the tension between individual informational rights and the use of personal data by large organisations, and, as we shall see, more recent regulatory activity has attempted to respond to the more diffuse and amorphous threat to individual privacy resulting from the use of computer networks.

Although regulation of this area within Europe is primarily dependent on legislative rules embodying the above principles of good data management, this approach is not confined to legislation and such principles are also a feature of the primarily self-regulatory regime in use in the USA. Business regulation in the USA is much more market-led and there is far less intervention in the private sector than there is in Europe. There are, however, informational privacy rules with legislative force at both federal and state levels that focus on specific issues such as health care, financial details, and so on,[55] but data protection in the private sector remains 'decentralized, fragmented, ad hoc and narrowly tailored to target specific sectors'.[56] This can create a very complex situation, which has resulted in 'a myriad of overlapping, and at times conflicting, state and federal laws'.[57] The differences in ethos and approach between the USA and Europe on this topic can be related to a number of things, including the contrasting approach to personal data privacy in the respective jurisdictions. In the USA, as implied above, this is regulated by a mixture of the **Constitution**, and federal and state laws, as well as the common law of tort. In Europe, on the other hand, data

---

53 See, eg, William Whitelaw (Home Secretary), Hansard HC, vol 40, col 554 (11 April 1983).
54 Viktor Mayer-Schönberger, 'Generational development of data protection in Europe', in PE Agre and Marc Rotenberg (eds), *Technology and Privacy: The New Landscape*, 1998, Cambridge, MA: MIT Press, ch 8.
55 For more precise details, see, eg, Liz Harding, 'Oceans apart: Overview of the US legal framework' (2010) 21(2) Computers and Law 27.
56 Tracie B Loring, 'An analysis of the informational privacy protection afforded by the European Union and the United States' (2002) 37 Tex Int'l LJ 421.
57 Susan Mann, 'Oceans apart: Data transfers between the EEA and USA' (2010) 21(2) Computers and Law 22, 23.

protection has been allied much more explicitly with fundamental human rights and is now incorporated in the **Treaty on the Functioning of the European Union (TFEU)** as a result of the coming into force of the **Lisbon Treaty** at the beginning of December 2009.[58]

At a basic level, it could appear that, notwithstanding the conceptual and philosophical differences, the fundamental principles do not differ dramatically. The 1998 report of the US Federal Trade Commission (FTC)[59] discussed five core principles of privacy protection by reference to the corresponding OECD guidelines – namely: notice/awareness; choice/consent; access/participation; integrity/security; and enforcement/redress. Beyond this apparent similarity, however, the regulatory regimes in Europe and the USA diverge markedly, and, as might be expected, the emphasis on individual rights in Europe appears to have been the prime catalyst to the legislative approach to data protection, whereas business needs have been set much more centre stage in the USA. The FTC noted consumer concern about privacy issues in its 1998 report, but nevertheless felt that these concerns could be resolved by the encouragement of self-regulation – even though it recognised that, at that time, there were severe deficiencies in the extent of regulatory protection.[60] A further report in July 1999 reiterated the philosophy of the previous report – that 'self-regulation is the least intrusive and most efficient means to ensure fair information practice, given the rapidly evolving nature of the internet and computer technology'.[61] It noted that, although there were still observable problems with compliance, there had been significant developments reflecting 'industry leaders' substantial effort and commitment to fair information practices'. This fact, together with other initiatives to protect individual privacy, suggested to the FTC that legislation to address online privacy was not appropriate at that time and there has been little substantive change in approach since – although, arguably, a stricter emphasis on enforcement has emerged, together with specific legislative response in a number of states to loss of personal data and other security breaches.[62]

These brief details of the contrasting approaches to regulation of data protection in Europe and the USA illustrate some of the points of conflict, but it would be misleading to imagine that these apparently opposing mechanisms are entirely mutually exclusive. The view is expressed in the recitals of the OECD's 1998 *Ministerial Declaration on the Protection of Privacy on Global Networks* that, although there are different approaches to privacy in member countries, these methods can, nevertheless, 'work together to achieve effective privacy protection on global networks'.[63] Although self-regulatory mechanisms are frequently invoked as a substitute for, or an avoidance of, legislation, they may also play a valuable role in both implementing and supplementing framework legislation by providing particular rules for specific sectors and/or purposes. Consider, for example, how a general framework for maintaining privacy might be put into effect in relation to direct marketing as opposed to the management of health records. In each of these cases, the risks and consequences of inappropriate processing are very different. Codes of practice (a common form of self-regulation) can be very effective at filling in the necessary detail to enable the framework requirements and guidance to be complied with in specific cases. The disadvantage, of course, is that too great a reliance on self-regulatory codes may result in divergence between the sectors, which, in turn, can lead to fragmentation at the implementation level.

---

58 Treaty on the Functioning of the European Union (TFEU), Art 16(1), amending Art 286, EC Treaty: Everyone has the right to the protection of personal data concerning them. See also Loring, op cit, and Mann, op cit.

59 Federal Trade Commission (FTC), *Privacy Online: A Report to Congress*, 1998, available online at www.ftc.gov/reports/privacy3/toc.htm

60 Ibid.

61 Federal Trade Commission (FTC), *Self-Regulation and Privacy Online*, 1999, available online at www.ftc.gov/os/1999/07/privacy99.pdf

62 See, eg, Christopher Wolf, 'New directions in enforcement and policy at the FTC and the impact on businesses' (2010) 1005 PLI/Pat 421.

63 OECD Working Party on Information Security and Privacy, *Ministerial Declaration on the Protection of Privacy on Global Networks*, DSTI/ICCP/REG(98)10/FINAL, 1998, Ottowa, ON: OECD, available online at www.oecd.org/dataoecd/39/13/1840065.pdf

Despite the possibilities for reconciliation, the two conflicting approaches in the USA and Europe appear entrenched within the existing regulatory frameworks, and it was apparent that there was likely to be a time when these would clash or would, alternatively, each have to find ways of accommodating the other. This eventually became an imperative with the adoption and implementation of **Directive 95/46/EC**, with its provisions requiring the adequacy of data protection in third countries to be assessed before transborder data flows will be allowed.[64] In May 2000, the European Union (EU) Member States approved an agreement with the USA concerning arrangements to safeguard individual privacy in transborder data flow that, in effect, attempt to reconcile the self-regulatory regime in the USA with the legislative approach in the EU (the so-called 'Safe Harbor Agreement', discussed in more detail below). Surprisingly, perhaps, in view of the content of the previous reports and the sometimes acrimonious nature of the Safe Harbor discussions, a further report from the FTC suggested that statutory intervention might be necessary in order to safeguard individual privacy in the USA;[65] however, there has been no follow-up activity in this respect and the regulatory mismatch between the two jurisdictions is still in evidence.

The Data Protection Directive 95/46/EC

Notwithstanding the fact that all of the EU Member States are also members of the Council of Europe, by the end of the 1980s, some Member States still had no data protection legislation and there were sufficient discrepancies between those that had to warrant further harmonisation. A further concern was that any differences in the protection afforded to data in each Member State might lead to restrictions on transborder data flow from those countries with a higher level of protection. This would obviously impede the functioning of the internal market – a crucial factor in the wake of the date of 31 December 1991 set by the **Single European Act 1986** for the completion of the single European market. Accordingly, in 1990, a proposal for a **Directive on the Protection of Individuals with regard to the Processing of Personal Data and on the Free Movement of such Data** was published.[66]

The centrality of the single market might suggest that a primary reason for harmonisation was business efficacy and the facilitation of free movement of data, but the competing interests endemic in this area are strongly represented in the Preamble to the original proposal, which refers not only to transborder data flows, but also to the importance of protecting the right of privacy. In the event, the final version was to be a long time in gestation – one problem was to devise legislation that would both ensure a high level of protection and yet not compromise that already in place in some Member States. In view of the different interpretations put on the various concepts in the different jurisdictions, the Economic and Social Committee was particularly concerned as to whether the proposal actually increased the level of protection or merely accentuated the differences between Member States. An amended proposal was published in 1992,[67] but although this was debated by the European Parliament and approved subject to amendments,[68] progress then seemed to come to a halt. Action was eventually precipitated by the Bangemann Report, which was produced for the Corfu Summit of 1994 and looked at all facets of the 'information society', but, in particular, noted that although Europe was a world leader in data protection, 'without the legal security of a Union-wide approach, lack of consumer confidence [would] undermine the rapid development of the information society', recommending that 'a fast decision' was required on the proposed Directive. This recommendation, from such an eminent source, proved the necessary boost to revive the

---

64 See the discussion on Arts 25 and 26 below.
65 FTC, 2000, op cit, p 44.
66 COM(1990)314 final, SYN 287 [1990]; [1990] OJ C 277/3.
67 COM(1992)422 final, SYN 287 [1992]; [1992] OJ C 311/30.
68 [1992] OJ C 94/198.

proposed Directive and the final version of the Directive was agreed using the codecision procedure in 1995.[69] The final version was a much-amended and augmented version of the original 1990 proposal, and contains a total of 72 Recitals in the Preamble. However, the fact that the final text only differs in very minor ways from the common position can probably be taken as an indication of the general agreement between Parliament and the Council on this issue.

Provisions of Directive 95/46/EC

Article 1 sets out the objectives of the Directive. First, and fundamentally, this Article refers to the protection of privacy with respect to the processing of personal data, signalling that, even though limited, data protection is part of the fundamental right of privacy. However, the provision also includes an important counterbalancing provision that requires Member States not to restrict or prohibit the free flow of data between them. Thus, as far as EU Member States are concerned, the free flow of personal data is envisaged for whatever purpose and this flow cannot be restricted, assuming that there is compliance with the provisions of the Directive. This is, of course, a necessary consequence of the harmonisation of data protection law throughout the EU and the situation is, as we shall see below, rather different for transborder data flow to third countries. Further, Arts 2 and 3 demonstrate that the scope of the Directive is independent of the mode of storage of the personal data. Although the discussion in the earlier part of this chapter focuses on the technological threat to privacy, so-called 'manual data' are also covered by the Directive as long as they are stored in a structured filing system.[70] Crucial concepts such as 'personal data' and 'processing' are defined in Art 2, and the interpretation of these will be considered in more detail below. These definitions also distinguish the 'controller' and the 'processor' of data. The 'controller' is the person who (alone or in conjunction with others) 'determines the purposes and means of processing personal data', whereas a 'processor' merely processes such data on behalf of the data controller. The distinction can be important, because the central responsibilities for complying with the data protection principles, discussed below, fall on the data controller. The provisions of the Directive extend only to the processing of data for purposes that fall within the areas of business, economic, and social activity that are within the EU competences set out in Art 6 **TFEU**. It will then be a question for individual Member States to decide whether or not to include other activities within the scope of the domestic legislation. Some of the first-generation data protection statutes were based on a concept of universal registration, but this had been criticised as unnecessarily bureaucratic and cumbersome to administer. Instead, the Directive requires notification of processing, which is intended to ensure transparency, rather than to create a method of control.[71]

The Data Protection Principles

In common with many other international and national instruments on this topic, the Directive lays down principles of good data management. Article 6 lists five of these:

● personal data should be processed fairly and accurately;
● personal data should be collected for specific purposes and not further processed for other purposes;
● personal data processed should be relevant and not excessive;

---

69 European Parliament and Council Directive 95/46/EC on the Protection of Individuals with regard to the Processing of Personal Data and on the Free Movement of Such Data, 24 October 1995, [1995] OJ L 281/31.
70 See also Recital 27.
71 See Arts 18–20.

- personal data should be accurate and kept up to date; and
- personal data should be kept no longer than is necessary.

Other matters, such as subject access and security, which are often included in lists of data protection principles are dealt with elsewhere in the Directive.

In support of the first of these principles, Art 7 lays down the basic criteria for the lawful processing of non-sensitive data. Compliance with this provision requires the data controller to comply with one of a number of options that will legitimise processing. These include where the data subject has 'unambiguously given consent' or where processing is for one of a list of reasons that include the performance of a contract to which the data subject is a party and the protection of the vital interests of the data subject. With respect to non-sensitive data, these alternative criteria to the consent of the data subject are all qualified by the use of the word 'necessary', which imports a strict construction and an objective standard beyond mere convenience and desirability for the data controller. In Case C-465/00 *Rechnungshof v Österreichischer Rundfunk & ors*,[72] the European Court of Justice (ECJ) considered the nature of the obligations in Arts 6 and 7 – specifically, Art 6(1)(c), which requires that personal data must be relevant and not excessive in relation to the purpose for which it was collected, and Art 7(c) and (e), which legitimise processing that is necessary for compliance with a legal obligation and for the performance of a task in the public interest or the exercise of official authority. The ECJ concluded that all of these provisions were directly effective, because they were sufficiently precise and unconditional to be relied upon by individuals in their national courts.[73] Because the other provisions of Arts 6 and 7 are couched in similar language, this decision suggests that they will also be directly effective.

Article 8 then prohibits the processing of sensitive data – that is, that which reveals racial or ethnic origin, political opinions, religious or philosophical beliefs, trade union membership, and health or sex life – unless one of a list of more stringent requirements applies. In comparison with the more general legitimising provisions in Art 7, the provisos in relation to sensitive data are mostly targeted at very specific situations in which there are other legitimate objectives to be attained by the processing of the data in question. For sensitive data to be processed, any consent given by the data subject must be 'explicit' rather than 'unambiguous', as required under Art 7. Consent is defined in Art 2(h) as 'any freely given specific and informed indication of his wishes by which the data subject signifies his agreement to personal data relating to him being processed'. What is the significance of the different qualifications placed on consent in these two Articles? Clearly, if consent is to be construed as unambiguous, then there must be no room for doubt, but explicit consent suggests a higher standard of proof, in that the consent is distinctly stated and cannot be implied, however unequivocal the implication. Before the adoption of the Directive, it was common to construe consent from the absence of objection, but, even for non-sensitive data, it seems that the Directive may require more positive action to legitimise processing of personal data. The presumption is thus changed from one under which further processing is permitted unless a contrary indication is notified to one under which it is not permitted unless there is definite evidence of consent. At a minimum, it would appear that even the qualification 'unambiguous' 'strengthens the argument that the consent must entail a clear indication of the agreement of the individual',[74] whereas the use of the qualification 'explicit' suggests that the fact that consent has been given must be established beyond doubt.

Given the commitment to individual rights to privacy with respect to the processing of data that is embedded in Art 1 of the Directive, it is not surprising that a number of its other provisions relate to specific rights to be enjoyed by the data subject. These rights can be divided loosely into the right

---

72 [2003] ECR I-4989.
73 Ibid, [100]–[101].
74 Rosemary Jay, *Data Protection Law and Practice*, 3rd edn, 2007, London: Sweet & Maxwell, p 154.

to information about the nature of the personal data held and the type of processing,[75] the right of access to data held by the data controller,[76] and the right to object to processing in certain situations.[77] However, there is no general right to object to data processing because this would be likely to be disproportionate to the internal market objective of maintaining the free flow of personal data.

As already mentioned, the Directive does not extend to personal data processed for purposes that fall outside of the competence of the EU to legislate and, in addition, Art 3(2) also provides that the Directive does not apply to processing of personal data 'by a natural person in the course of a purely personal or household activity'. These provisions together delineate the general scope of its application. However, there are also a number of other areas that may attract exemption from some or all of the provisions in recognition of the fact that there may be overriding reasons that will mitigate against disclosing what would otherwise be public information, or allowing access to what would otherwise be protected as personal. On occasions, this will mean a relaxation of the strict data protection rules if necessary to achieve an appropriate balance of interests: it may be that, at times, the public interest favours the data subject, whilst at others it favours the purpose of the processing. But in all cases, exemptions should be applied in a proportionate manner and should only go as far as is required to address the legitimate public interest at issue. The list of areas in the Directive that attract exemptions extends to national security, defence, public security, prevention, investigation, detection, and prosecution of criminal offences, or of breaches of ethics for regulated professions, important economic or financial interest of a Member State or of the EU, and monitoring, inspection, or regulatory functions, as well as the protection of the data subject or the rights and freedoms of third parties.[78] As well as the exemptions expressly referred to above, there are other limitations on the application of the Directive. These include the permissible derogations from the obligation to notify. It also appears, from Recital 29 and Art 6(1)(e), that it is expected that, under appropriate conditions, there should be an exemption provided for storage of personal data used for historical and statistical purposes, so that it can be kept for a sufficiently long time or perhaps indefinitely. A significant exemption is also contained in Art 9 regarding the potential tension between the processing of personal data and freedom of expression, particularly in the context of journalism and artistic or literary expression (the so-called 'special purposes'). There appears to be a tacit assumption behind Art 9 that the media should be treated differently, although on what basis is not explicitly stated.[79] Whether or not the media are a special case, it is axiomatic that upholding a right of privacy may at the same time be breaching the right to freedom of expression, and vice versa. Where the protection of one fundamental right may impinge on the enjoyment of another right, the problem of achieving a satisfactory balance is never amenable to easy solution. The Directive leaves it to Member States to achieve an appropriate balance in this context – a process that needs to be viewed within the wider debate of press freedom and privacy,[80] but which will, inevitably, be influenced by the distinctive cultures and legal traditions of the individual Member States.

Transborder Data Flows

In the discussion of individual rights, it must not be forgotten that the Directive, in common with other data protection regulation, has the dual objective of both safeguarding privacy in relation to

---

75 Articles 10 and 11.
76 Article 12.
77 Articles 14 and 15.
78 Article 13. The detailed list in this provision corresponds to the general list of areas of exemption set out in Art 9 of Council of Europe Convention 108.
79 See Perri 6, op cit.
80 See, eg, Department of National Heritage, *Review of Press Regulation*, Cm 2135, 1993, London: HMSO; Lord Chancellor's Department, *Infringement of Privacy*, Consultation Paper, 1993, London: Scottish Office; R Wacks, *Privacy and Press Freedom*, 1995, London: Blackstone; House of Commons Culture, Media and Sport Committee, *Press Standards, Privacy and Libel: Second Report of Session 2009–10*, 2010, London: HMSO.

processing of personal data and facilitating transborder data flow, as illustrated by Art 1.[81] The importance of the free flow of such data is further underlined by part of the first sentence of Recital 56: '... cross-border flows of personal data are necessary for the expansion of international trade.' Thus, there are no grounds for restricting the free flow of data, provided that the appropriate safeguards are in place. Indeed, it is the very necessity referred to in Recital 56 that makes protection of the individual so vital. In principle, given the expected harmonisation of protection created by the Directive, cross-border data flow between individual Member States would not be expected to create an additional threat to the privacy of individuals. The situation could be very different, though, in relation to the transfer of data to third countries that may not have data protection to the same extent, or at all. For this reason, Art 25, which proscribes the transfer of personal data to a third country unless that country ensures 'an adequate level of protection', is of extreme importance and its inclusion within the Directive has led many commentators to speculate on the potentially wide-reaching effect that its provisions may have. Thus Bennett has suggested that the 'Data Protection Directive now constitutes the rules of the road for the increasingly global character of data processing operations'[82] and Mayer-Schönberger predicts that the Directive will assist the drive to homogeneity of approach on a global scale.[83] Whether such speculation accords with the reality of the situation will be assessed in the subsequent discussion.

The question of whether or not personal data had actually been transferred to a third country was considered by the ECJ in Case C-101/01 *Bodil Lindqvist*.[84] Mrs Lindqvist had developed an internet home page as part of a course that she was following. She published on this site the personal data of a number of people who worked with her on a voluntary basis in a parish of the Swedish Protestant church for which she was a catechist. This included not only names and addresses, but also family circumstances, health issues, and other comments. Her colleagues were not informed of this and neither did she notify the relevant supervisory authority. She was subsequently charged with a number of offences relating to breaches of data processing rules and, as a result, a number of questions were referred to the ECJ. One of these asked:

> ... whether there is any transfer [of data] to a third country ... where an individual loads personal data onto an internet page which is stored on an internet site on which the page can be consulted and which is hosted by a natural or legal person ... thereby making those data accessible to anyone who connects to the internet, including people in a third country.

The question also went on to ask whether it made any difference to the answer if no one from a third country actually accessed the page.

The issue, of course, is that the Directive was not drafted with the transmission of personal data via the internet in mind and the ECJ noted that it could not be presumed that the provisions in question had been intended to apply to the loading of data onto an internet page, even if that process then made the data accessible to individuals in other jurisdictions.[85] It further pointed out that if there were a finding that there was a transborder data flow every time a website was accessed in another country, then the Directive would have global application and, further, even if only one of the countries were to fail to provide adequate protection (which would, of course, be very

---

81 Compare, eg, the Council of Europe Convention, which attempts, inter alia, to reconcile the notion of effective data protection with the ideal of free flow of information, as set out in the European Convention on Human Rights, Art 10. In pursuance of this, Art 12 of the Convention, on automatic processing of data, contains provisions allowing restriction of transborder data flows 'except where the regulations of the other Party provide an equivalent protection [for the personal data]'.

82 C Bennett, 'Convergence revisited', in PE Agre and M Rotenberg (eds), *Technology and Privacy: The New Landscape*, 1998, Cambridge, MA: MIT Press, p 111.

83 Mayer-Schönberger, op cit, p 223.

84 [2003] ECR I-12971.

85 Ibid, [68].

likely), the result would be that no personal data could lawfully be placed on the internet or web pages. With regard to the access to specific data such as that posted by Lindqvist in particular, the ECJ concluded that, to obtain that data, a user would have to take all of the necessary technical actions to locate and access the data – in other words, 'the internet pages did not contain the technical means to send that information automatically to people who did not intentionally seek access to those pages'.[86] The Court's overall conclusion with regard to transborder data flow was that when data was accessed on a website, that data was not directly transferred between those who had posted the information and those reading it, and that, in consequence, there was no transfer of data to a third country as a result of information posted on a web page being available for access in third countries.

This is perhaps not a surprising judgment given the potential impact, noted at [69] of the judgment, that a contrary finding could have. Conceptually, it can be likened to a finding that, in the virtual world, individuals accessing an internet page containing personal data 'visit' that page rather than that the data is sent to them. This is not dissimilar to the approach taken by Jacob J in *Euromarket Designs Inc v Peters*,[87] in relation to trade mark infringement, in which he likened browsing on commercial sites on the internet to looking into a shop or 'visiting' it. On the other hand, the approach taken in some defamation cases[88] equates publication on the internet with publication to the world – that is, something rather more active. Given the patchy development of the law in this respect, it is difficult to assess whether these apparently opposing approaches can be reconciled or whether it matters in either the practical or conceptual sense.[89]

Assuming that, in a particular case, there has actually been a transfer of personal data, the more difficult issue raised by Art 25 is the interpretation of 'adequate'. Should 'adequate' mean 'in conformity with the Directive'? Or 'functional similarity'? Or some lesser standard? How should, or can, this be assessed? The subsequent paragraphs of Art 25 attempt to provide guidance on this issue and give details of relevant factors including the nature of the data, and the purpose and duration of the processing, as well as the relevant legal, security, and professional rules in the country in question. However, this is of little help in providing any indication of clear priority amongst the criteria to be applied in assessment of adequacy and does not explicitly create a reference point by which adequacy may, or should, be determined. It was envisaged that there would be practical problems encountered in the assessment of adequacy and a number of possible methodologies were explored. One report prepared for the Commission used the concept of 'functional similarity', noting that Europe should not seek the direct transposition of its own principles and systems of protection into other countries.[90] Instead, adequacy might be determined in the presence of any element in the regulation of a third country providing the relevant requirements, even if this was accomplished in a completely different way. Such an approach permits better respect for local legal structures than the requirement for equivalent protection inherent in complete juristic similarity. The particular technique employed was to reduce the elements of data protection to 'risk factors' – namely, loss of control, reuse, non-proportionality, and inaccuracy – and assess the way in which they were protected. A further report referred to the problem of 'cultural and institutional non-equivalence', pointing out that a judgment of adequacy must appreciate and remain sensitive to

---

86 Ibid, [60].
87 [2001] FSR 20.
88 See, eg, *Dow Jones & Co v Gutnick* [2002] HCA 56.
89 For an alternative view of where actual publication takes place, see also *Moberg v 33T LLC* 666 F Supp 2d 415 (2009), discussed online at http://jolt.law.harvard.edu/digest/copyright/moberg-v-33t-llc. In a different context, the Court of Appeal has referred questions to the ECJ about whether publication on the internet takes place where it is uploaded or where it is accessed: *Football Dataco Ltd v Sportradar GmbH* [2011] EWCA Civ 330; now pending case C-604/10, [2011] OJ C 89/14.
90 Yves Poullet et al, *Preparation of a Methodology for Evaluating the Adequacy of the Level of Protection of Individuals with Regard to the Processing of Personal Data*, 1998, Luxembourg: OOPEC.

important cultural differences.[91] Despite the apparent convergence of data protection rules, privacy is still a variable concept, and different legal traditions still place different emphasis on protection and apportionment of rights. The report also submitted that 'assessment of adequacy will be incomplete to the extent that it cannot assess actual practices and the realities of compliance', and that 'a more empirical analysis of policies and practices, as well as rules, serves both to advance the debate and to anticipate the specific problems that will be encountered in the implementation of the Directive'.

The Article 29 Working Party,[92] which has produced a large number of opinions and recommendations,[93] has considered the concept of 'adequate protection' in the context of Art 25.[94] It suggested that, as noted earlier in this chapter, a 'core' of data protection principles and methods of application could be determined from a consideration of the provisions of both the **Data Protection Directive** and other international instruments on data protection, and that these could be used to formulate an appropriate minimum requirement for 'adequate protection'. It was pointed out that this was not the same as suggesting that 'adequate' in this context meant complete equivalence and that there would not be insistence on complete conformity with the Directive. Neither did it think that, because this standard originated in international conventions, it would prove particularly controversial for third countries. However, this view was to be severely challenged by the discussion on transborder data flow between the EU and the USA. Even before the entry into force of the Directive, the EU and USA had been discussing data protection issues and privacy, with the objective of creating a bridge between the EU legislative approach and the primarily self-regulatory approach in the USA. Building such a bridge, referred to by Leathers as 'an ambitious project',[95] was never likely to be simple and straightforward; in the event, it took two years to build, and involved discussions that were at times both heated and acrimonious. The, at times, turbulent history of the 'Safe Harbor' negotiations can be charted by an examination of successive documents of the Working Party,[96] which exposed the tension between the objectives of the various players involved. This included not only tension between the USA and EU, but also between the various EU bodies involved in the negotiations. Given the commercial power of the USA, there were clearly political motivations driving those who were directly participating in the discussions to work towards a negotiated, albeit inevitably compromised, settlement. On the other hand, the Working Party, with its independent yet only advisory status, showed itself keen to uphold standards, suggesting a potential criticism that it was actively trying to equate the term 'adequate' with the protection afforded under the Directive.

The starting point was the perceived inadequacy from the European perspective of the patchwork of narrowly focused sectoral laws and voluntary self-regulation that characterised the regulatory framework in the USA. In addition, the fact that the USA had ostensibly adopted the OECD Guidelines of 1980 was suggestive that an agreement on minimum requirements ought to be feasible. However, as already mentioned, stormy waters were encountered in the search for the safe harbour and it was some time before a mutually acceptable outcome was reached.

So that the USA would not be seen as a 'data haven', the adopted approach was to attempt to define a 'safe harbor' for personal data – a set of principles to which US companies would sign up

---

91 Charles Raab et al, *Application of a Methodology Designed to Assess the Adequacy of the Level of Protection of Individuals with Regard to Processing Personal Data*, 1998, Luxembourg: OOPEC.
92 For constitution and remit, see further Arts 29 and 31.
93 All available online at http://ec.europa.eu/justice/policies/privacy/workinggroup/wpdocs/2010_en.htm
94 Article 29 Working Party, *Transfers of Personal Data to Third Countries*, Opinion 12/98.
95 Daniel R Leathers, 'Giving bite to the EU–US data privacy safe harbor: Model solutions for effective enforcement' (2009) 41 Case W Res J Int'l L 193, 194.
96 Six separate Opinions and a Working Document on this topic were published from the beginning of 1999. These documents can be accessed via http://ec.europa.eu/justice/policies/privacy/workinggroup/wpdocs/1999_en.htm and http://ec.europa.eu/justice/policies/privacy/workinggroup/wpdocs/2000_en.htm

on a voluntary basis, but to which they would then be bound. Expanding on the metaphor, it has been suggested that 'the safe harbor is, figuratively, a place where US companies can find shelter from potentially damaging crosswinds caused by different privacy regimes in the US and EU'.[97] The advantage of this approach is that, whilst respecting the different regulatory cultures on both sides of the Atlantic, it is able to provide legal certainty for EU data controllers exporting data to 'safe harbor' participants, it does not impose a too onerous administrative burden, and it provides guidance to US companies and other organisations that wish to meet the 'adequate protection' standard specified in the Directive. It is these principles that had to be examined for 'adequacy' against the Directive's provisions. An agreement was eventually reached in the summer of 2000 and confirmed by a Commission Decision.[98] The rationale of the Safe Harbor is that organisations wishing to accept personal data from EU or European Economic Area (EEA) countries can agree to comply with the Safe Harbor principles by a self-certification method,[99] and the level of protection offered to that data will then be deemed to be adequate for the purposes of Arts 25 and 26. The Safe Harbor requirements consist of seven principles issued by the US Department of Commerce and contained in Annex 1 to Decision 2000/520, which give provisions relating to notice, choice, onward transfer, security, data integrity, access, and enforcement. To begin with, US companies did not rush to join and the uptake was very slow – although membership of the Safe Harbor is now much more widespread.[100]

As might be expected from the previous discussion, these principles broadly conform to those articulated in the Council of Europe Convention and the OECD Guidelines, although not to the more detailed requirements of the Directive.[101] Overall, the 'Safe Harbor' has had a mixed reception – particularly in relation to the perceived lack of redress for individuals and weak enforcement mechanisms. As pointed out by Palekar, the lack of effective enforcement mechanisms in particular has resulted in the Safe Harbor principles creating privacy protection 'more in form than function',[102] because the self-regulatory system in the USA provides little scope either for uniform enforcement or for the provision of effective remedies. Ultimately, the Safe Harbor principles are enforced by the Federal Trade Commission (FTC), but although that body could be said to be in 'an ideal position to create a stronger regulatory program for online privacy',[103] as yet there has been little evidence of significant activity in this respect. Although the FTC has the power to seek several remedies for consumers whose data have been compromised,[104] action by the FTC is the final stage in a multilayer approach to enforcement, which means that many complaints may never reach this final stage whether or not they have been satisfactorily resolved at an earlier stage. Although the FTC seems now to be prepared to take more formal action, this is a relatively recent development and comes some ten years after the inception of the 'Safe Harbor' agreement.[105]

For whichever country to which data are to be exported, the detailed rules in Art 25 can be ameliorated to a certain extent by derogations provided in Art 26(1), which are based primarily on

---

97 See E-Policy News, 'Privacy & data protection: Safe Harbor agreement approved by EU Member States' (2000) June, available online at http://ec.europa.eu/archives/ISPO/ecommerce/epolicy/2000-06.html; White House, 'Data Privacy Accord with EU (Safe Harbor)', Press release, 31 May 2000, available online at http://clinton4.nara.gov/WH/New/Europe-0005/factsheets/data-privacy-accord-with-eu.html
98 Decision 2000/520/EC of 26 July 2000 [2000] OJ L215/7.
99 For further details, see www.export.gov/safeharbor/
100 Schriver reports that, after six months, only twelve companies had signed up; this number increased very slowly, so that there were still only 168 organisations in the Safe Harbor in March 2002: RR Schriver, 'You cheated, you lied: The Safe Harbor agreement and its enforcement by the Federal Trade Commission' (2002) 70 Fordham L Rev 2777, 2793. The current list is available online at https://safeharbor.export.gov/list.aspx, although because there is a requirement to renew notification every twelve months, not all of those on the list are actually currently members.
101 See also M Ewing, 'The perfect storm: The Safe Harbor and the Directive on Data Protection' (2002) 24 Hous J Int'l L 315, 339.
102 Nikhil S Palekar, 'Privacy protection: When is "adequate" actually adequate?' (2008) 18 Duke J Comp & Int'l L 549, 550.
103 Ibid, 575.
104 See Leathers, op cit, 207.
105 For examples of FTC action in this area, see FTC, 'FTC approves final settlement order with Dave & Busters; FTC rejects COPPA Safe Harbor application' (2010) 6 August, available online at www.ftc.gov/opa/2010/06/davecoppa.shtm

the data subject's consent, the data subject's interest, or where transfer is from publicly available registers or documents. In addition, Art 26(2) provides for a contractual route to the assurance of adequate protection. This provision resulted in a further Commission Decision on standard contractual clauses for the transfer of personal data to third countries.[106] This decision sets out, in Annex 1, standard clauses for the protection of personal data that will conform to the requirements of the Directive. Further guidance has now been published by the Commission to take into account the expansion of data processing activities; these are also applicable to the increasingly common situation in which there is further outsourcing of processing to sub-processors.[107] Although the new rules leave the initial Decision in place, the new model clauses will apply to new transfers and to modifications of existing data processing operations. In addition, adequate protection may also be ensured by the use of 'binding corporate rules' (BCR). This is a system proposed and developed by the Article 29 Working Party[108] and requires organisations to develop a code of practice, which then has to be approved by every data protection authority in the jurisdictions in which they will be relied upon. Binding corporate rules might seem to be a more appropriate way of dealing with the practical issues that arise in relation to global data transfers and, especially for large multinational organisations, this system may prove to be an attractive alternative route to compliance with data protection rules. Nevertheless, their general adoption will clearly be a major undertaking; as yet, it is still at a relatively early stage of development and their use is not widespread.[109]

Data Protection in the UK: The Data Protection Act 1998

The **Data Protection Directive** was implemented in the UK by the **Data Protection Act 1998 (DPA 1998)**, which was finally brought into force on 1 March 2000. The structure of this statute is similar to that of its predecessor, the **Data Protection Act 1984**, but both are rather different from most other UK statutes. In relation to the 1984 Act, Stallworthy suggests that this arose because the main provisions follow the Council of Europe Convention and were therefore influenced by principles of statutory draftsmanship that are more usually associated with civil law systems.[110] The view of Aldhouse is that 'the Data Protection Act is unprecedented. Even the black letter criminal provisions make use of new concepts'.[111] Although both statutes are based on the premise of compliance with principles of good data management, the 'data protection principles' – which, as well as implementing the Directive, arguably have their origins in the Younger Report and can be discerned in the relevant international instruments on data protection – are not to found in the body of the statute, but are contained in a Schedule appended to the Act. The earlier statute was based on the notion of universal registration, but, unfortunately, the manner of drafting meant that these principles could only be enforced against those registered. This created a lacuna whereby the only action

---

106 Commission Decision 2001/497/EC of 15 June 2001 on standard contractual clauses for the transfer of personal data to third countries [2001] OJ L181/19.

107 Commission Decision 2010/87 of 5 February 2010 on standard contractual clauses for the transfer of personal data to processors established in third countries [2010] OJ L39/5; see discussion in Rohan Massey, 'Outsourcing: New standard contractual clauses for the transfer of personal data outside the EU' [2010] 16 CTLR 88.

108 See Article 29 Working Party, *Setting Forth a Co-operation Procedure for Issuing Common Opinions on Adequate Safeguards Resulting From 'Binding Corporate Rules'*, Working Document WP 107, and *Establishing a Model Checklist Application for Approval of Binding Corporate Rules*, Working Document WP 108, both available online at http://ec.europa.eu/justice/policies/privacy/workinggroup/wpdocs/2005_en.htm. The Working Party has subsequently published details of the operation of binding corporate rules (BCR) in *Setting up a Table with the Elements and Principles to be Found in Binding Corporate Rules*, Working Document WP 153, and *Setting up a Framework for the Structure of Binding Corporate Rules*, Working Document WP 154, both available online at http://ec.europa.eu/justice/policies/privacy/workinggroup/wpdocs/2008_en.htm

109 For further details of the operation of BCR, see Information Commissioner's Office (ICO), 'Binding Corporate Rules', available online at www.ico.gov.uk/for_organisations/data_protection/overseas/binding_corporate_rules.aspx; see also the discussion in Lingjie Kong, 'Data protection and transborder data flow in the European and global context' (2010) 21 EJIL 441.

110 Mark Stallworthy, 'Data protection: Regulation in a deregulatory state' [1990] Statute L Rev 130.

111 Francis GB Aldhouse, 'UK data protection: Where are we in 1991?' (1991) 5 LCT Yearbook 180, 184.

that could be taken against those not registered was a prosecution for non-registration, regardless of the degree to which the principles had apparently been flouted. This is no longer the case, because registration has now been superseded by a notification requirement and the principles can be enforced against all users regardless of whether notification has, in fact, taken place. The Information Commissioner[112] is given powers to enforce the principles with the aid of a range of enforcement notices. A number of criminal offences, and individual rights and remedies, are also created in the body of the statute.

Definitions

Although intended to implement the **Data Protection Directive**, Art 1 of which expressly refers to the privacy of the data subject, as already noted, the word 'privacy' appears nowhere in the **DPA 1998**. The Act applies to personal data, defined in s 1 as data relating to a living individual who can be identified from those data, or from a combination of those data and other information in the possession of the data controller. This includes expression of both opinion and intention. Further, the statute makes a distinction between sensitive and other personal data: the former being defined in s 2 as that pertaining to the data subject's racial or ethnic origin, his or her political opinions, religious or similar beliefs, trade union membership, physical or mental health or condition, sexual life, the commission or alleged commission of any offence, or related to any proceedings for such an offence. The data has to be 'processed' by means of 'equipment operating automatically' – that is, by computer – or be recorded as 'part of a relevant filing system'. This latter term refers to information not on computer, but manual files, which are structured either by reference to individuals or by reference to criteria relating to individuals in such a way that specific information relating to a particular individual is readily accessible. These statutory definitions of both 'personal data' and 'relevant filing system' were the subject of judicial discussion in *Durant v Financial Services Authority*.[113]

Durant's case arose out of a dispute with Barclays Bank that eventually led to him making a subject access request under **DPA 1998**, s 7, in order to obtain personal data about him held by the Financial Services Authority (FSA), which had been adjudicating his complaint with the bank. The FSA refused to provide all of the information to which Durant believed he was entitled, on the basis that it did not all constitute 'personal data' as defined or that, if it did, it was not contained within a 'relevant filing system'. As discussed later, the basic requirement in s 7 is to provide information constituting personal data, which means that the precise scope of this definition is vital in the assessment of the data subject's entitlement under the section. In addition, to the extent that some of the information might be contained in a 'relevant filing system' rather than on computer, the specific meaning of this phrase was also of significance. The argument for Durant was that both definitions suggested a 'wide and inclusive definition of "personal data"' and one that 'covered any information retrieved as a result of a search under his name, anything on file which had his name on it or from which he could be identified or from which it was possible to discern a connection with him'.[114] Although the Court of Appeal acknowledged the importance of interpreting the provisions of the Act in the light of the definition of personal data in Art 2 of the Directive, it came to the conclusion that the definition was not as wide as postulated by Durant. The fact that data might be retrieved from a search of a name was not sufficient to make it personal. Two further factors were needed: the first was whether the 'information is biographical in a significant sense'; the second was one of focus – that is, the data should not merely incidentally include reference to

---

112 The role of the Data Protection Commissioner created by the 1998 Act having been subsumed in the Office of Information Commissioner following the Freedom of Information Act 2000.

113 [2003] EWCA Civ 1746, [2004] FSR 28.

114 Ibid, [24].

the data subject. In sum, it needed to be 'information that affects his privacy, whether in his personal or family life, business or professional capacity'.[115]

Auld LJ went on to distinguish information about Durant and information about his complaints, and, in effect, said that the data Durant was trying to retrieve was not data about himself – that is, personal data – but data about his complaint and that this did not fall within the definition. He was also of the view that this narrow interpretation of personal data went 'hand in hand with a narrow meaning of "relevant filing system"'.[116] Having considered the provisions and objectives of the Act, and also of both the Directive and the Council of Europe Convention that preceded them, he was extremely influenced by the fact that, notwithstanding the Convention's provision permitting extension to manual data, the provisions of all of the instruments were substantially focused on computerised data and that the statutory provisions were only intended to be extended to manual records 'of sufficient sophistication to provide the same or similar ready accessibility as a computerised filing system'.[117] He therefore concluded that the term 'relevant filing system' referred to a system:

(1)   in which the files forming part of it are structured or referenced in such a way as clearly to indicate at the outset of the search whether specific information capable of amounting to personal data of an individual requesting it under s. 7 is held within the system and, if so, in which file or files it is held; and

(2)   which has, as part of its own structure or referencing mechanism, a sufficiently sophisticated and detailed means of readily indicating whether and where in an individual file or files specific criteria or information about the applicant can be readily located.[118]

Although it could be said that the definition of 'personal data' in Art 2 of the Directive does not seem to be limited in this way, as far as the data subject is concerned, the objective of the Directive is the protection of privacy rather than the provision of an unlimited right to control or retrieve every single mention of his or her name. Although more attention has subsequently been paid to the interpretation of the definitions of 'personal data' and 'relevant filing system' set out in *Durant*, the reference of Auld LJ to the fact that the statute should be construed to refer to 'information that affects his privacy' might be a more appropriate guide. This of itself could remove a number of references to data subjects from the ambit of 'personal data', although the subjectivity of the concept of privacy would inevitably create ambiguity and uncertainty in some cases. Certainly this could be construed as being in line with the view of the Article 29 Working Party on the subject, which pointed out that the data protection rules were designed to deal with situations in which the rights of individuals were at risk, and suggested that a balance should be achieved in which the data protection rules were not overstretched, but neither were they unduly restricted.[119] Durant was subsequently refused leave to appeal to the House of Lords,[120] and the Court of Appeal's interpretation of personal data and relevant filing system were subsequently applied in both *Johnson v Medical Defence Union*[121] and *Smith v Lloyds TSB Bank plc*.[122] Both Johnson and Smith argued in their individual cases that, because there was information that had been processed in the past on computer, it should be made available in response to the subject access request although it was no longer available in that format. Johnson, in particular, argued that even though the documentation in question no longer existed, it had been both recorded

---

115   Ibid, [28].
116   Ibid, [27].
117   Ibid, [48].
118   Ibid, [50].
119   Article 29 Working Party, Opinion 4/2007 on the concept of personal data.
120   Out-law.com, 'House of Lords ends Durant's data protection saga' (2005) *Out-law.com*, 30 November, available online at www.out-law.com/page-6405
121   [2004] EWHC 347.
122   [2005] EWHC 246 (Ch).

'with the intention that it is processed' and 'in a relevant filing system', and so fell within the definition of data in the **DPA 1998**.[123] Similarly, in *Smith*, the information sought had originally been kept on computer, but was no longer in that format when the request was made. In both cases, Laddie J declined to hold that this was personal data within the meaning of the 1998 Act[124] or that, on the facts, it was held in a 'relevant filing system'. For either claimant to succeed, it would have been necessary to show both that the information was personal data within the ruling in *Durant* and also that it was held in a relevant filing system at the time of the request.[125]

The House of Lords did, however, return to the issue of personal data in *Common Services Agency v Scottish Information Commissioner*,[126] a case under the **Freedom of Information Act (Scotland) 2002**. In this case, the Common Services Agency (CSA) refused to release information concerning the extent of childhood leukaemia, on the grounds that this might identify particular individuals, and that the data would therefore be personal data under the **DPA 1998** and so would fall within the exemption in s 38 of the Act. In response, the Scottish Information Commissioner required the CSA to 'barnadise' the data – a technique used to manipulate statistics prior to publication in order to reduce the possibility that any particular individual can be identified. As far as the Act was concerned, the question that had to be answered was whether or not the barnadised data was 'personal data' for the purposes of the Act so that the exemption in s 38 would be engaged. This could have been an opportunity to review the decision in *Durant*, but this was not to be. The Inner House of the Court of Session, using Auld LJ's two-factor approach, concluded that the effect of barnardisation was to move the focus of the information away from individual children so that it thus fell outside the definition of 'personal data'. In the House of Lords, however, Lord Hope said that although it may have that effect, that did not resolve the question, which required instead a consideration of the definition in **DPA 1998**, s 1(1), in the light of the provisions of the **Data Protection Directive**. In particular, this required a consideration of whether or not it was possible for the data controller or anyone else in possession of the barnadised data to identify a specific individual from either the data itself or in conjunction with other information. If not, then it was not information from which an individual could be identified, was therefore not personal data, and so fell outside the ambit of the Act. Which of these was the case was a question of fact for the Scottish Information Commissioner.[127] Lord Rodger further stated that there was no need to consider the kinds of issue addressed by the Court of Appeal in *Durant*; the significant issue was purely whether or not any individual was identifiable from the data.[128] The case thus leaves the *Durant* precedent in place, but without any review of the reasoning on which it is based.[129]

The Data Protection Principles

The eight data protection principles are listed in Pt I of Sch 1 to the 1998 Act and some guidance on their interpretation is contained in Pt II of that Schedule. Because some of the basic

---

123 [2004] EWHC 347, [30].
124 See also discussion in Case EA/2007/0058 *Harcup v Information Commissioner and Yorkshire Forward*, available online at www.informationtribunal.gov.uk/DBFiles/Decision/i37/harcupFinalDecision_050208.pdf
125 See also discussion in Usha Jagessar and Vicky Sedgwick, 'When is personal data not "personal data"? The impact of *Durant v FSA*' [2005] 21 CLSR 505.
126 [2008] 1 WLR 1550.
127 Ibid, [17]ff. The Scottish Information Commissioner subsequently concluded that, on the particular facts in question, the barnadised data were indeed personal data for the purposes of the DPA: Decision 021/2005, *Mr Michael Collie and the Common Services Agency for the Scottish Health Service* (26 May 2010), available online at www.itspublicknowledge.info/ApplicationsandDecisions/Decisions/2005/200500298.asp
128 Ibid, [74].
129 See also discussion in Richard Cumbley and Peter Church, 'What is personal data? The House of Lords identifies the issues – *Common Services Agency v Scottish Information Commissioner*' [2008] UKHL 47, [2008] 24 CLSR 565; Renate Gertz, 'Mr Collie Goes to London: The House of Lords decision in *Common Services Agency vs. The Scottish Information Commissioner*' (2009) 3(1) Studies in Ethics, Law, and Technology 4, available online at www.bepress.com/selt/vol3/iss1/art4

requirements contained in the 1998 data protection principles remain unchanged, a number of the cases decided under the 1984 Act remain of relevance.

Principle 1

1   Personal data shall be processed fairly and lawfully and, in particular, shall not be processed unless –

(a)   at least one of the conditions in Schedule 2 is met, and

(b)   in the case of sensitive personal data, at least one of the conditions in Schedule 3 is also met.

Scope of Processing

The definition of 'processing' in s 1(1) appears to envisage a wide meaning, encompassing the majority of acts that could be done during the life cycle of the data, starting with the initial obtaining, through to the final destruction. One question that arose was whether anonymising data – and, presumably therefore the barnadising referred to above in *CSA v Scottish Information Commissioner* – constituted processing and would therefore be subject to the requirements of the first principle. The problem was well illustrated by the facts of *R v Department of Health, ex p Source Informatics*.[130] Source Informatics provided software to pharmacists to record prescribing patterns of certain drugs by general practitioners (GPs), which could then be used by drug companies for marketing purposes. This was intended to be done with the consent and involvement of the GPs, and the information was all anonymised before being collated in this way. However, as a result of advice from the Department of Health that this information was subject to a duty of confidence, notwithstanding the fact of anonymisation, many pharmacists and GPs refused to participate. Source Informatics therefore sought judicial review of the decision of the Department of Health that the use of the data in this way would constitute a breach of confidence.

At first instance, Latham J was of the view both that the information was subject to a duty of confidence, whether or not it had been anonymised before being passed on, and that, absent the consent of the patient, there would be an offence (under the 1984 Act) for unauthorised use of data. He specifically rejected the 'sophistry' of a two-stage test.[131] The precise nature of the relationship between data protection and breach of confidence – and, indeed, between personal data and confidential data – has still to be fully explored, but a number of relevant points were made by the Court of Appeal that were in conflict with Latham J's reasoning concerning the potential application of the 1998 Act. The likely impact of the implementation of the 1995 Directive was considered, even though this post-dated the relevant policy information, and, specifically, whether the anonymising of data could be considered processing. If the answer were 'yes', then all of the conditions for lawful processing would apply, which might include the consent of the patients concerned; if the answer were 'no', then no consent or other conditions would be required. Simon Brown LJ, having considered the arguments for and against including anonymisation within the definition of processing, concluded that 'common sense and justice alike' favoured the proposition that it should not be included, and that such a finding would be 'unobjectionable'.[132]

The scope of processing has also been considered in a further case concerning Johnson's dispute with the Medical Defence Union (MDU).[133] Johnson was a consultant orthopaedic surgeon, whose professional indemnity cover was terminated by the MDU. In deciding both whether to

---

130 [2000] 1 All ER 786; see discussion in H Rowe, *Data Protection Act 1998: A Practical Guide*, 2000, Croydon: Tolley, pp 248ff.
131 [1999] 4 All ER 185, 192.
132 [2000] 1 All ER 786, 798.
133 *Johnson v Medical Defence Union (No 2)* [2007] EWCA Civ 262.

provide, refuse, or withdraw such cover, the MDU used risk assessment procedures based on the number of incidents or complaints on file about a subject, regardless of their severity or outcome. The number of such incidents relating to Johnson was such that a decision was made to terminate cover and this led to his litigation. In this second round, he sought compensation under the **DPA 1998**, s 13 (see later), on the grounds that, although the risk assessment had been carried out entirely according to the agreed rules, the policy of not taking into account whether any complaints had actually been substantiated led to unfair processing – in other words, that the Act effectively created a quasi-contractual right to a particular type of processing. At first instance, it was held that the procedure for reviewing his records that led to the adverse decision did not amount to actual processing of the data, but that even if it did, it had been carried out according to the agreed rules, of which Johnson was aware when he joined the MDU, and so could not be regarded as unfair.

Buxton LJ noted that the case raised issues that, in his view, had 'nothing or almost nothing to do with the protection of privacy and integrity of a person'.[134] In a lengthy decision, the majority found that a case officer had reviewed Johnson's records (that is, a human, not an automatic, judgment) and that her subsequent decision to make a recommendation to the risk assessment group that his cover should be withdrawn did not constitute processing of the data. This was so even though the case officer had downloaded the relevant files prior to review, which did constitute processing, and had then recorded her recommendation on computer. The act complained of was a human judgment based on the information extracted – something that the majority distinguished from 'processing' within the meaning of the Act. The dissenting judgment of Arden LJ carefully considered the definition of processing in the **DPA 1998** in the light of the Directive and concluded that all stages in the process, including the selection and judgment of the records, constituted processing. Buxton LJ had also considered the Directive's provisions, but had given particular weight to the Recitals at the expense of the actual provisions of the Directive, whereas Arden LJ's analysis arguably shows a greater understanding of the interpretation of European directives and also avoids the artificiality of dissecting the decision-making process. However, despite this difference in relation to processing, the judges were unanimous that Johnson's appeal failed, because, in any event, the 'processing' could not be regarded as unfair.[135]

Fairness

Assuming that there is processing as defined, then, by virtue of the first principle, this must be carried out both fairly and lawfully. Some of the cases on fairness under the 1984 Act remain relevant. An example is the decision of the Data Protection Tribunal[136] in *Innovations Mail Order v DPR*.[137] As well as supplying goods by mail order, this firm derived a significant amount of its income by trading in lists of customer names and addresses, and making these lists available to other companies for direct marketing purposes (so-called 'list rental'). The enterprise supplied goods in response to orders from its catalogues and in response to advertisements placed in the media. Customers ordering directly from the catalogues were advised of the possibility of their details being made available for other purposes, but those responding to the advertisements did not receive this information until after they had placed an order – that is, after they had supplied their personal details in response to the advertisement. The company argued that it was not practicable to provide notice of this practice in all other media advertisements, because of time and space constraints, and that later notification was more appropriate, because it would allow customers to be given more choice over the potential use of their information. The Data Protection Registrar, on the other hand, argued

---

134 Ibid, [1].
135 Ibid, [63], per Buxton LJ, and [149], per Arden LJ.
136 Subsumed into the jurisdiction of the Information Tribunal following the coming into force of the Freedom of Information Act 2000. This tribunal is now referred to as the 'First–tier Tribunal (Information Rights)'.
137 Case DA/92 31/49/1, available online at www.informationtribunal.gov.uk/DBFiles/Decision/i163/innovations.pdf

that if the obtaining were to be fair, the customer had to be aware of all of the potential uses of personal details at the time that the order was made. In the company's appeal against the notice, the Data Protection Tribunal found that the data could not be regarded as fairly obtained (now a part of processing) unless due notice was given to the customer as to the likely use of his or her data in advance of the data being, or at the point at which the data was, obtained.

Any assessment of whether processing is fair will need to take into account the purposes of processing, the type of processing, and the consequences to the data subject. Consideration of some of these issues arose out of a number of appeals under the 1984 Act against enforcement notices served against certain credit reference agencies. In each case, the important fact was that the method of processing was too wide – typically by address rather than by name, resulting in persons being judged to be bad credit risks on the basis of another person's record. This was illustrated, by what was agreed to be a representative complaint, in the case of CCN *Systems Ltd and CCN Credit Systems Ltd v Data Protection Registrar*.[138] J had bought a house from W. Three years later, J applied for a cheque guarantee card, but was refused and was told that CCN had provided the credit reference. A copy of his file (obtained under s 158 of the **Consumer Credit Act 1974**) showed a judgment against W. The only connection between J and W was that they had, at separate times, lived at the same address. Two important points were made in the Tribunal's decision that unfairness had been made out: first, that the purpose of the legislation is to protect the rights of the individual; and second, that the standard required is one of objective fairness. It is therefore irrelevant whether or not the data user had the motive or intention to process the data unfairly. A further case, *Infolink Ltd v Data Protection Registrar*,[139] discussed the 'extraction of information constituting the data'; although this is no longer part of the statutory definition, it is arguably the process that was at issue in *Johnson v MDU (No 2)*. In addition, it clarified the position in relation to balancing the competing interests of the individual and the processor. It was noted that the fact that, in CCN, the needs of the individual had been referred to as paramount did not mean that the applicant's interests prevailed over all other interests; it was necessary to balance various considerations in relation to both subject and user, but, in so doing, the Tribunal was entitled to give more weight to the interests of the individual, in line with the objectives of the legislation. The **DPA 1998** was subsequently to increase the emphasis on individual rights, which itself is likely to tip the balance in favour of the data subject in such cases.[140]

Criteria for Fair Processing

In addition to the general requirement of fair and lawful processing, the first data protection principle further stipulates that, in any event, data shall not be processed unless one of the conditions in either Sch 2 (for non-sensitive data) or Sch 3 (for sensitive data) is met.

The constraints on processing implement Arts 7 and 8 of the Directive (see above), and are based on a requirement of consent, unless the processing falls within one of the listed categories for which the process or its purpose is deemed necessary. As in the Directive provisions discussed above, a higher standard – that of *explicit* consent – is required for sensitive data. Further, the definition of 'consent' provided in the Directive is not transposed into the Act, but general approaches to statutory interpretation would suggest that the Directive provision would provide the definitive standard. Although there are different approaches to consent in different areas of law,[141] as discussed above, the extent to which implied consent might be effective is a moot point. Shaw LJ, in *Bell v Alfred*

---

138 Case DA/90 25/49/9, available online at www.informationtribunal.gov.uk/DBFiles/Decision/i166/ccn_systems.pdf
139 Case DA/90 25/49/6, available online at www.informationtribunal.gov.uk/DBFiles/Decision/i233/infolink.pdf
140 See also the assessment of fairness in Cases EA/2007/0096, 98, 99, 108, 127, *Chief Constables of Humberside, Staffordshire, Northumbria, West Midlands and Greater Manchester v Information Commissioner*, [161]–[166], available online at www.informationtribunal.gov.uk/ DBFiles/Decision/i200/Chief_Constables_v_IC_final_decision_2007081_web_entry[1].pdf
141 See discussion in Jay, op cit, pp 150–2.

Franks & Bartlett Co Ltd,[142] distinguished 'consent' from mere acquiescence, suggesting that the former required an active rather than a passive step – an action of a 'positive affirmative kind'. Such distinctions, and cases such as *Linguaphone v DPR*[143] and particularly *British Gas Trading Ltd v Data Protection Registrar*,[144] have resulted in a change from the use of opt-out boxes to opt-in boxes by which data subjects can notify their consent for their data to be passed on to other data controllers.

Principle 2

Personal data shall be obtained only for one or more specified and lawful purposes, and shall not be further processed in any manner incompatible with that purpose or those purposes.

The facts of *Macgregor v Procurator Fiscal of Kilmarnock*, a case under the 1984 Act,[145] provide an example of a violation of this principle. The neighbour of a police officer was concerned about the man with whom his 18-year-old daughter was living and asked the police officer if he could find out any information for him. Certain information about the man in question was obtained from both the Police National Computer and the Scottish Criminal Records Computer, and the police officer communicated some of this to the daughter in a telephone call, with the intention of trying to persuade her to return to her father. Although it was accepted that he had good motives, his actions could not be equated with policing purposes, and he was found to have used the information for another purpose.

Principle 3

Personal data shall be adequate, relevant and not excessive in relation to the purpose or purposes for which they are processed.

The interpretation of this principle has been discussed in a number of tribunal decisions prior to the 1998 Act. During the existence of the short-lived Community Charge, or 'Poll Tax', a number of complaints were received that information required by those administering the tax was in excess of that needed. The task of compiling and maintaining the register of those who were subject to the charge was the duty of the Community Charge registration officers (CCROs) in each area, who were provided with guidance by the then Data Protection Registrar about the minimum amount of information that they could hold that was compatible with their intended purposes. However, a number of CCROs continued to gather information about the type of property inhabited – a factor that was argued to have no relevance to the levying of a per capita tax and was found to breach this principle.[146] Another case arrived at the same conclusion in relation to the gathering of information regarding dates of birth, which could be relevant to certain categories of individual whose eligibility to pay the Community Charge was related to their age, but in other cases was far in excess of what was required to administer the Community Charge.[147]

---

142 [1980] 1 All ER 356.
143 Case DA/94 31/49/1, available online at www.informationtribunal.gov.uk/DBFiles/Decision/i164/Linguaphone_Institute.pdf
144 Case DA98 3/49/2, available online at www.informationtribunal.gov.uk/DBFiles/Decision/i162/british_gas.pdf
145 23 June 1993 (unreported).
146 Cases DA/90 24/49/3–5, *Community Charge Registration Officers of Runnymede BC, South Northamptonshire DC and Harrow BC v Data Protection Registrar*, available online at www.informationtribunal.gov.uk/DBFiles/Decision/i167/CCRO.pdf
147 Case DA/90 25/49/2 *Community Charge Registration Officer of Rhondda BC v Data Protection Registrar*, available online at www.informationtribunal.gov.uk/DBFiles/Decision/i168/CCRO2.pdf

Principle 4

Personal data shall be accurate and, where necessary, kept up to date.

Guidance on the interpretation of this principle is contained in Part II of Sch 1 to deal with the situation in which the data is found to be inaccurate, but nevertheless is an accurate representation of information supplied by a third party.

Principle 5

Personal data processed for any purpose or purposes shall not be kept for longer than is necessary for that purpose or those purposes.

The objective of this principle is to encourage data to be reviewed and destroyed at appropriate intervals, removing the possible temptation to process for further purposes, which might also fall foul of principles 1 and 2. One of the complaints in *Pal v General Medical Council & ors*[148] was that personal data had been kept longer than was justified. The case arose out of complaints made by Dr Pal to the General Medical Council (GMC) in the spring of 2000 about the treatment of elderly patients. Although the complaint was closed in October 2000, correspondence continued between the defendants in which were expressed personal views about Dr Pal's actions. There was no complaint about her from either colleagues or patients, but nevertheless, despite the GMC's retention policy, which required documentation in such cases to be destroyed after six months, relevant material was still available four years later. At a preliminary hearing, the argument that this was because the GMC was reconsidering its policy on document retention received little sympathy from the court, which concluded that the chances of Pal succeeding at trial were 'promising', because 'either [the GMC] is acting in compliance with the legislation or it is not. The fact that it may be spending several years deciding when, whether and how to comply cannot excuse or justify non-compliance'.[149]

A number of recent cases arose out of a number of complaints that criminal convictions frequently remained on the Police National Computer (PNC) even after more than twenty years of non-offending and when the offences themselves were not of a serious nature. While it was accepted that it was a police purpose to disclose conviction data held on the PNC to bodies such as the Criminal Records Bureau and Independent Safeguarding Agency for the carrying out of their statutory duties, this did not mean that there was a duty to retain data for this purpose when it was no longer required for core policing purposes. However, the Court of Appeal, in allowing appeals from the decision of the Information Tribunal that the data in question had been kept for longer than necessary, held that whether or not particular records could be regarded as still relevant was not a question for the Information Commissioner, but for the police themselves, taking all of the relevant circumstances into account.[150]

Principle 6

Personal data shall be processed in accordance with the rights of data subjects under this Act.

---

148 [2004] EWHC 1485.
149 Ibid, [31].
150 *Chief Constable of Humberside Police and ors v Information Commissioner (Secretary of State for the Home Department intervening)* [2010] 1 WLR 1136.

This principle will be complied with as long as data controllers comply with the substantive provisions dealing with the rights of the data subject contained in the body of the statute, covering the right of subject access, the right to prevent processing likely to cause damage or distress, the right to prevent processing for the purposes of direct marketing, and rights in relation to automated decision-making.

The Right of Access to Personal Data

The subject access right is found in **DPA 1998**, s 7, and, despite its length and detail, compliance with this section is not necessarily a straightforward matter. The first issue is the definition of personal data, since it is only that to which the data subject has a right of access. As discussed above, this definition has been construed narrowly by the Court of Appeal in *Durant v FSA*,[151] and neither were any significant questions raised as to its ambit by the ECJ in *Bodil Lindqvist*. Further, in *Durant*, Auld LJ pointed out that the purpose of s 7 was to allow a data subject to ascertain that any processing being carried out by the data controller was not unlawfully infringing his or her privacy, but that it was 'not an automatic key to any information readily accessible or not of matters in which he may be named or informed'.[152] Subject access requests may be quite burdensome for the data controller, especially in cases in which, as is not uncommon, the data subject requests all information that is held on him or her and/or has other motives for obtaining the information. This was the situation in *Ezsias v Welsh Ministers*,[153] in which Ezsias, who was in an employment dispute with the North Glamorgan NHS Trust, made a succession of data subject access requests to the National Assembly for Wales. He had been involved in voluminous correspondence about the issues raised in his dispute with a number of departments and the evidence was that there was extensive documentation, which had to be assessed to ascertain whether or not it could be released in response to the request. The facts and procedural history of the case are complex, but the judgment in the case points out that the wording of s 7 merely gives a right to know about whether personal data are being processed, for what purposes, and to what recipients disclosure is made. Although there was a requirement to communicate the information constituting the personal data that could be complied with by providing the actual document, the right itself was not 'coterminous with a right to disclosure of documents'.[154] The decision also considered the problems encountered by data controllers to voluminous requests such as this, and concluded that the duty on controllers was to make a 'reasonable and proportionate search'. A number of commentators believe this to be somewhat controversial.[155] Carey suggests that 'the judgment in this case seems to make assumptions about data protection law which are not immediately obvious from the wording of the relevant legal provisions',[156] although Rodway and Church find that the 'reasonable and proportionate search' requirement was 'clearly signposted by earlier decisions'.[157] It is true that there was some discussion of proportionality in *Durant*, although this was in the context of relevant filing systems rather than s 7.[158] Also **DPA 1998**, s 8(2), makes it possible for the data controller not to provide a copy of the data sought in permanent form if this would involve disproportionate effort, but this does not refer to the search to locate the personal data, which was one of the main issues in *Ezsias*.

---

151 [2003] EWCA Civ 1746.
152 Ibid, [27].
153 [2007] EWHC 815 (QB).
154 Ibid, [53]–[54].
155 See, eg, Suzanne Rodway and Peter Church, 'Wanting it all: Unreasonable subject access requests' (2008) 19(2) Comp & L 24, 25; Gary Brooks, 'Implications of *Ezsias'* Case for subject access: Proportionality may apply to searches of data' (2008) 8 PDP 5(3). The Court of Appeal granted leave to appeal on this point: [2008] EWCA Civ 874, [13]; but there have been no subsequent proceedings.
156 Peter Carey, *Data Protection: A Practical Guide to UK and EU Law*, 2009, Oxford: Oxford University Press.
157 Above n 154.
158 [2003] EWCA Civ 1746 [45]–[50].

However, because this statute implements the **Data Protection Directive**, the concept of proportionality should perhaps suffuse its more general interpretation – proportionality being one of the fundamental doctrines of EU law; as Brooks concludes, it would also be 'illogical for proportionality to only apply to the supply of a copy of the data, when the real difficulty and expense is in locating, retrieving and collating the information in the first place'.[159] There is, though, another approach allowed for in the statute to assist in locating data in response to a subject access request: s 7(3) provides that where data controllers reasonably require further information to locate the information sought by the data subject, then they are not obliged to comply unless provided with that further information. This envisages a dialogue between the data subject and data controller to assist in the retrieval of the relevant information, which could go some way towards alleviating the problems associated with large-scale searches of documents and data.

Beyond this, s 7(4)–(6) potentially raise considerable uncertainty for the controller regarding the circumstances in which personal data can be revealed when to do so might reveal data about a third party. Although such disclosure can clearly be legitimised by the consent of the third party, uncertainty arises when such consent cannot be obtained. Section 7(6) requires, amongst other things, the controller to have particular regard to any duty of confidentiality owed to the other individual, any steps taken to seek the consent of the other individual, whether the individual is capable of giving consent, and any express refusal of consent. Overall, though, an assessment has to be made as to whether, in the words of s 7(4)(b), it is nevertheless 'reasonable in all the circumstances' to comply with the subject access request. The balancing of interests that this entails was discussed in *Durant*. Auld LJ pointed out that the question was whether it was reasonable for the data controller to comply with the request rather than reasonable to refuse to comply, and that 'reasonableness' in the circumstances did not mean there was an explicit requirement to seek the third party's consent. It was also important to consider the legitimate interests of such third parties, including their right to privacy in making the decision. In conclusion, he suggested that:

> . . . it all depends on the circumstances whether it would be reasonable to disclose to a data subject the name of another person figuring in his personal data, whether that person is a source, or a recipient or likely recipient of that information, or has a part in the matter the subject of the personal data. . . . I believe that the courts should be wary of attempting to devise any principles of general application one way or the other.[160]

Rather than laying down any guidelines for the anxious data controller, this judgment serves only to underline the potential difficulties in deciding whether it is 'reasonable in all the circumstances' to disclose the information.

A further problem could arise with the potential clash between a putative duty of confidentiality and the data subject's right of access. This is illustrated most clearly by the issue of when a reference given in 'confidence' nevertheless may be disclosed to the data subject. References given by a data controller 'in confidence' are exempt from the subject access provisions by virtue of the miscellaneous exemption in s 7(1), but this appears to have no effect on the exercise of the subject access right to the data controller who receives such a reference. Can such references remain confidential? Briefly, the general requirement at common law is that an obligation of confidence will arise if the information is confidential in the sense that it is not known to others and is given in circumstances in which the receiver is made aware that there is an expectation of confidentiality. A party to whom information is given in confidence may not divulge it unless there are specific grounds for doing so; these are the consent of the confider, legal compulsion, or overriding public

---

159 Rodway and Church, op cit.
160 [2003] EWCA Civ 1746, [66].

interest. The only relevant one here would be consent, which, as in s 7(4), will obviously legitimise disclosure. Where third party data might be revealed, what role does this obligation play in the balancing act required by s 7(4)–(6)? One construction of the requirement in s 7(6) to have regard to any duty of confidentiality could be that a confidence is not overridden merely by the right of subject access. On the other hand, s 27(5), which provides that, but for the provisions on exemptions, the 'subject information provisions shall have effect notwithstanding any enactment or rule of law prohibiting or restricting the disclosure, or authorising the withholding, of information', could be construed as suggesting the opposite. In summary, consent will always validate the disclosure of third-party information, but in other cases, data controllers may be faced with a complex balancing exercise.[161]

Other Rights of the Data Subject

In line with the Directive, the 1998 Act now includes specific rights to prevent processing likely to cause damage or distress (s 10), to prevent processing for purposes of direct marketing (s 11), and in relation to automated decision-making (s 12). The right in s 11 was a central issue in *Robertson v Wakefield Metropolitan District Council*.[162] Robertson wished to have his name withheld from the electoral register because he objected to the practice of selling the register for use for direct marketing purposes. The electoral registration officer refused on the grounds that it was a legal requirement for electors to complete the requisite form and be included in the register. The court considered the provisions in Art 14(b) of the Directive and its implementation in **DPA 1998**, s 11, and found that s 11 implemented the requirement in Art 14(b) and that, even if it did not, Art 14(b) had direct effect, so that it could be relied on by an individual. It was therefore held that the legal rules concerning representation of the people must be construed 'in a manner which is Directive-compliant and consistent with the Data Protection Act 1998'. As a result, the electoral register is now in two parts: the full version lists the details of all those entitled to vote and cannot be used for direct marketing purposes; the edited version includes the details of those people who are willing for their data to be made available for other purposes.

The rights in ss 10–12 may all be exerted by application to court and the ability to claim compensation provided in s 13 is no longer restricted merely to cases of inaccuracy, loss, or unauthorised disclosure. In cases of inaccuracy, s 14 also gives the court the power to order rectification, blocking, erasure, and destruction of the relevant data.

Principle 7

> Appropriate technical and organisational measures shall be taken against unauthorised or unlawful processing of personal data and against accidental loss or destruction of, or damage to, personal data.

Again guidance on interpretation is given in Pt II of the Schedule, which suggests that what is an appropriate level of security depends on the state of technological development and the nature of the data to be protected. The data controller must also take reasonable steps to ensure the reliability of any employees who have access to the personal data. The specific reference to the state of

---

161 Note that there are certain cases in which consent is deemed to be given by virtue of the third party's professional status: see, eg, Data Protection (Subject Access Modification) (Health) Order 2000, SI 2000/413; Data Protection (Subject Access Modification) (Education) Order 2000, SI 2000/414; Data Protection (Subject Access Modification) (Social Work) Order 2000, SI 2000/415.
162 [2002] QB 1095.

technological development is an interesting one, because it is unclear to what extent technical solutions to privacy protection, such as the use of encryption, can be specifically required by the law on data protection. Where personal data is particularly sensitive or confidential, it may be that the seventh data protection principle will not be deemed to be complied with without the use of cryptography or other technical mechanism. Absence of encryption was the reason why an enforcement notice was issued against Marks & Spencer following the theft of a laptop containing details of 26,000 employees.[163] The overriding duty to ensure the security of the data is placed on data controllers even when there is outsourcing to a data processor.

Principle 8

> Personal data shall not be transferred to a country or territory outside the European Economic Area unless that country or territory ensures an adequate level of protection for the rights and freedoms of data subjects in relation to the processing of personal data.

The issues that arise from transborder data flow that are the subject of the eighth principle have already been discussed above in relation to Arts 25 and 26 of the Directive.

Exemptions

There is a long list of exemptions from some or all of the requirements of the Act. The so-called 'primary exemptions' are to be found in ss 28–36 and include: national security; four separate categories of crime; taxation; health; education and social work; regulatory activity; research, history and statistics; special purposes (that is, artistic, literary, and journalistic purposes); information made available to the public by law; disclosures required by law or in connection with legal proceedings; and domestic purposes. These broadly mirror the provisions of the Directive in Arts 3(2) and 13. In addition, Sch 7 contains the 'miscellaneous exemptions', specific to the **DPA 1998**, which include provisions relating to: preparation of confidential references (referred to above); armed forces; judicial appointments; Crown employment; management forecasts; negotiations; corporate finance; examination scripts and marks; legal professional privilege; and self-incrimination. The fact that a topic is apparently covered by an exemption does not necessarily imply that the exemption is from the requirements of the Act in toto and the precise terms of the exemption will need to be studied in each case; some examples are considered below.

The 'crime' exemption in s 29 exempts only from the first data protection principle (except to the extent that it requires compliance with the conditions in Schs 2 and 3) and s 7, the right of subject access. Further, this exemption only applies to the extent that the application of those provisions would be likely to prejudice the prevention or detection of crime. So, in many cases, the full force of the Act will apply, and, in all cases, the police will be required to process personal data in conformity with the majority of the principles; remedies are also available to those whose rights have been compromised.[164] In contrast, the exemption on the grounds of national security found in s 28 has the potential to exclude from data protection law all processing of personal data that could be construed to come under this head. The ambit of s 28 is very wide: it exempts from

---

163 See www.ico.gov.uk/upload/documents/library/data_protection/notices/m_and_s_sanitiseden.pdf. For further discussion of the role of cryptography in data protection, see, eg, SA Price, 'Understanding contemporary cryptography and its wider impact upon the general law' (1999) 13 Int Rev LC & T 95, 108ff. See further discussion of encryption in Chapter 6.

164 For application of the data protection principles to policing and crime data, see also Cases EA/2007/0096, 98, 99, 108, 127 *Chief Constables of Humberside, Staffordshire, Northumbria, West Midlands and Greater Manchester v Information Commissioner*, above.

compliance with the data protection principles as well as the provisions on the rights of the data subject, notification of processing and enforcement procedures. Given the non-applicability of the data protection principles to personal data processed for national security purposes, there can be no assurance that the processing will be fair or that other guarantees will be provided related, for example, to adequacy and relevancy. Removing the need to comply with the principles allows users to be cavalier with the personal data of others and, accepting that there might be corresponding problems with enforcement and the provision of remedies, it is difficult to see what would be lost by requiring adherence to the principles, especially those relating to fair and lawful processing for the purposes for which the data were collected. However, the precise wording of the exemption does suggest that exemption should not be granted if compliance with the Act is possible without prejudicing national security. In theory, therefore, there is no automatic blanket exemption.

Although s 28 only applies to data processed 'for the purpose of safeguarding national security', s 28(2) provides that a certificate signed by a relevant Minister is all that is required as 'conclusive evidence' of this fact. Section 28(4) and (5) then give a person 'directly affected' by such a certificate the right to appeal to the Information Tribunal, which may allow the certificate to be quashed if it is satisfied that the Minister did not have reasonable grounds for issuing it. The scope and effect of these provisions was considered in *Norman Baker MP v Secretary of State for the Home Department*.[165] The case arose out of a subject access request by the Member of Parliament (MP) Norman Baker for all of the information held on him by the security services. A certificate, as detailed in s 28(2), had been issued by the Home Secretary, which was both 'detailed and carefully drafted'.[166] Although there were differences between the treatment of personal data in different categories, the overall effect of the certificate could 'fairly be described as a blanket exemption for "any personal data that is processed by the Security Service" in the performance of its statutory functions'.[167] In particular, this meant that there was an exemption from s 7(1)(a) relating to subject access, which supported the use of a 'neither confirm nor deny' policy whereby data subjects would not be informed whether or not data was, in fact, held. Accordingly, Baker was informed that the security services would notify of processing of personal data for staff administration, building security CCTV, and commercial agreements, but that it held no information on him in those categories and that all other processing was exempt from the requirements of the **DPA 1998**. Baker subsequently appealed against this decision and, in its consideration of the matter, the Tribunal itemised a number of general considerations that applied to the work of the security services and the need for some of its work to remain secret. In particular, there was agreement that it was a necessary policy objective that some of this work should remain secret, even to the extent of not revealing that files existed, and that – in some cases at least – a 'neither confirm nor deny' policy was justifiable.[168] However, the point was made that the blanket exemption absolved the security services from any need to consider individual cases on either their particular merits or whether they actually do pose any threat to national security.

In its decision, the Tribunal, accepting that national security was obviously a legitimate aim, nevertheless considered that proportionality was of central importance – especially where individual rights were at stake and there was discretion in the review process. Having considered the relevant case law – notably, the decisions of the Privy Council in *De Freitas v Permanent Secretary of Ministry of Agriculture, Fisheries, Land and Housing*,[169] and the House of Lords in *R(Daly) v Secretary of State for the Home Department*[170] – the Tribunal concluded that 'where convention rights are engaged, judicial review

165 www.informationtribunal.gov.uk/Documents/nsap/baker.pdf
166 Ibid, [25].
167 Ibid.
168 Ibid, [35].
169 [1999] 1 AC 69.
170 [2001] 2 WLR 1622.

principles may require a more intrusive judicial attitude' and that this would always be sensitive to the context of the subject matter of the review. In the context of national security matters in particular, there was no area in which 'judges have traditionally deferred more to the executive view than that of national security; and for good and sufficient reason'.[171] Taking all of these issues into account, the Tribunal concluded, amongst other things, that the blanket exemption was wider than was necessary to protection national security and resulted in individual requests not being considered on their merits, and also that some personal data could be released without endangering national security and that the burden of responding to such requests would not be unduly onerous. The certificate issued under s 28(2) was quashed, but the Tribunal pointed out that this did not inevitably mean that all s 7 requests would need to be responded to, because a new certificate could be issued, provided that it took into account the points made in the decision.[172]

The 'Special Purposes'

The other exemption that has received judicial consideration is that relating to the special purposes contained in **DPA 1998**, s 32, which implements Art 9 of the **Data Protection Directive** relating to data protection and freedom of expression. To the extent that data protection is a facet of privacy, there is always going to be a tension between the rights guaranteed under the data protection legislation and the right to freedom of expression, in so far as that might involve discussion of an individual's personal details. Section 32 provides that where processing is for the publication of journalistic, artistic, or literary material and that the data controller reasonably believes that publication is in the public interest, then the processing is exempt from the provisions relating to the rights of the data subject in so far as these might be incompatible with that publication.

The application of this exemption was considered in *Campbell v MGN*. The case arose as a result of photographs published by the *Daily Mirror* of the model, Naomi Campbell, arriving at meetings of Narcotics Anonymous. The ensuing litigation was based on breach of confidence, privacy, and also the right in **DPA 1998**, s 13, to receive compensation for processing likely to cause damage or distress. Whether or not the publication was in the public interest was thus central to the adjudication. In the High Court,[173] Morland J found publication not to be in the public interest. In relation to the claim under the Act, he held that the published information constituted 'sensitive personal information' and that the newspaper had therefore failed to comply with the first data protection principle, because none of the relevant conditions in Schs 2 and 3 had been satisfied; neither could the newspaper rely in the exemption in s 32, because he held that this exemption applied up to – but not on or after – publication.

The Court of Appeal approached the application of the exemption in a different manner. It considered three specific questions: whether the Act applied to the publication of newspapers and other hard copies that had been subject to data processing; whether s 32 applied up to the moment of publication; and whether s 32 applied to the publication itself. In answer to the first question, an examination of the objectives of the legislation and the Directive that it implemented, the competing balance between the rights of privacy and freedom of expression given in the **European Convention on Human Rights (ECHR)** and referred to in the Recitals to the Directive, and the general scope of both the Directive and the Act resulted in the finding that 'the publication forms part of the processing and falls within the scope of the Act'.[174] An assessment of the relevant provisions did not, however, lead to the conclusion that s 32 only applied pre-publication. Indeed, the reverse was the

171 *Baker v Home Secretary*, [69]–[76].
172 Ibid, [113]–[116].
173 [2002] EWHC 499.
174 [2003] QB 633, [96]–[106].

case, for 'if these provisions apply only up to the moment of publication it is impossible to see what purpose they serve'.[175] In addition:

> it would seem totally illogical to exempt the data controller from the obligation, prior to publication, to comply with provisions which he reasonably believes are incompatible with journalism, but to leave him exposed to a claim for compensation under section 13 the moment that the data have been published.[176]

Having decided unequivocally that s 32 could, in general, be relied on at all stages of the publication process, the Court went on to consider whether or not the provisos in s 32(1) could be relied on in this particular case. In the High Court, Morland J had accepted the editor of the *Daily Mirror's* evidence regarding why he had decided to publish. This was deemed sufficient to satisfy the public interest test in s 32(2), based on the fact that Campbell was a role model for young people; she had nevertheless been involved in the use of drugs over a period of time despite public denials and had now 'admitted to drug addiction, chosen to seek help for it, and had demonstrated real commitment to tackling her problem by regular attendance at Narcotics Anonymous over a prolonged period'. The reason why it was not possible to comply with the data protection legislation was that Campbell had 'made it plain that there was no consent to the publication'. On this basis, the Court of Appeal decided that the public interest justified the publication of the article without Miss Campbell's consent.[177]

This decision was referred to with favour by the High Court in *Douglas v Hello* (No 5) as making 'an understanding of the Act easier than do the unvarnished provisions of the Act itself'.[178] This much-publicised case concerned the unauthorised publication of the wedding of Michael Douglas and Catherine Zeta-Jones by *Hello!* magazine when exclusive coverage had been granted to a rival publication. In that case, *Hello!* was not able to rely on the s 32 exemption, because there was 'no credible evidence' that the publication of the photographs could be in the public interest. However, the decision in favour of publication in *Campbell* was subsequently reversed by a divided House of Lords, which considered the balance between the rights guaranteed in Arts 8 and 10 of the **ECHR**, and concluded that:

> . . . looking at the publication as a whole and taking account of all the circumstances the claimant's right pursuant to [A]rticle 8 to respect for her private life outweighed the newspaper's right pursuant to [A]rticle 10 to freedom of expression; and that, accordingly, publication of the additional information and the accompanying photographs constituted an unjustified infringement of the claimant's right to privacy.[179]

However, there was no discussion of the interpretation of the **DPA 1998** as such, and it seems reasonable to assume therefore that the judgment of the Court of Appeal with respect to the application of s 32 to all stages of the publication process remains authoritative.

Administration and Enforcement

The **Data Protection Directive** refers to a 'supervisory authority', but is not prescriptive about the way in which its requirements should be enforced and administered. Most Member States have set

---

175 Ibid, [117].
176 Ibid, [119].
177 Ibid, [132].
178 [2003] EMLR 31, [230].
179 [2004] 2 AC 457.

up a specific commission and commissioner for this purpose.[180] In the UK, the role of Data Protection Commissioner established in the 1998 Act, which continued the role of Data Protection Registrar under the 1984 Act, has now been subsumed within the role of Information Commissioner. The functions and duties of this office are detailed in Pt VI of the Act and include: promoting good practice and observance of the Act by data controllers; producing codes of practice; reporting to Parliament; providing assistance to individuals who are bringing proceedings under certain sections of the Act; and participating in international cooperation. The Commissioner also has a role in enforcement and, inter alia, is empowered by s 40 to issue enforcement notices where he or she 'is satisfied that a data controller has contravened or is contravening any of the data protection principles'. However, the enforcement of the data protection principles has recently been enhanced by new ss 55A and 55B,[181] which give the Commissioner the power to impose monetary penalties for serious breaches. There are clearly potential conflicts of interest when the roles of policeman, judge, and jury – as well as sometimes lawgiver – are combined in the one office, but the original rationale was the need for best use of resources, together with consistency of approach.[182] This combination of responsibilities at the primary enforcement level is common to a number of other regulatory regimes; however, it is rare to have one individual responsible for such a range of activities. Whatever the conflicts between the varying roles of the Commissioner, the enforcement function is, arguably, of central importance, with other duties, such as dissemination of information, being ancillary to this. This is in contrast with data protection commissioners in some other jurisdictions, whose role can be likened more to that of an ombudsman.[183]

The Information Commissioner also has powers to bring criminal proceedings in relation to the commission of the offences created by the legislation. Most of these are regulatory offences of strict liability, all of which are qualified by a defence of due diligence. Thus, s 21 of the 1998 Act makes it an offence not to register particulars with the Commissioner or to fail to notify any changes in these particulars, and s 47 creates an offence for failure to comply with a notice. Section 55, on the other hand, creates a number of other offences relating to the unauthorised obtaining of personal data. The offences created by this section are all based on obtaining, disclosing, or procuring disclosure 'knowingly or recklessly' – a phrase that also qualified similar offences in s 5(5) of the 1984 Act. In *Data Protection Registrar v Amnesty International (British Section)*,[184] Amnesty was charged under both s 5(2)(b) and (d) of the 1984 Act in relation to two offences of trading in and disclosure of personal information for purposes and to persons not described in the Register. At first instance, Amnesty was acquitted, on the basis that the relevant factor was foreseeability of harm, rather than whether or not the user had been reckless as to the management of the data in a manner incompatible with the registration. Using this test, because the outcome of the action was merely an unsolicited mailing, it was held that Amnesty had not been reckless. On appeal to the divisional court by way of case stated, it was held that the seriousness of the consequences of the breach had been confused with the breach itself. In ruling that the appropriate definition of 'recklessness' for s 5 was an objective definition,[185] it had to be shown both that the circumstances were such that the ordinary prudent individual would realise that his or her act was capable of causing the kind of damage that the section was designed to prevent, that the risk could not justifiably be treated as negligible, and that the defendant had either given no thought to the possibility of that risk or had nevertheless continued with the act in question – in other words, the recklessness required was foresight of serious harmful consequences. This decision was criticised on the basis that the need

---

180 See http://ec.europa.eu/justice/policies/privacy/nationalcomm/index_en.htm
181 Inserted by the Criminal Justice and Immigration Act 2008 and brought into force on 6 April 2010.
182 William Whitelaw, Hansard HC, vol 46, col 556 (11 April 1983).
183 See, eg, Aldhouse (1991), op cit.
184 (1994) *The Times*, 23 November, [1995] Crim L R 633.
185 Often referred to as *Caldwell* or *Lawrence* recklessness: see *R v Caldwell* [1982] AC 341; *R v Lawrence* [1982] AC 510.

for such foresight 'seems entirely inappropriate in the context' and that to 'insist on the foresee-ability of serious consequences to constitute recklessness would be to make out the more serious form of the offence' – that is, more serious than knowingly disclosing personal data in contraven-tion of the legislation.[186] How the issue of recklessness – or, indeed, inadvertence – will be approached in this context following the subsequent overruling of *Caldwell* by the House of Lords in R v G remains to be seen.[187] However, the new powers to exact monetary penalties for breach of the data protection principles specifically provide (s 55A(3)) that the Commissioner must be satis-fied that either the controller knew, or ought to have known, that there was a risk of a contravention likely to cause substantial damage or distress, and yet failed to take reasonable steps to prevent it. 'Ought to have known' clearly imports an element of objectivity that is consonant with the approach to what are now breaches of s 55 in *DPR v Amnesty*.

The later case of *Information Commissioner v Islington London Borough Council*[188] also related to events that occurred when the 1984 Act was in force. Islington Borough Council had been registered in respect of a number of purposes for the use of personal data, but had let some of these registrations lapse without renewal. Reminders had been issued, which had not been acted upon, and personal data had continued to be processed in connection with purposes for which there was no longer a current registration. The Council was charged with the unauthorised use of personal data contrary to s 5 of the **Data Protection Act 1984**, and, as in the *Amnesty* case above, it had to be established that the Council had been reckless. One difficulty was that it was the Council that was the 'data controller', but the use of the personal data was by individual employees. In the statement of the case, one of the questions asked was how, in applying the test of recklessness, the 'actions and inferred responsibilities of the Council as a body through its servants or agents past and present' should have been approached, and whether an omission to ensure registration was enough to constitute recklessness. In essence, the decision suggested that, in order to find the requisite reck-lessness in the use of the data, it was possible to aggregate the acts of employees in using the data with the recklessness of the Council in failing to renew the registration. Although both of the above cases were brought under the 1984 Act, it seems unlikely that the approach under the 1998 Act would be any different.[189]

Section 55(2) of the **DPA 1998** provides defences in a number of situations when the person who obtains the data has a reasonable belief that either he or she had a lawful right or duty to disclose the data or that the data controller would have consented to the disclosure.[190] This defence could not be relied on in R v Rooney,[191] in which an employee in a human resources department, who was authorised to access the human resources databases for work purposes, gave information to her sister about the new address of her ex-partner and the person with whom he was living, who were also employed by the same organisation.

Data Protection and Electronic Communications

With data protection, as with other aspects of IT law, there is continual discussion regarding whether the law is sufficiently flexible to keep pace with technological change. Even prior to the

---

186 [1995] Crim LR 633, 634.
187 [2003] UKHL 50; see also discussion in Amirthalingam Kumaralingam, '*Caldwell* recklessness is dead, long live *mens rea*'s fecklessness cases' (2004) 67 MLR 491.
188 [2002] EWHC 1036.
189 See also Jay, op cit, pp 598 and 606.
190 The Criminal Justice and Immigration Act 2008 introduced a further head of defence (s 55(2)(ca)) specifically covering the situation in which a person reasonably believes that the data is subject to the special purposes exemption, but at the time of writing this new provision had not yet been brought into force. Arguably, a number of such circumstances might, in any case, be covered by the existing s 55(2)(b) and/or (d).
191 [2006] EWCA Crim 1841.

1998 Act, this was reflected in successive reports of the Data Protection Registrar, which included assessments of how the existing regime might be applied to technological advances.[192] Recital 14 of the **Data Protection Directive** reflects the fact that advances in the technology have now made it possible not only for personal data, as such, to be transmitted, manipulated, and processed, but also for visual and audio material to be used in such ways, and that the Directive also needs to be applicable to the processing of data by these means. However, it has become abundantly clear that although the original Directive might be fairly successful at responding to the issues caused by large-scale databanks, it is much less appropriate for application to the more diffuse use of personal data on global computer networks. The original fears expressed about the potential for the abuse of personal data were based on the existence of separate computer networks a fraction of the size of the internet. Although quantification of such matters cannot be exact, it is not an unreasonable presumption that the magnitude of this risk might increase supralinearly with the size of the network. The growth of the internet and world wide web, together with the functionality made possible by advances such as Web 2.0, has provided many more opportunities for the capture, retention, and subsequent processing of personal data. That such data is personal is indisputable, but it was a moot point as to how the original data protection legislation designed to deal with a much more static situation could be applied to the dynamic environment of the internet. How could, for example, the restriction on transborder data flows be applied? Can there be any guarantees of appropriate safeguards? How can the originator of the material know in which jurisdiction the resultant data might be used? If the information is made available by an individual, on, for example, a social networking site, does that mean that the processing attracts an exemption on the grounds of personal and domestic use? In short, can the original legislation on data protection cope with this phenomenon? Even if the capability is there, does enforcement and supervision become such a gargantuan task that it becomes impossible, for all practical purposes, to locate and deal with contraventions?

Some of these issues were touched upon in *Bodil Lindqvist*. In that case, Advocate General Tizzano suggested that including personal data about others on an individual's website could not be regarded as purely personal and domestic use, but that any consequent processing nevertheless fell outside the scope of the Directive on the grounds that it was not processing for economic gain and therefore could not be linked to the functioning of the internal market.[193] This was not the view of the ECJ: it noted that charitable and religious activities were not activities that were within the scope of what was then Community law, but neither could they be regarded as purely personal or household activities. This was 'clearly not the case with the processing of personal data consisting in publication on the internet so that those data are made accessible to an indefinite number of people'.[194] Instead, as discussed previously, the ECJ decision was based upon the fact that putting personal data on a home page should not be equated with transferring that data to a third country and that the Directive had not been drafted to apply to the internet.[195] Although providing a solution in the particular case, the facts and judgment serve to highlight the questions raised above.

The heart of the problem of personal data, and use of the internet and the web, is that users leave a trail everywhere they go on their journey through cyberspace. As discussed earlier,[196] there are a variety of ways in which personal data can be harvested as a user surfs the internet and so compromise privacy, including browsing trails, clickstream data and cookies, 'sniffers' (which can be used to capture data in transit on a network), 'intelligent agents' (which can be used to retrieve

---

192 See, eg, Data Protection Registrar, 1994, op cit, referring to the application of the 1984 Act to, inter alia, calling line identification, teleworking, smart cards, document image processing, and the internet.
193 [2003] ECR I-12971, [AG34]–[AG36], [AG44].
194 Ibid, [47].
195 Ibid, [68]–[71], discussed above.
196 Above pp 148–150.

required information), and also spyware and adware.[197] Indeed, it has been suggested that this gathering of data is an essential part of the survival of the web in its current form, albeit that it can 'ride roughshod over the whole idea of consent'.[198] Notwithstanding the inevitable difficulties, these more insidious and secretive ways of collecting personal data should not be immune from application of accepted legal rules and principles merely because they take place on global networks. When first adopted, the 1995 Directive could have reasonably been regarded as the 'state of the art' as far as data protection legislation was concerned, but the technology has developed considerably since then and, unsurprisingly, it has not proved a panacea to all privacy concerns raised by the use of computers and, especially, computer networks; neither has it provided a completely suitable privacy protection framework for e-commerce. The difficult issues are not so much the cases in which the data subject is aware that data has been collected and used, or even those in which this information is made available on the internet, since this is, arguably, the type of activity for which data protection law was designed; rather, the problems arising as a consequence of the traceability of operations online will be in situations in which the potential data subject may not be aware that data is being collected and retained.

How should the Directive and implementing legislation be applied in such cases? As already discussed, central to the requirements of **Directive 95/46/EC** is the need for the consent of the data subject, except in a restricted number of specific situations. A valid consent needs more than an affirmative response: it necessitates the data subject being made aware, at the time that the consent is given, of the intended purposes of processing, likely use of the data, possible disclosures, etc. Even where the collected data can be correlated with a specific identifiable individual, the invisibility of the collection leaves little opportunity for informed consent. An attempt to address some of these issues was made in **Directive 2002/58/EC**.[199] This Directive supplements the **Data Protection Directive** and attempts to clarify how the provisions of that Directive can be applied to later developments. Its provisions are intended to be as technology-neutral as possible, so that it is applicable to a wide range of communications technologies. However, this means that commonly recognised terms such as 'cookies' and spyware, for example, are not referred to in the body of the Directive, although it is made clear in the Preamble that these are a specific focus of its provisions.[200] It is possible for cookies, in particular, to be of benefit to the user: they can be used to verify identity and make certain applications more user-friendly. Some cookies automatically delete when the browser is closed ('session' cookies), whiles others are stored permanently. The Directive does not distinguish the two types and although the latter may, in principle, give rise to more privacy concerns, both can be used for legitimate purposes; this is recognised in Recital 24. Article 5, which refers to 'the use of electronic communications networks to store information or to gain access to information stored in the terminal equipment of a subscriber', can clearly be applied to cookies. However, Garvie and Wong point out that this provision may not apply to more general clickstream data that do not involve storage, as it is 'device specific'.[201] Such processing would presumable fall under the general provisions on data protection, although it is perhaps ironic that it was to remedy perceived deficiencies with the general regime that **Directive 2002/58/EC** was introduced. The original requirement in Art 5(3) was premised on the need for information about the purpose of

---

197 For more details on the technicalities, see, eg, Brian Keith Groemminger, 'Personal privacy on the internet: Should it be a cyberspace entitlement?' (2003) 36 Ind L Rev 827, PM Schwarz, 'Property, privacy and personal data' (2004) 117 Harv L Rev 2055; Frederic Debusseré, 'The EU E-Privacy Directive: A monstrous attempt to starve the cookie monster?' (2005) 13 IJLIT 70, 73–6.

198 Paul Bernal, 'Collaborative consent: Harnessing the strengths of the internet for consent in the online environment' (2010) 24 Int Rev LCT 287.

199 Directive 2002/58/EC of 12 July 2002 concerning the processing of personal data and the protection of privacy in the electronic communications sector [2002] OJ L201/37. The Directive has been implemented in the UK in the Privacy and Electronic Communications (EC Directive) Regulations 2003, SI 2003/2426.

200 See Recitals 24 and 25.

201 Daniel B Garrie and Rebecca Wong, 'The future of consumer web data: A European/US perspective' (2007) 15 Int Rev LTC 129.

storing or accessing information, together with an opportunity to refuse such processing. Article 5(3) has recently been amended by **Directive 2009/136/EC**,[202] which has to be implemented by 25 May 2011 and which introduces a requirement that the 'user concerned has given his or her consent, having been provided with clear and comprehensive information, in accordance with **Directive 95/46/EC**, inter alia, about the purposes of the processing'. But the provision nevertheless legitimises cookies where they are 'for the sole purpose of carrying out the transmission of a communication over an electronic communications network, or as strictly necessary in order for the provider of an information society service explicitly requested by the subscriber or user to provide the service'.

Although **Directive 2002/58/EC** responded to a number of concerns about the tracking of online users, some problems remain. One particular activity that has caused some difficulties is behavioural advertising, which allows advertisers to build up a profile of users' interests from their online journeys and so allows targeted advertising. The Article 29 Working Party published an extensive opinion in June 2010 about the application of both **Directive 95/46/EC** and **Directive 2002/58/EC** to this activity.[203] Although conceding the economic benefits of behavioural advertising, the opinion notes that such operators are bound by Art 5(3) and that, currently, browsers can only provide the capability for consent in limited situations. The opinion concludes that 'the nature of the practice of behavioural advertising, transparency requirements are a key condition for individuals to be able to consent to the collection and processing of their personal data and exercise effective choice', and recommends that, given the duty to comply with the regulatory regime, a dialogue should be initiated between the industry and the Working Party with a view to developing both technical and other means to ensure compliance. However, in the UK at least, the issues raised by this practice had already been brought to a head by the Phorm case. Phorm's system was more detailed than its predecessors, and, as a result, led to a number of protests from consumers and privacy groups – especially when it was revealed that BT had trialled the system without users' consent. The Article 29 Working Party opinion is of general application, but, with regard to the Phorm case, even before this opinion, the European Commission had begun action against the UK for failure to implement **Directive 2002/58/EC** properly in a way that would respond appropriately to this situation; as a result, the matter is to be referred to the ECJ.[204] The view of the Information Commissioner's Office (ICO) is that behavioural advertising is not 'intrinsically unfair', but that nevertheless website users should have the option to use website services without their personal details being recorded.[205]

The regulation of unsolicited commercial emails (UCE) – more popularly referred to as 'spam' – is also reliant on the provision of information and consent. Unsolicited email communications are dealt with generally by Art 13, which requires that these may only be sent for direct marketing purposes if the recipient has given consent and, further, proscribes any such emails that obscure the identity of the sender.[206] Spam has proved to be something of an intractable problem for internet users all over the globe. It has been described as one of the 'killer applications' that can prejudice security and reliability, and create a climate of distrust.[207] The problems caused by spam

---

202 Directive 2009/136/EC of the European Parliament and of the Council of 25 November 2009 amending Directive 2002/22/EC on universal service and users' rights relating to electronic communications networks and services, Directive 2002/58/EC concerning the processing of personal data and the protection of privacy in the electronic communications sector, and Regulation (EC) No 2006/2004 on cooperation between national authorities responsible for the enforcement of consumer protection laws, [2009] OJ L 337/11.
203 Article 29 Working Party, Opinion 2/2010 on online behavioural advertising.
204 European Commission, 'The European Commission refers UK to Court over privacy and personal data protection', Press release, 30 September 2010, available online at http://ec.europa.eu/unitedkingdom/press/press_releases/2010/pr1097_en.htm
205 See Information Commissioner's Office, *Personal Information Online: Code of Practice*, 2010, available online at www.ico.gov.uk/upload/documents/library/data_protection/detailed_specialist_guides/personal_information_online_cop.pdf
206 Spam is further regulated by Directive 2002/31 (the E-Commerce Directive), Art 7, implemented in the UK by the Electronic Commerce (EC Directive) Regulations 2002, SI 2002/2013, reg 8.
207 Abu Bakir Munir, 'Unsolicited commercial e-mail: Implementing the EU Directive' (2004) 10 CTLR 105.

have led to legislative activity not only in the EU, but in a number of other jurisdictions. In the USA, the **CAN-SPAM Act**[208] was passed at the end of 2003. In contrast to the perceived relationship between UCEs, direct marketing, and intrusions into personal privacy evident in **Directive 2002/58/EC**,[209] this statute arose in response to the perceived threat to the convenience and efficiency of electronic mail, additional costs, etc, together with concerns about, for example, the increasing use of misleading subject headers and the nature of the content of some UCEs. The statute makes it an offence, inter alia, not to give recipients information about how not to receive further communications; it nevertheless puts the onus on the recipient to opt out before any cause of action arises. The use of an opt-out rather than an opt-in approach,[210] together with the fact that the enterprise that adheres carefully to the statute can still lawfully send out unsolicited emails until an objection is received, has been severely criticised.[211] It may be that a technological solution to the problem of spam is likely to be both more effective and more appropriate, or that a combination of techniques is required,[212] whether the objective is the protection of privacy or wider concerns about the effects of spam.

One problem that appeared to require action was the apparently ever-increasing numbers of data security breaches involving a number of high-profile losses of personal data by both public and private organisations in many jurisdictions.[213] In the USA, concerns about these events led to legislation in a number of states making it mandatory to provide notice of personal data breaches. These laws incorporate 'elements of privacy regulation consumer protection and corporate governance mechanisms'.[214] These led eventually to proposals for action at the federal level; a series of Bills were debated from the end of 2009 and through 2010, the last being the Data Breach Notification Bill introduced in September 2010, but all failed to become law. Whether the 112th Congress, which began in January 2011, will return to this topic remains to be seen. There has, however, been legislative activity in Europe and **Directive 2009/136/EC**[215] introduces new provisions relating to personal data breaches into **Directive 2002/58/EC**. The Preamble notes that such breaches can result in both economic loss and social harm, as well as adversely affect privacy – especially where they lead to identity theft, for example.[216] 'Personal data breach' is defined as a breach of security leading to the accidental or unlawful destruction, loss, alteration, unauthorised disclosure of, or access to, personal data transmitted, stored, or otherwise processed in connection with the provision of a publicly available electronic communications service. On the occasion of such a breach, the new provisions require notification to the national data protection authority, together with notification of individuals concerned where the personal data breach is likely to adversely affect personal data or privacy, which should explain the nature of the breach and explain any steps to mitigate it. There is no need to do this if sufficient technological measures have been implemented to make the data unintelligible to a third party, but where the controller has not notified the individual, the authority can require it to do so if there are likely adverse effects.[217]

The discussion thus far has described regulatory activity at national and international level that has the objective of providing a suitable framework within which to safeguard users' privacy in

---

208 Controlling the Assault of Non-solicited Pornography and Marketing Act of 2003, 15 USC §§ 7701–7713 and 18 USC § 1037.
209 See, eg, Recital 40.
210 Compare Directive 2002/58, Art 13, and also the Australian Spam Act 2003, which contains a much clearer prohibition on UCEs together with strict rules concerning those commercial emails that are permitted.
211 See, eg, JD Sullivan and MB De Leeuw, 'Spam after CAN-SPAM: How inconsistent thinking has made a hash out of unsolicited commercial email policy' (2004) 20 CHTLJ 887; EA Alongi, 'Has the US canned spam?' (2004) 46 Ariz L Rev 263.
212 See, eg, Sullivan and De Leeuw, op cit, 931; cf A Mossoff, 'Spam: Oy, what a nuisance' (2004) 19 Berkeley Tech LJ 625.
213 See n 19 above and see discussion in, eg, Mark Burdon, Bill Lane, and Paul von Nessen, 'The mandatory notification of data breaches: Issues arising for Australian and EU legal developments' (2010) 26 CSLR 115.
214 Ibid.
215 See n 202 above.
216 Recital 61.
217 New Art 4(3) inserted in Directive 2002/58.

relation to their personal data, whether stored in databanks or collected via the internet. However, in 2000, the UK passed the **Regulation of Investigatory Powers Act (RIPA)**. This statute gives the government wide-ranging powers, allowing it to monitor all UK internet traffic in the name of 'law enforcement' and 'national interest'; there has therefore been significant criticism of this statute, which can be viewed as a clumsy tool when considering the delicate and diplomatic task of balancing rights and interests. Before the full effects of implementation of this statute could be appreciated, the UK, in common with a number of other jurisdictions in Europe and elsewhere, responded to the atrocities of 11 September 2001 ('9/11') by enacting legislation with the objective of addressing terrorist activities, including provisions on retention of communications data. Data retention in certain circumstances, over and above retention for declared business purposes, is permitted in some situations by Art 15 of **Directive 2002/58/EC**, but potentially raises significant privacy concerns. The extent to which this marks an erosion in the data protection rights that have been developed over two or three decades is open to debate and is discussed further in the next chapter.

Chapter 6

Surveillance, Data Retention, and Encryption

Chapter Contents

Introduction

In contrast to the laws relating to the protection of privacy and personal data are those laws that justify, formalise, and regulate state and private party actions likely to impact upon individuals' normal expectations of privacy, in the pursuit of other legitimate social, political, and economic goals. These include laws that influence the use of information technologies, such as telecommunications and the internet, by:

- facilitating the tracing of links between individuals – for example, permitting collection of 'traffic data' identifying when and with whom technology users communicate;
- facilitating the collection of information about the detail of individuals' interactions – for example, permitting interception of the content of their communications; or
- preventing the effective employment of surveillance countermeasures – for example, forbidding, or limiting the utility of, the use of encryption technologies.

The key pieces of legislation considered in this chapter are the **Regulation of Investigatory Powers Act 2000 (RIPA 2000)** and related statutory instruments,[1] and the **Data Retention (EC Directive) Regulations 2009, SI 2009/9870 (DERs)**.

In the digital information environment, the primary aim of UK state surveillance has been to ensure that law enforcement and national security agencies have suitable access and powers to maintain effective investigatory practices across the diverse range of public communications options. A secondary aim, motivated largely by external pressures – notably European Court of Human Rights (ECtHR) rulings – has been to place both access and investigatory powers within a legal framework. Such a framework, in theory, allows oversight of their lawful use, meaningful penalties for their abuse, and greater public transparency about their operation, without unduly compromising their effectiveness. While, on paper, considerable advances have been made toward this second aim, achieving and maintaining a proportionate balance between efficiency and legitimacy in an area in which technology is in a state of constant flux is far from a simple task. As a result, both legislators and judiciary have struggled to keep pace with developments.

A complicating factor is that powers granted to state agencies to access and collect digital information generated by the public often produce, or permit the production of, datasets relevant to commercial organisations. For example, internet traffic data can be valuable to content providers wishing to monitor potential infringements of their intellectual property, or to advertising companies seeking to deploy 'behavioural advertising'.[2] This can lead to pressure from commercial organisations for greater access to such datasets, or for the wider grant of access and investigatory powers to the private sector. Here, too, there is a delicate balancing act for legislature and judiciary to consider – that is, the extent to which the business interests of commercial organisations can be accommodated, without undue impact upon either the public interest, or the perceived legitimacy of state access and investigatory powers. Thus the requirement of a legal framework for the legitimate exercise of access and investigatory powers by state agencies is mirrored by the need for a similar framework for private entities – a need that, in the UK, is again being addressed mainly following adverse rulings from the ECtHR.

---

1 See http://security.homeoffice.gov.uk/ripa/legislation/ripa-statutory-instruments/

2 For example, behavioural advertising uses information about an individual's web-browsing behaviour, such as pages that he or she has visited, or searches that he or she has made, to determine which advertisements he or she is offered. See also discussion on p 186.

This chapter will examine the three key elements of the current regime for surveilling the digital environment:

● the legal framework for the interception of content in transit between parties – that is, the interception of communications;
● the requirement upon public telecommunications providers, including internet service providers (ISPs), to retain communications traffic data – that is, data retention; and
● the requirements placed on users of encryption technologies to make their communications accessible to the authorities upon demand – that is, decryption powers.[3]

It will also examine possible future developments, including the extent to which public concerns over the use of information technologies to surveil consumers may require further consideration of the regulatory framework with regard to the private sector.

Interception of Communications

The interception of communications by UK state agencies has a long and storied history, although the origin of the power to make such interceptions remains murky.[4] The interception of electronic communications was put on a formal, but non-statutory, footing in 1937 when it was decided that the Post Office should only intercept telephone conversations on the express warrant of the Secretary of State. The power to issue such warrants was perceived to flow from the same authority that permitted the interception of letters and telegrams on the basis of a warrant issued by the Secretary of State – a position long enshrined in statute.[5] However, unlike the interception of letters and telegrams, the power to authorise telecommunications interceptions was never formally incorporated into the various **Post Office Acts**.

In 1957, the government appointed a Committee of Privy Councillors to report on both the history and present state of communications interception. The Birkett Report, as it became known, was largely uncritical of the status quo. It did propose some relatively minor procedural and administrative changes – for example, no general warrants,[6] no warrants of indeterminate length,[7] periodic review of outstanding warrants,[8] and better records of warrants issued, cancelled and refused[9] – but it failed to press other pivotal issues:

● the lack of a clear legal basis for the Secretary of State to authorise phone taps was noted and the amendment of the **Post Office Act 1953** tentatively suggested, but no firm recommendation was made to put that power on a clear statutory footing; and
● little consideration was given to the question of whether it was appropriate for the Secretary of State, rather than the judiciary, to be issuing warrants in criminal (as opposed to national security) cases.

---

3 This chapter does not consider broader issues of electronic surveillance, such as bugging. For a broader survey, see Laura K Donohue, *The Cost of Counterterrorism: Power, Politics, and Liberty*, 2008, Cambridge: Cambridge University Press; Victoria Williams, *Surveillance and Intelligence Law Handbook*, 2005, Oxford: Oxford University Press.
4 See, for a brief history of pre-electronic interceptions, Home Office, *Report of the Committee of Privy Councillors Appointed to Inquire into the Interception of Communications* (the 'Birkett Report'), Cmnd 283, 1957, London: HMSO; also David Vincent, *The Culture of Secrecy: Britain, 1832–1998*, 1998, Oxford: Oxford University Press.
5 Birkett Report, para 41.
6 Ibid, para 56.
7 Ibid, para 75.
8 Ibid, para 74.
9 Ibid, para 84.

Two interesting issues raised were the issue of how intercepted communications should be used and whether tapping of telephones by unauthorised persons should be made an offence. In the case of use of interception material, the Committee felt that it should only be used for the purpose for which the warrant was obtained, and that private bodies and private persons should not have access to it. However, with regard to its use as evidence in court, the Committee saw:

> no reason why in a proper case the evidence should not be tendered, for when the occasion arises the admissibility of the evidence will be decided by a Court before whom the evidence is tendered, and the history of the law of evidence is proof enough of the immense care that is taken in the administration of justice to see that the evidence submitted both in civil and criminal cases is evidence that it is proper to admit in all the circumstances of the case.[10]

However, it was willing to defer to the Home Office, which argued that the power should be exercised for the purpose of detection only, primarily because using information obtained in this way in court would make the practice widely known, thereby destroying its efficacy to some degree.

This stance, as will be discussed below, remains firmly embedded in current law, under which intercept evidence is statutorily inadmissible in court. In the case of unauthorised interception of communications, the Committee suggested that Parliament might consider making this an offence.[11] In the event, it took another 28 years for an offence of unauthorised interception on public telecommunications service,[12] and 43 years for an offence of unauthorised interception on a private telecommunications service, to arrive.

In the 26-year period after the Birkett Report, despite occasional expressions of disquiet in Parliament and the media about the rising use of interception powers, often justified on national security grounds,[13] there was little evidence that successive governments had any intention of placing interception powers on a statutory footing, or indeed under any significant scrutiny. However, in 1980, following a series of articles on telephone tapping in The New Statesman, which resulted in questions in the Commons,[14] and the adverse judgment in Malone before the ECtHR (discussed below), the government produced a short White Paper, which aimed to update the Birkett Report on the interception of communications,[15] and also appointed Lord Diplock to be an 'independent judicial monitor' of interceptions.

The White Paper largely reaffirmed that little had changed since the government's adoption of the Birkett recommendations: 'serious offences' for the police had been widened slightly to include those for which there was 'good reason to apprehend the use of violence';[16] and the focus of interceptions for both police and customs had switched towards drug trafficking.[17] It also reiterated that established practice was that intercept material was not to be tendered in evidence.[18]

Lord Diplock's first report as judicial monitor, in 1981,[19] was similarly brief, examining whether:

---

10 Ibid, para 152.
11 Ibid, paras 129–131.
12 Telecommunications Act 1984, s 45, made it an offence for anyone running a public telecommunication service to disclose intentionally, other than in the course of his or her duty, either the contents of any message intercepted in the course of its transmission or information about the use made of the services by a third party.
13 Between 1958 and 1984, the number of warrants granted for telecommunications interceptions rose steadily from 129 to 352 per annum: Peter N Grabosky and Russell G Smith, Crime in the Digital Age, 1998, Annandale, NSW: Transaction Publishers, p 197.
14 HC Deb, vol 977, cols 1540–3 (31 January 1980).
15 Home Office, The Interception of Communications in Great Britain, Cmnd 7873, 1980, London: HMSO.
16 Ibid, para 4.
17 Ibid, paras 21–22.
18 Ibid, para 16.
19 Office of the Prime Minister, Communications Interception Standing Inquiry: The Interception of Communications in Great Britain, Cmnd 8191, 1981, London: HMSO.

. . . the following six conditions are observed:

(1) that the public interest which will be served by obtaining the information which it is hoped will result from the interception of communications is of sufficient importance to justify this step;

(2) that the interception applied, for offers a reasonable prospect of providing the information sought;

(3) that other methods of obtaining it such as surveillance or the use of informants have been tried and failed or from the nature of the case are not feasible;

(4) that the interception stops as soon as it has ceased to provide information of the kind sought or it has become apparent that it is unlikely to provide it;

(5) that all products of interception not directly relevant to the purpose for which the warrant was granted are speedily destroyed; and

(6) that such material as is directly relevant to that purpose is given no wider circulation than is essential for carrying it out.

He duly found that they were. However, despite the chorus of approval in successive official reports, public and parliamentary sentiment remained negative.[20]

Despite the appointment of a senior judge as 'independent monitor' of interceptions, neither the White Paper, nor Lord Diplock's report, considered the question of whether the continuing use of executive powers in criminal cases was appropriate. Nor, apparently, was Lord Diplock's existing role as Chairman of the Security Commission seen as potentially compromising his independence in that role.[21] Lord Diplock produced a second report in 1982, which was not publicly released, but which also concluded that 'the procedures for the interception of communications had continued to work satisfactorily and the principles set out in the White Paper . . . had been conscientiously observed by all Departments concerned'.[22]

However, the cosy arrangement whereby telecommunications interceptions were grounded in powers derived indirectly from the **Post Office Acts**, regulated by guidelines drawn up and altered at will by the Home Office, and overseen by an 'independent monitor' who reported to the Prime Minister and whose reports were only optionally made public, was on the verge of fundamental change.

The *Malone* Case

In 1977, during a trial of Mr James Malone for receiving stolen property (on which charges he was acquitted), it emerged by accident that his telephone conversations had been intercepted by the Metropolitan Police under the authority of a warrant issued by the Home Secretary.[23] Malone brought an action against the Metropolitan Police, claiming that:

- the interception, monitoring, or recording of confidential conversations on his telephone lines without his consent was unlawful, even if done under a warrant of the Home Secretary;

---

20 See, eg, 'Reassuring as far as it goes' (1981) *The Times*, 4 March, p 17.

21 The Security Commission was established in 1964 to '. . . investigate and report upon the circumstances in which a breach of security is known to have occurred in the public service, and upon any related failure of departmental security arrangements or neglect of duty; and, in the light of any such investigation, to advise whether any change in security arrangements is necessary or desirable': HC Deb, vol 687, cols 1271–3 (23 January 1964).

22 See HC Deb, vol 22, cols 95–6W (21 April 1982). Lord Diplock's second report on the interception of communications is annotated by Duffy [1982] Public Law 381.

23 As noted above, at this point, intercept material was customarily only used for investigative, and not for evidentiary, purposes: see Ian J Lloyd, 'The Interception of Communications Act 1985' (1986) 49(1) MLR 86.

- he had a right of property, privacy, and confidentiality in respect of telephone conversations on his telephone lines, which the interceptions breached;
- the interceptions and monitoring of his telephone lines violated his right under Art 8(1) of the **European Convention on Human Rights (ECHR)** to respect for his private and family life, his home and his correspondence, and could not be justified by Art 8(2) as being in accordance with the law; and
- contrary to Art 13 **ECHR**, there was no effective remedy before a national authority in the UK for any interceptions, monitoring, or recordings of conversations on his telephone lines, or for breaches of his Art 8 right.[24]

Megarry VC rejected all of Malone's arguments, holding that:

- the rights claimed under Art 8 were not legal or equitable rights (direct rights) and the court had no power to provide the declaration requested under Art 8, and chose not to do so with regard to Art 13;[25]
- telephone interceptions by the Post Office for use by the police to prevent or detect crime were not unlawful, because there was no law against such interceptions, and the **ECHR** could not be used as an 'aid in construction' (indirect rights) on the matter, because there was no statute, ambiguous or otherwise, for the court to construe;[26]
- although no statute directly authorised telephone interceptions, the **Post Office Act 1969**, s 80, gave the Home Secretary's warrant effective statutory function;[27]
- no property (apart from copyright) existed in words transmitted over the telephone;[28]
- there was no general right of privacy recognised by English law;[29]
- there was no contractual right of confidentiality arising from the provision of telephone services by the Post Office, nor was there a breach of any general right of confidentiality, and if there had been, then there was just cause and excuse for it;[30] and
- regardless of the other points, any claim for declarations against the Metropolitan Police must fail because the Post Office carried out the interceptions.[31]

Despite finding in favour of the defendants on all claims and ruling out the possibility of a solution derived from the common law, Megarry VC was clearly troubled by the lack of a legal framework to prevent abuses of the interception process, suggesting that while the complexity of regulating phone tapping meant that it was a matter best left to Parliament, rather than the courts, it was high time that Parliament addressed the matter[32] – not least because the UK appeared to be on a collision course with the ECtHR. The ECtHR had considered the issue of telephone interceptions in terms of Arts 8 and 13 at some length in *Klass v Germany*:[33]

> . . . the West German system that came under scrutiny in the *Klass* case was laid down by statute, and it contained a number of statutory safeguards . . . Not a single one of these safeguards is to be found as a matter of established law in England, and only a few corresponding

---

24 *Malone v Commissioner of Police for the Metropolis (No 2)* [1979] Ch 344, 344.
25 Ibid, 353–5.
26 Ibid, 367.
27 Ibid, 370.
28 Ibid, 357.
29 Ibid, 374–5.
30 Ibid, 375–8.
31 Ibid, 383–4.
32 Ibid, 380–1.
33 *Klass v Germany* (1979–80) 2 EHRR 214.

provisions exist as a matter of administrative procedure . . . it is impossible to read the judgment in the *Klass* case without its becoming abundantly clear that a system which has no legal
safeguards whatever has small chance of satisfying the requirements of that court, whatever
administrative provisions there may be . . . this is not a subject on which it is possible to feel any
pride in English law.[34]

Despite this clear judicial statement of concern, the government's response, in the form of the 1980
White Paper and the appointment of Lord Diplock as 'independent monitor', paid little heed to the
advice concerning the need to place communication interceptions on a statutory footing.[35] The
Royal Commission on Criminal Procedure, which reported in 1981, was also ignored when it
suggested, in regard to what it termed 'surreptitious surveillance', that:

> . . . although we have no evidence that the existing controls are inadequate to prevent abuse, we
> think that there are strong arguments for introducing a system of statutory control on similar
> lines to that which we have recommended for search warrants. As with all features of police
> investigative procedures, the value of prescribing them in statutory form is that it brings clarity
> and precision to the rules; they are open to public scrutiny and to the potential of Parliamentary
> review. So far as surveillance devices in general are concerned this is not at present so . . . We
> therefore recommend that the use of surveillance devices by the police (including the intercep-
> tion of letters and telephone communications) should be regulated by statute.[36]

Yet in 1981, even as Lord Diplock was declaring that all was well with the state of interceptions
in the UK, the European Commission of Human Rights declared that Malone's case was admissible
for hearing under the **ECHR** procedure.[37] It noted that the case raised significant questions
about the UK's administrative arrangements for the interception of communications, including
whether measures taken under such a system were 'in accordance with the law' for the purpose
of Art 8(2), and whether there were adequate and effective guarantees against abuse.[38] In 1982,
the Commission delivered its report on the case, holding that there were violations of both Arts 8
and 13:

- postal and telephone communications interceptions were an interference with Malone's right
  to respect for private life and correspondence under Art 8(1);
- while such interference could be justified by reference to the purposes of Art 8(2), the UK
  administrative process was inadequate, because warrants granted by the Secretary of State were
  subject to little or no legal restriction, their scope, form, content, and duration were not
  defined by law, and applications for warrants were not regulated by rules of law, nor was the
  handling of intercepted material; and
- while a statute, or comprehensive interception code, was not necessarily required, an
  interception system operating 'in accordance with the law' should be seen with reasonable
  certainty to permit interference only in precisely limited or defined circumstances, compatible

---

34 Ibid, 379–80.
35 See, eg, the words of the Home Secretary, Mr William Whitelaw, in HC Deb, vol 982, cols 205–8 (1 April 1980).
36 Royal Commission on Criminal Procedure, *Report of the Royal Commission on Criminal Procedure*, Cmnd 8092-I, 1981, London: HMSO,
    paras 3.56–3.60.
37 Three institutions originally dealt with complaints under the ECHR: the European Commission of Human Rights, which assessed
    individual applications, and decided which cases were forwarded to the ECtHR for judgment and which were declared
    inadmissible; the European Court of Human Rights; and the Committee of Ministers of the Council of Europe. In 1999, Protocol
    11 of the ECHR abolished both the Commission of Human Rights and the judicial function of the Committee of Ministers, and
    allowed individuals to bring actions directly before the Court.
38 *Malone v United Kingdom* (1982) 4 EHRR 330 (Commission, admissibility).

with the Art 8(2) purposes – mere statements of administrative practice were inadequate for this purpose.[39]

The ECtHR, which heard the case in plenary in 1984,[40] was equally forthright in its view that the UK administrative system for interception of communications was inadequate to provide UK citizens with adequate legal protection against abuses:

> . . . on the evidence before the Court, it cannot be said with any reasonable certainty what elements of the powers to intercept are incorporated in legal rules and what elements remain within the discretion of the executive. In view of the attendant obscurity and uncertainty as to the state of the law in this essential respect, the Court cannot but reach a similar conclusion to that of the Commission. In the opinion of the Court, the law of England and Wales does not indicate with reasonable clarity the scope and manner of exercise of the relevant discretion conferred on the public authorities. To that extent, the minimum degree of legal protection to which citizens are entitled under the rule of law in a democratic society is lacking.[41]

The ECtHR did not examine the content of the other guarantees required by Art 8(2) – that is, whether interceptions were 'necessary in a democratic society' in the defence of the recognised purposes – because its finding that the interceptions were not 'in accordance with the law' made that unnecessary.[42] Nor did it consider the issue of Art 13, holding that its decision with regard to Art 8 removed the need to do so.[43]

The Interception of Communications Act 1985

The UK government's reaction to *Malone* was not exactly a headlong rush to fundamentally change the process for authorising interceptions. It had begun preparing specific legislation in early 1984,[44] presumably on the basis that, given the tenor of the Commission's report in *Malone*, the pending action before the ECtHR was a lost cause. However, it soon became apparent that the new Interception of Communications Bill, while placing interception of telecommunications and mail on a statutory footing, was not, in practice, going to result in a significantly different regime; rather, it aimed to transport the existing mechanism for authorising interceptions, broadly unchanged, onto the statute book. As an editorial in *The Times* in 1985 succinctly put it: 'It is one of this Government's "dumb insolence" measures . . . in which the minimum action possible is grudgingly taken to comply with the letter of rulings under international agreements.'[45]

The resulting **Interception of Communications Act 1985 (IOCA 1985)** made it an offence, punishable by up to two years' imprisonment, to intercept communications by post, or through a public telecommunications system.[46] Interceptions could be made lawfully by warrant from the Secretary of State,[47] where the sender or recipient of the communication consented,[48] or where

---

39 *Malone v United Kingdom* (1983) 5 EHRR 385 (Commission, report).
40 *Malone v United Kingdom* (1985) 7 EHRR 14 (Court, decision).
41 Ibid, 44–5.
42 Ibid, 45–6.
43 Ibid, 47–8.
44 'Whitelaw pledge on Bill to control telephone tapping' (1984) *The Times*, 20 March, p 4; Home Office, *The Interception of Communications in the United Kingdom*, Cmnd 9438, 1985, London: HMSO.
45 'Tabs on the tappers' (1985) *The Times*, 6 March, p 13.
46 IOCA 1995, s 1(1).
47 Ibid, s 1(2)(a).
48 Ibid, s 1(2)(b).

interception occurred in the course of the normal operation of the communication service.[49] When considering the issue of a warrant, the Secretary of State was required to take into account much the same criteria as had been required under the long-standing administrative system.[50] Material collected under a warrant could be held only for the purpose of investigation, and had to be destroyed immediately this purpose had been achieved.[51] The **IOCA 1985** also formalised the scope, issuing, and duration of warrants,[52] and the procedure for modifying an existing warrant.[53]

The oversight of the interception process was also formalised and marginally enhanced. The Judicial Monitor was replaced by an Interceptions Commissioner – a person who held, or had held, 'high judicial office' – tasked with the role of overseeing the Secretary of State's use of the **IOCA 1985** powers, and the effectiveness of the statutory safeguards.[54] The Commissioner would work with a newly created Interception of Communications Tribunal. Any person believing that his or her communications had been intercepted could apply to the Tribunal for review of whether an interception warrant or certificate had been granted, and, if so, that the **IOCA 1985** procedural requirements had met.[55]

There were still significant limitations to the statutory oversight. The Tribunal's hearings were held in camera and no reasons for its decisions were given.[56] It was restricted to determining whether the Secretary of State's decisions met narrow judicial review standards – that is, that he or she had not acted illegally, irrationally, or improperly in issuing a warrant.[57] It was not given the power to determine whether entirely unauthorised interceptions had occurred. Where breaches were found, the Tribunal was to inform the applicant of those breaches, and report them both to the Prime Minister and the Interceptions Commissioner.[58] Additionally, in such circumstances, the Tribunal could, at its discretion, quash the warrant, require the destruction of material collected through the interception, and order compensation be paid.[59] However, in cases in which the Tribunal found no breaches of **IOCA 1985**, ss 2–5, it needed only to inform the applicant of that fact.[60] The Tribunal's own decisions were immune from judicial review.[61] Despite suggestions that technical expertise would be valuable on a tribunal that would increasingly be dealing with telecommunications interceptions, the five-member Tribunal was drawn exclusively from the legal profession.[62]

The Interceptions Commissioner was required to produce an annual report, but only to the Prime Minister (who also appointed the Commissioner).[63] Parliament was given no oversight role, nor any ability to review directly the activities of the bodies appointed to carry out the oversight.

These issues, whilst controversial, were arguably not the most significant changes in the **IOCA 1985**. That was to be found in s 9 – a statutory prohibition upon the admissibility of evidence obtained by interceptions, except in limited circumstances, such as prosecutions for unlawful interception under s 1:

---

49 Ibid, s 1 (3).
50 Ibid, ss 2 and 10(3). Commentators have argued that IOCA 1995 broadened the grounds on which interception warrants could be granted: see Adam Tomkins, 'Now you hear me, now you don't' (1994) 57(6) MLR 941, 961.
51 IOCA 1995, s 6(3).
52 Ibid, ss 3–4.
53 Ibid, s 5.
54 Ibid, s 8.
55 Ibid, s 7.
56 Ibid, Sch 1, s 4(2).
57 See *Council of Civil Service Unions v Minister for the Civil Service* [1985] AC 374; *R v Secretary of State for the Home Department, ex p Ruddock* [1987] 1 WLR 1482.
58 IOCA 1995, s 7(4).
59 Ibid, s 7(5).
60 See *Ruddock*, above. In the period 1985–2000, no complaints made to the Tribunal were upheld.
61 IOCA 1995, s 7(8).
62 Ibid, Sch 1, s 1(1).
63 Ibid, s 8.

9. (1) In any proceedings before any court or tribunal no evidence shall be adduced and no question in cross-examination shall be asked which (in either case) tends to suggest—

(a) that an offence under section 1 above has been or is to be committed by any of the persons mentioned in subsection (2) below; or

(b) that a warrant has been or is to be issued to any of those persons.

(2) The persons referred to in subsection (1) above are—

(a) any person holding office under the Crown;

(b) the Post Office and any person engaged in the business of the Post Office; and

(c) any public telecommunications operator and any person engaged in the running of a public telecommunication system.

Whether it was simply a continuation of the Home Office's long-held position that producing such material at trial would interfere with the effective use of interception, or an attempt to limit the effect of future inadvertent courtroom disclosures, as in *Malone*, the rationale for making a statutory exception out of 'established practice' is unclear. The 1985 White Paper stated only that:

The Bill will provide for controls over the use of intercepted material. By making such material generally inadmissible in legal proceedings it will ensure that interception can be used only as an aspect of investigation, not of prosecution.[64]

Although the **IOCA 1985** aimed to meet the basic requirements of the **ECHR**, and to modernise the law relating to the interception of post and telecommunications, it became apparent that the courts were having difficulty with (sometimes simultaneously) what constituted 'interception' on a public telecommunications service under s 1l, and the precise meaning of s 9. The case law relating to whether an interception took place on a public telecommunications network shows that the courts adopted a rather narrow interpretation. In R v *Ahmed*,[65] the defendants pled guilty to drugs charges after the judge at trial ruled that transcripts of telephone calls made by one of the defendants on a pay telephone at the police station, whilst in custody, were admissible in evidence. The calls were routed to the internal switchboard at the police station, which was connected to the public system. The court held that the public system ended at the junction box, where it connected to the private system of the subscriber. Thus interceptions made via a physical device attached to the private system before the junction box were not interceptions under the **IOCA 1985** and did not require a s 2 warrant. The judge did not discuss the admissibility of the transcript evidence, presumably because a private system interception fell entirely outside the **IOCA 1985** regime.

This was reinforced by the House of Lords in R v *Effik*,[66] in which Lord Oliver repeated with approval the judge's summary in *Ahmed*. In this case, the defendants were convicted of conspiracy to supply controlled drugs, based in part on evidence of incriminating telephone conversations made on a cordless telephone, which had been intercepted and taped by police, without a warrant. The Lords held that the interception was of the impulses transmitted through the air between the telephone base unit and the handset, as part of a telecommunication system 'run' by its owner, and not as part of the public telecommunication system run by BT. Thus no

---

64 Home Office, Cmnd 9438, op cit, p 7.
65 Unreported, 29 March 1994 (CA) (CD). See also *R v Allan* [2001] EWCA Crim 1027 CA (CD) – a prison telephone system was not a 'public telephone system' for the purposes of the Act.
66 [1994] 3 WLR 583 (HL). Also *R v Bray* (unreported), 26 June 1998; *R v Taylor-Sabori* [1999] 1 WLR 858, regarding radio pagers.

warrant under **IOCA 1985**, s 2, was necessary, and the issue of admissibility of evidence under s 9 did not arise.

Matters were more complicated in R v Preston,[67] in which the police obtained a warrant under **IOCA 1985**, s 2, in the course of surveilling the defendants who were suspected of drug smuggling. At trial, the prosecution introduced evidence about the frequency of calls made on the defendants' telephones, but gave no details of their content. This led the defence to question whether there had been interceptions. Preston was pursuing a 'duress' defence and argued that he should have access to any intercepted material in order, he claimed, to bolster that defence. Failure to provide it, he claimed, prejudiced his right to a fair trial. Alternatively, if there was no intercepted content, it was unfairly prejudicial to permit evidence about the calls' frequency. In effect, the issue was whether s 9 barred the defence from adducing evidence gathered by interception.

The House of Lords held that, on the plain words of the Act, it did. Additionally, because the evidence would not be admissible in court, the prosecution's normal duty to give complete disclosure of unused materials in the interest of a fair trial could be overridden.[68] Indeed, the prosecution could not have disclosed the intercept materials, as it emerged, during the appeals, that they had been destroyed after the information in them had been used to catch the defendants, as required by **IOCA 1985**, s 6. Prosecuting counsel helpfully volunteered that he had been informed by the police that the materials would not have helped Preston's defence.[69] The Lords also noted that while the Act might bar disclosure of intercept material to the defence, it did not bar disclosure by the police to the prosecution counsel to help in deciding whether a case should go forward to trial.[70]

The question of whether s 9 barred the use of evidence from all interceptions falling within **IOCA 1985** was initially addressed in R v Rasool,[71] in which the police had intercepted a telephone conversation between the defendant and a police informer. The informer had consented to the interception, meaning that, under s 1(2)(a), no warrant was required. The Court held that s 9(1) did not prevent the admission of the product of a telephone intercept to which **IOCA 1985** applied, unless it was a warranted intercept covered by s 9(1)(b). This was reversed in Morgans,[72] in which the House of Lords held that except where a communication had been intercepted for the purposes under s 1(3) (for example, provision of telecommunications services), s 9(1) always rendered inadmissible evidence of material obtained through interceptions of the kind described in s 1 (for example, warrant or consent), by the persons mentioned in s 9(2) (for example, police or telecommunications officials).

Interceptions lawfully made by foreign authorities were considered in R v Aujla,[73] in which calls made to the UK from the Netherlands were intercepted by the Dutch authorities. It was held that evidence from such interceptions was admissible in the UK courts, because the interceptions did not fall under the **IOCA 1985** regime.

---

67 [1993] 3 WLR 891 (HL).
68 Preston took this point to Strasbourg, arguing breach of Art 6 (right to a fair trial), but the European Commission of Human Rights accepted the UK's argument that IOCA 1995, s 9, placed the prosecution and defence on an equal footing, meaning that there was no 'inequality of arms': Preston v UK (App No 24193/94) 2 July 1997. See also Jasper v UK (2000) 30 EHRR 441 – there were circumstances in which it was appropriate to withhold evidence from the defence in the public interest so as to ensure the secrecy of police investigation methods, and it was for the national court to decide on admissibility of evidence and to weigh the public interest favouring non-disclosure against the defence's right to disclosure.
69 Given that police forces have not always distinguished themselves when it comes to representing accurately the weight of evidence in criminal investigations, this is not as much assurance as the Court appeared to surmise.
70 The bar on prosecution disclosure of intercept material to the defence in R v Preston was placed on a statutory footing in the Criminal Procedure and Investigations Act 1996, ss 3(7) and 8(6). The acceptability of disclosure of intercept material to prosecution counsel was placed on a statutory footing in the Regulation of Investigatory Powers Act 2000, s 18(7).
71 [1997] 1 WLR 1092 (CA) (CD).
72 Morgans v DPP [2000] 2 WLR 386.
73 [1998] 2 Cr App R 16 (CA) (CD). See also R v P [2001] 2 WLR 463 (HL) – foreign interceptions did not fall within the IOCA 1995 regime, the interference with the defendants' privacy under Art 8 ECHR was proportionate, and fair use of intercept evidence at a trial, even where such evidence was unlawfully obtained, did not breach Art 6 ECHR.

The weaknesses and contradictions of the **IOCA 1985** regime were highlighted in R v Sargent.[74] In this case, a telephone engineer intercepted, without authorisation, a telephone communication between his ex-wife and the defendant, whom he suspected of setting fire to his car. He gave a recording to the police, who arrested the defendant. The defendant denied involvement until confronted with the recording, when he confessed. At trial, the defendant claimed that evidence of the intercept was inadmissible since the engineer had been 'engaged in the running of a public telecommunication system' within s 9(2)(c) when carrying out the interception. It was held on appeal from his conviction that the engineer fell within s 9(2)(c) if he was an employee or other agent of a public telecommunications operator at the relevant time, whether or not he was acting within the scope of his authority, thus making the interception an unlawful one under **IOCA 1985D**s 1(11), and hence inadmissible under s 9(1). The corollary to this, however, appeared to be that s 9(2)(c) turned entirely on a person's office, status, or position. If the interception had been undertaken by an individual who did not fall precisely within the definitions in s 9(2), then, despite his or her interception being illegal, any materials obtained would still be potentially admissible in evidence.

It will be clear from the foregoing that the **IOCA 1985** regime was problematic on a number of levels. If the intent of the ECtHR in *Malone* had been to encourage the UK to provide a statutory framework for interceptions that was clear, consistent, and in conformity with Art 8 in terms of a proportionate interference with privacy rights, this had clearly not occurred. The narrow interpretation of 'public telecommunications network' meant that communications on cordless phone, pagers, and other new communications devices could fall outside the scope of statutory protection,[75] and organisations running private telecommunication systems, whether in hotels, prisons, or police stations, could still intercept communications on them at will. The degree of common understanding about permissible uses for, and admissibility of, intercept evidence was, if anything, worse under the statutory regime than it had been under the old administrative regime. It was almost inevitable therefore that the UK would find itself once more before the ECtHR.[76]

The *Halford* Case

Alison Halford was assistant chief constable with the Merseyside Police. However, her applications for promotion to a higher post were repeatedly denied. Eventually, she began proceedings in the Industrial Tribunal (later discontinued) against the Chief Constable of Merseyside Police and the Home Secretary on the ground of sex discrimination. Contemporaneously, the Merseyside Police brought disciplinary charges against her, which were eventually quashed by the courts.

During this time, Halford came to believe that the Merseyside Police were intercepting calls on her home and two office phones, and she complained to the Interception of Communications Tribunal. The Tribunal informed her that their investigation found no contravention of **IOCA 1985**, ss 2–5, with regard to her home phone, and refused to clarify whether an interception had taken place, or whether it had been authorised by the Home Secretary. In response to a question from her Member of Parliament (MP), the Home Office stated that any eavesdropping by the Merseyside Police on its own telephone system fell outside the scope of **IOCA 1985** and would not require a warrant. Halford then took her complaint to Strasbourg, where the European Commission on Human Rights declared her application admissible, expressing the opinion that there had been

---

74 [2001] UKHL 54 (HL).
75 As Prince Charles discovered when his private mobile phone calls to Camilla Parker Bowles were intercepted by journalists in the early 1990s ('Tampongate').
76 The government had successfully defended elements of the IOCA 1995 in Strasbourg: see, eg, Christie v United Kingdom (App No 21482/93) 27 June 1994; Matthews v United Kingdom (App No 28576/95) 16 October 1996; Preston v UK, above; Jasper v UK (2000) 30 EHRR 441. But see Liberty v United Kingdom (2009) 48 EHRR 1, discussed below.

violations of Arts 8 and 13 **ECHR** in relation to her office telephones, but no violation of Arts 8, 10, or 13 in relation to her home telephone.[77]

Before the ECtHR,[78] the UK government accepted that there was sufficient evidence that her office phones had been monitored, but disagreed with regard to her home phone.[79] However, it claimed that Halford had no reasonable expectation of privacy in telephone calls from her workplace, and that employers should, without the prior knowledge of employees, be able to monitor calls made by the latter on work telephones.[80]

The ECtHR agreed that there was sufficient evidence of interception of the office phones, but disagreed with the UK government's conclusions. It stated that, absent any warning that calls made on the internal telecommunications system might be intercepted, Halford had a reasonable expectation of privacy in such calls. This expectation was reinforced by a number of factors, such as that the phones were in a private office, that one was specifically designated for Halford's private use, and that she had been permitted to use her office telephone for the purposes of her sex discrimination case. That expectation had been subject to 'interference by a public authority', and the interference was not 'in accordance with the law' since UK law did not regulate interceptions of calls made on telecommunications systems outside the public network.[81] Because there was an arguable claim that Halford's Art 8 rights had been breached, she was entitled to an effective domestic remedy under Art 13. However, because there was no provision in UK law to regulate interceptions of telephone calls made on internal communications systems operated by public authorities, she could not seek a remedy, resulting in a breach of Art 13.[82]

While the *Halford* decision required another reconsideration of the statutory regime for interceptions, it was in any case a timely moment to re-evaluate the situation, because the economic and technical environment had moved on significantly from 1985. For example:

- there were 150 fixed-line telecommunications providers where previously there had been two;
- mobile telephones had come from nowhere to become mass-market items; and
- internet access and usage was developing rapidly.[83]

The government thus wanted to adopt wide-ranging new legislation. This would not only address the issue of interception of communications on private telecommunications, but also bring all communications within a statutory interception framework, alongside other forms of surveillance.

> The intention is to provide a single legal framework which deals with all interception of communications in the United Kingdom, regardless of the means of communication, how it is licensed or at which point on the route of the communication it is intercepted.
>
> . . .
>
> The Government believes that it should not make any difference how a communication is sent, whether by a public or non-public telecommunications or mail system, by wireless telegraphy or any other communication system. Nor should the form of the communication make

---

77 *Halford v United Kingdom* (1995) 19 EHRR CD43 (Commission, decision).
78 *Halford v United Kingdom* (1997) 24 EHRR 523.
79 Ibid, 543.
80 Ibid.
81 Ibid, 544–5.
82 Ibid, 548.
83 Home Office, *Interception of Communications in the United Kingdom: A Consultation Paper*, Cmnd 4368, 1999, London: HMSO; '. . . there was one completely dominant provider – BT – with Mercury barely off the ground, and only landlines. No pagers, no mobiles, no e-mail, no internet, no encryption': Home Office, 'Regulation of Investigatory Powers Bill published today', Press release 022/2000, 10 February 2000, London: HMSO.

any difference; all interception which would breach Article 8 rights, whether by telephone, fax, e-mail or letter, should all be treated the same way in law. A single authorising framework for all forms of lawful interception of communications will mean that each application will follow the same laid down procedure and will be judged against a single set of criteria.[84]

It would be part of the ongoing strategy for bringing state surveillance powers, and other elements of national security and law enforcement, onto a more harmonised statutory footing, alongside statutes such as the **Security Service Act 1989**, **Intelligence Services Act 1994**, **Security Service Act 1996**, **Criminal Investigations and Procedure Act 1996**, and **Police Act 1997**.

The Regulation of Investigatory Powers Act 2000

The result of the government's consultation and deliberations post-*Halford* was the **Regulation of Investigatory Powers Act 2000 (RIPA 2000)**. This repealed the **Interception of Communications Act 1985**, but still maintained much of the pre-existing public telecommunications interception regime, including the oversight mechanisms. The Act itself is split into seven parts covering the following:

- 'Communications';
- 'Interception';
- 'Acquisition and disclosure of communications data';
- 'Surveillance and covert human intelligence sources';
- 'Investigation of electronic data protected by encryption etc';
- 'Scrutiny etc of investigatory powers and of the functions of the intelligence services'; and
- 'Miscellaneous and supplemental'.

The remainder of this section will consider the interception provisions: the following two sections will consider acquisition and disclosure of communications data, and the investigation of electronic data protected by encryption. Surveillance and covert human intelligence sources are outside the scope of this chapter.

Under **RIPA 2000**, it is a criminal offence, punishable by up to two years' imprisonment, for a person 'without lawful authority' to intercept communications by post, or through a public telecommunications system.[85] It is also a criminal offence, punishable by up to two years' imprisonment, for a person without the express or implied consent of a person having the right to control the operation or the use of that system, and 'without lawful authority', to intercept communications through a private telecommunications system.[86]

Where communications are intercepted on a private telecommunications system, with the express or implied consent of a person having the right to control the operation or the use of that system, but without 'lawful authority', parties to the communication may bring a civil action. For example, if an employee believes that his or her employer has unlawfully intercepted their telephone conversation with a third party, either the employee or the third party may sue the employer.[87] The individual authorising, or carrying out, the interception in such circumstances would not, however, be guilty of a criminal offence.[88]

---

84 Home Office, 1999, op cit, paras 4.1 and 4.5.
85 RIPA 2000, s 1(1).
86 Ibid, s 1(2).
87 Ibid, s 1(3).
88 Ibid, s 1(6).

Interception takes place with 'lawful authority' where:

- all parties to the communication have consented to it, or it is reasonable to believe that they have consented;[89]
- one party has consented to it, and the interception is authorised under Pt II of the **RIPA 2000** as surveillance, rather than an interception;[90]
- it is necessary for the purposes of providing the telecommunications service, and carried out by the provider of that service, or on its behalf;[91]
- it is permitted under s 48 of the **Wireless Telegraphy Act 2006**;[92]
- it is permitted under an international mutual assistance agreement;[93]
- it is permitted under regulations made by the Secretary of State to permit certain kinds of interception in the course of lawful business practice;[94]
- it is permitted under prison rules, in hospital premises in which high security psychiatric services are provided, and in state hospitals in Scotland;[95]
- it is carried out under any statutory power that permits the obtaining of information or of taking possession of any document, or other property;[96] and
- an interception warrant has been issued by the Secretary of State.[97]

The Secretary of State may issue an interception warrant for the interception and disclosure of communications where the scope of the warrant is proportionate to the aim to be achieved, the information required could not reasonably be obtained by other means, and the purpose of obtaining the information is necessary to:

- protect the interests of national security; or
- prevent or detect serious crime in the UK, or in the context of any international mutual assistance agreement; or
- safeguard the economic well-being of the UK.[98]

Interception warrants may only be applied for by, or on behalf of, specific senior members of the intelligence services, police forces, and Commissioners for HM Revenue and Customs (HMRC); they may only be issued by the Secretary of State, except in limited circumstances.[99]

Warrants essentially fall into two categories: warrants for interception of domestic communications; and warrants for interception of telecommunications with an element external to the UK. Internal warrants are required to be limited in scope, in as much as they must refer to one person, or specific premises, as the subject of the interception, and must provide suitable information to be used for identifying the communications that may be, or are, to be intercepted.[100] External telecommunication warrants are considerably broader in scope. The Secretary of State may authorise

---

89 Ibid, s 3(1).
90 Ibid, s 3(2).
91 Ibid, s 3(3).
92 As per Wireless Telegraphy Act 2006, Sch 7, paras 21–24.
93 RIPA 2000, s 4(1).
94 Ibid, s 4(2).
95 Ibid, s 4(3)–(6).
96 Ibid, s 1(5)(c); see, eg, s 9 and Sch 1 of the Police and Criminal Evidence Act 1984 (PACE); see R (on the application of NTL Group Ltd) v Ipswich Crown Court [2002] EWHC 1585.
97 RIPA 2000, s 1(5)(b).
98 Ibid, s 5.
99 Ibid, ss 6–7. Emergency warrants of up to five days' duration can be issued by a senior official, eg a senior civil servant.
100 Ibid, s 8(1)–(2). Note, however, that s 81 defines 'person' as including 'any organisation and any association or combination of persons'.

intercepts on an external communications link (for example, commercial submarine cables having one terminal in the UK and carrying external commercial communications to Europe) on the basis of a certificate that sets out the categories of information to be extracted from the total volume of communications intercepted under a particular warrant, and the reason for the intercept, such as 'national security', 'preventing or detecting serious crime', or 'safeguarding the economic well-being of the United Kingdom'.[101]

The Act sets out limits for the duration of warrants, as well as their renewal and cancellation,[102] and provides a process for their modification.[103] Under **IOCA 1985**, the initial duration of warrants was two months, and renewals lasted for one month for the police, and up to six months for the security and intelligence services. Under **RIPA 2000**, the initial duration is increased to three months, and renewals for preventing or detecting serious crime increased to three months.[104] There is no limit on renewals if the perceived need for the warrant under s 5 remains.

Material obtained under general warranted interception, including communications data, must be held in accordance with specific safeguards. These are that:

- the number of people to whom the material/data is disclosed, the amount of data that is disclosed, and the amount of copying permitted are limited to the minimum required to meet the stated purpose of the interception;
- the material/data is destroyed as soon as there are no longer any grounds for retaining it to meet the stated purpose of the interception;
- the above points are overridden where the Secretary of State, the Interception of Communications Commissioner, or the Tribunal require the material/data to be retained/disclosed/copied to fulfil their functions under **RIPA 2000**, or a person conducting a criminal prosecution requires it to meet his or her duty to secure the fairness of the prosecution.

Material obtained under certificated warranted interception, including communications data:

- must be certified as necessary to be examined in the interests of national security for the purpose of preventing or detecting serious crime, or for the purpose of safeguarding the economic well-being of the UK; and
- cannot be intended to identify material contained in communications sent by, or intended for, an individual who presently in the British Islands, and has not been selected by reference to such an individual.

Anything to do with the existence or implementation of a warranted interception, including the content of the intercepted material and related communications data, must be kept secret by those to whom the warrant is addressed (for example, the applicant for an interception warrant), by those involved in the interception process (for example, civil servants, police officers), and by those undertaking the interception (for example, public telecommunications service providers and their employees, ISPs, anyone controlling part of a UK telecommunications system). Disclosure, unless specifically permitted under the Act, is a criminal offence.[105]

The bar on the use of evidence, or questioning or assertion, in legal proceedings likely to reveal the existence or absence of a warrant under **IOCA 1985**, s 9, which caused so much judicial

---

101 Ibid, s 8(4)–(5); originally contained in IOCA 1985, s 3(2).
102 Ibid, s 9.
103 Ibid, s 10.
104 Ibid, s 9(6).
105 Ibid, s 19.

confusion is retained in **RIPA 2000**, s 17. However, the Act attempts to clarify both when that bar does not apply, and when material may or may not be disclosed.

The bar is removed where:

- there is a 'relevant offence', including offences under **IOCA 1985**, **RIPA 2000**, the **Wireless Telegraphy Act 2006**, and the **Official Secrets Acts 1911 and 1989**, etc;[106]
- there are civil proceedings initiated by the Secretary of State under **RIPA 2000**, s 11(8), to require a person to give effect to a warrant;[107]
- there are proceedings before the Tribunal, or an appeal from the Tribunal permitted by order of the Secretary of State;[108]
- there are proceedings before, or arising out of proceedings before, the Special Immigration Appeals Commission or Proscribed Organisations Appeal Commission;[109] or
- anything is done in, for the purposes of, or in connection with, so much of any legal proceedings as relates to the fairness or unfairness of a dismissal on the grounds of any conduct breaching **RIPA 2000**, ss 1(1) or (2), 11(7), or 19, or **IOCA 1985**, s 1.[110]

Disclosure can be made:

- generally, where there is a lawful interception without a warrant under **RIPA 2000**, ss 1(5)(c), 3 or 4, including any disclosure needed to prove that this was the case;[111]
- generally, about the conduct of a person convicted of an offence under **RIPA 2000**, ss 1(1) or (2), 11(7) or 19, or **IOCA 1985**, s 1;[112]
- to a prosecutor, about the facts of and materials (where not destroyed) relating to an interception, to ensure that a prosecution is conducted fairly;[113]
- to a judge, in a case in which he or she has ordered the disclosure to be made to him or her alone on the ground that it is essential in the interests of justice;[114]
- in exceptional circumstances, following a disclosure to a judge, of such limited facts derived from interception by the prosecution as he or she thinks essential in the interests of justice, except for facts disclosing that an interception has taken place, where this is barred by **RIPA 2000**, s 17(1).[115]

In terms of providing oversight, **RIPA 2000** provides for an Interception of Communications Commissioner who holds, or has held, a high judicial office.[116] The Commissioner's role is, first, to review the processes for provision of interception warrants, acquisition of communications data, and decryption notices, and second, to review arrangements for the protection of intercepted material and encryption keys.[117] The Commissioner makes an annual report to the Prime Minister, and may additionally report on breaches of the Act within his or her remit, and failures in the protection

---

106 Ibid, s 18(1).
107 Ibid, s 18(1)(b).
108 Ibid, s 18(1)(c)–(d).
109 Ibid, s 18(1)(e)–(f); SIAC and POAC can see the intercept material in order to make their decision, but it cannot be disclosed to an organisation or individual in question, or to their legal advisers (s 18(2)).
110 Ibid, s 18(3).
111 Ibid, s 18(4)–(5).
112 Ibid, s 18(6).
113 Ibid, s 18(7)(a).
114 Ibid, s 18(7)(b); see *R v Gibbs* [2004] EWCA Crim 3431.
115 Ibid, s 18(8)–(10); see *R v Khachik* [2006] EWCA Crim 1272.
116 Ibid, s 57.
117 Ibid, s 57(2).

of intercepted material and encryption keys. The Prime Minister must lay the annual report before each House of Parliament, but can redact material that is contrary to the public interest, or prejudicial to national security, or that relates to the prevention or detection of serious crime, the economic well-being of the UK, or the operations of certain public authorities.[118]

The Act further provides for a Tribunal, which, amongst other tasks, considers complaints made with regard to the interception of communications – notably:

- proceedings concerning interception of communications in the course of their transmission that are incompatible with **ECHR** rights; and
- complaints by a person who believes that his or her communications have been intercepted in challengeable circumstances, or carried out by or on behalf of the intelligence services.[119]

The **RIPA 2000** Tribunal is restricted to application of the principles that would be applied by a court on an application for judicial review, although since the **Human Rights Act 1998**, this will include violations of an individual's human rights, including the principle of proportionality.[120] The Tribunal has the power to award compensation, quash or cancel any warrant or authorisation, and require the destruction of records of information. Where proceedings, complaints, or references are brought before the Tribunal, its public decision on the matter is confined to making a statement to the complainant that it has found in his or her favour, or not. No reasons will be given for the decision.[121] Decisions of the Tribunal cannot be appealed or questioned in any court.[122]

The Act also provides for the making of codes of practice in relation to the powers and duties in **RIPA 2000**. The Secretary of State is required to consult on any codes of practice, lay the drafts before Parliament, and bring them into force through an order. This requirement is largely designed to overcome criticisms that there was both a lack of clarity in, and public information about, the interceptions regime under **IOCA 1985**. The Home Office published a Code of Practice on Interception of Communications in 2002, and further Codes of Practice on Investigation of Protected Electronic Information, and Acquisition and Disclosure of Communications Data in 2007.[123] The Codes have no binding force, and there are no direct consequences for breaching them.

Following the passage of **RIPA 2000**, the **Telecommunications (Lawful Business Practice) (Interception of Communications) Regulations 2000 (LBPR)** were laid before Parliament under s 4(2). The aim of the Regulations was to authorise a range of interceptions of communications on private telecommunications systems (including those run by government departments and public authorities) that would otherwise be prohibited by **RIPA 2000**, s 1. Lawful interceptions must be carried out by, or with the consent of a person carrying on a business, for purposes relevant to that person's business, and using that business's own telecommunication system; the Regulations do not authorise private interceptions on public telecommunications systems. The controller of the telecommunications system must also have made all reasonable efforts to inform potential users that interceptions may be made.[124]

---

118 Ibid, s 58(2)–(7).
119 Ibid, s 65.
120 Ibid, s 67(2).
121 Ibid, s 67(7).
122 Ibid, s 67(8).
123 Home Office, *Interception of Communications: Code of Practice*, 2002, London: HMSO; Home Office, *Investigation of Protected Electronic Information: Code of Practice*, 2007, London: HMSO; Home Office, *Acquisition and Disclosure of Communications Data: Code of Practice*, 2007, London: HMSO.
124 The Regulations do not define 'users'. However, the government's intention is fairly clear: 'The persons who use a system are the people who make direct use of it. Someone who calls from outside, or who receives a call outside, using another system is not a user of the system on which the interception is made' (Department of Trade and Industry, *Notes for Business: Lawful Business Practice Regulations Information*, URN 06/1481, London: HMSO, p 15).

Where these criteria are met, interceptions are authorised for monitoring or recording communications:

● to establish the existence of facts, to ascertain compliance with regulatory or self-regulatory practices or procedures, or to ascertain or demonstrate standards that are or ought to be achieved (for example, quality control and training);[125]
● in the interests of national security;[126]
● to prevent or detect crime;[127]
● to investigate or detect unauthorised use of telecommunication systems;[128] or
● to secure, or as an inherent part of, effective systems operation.[129]

They are also authorised for monitoring, but not recording:

● received communications to determine whether they are business or personal communications;[130] or
● communications made to anonymous telephone helplines.[131]

Interception Post-RIPA 2000

RIPA 2000 was designed to harmonise the interception of communications across public and private telecommunications systems, to provide a technology-neutral approach to interception, to address some of the more problematic aspects of **IOCA 1985**, and to be **ECHR**-compliant.[132] Subsequent case law and debate suggests that the Act's approach to these issues has met with mixed results, not least because of its complexity and the lack of clarity in key definitions.[133]

Interception

The issue of when an 'interception' took place was initially at issue, because the definition in s 2(2) was felt to be unclear:

a person intercepts a communication in the course of its transmission by means of a telecommunication system if, and only if, he—

(a) so modifies or interferes with the system, or its operation,

(b) so monitors transmissions made by means of the system, or

---

125 LBPR 2000, SI 2000/2699, reg 3(1)(a)(i).
126 Ibid, reg 3(1)(a)(ii). Interception for this purpose can only be carried out by, or on behalf of, specific persons named in the RIPA 2000, s 6(2)(a)–(i), such as the Director-General of the Security Service: ibid, reg 3(2)(d)(i).
127 Ibid, reg 3(1)(a)(iii).
128 Ibid, reg 3(1)(a)(iv).
129 Ibid, reg 3(1)(a)(v).
130 Ibid, reg 3(1)(b).
131 Ibid, reg 3(1)(c).
132 It was also designed to implement Art 5 of the Telecommunications Data Protection Directive (Directive 97/66/EC), which required Member States to safeguard the confidentiality of communications. This has since been replaced by the Privacy and Electronic Communications Directive (Directive 2002/58/EC).
133 See also Gillian Ferguson and John Wadham, 'Privacy and surveillance: A review of the Regulation of the Investigatory Powers Act 2000' (2003) Special edn EHRLR 101; David C Ormerod and Simon McKay, 'Telephone intercepts and their admissibility' [2004] Crim LR 15; Hiral Bhatt, 'RIPA 2000: A human rights examination' (2006) 10(3) Int J Hum Right 285; Okechukwu B Vincents, 'Interception of internet communications and the right to privacy: An evaluation of some provisions of the Regulation of Investigatory Powers Act against the jurisprudence of the European Court of Human Rights' [2007] EHRLR 637; John R Spencer, 'Telephone-tap evidence and administrative detention in the UK', in M Wade and A Maljevic (eds), *A War on Terror? The European Stance on a New Threat: Changing Laws and Human Rights Implications*, 2009, Guildford: Springer.

(c)   so monitors transmissions made by wireless telegraphy to or from apparatus comprised in the system,

as to make some or all of the contents of the communication available, while being transmitted, to a person other than the sender or intended recipient of the communication.

In *Hardy*,[134] it was argued that tape recordings of a telephone conversation made by an undercover police officer who was a party to the call were interceptions. The Court disagreed, holding that the recording was not an interception under **RIPA 2000**, s 1(5)(b), for which an interception warrant would be required (and from which any evidence would be inadmissible under s 17(1)). If it had been an interception, it would fall under s 3(2), and would thus be authorised if one of the parties to the telephone call (the police officer) had consented and the surveillance/ interception was authorised under Pt II of the Act (and the evidence would be admissible under s18(4) as an unwarranted interception). However, the Court held that, because the contents of the calls were not made available, whilst being transmitted, to any third party, there was no interception at all.[135]

In R v E,[136] police installed a surveillance device in the defendant's car, which recorded his conversation with people in the car, as well as his side of conversations on his mobile phone. E sought to have the audio evidence collected excluded on the basis that it was an interception of his phone calls, that this required an interception warrant or was otherwise an unlawful interception by police officers, and that s 17(1) meant the evidence was inadmissible. He referred to the **RIPA 2000** Code on Covert Surveillance, which stated that:

> The use of a surveillance device should not be ruled out simply because it may incidentally pick up one or both ends of a telephone conversation, and any such product can be treated as having been lawfully obtained. However, its use would not be appropriate where the sole purpose is to overhear speech, which at the time of monitoring is being transmitted by a telecommunications system. In such cases an application should be made for an interception of communication warrant under s. 5 of the 2000 Act.[137]

The Court was unpersuaded by this, or by the argument that compliance with **Directive 97/66/ EC** and Art 8 **ECHR** required the interpretation of 'interception' to be considered much more broadly, stating that EU Member States must issue national regulations to protect the confidentiality of telecommunications. In particular, they must prohibit listening, tapping, storage, or other kinds of interception of communications by others without prior consent, except when legally authorised in accordance with Art 14(1).

It held that the Code of Practice went further than **RIPA 2000** required, and that, while the Directive clearly called for protection against infringement of confidentiality of communications by means other than simple interception, this did not justify the interpretation that E sought to place on the term 'interception' in **RIPA 2000**. Rather, the Court felt that:

134 R v Hardy [2002] EWCA Crim 3012 (CA) (CD). The Court relied upon the judgment in R v Hammond, McIntosh & Gray [2002] EWCA Crim 1243, decided under the IOCA 1985, for the proposition that interception did not include the recording of a telephone conversation by one party to the call. See also R v M [2003] EWCA Crim 3764; R v MacDonald, unreported (Woolwich Crown Court, 23 April 2002).
135 See Ormerod and McKay, op cit, 25–7, for discussion of this point.
136 R v E [2004] EWCA Crim 1243 (CA) (CD).
137 Home Office, *Covert Surveillance: Code of Practice*, 2002, London: HMSO, para 4.1, adopted under RIPA 2000, s 71(5).

The present case, in which nothing was recorded which had passed through any telecommunication system, even if the words did simultaneously go into it is, if anything, a clearer case of the absence of interception than are those cases of participant monitoring.[138]

It appears that the courts have adopted a strict technical test for interception under **RIPA 2000**, relating to considerations around securing the integrity of particular technologies (that is, the transmission mode is protected), rather than on the confidentiality of private communications (that is, the content is protected).[139]

Control

The question of the meaning of ' "control" of the operation, or the use of, a private telecommunications system' under s 1(6)(a)–(b) was addressed in *Stanford*,[140] in which the defendant had either personally intercepted emails, or had had emails intercepted on his behalf, via a mirroring service set up on a mail server owned by a company of which he had been deputy chairman.

> 1. . . .
>
> (6) The circumstances in which a person makes an interception of a communication in the course of its transmission by means of a private telecommunication system are such that his conduct is excluded from criminal liability under subsection (2) if—
>
> (a) he is a person with a right to control the operation or the use of the system; or
> (b) he has the express or implied consent of such a person to make the interception.

Stanford's argument was that a third party, X, an employee of the company, had been given and permitted to use an administrator username and password for the company server by Y, who was authorised to use an administrator username and password on that system. X was not given any limits to his use of the system, but was not expressly permitted to set up the mirroring processes that he then used to divert email messages to a server operated by himself and Stanford. Because X had been given the administrator username and password, Stanford suggested, either X was a person who had a right to control the operation or use of the system (s 1(6)(a)), or X had the express or implied consent of such a person to make the interception (s 1(6)(b)).

The judge at first instance rejected this line of argument, holding that 'right to control' for the purposes of s 1(6) meant 'more than merely "the right to access or to operate the system"'. It meant the right to authorise or forbid the operation or the use of the system'. Even if X had a general authorisation to operate or use the system, this would not include authorisation to 'make the interception' for the purposes of s 1(6)(b), which would only apply if X had authority to make the

---

138 R v E, [30]. See also R v Smart and Beard [2002] EWCA Crim 772 (under the IOCA 1985); R v Allsopp [2005] EWCA Crim 703 (under the RIPA 2000).
139 Both Ormerod and McKay, op cit, 24–7, and Ian Walden, 'Communication service providers: Forensic source and investigatory tool' (2006) 11(1) Inform Secur Tech Rep 10, 13, suggest that this is too narrow an interpretation to provide the privacy protections required under the ECHR, which are premised on the suspect's ability to foresee, with a reasonable degree of certainty, the consequences of his or her actions.
140 R v Stanford [2006] EWCA Crim 258. See also David C Ormerod, 'Interception of communications: Meaning of "control" of the operation or the use of a private telecommunications system' [2006] Crim LR 1069; Clive Walker, 'Email interception and RIPA: The Court of Appeal rules on the 'right to control' defence' (2006) 11(1) Communications Law 22; Fiona Mares, 'The Regulation of Investigatory Powers Act 2000: Overview of the case of R v Clifford Stanford (CA (Crim Div) 1 February 2006) and the offence of unlawfully intercepting telecommunications on a private system (section 1(2) offence)' (2006) 22(3) CLSR 254.

specific interceptions. The judge drew the reasoning for this from the House of Lords' judgment in *Allison*,[141] in which the court addressed s 17 of the **Computer Misuse Act 1990**:

> Access of any kind by any person to any programme or data held in a computer is unauthorised if –
>
> > (a) he is not himself entitled to control access of the kind in question to the programme or data.

Lord Hobhouse stated that 'the word "control" in this context clearly means authorise and forbid ... it is plain that [the subsection] is not using the word "control" in a physical sense of the ability to operate or manipulate the computer'.

Faced with this interpretation, the defendant pleaded guilty, but sought leave to appeal on the ground that the judge had misinterpreted the meaning of 'control'. This was refused by the Court of Appeal, which held that:

- the purpose of **RIPA 2000** was to protect the privacy of private telecommunications;
- this purpose was primarily to be achieved by the criminal sanctions in s 1;
- if anyone with unrestricted physical ability to operate and use a telecommunications system were to be exempt from criminal liability for intercepting communications, this would wholly undermine s 1;
- s 1(6)(b) made provision for the grant of express authority to make intercepts; and
- the grant of express authority to make intercepts must come from a person with a right to control the operation or the use of the system (for example, a senior manager), but such persons would not necessarily have the ability physically to operate and use a telecommunications system.

Thus, for s 1(6)(b) to make sense, 'control' had to mean 'authorise and forbid', not 'the ability physically to operate and use a telecommunications system'.

Admissibility of Intercept Evidence

Despite the attention paid in **RIPA 2000**, ss 17 and 18, to the question of the admissibility of intercept evidence, several issues remained unclear. In *Scotting*,[142] the appellant was a serving prisoner. His telephone calls from prison were monitored and recorded by the prison authorities, as was general practice. He telephoned his girlfriend and arranged for her to smuggle drugs into the prison. Following the interception of these calls, they were arrested and charged. At trial, it was argued that the interceptions were inadmissible under s 17(1) and did not fall under any of the s 18(4) exceptions. The Court held that:

- s 17(1) was not relevant, because there was no interception falling within s 17(2) – that is, an interception under warrant, or an interception that should have been under warrant;
- s 18(4) permitted the disclosure of the contents of a communication if the interception of that communication was lawful by virtue of ss 1(5)(c), 3, or 4.

---

141 R v *Bow Street Metropolitan Stipendiary Magistrate and Allison, ex p Govt of the United States of America* [2000] 2 AC 216; cf *Bignell v DPP* [1998] 1 Cr App R 1. See also discussion in Chapter 4.
142 R v *Scotting* [2004] EWCA Crim 197; see also R v *Abiodun* [2005] EWCA Crim 9.

Under **RIPA 2000**, s 4(4), interceptions taking place in prisons are authorised if they are in conformity with the Prison Rules made under s 47 of the **Prison Act 1952**, and r 35(a)(iv) of **Prison (Amendment)(No 2) Rules 2000, SI 2000/2641**, permitting interceptions of telecommunications from prison for the prevention, detection, investigation, or prosecution of crime. If disclosure was not statutorily barred, then interceptions were admissible under the ordinary rules of evidence.

Harder questions were raised in *Attorney General's Reference* (No 5 of 2002),[143] in which the Attorney General requested an opinion as to whether – and, if so, to what extent – a criminal court might investigate whether intercept material relied on by the Crown was obtained by tapping a private, as opposed to a public, telecommunications system. The questions arose from a case in which police officers were believed to be supplying confidential and sensitive information to a known criminal, and to journalists. Authorisation was given by the chief constable to intercept communications on several telephone extensions used by the officers. The interceptions were made on a telecommunications system, which linked several police stations. This was made up of several private automated branch exchanges (PABX) linked by telecommunications lines, which were part of a public telecommunications system. A telephone call received on, or made from, the relevant telephones activated the interception equipment, which created a duplicate call. This was relayed through a BT telephone line to another police station, where recording equipment had been installed. Evidence was gathered confirming the supply of confidential information to unauthorised persons, and the police officers and another person were prosecuted on the basis of it.

The prosecution claimed that the interceptions had occurred within a private telecommunications system and it served evidence on the defence pre-trial to prove that fact. The defence countered that the interceptions had taken place on a public telecommunications system and, before presenting its evidence, argued that **RIPA 2000**, s 17, prevented any investigation into the circumstances of the interception, including its claim that the interceptions took place on the public side of the telecommunications system. The judge agreed that this was so, and also that, under **RIPA 2000**, the prosecution could present evidence that the interception had occurred on the private side. This, the defence argued, was unfair and all of the interception evidence should thus be excluded under s 78 of the **Police and Criminal Evidence Act 1984 (PACE 1984)**. The judge agreed. Because the prosecution's case was based on the interception material, it collapsed, and the defendants were acquitted.

The Attorney General sought answers to the following questions.

- Does **RIPA 2000**, s (1), prevent, in criminal proceedings, any evidence being adduced, question asked, assertion or disclosure made, or other thing done in order to ascertain whether a telecommunications system is a public or a private telecommunications system?
- Where interception of a communication takes place on a private telecommunications system, is it permissible in criminal proceedings to ask questions or adduce evidence, etc, to establish that the interception has been carried out by, or on behalf of, the person with the right to control the operation or use of the system?[144]

In its opinion, the Court of Appeal distinguished the previous case law in *Preston* (decided under **IOCA 1985**, s 9), and stated that its answers to these questions would be, respectively, 'No' and

---

143 *Attorney General's Reference* (No 5 of 2003); Re R v W [2003] EWCA Crim 1632 – a reference under Criminal Justice Act 1972, s 36(1); [2004] UKHL 40 – a reference under Criminal Justice Act 1972, s 36(3).
144 The AG asked these questions with regard to interceptions that took place before and after the coming into force of RIPA 2000, because the events in the case took place under the IOCA 1995 regime. This discussion only covers the post-RIPA questions.

'Yes', but referred the questions to the House of Lords for further consideration. Both the Court of Appeal's and Lords' rationales for reaching their judgments are compelling testimony to the complexity of the **RIPA 2000** exclusionary rule.

After examining the statutory provisions at length, their Lordships concluded that:

> Given the obvious public interest in admitting probative evidence . . . and the absence of any public interest in excluding it, I am satisfied that a court may properly enquire whether the interception was of a public or private system and, if the latter, whether the interception was lawful. If the court concludes that it was public, that is the end of the enquiry. If the court concludes that it was private but unlawful, that also will be the end of the enquiry. If it was private but lawful, the court may (subject to any other argument there may be) admit the evidence.[145]

. . .

> Before the statute of 2000 was enacted the clear understanding was that a court may examine whether an interception was made within a public or private system. . . . Neither the text of the 2000 Act, nor any of the external aids to its construction, give any indication that such a radical change of policy was intended.[146]

Thus the position with regard to admissibility of evidence obtained by interception under **RIPA 2000** currently remains that it is broadly inadmissible, except in limited statutorily defined circumstances, or where it is necessary to determine whether an interception took place on a public or private telecommunications system.

External Warrants

The compliance of the arrangements for external warrants under both **IOCA 1985** (s 3(2)) and **RIPA 2000** (s 8(4)–(5)) with the **ECHR** was challenged in *Liberty v UK*.[147] During the 1990s, the Ministry of Defence routinely intercepted all telephone, facsimile, and email communications transmitted between BT's radio stations at Clwyd and Chester, including the majority of electronic communications between Ireland and England and Wales. The interception system could intercept 10,000 simultaneous telephone channels and operated from 1990 until 1997. The claimants, Liberty, British Irish Rights Watch, and the Irish Council for Civil Liberties, noted that, during this period, they were in regular telephone contact with each other and also provided legal advice, via telephone, to those who sought their assistance. Many of their communications would have passed between the BT radio stations and would thus have been intercepted.

Interception was, it was alleged, a five-stage process, as follows.

(1) A broad warrant would be issued, specifying an external communications link, or links, to be physically intercepted.
(2) The Secretary of State would issue a certificate, describing the categories of information that could be extracted from all of the communications intercepted under a particular warrant. These would be based on the broad classes of information specified in **IOCA 1985**, such as

145 [2004] UKHL 40, [20], *per* Lord Bingham.
146 Ibid, [30], *per* Lord Steyn.
147 *Liberty v United Kingdom* (2009) 48 EHRR 1. See Benjamin Goold, '*Liberty and others v The United Kingdom*: A new chance for another missed opportunity' [2009] Public Law 5.

'national security', 'preventing or detecting serious crime', or 'safeguarding the economic well-being of the United Kingdom'. The combination of a certificate and a warrant formed a 'certified warrant'. All communications falling within the specified category would be physically intercepted.

(3)   Once communications were intercepted, they would be filtered using an automated process operating under human control, looking for specific search terms. Search terms and filtering criteria were not specified in certificates, but were selected and administered by state officials without judicial scrutiny or ministerial oversight.

(4)   Communications intelligence reports were then reviewed to remove names or material identifying individuals or organisations, where their inclusion in the final report was not proportionate or necessary for the lawful purpose of the warranted interception.

(5)   Information obtained by an interception would then be disseminated to recipients whose purpose(s) for receiving the information was proportionate and necessary in the circumstances.[148]

This process, the organisations claimed, breached Art 8 **ECHR**, because it constituted an interference with their rights under Art 8(1), and was not 'in accordance with the law' under Art 8(2), because it did not have a basis in domestic law that was adequately accessible and formulated with sufficient precision as to be foreseeable.

The claimants had initially sought to investigate the lawfulness of any warrants that had been issued in respect of their communications between England and Wales and Ireland, via the Interception of Communications Tribunal (under **IOCA 1985**, s 7) in September 1999. The Tribunal investigated their complaint and, in December 1999, ruled that there was no contravention of **IOCA 1985**, ss 2–5, in relation to a relevant warrant or certificate. The problem that claimants faced was that the Tribunal's ruling, whilst meeting the statutory criteria for a response under **IOCA 1985**, left them without any definitive statements as to whether a warrant had been issued or, if it had, whether it had been complied with. The claimants also complained to the Director of Public Prosecutions (DPP) about an unlawful interception and requested that those responsible be prosecuted. The DPP passed the matter to the Metropolitan Police for investigation. In April 2000, the police reported that their enquiries had not revealed an offence contrary to **IOCA 1985**, s 1.

In December 2000, **IOCA 1985** was replaced by **RIPA 2000**, and the Investigatory Powers Tribunal was created, incorporating the former functions of the Interception of Communications Tribunal. In August 2001, the complainants began proceedings in the Investigatory Powers Tribunal complaining of interferences with their rights to privacy for their telephone and other communications from 2 October 2000 onwards.[149] During the proceedings, the key question became whether the interception of communications between the UK and an external source, captured under a warrant under **IOCA 1985**, s 3(2), or later **RIPA 2000**, s 8(4), in order to filter them for intelligence data was 'in accordance with the law'. In December 2004, the Investigatory Powers Tribunal ruled on the issue of accordance with the law, stating that:

The selection criteria in relation to accessing a large quantity of as yet unexamined material obtained pursuant to a s8(4) RIPA 2000 warrant . . . are those set out in s5(3) RIPA 2000. The

---

148 Before the ECtHR, the UK government refused to confirm or deny that this was the process, but conceded that, in principle, any person who sent or received any form of telecommunication outside the British Islands during the period in question could have had it physically intercepted under an s 3(2) (IOCA 1985) warrant. It insisted, however, that if interception of the applicants' communications occurred, it was lawfully sanctioned by an appropriate warrant.
149 British-Irish Rights Watch and ors v The Security Service and ors, IPT/01/62/CH.

Complainants' Counsel complains that there is no 'publicly stated material indicating that a relevant person is satisfied that the [accessing] of a particular individual's telephone call is proportionate'. But the Respondents submit that there is indeed such publicly stated material, namely the provisions of s6(1) of the Human Rights Act which requires a public authority to act compatibly with Convention rights, and thus, it is submitted, imposes a duty to act proportionately in applying to the material the s5(3) criteria.

To that duty there is added the existence of seven safeguards listed by the Respondents' Counsel, namely (1) the criminal prohibition on unlawful interception (2) the involvement of the Secretary of State (3) the guiding role of the Joint Intelligence Committee ('JIC') (4) the Code of Practice (5) the oversight by the Interception of Communication Commissioner (whose powers are set out in Part IV of the Act) (6) the availability of proceedings before this Tribunal and (7) the oversight by the Intelligence and Security Committee, an all-party body of nine Parliamentarians created by the Intelligence Services Act 1994 . . .

It is plain that, although in fact the existence of all these safeguards is publicly known, it is not part of the requirements for accessibility or foreseeability that the precise details of those safeguards should be published . . .

. . . [F]oreseeability is only expected to a degree that is reasonable in the circumstances, and the circumstances here are those of national security . . . In this case the legislation is adequate and the guidelines are clear. Foreseeability does not require that a person who telephones abroad knows that his conversation is going to be intercepted because of the existence of a valid s. 8(4) warrant . . .

The provisions, in this case the right to intercept and access material covered by a s. 8(4) warrant, and the criteria by reference to which it is exercised, are in our judgment sufficiently accessible and foreseeable to be in accordance with law. . . . In this difficult and perilous area of national security, taking into account both the necessary narrow approach to Article 8(2) and the fact that the burden is placed upon the Respondent, we are satisfied that the balance is properly struck.[150]

However, the ECtHR was unconvinced by this reasoning and the UK government's arguments. In its ruling in 2008, which assessed the **IOCA 1985** external warrant system, the Court reiterated that:

the mere existence of legislation which allows a system for the secret monitoring of communications entails a threat of surveillance for all those to whom the legislation may be applied. This threat necessarily strikes at freedom of communication between users of the telecommunications services and thereby amounts in itself to an interference with the exercise of the applicants' rights under Article 8, irrespective of any measures actually taken against them.[151]

With regard to **IOCA 1985**, the Court noted that:

66 Under s. 6 . . . the Secretary of State, when issuing a warrant for the interception of external communications, was called upon to 'make such arrangements as he consider[ed] necessary' to ensure that material not covered by the certificate was not examined and that material that

---

150 Cited in *Liberty v United Kingdom*, above, [15].
151 Ibid, [56], citing *Weber and Saravia v Germany* (Dec) No 54934/00, §77, 29 June 2006.

was certified as requiring examination was disclosed and reproduced only to the extent necessary. The applicants contend that material was selected for examination by an electronic search
engine, and that search terms, falling within the broad categories covered by the certificates,
were selected and operated by officials . . . According to the Government . . ., there were at the
relevant time internal regulations, manuals and instructions applying to the processes of
selection for examination, dissemination and storage of intercepted material, which provided a
safeguard against abuse of power . . . however, details of these 'arrangements' made under
s. 6 were not contained in legislation or otherwise made available to the public.

67 The fact that the Commissioner in his annual reports concluded that the Secretary of State's
'arrangements' had been complied with . . ., while an important safeguard against abuse of
power, did not contribute towards the accessibility and clarity of the scheme, since he was not
able to reveal what the 'arrangements' were . . .

68 The Court notes the Government's concern that the publication of information regarding the
arrangements made by the Secretary of State for the examination, use, storage, communication and destruction of intercepted material during the period in question might have damaged
the efficacy of the intelligence-gathering system or given rise to a security risk. However, . . .
the German authorities considered it safe to include in the G10 Act, as examined in *Weber and
Saravia* . . . express provisions about the treatment of material derived from strategic interception as applied to non-German telephone connections . . . The G10 Act further set out detailed
provisions governing the transmission, retention and use of data obtained through the interception of external communications . . . In the United Kingdom, extensive extracts from the
Code of Practice issued under s. 71 [**RIPA 2000**] are now in the public domain . . . which
suggests that it is possible for a State to make public certain details about the operation of a
scheme of external surveillance without compromising national security.

This led the Court to conclude that **IOCA 1985** failed to indicate sufficiently clearly to individuals
the scope of the powers available under the external warrant process, or the degree of discretion
available over the ways in which they could be exercised. In particular, it failed to follow ECtHR case
law in providing, in a publically accessible form, an overview of the procedures used when selecting
intercepted material for examination, sharing, storage, and destruction. This meant that the interference with the claimants' rights under Art 8(1) could not be justified as being 'in accordance with
the law', as required by Art 8(2).

The judgment has implications for the **RIPA 2000** external warrant system, because it is based
on the **IOCA 1985** system. It appears that, to meet the ECtHR's test for acceptability, further amendments to the existing system will be required, and the ECtHR has given clear indication of the types
of safeguard that it will expect, in its reference to the German **G10 Act**.[152] The **G10 Act** provides a
clearly defined set of legal checks and balances, including the following.

- There are different rules for individual targeted interceptions and 'strategic' interceptions, the
  latter of which can be conducted only for specific types of criminal offence (for example, drug
  trafficking or international terrorism), and when authorised by the Parliamentary Control
  Panel and G10 Commission.
- The nine-member Parliamentary Control Panel (PCP), with general oversight of postal and
  telecommunications monitoring, receives six-monthly reports from the Federal Minister and

---

152 Law on the restriction of the privacy of posts and telecommunications, Gesetz zu Artikel 10 Grundgesetz v 26 June 2001
(BGBl I S 1254), as amended 9 January 2002 (BGBl I S 361).

appoints G10 Commission members. The PCP can request intelligence service documents and files, question staff, and conduct on-site visits to the intelligence services. It can receive information from intelligence service members and ordinary citizens. It reports to the Bundestag and provides information to the general public.

● The four-member G10 Commission examines requests by the intelligence services for specific surveillance operations to ensure that they are legal, necessary, and proportionate. Where filtering of intercepted communications is used, it approves the search terms. Its decisions to permit or deny authorisation are binding. The Commission's staff can demand information, inspect government documents, and conduct on-site visits, and can receive complaints from the public.[153] The Commission is also responsible for notifying subjects of monitoring once the purpose of the monitoring, or use of the data obtained, has ended.[154]

While the **G10 Act** framework has itself been criticised as too secretive, and the G10 Commission is said to be too overstretched to undertake intensive investigations into the activities of the intelligence services,[155] it appears more open and democratically robust than the current **RIPA 2000** regime.

Communications Data, Traffic Data, and Data Retention

Even where the content of messages is not intercepted and accessed, a considerable amount of information can be gathered, or extrapolated, from communications data. Communications data can be broadly divided into three main types:

● *traffic data* – information about a communication, such as the location of a person when using his or her mobile phone;
● *service use data* – information about the use of a communications service, such as itemised telephone call records showing the numbers called; and
● *subscriber information* – information about the user of a communications service, such as the identity of the subscriber to a particular telephone number.[156]

However, the line dividing what is 'content data' and what is 'communication data' is not always clear-cut, because modern communications systems, such as internet services, have rarely been developed with monitoring in mind. Consider, for example, a URL such as www.bristol.ac.uk/

● Click on a link containing that URL on a third-party web page and the browser will access the computer at that location – this is *communication data* (Computer A accessed www.bristol.ac.uk/ at Computer B).
● Visit the Google search engine and key in the search 'University of Bristol'; the search engine will return a list of websites including URLs, one of which will be (the University of Bristol

153 See further Christian Heyer, 'Parliamentary oversight of intelligence: The German approach', in S Yui-Sang Tsang (ed), *Intelligence and Human Rights in the Era of Global Terrorism*, 2007, Westport CN: Praeger, pp 67–77.

154 Goold, op cit, p 10.

155 Heyer, op cit, p 77. Recent scandals suggest that those critics may have a point: 'German spies caught reading journalist's e-mails' (2008) *Deutsche Welle*, 21 April.

156 It is worth noting that there does not appear to be a widely agreed terminology: eg, OECD *Convention on Cybercrime*, Ch 1, Art 1(d), defines 'traffic data' as 'any computer data relating to a communication by means of a computer system, generated by a computer system that formed a part in the chain of communication, indicating the communication's origin, destination, route, time, date, size, duration, or type of underlying service'. See further on this point Lilian Mitrou, 'Communications data retention: A Pandora's Box for rights and liberties?', in A Acquisti and S Gritzalis (eds), *Digital Privacy: Theory, Technologies, and Practices*, 2007, Abingdon: CRC Press, pp 412–13.

webmaster hopes) www.bristol.ac.uk/ – this is *content data* (Computer A asked Computer B for information relating to the University of Bristol).

Both content data and communication data may be capable of being analysed to permit identification of the individual involved in the communication, as well as to provide information about the social group with which the individual communicates (for example, by social network analysis/ subject-based data mining), and the individual's behaviour (for example, by pattern-based data mining).

A key difference between 'content data' and 'communication data', both in technological operation and practical use, is that content data is rarely retained by the operator of the communications system in routine operations. A telephone company does not keep a recording of the content of a conversation and an ISP does not keep a copy of an email (although an email may be temporarily stored at various points in the ISP's email system – not so that the ISP can access and read it, and the user and not the ISP has control over its retention). Communications data is usually collected and stored for a period of time to allow the communications provider to provide services (for example, location-based services, personalised phone tariffs), to record transactions for billing purposes (for example, itemised phone or text bills), and to identify individuals using their services (for example, to ensure authorised use). It may also be used by providers to identify further marketing opportunities through behavioural analysis (for example, personalised advertisements on web pages based on browsing history).

Thus there is an expectation that communication data will be collected, held, and used for a limited period of time, and for specific purposes, by communications providers. There is also an expectation that content data will not be treated in that fashion. This has been reflected in the legal frameworks relating to each type of data, in which communication data has, until recently, received significantly less protection than content data. However, as modern communications technology has developed, it is clear that the significance of communications data for individual privacy has increased:

> Traffic data is directly linked to our identity and can be automatically processed and evaluated. Whom we know, where we go and what we do on the Internet reflects our personalities, our preferences and our weaknesses in unprecedented detail.[157]

This change was recognised in the EU **Directive on Privacy and Electronic Communications**,[158] which extended privacy protection beyond the content of the communication to include associated traffic and location data.[159] The Directive required that:

- traffic data relating to subscribers and users be erased or made anonymous when it was no longer needed for the purpose of the transmission of a communication;[160]
- processing of traffic data for the purposes of subscriber billing and interconnection payments could only take place in the period during which the bill could lawfully be challenged or payment pursued;[161]

---

157 Working Group on Data Retention, 'Position on the processing of traffic data for "security purposes" ' (2009) 21 March, available online at www.statewatch.org/news/2009/mar/eu-dat-ret-wg-e-security-position-paper.pdf

158 Directive 2002/58/EC of the European Parliament and of the Council of 12 July 2002 concerning the processing of personal data and the protection of privacy in the electronic communications sector, [2002] OJ L201/37.

159 Article 2(b): ' "traffic data" means any data processed for the purpose of the conveyance of a communication on an electronic communications network or for the billing thereof'; Art 2(c): '"location data" means any data processed in an electronic communications network, indicating the geographic position of the terminal equipment of a user of a publicly available electronic communications service'.

160 Directive 2002/58/EC, Art 6(1).

161 Ibid, Art 6(2).

- traffic data could only be processed for marketing electronic communications services or for the provision of value added services with the subscriber or user's consent, which could be withdrawn at any time;[162]
- subscribers or users had to be informed of the types of traffic data processed, the purpose of the processing, and its duration;[163] and
- processing of traffic data must be carried out by authorised persons handling billing or traffic management, customer enquiries, fraud detection, marketing electronic communications services, or providing a value-added service, and must be restricted to what is necessary for the purposes of such activities.[164]

The Directive prohibited Member States from permitting the listening, tapping, storage, or other kinds of interception or surveillance of communications and the related traffic data by persons other than users, without the consent of the users concerned, except where these actions are permitted by domestic law.[165] Any such law had to be a necessary, appropriate, and proportionate measure within a democratic society to safeguard national security, defence, and public security, and for the prevention, investigation, detection, and prosecution of criminal offences or of un-authorised use of the electronic communication system.[166] The Directive also permitted Member States to adopt legislative measures providing for the retention of data for a limited period for those purposes.[167]

The political environment after the Madrid bombings in 2004 and the London subway bombings in 2005 led to a reassessment of the data retention provisions in the EU, and a new **Data Retention Directive** was proposed as part of a package of measures during the UK presidency of the EU, at the end of 2005.[168] The EU adopted the **Data Retention Directive**[169] in March 2006.[170]

While the terrorist attacks were a key motivator, the stated purpose of the Directive was to achieve EU-wide harmonisation of national requirements for mandatory retention of communications data. It aimed to prevent Member States from, accidentally or deliberately, creating barriers to the cross-border supply of electronic communications services via legal and technical differences in national provisions for data retention designed to aid the prevention, investigation, detection, and prosecution of criminal offences. For example, prior to the Directive, a mobile phone service provider might find that, in order to provide services to customers in multiple Member States, it would be legally required to retain different types of communications traffic data, under different conditions, and for different time periods in each of those Member States. This would be a potential disincentive to entering other Member State markets, and thus protect existing national providers from external competition.

---

162 Ibid, Art 6(3).
163 Ibid, Art 6(4).
164 Ibid, Art 6(5).
165 Ibid, Art 5.
166 Ibid, Art 15(1).
167 Ibid.
168 A draft framework Decision on Data Retention had been proposed in 2004, suggesting retention periods of one to three years, but this was rejected by the European Parliament.
169 Directive 2006/24/EC of the European Parliament and of the Council of 15 March 2006 on the retention of data generated or processed in connection with the provision of publicly available electronic communications services or of public communications networks and amending Directive 2002/58/EC, [2006] OJ L105/54.
170 The Directive's legal basis was questioned by Ireland and Slovakia (Case C–301/06, OJ 2006 C 237), which argued unsuccessfully that its purpose was not ensuring the functioning of the internal market (Art 95 EC), but the investigation, detection and prosecution of crime (Title VI TEU – in particular Arts 30, 31(1)(c), and 34(2)(b)). See Monica Vilasau, 'Traffic data retention v data protection: The New European Framework' (2007) 13(2) CTLR 52.

Access to Retained Communications Data in the UK

In the UK, since 2004, access to communications data has been largely controlled by Ch II of Pt I of **RIPA 2000**.[171] Prior to this, access by a range of agencies was premised on the basis of powers derived from the common law and various legislation.

The Act permits access to communications data[172] in the form of traffic data,[173] service use information,[174] and subscriber information.[175] The Home Office gives examples of these in its Code of Practice. Communications data can be accessed if a public authority can demonstrate that it is necessary and proportionate, and required:

● in the interests of national security;
● for the purpose of preventing or detecting crime or of preventing disorder;
● in the interests of the economic well-being of the UK;
● in the interests of public safety;
● for the purpose of protecting public health;
● for the purpose of assessing or collecting any tax, duty, levy or other imposition, contribution or charge payable to a government department;
● for the purpose, in an emergency, of preventing death or injury or any damage to a person's physical or mental health, or of mitigating any injury or damage to a person's physical or mental health; or
● for any purpose, not already covered, which is specified for the purposes of this subsection by an order made by the Secretary of State.[176]

A wide range of public authorities can lawfully obtain communications data, including:

● intelligence and law enforcement agencies – such as the security services, police, the Serious Organised Crime Agency (SOCA), and HMRC;
● emergency services – such as ambulance services, fire authorities, and HM Coastguard; and
● other public authorities – such as the Financial Services Authority (FSA), local councils, and the Home Office UK Border Agency.[177]

'Authorisations' to obtain communications data are granted by a 'designated person' within each of these authorities.[178] A formal authorisation or notice must be completed by the relevant senior official of that authority, stating the necessity and proportionality of obtaining specific information about a given individual.[179] This notice or authorisation has an authorisation period of one month,

---

171 Relevant public authorities for the purposes of Ch II of Pt I of the Act may only use other statutory powers to obtain communications data from a postal or telecommunications operator if that power provides explicitly for obtaining communications data, or is conferred by a warrant or order issued by the Secretary of State or a person holding judicial office: Home Office, 2007, op cit, p 5.
172 RIPA 2000, s 21(4).
173 Ibid, s 21(6).
174 Ibid, s 21(4)(b).
175 Ibid, s 21(4)(c).
176 Ibid, s 22(2). See the Regulation of Investigatory Powers (Communications Data) Order 2010, SI 2010/480, which adds 'to assist investigations into alleged miscarriages of justice; and for the purpose of assisting in identifying any person who has died as a result of a crime or who is unable to identify himself because of a physical or mental condition, other than one resulting from crime, or obtaining information about the next of kin or other connected persons of such a person or about the reason for his death or condition'.
177 In 2009, the Interception Commissioner noted that 52 police forces, the three security agencies, 474 local authorities, and 110 other authorities were able to request communications data: Interception of Communications Commissioner (ICC), *Report of the Interception of Communications Commissioner for 2008*, 2009, London: HMSO.
178 See SI 2010/480.
179 RIPA 2000, s 23.

unless renewed.[180] These powers are self-authorised by the body concerned, with no direct external or judicial oversight, although the Interception of Communications Commissioner maintains general oversight, notably by a system of periodic inspection.[181] A Code of Practice on the Acquisition and Disclosure of Communications Data was published by the Home Office in 2007, and provides guidance for public authorities on how to meet the requirements for acquisition of data. While the Code is not legally binding, it is likely to be taken as a benchmark by the courts for deciding whether authorisations and notices by public authorities are lawful. In 2007, there were 519,260 requisitions of communications data from telephone companies and ISPs; this dropped slightly to 504,073 in 2008.[182]

The UK Code of Practice for Voluntary Retention of Communications

When the **Data Retention Directive** was adopted, the UK was already operating a voluntary system of data retention of communications traffic data via the Code of Practice for Voluntary Retention of Communications.[183] The Code was provided for in Pt 11 of the **Anti-Terrorism, Crime and Security Act 2001 (ATCSA 2001)**, and came into force in January 2004. Although the Code was, in principle, a voluntary system, there was considerable pressure from government on the telecommunications industry to accede to it, with the threat of a mandatory scheme being imposed via statutory instrument. The Code was unpopular with communications providers, partly because of industry concern that compliance with a voluntary code – as opposed to a legal obligation – could breach human rights and data protection legislation, and partly because of concerns about the expense attached to developing permanent retention processes.

The Code only applied to communication service providers who provided a public telecommunications service in the UK, as defined in **RIPA 2000**, s 2, and who retained communications data in line with the provisions of the **ATCSA 2001**. It did not apply to individuals and organisations that did not provide a public service (for example, corporate telecommunications and computer networks).

The Code did not require telecommunications service providers and ISPs to retain communications data, but it was designed to suggest agreed time periods for the retention of certain types of communications data, and to provide a basis for the retention of communications data beyond normal business operations for national security purposes, and the prevention or detection of crime, or the prosecution of offenders relating to the national security. The Code did not require that service providers collect information that they would not have collected in their business activities. The maximum retention period for communications data held under the Code was twelve months. However, if the communication service provider's business practices required a longer retention period, the Code did not prevent this.

The voluntary Code was replaced for fixed network telephony and mobile telephony communications providers in 2007, and for internet access, internet email, or internet telephony in 2009, by secondary legislation, based on the **Data Retention Directive**.

The EU Data Retention Directive

Like the Code, the **Data Retention Directive** is only concerned with the traffic and location data of legal entities and natural persons, and any related data necessary to identify a subscriber or regis-

---

180 Ibid, s 23(5).
181 Ibid, s 57(b). The Commissioner carried out only one inspection of a large local authority in 2008, and only eight inspections of local authorities in total, due to 'a temporary shortage of staff': ICC, op cit, p 18.
182 ICC, *Report of the Interception of Communications Commissioner for 2007, 2008*, London: HMSO; ICC, 2009, op cit.
183 See further Edgar A Whitley and Ian Hosein, 'Policy discourse and data retention: The technology politics of surveillance in the United Kingdom' (2005) 29(11) Telecommunications Policy 857.

tered user. It explicitly states that the retention of the content of electronic communications, including information consulted using an electronic communications network, is outside its scope – but while it does not require such retention, it does not explicitly bar it.

The Directive does not apply to all communications networks; instead it refers to a limited subset of communications networks. It requires that certain data are to be retained where those data are generated or processed by providers of publicly available electronic communications services, or by providers of a public communications network, in the process of supplying the communications services concerned. Determining what activities will cause an organisation to be deemed to be a 'provider of publicly available electronic communications services' or 'a provider of a public communications network' is left to the Member States. There is no requirement in the Directive for communications service providers to create new data for retention purposes; merely a requirement to retain existing data generated or produced in the course of their service provision.[184]

Questions were raised about the Directive's statement that all data 'generated or processed' by a communications service provider would be covered. Whilst nominally technology-neutral, this phrase seems more applicable to point-to-point telecommunications than to internet services. There were suggestions that this could mean that internet service providers might be required not only to retain only data of their own subscribers, but also the data of users whose communications simply pass over their network. However, in practice, it seems that the former, pragmatic, interpretation has been applied by Member States.[185]

The Directive sets out several categories of data that must be retained. These are data necessary to:

- trace and identify the source of a communication, such as the telephone number and subscriber name and address (telecoms), or user ID and name and address of the subscriber or registered user (internet);
- identify the destination of a communication, such as the number called, any number to which a call is rerouted, name and address of subscriber/user (telecoms), or user ID or telephone number of the intended recipient(s) of an internet telephony call, and name and address of subscriber/user (internet);
- identify the date, time, and duration of a communication;
- identify the type of communication, such as the telephone or internet service used;
- identify users' communication equipment, or what purports to be their equipment; and
- identify the location of mobile communication equipment, such as cell ID and the geographic location of cell.

The Directive also requires the retention of data relating to unsuccessful call attempts where those data are generated or processed, and stored (for example, telephony data) or logged (for example, internet data). This is not data that would normally be held, for example, by telecommunications companies for billing purposes.[186] As far as retention periods are concerned, the Directive states that Member States may set a retention period of not less than six months and not more than two years from the date of the communication. However, Member States can, if circumstances dictate and for a limited period of time, extend the maximum period as long as they inform the other Member States and the Commission that they have done so, and of their reason for doing so. The Commission will then check after six months to ensure that the extended retention period is not being used as a disguised trade restriction. It appears that where such an extension is approved by the Commission,

---

184 Eleni Kosta and Peggy Valcke, 'Retaining the Data Retention Directive' (2006) 22(5) CLSR 370, 374.
185 Gareth Davies and Gayle Trigg, 'Being data retentive: A knee jerk reaction' (2006) 11(1) Communications Law 18.
186 Ibid.

it may be continued indefinitely. Previous experience, in areas such as data privacy, suggests that the broad scope of the discretion over time periods may not bode well for uniformity of retention and the harmonisation process.

The Directive indicates that data retained must be kept subject to appropriate technical and organisational measures to ensure that they can be accessed by specially authorised personnel only; except for data that has been accessed and preserved (presumably for the purposes specified under the Directive), retained data must be destroyed at the end of the period of retention. With regard to the former point, it was suggested that, given that data generated or processed by communications service providers in the process of supplying communications services is likely to include items such as billing data, this might mean either designating billing clerks as 'specially authorised personnel', or requiring separate systems for business-purpose data and data retained pursuant to the Directive.[187] In practice, it seems that, at least while the data is still being used for business purposes communications, service providers in the UK will continue with their existing operational practices.

A final area of interest lies with the use of the retained data. The Directive provides that data retained under the Directive is to be provided only to 'the competent national authorities in specific cases and in accordance with national law'. It does not specify any criteria for 'competent authorities' – which means that some Member States may choose to widen access beyond law enforcement agencies – nor does it provide guidance as to the reasons for which retained data may be accessed – again leaving this to the discretion of the Member States.[188]

UK Data Retention (EC Directive) Regulations 2007 and 2009

The UK implemented the Directive via secondary legislation in two stages. The first piece of legislation, the **Data Retention (EC Directive) Regulations 2007**, covered fixed network telephony and mobile telephony communications providers.[189] The **Data Retention Directive** permitted Member States to postpone application of that Directive to the retention of communications data relating to internet access, internet telephony, and internet email,[190] and the UK delayed implementation in those areas until the **Data Retention (EC Directive) Regulations 2009**, which then replaced and repealed the 2007 Regulations.[191]

The 2009 Regulations require any public communications provider generating or processing communications data in the UK to retain the specific categories of data pertaining to its type of network or service[192] for up to twelve months.[193] Where a communications provider fails to co-operate with this requirement, the Secretary of State may take civil action to seek an injunction, or specific performance of a statutory duty under s 45 of the **Court of Session Act 1988**, or other appropriate relief.[194]

Fixed network telephony communications providers have to provide the:

- calling telephone number;
- name and address of the subscriber or registered user of any such telephone;

---

187 Ibid.
188 See Gerrit Hornung and Christoph Schnabel, 'Data protection in Germany II: Recent decisions on online-searching of computers, automatic number plate recognition and data retention' (2009) 25(2) CLSR 115.
189 SI 2007/2199. See Richard Jones, 'UK Data Retention Regulations' (2008) 24(2) CLSR 147.
190 Directive 2006/24/EC, Art 15(3).
191 SI 2009/9780. See Claire Walker, 'Data retention in the UK: Pragmatic and proportionate, or a step too far?' (2009) 25(4) CLSR 325.
192 Data Retention (EC Directive) Regulations 2009, reg 4.
193 Ibid, reg 5.
194 Ibid, reg 10(6).

- telephone number dialled and any telephone number to which the call is forwarded or transferred;
- name and address of the subscriber or registered user of any such telephone;
- date and time of the start and end of the call; and
- telephone service used.[195]

Mobile telephony communications providers must provide the:

- calling telephone number;
- name and address of the subscriber or registered user of any such telephone;
- telephone number dialled and any telephone number to which the call is forwarded or transferred;
- name and address of the subscriber or registered user of any such telephone;
- date and time of the start and end of the call;
- telephone service used;
- international mobile subscriber identity (IMSI) and the international mobile equipment identity (IMEI) of the telephone from which a telephone call is made;
- IMSI and the IMEI of the telephone dialled;
- the date and time of the initial activation of the service and the cell ID from which the service was activated, for prepaid anonymous services;
- cell ID at the start of the communication; and
- data identifying the geographic location of cells by reference to their cell ID.[196]

Internet access, email, and telephony providers must provide the:

- user ID allocated;
- user ID and telephone number allocated to the communication entering the public telephone network;
- name and address of the subscriber or registered user to whom an internet protocol (IP) address, user ID, or telephone number was allocated at the time of the communication;
- user ID or telephone number of the intended recipient of the call (internet telephony);
- name and address of the subscriber or registered user and the user ID of the intended recipient of the communication (internet email or internet telephony);
- date and time of the log in to and log off from the internet access service, based on a specified time zone (internet access);
- IP address, whether dynamic or static, allocated by the service provider to the communication (internet access);
- user ID of the subscriber or registered user of the service (internet access);
- date and time of the log in to and log off from the service, based on a specified time zone (internet email or internet telephony);
- internet service used (internet email or internet telephony);
- calling telephone number (dial-up access); and
- digital subscriber line (DSL) or other end point of the originator of the communication.[197]

---

195 Ibid, Sch 1.
196 Ibid, Sch 2.
197 Ibid, Sch 3.

The data retained must be stored in such a way that it can be transmitted without undue delay in response to requests.[198] However, such storage must be consistent with the requirements of the **Data Protection Act 1998** (and is subject to review by the Information Commissioner),[199] and the data retained may only be released for a specific purpose permitted or required by law, such as a properly constituted request under **RIPA 2000**, s 22.[200] The government can reimburse any expenses incurred by a public communications provider in complying with the Regulations that are agreed in advance.[201]

Encryption

Encryption involves turning ordinary information (or plaintext), such as letters or emails, into apparent random strings of characters (or ciphertext). Decryption is the reversal of this process. Both encryption and decryption require the use of specific algorithms and a 'key'. Symmetric-key cryptography refers to encryption in which both the sender and receiver share the same key; asymmetric key cryptography refers to encryption in which two different but mathematically related keys are used – a public key and a private key. In asymmetric systems, the public key is typically used for encryption, while the private key is used for decryption. Thus if Alice wants to send Bob a secret message, she uses her private key to generate a public key, which she passes to Bob. Bob uses the public key to encrypt the message to send to Alice, who decrypts it with her private key. Even if a third party, Eve, intercepts the public key, she cannot decrypt the message from Bob to Alice, because the private key cannot be generated from the public key.[202]

The use of encryption is not a new phenomenon. Long before the development of computers, various groups, including the military, spies, diplomats, and powerful elites, were using encryption techniques to try to protect individual and group secrets in communications. Equally, other parties were constantly seeking to decrypt their ciphers. The trial and execution of Mary Queen of Scots in 1587 were, in part, precipitated by the interception and decryption by cryptographers in the employ of Elizabeth I of Mary's encrypted communications with the members of the Babington Plot. During the Second World War, the ability of Polish and UK cryptographers to decrypt messages enciphered using the Enigma machines conferred a significant advantage to the Allied forces.[203] However, the widespread availability of strong encryption for personal privacy protection is a relatively recent phenomenon, driven by the rise of ubiquitous access to personal computing facilities.

Since the development of significant open academic/commercial research into encryption in the 1970s, the problem that has faced national governments has been how to ensure a balance between public access to, and use of, strong encryption, whilst maintaining the ability of national security and law enforcement agencies to access private communications.[204] Initially, this tended to take the form of direct or indirect prohibitions on public access to encryption. In the USA and UK, for example, public research into the development and use of encryption technologies was not barred, but was subject to national security restrictions, such as patent secrecy orders and classifica-

---

198 Ibid, reg 8.
199 Ibid, reg 6.
200 Ibid, reg 7. This is not necessarily a very restrictive definition, as Parliament (and possibly the courts, through disclosure orders such as Norwich Pharmacal orders) may permit or require that further public and private bodies be granted access to retained data.
201 Ibid, reg 11.
202 For a detailed discussion of cryptography, see HX Mel and Doris M Baker, *Cryptography Decrypted*, 5th edn, 2002, Indianapolis, IN: Addison-Wesley Professional; Friedrich L Bauer, *Decrypted Secrets: Methods and Maxims of Cryptology*, 4th edn, 2006, Berlin: Springer.
203 For a definitive history of cryptography, see David Kahn, *The Codebreakers: The Comprehensive History of Secret Communication from Ancient Times to the Internet*, 1996, New York: Scribner.
204 See further, Andrew Charlesworth, 'Munitions, wiretaps and MP3s: The changing interface between privacy and encryption policy in the information society', in K De Leeuw and JA Bergstra (eds), *The History of Information Security*, 2007 Amsterdam: Elsevier; Aaron Perkins, 'Encryption use: Law and anarchy on the digital frontier' (2005) 41 Hous L Rev 1625.

tion of research. In France, the use of encryption in communication was prohibited without authorisation by the government.

However, there were a number of problems with these approaches. The primary problem was that as information technologies were taken up by the commercial sector, the need for widespread access to strong encryption to provide adequate security for the use of those technologies – notably in sectors such as banking and online services – became increasingly obvious. Additionally, some countries, such as the USA, found it difficult, on constitutional grounds, to justify barring their citizens from securing their communications, should they wish to do so. Indeed, arguments based on the US First Amendment played a significant role not only in the spread of strong encryption technology to the American public, but also in the export of such technology overseas.

Even as national governments were losing the battle to restrain the use of encryption technologies by their own citizens, they were also discovering that it was difficult to prevent the spread of such technologies outside their borders. An international arrangement, negotiated amongst Western countries led by the USA, during the period immediately after the Second World War, and which remained in place throughout the Cold War, sought to limit the spread of strong encryption. Initially, this was because it was seen to be of purely military application, then because it was a 'dual-use' technology, in that it had legitimate civilian uses, but also still had military applications. However, by the 1990s, with the effective end of the Cold War, the united position began to fragment and, despite attempts led by the USA to build a new consensus on restriction of encryption technologies, many countries began openly selling strong encryption products into the international marketplace.[205] This led to increased pressure on the US government to relax its export position, as US companies complained that they were losing significant competitive advantage by only being able to sell products with weak encryption.

The economic pressures to permit public use of strong encryption in support of widening public take-up of internet technologies, including email communication, web-browsing, and e-commerce, left governments looking for a viable fallback position. It was no longer economically tenable (particularly in laissez-faire Western economies) to use legal measures to directly ban or inhibit such uses of encryption. Equally, it was politically problematic to be seen to be permitting the widespread use of a technology that could potentially damage national security or hinder law enforcement. How could this circle be squared?

One possible avenue that suggested itself was to mandate a government-approved encryption standard under which national security agencies and law enforcement bodies were provided with a back door, or with access via 'escrowed' encryption keys. Attempts to implement this approach dominated government encryption policy and lawmaking in the USA and Europe through the late 1990s. Such a policy approach, however, provided the potential for future wholesale public surveillance by government bodies and law enforcement agencies. This possibility, combined in many jurisdictions with the proposed provision of relatively weak protections to deter abuse, was to provoke a furious backlash from privacy organisations and the commercial sector alike.[206]

By the early 2000s, it was clear that, at the international level, even states such as France, which had fought a long rearguard action alongside the USA to prevent strong encryption gaining a foothold amongst the general public, had been largely defeated. Although they might not have totally liberalised their policies on encryption, they had been forced by market pressures to accept that the use of regulatory tools, such as export controls and the various iterations of key escrow, were no

205 Charlesworth, op cit, pp 782–8.
206 Ibid, 794–7.

longer effective means of controlling the use of encryption technologies by the public.[207] The Cold War national security arguments that had held sway for half a century were unpersuasive in a globalised commercial marketplace that was increasingly dependent upon secure telecommunication and computer network services. However, if the requirements of national security were diminishing as a justification for government intervention in the public use of encryption, their place was being rapidly overtaken by the perceived requirements of law enforcement. The 'Red Menace' was replaced in the rhetoric of those promoting greater powers for law enforcement agencies to combat criminal use of encryption by the 'Three Horsemen of the Internet' – that is, child pornographers, drug dealers, and terrorists.

UK Encryption Controls

The UK government tested the water with regard to internal encryption controls (as opposed to export restrictions) in the late 1990s, when it sought to garner support for key escrow in the form of a system of trusted third parties (TTPs).[208] The Labour Party had been, in Opposition, opposed to encryption controls, including key escrow.[209] In power, the new Labour government largely continued the policy approach that the Department of Trade and Industry (DTI) had adopted prior to the 1997 election.[210] This envisaged the introduction of licensing arrangements for TTPs, possibly modelled on the licensing of telecommunications providers, and specifying the competence criteria that TTPs (offering services to the public) would have to meet, as well as what legal access arrangements (to client's encryption keys) would be required by law enforcement agencies. In April 1998, the DTI announced, in its secure Electronic Commerce Statement, that it would introduce legislation to license those bodies providing, or facilitating the provision of, cryptography services and to enable law enforcement agencies to obtain a warrant for lawful access to information necessary to decrypt the content of communications or stored data

The government did, indeed, pass legislation providing for the registration and requirements of cryptography service providers in ss 1–6 of the **Electronic Communications Act 2000 (ECA 2000)**. However, these required a further statutory instrument to be made by the Secretary of State to bring them into force,[211] and when this did not occur, they were repealed on 25 May 2005 under a 'sunrise provision'.[212]

National Security and Criminal Investigations

This left the issue of law enforcement and national security-related access to encrypted materials, and that was duly addressed in **RIPA 2000**, Pt III, headed 'Investigation of Electronic Data Protected by Encryption'.[213]

The Act applies where any encryption-protected information:

---

207 It is worth noting, however, that certain types of cryptographic product still remain subject to export controls: see Department for Business, Enterprise and Regulatory Reform (BERR), *UK Strategic Export Control Lists*, 2009, London: HMSO.

208 See further, Yaman Akdeniz and Clive Walker, 'UK government policy on encryption: Trust is the key' (1998) 3 Journal of Civil Liberties 110.

209 Labour Party, *Communicating Britain's Future: Labour Party Policy on the Superhighway*, 1995, London: Labour Party.

210 Department of Trade and Industry (DTI), *Paper on Regulatory Intent concerning Use of Encryption on Public Networks*, 1996, London: HMSO; DTI, *Licensing of Trusted Third Parties for the Provision of Encryption Services: Public Consultation Paper on Detailed Proposals for Legislation*, 1997, London: HMSO.

211 ECA 2000, s 16(2).

212 Ibid, s 16(4).

213 See further Alan S Reid and Nicholas Ryder, 'For whose eyes only? A critique of the United Kingdom's Regulation of Investigatory Powers Act 2000' (2001) 10(2) ICTL 179; Yaman Akdeniz and Clive Walker, 'Whisper who dares: Encryption, privacy rights and the new world disorder', in Y Akdeniz, C Walker, and D Wall (eds), *The Internet, Law and Society*, 2000, London: Longman.

- comes into the possession of any person (or is likely to do so):

  o via a statutory power to seize, detain, inspect, search, or otherwise to interfere with documents or other property;
  o by means of the exercise of any statutory power to intercept communications;
  o as a result of having been provided or disclosed in pursuance of any statutory duty; or

- has, by any other lawful means not involving the exercise of statutory powers, come into the possession of any of the intelligence services, the police, or HMRC.[214]

In such circumstances, where permission is granted by court order, by warrant, by statute, or (in certain circumstances) by the Secretary of State,[215] that person can require a third party in possession of an encryption key to disclose that key where it is necessary:

- for the exercise or proper performance by any public authority of any statutory power or statutory duty;
- in the interests of national security;
- for the purpose of preventing or detecting crime; or
- in the interests of the economic well-being of the UK.[216]

The disclosure requirement must be proportionate to achieve the aims to be achieved, and the protected information must not be reasonably accessible by other means.[217] No public authority may serve any notice under **RIPA 2000**, s 49, or, when the authority considers it necessary, seek to obtain appropriate permission without the prior written approval of the National Technical Assistance Centre (NTAC) to do so. The NTAC provides technical support to public authorities, particularly law enforcement agencies and the intelligence services. It may grant approval in specific cases, or it may give approval generally to a public authority if it assesses that authority as competent to exercise the powers in **RIPA 2000**, Pt III.[218]

Where a disclosure notice is made, it must:

- be in writing, or in some other permanent record;
- describe the protected information, state the grounds for disclosure, specify the office, rank, or position held by the person making it, specify the office, rank, or position of the person who gave permission for it, and specify a reasonable time period in which it must be complied with; and
- set out the disclosure that is required by the notice, and the form and manner in which it is to be made.[219]

Where a disclosure notice is given to an officer or employee of a corporation, it must, unless impracticable, be given to the most senior employee or officer available, unless this would defeat the purpose of the notice.[220]

When a disclosure notice is issued, if the person receiving it holds both the protected information and a means of obtaining access to the unencrypted information, he or she may use any key in

---

214 RIPA 2000, s 49 (1)(a)–(e).
215 Ibid, Sch 2.
216 Ibid, s 49(2)(b) and (3).
217 Ibid, s 49(2)(c)–(d).
218 Home Office, 2007, op cit, paras 3.09–3.11.
219 RIPA 2000, s 49(4).
220 Ibid, s 49(5)–(6).

his or her possession to obtain access to the information and make a disclosure of the information in an intelligible form, or he or she may disclose the key to the issuer of the notice. If he or she holds only the key, he or she must disclose that. If he or she no longer holds the key, he or she must disclose all information that would facilitate the obtaining or discovery of the key, or the putting of the protected information into an intelligible form.[221] Failure to make necessary disclosures is a criminal offence carrying a penalty of up to two years' imprisonment and the burden of proof is on the individual to demonstrate that he or she no longer had access to the encryption keys when the notice was given.[222]

In certain circumstances, a disclosure notice may require the person to whom the notice is given and any other person who becomes aware of it, or of its contents, and who knows, or has reasonable grounds for suspecting, that the notice contains a secrecy requirement to keep secret the giving of the notice, its contents, and any actions taken under it. Breaching this requirement (that is, 'tipping off') is also a criminal offence, carrying a penalty of up to five years' imprisonment.[223]

The Act also requires that:

- those who issue disclosure notices and those who operate on their behalf only use disclosed keys for obtaining access to, or putting into an intelligible form, the protected information covered by the notice;
- the uses to which the keys are put are reasonable and proportionate in the context of the case; and
- the keys are stored in a secure manner and that all records of the key are destroyed when no longer required.[224]

Persons making disclosures under **RIPA 2000** can be compensated by the government for any costs incurred in complying with a disclosure order.[225] The Home Office has provided a Code of Practice for the Investigation of Protected Electronic Information. This provides guidance to be followed when requiring the disclosure of protected electronic information in an intelligible form, or acquiring the means by which protected electronic information may be accessed or put into an intelligible form.[226]

The disclosure powers under **RIPA 2000**, s 49, did not come into force at the same time as the main **RIPA 2000** provisions, and their implementation was delayed until October 2007. Relatively few disclosure orders have been sought.[227] The requirement to disclose was challenged in R v S & A,[228] in which the defendants, having been served notices under s 49 of the Act by the police and refused to comply with them, were each charged with an offence under s 53(1). The defendants claimed that the requirement to provide information to the police under ss 49 and 53 was an infringement of the privilege against self-incrimination and contravened Art 6 **ECHR**. The Court of Appeal, in rejecting their claim, noted that the principle that evidence existing 'independent of the will of the subject' does not normally engage the privilege against self-incrimination is clearly

---

221 Ibid, s 50.
222 Ibid, s 53.
223 Ibid, s 54.
224 Ibid, s 55; see further Nicko van Someren, 'RIPA Part III: The intricacies of decryption' (2007) 4(3–4) Digital Investigation 113.
225 Ibid, s 52
226 Home Office, 2007, op cit.
227 Between April 2008 and March 2009, NTAC approved 26 applications for service of a notice under s 49, RIPA 2000. Seventeen notices were then judicially authorised (no notice placed before a judge was refused) and 15 notices were served. Eleven individuals failed to comply, resulting in seven charges and two convictions: Office of Surveillance Commissioners, *Annual Report of the Chief Surveillance Commissioner to the Prime Minister and to Scottish Ministers for 2008–2009*, 2009, HC 704 SG/2009/94, London: HMSO, p 12.
228 R v S(F) and A(S) [2008] EWCA Crim 2177; R Pattenden, 'Privilege against self-incrimination' (2009) 13(1) IJEP 69; Andrew J Roberts, 'Evidence: privilege against self-incrimination: Key to encrypted material' [2009] Crim L Rev 191.

established in domestic law[229] and, comparing the encryption key to the key to a locked drawer, concluded that the encryption key was 'independent of the will of the subject'. The Court further noted that if the encrypted item did prove to contain incriminating evidence, then the fact that the defendant knows the encryption key is itself incriminating, and this might trigger the privilege against self-incrimination. However, even were the privilege to be triggered, it was not an absolute privilege, and could be legitimately overridden by a statutory provision, without breaching Art 6 **ECHR**, where the purpose for doing so was legitimate and proportionate.[230]

Other states have since adopted a similar approach to obtaining access to encrypted materials. The Council of Europe's **Cybercrime Convention** requires that all parties to it to 'adopt such legislative and other measures as may be necessary to empower its competent authorities to order any person who has knowledge about the functioning of the computer system or measures applied to protect the computer data therein to provide, as is reasonable, the necessary information' to permit search or access to computer systems and computer storage media in their jurisdiction. Citing the **Cybercrime Convention** as a model, the Australian government introduced a new federal law, the **Cybercrimes Act 2001 (Cth)**, which as one of its measures amended the federal **Crimes Act 1914 (Cth)**, inserting a new section allowing law enforcement agencies to compel individuals to reveal private encryption keys, ID numbers, or passwords for the purpose of prosecuting computer-related offences. Failure to comply is a criminal offence.[231]

Developing Areas

The changes in the UK legal framework surrounding the collection of information by interception and data retention, and the control of methods by which the public might seek to obscure communication content, have tended to reflect two main objectives. The first is to preserve the legitimate need of government and law enforcement agencies to retain and enhance access to such information in a changing technological environment, to fulfil mandates such as preserving national security and fighting crime. The second is the requirement, in a democratic society, to ensure that the scope of the powers – and the extent of political and administrative discretion in undertaking such collection – is clearly known to the public, that the uses of such powers are necessary, proportionate, and subject to meaningful oversight, and that any abuses of those powers are exposed and appropriately remedied.

There will always be a tension between these two objectives, influenced by ongoing political, social, and technological developments. As a result, the balance between the power of the state to engage in communications surveillance and the ability of the citizen to prevent, or exert influence to control, excessive use or abuse of those powers is in constant flux. It is a measure of the importance of both objectives that, when it comes to drafting laws, granting administrative powers, and designing practical processes, rational analysis of that balance can easily be lost amidst polemic. Measured assessment and appropriate balancing often comes only later.

The **RIPA 2000** framework, across its provisions on interception powers, access to retained data, or control of public use of encryption, provides a salutary example of this. A decade after its inception, the *Liberty* case (discussed above) will require the government to reconsider its transparency and oversight mechanisms. Criticisms of the use of **RIPA 2000** powers, including access to communications data by public authorities, led to a consultation of which public authorities should

---

229 Citing *Attorney-General's Reference (No 7 of 2000)* [2001] EWCA Crim 888, *R v Kearns* [2002] EWCA Crim 748, and *R v Hundall and Dhaliwal* [2004] EWCA Crim 389.

230 *Brown v Stott* [2001] 2 WLR 817.

231 Nickolas J James, 'Handing over the keys: Contingency, power and resistance in the context of section 3LA of the Australian Crimes Act 1914' (2004) 23 U Queensland LJ 10.

have those powers and the level of authorisation required to employ their use in local authorities.[232] Perhaps unsurprisingly, this resulted in little change.[233] Even the limited use of the **RIPA 2000** decryption powers has also led to criticism that they are being used for purposes that are disproportionate to the original goal of the legislation in tackling serious crime and threats to national security.[234] The inadmissibility of interception material as evidence in court (s 17) also continues to stir controversy, as two government reviews published in 2005 and 2008 disagreed on the possibility of changing the current position. The report of the former led the government to conclude that the risks of using intercept evidence outweighed the benefits of doing so,[235] while the latter review, headed by Sir John Chilcot, felt that 'it would be possible to provide for the use of intercept as evidence in criminal trials in England and Wales by developing a robust legal model, based in statute and compatible with [the] ECHR'.[236] While the government broadly accepted the Chilcot Review's findings in early 2008, signs of progress on implementing law reform in this area have been limited.[237]

Meanwhile, there have been interesting developments in the private sector. As noted at the outset of this chapter, companies are keenly interested in collecting information about consumer habits, particularly in order to target marketing more efficiently. For large UK communications service providers, which will be required to retain communications data under the **Data Retention Regulations 2009**, building the necessary data retention capability will potentially offer the opportunity to gather more information about their subscribers/users. While the use of communications data held under the Regulations is subject to strict restrictions under privacy legislation, there will inevitably be pressure from the commercial sector to grant wider access to it. Even if this pressure is resisted by government, companies may either seek to take advantage of the wide category of conditions available for lawful processing under the **Data Protection Act 1998**, or may seek to collect and use subscriber information in ways that purport not to trigger data privacy laws.

Major internet service providers in the UK, such as BT, TalkTalk, and Virgin Media, have openly considered adopting, via a third-party service supplier, a technique called 'deep-packet inspection' to inspect and sort their users' data as it travels through their systems, and to use the data gathered (web pages visited, etc) to send targeted advertising based on their users' web activity. Suppliers of such ISP-based behavioural targeting, such as NebuAd and Phorm, claim that their systems do not allow them to know exactly where an individually identifiable user has been or what they have done. As a result, they say, such systems do not breach privacy laws such as the 1998 Act.[238] However, other nominally anonymous data collections, such as search engine search terms, have been shown to be capable of being data-mined in ways that identify individuals, and at present there appears to be limited independent research on the possibility of deriving personally identifiable data from behavioural targeting systems. There has also been some question as to whether such deep-packet inspection would be caught by the interception provisions of **RIPA 2000**.[239] Currently, the situation is uncertain, although the Home Office did release a document (the precise legal status of which is

---

232 Home Office, *Regulation of Investigatory Powers Act 2000: Consolidating Orders and Codes of Practice – A Consultation Paper*, 2009, London: HMSO; Home Office, *Regulation of Investigatory Powers Act 2000: Consolidating Orders and Codes of Practice – Summary of Responses to the 2009 Consultation Paper*, 2009, London: HMSO.

233 The Regulation of Investigatory Powers (Communications Data) Order 2010, SI 2010/480, made adjustments to some public authorities' powers, but did not significantly reduce the number of authorised public authorities.

234 For example, s 49 RIPA notices used against animal rights activists: Mark Ward, 'Campaigners hit by decryption law' (2007) *BBC News*, 20 November, available online at http://news.bbc.co.uk/1/hi/technology/7102180.stm

235 Statement by Home Secretary, HL Deb, vol 668, cols 52–3WS (26 January 2005). The report was not made public.

236 Home Office, *Privy Council Review of Intercept as Evidence*, Cmnd 7324, 2008, London: HMSO.

237 Letter from Sir John Chilcot to the Prime Minister, 9 February 2009, available online at www.parliament.uk/deposits/depositedpapers/2009/DEP2009-0429.pdf

238 Richard Clayton, 'The Phorm "Webwise" system' (2008) 18 May, available online at www.cl.cam.ac.uk/~rnc1/080518-phorm.pdf See also discussion in Chapter 5.

239 Nicholas Bohm, 'The Phorm "Webwise" system: A legal analysis' (2008) 23 April, available online at www.fipr.org/080423phormlegal.pdf

unclear) in response to a request from Phorm, which suggested that 'targeted online advertising' would not be considered to be performing an illegal interception under **RIPA 2000**.[240]

Regardless of the outcome of a comprehensive legal evaluation of the conformity of ISP-based behavioural targeting with current UK data protection or interception law, such activity raises important questions. What impact will developing and future technologies have on the communications surveillance framework in the UK? To what extent should the state or private organisations be able to deploy them in circumstances that may impact negatively on individual citizens? What safeguards should be required in order that the balance between state interests and individual rights is maintained? And are such safeguards appropriate in circumstances in which private interests and individual rights are in the balance?

240 See Home Office, 'Targeted online advertising', FOI Release 9187, 29 April 2009, available online at www.homeoffice.gov.uk/about-us/freedom-of-information/released-information/foi-archive-crime/9187_targeted_online_advertising

Chapter 7

Electronic Commerce

Chapter Contents

Introduction*

Electronic commerce, or commerce taking place via electronic communication media, ranges from the traditional electronic data interchanges on closed networks and commerce via fax or telex, to the modern forms of online commerce via the web, email, and mobile phones. The focus of this chapter is on the latter, and in particular the online selling and buying of goods and services, as opposed to the provision of ancillary services to enable internet access, retrieve data, or host material. The spectrum of the goods or services sold online is wide, encompassing goods and services delivered physically, as well as the new digital intangible goods, such as films, music, software, books, news, financial data, and pornography, and services, such as online banking, internet telephony, or the provision of recreational activities, such as gambling and gaming in virtual worlds. In these latter instances, the contract is not only made, but also performed, electronically. The vast majority of these online transactions are relatively low-value business-to-consumer (B2C) or consumer-to-consumer (C2C) transactions (for example, eBay transactions) rather than business-to-business (B2B) transactions, and so the legal protection of consumers forms a central part of the regulatory landscape.

There is no single legal definition of 'electronic commerce' and indeed, in most legal contexts, none is needed; when electronic transactions are treated the same as comparable offline transactions, there is no need to define electronic commerce. Such a legal position accords perfectly with the notion of 'technological neutrality'[1] according to which legal rights and obligations ought to be dependent solely on the substance of the transaction and not on the underlying technology used to carry it out – whether the 'technology' is the voice, paper, fax, or the phone, or electronic channels. In some ways, the discussion in this chapter (and indeed book) focuses on the areas of law that cannot be applied to the online environment in straightforward fashion and, by definition, this is because the law is or was not sufficiently technologically neutral. However, the notion of technological neutrality – which has figured prominently in the regulatory debate on electronic commerce in the European Union (EU) – tends to be understood more narrowly than described above. For example, in the lead-up to the 2002 EC **Directive on Privacy and Electronic Communications**, the Commission stated that '[t]he aim is to cover *all electronic* communication services in a technology neutral fashion'.[2] In other words, technological neutrality becomes relevant only after a decision has been made that 'electronic communication services' require special regulation. But once within the electronic sphere, it ought not to matter legally whether a film or music file is downloaded onto a computer, a TV set, a mobile phone, or one's coffee machine. This approach then requires a definition of 'electronic commerce', but it also begs the question whether electronic communications indeed require such special regulation and, if so, why. The discussion below shows that much of the special regulation created for electronic commerce is designed to create no more than a level playing field for online and offline transactions, to fill gaps created by the characteristics of the electronic communications. These characteristics of the electronic networked environment may, depending on the context, be the speed and ease of transacting, its low cost, its anonymity, or its irreverence for national boundaries. However, in the final analysis, the rationale for special electronic commerce regulation is substantive technological neutrality: consumers or businesses ought not to prefer one medium over another for transacting on the basis of fearing its increased risks and inadequate remedies. And this aim of substantive neutrality ultimately provides the yardstick for assessing the wisdom or otherwise of the particular regulatory approaches taken to electronic commerce.

---

*   Thank you to David Poyton, Aberystwyth University, for some useful feedback.
1   Chris Reed, 'Taking sides on technology neutrality' (2007) 4:3 SCRIPTed 263, available online at www.law.ed.ac.uk/ahrc/script-ed/vol4-3/reed.asp
2   Proposal for a Directive of the European Parliament and of the Council Concerning the Processing of Personal Data and the Protection of Privacy in the Electronic Communication Sector, COM(2000)385 final, 12 July 2000, Brussels, p 29.

Much of this book, not only this chapter, is concerned with the regulation of electronic commerce, given that online trading potentially triggers a multitude of regulation of both civil and criminal nature. On the civil front, electronic trading often raises implications under intellectual property laws or tort, such as negligence, defamation, or privacy. In the criminal sphere, electronic commerce may be affected by laws regulating data protection or laws regulating certain industries, such as pharmaceutical products, gambling, or banking activities, as well as by consumer protection laws or anti-terrorist, anti-racism, or obscenity regulation. This chapter does not deal with these regulatory concerns. Its focus is broadly contract law, and any regulation that either directly affects contractual rights and obligations or is integral to the contractual process, such as electronic signatures.

A fundamental canon underlying contract law is contractual autonomy – that is, that individuals are free to decide whether to contract or on what terms. The flipside of the freedom to contract on terms mutually agreed is the freedom from state interference with those terms.[3] In practice, however, contractual autonomy never amounts to a total freedom from the state even when it is treated with utmost sanctity. Contractual autonomy interacts with the laws of the land in two fundamental ways. First, it is not a principle that exists over and above the regulatory sphere of a state; its very existence is dependent upon its recognition by the relevant legal order, and in cases of disputes reliant upon the state's enforcement mechanisms, states invariably recognise contractual autonomy, albeit subject to certain limitations, often to protect the consumer, which vary from state to state. For example, under Islamic law, a contract that provides for the payment of interest on a loan is void, and in most legal systems, contracts entered into with minors are not enforceable. Second, contractual parties cannot contract out of the criminal laws or public regulation of a state. This reflects the 'superiority' of public regulation and criminal laws over any terms agreed by private parties, and foreshadows the not-infrequent legitimate interferences of public regulation in private bargains. The above points deserve a special mention in the context of online contracts, given that online terms and conditions have often the appearance of standing over and above any state law. This mistaken perception may partly be explained by the now less common view of cyberspace as being separate from the 'real' world, and partly by the over-regional dimension of online transactions and interactions. But a mistaken perception it is nonetheless.

Online Contracting

Online Advertising and Remedies against Spam

The internet provides a perfect platform for advertising given that it allows for an international market to be reached relatively cheaply. Such advertising occurs in numerous ways: on third-party websites, via banner ads, via email, and more recently via messages sent over social networking sites. Mass-marketing email – which is, 'spam' – in particular has been problematic around the globe. According to some surveys, it accounts for half, or even more than half, of all email traffic. Quite apart from fraudulent and unsavoury spam, even 'innocent' spam has caused huge losses: it clogs up networks and slows down legitimate traffic, forcing businesses and consumers to use anti-spam software and waste hours deleting messages. Most states have responded to spam with restrictive legislation – unfortunately, not with a harmonised solution.[4] The legislative responses fall broadly into two categories: the opt-in approach and the opt-out approach.

The EU has chosen the more restrictive opt-in approach in Art 13(1) of the **Directive on Privacy and Electronic Communications**:[5]

---

3 As an often-forgotten adjunct, party autonomy also entails personal responsibility for one's own decision and thus no protection against unwise decisions.
4 For the competence approaches taken to spam, see Chapter 2.
5 Directive 2002/58/EC. (OJ L212, 7.8.2001).

The use of automated calling systems without human intervention (automatic calling machines), facsimile machines (fax) or electronic mail for the purposes of direct marketing may only be allowed in respect of subscribers who have given their prior consent.

Furthermore, where a customer of a business does not object to the use of his or her email address for marketing purposes at the time that it was collected, he or she must be able to opt out of such use whenever he or she receives a marketing email.[6] Like the EU legislation, the Australian **Spam Act 2003 (Cth)** adopts the opt-in approach, by prohibiting commercial electronic messages unless the receiver consented to the message being sent.[7] In contrast, in the USA, under the **Controlling the Assault of Non-Solicited Pornography and Marketing Act of 2003** (known as the **CAN-SPAM Act**), unsolicited email is not prohibited per se, but must provide the receiver with an opportunity to opt out of receiving advertising messages.[8] In light of these varying stances taken on spam, and given that online businesses cannot always be sure of the location of the recipient, they are best advised to conform to the more restrictive opt-in approach and only send advertising messages to willing participants.

Whether the sanctions to enforce these provisions are sufficient to deter businesses from exploiting email illegitimately is questionable. In the EU, a breach of the prohibition entitles the 'victim' to a judicial remedy (for example, an injunction) and compensation if he or she suffered damage, and may also result in penal sanctions.[9] The problem with spam is that while it is intrusive and annoying, it rarely, on an individual level, gives rise to any damage and is unlikely to justify individual litigation (apart from civil actions concerning the fraudulent content of much spam). This may explain why, in the USA, the **CAN-SPAM Act** makes ISPs (which are widely defined) the only private parties that can take advantage of the civil cause of action for damages.[10] While penal enforcement actions – which are, in the UK, taken by the Information Commissioner – are a more robust sanction for a spammer, they are an onerous enforcement tool considering the number of spammers, and indeed impossible where the spam comes from abroad, especially outside the EU. For these reasons, most regulatory authorities heavily rely upon educational campaigns and self-help mechanisms, in tune with Lessig's four-pillar conception of regulation.[11]

See Chapter 5

See Chapter 1

The statutory availability of civil remedies against spammers in the EU makes the search for remedies within traditional causes of action, such as trespass to goods or intellectual property actions, redundant. In the USA, such actions may, however, still provide a possible avenue for individuals other than ISPs against spammers, given that they cannot take advantage of the statutory tailor-made remedy.[12] The adaptation of trespass to the digital environment illustrates both the potentials and problems of the old law in the online environment. In the early case of *CompuServe v Cyber Promotions Inc*,[13] the court dealt with the requirement for a 'physical contact with the chattel' by stating that that 'electronic signals generated and sent by computer [are] . . . sufficiently physically

---

6 Article 13(2).

7 Section 16.

8 Section 5(a)(4).

9 Article 15(2), which refers to Ch III of the Data Protection Directive 95/46/EC. Note that, in the UK, it is only the Information Commissioner that can ask for an injunction.

10 Successfully applied in *MySpace Inc v Wallace* 498 F Supp 2d 1293 (CD Cal, 2007), in which the defendant had created 11,000 MySpace profiles to disseminate spam to other MySpace.com users.

11 Lawrence Lessig, *Code: And Other Laws of Cyberspace*, 1999, New York: Basic Books. and see discussion in Chapter 1. See also the spam advice provided by the Information Commissioner's Office, available online at www.ico.gov.uk

12 *America Online, Inc v IMS* 24 F Supp 2d 548 (ED Va, 1998); *America Online, Inc v LCGM, Inc* 46 F Supp 2d 444 (ED Va, 1998); *America Online v Prime Data Systems* [1998] US Dist LEXIS 20226.

13 962 F Supp 1015 (SD Ohio, 1997). See also *Cyber Promotions Inc v American Online Inc* 948 F Supp 436 (ED Pa, 1996); *America Online Inc v IMS* 24 F Supp 2d 548 (ED Va, 1998); Mark D Robins, 'Electronic trespass: An old theory in a new context' (1998) 15 Computer Law 1.

tangible to support a trespass cause of action'.[14] The requirement of the chattel being 'impaired as to its condition, quality, or value' was satisfied:

> . . . to the extent that defendants' multitudinous electronic mailings demand the disk space and drain the processing power of plaintiff's computer equipment, those resources are not available to serve CompuServe subscribers. Therefore, the value of that equipment to CompuServe is diminished even though it is not physically damaged by defendants' conduct.[15]

Thus the requirement of physical damage was reinvented to suit the intangible world of bits.

Clickwrap and Browsewrap Agreements

Under English law, a valid contract requires an offer, an acceptance, consideration, and an intention to create legal relations. Whether these elements are satisfied depends to some extent on the type of the online contract. The main types of online contract are 'clickwrap' and 'browsewrap' agreements, and rather more rarely contracts by exchange of emails. In a 'clickwrap' agreement, the customer clicks on an 'I agree', or 'I accept', button close to the terms of the agreement, or a link to them to indicate his or her assent to them. A 'browsewrap', or 'click-free', agreement is one of which most internet users are not aware, or only vaguely so. These agreements are generally found behind links such as 'Terms of use' or 'Legal' at the bottom or top of the website, to which users agree by virtue of their conduct, such as browsing or downloading or using software. For example, the 'Terms and conditions' of GuardianOnline state: 'By using the network, you are deemed to have accepted these conditions.'[16]

Although clickwrap agreements are legally 'safer', many sites still opt for browsewrap agreements, because they are both visually and practically less intrusive. In most (but, as seen below, by no means all) browsewrap agreements neither products nor money change hands, and thus many of the issues and disputes discussed below in relation to clickwrap agreement and contracts entered into by email have often no application or urgency for the parties to browsewrap agreements. The difference between both types of agreement is often legally one of degree only, which explains why courts have not paid much attention to these two different types.

Offer and Acceptance

As indicated, for a contract to be formed, there has to be an offer and an acceptance of that offer. Internet contracts have raised the questions, first, whether a website is an offer or merely an 'invitation to treat', and second, whether an acceptance via email or web-based communications occurs upon sending it or only upon its actual communication to the offeror. Neither of these questions is problematic in browsewrap agreements, because here the acceptance by the user/offeree occurs at the time and place of his or her use, as stipulated by the terms of the agreement.

In relation to clickwrap agreements, both of these questions appear to be answered by Art 11(1) of the **Electronic Commerce Directive**:[17]

> Member States shall ensure . . . that in cases where the recipient of the service places his order through technological means the following principles apply:

---

14 *CompuServe v Cyber Promotions Inc* 962 F Supp 1015, 1021 (SD Ohio, 1997).
15 Ibid, 1022. Note that, because trespass to chattel is not actionable per se, actual damage is necessary both in the USA and in England and Wales.
16 www.guardian.co.uk/help/terms-of-service
17 2000/31/EC, [2000] OJ L 175/1.

- the service provider has to acknowledge the receipt of the recipient's order without undue delay and by electronic means
- the order and the acknowledgment of receipt are deemed to be received when the parties to whom they are addressed are able to access them.

The first paragraph seems to suggest that the supplier of online services *accepts* the customer's *offer* when he *acknowledges* the costumer's *order*. This assumes that the term 'order' equates with the legal concept of 'offer' and the term 'acknowledgment' with the legal concept of 'acceptance'. In the UK, reg 12 of the **Electronic Commerce (EC Directive) Regulations 2002** validates such an assumption only with respect to the second paragraph and only in relation to the 'order'.[18] Thus even in respect of the above second paragraph, it cannot be assumed that the acknowledgement of the order is an acceptance. Although such assumptions would be helpful in providing answers to the online contracting analysis, they are not justified. First, the language of the Article and its meaning in plain English does not support such an interpretation: an 'acknowledgment' of an order does not convey whether the supplier is willing to accept it or not. Second, the provisions are, on their face, intended to give additional safeguards (in the form of confirmations of messages) to online contractual parties in view of the perceived unreliability of cyberspace – consistent with the other provisions in the Directive.[19] So quite regardless of whether the order is, in legal terms, an offer or an acceptance, under the Article, the receipt of the order must still be acknowledged. So the Directive does not offer any guidance as to the proper contractual analysis of offers and acceptances online.

Of some help is Art 10 of the **Electronic Commerce Directive**, which requires that the service provider must, at least in consumer contracts, give the recipient of the service prior notice of the 'different technical steps to follow to conclude the contract'.[20] Thus, under Art 10, the service provider must make it clear when the deal is struck. Unfortunately, this requirement does not apply to contracts concluded 'via electronic mail or by equivalent individual communications'[21] and not at all to providers outside the ambit of the Directive – that is, non-EU providers.

Offer or Invitation to Treat

The issue of whether a website offering goods or services is legally an offer or a mere invitation to treat is significant because it determines whether and, if so, when a contract was concluded, preventing the parties from withdrawing from the bargain. If a website constitutes an offer, the order by the customer concludes the contract and the supplier cannot reject it. If, however, the site is a mere invitation to treat, the customer's order constitutes the offer that he or she can withdraw until the provider accepts it.

Whether a communication constitutes an offer or a mere invitation to treat is a question of the intention of the offeror as communicated to the offeree and as objectively ascertainable from all of the circumstances (hereafter 'objective intention'): did he or she intend to be bound by it or did he or she merely intend to elicit an offer or negotiations with the view to an offer?[22] Although, ultimately, this is a question of fact to be decided in the particular circumstances of the case, traditionally, shop-window displays, supermarket shelves, and advertisements have been treated as invitations to treat,[23] while automatic vending and ticket machines make offers that the customer accepts by putting money in the machine.[24] So far, there has been no judicial pronouncement by an English

---

18 SI 2002/2013. Regulation 12 states: 'Except in relation to regulation 9(1)(c) and regulation 11(1)(b) where "order" shall be the contractual offer, "order" may be but need not be the contractual offer for the purposes of regulations 9 and 11.'

19 Article 5 ('General Information to be Provided') and Art 6 ('Information to be Provided').

20 Article 10(1)(a), which is also applicable to non-consumer contracts unless agreed otherwise.

21 Article 10(4).

22 See, eg, *Gibson v Manchester CC* [1979] 1 WLR 294.

23 *Fisher v Bell* [1961] 1 QB 394; *Pharmaceutical Society of GB v Boots Cash Chemists* [1953] 1 QB 401; *Partridge v Crittenden* [1968] 2 All ER 421.

24 *Thornton v Shoe Lane Parking* [1971] 2 QB 163.

court on online contracts, but academia on the whole supports the shop-window analogy for the following two reasons.[25]

- In the case of non-digital goods, the online business may have a finite supply of those goods and would not want to be exposed to a situation in which the acceptances outstrip the number of goods in its possession.[26] (Note that this argument is generally inapplicable to digital goods, although exceptionally a business may have a licence to supply only a limited number of them.[27] Generally, the limited supply concern can be addressed by making the offer subject to availability.)
- An online business may want to be able to weed out certain customers – for example, customers from legally inhospitable jurisdictions or customers below a certain age.

Although these arguments are persuasive prima facie, they cannot by themselves be decisive, if they are not consistent with the objective intention of both parties as ascertainable by the circumstances of the case.

In clickwrap agreements, in which the customer has to click a 'Proceed', 'Place your order', 'Confirm', or 'Purchase' button after ticking a box with the terms and conditions, it would be reasonable for him or her to expect that this act constitutes the acceptance, not the offer – contrary to academic opinion.[28] The wording and the contractual process of compiling all of the relevant data (such as the name, delivery address, and the payment details), and securing the customer's consent to the terms before his or her final click, all suggest that this click is the last act needed to conclude the contract once and for all, and that any subsequent web notice or email notification merely confirms the details of that contract. From the customer's perspective, because the whole order is on the supplier's terms, why would the supplier need to consent to it? Noteworthy, under German law (interpreting § 145 of the **German Civil Code**), a declaration is an offer if it is clear and complete as far as all of the essential terms of the contract are concerned, so that the other party simply needs to say 'yes' to conclude the contract.[29] That 'yes', it would seem, comes from the online customer after being presented with all of the terms of the agreement. While an online business may analyse orders with a view to rejecting unsuitable ones, if that is not obvious to the customer, it cannot alter his or her reasonable expectation of finality. In that sense, many online contract formation scenarios are comparable to those with traditional vending machines, in which the machine makes the offer and the customer accepts by putting money into it. As Lord Denning stated in *Thornton v Shoe Lane Parking*: 'The offer is made when the proprietor of the machine holds it out as being ready to receive the money. The acceptance takes place when the customer puts his money into the slot.'[30] So even if there are business considerations that support a different conclusion, these will be irrelevant if the customer is not made aware of them.

Because it is in the interest of suppliers to have the power of finally concluding the contract, online businesses may expressly alter what would otherwise be the customer's reasonable expectations, and indeed many do. Amazon.co.uk's 'Conditions of use & sale' state (at Term 14):

---

25 For example, Christoph Glatt, 'Comparative issues in contract formation' (1998) 6 Int JLIT 34, 49ff; Graham Smith (ed), *Internet Law and Regulation*, 4th edn, 2007, London: Sweet and Maxwell, pp 811ff.
26 *Grainger & Son v Gough* [1896] AC 325.
27 Glatt, op cit, 50.
28 Most academic treaties argue for the opposite, but note, in the typical software licence agreements: Andres Guadamuz-González, 'The licence/contract dichotomy in open licenses: A comparative analysis' (2009) 30 U La Verne L Rev 296, 301; Lawrence E Rosen, *Open Source Licensing: Software Freedom and Intellectual Property Law*, 2004, London: Prentice Hall, p 60.
29 Peer Zumbansen, 'Contracting in the internet: German contract law and internet auctions' (2001) 2(7) NJW, available online at http://germanlawjournal.com/index.php?pageID=11&artID=65
30 [1971] 2 QB 163, 169.

> When you place an order to purchase a product from Amazon.co.uk, we will send you an e-mail confirming receipt of your order and containing the details of your order. Your order represents an offer to us to purchase a product which is accepted by us when we send e-mail confirmation to you that we've dispatched that product to you . . .

Alternatively, bmibaby's 'Terms and conditions' simply provide (at Term 5.1.2):

> A reservation is not made until you have received a confirmation number and payment has been received by us.

In both of these cases, the express terms stipulate that it is the business that accepts and thereby concludes the contract.[31] Such contractual classification is likely to be upheld provided that the parties enjoy the rights that are consistent with the classification[32] – that is, the customer is an offeror if he or she is able to withdraw the offer at any time after clicking the 'Confirm' or 'Accept' button, but before the acceptance, and the seller is the offeree provided that he or she is not, by the terms of the contract, bound to accept the offer regardless of his or her wish to do so (as is often the case in online auctions). If that is not the case, the 'labels' in the contractual terms must be taken as wrong in light of the objective intention of the parties.[33]

The above clauses are particularly important to avoid contracts based on pricing errors that have so often made the headlines in recent years. If, in addition, a vendor uses software to pick up unusual buying patterns, it may be able to pick up pricing errors before its acceptance. Once this acceptance has occurred, the situation becomes trickier. For example, in the Singaporean case of *Chwee King Keong v Digilandmall.com Pte Ltd*,[34] the online seller of laser printers worth $3,854, mistakenly priced at $66, tried to get out of 1,600 orders made by six buyers. At the trial stage, the vendor unsuccessfully argued that no contracts came into existence given that the placing of the order was followed by an automated message and email confirming the 'successful transaction'.[35] He succeeded on a different ground: namely, that the orders were void under the common law doctrine of unilateral mistake. On appeal, the court rejected the lower court's reasoning that constructive, and not only actual, knowledge of the mistake by the non-mistaken party is sufficient for the common law doctrine of unilateral mistake, but held that, in equity, constructive knowledge plus an impropriety would suffice to allow the vendor to avoid the contract:

> . . . constructive knowledge [of the mistake by the non-mistaken party] alone should not suffice to invoke equity. There must be an additional element of impropriety. The conduct of deliberately not bringing the suspicion of a possible mistake to the attention of the mistaken party could constitute such impropriety.[36]

---

31 For a discussion (in the context of shrink-wrap licences) on why the acceptance of the contract can occur long after the payment was accepted, see *ProCD Inc v Zeidenberg* 86 F 3d 1447 (7th Cir, 1996).

32 For other form-versus-substance debates in contract law, see, eg: (employee or independent contractor) *Autoclenz Ltd v Belcher and ors* [2009] EWCA Civ 1046; (condition or warranty in insurance contracts) *Kler Knitwear Ltd v Lombard General Insurance Co Ltd* [2000] Lloyd's Rep IR 47; (fixed or floating charge in debentures) *National Westminster Bank plc v Spectrum Plus Ltd* [2005] UKHL 41, [119]: 'Its right to do so was inconsistent with the charge being a fixed charge and the label placed on the charge by the debenture cannot, in my opinion, be prayed-in-aid to detract from that right.'

33 By the same token, regardless of whether the parties label a communication an acceptance, it will not be an acceptance (but a counteroffer), if it is not on the same terms as the offer, because this is a fundamental aspect of an acceptance: *Hyde v Wrench* (1840) 3 Beav 334. On the use of the word 'offer', see also *Spencer v Harding* (1870) LR 5 CP 561.

34 [2005] 1 SLR 502 (CA); aff'd *Chwee King Keong v Digilandmall.com Pte Ltd* [2004] 2 SLR 594. See also German cases in which price errors were not binding on vendors: *Anfechtung wegen Übermittlungsfehlers* (OLG Hamm, 12 January, 2004, 13 U 165/03); *Irrtumsanfechtung bei falscher Preisangabe* (AG Lahr, 21 December 2004, 5 C 245/04).

35 *Chwee King Keong v Digilandmall.com Pte Ltd* [2005] 1 SLR 502, [29], also [104].

36 Ibid, [80].

The holding clearly depended on the price being very obviously erroneous. In scenarios in which the mistake is of a lesser order, it would be much more difficult to prove some form of bad faith.

Delaying acceptance via the terms of the contract and using software to detect pricing unusual buying patterns, as well as addressing pricing errors in the terms and conditions, should go a long way towards minimising the risk of pricing accidents.

Offer or Invitation to Treat in Online Auctions

Contract formation is complicated in auction scenarios, given the presence of a third party, the auctioneer, and the competing bidders. According to ordinary contract law on auctions (partly codified in s 57 of the **Sale of Goods Act 1979**, which is presumptive, not mandatory), the offer is made by the bidding parties;[37] each offer lapses if overtaken by a higher offer and can be withdrawn any time before the hammer falls, which indicates the seller's acceptance. The auctioneer (as an agent for the seller) is free to accept or reject the final bid. However, in auctions without a reserve price, there is a collateral contract between the highest bidder and the auctioneer pursuant to which the auctioneer promises to sell to the highest bidder no matter how low the bid is. If the auctioneer fails to honour the highest bid, there is no contract between the bidder and the seller, but the bidder can sue the auctioneer for the difference in market value and the value of the bid.[38]

How does this apply to online auctions? First, the providers of online auctions, such as eBay, are unlikely to be seen to step into the shoes of the traditional auctioneer. In contrast to auctioneers, eBay does not play an active role in the bidding process and merely provides an auction venue, and broadly 'supervises' the transaction. eBay.co.uk requires users to accept its facilitatory background role in its user agreement:

> You acknowledge that we are not a traditional auctioneer. Instead, our sites are a venue to allow anyone to offer, sell, and buy just about anything, at anytime, from anywhere . . .

So instead of the triangular relationship of traditional auctions, there appears to be only a two-way relationship between the buyer and the seller in online auctions. Does this mean that online auctions fall outside the traditional rules for auctions? The answer to this question must depend on the legal issue at stake and to what extent the presence of a third-party auctioneer is critical in that context. As argued below, it should not matter to the right of withdrawal (see below), but the different contracting process is likely to impact on the contract formation analysis.

Returning to the issue of offer and acceptance, although s 57 of the **Sale of Goods Act 1979** seems prima facie applicable to online auctions, eBay's terms largely override it.[39] According to those terms – and in contrast to the default auction rules – bidders cannot, or only very exceptionally may, retract their 'offers' (not used in the legal sense). In its terms relating to 'Invalid bid retraction', eBay states:

> When you bid on an item you enter into a binding contract with the seller to purchase them if you are the highest bidder at the end of the listing . . . You are only permitted to retract your bid under the following special circumstances . . . [for example,] the seller changed the item description.

---

37 *Payne v Cave* (1789) 3 Term Rep 148; *British Car Auctions Ltd v Wright* [1972] 1 WLR 1519.
38 *Barry v Heathcote Ball & Co (Commercial Auctions) Ltd* [2001] 1 All ER 944; *Warlow v Harrison* (1859) 1 E & E 309. This rule would presumably extend to auctions with a publicly known reserve.
39 These terms imposed by eBay on the participants affect the contract between sellers and buyers vis-à-vis each other by informing their reasonable expectations towards each other; under English law, these terms would be implied terms of the contract between the seller and the highest bidder.

Sellers can end their listings early without much ado, in which case, all bids are cancelled automatically ('Ending your listing early'). But once the time is up, the seller's 'acceptance' occurs automatically and he or she cannot refuse to honour the highest bid. So although the seller steps into the shoes of the auctioneers, unlike traditional auctioneers, he or she cannot reject the highest bid.

Both German and Australian courts have had the opportunity to consider the contract formation of online auctions. In the German *VW* case,[40] the seller was unhappy with the highest bid that he got for a new VW-Passat (about half the list price) and sought to reject it on the basis that it was up to him to accept or reject the highest bid. This indeed seemed consistent with the terms and conditions of the online auction site (ricardo.de), which all participants had to accept during the registration process, and which stated that posting merchandise on the site served as an invitation to treat. Yet these terms also required the seller to accept the highest bid and required his express declaration to that effect when he uploaded his post to the site. The court at first instance[41] agreed with the seller's argument that no acceptance had taken place; in fact, according to the court, his protest proved his non-acceptance – consistent with German (and English) default position, which does not require the auctioneer to accept the highest bid.[42] The automatic mail sent to the buyer by the auction site at the end of the auction did not bind the seller, despite the standard term of the auction site. According to the court, these terms were 'too abstract' to qualify as the seller's specific contractual intent. The parties could not possibly have intended to enter into an agreement for the sale of a car so substantially below the list price. Fortunately, the appeal court reversed the holding.[43] It upheld the standard terms of the auction site as the basis for the creation of a binding contract between the parties. The court viewed the initial offering by the seller as the offer (and not an invitation to treat or a pre-offer acceptance, as stipulated in the auction house's terms) and the highest bid as the acceptance. Given the completeness of the initial offering – in terms of stating all of the essential terms – and the lack of any danger of over-acceptances, the contract was concluded by the highest bidder at the time when the auction ended. The court also reasoned that even in disregard of the auction terms, considering all of the surrounding circumstances, including the nature of the auction, one would still have to conclude that the seller intended to sell at any price whatsoever. On appeal, the German Federal High Court[44] again upheld the contract, but left open – because it made practically no difference – whether the acceptance was made by the highest bidder or came in form of a pre-offer acceptance by the seller made via his declaration to the system at the time of uploading his posting. Consistently, other German cases have held that for the seller/auctioneer not to make a binding offer, he or she must have made that clear: for example, a request not to bid and take the stated price as a basis for negotiations only, or a statement inviting expression of interests only and not bids.[45]

Virtually the same scenario was the basis of the Australian dispute in *Peter Smythe v Vincent Thomas*.[46] In this case, the seller wanted to get out of a finished eBay transaction for a WWII aircraft (for AU$150,000) for which he had received a significantly better offer offline after the end of the auction. The court, referring to the German judgment, adopted the same contractual analysis of the posting being the offer and the highest bid the acceptance, and refused to allow the seller to weasel

---

40 *Ricardo.de* (BGH, 7 November 2001, Az VIII ZR 13/01); Peer Zumbansen, 'Contracting in the internet: German contracting law and internet auctions' (2001) 2(7) NJW, available online at www.germanlawjournal.com/article.php?id=65; Jan-Malte Niemann, 'Online auctions: Germany – Online auctions under German contract' (2001) 17(2) CLSR 114.

41 *Ricardo.de* (LG Münster, 21 January 2000, 4 O 429/99), (2000) Juristen Zeitung 730.

42 German Civil Code, § 156.

43 *Ricardo.de* (OLG Hamm, 14 December 2000, 2 U 58/00, (2001) Juristen Zeitung 764; (2001) NJW 1142.

44 *Ricardo.de* (BGH, 7 November 2001, Az VIII ZR 13/01).

45 *Preisangabe in Internetauktion als Verhandlungsbasis* (AG Kerpen, 25 May 2001, 21 C 53/01); *Umfrage statt Verkauf auf Internet-Auktionsplattform* (LG Darmstadt, 24 January 2002, 3 O 289/01).

46 [2007] NSWSC 844.

out of the deal.[47] Understanding the seller's post as the offer and not only an invitation to treat, and the highest bid at the end of the auction as the acceptance, neatly reflects the objective intention of the parties in an ordinary eBay transaction, as informed by the site's standard terms. It would explain why the seller can withdraw his or her post, but the bidder cannot generally retract his or her bid, and why the seller is not at liberty to reject the highest bid.[48]

Receipt or Postal Rule

Another contract formation issue is whether the internet contract is concluded upon the receipt of the acceptance by the offeror or already upon the sending of it by the offeree. The answer to this question is important because, first, it again determines the point of no return for the parties, and is likely to be a bone of contention where the acceptance was lost or damaged. Second, the timing of the conclusion of the contract may also have implications on *where* the contract is considered to be concluded – an issue that is of importance in transnational contracts (see below).

The traditional standard rule is the receipt rule – that is, the contract is concluded when the acceptance is communicated to the offeror.[49] The receipt rule is straightforward in face-to-face transactions in which the acceptance being spoken by the offeree coincides perfectly with it being heard by the offeror – freak circumstances apart. Yet, in distance contracts, there is always the risk of a break in the communications. And then it needs to be decided which party should bear the risk of loss. In contracts formed using the post, the main rule was displaced in favour of the 'postal rule', according to which a posted acceptance is already effective upon posting.[50] Thus, provided that the letter was properly addressed and posted, the risk of it going astray lies with the offeror.[51] The question much debated in the internet context is whether online contracts should be governed by the standard or the postal rule.[52]

First of all, contractual parties may avoid uncertainties by addressing this issue expressly in their terms, as many online businesses in fact do. In Term 14 of its 'Conditions of use and sales', Amazon.co.uk opts for the postal rule:

> That acceptance will be complete at the time we send the Dispatch Confirmation E-mail to you.

Yet Art 2.1.3. of Easyjet.com's terms and conditions favours the receipt rule:

> Once you have received an email from us confirming our acceptance of your booking there is a binding contract in place . . .

If there is no such express provision,[53] the question remains whether the standard or the postal rule govern the online contract.

According to traditional common law rules, the answer is as good as cut-and-dried given that courts have shown a strong reluctance to extend the postal rule to other modern forms of communications. The postal rule has been applied to telegrams,[54] but not to telephone and telex acceptances,[55] and will almost certainly be rejected for online contracts, whether effected by email or web

47 *Peter Smythe v Vincent Thomas* [2007] NSWSC 844, [39].
48 Contrast Smith, op cit, 825ff.
49 *Entores v Miles Far East Corp* [1955] 2 QB 327 (CA).
50 *Adams v Lindsell* (1818) 1 B & Ald 681.
51 *Household Fire Insurance v Grant* (1879) 4 Ex D 216.
52 Valerie Watnick, 'The electronic formation of contracts and the common law "mailbox rule"' (2004) 56 Baylor L Rev 175; Marwan Al Ibrahim, Al'eldin Ababneh, and Hisham Tahat, 'The postal acceptance rule in the digital age' (2007) 2 JICLT 47.
53 In most online consumer contracts, such express provisions are required under Art 10 of the Electronic Commerce Directive.
54 *Cowan v O'Connor* (1888) 20 QBD 640.
55 *Entores v Miles Far East Corp* [1955] 2 QB 327 (CA); app'd in *Brinkibon Ltd v Stahag Stahl* [1983] 2 AC 34 (HL).

contracting in clickwrap contracts. The reasons for this reluctance are not entirely clear, which is not surprising given the disagreements about the rationale for the postal rule and, by implication, for the standard receipt rule. In *Entores Ltd v Miles Far Eastern Corp*,[56] Lord Denning favoured the standard rule for an acceptance by telex because, according to him, in these scenarios, 'the man who sends the message of acceptance knows that it has not been received or he has reason to know it'.[57] His reasoning suggests that, unlike in the case of the post, the instantaneity of the media helps to alert the sender to any malfunction in the media. So if a line goes dead, the telephone conversation will be interrupted or the teleprinter motor will stop working – matters that would be obvious to the offeree and thereby within his or her control. But if, according to Lord Denning, the offeror is at fault for knowing that the acceptance was in some ways compromised and failed to alert the offeree of that fact, he or she 'is clearly bound, because he will be estopped from saying that he did not receive the message of acceptance'.[58] Lord Denning's reasoning is not particularly helpful in situations in which the acceptance is not effectively communicated, but neither party knew or could have known this, and thus neither is at fault – a matter well within the realm of possibilities in respect of telex, and certainly email or web-based communications.

Lord Denning's reasoning was slightly tweaked by Lord Fraser in the House of Lords' decision in *Brinkibon Ltd v Stahag Stahl*,[59] in which he framed the inquiry less in terms of fault and more in terms of which party is in a better position to guard against loss:

> a party (the acceptor) who tries to send a message by telex can generally tell if his message has been received on the other party's (the offeror's) machine, whereas the offeror, of course, will not know if an unsuccessful attempt has been made . . . It is therefore convenient that the acceptor, being in the better position, should have the responsibility for ensuring that his message is received.[60]

This more general rationale avoids the fruitless search for fault where there is none, by insisting that the greater control of the offeree over the communicative act justifies imposing on him or her the burden of ensuring that his or her message is received. It also brings to the forefront why the standard rule on acceptances is there to start with: the contractual notion of a 'meeting of two minds' occurs only upon the offeror receiving the offeree's acceptance, and ensuring the effectiveness of that communication cannot but rest with the communicator himself or herself. The above rationale also helps to explain why posted acceptances are treated as an exception (apart from the practical reason of avoiding unnecessary delays and a never-ending chain of confirming communications): the acceptor loses control over the communicative act once the letter is posted, with nothing to alert him or her to possible mishaps. In the postal context, the problem is not so much that control is surrendered to a third party or the lack of instantaneity per se, but rather that the post as a communication channel does not give automatic feedback on its operability, unlike the telephone or telex.[61] If anything, the offeror would be the first party to wonder about a non-forthcoming acceptance. Considering the not-infrequent occurrences of electronic messages (email or otherwise) being lost without a trace in cyberspace, the postal rule would seem appropriate in the digital context.

And yet, courts have been unwilling to extend the postal rule exception and are unlikely to do so in the future.[62] The explanation for this must partly be that the postal rule flies in the face of the

---

56 Ibid.
57 Ibid, 333.
58 Ibid.
59 [1983] 2 AC 34 (HL).
60 Ibid, 43.
61 Ibid, 43.
62 Contrast Smith, op cit, 816, in which the author suggests that neither rule 'can slavishly be applied to the Internet'.

foundational contract notion of the meeting of two minds, as well as the more general idea that the onus is on the communicator to ensure that his or her communication is effective. Interrelatedly, but more importantly – particularly where an acceptance is lost or delayed in transport – the postal rule suffers from the serious flaw that the offeror is contractually bound without his or her knowledge, which is a position infinitely less desirable than that created by the standard rule – that is, that the offeree is *not* bound by a contract by which he or she believes he or she is bound.

Finally on the issue of acceptance, an effective communication does not require that the offeror has actually read it as long as he or she is capable of doing so – consistent with Lord Fraser's statement in *Brinkibon* that it is the offeror's 'responsibility to arrange for the prompt handling of messages in his own office'.[63] This would also be consistent with the spirit of Art 11(1) of the **Electronic Commerce Directive** ('the order and the acknowledgement of receipt are deemed to be received when the parties to whom they are addressed are able to access them'), although, as explained above, the Article only deals to a very limited extent with the legal concepts of offer and acceptance. So in terms of timing, the acceptance is effectively communicated when it can be accessed, assuming access within ordinary business hours.[64] As to *where* the acceptance must be deemed to be received, see below.

Intention to Contract

Automated Contracting

A contract is a bargain that is *voluntarily* entered into between two or more persons with legal capacity. In the technological age, one question raised by the notion of volition (implicit in the requirement of the intention to create legal relations) is whether a contract can be struck by computers programmed to make offers or acceptances without any further human intervention or the possibility thereof in the particular contract (that is, electronic agents). In other words, is automation compatible with the notion of a *voluntary* agreement? The answer is 'yes'.

Even before the advent of computer technology, courts have accepted automated responses by machines as valid contractual communications. In *Thornton v Shoe Lane Parking*,[65] Lord Denning held that a user of a vending machine accepts the offer made by the machine 'at the very moment when he put his money into the machine. The contract is concluded at that time'.[66] By the same token, and more importantly, the proprietor of the machine is also bound by the offer made by his or her machine even if – had he or she known the particular circumstances of the intended transaction – he or she would not have made the offer.[67] The arguments in favour of accepting the contractual validity of automated responses by machines, computers, websites, etc, are, first, that it gives legal recognition to an ever-more-pervasive commercial reality that favours the efficiency and convenience of automated transacting, and second, that machines – whether they are relatively simple vending machines or highly sophisticated computer systems (capable of making 'intelligent' decisions on behalf of their owners) – are only tools in the hand of their owners or users. Their actions and 'intentions' are no more than the prior intention of their human or corporate owners put into a programmed form. The owners or users have legal responsibility for their actions and are bound by them.[68] Thus sellers on auction sites are bound by the site's automatic acceptance of the highest

---

63 *Brinkibon Ltd v Stahag Stahl*, 43.
64 *Schelde Delta Shipping BV v Astare Shipping Ltd (The Pamela)* [1995] 2 Lloyd's Rep 249, in which receipt of the telex received at midnight on a Friday was held to be effective Monday morning.
65 [1971] 2 QB 163 (CA).
66 Ibid, 169.
67 For a discussion for liability for pricing errors, see above.
68 Guide to Enactment of the UNCITRAL Model Law on Electronic Commerce, para 35: 'Data messages that are generated automatically by computers without human intervention should be regards as 'originating' from the legal entity on behalf of which the computer is operated.'

bid even if it is not to their liking, because that is what everyone agreed upon registration (discussed above). Similarly, bidders in such auctions are committed by the acts of any automated bidding agent that they employ.[69] More controversially, according to US jurisprudence, search engines are bound by the browsewrap agreements of the sites that their electronic agents access while gathering information.[70] The message is clear: you cannot hide behind your not-very-bright electronic agent. The debate on automation will have to be revisited if, or when, true artificial intelligence is invented.

Contractual Intention in Browsewrap Agreements?

Whether, in browsewrap agreements, the required contractual *mens rea* – that is, the intention to create legal relations – is present may often be questionable. For many surfers, it may come as a surprise that their act of surfing is legally significant and makes them parties to the site's user agreements.[71] One legal issue is whether, despite the user's ignorance of the offer made in the site's terms, his or her conduct can amount to an acceptance. Overlapping issues are whether surfers have sufficient notice of the terms for them to be incorporated into the contract, and whether there is any consideration in such agreements (see below).

There is no English internet case on the validity of acceptances by conduct in ignorance of a site's terms/offer. However, according to existing jurisprudence, performance of an act cannot amount to an acceptance unless the party performing the act did so with knowledge of the existence of an offer; so the conduct must occur in the knowledge of its contractual effect as an acceptance.[72] Where a surfer has no awareness of the site's terms of use, the offer in those terms will not be accepted upon the surfer's conduct and thus there is no contract. Having said that, the critical issue in many browsewrap agreements must be whether the user had no such awareness, as objectively ascertained.

Browsewrap agreements have been subject to judicial scrutiny in the USA,[73] and upheld when the user had sufficient awareness of the terms and thereby of the legal significance of his actions. In *Specht v Netscape Communications Corp*,[74] Netscape tried to enforce an arbitration clause contained in its software licence agreement applicable to the free software that Netscape encouraged users to download via a 'Download' button on the site. One reason why the consumers could not be bound by the agreement was, according to the court, that 'a consumer's clicking on a download button does not communicate assent to contractual terms if the offer did not make clear to the consumer that clicking on the download button would signify assent'.[75] Similarly, in *Feldman v United Parcel Service Inc*,[76] United Parcel sought to rely upon a limitation-of-liability clause contained in its terms behind a hyperlink immediately below a 'Print' button with the following instructions: 'Review everything carefully and then click "Print" to print your shipping request.' According to the court, this statement did not make it sufficiently clear that 'Print' – unlike 'I Agree' – would amount to an acceptance of the terms; '[r]ather, for example, one might interpret the directions to mean that the shipper is being asked to confirm and carefully review the addresses before printing the shipping label.'[77]

---

69 *Einsatz eines Bietagenten* (AG Hannover, 7 September 2001, Az 501 C 1510/01).

70 *Cairo Inc v Crossmedia Services Inc* WL 756610 (ND Cal, 1 April 2005); see also *Register.com Inc v Verio Inc* 356 F3d 393 (2d Cir 2004), discussed below.

71 Note exceptionally that the business itself may not want the terms to have binding effect: *Re JetBlue Airways Corp Privacy Litigation* 379 F Supp 2d 299 (EDNY, 2005).

72 *Tinn v Hoffman & Co* (1873) 29 LT 271 (concerning identical cross-offers). An exception to this rule is the unilateral contract, such as offers of rewards: *Gibbons v Proctor* (1891) 64 LT 594.

73 American Bar Association (ABA) Joint Working Group on Electronic Contracting Practices, 'Browse-wrap agreements: Validity of implied assent in electronic form agreements' (2003) 59 Business Lawyer 279.

74 306 F3d 17 (2d Cir 2002), aff'ing 150 F Supp 2d 585 (SDNY 2001); see also below.

75 *Specht v Netscape Communications Corp* 306 F3d 17, 29f (2d Cir 2002), relying on § 2204(1) of the Californian Commercial Code: 'A contract for sale of goods may be made in any manner sufficient to show agreement, including conduct by both parties which recognizes the existence of such a contract.'

76 WL 800989 (SDNY, 24 March 2008).

77 Ibid, 16.

In contrast, in *Druyan v Jagger*,[78] a Rolling Stones fan brought a class action against Ticketmaster, an online ticket agency, and Mick Jagger for breach of contract for failing to provide timely notice of the postponement of a concert, which caused the plaintiffs to incur travel, food, and other costs. Because, under its agency's terms of use, Ticketmaster was relieved from any liability for the cost incurred on postponement of an event, the question was whether these terms were binding. To purchase her ticket, the plaintiff had to click on a 'Look for tickets' button supported by the statement: 'By clicking on the "Look for Tickets" button or otherwise using this web site, you agree to the Terms of Use [hyperlinked] . . .' This sentence not only put the plaintiff on notice of the terms, but put beyond doubt the contractual effect of clicking on the 'Look for Tickets' button as acceptance.

Notice of Contractual Terms

A basic rule of contract law is that contractual parties are only subject to those terms and conditions of which they had notice. Such notice can be established either by showing a signature under the relevant terms or by proving 'reasonably sufficient notice'[79] of them before the contract was concluded. There has been much debate over how the traditional law on incorporation of terms should be transplanted to online contracts, but in the final analysis, offline as well as online, notice is always a question of fact to be decided in the particular circumstances of the case.

Incorporation by Signature[80]

The traditional position is that a signature under the terms of the contract means that these terms are incorporated into the contract. In *L'Estrange v F Graucob Ltd*,[81] it was held that '[w]hen a document containing contractual terms is signed, then, in the absence of fraud, or . . . misrepresentation, the party signing it is bound, and it is wholly immaterial whether he has read the document or not'.[82]

The first question in the internet context is whether clicking on an 'I Agree' or 'Place your Order' button, as in a typical clickwrap agreement, is the equivalent to the traditional signature for the purposes of showing intention to contract and acceptance of the terms provided. Although such a click does not satisfy the requirements of an 'advanced electronic signature' (discussed below), it is still sufficient to show the contractual intention and acceptance of terms. According to the Law Commission, 'it satisfies the principal function of a signature: namely demonstrating an authenticating intention. We suggest that the click can reasonably be regarded as the technological equivalent of a manuscript "X" signature', which has long been accepted as valid for that function.[83]

Provided that the title of the button is unambiguous – unlike, for example, 'Print' (see above) – a click demonstrates the intention of the signer to be bound by the contract. But because a click is – like the 'X' or a stamp – a non-personalised signature,[84] it cannot reliably establish who the signer was, which may render it invalid as a signature where the clickee's identity is disputed and there is no extrinsic evidence to establish it.[85] Arguably, however, the password-protected use of a

---

78 508 F Supp 2d 228 (SYNY 2007).
79 *Parker v South Eastern Railway Co* (1877) 2 CPD 416 (CA); *Thornton v Shoe Lane Parking Ltd* [1971] 2 QB 163 (CA); *Interfoto Picture Library Ltd v Stiletto Visual Programmes Ltd* [1989] QB 433 (CA).
80 See also discussion below.
81 [1934] 2 KB 394; see also *Levison v Patent Steam Carpet Cleaning Co Ltd* [1978] QB 69 (CA).
82 Ibid, 403.
83 Law Commission, *Electronic Commerce: Formal Requirements in Commercial Transactions*, 2001, London: HMSO, paras 3.36ff.
84 *Goodman v J Eban Ltd* [1954] 1 QB 550 (rubber stamp); *Brydges (Town Clerk of Cheltenham) v Dix* (1891) 7 TLR 215 (printed signature).
85 German cases: *Internet-Versteigerung* (AG Erfurt, 14 September 2001, 28 C 2354/01); *Auktion durch Trojaner* (LG Konstanz, 19 April 2002, 2 O 141/01); *Beweisfragen bei Vertragsschluss in der Internet-Auktion* (OLG Köln, 6 September 2002, 19 U 16/02); discussed in Smith, op cit, 825.

site ensures that the click is reasonably reliably linked to the owner of the password and thus 'personalises' the click. In general, because English law takes a functional approach to signatures, a mark or act may or may not be recognised as a valid signature depending on the legal requirements and circumstances of the case. The validity of the click as the functional equivalent of a signature to indicate contractual intention will remain a subject of residual doubt in England and Wales given the absence of a clickwrap case to that effect. The Court of Appeal in *Midasplayer.com Ltd v Watkins*[86] came close to that decision when it upheld the 'Terms and conditions' of King.com on the basis that '[w]hen a visitor accesses the King.com site the visitor is provided with a set of terms and conditions'.[87] Unfortunately, Judge Norris did not consider whether these terms were incorporated through a click or otherwise.

The issue has been settled by the US judiciary: when online users click on 'I Agree' or equivalent icons, the contractual terms behind a hyperlink near the icon are incorporated into the contract. For example, in *AV v iParadigms LLC*,[88] the defendants owned a software system that checked essays for plagiarism and archived them for comparison with later submissions. The plaintiffs were students and required by their university to submit their work to the defendant's system to confirm its originality. Before submitting their work, they had to click the 'I Agree' icon that appeared directly below the contractual terms of the defendant's site. Because the plaintiffs did not want their essays to be archived, they put a disclaimer to that effect on their essays. When the defendant then still archived the plaintiffs' work, they brought an action for copyright infringement. The court found that, under Virginian law, the students' disclaimer was ineffective, because by clicking the 'I Agree' button, they had given their consent to the full terms of use, including the very first term – according to which the defendant's offer was 'conditioned on your acceptance, without modification of the terms … contained therein'. The students had been given a clear choice of either accepting the terms or not accepting them; modifying them was not an option, and their click confirmed the choice they had made. On a critical note, it is not clear why the students' submission was not treated as a counter-offer (rather than an acceptance, given that they disagreed with one of the proposed terms), which in turn was impliedly accepted by the site operator by retaining the essays and checking them for plagiarism.

Clickwrap agreements have also been validated in Canada. In *Rudder v Microsoft Corp*,[89] two law school graduates attempted to bring a class action (the class consisted of the 89,000 Canadian MSN members) against Microsoft, claiming damages for breach of contract, breach of fiduciary duty, misappropriation, and punitive damages, totalling $75 million. They tried to bring the claim in Canada, despite a forum selection clause – pointing to the law and courts of the state of Washington – in the membership agreement to which they had indicated their consent by clicking on an 'I Agree' button. The judge held that this 'Membership Agreement must be afforded the sanctity that must be given to any agreement in writing'.[90]

What is noteworthy about the above decisions is that the judges do not attach magical weight to the click-come-signature issue,[91] but treat the issue of incorporation of the terms within the broader question as to whether and to what extent users were given the opportunity to familiarise themselves with the terms. So, in *Rudder*, Justice Winkler notes that, during the sign-up process, users were given twice the chance to view and accept or reject the terms, the terms themselves were

---

86 [2006] EWHC 1551 (Ch).
87 *Midasplayer.com Ltd v Watkins* [2006] EWHC 1551 (Ch), [2]; see also [16].
88 544 F Supp 2d 473 (ED VA 2008). See also one of the first cases upholding clickwrap agreements: *Caspi v Microsoft Network LLC* 732 A2d 528 (NJ Super Ct App Div 1999).
89 2 CPR (4th) 474 (1999).
90 *Rudder v Microsoft Corp* (1999) 2 CPR (4th) 474, [17] (Ont SC).
91 Juliet M Moringiello and William L Reynolds, 'Survey of the law of cyberspace: Electronic contracting cases 2006–2007' (2007) 63 Business Lawyer 219; Juliet M Moringiello and William L Reynolds, 'Survey of the law of cyberspace: Electronic contracting cases 2007–2008' (2008) 64 Business Lawyer 199.

in plain English and the agreement was viewable much like 'a multi-page written document which requires a party to turn the pages'.[92] The explanation for this approach is either that a click is not treated as the equivalent of a signature or, even if it is, incorporation by signature is treated as part of the broader incorporation-by-reasonable-notice inquiry.[93] This general approach is helpful in scenarios in which the click is not unambiguously the functional equivalent of a signature as, for example, where the button said 'Look for Tickets'[94] or 'Print' (rather than 'I Agree' or 'I Accept'), or where the terms are not unambiguously linked to the click in borderline clickwrap/browsewrap agreements,[95] or where the terms in browsewrap seeks to make visiting a site the legal equivalent of a signed written contract (as discussed below). In such scenarios, the broader and helpful question would have to be whether the user had reasonable notice of the terms, and not whether the contract was signed or not.

Incorporation by 'Reasonable Notice'

Under English law, terms in unsigned contracts are incorporated provided that reasonable steps were taken to bring them to the attention of the other party before the conclusion of the contract.[96] Again, this inquiry comes down to the facts of each case. In the past, it has been held that a reference to the terms on the front of a ticket provides reasonable notice of them.[97] Conversely, a notice at the back of a document with no further reference at the front, or one made illegible by a stamp, does not satisfy the 'reasonable notice' test.[98] Furthermore, the more onerous or unusual the term, the more effort must be made to bring it to the attention of the other party: '. . . if one condition . . . is particularly onerous or unusual, the party seeking to enforce it, must show that particular condition was fairly brought to the attention of the other party.'[99] And last but not least, notice of the terms may be provided by the regular and consistent course of dealing between the parties, or any 'common understanding' derived from the custom in a particular trade – a basis that is generally confined to B2B transactions.[100]

There is no doubt that these rulings can be applied to online contracts and, in particular, browsewrap agreements. The cases already decided in the USA, following a similar notice concept to the English one, show that there is a spectrum of such agreements in terms of their enforceability.[101] At one end of the spectrum are cases such as *Register.com Inc v Verio Inc*[102] – often concerning competing businesses – in which browsewrap agreements have been upheld. Register.com, an internet domain name registrar, sought an injunction against Verio enjoining it from using its search robot to access and collect information of registrants from Register.com's online interactive WHOIS database contrary to Register.com's terms of use posted on its site. Verio used this information for marketing its services to those registrants (in direct competition with Register.com). To add insult to injury, Register.com had refrained from marketing its services to the registrants who had opted out of receiving sales and marketing communications during the registration process, and who now complained to Register.com about the spam and telemarketing by Verio. Verio argued, inter alia, that it was not bound by the terms of use, because it had not clicked on an 'I Accept' icon.

92 Rudder v Microsoft Corp, [14].
93 The traditional strict division of incorporation by notice and incorporation by signature has also shown some cracks in England and Wales: see dicta in McCutceon v David MacBrayne [1964] 1 WLR 125, 133; Ocean Chemical Transport Inc v Exnor Craggs Ltd [2000] 1 All ER 519, 530.
94 Druyan v Jagger 508 F Supp 2d 228 (SYNY 2007).
95 Specht v Netscape Communications Corp 306 F3d 17 (2d Cir 2002).
96 Parker v South Eastern Railway Co (1877) 2 CPD 416 (CA); in relation to timing, see Thornton v Shoe Lane Parking [1971] 1 All ER 686 (CA); Beta Computers (Europe) Ltd v Adobe Systems (Europe) Ltd [1996] FSR 37.
97 Thompson v London, Midland and Scottish Railway Co [1930] 1 KB 41.
98 Henderson v Stevenson (1875) 1 All ER 172, and Sugar v London, Midland and Scottish Railway Co [1941] 1 All ER 172, respectively.
99 Interfoto Picture Library Ltd v Stiletto Visual Programmes Ltd [1989] QB 433, 439 (CA).
100 British Crane Hire Corp v Ipswich Plant Hire Ltd [1975] QB 303.
101 For excellent case summaries, see Moringiello and Reynolds, op cit.
102 126 F Supp 2d 238 (SDNY, 2000), aff'd in 356 F3d 393 (2d Cir 2004). See also discussion above on 'Automated Contracting'.

In rejecting this submission, the New York court reasoned that because the terms stated that, by using the site, the user agrees to abide by the terms, by using the site, Verio 'manifested its assent to be bound by Register.com's terms of use'.[103]

At the other end of the spectrum is *Specht v Netscape Communications Corp*[104] – a consumer action against an online business – in which a browsewrap agreement was not upheld. In this case, the consumers brought a class action against Netscape on the basis that the free software downloaded from Netscape violated their right to privacy because, unbeknown to them, it enabled Netscape to carry out electronic surveillance of their online activities through cookies. The court found that the arbitration clause in the licence agreement far below the 'Download' button was not enforceable: '. . . an offeree . . . is not bound by inconspicuous contractual provisions of which he is unaware, contained in a document whose contractual nature is not obvious.'[105] The consumers were not put on inquiry or constructive notice of those terms.[106] *Specht* was followed in *Defontes v Dell Computers Corp*,[107] in which it was held that 'the terms via a hyperlink, inconspicuously located at the bottom of the webpage' could not bind the consumer. The general position in the USA (and likely to be similar in the UK) is that the terms must not be hidden or be so inconspicuous that a reasonably prudent user would not become aware of them.[108] The common practice adopted by many online businesses of inserting a small link to its terms at the bottom of the screen is by itself unlikely to provide adequate notice.

Interestingly, in a number of cases,[109] the court considered as a point in favour of the existence of notice that the plaintiff was a long-term user of the site – comparable to the English concept of notice through a regular and consistent course of dealing between the parties. This argument is dubious, because an inconspicuous notice would not become any more conspicuous simply through a user's regular access of the site. Having said that, a growing familiarity with the internet and the universal custom of site providers to have terms of use makes it now more difficult to argue that a reference to the terms at the bottom of the screen is inconspicuous.[110]

A variation of the notice problem occurs when the terms of use or of the service contract get changed after the initial contract conclusion – for example, where users have entered into a long-term relationship with the site provider, such as on social networking or email account sites. In contractual terms, this scenario presents essentially the same notice issue as the one at the formation stage: a variation of the terms by one contractual party amounts to an offer that the other party may or may not accept, and again acceptance is premised on reasonable notice of the varied terms. Thus, in the US case of *Douglas v District Court, ex rel Talk America Inc*,[111] even a conspicuous notice of the change of terms on the website was held to be insufficient to put the plaintiff on notice of the change of terms of his agreement with his telephone service provider, because he simply had no reason to visit the site in the meantime. An English court would have to come to the same conclusion.

---

103 *Register.com Inc v Verio Inc* 126 F Supp 2d 238, 248 (SDNY, 2000).
104 306 F3d 17 (2d Cir 2002).
105 *Specht v Netscape Communications Corp* 306 F3d 17, 29 (2d Cir 2002).
106 Ibid, 32.
107 WL 253560 (RI Super, 29 January 2004).
108 See also *AV v iParadigms LLC* 544 FSupp 2d 473 (ED Va, 2008), in which the usage policy, unlike the clickwrap agreement, was not binding on the student users of the plagiarism service.
109 *Druyan v Jagger* 508 F Supp 2d 228 (SDNY, 2007); *Southwest Airlines Co v BoardFirst LLC* LEXIS 96230 (ND Tex, 12 September 2007); *Register.com Inc v Verio Inc*, above; *Cairo Inc v Crossmedia Services Inc* WL 756610 (ND Cal, 1 April 2005).
110 *Alexander v Railway Executive* [1951] 2 KB 882, 886, noting inter alia: 'After all, most people nowadays know that railway companies have conditions subject to which they take articles into their cloakrooms.'
111 495 F3d 1062 (9th Cir, 2007).

Accessibility and Readability of the Terms

It is perhaps self-evident that, even if a user is on notice about the existence of the terms of the agreement in notice-by-reference cases, for those terms to be binding, they must also be relatively easily accessible. But what does that actually mean?

Again, there are US cases illustrating this notion of accessibility. In *Greer v 1-800-Flowers.com Inc*,[112] it was held that if a contract concluded via one means of communications, such as telephone, makes an express reference to the terms of the agreement accessible via another communication medium, such as the internet, the terms are easily enough accessible to be incorporated. Ultimately, whether this is the case or not depends on the peculiar facts of the case. In *Trujillo v Apple Computer Inc, and AT&T Mobility LLC*,[113] it was not enough that, prior to buying an iPhone, the purchaser was told in an Apple store that the AT&T mobility service agreement could be accessed on the internet. Similarly, in *Feldman v United Parcel Service Inc*,[114] the I-Ship kiosk, which the plaintiff used to conclude the shipping agreement with UPS, was connected to the internet, when in fact the terms of the agreement were accessible online. Thus those terms were not incorporated into the contract. Accessibility is a matter of degree, depending on what is reasonable and feasible in the circumstances – and this would equally be the case in the UK.

Finally, and interrelated, is the question how readable the terms must be. The problem concerning the unreadability and unreality of standard-form contracts is, of course, far from peculiar to the internet. However, the internet exacerbates the artificiality of standard-form agreements given that almost every site purports to create contractual relations with lengthy convoluted terms. While this has again been acknowledged in various US cases, judges have predictably shied away from declaring them non-binding, which would have had major ramifications for the vast majority of online providers. For example, *Scarcella v America Online*[115] concerned AOL's sign-up process, which involved viewing 91 computer screens and which was described by the court as lulling customers 'into a trance of lethargy and inattentiveness from the seemingly endless presentment of useful and inconsequential information'.[116] Yet it still upheld the maxim that a signatory to a contract is presumed to know its content, but left open the possibility that the consent was procured by deceit, because, according to the plaintiffs, AOL, like many other online businesses, 'encourages its customers to skip the [member agreement] with no expectation that you will actually go back and read it, yet comforted in their knowledge that you clicked the correct box in order for them to cloak themselves in the protection of the contract they drafted'.[117] In the end, the court found the agreement unenforceable for other reasons.

Despite the stronger consumer protection tradition in Europe, it is unlikely that UK consumers would fare any better. In the UK, under the **Unfair Terms in Consumer Contracts Regulations 1999** (implementing the EU Directive of the same name),[118] terms in standard-form consumer contracts shall be regarded as unfair and thus non-binding 'if, contrary to the requirement of good faith, it causes a significant imbalance in the parties' rights and obligations arising under the contract, to the detriment of the consumer'.[119] Such a term may be one that has 'the object or effect of irrevocably binding the consumer to terms with which he had no *real opportunity* of becoming acquainted before the conclusion of the contract'.[120] On a wide interpretation of this regulation, and taking into account the length and language of most online terms and conditions, and the

---

112 *Greer v 1–800-Flowers.com Inc* LEXIS 73961 (SD Tex, 3 October 2007).
113 No 07 C 4946 (ND Ill, 18 April 2008).
114 WL 800989 (SDNY, 24 March 2008); see also *Treiber & Straub v United Parcel Service Inc* 474 F3d 379 (7th Cir 2007).
115 WL 2093429 (NY City Civ Ct 2004); see also *Novak v Overture Services Inc* 309 F Supp 2d 446 (EDNY 2004).
116 *Scarcella v America Online* WL 2093429 (NY City Civ Ct, 8 September 2004), 1.
117 Ibid, 2.
118 SI 1999/2083, which implements Council Directive 93/13/EEC on Unfair Terms in Consumer Contracts.
119 Ibid, regs 5(1) and 8(1).
120 Schedule 2(1)(i), emphasis added.

frequency of being required to read them and the low risk associated with not reading them, it would seem that the opportunity to become acquainted with any particular set of online terms is *unreal* indeed. However, such wide interpretation is unlikely in view of the restrictive approach taken to 'good faith' by the House of Lords in *Director General of Fair Trading v First National plc*.[121] The Lords rejected that a term that would take a consumer by surprise – that is, assuming a normal consumer who had not read the terms – would be contrary to 'good faith'. According to the Lords, a term is in 'good faith' as long as that term was 'expressed fully, clearly and legibly, containing no concealed pitfalls or traps'[122] – irrespective of its substance. The emphasis is on the wording of the terms, rather than their length or existence. This is reinforced by reg 7, according to which a seller must use plain, intelligible language, and ambiguities are resolved in favour of the consumer.

Some more realistic scope for overriding certain terms in online contracts may lie in the **Unfair Contract Terms Act 1977**, which provides for the ineffectiveness of exemption clauses based on unreasonableness,[123] taking into account, for example, 'whether the customer knew or ought reasonably to have known of the existence and the extent of the term (having regard, among other things, to any custom of the trade and any previous dealing between the parties)'.[124] And to judge what is reasonable 'it is necessary ... to consider to what extent the party has actually consented to the clause'.[125] While it is debatable whether it is indeed actual, rather than constructive, knowledge of the terms that should be decisive,[126] even taking the test of a reasonable person, it would often be possible to argue that a lack of knowledge of the online terms of browsewrap agreements is well within the realms of reasonableness.

Additional Transparency Requirements

While traditional contract law expects internet businesses, just like any other business, to put their customers on reasonable notice of the contractual terms, various EU Directives[127] impose additional transparency requirements in long-distance and/or electronic transactions. These informational obligations are designed to give consumers more leverage against distant/online businesses that might otherwise be difficult to trace and hold accountable, and thus inspire more confidence in them. For example, Art 4 of the **Distance Selling Directive**[128] (which is applicable to most electronic transactions other than, for example, financial services)[129] provides that a distant vendor must provide the consumer with information about:

(a) his identity and, the case of contracts the contract requiring payment in advance, address

(b) the main characteristics of the goods or services

(c) the price of the goods or services

(d) the delivery costs

(e) the arrangements for payment, delivery or performance

(f) the existence of a right of withdrawal

(g) the cost of using the means of communications, if it is not at the basic rate

(h) the period for which the offer or the price remains valid.

---

121 [2001] UKHL 52.

122 Ibid, [17].

123 Reasonableness (s 11) is not always required to trigger the ineffectiveness of the exemption – see, eg, s 2(1) – but is required under ss 2(2), 3, 6(3), and 7(3).

124 Unfair Contract Terms Act 1977, Sch 2(c).

125 *AEG (UK) Ltd v Logic Resources Ltd* [1996] CLC 265, 279.

126 Laurence Koffman and Elizabeth Macdonald, *The Law of Contract*, 7th edn, 2010, Oxford: Oxford University Press, p 232.

127 Distance Selling Directive 97/7/EC; Electronic Commerce Directive 2000/31/EC; Unfair Commercial Practices Directive 2005/29/EC.

128 Directive 97/7/EC, implemented in the UK by the Consumer Protection (Distance Selling) Regulations 2000, SI 2000/2334.

129 On the scope of the Directive, see Art 3. See also Distance Marketing of Financial Services Directive 2002/65/EC.

The information must be provided 'in good time prior to the conclusion of any distance contract' and 'in a clear and comprehensible manner in any way appropriate to the means of distance communication used'.[130] This requirement came under the spotlight in a German case in which the court held that the provision of the required information via a 'Contact' link was insufficient to bring it to the attention of the user.[131]

The **Electronic Commerce Directive**[132] imposes overlapping informational requirements in Arts 5–7, 10, and 11 – all broadly designed to put online consumers on a level playing field with consumers in a face-to-face or other long-distance transactions. They add to the distance selling obligations by focusing more strongly on the intangible and ephemeral nature of electronic communications.[133] So, for example, under Art 5, service providers have to give users information about their geographical address; under Art 10, information on the technical means of identifying and rectifying input errors;[134] and under Art 11, service providers have to confirm transactional communications.

Despite, or perhaps because of, the wide range of the transparency requirements, the European Commission found in a Europe-wide survey of online electronics retailers[135] that 55 per cent of the surveyed sites showed irregularities particularly relating to consumer information; of those, two-thirds completely failed to inform consumers of their rights, such as the 'right of withdrawal' (discussed below), 45 per cent gave misleading information about the total price, and 33 per cent gave incomplete or no contact details of the trader. The survey focused on the biggest websites selling consumer electronics. Following the survey, national authorities will have to take enforcement actions, first, by contacting the relevant sites and requiring corrections, and second, in case of failure, by bringing legal actions leading to fines and possible closure of the site.[136] The low compliance level with both Directives may at least partly be due to the fact that non-compliance does not affect the contracts made, and gives users at the most a statutory right to seek compliance or damages.[137]

Right of Withdrawal

In the EU, traditional contract law has been changed quite dramatically with the creation of the right of withdrawal in distance-selling contracts. Article 6(1) of the **Distance Selling Directive** states:

> For any distance contract the consumer shall have a period of at least seven working days in which to withdraw from the contract without penalty and without giving any reason. The only charge that may be made to the consumer because of the exercise of his right of withdrawal is the direct cost of returning the goods.[138]

---

130 Article 4(2).
131 *Wetten über Internet-Lottospielgemeinschaft als Fernabsatzgeschäft* (OLG Karlsruhe, 27 March 2002, 6 U 200/01).
132 Directive 2000/31/EC.
133 But see also Recital 13 of the Distance Selling Directive 97/7/EC.
134 This is the only section in the Directive that allows the customer to rescind the contract.
135 European Commission, *Consumer: EU Crackdown on Websites Selling Consumer Electronic Goods*, IP/09/1292, 9 September 2009, Brussels: European Commission.
136 For example, Arts 18 and 20 of the Electronic Commerce Directive 2000/31/EC, dealing respectively with legal actions and sanctions; see also Injunctions for the Protection of Consumers' Interests Directive 98/27/EC.
137 For example, Electronic Commerce (EC Directive) Regulations 2002, SI 2002/2013, reg 13.
138 Even the cost of delivery may not be charged to the consumer who exercises the right of withdrawal: *Verbraucherzentrale Nordrhein-Westfalen eV v Handelsgesellschaft Heinrich Heine GmbH* C511/08 ECJ (15 April 2010) concerning the validity of German law allowing online sellers not to refund delivery costs incurred by the consumer when excising the right of withdrawal. See also *Messner v Firma Stefan Kruger* C–489/07 ECJ (3 September 2009) and *Voraussetzungen des Wertersatzanspruchs bei Widerruf im Fernabsatzkauf* (BGH, 3 November 2010, VIII ZR 337/09) concerning the seller's right to claim compensation for the value of their use before the right of withdrawal was excised.

The right of withdrawal starts ticking when the goods are received or, in the case of services, either when the contract is concluded or when the written information concerning the contract and the right of withdrawal has been received by the consumer.[139] If this latter information has not been provided, the right of withdrawal extends to three months.[140] This radical departure from the traditional sanctity of contract doctrine reflects that distance consumers cannot 'see the product or ascertain the nature of the service provided before concluding the contract'.[141]

One disputed issue in the electronic environment has been the scope of the Directive and the application of the right of withdrawal to online auctions. The Directive expressly excludes from its scope contracts concluded at an auction (Art 3) and contracts between private sellers.[142] The rationale for the auction exception lies in the nature of auctions. Given the gaming or speculative character of auctions, the finality of the highest bid adds to the tension of the bidding process and is critical for its success: 'If buyers are enabled to revoke their contracts after the end of an auction there would be no risk for a buyer in making the highest possible bid, thus rendering the auction a farce.'[143] Thus a right of withdrawal – that is, a *cooling-off* period – would sit uncomfortably with auction transactions, the essence of which is the *heated* competition between the buyers. Also, '[t]he seller would lose all advantages if a bidder could revoke his or her contract freely. The situation of the auction before the final bid cannot be reinstalled; the seller cannot take resort to the next highest bid because the auction has already been terminated'.[144]

In respect of eBay and comparable online auctions, the situation is complicated by the fact that eBay disputes its role as auctioneer as opposed to being a mere provider of an auction platform, as discussed above. As also discussed above, there are good grounds for arguing that online auctions do not follow the ordinary pattern of offer and acceptance in traditional auctions. But does it follow that eBay auctions are not auctions at all, or not auctions for the purposes of the right of withdrawal? The answer is that eBay auctions (unlike 'Buy It Now' sales) rely – just like ordinary auctions – upon the heat of the auctions for their success and thus cannot accommodate a cooling-off period. For this reason, the controversial judgment by the highest German court,[145] according to which commercial sellers on eBay are bound to grant their customers the right of withdrawal, is unlikely to be followed by other national courts or the European Court of Justice (ECJ).[146] Just because there is no auctioneer and no fall of the hammer does not mean that that eBay auctions are not auctions with the attendant heated competition, as any respectable eBayer will know. And to argue that the absence of a right of withdrawal on eBay auctions would allow online traders to avoid their statutory obligation by offering their wares on eBay misses the point that this argument is not peculiar to eBay or the internet, and that auctions are a sales strategy with distinct advantages and disadvantages.

Subject Matter of the Contract

Consideration in Gratuitous Agreements?

As any first-year student of English common law knows, a contract is only a contract, rather than a gift, if there is consideration – a doctrine that has remained intact despite various criticisms,[147] and

---

139 Article 6. Where the services are, with the consent of the consumer, performed in the cooling-off period, then there is no right of withdrawal.
140 Article 6(1).
141 Recital 14.
142 See the definitions of 'distance contract' and 'supplier' in Art 2(1).
143 Gerald Spindler, 'Internet-auctions versus consumer protection: The case of the Distant Selling Directive' (2005) 6(3) GLJ, available online at www.germanlawjournal.com/article.php?id=585
144 Ibid.
145 Vertragsschluss bei Online-Auktionen (BGH, 3 November 2004, VIII ZR 375 03); for criticism, see Spindler, op cit.
146 Contrast Smith, op cit, 782.
147 *Johnson v Gore Wood & Co* [2001] 1 All ER 481, 507.

its discrepancy with civil law systems. Although consideration can come in all forms and sizes, ultimately something of value must be exchanged.[148] This raises the question of whether there is any value being exchanged in most browsewrap agreements or in the many clickwrap agreements in which the user gets a free product or service, such as free software downloads, or access to email, or social networking sites. Does the user pass a benefit to the site provider that would be sufficient to amount to 'valuable consideration' in return for the use of the site, product, or service? That the providers benefit from their site being accessed by the user by, for example, delivering the surfer to advertisements of the provider's or third parties' products is unquestionable, but does that benefit count? Some free sites attempt to fulfil the notion of reciprocal consideration by statements such as Yahoo's in the terms of its UK site:

> In consideration of your use of the Services, you agree to: (a) provide true, accurate, current and complete information about yourself as prompted by the Services' registration form (such information being the 'Registration Data') and (b) maintain and promptly update the Registration Data to keep it true, accurate, current and complete.

This consideration could either be attacked for being too discretionary[149] (that is, because Yahoo has no way of checking the veracity of the data, complying with it is entirely within the discretion of the user), or for being an uninduced performance[150] (that is, the user would have given the data in any event). Some providers suggest that the consideration for the use of the site is being bound by the agreement. The terms and conditions of timesonline.co.uk state that:

> By using the Services, and in consideration of Provider providing the Services to you, you agree to be bound by this Agreement, whether you are a 'Visitor' (which means that you have not registered with the Website) or you are a 'Member' (which means that you have registered with the Website).

Here, the consideration purports to be 'being bound', which would also be the result of its presence – a circular provision and thus the consideration would again appear to be illusory.[151]

Despite these academic difficulties concerning gratuitous internet agreements, they have been upheld in the USA (see above), and are likely to be upheld in England and Wales (assuming no other default, such as lack of notice or lack of an intention to create legal relations), given that the doctrine of consideration has lost some of its restrictiveness and been supplemented by the doctrine of estoppel. Also, the non-recognition of such agreements would be out of sync with the pragmatism of common law judges to follow and facilitate commercial practice; in Lord Steyn's words, judges have shown a 'readiness to hold that the rigidity of the doctrine of consideration must yield to practical justice and the needs of modern commerce'.[152] Clearly commercial providers of 'free' online services, such as eBay, Hotmail, Facebook, or Google, derive significant benefits from their non-paying customers, as do the customers; a court that struck down agreements that legitimise and regulate mutually beneficial exchanges would be a foolish one indeed.

Finally, the above debate has some parallels with the discussion on the contractual force of open source or free software licence agreements,[153] given that here the software is often (albeit not always) freely available, but subject to conditions on how subsequent modified versions must be

---

148 *Thomas v Thomas* (1842) 2 QB 851, 859.
159 *Powell v Braun* [1954] 1 WLR 401.
150 *Arrale v Costain Civil Engineering Ltd* [1976] 1 Lloyd's Rep 98.
151 Consideration in the form of performance of pre-existing contractual duties: *Stilk v Myrick* (1829) 6 Esp 129, 2 Camp 317; cf *The Eurymedon* [1975] AC 154.
152 Lord Johan Steyn, 'Contract law: Fulfilling the reasonable expectations of honest men' (1997) 113 LQR 433, 437.
153 Guadamuz-González, op cit.

redistributed, generally requiring equally generous rights to access the source code of the software, and to modify and share it. Do these conditions have contractual force even where the software is acquired gratuitously? Regardless of whether they do or do not, licences in the copyright context provide valid permissions for what would otherwise amount to breaches of copyright – quite independent of any contract notions. However, to the extent to which browsewrap agreements go over and beyond permitting and limiting intellectual property rights, they cannot be explained and enforced as such licences, and would need resort to contract law – unless courts were prepared to treat them as analogous to physical premises, treating cyberspace like a physical space. The law of trespass means that visitors of physical premises have a limited licence to enter and to explore – always subject to the rules of the owner. By the same token, a browsewrap agreement could be treated as providing users with a licence to 'enter' and explore the site, subject to the owner's rules. An action for breach of these terms would then give rise to 'electronic trespass' (see above).

Goods or Services

For most legal purposes, it is irrelevant whether the subject matter of the contract is one for goods or services. However, it matters when it comes to quality control. Current legislation imposes more onerous implied terms into contracts for goods than for services. Goods must be of 'satisfactory quality' under the **Sale of Goods Act 1979**.[154] With services, such quality is not required; under the **Supply of Goods and Services Act 1982**, the provider must have exercised reasonable care and skill to the degree expected of a professional man of ordinary competence and experience[155] – so what matters is effort and not outcome. Because many digital products, such as software, films, books, news, financial data, etc, are not easily categorised as either goods or services, there is an ongoing debate as to their proper categorisation, as discussed in relation to contracts for the supply of software elsewhere in this book.

See Chapter 12

Transnational Online Contracting

The internet has opened up transnational trade to the ordinary consumer. The incidence of cross-border B2C transactions has drastically increased. Although, in practical terms, it often makes little difference whether you buy something from someone in your own jurisdiction or from abroad, legally it does make a difference.[156] The respective rights and obligations of the parties to a transnational contract are complicated by questions of competence. The first issue is which court has the right to hear the dispute (the jurisdictional inquiry); the second, which law applies to the dispute (the applicable law inquiry); and the third, whether the judgment can be enforced against the foreign defendant (that is, enforcement jurisdiction). What sets a transnational contractual dispute apart from other civil disputes is that the parties have frequently contractually agreed the answer to the first two questions in the form of a 'choice of forum' and 'choice of law' clause. For example, Term 14 of Facebook's terms and conditions states:

See Chapter 2

See Chapter 2

> You will resolve any claim . . . you have with us arising out of or relating to this Statement of
> Facebook in a state or federal court located in Santa Clara County. The laws of the State of

---

154 Section 14 of the Act, as amended by the Sale and Supply of Goods Act 1994.
155 Contrast the approach taken in *St Albans City and District Council v International Computers Ltd* [1996] 4 All ER 481 (CA) (requiring 'goods' to be tangible and thereby excluding digital products).
156 This is not necessarily the case, because it may turn out that the contract is simply governed by the terms agreed by the parties or that the dispute is resolved entirely by reference to local laws and procedures.

> California will govern this Statement, as well as any claim that might arise between you and us, without regard to conflict of law provisions . . .

The question is: when would such a term be enforceable and what happens if the parties have not agreed on such a clause? For online businesses, particularly with a worldwide clientele, such clauses provide significant protection and certainty; not enforcing them discourages such trade. Conversely, for consumers, they are troublesome, because they often deprive them of a realistic chance of a remedy; thus enforcing them is likely to undermine consumer confidence in transnational online trade.

Jurisdiction

The enforceability of jurisdiction clauses and, more generally, the issue of which court settles the dispute are significant both in practical and substantive terms. In practical terms, it means the difference between being able to bring or defend proceedings in your home jurisdiction, on the one hand, or having to go abroad, on the other hand, and thus face the cost of travelling and unfamiliarity with the foreign legal system, customs, and possibly the language. Substantively, the choice of the court is also likely to have an impact on the substantive outcome of the case because the court deciding the case always applies its own procedural law to the matter,[157] will generally favour local substantive law as the applicable law, and will not allow the exclusion of local mandatory rules even where foreign substantive law is otherwise applicable. For these reasons, the choice of the court is often a hotly disputed issue.

Jurisdiction in the EU

Contractual Choice

In the EU, choice-of-forum clauses are principally validated by Art 23 of the EC **Regulation on Jurisdiction and the Recognition and Enforcement of Judgments in Civil and Commercial Matters**:[158]

> If the parties . . . have agreed that a court or the courts of a Member State are to have jurisdiction to settle any disputes which have arisen or which may arise in connection with a particular legal relationship, that court or those courts shall have jurisdiction. Such jurisdiction shall be exclusive unless the parties have agreed otherwise.

The only preconditions are that at least one of the parties is domiciled in a Member State (as an exception to Art 4, which otherwise extends the Regulation only to defendants domiciled in the EU) and that the agreement is in writing or in another form consistent with the practices of the parties or usage within the industry. Electronic communications are covered in Art 23(2), which provides that 'any communication by electronic means which provides a durable record of the agreement shall be the equivalent to "writing"'. What exactly 'durability' entails is discussed below, but for the moment, it suggests the accessibility and integrity of the record over time.

---

157 That may include matters such as discovery or the quantification of damages.
158 Regulation on Jurisdiction and the Recognition and Enforcement of Judgments in Civil and Commercial Matters 44/2001/EC. For a commentary of the Regulation, see Ulrich Magnus and Peter Mankowski (eds), *Brussels I Regulation*, 2007, Brussels: Sellier European Law Publishers. See also Arts 1 and 2 of the Hague Conference on Private International Law's Convention on Choice of Court Agreements (2005), which, by virtue of Art 2(1), does not apply to consumer contracts and thus is not applicable to most online clickwrap agreements.

Contractual autonomy, as upheld in Art 23, is limited by the consumer protection provisions in Arts 15–17 of the Regulation (see below). But even if a choice-of-forum clause survives these consumer provisions, it may still be invalidated under the **Unfair Terms in Consumer Contracts Directive**,[159] which has priority over the Regulation.[160] In a preliminary ruling, the ECJ decided in *Océana Grupo Editorial SA v Roció Murciano Quintero, Salvat Editores SA v José M Sánchez Alcón Prades et al*[161] that choice-of-forum clauses in consumer contracts are unfair under Art 3 of the Directive if the clause was not individually negotiated and confers exclusive jurisdiction on the court where the seller or supplier is established, as is usually the case.[162] Consistently, the Guidelines by the UK's Office of Fair Trading treat jurisdiction clauses unfavourable to the consumer as unfair almost as a matter of presumption.[163]

In the Absence of Contractual Choice

Where the parties to a contract have not agreed on the court that should be the venue for their dispute resolution, the general rules in Arts 2 and 5 would kick into play. Article 2(1) provides the default position: the defendant must be sued where he or she is domiciled. This rule accords with notions of fairness and practicalities: it is fair, all things being equal, that the plaintiff has to bring the complaint to the so-far 'innocent' defendant, and it is practical, because if the defendant is found liable, the judgment is more easily enforceable against him or her in his or her home jurisdiction.

Article 5 provides rules of 'special' jurisdiction basing jurisdiction on the close connection between the dispute and a particular court. Pursuant to Art 5(1), the defendants in a contractual dispute may be sued in the place in which the contract was or should have been performed – that is (unless the parties agreed otherwise), where the goods or services were or should have been delivered, or performed, respectively.[164] Although there may be difficulty in categorising an electronic contractual subject matter as either 'goods' or 'services', such categorisation would not appear to be critical in this context given the focus of the Article on the place of the performance of the contract. Again, the term 'place' is ambiguous where a digital good or service is involved, because it may or may not be said to be delivered or performed in any particular physical place. Yet, as the terms 'delivery' and 'performance' focus on the receipt of the goods or services, it would appear reasonable that, in most cases, the place of business or domicile of the buyer is the place of performance. In view of that, online sellers do well to remember to include a choice-of-court clause in their terms, even it is struck down in some consumer contracts.

Consumer Protection Provisions

Consumer contracts are governed by Arts 15–17 of the Regulation.[165] Provided that the contract is within the scope of one of the exceptions, the internet business loses the benefit of the forum selection clause (although not necessarily other contractual clauses) as well as of the default position in

---

159 93/13/EEC, implemented in the UK by the Unfair Terms in Consumer Contracts Regulations 1999, SI 1999/2083. See Sch 2, regs 5(1) and 1(q), but note that the Schedule lists the terms 'that *may* be regarded as unfair'. See also Consumer Credit Act 1974, s 141.

160 See Art 67 of the Jurisdiction Regulation, and discussion in Magnus and Mankowski, op cit, pp 322ff.

161 *Océana Grupo Editorial SA v Roció Murciano Quintero, Salvat Editores SA v José M Sánchez Alcón Prades, José Luis Copano Badillo, Mohammed Berroane and Emilio Viñas Feliù*, Joined Cases C-240/98, C-241/98, C-242/98, C-243/98, C-240/98 [2000] ECR I–4941, I–4971, and I–4973.

162 See also Art 6 and Annex 1(q) of the Unfair Terms in Consumer Contracts Directive 93/13/EEC.

163 Office of Fair Trading (OFT), *Unfair Contract Terms Guidance*, OFT 311, 2008, London: HMSO, pp 67ff.

164 See also Art 5(5): '. . . a person domiciled in a Member State may, in another Member State, be sued, as regards a dispute arising out of the operations of a branch, agency or other establishment in the court for the place in which the branch, agency or other establishment is situated.'

165 Given the uncertainties created by the consumer protection provisions for businesses, one may question whether they are still needed in the online environment: Arnold Roosendaal and Simone Van Esch, 'Commercial websites: Consumer protection and power shifts' (2007) 6(1) JITLP 13.

Art 2. Under Art 15(1), a consumer contract is one that is 'concluded by a person . . . for a purpose outside his trade or profession'. The Article is silent on the status of the other party to the contract; it is, however, unlikely that C2C transactions, such as via online auctions, are within the Article's ambit given its underlying idea of protecting the vulnerable party in an unequal bargaining scenario.[166]

Extended Scope in Consumer Cases: Branch, Agency, or Establishment in the EU

Like the rest of the Regulation, the protective provisions only apply where the defendant is domiciled in an EU Member State, and thus a contractual dispute instigated by a European consumer against a US online provider would generally be outside the scope of Regulation, including its consumer provisions.

However, the scope of the Regulation is extended in consumer contracts by virtue of Art 15(2) (which is not a substantive provision) to certain non-EU defendants:

> Where a consumer enters into a contract with a party who is not domiciled in the Member State but has a branch, agency or other establishment in one of the Member States, that party shall, in disputes arising out of the operations of the branch, agency or establishment, be deemed to be domiciled in that State.

Thus a US online business with European headquarters would fall within the scope of the Regulation (including its consumer protection provisions), provided that the dispute arose out the activities of the European headquarters. This means that the business can be sued either in the place of its establishment in the EU,[167] or, possibly, within the consumer's domicile, depending on whether Art 15(1) is also satisfied (see below). Article 15(2) catches many of the larger online providers that have a corporate presence in Europe. For example, Facebook, although headquartered in California, has its European headquarters in Dublin, and thus any contractual dispute arising out of Facebook's Dublin operations falls within the Regulation.[168]

Beyond such clear-cut cases, there has also been some debate over whether the mere presence of a local server hosting a site or a local electronic agent amounts to an 'establishment'.[169] Such a position is expressly rejected in the **Electronic Commerce Directive**, defining an 'established service provider' as:

> a service provider who effectively pursues an economic activity using a fixed establishment for an indefinite period. The presence and use of the technical means and technologies required to provide the service do not, in themselves, constitute an establishment of the provider.[170]

Although the Regulation does not provide for a comparable definition, a comparable position is likely to be favoured for a number of reasons. First, the location of a server or other technology can easily be manipulated by the parties and is an entirely fortuitous event that need not reflect at all the real connection of the parties or the dispute with the forum. Second, the Regulation is the more

---

166 Magnus and Mankowski, op cit, pp 312ff. See also the wording of Art 15(3)(c) ('pursuing commercial or professional activities in the Member State') and *Rudolf Gabriel* Case C-96/00 [2002] ECR I–6367, [39].

167 Article 2(1) of the Regulation. Note the difference from Art 5(5), which also deals with the right to sue in the place of a business' branch, agency, or other establishment, is that it is only applicable if the business itself is domiciled in a Member State (Art 4(1)).

168 Provided that the dispute arises out of the activities of that 'branch, agency or other establishment'.

169 Joakim ST Øen, 'Electronic agents and the notion of establishment' (2001) 9 Int JLIT 249; M Foss and L Bygrave, 'International consumer purchases through the internet: Jurisdictional issues pursuant to European law' (2000) 8 Int JLIT 99.

170 Article 2(c) (and also Recital 19) of the Directive.

general instrument that can draw, for more specific queries, upon more specific instruments, such as the Directive, with its focus on electronic commerce.

Finally, let us turn to traditional ECJ jurisprudence on the matter.[171] The phrase 'agency, branch or other establishment' is understood to refer:

> to a *place* of business which has the *appearance* of permanency, such as the extension of a parent body, has a *management* and is materially equipped to *negotiate* businesses with the third parties so that the latter, although *knowing* that there will if necessary be a legal link with the parent body . . . abroad, do not have to deal directly with such parent body but may transact business at the place of . . . the extension.[172]

It may be arguable that business transacted via a local server, using an electronic agent, 'negotiates' business and is thus an 'establishment'. However, the above definition is also concerned with the perception of the extension through the eyes of the customer. Where the business of a foreign provider is simply transacted via a local server, this would not create any expectations in the mind of the customer that there is a local extension of the foreign business given that the location of the server would be invisible to all but the most computer-savvy clients. This situation may be different where the local server hosts a country-specific website of an international well-known company, such as amazon.fr or ebay.fr, which then might create the expectation of a locally supported corporate base, and thus would seem to satisfy the appearance test. Some academics have gone further and argued that 'place of business' does not necessarily refer to a physical place, and would thus include even country-specific websites not supported by local servers.[173] Certainly, such a wide interpretation of 'establishment' would accord with the consumer's legitimate expectations. Yet it must be remembered that the phrase 'agency, branch or other establishment' is also used outside the consumer context in Art 5(5) and thus consumer expectations by themselves cannot be sufficient to justify it. Furthermore, making local personnel a necessary requirement of any 'establishment' (note the reference to 'management') – and thereby excluding lonely servers hosting sites and electronic agents of any kind – makes good sense in practical terms. One rationale for the 'establishment' exception is to serve the interest of the due administration of justice. The personnel of a local establishment are likely to have knowledge of the dispute and can thus be called before a local court without unduly inconveniencing the defendant.[174]

Substantively, Art 15 sets out two types of consumer contracts that fall within the protective regime.[175] A consumer may sue, and must be sued by, a foreign business in the consumer's domicile,[176] regardless of any 'choice of forum' clause,[177] provided that the conditions in Art 15(1)(c) are satisfied:

● the contract has been concluded with a person who pursues commercial or professional activities in the Member State of the consumer's domicile or,

---

171 Most of the jurisprudence concerns Art 5(5) of the Regulation or its identically worded predecessor. The only case decided under the consumer protection provision is *Wolfgang Brenner and Peter Noller v Dean Witter Reynolds Inc* C-318/93 [1994] ECR I-4275.

172 *Somafer v Saar-Ferngas* C-33/78 [1978] ECR 2183, [12] (emphasis added); *Lloyd's Register of Shipping v Société Campenon Bernard* [1995] ECR I-961. In certain circumstances, establishment may not even be an extension of the foreign company, but a legally independent business entity: *SAR Schotte GmbH v Parfums Rothschild Sarl*, C–218/86 [1987] ECR 4905, [15]. See also Magnus and Mankowski, op cit, pp 224ff.

173 Øren, op cit, 258ff.

174 Foss and Bygrave, op cit, 132.

175 Joakim ST Øren, 'International jurisdiction over consumer contracts in e-Europe' (2003) 52 ICLQ 665.

176 See also Arts 16(1) and (2), and 17, of the Regulation.

177 Article 17 of the Regulation.

- by any means, directs such activities to that Member State or to several States including that Member State,

and the contract falls within the scope of such activities.

Consumer Exception: Pursuing Commercial or Professional Activities

In relation to the first of these conditions, the question is whether an online business that advertises and sells its products via its site in the consumer's state would thereby 'pursue commercial activities' there. While the phrase by itself would appear to allow for that possibility, the very scenario is already and more neatly covered by the second exception (see below). Thus it seems that 'pursues commercial or professional activities in the Member State' suggests more substantial activities in the state than mere web presence, probably requiring the physical presence of the trader in the state.[178]

Consumer Exception: Directing Activities

The second exception was specifically drafted with e-commerce in mind. It gives a consumer the benefit of litigating at home, whenever the foreign trader specifically directed its products at the consumer's state and the consumer entered into a contract on the basis of those activities. The rationale underlying it is the same as that endorsed by its predecessor – namely, that businesses cannot expect to take the benefit of the custom of foreign markets that they specifically seek out (previously, for example, through mail order catalogues or doorstep selling) and then not take the burden of defending suits in those markets.[179]

A question that has remained wide open is when an online business should be held to have 'directed' its online activities to a Member State. Perhaps every website is directed to every state? To avoid this position, as well as any uncertainty, the European Parliament proposed amending Art 15 to make it clear that:

> [t]he expression 'directing such activities' shall be taken to mean that the trader must have purposefully directed his activity in a substantial way to that other Member State or to several countries including that Member State. In determining whether a trader has directed his activities in such a way, the courts shall have regard to all the circumstances of the case, including any attempts by the trader to ring-fence his trading operation against transactions with consumers domiciled in particular Member States.[180]

So just because a trader has an isolated contact with a resident in a Member State does not mean that he or she is subject to the court processes of that Member State. However, the European Commission rejected this amendment, which, in its opinion:

> runs counter to the philosophy of the provision. The definition is based on the essentially American concept of business activity as a general connecting factor determining jurisdiction, whereas that concept is quite foreign to the approach taken by the Regulation. Moreover, the existence of a

---

178 Øren (2003), op cit, 677.
179 This was not satisfied in *Rayner v Davies* [2003] 1 All ER 394, but was satisfied in *Gabriel v Schlank & Schick GmbH* C96/00 [2002] ECR I–6367 on the basis of a number of personalised letters being sent to the consumer inviting him to enter into the contract. Both cases were decided under Art 13(3) of the Brussels Convention on Jurisdiction and the Enforcement of Judgments in Civil and Commercial Matters (1968). There are clear parallels to the US 'purposeful availment' test generally adopted in civil matters: see Chapter 2.
180 Amendment 37 (OJ C 146/98, 2001) to the Proposal for a Council Regulation on Jurisdiction and the Recognition and Enforcement of Judgments in Civil and Commercial Matters (OJ C 376/17, 1999).

consumer dispute requiring court action presupposes a consumer contract. Yet the very existence of such a contract would seem to be clear indication that the supplier of the goods or services has directed his activities towards the state where the consumer is domiciled.[181]

The Commission also noted that 'the language or currency which a website uses does not constitute a relevant factor'[182] in determining whether the activities were directed at the state or not. According to the Commission, if there is a contract with a consumer, then the business is presumed to have targeted the consumer's residents.

This interpretation by the Commission is not reconcilable with the existence of Art 15.[183] Article 15 is only ever invoked if there is a consumer contract. However, Art 15 limits the privilege of the consumer to litigate at home to certain consumer contracts; otherwise it could simply have stated that, whenever there is a consumer contract, the consumer can sue the foreign defendant in his or her home jurisdiction. In short, it envisages the possibility that sometimes, despite there being a consumer contract, the consumer will fall outside the privileged exceptions – contrary to the position of the Commission.

The better approach to 'directing' was recently adopted by the ECJ in *Peter Pammer v Reederei Karl Schlüter GmbH & Co KG and Hotel Alpenhof GesmbH v Oliver Heller*,[184] in which the court held that the mere use of a website by a trader in order to engage trade does not by itself mean that the site is 'directed to' other Member States; other evidence is needed to show the trader's manifest intention to establish commercial relations with those foreign consumers. Such evidence may come in the form of an express mentioning of the targeted Member States, or paying search engines to advertise the goods and services there, or through more indirect and subtle factors, such as:

- the international nature of the activity at issues, such as tourism;
- the use of telephone numbers with the international code;
- the use of a top-level domain name other than that of the Member State in which the trader is established, such as .de or .fr, or the use of neutral top-level domain names, such as .com or .eu;
- the description of itineraries from one or more other Member States to the place where the service is provided;
- the mention of an international clientele composed of customers domiciled in various Member States, in particular by presentation of accounts written by such customers; and/or
- the use of a language or a currency other than that generally used in the trader's Member State, and the possibility of translations.

In short, the ECJ quite rightly adopted the holistic approach, looking at the overall business activity, which the European Commission had rejected as 'too American'. This approach also means that an isolated contract with a consumer from a Member State will not in itself be sufficient to amount to 'directing'.

Jurisdiction under English Common Law: Defendants outside the EU

The rules of jurisdiction under English common law potentially have a significant role to play in the electronic environment, because they govern contracts with defendants from outside the EU, such

---

181 Amended Proposal for a Council Regulation on Jurisdiction and the Recognition and Enforcement of Judgments in Civil and Commercial Matters (OJ 062 E, 27.2.2001 P.0243–0275), para 2.2.2.
182 Joint Council and the Commission Statements (14 December 2000), 5.
183 Frederic Debusseré, 'International jurisdiction over e-consumer contracts in the European Union: *Quid novi sub sole?*' (2002) 10 Int JLIT 344. See also Magnus and Mankowski, op cit, p 317.
184 *Peter Pammer v Reederei Karl Schlüter GmbH & Co KG* (C–585/08), *and Hotel Alpenhof GesmbH v Oliver Heller* (C–144/09) [2005] ECR 1-481.

as US defendants.[185] Although, on the face of it, they provide for a very different regime from that of the European rules, there are significant similarities. Under English law, a foreign defendant – not present in England or Wales – may be sued in a local court in contractual disputes in five situations:[186]

> a claim form may be served out of the jurisdiction with the permission of the court, if—
>
> a claim in made in respect of a contract, where the contract—
>
> (1)   was made within the jurisdiction
> (2)   was made by or through an agent trading or residing within the jurisdiction
> (3)   is governed by English law
> (4)   contains a term to the effect that the court shall have jurisdiction to determine any claim in the contract
> (5)   a claim in respect of a breach of contract committed within the jurisdiction

Let us briefly consider the relevance of each of these heads to transnational electronic contracts.

Contractual Choice

Starting with the fourth head, English courts will generally uphold a forum selection clause in favour of the local court, because the defendant has thereby submitted to its jurisdiction.[187] What this head does not address is whether a court may also assume jurisdiction *despite* a forum selection clause in favour of a foreign court, such as when a UK consumer enters into an online contract with a US business and the jurisdiction clause refers the dispute to a US court (à la Facebook). Despite the underlying principle that parties are made to comply with their bargain, such a clause may be struck down as 'unfair' under the **Unfair Terms in Consumer Contracts Regulations 1999** (as discussed above). Striking down a forum selection clause referring the dispute to a foreign court may also be necessary to override a choice-of-law clause that invalidly purports to exclude local mandatory rules, given that a foreign tribunal is unlikely to apply those mandatory rules (see below).[188]

Location of the Contract

In the absence of a choice-of-law clause, the other four heads assume relevance. The first requires a decision on *where* an electronic contract is concluded. A contract is concluded where the last act necessary for its conclusion has occurred. Assuming the applicability of the receipt rule to online contracts (see above),[189] this would be where the electronic acceptance is received by the offeror – or, more specifically, where he or she is capable of accessing it (see above). In this context, it should not matter where the offeror's mail is stored or where he or she happens to checks it – these are fickle indicators. A more stable criterion for fixing the location of the contract is the offeror's place of business or residence, with one proviso: when the offeror's actual location – either his or her residence or place of business – is different from that reasonably communicated to the offeree, the parties must be considered to have objectively intended to conclude the contract in the second

---

185 But for Art 23, discussed above. See generally Lorna E Giles, *Electronic Commerce and Private International Law*, 2008, Aldershot: Ashgate, ch 6. In Scotland, the rules are provided in Sch 8 of the Civil Jurisdiction and Judgments Act 1982.
186 CPR 6.20(5) and (6). For their interpretation, see Lawrence Collins (ed), *Dicey, Morris and Collins on the Conflicts of Laws: Vol 1*, 14th edn, 2006, London: Sweet and Maxwell, pp 375ff.
187 *Attock Cement Co v Romanian Bank for Foreign Trade* [1989] 1 WLR 1147. It is within the discretion of the court to grant a stay of proceedings on *forum conveniens* grounds: *Donohue v Armco Inc* [2001] UKHL 64.
188 This would fall with *The Eleftheria* [1970] P 94, in which the court laid down the factors that may be taken into account in its discretionary exercise whether to override a jurisdictional clause, including the law governing the contract.
189 *Entores v Miles Far East Corp* [1955] 2 QB 327 (CA); *Brinkibon Ltd v Stahag Stahl* [1983] 2 AC 34 (HL); see above.

location.[190] For example, if I were to buy a book through amazon.de using a German credit card and providing a German delivery address, it would be concluded that Amazon and I have objectively intended to conclude the contract in Germany, even if I am resident in the UK.

An Agent within the Jurisdiction

The second head – that is, 'an agent trading or residing within the jurisdiction' – is the broad equivalent of the 'agency, branch or other establishment' head of jurisdiction in Arts 5(5) and 15(2) of the **Jurisdiction Regulation** (see above), and thus local technology supporting online services should not by itself be treated as an 'agent'.

Contracts Governed by English Law

The third ground – that is, the contract is governed by English law – is addressed below. At this stage, suffice to say that while a finding in favour of English law is not a conclusive factor in favour of an English court hearing the dispute,[191] it carries material weight where the foreign law is significantly different from English law or it would defeat a valid claim under English law, such as where the foreign court would not apply local mandatory consumer protection provisions.[192]

Location of the Breach

The 'location of the breach' is perhaps the most ambivalent basis for the court's jurisdiction, both in offline and electronic contracts. To start with, whether a contract is breached within the jurisdiction depends on the type of breach. If the breach occurs by an express repudiation (for example, an email in which one party informs the other that he or she does not intend to perform the contract), then, according to traditional case law, the repudiation occurs where the email was sent and not where it was received.[193] Where, on the other hand, the breach takes the form of a failure to perform the contract, the focus is on the location where the performance ought to have occurred (reminiscent of Art 5(1) of the Regulation – see above).[194] Again, in the electronic context, it might be tempting to look at the location of the technology involved in the transaction, but traditional rules support more stable factors, such as the place of business or residence of the parties, as the default position.[195]

In respect of non-payment, *The Eider*[196] established long ago that '[t]he general rule is where no place is specified, either expressly or by implication, the debtor must seek out his creditor'.[197] In most electronic contracts, the buyer is expressly required to pay the outstanding sum into the seller's account, often via intermediaries such as PayPal. While that account could be anywhere, in the absence of any contrary indication, it would be inferred that the account is where the place of business or residence of the seller is located. Conversely, when the breach of an electronic contract consists of a non-delivery of the promised goods or services, the place of the performance would generally be the buyer's place of business or residence. This is not inconsistent with s 29(2) of the **Sale of Goods Act 1979**, which provides that – bar any express or implied contractual provision to the contrary – 'the place of delivery is the seller's place of business if he has one, and if not, his

---

190 For similar reasoning, see below discussion on 'Location of the Breach'.
191 *Amin Rasheed Shipping Corp v Kuwait Insurance Co* [1984] AC 50.
192 Collins, op cit.
193 *Cherry v Thompson* (1872) LR 7 QB 573; *Holland v Bennett* [1902] 1KB 867 (CA); *Martin v Stout* [1925] AC 359 (PC); *Atlantic Underwriting Agencies Ltd v Compagnia di Assicurazione di Milano* [1979] 2 Lloyd's Rep 240; *Stanley Kerr Holdings Pty Ltd v Gibor Textile Enterprises Ltd* [1967] 2 NSWLR 372.
194 The difference here is that, unlike in the Regulation, the focus is not only on the substantive obligation concerning the delivery of the goods or the performance of the service, but also equally on the monetary obligation.
195 *Thompson v Palmer* [1893] 2 QB 80 (CA); *Bremer Öltransport GmbH v Drewy* [1933] 1 KB 753.
196 [1893] P 119.
197 Ibid, 136.

residence'. In the electronic context, most contracts would have an implied or express term providing for the delivery of the goods to the buyer.[198] Again, in the case of digital goods or services, the place of delivery is not as straightforward, but might follow a similar line of argument as that advanced above in relation to the 'performance of the contract' under Art 5(1) of the **Jurisdiction Regulation**.

Jurisdiction in the USA

The greater US deference for party autonomy means that choice-of-forum clauses are upheld not only in B2B contracts, but also frequently in B2C contracts. In *Carnival Cruise Lines Inc v Shute*,[199] the US Supreme Court held that even in adhesion contracts – that is, standard-form contracts – such clauses are enforceable unless there is a finding of unfairness or unconscionability. While this appears to echo the European position under the **Unfair Terms in Consumer Contracts Directive**,[200] the devil sits in the detail. According to the Supreme Court, a clause is not simply unfair because it is onerous to the consumer; it will nonetheless stand provided that it serves legitimate reasons (rather than simply trying to discourage legitimate claims by customers), such as protecting the business from being exposed to proceedings in the innumerable locations of its customer, wishing to bring proceedings in a place to which the business has a link, eliminating *ex ante* uncertainty and argument as to the forum, and thus saving costs that may even have been passed onto the consumers. Apply this to the online world and most choice-of-forum clauses would withstand US judicial scrutiny. Having said that, *Carnival Cruise* concerned an intra-national case and, in an international scenario, US courts might be more sympathetic to its local consumers' plight. Where the parties to the electronic contract have not agreed on a choice-of-forum clause, the US default rules on jurisdiction come to bear.

See Chapter 2 →

The Applicable Law

The rules determining the law applicable to contractual disputes have, in the Member States of the EU, only one provenance (unlike the dual system in place for jurisdictional questions): the EC **Regulation on the Law Applicable to Contractual Obligations**,[201] commonly referred to as **Rome I**. The Regulation applies regardless of the connection of the parties with any Member States, and may well lead to the application of the law of a non-Member State to the dispute (Art 2). Although the Regulation is thus broader in its catchment area than the **Jurisdiction Regulation**, it generally mirrors the contractual provisions in the latter Regulation.

Another point worth noting is that different aspects of a contract may be governed by different laws, such as if so agreed by the parties (Art 3(1)). While the contractual dispute may be governed by Greek law, the validity of a party's consent may be determined by reference to Spanish law, if that is the law of the country in which he or she is habitually resident (Art 10(2)). While the court may uphold the parties' choice of law for most purposes, it may not do so for all purposes (for example, Art 3(3)). Certainly, parties cannot exclude any public, criminal, or other mandatory laws of any state, which – if the contract falls within their scope – will take priority over the 'applicable law' (Art 9, discussed below).

---

198 Generally, if the buyer is expected to collect the goods from the seller, this would be expressly stated given its exceptional nature.
199 499 US 585 (1991).
200 Directive 93/13/EEC, discussed above.
201 Regulation 593/2008/EC, replacing the Rome Convention on the Law Applicable to Contractual Obligations (1980); see Nils Willem Vernooij, 'Rome I: An update on the law applicable to contractual obligations in Europe' (2009) 15 Colum J Eur L 71. There is no room for the residual application of the national choice of law rules. Article 1(1) provides that the 'Regulation shall apply, in situations involving a conflict of laws, to contractual obligations in civil and commercial matters'.

Contractual Choice and its Limits

The starting point under the Regulation for determining the applicable law is the contract between the parties. Article 3(1) upholds contractual autonomy:

> A contract shall be governed by the law chosen by the parties. The choice shall be made expressly or clearly demonstrated by the terms of the contract or the circumstances of the case. By their choice the parties can select the law applicable to the whole or to part only of the contract.

Most frequently, online businesses include an express choice-of-law clause that, according to the above provision, binds the parties – a matter of utmost importance for online businesses that may otherwise potentially be exposed to the multiple sets of contract law of the countries of their customers. Where the existence or validity of the contract or any of its terms (such as the choice-of-law clause) is in dispute, the validity issue is decided by reference to the law that would be applicable if the contract or term were valid (Art 10(1)).

However, Art 3 already creates a significant inroad into the sanctity of choice-of-law clauses. Article 3(3) provides that parties cannot avoid mandatory provisions of a state with which a contract is closely connected by choosing the laws of another state:

> Where all other elements relevant to the situation at the time of the choice are located in a country other than the country whose law has been chosen, the choice of the parties shall not prejudice the application of provisions of the law of that other country which cannot be derogated from by agreement.

This provision prevents the evasion of regulation often protective of the weaker contractual party and stops contractual parties from a wholesale buying out of regulatory requirements of a state by choosing the laws of another state. Both the **Unfair Contract Terms Act 1977** and the **Unfair Terms in Consumer Contract Regulations 1999** provide examples of laws that may not be derogated from by agreement. According to s 27(2)(a) of the **Unfair Contract Terms Act 1977**:

> This Act has effect notwithstanding any contract term which applies or purports to apply the law of some country outside the United Kingdom where . . . the terms appear to the court or arbitrator or arbiter to have been imposed wholly or mainly for the purpose of enabling the party imposing it to evade the operation of the Act.

Similarly, reg 9 of the **Unfair Terms in Consumer Contracts Regulations 1999** states that the Regulations apply 'notwithstanding any contract term which applies or purports to apply the law of a non-Member State, if the contract has a close connection with the territory of the Member States'. The reference to the law of a *non-Member State* simply reflects that the 1999 Regulations implement the EC **Directive on Unfair Terms in Consumer Contracts** and thus the laws of other Member States should be as protective of consumers as UK law. While both pieces of legislation are principally aimed at the weaker contractual parties, the 1977 Act is not confined to consumers. Similarly, Art 3(3) is also not an exclusive consumer protection provision, and thus may extend protection to small online businesses not shielded by Art 6 (discussed below).

Article 9 of the Regulation goes further than Art 3(3) by validating a state's overriding mandatory provisions necessary 'for safeguarding [a state's] public interests, such as its political, social or economic organisation . . . irrespective of the law otherwise applicable to the contract under this Regulation'. So even if there is no attempt to evade regulatory provisions and even if the law of the relevant state would not be the 'applicable law', the contract may still be subject to those mandatory laws depending on their scope. Article 9 affirms the superiority of regulatory law – such as rules on cartels, competition, restrictive practices, and rules regulating certain industries, such as the banking, insurance, and investment sectors – which is unaffected by the applicable contract law. By the same token, states also retain a residual power to refuse to enforce the otherwise applicable law of another state 'if such application is manifestly incompatible with the public policy . . . of the forum' (Art 21).

So although choice-of-law clauses are a valuable tool for online businesses to reduce their exposure to unwanted laws vis-à-vis their contracting parties, their ambit is limited in two signifi-cant respects: first, these clauses are only enforceable against those who consented to them, but not strangers to the contract, such as those alleging violations of intellectual property rights or defamation; second, their effectiveness is also circumscribed by not preventing the application of certain non-derogatory or mandatory laws of the states affected.

See Chapter 2 →

In the Absence of Contractual Choice

Where the parties have failed to agree on the law applicable to their contract, Art 4(1)[202] provides that:

(a) a contract for the sale of goods shall be governed by the law of the country where the seller has his habitual residence;

(b) a contract for the provision of services shall be governed by the law of the country where the service provider has his habitual residence;

. . .

(g) a contract for the sale of goods by auction shall be governed by the law of the country where the auction takes place, if such a place can be determined; . . .

It then continues to provide two wider default rules that are intended to catch any ambiguous cases – that is, those that are covered by more than one of the above heads, or by none. In those cases, the law governing the contract is 'the law of the country where the party required to effect the characteristic performance of the contract has his habitual residence' (Art 4(2)). Because the 'char-acteristic performance' is the non-monetary consideration, again this rule leads to the law of the place of residence of the seller or service provider. Finally, if that rule fails to yield a suitable appli-cable law, then it is the law of the country that is most closely connected to the contract that shall prevail (Art 4(4) and (5)).

The Regulation makes the 'habitual residence' of one of the parties the reference point for fixing the applicable law. 'Habitual residence' means, in the case of companies, the place of its central administration,[203] in the case of natural persons acting in the course of business, their prin-cipal place of businesses, and finally, in the case of operations of a branch, agency, or any other establishment, the place of that branch, agency, or establishment (Art 19). As in respect of the Regulation's predecessor, the 1980 **Rome Convention on the Law Applicable to Contractual Obligations**, there may be some who argue that a web server by itself may amount to a 'place of business'.[204] Given the fortuitous nature of the location of servers, such arguments should meet as

---

202 Article 4 reverses the approach taken under its predecessor, the Rome Convention on the Law Applicable to Contractual Obligations (1980), by opting for specific rules supplemented by more general default tests, rather than, as previously, providing for a very general test as the main rule, which was then given substance by more specific presumptions: see Vernooij, op cit, 73ff.

203 Contrast Art 60(1) of the Jurisdiction Regulation, which provides for a choice of three criteria to determine a company's domicile; see also below.

204 Michael Chissick and Alistair Kelman, *Electronic Commerce: Law and Practice*, 3rd edn, 2000, London: Sweet & Maxwell, p 120.

much resistance as arguments that a web server may be treated as an agent or a fixed establishment in the jurisdiction enquiry (see above).

Consumer Protection Provisions

Finally, Art 6 of the Regulation deals specifically with consumer contracts and thus has a narrower ambit than Arts 3 and 9 in terms of the contracts to which it applies. However, in respect of these contracts – provided that certain preconditions are satisfied – Art 6 confers wider benefits: it applies the law of the country of the consumer's habitual residence to the contract and not only the mandatory laws (Art 6(1)).

Where there is a choice-of-law clause, Art 6(2) states that the choice will stand in so far as it does not have 'the result of depriving the consumer of the protection afforded to him by provisions that cannot be derogated from by agreement by virtue of the law which, in the absence of choice, would have been applicable on the basis of paragraph 1'. In other words, the court will examine the law of the consumer's residence and apply any mandatory rules from that body of law. Unlike Art 3(3) of the Regulation, there is no need to further show that the contract was otherwise closely connected to the consumer's residence. Again, the **Unfair Contract Terms Act 1977** provides an example of such a mandatory provision. Section 27(2)(b) states:

> This Act has effect notwithstanding any contract term which applies or purports to apply the law of some country outside the United Kingdom, where ... in the making of the contract one of the parties dealt as consumer, and he was then habitually resident in the United Kingdom, and the essential steps necessary for the making of the contract were taken there.[205]

The preconditions that must be satisfied before the consumer exception in the Regulation kicks into place are spelled out in Art 6(1):

> [A] contract concluded by a natural person for a purpose which can be regarded as being outside his trade or profession (the consumer) with another person acting in the exercise of his trade or profession (the professional) shall be governed by the law of the country where the consumer has his habitual residence, provided that the professional:
>
> (a)   pursues his commercial or professional activities in the country where the consumer has his habitual residence, or
>
> (b)   by any means, directs such activities to that country or to several countries including that country

Because this Article is virtually identical to Art 15(1)(c) of the **Jurisdiction Regulation**,[206] it means that if the court of the consumer's habitual residence has the power to hear the dispute, then that court can also apply the substantive law of the forum to the dispute. This creates consistency and simplicity that is advantageous to both consumers and businesses, particularly in the online world.

Regarding the interpretation of Art 6(1)(a) and (b) in the online context, the arguments are the same as those discussed above and need not be repeated here, beyond saying that para (b) in

---

205 Note that this section is still modelled on the formulation of Art 5(2) of the Rome Convention on the Law Applicable to Contractual Obligations (1980).

206 The Rome Regulation uses the concept of 'habitual residence' rather than 'domicile' used in the Jurisdiction Regulation. On the difference of those terms, see Pippa Rogerson, 'Habitual residence: The new domicile?' (2000) 49 ICLQ 86.

See Chapter 2 →

particular again arguably adopts the 'targeting' approach to jurisdiction. This approach is by no means new; it simply applies to the internet what was previously applied to offline communications:

> Thus the trader must have done certain acts such as advertising in the press, or on radio or television, or in the cinema or by catalogues aimed specifically at that country, or he must have made business proposals individually through a middleman or by canvassing. If, for example a German makes a contract in response to an advertisement published by a French company in a German publication, the contract is covered by the special rule. If, on the other hand, the German replies to an advertisement in an American publication, even if they are sold in Germany, the rule does not apply unless the advertisement appeared in special editions of the publication intended for European countries. In the latter case the seller will have made a special advertisement intended for the country of the purchaser.[207]

Although the targeting approach is not new, its application to the internet is likely to produce many boundary cases in which it will not be clear – on the basis of the site's language, currency, the site's names, or products – who is the site's intended clientele. While a willingness to deliver products to a particular country is likely to be taken as a confirmation that the country is part of the site's target, this indicator is often absent in respect of digital products (see above).

Regulatory Requirements: Electronic Commerce Directive

Within the EU, transnational electronic commerce is substantially affected by the allocation principle of the **Electronic Commerce Directive**.[208] This Directive provides – within the sphere of the EU – the origin principle[209] as a basis for sharing out certain regulatory space over electronic commerce between the Member States, online providers are only subject to the law of their state of origin. Article 3 of the Directive provides:

1. Each Member State shall ensure that the information society services provided by a service provider established on its territory comply with the national provisions applicable in the Member State in question which fall within the coordinated field.
2. Member States may not, for reasons falling within the coordinated field, restrict the freedom to provide information society services from another Member State.

So while Art 3(1) establishes a duty on Member States to regulate online providers established on their territory,[210] under Art 3(2), Member States are prohibited from regulating services by providers from other Member States. In short, online service providers are subject to one set of rules (the rules of their state of origin), rather than the multiple sets of rules from all of the states in which they offer their online services. This approach to regulatory competence is highly desirable (particularly for online businesses) and also rather exceptional.

See Chapter 2 →

---

207 Mario Giuliano and Paul Lagarde, 'Council report on the Convention on the Law Applicable to Contractual Obligations' (1980) OJ C282, 24.
208 Directive 2000/31/EC, implemented in the UK by the Electronic Commerce (EC Directive) Regulations 2002, SI 2002/2013. See Lokke Moerel, 'The country-of-origin principle in the E-Commerce Directive: The expected one-stop shop' (2001) 7 CTLR 184.
209 For the reasons behind the acceptability of the origin approach in the EU, see Chapter 2.
210 See Art 2(c) of the Directive, which defines 'established service provider' as a service provider who effectively pursues an economic activity using a fixed establishment for an indefinite period. The presence and use of the technical means and technologies required to provide the service do not, in themselves, constitute an establishment of the provider.

The question is how far-reaching it is: what is the scope of the origin rule under the **Electronic Commerce Directive**? While it does not apply across the field of civil and criminal law, equally it is not only limited to the substantive law harmonised in the Directive, which is a novelty and is perhaps to blame for the resulting complexity of the rules on its scope. The starting position is very broad. The origin rule applies to all 'information society services', which are defined as 'any service normally provided for remuneration at a distance by electronic means and at the individual request of a recipient of services'[211] – covering any commercial activity by online actors and facilitators, such as ISPs, including free services, such as search engines, which are financed by third parties, such as advertisers.[212]

Second, the law that comes within the ambit of the origin approach may be general or specifically designed for online providers, but must fall with within the 'coordinated fields', defined as requirements concerning:

- the taking up of the activity of an information society service, such as requirements concerning qualifications, authorisation, or notification; or
- the pursuit of the activity of an information society service, such as requirements concerning the behaviour of the service provider, requirements regarding the quality or content of the service, including those applicable to advertising and contracts, or requirements concerning the liability of the service provider.[213]

Excluded from the 'coordinated fields' are requirements applicable to goods, to the delivery of goods, and to services not provided by electronic means.[214]

The best way in which to understand the above provisions is to see them as an attempt to deal with the matters that are peculiar to electronic commerce only and to avoid accidentally regulating commercial activities that happens to have some electronic aspect. So, for example, while legal or medical advice provided online triggers the origin rule of the Directive (concerning qualification requirements), any such advice provided offline following an online advert would be outside its scope – although the online advert would again be within its scope. Similarly, when it comes to 'goods' (which appear to encompass only tangible goods, with intangible products being treated as a 'service'),[215] any legal requirement relating to advertising and selling them online falls within the coordinated fields, but any requirements relating to the tangible good itself (for example, its legality, safety standards, labelling requirements, or liability for it) or to its delivery (for example, medicine with or without prescription) is outside the origin rule. This aim of separating the ordinary offline aspects of electronic commerce from its true electronic core makes good sense, because the Directive would otherwise apply far beyond its intended electronic sphere. Nevertheless, such separation is still problematic and ambiguous in the borderline scenarios and overlapping areas. In the final analysis, it illustrates the difficulties created by regulation that is not technologically neutral (see above). For example, does it make sense to apply a different set of rules to an electronic book than to its old-fashioned paper variant? Similarly, labelling requirements of medicine are outside the origin rule, but rules on advertising of medicine online are within it: how are these positions reconcilable when the online advert reproduces the label?

Excluded from the entire Directive are also significant areas of law in respect of which states were not prepared to surrender control: taxation; data protection; cartel law; activities of notaries;

---

211 Ibid, Art 2(a), which refers to the definition in Art 1(2) of Directive 98/34/EC (as amended by Directive 98/84/EC).
212 Ibid, Recital 18.
213 Ibid, Art 2(h)(i).
214 Ibid, Art 2(h)(ii).
215 On the categorisation of goods and services, see discussion above and Chapter 12.

legal representation before the court; gambling, lotteries, and betting.[216] Further, the origin rule also does not apply to copyright and some other intellectual property rights, electronic money, the contractual freedom to choose the law applicable to a contract, contractual obligations concerning consumer contracts, formal validity of contracts creating or transferring rights in real estate or the permissibility of unsolicited commercial communications by electronic mail.[217] Thus, in respect of electronic contracting, the Directive appears to preserve ordinary competence rules (as discussed above) only in two areas: choice-of-law clauses and consumer contracts. Having said that, Art 1(4) states rather more broadly: 'This Directive does not establish additional rules on private international law nor does it deal with the jurisdiction of Courts.'[218] If the Directive does not intend – by virtue of its origin rule – to supplant any rules on private international law, the origin rule cannot apply to any civil law at all, given that private international law lays down the allocation principles for private/civil law.[219] This would limit the origin rule's application to regulatory and criminal law.[220] Whether this was intended is doubtful in light of the specific exclusion of certain civil law competence rules (for example, contractual choice) and in light of Recital 23: '. . . provisions of the applicable law designated by rules of private international law must not restrict the freedom to provide information society services as established in this Directive.' This provision suggests that the origin rule may operate as a check on restrictive choice-of-law rules. However, until the ECJ rules on the matter, the scope of the origin rule and its relationship to private international law will remain foggy.[221]

Finally, even when the origin rule is applicable, Member States can derogate, under Art 3(4), where it is perceived to be necessary for reason of: public policy – in particular the prevention, investigation, detection, and prosecution of criminal offences; the protection of public health; public security; and the protection of consumers.[222] In light of the complexity of the above, it might have been more desirable to define the ambit of the application of the origin rule with specificity, such as by referring to particular rules or legal fields. However, the virtue of the adopted approach is that it leaves the door open for future developments in substantive law at both national and EU levels.

Formalities and Signatures
Requirement of Writing and Durability
Although there are few contracts that, under English law, must be in writing in order to be binding,[223] a written contract is desirable, and thus frequently adopted, because it provides parties with greater certainty as to their rights and obligations, and it gives them a reliable record of the transaction useful for evidentiary purposes. The law implicitly acknowledges these benefits by

---

216 Article 1(5) of the Directive.
217 Ibid, Art 3(3) and Annex.
218 This statement is misleading in so far as rules governing the jurisdiction of the courts are part of private international law.
219 For a different interpretation, see Department of Trade and Industry (DTI), *A Guide for Business to the Electronic Commerce (EC Directive) Regulations 2002 (SI 2002/2013)*, London: HMSO, para 4.8.
220 There is some debate whether the Directive extends to criminal as opposed to regulatory law. Because criminal law is not specifically excluded and because, under Art 3(4), derogation in criminal matters may under certain circumstances be justified, it would appear that the origin rule is applicable to criminal law.
221 Mark Turner, Mary Traynor, and Herbert Smith, 'E-Commerce Directive: UK implementation – Electronic Commerce (EC Directive) Regulations 2002: Worth the wait?' (2002) 18(6) CLSR 396, section 8.
222 Other conditions for the justified derogation are that: the information society service against which it is directed prejudiced, or was highly likely to prejudice, the above objectives; the measure taken must be proportionate to the objective; the origin state failed to take the required measures after being asked to do so; and the Commission was informed of the Member State's intention to take such measures.
223 For example, contracts for the sale or transfer of law must be in writing, according to s 2 of the Law of Property (Miscellaneous Provisions) Act 1989, and guarantees under s 4 of the Statute of Frauds 1677.

frequently requiring, or entitling the parties to, a written record of the agreement.[224] There are also wide-reaching statutory requirements concerning instruments, documents, notices, and records – which were invariably assumed to be paper-based.[225] The shift from paper-based communications to electronic communications has raised two interrelated issues in respect of all of these requirements:

(1) Does an electronic record satisfy the legal requirements of writing – that is, is the law technologically neutral?

(2) What are the characteristics that an electronic record must have to be functionally equivalent to a paper-based record?

In relation to the first question, one of the earliest international attempts to facilitate electronic commerce by validating electronic records is the United Nations Commission on International Trade Law (UNCITRAL) Model Law on Electronic Commerce (1996), which provides in Art 5 that '[i]nformation shall not be denied legal effect, validity or enforceability solely on the ground that it is in the form of a data message'. This general axiom is then spelled out more explicitly with reference to the requirement of writing in Art 6:

1. Where the law requires information to be in writing, that requirement is met by a data message if the information contained therein is accessible so as to be usable for subsequent reference.

2. Paragraph 1 applies whether the requirement therein is in the form of an obligation or whether the law simply provides consequences for the information not being in writing.

Where the law requires the 'original' document, according to Art 8, data messages are valid as long as there is 'a reliable assurance as to the integrity of the information': has the information remained complete and unaltered? The standard of reliability varies depending on the purpose for which the information was generated, but may require encryption of the message (discussed below). The effect of these provisions for evidential purposes is governed by Art 9, according to which a data message cannot be denied admissibility solely because it is a data message, and the evidentiary weight attached to any such message varies depending on its reliability, such as how was it created, stored, communicated, or maintained.

Of a mandatory character in the UK[226] are the provisions of the **Electronic Commerce Directive** and, in particular, Art 9, which requires Member States to ensure the legal effectiveness and validity of electronic contracts, and to remove any obstacles to the use of such contracts. Such obstacles would be '[r]equirements that a contract (or any steps required to be taken under or in relation to a contract) be in writing, evidenced in writing, or signed . . .'.[227] Unlike the Model Law, the requirement is restricted to electronic contracts (with some exceptions, such as real estate transactions).

How then are these requirements implemented in UK law? On a very general, all-encompassing level, they are implemented via the definition of 'writing' in Sch 1 of the **Interpretation Act 1978**:

---

224 For example, Art 13 of Commercial Agents Directive 86/653/EEC, Art 6(3) of the Consumer Sales Directive 1999/44/EC, or Art 23 of the Jurisdiction Regulation.

225 Such as communications of individuals and companies with government departments, such as Company House.

226 A Model Law, unlike a Convention, creates no binding legal obligations. It is designed to provide useful guidance on the area of law covered. In incorporating a Model Law into national law, states may make any modifications that they like, and thus it is inherently more flexible, but less harmonising, than a Convention.

227 Law Commission, op cit, para 3.48.

'"Writing" includes typing, printing, lithography, photography and other modes of representing or reproducing words in a visible form, and expressions referring to writing are construed accordingly.' Although there was some early disagreement whether electronic writing that relies on a series of electronic impulses is in essence visible, the general consensus now is that if electronic writing is visible on a computer screen, it satisfies the above definition and, by implication, most legislative writing requirements.[228]

Nevertheless, to forestall any arguments, the **Electronic Communications Act 2000** was enacted. Section 8 of the Act allows for the 'appropriate Minister' to modify (via Orders) existing law 'in such manner as he may think fit for the purposes of authorising or facilitating the use of electronic communications or electronic storage' for a multitude of specified purposes (s 8(1) and (2)) – going far beyond the contractual context, in line with the Model Law. To do so, the Minister must be satisfied that the records based on electronic communications and storage will be no less satisfactory than previous records (s 8(3)) – in other words, the section does not support the wholesale conversion of traditional records into electronic records, but requires the comparability of the electronic communications with paper-based communications in the circumstances. Such comparability may be achieved by the conditions that the Minister can put on the form or use of the electronic communication or storage under s 8(4). In respect of the use of electronic communications in court proceedings, conditions may be imposed for determining and proving whether an electronic communication has taken place and, if so, when, by whom, and its content (s 8(4) (g) and (5)). Although s 8 potentially provides for the wide-ranging incorporation of electronic communications into existing law, in fact it requires further actions by the appropriate Ministers in the form of Orders, of which there have been few so far.[229] There has so far been no Order that implements Art 9 of the **Electronic Commerce Directive** (dealing with electronic contracts generally).[230] This may partly be explained by reference to the fact that writing requirements are 'very rare in English Law [and i]n those rare cases . . . the form requirements are . . . capable of being satisfied by email or website trading'.[231]

Finally, a number of recent EU instruments address either how the term 'writing' should be understood in the electronic era or, more generally, how information must be disseminated. For example, Art 23(2) of the **Jurisdiction Regulation** states that 'any communication by electronic means which provides a durable record of the agreement shall be the equivalent to "writing"'. Similarly, Art 5(1) of the **Distance Selling Directive** stipulates that '[t]he consumer must receive written confirmation or confirmation in another durable medium available and accessible to him of the [specified] information . . .'.[232] A term that reappears in these definitions is 'durable'. While it is not always defined, it is defined in Art 4(25) of the **Payment Services Directive**:[233]

> 'durable medium' means any instrument which enables the payment service user to store information addressed personally to him in a way accessible for future reference for a period of time adequate to the purposes of the information and which allows the unchanged reproduction of the information stored.

---

228 Ibid, para 3.8. For a general early discussion on the writing requirement, see also DTI, *Building Confidence in Electronic Commerce: A Consultation Document*, URN 99/642, 1999, London: HMSO; Chris Reed, *Digital Information Law: Electronic Documents and Requirements of Form*, 1996, London: Centre for Commercial Law Studies, Queen Mary and Westfield College, University of London.

229 An early example was the Companies Act 1985 (Electronic Communications) Order 2000, SI 2000/3373.

230 The Electronic Communication (EC Directive) Regulations 2002, SI 2002/2013, which implements much of the Electronic Commerce Directive 2000/31/EC, do not cover Art 9.

231 Law Commission, op cit, para 3.48.

232 See also Art 6(3) of the Consumer Sales Directive 1999/44/EC; Art 10(3) of the Electronic Commerce Directive 2000/31/EC; Art 2(3) of the Financial Collateral Arrangements Directive 2007/64/EC.

233 Directive 2007/64/EC; same definition adopted in Art 2(f) of the Distance Marketing Financial Services Directive 2002/65/EC and Art 2(12) of the Insurance Mediation Directive 2002/92/EC.

Recital 24 of the same Directive provides examples of what such durable medium may be: '... printouts by account printers, floppy disks, CD-ROMs, DVDs and hard drives of personal computers on which electronic mail can be stored, and internet sites, as long as such sites are accessible for future reference.' From this, it seems clear that 'durable' is not a term of art that requires encryption to guarantee absolutely the inalterability of the information in question – in tune with the facilitative, rather than restrictive, objective of the Directive. Yet, on the other hand, the term 'durable' itself, as well as the reference to 'future reference', suggest a certain reliability of the record over time – a notion confirmed by the requirement of the 'unchanged reproduction of the information stored'. Thus terms and conditions of online content providers would prima facie not be durable, because they can easily be changed by the provider – unless users are given access to relevant historic versions, or are specifically encouraged to print and/or retain an electronic copy of these online sources, or are sent a copy of them by email.[234] This interpretation would also be in line with Art 10(3) of the **Electronic Commerce Directive**, which simply provides that '[c]ontract terms and general conditions provided to the recipient must be made available in a way that allows him to store and reproduce them'.[235]

Signatures[236]

Although signatures (like writing) are not a legal requirement for the vast majority of commercial transactions,[237] they are nevertheless commonplace, because they unequivocally indicate (or are in law taken to do so) that the signer adopts or approves the content of the document, i.e. its acceptability or its veracity. The purpose of a signature is broadly threefold:

(1) *Identification and authentication of the signatory* A signature identifies a person and confirms that he or she is who he or she claims to be. So a signature establishes a person's association and personal involvement with the document at a particular time and place with certainty – that is, it provides certainty as to the personal involvement of a person in the act of signing the document.

(2) *Acceptance of the content as it is by the signatory* A signature confirms that the signer accepts, adopts, or endorses the document as it stands – that is, it is an accurate reflection of what is/was agreed.

Integrity/authenticity of the document/data It is in this way that the signatory authenticates the data: '... the document is the "original" support of the information it contains, in the form it was recorded and without any alteration.'[238] This function relies upon the relative difficulty of altering a document without detection.

(3) *Legal intention of signatory* Finally, because signatures are known to be legally significant,[239] a signature shows the signer's intention to engage in a legally significant act: the signer does

---

234 See also OFT/DTI, *A Guide for Businesses on Distance Selling*, OFT698, 2006, London: HMSO, para 3.10.

235 Implemented in Electronic Commerce (EC Directive) Regulations 2002, reg 9(3).

236 On electronic signatures, see: UN Commission on International Trade Law (UNCITRAL), *Promoting Confidence in Electronic Commerce: Legal Issues on International Use of Electronic Authentication and Signature Methods*, 2009, Vienna: United Nations, available online at www. uncitral.org/pdf/english/texts/electcom/08-55698_Ebook.pdf; UNCITRAL, *UNCITRAL Model Law on Electronic Signatures with Guide to Enactment*, 2001, Vienna: United Nations, available online at www.uncitral.org/pdf/english/texts/electcom/ml-elecsig-e.pdf; Chris Reed, 'What is a signature?' 2000 (3) JILT, available online at www2.warwick.ac.uk/fac/soc/law/elj/jilt/2000_3/reed/; Law Commission, op cit; Attorney General of Australia, *Electronic Commerce: Building the Legal Framework – Report of the Electronic Commerce Expert Group to the Attorney-General*, 1998, Canberra: Government of Australia.

237 Exceptions, such as s 4 of the Statute of Frauds 1677, which makes guarantee unenforceable in the absence of writing and signature: see *Mehta v J Pereira Fernandes SA* [2006] EWHC 813 (Ch).

238 UNCITRAL, 2009, op cit, p 5.

239 Where a signed document is not intended to be legally binding (eg, a book signed by the author or a signed mediation agreement), the lack of the legal intention arises by virtue of the substance of the document or the transaction, rather than by virtue of the signature.

not sign unless he or she really means it. A signature thereby also encourages reflection before the act of signing.

These three aspects of a signature bolster the reliability and security of contracts, which makes them highly useful in the commercial world. As will be seen, these three functions of a signature, fulfilled to varying degree by different types of signature, also go towards defining them.

Electronic Signatures under Common Law

What constitutes a signature generally in law? They are defined neither in the statutes that require a signature, nor in the **Interpretation Act 1978**. Under common law, the paradigm signature would be a person writing by hand his or her full name (that is, a handwritten or manuscript signature). However, 'lesser' signatures have long been accepted, such as an 'X' or a person's initials, as well as non-personalised marks in the form of stamps, or printed or typed names.[240] Common law courts have taken a pragmatic approach to signatures by examining whether the particular mark fulfilled the function of the signature under the particular legislation or contractual provision in question. Thus the legal validity of a signature has not been set in stone, but has been made dependent on the circumstances of the case and the reason for its requirement. An 'X' or stamp would often be a valid signature as long as there was evidence that identified the signatory and showed that he or she intended for the writing or mark to be his or her signature. Broadly, a signature is 'any name or symbol used by a party with the intention of constituting it his signature'.[241]

In light of the functional definition of signatures at common law, various electronic ways of indicating assent seem to satisfy the traditional test of signing. The modern electronic equivalent of 'X' is the click on the 'I Agree', 'I Accept', or similar icon in clickwrap agreements (see above); a printed name at the end of an email or an instant message is no different from a printed or typed name at the end of paper document, and a scanned manuscript signature at the end of an electronic message is comparable to the traditional stamp.

This is borne out by the case law on the subject. In the employment case of *Hall v Cognos Ltd*,[242] it was held that a term in an employment contract was effectively varied – in accordance with a term requiring a variation to be in writing and signed by the parties – by an email exchange between Hall and his line manager, Keith Schroeder, and Sarah McGoun from personnel. When the latter two signed their emails 'Keith' and 'Sarah', respectively, the signature requirement under the contractual term was satisfied. By the same token, a personal guarantee provided by email in *Mehta v J Pereira Fernandes SA*[243] was not signed for the purpose of s 4 of the **Statute of Frauds 1677**, because the sender's name only appeared in the email address and not at the bottom of the text:

> . . . the inclusion of an e mail address in such circumstances is a clear example of the inclusion of a name which is incidental in the sense identified by Lord Westbury in the absence of evidence of a contrary intention. Its appearance divorced from the main body of the text of the message emphasises this to be so. Absent evidence to the contrary, in my view it is not possible to hold that the automatic insertion of an e mail address is, to use Cave J's language, '. . . *intended for a signature* . . .'. To conclude that the automatic insertion of an e mail address in the circum-

---

240 *Phillimore v Barry* (1818) 1 Camp 513 (initals); *Ex p Dryden* (1893) 14 NSWR 77, *Goodman v J Eban LD* [1954] 1 QB 550, and *British Estate Investment Society Ltd v Jackson* (HM Inspector of Taxes) [1956] TR 397 (stamping); *Brydges* (Town Clerk of Cheltenham) *v Dix* (1891) 7 TLR 215 (printing); *Newborne v Sensolid* (Great Britain) LD [1954] 1 QB 45, *Evans v Hoare* [1892] 1 QB 593, and *Leeman v Stocks* [1951] Ch 941 (typewriting).
241 *Alfred E Weber v Dante de Cecco* 1 NY Super 353, 358 (1948).
242 Hull Industrial Tribunal 1803325/97; discussed in Stephen Mason, 'Lawyers and electronic signatures' (2005) July/Aug Internet Newsletter for Lawyers, available online at www.venables.co.uk/n0507signatures.htm
243 [2006] EWHC 813 (Ch); see also *Firstpost Homes Ltd v Johnson* [1995] 1 WLR 1567.

stances I have described constituted a signature for the purposes of Section 4 would I think undermine or potentially undermine what I understand to be the Act's purpose . . .[244]

Similarly, it is questionable whether the automatic inclusion of a signature line in every email should be taken to mean that these emails are signed, rather they provide contact details for the addressee.[245] These examples highlight that although the functional approach to signatures allows for a range of marks and acts (for example, clicks) to amount to signatures, it is certainly always critical that the signatory is conscious of the mark's or act's symbolic legal significance – as a signature. In that sense, the legal intention function is a necessary attribute – a *sine qua non* – of any signature.[246] Such awareness would not normally be present in respect of browsewrap agreements, which purport to make the act of browsing the equivalence of a signature:

> By visiting the Site, you, the User, indicate that you understand these Terms and Conditions and intend them to be the legal equivalent of a signed, written contract and equally binding, and that you accept such Terms and Conditions and agree to be legally bound by them.[247]

Unless the user has actual, and not only constructive, knowledge of the symbolic legal effect of visiting the site, his or her conduct in form of visiting the site lacks the legal intentionality that, by definition, accompanies a signature. In any event, the argument to support the binding effect of the above term is circular: the term is only binding if it is incorporated into the contract and it is only incorporated if it is binding. On the other hand, where a surfer is left in no doubt that the act of entering a site is taken as an implicit acceptance of the terms, then that act would certainly have the legal intentionality required for a signature. For example, before accessing Beefeatergin.com, the user is presented with the following prominent notice:

> If you visit us at this Site, by clicking a flag on our home page to enter the Site, you are confirming to us that you understand and accept these Terms, and that you intend and agree that they will apply to you and your use of the Site in the same way as any signed, written contract.

In these circumstances, there is a stronger case for arguing that entering the site is equivalent to signing the terms and conditions – although it still stretches the ordinary meaning of signature beyond recognition. Certainly, in neither clickwrap nor browsewrap agreements is there any 'mark' or 'marking' to speak of, comparable to stamps, printed, typed, or manuscript signatures,[248] but the same would also apply to digital signatures (discussed below). For many statutory provisions, in which a signature goes hand in hand with the requirement of writing or visible equivalent, such as s 4 of the **Statute of Frauds 1677**, it is doubtful whether these signatures that are neither visible nor personal would be sufficient. And for all of those instances in which a signature is not a legal requirement, little is gained by arguing that the conduct in question equates with a signature rather than what the signature is designed to signify – that is, generally, notice or acceptance of the document.

---

244 Ibid, [29], emphasis added.

245 Alan L Tyree, 'Electronic signatures' (2008), available online at http://austlii.edu.au/~alan/electronic-signatures.html

246 See *Jenkins v Gaisford & Thring, In the Goods of Jenkins* (1863) 3 Sw & Tr 93, 164 ER 1208: 'Now whether the mark is made by pen or by some other instrument cannot make any difference . . . [it] was intended to stand for and represent the signature of the testator.' An exception to this rule (driven by pragmatic considerations) was the 'authenticated signature fiction', which allowed unsigned documents to be considered signed if the name appeared in the document prepared by the 'non-signer' and there was evidence that he or she considered it a complete and final document that becomes binding upon the signature of the other party: *Leeman v Stocks* [1951] 1 Ch 941; cf *Firstpost Homes Ltd v Johnson* [1995] 1 WLR 1567.

247 See www.ecfmg.org. Going even further, some sites state: 'You further agree that your use constitutes an electronic signature . . .' (Term 13, www.parkplaza.com/).

248 For references to a mark, see, eg, *Jenkins*, above, and *Re a Debtor (No 2021 of 1995)* [1996] 2 All ER 345.

The weakness of all of the above non-personalised signatures is their failure to authenticate along the lines of a hand-written signature, which provides assurances as to the identity of the signatory. Thus their authentication functionality is weak and so, where the alleged signatory's identity is disputed (for example, in cases of identity theft), extrinsic evidence would be required to prove it.[249] The equivalence of a handwritten signature that fulfils all three of the above functions of a signature would be satisfied by more sophisticated electronic signatures, such as digital signatures (discussed below), or the much more common forms of online signatures, such as pin numbers or passwords used for online or ATM banking, shopping, or utility or e-government transactions. Other less-prevalent personalised signatures that further minimise the risk of forgeries are biometric signatures based, for example, on fingerprints or retinal patterns, or biodynamic signatures that measure and analyse the physical activity of signing, the pressure applied, the speed, and the stroke order.

That these personalised electronic signatures are prima facie validated like handwritten signatures is implicit in the judgment of *Standard Bank London Ltd v Bank of Tokyo Ltd*[250] concerning a forerunner of today's sophisticated electronic signatures. In this case, Standard Bank received from the Bank of Tokyo three letters of credit issued by 'tested telexes' (which contain a secret code confirming the authenticity of letters of credit) with a total face value of US$19.8 million. When it later transpired that those telexes had been sent by a fraudster, it was held that Standard Bank was entitled to rely on the telexes, as it in fact had. The Bank of Tokyo was liable for negligent misrepresentation, because the fraud could only have occurred if the Bank was negligent. So, here, the law of negligence tempered the default legal position that a forged signature is a nullity and thus a risk placed on the recipient.[251] Negligence, particularly on the part of the signer, is likely to play a greater role in electronic signatures, such as pin numbers and passwords, because these can be more easily misappropriated than handwritten signatures and, once used by the fraudster, cannot easily be detected by the recipient.[252] Ultimately, contracting parties that use electronic signatures are free to allocate the risk of any fraudulent or unauthorised use amongst themselves, as they often do. So where, as in the case of digital signatures, the use of the electronic signature between two parties entails reliance on the assurances of a third party, this third party could contractually shift the risk of forgery to the signer and/or the recipient of the signature[253] – subject to the rules laid down in the **Electronic Signature Directive**.

Electronic Signatures under the Electronic Signatures Directive

The wide and flexible common law position is, in the context of electronic signatures, complemented by the **Electronic Signature Directive**,[254] which creates a dualist regime of 'electronic signatures', on the one hand, and 'advanced electronic signatures', on the other.[255] Although the Directive was designed to be technologically neutral, the two types of signature are not exclusively divided by their functionality, but also by the type of technology used. The result is that the definition of 'advanced electronic signatures' favours digital signatures, which are then accorded a special legal status not given to other functionally equivalent signatures, such as pin numbers and passwords. This

---

249 There are German cases: *Internet-Versteigerung* (AG Erfurt, 14 September 2001, 28 C 2354/01); *Auktion durch Trojaner* (LG Konstanz, 19 April 2002, 2 O 141/01); *Beweisfragen bei Vertragsschluss in der Internet-Auktion* (OLG Köln, 6 September 2002, 19 U 16/02); discussed in Smith, op cit, 825. Note that the authenticity of a signature is in the offline world rarely routinely checked; cheques and cheque guarantee cards provide one example.
250 [1995] CLC 496; [1996] 1 CTLR T–17, discussed in Stephen Mason, 'Electronic signatures explained' (2002) Jan/Feb Internet Newsletter for Lawyers, available online at www.venables.co.uk/n0201signatures.htm
251 *Brook v Hook* (1871) LR 6 Exch 89.
252 See, eg, pin number case *Job v Halifax plc* (unreported, 4 June 2009), applying s 24 of the Bill of Exchange Act 1882; cf Payment Services Regulations 2009, SI 2009/209, reg 60, implementing Art 59 of the Payment Services Directive 2007/64/EC.
253 For an analogy with cheque guarantee cards, see *First Sport Ltd v Barclays Bank plc* [1993] 3 All ER 789.
254 Directive 1999/93/EC.
255 A third type is the qualified electronic signature in Art 5 of the Directive.

is unfortunate, because it creates legal differences where none should be. Also, because digital signatures have not been taken up by the market as envisaged by the European regulator, the 'advanced electronic signature' provisions have seen little use. Both factors underscore the importance of technologically neutral regulation – especially when dealing with rapidly evolving technology.

Indeed, it was the technological neutrality of the traditional English common law position that prompted many to argue that the **Electronic Signature Directive** required no implementation in the UK.[256] The Directive seeks to ensure the equality between electronic and traditional signatures, and, as shown above, English common law caters for this already. Still, implementing action was taken in the form of s 7 of the **Electronic Communications Act 2000** and the **Electronic Signatures Regulations 2002**,[257] but with doubtful success in terms of creating greater clarity. As neither piece of legislation is intended to be restrictive, the damage that they can do seem limited to being superfluous. Having said that, any facilitating/enabling provision creates the danger of being restrictive both through laying down certain conditions of application and through exclusion by omission.

Electronic Signatures
The Directive defines 'electronic signatures' as 'data in electronic form which are attached to or logically associated with other electronic data and which serve as a method of authentication' (Art 2(1)). The effect of a signature being an electronic signature is that it must not be 'denied legal effectiveness and admissibility as evidence in legal proceedings solely on the grounds that it is in electronic form' or on the ground that it does not have some of the reliability factors required of an advanced electronic signature, such as being created by a secure signature-creation device (Art 5(2)). Yet, even if admissible, the Directive does not further stipulate the evidential weight to be attached to the signature and the data, or how 'legal effectiveness' should be understood. This is thus a matter for the court's discretion.

The main uncertainty of Art 2(1) is the ambit of the definition of 'electronic signature', particularly considering the requirement that it must have been used as a 'method of authentication'. Although the Directive does not define 'method of authentication', Recitals 4 and 8 suggest that the authentication must be related to the data rather than the signatory – that is, the signature must be used to confirm the genuineness and accuracy of the data (see above). The European Commission, on the other hand, states that an electronic signature could be 'as simple as signing an e-mail message with a person's name or using a PIN-code. To be a signature the authentication must relate to data and not be used as a method or technology *only* for entity authentication'.[258] This statement is noteworthy for two reasons: first, the Commission considers that, to be an 'electronic signature', the signature must be used both for data *and* signatory authentication; and second, signing an email falls within the Directive's definition given the relative unreliability of emails. Consider a typical phishing email, in which a fraudster masquerades as a well-known bank or other business: in this instance, the signed email message does not at all guarantee that either the message or the signer is what it purports to be. Even if this is not applicable to all, or even most, emails, one must conclude that email by itself is weak in terms of authenticating the signatory or the data. If the Commission's view is correct, then, for the purposes of the Directive, any purported signature is an 'electronic signature' no matter how weak its authentication functionality. Perhaps stating that the purported signature 'serves as a method of authentication' simply requires that the signature/data must have

---

256 For example, Smith, op cit, 833.
257 SI 2002/318.
258 European Commission, *Report on the Operation of Directive 1999/93/EC on a Community Framework for Electronic Signatures*, COM(2006)120final, 2006, Brussels: European Commission, para 2.3.2 (emphasis added).

been intended to be a signature? If that is the case, Art 2(1) creates an all-inclusive signature definition, possibly even including clicks and other non-personalised electronic signatures.

The definitional uncertainties in Art 2(1) are not alleviated by s 7 of the **Electronic Communications Act 2000**, which seeks to implement it in the UK. According to s 7(2), an electronic signature is as much of anything in electronic form as:

(a) is incorporated into or otherwise logically associated with any electronic communication or electronic data; and

(b) *purports* to be so incorporated or associated *for the purpose of* being used in establishing the *authenticity of the communication or data*, the *integrity of the communication or data*, or both. [Emphasis added]

In relation to s 7(2)(b), 'authenticity' is then defined in terms of establishing the source of the communication – which is, the signer – and in terms of establishing his or her legal intention (s 15(2)). In other words, under s 7, a signature/data is an electronic signature if it was intended to be a signature and purports to establish the authenticity of the signatory or the integrity of the data. Comparable to the Directive, s 7 does not require the signature to be successful in fulfilling these functions and neither does it specify the evidential weight that should be given to such signatures once admitted in evidence (s 7(1)). What is anomalous is that s 7, in conjunction with s 15(2), may validate as an 'electronic signature', a signature that was not intended to have legal effect, given that the phrase 'or both' in s 7(2)(b) may allow for a situation in which the 'authenticity' purpose (that is, here, inter alia, 'legal intention') is absent. This seems an unwise departure from the common law. Yet it hardly matters given the limited effect of falling within the 'electronic signature' definition.

Advanced Electronic Signature

As noted above, the treatment of 'advanced electronic signatures' in the Directive (as implemented in the UK by the **Electronic Signatures Regulations 2002**) favours digital signatures over other functionally equivalent signatures. Article 2(2) is, by itself, technologically neutral, because it requires 'advanced electronic signatures' to be:

(a) uniquely linked to the signatory;

(b) capable of identifying the signatory;

(c) created using means that the signatory can maintain under his sole control; *and*

(d) linked to the data to which it relates in such a manner that any subsequent change of the data is detectable.

While the first three points focus on the authentication function of signatures, the last one addresses the integrity function.[259] This functional definition is followed in Art 5(1) by a legal effect premised on more technology-specific requirements:

Member States shall ensure that advanced electronic signatures which are based on a *qualified certificate* and which are created by a *secure-signature-creation device*:

(a) satisfy the legal requirements of a signature in relation to data in electronic form in the same manner as a handwritten signature satisfies those requirements in relation to paper-based data; and

(b) are admissible as evidence in legal proceedings. [Emphasis added]

---

259 Note that the Directive explicitly excludes from its scope the 'legal intention function' discussed above.

In other words, these are the only signatures that Member States must treat like handwritten signatures, although there is nothing to prevent them from extending this treatment to other electronic signatures – as occurs, in fact, under English common law.

Concepts of 'qualified certificate' and 'secure-signature-creation device' are intimately linked to digital signature technology.

Briefly, a digital signature relies, quite unlike any ordinary signature, not upon any marking or writing as such, but upon a mathematical formula attached to a message. It uses asymmetrical encryption, also known as 'public key encryption', which requires a matching public and a private key, and an intermediary, known as 'trusted third party' (TTP), which provides assurances as to the identity of the signatory.[260] If Anna were to want to sign digitally an electronic message to Brian, she would send him the message with the digital signature either attached to it or sent separately. To create the digital signature, Anna would use the private key to encode the message (that is, to transform it into a seemingly unintelligible form), which would be decoded by Brian using a public key. While the private key is like a pin number or password that Anna keeps secret, the matching public key is more widely known, but cannot be used to work out the private key (thus asymmetrical encryption). The TTP, also known as the 'certification services provider' (CSP), issues certificates that state the public key and the certificate subscriber – that is, the signatory. Thus these certificates link a public key with a particular signatory and thereby verify the signature. Brian, by using the public key, would be reassured that the contract was signed by the person mentioned on the certificate – hopefully, Anna (that is, the authentication function). In addition, there is also what is known as the 'hash function', which allows Brian to be certain that the message he received is exactly the same message as that which Anna sent (the integrity function). The hash function is a mathematical process that creates a 'hash value' unique to the message (also referred to as a 'fingerprint' of the message, or the 'message digest'); thus any alteration of the message would yield a different hash value. In fact, Anna does not attach her digital signature to the message itself, but rather to the hash value of her message. Brian can verify the hash value by going through the same process as Anna – that is, by using the same hash function on the original message.

From the above description, it becomes clear that digital signatures are a functional match for handwritten signatures – in fact, in some ways, they outperform them. A digital signature has verification of the authenticity of the signatory built into it – unlike a handwritten signature, which, by itself, without a signature for comparison, cannot guarantee its authenticity. However, what is critical in ensuring the reliability of digital signatures is that the TTP is indeed trustworthy – given that the recipient is entirely dependent on the accuracy of the certificates. This imperative is reflected in two ways in the **Electronic Signatures Directive**: first, the Directive lays down detailed requirements with which the CSP, the certificate itself and the secure-signature-creation device must comply;[261] second, the Directive imposes on CSPs civil liability for damages caused by inaccurate certificates to anyone who reasonably relied on them, unless the CSP can prove that it was not negligent (Art 6(1)) However, it also allows CSPs to limit their liability by putting restrictions on the use of digital signatures and on the value of the transactions (Art 6(3) and (4)).

Despite both the technical and regulatory advantages, digital signatures have enjoyed little popularity and this is not likely to change in the near future. The reasons are numerous, but include the complexity of encryption technology and the lack of interoperability standards at national and cross-border levels, the lack of interest by service providers, such as banks, to allow their customers to use their authentication device, such as passwords, and the complexity and cost of archiving electronically signed documents for periods as long as thirty years.[262]

---

260 For an extensive and clear discussion, see UNCITRAL, 2009, op cit. and see also discussion in Chapter 6.
261 Annexes I, II, and III of the Directive.
262 European Commission, op cit, para 3.3.2.

Chapter 8

Domain Names

Chapter Contents

Introduction

A domain name can be likened to an address on the global computer network, which both identifies and gives other information about a specific internet site. A web domain name permits web users to use unique alphanumeric website addresses rather than to have to remember numeric IP addresses.[1] For example:

bris.ac.uk	Registered domain name used by the University of Bristol
http://www.bris.ac.uk	Uniform resource locator (URL) that refers to the front page of the University of Bristol website
137.222.10.86	Internet protocol (IP) address of http://www.bris.ac.uk

The domain name system is overseen by a non-profit corporation, the Internet Corporation for Assigned Names and Numbers (ICANN), which was created in October 1998 and is based in California.[2] ICANN has, amongst other roles, policy responsibility for coordinating the assignment of internet domain names.[3] The technical operation of the domain name system is performed by the Internet Assigned Numbers Authority (IANA), which 'allocates and maintains the unique codes and numbering systems that are used in the technical standards ("protocols") that drive the Internet'.[4]

The term 'top-level domain' (TLD), or 'first-level domain', refers to the final segment of the domain name. In the example given above, the TLD is '.uk'. IANA recognises five different types of TLD, as follows.[5]

Infrastructure top-level domains	.arpa
Country-code top-level domains (ccTLD)	For example, .br (Brazil); .ca (Canada); .fr (France); .eu (European Union)
Sponsored top-level domains (sTLD)	.aero; .asia; .cat; .coop; .edu; .gov; .int; .jobs; .mil; .mobi; .museum; .tel; .travel
Generic top-level domains (gTLD)	.com; .info; .net; .org
Generic restricted top-level domains	.biz; .name; .pro

ICANN delegates control over each TLD to a domain name registry. It retains direct governance control over the generic top-level domains (gTLDs), and can thus define the terms and conditions to be applied by each gTLD registry. For sTLDs, a sponsor representing the narrower community that is most affected by the TLD is responsible for appointing the domain name registry, and for establishing the terms and conditions to be applied, in conjunction with ICANN. For ccTLDs, the domain name registry is usually appointed or controlled by the government of the state or territory, and ICANN does not control the terms and conditions applied by ccTLDs.

Within each TLD, the domain name registries manage the registration of domain names, administer the policies of domain name allocation, and control the technical operations. Some

---

1 See further Graham JH Smith, *Internet Law and Regulation*, 4th edn, 2007, London: Sweet & Maxwell, pp 148–58.
2 Internet Corporation for Assigned Names and Numbers (ICANN), online at www.icann.org/
3 For a more wide-ranging analysis of the role of ICANN than is possible here, see, eg, Milton L Mueller, *Ruling the Root: Internet Governance and the Taming of Cyberspace*, 2002, Cambridge, MA: MIT Press; David Lindsay, *International Domain Name Law*, 2007, Oxford: Hart Publishing.
4 Internet Assigned Numbers Authority (IANA), online at www.iana.org/about/
5 IANA, 'Root Zone Database', available online at www.iana.org/domains/root/db/

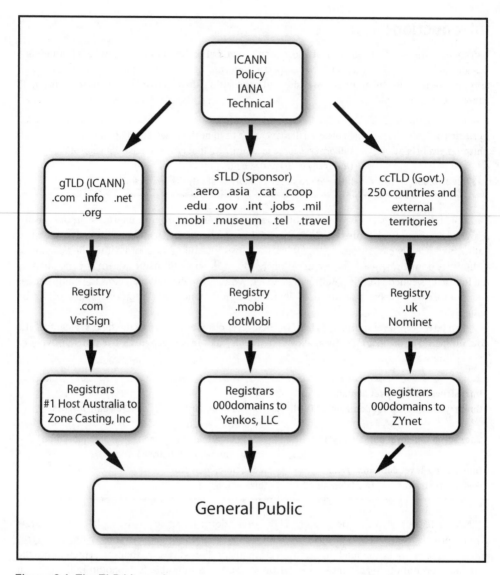

Figure 8.1 The TLD hierarchy

domain name registries are government departments; others are cooperatives of internet service providers or not-for profit companies. Each registry may sell domain names directly or via other organisations, or registrars. A domain name registrar is a company accredited by ICANN, and/or by a national ccTLD authority or sTLD sponsor, to register internet domain names. Individuals cannot obtain domain names directly from ICANN, but must obtain them either through a registry, or a registrar, as applicable within the TLD in which the domain name is sought.

Under UK law, it appears still unresolved whether domain names are actually owned by the registrant. Nominet's 'Terms and Conditions of Domain Name Registration' state that:

10 A domain name is not an item of property and has no 'owner'. It is an entry on our register database reflected by our nameservers which we provide as part of this contract . . .[6]

This suggests that a domain name should be considered a licence from the registrar to use the domain name during the period of registration, and that title for the domain name thus ultimately belongs to the registrar. Bettinger suggests that this has little practical implication for the commercial use of domain names, because, regardless of whether they are treated as items of property or simply as contractual rights, domain names can still be bought, sold, or licensed.[7]

A second-level domain name (SLD) then gives further information, which may be the name of the site in the case of the generic TLD (for example, 'routledge.com') or further information about the type of site in the case of country TLDs. In the ccTLD '.uk', there is a restricted list of SLDs available,[8] although a procedure exists for proposing additional SLDs.[9]

ac.uk	Higher and further education and research institutions
co.uk	Commercial entities and purposes
gov.uk	National, regional, and local government bodies and agencies
ltd.uk	Private limited companies
me.uk	Personal names
mod.uk/mil.uk	Military and related purposes
net.uk	ISPs' infrastructure
nhs.uk	National Health Service
nic.uk	Network use only
org.uk	Not-for-profit entities
plc.uk	Public limited companies
police.uk	Police forces
sch.uk	Schools

In cases in which the SLD is restricted, or provides another layer of general information, a further domain level will then identify the actual site (for example, 'bris.ac.uk'). Each domain name can identify only one site and is unique to that site, so that two companies who might trade under the same name quite successfully in the 'real world' cannot have exactly the same domain name in cyberspace.[10] There are many organisations that, for example, use the initials 'FSA'. Only one of these can have the domain name 'fsa.com', although there are, of course, other possible registrations and 'fsa.gov.uk', 'fsa.co.uk', 'fsa.org', and 'fsa.org.uk' are all owned by different concerns.[11] Conversely, it is common for the same company to register in more than one TLD: for example, a small fraction of Amazon.com Inc's (or its subsidiaries') registrations include the following.[12]

---

6 Nominet, 'Terms and conditions of domain name registration', available online at www.nominet.org.uk/registrants/aboutdomainnames/legal/terms/

7 Torsten Bettinger (ed), *Domain Name Law and Practice*, 2005, Oxford: Oxford University Press, p 871.

8 Nominet, 'Rules of registration and use of domain names', available online at www.nominet.org.uk/registrants/aboutdomainnames/rules/

9 Nominet, 'Procedure for new second level domains', available online at www.nominet.org.uk/policy/newslds/procedure/

10 The courts have provided agreed explanations of the operation of domain names in, eg, *Pitman Training Ltd v Nominet UK* [1997] FSR 797; *Panavision International LP v Toeppen* 141 F 3d 1316 (9th Cir 1998). See also descriptions in, eg, Bettinger, op cit; Lindsay, op cit.

11 See Findlay Steele Associates (www.fsa.co.uk) and further discussion below at p 289. Findlay Steel Associates succeeded in retaining this registration in an acrimonious dispute with the Financial Services Authority (www.fsa.gov.uk). Compare the situation in *WWF–World Wide Fund for Nature v World Wrestling Federation Entertainment Inc* [2002] FSR 33.

12 'Bank of America owns more than 630 active, registered trade marks in the United States and approximately 700 trade mark registrations in other jurisdictions. In addition, the Corporation owns more than 11,500 domain name registrations. However, only available online at http://www.bankofamerica.com provides access to Bank of America N.A.'s award-winning online banking services. Three other domains are authorized portals to other lines of business. All other domain names are defensively registered or were acquired through successful UDRP actions . . .': E Thomas Watson, Assistant General Counsel, Bank of America Corporation, Comment to ICANN on new gTLD Draft Applicant Handbook, 15 December 2008.

Main website	amazon.com
International subsidiaries	amazon.ca; amazon.cn; amazon.fr; amazon.de; amazon.co.jp; amazon.co.uk
Gateway/referring domain name	amazon.eu; amazon.gr
Redirect to Amazon main websites	amazon.info; amazon.biz; amazon.cd
Alternative spellings – redirect to Amazon main websites	amaon.com; amazom.com; ajmazon.com; akazon.com; akmazon.com; amaozon.com; amamzon.com; wwamazon.com; smszon.com; zamazon.com, amazong.com; ammazon.com
Other – redirect to Amazon main websites	amazonbooks.net; amazonbooks.org; amazonpic.com; amazonoutletstores.com; amazon-sales.com; amazon119.com
Registered, but not in use	amazon.us; amazon.tv; amazon.hk; amazon.pro; amazonfire.com; amazonisrael.com; amazon-order.com

Thus domain names have long posed a problem for trade mark holders.[13] They would like to reduce costs by only registering high-profile domain names containing their trade mark: for example, <their trade mark>.com, or <their trade mark>.co.uk. However, the nature of the internet means that unless they can control the use of their trade mark in domain names registered in all of the international registries, then a potential competitor or other third party may be able to register and use those names.

While it is possible to use trade mark law via traditional legal avenues to prevent abuses at the national level, this has proven difficult internationally. This has led to the development of alternative methods of applying trade mark-like rules to the registration and use of domain names, usually through contractual mechanisms built into the registry system. As this chapter will demonstrate, while it still remains possible in certain circumstances for a third party to register a domain name that contains another's trade mark or 'well-known trade name',[14] the ability both to register and to use such domain names is increasingly subject to restriction, either under national law or, more commonly, via registry practices and procedures.

As trading and/or advertising on the web has become an integral part of many commercial enterprises' business strategies, some domain names have the potential to be highly valuable, either because they contain trade marks or brand names; or because they contain a generic term that consumers are likely to seek out, either by direct search or via search engines.[15] Large corporations, such as Proctor and Gamble, will often register not only product names as domain names, but also the things for which its products may be used. It is thus the proud owner of 'diarrhea.com', which, when consumers type it into a browser, redirects them to 'pepto-bismol.com' – Proctor & Gamble's medicine for digestive complaints.

However, while some generic terms have caused major legal battles,[16] the primary triggers for dispute are domain names containing, or similar to, trade marks, brand names, and famous names.

13 See, eg, Dawn Osborne, 'Domain names, registration and dispute resolution and recent UK cases' (1997) EIPR 644.
14 At the time of writing, the domain names 'amazon.net' and 'amazon.org' are not held by Amazon.com Inc (or its subsidiaries).
15 'Sex.com broke the eight-figure barrier in 2005 by nabbing $12 million, . . . Porn.com came in next, at $9.5 million last month, followed by Business.com ($7.5 million in 1999), Diamond.com ($7.5 million in 2006) and Beer.com (a reported $7 million in 1999)': Lisa LaMotta, 'The most expensive web addresses' (2007) Forbes.com, 29 June, available online at www.forbes.com/2007/06/28/google-news-corp-ent-tech-cx_ll_0629webaddresses.html
16 Legal actions relating to the disputed ownership of the domain name 'sex.com' ran for over five years: see Kieren McCarthy, Sex.Com: One Domain, Two Men, Twelve Years and the Brutal Battle for the Jewel in the Internet's Crown, 2007, London: Quercus.

Whereas a large number of trade marks containing the same name can comfortably coexist because they are associated with different products, belong to business in different jurisdictions, etc, the distinctive nature of the domain name in providing global exclusivity has been much sought after, with '.com' addresses in particular demand.[17] This has led to disputes between those who wish to claim sole entitlement to use a particular domain name, and also to the emergence of 'cybersquatting', whereby domain names incorporating famous names are registered by third parties solely to seek to extract payments from the 'rightful owners'.[18]

The introduction of new TLDs (for example, '.eu' in 2005, '.mobi' in 2006, '.asia' in 2007) has often led to surges in disputes, as would-be domain name speculators attempt to obtain potentially high-value domain names.[19] As a result, new TLD registries have adopted a number of measures designed to limit disputes, often by giving trade mark holders and others the ability to reserve domain names in new TLDs before domain name registration is made more generally available (discussed further below).

As disputes over the registration and use of domain names proliferated, litigants and potential litigants initially looked to the law for a suitable remedy. Many disputes in the commercial sector arose from the use of trade marks and trade names, and so answers were sought in the trade mark law, unfair competition, and passing off. Those cases that reached the courts can basically be divided into two types: those in which both parties have some legitimate interest in the name; and the more common 'cybersquatting' cases. The latter category includes those cases in which the defendant merely shelved the acquired domain names in order to block use by the 'rightful owner' and extract a high price for the transfer, and those in which the defendants used the name to maximise visits to their own sites, or to cause damage to the plaintiff as a result of the confusion created.[20]

In recent years, the alternative dispute resolution (ADR) procedures introduced by the registries, such as the Uniform Domain Name Dispute Resolution Policy (UDRP) that all registrars of the generic top level domains must follow, have diverted most domain name disputes concerning trade marks away from national courts, thus reducing the opportunities for significant development of legal precedents in this area, and limiting the perceived need for legislative intervention.

Trade Marks and Domain Names

It is understandable that companies that own trade marks in different jurisdictions will want to register the same name as a domain name. However, it has to be borne in mind that, when a word is used as a domain name, it is not performing the same function as when it is used as a trade mark. At the most basic level, a domain name is an address used to facilitate access to an internet site, whereas a trade mark is a jurisdictionally based intellectual property right that enables consumers to distinguish between different products and services. They should not, therefore, be regarded as serving the same purpose.

Nevertheless, given that many companies are closely associated with either their trade marks or products, it is not surprising that there is some blurring of function. As Froomkin notes, 'a system that relies on geographic distance and sectoral differentiation maps badly to a borderless

---

17 In 1998, there were 100,000 trade marks in the world that used the word 'Prince', but only one of these could have the domain name 'prince.com': TW Krieger, 'Internet domain names and trade marks: Strategies for protecting brand names in cyberspace' (1998) 32(1) Suffolk UL Rev 47.

18 For further discussion of how such disputes arise, see, eg, Bettinger, op cit; Lindsay, op cit.

19 See, eg, CAC-4014/2007 *Game Group Plc v First Internet Technology Ltd* [2007] ETMR 78 (concerning game.eu), in which the respondent had registered 52 '.eu' domain names, including 'business.eu', 'computer.eu', 'hotels.eu', 'fashion.eu', 'finance.eu', and 'mortgage.eu'.

20 The issue of confusion has also been discussed in actions for trade mark infringement in relation to the unauthorised use of trade marks as metatags. For a consideration of the difference in the relevant factors suggesting confusion in metatag and domain name cases, see, eg, *Brookfield Communications Inc v West Coast Entertainment Corp* 174 F 3d 1036 (9th Cir 1999).

world in which every participant on the global network needs a unique address'.[21] Generally, trade mark law can still be applied where a word used as a domain name is also used as a trade mark. If, then, a trade mark registered in one jurisdiction is incorporated into a website in another jurisdiction, can this constitute 'use' in the course of trade, so that the website owner becomes liable for trade mark infringement?

In theory, a website could be taken as an indication of trading in a worldwide market, whereas, in fact, for most undertakings, the actual market now is very little different geographically from how it was before the internet. In *Euromarket Designs Inc v Peters*,[22] the claimant had stores in the USA called 'Crate and Barrel', had a UK-registered trade mark from 1988 for household goods, and also held a (then) Community mark. Peters had a store in Dublin with the same name. Peters had created a website initially at 'crateandbarrel-ie.com' and then at 'createandbarrel.ie'. The dispute centred on whether the name 'Crate and Barrel' was *used* in the UK, although in substance neither of the parties traded in the UK. Jacob J was of the opinion that neither the domain name, nor the content of the site, would encourage the average person in the UK to assume that the site was directed at them.[23] He further reasoned that there was little evidence that the defendants were using the words 'Crate & Barrel' in the course of trade in goods that was specifically targeted at the UK consumer.[24] Thus, the mere accessibility of a site in the UK was insufficient for that site to be regarded as making 'use' of a trade mark in the UK. The website was effectively only visible to UK web-surfers because they had taken the initiative of reaching out to access it. As Edwards notes: '. . . in this view of the internet, websites are seen as essentially passive, and web-surfers (or consumers) as the active agents.'[25]

In *1-800-Flowers Inc v Phonenames*, also heard at first instance by Jacob J,[26] the key issue was the question of whether the name '800 FLOWERS', which, on an alphanumeric phone, connected to a service providing flowers, was sufficiently distinctive, as opposed to merely descriptive. However, there was also discussion of whether there had been use in the UK and, in particular, whether inclusion of the name on a website hosted in the USA would constitute 'use' in the UK if accessed from this jurisdiction. Jacob J, prefiguring his later judgment in *Euromarket Designs Inc v Peters*, suggested that, while there might be areas of law in which publication on a website could be considered to be a publication aimed at the world and thus trigger legal consequences (for example, defamation law), UK trade mark law required regard to particular circumstantial criteria, such as the intention of the website owner and the likely effect on the consumer, and that in this case examination of these did not suggest compelling evidence of 'use' in the UK.[27] The Court of Appeal was equally unconvinced that mere accessibility of a website automatically equated to trade mark 'use' despite the applicant's attempts to link trade mark 'use' on the internet with the jurisdictional rules then developing in defamation law.[28]

Since the *Euromarket* and *1-800-Flowers Inc* cases, the UK courts have had little opportunity to expand further upon the issue of 'use' as it pertains to the internet. In *Bonnier Media Ltd v Greg Lloyd Smith and Kestrel Trading Corp*,[29] a Scottish case concerning an appeal against an interdict (that is, injunction) preventing the defender from setting up websites using domain names containing the

---

21 AM Froomkin, 'Semi-private international rule-making', in C Marsden (ed), *Regulating the Global Society*, 2000, London: Routledge.
22 [2001] FSR 20.
23 Ibid, [22].
24 Ibid, [23]–[24].
25 Lilian Edwards, 'The Scotsman, the Greek, the Mauritian company and the internet: Where on earth do things happen in cyberspace?' (2004) 8 Edin LR 99, 104. In the US litigation, *Euromarket Designs, Inc v Crate & Barrel Ltd* 96 F Supp 2d 824 (ND Ill, 2000), the District Court found that there was 'use in commerce' in Illinois for the purposes of the Lanham Act, that the Irish firm was operating an interactive website, and that, through both its internet and non-internet activities, had deliberately developed and maintained not only minimum, but significant, contacts with Illinois, thus grounding jurisdiction.
26 [2000] FSR 697.
27 [2000] IP&T 325, 332–3.
28 [2002] FSR 12, [136]–[138].
29 2003 SC 36, [18]–[19].

pursuer's trade marks, Lord Drummond Young held that although a business website established on the internet was clearly intended for commercial communication and the form of such communication might create liability in countries in which the website was accessible, it should not be deemed to automatically do so; rather a judge should look to both the content and the context of the website in order to determine whether a legally significant impact was occurring.

While sparse, the existing UK case law appears consistent with holdings elsewhere in the world. In the USA, while there is no single USA-wide test for jurisdiction in cases involving trade mark infringement on the internet, the test arising from *Zippo Manufacturing Co v Zippo Dot Com Inc*[30] has been highly influential, if not always enthusiastically adopted. In *Zippo*, the Federal District Court of Pennsylvania recognised three categories of internet presence: active, passive, and interactive.

- An *active* site is clearly doing business over the internet in a jurisdiction by having an interactive website and making contracts with residents in that jurisdiction, involving the deliberate and repeated transmission of computer files over the internet – and it will clearly subject the defendant to personal jurisdiction.
- A *passive* site will do 'little more than make information available to those who are interested in it', and is not sufficient to justify the exercise of personal jurisdiction, even if the site is accessed frequently by residents of the forum state, in the absence of further 'minimum contacts'.[31]
- An *interactive* site is one through which the product or service being sold cannot be directly transmitted via the internet, but the site itself allows for the exchange of information between the visitor to the site and the site's owner. Here, 'the exercise of jurisdiction is determined by examining the level of interactivity and commercial nature of the exchange of information that occurs on the website'.[32]

An alternative test with similar effect can be seen in *Pebble Beach Co v Caddy*,[33] in which the US Court of Appeals for the Ninth Circuit applied the '*Calder* effects' test.[34] This test requires the defendant to have '(1) committed an intentional act which was (2) expressly aimed at the forum state, and (3) caused harm, the brunt of which is suffered and which the defendant knows is likely to be suffered in the forum state'.[35] Caddy, a citizen and resident of the UK, ran a bed and breakfast (B&B) in southern England, overlooking a pebbly beach, and used a website (www.pebblebeach-uk.com) to advertise the premises. The Californian golf course and resort, Pebble Beach, which had used 'Pebble Beach' as its trade name for fifty years and owned the website www.pebblebeach.com alleged that Caddy's domain name infringed and diluted its trade mark rights. However, the Court concluded that:

> Caddy did not expressly aim his conduct at California or the United States and therefore is not subject to the personal jurisdiction of the district court. A passive website and domain name alone do not satisfy the *Calder* effects test, and there is no other action expressly aimed at California or the United States that would justify personal jurisdiction.[36]

---

30 952 F Supp 1119 (WD Pa, 1997). See also discussion in Chapter 2.
31 See, eg, *Bensusan Restaurant Corp v King*, 126 F 3d 25 (2d Cir 1997).
32 See, eg, *Maritz, Inc v Cybergold, Inc*, 947 F Supp 1328 (ED Mo, 1996).
33 *Pebble Beach Co v Caddy* 453 F 3d 1151 (9th Cir 2006).
34 Derived from the US Supreme Court judgment in *Calder v Jones* 104 S Ct 1482 (1984).
35 *Bancroft & Masters, Inc v Augusta Nat. Inc* 223 F 3d 1082, 1088 (9th Cir 2000).
36 *Pebble Beach Co v Caddy* 453 F 3d 1151, 1160 (9th Cir 2006).

Domain Name Disputes in the Courts
UK

Competing Trade Mark Rights

Pitman Training Ltd v Nominet UK Ltd[37] concerned a dispute between Pitman Training and Pitman Publishing over the use of the name 'Pitman'. Pitman Publishing had been using the name 'Pitman' in association with publishing since 1849. The business had originally been a training business, which was sold in 1985 to Pitman Training Ltd. Pitman Publishing became one of the divisions of Pearson Professional Ltd, a wholly owned subsidiary of Pearson plc. By virtue of an agreement made when the businesses were divided, both Pitman Training and Pitman Publishing were allowed to use the name 'Pitman' in connection with their respective businesses, as long as Pitman Training used it only in connection with training and correspondence courses, and agreed not to publish books or engage in any other trade under that name.

The dispute arose when Pitman Publishing applied to Nominet, which administers registrations for the '.uk' domain, for use of the domain name 'pitman.co.uk', which was allocated to it on the usual 'first come, first served' basis in February 1996. It was intended that a website would be designed and constructed, but would not be ready for launch until December 1996. The domain name was not used in the interim except for advertising in connection with promotions. In March 1996, Pitman Training was told that 'pitman.co.uk' was still unallocated; its ISP therefore procured the name and began to use the email address 'enquiries@pitman.co.uk'. As noted by the court, the question of how this dual registration could have occurred was never resolved.[38]

Pitman Publishing became aware of the situation in December 1996 and requested immediate restoration of the domain name from Nominet, which acceded. Pitman Training commenced proceedings. Scott VC was not impressed by the argument that the actions of Pitman Publishing could constitute passing off:

> This strikes me as a strange proposition given that Pitman Publishing has traded under the style Pitman for nearly 150 years . . . The evidence does not even begin to support the contention that the public associates the domain name pitman.co.uk with PTC . . . That there may be some confusion by some members of the public is undoubtedly so. But that confusion results from the use by both companies . . . of the style 'Pitman' for their respective trading purposes.[39]

So, although the court appeared to accept that inappropriate use of a domain name might sometimes constitute passing off, that was not the case in these particular circumstances; any confusion that might have arisen had its origin in another source – namely, the agreement voluntarily entered into by both parties concerned.

Another case in which, as in *Pitman*, the dispute had arisen because both parties felt that they had a legitimate entitlement to the use of the domain name in question was *Prince plc v Prince Sportswear Group Inc*.[40] When the US firm, Prince Sports Group Inc, the owner of the trade mark 'Prince' for sporting goods in the UK, tried to register the domain name 'prince.com', it found that it had already been registered by Prince plc, a UK computer services firm, which had also registered the domain name 'prince.co.uk'. The dispute led to proceedings being filed in both the USA and the UK. In the UK, Prince plc sought a ruling that the allegations of Prince Sports Groups that its

---

37 [1997] FSR 797.
38 Ibid, 804.
39 Ibid, 807.
40 [1998] FSR 21; Annette Orange, 'Developments in the domain name system: For better or for worse' (1999) (3) JILT, available online at www2.warwick.ac.uk/fac/soc/law/elj/jilt/1999_3/orange

registration of the domain name had resulted in trade mark dilution were unfounded and constituted groundless threats in relation to s 21 of the **Trademarks Act 1994**. The High Court found for Prince plc and issued an injunction preventing Prince Sports from continuing with the threats, but there was no discussion of whether the UK trade marks held by Prince Sports were being infringed. The parties subsequently agreed a settlement in which Prince plc retained the domain name, and so the legal arguments went no further.

In most cases in which there is entitlement on both sides to use the name, the significant factor will be first use. It was for this reason that the dispute between Findlay Steele Associates and the Financial Services Authority was decided in favour of Findlay Steele.[41] Findlay Steele had registered the domain name 'fsa.co.uk' in 1997. A website was not launched until 2002, but the domain was used for email communications. The Financial Services Authority, which has the domain name 'fsa.gov.uk', was created six months after Findlay Steele's registration of its domain name. It subsequently sought to obtain 'fsa.co.uk' on the grounds that the similarity between the domain names might lead to confusion for the consumer who was trying to contact the Financial Services Authority.

Thus, in the absence of evidence of bad faith, the first-use principle will be the usual determinant. This principle has been adhered to in cases in which the choice of domain name registered was more dubious. An example of this is found in the case of *French Connection v Sutton*.[42] In 1997, French Connection began the advertising campaign that established the use of 'fcuk' as representing the company. Around the same time, Sutton registered the domain name 'fcuk.com'. He alleged that he intended to use in connection with his IT consultancy business, First Consultants UK. His evidence was that he thought he would get more hits as a result of the use of this abbreviation. Subsequently, French Connection – which had registered the trade mark, but had overlooked registration of the domain name – sought to have the domain name transferred. Although the judge found the facts of the case from both parties 'unpalatable in the extreme', there was no evidence of bad faith. Sutton had not offered to sell fcuk.com to French Connection for vast sums of money and neither had he acquired any other domain names, which might have been indicative of cybersquatting (see below).

Breach of Registered Trade Mark Rights and Passing Off

In cybersquatting cases, the typical behaviour is to register numerous domain names corresponding with well-known names and marks, and then attempt to sell them to the rightful owner.[43] On occasions, the names are merely shelved rather than used. Cases in a number of jurisdictions demonstrate that this behaviour is not viewed sympathetically by the courts. The first cybersquatting case in the UK was that of *Harrods plc v UK Network Services Ltd*.[44] The domain name 'harrods.com' was registered, but not used, by unrelated third parties, with the intention of selling the name to Harrods at an inflated price. Harrods sued for trade mark infringement, passing off, and conspiracy. In agreeing to issue an injunction, the legal arguments were not aired extensively, but Lightman J accepted the principle that the law relating to trade marks and passing off could be applied to domain names. He referred, by analogy, to the case of *Glaxo plc v Glaxowellcome Ltd*,[45] in which a company called 'Glaxowellcome' was registered in anticipation of the merger of Glaxo and Wellcome, and a sum of £100,000 was demanded for transfer of the name. Even though the company had not traded, the court in that case was not prepared to tolerate a price being demanded for a name in which another party had goodwill. In both cases, the court appeared to be heavily influenced by the perceived dishonest intentions of the defendants. In the *Harrods* case itself, the defendant had accumulated a range of domain names corresponding to famous

41 Adjudicated by Nominet under the Uniform Dispute Resolution Policy (UDRP).
42 (Ch D) December 1999, unreported; also *MBNA America Bank v Freeman*(Ch D) July 2000, unreported.
43 See further Abida Chaudri, 'Internet domain names and the interaction with intellectual property' (2008) 24(4) CLSR 360.
44 [1997] 4 EIPR D-106, discussed in, eg, J Morton, 'opinion.com' (1997) 19(9) EIPR 496; Osborne, op cit.
45 [1996] FSR 388 (Ch D); see also *Direct Line Group Ltd v Direct Line Estate Agency Ltd* [1997] FSR 374 (Ch D).

names. Policy issues clearly play a part in these cases, since 'most would agree that some remedy should exist against a domain name pirate seeking to extract payment from the "rightful owner" in return for a domain name which the pirate possesses'.[46]

The issues were aired more extensively in the *One in a Million* case, which remains the leading case in the UK. One in a Million had registered domain names associated with a number of famous enterprises, including Marks & Spencer, Ladbrokes, Sainsbury, Virgin Enterprises, and British Telecommunications, for the apparent purpose of extracting a high price for transferring them. The domain names were not placed in use as active websites, but some were offered to the trade mark holders for significant sums of money. Actions were brought on behalf of all of the companies concerned, on the basis that the registration of the domain names was the equivalent of the creation of instruments of deception, and constituted actual or threatened passing off and trade mark infringement under s 10(3) of the **Trademarks Act 1994 (TMA 1994)**. In the High Court, Sumption J was faced with several important issues:

- the defendants claimed that trade mark infringement under **TMA 1994**, s 10(3), required use of the trade mark 'in the course of trade' and a likelihood of confusion on the part of the public, and that neither element was present;
- there was the question of whether mere creation of an 'instrument of deception' – that is, the registration of a trade mark – could constitute passing off, in the absence of a deceptive use, or the intent to supply it to someone else for deceptive use.

On the issue of trade mark infringement, the judge held that the use that the defendants were making of the trade marks in question – that is, of selling domain names containing the trade marks to the trade mark owner for a higher price than the cost of registration – was a use in the course of trade;[47] they did not have to be using the trade marks *qua* trade marks.[48] Regarding 'likelihood of confusion', he did not propose to decide whether **TMA 1994**, s 10(3), required a likelihood of confusion, but that if it was required, then the facts of the case – not least the defendants' own behaviour in registering the names – demonstrated its existence.

On the issue of passing off, the judge noted that the tort of passing off consisted of a misrepresentation to the public, intentional or otherwise, which would be likely to lead the public to assume that goods and services so denoted represented, or were, those of the plaintiff. The tort could also be committed by a party who provided, or authorised the provision of, an 'instrument of deception' to others. However, simply creating an 'instrument of deception' – for example, registering a domain name containing a third party's trade mark – did not involve deception, nor did it by itself constitute placing such an instrument in the hands of others, thus it could not be passing off.[49]

In this case, however, the judge held that it was clear that any party, other than the plaintiffs themselves, could only have one purpose for registering the domain names containing the plaintiff's trade mark – that being to pass off their website and/or products as the plaintiff's.[50] This fact, taken in conjunction with the defendants' previous history of registering domain names similar to the names and marks of third parties with the intention of deception, meant that while there was no evidence as such that there had been any trading, or even any other activity via these domain names, the potential for passing off, rather than a demonstration of genuine threat, was sufficient to allow an injunction to be granted.[51] As in the *Harrods* case, there was clearly little judicial sympathy for the business practices adopted by the would-be cybersquatters.

---

46 R Meyer-Rochow, 'The application of passing off as a remedy against domain name piracy' (1998) EIPR 405.
47 *Marks & Spencer plc v One in a Million Ltd* [1998] FSR 265, 272.
48 Referring to *British Sugar Plc v James Robertson & Sons Ltd* [1996] RPC 281, 290–2.
49 Ibid, 270–1.
50 Ibid.
51 Ibid, 273.

In the Court of Appeal,[52] One in a Million sought to appeal the earlier decision and overturn the negative injunctions restraining it from engaging in passing off and infringement, and the mandatory injunctions requiring them to assign the disputed domain names to the plaintiffs. The Court, however, gave the company relatively short shrift, approving the reasoning of the first-instance judge with regard to **TMA 1994**, s 10(3), with little additional explanation. As regards the issue of passing off, Aldous LJ first reviewed the history of the action for passing off, noting the five familiar characteristics itemised by Lord Diplock in *Erven Warnink BV v J Townend and Sons (Hull) Ltd*.[53]

He then analysed the position with regard to distinctive names, such as 'Marks and Spencer' and non-distinctive names such as 'Virgin'. In the case of the former, he held that Marks and Spencer was clearly distinctive of Marks & Spencer plc. Thus, where a third party registered a domain name including the name 'Marks & Spencer', there was a clear misrepresentation that the third party was affiliated in some way with Marks & Spencer plc, which amounted to passing off. Neither One in a Million, nor any party to which it sold domain names comprising the name 'Marks & Spencer', could use those domain names without engaging in passing off, and therefore the domain names were fairly characterised as 'instruments of deception'. Thus an injunction preventing their use by One in a Million or their transfer to other third parties was justified.[54]

With regard to the non-distinctive names, Aldous LJ held that registering a domain name consisting of a well-known 'household name' that was not distinctive would not inevitably lead to passing off, and thus the domain name would not necessarily be an instrument of fraud. In the latter case, it would be up to the court to consider the circumstances surrounding registration of the domain name, including the intentions of the person registering the name, to determine whether the purpose of registration was to enable passing off; if it were so, then the domain name would become an instrument of fraud. If the circumstances led the court to believe that the domain name was intended to be used for passing off and was likely to be used fraudulently, then an injunction could legitimately be granted.[55]

As can be seen in *Tesco Stores Ltd v Elogicom Ltd*,[56] the *One in a Million* decision has been followed in a line of cases – primarily applications for summary judgment or interim injunction. In the *Tesco* case, the defendant registered 24 domain names, all of which included the word 'tesco' – for example, 'tesco2u.co.uk', 'tesco2u.com', 'tesco2you.co.uk' – for use in an internet affiliate program. Tesco had entered into a contractual arrangement with a firm called TradeDoubler through which other website providers could become Tesco affiliates. Affiliates placed a link on their websites that, when clicked, took them to Tesco's website, and Tesco paid commission to the affiliate via TradeDoubler based on resulting sales. The defendant registered two general websites, 'Avon4me. co.uk' and 'Avonlady.co.uk', as affiliate sites with TradeDoubler after approval by a Tesco employee. However, TradeDoubler allowed the affiliates to group other domain names under the general websites, which also directed traffic to Tesco's website. These domain names were not visible to

---

52 [1999] 1 WLR 903.
53 [1979] 2 All ER 927, 932. (1) There must be a misrepresentation. (2) The misrepresentation must have been made by a trader in course of trade. (3) The misrepresentation must have been made to the trader's prospective customers or to ultimate consumers of goods or services supplied by him or her. (4) The misrepresentation must be calculated to injure the business or goodwill of another trader ('calculated to injure' means, in this sense, that injury is a reasonably foreseeable consequence). (5) The misrepresentation must cause actual damage to a business or goodwill of the trader by whom the action is brought (or in the case of a *quia timet* action, it must be probable that the misrepresentation will cause damage to a business or goodwill of the trader by whom the action is brought).
54 [1999] 1 WLR 903, 924–5.
55 Ibid.
56 [2007] FSR 4; see also *Britannia Building Society v Prangley & ors* (Ch D) June 2000, unreported; *Metalrax Group Plc v Vanci* [2002] EWHC 167 (Ch D); *Easyjet Airline Co and ors v Tim Dainty* [2002] FSR 6; *Easygroup IP Licensing Ltd v Sermbezis* [2003] All ER (D) 25; *Global Projects Management Ltd v Citigroup Inc* [2006] FSR 39; *Phones 4U Ltd v Phone4U.co.uk Internet Ltd* [2006] EWCA Civ 244 (CA). For similar results in another common law jurisdiction, see the New Zealand cases of *Oggi Advertising Ltd v McKenzie* [1999] 1 NZLR 631; *Post v Leng* [1999] 3 NZLR 219. See also Clive Elliott and Breon Gravatt, 'Domain name disputes in a cross-border context' (1999) 21(8) EIPR 417.

Tesco, but visitors entering those domain names into their browser would be taken directly to a website operated by Tesco without entering a website run by the defendant. The defendant grouped his 24 'Tesco-related' domain names under the 'Avon4me.co.uk' website, and TradeDoubler recorded traffic to Tesco's websites generated through these 'tesco'-related domain names and included it with the Avon4me website for commission payable by Tesco to the defendant. Tesco caught wind of the scam when its commission bill for Elogicom soared (from a monthly average of £60–70 to over £26,000). On investigation, Tesco discovered the registration and use of the domain names that incorporated the word 'tesco'. Tesco sought an injunction to restrain the defendants from infringing Tesco's registered trade marks and from passing off any goods or services as associated with Tesco by use of the sign 'Tesco' or similar, and an order that the defendants transfer to Tesco each of the domain names. The court, following the test in *One in a Million*, held in regard of the trade mark claim 'that the 'tesco'-related domain names registered by Elogicom were inherently fraudulent, like the 'Marksandspencer'-related name in *One in a Million* – but that even if this were not the case, then 'the relevant test in relation to the other names (such as "Sainsbury") considered in that case would also be satisfied in the circumstances of the present case, so that injunctive relief would be warranted on that basis'.[57] Equally, with regard to the passing-off claim, the court held:

> . . . Elogicom, by its registration and use of the 'tesco' related domain names, has sought to associate itself with and trade upon the considerable goodwill which attaches to the name 'Tesco' for the benefit of Tesco. There is also no doubt that Elogicom continues to threaten to make use the Tesco name, so damaging Tesco's goodwill, both by retaining those domain names with the option of starting to use them again at some point in the future and by virtue of maintaining their registration against Elogicom's name in the register. Therefore, for the same reasons as I have given above in relation to Tesco's trade marks claim and by application of the principles in One in a Million, Tesco is entitled by way of summary judgment to the *quia timet* injunctive relief which it seeks . . .[58]

The result of the UK case law is that the practice of registering domain names that are the same as, or confusingly similar to, the distinctive name/trade mark of another party will, upon action by a claimant, inevitably result in the courts granting both injunctive relief and reassignment of the domain names. Registering domain names that are the same as, or confusingly similar to, a non-distinctive name/trade mark of another party may lead to the courts granting injunctive relief and reassignment of the domain names where it is clear from the context of the dispute that the party that registered the names did so with the clear intent of using them to appropriate the goodwill of the claimant, or to allow others to do so. While the ADR procedures introduced by the registries may now offer potential claimants a swifter and cheaper alternative to legal action, claimants are likely to still bring actions to the courts where they feel that the broader scope of protection afforded by injunctive relief is necessary to protect their future position.[59]

USA

The USA is one of the few jurisdictions to enact specific legislation regarding the registration and use of internet domain names, in the form of the federal **Anti-Cybersquatting Consumer Protection Act of 1999 (ACPA)**. The legislation is an addition to the federal legislation dealing with trade mark law, the **Trademark Act of 1946** (known as the **Lanham Act**).[60] In the USA, trade

---

57 *Tesco Stores Ltd v Elogicom Ltd* [2007] FSR 4, 102.
58 Ibid, 102–3.
59 Ibid, 99.
60 Codified within Title 15 of the US Code §§ 1051–1127.

marks may be protected both at the federal level, under the **Lanham Act**, and the state level, under states' statutory and/or common laws. This chapter will deal solely with the federal level.

The US legislation has particular significance, because the registries of the key .com, .org, and .net TLDs are based in the USA. Under the US **ACPA** legislation, legal actions may be taken against a registrant of a potentially infringing domain name (an *in personam* action) or, where the registrant is out of jurisdiction or is otherwise untraceable by the trade mark owner, against the domain name (an *in rem* action), when the action must be brought in the judicial district in which the domain name registrar is located, or in which the registry is located.[61] The registries for .com, .net (VeriSign Global Registry Services), .org (Public Interest Registry), and .biz (NeuLevel) are all based in a judicial district in Virginia. As a result, the reported cases from the federal courts connected to Virginia outnumber those from any other state.[62]

In the US federal courts, trade mark holders involved in domain name disputes have three main courses of action available to them:

- trade mark infringement litigation – in which the trade mark holder has to establish likelihood of confusion between its mark and a third party's domain name;
- trade mark dilution litigation – in which the trade mark holder has to establish that its mark is 'famous' and that the defendant's use of it in a domain name is devaluing the mark; or
- **ACPA** litigation – in which the trade mark holder has to show a bad faith intent to profit from use, registration, or trafficking in a domain name.

Under the **Lanham Act**, the term 'trademark' includes any word, name, symbol, or device, or any combination thereof that is (1) used by a person, or (2) that a person has a bona fide intention to use in commerce and applies to register on the principal register established under the Act, to identify and distinguish his or her goods, including a unique product, from those manufactured or sold by others, and to indicate the source of the goods, even if that source is unknown.[63] Registered and non-registered trade marks are both eligible for protection.

Trade Mark Infringement

Federal trade mark infringement actions require that there must be 'use in commerce' of the infringing mark.[64] However, the federal courts have often interpreted the meaning of 'use in commerce' quite broadly.[65] If 'use in commerce' is found, a basic trade mark infringement suit will involve the court determining whether the use of an existing trade mark by a later party (a 'junior mark') will create a 'likelihood of confusion' with the goods provided by an existing party (a 'senior mark'). The federal circuit courts have come up with several similar, but not identical, tests

---

61 See, eg, *Standing Stone Media, Inc v Indiancountrytoday.com* 193 F Supp 2d 528 (NDNY 2002); *Cable Network News LP v Cnnews.com* 177 F Supp 2d 506 (ED Va, 2001).

62 When examining case law under the US Anti-Cybersquatting Consumer Protection Act of 1999 (ACPA), it is important to understand the structure of the US federal courts. The federal courts have jurisdiction to hear ACPA-based cases, because the ACPA is an Act of Congress. The lower federal courts, or district courts, are the federal trial courts for their particular districts. The judicial districts are organised into twelve regional circuits, each of which has a US Court of Appeals. A Court of Appeals will hear appeals from the district courts located within its circuit. It is important to remember that the judgments of a particular Court of Appeal are binding precedent only upon the courts within that circuit. It is possible, and indeed not uncommon, for different circuits to have conflicting precedents.

63 15 USC § 1127.

64 15 USC § 1114(1)(a).

65 See, eg, *Planned Parenthood Federation of America, Inc v Bucci* 42 USPQ 2d 1430 (SDNY 1997) (the registration of domain name 'plannedparenthood.com' and creation of website using that title, which contained information contrary to Planned Parenthood's views, was a use 'in connection with' commerce); cf *555-1212.com, Inc v Communication House Intern, Inc* 157 F Supp 2d 1084 (ND Cal, 2001) (simply reserving the domain name '5551212.com', without use in connection with any commercial enterprise, did not constitute use of allegedly infringing trade mark 'in commerce'); also *Bird v Parsons* 289 F 3d 865 (6th Cir 2002); *Taubman Co v Webfeats* 319 F 3d 770 (6th Cir 2003); *Bosley Medical Institute, Inc v Kremer* 403 F 3d 672 (9th Cir 2005).

in order to reach such determinations.[66] It appears, however, that there is less uniformity in opinion between the circuits as regards the appropriate test for 'likelihood of confusion' on the internet than there is in the off-line environment.[67]

Some federal circuits have examined the issue of likelihood of confusion as regards domain names by reference to the theory of 'initial interest confusion'. This theory suggests that, where a party lures potential customers away from a producer, by initially passing off its goods as those of the producer's, even if the confusion as to the source of the goods is dispelled by the time of a sale, this is sufficient to demonstrate actionable confusion. The primary consideration has been whether the mere fact that a user is drawn to a website that has used another party's trade mark should be the only criteria to be used. Early case law in the district courts suggested that it was. In those cases, the fact that the actual content of the website was clearly not related to the goods and services of the trade mark holder, and the fact that the website owner was clearly not seeking to profit from the mark, were held to be irrelevant.[68] On the other hand, in later case law, the appellate courts appear to require that there be some intention to capitalise financially on the misdirection of consumers.[69]

Trade Mark Dilution

As well as bringing an action for infringement, owners of trade marks can also bring an action for trade mark dilution under federal law. Dilution essentially extends trade mark law to forbid the use of a trade mark, or a mark similar to it, in a way that would lessen the senior trade mark's effectiveness in functioning as a unique indication of the trade mark holder's goods or services.

The **Trademark Dilution Revision Act of 2006 (TDRA)**, amending the **Federal Trademark Dilution Act of 1996 (FTDA)**, provides remedies for trade mark dilution. It permits a dilution claim to be brought where the mark is 'famous', and the use made of the mark by a third party began after the senior mark became famous and was 'commercial use in commerce'. The **TDRA** defines a 'famous' mark as one that is 'widely recognized by the general consuming public of the United States as a designation of source of the goods or services of the mark's owner'.[70]

The **TDRA** permits owners of marks that are distinctive, either 'inherently or through acquired distinctiveness', to assert a claim. The Act also provides that it covers both 'dilution by blurring' and 'dilution by tarnishment', and defines the two distinct types of dilution:

- 'dilution by blurring' is defined as 'association arising from the similarity between a mark or trade name and a famous mark that impairs the distinctiveness of the famous mark'; and
- 'dilution by tarnishment' is defined as 'association arising from the similarity between a mark or trade name and a famous mark that harms the reputation of the famous mark'.

The **TDRA** also clarifies those activities that are not actionable as dilution by blurring or dilution by tarnishment, including:

- fair use, such as comparative advertising or promotion of goods or services; or identifying and parodying, criticising, or commenting upon the famous mark owner or the goods or services of the famous mark owner;
- all forms of news reporting and news commentary; and
- any non-commercial use of a mark.

---

66 See, eg, *Polaroid Corp v Polarad Electronics Corp* 287 F 2d 492, 495 (2d Cir 1961); *AMF Inc v Sleekcraft Boats* 599 F 2d 341, 348–9 (9th Cir 1979); *Interpace Corp v Lapp, Inc* 721 F 2d 460, 463 (3d Cir 1983); *Eli Lilly & Co v Natural Answers, Inc* 233 F 3d 456, 462 (7th Cir 2000).
67 See, eg, *Planned Parenthood*, above; *Brookfield Communications Inc v West Coast Entertainment Corp* 174 F 3d 1036 (9th Cir 1999).
68 See, eg, *Planned Parenthood*, above; *Jews for Jesus v Brodsky* 993 F Supp 282 (DNJ 1998), aff'd 159 F 3d 1351 (3d Cir 1998).
69 See, eg, *Lamparello v Falwell* 420 F 3d 309 (4th Cir 2005); *Interstellar Starship Servs, Ltd v Epix, Inc* 304 F 3d 936, 946 (9th Cir 2002); *PACCAR Inc v TeleScan Techs, LLC* 319 F 3d 243, 253 (6th Cir 2003).
70 15 USC § 1125(c)(2)(A).

Prior to the enactment of the **ACPA**, the **FTDA** was used in a number of high-profile domain name cases.[71] In early case law, the courts applied a broad definition of whether a mark was 'famous', possibly because of the lack of other trade mark remedies for cybersquatting in the absence of obvious trade mark infringement.[72] Since the passage of the **ACPA** in 1999, the courts have taken a more restrictive approach towards the use of federal dilution law in domain name cases.[73] However, actions against holders of domain names for dilution where the trade mark incorporated in the domain name is 'famous' remain an option for trade mark holders.[74] As with trade mark infringement actions, federal dilution actions require a showing that the trade mark is being 'used in commerce'[75] and the statute explicitly states that the '[n]oncommercial use of a mark' is not actionable.[76]

The Anti-Cybersquatting Consumer Protection Act of 1999

The **ACPA** came into force in November 1999. Its application is solely to domain names.[77] It contains both trade mark-related provisions and non-trade mark provisions. The trade mark-related provisions are:

- outlawing of registration, with the bad faith intent to profit, of a domain name that is confusingly similar to a registered or unregistered mark or dilutive of a famous mark;[78] and
- limiting the liability of, and remedies against, domain name registrars for registering an infringing domain name and for refusing to register, cancelling, or transferring a domain name in furtherance of a dispute resolution policy.[79]

The non-trade mark provisions relate to protection against the use of non-trade marked personal names by cybersquatters.[80]

Under the Act,[81] a person is liable in a civil action by the owner of a mark (including a personal name protected as a mark) if, without regard to the goods or services of the parties, the defendant has a bad faith intent to profit from that mark, and registers, traffics in, or uses a domain name that is:

- identical, or confusingly similar to, a mark that is distinctive at the time of registration of the domain name;
- identical, or confusingly similar to, or dilutive of, a famous mark that is famous at the time of registration of the domain name; or
- a trade mark, word, or name protected under 18 **USC** § 706 (the 'Red Cross', the 'American National Red Cross', or the 'Geneva Cross'), or 36 **USC** § 220506 (Olympic symbols, including the words 'Olympic', 'Olympiad', and 'Olympia').

---

71 See, eg, *Hasbro, Inc v Internet Entertainment Group, Ltd*, 40 USPQ 2d 1479 (WD Wash, 1996), in which the use of 'candyland.com' as a domain name for a sexually explicit website diluted the value of the game company Hasbro's 'Candy Land' mark; also *Toys 'R' Us, Inc v Akkaoui* 40 USPQ 2d 1836 (ND Cal 1996); *Panavision International LP v Toeppen* 141 F 3d 1316 (9th Cir 1998).

72 See, eg, *Teletech Customer Care Management, Inc v Tele-Tech Company, Inc* 977 F Supp 1407 (CD Cal 1997); cf *Washington Speakers Bureau, Inc v Leading Authorities, Inc* 33 F Supp 2d 488 (ED Va 1999).

73 See, eg, *Avery Dennison Corp v Sumpton* 189 F 3d 868 (9th Cir 1999), in which it was held that to be 'famous', a mark must be truly prominent and renowned, and may not be merely distinctive (worldwide use of a non-famous trade mark does not establish fame); also *Hasbro, Inc v Clue Computing, Inc*, 66 F Supp 3d 117 (D Mass, 1999).

74 See, eg, *Ford Motor Co v Lapertosa* 126 F Supp 2d 463 (ED Mich 2000) (registration and use of the domain name 'fordrecalls.com' for selling pornography diluted the Ford trade mark).

75 15 USC § 1125(c)(1). See, eg, *Bally Total Fitness Holding Corp v Faber* 29 F Supp 2d 1161 (CD Cal 1998).

76 15 USC § 1125(c)(4). See, eg, *Northland Ins Companies v Blaylock* 115 F Supp 2d 1108 (D Minn 2000).

77 See, eg, *Bihari v Gross* 119 F Supp 2d 309 (SDNY 2000).

78 15 USC § 1125(d).

79 15 USC § 1114(2)(D).

80 15 USC § 1129.

81 15 USC § 1125 (d)(1)(A).

The term 'mark' covers both registered and unregistered marks. The term 'confusingly similar' in this context means that the plaintiff's mark and the defendant's domain name are so similar in sight, sound, or meaning that the reasonable user would be confused. Thus simply including some generic or descriptive term in the domain name along with the mark is unlikely to overcome this test.[82] Equally, misspellings of the plaintiff's marks are also likely to be held to be confusingly similar.[83]

The fact that confusion about a website's source could be overcome by visiting the website at the defendant's domain name will not necessarily sway a court.[84] This is in line with the **ACPA**'s purpose of combating cybersquatting, in as much as cybersquatters may not actually use the domain name for a website, but may simply 'warehouse' it prior to sale to another party. The use of potentially negative terms (for example, 'sucks', 'fuck') in the domain name may persuade a court that there is little risk of confusion.[85] However, it appears that, in such cases, an 'unequivocal negative message' will be required.[86]

Because there has to be a 'use in commerce' for there to be trade mark infringement, courts have often rejected attempts by mark holders to prevent 'gripe sites' from using domain names that are very similar to their marks.[87] However, in *Bosley Medical Institute, Inc v Kremer*, the Ninth Circuit held that the important test within the **ACPA** was the 'bad faith' test, and that:

> The non-commercial use exception . . . is in direct conflict with the language of the ACPA. The ACPA makes it clear that 'use' is only one possible way to violate the Act ('registers, traffics in, or uses'). Allowing a cybersquatter to register the domain name with bad faith intent to profit but get around the law by making noncommercial use of the mark would run counter to the purpose of the Act. . . . Additionally, one of the nine factors listed in the statute that courts must consider is the registrant's 'bona fide noncommercial or fair use of the mark in a site accessible under the domain name.' . . . This factor would be meaningless if the statute exempted all noncommercial uses of a trade mark within a domain name.[88]

The meaning of the terms 'distinctive', 'dilutive', and 'famous' are the same as those applied under the **TDRA**. Failure by a plaintiff to demonstrate that their mark is distinctive or famous will result in the rejection of the plaintiff's **ACPA** claims.[89]

Bad Faith under the ACPA

The Act lists nine non-exclusive, non-exhaustive factors for determining bad faith:[90] As the Second Circuit noted in an early judgment, often cited by other circuit courts, the most important grounds for finding bad faith 'are the unique circumstances of th[e] case which do not fit neatly into the specific factors enumerated by Congress, but may nevertheless be considered under the statute'.[91]

---

82 See, eg, *PACCAR Inc*, above, 252 (defendant's domain names, such as 'www.peterbiltnewtrucks.com', had the same appearance as plaintiff's domain name 'www.peterbilt.com'); also *DaimlerChrysler v The Net Inc* 388 F 3d 201 (6th Cir 2004); *Audi AG v D'Amato* 2006 WL 3392623 (6th Cir 2006).

83 See, eg, *Shields v Zuccarini* 254 F 3d 476 (3d Cir 2001) (intentional registration of domain names that were misspellings of distinctive or famous names, causing an internet user who made a slight spelling or typing error to reach an unintended site, were confusingly similar).

84 See, eg, *Coca-Cola Co v Purdy* 382 F 3d 774 (8th Cir 2004) (internet domain names for anti-abortion websites that differed from famous marks only by the addition of generic terms such as 'my', 'says', or 'drink' were confusingly similar to those marks).

85 *Ford Motor Co v 2600 Enterprises* 177 F Supp 2d 661 (ED Mich 2001).

86 See, eg, *Sunlight Saunas, Inc v Sundance Sauna, Inc* 427 F Supp 2d 1032 (D Kan 2006) (use of 'www.sunlightsaunas-exposed.com', which contained the plaintiff's mark SUNLIGHT SAUNAS, did not send the same unequivocal negative message as 'sucks'; it might not immediately alert an internet user that he or she was entering a 'gripe site').

87 See, eg, *Lamparello v Falwell* 420 F 3d 309 (4th Cir 2005) (registration of 'www.fallwell.com' domain name for website expressly critical of Reverend Jerry Falwell's views on homosexuality did not violate ACPA); see also *TMI, Inc v Maxwell* 368 F 3d 433 (5th Cir 2004); *Lucas Nursery & Landscaping* 359 F 3d 810 (6th Cir 2004).

88 *Bosley Medical Institute, Inc v Kremer* 403 F 3d 672, 680–1 (9th Cir 2005).

89 See, eg, *Bavaro Palace, SA v Vacation Tours, Inc* 2006 WL 2847233 (11th Cir 2006).

90 15 USC § 1125(d)(1)(B).

91 *Sporty's Farm LLC v Sportsman's Market, Inc* 202 F 3d 489, 499 (2d Cir 2000).

- *The trade mark or other intellectual property rights of the person, if any, in the domain name.* This recognises that, under trade mark law, there may be concurring uses of the same name that are non-infringing, due to their use in conjunction with different types of product or service, or in different national markets.[92]

- *The extent to which the domain name consists of the legal name of the person or a name that is otherwise commonly used to identify that person.* This recognises that a person should be permitted to register his or her legal name or widely recognised nickname as the domain name of his or her website.[93]

- *The person's prior use, if any, of the domain name in connection with the bona fide offering of any goods or services.* This recognises that the legitimate use of the domain name in commerce is a good indicator of good faith intent.[94]

- *The person's bona fide non-commercial or fair use of the mark in a site accessible under the domain name.* This recognises the line of case law developed prior to the **ACPA** that held that the non-confusing use of a company name or mark in a domain name on a website used solely to criticise the goods or policies of that company was a fair use and thus could not be infringement.[95] The courts are likely, however, to be unpersuaded by supposedly critical sites upon which criticism only appears after the domain name dispute arises.[96]

- *The person's intent to divert consumers from the mark owner's online location to a site accessible under the domain name that could harm the goodwill represented by the mark, either for commercial gain or with the intent to tarnish or disparage the mark, by creating a likelihood of confusion as to the source, sponsorship, affiliation, or endorsement of the site.* This recognises that cybersquatters who actually create a website under the domain names that they have registered using other parties' trade marks often intend to divert internet users to their own sites under false pretences.[97]

- *The person's offer to transfer, sell, or otherwise assign the domain name to the mark owner or any third party for financial gain without having used, or having an intent to use, the domain name in the bona fide offering of any goods or services, or the person's prior conduct indicating a pattern of such conduct.* This is premised on the basis that cybersquatters often intend to trade on the value of trade mark owners marks by engaging in the business of registering domain names consisting of or incorporating those marks and selling them to the rightful trade mark owners. However, Congress did not intend any offer to sell a domain name to a trade mark holder to be automatically indicative of bad faith.[98]

- *The person's provision of material and misleading false contact information when applying for the registration of the domain name, the person's intentional failure to maintain accurate contact information, or the person's prior conduct indicating a pattern of such conduct.* Cybersquatters will often take great pains to avoid contact with trade mark holders, particularly if they are using the relevant domain names to divert internet

---

92 See, as an example of 'bad faith', *Virtual Works, Inc v Network Solutions, Inc* 106 F Supp 2d 845 (ED Va, 2000), aff'd 238 F 3d 264 (4th Cir 2001) (defendant registered and used the domain name 'vw.net' for two years in its business, but never did business as VW nor identified itself as such and knew that it was registering a domain name bearing strong resemblance to a federally protected trade mark, and did so, at least in part, with the idea of selling the site 'for a lot of money' to the mark's owner).

93 See, eg, *Nissan Motor Co v Nissan Computer Corp* 2002 WL 32006514 (CD Cal, 7 January 2002); also *Lewittes v Cohen* 2004 WL 1171261 (SDNY 2004).

94 See, eg, *Sloan v Auditron Electronic Corp* 68 Fed Appx 386 (4th Cir 2003); cf *Sporty's Farm LLC*, above.

95 See, eg, *Bally Total Fitness Holding Corp v Faber* 29 F Supp 2d 1161 (CD Cal 1998); *TMI, Inc v Maxwell* 368 F 3d 433 (5th Cir 2004); *Bosley Medical Institute, Inc v Kremer* 403 F 3d 672, 680–1 (9th Cir 2005).

96 See, eg, *Shields v Zuccarini* 254 F 3d 476 (3d Cir 2001).

97 See, eg, *Planned Parenthood Federation of America, Inc v Bucci* 42 USPQ 2d 1430 (SDNY 1997); *Jews for Jesus v Brodsky* 993 F Supp 282 (DNJ 1998), aff'd 159 F 3d 1351 (3d Cir 1998); *Coca-Cola Co v Purdy* 382 F 3d 774 (8th Cir 2004); *Faegre & Benson LLP v Purdy,* 70 USPQ 2d 1315 (D Minn 2004); *March Madness Athletic Ass'n, LLC v Netfire, Inc* 310 F Supp 2d 786 (ND Tex 2003); *Venetian Casino Resort, LLC v Venetiangold.Com* 380 F Supp 2d 737 (ED Va, 2005).

98 Contrast *Virtual Works, Inc v Network Solutions, Inc* 106 F Supp 2d 845 (ED Va, 2000), aff'd 238 F 3d 264 (4th Cir 2001), and *Ford Motor Co v Catalanotte* 342 F 3d 543 (6th Cir 2003), with *Interstellar Starship Servs, Ltd v Epix, Inc* 304 F 3d 936, 946 (9th Cir 2002). However, the profoundly negative connotations that the courts often appear to attach to such offers, and the apparent willingness of plaintiffs to allege bad faith on the grounds of any offer to sell, means that it is probably unwise for a registrant of a domain name consisting of, or incorporating, a third party's mark to make such an offer or, potentially, even to enter into negotiations with the trade mark holder in a dispute scenario.

users to their own sites by creating confusion as to the source, sponsorship, affiliation, or enforcement of the site.[99]

- *The person's registration or acquisition of multiple domain names that the person knows are identical or confusingly similar to marks of others that are distinctive at the time of registration of such domain names, or dilutive of famous marks of others that are famous at the time of registration of such domain names, without regard to the goods or services of the parties.* This addresses the 'warehousing' of domain names whereby a cybersquatter has amassed hundreds of domain names identical or confusingly similar to the marks of others.[100] While the warehousing of many domain names, particularly where some of those domain names resemble well-known trade marks, tends to be viewed with suspicion by the courts,[101] 'warehousing' by itself (even including domain names that resemble well-known trade marks) is not definitive proof of bad faith.[102]

- *The extent to which the mark incorporated in the person's domain name registration is or is not distinctive and famous, as defined within the amended dilution section of the* **Lanham Act**. This provides that the court should have regard to the strength of the plaintiff's mark. The stronger the mark is, the more chance there is for the possibility of confusion, and the less likely it is that the defendant could have registered the domain name in good faith in the absence of knowledge of the mark.

The **ACPA** contains a 'safe harbour' provision that bad faith intent 'shall not be found in any case in which the court determines that the person believed and had reasonable grounds to believe that the use of the domain name was fair use or otherwise lawful'.[103] Some concerns have been expressed about its breadth.[104] However, while some defendants have successfully argued that they had reasonable grounds to believe that their use was lawful,[105] the courts have been quick to rule out such arguments in the light of actual fact situations.[106] Thus the safe harbour is a relatively narrow one, because it requires the registrant to have an objectively 'reasonable' basis for believing that he or she is making fair or lawful use of the domain name.

In Personam and In Rem Actions

Under normal circumstances, an action by a plaintiff under the **ACPA** would be an *in personam* action – that is, it would be against the domain name registrant, or his or her licensee. As already noted, in an *in personam* action, the defendant will be liable if he or she has a bad faith intent to profit from the mark, and register, traffic in, or use a domain name that is identical, confusingly similar, or dilutive to, or of, a distinctive or famous mark. When filing an *in personam* **ACPA** case, the normal rules of personal jurisdiction apply.[107]

Remedies in an *in personam* case under the **ACPA** can include both injunctive relief and monetary relief. Injunctive relief may simply be the transfer or cancellation of the domain name, but may also involve injunctions barring defendants from engaging in other action, such as registering any other plaintiff's other mark.[108] Monetary relief can be requested in the form of defendant's profits, plaintiff's damages, and, in exceptional cases, reasonable attorneys' fees.[109] In lieu of actual damages and

---

99 John Zuccarini appears routinely to have provided inaccurate or false contact information when registering websites for use in his 'mousetrapping' schemes: eg, WIPO Case No D2002-0950 *Wal-Mart Stores, Inc v John Zuccarini d/b/a RaveClub Berlin*.

100 See, eg, *Panavision Int'l LP v Toeppen* 945 F Supp 1296 (CD Cal 1996).

101 See, eg, *E & J Gallo Winery v SpiderWebs Ltd* 286 F 3d 270 (5th Cir 2002).

102 See, eg, *Avery Dennison Corp v Sumpton* 189 F 3d 868 (9th Cir 1999).

103 15 USC S 1225(d)(1)(B)(ii).

104 *Virtual Works, Inc v Volkswagen of America, Inc*, 238 F 3d 264, 270 (4th Cir 2001).

105 See, eg, *Cello Holdings, LLC v Lawrence-Dahl Companies* 89 F Supp 2d 464 (SDNY 2000); *Interstellar Starship Services, Ltd*, above; *Mayflower Transit, LLC v Prince* 314 F Supp 2d 362 (DNJ 2004); *Rohr-Gurnee Motors, Inc v Patterson* 2004 WL 422525 (ND Ill, 9 February 2004).

106 See, eg, *Shields v Zuccarini* 254 F 3d 476 (3d Cir 2001); *Coca-Cola Co v Purdy* 382 F 3d 774 (8th Cir 2004); *Audi AG v D'Amato* 2006 WL 3392623 (6th Cir 2006).

107 See, eg, *Alitalia-Linee Aeree Italiane SpA v Casinoalitalia.Com*, 128 F Supp 2d 340 (ED Va, 2001).

108 See, eg, *Mattel, Inc v Internet Dimensions Inc* 2000 WL 973745 (SDNY 2000).

109 15 USC § 1117.

profits, however, the plaintiff may elect, at any time before the trial court renders final judgment, an award of statutory damages ranging from US$1,000 to US$100,000 per domain name.[110]

The **Fraudulent Online Identity Sanctions Act of 2004 (FOISA)**, part of the **Intellectual Property Protection and Courts Amendments Act of 2004**, creates a rebuttable presumption of wilfulness where a defendant knowingly provides materially false contact information in a domain name registration and then uses the website accessed by that domain name in infringing another party's copyright or trade mark. The presumption that the defendant committed wilful infringement can, at the court's discretion, lead to significantly increased damages – in trade mark cases, the statutory damages upper limit is increased to US$1 million in cases in which infringement is wilful.[111]

However, in a significant percentage of domain name cases, the trade mark owner may find itself unable to either identify, or serve notice of process upon, the owner of the domain name. This may be because the domain name registrant has registered domain names under aliases or otherwise provided false information in his or her registration applications. It may also be the case that personal jurisdiction cannot be established over the domain name registrant – for example, when a non-US resident has registered a domain name that infringes upon a US trade mark.

In such circumstances, the **ACPA** provides for in rem jurisdiction permitting the trade mark holder to file an in rem action against the name itself. The trade mark holder can only do this having first either:

- exercised due diligence in trying to locate the owner of the domain name, including publishing notice, but having been unable to do so, or been unable to effect service; or
- demonstrated that personal jurisdiction cannot be established over the domain name registrant because he or she is outside the USA.[112]

In other words, the plaintiff must show that he or she cannot obtain in personam jurisdiction over a person who would have been a defendant in an in personam action in any judicial district in the USA.[113] Both 'due diligence' and constitutional due process require that the plaintiff waits a 'reasonable time' after publishing notice; failure to do so may result in an in rem action being rejected due to the availability of an in personam defendant.[114]

In rem jurisdiction still requires a nexus based upon a US registry, or registrar, and jurisdiction does not extend to any domain name registries existing outside of the USA. An in rem action under the **ACPA** can be (and must be) filed in any district in which the domain name registrar, registry, or other domain name authority is located.[115]

Under an in rem action, the trade mark owner effectively has the following options:

- action for infringement of a registered mark;
- action for infringement of an unregistered mark;
- action for dilution of a famous mark; or
- action for cyberpiracy of a registered mark.[116]

---

110 15 USC § 1117(a) and (d).
111 15 USC § 1117(e).
112 See, eg, *Heathmount AE Corp v Technodome.Com*, 106 F Supp 2d 860 (ED Va, 2000) (no personal jurisdiction in the Eastern District of Virginia over Canadian citizen).
113 See, eg, *Alitalia-Linee Aeree Italiane SpA*, above (in rem and in personam provisions are mutually exclusive avenues for cybersquatting relief).
114 See, eg, *Lucent Technologies, Inc v Lucentsucks.com* 95 F Supp 2d 528 (ED Va, 2000).
115 See, eg, *Fleetboston Financial Corp v Fleetbostonfinancial.com* 2001 US Dist LEXIS 4797 (D Mass, 27 March 2001).
116 15 USC§ 1125(d)(2)(A)(i).

While some district courts have required evidence of 'bad faith' under an *in rem* case, the Fourth Circuit has held that 'bad faith' is not always required.[117] The remedy in an *in rem* action is limited to a court order for forfeiture or cancellation and transfer of the domain name.

Abuse of a Dispute Resolution Procedure.

If a registrar, registry, or other registration authority refuses to register, removes from registration, transfers, temporarily disables, or permanently cancels a domain name based on a knowing and material misrepresentation by any other person that a domain name is identical to, confusingly similar to, or dilutive of a mark, the person making the knowing and material misrepresentation shall be liable for any damages, including costs and attorney's fees, incurred by the domain name registrant as a result of such action.[118]

A court may also grant injunctive relief to the domain name registrant, including the reactivation of the domain name or the transfer of the domain name to the domain name registrant. This provision is designed to protect the rights of domain name registrants against overreaching trade mark owners; it is in essence a statutory reverse domain name hijacking provision.[119]

The ACPA and Domain Name Registrars

Prior to the **ACPA**, the US federal courts had already determined that Network Solutions, Inc (NSI) – at the time, the only domain name registrar – could not be held liable for registering domain names to alleged cybersquatters.[120] The **ACPA** provides domain name registrars with immunity from monetary and injunctive relief for the acts of:

- refusing to register, cancelling, or transferring a domain name in compliance with a court order pursuant to the **ACPA**; or
- in the implementation of a reasonable policy of the registrar, prohibiting the registration of a domain name that is identical to, confusingly similar to, or dilutive of another's mark.[121]

The ICANN Uniform Dispute Resolution Procedure (UDRP) that has been adopted by the gTLD registrars is an example of a 'reasonable policy' for the purposes of the **ACPA**.[122] Thus, if a UDRP dispute resolution panel decides that a trade mark holder has good grounds to challenge the registration of a domain name as being identical or confusingly similar to a trade mark or service mark in which the trade mark holder has rights, that the respondent has no rights or legitimate interest in respect of the domain name, and that the domain name has been registered and is being used in bad faith, the panel may order the cancellation or transfer of the domain name. Under the **ACPA**, even where a court later decides that the respondent was entitled to the domain name and that the registrar should not have transferred or cancelled the domain name, the registrar will be immune from suit.

Registrars thus cannot be:

- liable for trade mark infringement, or dilution, or a violation of the **ACPA** for registering domain names that infringe trade marks;

---

117 See, eg, *Harrods Ltd v Sixty Internet Domain Names* 302 F 3d 214 (4th Cir 2002) (the *in rem* provision of the ACPA is not limited to claims of bad faith registration with the intent to profit under the ACPA, but also authorises *in rem* actions for certain federal infringement and dilution claims).
118 15 USCA § 1114(2)(D)(iv).
119 See *Hawes v Network Solutions, Inc* 337 F 3d 377 (4th Cir 2003); *Barcelona.com, Inc v Excelentisimo Ayuntamiento De Barcelona* 330 F 3d 617 (4th Cir 2003).
120 *Panavision Int'l LP v Toeppen* 945 F Supp 1296 (CD Cal 1996); *Lockheed Martin Corp v Network Solutions, Inc* 985 F Supp 949 (CD Cal 1997), aff'd, 194 F 3d 980 (9th Cir 1999).
121 USC § 1114 (2)(D)(i)(I).
122 *Barcelona.com, Inc*, above; *Storey v Cello Holdings, LLC* 347 F 3d 370 (2d Cir 2003).

- joined as a party to a lawsuit by a respondent/complainant who wishes to attack the result of a dispute resolution procedure; or
- liable for damages for the registration or maintenance of a domain name for another party in the absence of a showing of bad faith intent to profit from the domain on the registrar's part.

Registrars can be exposed to injunctions if they refuse to comply with their obligations in an *in rem* lawsuit – that is, if they:

- do not expeditiously deposit with a court such documents as are necessary to establish the court's control and authority over the domain name;
- transfer, suspend, or otherwise modify the domain name before an *in rem* action is decided; or
- wilfully fail to comply with a court order to do or not do the above acts.[123]

The ACPA and Personal Names

Beyond US federal trade mark law, the **ACPA** also provides for civil liability for the registration of a domain name that consists of the name of another living person, or a name that is substantially and confusingly similar, without that person's consent, with the intent to profit by selling the domain name for financial gain to that person or any third party.[124]

A plaintiff must demonstrate that the defendant has:

- registered a domain name that consists of, or is confusingly similar to, the name of the plaintiff, who is a living person – there is no reference to 'traffics in or uses', as with the trade mark provisions;
- registered that domain name without the plaintiff's consent; and
- done so with the specific intent to profit from the plaintiff's name by selling the domain name for financial gain to the plaintiff or to a third party – 'bad faith intent' and the nine, non-exhaustive factors for determining bad faith under the trade mark provisions do not apply.

The Act does not define what is meant by a 'name', although the Congressional Record shows that it was intended to cover at least '. . . the registration of full names (e.g., "johndoe.com"), appellations (e.g., "doe.com"), and variations thereon (e.g., "john-doe.com" or "jondoe.com") . . .'.[125] Other commentators have suggested that it may also 'include pen names, stage names or widely recognized nicknames . . . if they are widely used and understood as the identifier of a specific person'.[126]

The provision appears to be aimed at circumstances such as those in *Jeanette Winterson v Mark Hogarth*,[127] in which the respondent registered domain names consisting of about 130 famous writers' names, allegedly in order to develop websites devoted to them containing book extracts, reviews, biographies, signings, forthcoming works, and links to an e-book seller such as amazon. com, but offered at least some of the domain names for sale to the relevant writers or their agents. In such circumstances, the defendant in an **ACPA** personal name action whose name was different from the name contained in the domain name would clearly have a specific intent to profit from the name of another living person.

The use of a personal name in a domain name, where the defendant is using the website under the domain name to comment on the individual in question, is likely to fall outside the scope of

---

123 USC § 1114(D)(i)(I). It appears likely that 'court' within this section of the ACPA refers only to US courts: *Hawes*, above.
124 15 USC § 1129.
125 Congressional Record (1999) 17 November, p S14715.
126 J Thomas McCarthy, *McCarthy on Trademarks and Unfair Competition*, 4th edn, 1998–2009 (looseleaf), Eagan, MN: West Publishing.
127 WIPO Case No D2000-0235.

the **ACPA**.[128] Equally, a domain name registrant whose name was 'Octavius Xavier' would not fall foul of the legislation if he were to register 'octaviusxavier.com', even if there were a famous person whose name was also 'Octavius Xavier' who wanted that domain name and the former party offered to sell it to the latter. Where a party has registered many common surnames as domain names and is offering them for sale, or is intending to use them for provision of services such as vanity email addresses, the fact that one of those domain names consists of, or is confusingly similar to, the name of another party, even a famous party, will be in itself insufficient to trigger the **ACPA** personal name provision in the absence of clear evidence of specific intent to profit from the plaintiff's name.

The **ACPA** exempts from its provisions regarding personal names (and only those provisions) a person who in good faith registers a domain name consisting of the name of another living person, or a confusingly similar name, if the domain name is used in, affiliated with, or related to, a work of authorship protected under Title 17 (the **Copyright Act**), provided that:

- the person registering the domain name is the copyright owner or licensee of the work;
- the person intends to sell the domain name in conjunction with the lawful exploitation of the work; and
- the registration is not prohibited by a contract between the registrant and the named person.

The purpose of this exemption is to permit the registration of a domain name in good faith by an owner or licensee of a copyrighted work, such as an audiovisual work, a sound recording, a book, or other work of authorship, where the personal name is used in, affiliated with, or related to that work, where the person's intent in registering the domain is to sell the domain name as part of the lawful exploitation of the work – for example, 'the registration of a domain name containing a personal name by the author of a screenplay that bears the same name, with the intent to sell the domain name in conjunction with the sale or license of the screenplay to a production studio'.[129] A defendant to an action under this provision is entitled to any defence that is available to him or her under the **Lanham Act**, including any defence under s 43(c)(4) or relating to fair use, and to consideration of his or her right of free speech or expression under the First Amendment of the US **Constitution**.

A successful plaintiff under this provision may obtain injunctive relief, including forfeiture, cancellation, or transfer of the offending domain name. There is no provision for monetary damages to either party beyond costs and attorney fees, and award of these is at the court's discretion.

Both US citizens and citizens of other nations have standing to invoke the **ACPA** provisions relating to personal names.[130] At least two URDP dispute panels have made reference to the availability of the **ACPA** personal names provision to complainants with a connection to the USA, whilst denying them relief under the UDRP.[131]

The Truth in Domain Names Act of 2003

While there are a range of trade mark-related actions that can be brought by a trade mark holder against a party who has registered a domain name that is identical to, or confusingly similar to, its own mark, neither those actions nor other non-trade mark legal approaches, such as the use of consumer protection legislation, may discourage the hardened cybersquatter.

The classic example is the case of US cybersquatter, John Zuccarini. Zuccarini was the subject of numerous World Intellectual Property Organization (WIPO) dispute resolution proceedings

---

128 See, eg, *Ficker v Tuohy* 305 F Supp 2d 569 (D Md 2004).
129 Congressional Record (1999) 17 November, p S14715.
130 See, eg, *Schmidheiny v Weber* 146 F Supp 2d 701 (ED Pa, 2001).
131 See WIPO Case No D2002-0030 *Kathleen Kennedy Townsend v BG Birt*; WIPO Case No D2002-0184 *The Reverend Dr Jerry Falwell and The Liberty Alliance v Gary Cohn, Prolife.net, and God.info.*

alleging cybersquatting or typosquatting,[132] and was successfully sued under the **ACPA** on two occasions.[133] He was also pursued by the US Federal Trade Commission (FTC) for violations of s 5 of the **Federal Trade Commission Act of 1914** relating to unfair or deceptive acts or practices in or affecting commerce,[134] for redirecting consumers from their intended destinations on the internet to his own web pages, where he then obstructed them from leaving those pages using web pages displaying advertisements for goods and services for his financial gain (a process known as 'mouse-trapping').[135] None of these legal setbacks dissuaded Zuccarini from engaging in his cybersquatting/typosquatting/mousetrapping activities, not least because the financial rewards from such activities were considerably greater than the costs of legal fees and damages.

In 2003, however, Congress passed the **Truth in Domain Names Act of 2003 (TDNA)**.[136] This makes knowingly using a misleading domain name on the internet with the intent to deceive a person into viewing material constituting obscenity a criminal offence, punishable by a fine and/or imprisonment of up to two years. Where a party knowingly uses a misleading domain name on the internet with the intent to deceive a minor into viewing material that is harmful to minors on the internet, this is punishable by a fine and/or imprisonment of up to four years. In late 2003, Zuccarini was arrested and charged with offences under the Act relating to his use of domain names with spellings such as 'Dinseyland.com', 'Bobthebiulder.com', 'Teltubbies.com', and 'Britnyspears.com'. A person accessing Zuccarini's websites was presented with advertisements for free access to pornography, including numerous images of hardcore pornography. Zuccarini pled guilty to 49 counts of violating the **TDNA** and, in February 2004, was sentenced to 30 months' imprisonment.

Arbitration

The Generic TLDs (gTLDs): The ICANN Uniform Dispute Resolution Policy (UDRP)

In the mid-to-late 1990s, as the commercialisation of the internet gathered pace, two key issues became apparent to those responsible for running the registry services for the domain name system. First, given the jurisdictional nature of trade marks, and the international nature of the web, there were likely to be a lot of trade mark-based disputes over domain names that the registries were not in a position to handle effectively. Second, in the absence of some form of legal immunity or other way of avoiding involvement, they were going to find themselves caught up as reluctant parties to trade mark litigation over decisions to allocate, reallocate, or put on hold domain names. A solution needed to be developed that would reduce the registries' exposure to such involvement. Initially, NSI (the forerunner to ICANN)[137] developed the NSI Domain Name Dispute Policy, which

---

132 WIPO Case No D2000-0330 *Encyclopaedia Britannica, Inc v Zuccarini*; WIPO Case No D2000-0996 *Diageo plc v Zuccarini*; WIPO Case No D2001-0489 *Disney Enterprises, Inc v Zuccarini*; WIPO Case No D2001-0700 *Lucasfilm Ltd and Lucas Licensing Ltd v Zuccarini*; WIPO Case No D2001-0654 *Backstreet Productions, Inc v Zuccarini*; WIPO Case No D2002-0666 *AT&T Corp v Zuccarini*; WIPO Case No D2002-0827 *AOL Time Warner Inc v Zuccarini*.

133 *Shields v Zuccarini* 254 F 3d 476 (3rd Cir 2001); *Electronics Boutique Holdings Corp v Zuccarini* 56 USPQ 2d 1705 (ED Pa, 2000).

134 15 USC § 45.

135 *FTC v Zuccarini* 2002 US Dist LEXIS 13324 (ED Pa, 10 April 2002).

136 18 USCA § 2252B. See further CG Clark, 'The Truth in Domain Names Act of 2003 and a preventative measure to combat typosquatting' (2004) 89 Cornell L Rev 1476.

137 The NSI was named as a defendant in several lawsuits during the period 1994–99, including *Knowledge-Net v Boone* No 1-94-CV-7195 (ND Ill, filed 2 December 1994); *Roadrunner Computer Systems, Inc v Network Solutions, Inc* No 96-413-A (ED Va, filed 26 March 1996); *Giacalone v Network Solutions, Inc* No C-96 20434 RPA/PVT, 1996 US Dist LEXIS 20807; *Network Solutions, Inc v Clue Computing, Inc* 946 F Supp 858 (D Colo 1996); *Panavision International v Toeppen* 945 F Supp (CD Cal 1996), aff'd 141 F 3d 1316 (9th Cir 1998); *Lockheed Martin Corp v Network Solutions, Inc* 985 F Supp 949 (CD Cal 1997); *Academy of Motion Picture Arts and Sciences v Network Solutions, Inc* 989 F Supp 1276 (CD Cal 1997); *Data Concepts Inc v Digital Consulting Inc* 150 F 3d 620 (6th Cir 1998). See further Sally M Abel, 'Trademark issues in cyberspace: The brave new frontier' (1999) 5 MTTLR 91.

sought to provide clarity to the dispute process, but which still left NSI to make decisions under it – unfortunately, rather than preventing legal actions, this appears to have increased them.[138]

However, by 1998, the US government was in the process of devolving the administration of the domain name system to a wholly non-governmental entity, which would be a non-profit, US-based company. This process resulted in the creation of ICANN. As part of the process, the US government issued a White Paper, part of which stated that the WIPO was to conduct a consultative study on domain name/trade mark issues. The WIPO report was submitted to ICANN in early 1999 and recommended the establishment of a Uniform Domain Name Dispute Resolution Policy (UDRP) to be followed by all registrars in the .com, .net, and .org TLDs. The UDRP was agreed by late 1999, and the first proceeding under the UDRP took place in December 1999.[139] While it is difficult to obtain precise statistics, it appears that in the region of 20,000 proceedings had been initiated by mid-2007.

At present, the UDRP[140] has been adopted by ICANN-accredited registrars in all gTLDs (.aero, .asia, .biz, .cat, .com, .coop, .info, .jobs, .mobi, .museum, .name, .net, .org, .pro, .tel, and .travel). The UDRP is a contractual policy between a registrar and its customers, and is included in registration agreements for all ICANN-accredited registrars. The UDRP provides that cancellation, transfer, or other changes to domain name registrations will only take place:

- where the registrar is instructed by the registrant or its authorised agent;
- on receipt of an order from a court or arbitral tribunal of competent jurisdiction, requiring such action;
- on receipt of a decision of an administrative panel requiring such action in any administrative proceeding to which the registrant was a party and which was conducted under the UDRP; and
- in accordance with the terms of the registrant's registration agreement or other legal requirements.[141]

The UDRP is aimed squarely at the abusive registration of domain names; as such, it cannot provide a solution where both parties have legitimate claims to the domain name. In such circumstances, the 'first to register' rule will normally apply. Registrants agree that, in the event of a complaint by a third party that the domain name is identical or confusingly similar to a trade mark in which the complainant has rights, the respondent holder has no rights or legitimate interests in respect of the domain name, and the domain name has been registered and is being used in bad faith,[142] they will be subject to a mandatory administrative proceeding before one of ICANN's approved ADR service providers.[143]

At the administrative proceeding, the complainant has to prove each of the above elements in order to obtain ruling in his or her favour. It is worth noting that the UDRP does not operate on a strict doctrine of precedent. This means that different panels can come to different conclusions on similar fact scenarios. This can make definitive statements about what will happen in particular fact circumstances hazardous. The following points are derived from the WIPO 'Overview of WIPO Panel Views on Selected UDRP Questions'[144] and reflects trends in what is the largest of the UDRP providers.

---

138 Abel, ibid, 100.
139 WIPO Case No D1999-0001 *World Wrestling Federation Entertainment, Inc v Bosman*.
140 ICANN 'Uniform Domain Name Dispute Resolution Policy' (UDRP), as approved by ICANN on 24 October 1999, available online at www.icann.org/en/udrp/udrp-policy-24oct99.htm
141 Ibid, para 3.
142 Ibid, para 4(a).
143 'Approved Providers for Uniform Domain-Name Dispute-Resolution Policy', available online at www.icann.org/en/dndr/udrp/approved-providers.htm
144 'WIPO Overview of WIPO Panel Views on Selected UDRP Questions', available online at www.wipo.int/amc/en/domains/search/overview/index.html

- *The domain name is identical or confusingly similar to a trade mark in which the complainant has rights.* It appears well established that:

> The UDRP does not require that a Complainant must hold rights specifically in a registered trademark or service mark. Instead, it provides only that there must be 'a trademark or service mark in which the Complainant has rights,' without specifying how these rights are acquired.[145]

This can be seen in the *Jeanette Winterson v Mark Hogarth*[146] and *Julia Fiona Roberts v Russell Boyd*[147] panel decisions, in which the panel held that 'trade mark' includes unregistered marks recognised by the laws of unfair competition. Where the domain name is identical to the trade mark, there is no need to demonstrate likelihood of confusion; for this purpose, the gTLD suffix is ignored (for example, '.com').[148] Where there is a significant addition to the trade mark, the complainant is likely to have to prove likelihood of confusion; however, a domain name consisting of an entire trade mark with the addition of other terms, even derogatory ones, is likely to be found confusingly similar to the complainant's mark.[149] The content of a website (whether it is similar to or different from the business of a trade mark owner) will be considered irrelevant in the finding of confusing similarity.[150]

- *The respondent holder has no rights or legitimate interests in respect of the domain name.* The overall burden of proof rests with the complainant, but because this may, in some circumstances, effectively require the respondent to prove a negative, the general rule appears to be that the complainant is required to make out a prima facie case that the respondent lacks rights or legitimate interests, at which point the respondent assumes the burden of demonstrating rights or legitimate interests in the domain name.[151] If a domain name is being used for the purpose of a genuine non-commercial free speech website, there are two schools of thought exemplified in the panel decisions: first, the right to criticise does not extend to registering a domain name that is identical or confusingly similar to the owner's registered trade mark or conveys an association with the mark;[152] second, irrespective of whether the domain name as such connotes criticism, the respondent has a legitimate interest in using the trade mark as part of the domain name of a criticism site if the use is fair and non-commercial.[153] There are also two schools of thought exemplified in the panel decisions about 'fan sites': first, that an active and clearly non-commercial fan site may have rights and legitimate interests in the domain name that includes the complainant's trade mark, but it must be non-commercial and clearly distinctive from any official site;[154] second, a respondent does not have rights to express its view, even if positive, on an individual or entity by using a confusingly similar domain name, because the respondent is misrepresenting itself as being that individual or entity. In particular, where the domain name is identical to the trade mark, the respondent,

---

145 *Report of the Second WIPO Internet Domain Name Process,* 3 September 2001, para 182.
146 WIPO Case No D2000-0235.
147 WIPO Case No D2000-0210.
148 See, eg, WIPO Case No D2000-1838 *Celine Dion v Jeff Burgar.*
149 Hence the transfer to complainants of many domain names containing words such as 'suck'. However, the respondent may still prevail under the remaining two heads: see, eg, WIPO Case No D2008-0647 *Sermo, Inc v CatalystMD, LLC;* WIPO Case No D2008-0430 *Southern California Regional Rail Authority v Robert Arkow.*
150 WIPO Case No D2000-1698 *Arthur Guinness Son & Co (Dublin) Ltd v Dejan Macesic.*
151 WIPO Case No D2001-0121 *Julian Barnes v Old Barn Studios;* WIPO Case No D2004-0110 *Belupo dd v WACHEM doo.*
152 WIPO Case No D2004-0136 *Kirkland & Ellis LLP v DefaultData.com, American Distribution Systems, Inc.*
153 WIPO Case No D2000-0536 *TMP Worldwide Inc v Jennifer L Potter;* WIPO Case No D2004-0014 *Howard Jarvis Taxpayers Association v Paul McCauley.*
154 WIPO Case No D2004-0001 *2001 White Castle Way, Inc v Glyn O Jacobs.*

in its actions, prevents the trade mark holder from exercising the rights to its mark and managing its presence on the internet.[155]

- *The domain name has been registered and is being used in bad faith.* If a domain name is registered before a trade mark right is established, the registration of the domain name is not in bad faith because the registrant could not have contemplated a non-existent right,[156] unless the respondent is clearly aware of the complainant, and it is clear that the aim of the registration was to take advantage of the confusion between the domain name and any potential complainant rights.[157] The lack of active use of the domain name does not as such prevent a finding of bad faith; a panel should examine all of the circumstances of the case to determine whether the respondent is acting in bad faith.[158] The existence of a disclaimer cannot cure bad faith, when bad faith has been established by other factors.[159] Evidence of offers to sell the domain name in settlement discussions can be used to show bad faith, because many cybersquatters wait until a trade mark owner launches a complaint before asking for payment. Panels can decide whether settlement discussions represent a good faith effort to compromise or a bad faith effort to extort.[160]

The UDRP provides specific, but non-exclusive, examples of evidence of the registration and use of a domain name in bad faith, including:

- circumstances indicating registration or acquisition of the domain name primarily for the purpose of selling, renting, or otherwise transferring the domain name registration to the complainant who is the owner of the trade mark or service mark, or to a competitor of that complainant, for valuable consideration in excess of the documented out-of-pocket costs directly related to the domain name;
- registration of the domain name in order to prevent the owner of the trade mark or service mark from reflecting the mark in a corresponding domain name, where there is a pattern of such conduct;
- registration of the domain name primarily for the purpose of disrupting the business of a competitor; or
- using the domain name to attempt intentionally to attract, for commercial gain, internet users to a website or other online location, by creating a likelihood of confusion with the complainant's mark as to the source, sponsorship, affiliation, or endorsement of the website or location or of a product or service on the website or location.[161]

The UDRP also provides specific, but non-exclusive, examples of ways in which a respondent might demonstrate rights or legitimate interests to a domain name, including that:

- before any notice to the respondent of the dispute, he or she used, or made demonstrable preparations to use, the domain name or a name corresponding to the domain name in connection with a bona fide offering of goods or services;
- he or she (as an individual, business, or other organisation) has been commonly known by the domain name, even if he or she has acquired no trade mark or service mark rights; or

---

155 WIPO Case No D2000-1459 *David Gilmour, David Gilmour Music Ltd and David Gilmour Music Overseas Ltd v Ermanno Cenicolla.*
156 WIPO Case No D2001-1182 *PrintForBusiness BV v LBS Horticulture.*
157 WIPO Case No D2003-0598 *Madrid 2012, SA v Scott Martin-MadridMan Websites.*
158 WIPO Case No D2002-0131 *Ladbroke Group Plc v Sonoma International LDC.*
159 WIPO Case No D2003-0316 *Pliva, Inc v Eric Kaiser.*
160 WIPO Case No D2004-0078 *McMullan Bros., Ltd, Maxol Ltd, Maxol Direct Ltd, Maxol Lubricants Ltd, Maxol Oil Ltd, Maxol Direct (NI) Ltd v Web Names Ltd.*
161 UDRP, para 4(b).

● he or she is making a legitimate non-commercial or fair use of the domain name, without intent for commercial gain to misleadingly divert consumers, or to tarnish the trade mark or service mark at issue.[162]

Complaints will be heard by a panel consisting of one or three panellists. The default is a single panellist, but either party can request a three-person panel. The complainant pays the fee for the panel, except where the respondent requests a three-person panel, in which case the fee is split equally.[163] A panel normally accepts only written submissions; in-person hearings are at the sole discretion of the panel.[164] The panel decides complaints on the basis of the statements and documents submitted, and in accordance with the UDRP, UDRP Rules, and any rules and principles of law that it deems applicable.[165] This avoids charges of, for example, US-centricism, but has the disadvantage that different panels may decide similar cases under different national legal rules.

The panel's decision is a summary one; there is no appeal through the UDRP. The result of a successful complaint is limited to requiring the cancellation of the respondent's domain name, or the transfer of the domain name registration to the complainant. As noted earlier, complainants fearing damage in the short term, seeking a broader range of protection, or wanting compensation may thus be inclined to seek injunctions or other remedies in the courts. The UDRP explicitly allows for recourse to the courts before, during, or after a UDRP panel hearing,[166] and a party who is unhappy with a panel decision can seek to overturn it in the courts. Cases have been brought in both the USA and UK to this end, although it appears that, in the UK courts, at least, losing respondents may find it difficult to identify a cause of action upon which the panel's decision can be challenged.

In *Patel v Allos Therapeutics Inc*, the judge noted that the UDRP could not provide the court with a jurisdiction that it did not already have and that the court had no appellate or judicial review function with regard to the UDRP. Any claimant thus had to demonstrate a right of action that the court could consider. In the case of a UDRP complainant, he or she could clearly bring a trade mark infringement action before the court if the UDRP panel had rejected the complaint. In the case before the court, however, Mr Patel, as a registrant, had not identified a cause of action on which the court could adjudicate.[167]

In the USA, the position of losing respondents seems stronger, as the court in *Excelentisimo Ayuntamiento de Barcelona v Barcelona.com Inc* outlined:

> The ACPA recognizes the UDRP only insofar as it constitutes a part of a policy followed by registrars in administering domain names, and the UDRP is relevant to actions brought under the ACPA in two contexts. First, the ACPA limits the liability of a registrar in respect to registering, transferring, disabling, or cancelling a domain name if it is done in the 'implementation of a reasonable policy' (including the UDRP) that prohibits registration of a domain name 'identical to, confusingly similar to, or dilutive of another's mark.' . . . Second, the ACPA authorizes a suit by a domain name registrant whose domain name has been suspended, disabled or transferred under that reasonable policy (including the UDRP) to seek a declaration that the registrant's registration and use of the domain name involves no violation of the Lanham Act as well as an injunction returning the domain name.[168]

---

162 Ibid, para 4(c).
163 ICANN Rules for Uniform Domain Name Dispute Resolution Policy, para 6.
164 Ibid, para 13.
165 Ibid, para 15(a).
166 UDRP, para 4(k).
167 *Patel v Allos Therapeutics Inc* [2008] ETMR 75 (Ch D), [15].
168 330 F 3d 617, 625 (4th Cir 2003); see also *Sallen v Corinthians Licentiamentos LTDA* 273 F 3d 14, 28 (1st Cir 2001).

Opinion is divided on how successful ICANN and the UDRP have been to date. The UDRP has certainly proved popular with those seeking to resolve disputes over domain names and many more cases are decided by this mechanism than by national courts. There have, however, been criticisms of the procedural aspects of the policy,[169] and of the reasoning and outcomes of the panels.[170] However, as the process has 'bedded in' and an informal system of precedent has developed amongst the panels (albeit with some notable disagreements), leading to greater certainty, such complaints appear to have diminished.

The Country Code TLDs (ccTLDs): The .eu TLD

The ccTLDs are not obliged to adopt the UDRP, or to agree to its recognition in binding form in customer contracts for domain registration, although some have done so. Most ccTLDs have adopted their own ADR procedures, although these often do not vary greatly from those of the UDRP. A key variation amongst ccTLDs is often the expansion of the rights under which a complainant can base a complaint. This section will consider the .eu TLD as an example of a ccTLD.

The .eu TLD is a relatively recent addition to the TLDs. In February 2000, the Commission issued a Working Paper, *The Creation of the .EU Internet Top Level Domain*, which discussed the creation of a .eu registry. In September 2000, the ICANN board passed a resolution essentially approving the delegation of a .eu TLD. In December 2000, the Commission proposed a Regulation that would provide a legal basis for the creation of the .eu TLD, and this Regulation was finally adopted in April 2002.[171] The Regulation stated that the new TLD should be managed and operated by a private, non-profit organisation to be known as the '.eu Registry'. This was followed by a further Regulation in 2004, which provided the public policy rules to deal with issues such as speculative and abusive registrations of domain names, intellectual property and other rights, issues of language and geographical concepts, and the extrajudicial settlement of conflicts.[172]

While it is considered a country code TLD (ccTLD), the .eu TLD is not designed to replace the existing national ccTLDs for the EU Member States, but rather exists in parallel with them. There are eligibility restrictions upon who may register a .eu domain name. Those eligible to register a name under the .eu TLD are:

- undertakings having their registered office, central administration, or principal place of business within the EU;
- organisations established within the EU, without prejudice to the application of national law; or
- natural persons resident within the EU (regardless of nationality).[173]

Certain .eu domain names are reserved or blocked. Examples of blocked names that may not be registered as .eu domain names include geographical or geopolitical concepts (for example, ellinikou, 3reich), and two-letter codes representing countries (for example, uk, be, de, es). Examples of reserved names include those that are reserved for:

---

169 Christopher T Varas, 'Sealing the cracks: A proposal to update the anti-cybersquatting regime to combat advertising-based cybersquatting' (2008) 3(4) JIPLP 246.

170 See, eg, O Armon, 'As good as it gets? An appraisal of the Uniform Domain Name Dispute Resolution Policy' (2003) 20(12) Computer & Internet Law 1; Juan Pablo Cortés Diéguez, 'An analysis of the UDRP experience: Is it time for reform?' (2008) 24(4) CLSR 349.

171 EC/733/2002 of the European Parliament and of the Council on the implementation of the .eu Top Level Domain.

172 Regulation EC/874/2004 laying down public policy rules concerning the implementation and functions of the .eu Top Level Domain and principles governing registration, as amended by Regulation EC/1654/2005.

173 EC/733/2002, Art 4 (2)(b). See, eg, CAC-370/2006 *Kane International Ltd v EURid* (complainant successfully contested the registration of the domain name KANE by World Wrestling Entertainment Inc, because it did not meet the general eligibility requirements for registration).

- registration only by the government of a Member State (for example, algarve, allemagne, alsace);
- use by the EU institutions (for example, unitedeurope, ted, schengen); and
- the use of the .eu Registry (for example, registry, nic, dns, internic, whois).

Applications to register domain names are not made directly to EURid ('the Registry'), but to one of its accredited 'registrars'.[174] Registrars do not have to be established within the EU; indeed of the 1560 accredited registrars in June 2006, 624 were based in the USA.[175]

The ADR procedure for .eu domain name disputes is provided by the Prague-based Arbitration Court attached to the Economic Chamber of the Czech Republic and Agricultural Chamber of the Czech Republic (the 'Czech Arbitration Court', or 'CAC'), which is currently the sole provider. The CAC administers ADR proceedings according to a set of .eu ADR Rules and .eu ADR Supplemental Rules, and in accordance with the public policy rules for the .eu domain set out in **Regulation EC/874/2004**. Under the Rules, complaints are examined by independent panels appointed by the CAC. All necessary information related to the .eu ADR process, including an online arbitration platform, can be located via the ADR .eu website.[176]

The .eu ADR Rules ('.eu ADRR') are based to a considerable extent on the ICANN UDRP, but there are several significant differences. Participation in the .eu ADR process is compulsory for the EURid Registry and for all holders of .eu domain names.[177] The ADR procedure can be initiated by any third-party complainant, against either a registrant whose registration of a .eu domain name is speculative or abusive,[178] or the EURid Registry, if its decisions breach the public policy rules contained in **Regulation EC/874/2004**, or **Regulation EC/733/2002** on the implementation and functions of the .eu TLD.[179] Until a domain name is registered and activated, a proceeding may only be brought against EURid.

The requirements of a valid complaint against EURid under the .eu ADRR are that EURid has made a decision with regard to the registration or non-registration of a domain name that is contrary to the public policy rules contained in **Regulation EC/874/2004**, or **Regulation EC/733/2002**, such as a decision that breaches the 'first come, first served principle',[180] or a decision to revoke a domain name under the grounds contained in Art 20(1)(a)–(c), **Regulation EC/874/2004**.

The requirements of a valid complaint against registrants under the .eu ADRR are:

- the complainant has rights in respect of a name or mark that is recognised or established by the national law of a Member State and/or EU law, and that is identical or confusingly similar to the contested domain name;[181] *and*
- the respondent has no rights or legitimate interest in the name;[182] *or*
- in the hands of the respondent, the domain name is a bad faith registration – that is, one that was registered or otherwise acquired, or has been used in a manner that took unfair advantage of, or was unfairly detrimental to, the complainant's rights.[183]

The first requirement is similar, but not identical, to the first requirement of the UDRP (that the domain name is identical or confusingly similar to a trade mark in which the complainant has

---

174 EC/733/2002, Art 3(4); EC/874/2004, Arts 4 and 5.
175 EURid's quarterly progress report to the European Commission, Second quarter 2006.
176 ADR.eu, online at www.adreu.eurid.eu/
177 EC/874/2004, Art 21(2); and .eu Domain Name Registration Terms and Conditions, s 16(2).
178 EC/874/2004, Art 21(1)(a).
179 Ibid, Art 21(1)(b).
180 Ibid, Art 2.
181 ADRR, para B11(d)(1)(i).
182 Ibid, para B11(d)(1)(ii), in conjunction with para B11(e)(1)–(3)
183 Ibid, para B11(d)(1)(iii), in conjunction with para B11(f)(1)–(5)).

rights). Rights that can be relied upon are those recognised or established by the national law of a Member State or by EU law. These will include, but are not necessarily limited to:

> registered national and community trademarks, geographical indications or designations of origin, and, in as far as they are protected under national law in the Member-State where they are held: unregistered trademarks, trade names, business identifiers, company names, family names, and distinctive titles of protected literary and artistic works.[184]

Where a holder of a right recognised or established by the national law of a Member State or by Community law does not meet the general eligibility requirements for registration, it may use the .eu ADR proceedings to have the domain name revoked, even though it cannot request transfer of the domain name.[185] The question of what is meant by 'confusingly similar' is left unaddressed by Art 21, **Regulation EC/874/2004**, and the ADR Rules. It appears, however, that the ADR panels are inclined to follow the general approach adopted by the UDRP panels. This, as noted above has, after a few fits and starts, in that some WIPO panels flirted with 'likelihood of confusion' and 'initial interest confusion' tests derived from US trade mark law, broadly settled into a straight comparison between the name in which a right is being claimed and the alphanumeric string making up the domain name.[186] It also seems settled that the '.eu' suffix should be disregarded for determining whether the domain name is identical or confusingly similar to the trade mark.[187]

The second requirement largely mirrors that of the second requirement of the UDRP (that the respondent has no right or legitimate interest in respect of the domain name).

The third requirement is broadly similar to that of the third requirement of the UDRP (that the domain name has been registered and is being used in bad faith). However, unlike the UDRP provisions in which the two requirements must both be shown, the second and third requirements are each independently capable of grounding a valid complaint.[188]

There is evidence that panels are going to be willing to look behind certain types of right – particularly Benelux (that is, Belgium, the Netherlands, and Luxembourg) trade marks obtained through the expedited process. In British Olympic Association v Van der Velden Beheer BV,[189] the respondent had registered more than 280 word marks, mainly generic terms, through the Benelux fast-track application procedure. Most of such trade marks were filed for rope ladders and fishing nets in Class 22, which did not show any connection with the respondent's commercial activities. In IAC Search & Media Europe Ltd v First Internet Technology Ltd,[190] the respondent obtained at least 47 marks through the Benelux fast-track application procedure, mostly consisting of an English word for associated goods and services that were generally plectrums. In both cases, the panels refused to accept that the respondents' Benelux trade mark registrations were of themselves sufficient to show a legitimate interest in the registered domain names, and the fact that the respondents' were not using, nor obviously planning to use, the domain names in connection with the offering of goods and services demonstrated that they had no such legitimate interest.

Domain name holders are given some directions on how to show that they have a right or legitimate interests in ADRR, para B11(e)(1)–(3), in which it is stated that if they can demonstrate one of the following criteria to the satisfaction of the panel, based on its evaluation of the available evidence, this will meet their burden under para B11(d)(1)(ii). This list, like UDRP, para 4(c), is

184 Ibid, para B11(d)(1)(i), based on EC/874/2004, Art 21(1).
185 CAC-2300/2006 Seven For All Mankind LLC v Riazul Quadir.
186 CAC-2781/2006 Tempus Enterprises Ltd Stadt Koeln; CAC-1954/2006 Volvo Trademark Holding AB v Tema Syd.
187 CAC-387/2006 Global Network Communication v Holland and Barrett Holdings Ltd; CAC-475/2006 Helsingin Kaupunki v Traffic Web Holding BV.
188 CAC-2727/2006 JS Staedtler GmbH & Co KG v David Fishman.
189 CAC-1369/2006.
190 CAC-2438/2006.

not exhaustive, and thus panels may find a right or legitimate interest to exist based on behaviour outside the three listed criteria – that is, that:

- prior to any notice of the dispute, the domain name holder has used the domain name or a name corresponding to the domain name in connection with the offering of goods or services, or has made demonstrable preparation to do so;
- the domain name holder, being an undertaking, organisation or natural person, has been commonly known by the domain name, even in the absence of a right recognised or established by national and/or EU law; or
- the domain name holder is making a legitimate and non-commercial or fair use of the domain name, without intent to mislead consumers or harm the reputation of a name in which a right is recognised or established by national law and/or EU law.

While the ADRR's right or legitimate interest provisions may have similarities to UDRP, para 4(c), in terms of their respective texts, it would seem that there are some key differences, as follows.

- Under UDRP, para 4(c)(i), rights or legitimate interests to a domain name may be demonstrated by 'before any notice to you of the dispute, your use of, or demonstrable preparations to use, the domain name or a name corresponding to the domain name in connection with a *bona fide* offering of goods or services'.
- Under ADRR, para B1(e)(1), the *bona fide* requirement is omitted, which may leave a loophole for potential cybersquatters.
- Under UDRP, para 4(c)(i), rights or legitimate interests to a domain name may be demonstrated by 'making a legitimate noncommercial or fair use of the domain name, without intent for commercial gain to misleadingly divert consumers or to tarnish the trade mark or service mark at issue'.
- Under ADRR, para B1(e)(3), the last element is replaced by 'harm the reputation of a name in which a right is recognized or established by national law and/or Community law'. This would seem to be a far broader formulation, which could easily be read as excluding non-commercial criticism of the right holder under pejorative domain names, such as 'walmartsucks.com', notwithstanding a fair use, which would be permissible under the UDRP (and the US **ACPA**).

Bettinger also criticises the fact that Art 21(2)(a) of **Regulation EC/874/2004** requires the domain holder to demonstrate a legitimate interest in the domain name, in the form of the offering of goods or services or demonstrable preparation to do so, 'prior to any notice of an alternative dispute resolution (ADR) procedure'. In contrast, UDRP, para 4(c)(i), requires use of, or demonstrable preparations to use, the domain name or a name corresponding to the domain name before any notice of a dispute more generally. Bettinger notes that this would allow a domain holder to use the domain name despite knowing of a dispute with the aim of establishing a 'legitimate interest' prior to the start of a .eu ADR proceeding.[191]

The ADR Rules list five non-exhaustive factors that a panel may consider when assessing whether a domain name has been registered or used in bad faith:

(1) circumstances indicating that the domain name was registered or acquired primarily for the purpose of selling, renting, or otherwise transferring the domain name to the holder of a name, in respect of which a right is recognised or established by national and/or EU law, or to a public body; or

---

191 Bettinger, op cit.

(2)   the domain name has been registered in order to prevent the holder of such a name in respect of which a right is recognised or established by national and/or EU law, or a public body, from reflecting this name in a corresponding domain name, provided that:

    (a)   the respondent has engaged in a pattern of such conduct; or

    (b)   the domain name has not been used in a relevant way for at least two years from the date of registration; or

    (c)   there are circumstances in which, at the time that the ADR proceeding was initiated, the respondent has declared its intention to use the domain name, in respect of which a right is recognised or established by national and/or EU law or which corresponds to the name of a public body, in a relevant way, but failed to do so within six months of the day on which the ADR proceeding was initiated; or

(3)   the domain name was registered primarily for the purpose of disrupting the professional activities of a competitor; or

(4)   the domain name was intentionally used to attract internet users, for commercial gain, to the respondent's website or other online location, by creating a likelihood of confusion with a name in respect of which a right is recognised or established by national and/or EU law, or it is a name of a public body, such likelihood arising as to the source, sponsorship, affiliation, or endorsement of the website or location or of a product or service on the website or location of the respondent; or

(5)   the domain name is a personal name for which no demonstrable link exists between the respondent and the domain name registered.[192]

The first factor is aimed squarely at the issue of cybersquatting. Although the factor suggests that the domain name should have been registered or acquired primarily for the purpose of selling, renting, or otherwise transferring the domain name to a rights holder of a name, or to a public body,[193] it appears that a general offer of sale may be considered sufficient by a panel to demonstrate bad faith.[194]

The second factor is aimed at preventing 'blocking'.

The third and fourth factors map reasonably well to UDRP, para 4(b)(iii)–(iv), with the exception that para 4(b)(iv) only protects trade marks, whereas para B11(f)(4) covers all names in which rights are recognised or established by national and/or EU law, or which correspond to the name of a public body.

The fifth factor has no direct parallel in the UDRP, because it deals with personal names and the UDRP is, in principle, concerned with trade mark rights. It bears a superficial similarity to the provision concerning personal names in the US **ACPA**,[195] but is potentially considerably broader in scope, because it covers both registration and use, and contains none of the provisos that surround the **ACPA** provision.

It will be apparent that there is at least some overlap between the factors for determining whether a domain name holder has a right or legitimate interest in the domain name, and whether he or she has registered or is using the domain name in bad faith, especially with regard to the use made of the domain name. This factor could be used to determine either a lack of a right or legitimate interest in the domain name, or bad faith registration and usage.

Complaints must be decided by the panel on the basis of the statements and documents submitted, and in accordance with the procedural rules, which consist of the .eu ADRR, the

---

192 ADDR, para B11(f)(1)–(5), based on EC/874/2004, Art 21(3)(a)–(e).
193 CAC-2684/2006 NV Raymond Van Marcke v Citizen Engineering Services Ltd.
194 CAC-1644/2006 Dansk Internet Forum v Zhonglan.
195 15 USC § 1129, see above at p 301.

Supplemental ADRR, and EU Regulations. In the event of a conflict between the elements of the procedural rules, the EU Regulations must take precedence.[196] If the panel concludes that a complaint against a decision of EURid satisfies the requirements specified in the policy, it directs that the decision be annulled; if not, the complaint is rejected. If the panel concludes that a complaint against a registrant satisfies the requirements specified in the policy, it directs that the domain name should be revoked or transferred to the complainant; if not, the complaint is rejected.

Developing Areas

Preventative Domain Name Registration Mechanisms: 'Sunrise Periods'

As new gTLDs (for example, '.info', '.mobi') and ccTLDs (for example, '.pk', '.eu') have been created, their registries have attempted to tackle the problem of cybersquatting by allowing organisations, companies, and individuals to protect their trade marks and other legally protected names against abusive registration by cybersquatters through a phased registration process, or 'sunrise period'.

For example, for the .eu ccTLD, a two-phase 'sunrise period' was established.[197] During this period, registration was limited to particular categories of applicant. Only after the expiry of the sunrise period did open registration – often referred to as the 'landrush period' – begin.

Phase 1 of the sunrise period began on 7 December 2005 and ran until 6 February 2006. During this phase, the following categories of applicant could register .eu domain names:

- anyone who met the EU eligibility criteria, and was:
    - a public body; or
    - a holder/licensee of a trade mark; or
    - a holder of a geographical indication or denomination of origin.

Phase 2 began on 7 February 2006 and ran until 6 April 2006. During this phase, the following categories of applicant could register .eu domain names:

- anyone who met the EU eligibility criteria, and was:
    - eligible to apply under Phase 1; or
    - a holder of any other prior right protected under the national law of the Member State in which it was held.

All applications during the sunrise period were subject to prior validation by EURid's appointed validation agent – PricewaterhouseCoopers – and applicants were required to provide a range of mandatory information for this purpose. It was clear that, even within the sunrise period, there were likely to be multiple applicants for many domain names, because more than one party may hold an identical, or very similar, registered or unregistered mark due to their use of the mark in conjunction with different types of product or service, or in different national markets. Thus, within the sunrise period, legitimate applications were dealt with on a first-come, first-served basis: for example, if three parties claimed registered trade marks on the word 'merlin', the fastest one to apply would be given first chance to validate its right to the domain name 'merlin.eu'. In the event

---

196 ADRR, para B11(a), in conjunction with para A1 'Procedural Rules'.
197 EC/874/2004, Art 10.

that the first applicant failed to present adequate documentation to authenticate its trade mark within a 40-day period, the second-fastest applicant's documentation would be examined, and so on, until an adequately authenticated registration was accepted. Once a registration was accepted, there was then a 40-day 'sunrise appeal period' during which other applicants were able to initiate an ADR procedure against the decision of EURid to effect registration. Therefore, a domain name, even when already applied for, remained open for continuing application by other parties until its actual activation.

During the sunrise period, a total of 346,218 applications were filed for 245,908 different domain names. It will be obvious, therefore, that, in many cases, two or more applicants were claiming a prior right in relation to the same domain name. Indeed, in some cases, the difference between a successful registration and failure could be measured in seconds under the first-come, first-served principle. The scope for disputes was obvious, even in the absence of attempts at cyber-squatting. Despite the use of the sunrise period, it is clear that the .eu registration process failed to prevent significant numbers of problematic registrations, even during the restricted registration periods. This was essentially due to the wide scope of prior rights that could be used to claim eligibility to register domain names during the period of phased registration,[198] and to textual ambiguities in **Regulation EC/874/2004**.

There was clear evidence of cybersquatting and warehousing by registrants of both generic domain names, and domain names identical to, or very similar to, names or marks in which a third party had rights recognised or established by the national law of a Member State and/or EU law. A large part of the problem arose from the expedited process for registration of a Benelux trade mark, available via the Benelux Trademark Office, which saw a flood of expedited 'bad faith' trade mark registrations at the end of 2005 in anticipation of the .eu launch. This process permitted would-be cybersquatters and warehousers to obtain Benelux trade marks in periods as short as 48 hours, and in full knowledge of the potential loopholes in the registration rules, either for the sunrise period, or generally.[199]

An example of a loophole in the registration rules is the lack of clarity in **Regulation EC/874/2004**, Art 11, regarding the registration of domain names based on trade marks that include special characters, spaces, or punctuations. This led to the registration, during the sunrise period, of hundreds of domain names such as barcelona.eu, frankfurt.eu, and petrom.eu, on the basis of Benelux word trade marks of, respectively, BARC & ELONA (trade mark applied for on 28 November 2005, granted on 30 November 2005), FRANKF & URT (trade mark applied for on 30 November 2005, granted on 2 December 2005), and PET & ROM (trade mark applied for 20 March 2006, granted 22 March 2006), in relation to which the holder of the Benelux mark claimed to have the right under Art 11 to decide whether the ampersand, as a special character, should be 'eliminated entirely from the corresponding domain name, replaced with hyphens, or, if possible, rewritten'. There can be little doubt as to the motives of some of the registrants in registering the Benelux trade marks, where hundreds of marks were registered and then almost immediately used to file applications for .eu domain names identical to the names of cities and existing famous brands. Many of these domain names have since been transferred via .eu ADR decisions to legitimate trade mark holders.[200]

---

198 Ibid, Art 10(2).
199 See, eg, CAC-35/2006 *Leonie Vestering v EURid*.
200 See above at p 309. A key difficulty in the .eu process was that the ADR process during the sunrise period (the sunrise appeal period) was restricted to challenges to decisions of EURid to register or not to register a domain name – actions could not be begun against registrants. The .eu ADR panels were not given direct jurisdiction to deal with obvious 'bad faith' applications and, where those applications had followed the letter of the registration requirements in EC/874/2004, it was hard for complainants to argue convincingly that EURid had unreasonably registered the relevant domain names. EURid claimed, not without some justification, that the Regulations did not oblige it, or its validation agent, to look behind the registration formalities for evidence of bad faith. Complainants thus had to wait until the sunrise appeal period ended to initiate an ADR proceeding against the registrant, based on violation of EC/874/2004, Art 21.

Later gTLDs appear to have learned from the .eu registration process, and have taken steps to reduce the Benelux trade mark problem with respect to their sunrise periods. For example, in order for their holders to participate during the .mobi sunrise period, trade marks had to have been registered before 11 July 2005 (the date on which dotMobi signed its contract with ICANN), or have been applied for before that date, and registered by the time of domain name registration. However, many trade mark holders remain dissatisfied with the protection that they are granted.

> ... the 'sunrise' registration period employed by some registries is nothing more than an extremely expensive method of defensively registering brand names. Where a brand owner owns dozens of brands or more and there are hundreds of new gTLDs, sunrise registrations will be too expensive to even contemplate.[201]

Internationalised Domain Names (IDNs)

Because much of the initial development of internet services was carried out either by English speakers, or by formal or informal groups for whom the *lingua franca* was English, the character encoding scheme that was adopted for computer communications was the American Standard Code for Information Interchange (ASCII) based on the English alphabet. ASCII includes definitions for 94 printable characters; of these, a subset of 37 were adopted for use in the domain name system (26 letters of the Latin alphabet, ten digits, the hyphen, and the dot). Domain names are case-insensitive. Since the original implementation, two factors have driven a demand for a wider range of characters to be available. The first is the fact that while English remains the largest single language in use on the internet, the percentage of internet users for whom English is a first language is estimated to be about 25–30 per cent of the general internet user population, with users for whom Chinese is their first language between 15–20 per cent. Thus, the greater proportion of internet users are non-native English speakers. The second factor is that using the original ASCIII subset provides a limited number of viable domain names.

With this in mind, work was undertaken to develop a system that is capable of dealing with domain names containing non-ASCII characters. Making significant changes to the existing domain name system, including entirely reconfiguring how browsers and email packages handle domain names, was seen as impractical. The solution, adopted in 2003, is called 'Internationalizing Domain Names in Applications' (IDNA).[202] IDNA extends the number of characters that can be used in domain names to include Unicode characters (with some restrictions),[203] by using an ASCII representation of the non-ASCII elements of a domain name. An IDNA-enabled application can convert between the restricted-ASCII and non-ASCII representations of a domain, using the ASCII form in cases in which it is needed – such as for domain name server (DNS) lookup – but presenting the more readable non-ASCII form to users.[204] This allows a business that operates in a particular region (or wants to reach a community from that region) that does not use ASCII characters to represent its domain name on the internet using its native character set.

---

201 E Thomas Watson, Assistant General Counsel, Bank of America Corporation, Comment to ICANN on new gTLD Draft Applicant Handbook, 15 December 2008, available online at http://forum.icann.org/lists/gtld-guide/pdfynPfMoj3Jy.pdf
202 See further FAQs.org, 'Internationalising domain names in applications (IDNA)', RFC3490, available online at www.faqs.org/rfcs/rfc3490.html
203 Unicode contains more than 100,000 characters, and covers almost all writing systems in current use: see further The Unicode Consortium, online at http://unicode.org/
204 Punycode is a computer programming encoding syntax by which a Unicode string of characters can be translated into the more limited character set permitted in network host names. The encoding syntax is published on the internet in 'Request for Comments 3492', RFC 3492.

> The domain name to be encoded is Zürich.com. This has two 'labels': 'Zürich' and 'com'. The second label is entirely ASCII and so is left unchanged. The first label is processed using the IDNA process to become 'zrich-kva', and then has 'xn–' prepended to give 'xn--zrich-kva'. The final domain suitable for use with the DNS is therefore 'xn--zrich-kva.com'.

Domain name input by user	Non-ASCII	zürich.com
IDNA-processed domain name	Restricted ASCII	xn--zrich-kva.com
Domain name input by user	Non-ASCII	tūdaliņ.lv
IDNA-processed domain name	Restricted ASCII	xn--tdali-d8a8w.lv/
Domain name input by user	Non-ASCII	中国互联网络信息中心.cn
IDNA-processed domain name	Restricted ASCII	xn--fiqa61au8b7zsevnm8ak20mc4a87e.cn

By early 2009, internationalised domain names (IDNs) were only available in some of the existing TLDs. Of those TLDs, many restricted the types of IDN available.[205] The establishment of new internationalised country code TLDs in 2010 means that IDNs will become more prevalent in the future.

As noted by several commentators,[206] IDNs can pose a number of potential legal problems, not least because several characters (glyphs) in non-Latin scripts are identical to glyphs in the Latin alphabet, but have a different Unicode character encodings, for example:

Domain name (Latin)	Non-ASCII	microsoft.com
IDNA-processed domain name	Restricted ASCII	microsoft.com
Domain name (Latin + *Cyrillic*)	Non-ASCII	microsoft.com
IDNA-processed domain name	Restricted ASCII	xn--mirsft-yqfbx.com

The possibility of confusion between phonetically similar or visually similar IDNs may be used for spoofing or phishing, as well as cybersquatting. However, to date, no cases appear to have come before UDRP panels.

Equally, registrants can register domain names in non-Latin alphabets that are identical to a famous name or trade mark. An example of this can be seen in *Citizen Watch (China) Co Ltd v Cheng Zhi Gang*,[207] in which a Chinese citizen registered the domain name 西铁城.com, the complainant having registered '西铁城' ('CITIZEN' in normal Chinese characters) as a trade mark in China. This means that trade mark holders may have to register yet more domain names to cover all possible language variations of their marks.

While the number of UDRP panel decisions involving IDNs remains relatively small at present, and almost entirely related to direct trade mark infringement, as more TLDs accept IDNs, or widen the range of characters sets that they will accept, it is likely that such issues will become more common. ICANN is also currently testing IDN TLDs in eleven different scripts, with the aim of introducing them as new gTLDs.[208]

---

205 The .com gTLD provides IDNs in 113 different languages, using the following character sets: Arabic; Armenian; Bengali; Bopomofo; Cherokee; Cyrillic; Devanagari; Ethiopic; Georgian; Greek; Gurmukhi; Han (Chinese, Japanese, and Korean ideographs); Hangul; Hebrew; Hiragana; Kannada; Katakana; Khmer; Lao; Latin; Malayalam; Mongolian; Myanmar; Oriya; Sinhala; Syriac; Tamil; Telugu; Thaana; Thai; Tibetan; Yi (Unicode 3.2). The .org gTLD provides IDNs in ten different languages. The .uk ccTLD does not currently register IDNs.

206 Evgeniy Gabrilovich and Alex Gontmakher, 'The homograph attack' (2002) 45(2) Commun ACM 128; Caroline Wilson, 'Internationalised domain names: Problems and opportunities' (2004) 10(7) CTLR 174; Oleksandr Pastukhov, 'Internationalised domain names: The window of opportunity for cybersquatters' (2006) 4 IPQ 421.

207 WIPO Case No D2001-1305; see also WIPO Case No D2002-0357 *Iwasaki Corp and Iwasaki Hotels*; NAF Claim No FA0305000158427 *TÜV Rheinland eV v Hamdan GmbH Corp v Mitaden Co Ltd* (2003); NAF Claim No FA0804001176666 *Yahoo! Inc v Sergey Korshunov* (2008).

208 Simplified Chinese; traditional Chinese; Japanese; Hindi; Russian; Yiddish; Persian; Greek; Arabic.

Additional TLD Names

In June 2008, ICANN approved the introduction of a new range of gTLDs, with the aim of accepting applications in mid-2009. ICANN stated that the new gTLDs would provide more innovation, choice, and competition on the internet, especially for non-English language domains. The new gTLDs would be anywhere from three to 63 characters in length, and could support Chinese, Arabic, and other scripts. ICANN suggested that applications for new gTLDs would be accepted in the first quarter of 2012. New internationalised ccTLDs were launched in June 2010, allowing the use of non-ASCII ccLDs, such as one using Cyrillic, .рФ (for Russia).

The proposal could potentially permit the creation of as many new gTLDs as there are presently domain names in the .com TLD. It could allow, for example, Amazon.com Inc to own a gTLD '.amazon' with second-level domains such as '.uk.amazon' and '.france.amazon' instead of its current '.amazon.co.uk' and '.amazon.fr', or perhaps '.books.amazon' and '.cds.amazon'. In parallel with the development of IDNs, it could also permit '.中国.amazon' (or even '.中国.阿玛逊') instead of '.amazon.cn'.

However, the proposal does not mean that anyone will be able to register a gTLD – there are two main barriers. The first is likely to be the cost. ICANN has suggested that the cost of registering a gTLD will be about US$185,000 and that there will then be an annual charge of US$75,000 to keep that gTLD in the DNS root zone. The second is the administrative process that ICANN has proposed to which each new gTLD application would be subjected. Under the draft procedure, each application would be posted for public comment; during this period, the 'string' (for example, '.amazon') would be subject to initial evaluation, comprising TLD string evaluation of:

- *DNS stability* – that is, whether an applied-for gTLD string might cause instability to the DNS;
- *string confusion* – that is, whether an applied-for gTLD string might create a probability of detrimental user confusion against existing TLDs and against other applied-for gTLD strings; and
- *geographical names* – that is, whether an applied-for gTLD might represent a geographic name, in which case the applicant must provide a letter of support or non-objection from the relevant government.

It would then be subject to applicant evaluation covering:

- *financial capability* – that is, the provision of adequate information about an applicant's financial capabilities to operate a gTLD registry business and its financial planning in preparation for long-term operation of a new gTLD;
- *technical and operational capability* – that is, a demonstration of a clear understanding of the key technical and operational aspects of running a gTLD registry, and some evidence of preparation; and
- *registry services* – that is, determination of whether a proposed registry service requires further consideration based on whether the registry service may raise significant security or stability issues.

If the application were to fail initial evaluation, then the applicant could apply for extended evaluation. If it were to pass initial evaluation, the application would be subject to objection proceedings on the following grounds:

- *string confusion* – that is, an applied-for gTLD string is confusingly similar to an existing TLD or to another applied for gTLD string;
- *legal rights* – that is, an applied-for gTLD string infringes existing legal rights of the objector;
- *morality and public order* – that is, an applied-for gTLD string is contrary to generally accepted legal norms of morality and public order that are recognised under international principles of law; or

- *community objection* – that is, there is substantial opposition to the gTLD application from a significant portion of the community to which the gTLD string may be explicitly or implicitly targeted.

If the applicant were to pass objection proceedings, the application would be subject to a string contention process. 'String contention' refers to the scenario in which there is more than one qualified applicant for the same gTLD or for gTLDs that are so similar that they create a probability of detrimental user confusion if more than one is delegated. ICANN has proposed to resolve cases of string contention either through comparative evaluation or through an alternative mechanism for efficient resolution, such as an auction. Only if all of these stages were passed successfully would the gTLD be registered.

ICANN's decision to move ahead with the expansion of gTLDs was not uncontroversial. Significant numbers of high-profile companies expressed major concerns about the implications of the proposed expansion – for example:

> We do not believe there is significant demand from businesses or consumers for additional gTLDs to host commercial sites . . . Additional top level domains, will, however, offer unprecedented opportunities for the registration of new second level domain names that are deliberately confusingly similar to existing second level registrations or to legally protected brand names, without offering any countervailing benefits . . . Brand owners have found it necessary to 'defensively' register their brands, common misspellings and variations of their brands in existing gTLDs in order to prevent consumer confusion between sites legitimately associated with their products and services and those that are not. As pointed out in our introduction, we currently own a portfolio of over 11,500 essentially useless domain names. For the most part, their existence benefits only the registrars that maintain them and the registries that host them.[209]

The US government also intervened with a response from the Commerce Department's National Telecommunications and Information Administration (NTIA), citing various concerns including over 'how ICANN will conduct legal reviews of applications, consider legal objections from third parties, and discharge its responsibility to ensure that the process of introducing new gTLDs respects all relevant national and international law, including intellectual property rights'.

It appears that these concerns will lead to, at the very least, a rethink of how further TLDs will be created and allocated, and may, in fact, halt significant expansion of gTLDs for the foreseeable future.

---

209 E Thomas Watson, Assistant General Counsel, Bank of America Corporation, Comment to ICANN on new gTLD Draft Applicant Handbook, 15 December 2008, available online at http://forum.icann.org/lists/gtld-guide/pdfynPfMoj3Jy.pdf

Chapter 9

Copyright and the Internet

Introduction

The internet has created new methods of delivering and disseminating creative content online that has had a significant impact on the market in creative works. The rate of change can be appreciated by considering that, in 2007, it was forecast that, by 2010, revenue in Europe from online content would reach €8.3 billion, representing a growth of 400 per cent in five years.[1] However, just as computer networks created new ways of committing traditional crime, so they provided new ways of infringing copyright. Some of these issues are the generic ones that have already been identified such as jurisdiction, detection, and enforcement, but others are specific to the law of copyright. Cornish and Llewellyn have referred to the internet and copyright as 'the most inflamed issue in current intellectual property',[2] and developing uses of this medium continue to challenge the traditional principles of copyright; as Ganley has commented, 'the internet has ruffled the feathers of copyright law'.[3] Indeed, the phrase 'digital copyright' is sometimes used misleadingly as an indication of another species of copyright with different rules, rather than an application of the existing rules to the digital environment, together with an attempt to draw an appropriate balance between authors' and users' rights in this context. This chapter will consider, in particular, some of the general issues relating to the application of copyright principles to a new medium, together with associated changes in the law in both Europe and the USA, using the practical examples of hypertext links, the operation of search engines and file-sharing. Before considering how the law has responded to the issues, we will consider the origins of the problems that have been encountered.[4]

As every student knows, copying of material from the vast information source that is the internet is a trivial matter; similarly, the technology also makes it a trivial matter to make existing copyright works available on the internet. Examples of the latter range from individuals putting copyright works on YouTube, to major initiatives such as the Google Print Library Project,[5] but application of the law of copyright to these issues has not always proved to be straightforward and has frequently been controversial. The conundrum at the heart of traditional copyright law is how to balance the respective rights of the creator and user of copyright material. As noted in the Preamble to the **Information Society Directive**, 'a fair balance of rights and interests between the different categories of rightholders, as well as between the different categories of rightholders and users of protected subject matter must be safeguarded'.[6] It goes without saying that there is an inherent tension between these rights – that 'conflict is at the heart of copyright'.[7] How should this balance be struck on the internet? There are those who suggest that the ethos and culture of the internet is radically different from previous media to the extent that copyright is no longer an appropriate vehicle for protecting the rights of authors and creators; because copyright originated and developed in a very different era, it may have outlived its usefulness.[8] One problem with this approach is that although the original culture of the internet may have been one of openness and

---

1 See Communication from the Commission to the European Parliament the Council, the European Economic and Social Committee, and the Committee of the Regions on Creative Content Online in the Single Market, COM(2007)836 final, and also European Commission, *Creative Content in A European Digital Single Market: Challenges for the Future*, A Reflection Document of DG INFSO and DG MARKT, 22 October 2009, available online at http://ec.europa.eu/avpolicy/docs/other_actions/col_2009/reflection_paper.pdf

2 WR Cornish and D Llewellyn, *Intellectual Property*, 6th edn, 2007, London: Sweet and Maxwell, p 842.

3 Paul Ganley, 'Digital copyright and the new creative dynamics' (2004) 12 IJLIT 282.

4 For a more detailed review of the major issues relating to intellectual property on the internet, see, eg, World Intellectual Property Organization (WIPO), *The Impact of the Internet on Intellectual Property Law*, 2002, Geneva: WIPO, available online at www.wipo.int/copyright/en/ecommerce/ip_survey/chap3.html, ch 3 of which is devoted to copyright matters.

5 See further discussion on p 332.

6 Directive 2001/29/EC of the European Parliament and of the Council on the harmonisation of certain aspects of copyright and related rights in the information society [2001] OJ L167/10, Recital 31.

7 Karla M O'Regan, 'Downloading personhood: A Hegelian theory of copyright law' (2009) 7 Can J L & Tech 1, 11.

8 For representative arguments, see, eg, JP Barlow, 'Selling wine without bottles: The economy of mind on the global net', in P Bernt Hugenholtz (ed), *The Future of Copyright in a Digital Environment*, 1996, The Hague: Kluwer; C Kergévant, 'Are copyright and *droit d'auteur* viable in the light of information technology?' (1996) 10 Int Rev LCT 55.

inclusivity, the vast and diverse spectrum of both uses and users of the internet now make identification of a prevailing ethos far more problematic. Others support a relaxation of traditional copyright rules for the purely pragmatic reason that jurisdictional issues and problems of detection make copyright law difficult to enforce in practice. In contrast to this, others are of the view that copyright still has a role to play in encouraging imagination and originality in whatever medium is at issue, simply because material continues to be created that is the proper subject matter of copyright protection.[9] In other words, the concept of copyright is still a necessary one, albeit with a recognition that it may need modification or amendment if it is to be able to respond appropriately to contemporary challenges. Schønning[10] points out that the internet is no more likely to lead to a mass breakdown in the copyright system any more than happened when it had to deal with other forms of piracy and illicit copying of easy-to-copy media, such as videos, audiotapes, computer software, etc, and simply concludes thus: '. . . surely copyright will survive even this legal and technological challenge.' Wiese,[11] having reviewed the arguments on both sides, came to the conclusion that there are still reasons to rely on copyright law, that it should not be regarded as a threat to the internet society, and that an appropriate balance between competing interests was possible. He came to the conclusion that a concept that had been developed over decades should be adjusted to fit the new circumstances rather than abolished – 'the question is not so much whether copyright can adapt at all but rather how it should adapt'.[12]

The existence of copyright protection is assumed to stimulate the creative process and, in this vein, a clause was included in art 1 of the US **Constitution** giving Congress the power 'to promote the progress of science and useful arts, by securing for limited times to authors and inventors the exclusive right to their respective writings and discoveries'. But it has always been the case that there is a wider public interest, not only in the creation of copyright works, but also in such works being available for the use and enjoyment of citizens at large. It is commonly stated that the purpose of intellectual property protection in general, and of copyright in particular, is to provide an incentive for creativity by ensuring that creators are justly rewarded for their creativity and that a remedy is available in cases of infringement. In providing creators with control over dissemination and reproduction, the resources that went into the creative process can be recompensed. At the same time, authorised acts and exceptions provide lawful users with certain rights to utilise the material. Taking such factors into account, the law of copyright seeks to balance the rights of the user and the rights of the creator in an optimum fashion. However, what is an appropriate balance in relation to traditional means of dissemination may not be appropriate for the digital environment, in which the distinction between users and creators has been blurred. Materials in a whole host of formats – text, audio, video etc – can now be distributed and copied 'with extraordinary ease and accuracy'.[13]

This chapter will concentrate in the main on issues that have no straightforward parallel in traditional media, including the copyright issues generated by the use of hyperlinks, search engines, file-sharing, and including liability issues in relation to both individuals and ISPs. A number of these issues are interrelated and those specific to intermediary liability have been examined elsewhere. The discussion in this chapter focuses purely on the application and interpretation of copyright principles in the context of the internet; a fuller picture will be obtained by reading both chapters in conjunction. Disputes that have arisen include those between

See Chapter 3

---

9 See, eg, Ejan Mackaay, 'The economics of emergent property rights on the internet', in P Bernt Hugenholtz (ed), *The Future of Copyright in a Digital Environment*, 1996, The Hague: Kluwer, p 18.

10 Peter Schønning, 'Internet and the applicable copyright law: A Scandinavian perspective' [1999] EIPR 45. For a summary of the challenges facing copyright law, see also JAL Sterling, 'Philosophical and legal challenges in the context of copyright and digital technology' (2000) 31 IIC 508; Simon Fitzpatrick 'Copyright imbalance: US and Australian responses to the WIPO Digital Copyright Treaty' [2000] EIPR 214, esp 214–18.

11 Henning Wiese, 'The justification of the information society in the digital age' [2002] EIPR 387.

12 Ibid, 393.

13 Cornish and Llewelyn, op cit, p 842.

traditional newspapers and news websites involving linking to news reports, complaints relating to file-sharing by means of software such as Napster, Grokster, and KaZaa, and complaints against search engines and ISPs for facilitating access to copyright material. The burgeoning quantity of user-generated content on the internet on sites such as YouTube, social networking sites, and blogs includes the whole spectrum from content generated by the individuals themselves, which they make available for free to copyright material, or modified copyright material, which is made available in breach of copyright, performing rights, etc. It is perhaps thus not surprising that many users perceive that the internet provides a repository of freely available material and pay scant attention to the rights of copyright holders, if indeed they are even aware that there are such rights holders. How is an equitable balance of rights to be determined in an environment in which a dominant ethos is one of free, and freely shared, material, but also one that has become colonised by commercial operators and those whose living is made by creating and/or trading in copyright works? Digitisation of major collections of papers and books, etc, for example, may be in the interests of those who wish to access their contents, but may not always be in the interests of the copyright holders, especially if the ability to control dissemination would otherwise provide a significant part of their income.[14] Popular opinion may not sympathise with large record companies and publishing houses,[15] but may be more understanding of the plight of the struggling author or musician. The technology itself may provide a means of control and the use of copy protection devices has been enshrined in law in some jurisdictions although not without controversy.[16] Although there are a number of international treaties and conventions on copyright, copyright law is a matter for individual jurisdictions. This raises further questions of how copyright principles that are already enshrined in national laws should be applied and how any lack of global harmonisation is to be dealt with when the medium, itself, is a global one. Millé[17] indicates that the solution itself must necessarily be global; that copyright law needs to find answers to the questions posed by the presence of new modes of intellectual creation, of distribution to the public, and of use and enjoyment of the works; that there is a need to make the treatment given to intangible property uniform at world level; and that administration by an international organisation appears essential. However, some other commentators, having considered the various arguments, have sounded a note of caution about the consequences of being in too much haste to introduce new or amended legislative rules.[18]

Hyperlinks

The phenomenon of hypertext linking, which allows the user to move from site to site, is now so familiar as to have lost all remaining vestiges of novelty, but is indisputably crucial to the existence and operation of the world wide web. A hyperlink has been judicially referred to as a 'cross-reference . . . appearing on one page that, when activated by the point-and-click of a mouse, brings onto the computer screen another web page'.[19] Linking provides the way in which information is retrieved via search engines and is the way in which users move from site to site. The web pioneer,

---

14 Many major libraries have digitisation projects: see, eg, details of the British Library digitisation project available online at www.bl.uk/aboutus/stratpolprog/digi/digitisation/index.html. The National Library of Wales digitisation project caused some controversy: see, eg, www.literaturewales.org/libraries-in-wales/i/134826/. See also the Google Books project litigation discussed below at p 332.

15 See, eg, Konstantinos Stylianou, 'ELSA Copyright Survey: What does the young generation believe about copyright?' [2009] IPQ 391.

16 See later discussion at pp 348–351.

17 Antonio Millé 'Copyright in the cyberspace era' [1997] EIPR 570.

18 See, eg, Lionel Bently and Robert Burrell, 'Copyright and the information society in Europe: A matter of timing as well as content' (1997) 34 CMLR 1197, 1208.

19 *Universal City Studios v Corley* 273 F 3d 429, 455 (2nd Cir 2001).

Berners-Lee, suggested that it should be possible to link to any piece of information as 'universality is essential to the Web: it loses its power if there are certain types of things to which you can't link'.[20] At a practical level, a site with few links is less likely to be found by other users and its worth will also be diminished to the user if he or she cannot travel from that site to another. Conversely, many people will bookmark sites to compile a collection of links to sites relevant to their interests. The number of times different users arrive at a site (the number of 'hits') is a useful way of gauging the site's appeal and popularity, as well as the efficiency of its links; for commercial sites in particular, the number of hits may be an important way of raising advertising revenue. Given the fact that the world wide web cannot function without links, does the fact of launching a website create an implied licence to link to it? Or could there be something akin to a right to link?[21] Various real-world analogies have been suggested for hypertext links. In *Universal City Studios v Reimerdes*,[22] it was said that 'links bear a relationship to the information superhighway comparable to the relationship that roadway signs bear to roads but they are more functional. Like roadway signs, they point out the direction'. An alternative analogy is that of the footnote or reference. Burk explains that 'the hypertext link is in essence an automated version of a scholarly footnote or bibliographic reference: it tells the reader where to find the referenced material',[23] and Deveci has made the categorical comment that 'a link is no different from a citation in hard copy'.[24] However, although a link may conceptually perform both of these apparently disparate purposes, in each case it goes beyond the functionality of the corresponding real-world analogy. As the court in *Reimerdes* went on to say, 'unlike roadway signs, [links] take one almost instantaneously to the desired destination with the mere click of an electronic mouse'. The same is clearly true for the citation/reference analogy as graphically explained by Burk: '. . . the user's browser . . . can then retrieve the material from its location, a process that is not only hidden from the user, but far more convenient than physically venturing into library stacks to retrieve hardcopy referenced in a plain footnote.' The adoption of such analogies could have a potential impact on the liability of the linkor. If a link is merely a pointer that the user may or may not choose to follow, the question is whether the linkor should be liable if the link provides access to unlawful material – specifically, in the context of this chapter, to material that infringes copyright. If a link is merely a reference, writers would not expect to find themselves liable for copyright infringement on the basis of an infringement in a work cited in a footnote; why should a different situation pertain in relation to links? To what extent should any additional functionality that links provide affect the potential liability of the linkor?

There have been a number of cases on linking and intellectual property rights; some of these, such as *Reimerdes* above, concern direct links to allegedly infringing material, and these will be considered further below in relation to file-sharing cases. Other disputes involve whether there is a right for third parties to link to a site, or whether the manner in which this is accomplished can infringe the copyright or other intellectual property rights of the host site. Typically, such cases involve so-called 'deep' linking, whereby the link bypasses the home page and directs the user to another page hosted by the site, or 'framing', in which the linked-to site opens within the 'frame' provided by the linking site and so, at first glance, can easily appear to be material created by or hosted on the original site. Few non-commercial sites and users seem to complain about links – probably because such sites are keen to take advantage of the intrinsic functionality of the web both

---

20 Tim Berners-Lee, 'Realising the full potential of the Web', Presentation at W3C meeting, London, 3 December 1997, available online at www.w3.org/1998/02/Potential.html
21 See comment from Berners-Lee, in an online article, that 'the ability to refer to a document . . . is in general a fundamental right of free speech to the same extent that speech is free. Making the reference with a hypertext link is more efficient but changes nothing else': 'Links and law: Myths', 1997, available online at www.w3.org/DesignIssues/LinkMyths.html
22 111 F Supp 2d 294 (SDNY 2000).
23 Dan L Burk, 'Proprietary rights in hypertext linkages' (1998) 2 JILT, available online at www2.warwick.ac.uk/fac/soc/law/elj/jilt/1998_2/burk/
24 Hasan A Deveci, 'Hyperlinks oscillating at the crossroads' (2004) 10 CTLR 82, 84.

to link and to be linked to in order to disseminate their information more efficiently and effectively. However, commercial actors, although obviously wishing to use the same functionality, are often equally concerned to be able to exert some control over how and in what circumstances links are created, resulting in a number of cases in which the manner in which links are made has been challenged. Deep links are often not popular with commercial sites for a number of reasons. Revenue may be generated by the number of 'hits' on adverts hosted on the home page that will be lost if the home page is bypassed. A number of cases have involved deep links to underlying databases – the commercial site may typically be trading in tickets for entertainment, flights, or whatever, which it sources via access to its database. Clearly, the contents of the database have significant commercial value that will be lost if other websites can link directly to the database, rather than deal with the business via its home page in the intended manner.[25] An early example is provided by the US case of *Ticketmaster Corp v Microsoft Corp*,[26] in which a website containing a city guide to Seattle linked directly to Ticketmaster pages providing details of events and tickets, bypassing the home page. In tandem with this line of cases are disputes involving the operation of search engines, another intrinsic feature of the internet and world wide web facilitated by linking technology.

See Chapter 3 →

The first case to consider such matters was *Shetland Times v Wills*,[27] which, unsurprisingly, received substantial debate and comment despite being only an interlocutory hearing.[28] The *Shetland Times* is an old established newspaper, serving the Shetland Islands. Wills, an ex-employee of the *Shetland Times*, started an electronic newspaper, the *Shetland News*. When its site was accessed, the reader would see a selection of headlines, on which he or she could click to read the full story. Some of these headlines were reproduced verbatim from the *Shetland Times* website and, when these particular hypertext links were followed, the reader would be taken directly to the story on the *Shetland Times* site, bypassing the *Shetland Times* home page, using a deep link. There was no suggestion that the actual stories had been copied from one site to the other, but the *Shetland Times* alleged that its copyright in both the headlines and the stories themselves had been infringed. The bulk of the discussion was whether or not the accessing of material via the web could be likened to a cable programme and an injunction was issued on the basis that the information could be deemed to be *sent* from the *Shetland Times* website rather than wait passively to be accessed. Although this reasoning is no longer current, the court additionally considered that the copyright in the headlines could be infringed. Whilst not all headlines will attract copyright protection, it was noted that some of them 'involve eight or so words designedly put together for the purpose of imparting information'[29] and so were therefore a proper subject for copyright protection. Although not a case about linking as such, it may be noted in passing that similar reasoning was employed both in the European Court of Justice (ECJ)'s judgment in *Infopaq International v Danske Dagblades Forening*[30] and in the Belgian Court of First Instance in *Copiepresse SCRL v Google*. In the Belgian case, the Court found that the headlines and first few lines of articles from newspapers, which had been aggregated with articles on the same news stories from other sources to supply the Google News service, could

---

25 Such information can also be extracted by 'bots', 'spiders', or 'webcrawlers': see, eg, the facts of *eBay v Bidders Edge* 100 F Supp 2d 1058 (ND Cal 2000).
26 See http://legal.web.aol.com/decisions/dlip/tickcomp.html
27 1997 SLT 669; [1997] FSR 604.
28 See, eg, KJ Campbell, 'Copyright on the internet: The view from Shetland' [1997] EIPR 255; James P Connolly and Scott Cameron, 'Fair dealing in webbed links of Shetland yarn' [1998] JILT, available online at www2.warwick.ac.uk/fac/soc/law/elj/jilt/1998_2/connolly/; Hector L MacQueen, 'Copyright in cyberspace: *Shetland Times v Wills*' [1998] JBL 297. For comparison with other linking cases, see, eg, Chris Reed, 'Controlling world wide web links: Property rights, access rights and unfair competition' (1998) 6 Indiana J Global LS 167; Mark Sableman, 'Link law revisited: Internet linking law at five years' (2001) 16 Berkeley Technology LJ 1273; Diane Rowland and Andrew Campbell, 'Content and access agreements: An analysis of some of the legal issues arising from linking and framing' (2002) 16 Int Rev LCT 171.
29 1997 SLT 669, 671.
30 Case C-5/08 [2009] ECR I-6569.

feasibly be eligible for copyright protection.[31] In the *Infopaq* case, copyright infringement was alleged against Infopaq for producing customised summaries of selected articles from newspapers on the basis of previously specified search criteria. Customers were then emailed the publication details of all of the relevant pages from the search, which provided the context of the story by including the five words immediately before and after the search term. Article 2(a) of **Directive 2001/29/EC**[32] provides that authors shall be given the 'exclusive right to authorise or prohibit direct or indirect, temporary or permanent reproduction by any means and in any form, in whole or part' of their works. Article 5 then provides for certain exemptions, which the ECJ pointed out should be construed strictly, including for 'temporary acts of reproduction which are transient and incidental [and] an integral and essential part of a technological process'. A total of thirteen questions were referred to the ECJ on the application of Arts 2 and 5, but for the purposes of this discussion, the salient point was that it was entirely possible for the eleven words to express the author's creativity and so they could be protected as a part of the work by virtue of Art 2. Whether or not the words did in fact express creativity was a matter for the national court to determine.

Other cases seem to suggest that the mere fact of providing a simple link without more is not sufficient in itself to constitute copyright infringement by the linkor.[33] So-called deep links have continued to be the subject of litigation. In an early dispute between Ticketmaster and Microsoft, Microsoft had created deep links that bypassed the Ticketmaster home page.[34] The case settled apparently by agreeing a licence that required any links to be to the home page; this may be indicative of the fact that the main issue for commercial sites is often not the linking as such, but the fact that bypassing the home page results in a loss of revenue as a result of loss of advertising and/or access to or extraction of commercially valuable information. In addition, the deep link may access material for which a password or some form of registration would normally be required, but this technology can also be used to prevent links completely, other than to the home page. In the *Ticketmaster Corp v Tickets.com* litigation,[35] both parties provided information and sold tickets for a variety of entertainment and sporting events. For events for which it did not sell tickets itself, Tickets.com listed alternative vendors and often deep-linked to other similar sites, such as that of Ticketmaster. On the copyright issue, the court applied the decision of the Supreme Court in *Feist*[36] and reasoned that there was no copyright protection for facts or raw data. This limited the information that could be protected and, further, the four elements of the fair use doctrine[37] favoured Tickets.com. Tickets.com made temporary copies of the material from Ticketmaster's pages and the final webpage did not contain any infringing material. Ticketmaster thus gained very little assistance from the law of copyright in trying to prevent the deep links to its site.

See Chapter 10

A number of cases from Europe do not suggest that copyright law is a major tool in the regulation of hyperlinks. In *Algemen Dagblad BV & ors v Eureka Internetdiensten*,[38] Eureka operated a website, www.kranten.com, containing a page of national newspapers that listed news reports and articles matching those provided on the papers' own websites. These were deep links taking the user straight to the story and bypassing the home page. In addition, Eureka also provided a daily email service

---

31 At the time of writing, this litigation is still ongoing. Google has appealed the original decision, but, as yet, no date has been set for the hearing. In addition, because attempts to negotiate a settlement have been unsuccessful, Copiepresse has initiated an action in damages based on the injunction: see www.copiepresse.be for the history of the litigation and links to the judgment in English.

32 [2001] OJ L 167/10.

33 This was assumed to be the case in *Copipresse v Google*, above, and see also further discussion of *Reimerdes*, below at p 327.

34 No 97-3055 DDP (CD Cal 1997).

35 For discussion of the copyright issues, see 2003 WL 21406289 (CD Cal) and see discussion in Tarra Zynda, 'Ticketmaster corp v Tickets.com Inc: Preserving minimum requirements of contract on the internet' (2004) 19 Berkeley Tech LJ 495. Subsequent litigation focused on issues of unfair competition: see, eg, 2003 WL 21397701 (CD Cal).

36 113 L Ed 2d 358 (1991). See also discussion in Chapter 10.

37 See below at p 329 n.62.

38 Case 139609/KGZA 00-846 (District Court of Rotterdam, 22 August 2000) (the *Kranten.com* case), an informal translation of which is available online at www.ivir.nl/rechtspraak/kranten.com-english.html

with the latest news stories in the form of a list of these deep links. The court was unconcerned about the effect of deep-linking, noting that the home pages of the newspapers were not made inaccessible by the deep link, that kranten.com did not take over the function of these home pages, and nor did it prejudice the exploitation of the home pages. Its view was that, for the purposes of copyright law, adding a deep link could not be regarded as a reproduction of the works contained on the linked-to page. Although the complete taking of the list of stories might be afforded copyright protection, it would be subject to an exception for freedom of quotation for press surveys. On similar facts to those in *Kranten.com*, the Bundesgerichthof (Federal Court of Germany) did not find that copyright was infringed by deep links. In *Handelsblatt Publishers Group v Paperboy*,[39] Paperboy provided access to a large number of news sites, including those of newspapers, radio stations, political parties, etc, by means of deep links, together with a daily email service allowing users to create a personalise news service. Reproduction of the small parts necessary to make the links did not constitute copyright infringement, because they were not sufficiently original, in themselves, to be copyrightable. Specifically on the functionality of links, the court said that the links provided by Paperboy merely made access easier – that is, they were not a prerequisite to access that could be obtained directly if the user knew the URL. Further, the court suggested that, given that there was no liability for the link if a URL was published as a footnote in a hardcopy publication, the situation should be no different if the URL was effectively made available via a deep link. Although the focus of this discussion is the application of copyright law to linking, the majority of deep-linking cases base their actions on a number of claims. In Europe, these have usually been infringement of database rights[40] and unfair competition, whereas in the USA, where there is at present no separate protection for databases, the more tortuous avenue of trespass has been attempted.[41]

See Chapter 10 →

Slightly different issues arise when the links and references to other sites are made via the techniques of inline linking, in which images can appear as part of the viewed web page even though they originate elsewhere, or framing, in which the viewed web page will appear divided into multiple, independently scrollable, windows, some of which may come from other sites although appearing within the frame of the first site. These avoid the issues of bypassing the home page seen in deep-linking cases, but instead give rise to other problems. Sableman suggests that this is 'a little bit like painting a picture of a gallery at the Louvre, simply by importing onto your canvas the Louvre's own digital reproductions of those drawings. At the very least, it seems sneaky'.[42] He refers to the case of *Washington Post Company v Total News Inc*,[43] in which a number of publishers objected to the way in which Total News used framing technology to set a news story from another site within the overall Total News frame – in particular by blocking banner advertisements and other distinguishing features. The objection here was not to the link per se, but to the way in which the link was accomplished and presented. In common with many linking cases, the issue was settled by agreement between the parties, originating the notion of the 'linking licence' whereby Total News agreed to link to other sites only in certain specified ways.

---

39 BGH, 17 July 2003, I ZR 259/00. See BC Müller, 'Case comment' (2003) 8 Comm L 375; also discussion in Susanne Klein, 'Search engines and copyright: An analysis of the Belgian *Copiepresse* decision in consideration of British and German copyright law' (2008) 39 IIC 451, 457ff.

40 For example, in *DDF v Newsbooster* [2003] ECDR 5, again on similar facts to the *Kranten.com* case, an injunction to prevent Newsbooster creating deep links to newspaper articles was upheld, but on the basis of a violation of the database right rather than copyright infringement. In this context, see also Andrew L Dahm, 'Database protection v deep linking' (2004) 82 Tex L Rev 1053.

41 See, eg, *Register.com v Verio* 00 Civ 5747 (BSJ) (SDNY 2000); *Ticketmaster v Tickets.com Inc*, above; *eBay v Bidder's Edge* 100 F Supp 2d 1058 (ND Cal 2000), all of which involved, inter alia, the collection of data from other websites by means of an automated software robot or 'spider'. See also discussion in Rowland and Campbell, op cit, 181; Michael E Dockins 'Internet links: The good, the bad, the tortious and a two-part test' (2005) 36 U Tol L Rev 367, 395ff.

42 Mark Sableman, 'Link law: The emerging law of internet hyperlinks' (1999) 4 Comm L & P 557.

43 97 Civ 1190 (PKL) (SDNY filed 20 February 1997).

Aside from the potential loss of advertising, etc, the question in the *Total News* case was essentially whether framing led to the creation of derivative works. This same issue also arose in *Futuredontics Inc v Applied Anagramics Inc.*[44] Applied Anagramics linked to the Futuredontics website in such a way that Futuredontics material appeared within frames on the Anagramics site. Futuredontics claimed that this was a copyright infringement and sought an injunction to restrain the link. The district court found insufficient reasons for granting an injunction, as Futuredontics had not demonstrated conclusively that the 'balance of hardships tips sharply in its favor' and no real evidence of significant injury had been presented. The US Court of Appeals for the Ninth Circuit affirmed this denial of injunctive relief, agreeing with the lower court on the application of the 'balance of hardships' test. Because of these factors, the question of whether the material on the Anagramics site constituted a derivative work was not considered in any detail, but the district court suggested that the 'cases cited by the parties do not conclusively determine whether the defendant's frame page constitutes a derivative work' and no actual decision was made on this issue.

There have been many cases filed in the USA and elsewhere on matters associated with linking and framing,[45] and the majority appear to have reached a settlement based on an agreement related to the manner of framing. However, framing is arguably a special case because of the ease of confusion as to the origin of the material. Nonetheless, a number of other cases have also settled by agreeing a licence to link, despite the fact that there does not appear to be a strong case that links are likely to be unlawful, other than in the comparatively rare cases in which the connection is made with knowledge, and indeed perhaps with intent, to connect the user to infringing material of some sort. Although an implied or actual licence to link may be a useful device that helps to ameliorate any friction between the parties concerned, it is a moot point whether it is a necessary or essential device.[46] Afori suggests that, even where American courts allow linking without reference to an implied licence, 'their decisions are clearly motivated by it',[47] and that a rule presuming consent to link by virtue of posting material on the internet would infuse 'reasonableness into Internet activity'.[48] While it is difficult to argue with the latter point, the former seems debatable: if there is actually some hidden subtext, such decisions could equally be motivated by the existence of a general freedom to link provided that it did not adversely affect another's interests. Allgrove and Ganley point out that the implied licence device offers no more certainty to internet users since liability will still be dependent on the facts of the case. However, in their view, its utility could be to protect works for public policy reasons.[49] In contrast, the alternative view is that, far from requiring a licence from the linkee, the manner in which the internet and world wide web have developed suggests that the linkor may have a right to link, which some have construed as part of the right of free expression.[50]

The case of *Reimerdes et al*[51] arose because the defendant had made available the decryption code for DVD recordings on his website. After removing this information, he continued to maintain links to other sites where the relevant code could be found. In the USA, trafficking in anti-circumvention technology is prohibited by the **Digital Millennium Copyright Act of 1998 (DMCA)** and the question for the district court was whether maintaining such links could be equated with

44 45 USPQ 2d (BNA) 2005 (1998), aff'd 152 F 3d 925 (9th Cir 1998); see Robert L Tucker, 'Information superhighway robbery: The tortious misuse of links, frames, metatags and domain names' (1999) 4 Va JLT 8.

45 See also the decision of the Landgericht (Cologne, 2 May 2001), in which a poetry website was framed by the defendant. This had the result of circumventing banner advertisements and was deemed to cause damage to the website owner: see www.netlaw.de/urteile/lgk_19.htm

46 For further discussion on this point, see Rowland and Campbell, op cit, 183. On the use of implied licences generally in copyright law, see, eg, Lionel Bently and Brad Sherman, *Intellectual Property Law*, 3rd edn, 2009, Oxford: Oxford University Press.

47 Orit Fischman Afori, 'Implied license: An emerging new standard in copyright law' (2009) 25 CHTLJ 275, 304.

48 Ibid, 305.

49 Ben Allgrove and Paul Ganley, 'Search engines, data aggregators and UK copyright law: a proposal' [2007] EIPR 227, 234.

50 See, eg, Berners-Lee, 'Links and Laws: Myths', op cit.

51 *Universal City Studios v Reimerdes* 111 F Supp 2d 294 (SDNY 2000).

trafficking. A significant factor in this case was that the linked-to sites contained no other material and, indeed, activating the link initiated an automatic download. In these circumstances, the court had no difficulty in finding liability for the links, although it conceded that the situation might not have been so simple if the linked-to sites had contained other material in addition to the infringing matter. Liability under the **DMCA** itself will be considered further below, but the court also discussed more general issues of linking noting that:

> Links are . . . often used in ways that do a great deal to promote the free exchange of ideas and information that is a central value of our nation. Anything that would impose strict liability on a web site operator for the entire contents of any web site to which the operator linked therefore would raise grave constitutional concerns, as web site operators would be inhibited from linking for fear of exposure to liability.[52]

Using the classic vocabulary of First Amendment discussion, the court found that imposing strict liability on website operators for links to sites containing infringing content could raise constitutional concerns about freedom of expression because of the potential 'chilling effects',[53] and, in consequence, ruled that, in the particular circumstances of the case, there should be no liability unless it could be shown that those responsible for the link:

(a)   know at the relevant time that the offending material is on the linked-to site,
(b)   know that it is circumvention technology that may not lawfully be offered, and
(c)   create or maintain the link for the purpose of disseminating that technology.[54]

It is arguably implicit in this test that, absent a known link to infringing material, the linkor would have had a 'right', or at least a freedom, to make the link. The question of whether or not there is the requisite knowledge is therefore crucial and such a test could, in principle, be extended to other cases of direct linking in which the linkor was both aware of the existence of unlawful content and was also, perhaps, making the link for that purpose. The decision in *Reimerdes* was subsequently affirmed by the Second Circuit in *Corley*, but the court stopped short of propounding a general test because 'it is not for us to resolve the issues of public policy implicated . . . Those issues are for Congress'.[55]

Notwithstanding the discussion on linking in *Reimerdes*, it is a case in which the functionality of the link was crucial to the outcome and the extent to which it can be applied to the more general case of a direct link is doubtful. Whether the knowledge test can be used if the linkor knows that the link may result in a breach of copyright ultimately depends on an adjudication of the function of links and whether there exist legitimate restrictions on making links or whether there is something akin to a 'right to link'. On the latter, as evidenced by comments in cases such as *Kelly v Arriba*,[56] there is evidence that the courts may not wish to inhibit unduly the use and utility of the new technology. In addition, any knowledge test must necessarily be circumscribed if the linkor is not to run the risk of either being found liable for additional linked sites or liable at a future date because the content of the linked-to site has changed.

Whereas common law countries provide fair use or fair dealing exceptions to copyright, the majority of civil law countries instead list a number of public interest exceptions to copyright, which, in keeping with their status as exceptions, are generally construed quite strictly. This has

52 Ibid, 340.
53 But noted that this was unique to neither links nor to copyright.
54 Ibid, 341.
55 *Universal City Studios v Corley* 273 F 3d 429, 458 (2nd cir 2001).
56 336 F 3d 811 (9th Cir 2003), discussed further below.

meant that unless such jurisdictions are willing to invoke a right to link, the linkor can only feasibly rely on the presumption of the existence of an implied licence discussed earlier – a device that has also been invoked in relation to the operation of search engines, as discussed in the next section.

Search Engines

If links are an essential contributing factor to the universality of the internet, the user would not be able to enjoy the maximum benefit from their functionality without that other indispensible feature of internet technology – the search engine. Indeed, search engines are now recognised as 'essential sources of vital information for individuals, governments, non-profits, and businesses who seek to locate information'.[57] Links and search engines could be said to have a symbiotic relationship: while links create the vast web of information that is the world wide web, search engines enable that web to be navigated more purposefully and, of course, they also rely on link technology to connect search engine users with the results of their searches. For this reason, some of the same issues arise in these cases as those on linking, such as whether or not there is a need to invoke an implied licence or whether freely available content can both be linked to and retrieved by search engines with impunity. Aside from email, search engines are the most commonly used application on the internet[58] and they have been described as 'managers of information, organizing and categorizing content in a coherent, accessible manner thereby shaping the Internet user's experience'.[59] Search engines basically rely on three processes: trawling the internet or world wide web by means of an automated program (variously referred to as a 'spider', 'robot', or crawler); analysing and prioritising the information returned; and then compiling a list of the information for the user.[60] Not surprisingly, in view of their ubiquity and the extent of the information that they are able to make available by use of a variety of search technologies, they have also posed some questions for the application of the law of copyright.

A good example of this was found in the early case of *Kelly v Arriba Software*.[61] Kelly, a professional photographer, had uploaded original photographs to his website. Arriba operated an image search engine based on a database containing images copied from websites. The images were first copied at full size and were then converted to low-resolution 'thumbnails' for storage and retrieval, after which the first copies were deleted. The Court of Appeals for the Ninth Circuit considered the application of the four fair use factors in the US **Copyright Act of 1976**[62] to the creation and use of these thumbnails. It found that even though the images were reproduced exactly and entirely, it was for a completely different purpose. Although the search engine used exact replicas of the original image, they were much smaller, lower-resolution images, which could not be enlarged to the size of the original without significant loss of clarity.[63] The fact that Arriba was using the images commercially did not automatically negate a finding of fair use; instead, as part of the first factor, the court had to consider the extent to which the new use was 'transformative'.[64] In this case, it was not merely a question of retransmission of the work in a different form; rather, Arriba's use served a different function to that of Kelly. Arriba's use of the thumbnails was neither for artistic purposes, nor did it 'supplant the need for the originals', and, in addition, it also served the purpose of

---

57 *Perfect 10 v Google* 416 F Supp 2d 828, 849 (CD Cal 2006).
58 See discussion in Eszter Hargittai, 'The social, political, economic, and cultural dimensions of search engines: An introduction' (2007) 12 Journal of Computer-Mediated Communication 769.
59 Emily B Laidlaw, 'Private power, public interest: An examination of search engine accountability' (2009) 17 IJLIT 113.
60 For further discussion of the technology, see, eg, Allgrove and Ganley op cit, and descriptions in the relevant case law, eg, *Field v Google* 412 F Supp 2d 1109, 1110ff; *Perfect 10 v Google*, above, 832.
61 336 F 3d 811 (9th Cir 2003).
62 17 USC § 107. The fair use factors are: the purpose and character of the use; the nature of the copyrighted work; the amount and substantiality of the portion used; and the effect on the potential market or value of the copyrighted work.
63 336 F 3d 811, 818 (9th Cir 2003).
64 See further *Campbell v Acuff-Rose* 510 US 569 (1994).

'enhancing information-gathering techniques on the internet'.[65] Although the works at issue were entitled to strong copyright protection, there was no evidence that the use of the thumbnails would damage the market for the original works and it was found that, overall, the use was fair. *Kelly* first came to the District Court in 1999,[66] at a relatively early point in the history of the internet, but the court explicitly recognised the 'established importance of search engines'.[67] It suggested that, given the developing nature of the technology, the transformative nature of the use was the most important factor, commenting that where 'a new use and new technology are evolving, the broad transformative purpose of the use weighs more heavily than the inevitable flaws in its early stages of development'.[68]

In the early days of the internet, although there were a number of different search engines available, arguably none could really be said to dominate the market. This situation has changed over the years with the rise and rise of Google, which now has an overwhelming share of the available custom.[69] Unsurprisingly perhaps, this success story has been accompanied by a number of legal challenges, including some concerning the way in which Google deals with the copyright works of others via its search methods and mechanisms. As mentioned, search engines glean their information via automated programs that crawl the web. Website owners can both optimise their websites so that they are more likely to be indexed by search engines, and therefore more likely to come to the attention of users, or, conversely, robot crawlers can also be instructed not to index sites.[70] In *Field v Google*,[71] the issue was not that Google's use of web crawlers to make copies of Field's documents infringed copyright, but that copyright was infringed by copying or distribution when a user clicked on the Google cache to view the documents in question. With respect to fair use, the court found that, as in *Kelly* above, Google's cache did not serve the same purpose as the original, but allowed users to access the document when the original source was, for whatever reason, inaccessible. It also enabled users to ascertain whether changes had been made to the document and to check why it was returned in response to their search. In other words, it was a transformative use; an explicit comparison was drawn with *Kelly* pointing out that the cache served 'multiple transformative and socially valuable purposes'.[72] Taking all of the relevant factors into account led to the decision that Google could rely on the fair use defence. In addition, there were further factors that had not appeared in *Kelly*: Field provided free access to all of his materials on the web, and had also used a robots.txt file to optimise his site for search engines and was thus well aware of technology that would inhibit search engines. Under these circumstances, Google was also entitled to rely on an implied licence to index Field's site.[73] As Kociubinski has commented, this decision, together with *Kelly*, 'establishes a seemingly broad sphere of protection around the activities of Internet search engines'.[74] However, the fact that search engines might not enjoy completely unfettered freedom of operation appeared to be illustrated subsequently by *Perfect 10 v Google*.[75]

Perfect 10 concerned thumbnail images that had been copied from websites by a robot crawler and indexed for use as part of Google's popular image search. Distinctions between this and the situation in *Kelly* were that Perfect 10 was a subscription site and so the images were obtained from

---

65 336 F 3d 811, 820 (9th Cir 2003).
66 77 F Supp 2d 1116 (CD Cal 1999).
67 Ibid, 1121.
68 Ibid.
69 See, eg, ComScore, 'Global search market draws more than 100 billion searches per month', Press release, 31 August 2009, available online at www.comscore.com/Press_Events/Press_Releases/2009/8/Global_Search_Market_Draws_More_than_100_Billion_Searches_per_Month. See also Chapter 3 for discussion of other litigation involving Google.
70 Typically by the use of metatags or a robots.txt file. For further information, see, eg, www.robotstxt.org/
71 412 F Supp 2d 1106 (DC Nev 2006).
72 Ibid, 1121.
73 See also above discussion at p 327.
74 Ben Kociubinski, 'Copyright and the evolving law of internet search' (2006) BU J Sci & Tech L 372, 377.
75 416 F Supp 2d 828. (DC Cal 2008).

third-party sites, and that Google also used a program (Adsense), which allowed third parties to have advertising space and share any subsequent revenue based on the number of hits and 'click-throughs'. In addition, although, as with Arriba's thumbnails, there was a consequent resolution reduction as compared with the original, the thumbnails produced by Google's image search could also be downloaded to mobile phones. This practice effectively superseded Perfect 10's own licence with a company for sale and distribution of its images via mobile phones. These factors made Google's use both more commercial and less transformative than Arriba's, and were the major factors that tipped the balance in Perfect 10's favour and led to a finding that Google could not rely on fair use as a defence. In the light of the 'enormous public benefit that search engines such as Google provide',[76] the court expressed itself to be 'reluctant to issue a ruling that might impede the advance of internet technology',[77] but nevertheless was of the view that this should not be allowed to 'trump a reasoned analysis of the four fair use factors'.[78]

This apparent restriction on the operation of search engines was fairly short-lived, as the Ninth Circuit subsequently found that the use was fair using substantially the same reasoning as it had used in *Kelly*. In particular, it concluded that:

> . . . the significantly transformative nature of Google's search engine, particularly in light of its public benefit, outweighs Google's superseding and commercial uses of the thumbnails in this case. In reaching this conclusion we note the importance of analyzing fair use flexibly in light of new circumstances.[79]

While it has been acknowledged that the decisions of the Ninth Circuit in *Kelly* and *Perfect 10* are practical outcomes for the technology, it has been pointed out that they rely on the fact that the new use is transformative rather than the subject of the copyright being transformed into a new creation.[80] It has also been suggested that a finding of fair use is problematic when the original work is copied in its entirety, although there are other areas in which copying of an entire work has not necessarily militated against fair use.[81] In addition, although paying lip service to policy reasons concerning the importance of search engines, the reasoning in both cases was 'based on a "micro" fair use calculus and not on "macro" policy grounds'.[82] On the other hand, other commentators are of the view that the copying that is a necessary part of search engine technology should be taken out of the discussion of copyright infringement and 'recognized as an orthogonal use, rather than being characterized as transformative'.[83]

In Europe, similar issues concerning the Google image search have been raised in the German courts, but with no conclusive outcome as to the reasoning. As in *Kelly*, the fact that thumbnails could not be enlarged without loss of quality was a relevant factor for the District Court of Erfurt in deciding that there was implied consent to the operation of search engines, because there was an actual benefit to the copyright holder in having the thumbnails retrieved by a visual search engine, which would help people to locate the works and make them available to a larger audience.[84] However, on appeal, the Thuringian Higher Regional Court did not follow this reasoning, but found that mere uploading of a work to a website should not be taken to imply consent to the

---

76 Ibid, 851.
77 Ibid.
78 Ibid.
79 *Perfect 10 v Amazon* 487 F 3d 701, 723 (9th Cir 2007).
80 See, eg, Kathleen K Olson, 'Transforming fair use online: The Ninth Circuit's productive-use analysis of visual search engines' (2009) 14 Comm L & Pol'y 153.
81 See, eg, *Sony v Universal Studios* 464 US 417, 78 Led 2d 574 (1984), discussed further below.
82 Fischman Afori, op cit, 308.
83 Pamela Samuelson, 'Unbundling fair uses' (2009) 77 Fordham L Rev 2537.
84 Case No 3 O 1108/05, decision of 15 March 2007, full text available (in German) online at www.linksandlaw.de/urteil171-bildersuche-thumbnails.htm

indexing of the images by search engines. On the particular facts of the case, however, the site had been optimised for search engines and so the court found that the complainant was estopped from bringing a complaint about the manner in which search engines operated.[85] This decision was subsequently upheld by the Federal Supreme Court, the Bundesgerichtshof, which has held that Google's image search does not amount to copyright infringement.[86]

A number of the issues raised by search techniques, together with the more general problem of locating an appropriate balance of rights between author and user in the digital environment, were brought sharply into focus by the furore surrounding the Google Book Project launched at the end of 2004. Working with a number of major libraries, including some major university libraries, Google announced its intention to digitise all of the world's books to make them both accessible and searchable – in other words, those with internet access would potentially have the literary resources of the world available to them from their desks or wherever else they happened to be online. As Bracha has noted, 'digital technology has the potential of empowering many members of society by providing them access to gigantic quantities of information in highly retrievable and manipulable forms. Books are just the beginning'.[87] In brief, the project is in two parts: those books that Google has been given permission to copy (the 'Partner Program'); and the Library Project itself, which potentially includes all other books. Unless permission has been given for more material to be accessible, a search will typically provide users with 'snippets' – that is, a few sentences either side of the search term(s). In addition, Google provides an opt-out facility for copyright owners who do not wish their publications to be made available in this way.[88] This project was rapidly challenged as a copyright infringement by a number of authors and publishers.[89] Subsequent negotiations led to a settlement being agreed, which was given preliminary approval in 2009.[90] While this settlement only covers the USA, if adopted, it may well have wider ramifications, although for the purposes of this discussion, the precise outcome may be less important than the questions that the dispute raises for copyright in the digital age.[91] More recently, a further court hearing has declined to uphold a revised settlement that took into account points raised in the 2009 hearing and so the future of the project now faces uncertainty.[92]

Unsurprisingly, there has been significant academic discussion about issues raised by the case. This includes, amongst other things, assessment of the wider public benefit of increased accessibility, the practicability of obtaining consent from all copyright owners, and the question of whether the 'opt-out' turns copyright law on its head in that instead of copyright owners being asked to give an explicit permission, permission is implied or assumed unless the copyright owner expressly opts out of the system. The most extensive academic scrutiny has been about the potential application of the four fair use factors in the US **Copyright Act of 1976** to these activities. It is beyond the scope of this work to provide a detailed analysis of this issue; arguably, the prevailing view is that Google might succeed in a fair use defence, but this opinion is by no means unanimous and neither do those who are in overall agreement necessarily agree about how each of the fair use

---

85 Case No 2 U 319/07, decision of 27 February 2008, full text available (in German) online at www.linksandlaw.de/urteil228-olg-thumbnails-urteil.htm

86 *Vorschaubilder* Case I ZR 69/08 BGH, 29 April 2010; see Out-law.com, 'Google image search results do not infringe copyright, says German court' (2010) Out-law.com, 30 April, available online at www.out-law.com/page-10980

87 Oren Bracha, 'Standing copyright law on its head? The googlization of everything and the many faces of property' (2007) 85 Tex L Rev 1799, 1803.

88 For further details and discussion of the project, see, eg, Jonathan Band, 'Copyright owners v the Google Print Library Project' (2006) 17 Ent L Rev 21; Joseph Savirithmu, 'Legal reflections on the Google Print Library Project' (2006) 1 JIPL&P 801.

89 *The Authors Guild, Inc, et al v Google Inc*, Case No 05 CV 8136 (SDNY); see also http://fl1.findlaw.com/news.findlaw.com/nytimes/docs/google/aggoog92005cmp.pdf

90 See www.googlebooksettlement.com/

91 See Caroline Turner, 'Google Library Project settlement agreement' (2009) 20 Ent LR 183.

92 *The Authors Guild, Inc, et al v Google Inc*, Case No 05 CV 8136 (SDNY) 22 March 2011; see commentary online at http://jolt.law.harvard.edu/digest/copyright/authors-guild-v-google-2

factors should be applied or what weighting each should be given.[93] In brief, those supporting a finding of fair use tend to focus on the transformative nature of the use – namely, that Google is creating a tool that is not for reading books, but for finding them – and that the new use does not adversely affect the market for the originals, and may even stimulate and encourage it. In addition, most also mention the educational benefits of the Google Book Search facility, concluding that it 'has important social objectives that must be encouraged',[94] that it is 'an innovative contribution to the public's benefit by facilitating research and promoting scholarship',[95] and that there would, in consequence, be an immense benefit to both authors and the public.[96] Those who take a more circumspect stance focus particularly on Google's commercial activities and commercial use, and, instead of considering the project as a whole, often apply the fair use factors separately to the individual stages of the project, concluding overall that a finding of fair use could 'significantly diminish authors' and inventors' exclusive rights'.[97]

Even though academic opinion generally seems to suggest that Google may be able to rely on the fair use defence, the case-by-case approach to fair use, together with a lack of appropriate precedent, means that it is difficult to predict exactly how a court might weigh and balance the respective factors. A number of commentators have concluded that, because of the perceived public interest advantages, there is a case for legislative intervention to allow published works to be available in this form.[98] Copyright law has two strands: the fact of unauthorised copying in the absence of permitted fair use or fair dealing provisions; and also more severe provisions for those who, as well as copying the work, distribute it to the public. Proskine suggests that copyright law should be revisited to focus solely on distributing to the public: in the Google Books context, this would presumably mean that a whole book scanned onto Google's database would not infringe because it was not available in that form for general consumption (in the absence of specific permission or for public domain material), but only as snippets, which would qualify as fair use.[99] There are many policy factors that could be used to make a case for a variation of copyright in this context based on the benefit to the public, including the fact that, although the whole of the work may be copied, the end user can never access it in this form, together with the ongoing issue of whether rules that have their origins in print and hard copy should continue to be applied without amendment in the digital age.[100] Similar factors are also relevant in the analysis of the next topic – namely, the legal response to another activity made possible by digital technology: peer-to-peer (P2P) file sharing.

File Sharing

Given the quality of the copies that can be obtained by digitisation, it is not surprising that ever-more-inventive ways have been found both to copy and to deal in copyright material, leading Helmer and Davies to remark that 'the staggering pace of development of the internet has fundamentally

---

93   For example, the following authors have come to the conclusion that a finding of fair use could be supported: Nari Na, 'Testing the boundaries of copyright protection: The Google Books Library Project and the fair use doctrine' 16 Cornell JL & Pub Pol'y 417; Melanie Costantino, 'Fairly used: Why Google's Book Project should prevail under the fair use defense' 17 Fordham Intell Prop Media & Ent LJ 235; Kinan H Romman, 'The Google Book Search Library Project: A market analysis approach to fair use' 43 Hous L Rev 807; whereas the following are rather more circumspect: Aundrea Gamble, 'Google's Book Search Project: Searching for fair use or infringement' 9 Tul J Tech & Intell Prop 365; Steven Hetcher, 'The half-fairness of Google's plan to make the world's collection of books searchable' 13 Mich Telecomm & Tech L Rev 1; Ari Okano, 'Digitized book search engines and copyright concerns' 3 Shidler JL Com & Tech 13.

94   Costantino, op cit, 277.

95   Na, op cit, 435.

96   See, eg, Romman, op cit, 831.

97   Gamble, op cit, 384.

98   See, eg, Okano, op cit.

99   Emily Anne Proskine, 'Google's technicolor dreamcoat: A copyright analysis of the Google Book Search Library Project' 21 Berkeley Tech LJ 213.

100 See also discussion in Savirimuthu, op cit.

changed the rules of engagement with [intellectual property] infringers, who now operate in a virtual world that cannot be policed using conventional means'.[101] There are many ways in which copyright can be infringed online, but the growth in both sophistication and usage of P2P file-sharing software has arguably caused the greatest challenges for the application of traditional copyright principles. Although there are many entirely lawful ways for using this technology, it also facilitates the easy dissemination, distribution, and sharing of copyright material. Historically, copyright infringement was rarely pursued against individual infringers not only because of difficulties of detection, but also because both the amount of copying and its economic impact were relatively insignificant.[102] The advent of the perfect copy that could be easily and simultaneously made available to multitudes of users has moved the focus of litigation onto both the individual infringer, and the means by which the infringement can occur – that is, those who facilitate individual copying and file sharing. According to certain figures, rights holders lose significant revenue as a result of the activities of file sharers. The most recent figures quoted by the BPI suggested that online copyright infringement cost the UK music sector an estimated £200 million in 2009.[103] This has resulted in copyright owners – notably the music recording industry – taking action in a number of jurisdictions against not only those who make available various types of P2P file-sharing software, but also individual infringers.

This litigation represents far more than merely a dispute over the application of copyright to new activities made possible by internet technology, but has been presented as a battle between corporate interests and those – usually individuals – who espouse the freedom to access information that the internet provides. As Cornish and Llewelyn remark, 'the *Napster* judgment in the US [see discussion below] has become a bleeding image much paraded in the campaigns to preserve the internet as an unfettered instrument of free exchange'.[104] In similar vein, Sookman suggests that not only does the technology present a threat to rights holders, but that it also is 'changing philosophical views about the purpose and value of copyrights'.[105] Nevertheless, there is little evidence that any new model of regulation is being sought to respond to the challenges posed to copyright law by digital technology. It is certainly true that copyright law has proved able to evolve through its history to cope with technological change, and that its general ethos and provisions have not changed substantially during that time. On the other hand, one of the objectives of intellectual property law in general, and copyright law in particular, is popularly supposed to be the encouragement of creativity and innovation – yet the development of the technology that has produced P2P networks is more often viewed negatively for its perceived fostering of infringement, rather than celebrated for its innovatory qualities.[106] There seem to be no proposals for revision of the

---

101 Stuart Helmer and Isabel Davies, 'File-sharing and downloading: Goldmine or minefield?' (2009) 4 JIPL 51.

102 See, eg, Jane C Ginsburg, 'Putting cars on the information superhighway: Authors, exploiters and copyright in cyberspace' (1995) 95 Colum L Rev 1466, 1488–9; Tim Wu, 'When code isn't law' (2003) 89 Va L Rev 679, 711–16; Mark A Lemley and R Anthony Reese, 'Reducing digital copyright infringement without restricting innovation' (2004) 56 Stan L Rev 1345, 1373–9.

103 See www.bpi.co.uk/digital-music/article/online-faqs.aspx, in which the BPI also reports research suggesting that the total loss to the music industry between 2007 and 2012 will be £1.2 billion. However, trends seem difficult to establish: although the BPI figure for 2009 shows a slight increase on that for 2008 (see Department for Culture, Media and Sport (DCMS)/ Department for Business, Innovation and Skills (BIS), *Digital Britain*, Cm 7650, 2009, London: HMSO, ch 4, para 17), it should be noted that the figure of £200 million for 2009 is actually a reduction on the figure of £414 million quoted for 2005 (Chancellor of the Exchequer, *Gowers Review of Intellectual Property*, 2006, London: HMSO, available online at www.hm-treasury.gov. uk/gowers_review_index.htm, para 2.18). For discussion of file-sharing behaviour, see also Tracy A Suter, Steven W Kopp, and David M Hardesty, 'The effect of consumers' ethical beliefs on copying behaviour' (2006) 29 J Consum Policy 190; Stylianoue, op cit; www.ukmusic.org/research

104 Cornish and Llewellyn, op cit, 851.

105 Barry B Sookman, 'Technological protection measures (TPMs) and copyright protection: The case for TPMs' (2005) 11 CTLR 143.

106 See, eg, *Digital Britain*, op cit, ch 4, para 18; see also Mark Sweney, 'Lord Mandelson sets date for blocking filesharers' internet connections' (2009) *GuardianOnline*, 28 October, available online at www.guardian.co.uk/technology/2009/oct/28/ mandelson-date-blocking-filesharers-connections; Lord Mandelson, 'Keynote address', Cabinet Conference, 26–28 October 2009, available online at www.cabinetforum.org/conference/archive/l._keynote_address_-_rt_hon_lord_mandelson/; see also Lord Mandelson, 'The future of the creative industries' (2009) 29 October, available online at www.bis.gov.uk/News/ Speeches/creative-industries

regulatory framework that would embrace the functionality of the technology; instead, as we shall see in the subsequent discussion, the response has been to preserve traditional copyright principles and to enhance enforcement against individual infringers. Although new business models that respond to the technology by diversifying the modes of delivery of copyright material are welcomed,[107] it seems that new regulatory modes are not on the agenda.[108]

It is beyond the scope of this text to enter into a detailed explanation of the technology that has enabled file sharing over the internet, but some brief account of the modus operandi of the technology and the way in which it has developed over time will be of assistance. Readers who require more technical detail will find it in commentary by legal scholars and also in judicial discussion.[109] Before the advent of P2P, different computers on a network could only communicate through a central server, but, in simple terms, P2P software now allows computers connected to a network to communicate both ways with other computers on the network without those communications necessarily being routed through a central server. Napster was one of the earliest examples of this in which, although the actual file transfers took place between individual users, there was an element of centralisation in that the requests for the files passed through a central server. Later applications, such as Grokster and Kazaa, were examples of the 'purest form of P2P network'[110] – that is, ones in which individual computers communicated without the need for a central server. Thus Grokster was an example of a P2P sharing network based on the 'supernode' model in which a number of select computers on the network are designated as indexing servers. The user initiating a file search connects with the most easily accessible supernode; this conducts the search of its index and supplies the user with the results. Any computer on the network could function as a supernode if it met the technical requirements, such as processing speed.[111] In the first instance, such applications spawned a number of cases of alleged copyright infringement against the providers of the P2P software that enabled materials – usually music files – to be shared between users. Those bringing the challenges were typically record companies and organisations, which protected the rights of the creators of copyright material. The first of these was the decision of the US Court of Appeals for the Ninth Circuit in *Napster*.[112]

Actions against P2P Network Providers

Use of the Napster system had increased during the late 1990s, and, eventually, a number of record companies and music publishers brought various claims, including contributory and vicarious liability for copyright infringement under US law. Napster, for its part, responded that its users could avail themselves of the fair use defence, first on the basis of sampling the music before buying, and second, on the basis of space-shifting – that is, using the Napster system to make a copy of an audio CD of which they were already the legitimate owner. The latter reasoning was by analogy with the seminal case of *Sony v Universal City Studios*[113] in relation to video recordings made for time-shifting purposes. The court considered the four fair use factors. In terms of the purpose and character of the use, the court found that a commercial use 'weighs against a finding of fair use but is not conclusive'.

---

107 In the final debates on the Digital Economy Bill, the Secretary of State reminded Parliament that 'we have stressed all along the importance of developing legitimate paid-for downloading models. The problem, however, is that those will become widespread and sustainable only if there is a proper legal framework to tackle unlawful downloading': HC Debs, vol 508, col 840 (6 April 2010); see also *Digital Britain*, op cit, ch 4, paras 13ff; European Commission, op cit.

108 For a quirky comment on this, see Lord Whitty, Hansard HL, vol 718, col 1725 (8 April 2010).

109 See, eg, Richard Swope, 'Peer-to peer file sharing and copyright infringement: Danger ahead for individuals sharing files on the internet' (2004) 44 Santa Clara L Rev 861; *MGM v Grokster* 259 F Supp 2d 1029, 1032 (2003).

110 Maureen Daly, 'Life after *Grokster*: Analysis of US and European approaches to file-sharing' [2007] EIPR 319.

111 *MGM v Grokster* 380 F 3d 1154, 1159 (9th Cir 2004); see also the extensive explanation and discussion of the Kazaa file-sharing application in *Universal Music Australia Pty Ltd v Sharman License Holdings Ltd* [2005] FCA 1242.

112 *A&M Records v Napster* 239 F 3d 1004 (9th Cir 2001).

113 464 US 417, 78 LEd 2d 574 (1984).

Although 'direct economic benefit was not required to demonstrate a commercial use', in relation to Napster, 'commercial use is demonstrated by a showing that repeated and exploitative unauthorized copies of copyrighted works were made to save the expense of purchasing authorized copies'.[114] In addition, merely retransmitting in a different format was not a 'transformative' use.[115] Given the creative nature of the works copied, the second fair use factor, 'nature of the use', militated against a finding of fair use. The third factor requires a consideration of the portion used. Although copying a whole work can amount to fair use in certain situations (under the *Sony* doctrine, for example), in general it militates against fair use. The final factor is the effect of the alleged fair use on the market. To assess this, the court considered a number of reports on the use of Napster and its effect on the sale of recorded music, and concluded that 'having digital downloads for free on the Napster system necessarily harms the copyright holders' attempts to charge for the same downloads'.[116] The cumulative effect of these findings was that file sharing was not protected by the fair use provisions. Applying this reasoning to sampling, the court upheld the previous findings that 'sampling remains a commercial use even if some users eventually purchase the music . . . even authorized temporary downloading of individual songs for sampling purposes is commercial in nature'.[117] This was not affected by the fact that record companies themselves sometimes provide samples for users to try before purchase, because 'free downloads provided by record companies consist of thirty to sixty-second samples or are . . . programmed to . . . exist only for a short time on the downloader's computer'.[118] In comparison, Napster users download a full, free, and permanent copy of the recording. Overall, Napster was found to have 'an adverse impact on the audio CD and digital download markets'.[119] In relation to the space-shifting argument, the court noted that, in *Sony*, it was held that time-shifting was fair use, but the same argument was held not to be applicable to Napster because, in *Sony*, there was no question of also simultaneously making the copyright materials available to other members of the public: 'It is obvious that once a user lists a copy of music he already owns on the Napster system in order to access the music from another location, the song becomes available to millions of other individuals, not just the original CD owner.'[120]

Having ascertained that there was no fair use and that Napster users were directly infringing copyright, the court went on to consider whether Napster could be liable for contributory infringement; this required an assessment of whether it knew, or had reason to know, of the direct infringement. In *Sony*, there had been no evidence of actual knowledge of specific cases of infringement, and neither did the Supreme Court assign constructive knowledge to Sony for infringing uses of its video recorders on the grounds that the equipment could be used for both infringing and 'substantial noninfringing' uses. The lower court in *Napster* had based liability on the fact that Napster had 'failed to demonstrate that its system is capable of commercially significant noninfringing uses', but the Court of Appeals departed from this reasoning, and instead found that Napster had 'actual knowledge that specific infringing material is available using its system, that it could block access to the system by suppliers of the infringing material, and that it failed to remove the material'.[121] Neither was it willing to countenance Napster's attempt to avail itself of the **DMCA** 'safe harbor' for ISPs.[122]

The outcome was that Napster, in its original incarnation, was closed down – although it has since been resurrected as a subscription service. The reason for Napster's demise was primarily due to its centralised architecture, and its consequent ability to both control and to block access.

---

114 *Napster*, above, 1015.
115 Following the judgment of the Supreme Court in *Campbell v Acuff-Rose* 510 US 569, L Ed 2d 500 (1994).
116 *Napster*, above, 1017.
117 Ibid, 1018.
118 Ibid.
119 Ibid.
120 Ibid, 1019.
121 Ibid, 1022.
122 For consideration of the DMCA 'safe harbor' provisions for ISPs, see discussion below at p 341. and also further discussion in Chapter 3.

As Wu has commented: 'Napster taught peer network designers that both lack of control and general functionality had to be comprehensive and credible to avoid contributory liability.'[123]

In the later case of *Aimster*,[124] neither did a decentralised system escape liability. Although there was no finding of direct infringement, the court was critical of the Ninth Circuit's interpretation of *Sony*, since the evidence showed that the technology was being used for both infringing and non-infringing uses, and the court did not wish to deny non-infringing users the benefit of the technology. It therefore disagreed with the suggestion that actual knowledge of specific infringing uses was a sufficient condition for a finding of contributory infringement. Instead, it took the view that 'when a supplier is offering a product or service that has noninfringing uses as well as infringing uses, some estimate of the respective magnitudes of these uses is necessary for a finding of contributory infringement'.[125] Although the Aimster system could, in principle, be used for entirely innocuous purposes, in fact the only examples given in the explanatory tutorial about Aimster involved the sharing of copyrighted material. As 'wilful blindness is knowledge in copyright law',[126] neither was the argument that encryption prevented the operators from knowing what was being copied persuasive and neither was there evidence that the service was ever used for non-infringing uses: '. . . its ostrich-like refusal to discover the extent to which its system was being used to infringe copyright is merely another piece of evidence that it was a contributory infringer.'[127] Further, even if it could be shown that there were substantial non-infringing uses, to avoid liability, it would still be necessary to show that preventing, or at least substantially reducing, the infringing uses would have been disproportionately costly.

At this point, it appeared that whether the system was centralised or decentralised, absent genuine evidence that a file-sharing system both could have, and did have, non-infringing uses, the courts were likely to find liability for contributory infringement. This application of the law was criticised as having the potential to restrict innovation, especially in cases of dual-use technology,[128] but it appeared that this situation might be clarified when the Ninth Circuit gave a further judgment on file-sharing in the *Grokster* case referred to above. The use of the Grokster 'supernode model' was described by the lower court as being 'novel in important respects', but nevertheless operating in 'a manner conceptually analogous to the Napster system'.[129] On appeal, the Ninth Circuit, referring to both its previous judgment in *Napster* and that of the Supreme Court in *Sony*, concluded that there was no liability for contributory infringement on the basis that it had been shown that not only could there be substantial non-infringing uses, but that those uses also had commercial viability. The technology employed in *Grokster* was specifically distinguished from that in *Napster*; it was pointed out that it had 'numerous other uses, significantly reducing the distribution costs of public domain and permissively shared art and speech, as well as reducing the centralized control of that distribution'.[130] The court went on to discuss the difficulties for the law in responding to fast-moving technologies, noting that 'we live in a quicksilver technological environment with courts ill-suited to fix the flow of internet innovation' and suggesting that although new technology might be 'disruptive to old markets . . . market forces often [provided] equilibrium in balancing interests, . . . it is prudent for courts to exercise caution before restructuring liability theories for the purposes of addressing specific market abuses, despite their apparent present magnitude'.[131] However, this was to prove a short-term victory for distributors of file-sharing

---

123 Wu, op cit, 730.
124 *In Re: Aimster Copyright Litigation* 334 F 3d 643 (7th Cir 2003).
125 Ibid, 649.
126 Ibid, 650.
127 Ibid, 655.
128 Lemley and Reese, op cit, 1362.
129 *MGM v Grokster* 259 F Supp 2d 1029, 1032 (CD Cal, 2003).
130 *MGM v Grokster* 380 F 3d 1154, 1160 (9th Cir 2004).
131 Ibid, 1167.

software, because the decision was overturned by the Supreme Court on the basis that *Sony* had been misapplied.[132] Instead, the Supreme Court said that the ruling in *Sony* meant that there would be no liability for the mere distribution of products that were capable of both infringing and non-infringing uses, but this did not mean that liability could not be found in cases in which 'there is no injustice in presuming or imputing an intention to infringe'.[133] It found that 'one who distributes a device with the object of promoting its use to infringe copyright, as shown by clear expression or other affirmative steps taken to foster infringement, is liable for the resulting acts of third parties'.[134] In the circumstances of *Grokster*, there was ample evidence that there had been both intent to promote, and actual promotion of, infringing use sufficient to find Grokster liable for contributory infringement.

The USA was not the only jurisdiction in which such cases were being heard, although not always with the same outcome. The supernode architecture, of which Grokster is an example, had been developed by a Dutch company, KaZaa, which itself distributed file-sharing software via its website. This resulted in an action brought by the licensing organization BUMA-STEMRA, in which the Amsterdam Appeal Court found that, although individual users might infringe copyright when file sharing, the distributor of the software, KaZaa, was not liable on the basis that, because there was no central server, there could be no control over the files that were shared once the software had been installed on a user's computer. As in *Grokster*, it was also the case that the software could be, and was being, used for legal purposes, including the exchange of both copyright material with the permission of the copyright owner and also non-copyright material. This reasoning was subsequently upheld by the Dutch Supreme Court in December 2003.[135] The licence to distribute KaZaa was subsequently transferred to an Australian company[136] (and renamed 'Kazaa'), leading to further litigation. The US cases had been decided on the basis of secondary and contributory copyright infringement according to the provisions of the US **Copyright Act**. The differences between the operation of Kazaa and, say, Grokster, together with the differences in copyright law between the USA and Australia, meant that the US judgments were of little assistance to the Federal Court of Australian in *Universal Music Australia Pty Ltd v Sharman License Holdings Ltd*.[137] The Australian Court found that it could not be said that the owners of Kazaa themselves communicated the copyright works; instead, the more realistic argument was that they authorised individual users to infringe copyright in the sound recordings in question. The Court acknowledged that the software could be used for non-infringing purposes, but was not convinced that such use could account for more than a small proportion of the traffic on the Kazaa website.[138] In a long and detailed judgment, Wilcox J found that those in the company were well aware that Kazaa was widely used to share copyright files, that they had technical measures at their disposal that, had they been implemented, might have curtailed these activities, and that, although falling short of actual endorsement of file sharing, information on the Kazaa website was nevertheless critical of record companies that opposed it. However, Wilcox J was also anxious that any remedy would reflect the balance of rights at the heart of copyright law:

---

132 *MGM v Grokster* 125 S Ct 2764 (2005).
133 Ibid, 2777.
134 Ibid, 2780.
135 See Out-law.com, 'Kazaa is legal, says Dutch Supreme Court' (2004) *Outlaw.com*, 5 January, available online at www.out-law.com/page-4169
136 The company, Sharman Networks Ltd, was originally organised in the Netherlands as Kazaa.com, but using software from Estonian companies. It was subsequently incorporated in Vanuatu, but had its headquarters in Australia. The first 'KaZaA' software was provided free of charge from a website in Estonia through internet servers located, at one time, in Denmark. The RIAA was apparently unsuccessful in pursuing Kazaa through the Estonian courts: Slyck News, 'US court loses case in Estonia over KaZaA' (2002) *Slyck News*, 21 December, available online at www.slyck.com/story306_US_Court_Loses_Case_in_Estonia_Over_KaZaA
137 [2005] FCA 1242, [30].
138 Ibid, [184].

> I am anxious not to make an order which the respondents are not able to obey, except at the unacceptable cost of preventing the sharing even of files which do not infringe the applicants' copyright. There needs to be an opportunity for the relevant respondents to modify the Kazaa system in a targeted way, so as to protect the applicants' copyright interests (as far as possible) but without unnecessarily intruding on others' freedom of speech and communication.[139]

Notwithstanding this attempt at balancing the rights of copyright holders and users, one critical issue that differentiates the legal framework in the USA from that in Australia is that, in the former, the *Sony* judgment provides a general defence for the distributor of technology that has 'substantial non-infringing uses', whereas the Australian decision focused more explicitly on the fact of the actual use of the software in question; the reasoning has thus the potential to be more far-reaching that that in *Grokster*.[140] There have, as yet, been no major cases taken against the distributors of file-sharing software in the UK, although there has been speculation as to whether the courts would follow the approach in *Sharman* or whether they would use a *Sony*-type approach based on the case of *CBS Songs v Amstrad*,[141] in which the House of Lords held that Amstrad's production of twin-deck tape recorders did not, of itself, indicate that Amstrad authorised copyright infringement, because the devices could be used for both infringing and non-infringing purposes.[142]

What could be called the 'third generation' of file-sharing technology, based on the use of BitTorrent software, raises some slightly different legal issues. BitTorrent software enables users to download large files in smaller portions (bits) from multiple sources, thereby making economies on the required bandwidth. This makes it possible to share and swap much larger files than would be possible with earlier file-sharing software. BitTorrent software was originally developed by Bram Cohen[143] and can now be downloaded from a number of sources. This software alone merely permits the requisite files to be downloaded; it does not itself provide search facilities and so, if it is to be used for illicit file sharing, needs to be used in conjunction with another file, the tracker. The tracker is often obtained from another website that allows users to search for the files they want, which can then be downloaded using BitTorrent.[144] There is no doubt that BitTorrent itself provides an extremely effective and efficient way of transferring files, and has substantial non-infringing uses. Because it also does not itself provide users with the tools to actually locate files, it is very likely that a *Sony*-type defence would succeed if any action were to be brought against sites that merely allow downloading of the BitTorrent software and on which there was no evidence of intent to induce users to breach copyright.[145] However, the situation regarding tracker websites is more complex. If litigation were to be pursued against a site that merely provided search facilities, then it would arguably be difficult to support an argument that it has facilitated or authorised copyright infringement given that it does not actually provide the wherewithal for the user to download the file; to take advantage of the pure tracker site, the user would have already had to have installed the BitTorrent application. On the other hand, some sites, of which the most famous is probably Pirate Bay, not only provide search facilities, but also link to sites from which BitTorrent can be

---

139 Ibid, [520].
140 Jeffrey CJ Lee, 'The ongoing design duty in *Universal Music Australia Pty Ltd v Sharman License Holdings Ltd*: Casting the scope of copyright infringement even wider' (2007) 15 IJLIT 275.
141 [1988] AC 1013.
142 See also discussion in Haflidi Kristjan Larusson, 'Uncertainty in the scope of copyright: The case of illegal file-sharing in the UK' [2009] EIPR 124.
143 http://bramcohen.com/BitTorrent/
144 For more detailed explanation, see, eg, Rhys Boyd-Farell, 'Legal analysis of the implications of *MGM v Grokster* for BitTorrent' (2006) 11 Intell Prop L Bull 77, 78; Okechukwu Benjamin Vincents, 'Secondary liability for copyright infringement in the BitTorrent platform: Placing the blame where it belongs' [2008] EIPR 4, 6; Mikko Manner, Topi Siniketo, and Ulrika Polland, 'The Pirate Bay ruling: When the fun and games end' (2009) 20 Ent L R 197, 198.
145 See, eg, discussion in Boyd-Farell, op cit, 81ff.

downloaded.[146] In the case of Pirate Bay, it also made no secret of the fact that it supported illicit file sharing and had little respect for the rights of copyright holders.[147] On this basis, Touloumis, referring to the 'legal slipperiness' of BitTorrent technology, suggests that there is 'little doubt' that Pirate Bay would be held liable for secondary infringement under US copyright law.[148]

The concept of secondary infringement discussed in the high-profile cases of *Napster* and *Grokster* does not feature in the majority of the civil law countries in Europe, and Pirate Bay was, of course, not operating out of the USA, but out of Sweden. It had been founded in 2003 and had apparently become the most extensively used file-sharing website. Files downloaded were not limited to music, but also included films, books, and TV programmes.[149] Under Swedish copyright law, it is a criminal offence to infringe copyright; further, the **Swedish Criminal Code** also criminalises any act that contributes to a criminal offence whether by words or actions.[150] So, although Swedish law contains no provisions that parallel secondary or contributory infringement, the possibility of criminal liability in this context arises if it can be established that those accused of contributing to, or facilitating, a copyright infringement had knowledge of the infringements, knew that their actions contributed to that infringement, and were doing so for financial gain.[151] On this basis, charges were brought against the three individuals operating the Pirate Bay website and its financier, together with a civil claim for damages on behalf of the copyright holders affected by their activities. The Stockholm District Court found that file sharing was an illicit communication to the public of copyright works and would be a criminal offence in Sweden, provided that it took place in that jurisdiction. This could clearly be established by the fact that the copyright materials were available to users in Sweden, the website was available in Swedish, and the servers were in Sweden. The primary offence was therefore deemed to have occurred in Sweden. Further, the defendants had contributed to the copyright infringement 'by providing a user-friendly interface and search engine, simple upload and download procedures and by administering contacts between users by its tracker or torrent files'.[152]

The eventual outcome attracted intense publicity when the court gave custodial sentences of one year to each of the defendants.[153] An important factor in the perceived severity of these sentences is likely to have been the attitude of the defendants to file sharing and copyright infringement evidenced by their comments on the website and their general attitude to the rights of copyright holders; they had 'made it clear that they were not going to put an end to such dissemination, even in cases whether there could be no doubt that it was in violation of individual identified rights'.[154] Edstrom and Nillson refer to the decision as 'a minor milestone in society's quest to come to terms with the effects of digitalisation of products and the disruptive efficiency of the internet in the distribution of these digitalised products'.[155] In the *Pirate Bay* case, it was not at all difficult to infer intent from the surrounding circumstances, but a clearer exposition of what is required might be desirable for cases that are less equivocal. The case has been appealed, so further developments along these lines remain possible.

---

146 For an overview of the operation of Pirate Bay, see, eg, Jerker Edstrom and Henrik Nillson, 'The Pirate Bay: Predictable and yet . . .' [2009] EIPR 483.
147 See, eg, Manner et al, op cit, 198.
148 Tara Touloumis, 'Buccaneers and bucks from the internet: Pirate Bay and the entertainment industry' (2009) 19 Seton Hall J Sports and Ent L 253, 262–6.
149 Henrik Wistam and Therese Andersson, 'The Pirate Bay trial' (2009) 15 CTLR 129.
150 Edstrom and Nillson, op cit.
151 Manner et al, op cit, 198.
152 Wistam and Andersson, op cit, 130.
153 However, it was not the first case in Scandinavia in which criminal liability had been imposed on the administrators of a file-sharing service. In June 2008, the Turku Court of Appeal in Finland upheld the decision against the 'Finreactor' BitTorrent-based P2P network. For further discussion, see Mikko Manner, 'A BitTorrent P2P network shut down and its operation deemed illegal in Finland' (2009) 20 Ent LR 21.
154 Edstrom and Nillson, op cit, 487.
155 Ibid.

The effect that this litigation has had on illicit file-sharing activities is difficult to ascertain and evaluate. Since the *Napster* case, there have been an increasing number of sites providing lawful downloading services, such as Spotify and the resurrected Napster itself. Although, as noted above, figures continue to be quoted about the extent and effect of file sharing, Koempel reports that, following the *Pirate Bay* case, internet traffic in Sweden has reduced by 30 per cent compared to its value before April 2009, and further that 'the latest IFPI figures show that sales of recorded music rose 14 per cent with digital sales up 57 per cent',[156] which could be taken to suggest that the number of users who opt to download lawfully rather than to engage in illicit file sharing is increasing.

Actions against ISPs

The examples referred to above have been cases against those who make available file-sharing software. In the bid to constrain unlawful file sharing, the music industry and associations representing the rights of copyright holders have not only pursued distributors of file-sharing applications, but have also initiated actions against both ISPs that are perceived to allow access to file-sharing applications via their networks and, as discussed below, individual file sharers. ISPs have been a popular target for those wishing to gain some recompense for violation of their rights in situations in which they cannot identify or cannot locate the offending parties, or in which there are other problems in bringing suit. ISPs, in contrast, are in line because they fulfil all of these criteria, being identifiable, locatable, and frequently situated in the same jurisdiction. There are some very different approaches to the question of the extent of ISPs' liability for copyright infringement, which, to a great extent, depends on whether they are acting merely as a communications carrier, providing the means of transmission between provider and user, or whether they have, or are capable of having, some input and control over at least some of the material to which they provide access. It has been fairly widely recognised that, when acting as a mere communications carrier, there is a very strong case for exemption 'from any type of copyright liability in respect of the provision of Internet infrastructure',[157] but that the situation may not be so clear-cut for ISPs that retain some control. The liability of ISPs for copyright infringement is governed in the USA by the **DMCA**, in the European Union (EU) by the provisions of the **E-Commerce Directive**[158] and the **Copyright Directive**,[159] implemented in the UK by the **Copyright and Related Rights Regulations 2003**.[160] Both the EU and US provisions purport to provide ISPs with immunity from suit (a 'safe harbor') provided that they are not acting as a content provider and have no involvement with the actual information transmitted via their networks – that is, that they are acting as a 'mere conduit'.[161] In both cases, immunity can be lost if there is evidence that the ISP had knowledge (actual or constructive) of the infringement. The provisions of the **DMCA** and the European Directives provide immunity from liability not only for transient and temporary copies, but also for the actual hosting of material that is in breach of copyright, provided that where there is knowledge of infringing material, that material is removed 'expeditiously'. The **DMCA** clarifies this duty with a very detailed 'takedown' procedure, whereas the parallel provision in Art 14(3) of the **E-Commerce Directive** allows Member States a discretion to use such a procedure.

See Chapter 3

---

156 Florian Koempel, 'Digital Economy Bill' (2010) 16 CTLR 39, 42.

157 See, eg, F Macmillan and M Blakeney, 'The internet and communication carriers' liability' [1998] EIPR 52.

158 Directive 2000/31/EC of the European Parliament and of the Council of 8 June 2000 on certain legal aspects of information society services, in particular electronic commerce, in the Internal Market [2000] OJ L178/1.

159 Directive 2001/29/EC of the European Parliament and of the Council of 22 May 2001 on the harmonisation of certain aspects of copyright and related rights in the information society [2001] OJ L167/10.

160 SI 2003/2498.

161 See, in particular, E-Commerce Directive, Art 12, and DMCA § 512(a). ISPs can also take advantage of safe harbours in relation to the activities of caching and hosting.

Although, in Europe, the substantive provisions relating to ISPs are found in the **E-Commerce Directive**, Art 8(3) of the **Copyright Directive** requires Member States to ensure that injunctions are available against intermediaries whose services are used by a third party to infringe copyright. In *SABAM v Tiscali*, this provision was relied on in November 2004 by the Court of First Instance of Brussels in an action by a Belgian society of authors, composers, and publishers against an ISP for allowing the file sharing of infringing music files via its service, even though the Directive had not yet been transposed into Belgian law.[162] Controversially, when the case came to full trial in 2007,[163] the Court, having taken technical advice, ordered Tiscali Belgium (renamed 'Scarlet') to install filtering software to prevent users from accessing infringing downloaded files by means of P2P file-sharing applications, having concluded from the expert evidence provided that it would not be disproportionately expensive to do so.[164] The appeal against this decision has led to two questions being referred from the Belgian Court of Appeal to the ECJ.[165] The first concerns the scope of the ability both to issue an injunction against ISPs whose services are used to infringe copyright, and to require filtering as a preventive measure. If such orders are permissible, the second question further asks about the application of the principle of proportionality when deciding on the effectiveness and the dissuasive effect of the measure sought. The outcome of this case will be awaited with interest: on the one hand, although a 'safe harbor' provision is easier to implement, it may not necessarily provide the most appropriate balance of rights; on the other hand, requiring a proportionate response will depend on the particular facts of an individual case, which will need to be adjudicated by the national courts and might lead to inconsistency of approach across jurisdictions.

The most frequent action by rights holders against ISPs, though, is to attempt to require them to provide details of individual clients who are suspected of illicit file sharing in order that the right holders – or, more usually, organisations acting on their behalf – can initiate action against the individuals concerned. Examples of this type of litigation can be found in a large number of jurisdictions, and have generated significant discussion over where the balance should be drawn between the right to uphold copyright, on the one hand, and, on the other, the individual user's right to privacy. The latter may ostensibly be protected by the contract with the ISP and/or specific data protection law, depending on the jurisdiction in question. In Europe, the issue had already arisen in a number of jurisdictions[166] before being considered by the ECJ in *Promusicae*.[167] The facts of the case were not unusual: Promusicae, a non-profit-making association seeking to uphold the intellectual property rights of its members, was contesting the refusal of the ISP, Telefonica, to disclose names and addresses of certain of its customers. Promusicae was in possession of known IP addresses, data, and patterns of use that suggested file sharing using Kazaa, but did not have specific names and contact details. Questions were referred to the ECJ from the court in Madrid concerning the clash between, and the required balance of, intellectual property rights, specifically copyright, and the right to privacy in the form of data protection rights.[168] At the heart of these cases was the apparently simple question of whether data can be acquired without consent if it is needed to trace an intellectual property violation. The ECJ in *Promusicae* considered the provisions of

---

162 For details, see, eg, Stibbe ICT Law Newsletter No 18, January 2005, p 7, available online at www.stibbe.be/assets/publications/newsletters/stibbe_ict_law_newsletter_no_18.pdf

163 *SABAM v SA Scarlet*, District Court of Brussels, No 04/8975/A, Decision of 29 June 2007, published in CAELJ Translation Series #001, trans Mady, Bourrouilhou, and Hughes (2008) 25 Cardozo Arts & Ent LJ 1279; see further discussion in Chris Watson, Tom Scourfield, and Scott Fairbairn, 'Why the *SABAM v Tiscali* questions matter' (2010) 21 Computers and Law 22.

164 See also *Roadshow Films Pty Ltd v iiNet Ltd* [2009] FCA 332.

165 Case C-70/10 *Scarlet Extended SA v SABAM* [2010] OJ C113/20. On 14 April 2011, the Advocate General proposed that an order requiring filtering was not compatible with EU law.

166 See, eg, *SCPP v Anthony G* (Court of Appeal of Paris, 27 April 2007), available online at www.legalis.net/jurisprudence-decision.php3?id_article=1954 (in French); *Peppermint Jam v Telecom Italia*, discussed in Eugenio Prosperetti, 'The Peppermint "Jam": Peer to peer goes to court in Italy' (2007) 18 Ent LR 280; *KPN v Brein* (District Court of the Hague 2007), discussed in Diderik Stols, 'Brein v KPN Telecom and the Dutch Civil Code: ISPs under pressure' (2007) 18 Ent LR 147; see also (2007) 23 CLSR 317.

167 Case 275/06 *Productores de Musica de Espana v Telefonica de Espana* [2008] ECR I-271, and see discussion in Helmer and Davies, op cit.

168 For further discussion of data protection law in Europe, see Chapter 5.

a number of relevant directives on data protection, e-commerce, and intellectual rights.[169] Advocate General Kokott pointed out that, although rights of privacy were fundamental, the protection of copyright was also an interest of society the importance of which had been repeatedly emphasised by the Community,[170] so that, even though the interests of rights holders are private rather than public, they can still be categorised as a fundamental interest of society. However, the Advocate General was not certain that private file sharing threatened copyright protection to the extent that it should take precedence over data protection.[171]

The ECJ judgment itself raised the need to reconcile privacy with property rights,[172] but was very vague as to how this balance should be struck; having set out the overarching principle of reconciliation, it then left the matter for the national court to ensure that implementation of the relevant directives allowed a fair balance to be struck. No explicit guidance was provided on how this might be assessed, but, in the particular case, both the Advocate General and the ECJ found that the combination of the respective provisions did not require personal data to be divulged when the illegal act being pursued did not attract criminal sanctions in the home state. Nevertheless, the judgment leaves it open to Member States to make such provision, assuming that the balance between data protection and copyright is addressed in a proportional manner.

Attempts to pursue individual file sharers by obtaining their details from ISPs have continued in Europe and similar examples can be found in a number of other jurisdictions.[173] In all cases, though, courts seem to consider that file sharers should not be able to use privacy rights to prevent or inhibit them from being pursued for copyright infringement, even though the ethos of the technology is to foster and encourage the availability of such material. The prevailing legal response is encapsulated in the following comment of Poon J in the Hong Kong case of *Cinepoly Records Co Ltd v Hong Kong Broadband Network Ltd*:

> The Internet is invaluable and even indispensable, some would suggest, to the free communication, dissemination and sharing of information in modern societies . . . I have no intention whatsoever to restrict, obstruct or otherwise frustrate the free flow of communication and information on the Internet. . . . Users of the Internet, like any individuals, must abide by the law. And the law protects the users' rights as much as others' legitimate rights, including those of the copyright owners. Some online copyright infringers may well think that they will never be caught because of the cloak of anonymity created by the P2P programs. They are wrong. . . . For protection of privacy is never and cannot be used as a shield to enable them to commit civil wrongs with impunity.[174]

---

169 Specifically: Directive 95/46 of the European Parliament and of the Council on the protection of individuals with regard to the processing of personal data [2005] OJ L281/31; Directive 2002/58/EC of the European Parliament and of the Council concerning the processing of personal data and the protection of privacy in the electronic communications sector [2002] OJ L 201/37; Directive 2000/31/EC of the European Parliament and of the Council on certain legal aspects of information society services, in particular electronic commerce, in the Internal Market [2000] OJ L178/1; Directive 2001/29/EC of the European Parliament and of the Council on the harmonisation of certain aspects of copyright and related rights in the information society [2001] OJ L167/10; and Directive 2004/48/EC of the European Parliament and of the Council on the enforcement of intellectual property rights [2004] OJ L 157/45.
170 [2008] ECR I-271, [105].
171 Ibid, [106].
172 Ibid, [65].
173 See, eg, *Cinepoly Records Co Ltd v Hong Kong Broadband Network Ltd* HCMP002487/2005, available online at http://legalref.judiciary.gov.hk/lrs/common/ju/ju_body.jsp?DIS=51414&AH=&QS=&FN=&currpage=, and discussed further in Jojo Mo, '*Cinepoly Records Co Ltd v Hong Kong Broadband Network Ltd*' [2009] EIPR 48; *Odex Pte Ltd v Pacific Internet Ltd* [2007] SGDC 248, discussed in Susanna HS Leong, 'Pre-action discovery against a network service provider and unmasking the John Does of alleged online copyright infringements in Singapore' [2009] EIPR 185. See also John Leitner, 'A legal and cultural comparison of file-sharing disputes in Japan and the Republic of Korea and implications for future cyber-regulation' (2008) 2 Colum J Asian L 1; Matthew Starmer, 'Video game company hunts down individual gamers in clampdown on illicit peer to peer file sharing' (2009) Ent L Rev 20. For a more US-centred discussion, see, eg, Weixiao Wei, 'ISP indirect copyright liability: Conflicts of rights on the internet' (2009) 15 CTLR 181.
174 *Cinepoly Records*, above, [78].

Actions against Individual File Sharers

Whilst there are certainly some proponents of a freer exchange and dissemination of information via the internet, an increasingly hard line is also being taken against file sharers. Henslee reports that, in its attempts to stop unlawful file sharing, the Recording Industry Institution of America (RIAA) has initiated suit against over 35,000 file sharers since 2003.[175] In the first instance, RIAA and parallel institutions in other jurisdictions typically send 'cease and desist' letters to alleged file sharers, as a result of which most agree to settle for some agreed sum without formal action being taken.[176] The controversial and potentially far-reaching implications of a policy of aggressive pursuit of individual file sharers are highlighted by the ongoing litigation in the US case of *Capitol Records v Thomas Rassett*. Although not brought by the RIAA itself, *Capitol v Thomas* began in exactly the same way, but was the first such action to go to trial before a jury. At the initial trial,[177] the jury was directed that the copyright holders' right to control distribution of their works was infringed, even in the absence of evidence of actual distribution, merely by the act of 'making available'. The jury found Thomas liable for wilful infringement and she was required to pay statutory damages of US$222,000 (US$9,250 for each of 24 songs). However, a retrial was subsequently ordered on the basis that the above instruction to the jury was 'erroneous' and that *actual* dissemination, rather than merely 'making available' for dissemination, was required to establish distribution. In making the order for the retrial, Chief Judge Michael Davis suggested there was a need for congressional action to amend the **Copyright Act** in response to liability and damages in P2P file-sharing cases. Whilst not condoning Thomas' actions, he acknowledged that they were for purely personal reasons and could not be compared with the actions of those who engaged in widespread piracy for profit. Although 'cumulatively, illegal downloading has far-reaching effects . . . the damages awarded in this case are wholly disproportionate to the damages suffered' and this comment was obviously before the award was increased almost tenfold. He went on to summarise as follows:

> In the case of commercial actors, the potential gain in revenues is enormous and enticing to potential infringers. In the case of individuals who infringe by using peer-to-peer networks, the potential gain from infringement is access to free music, not the possibility of hundreds of thousands – or even millions – of dollars in profits. This fact means that statutory damages awards of hundreds of thousands of dollars is certainly far greater than necessary to accomplish Congress's goal of deterrence. . . . Her status as a consumer who was not seeking to harm her competitors or make a profit does not excuse her behavior. But it does make the award of hundreds of thousands of dollars in damages unprecedented and oppressive.[178]

However, on the retrial, the same verdict was returned, with increased statutory damages of US$1.92 million (that is, US$80,000 per song).[179] This apparently punitive award raised a number of issues relating to both the award and the assessment of distribution. Thomas is a single mother, with limited means, who was clearly unable to pay the damages; neither was the sum a reflection of the 'damage' that she inflicted, but rather the award was a result of the fact that the US **Copyright Act** makes provision for statutory damages of US$750–US$150,000 per work to be payable to those who register their works prior to infringement, and the higher end of the spectrum of possible charges can be applied to those who are deemed, as Thomas was, to make a 'wilful'

---

175 William Henslee, 'Money for nothing and music for free? Why the RIAA should continue to sue illegal file-sharers' (2009) 9 J Marshall Rev Intell Prop L 1; see also http://recordingindustryvspeople.blogspot.com/

176 In this context, see also the discussion of the practice and effect of volume litigation in Andrew Murray, 'Volume litigation: More harmful than helpful?' (2010) 20 Computers and Law 46.

177 579 F Supp 2d 1210 (DC Minnesota 2008).

178 Ibid, 1227.

179 See Nate Anderson, 'Thomas verdict: Willful infringement, $1.92 million penalty' (2009) *arstechnica.com*, 18 June, available online at http://arstechnica.com/tech-policy/news/2009/06/jammie-thomas-retrial-verdict.ars

infringement.[180] The magnitude of this award led to specific criticism of the inequity of the use of statutory damages in such cases. As Samuelson and Wheatland's extensive analysis demonstrates,[181] statutory damages may be punitive in both intent and effect, and they proposed that reform was needed since such damages can be 'applied in a manner that often results in arbitrary, inconsistent, unprincipled, and grossly excessive awards'.[182] On the other hand, there were also those who believed that the deterrent value of making such awards against individual file sharers should not be overlooked and suggested that *Capitol Records v Thomas* served as 'an example of how well litigation works to spread the word that downloading is illegal'.[183]

The second trial was itself overturned on the amount of the award and, at a further hearing in January 2010,[184] the damages award was reduced to US\$2,250 per song, with Chief District Judge Davis again making some categorical statements about the need to justify the amount awarded. In particular, he was of the view that the need for deterrence could not justify the damages awarded at the second trial, and that there had to be some relation between statutory damages and the actual loss suffered by the plaintiffs. In particular, he pointed out that it was a considerable task to find an amount that balanced the jury's wide discretion to address wilful violations, the plaintiffs' 'far-reaching but nebulous damages', the need to deter online piracy, and the 'outrageousness' of the award of US\$2 million. In his view, even the amount of the reduced award was 'significant and harsh', but was 'the maximum amount that is no longer monstrous and shocking'.[185] The reduction in the award was not accepted by the plaintiffs and a further trial purely on the measure of damages has been scheduled for October 2010.

The ongoing discussion in *Capitol v Thomas* thus relates purely to the appropriate amount of compensation in file-sharing cases, and the decision has still left some confusion over whether or not merely 'making available' is sufficient to ground an action for infringement or whether there needs to be evidence of 'actual dissemination'. Espousing the 'making available' approach would radically change the balance of copyright law, since rights holders would not even need to prove that any files had actually been transferred to establish a case of primary infringement. The reasoning on this point has been criticised by academic commentators and has not been uniformly accepted by all US court circuits.[186]

In contrast, in France in 2005, the Tribunal de Grande Instance de Paris held file sharing to be legal based on an exception relating to copying for private use. However, the French Supreme Court, in a later decision, did not allow a student who shared files downloaded from the internet onto CDs to benefit from this exemption.[187] But decisions such as these have now been overtaken by a legislative response to the growing threat of piracy. In June 2009, France enacted the controversial **Creation and Internet Law**, with the objective of both providing sanctions for illegal downloading, and also encouraging the development of legal downloading. Amongst other things, the law established an administrative authority to deal with the protection of creative works online: *Haute Autorité pour la Diffusion des Oeuvres et la Protection des Droit sur Internet* (HADOPI – now usually adopted as the acronym for the law itself). The provisions of this law were based on a 'three-strikes model' and gave the authority the power to suspend internet access for up to a year on the third strike.

---

180 See discussion in Pamela Samuelson and Ben Sheffner, 'Unconstitutionally excessive statutory damage awards in copyright cases' (2009) 158 U Pa L Rev PENNumbra 53.

181 Pamela Samuelson and Tara Wheatland, 'Statutory damages in copyright law: A remedy in need of reform' (2009) 51 Wm & Mary L Rev 439.

182 Ibid, 497.

183 Henslee, op cit.

184 680 F Supp 2d 1045 (DC Minnesota, 2010).

185 Ibid, 1049.

186 See, eg, John Horsfield-Bradbury, 'Making available as distribution: File sharing and the Copyright Act' (2008) 22 Harv JL & Tech 273; Shana Dines, 'Actual interpretation yields actual dissemination: An analysis of the make available theory argued in peer-to-peer file sharing lawsuits and why courts ought to reject it' (2009) 32 Hastings Comm & Ent LJ 157.

187 *Ministere Public v Aurelien*, discussed in Christophe Geiger, 'Legal or illegal? That is the question! Private copying and downloading on the internet' (2008) 39 IIC 597.

However, the law, as originally enacted (**HADOPI 1**), was immediately challenged, and parts were ruled unconstitutional on the basis that there was an insufficient balance between copyright and data protection rights,[188] that the sanctions were disproportionate to the user's freedom of expression, and that the burden of proof was placed on the user to show that he or she was not responsible for any alleged piracy. The consequent revisions resulted in the adoption of **HADOPI 2**, in which the function of the authority was reduced to monitoring illegal downloads and warning individuals when illegal downloads are detected. The power to impose sanctions, including suspension of internet accounts and custodial sentences in appropriate cases, was passed to judges,[189] but users could also be liable if third parties were to make illegal downloads from their accounts. **HADOPI 2** was itself subject to a constitutional challenge, but the Constitutional Council, in a decision on 22 October 2009, upheld the law as it stood – a decision described by the lobbying group La Quadrature du Net as 'sad news for democracy and the rule of law'.[190] Given that the **HADOPI** law envisages custodial sentences, it may be that individual users will follow the path taken by the providers of file-sharing software in the *Pirate Bay* case.

In 2006, in the UK, the *Gowers Review*, in its review of the current state of intellectual property law, recommended that the industry agreement of protocols for sharing data between ISPs and rights holders should be observed in order to remove and disbar users engaged in 'piracy', with the additional proviso that if this approach had not proved successful by the end of 2007, then the government should consider whether to legislate.[191] In the subsequent *Digital Britain* report, produced after extensive consultation, the government noted that 'unlawful downloading or uploading, whether via peer-to-peer sites or other means, is effectively a civil form of theft', together with its belief that a reduction of 70–80 per cent was needed in the incidence of unlawful file sharing.[192] In consequence, it set out the following intentions in relation to internet downloads:

> Firstly, to provide a framework that encourages the growth of legal markets for downloading that are inexpensive, convenient and easily accessible for consumers. Secondly, through encouraging suitable information and education initiatives, to ensure that consumers are fully aware of what is and is not lawful. And thirdly . . . to provide for a graduated response by rights-holders and ISPs so that they can use the civil law to the full to deter the hard core of users who wilfully continue unlawful activity.[193]

See Chapter 3 → Legislative provisions dealing with the last of these points are now contained in the **Digital Economy Act 2010 (DEA 2010)**, which, inter alia, inserts new ss 124A–O into the **Communications Act 2003 (CA 2003)** providing for a 'graduated response' to illicit file sharing and copyright infringement on the internet. The Act, passed eventually in the 'wash-up' of Bills before Parliament was dissolved for the 2010 general election, went further than *Digital Britain* and a number of its more controversial provisions were introduced at a later date. The Act has already been the subject of trenchant criticism both for its provisions relating to online copyright infringement and the manner of its enactment.[194] Indeed, the High Court allowed an application for judicial review of the statute on behalf of two ISPs, TalkTalk and BT, on the basis that there was

---

188 See also Case 275/06 *Productores de Musica de Espana v Telefonica de Espana* [2008] ECR I-271 (*Promusicae*).
189 This could include a fast-track procedure in which a single judge could issue a sanction without a hearing on an *ex parte* basis: see LinkLaters, 'France: The Hadopi Law and France's controversial fight against piracy' (1009) *LinkLaters.com*, 16 October, available online at www.linklaters.com/Publications/Publication1403Newsletter/20091016/Pages/FranceTheHadopiLaw.aspx
190 La Quadrature du Net, 'HADOPI 2 validated: A defeat for the rule of law' (2009) *Laquadature.net*, 24 October, available online at www.laquadrature.net/en/hadopi-2-validated-a-defeat-for-the-rule-of-law
191 *Gowers Review*, op cit, Recommendation 39.
192 *Digital Britain*, para 18.
193 Ibid, paras 45–6.
194 On the latter, see, eg, Out-law.com, 'The legislative farce of the Digital Economy Bill' (2010) *Out-law.com*, 7 April, available online at http://out-law.com/page-10900

insufficient scrutiny of the provisions dealing with file sharing discussed below, but the majority of claims were dismissed.[195] The provisions relevant to file sharing are both detailed and complex, but the following discussion provides a summary. New ss 124A and 124B, **CA 2003** (ss 3 and 4, **DEA 2010**) provide details of the 'initial obligations' placed on ISPs, and provide certain rights for the copyright owner that the ISP must implement. These obligations are to be governed by an 'initial obligations code' (IOC), as provided for in new ss 124C and 124D (ss 5 and 6, **DEA 2010**). A new s 124E (s 7 **DEA 2010**) details the contents of such codes. In brief, s 124C allows UK communications regulator Ofcom to approve IOCs that have been drafted by specific ISPs, or the industry generally, to comply with their obligations under these new provisions. Section 124D further allows Ofcom to make a code to regulate the initial obligations in the event that there is no pre-existing approved IOC.

If an IOC is in force, then a copyright owner can make a copyright infringement report (s 124A(2)) to the ISP if it *appears* to a copyright owner that either a subscriber of an internet access service, or someone who he or she has allowed to use the service, has infringed the owner's copyright (s 124A(1)). 'Who [he or she has] allowed' has a potentially wide interpretation, and it has been speculated that this section could apply, for example, to businesses that provide wi-fi as a service and also to domestic unsecured wi-fi networks. Similarly, organisations (such as universities, pubs and cafes, for example), which provide access to the internet to large numbers of individuals, may also fall within the ambit of this section. Any such copyright infringement report must, inter alia, state that there appears to have been a copyright infringement, and offer both a description of that apparent infringement and evidence of it, including the subscriber's IP address and the time at which the evidence was gathered. Any ISP receiving such a notice must then, if required by the IOC, notify the subscriber in question within a month. These new provisions are based solely on the existence of an *apparent* infringement and contain no provisions that deal with reckless, negligent, speculative, malicious, or vexatious notifications. It has already been widely reported that subscribers have been mistakenly accused of file sharing, and it seems unlikely that this trend will be reduced by the enactment of this statute.[196]

The required contents of any such notification are detailed in s 124A(6). In addition to expected details, such as the description and evidence of the apparent infringement, the name of the copyright holder, etc, the notification must also include 'information about copyright and its purpose'. Given that the purpose of copyright can be a contentious topic and not infrequently features in essay topics for those studying the subject, it will be interesting to see what is included in the notification in this respect. Section 124A(6)(i) includes the catch-all that the notification must also include anything else that might be required by the IOC. Examples of what this could refer to are suggested in s 124A(8) and include, inter alia, that the copyright owner might apply to a court to both find out the subscriber's identity, and also bring proceedings for copyright infringement. Section 124B then further requires that, if requested, an ISP must supply a copyright owner with a copyright infringement list that 'sets out in relation to each relevant subscriber which of the copyright infringement reports relate to the subscriber but does not enable any subscriber to be identified'.[197]

The intention is that the notification process will itself deter online copyright infringement, but ss 124F–J then make provision for subsequent action in the event that the desired reduction in online copyright infringement is not achieved. Ofcom is charged with the general oversight of the new regime and s 124F imposes a duty on Ofcom to prepare reports on the extent of infringement of copyright by internet users. Once an IOC has been in force for twelve months, 'technical obligations' may be imposed on ISPs to take 'technical measures' for the purpose of preventing or reducing

---

195 [2011] EWHC 1021.
196 Dan Sabbagh, 'Digital Economy Act likely to increase households targeted for piracy' (2010) *GuardianOnline*, 12 April, available online at www.guardian.co.uk/media/2010/apr/12/digital-economy-bill-households-piracy; see also Murray, op cit.
197 Compare the ECJ discussion in *Promusicae*, above.

infringement of copyright by means of the internet (ss 124G and 124H). A 'technical measure' in this context is something that may limit the speed of the internet connection, prevent access to particular sites, suspend the service, or otherwise limit what is provided to the subscriber. These provisions that allow for the introduction of punitive action with very little opportunity for external scrutiny, albeit subject to a code of practice (ss 124I and 124J) and an appeals process (s 124K), are probably the most controversial elements of the new regulatory framework, but it is clearly too early to be able to state with any confidence exactly how this will operate in practice.

Technological Protection Mechanisms and Digital Rights Management

Digital technology allows the creation of multiple copies of works that are indistinguishable from the original and also copies of copies with no subsequent deterioration in quality. As Lemley and Reese comment, 'the great promise of digital dissemination – the virtual elimination of the costs of copy production and distribution – is a mixed blessing for copyright owners'.[198] It is hardly surprising, therefore, that as digital dissemination has increased, so have systems of digital rights management (DRM). DRM systems may be used both to prevent actual access to copyright works to prevent infringing copying, or to control the use of a copyright work, which the user has been authorised to access. In principle, therefore, they allow new methods of delivering content, while still maintaining protection for the right holder's copyright and so, from a rights holder perspective, look like an effective model for the control and dissemination of digital content. DRM systems have been made possible by the development of technological protection mechanisms (TPMs), which prevent copying, thereby providing an additional method of protection for an author's works that are disseminated online. The use of DRMs and TPMs has been paralleled by legal provisions supporting their use in both the EU and the USA, although these have proved to be a controversial addition to the law on copyright. In particular, these provisions proscribe anti-circumvention technologies, as required by Art 11 of the World Intellectual Property Organization (WIPO) **Copyright Treaty 1996**. Importantly, this Article implicitly allows circumvention of anti-copying measures for acts that would be permitted by law, but, in the nature of the Treaty provision, gives no practical guidance as to how this should or could be accomplished. The new approach targets the actual prevention of copying, together with those who provide the technology to circumvent this prevention. The circumvention of anti-copying devices raises specific issues in relation to the ability to, and the legality of, decompilation or disassembly of a computer program, but also has wider implications for the dissemination of copyright works on the internet.

See Chapter
10 →

In the EU, such provisions were introduced in the **Copyright Directive**. Although asserting in Recital 5 that 'no new concepts for the protection of intellectual property are needed', but that 'the current law on copyright and related rights should be adapted and supplemented to respond adequately to economic realities such as new forms of exploitation', the Preamble contains many references to the appropriate balance of rights that needs to be achieved. The need for incentives, and appropriate regard for creative and intellectual endeavour, is emphasised in Recitals 9–11. Recital 14 notes the simultaneous need to 'seek to promote learning and culture . . . while permitting exceptions or limitations in the public interest', and Recital 31 states explicitly that 'a fair balance of rights and interests between the different categories of right holders, as well as between the different categories of right holders and users of protected subject-matter must be safeguarded'. These provisos are then given legal effect in Art 6 of the Directive. The extent to which this

---

198 Lemley and Reese, op cit, 1375.

provision is successful at balancing these competing interests is open to question, and the fact that the wording does not lend itself to easy apprehension is highlighted by the comment that 'the InfoSoc Directive's eventual provision on the subject, Art 6, became during the legislative process so twisted by conflicting demands as to resemble Laocoon wrestling with the serpents. Legislation should never be so hideously contorted but here it writhes'.[199] Unfortunately, the effect of Art 6(4) in no way encompasses all possible exceptions and limitations to the exclusive rights granted to copyright holders, such as the right to use material for the purposes of criticism or review, for example, suggesting that for fair dealing rights not included in Art 6(4), the Directive does not assist in maintaining a fair balance between authors' and users' rights.[200] Foged, in particular, discusses a number of instances in which public user privileges may be diminished, including when anti-circumvention measures operate to prevent rights given by fair use provisions and the fact that access may, incidentally, be prevented to works that are not subject to copyright protection, such as ideas, facts, and scènes à faire.[201]

The provisions of Art 6 are very similar in essence to those of the US **DMCA** §1201, which has also been criticised both for its complexity and on a more general basis. Although the **DMCA** purports to leave the usual fair use exceptions in place, it is difficult to see how compatible fair use is with the **DMCA**. A number of commentators immediately expressed concern at this apparent disturbance of the traditional balance of copyright law.[202] Fair use is threatened because, even where DRM is used to control rights, it is the copyright holder's interpretation of what rights can be granted (particularly with regard to fair use) rather than any accepted legal interpretation. In particular, copyright owners might, by DRM, grant themselves more protection than copyright law allows them – as Lemley and Reese have remarked, 'copyright owners have a history of trying to enforce the law beyond its bounds'.[203] Given that fair use and fair dealing exceptions are a primary mechanism whereby copyright law balances the rights of the creator and the public interest, DRM has the capacity to cause fundamental changes in the application of copyright law in the digital environment; as Ottolia has suggested, DRM systems can be regarded as 'technical systems enforcing (il?)legal rules'.[204]

Samuelson suggests that, notwithstanding the US commitment to the WIPO Treaty that it had been instrumental in drafting, it might not have been necessary to create such elaborate statutory provisions to give effect to the Treaty's intentions, because the pre-existing law could be construed appropriately.[205] Further, she concluded that, although the way in which the USA implemented the WIPO **Copyright Treaty** generally conformed to the spirit of the Treaty, which provided a 'predictable, minimalist, consistent and simple legal environment', this could not be said of the anti-circumvention provisions, which were:

> . . . unpredictable, overbroad, inconsistent, and complex. The many flaws in this legislation are likely to be harmful to innovation and competition in the digital economy sector, and harmful to the public's broader interests in being able to make fair and other non-infringing uses of copyrighted works.[206]

---

199 Cornish and Llewelyn, op cit, 857.
200 See also the more detailed discussion of this point in Terese Foged, 'US v EU anti-circumvention legislation: Preserving the public's privileges in the digital age' [2002] EIPR 525, 536–8; Michael Hart, 'The Copyright in the Information Society Directive: An overview' [2002] EIPR 58, 63–2.
201 Foged, op cit, 526.
202 See, eg, Pamela Samuelson, 'Intellectual property and the digital economy: Why the anti-circumvention regulations need to be revised' (1999) 14 Berkeley Tech LJ 519; David Nimmer, 'A riff on fair use in the Digital Millennium Copyright Act' (2000) 148 U Pa L Rev 673.
203 Lemley and Reese, op cit, 1384.
204 Andrea Ottolia, 'Preserving users' rights in DRM: Dealing with juridical particularism in the information society' (2004) 35 IIC 491, 492.
205 Samuelson (1999), op cit, 530. For application of Art 11 to free software, see Chapter 11.
206 Ibid, 563.

The issues raised by this latter point have also been the subject of discussion by other commentators, who are concerned that such provisions have the potential to effect a drastic change on the traditional balance between copyright owners' rights and public user privileges in favour of the copyright owner.[207] The fact that such rules may provide blanket protection preventing not only infringing use, but also lawful use under fair use and fair dealing exemptions, has thus arguably reinvigorated the old debate about how copyright law should preserve the balance between the rights of the copyright holder and the public interest in the dissemination of copyright works.

A particular argument is that the overuse of TPM effectively 'locks up' the copyright work so that it is virtually removed from the public domain, notwithstanding provisions detailing permitted acts such as use in research, criticism review, etc. Technology has no way of divining the difference between copying that is an infringement of copyright and that which is not because, for example, it falls within one of the exceptions to copyright, such as fair use or fair dealing. Although they can be used in a permissive way, technological devices, on their face, thus have the potential to prevent copying in an indiscriminate way. This fact is probably the factor most capable of creating significant perturbations in the traditional balance that copyright law has tried to establish between the rights of the copyright holder and the public interest in providing and maintaining access to copyright works. From this perspective, the balance is too heavily in favour of the right holder and neglects the rights given to users under copyright regimes. As Calandrillo and Davison remark, 'copyright scholars characterize the circumvention rule . . . as a "paradigm shift" away from a three century old focus on the activities of individuals who make unauthorized copies'.[208] On the other hand, proponents of TPM will suggest that there is no incentive to develop new methods of distributing content for the digital age without the use of reliable TPMs to prevent unauthorised downloads. Sookman, writing from a Canadian perspective, points out that 'the evidence is overwhelming that only a small portion of downloading does not involve infringement or illegal activity'[209] and that rights holders who try to establish legitimate payment-based digital delivery mechanisms are unable to compete with freely available content based on pirated copies. Sookman acknowledges that technological protection could potentially limit fair use, but suggests that the more significant issue is whether not providing sufficient protection for digital works will lead to a decline in innovation and creativity, and cites the **DMCA** provisions as demonstrating that the use and regulation of TPMs have not had a detrimental impact.[210] Overall, he concludes that TPMs are essential to counter the threat to rights holders from unauthorised downloading.

It is beyond the scope of this chapter to examine in detail the voluminous case law that there has now been on anti-circumvention provisions in the **DMCA**, but in their review of the history of the judicial interpretation of this case law, Calandrillo and Davison suggest that the approach has evolved from one in which the courts were 'blindly intent on preventing piracy and protecting copyright holders' through the nadir of an apparent abandonment of an accurate application of the Sony principle, to a more balanced approach in which courts have begun to recognise that 'a weak TPM does not outweigh the substantial public interest in information access'.[211] As well as the technical discussion about the relationship of the **DMCA** provisions with traditional copyright principles, the **DMCA** anti-circumvention measures have also been attacked as unconstitutional and constituting an unacceptable restriction on freedom of speech.[212] Mitchell, for example, points out

---

207 See, eg, Fitzpatrick, op cit, 219; Foged, op cit, 526.
208 Steve P Calandrillo and Ewa M Davison, 'The dangers of the Digital Millennium Copyright Act: Much ado about nothing?' (2008) 50 Wm & Mary L Rev 349, 363.
209 Sookman, op cit, 145.
210 Ibid, 152.
211 Calandrillo and Davison, op cit, 414–15.
212 TA Mitchell, 'Copyright, Congress and constitutionality: How the Digital Millennium Copyright Act goes too far' (2004) 79 Notre Dame L Rev 2115; GM Schley, 'The Digital Millennium Copyright Act and the First Amendment: How far should courts go to protect intellectual property rights?' (2004) 3 J High Tech L 115.

that the goal of the copyright clause in the US **Constitution** is defined as promoting the 'progress of science and the useful arts', and that the widespread dissemination of information via the internet points is capable of fulfilling this objective by generally promoting learning. This issue of constitutionality was considered by the US courts in the case of *Reimerdes*.[213] The case arose because the defendant website owners, Reimerdes, Corley, and Kazan, had made available the decryption code for DVD recordings (DeCSS) on their websites. DeCSS was designed to circumvent the encryption technology (CSS) that prevented unauthorised viewing and copying of films. One of the arguments presented was that because computer code is protected speech, in so far as the **DMCA** prohibited the dissemination of DeCSS, it violated the First Amendment. It was held that computer code was not exempted from the protection of the First Amendment because it was 'abstract and, in many cases, arcane', and neither because the instructions within a program required a computer to execute them.[214] However, it was found that the provisions of the **DMCA** at issue were content-neutral and, because they were not intended to suppress the ideas of programmers, any impact of the dissemination of programmers' ideas was purely incidental. Congress can enact content-neutral regulation provided that there is a sufficiently important governmental interest; this need not involve the least restrictive means of achieving the desired objective as long as, in the process, it did not substantially overburden more speech than was necessary.[215] As a result, no violation of First Amendment rights was found.

Conclusion

A pervasive theme throughout this chapter has been the need to balance the rights of the creators of copyright material with the rights of the users of that material. Whilst this is not a novel dilemma for copyright law, it may be that the balance requires rather different considerations online to offline. To what extent does copyright law need a root-and-branch reconfiguration for the digital age? Is copyright really so flexible a concept that it can accommodate the challenges of the digital age without contradicting the apparent precepts on which it was originally based? On the other hand, according to Deazley, copyright was initially based not on the rights of the individual, but on an intention to encourage and spread education, and to make information available to the reading public for the general benefit of society.[216] If, then, a digital copyright were to emerge in which the balance moved towards the user of copyright material, this could be viewed as returning copyright to its roots rather than a radical development. One solution may depend not on redrafting copyright law, but on creating and accepting new business models for the delivery of online content; as we have seen, however, such proposals do not envisage any modification of the copyright regime, but would take their place alongside it. Indeed, Turner and Callaghan have suggested that the growth of search tools, hyperlinkers, and content aggregators '[do] not necessitate a radical rewriting of current copyright laws', but propose instead that there should be rapid action at EU level to safeguard the providers of these tools by the provision of new mandatory exemptions.[217] Further, the

---

213 *Universal City Studios v Reimerdes et al* 111 F Supp 2d 294 (SDNY 2000), aff'd *Universal City Studios v Corley* 273 F 3d 429 (2nd Cir 2001), discussed above at pp 327–8.

214 *Reimerdes*, 327; *Corley*, 447.

215 *Corley*, 454–5.

216 Ronan Deazley, *On the Origins of the Right to Copy*, 2005, Oxford: Hart Publishing.

217 Mark Turner and Dominic Callaghan, 'You can look but don't touch! The impact of the *Google v Copiepresse* decision on the future of the internet' [2008] EIPR 34, 38. During the passage of the Digital Economy Bill, Lord Lucas proposed an amendment that would have introduced new sections in the Copyright, Designs and Patents Act 1988, which would have provided search engines with immunity from copyright infringement in certain circumstances. Although not adopted, it demonstrates the concern in some quarters to protect the fundamental operation of the internet from excessive litigation. For details see Out-law. com, 'Peer proposes copyright exemption for search engines' (2010) Out-law.com, 12 January, available online at www.out-law. com/page-10658; for the full text of the amendment, see www.publications.parliament.uk/pa/ld200910/ldbills/001/ amend/ml001-iie.htm

European Commission has noted that some rights holders prefer to protect existing revenue streams rather than actively to license their rights on new platforms, and that DRM and TPM have sometimes been perceived in a negative way, as technology used to restrict copying and competition.[218] Further, and more widely accepted, progress might occur if consensus and cooperation could be achieved on the development of both an appropriate rights regime and appropriate business models for the digital environment, rather than the apparent entrenchment favoured by some rights holder associations and user groups.

The fact that the technology produces such perfect copies may be the driving force behind the sometimes overzealous pursuit of copyright infringers – especially private individuals who historically have not usually been a major target for enforcement activity. However, as Lemley and Reese remark, 'the content industries have never had or needed perfect control over infringement',[219] which suggests that the goal should be sufficient, rather than total, control of infringement. (It would be a rare area of law in which 100 per cent compliance was expected, much less achieved.) Recent legal developments in case law, such as *Capitol Records v Thomas*, and legislative developments, such as the French **HADOPI** law and the UK **Digital Economy Act 2010**, represent serious steps towards dealing with individual infringers. As Watson et al point out, 'it still remains to be seen how measures designed to protect rights holders, but seen by opponents as draconian, can be objectively justified as proportionate'.[220] Although this was written in the context of the case of *Scarlet v SABAM*, the same sentiment could equally be applied to the provisions of the **DEA 2010**. Powell's view is that the law is 'increasingly modified for the benefit of the major content holders'.[221] In this context, the outcome of *Scarlet v SABAM* itself will be important, because, notwithstanding the above, there often appears to be a quandary amongst rights holders as to whether to pursue those who infringe copyright or those who provide them with the wherewithal to do so, whether that is the P2P service itself or an ISP that provides access to that service. Rights holders may well prefer to target P2P network providers and ISPs, because they are easily identifiable, locatable, and (presumably) solvent. On the other hand, this could be seen as allowing those who infringe to escape liability. The abortive attempts at volume litigation underline some of the problems with pursuing individual infringers and, even with the assistance of measures such as those in the **HADOPI** law and the **DEA 2010**, individuals may be much less worth pursuing. Although commentators such as Lemley and Reese have suggested that the problems of enforcement against individuals, including issues of cost, could be reduced by introducing a cheap and speedy alternative dispute resolution (ADR) mechanism, rather than engaging the formalities of litigation,[222] this approach is not currently under serious consideration.

Other copyright modifications in the USA and Europe in response to the digital and online environment, including the US **DMCA** and the EU **Copyright Directive**, do not prevent standard copyright principles being applied to activities on the internet. Both of these have provided ISPs with immunity from liability for copyright infringement, but there is evidence that opinion is turning on the wisdom of a complete blanket immunity. The House of Lords Science and Technology Committee, in its report on *Personal Internet Security*,[223] concluded that although it would not wish to see the abandonment of the 'mere conduit' defence, it might now be appropriate to 'take a nibble out of the blanket immunity'. More recently, in contrast, as the amendments introduced by the **DEA 2010** bite, ISPs will become an essential component of the enforcement process against individual infringers rather than being the neutral entity suggested by the term 'mere conduit'.

---

218 COM(2007)836 final.
219 Lemley and Reese, op cit, 1394.
220 Watson et al, op cit.
221 Aaron Ross Powell, 'Creators, consumers and distributors: Understanding the moral structure of digital copyright' (2009) 5 ISJLP 383, 405.
222 Lemley and Reese, op cit, 1351–2.
223 House of Lords Science and Technology Committee, *Fifth Report of Session 2006-07: Personal Internet Security*, 2007, London: HMSO.

As yet, therefore, there is no emerging consensus on how digital copyright should develop and it is clear that, in addition to the debate over which direction should be taken in the future, there will be continuing debate over the developments so far: as concluded by Cornish and Llewelyn, 'How far the results have been effective in real terms, how far therefore they have been fair, is a debate for the moment that can only rage'.[224]

---

224 Cornish and Llewelyn, op cit, 805.

Chapter 10

Intellectual Property Rights in Software

Chapter Contents

Introduction

In *University of London Press Ltd v University Tutorial Press Ltd*, Petersen J remarked that what is worth copying is prima facie worth protecting.[1] The truth underlying this statement is demonstrated nowhere so strikingly as in the commercial exploitation of computer software. Although computers have now been in existence for well over half a century, the protection of the intellectual property rights in computer programs and software only really became a legally significant issue with the later advent of microcomputers. In the early stages of development of the industry, computer systems were large, custom-built affairs, used primarily by large institutions, whether commercial, industrial or educational. If there was a need for protection of the intellectual property rights in the software and programs, then this could easily be accommodated in contractual terms, supplemented by actions for breach of confidence if appropriate.[2] As microprocessors and personal computers became commonplace, their use became widespread and was no longer confined to large institutions. This, together with the accompanying trend towards general applications programs, rather than specific bespoke software, meant that it rapidly became impossible to rely purely on contract and confidence to protect intellectual property rights in computer programs. As a considerable amount of research and development time and money may be devoted to the creation of new computer software, it is not surprising that those engaged in this activity look for assurance that their intellectual property rights are protected. Although desirable for commercial reasons and the familiar justification of intellectual property law as an incentive to innovation, providing such legal protection has not proved to be straightforward. A property of computer software, and a significant difference from other forms of intellectual property, is its extreme vulnerability to copying. This is a direct consequence of the nature of the technology – the actual functioning of a computer is dependent on copying code backwards and forwards. It is a trivial matter therefore to make copies of software and widespread piracy is easy. In contrast to the previous chapter, this chapter will consider the way in which the intellectual property rights in computer programs have developed and the scope of the legal protection available using traditional forms of intellectual property protection.

Choice of Intellectual Property Protection

Once intellectual property rights could no longer be protected by contract, the question arose as to what was an appropriate form of protection. The obvious contenders were copyright and patents. In principle, copyright appears to be suitable given that a program can be expressed in written form and copyright protects the form or expression of an idea rather than the idea itself. This should provide protection for the form of the program rather than the ideas that lie behind it and therefore leave it open to another programmer to write an independent program performing the same function without infringing copyright in the first program. In addition, copyright protection arises automatically on creation of the work and generally requires no fundamental creativity or originality as long as it is the author's own individual handiwork – albeit that the need for some minimal creativity/originality can create difficulties in respect of some utilitarian or functional works.[3] When a work is subject to copyright protection, the law gives a copyright owner certain rights to control the dissemination and use of the material that is subject to the copyright, including, of course, the rights to allow or prevent copying. This is intended to be balanced by certain rights for users that allow a certain amount of copying for certain specified reasons and under certain

---

1 [1916] 2 Ch 601, 610, per Petersen J.
2 These methods may still provide a useful remedy in certain cases. As an example, *Ibcos Computers Ltd v Barclays Mercantile Highland Finance Ltd* [1994] FSR 275 (discussed below) concerned an action for breach of confidence, as well as an action for copyright infringement.
3 See, eg, *Baker v Selden* 101 US 99 (1879), discussed later.

specified conditions, referred to as 'fair dealing' in UK law and 'fair use' in the USA. Copyright is long-lasting. The term of copyright protection under Art 7 of the **Berne Convention** is the life of the author plus 50 years, and this has been extended in many jurisdictions.[4] Computer programs can become obsolete in very short times and so could equally well be protected by a shorter term, but neither is the longer term available under current copyright law particularly detrimental. Overall, therefore, copyright could clearly be a suitable method of protection as long as any issues arising out of the functional or utilitarian nature of computer programs can be accommodated.

While copyright is the principle method of protecting creative works, in contrast, patent protection is usually considered the appropriate method of protecting intellectual property rights in functional works. Whereas copyright only protects form and expression, patents also protect the underlying ideas. Unlike copyright, patents do not arise automatically, but must be applied for and examined for compliance with the essential attributes of the patent – that is, novelty, inventiveness, and industrial application. Once a patent has been granted, it confers a monopoly on the holder for a limited period of time; this may appear to be more suitable for computer technology. On the other hand, it would, of course, mean that an independently produced program based on the same idea would violate the patent – the opposite situation to that pertaining to copyright protection. The application of patent law to computer programs will be considered in much more detail later in the chapter, but for now it should be pointed out there are two major obstacles to granting patent protection to computer programs. The first is the requirement of inventiveness: as pointed out by Karjala, 'most programs are simply an application of well known techniques to a well defined problem'.[5] The majority of programs are incremental changes to existing programs and do not exhibit the inventive step that is an essential prerequisite for patent protection. Second, in the UK and Europe at least, computer programs have been the subject of statutory exclusions from patent protection, as detailed in **European Patent Convention (EPC)**, Art 52(2), and the UK **Patents Act 1977**, s 1. Although other jurisdictions have developed a more relaxed approach to patenting software, as discussed later in the chapter, this exclusion is still a controversial one in Europe.

As early as the beginning of the 1970s, well before the use of computers was as ubiquitous as it is today, the World Intellectual Property Organization (WIPO) considered the above issues, and reviewed the most appropriate and effective method of protecting the intellectual property rights in computer software and programs.[6] It identified with accuracy a number of issues that were to trouble the courts. In particular, it noted the legal difficulties in patenting software and estimated that perhaps only 1 per cent of computer programs would exhibit the necessary inventiveness to qualify for patent protection. In contrast, copyright protection was, on balance, considered to be far more appropriate, taking into account the fact that a computer program could be regarded as a form of expression of the ideas behind it. The problems that some jurisdictions would encounter with according copyright protection to such a utilitarian work were noted, but, overall, copyright was thought to have more advantages than disadvantages. This initial study proved to be very influential and the approach that has been taken subsequently, both in individual jurisdictions and by global consensus, is to protect computer programs 'as literary works' and, on the whole, absorb the protection of intellectual property rights in computer programs into existing copyright principles.

In many ways, this appeared to be a sensible and pragmatic response. The copyright system was already well established and internationally recognised; copyright arises automatically on creation of a work and clearly provides protection against the more blatant forms of line-by-line copying and piracy. But in relation to both the philosophical and pragmatic objectives, the choice of

---

4 In Europe, the standard copyright duration for literary works was harmonised in the 1990s. The relevant provisions are now to be found in Directive 2006/116/EC of the European Parliament and of the Council of 12 December 2006 on the term of protection of copyright and certain related rights (codified version) [2006] OJ L 372/12.

5 Dennis S Karjala, 'Copyright protection of computer software in the United States and Japan: Part 1' [1991] EIPR 195.

6 World Intellectual Property Organization (WIPO) Model Provisions for the Protection of Intellectual Property Rights in Computer Software, 1978.

copyright can, at times, seem to raise as many problems as it solves. What is it about computer programs and computer technology that might cause problems for traditional copyright law? In simple terms, there are two broad areas that need to be considered. The first, and simplest in conceptual terms, if not in solution, is the mode of operation of computers and the ease of copying. Computer programs were made to be copied. It is impossible to run a computer program and avail oneself of its useful effects without copies being made, however transient, within the depths of the computer. Also, because programs may be corrupted or inadvertently erased, it is good computing practice to take and keep a back-up copy of each computer program. Whilst even this level of copying could constitute a technical breach of copyright unless express provision is made, such copying does not, on the whole, threaten the commercial exploitation of that program. However, it is precisely the fact that the success of computer technology relies heavily on the ease with which programs can be copied that also makes it a trivial matter to produce multiple illicit copies, whether for private use, use within a commercial organisation, or for selling on the open market. This is not an issue as far as the actual application of copyright law is concerned, but causes significant problems for the enforcement of such law in relation to straight disk-to-disk copying and piracy of computer programs.[7] No special equipment is needed to make copies, and multiple copies can be made quickly and for minimal capital outlay. These can then be marketed at much lower prices than the authentic version. Even the widespread copying of software within an organisation can also have a severely prejudicial effect on the rights of the copyright owner. This problem of enforcement in relation to direct copying has been further exacerbated by the growth of the internet and the consequent ease with which software can be downloaded from remote sites.

The second general difficulty is that application of traditional copyright rules to the process of copying at the stage at which the computer program is written by the programmer has not been straightforward. Copyright was originally developed to protect the authors of literary, artistic, and other works from those who might copy the way in which their ideas had been expressed, especially where this was done for commercial gain. On the face of it, therefore, protecting computer programs as literary works would seem to be an appropriate method. However, as discussed in the next section, computer programs differ from conventional literary works in a number of important and fundamental ways, bringing into question the suitability of copyright for this purpose. A number of commentators are still of the view that, given the differences between computer programs and traditional literary works, a *sui generis* scheme would be more appropriate, tailored to take into account the particular properties of computer programs.[8] In such a global market as that for computer programs, one further benefit of the copyright system is the level of international consensus; it is debatable whether such consensus could be achieved on the form of a *sui generis* protection for computer software. There have been *sui generis* schemes in place for some time to protect the topography of semiconductor chips, although in this context, the USA was the dominant actor in the market and easily able to enforce its standards on other jurisdictions, and so global consensus proved not to be a major issue.[9] In contrast, the European **Database Directive** provides for a *sui generis* database right for databases that do not qualify for copyright protection,[10] but this is controversial in the USA, which continues to make no such provision.

---

7 In an early note, now of only historical significance, it was nevertheless recognised that widespread piracy was likely to be a problem in the industry, even in an age in which *only those large enough to own computers are well established businesses*: see John Banzhaf, 'Copyright protection for computer software' (1964) 64 Colum L Rev 1274.

8 Lawrence Diver, 'Would the current ambiguities with the legal protection of software be solved by the creation of a *sui generis* property right for computer software?' (2008) 3 JIPLP 125.

9 See, eg, US Semiconductor Chip Protection Act of 1984 (SCPA) 17 USC §§ 901–914; European Council Directive 87/54/EEC of 16 December 1986 on the legal protection of topographies of semiconductor products [1987] OJ L 24/36.

10 See later discussion below at pp 386–393.

Computer Programs as Literary Works

Given that computer programs have now 'joined books, poems and plays as full members of the literary work club',[11] they should be subject to the usual copyright regime. But even on a cursory examination it is apparent that there are significant differences between computer programs and more traditional literary works. Indeed, Karjala goes as far as to suggest that the 'decision to protect computer programs under copyright was in fact a radical departure from traditional intellectual property principles ... Software is not art, music or even literature'.[12] Neither can programs, in their 'literary form', be readily understood other than by a person skilled in the particular programming language employed. Indeed, end users of the program will often have no knowledge of the underlying program that is causing their computer to perform a particular task or function, nor will they have any need for such knowledge. Such characteristics are not shared by other literary works, even those of a utilitarian nature. This section will examine the extent of the similarities and differences, and begin to consider whether or not any differences are legally significant.

Expressed in Writing

The choice of copyright may seem obvious at first sight because of the fact that programs can be represented in 'writing'. In written form, computer programs can be expressed as both *source code* and *object code*. The former is the program as written by the programmer and may be in any one of a host of different languages. Many of these are the so-called *high-level languages* (HLL) that bear a certain resemblance to literary language, and have their own rules of syntax and grammar. As with any language, if readers have no specialist knowledge of the language, they will not understand what is written, because there may be no explicit clue as to the purpose and function of the program. On occasions though, programmers may annotate source code with comments in literary language. It is rare to be given the actual source code when acquiring software, whether off-the-shelf or bespoke – the usual situation is that the end user has neither knowledge of, nor need for knowledge of, the underlying program that causes the computer to perform the particular function.

These HLLs have similarity with literary languages, but as with spoken language, it is evident that, without specialist knowledge, they will only be understood by those conversant in the language in question. Nonetheless, Brennan J in *Computer Edge v Apple Computer Inc*[13] was even sceptical about classifying them as 'languages' since, in his view, 'it is difficult to divorce "language" from human speech, and a means of communicating ideas which does not consist of words is not properly described as a language'.

This view can, however, be contrasted with the following:

> If someone chose to write a novel entirely in computer object code by using strings of 1's and 0's for each letter of each word, the resulting work would be no different for constitutional purposes than if it had been written in English. The 'object code' version would be incomprehensible to readers outside the programming community (and tedious to read even for most within the community), but it would be no more incomprehensible than a work written in Sanskrit for those unversed in that language. The undisputed evidence reveals that even pure object code can be, and often is, read and understood by experienced programmers. And source code (in any of its various levels of complexity) can be read by many more.[14]

---

11 Pheh Hoon Lim and Louise Longdin, 'Fresh lessons for first movers in software copyright disputes: A cross-jurisdictional convergence' (2009) 40 IIC 374, 376.
12 Karjala, op cit.
13 (1986) 161 CLR 171, 204, and see later discussion.
14 *Universal City Studies v Corley* 273 F 3d 429, 446 (2nd Cir 2001).

This commentator preferred to use the term 'code' rather than 'language' – a term that is, of course, commonly used in this connection. Leaving such semantic arguments aside, although the source code, at least, may be intelligible to a programmer, the computer cannot respond to the source code in HLL as it can only recognise a stream of electrical pulses. So, in order for the computer to perform the intended function, the source code, as written by the programmer, has to be translated, or *compiled*, into a version that can be 'understood' by the computer. This version of the program is referred to as the 'object code' and can be represented on paper by a list of binary instructions – a series of '0's and '1's reflecting the presence or absence of an electrical pulse. This conversion is normally carried out by another program referred to as the 'compiler'. Notwithstanding the comments in *Corley*,[15] even experienced programmers often find difficulty in reading and following object code; however, some of the simpler programming languages, such as machine and assembly code, do approach simple binary form and are favoured by some programmers.[16]

Already, it can be seen that computer programs exhibit a number of differences from traditional literary works. Programs in their literary form are not readily understood other than by a person skilled in that programming language, but the program cannot achieve its ultimate objective unless it can be understood by the computer. Such characteristics are not shared by other literary works, even those of a utilitarian nature, as succinctly expressed by the High Court in *Navitaire v EasyJet*:

> Computer programmes are curious literary works in that they are the prescriptive expression
> of the manner in which a completely deterministic machine is required to operate. Something
> more different from an imaginative work of fiction which attracts exactly the same protection it
> is difficult to imagine.[17]

Because of such issues, some of the early cases questioned whether copyright protection could actually be extended to both source and object code. Comparisons with literary works notwithstanding, it has been accepted for a long time that copyright can subsist in code – that is, that a code could be construed as an original literary work.[18] The debate initiated by the question of whether copyright could subsist in both source and object code is highly illustrative of the way in which intellectual property law has been used to argue both for and against copyright protection for computer programs. US copyright law required the subject of copyright protection to be a 'writing' and also denied copyright protection to works of a utilitarian nature. This led to the suggestion that, although there might be copyright in the source code, this could not be true of the object code, which could not be construed as a 'writing'. Further credence was given to this view by the argument that object code was created not by a person, but by a machine, referring to the process of compilation described above. On the other hand, computer programs are contained within the definition of 'literary work' in the US **Copyright Act of 1976**, and amendments introduced in 1980 included the definition 'a set of statements or instructions to be used directly or indirectly in a computer in order to bring about a certain result'. In addition, in cases such as *Apple Computer Inc v Franklin Computer Corp*,[19] the US courts began to recognise that object code was subject to copyright protection. These developments were mirrored in other jurisdictions, as, for example, in the UK in *SEGA Enterprises v Richards*.[20] Whilst the court was happy to accept in principle that computer programs could be the subject of copyright, there was some discussion as to whether copyright could subsist in both the source code and the object code. At the heart of this discussion was the supposition that

---

15 Ibid.
16 This was true in the case of *John Richardson Computers Ltd v Flanders* [1993] FSR 497, which will be discussed in more detail later in the chapter.
17 [2004] EWHC 3487(Ch), [13].
18 *DP Anderson & Co v Lieber Code Co* [1917] 2 KB 469.
19 714 F 2d 1240 (3rd Cir 1983).
20 [1983] FSR 73.

copyright protection could be extended to software either because of the writing requirement or because a computer program is a form of 'literary work', as opposed to any other type of creation attracting copyright protection. However, even this view was challenged in the Australian case of *Apple Computer v Computer Edge Pty Ltd*.[21] The initial decision declined to extend copyright protection to computer programs because the purpose of literary works was for enjoyment and, in the view of the court, this was not the function of computer programs.[22] The Federal Court reversed this decision, holding that the source programs were protected by copyright as new and original literary works, and that the object programs were protected in consequence as adaptations of the source programs.[23] On a further appeal, the High Court of Australia[24] concluded, albeit not without difficulty, that the source programs could be protected as literary works. There was, however, a division of opinion as to whether there was any basis for affording protection to the object code. Gibbs J, for example, found that nothing had persuaded him that 'a sequence of electrical impulses in a silicon chip, not capable itself of communicating anything directly to a human recipient, and designed only to operate a computer, is itself a literary work, or is the translation of a literary work'.[25] Brennan J suggested that although these electrical impulses could be represented in writing, 'the written representation must not be confused with what is represented not written'.[26] Since the object codes could neither be detected by, nor had any meaning for, humans, they could not, in the view of the majority, be construed as literary works. Neither, again in the view of the majority, could the object code be protected as an adaptation of the source program. This decision led to some consternation in the common law world based on both the theoretical and conceptual issues raised, and also the practical issue of whether object code could be protected by copyright. This led directly to statutory action being taken in the UK: the **Copyright (Computer Software) Amendment Act** was passed in 1985 and its provisions have now been re-enacted in the **Copyright, Designs and Patents Act 1988 (CDPA 1988)**, putting the matter beyond doubt for all practical purposes.[27] Since then, a number of international instruments have made it clear that computer programs are protected as literary works within the meaning of the **Berne Convention**.[28]

The Boundary between Idea and Expression

The general concept of copyright and the application of copyright law in particular is bedevilled by the 'nothing new under the sun' problem. Even the most creative mind often borrows from, reworks, adapts, or is inspired by the ideas and work of others. Prohibiting such processes would be to stifle the very innovation and creativity that intellectual property protection is said to encourage. But this, of course, results in a conundrum: how to distinguish what is acceptable use of the ideas and work of others from copyright infringements. One approach to this is reflected in the fact that copyright protects the form in which authors or artists create their work rather than the idea itself. This explanation has its advocates and its opponents, but the premise recognises that different creators and authors may well have the same or similar ideas, but that these are likely to be expressed in very different ways; thus it is the particular expression that should be protected. Although, as we shall see, approaches to this distinction have varied between both courts and jurisdictions, some of the issues raised have been in the context of the scope of software copyright protection and so a brief discussion is pertinent here.

---

21 (1983) 50 ALR 581; [1984] FSR 246.
22 A view that echoes the dictum of Davey LJ in *Hollinrake v Truswell* [1894] 3 Ch 420, 428.
23 (1984) 53 ALR 225.
24 (1986) 161 CLR 171.
25 Ibid, [18].
26 Ibid, 201.
27 Nevertheless the arguments about the relevance of the 'literary' differences between source and object code have not disappeared: see, eg, Susan Corbett, 'What if object code had been excluded from protection as a literary work in copyright law? A New Zealand perspective' (2008) Mich St L Rev 173.
28 See, eg, Art 10(1) of the Trade-related Aspects of Intellectual Property Rights (TRIPS) Agreement; Art 4 of the WIPO Copyright Treaty; Art 1(1) of the Software Directive (discussed below at p 371).

The 'idea' of a work includes, most obviously, the original notion behind the work, but can also encompass the subject matter or the general style of the composition.[29] This has two broad consequences. The most obvious is that the underlying idea is not protected, and so other authors and creators can incorporate and build upon ideas behind existing copyright works within their own works. Additionally, or alternatively, many works may be based on well-recognised general themes. Both *Romeo and Juliet* and *West Side Story* tell similar tragic tales of star-crossed lovers. But although *West Side Story* clearly borrows from *Romeo and Juliet*, there the similarity ends. The general idea of feuding gangs and forbidden love might be the same, but the expression and detailed development of that idea is dramatically different. However, the more detailed an idea becomes, the more difficult it is to distinguish between idea and protectable expression.

In *Ibcos v Barclays*,[30] Jacob J suggested that the distinction had no real relevance in English law, but whether or not it is specifically articulated as such, the distinction does exist in the UK. Thus, in *Donoghue v Allied Newspapers Ltd*,[31] Farwell J said: '. . . there is no copyright in an idea or ideas . . . If the idea, however original, is nothing more than an idea, and is not put into any form of words, or any form of expression . . . then there is no such thing as copyright at all.' This notion was also taken up by Baker J in *Total Information*: '. . . stemming from the principle that copyright does not exist in ideas but in the expression of them, is the line of authorities commencing with *Kenrick and Company v Lawrence and Company*[32] that if there is only one way of expressing an idea that way is not the subject of copyright.'[33] Lord Hailsham, in *LB Plastics Ltd v Swish Products Ltd*, commented that 'it is trite law that there is no copyright in ideas . . . But, of course, as the late Professor Joad used to observe, it all depends on what you mean by "ideas" '.[34]

The problems of separating idea and expression were discussed most recently in *Baigent & anor v The Random House Group*.[35] This was the high-profile case in which Baigent and his co-authors were alleging copyright infringement in their work *The Holy Blood and the Holy Grail* by Dan Brown in his now-famous book *The Da Vinci Code*. Although the claimants' work was referred to and recognised explicitly in Brown's book, the claimants' submission was that their work had been appropriated to such an extent as to constitute copyright infringement. The case is complex, but is concerned with the extent to which both general themes and more specific, well-documented detail can be the subject of copyright protection. After some examination, the court found that what had been taken were general themes and ideas that were either at too high a level of abstraction or were already sufficiently well known that they did not qualify for protection. Although *The Holy Blood and the Holy Grail* was clearly one of the sources for *The Da Vinci Code*, as indeed was acknowledged within the work, there were also many ideas and themes within *The Da Vinci Code* that did not originate in *The Holy Blood and the Holy Grail*. For a combination of these reasons, no infringement was found, but the court found itself unable to lay down any general principle to distinguish ideas and expression:

> What is said to have been copied is a theme of the copyright work. Copyright does not subsist in ideas; it protects the expression of ideas, not the ideas themselves. No clear principle is or could be laid down in the cases in order to tell whether what is sought to be protected is on the ideas side of the dividing line, or on the expression side.[36]

Baigent v Random House is a case involving many ideas and many ways of expressing of those ideas. What of the situation in which there are only a few ways, or perhaps only one way, of expressing a

---

29 See further Lionel Bently and Brad Sherman, *Intellectual Property Law*, 3rd edn, 2007, Oxford: Oxford University Press, pp 181ff.
30 [1994] FSR 275 discussed in more detail below.
31 [1938] Ch 106, 109, 110.
32 (1890) 25 QBD 99.
33 [1992] FSR 171, 181.
34 [1979] FSR 145, 160.
35 [2007] EWCA Civ 247.
36 [2007] EWCA Cov 247, [5].

particular idea? Arguably, this is not very likely in creative and artistic works, but is much more feasible in relation to factual works or computer programs. The function that the computer program is required to perform may restrict the way in which it can be written to the extent that, if two programmers independently both create programs for the same purpose, they may have a number of, or even many, similar features. If there is only one way in which the program or part of the program can be written, can this reasonably be treated as the expression of an idea, or has the expression merged with the idea, so that the whole cannot be protected by copyright? The issue of when ideas merge with actual expression has caused particular problems in determining the scope of copyright protection for computer programs, which will be explored in more detail below.

There are thus a number of difficulties in distinguishing idea and expression, which has led to some criticism of the concept, particularly in the UK. Cornish and Llewelyn refer to it as a 'distinction with an ill-defined boundary',[37] while Laddie et al, in a discussion of what they refer to as the idea/expression fallacy, comment that 'a moment's thought will reveal that the maxim is obscure, or in its broadest sense suspect'.[38] The expression/idea distinction is more specifically entrenched in the copyright law of the USA, where the issues was first examined in the now-famous case of *Baker v Selden*.[39] It has subsequently been enshrined in s 102 of the US **Copyright Act of 1976**, which sets out the categories of work to which copyright can be applied and then goes on to state explicitly that copyright protection does not extend to 'any idea . . .'. That is not to say that the US courts have always found the distinction an easy one to identify. In *Nichols v Universal Pictures Ltd*, Learned Hand J enunciated his frequently quoted 'levels of abstraction' test in an attempt to elucidate the demarcation between idea and expression,[40] but nevertheless went on to conclude that: 'Nobody has ever been able to fix that boundary, and nobody ever can.'

Nonetheless, the distinction between idea and expression has been recognised internationally in both the **Trade-related Aspects of Intellectual Property Rights (TRIPS) Agreement**[41] in Art 9(2) ('Copyright protection shall extend to expressions and not to ideas . . . as such') and also in the European **Software Directive**.[42] The original version of this Directive purported to be implemented into UK law by the **Copyright (Computer Programs) Regulations 1992**,[43] amending the **CDPA 1988**, but has no express provision that reflects Art 1(2), which provides that the expression in any form of computer program is protected by copyright, but not the ideas and principles underlying any elements of it. However, notwithstanding the implicit acceptance of the idea/expression distinction in these provisions, neither instrument gives any guidance on its practical implementation.

The idea/expression distinction is thus both controversial in some quarters and also difficult to apply. As Ginsburg has succinctly pointed out, separating idea from expression is 'one of the hardest tasks in traditional copyright analysis. It remains difficult, but not necessarily more so, when computer programs are at issue'.[44] However, it should be remembered that the reason it is invoked is to identify what elements of a work qualify for protection or to ascertain whether an alleged copyright infringement actually involved copying part of an author's work that was protected by copyright. Such an adjudication will always have to be made by some means and it may be that invoking the idea/expression distinction is helpful in some cases, but not in others. As we shall

---

37 William Cornish and David Llewelyn, *Intellectual Property Law*, 6th edn, 2007, London: Sweet and Maxwell, p 455.
38 Hugh Laddie, Peter Prescott, Mary Vitoria, Adrian Speck, and Lindsay Lane, *The Modern Law of Copyright and Designs: Vol 1*, 2000, London: Butterworths, pp 97ff.
39 101 US 99 (1879).
40 *Nichols v Universal Pictures* 45 F 2d 119, 121 (2nd Cir 1930).
41 TRIPS Agreement; see www.wto.org/english/tratop_e/trips_e/t_agm0_e.htm
42 Directive 2009/24/EC of the European Parliament and of the Council of 23 April 2009 on the legal protection of computer programs [2009] OJ l111/16. This Directive repeals and codifies Council Directive 91/250/EEC [1991] OJ L 122/42; references to the repealed Directive are to be construed as references to Directive 2009/24. On this point, see also *Nova Productions Ltd v Mazooma Games Ltd* [2007] EWCA Civ 219, [31]ff, and further discussion of the provisions of the Directive below at pp 371–375.
43 SI 1992/3233.
44 Jane C Ginsburg, 'Four reasons and a paradox: The manifest superiority of copyright over *sui generis* protection of computer software' (1994) 94 Colum L Rev 2559, 2569.

explore further later in the chapter, identification of the particular idea behind a computer program has provided particular challenges, as has, on occasions, extricating the expression from the idea.

Structure, Sequence, and Organisation

The basic explanation given above of the design of a computer program in terms of source and object code oversimplifies the task of creating a workable computer program. In practice, many computer programs are constructed in a modular fashion by using standard instructions (code) obtained from libraries of tried-and-tested software. Generally, a program is not created in a linear fashion, but has a particular structure at the level at which the computer operates. In addition to this, it will also have a certain structure at the higher level – that is, the level at which the user interacts with the program via the user interface. It is this higher-level structure that creates the so-called 'look and feel'[45] of the program. The 'look' includes the screen display and the 'feel' refers to the way in which it is used. The familiar dropdown menus used by Microsoft are part of the 'feel' of Microsoft office. The generic term 'look and feel' recognises that these concepts may frequently overlap or be interdependent. The 'look and feel' of a program is often the factor that may give a particular program a competitive edge over its rivals, and therefore may be the element that the originators of the program most want to protect and competitors most want to emulate.[46] The extent to which the non-literal elements of a program – the structure, sequence, and organisation (SSO) – can be protected by copyright has, arguably, caused the most difficulties for the application of copyright principles, accentuated by the issues raised in identifying the boundary between idea and expression referred to above. Does, or could, the particular structure of a computer program represent the idea behind the program – or is it merely part of the expression? The consideration of the extent to which non-literal elements of a computer program can be protected by copyright law, together with the formulation of a suitable test for ascertaining whether non-literal copying has actually occurred, have arguably been the aspects of software copyright that have caused the most challenges for the courts and for which there are few parallels in more traditional literary works.

Functionality and Behaviour

Notwithstanding the fact that computer programs can be expressed in a written form, one important difference between computer programs and other literary works is that the program is written not for its own sake, but in order to make the computer perform some task or function either within the computer system itself or in the real world. In other words, the literary is combined with the technical, causing technology to operate to produce a defined result. In Karjala's words: '. . . computer programs are literary works only in form . . . In operation, they are pure works of function, that is, of technology.'[47] Samuelson et al[48] explain this characteristic in terms of the 'behaviour' of software, a property that, they suggest, means that programs cannot be regarded merely as texts: '. . . a crucially important characteristic of programs is that they behave; programs

---

45   A concept that originated in relation to greetings cards and children's books, and entered the analysis of copyright infringement of computer programs in cases involving video games: see, eg, JWL Ogilvie, 'Defining computer program parts under Learned Hand's abstractions tests in software copyright infringement cases' (1992) 91 Mich L Rev 526; J Velasco, 'The copyrightability of non-literal elements of computer programs' (1994) 94 Col L Rev 242.

46   A number of the court decisions discussed in this chapter provide more detailed explanations of the design and construction of computer programs, which have the advantage for legal analysis that they have usually been accepted by both sides. In particular, useful basic explanations are provided in the following: *John Richardson Computers Ltd v Flanders*, [1993] FSR 497, 503–4, per Ferris J; *Ibcos v Barclays Bank*, [1994] FSR 275, 285–8, per Jacob J; *Computer Edge v Apple Ltd* (1986) 161 CLR 171, 178–9, per Gibbs CJ, and 199, per Brennan J. A more recent, but rather more technical, explanation can be found in *Cantor Fitzgerald v Tradition Ltd* [2000] RPC 95, 145, Appendix A 'An introduction to computers and programming languages'. For a discussion of the significance of this for the application of copyright concepts, see, eg, Steven R Englund, 'Idea, process or protected expression? Determining the scope of copyright protection of the structure of computer programs' (1990) 88 Mich L Rev 866, 867–72; more recently, Daniel B Garrie, 'The legal status of software' (2005) 23 J Marshall J Computer & Info Law 711.

47   Karjala, op cit, 198.

48   P Samuelson, R Davis, MD Kapor, and JH Reichman, 'A manifesto concerning the legal protection of computer programs' (1994) 94 Colum L Rev 2308.

exist to make computers perform tasks.' Since this attribute is central to the essential nature of programs, it gives them a 'dual character': they can be regarded simultaneously as both 'writings and machines'. This means that, in Samuelson et al's view, neither copyright nor patent law are suitable for protecting software innovation. Other commentators have, however, pointed out that computer programs are not the only works that are protected by copyright that can be said to exhibit 'behaviour'; this is also true of a range of creative and more functional works, ranging from music manuscripts, to architectural drawings. If there are a number of ways of achieving the ultimate purpose of a work, then it can be afforded copyright protection without subsequent creativity of innovation being stifled.[49]

Interoperability Requirements

One feature that may be desirable in a computer program, but which has no clear parallel in relation to more conventional literary works, is the need for interoperability – that is, the capacity of the computer program to be compatible with other computer programs or hardware elements in a system, such as a printer, for example. The copyright in a more traditional work does not depend on the medium in which it is stored; neither does a traditional work have to interact with other works.[50] In contrast, compatibility between different programs – and particularly between applications and systems software – is of central importance to the software market. It would be no good purchasing the latest games software produced by one manufacturer only to find that it would not operate on a PC produced by another manufacturer. However, if a computer program is to be interoperable with another, it will need to contain some of the same features, at least at the interface between the two. If the code of the other program is not available, one way of producing a computer program that is interoperable with other programs is by decompiling (that is, compiling in reverse), or reverse engineering, the object code of the program with which interoperability is desired, to obtain the source code in an HLL. The features that are required to ensure interoperability are then duplicated – that is, copied – in order to create the interface between the existing and the new or proposed program. Where the creator of the new program does not have the copyright in the other program, this can lead to allegations of copyright infringement as a result of the decompilation and subsequent development of the new program.[51] There is no exact parallel to this process for other works that are eligible for copyright protection and so, inevitably, questions have arisen as to the extent to which copyright law allows decompilation for these purposes.

Scope of Protection

Having considered some of the differences between computer programs and traditional literary works, or factors that may create challenges for courts trying to protect computer programs as literary works, we move on to a consideration of the actual legal response to these issues. Of those differences identified, some actually have little legal significance. Thus, although there was a preliminary controversy over the issues of whether copyright could actually subsist in both source and object code, as we have seen, this matter is no longer contentious, and the majority of jurisdictions make it clear that copyright protection is extended to both source and object code. However, there are a number of other issues that continue to be raised in the courts surrounding both the extent and scope of protection, and the test for copying.

Many aspects of a computer program can be copied from straight line-to-line copying of both source and object code – so-called 'literal' copying – to copying of the structure of the program –

---

49 See further Ginsburg, op cit, 2566.
50 See further Dennis S Karjala, 'Copyright protection of computer software in the United States and Japan: Part 2' [1991] EIPR 231, 233.
51 See, eg, the facts of *SAS Institute Inc v World Programming Ltd* [2010] EWHC 1829.

often referred to as 'non-literal' copying, although 'non-textual' copying might be a more accurate description. Should all of these aspects of copying be protected by the law of copyright, or only those that correspond to literal copying of the work, by analogy with a literary work? How far can computer programmers use the work done by others in their own creation of new programs without infringing the original developer's rights? How can compatibility with another program be ensured without infringing copyright. At what point does the code for a commonly used routine enter the public domain? These, and other issues, have resulted in discussion in many jurisdictions regarding the extent of the scope of copyright protection for computer programs and the literature on the subject is now voluminous.

How much needs to be copied before an infringement occurs is defined differently in different jurisdictions. In the UK, the concept is one of taking a substantial part, whilst the law in the USA considers the amount and substantiality of the portion used, often interpreted by the courts in terms of substantial similarity.[52] While the detail of these may differ, they both require some assessment of what and how much has been copied in comparison with the whole. However, the US test for substantial similarity requires much more wrestling with the idea/expression dichotomy than the UK test of establishing whether there has been copying of a substantial part. A consideration of the manner of constructing computer programs, to which reference has already been made, will reveal that many aspects of a program can be copied, from straight, line-by-line copying of the source or object code (literal copying), to copying of the SSO of the program (non-literal copying). Whereas line-by-line copying is both easy to identify and fit within the framework of copyright protection, the formulation of a suitable test for non-literal copying has not been quite so amenable to accepted and acceptable solution. It has been established, in relation to other areas of copyright law, that the test of substantial taking may be either quantitative or qualitative.[53] Thus, if part of a work is copied that is small in quantity, but highly significant in terms of its overall contribution to the work, then an action will lie.[54] Copying can be detected by, for example, including spurious lines of code that are not essential to the execution of the program. Other evidence may also raise a strong presumption of literal copying. Thus, in MS Associates v Power,[55] it was noted that there were a number of similarities in the names of the variables in the defendants' and plaintiffs' programs – names that would be expected to be decided quite arbitrarily. It was also noted that the function 'vtprs' appeared in both the defendants' and the plaintiffs' list of variables, although the facts showed that the function was not actually used in the defendants' program.

If there are similar errors in two programs, this can raise a strong presumption of copying. However, this may be capable of rebuttal because of another difference between computer programs and other forms of literary work. Whereas it is statistically improbable that, if two authors independently have the same idea for a novel, they will write it in the same words and sentence construction, this is not necessarily such a remote possibility in the case of a computer program. If two programmers independently write a program to perform the same task, especially if this is a relatively simple task or subroutine, it may be very likely that they will write the same, or a similar, program. It is also equally possible that they may make the same errors. If such programs contain the same errors, then, although this may provide persuasive evidence, copying will not be a foregone conclusion, because some errors are more frequent and obvious than others. Illustrations of these issues are again to be found in MS Associates v Power, in which the same errors were noted in one part of the program, but, in relation to another part, it was perhaps possible to explain the observed similarities. Such factors have not really caused major headaches for the courts in

---

52 CDPA 1988, s 16(3); 17 USC § 107(3).
53 See, eg, *Hawkes & Son (London) Ltd v Paramount Film Services Ltd* [1934] Ch 593; *Ladbroke (Football) Ltd v William Hill (Football) Ltd* [1964] 1 WLR 273, in which Lord Pearce said: 'Whether a part is substantial must be decided by its quality rather than its quantity.' This latter case was relied upon by Ferris J in *John Richardson Computers v Flanders* [1993] FSR 497 (see below).
54 See, eg, the cases reviewed in Nancy J Mertzel, 'Copying 0.03% of software code base was not *de minimis*' (2008) 3 JIPLP 547.
55 [1987] FSR 242.

contrast with the challenges created by the attempts to accommodate non-literal copying and decompilation within the existing copyright regime. The following sections will examine some of the case law on this topic primarily from US and UK perspectives.

Copyright and Non-literal Copying in the USA

The first case to consider the issue of both non-literal copying and issues surrounding the idea/expression boundary was *Whelan Associates v Jaslow Dental Laboratory Inc.*[56] The case concerned two computer programs for the organisation of dental laboratory records created by the same programmer whilst in different employment. It was accepted that the functionality of both programs was the same, but the coding was different and internal similarities were absent. Given that the programs had similar structures, the defendant's argument was that the structure was the idea, rather than the expression, of the programs and was thus beyond the scope of copyright protection. The judgment considered various copyright precedents, including the much-quoted authority *Baker v Selden*,[57] and concluded that 'the purpose or function of a utilitarian work would be the work's idea, and everything that is not necessary to that purpose or function would be part of the expression of the idea'.[58] The necessary corollary was that if there were only limited ways in which to express the function, then these would be construed as part of the idea. The judgment refers to Learned Hand's dicta on the delineation of idea and expression, but does not build on his famous abstractions test; instead, it relies on another line of case law and also on statute to show that the SSO of the program, the non-literal elements, should be afforded copyright protection. In brief, the court found that the purpose of the program at issue was the organisation of the dental laboratory records, and that the structure of the program was not necessary to that purpose and so was entitled to copyright protection.

Velasco makes the point that the ideal test would be one that is both simple and accurate,[59] and one significant aspect of the test in *Whelan* is that it is both straightforward and easy to apply.[60] However, in such a technically complex area as computer software, it has proved difficult to pursue either of these aims without compromising the other and it is unsurprising, therefore, that certain inadequacies have been identified in the straightforward test enunciated in *Whelan*. It can thus be criticised as being over-simplistic in its suggestion that it may be possible both to define and isolate a single purpose for a particular program. An obvious consequence of this is that if programmers are to be able to devise other programs that perform the same function, but do not infringe copyright, then there has to be a number of other possible structures for the program that could, reasonably and efficiently, fulfil that same purpose. If not, the *Whelan* formulation is capable of conferring an almost patent-like protection on the first programmer to develop a suitable structure. Given that 'many aspects of application code are dictated by basic principles of software engineering',[61] this is a very real consequence of adherence to the test in *Whelan*. Also, it is difficult, if not impossible, to identify a single purpose behind many, if not most, commercially important programs, because the reality is that they usually consist of a number of subroutines and modules, each of which could, validly, be considered as an idea. It thus has the propensity to stifle, rather than stimulate, innovation by giving preferential protection to the first comer on the market.[62]

The US Court of Appeals Second Circuit recognised some of these problems in the later case of *Computer Associates v Altai*,[63] noting that the decision in *Whelan* had received a 'mixed reception' in the

---

56 797 F 2d 1222 (3rd Cir 1987), [1987] FSR 1.
57 101 US 99 (1879).
58 797 F 2d 1222, 1236.
59 Velasco, op cit.
60 See further Englund, op cit.
61 PS Menell, 'An analysis of the scope of copyright protection for application programs' (1989) 41 Stan L Rev 1045, 1082.
62 Ibid.
63 982 F 2d 693 (2nd Cir 1992).

courts and that 'Whelan has fared . . . poorly in the academic community where its standard . . . has been widely criticised for being overbroad',[64] and going on to use rather different reasoning. Again, the case concerned a programmer developing similar software for two different employers. In the first program produced for Altai, there had been literal copying of 30 per cent of Computer Associate's code. Another program was then produced using new programmers, but Computer Associates then alleged that this version still made use of the non-literal elements of the original program. This led to the Second Circuit formulating what has become known as the 'abstraction–filtration–comparison' test as it struggled to articulate a suitable method for determining the extent to which the non-literal elements of a computer program could be protected by copyright and, in particular, how 'substantial similarity' could be adjudicated. It was accepted in the case that copyright protection of computer programs extends beyond literal similarities in code and also includes similarities in structure. In contrast to the decision in Whelan, the judgment of the Second Circuit utilised Learned Hand's famous abstractions approach, at least for the first part of the test, and the Whelan formulation, that the overall purpose of the program can be equated with its idea, was roundly criticised on the basis already mentioned that the majority of programs do not consist of a single 'idea', but are more accurately described as composites.

The new three-stage test comprises breaking down the work into its constituent parts, separating out the elements that are not protected by copyright, and then comparing what remains (the 'kernel' of creative expression) with the allegedly infringing program.[65] The first step – the abstraction – essentially replicates Learned Hand's levels of abstractions approach in Nichols v Universal Pictures. The second stage – filtration – involves identifying, at each level of abstraction, the constituent elements and, in particular, whether they are dictated by efficiency, external factors, or are taken from the public domain. The first of these reflects the fact that, as discussed above, there may be only one way of accomplishing a given task, so that the only efficient way in which to construct the program is to replicate these elements. The court suggested that, 'since evidence of similarly efficient structure is not particularly probative of copying, it should be disregarded in the overall substantial similarity analysis'.[66] The second category of element to be filtered out is those that are dictated by external constraints, such as the specification of the system on which the program has to run, necessary compatibility with other programs, etc. Finally, this stage of the test requires any material already in the public domain to be disregarded in assessing substantial similarity. The result of the filtration stage is to leave behind what the court referred to as 'a core of protectable expression. In terms of a work's copyright value, this is the golden nugget . . .'.[67] It is only at this stage that there is a comparison with an alleged infringing program to ascertain whether or not there is 'substantial similarity' between the two.

The court recognised that the decision narrowed the scope of protection and so was more favourable to the defendant than Whelan, but asserted that it was merely the outcome of applying standard copyright principles to computer programs.[68] The judgment was generally well received as demonstrating a good understanding of the way in which computer programs are designed and written. It was acknowledged by some writers that the decision was also able to deal with constraints of interoperability and compatibility.[69] On the other hand, some reservations were expressed that it would leave non-literal elements underprotected, and it was also suggested that 'the court was unduly constrained by a uniquely literary view of the creative process and thus failed to recognise its own ability to "keep pace" with technological change within the traditional copyright framework', even though, despite its imperfections, the test was 'arguably a "practical necessity" in the computer

64 Ibid, 705.
65 Ibid, 706.
66 Ibid, 709.
67 Ibid, 701.
68 Ibid, 712.
69 See, eg, TS Teter, 'Merger and the machines: An analysis of the pro-compatibility trend in computer software copyright cases' (1993) 45 Stan L Rev 1061, 1084. Interoperability issues are explored in more detail below at pp 373–375.

program context'.[70] A practical example of a situation in which there could be said to be under-protection occurred in *Apple Computer Inc v Microsoft Corp*.[71] In this case, applying the abstraction–filtration–comparison test resulted in there being little to compare, because the program had been constructed from existing subroutines already in the public domain or dictated by efficiency requirements, with a consequent denial of copyright protection. In such cases, whether or not there is any copyright protection will depend on an assessment of the way in which the subroutines have been assembled and interlinked. In these situations, another strand of case law – that on the copyright of compilations – may become very relevant.[72]

In different ways, both *Whelan* and *Altai* have been influential, have generated much debate, and have subsequently been referred to in cases in the UK and other jurisdictions. In some ways, they can be viewed as two ends of the spectrum of copyright protection for computer programs, because 'both approaches are rooted in and use the language and legal precedent of copyright law but with vastly differing results'.[73] *Whelan*, with its almost patent-like protection, operates in favour of the original developer of the program, whereas application of the test in *Altai* changes the balance considerably. Where the balance lies may be significant for certain sectors of the industry, depending on whether they produce primarily systems or applications software. Different commentators have both supported and opposed the decision in *Altai*, but Miller suggests that the differences between the two have been overstated because the decisions can be reconciled by viewing *Altai* as a further refinement of the approach begun in *Whelan*.[74]

Whatever view is taken of the relationship between the decisions in these two cases, the situation in the US courts has been more complex than the analysis above might suggest. As we have seen, both *Whelan* and *Altai* were decided in different circuits of the US Court of Appeals and, despite the criticisms of *Whelan* contained in the court's judgment in *Altai*, it was certainly not the case that the test in *Altai* immediately eclipsed that in *Whelan*. In addition, other tests were devised sometimes based in part on either of these tests. This resulted, at times, in certain contradictions and confusions, and, in the words of the court in *Altai*, 'many of the decisions in this area reflect the courts' attempt to fit the proverbial square peg in a round hole'.[75] The Ninth Circuit, for example, developed its own test (the intrinsic/extrinsic test) for copyrightability of computer programs in *Brown Bag Software v Symantec Corp*.[76] The proliferation of such tests and their subsequent modification led one commentator to state: 'The "look and feel" cases . . . can fairly be characterised as a mess.'[77] Thus the situation with regard to copyrightability of computer software in the US courts has been more confused than is sometimes presented,[78] although the *Altai* test now appears to be generally accepted.[79]

Copyright and Non-literal Copying in the UK

John Richardson Computers Ltd v Flanders[80] was the first case in the UK to consider these issues. The facts of the case are complex, but, in brief, both parties developed and marketed programs to print labels for prescriptions at pharmacists, and to keep details of the stock of drugs; the same programmer, Flanders, was involved in each. There was no evidence of substantial taking of literal parts of the

---

70 'Case note on *Computer Associates v Altai*' (1992) 106 Harv L Rev 510.
71 35 F 3d 1435 (9th Cir 1994); see also Steve S Moutsatsos and John CR Cummings, '*Apple v Microsoft*: Has the pendulum swung too far?' (1993) 9 CL & P 162.
72 In the USA, see *Feist Publications Inc v Rural Telephone Service Co* 113 L Ed 2d 358 (1991), cited in *Altai*, and discussed in the context of databases below at p 386. In the UK, see the discussion of *Richardson v Flanders* [1993] FSR 497, below.
73 Moutsatsos and Cummings, op cit.
74 AR Miller, 'Copyright protection for computer programs, databases and computer-generated works: Is anything new since CONTU?' (1993) 106 Harv L Rev 977.
75 982 F 2d 693, 712 (2nd Cir 1992).
76 960 F 2d 1465 (9th Cir 1992).
77 DL Hayes, 'What's left of look and feel? A current analysis' (1993) 10 CL 1.
78 A more detailed analysis is beyond the scope of this publication: see, eg, ibid; Miller, op cit; Velasco, op cit; Karjala, '. . . Part 2', op cit; J Drexl, 'What is protected in a computer program? Copyright protection in the US and Europe' (1994) 15 IIC.
79 S Lai, *The Copyright Protection of Computer Software in the United Kingdom*, 2000, Oxford: Hart Publishing, ch 2.
80 [1993] FSR 497.

code; rather what was alleged was that parts of the general 'scheme' of the program, including some rather idiosyncratic subroutines, had been copied. Ferris J noted that the *Altai* approach had already been adopted in two federal circuits in the USA and that there was nothing to suggest that the *Whelan* approach should be preferred.[81] However, Ferris J did not adopt the *Altai* approach verbatim, but instead first assessed whether or not under English copyright law the program in question was, as a whole, entitled to copyright protection by considering it as a compilation by analogy with the *William Hill* case.[82] Only after establishing that the non-literal elements were protectable as a compilation did Ferris J go on to apply the *Altai* test, concluding that the copyright infringement was minor and limited. The steps in his analysis can perhaps be summarised by the following:

(1)   Is the claimant's program as a whole entitled to copyright protection?
(2)   Are there similarities to the claimant's program in the defendant's program?
(3)   Is any similarity attributable to copying?
(4)   Do any such similarities amount to the copying of a substantial part of the claimant's program assessed by application of the abstraction–filtration–comparison test of *Computer Associates v Altai*?

Whether or not this is an appropriate approach,[83] it is difficult to apply – a fact that was recognised in the judgment itself.

Richardson v Flanders *was soon followed by another case, that of* Ibcos Computers Ltd v Barclays Finance Ltd.[84] Again, the facts are rather complex, but basically centred around an ex-employee continuing to develop and rewrite software on which he had been working during employment. Copyright infringement was claimed in the individual programs and subroutines, the general structure, and certain general features of the system. Jacob J first considered whether the work in question attracted copyright protection. He found it generally unhelpful to focus on the idea/expression distinction, but did suggest that '[t]he true position is that where an "idea" is sufficiently general, then even if an original work embodies it, the mere taking of that idea will not infringe. But if the "idea" is detailed, then there may be infringement. It is a question of degree'.[85]

Jacob's notion of a detailed idea that might be protected by copyright is, presumably, in the context of computer programs, that found when a number of subroutines are put together to form one program. This would be the result of the intellectual effort, skill, and judgment of the software writer, as opposed to a general idea, which would not be protected by copyright, and presumably might equate with the 'function' in the *Whelan* sense. He was generally dismissive of reliance on US copyright cases, particularly in the light of the fact that the idea/expression distinction is treated differently in the two jurisdictions, and held that the question of judging a substantial part was a matter of applying the standard principles of copyright law in the UK. Although the decision suggests that non-literal elements can be protected by copyright, this was a case in which there was evidence of literal copying of the code and so an assessment of what might constitute a substantial part of the non-literal elements was not a critical part of the decision.

Although not actually concerned with the copying of non-literal aspects of a program, what constitutes a substantial part was nevertheless a focus for the discussion in *Cantor Fitzgerald v Tradition*.[86] Pumfrey J, agreeing with the general approach in *Ibcos*, went on to consider 'the interrelationship of the originality of the work (the prerequisite for the subsistence of copyright) and substantiality of

---

81 General references had been made to the *Whelan* judgment in the interlocutory hearings in both *Computer Aided Design v Bolwell*, 23 August 1989, unreported, and *Total Information Processing Systems Ltd v Daman Ltd* [1992] FSR 171.
82 *Ladbroke (Football) Ltd v William Hill (Football) Ltd* [1964] 1 WLR 273.
83 See further Richard Arnold, 'Infringement of copyright in computer software by non-textual copying: First decision at trial by an English court' [1993] EIPR 250.
84 [1994] FSR 275.
85 Ibid, 291.
86 [2000] RPC 95.

the part of the work copied (the prerequisite for infringement)'.[87] He pointed out that the correct approach to substantiality was straightforward: there would be a copyright infringement if a part of a work were appropriated 'upon which a substantial part of the author's skill and labour were expended'.[88] Using the analogy of a novel or a play, he concluded that the 'architecture'[89] of a computer program could be protected by copyright if it resulted from the expenditure of a substantial part of the programmer's skill, labour, and judgment.[90]

Pumfrey J returned to the issue of software copyright in *Navitaire v Easyjet*, in which the claimant was alleging that the defendants had created software for an airline booking system by observing and studying the original.[91] The claimant alleged copying of the overall 'look and feel', detailed copying of individual commands, and copying of certain screen displays showing the results. At the preliminary hearing, Pumfrey J made reference to some of the unexpected outcomes of classifying computer programs as literary works for the purposes of copyright, but suggested that analogies with, for example, literary plots may provide 'a valuable jumping off point for the formulation of a modern system of protection for computer programmes [sic] . . .'.[92] He cautioned, however, that English law had not yet worked out how copyright protection for computer programs should operate beyond literal copying.[93] He returned to the problem of distinguishing computer programs from other literary works at full trial,[94] explaining that:

> . . . two completely different computer programs can produce an identical result: not a result identical at some level of abstraction but identical at any level of abstraction. This is so even if the author of one has no access at all to the other but only to its results.[95]

In a lengthy discussion of the problems of trying to protect functional elements of computer programs by copyright,[96] no assistance was found from the decisions in *Flanders* and *Ibcos*, and overall it was held that the claim failed for both a lack of substantiality and the nature of the skill and labour to be protected, and that neither was any of the code read or copied by the defendants. Thus copyright protection could not be relied on to prevent the creation of a competing product. However, this is not necessarily an unusual position and, although the US authorities were not relied upon, it seems likely that, on these facts, a similar result would be obtained by applying the *Altai* test.[97] In other words, in the absence of access to the original code, if a programmer writes a program that is based on the general idea of a program written by another person, that will be insufficient to establish copyright infringement. This was subsequently confirmed by the Court of Appeal in *Nova v Mazooma Games*,[98] upholding the reasoning in *Navitaire*, which has since been referred to as the 'leading case on the copyright protection of computer programs'.[99] This decision seems to have been generally welcomed as providing a coherent approach to the application of copyright principles to the production of similar programs[100] that has 'blown away the fog of technical obfuscation'.[101]

---

87 Ibid, [73].
88 Ibid, [76].
89 Pumfrey J explained that this term could encompass either the overall structure of the system at a high level of abstraction or the allocation of functions between various programs.
90 Ibid, [77].
91 [2004] EWHC 1725 (Ch).
92 Ibid, [12].
93 Ibid, [14].
94 [2004] EWHC 1725 (Ch), [2006] RPC 3.
95 Ibid, [125].
96 Ibid, [118]ff.
97 See also discussion in R Marchini, 'Navitaire v easyJet: What now for look and feel?' (2005) 15(6) Comp and Law 31.
98 [2007] EWCA Civ 219.
99 SAS v World Programming [2010] EWHC 1829 (Ch), [174], in which Arnold J also lists the reasons why Pumfrey J was in a good position to decide the case.
100 See, eg, Simon Miles and Emma Stoker, 'Nova Productions Ltd v Mazooma Games Ltd' (2006) 17 Ent L Rev 181; Andrew Clay, 'Nova Productions Ltd v Mazooma Games Ltd: Game over for Nova' (2007) 18 Ent L Rev 187.
101 Lim and Longdin, op cit, 375.

The Software Directive and its Implementation

Around the time that *Flanders* was under consideration, legislative action was also being taken with respect to intellectual property rights in computer programs in the form of the **Software Directive**. This Directive was a recognition of the issues that had caused debate in relation to the protection of intellectual property rights in computer programs, and also of the fact that, without harmonisation of these provisions, the completion and operation of the single European market in goods and services might be compromised. This was particularly necessary in view of the fact that different Member States had adopted quite different attitudes to the legal protection of computer programs. Thus, notwithstanding that many other jurisdictions, both inside and outside Europe, were basing their protection on copyright principles, this was not possible in Germany, for example, where computer programs were viewed as technical and scientific products, rather than literary works.[102] The fact that such states might be signatories to the **Berne Convention** was of little relevance, because the issue was one of the categorisation of computer programs as copyright material. The Directive was adopted in 1991, with an implementation date of 1 January 1993, and its provisions seem to have stood the test of time. A subsequent report from the European Commission on its implementation found that overall implementation by Member States was satisfactory and that the effects of the implementation were beneficial. It therefore concluded that 'experience to date does not lead to the view that the substantive copyright provisions of the Directive should be revisited at this time'.[103] This view was effectively endorsed by the fact that no amendments to this Directive were included in the later **Copyright Directive**, which notes that it is 'based on principles and rules already laid down in the directives currently in force in this area, in particular Directive 91/250/EEC ...'.[104] In 2009, the provisions of the original Directive were codified in **Directive 2009/24/EC**, but the substantive requirements remain unchanged.[105]

Scope of the Directive

As already mentioned,[106] Art 1(1) protects computer programs as literary works and this is deemed to extend to any preparatory design material; however, the protection only extends to the expression and does not include any underlying ideas (Art 1(2)). Questions on the interpretation of Art 1(2) have recently been referred to the European Court of Justice (ECJ) by the High Court in *SAS v World Programming*.[107] SAS had developed a series of applications to carry out statistical analysis. The functionality of the basic package could be extended by using additional SAS applications. All of these programs were written in SAS language – a proprietary language developed by SAS for this purpose. World Programming created alternative programs that had similar functionality to the SAS applications programs. SAS alleged that World Programming's software infringed its copyright and also that its manuals had been copied, which itself constituted indirect copying of the applications programs. The reasoning in *Navitaire* and *Nova* above would not lead to a finding of copyright infringement, but in a long and detailed judgment that, amongst other things, reviews the earlier case law and considers the provisions of the Directive and its implementation, although apparently not disagreeing with *Navitaire*, it was decided that Art 1(2) was neither reasonably clear

---

102 See, eg, Andreas Wiebe, 'European copyright protection of software from a German perspective' (1993) 9 CL & P 79.
103 Report from the Commission to the Council, the European Parliament and the Economic and Social Committee, COM(2000)1999 final.
104 Directive 2001/29/EC of the European Parliament and of the Council of 22 May 2001 on the harmonisation of certain aspects of copyright and related rights in the information society, [2001] OJ L 167/10, Recital 20.
105 Directive 2009/24/EC of the European Parliament and of the Council of 23 April 2009 on the legal protection of computer programs (Codified version) [2009] OJ L 111/16.
106 Above p 362.
107 Case C–406/10 [2010] OJ C 346/26.

nor free from doubt leading to the questions referred to the ECJ.[108] These questions are specifically targeted at the situation in which a competing program is produced that reproduces the functionality of the first program, but without accessing any of its code. The questions are detailed and technical, but included are such issues as the relevance of the functionality of the first program, and the skill and judgment that resulted in its creation, the level of detail of this functionality that has been reproduced, and whether it makes a difference if the second program has been produced as a resulting of observing and studying the first program and/or reading the manual. Given the existing clarity of the approach in *Navitaire* and *Nova*, it is hoped that the response of the ECJ will continue the clarification rather than generate further obfuscation.

Article 1(3) further requires that the program must be original in the sense of 'the author's own intellectual creation'. This requirement hides a clash between the civil law and common law approach to originality. The former looks for some innovative or creative quality specific to the author, whereas the latter merely uses a test based on the author's own endeavours. As would be expected, cases on computer programs in Germany, France, Belgium, and the Netherlands prior to the Directive looked for evidence of some aspect of the author's personality to sustain a finding of originality.[109] The Directive sought to harmonise this 'mosaic of originality interpretations',[110] but the conflict between the approaches persists because the phrase 'own intellectual creation' can be interpreted in conformity with either approach. Given this possibility, and in the light of recent case law in Belgium, Deene calls for referrals also to be made to the ECJ to establish a uniform interpretation of originality with respect to computer programs.[111]

Restricted Acts and their Exceptions

The Directive reserves the usual rights to copyright holders. An application of traditional copyright principles would suggest that non-infringing use is then possible with express authorisation of the copyright holder or within one of the general 'fair use' exceptions. The 1991 **Software Directive** introduced for the first time a new category of acts that, rather than being generally available, are reserved for a person with a 'right to use the program' – that is, introducing a concept of a 'lawful user'. The substance of these exceptions reflects some of the differences between computer programs and traditional literary works. They are contained in Art 5 and include anything necessary for the use of the computer program by the lawful acquirer for its intended purpose, including: error correction; the making of a back-up copy; and a right for the lawful user to 'observe, study or test the functioning of a program in order to determine the ideas and principles underlying any element of the program', as long as this is done whilst performing acts that are otherwise permitted by copyright law. Further, most of these exceptions to the restricted acts are obligatory and cannot be excluded by contract.[112] It has been suggested that these new exceptions 'mark the advent of a more active approach to copyright exceptions', which creates 'rights' that are 'legal hybrids between exceptions and rights'.[113] Section 50C of the **CDPA 1988**,

See Chapter 11 →

---

108 In total, nine questions were referred: the first five of these refer to the interpretation of Art 1(2); questions 6 and 7 to Art 5(3), discussed below at p 373; the remaining two questions concern the interpretation of Directive 2001/29. There had been requests to make a reference to the ECJ in *Nova*, but this was turned down by the Court of Appeal on the grounds that it would be possible to decide the appeal without the need to interpret the provisions of the Directive (as in fact turned out to be the case), and that if such an interpretation were to prove necessary, it would be possible to make the referral at that stage when the precise nature of the questions could be more easily ascertained: [2006] EWCA Civ 1044.

109 Discussed in Joris Deene, 'Originality in software law: Belgian doctrine and jurisprudence remain divided' (2007) 2 JIPLP 692, 693.

110 Ibid.

111 Ibid, 698.

112 Directive 91/250, Art 9; now Directive 2009/24, Art 8. The provisions have been implemented in the UK by introducing new ss 50A, 50BA, 50C, and 296A into the Copyright, Designs and Patents Act 1988 (CDPA 1988). These should be read in conjunction with the new s 21(3)(ab), which introduces a new element into the definition of 'adaptation' – namely, 'an arrangement or altered version of the program or a translation of it'.

113 Tatiana-Eleni Synodinou, 'The lawful user and a balancing of interests in European copyright law' (2010) 41 IIC 819, 826.

giving effect to Art 5(1), speaks in terms of 'lawful use'. There is no definition of either lawful use or the 'lawful user', but it seems clear that it does not equate with all people who use the program, but is more akin to the term 'lawful acquirer' that is used in Art 5(1). The effect of the above provisions on the permissible use of software is considered in more detail elsewhere in the book.

Navitaire, Nova, and SAS v World Programming all involved the observation of the functionality of programs and the subsequent creation of a similar one, but only in the last of these is there any discussion of Art 5(3).[114] Arnold J reviewed the arguments on both sides.[115] These included: whether or not Art 5(3) complied with the **Berne Convention** 'three-step test'; whether it was an 'avoidance of doubt' provision; the effect of any licence provisions; and the effect of the legislative history and relevant recitals. His provisional view was that, as an exception, Art 5(3) should be interpreted as a positive defence not an avoidance of doubt measure; that it was significant that it could not be overridden by contract – that is, by standard licence terms – and that its provisions should be interpreted broadly. Nevertheless, he concluded that the matter was not free from doubt and that this was also a matter that should be referred to the ECJ.[116]

Decompilation and Fair Use

One feature that may be desirable in a computer program, but which has no clear parallel in relation to more conventional literary works, is the need for interoperability – that is, the capacity of the computer program to be compatible with other computer programs or hardware elements in a system, such as a printer. This means that the interoperable program will need to contain some of the same features as the original, at least at the interface between the two. One way of accomplishing this is to decompile (that is, to compile in reverse), or reverse engineer, the object code of the program with which interoperability is desired, to obtain the source code. This can then be used in the creation of the interface between the existing and the new or proposed program. Those sections of the industry that create software primarily for running on operating systems created by others clearly have a vested interest in allowing decompilation to the maximum extent without fear of infringement, whereas other sectors of the industry, such as those that produce complete systems, are less likely to wish to permit decompilation, or any other form of reverse engineering or analysis. Until the advent of the **Software Directive**, such activity was likely to breach copyright unless it could be brought within the fair use or fair dealing exceptions, and this led to much discussion about how these provisions could be applied to reverse engineering and decompilation, but with no unanimity of opinion.[117]

The court in Atari Games Corp v Nintendo of America Inc concluded that reverse engineering object codes to discern the unprotectable ideas in a computer program was 'fair use'.[118] In SEGA Enterprises v Accolade,[119] the Court of Appeals for the Ninth Circuit, reversing the decision of the district court, seemed to suggest that decompilation may be permissible in certain circumstances and found its reasoning to be compatible with that in Atari. In particular, there was likely to be fair use where the end product did not contain copyright material and the copying was necessary to obtain access to

---

114 CPDA 88, s 50BA, which must be interpreted in conformity with Art 5(3): [2010] EWHC 1829, [163].
115 Ibid, [291]–[315].
116 For precise terms of the questions referred, see Case C–406/10 [2010] OJ C 346/26.
117 Compare, eg, the views expressed in Susan A Dunn, 'Defining the scope of copyright protection for computer software' (1986) 38 Stan L Rev 497, 518, and Miller, op cit, 1026.
118 975 F2d 832, 843 (Fed Cir 1992).
119 977 F 2d 1510 (9th Cir 1992). Compare the views of Miller, op cit, 1014ff; RH Stern, 'An ill-conceived analysis of reverse engineering of software as copyright infringement: Sega Enterprises v Accolade' [1992] EIPR 107, discussing the district court's decision; RH Stern, 'Reverse engineering of software as copyright infringement: An update – Sega Enterprises v Accolade' [1993] EIPR 34, following the judgment of the Court of Appeals. Hunter notes that the Australian courts would not arrive at the same conclusion: 'Reverse engineering computer software: Australia parts company with the world' (1993) 9 CL & P 122. See also P Waters and PG Leonard, 'The lessons of recent EC and US developments for protection of computer software under Australian law' [1991] EIPR 125.

the functional elements of the program. The application of the fair use factors to acts of decompilation was considered again in *Sony v Connectix*.[120] Connectix created 'emulator software' that allowed Sony games to be used not only on the proprietary Playstation console, but also on a standard PC. During the development process, Sony was contacted for 'technical assistance', but the request was declined; Connectix then decompiled Sony's software in order to ensure compatibility, but the final product contained none of the original code. The Ninth Circuit, applying the fair use provisions, found that decompilation was necessary to provide access to the unprotected functional elements; although the whole of Sony's software had been copied, there was no infringing material in the final product and so this factor could be accorded little weight. Connectix's use was 'modestly transformative' in that a wholly new product had been produced and the new product was a 'legitimate competitor'. The decompilation was thus protected by the fair use provisions.

Further developments in the USA have centred around the extent to which decompilation and reverse engineering of software can be controlled or precluded by contractual provisions. The **Digital Millennium Copyright Act of 2000 (DMCA 2000)** introduced a new s 1201 into the US **Copyright Act of 1976**, which generally prohibits the circumvention of copyright protection systems. Section 1201(f) appears to allow reverse engineering along similar lines to that developed by the judiciary, but it still appears to be the case in the USA that decompilation or reverse engineering can be prohibited by contractual terms. Indeed, this situation appears to have been underlined in *Davidson & Assocs v Jung*.[121] Despite such decisions, the official comment to s 105 of the proposed Uniform Computer Information Transactions Act (UCITA) noted recognition of 'a policy not to prohibit some reverse engineering where it is needed to obtain interoperability',[122] but this enactment, which was intended to modify the **Uniform Commercial Code** in relation to contracts for, for example, software, remains controversial and has not been implemented in most states.

See Chapter 9 →

The issue of decompilation has not been discussed by the UK courts in the context of the fair dealing provisions in s 29 of the **CDPA 1988**. Indeed, the exception for research and private study in s 29(1) now only applies to non-commercial research, so, without the decompilation provisions of the **Software Directive** discussed below, it seems unlikely that the fair dealing provisions would 'save' decompilation.[123] Similar fair dealing provisions in the Singapore **Copyright Act of 1988** were discussed in *Aztech Systems Pty Ltd v Creative Technology Ltd*. The case concerned the development of computer sound cards that would be interoperable with the 'Sound Blaster' card – the market leader. On the evidence, there had actually been no decompilation, because the new application had been created by non-invasive methods, together with trial and error, until the new product was compatible with the 'Sound Blaster' card. Research for industrial purposes or by companies was expressly excluded by s 35 of the Singapore **Copyright Act of 1988** and so Aztech sought to rely on fair dealing for private study. Although this argument succeeded at first instance,[124] this was reversed by the Singapore Court of Appeal,[125] which held that extending the meaning of 'private study' would 'render otiose the specific exclusion of commercial research under s 35(5)'.[126] The

---

120 203 F3d 596 (9th Cir 2000); see also discussion in D Prestin, 'Where to draw the line between reverse engineering and infringement: *Sony Computer Entertainment Inc v Connectix Corp*' (2002) 3 Minn Intell Prop Rev 137.

121 422 F 3d 630 (8th Cir 2005); see also discussion in Benjamin I Narodick, 'Smothered by judicial love: How *Jacobsen v Katzer* could bring open source software development to a standstill' (2010) 16 BU J Sci & Tech L 264.

122 Further discussion of this point is beyond the scope of this chapter, but for a more complete consideration, see, eg, E Douma, 'The Uniform Computer Information Transactions Act and the issue of preemption of contractual provisions prohibiting reverse engineering, disassembly or decompilation' (2001) 11 Alb LJ Sci & Tech 249; *Bowers v Baystate Technologies* 320 F 3d 1317 (Fed Cir 2003); DL Kwong, 'The copyright–contract intersection: *Softman Products Co v Adobe Systems Inc & Bowers v Baystate Technologies Inc*' (2003) 18 Berkeley Tech LJ 349; JA Andrews, 'Reversing copyright misuse: Enforcing contractual prohibitions on software reverse engineering' (2004) 41 Hous L Rev 975; S Son, 'Can black dot (shrinkwrap) licenses override federal reverse engineering rights?: The relationship between copyright, contract and antitrust laws' (2004) 6 Tul J Tech & Intell Prop 63.

123 For a discussion of how the UK fair dealing provisions might be applied to copyright of computer programs, see Chris Reed, 'Reverse engineering computer programs without infringing copyright' [1991] EIPR 47.

124 [1996] FSR 54.

125 [1997] FSR 491.

126 Ibid, 505.

High Court of Australia also found reverse engineering of software not to be legitimised by the fair dealing provisions in the case of *Data Access v Powerflex Services*.[127] The Court noted the potential effect this interpretation could have on the software market, but felt that this was something that had to be addressed by the legislature rather than the judiciary. In Europe, this was effectively what happened with the adoption of the **Software Directive**.

Difficulty in delineating the circumstances in which decompilation would be acceptable to all sectors of the industry was one of the main reasons for the protracted gestation of the Directive.[128] Article 6(1) provides that, subject to certain conditions, decompilation is permissible where it is 'indispensable to obtain the information necessary to achieve the interoperability of an independently created computer program with other programs'. As for the exceptions in Art 5, this right is reserved for the 'lawful user'; it cannot be used if the relevant information has already been made available, and it only extends to those parts of the program necessary to ensure compatibility, not to the program in total. Article 6(2) further provides that any information obtained in this way cannot be used for other purposes, given to others unless for the purposes of making an interoperable program, or used to create a computer program that is substantially similar in its actual expression. This provision is a compromise that tries to reconcile the needs and interests of the various sectors in the industry. It appears to be aimed at allowing products to be developed that are compatible with the original, rather than those that might be viewed as being in direct competition with the original.[129] This is a fine line to draw.

This right was implemented in the UK by removing decompilation from the ambit of the fair dealing provisions relating to research and private study contained in s 29 **CDPA**, and introducing it as a new permitted act in s 50B. In these provisions, 'decompilation' refers to the conversion of a computer program in a low-level language to one in an HLL. It is by no means clear that this definition coincides with the one in the Directive.[130] The Directive refers to decompilation as 'reproduction of the code and translation of its form', which appears to represent a much wider view of its scope. The new s 50B(2) provides that decompilation will be allowed where it is 'necessary to create an independent program which can be operated with the program decompiled or another program'. This, taken together with s 50B(3), suggests that it may be lawful to create a competing program, provided that it is not substantially similar to the original program, but that it would be impermissible to devise modifications to an existing program to make it interoperable with another. This latter act would, apparently, be permitted under the Directive, which allows decompilation where it is 'indispensable to obtain the information necessary to achieve the interoperability of an independently created computer program with other programs'.

Patents and Computer Software

Whereas copyright has evolved primarily as a device for protecting the literary and the creative, patents are associated with inventions and technical products. While the aim of copyright is to stimulate creativity while respecting the rights of the creator, patents are intended to encourage innovation, while also providing rights to the inventor or developer. Unlike copyright, a patent does

127 [1999] HCA 49, available online at www.austlii.edu.au/au/cases/cth/HCA/1999/49.html

128 For details of the discussions both before and after the adoption of the Directive, see eg, the debate between Cornish, Lake et al, and Colombe and Meyer in [1989] EIPR 391, [1989] EIPR 43, [1990] EIPR 79, [1990] EIPR 129, [1990] EIPR 325; Jerome Huet and Jane Ginsburg, 'Computer programs in Europe: A comparative analysis of the 1991 EC Software Directive' (1992) 30 Col J Transnat L 327; J Haaf, 'The EC Directive on the Legal Protection of Computer Programs: Decompilation and security for confidential programming techniques' (1992) 30 Col J Transnat L 401; PG Hidalgo, 'Copyright protection of computer software in the European Community: Current protection and the effect of the adopted Directive' (1993) 27 Int Lawyer 113; David Bainbridge, 'Computer programs and copyright: More exceptions to infringement' (1993) 56 MLR 591.

129 For a discussion of the balance of rights in the Directive specifically in relation to decompilation, see ER Krocker, 'The Computer Directive and the balance of rights' [1997] EIPR 247.

130 See also criticism in COM(2000)199 final, pp 13–14.

not arise spontaneously on creation, but a claim has to be made[131] and important criteria fulfilled – namely, that the invention is new, involves an inventive step, and is capable of industrial application.[132] Once granted, a patent is valid for a shorter period (up to a maximum of 20 years) than copyright, but, during the term of its validity, it gives the owner of the patent the exclusive right to control the production and use of the invention. Although many programmers have relied on copyright protection for software, that in no way means that patents have not also been employed in this respect. As we have seen above, the protection that copyright can afford to the functional elements of computer programs is both limited and uncertain. Patent law, on the other hand, is able to protect ideas, and therefore the functional aspects of a program, provided that the other criteria for the grant of a patent are met. The exclusive rights granted mean that patent protection is far stronger than copyright and can prevent the development of a similar independently produced product.[133] A patent can be extremely valuable in providing the opportunity to those developing the programs to recoup their research and development costs, and in facilitating control over exploitation of the patented matter, especially in the early stages of the product. This value is demonstrated by the extent of the lobby from software producers, although this is matched by an equally vociferous lobby from programmers and users who believe that patent protection will, amongst other things, stifle the technology.[134] Guadamuz, on the other hand, has remarked that, if the arguments for the use of patents are accepted, 'society can only benefit from the patentability of some software inventions'.[135]

The 'As Such' Exclusion

But the above does not tell the whole story: under the **European Patent Convention (EPC)**, and therefore under the law of those states that are signatories to that convention, there are a number of exclusions from patentability. So, although Art 52(1) **EPC** allows patents to be granted subject to the criteria above for 'any inventions, in all fields of technology', Art 52(2) subsequently lists things that are not deemed to be inventions for these purposes and so are excluded from patentability in so far as the claim relates to any of these 'as such'. The list includes, amongst other things, mathematical methods, business methods, and computer programs.[136]

Clearly, the interpretation of 'as such' will then be a key issue in determining the patentability or otherwise of what are frequently referred to as 'computer-implemented inventions'. A crucial question would seem to be whether the claim for a patent for an invention involving a computer program can be regarded as an application for a patent for a program 'as such' – that is, does the inventiveness and non-obviousness lie solely in the computer program itself, or, rather, is the effect to create an entirely new product or process within which the computer program can merely be regarded in the same light as any other component might be? In the USA, views on this matter have, arguably, polarised more distinctly. Many have expressed the view that claims for patents involving computer software should be treated in the same way as those concerning computer hardware; others advocate the opposite view on the basis that software technology is significantly different from that which applies to hardware.[137]

Some of the perceived difficulties appear to have arisen from definitional difficulties. Since the statutory exclusion is for a computer program as such, a uniform interpretation of the exclusion is

131 To the relevant awarding body. In the UK, this is the Intellectual Property Office, online at www.ipo.gov.uk. The European Patent Office (EPO), online at www.epo.org, administers the European Patent Convention and provides a uniform application process for obtaining patents in up to forty countries in Europe.
132 See European Patent Convention, Art 52(1); Patents Act 1977, s 1(1).
133 See further Daehwan Koo, 'Patent and copyright protection of computer programs' [2002] IPQ 172, 199ff.
134 Andres Grosche, 'Software patents: Boon or bane for Europe' (2006) 14 IJLIT 257, 259.
135 Andrés Guadamuz Gonzáles, 'The software patent debate' (2006) 1 JIPLP 196, 202.
136 In the UK, these provisions are given effect by Patents Act 1977, s 1.
137 For a more conceptual discussion of the nature of technology, and the purpose and application of both patents and exclusion from patentability, see, eg, A Von Helfeld, 'Protection of inventions comprising computer programs by the European and German Patent Offices: A confrontation' (1986) 3 CL & P 182.

very dependent on an accepted and acceptable definition, and yet this is not something that has ever been decisively defined in law. What is a computer program? Since computer programs can be expressed in the form of algorithms, the origin of the exclusion appears to derive from the same source as the exclusion for mathematical methods. For some time, there have been arguments that such an exclusion is unnecessary, and that any bar to patentability should rest merely on the basic requirements of novelty and non-obviousness. Article 27 of the **TRIPS Agreement**, for example, although allowing exclusions in order to restrict the exploitation of, for example, human and animal tissue, seems to envisage no other exclusions and merely requires that 'patents shall be available for any inventions, whether products or processes, in all fields of technology'. In this vein, Chisum poses the question: 'Why are new and useful developments in mathematics with direct industrial applications per se excluded from the patent system when developments in all other areas of applied technological knowledge are included?'[138] In his view, the confusion over patentability in the USA was entirely due to the decision of the Supreme Court in *Gottschalk v Benson*, which had held that a mathematical algorithm could not be patented, no matter how new and useful, and that 'policy considerations' indicated that patent protection was as appropriate for mathematical algorithms that are useful in computer programming as for other technical innovations.[139] Harrington has suggested that the crux of the problem lies in different approaches to the meaning of 'computer program' between lawyers and electronic or electrical engineers. Whereas lawyers tend to define a computer program in terms of instructions, creating a prima facie impression of non-patentability, electrical engineers are more likely to think in terms of 'a process for performing a specific function or a means for creating circuitry in a block of silicon'.[140] This carries echoes of the bifurcated nature of software noted by Samuelson et al,[141] and sounds much more like the substance of a patent claim. He cites with approval *In re Alappat*,[142] in which Judge Rich said that it was 'inaccurate and confusing to speak in terms of a mathematical algorithm as excluded subject matter when assessing the patentability of a computer related invention' and used an approach that was much more in accordance with engineering definitions of 'computer program'. In Harrington's view, this approach 'recognises the reality of what actually occurs when a program is run on a computer and the utility of the mathematical sciences as a powerful vehicle for applied technology'.

Some of the propensity for confusion over matters of definition can be observed in *Data Access v Powerflex*, in which, albeit for the purposes of copyright law rather than the granting of a patent, it was vital to ascertain whether the user interface commands could be classified as 'computer programs' using a legal definition of a computer program as a set of instructions. The lower courts had conflicting views on whether, on the facts, the particular features at issue could be construed as a computer program, but, for the purposes of this discussion, the High Court of Australia noted that 'the definition of a computer program seems to have more in common with the subject matter of a patent than a copyright'.[143]

As will be discussed further below, there is an ongoing debate over the interpretation of the exclusions. As might be expected, it has proved a relatively simple task to identify cases that fall at either end of the spectrum: no patent will be granted, for example, where the application relates merely to the operation of the computer under the control of the program. However, there is no bright line between what is, or what is not, within the exclusions and the border between the two has proved difficult to delineate. Given that the statutory exclusions are well known, there have been many attempts to associate the patent claim with some technical effect made possible by the

138 DS Chisum, 'The patentability of computer algorithms' (1986) 47 Pitt UL Rev 959, 1007, following In re Pardo 684 F 2d 912 (1982).
139 409 US 63 (1972). But note the comment on the nature of algorithms in response to Chisum's article in A Newell, 'The models are broken, the models are broken' (1986) 47 Pitt UL Rev 1023.
140 D Harrington, 'The engineers have it! Patenting computer programs in the USA' (1996) 1 Comm L 232.
141 Op cit.
142 33 F 3d 1526 (Fed Cir 1994); see below p 378; see also AD Lowrie, 'Developments in US case law' (1997) 28 IIC 868.
143 [1999] HCA 49, [20].

novelty of the invention as a whole. The fact that, subject to these provisos and the general requirements for patentability, patents are available for computer-implemented inventions has led to a
steady increase in the number of patent applications relating to computer-implemented inventions.
This has only exacerbated the difficulties in drawing a line between what is, and is not, patentable
subject matter and the subsequent outcomes have been neither straightforward nor uncontroversial. A key issue for both the Technical Board of Appeal (TBA) of the European Patent Office (EPO)
and the courts in contracting states of the **EPC** has been to attempt to clarify the criteria governing
the interpretation and application of the exclusions in Art 52(2) **EPC** – in particular, whether or
not the invention exhibits any technical effect outside of the operation of the computer.

The Approach of the European Patent Office

An important early decision of the TBA was that of *Vicom*.[144] The application concerned a claim for a
method of digitally processing images in the form of a two-dimensional array that could be used to
enhance or restore the technical quality of such images. It was the computer program that embodied
the inventive idea that both controlled the process and gave it its value, but it was held that the
application was not for the program 'as such', but for the invention that it was used to perform. A
decisive point was that the application was susceptible of industrial application, since it could be
used for investigating the properties of a real or simulated object, or for designing an industrial
article. The requisite technical effect was therefore found in the operation of the computer rather
than in the actual program. In relation to the exclusion, the TBA stated that the exclusion should not
only be related to the fact that a computer program is used to implement an invention; the decisive
point was the 'technical contribution the invention . . . when considered as a whole makes to the
known art'.[145] The *Vicom* decision provided a strict test for patentability and, for a number of years,
was treated as the standard approach to computer-implemented inventions by the TBA.

Criticisms of this interpretation developed for a number of reasons. First was that it did not
represent a true picture of the technology, because the 'description of computer programs as non-
technical sits uncomfortably with the reality that many programs are of technical "real world"
significance'.[146] Second, and arguably more significant, was the argument that, during the 1990s,
the European practice on computer-implemented inventions diverged from that of two major
trading partners, the USA and Japan, both of which had become more flexible over the grant of
'software patents'.[147] In the USA, by virtue of 35 **USC** §101, patents are available for 'any new and
useful process, machine manufacture, or composition of matter or any new and useful improvement thereof'. However, the exclusion of algorithms from patentability in *Gottschalk v Benson*, referred
to earlier in the chapter, originally ruled out computer program claims. But the turning point for
software patentability in the USA still came as early as 1981, with the case of *Diamond v Diehr*,[148] and
as long as the whole system could be considered the subject matter of the claim, tests for the patentability of software could be based on the overall functioning of the system. The reasoning was
relaxed further in *Re Alappat*,[149] in which the approach taken was to consider the computer as a
machine so that a program could be construed as a 'new and useful improvement thereof' within
the meaning of §101. In later cases such as *State Street Bank v Signature*[150] and *AT & T Corp v Excel
Communications*,[151] the US courts have enunciated a test that is based on the identification of a 'useful

144 T208/84 [1987] EPOR 74.
145 Ibid, [16].
146 J Newman, 'The patentability of computer-related inventions in Europe' [1997] EIPR 701.
147 S Davies, 'Computer program claims' [1998] EIPR 429.
148 450 US 175 (1981).
149 33 F 3d 1526 (Fed Cir 1994).
150 149 F 3d 1368 (Fed Cir 1998).
151 172 F 3d 1352 (Fed Cir 1999).

concrete and tangible result'. This represents a considerable departure from the early approaches and has resulted in a consequent liberalisation of the criteria for patentability of computer software in the USA.[152] The third issue was the lack of a similar exclusion in Art 27 of the **TRIPS Agreement**.

Whether or not as a response to these factors, two decisions of the TBA – the so-called IBM 'Twins',[153] in which the applicant referred to both the **TRIPS Agreement**, and the situation in the USA and Japan – were to provide the opportunity for a review of the approach to the 'as such' exclusion. With regard to **TRIPS**, the TBA, in T1173/97, was not convinced that it applied to the **EPC**, but even so it was 'appropriate to take it into consideration'. With regard to the comparison with the USA and Japan, it emphasised the difference in the respective legal systems, but pointed out that 'nevertheless ... these developments represent a useful indication of modern trends'. Having pointed out that the only applicable law that the Board could be bound to consider was the **EPC**, it continued in its review of the interpretation of the exclusions, noting that the main problem was the definition of 'technical character'. Having considered this in some detail, it reached the overall conclusion that:

> ... a computer program claimed by itself is not excluded from patentability if the program, when running on a computer or loaded into a computer, brings about, or is capable of bringing about, a technical effect which goes beyond the 'normal' physical interactions between the program (software) and the computer (hardware) on which it is run.[154]

The TBA acknowledged that its decision was 'based on a slightly different approach in thinking and reasoning' from previous case law, but did not feel that there was any real inconsistency.[155] Although the decision had been reached 'in the light of developments in information technology', it had 'not gone beyond the ordinary meaning given to the terms of the EPC'.[156] An essentially similar judgment and outcome occurred in T935/97. The wording of Art 52 **EPC** was subsequently amended in 2000 and now, in common with Art 27 **TRIPS**, includes the phrase 'in all fields of technology'.

Following these decisions, the TBA again revisited the nature of technicality in T931/95 *Pension Benefit Systems Partnership*.[157] One of the other exclusions from patentability 'as such' is a claim for a 'business method'. Because most business methods are now effected by computer, these two issues are often discussed together. Even where they are not, similar concepts are involved – notably, the need for a technical contribution. T931/95 contained a claim for a process for managing and controlling a pension benefits program, and also for an apparatus for performing this process. The former was rejected as being purely a claim for a business method. In relation to the latter, the TBA decided that 'a computer system suitably programmed for use in a particular field, even if that is the field of business and economy' could be an invention because it 'has the character of a concrete apparatus in the sense of a physical entity, manmade for a utilitarian purpose'.[158] It was critical of the 'contribution approach' to technicality that had been used in a number of previous cases, since if this contribution were not of a technical character, then, on the previous reasoning, there would be no invention. Referring to both of the IBM cases, the TBA concluded that possession of technical character was an implicit requirement of an invention, and there was no basis for distinguishing

---

152 For further discussion, see, eg, J Fellas, 'The patentability of software-related inventions in the US' [1999] EIPR 330; DM Attridge, 'Challenging claims! Patenting computer programs in Europe and the United States' [2001] IPQ 22; Koo, op cit; Jack George Abid, 'Software patents on both sides of the Atlantic' (2005) 23 J Marshall J Computer & Info L 815. At the time of writing, it is as yet uncertain whether a further liberalisation of the patentability of software will result following the ruling of the Supreme Court in *Bilski v Kappos* 130 S Ct 3218 (2010). This decision relates primarily to business methods, but is capable of wider application: see, eg, 'Patent-eligible subject matter' (2010) 124 Harv L Rev 370.
153 T935/97 [1999] EPOR 301; T1173/97 [2000] EPOR 219.
154 T1173/97, [11.5].
155 Ibid.
156 Ibid, [10.2].
157 [2002] EPOR 52.
158 Ibid, [5].

between 'new features' of an invention and features of that invention that are known from the prior art. This approach, which has subsequently been dubbed the 'any hardware' approach, appears to focus less on the exclusion of a computer program and more on whether or not the claim in question relates to an invention. The focus, therefore, is on the identification of the inventive step. Likhovski has remarked that this decision 'elevates the form of the claim over its substance' and 'sanctions what seem to be almost automatic findings of technicality for apparatus claims',[159] while Laakkonen and Whaite suggest that the ruling was intended to 'end the discussion on the patentability of programs for computers' and that it 'appears to remove practically all restrictions derived from patentability of programs as such'.[160]

The reasoning in T931/95 was developed further in T258/03 *Hitachi/Auction Method*. Noting that the term 'invention' was to be construed as 'subject matter having technical character', the TBA appeared to respond to some of the criticism by deciding that, where there was a mix of technical and non-technical features, 'a compelling reason' for not engaging Art 52(2) was that the 'technical features may in themselves turn out to fulfil all the requirements of Article 52(1) EPC'.[161] Although, on the facts, Hitachi's claim failed for lack of inventive step, the TBA nevertheless extended the application of technicality in T931/95 to methods, as well as to systems, claims noting that 'this reasoning is independent of the category of claim'. In focusing again on the inventive aspects of the claim, the TBA acknowledged that it was now using a comparatively broad interpretation of the term 'invention', but argued that this did not lead inexorably to the conclusion that all methods involving technical means would be granted patents; they still had to satisfy the standard criteria of novelty, inventiveness, and industrial application.

This line of decisions saw further development in the *Microsoft (Clipboard format)* cases.[162] The claims concerned clipboard applications for transferring non-filed data between software applications. The TBA distinguished the claim category of a computer-implemented method from that of a computer program on the basis that a claim relating to a method of operating a computer put into practice with the help of a computer program does not claim a computer program 'as such'.[163] The claim provided an additional functionality for an existing computer that was both new and involved an inventive step. This 'trio' of decisions has been followed in subsequent EPO cases such as *Sharp/Graphical user interface*, in which it was said that the exclusion would be unlikely to be engaged where the 'technical effect relates to functional features rather than cognitive aesthetic content'.[164] The above cases represent a significant move away from the test in *Vicom* and have proved to be controversial in the UK.

The European Patent Convention and National Courts

The **EPC** was implemented in the UK by the **Patents Act 1977**, s 130(7) of which declares that a number of its provisions, including the criteria for patentability and the exclusions in s 1 are 'so framed as to have, as nearly as practicable, the same effects in the United Kingdom as the corresponding provisions of the European Patent Convention'. Further, s 91(1)(c) requires 'judicial notice' to be taken of 'any decision of, or expression of opinion by, the relevant convention court on any question arising under or in connection with the relevant convention'. In addition, the **EPC** is a multilateral international treaty and so should be construed in the light of the corresponding international law — in particular, Art 31(1) of the **Vienna Convention**, which

---

159 M Likhovski, 'Fighting the patent wars' [2001] EIPR 267, 270; see comments in *Hutchins' Application* [2002] RPC 8, [33] and [34], discussed below at p 381.
160 A Laakkonen and R Whaite, 'The EPO leads the way, but where to?' [2001] EIPR 244.
161 [2004] EPOR 55, [3.5].
162 T424/03 and T411/03 [2006] EPOR 39 and 40.
163 [2006] EPOR 39, [5.1].
164 T 1188/04 [2008] EPOR 32, [14].

requires the provisions of a treaty to be interpreted in good faith, taking into account the meaning of the words in context, and having regard to the object and purpose of the provisions in question. Evidence of such a purposive construction can perhaps be identified in some of the decisions made under the **EPC**. The discussion of the decisions in UK courts needs to be set against this background. Notwithstanding Aldous LJ's remark in *Fujitsu's Application* that 'the intention of Parliament was that there should be uniformity in this regard and that any substantial divergence would be disastrous',[165] as we shall see, there has indeed been a divergence between the UK courts and the TBA. This appears to have resulted partly from a less purposive interpretation of 'as such' and also from a perceived need for strict adherence to previous precedents.[166]

The UK Situation

An early case to reach the Court of Appeal was that of *Merrill Lynch's Application*. The original examiner had declined to grant a patent on the basis that the 'as such' exclusion meant that excluded matter could not be considered to contribute to either novelty or inventive step. The Court of Appeal noted that it was required to take 'judicial notice' of *Vicom* and thus ruled that matter excluded from patentability could, nevertheless, contribute to the inventive step required to make an invention patentable. However, it could not be permissible to patent an item excluded by s 1(2) under the guise of a claim for an article that included it; there had to be something more – and that something, applying *Vicom*, was 'a technical advance on the prior art in the form of a new result'.[167]

However, this test proved difficult to apply. As Nicholls LJ succinctly put it in *Re Gales' Application*: 'I confess to having difficult in identifying clearly the boundary between what is and what is not a technical problem.'[168] Even so, the centrality of this basic test was subsequently affirmed in *Fujitsu Ltd's Application*, in which Laddie J summarised the requirements for patentability of computer programs.[169] The effect of these cases was to allow claims where the advance on the prior art was achieved in software. What mattered was what the computer control was accomplishing: as long as it was not performing one of the activities in s 1(2), then it could still be eligible for patent protection. However, these cases gave no real clarification of the meaning of technical contribution; on appeal, Aldous LJ found little help from *Vicom* and declared that he had 'difficulty in identifying clearly the boundary line between what is and what is not a technical contribution'.[170]

The later case of *Hutchins' Application* was heard after the evolving reasoning in the IBM 'Twins' and *Pensions Benefit*. These decisions were criticised on the basis that the new 'any hardware' approach conflicted with the 'long established practice of the United Kingdom courts originating from the *Merrill Lynch* judgment' and suggesting that the TBA was 'adopting an approach that was accepted as erroneous' in *Merrill Lynch*.[171] The court concluded that it was bound to follow the UK decisions, but that, in any case, their approach was preferable. Subsequent cases have all had to get to grips with this divergence of approach. In *CFPH LLC's Application*, Prescott QC observed that the jurisprudence of the EPO was not constant, but that the UK courts were bound by earlier decisions, even though they might follow decisions of the EPO that the EPO itself no longer applied. However, he observed that it was not good that the law should be applied differently and suggested that 'in practice it may not

165 [1997] RPC 608, 611.
166 Although the discussion in this chapter focuses on the situation in the UK, other jurisdictions have struggled with the same issues – notably Germany (the majority of software patents in Europe are claimed in the UK or Germany): see, eg, *Re IBM's Patent Application* ('search for incorrect strings') [2003] ENPR 2; Bundesgerichtshof X ZR 27/07 *Windows-Dateiverwaltung*, 20 April 2010; Bundesgerichtshof Xa ZB 20/08 '*Dynamische Dokumentengenerierung*', 22 April 2010. The last two are discussed in Phillip Ess, 'Bundesgerichtshof clarifies software patentability prerequisites: First step towards legal certainty in Europe?' (2010) 5 JIPIL 827.
167 [1989] RPC 561, 569.
168 [1991] RPC 305, 327.
169 [1996] RPC 511, 530.
170 [1997] RPC 608, 616.
171 [2002] RPC 8, [25] and [28].

be useful to consider whether something is an invention without considering whether it is new and non-obvious',[172] and went on to suggest the 'little man' test:

> The question to ask should be: is it (the artefact or process) new and non-obvious merely because there is a computer program? Or would it still be new and non-obvious in principle even if the same decisions and commands could somehow be taken and issued by a little man at a control panel, operating under the same rules? For if the answer to the latter question is 'Yes' it becomes apparent that the computer program is merely a tool, and the invention is not about computer programming at all.[173]

This decision led to an immediate change in approach to the examination of computer-implemented inventions that acknowledged the usefulness of the 'little man' test and stated that, 'in identifying the advance in the art that is said to be new and non obvious, examiners will look at the claim as a whole, including aspects that might fall within s 1(2)'.[174]

But the most significant influence on the patenting of computer-implemented inventions in the UK is now *Aerotel Ltd v Telco Holdings Ltd, Macrossan's Patent Application*.[175] In this case, the Court of Appeal noted that a number of contradictory approaches had been used in both the EPO and national courts. These were referred to as the 'contribution' approach, the 'technical effect' approach, and the 'any hardware' approach, the last of which had three variants displayed in *Pensions Benefit*, *Hitachi*, and *Microsoft* (the 'trio'). Having decided that the reasoning in *Pensions Benefit* and *Hitachi* was 'not intellectually honest',[176] Jacob LJ reformulated the statutory test in a way that effectively required answers to the following questions.

(1) What is the proper construction of the claim?
(2) What is the actual contribution?
(3) Does it fall solely within the excluded subject matter?
(4) Is the actual or alleged contribution actually technical in nature?[177]

The UK Intellectual Property Office (UKIPO) subsequently declared that this four-step test must be treated as a definitive statement, and that it should rarely be necessary to refer back to previous UK and EPO case law. Nonetheless, although it severely limited the occasions on which computer-implemented inventions would be patentable, the decision was not believed to make any major changes to the boundaries of patentability. Although the reasoning was undoubtedly different to that of the EPO, it was suggested that, in most cases, the actual outcome would be the same.[178]

Cases following *Aerotel*, including *Raytheon*,[179] *Astron Clinica Ltd v Comptroller General of Patents, Designs and Trade Marks*,[180] and *Autonomy Corporation Ltd's Patent Application*,[181] have all applied the four-step test. In *Astron Clinica*, Kitchin J expressed the view that it was 'highly undesirable that provisions of the EPC are construed differently in the EPO from the way they are construed in the national courts of a Contracting State'.[182] Although he felt obliged to follow the *Aerotel* four-step test, he thought that a

---

172 [2006] RPC 5, [94].
173 Ibid, [104].
174 Practice Note [2006] RPC 6, [9] and [10].
175 [2006] EWCA Civ 1371, [2007] RPC 1.
176 Ibid, [27].
177 Ibid, [40].
178 Practice Direction [2007] RPC 8. The Aerotel patent was litigated again in *Aerotel Ltd v Wavecrest Group Enterprises* [2008] EWHC 1180 (Pat) and upheld by the Court of Appeal in [2009] EWCA Civ 400; however, these infringement proceedings have no bearing on the four-step test and its application.
179 [2007] EWHC 1230 (Pat), [2008] RPC 3.
180 [2008] EWHC 85 (Pat), [2008] RPC 14.
181 [2008] EWHC 146 (Pat) [2008] RPC 16.
182 [2008] EWHC 85 (Pat), [2008] RPC 14, [50].

consistent result could be produced despite the apparent disparity in approach and concluded overall that 'claims to computer programs are not necessarily excluded by Article 52'.[183] Recognising a range of different nuances on the basic test, the court in *Autonomy* set out in great detail how the tests from the various cases should be applied.[184] In *Symbian Ltd v Comptroller General of Patents*, it was agreed that 'it was manifestly difficult to formulate a precise test . . . and it would also be dangerous to suggest that there was a clear rule available to determine whether or not a program was excluded by Art 52(2)'.[185] This was important because the claim in *Symbian* was effectively for a computer program that improved the performance of a computer. If it were to have improved the performance of any other apparatus or device, the whole would clearly be patentable, and Symbian's main point was that it should not be excluded merely because that device was a computer and not something else. In this case, a differently constituted Court of Appeal produced a more conciliatory judgment than *Aerotel*, attempting to find common ground between earlier Court of Appeal judgments and the current EPO approach rather than accentuating differences. Interestingly, the *Symbian* appeal was heard after the EPO's decision in T 154/04 *Duns Licensing Associates LP*, in which the TBA, while appreciating that the *Aerotel* decision might be understandable given the previous case law, found it not to be consistent 'with good faith interpretation of the EPC'.[186] *Symbian* was applied in the subsequent cases of *AT&T Knowledge Ventures LP*[187] and *Gemstar-TV Guide International v Virgin Media Ltd*.[188] The former sets out what it believed to be useful 'signposts' to assist with the meaning of 'technical effect',[189] but both use the *Aerotel* four-step test as the starting point.

Despite the concerns expressed in some of the UK decisions and in the EPO, there has still been no resolution of the divergence of approach to patentability of computer-implemented inventions even if, in practical terms at least, the outcome might be similar. For its part, the President of the EPO referred questions on the issue to the Enlarged Board of Appeal (EBA).[190] These were ruled inadmissible on the grounds that the EPO jurisprudence on the matter was clear, did not contain any significant inconsistencies on the substance, and exhibited a legitimate development of the case law.[191] Nevertheless, on the substance, the EBA did concede that although there was no actual divergence, there was 'at least the potential for confusion, arising from the assumption that any technical considerations are sufficient to confer technical character on claimed subject-matter'.[192] As far as the UK courts are concerned, the difference seems to lead most decisions to provide extensive reviews of the existing case law, notwithstanding the UKIPO's Practice Statement post-*Aerotel*. But is the Court of Appeal as strictly bound by its own rulings as these cases would have us believe? As is well known, the rule on Court of Appeal precedents and the permissible exceptions was set out in *Young v Bristol Aeroplane*.[193] In a recent patent dispute in a different area of claim, the Court of Appeal in *Actavis UK Ltd v Merck & Co Inc* considered this issue in great detail and noted that, because that Court created the rules in the first place, it could also rule on whether there should be further exceptions.[194] Overall, it concluded that, given the developing nature of new technologies and the importance of patents to the economy, there 'ought to be, and is, a specialist and very limited exception to the rule'.[195] Perhaps the real problem is not that the Court of Appeal is not at liberty to follow the EPO rulings, but that it thinks that they are wrong.[196]

183 Ibid, [51].
184 [2008] EWHC 146 (Pat), [2008] RPC 16, [29].
185 [2008] EWCA Civ 106, [2009] RPC 1, [52].
186 [2007] EPOR 349, [12].
187 [2009] EWHC 343 (Pat), [2009] FSR 19.
188 [2009] EWHC 3068 (Ch), [2010] RPC 10.
189 [2009] EWHC 343 (Pat), [2009] FSR 19, [40].
190 G03/08 *President's Reference/Computer program exclusion* [2009] EPOR 9.
191 [2010] EPOR 36.
192 Ibid, [13.5].
193 [1944] KB 718, 729–30.
194 [2008] EWCA Civ 444, [2009] 1 WLR 1186, [92].
195 Ibid, [107].
196 *Symbian*, [36].

Sui Generis Rights Revisited

The beginning of this chapter contained a discussion about the appropriate intellectual property protection for computer programs. As we have seen, the law in a number of jurisdictions has, on occasions, struggled to accommodate the particular properties of software and has sometimes needed to modify traditional copyright principles in order to apply them satisfactorily to computer programs. In Europe, a *sui generis* right for computer programs was rejected under the influence of the observed case law trend towards copyright already formulated by the courts in a number of jurisdictions. Nonetheless, it could be argued that some of the modifications that were negotiated for inclusion in the **Software Directive** and which have led to new derogations with respect to decompilation rights, for example, modify traditional copyright principles to such an extent that the resulting protection is, more accurately, described as a *sui generis* right.[197] Because copyright emphasises the literal, a copyright-type protection might be seen as the appropriate form of protection for the expression and writing of computer programs. Patents, on the other hand, emphasise the functional, but in this respect too there has been no agreed solution. Campbell-Kelly discusses the divided debate over software patentability, observing that members of the open source community are often hostile to software patents, whereas the academic discussion encompasses all shades of opinion. He concludes, however, that patents have the propensity to encourage more investment in reinvention and software components, while in contrast 'trade secrecy is antithetical to cooperation' and 'copyright is wholly inadequate in this context'.[198] Nonetheless, software patents remain controversial; there might be a relaxed regime in the USA and Japan, but this does not prevent some commentators from asserting that 'computer programs are texts, not machines as some lawyers have confused themselves into believing, and thus they may be copyrighted . . . but they are not patentable as machines'.[199]

 See Chapter 11 →

It is perhaps not surprising either, that the European patent system has been stricter over the computer program claims than its counterparts in the USA and Japan, given the focus and activity on copyright, as evidenced by the **Software Directive**. An attempt to harmonise the patentability of computer programs in the European Union (which includes most of the contracting states to the **EPC**), and to bring it more into line with US and Japanese trading partners, had a stormy ride through the various stages of the codecision procedure. The text finally adopted ignored most of the European Parliament's amendments, which, not surprisingly perhaps, led to its rejection by that institution.[200]

So we see that neither copyright nor patents have provided a perfectly tailored solution. Would a bespoke *sui generis* solution have been an improvement? Could this take into account the dual nature of software – namely, that it can be regarded as both writing and machine?[201] Opponents of *sui generis* protection stress both the unknown and potentially unpredictable effects of new provisions, and the fact that intellectual property law has, in the past, often proved flexible in adapting to changing technological environments. Indeed, this very evolution has been likened to a type of *sui generis* protection in the way that it allows a new approach to the intellectual property in software. On the other hand, nearly twenty years ago, Stern remarked that:

> We need a system that borrows appropriately from copyright law, patent law, and utility model law – perhaps slavish imitation law as well – and combines selected features of each, and new features where the nature of software dictates it, to provide a form of legal protection congruent

197 See, eg, the views expressed by Wiebe, op cit. See also discussion in P Goldstein, 'The EC Software Directive: A view from the USA', in M Lehmann and CF Tapper (eds), *Handbook of European Software Law*: Pt 1, 1993, Oxford: Clarendon.

198 Martin Campbell-Kelly, 'Not all bad: An historical perspective on software patents' 11 Mich Telecomm & Tech L Rev 191, 248.

199 Peter D Junger, 'You can't patent software: Patenting software is wrong' 58 Case W Res L Rev 333, 481.

200 European Commission, 'European Parliament sends software patent packing' (2005) *European Research Headlines*, 20 July, available online at http://ec.europa.eu/research/headlines/news/article_05_07_20_en.html

201 See, eg, Samuelson et al, op cit; Diver, op cit.

to the subject matter, the commercial needs of industry, software professionals, and software users, and the interests of the public.[202]

Arguably, we are no closer to this utopian vision. The debate over the appropriate form of protection for software will doubtless continue to ebb and flow. The following sections will illustrate some of the advantages and disadvantages when a *sui generis* right is created, albeit not in relation to computer programs themselves, but to a product the development of which has been facilitated by computer technology – the database.

Intellectual Property Rights in Databases

Computer technology has revolutionised information storage and retrieval, and this has facilitated the creation and commercial exploitation of databases, providing ready access to information on a wide range of subject matter. Collections and compilations are not new, but the ease of search and correlation made possible by computerisation of such products has had a dramatic effect on both their ease of use and their ultimate usefulness. It is frequently the case that the value of the database lies not in the individual entries per se, since, depending on the nature of the database, these may be obtained from public domain material, or may be brief facts that are not individually subject to copyright protection; rather, the value lies in the way in which this material is available for retrieval, the sheer volume and comprehensive nature of the material that may be accessed, and the manner in which it is presented to the user. Electronic databases are important tools for users in many segments of the economy and the fact that they can be copied in a minute with almost no effort suggests that some consideration of the way in which intellectual property rights in databases can be protected is essential.[203]

Even prior to the burgeoning of the market in databases, many jurisdictions had found difficulty in extending copyright protection to collections, compilations, and directories.[204] There was a marked division also between the common law and civil law approaches to copyright, based on a different view of originality and its role in imparting copyrightability.[205] The acceptable standard of originality in the civil law *droit d'auteur* reflects the fact that the material should exhibit something of the author's personality and creativity, or demonstrate original – in the sense of novel – intellectual activity. Such a standard will, inevitably, exclude many databases from being protectable by copyright.[206]

The common law approach, on the other hand, is based on a literal 'copyright' – a legal method of safeguarding work against commercial exploitation arising as a result of copying by a third party. This requires only a low threshold of originality. It may be sufficient merely that the work is the author's independent creation and not copied from elsewhere, rather than the necessity of a finding of particular novelty. Instead of novelty, the common law courts have tended to look for a 'sweat of the brow' test for the subsistence of copyright. As Lord Atkinson said: '. . . it is necessary that labour, skill and capital should be expended sufficiently to impart to the product some quality or character which the raw material does not possess and which differentiates the product from the raw material.'[207] Lord Pearce agreed with this reasoning, commenting that 'the courts have looked to see whether the compilation of the unoriginal work called for work or skill or expense. If it did,

---

202 Richard H Stern, 'Is the centre beginning to hold in US copyright law?' [1993] 2 EIPR 39, 40.
203 See further P Cerina, 'The originality requirement in the protection of databases in Europe and the United States' (1993) 24 IIC 579; Neeta Thakur, 'Database protection in the European Union and the United States: The European Database Directive as an optimum global model' [2001] IPQ 100.
204 For a review of the situation in a number of jurisdictions at the beginning of the 1990s, see EJ Dommering and PB Hugenholtz (eds), Protecting Works of Fact: Copyright, Freedom of Expression and Information Law, 1991, The Hague: Kluwer.
205 See also Diane Rowland, 'The EC Database Directive: An original solution to an unoriginal problem?' [1997] Web JCLI, available online at http://webjcli.ncl.ac.uk/1997/issue5/rowland5.html
206 See, also Cerina, op cit. For a review of the treatment of originality in relation to fact-based compilations in a number of jurisdictions, see, eg, Hasan A Devici, 'Databases: Is *sui generis* a stronger bet than copyright?' (2004) 12 Int'l JL & Info Tech 178.
207 *Macmillan & Co Ltd v Cooper* (1924) 40 TLR 186, 188.

it is entitled to be considered original and to be protected against those who wish to steal the fruits of the work or skill or expense by copying it'.[208]

However, the 'sweat of the brow' test became controversial, even in the common law world, as can be seen from the US case of *Feist Publications Inc v Rural Telephone Service Company Inc*, in which the Supreme Court did not extend copyright protection to a telephone directory.[209] Despite earlier decisions that had found copyrightability in a 'sweat of the brow' or 'industrious collection test', the Court held that originality was the only standard for deciding whether or not a factual compilation is protectable by copyright. Factual compilations may be protected by copyright, but only if the selections 'are made independently by the compiler and entail a minimal degree of creativity' and 'are sufficiently original that Congress may protect such compilations through the copyright laws'.[210] *Feist* makes it clear though that this standard of originality is somewhat lower than the civil law standard and is related purely to independent creativity.

According to Thakur, '*Feist* caused ripples of alarm in Europe',[211] and it was against this general background of inconsistency and doubt over both the existence and scope of copyright protection for databases and factual and other compilations that the EC **Database Directive** was drafted and adopted. The main impetus was a desire to harmonise the legal protection provided for databases and, as an adjunct, to ensure that there was no impediment to the free market in both information products and information services. Even before the judgment in *Feist*, some commentators[212] had expressed concern that insistence on a high threshold of originality for copyright protection would cause problems for modern informational works and that copyright, at least in its common law manifestation, had always needed to balance creative aspects of the work with commercial demands. Ginsburg's suggested solution was to recognise a differential between works of 'high' and 'low' authorship, and to provide corresponding protection.[213] In essence, this could be said to be what the **Database Directive** does by extending conventional copyright protection to those works that satisfy the requisite originality requirement and also by providing a *sui generis* right for those databases that do not satisfy this test, but are, nevertheless, the result of considerable investment.

The Database Directive[214]

The Directive applies to both electronic and non-electronic databases, but not to the underlying computer programs. It defines 'database' in Art 1(2) as 'a collection of independent works, data or other materials arranged in a systematic or methodical way and individually accessible by electronic or other means'. It retains copyright protection for those databases that reach the requisite standard of originality (Art 3), but also provides a *sui generis* database right for those databases that fall short of this standard. The standard required for copyright protection is higher than the 'sweat of the brow' test and so there may be room for debate as to whether a database is sufficiently original to qualify for this protection.[215]

The *sui generis* right is independent of copyright eligibility; its scope is delineated in Arts 7–9, together with the rights and obligations of lawful users and exceptions to the right. Databases qualify for the *sui generis* right if the maker of the database can show that 'there has been qualitatively

---

208 *Ledbroke (Football) Ltd v William Hill (Football) Ltd* [1964] 1 WLR 273, 291. For a comprehensive review of the relevant cases, see *Desktop Marketing Systems Pty Ltd v Telstra Service Company Inc* [2002] FCAFC 112, [20]–[160].
209 113 L Ed 2d 358 (1991).
210 Ibid, 370.
211 Op cit, 110.
212 See, eg, Jane Ginsburg, 'Creation and commercial value: copyright protection of works of information' (1990) 90 Col L Rev 1865.
213 Ibid.
214 Directive 96/9/EC of the European Parliament and of the Council of 11 March 1996 on the legal protection of databases [1996] OJ L77/20.
215 See discussion of *Football Dataco Ltd v Brittens Pools Ltd* [2010] EWHC 841 (Ch) below.

and/or quantitatively a substantial investment in either the obtaining, verification or presentation of the contents to prevent extraction and/or re-utilization of the whole or of a substantial part, evaluated qualitatively and/or quantitatively, of the contents of that database'. The terms 'extraction' and 'reutilization' are themselves defined in Art 7(2). Article 9 provides exceptions to the *sui generis* right in respect of use for private purposes, for teaching and scientific research, and for the purposes of public security or an administrative or judicial procedure. However, 'the repeated and systematic extraction and/or re-utilization of insubstantial parts of the contents of the database implying acts which conflict with a normal exploitation of that database or which unreasonably prejudice the legitimate interests of the maker of the database' is not permitted (Art 7(5)).

In many European jurisdictions, databases that satisfy the requirements of Art 3(1) with regard to eligibility for copyright protection would, in any case, be likely to be protected by the law of copyright even in the absence of the Directive, but, in the UK in particular, there are likely to be many databases that would have qualified for copyright protection under the old 'sweat of the brow' test that will now be denied that protection. However, as long as these fulfil the requirement of 'substantial investment', which is not defined in the Directive, they will still qualify for the *sui generis* database right in Art 7, although this has a duration of only 15 years (Art 10) compared with the standard term for copyright protection of 70 years. This approach has been criticised on the basis that a 'two-tier' system has implicit connotations of a higher and lower mode of protection, and there have also been expressions of doubt as to whether the compromise solution of the combination of a traditional copyright with a new form of right is the correct model.[216] It may be misguided, though, to view the protection afforded by the *sui generis* right as second rate. A major threat to large databases is that of piracy and a 15-year term of protection against copying is, in most cases, likely to be sufficiently extensive to accommodate the shelf life of even the most enduring database. This should not be divorced from the fact that any further substantial investment, such as might be required by necessary revision and updating, will generate a further term of protection. It can thus be said that the two-tier system, rather than providing a superior and an inferior protection, instead maintains the necessary balance between creativity and investment.

That is not to say, however, that the line between creative and non-creative databases will be an easy one to draw. Smith Ekstrand's consideration of the similar problem confronting the US courts post-*Feist* revealed judicial analysis that 'bordered on hair-splitting, infinitesimal detail, as courts attempted to peel back each layer of the work, attempting to find its creativity or lack thereof'. She concludes that a flexible test is needed to determine when a compilation is sufficiently creative, because 'a creative database may be comprised of creative parts but uncreative selection, arrangement or coordination; or it may be comprised of creative selection, coordination and arrangement with uncreative parts. Databases may lie anywhere along the continuum'.[217]

The **Database Directive** was implemented in the UK by the **Copyright and Rights in Databases Regulations 1997 (the Database Regulations)**,[218] amending the **CDPA 1988** in relation to copyright, by inserting definitions of 'database' and 'originality in databases' (new s 3A), making relevant amendments to ss 29 (fair dealing) and 50 (permitted acts), and also inserting a new s 296B, which provides that acts permitted by virtue of the amended s 50 cannot be excluded by contract. The new database right contained in Pt III of the Regulations, not being a copyright as such, has not been subsumed within the text of the 1988 Act, although certain of the available rights and remedies are, nevertheless, those contained in that statute (see reg 23).

---

216 There have also been criticisms based on the fact that a 'neighbouring rights' regime would have provided a suitable solution without necessitating the creation of a specific *sui generis* right: see, eg, CC Garrigues, 'Databases: A subject matter for copyright or for a neighboring rights regime?' [1997] EIPR 3. Cornish, on the other hand, suggests that the *sui generis* right is to take account of the fact that there is no harmonised law of fair competition in the EU: Cornish and Llewelyn, op cit, p 833.
217 V Smith Ekstrand, 'Drawing swords after Feist: Efforts to legislate the database pirate' (2002) 7 Comm L & Pol'y 317.
218 SI 1997/3032.

Although the Directive only provides a definition of 'extraction and re-utilisation', the Regulations provide explicit definitions of both 'substantial' and 'investment'. 'Substantial', the meaning of which is implicit within the Directive with regard to extraction and reutilisation, includes substantial in respect of both quality and quantity or a combination. Any use of financial, human, or technical resources can qualify as 'investment'.

Interpretation of the Scope of the Database Right

The first UK case to take note of the new provisions concerned none of the more fundamental issues that were to be the subject of later litigation. For the purposes of the relevant discussion in *Mars UK Ltd v Teknowledge Ltd*,[219] the pertinent question was whether there was any right of repair that could be read into the **Database Regulations**. Having decided that, notwithstanding the rights of error correction, etc, the permitted acts in relation to computer programs themselves revealed no such defence, Jacob J went on to consider the Regulations. He pointed out that the situation with respect to databases could be distinguished from that for software because the **Database Directive** itself allowed, in Art 6(2)(d), a defence 'where other exceptions to copyright which are traditionally authorised under national law are involved'. This, in Jacob J's view, gave Parliament a right to impose limitations on the scope of rights, but, in the absence of such legislative activity, gave no discretion to the courts in lieu. A steadily increasing number of cases for alleged infringement of the database right have come to the courts in a number of the EU Member States. A comprehensive review of this litigation is beyond the scope of this chapter, but it is instructive to consider a representative selection of the cases highlighting the approach to some of the essential elements of the *sui generis* right.

Substantial Investment and the 'Spin-off' Doctrine

The interpretation of 'substantial investment' has, perhaps predictably, been a key issue in much of the litigation, especially in relation to so-called 'spin-off' databases – those in which compilations of data arise incidentally to the main activities of the database owner. Typical examples include travel timetables, television programme listings, details of sports fixtures, etc. In such cases, the primary investment is in the activities, rather than the database that catalogues those activities, or their results or outcomes. There is a school of thought – sometimes referred to as the 'spin-off' theory – that suggests that the database right should not protect such databases. The relevant arguments include the fact that the database right is based on utilitarian reasoning in order to promote investment in databases. On this basis, there would be no need to extend protection to databases that were the (inevitable) by-product of other activities. This also makes it difficult to establish a direct link between the investment and the database at issue. An alternative argument is that investment costs should be recouped from primary, rather than incidental, activities – that is, from the television programmes, sports fixtures, etc, themselves. Laddie J, in the first-instance decision in *British Horseracing Board v William Hill*,[220] distinguishes 'creating' and obtaining', the latter implying an object with a prior existence. Whereas 'creating' implies at the least labour and effort, 'obtaining' can arise much more easily – in some cases, even automatically.

The spin-off doctrine is unlikely to be popular with database producers because it severely restricts the scope of protection, but the obverse of this argument is that it fosters a 'broader public domain'.[221] Given that the doctrine apparently originated in the Netherlands, it was entirely foreseeable that it should be referred to in decisions in that jurisdiction and, in *NV Holdingmaatschappij de Telegraaf v Nederlandse Omroep Stichting*,[222] the court found that there was no evidence of substantial

219 [2000] FSR 138.
220 [2001] 2 CMLR 12.
221 Estelle Derclaye, 'Databases *sui generis* right: Should we adopt the spin-off theory?' [2004] EIPR 402.
222 [2002] ECDR 8.

investment when information about television programmes was gathered merely as a spin-off of broadcasting activity. Similar reasons have been used in other courts in the Netherlands. In *Algemeen Dagblad v Eureka Interntdiensten* (the *Kranten.com* case), for example, the District Court of Rotterdam declined to offer the protection of the database right to a list of headlines from newspapers,[223] but other Member States have not embraced the theory so readily. In *Danske Dagblades Forening (DDF) v Newsbooster*, the Copenhagen City Court, on similar facts to those in *Kranten.com*, did extend protection to a collection of headlines and articles.[224]

A number of cases in which the spin-off theory could be deemed to be relevant involved Fixtures Marketing Ltd, and concerned a database created by the English and Scottish Football leagues and containing lists of football fixtures. The information on football fixtures in this database was used, inter alia, by companies in Sweden, Finland, and Greece, which organised pools games or other gambling activities based on forecasting the results of these matches. Applying the spin-off theory, it could be concluded that the lists were a mere by-product of the Football Leagues' main activity, but all three disputes led to questions being referred to the ECJ concerning the nature of the substantial investment required. The Advocate General, in C-444/02 *Fixtures Marketing Ltd v Organismos prognostikon agonon podosfairou AE*, considered the spin-off theory, but, after analysing the factors relevant to obtaining, concluded that it did not apply. Databases could also be protected where 'the obtaining was initially for an activity other than the creation of a database'.[225] The ECJ itself, in C-338/02 *Fixtures Marketing v Svenska Spel*,[226] paid lip service to the fact that such databases could involve substantial investment – that is, there could be no automatic conclusion that a spin-off database could not be protected by the database right. However, in these particular cases, no additional investment was required to constitute the database and so the database could not benefit from that protection. In other words, the same result was obtained as if the spin-off doctrine had been applied. As the judgment allows for the possibility of such databases to be subject to the database right, each case has to be considered on its merits; in the cases above, it is a fairly simple matter to distinguish creating and obtaining, but this may not always be so.[227]

At the same time as the *Fixtures Ltd* cases, the ECJ also gave judgment in a similar, albeit rather more complex, case, C-203/02 *British Horseracing Board v William Hill*.[228] BHB operated a database of various facts related to horse racing. The size of this database was significant and the estimated annual cost of keeping the 20 million records up to date was £4 million. The information was made available to other interested organisations and was licensed to a number of bookmakers, including William Hill. William Hill also provided online betting services and BHB alleged that this process used information derived from the BHB database without the requisite licence. Laddie J, at first instance, gave a wide interpretation to the Directive, leading to questions being referred by the Court of Appeal to the ECJ.[229] The ECJ reiterated its view in the *Fixtures* cases that, in this case, there was no substantial investment in the obtaining or verifying the contents of a database.[230] None of these cases, however, provide any real guidance on the *quantum* that would be considered 'substantial' in terms of investment, because, in all of the cases, the investment was judged to be minimal.

Substantial Part

A further issue in the *William Hill* case was the meaning of 'substantial part' of a database. The ECJ concluded that 'substantial part, evaluated quantitatively', referred to the volume of data involved,

---

223 [2002] ECDR 1.
224 [2003] ECDR 5. Both of these cases also involved the legality of hypertext links to the websites containing the lists of headlines and articles – see Chapter 9.
225 Case C–444/02 [2004] ECR I–10549, [2005] 1 CMLR 16, [AG73].
226 Case C–338/02 [2004] ECR I–10497; see also Case C–46/02 *Fixtures Marketing Ltd v Oy Veikkaus AB* [2004] ECR I–10365.
227 See examples in Mark J Davison and P Bernt Hugenholtz, 'Football fixtures, horseraces and spinoffs: The ECJ domesticates the database right' [2005] EIPR 113, 115.
228 Case C–203/02 [2004] ECR I–10415.
229 [2001] 2 CMLR 12 (High Ct), [2002] ECC 24 (CA).
230 [2004] ECR I–10415, [29]–[41].

whereas 'substantial part, evaluated qualitatively', referred to the scale of investment in obtaining the contents. The intrinsic value of the contents was irrelevant to this assessment; anything that did not fall within it could be regarded as insubstantial. The rejection of the notion that 'substantial part' bears any relation to the intrinsic value of the data[231] is especially significant. Holding otherwise would be to afford a very wide protection to database owners, who could presumably usually argue that the data was valuable to them. The judgment then goes on to discuss the interpretation of 'repeated and systematic extractions of insubstantial parts', and concludes that these will only infringe if they are sufficient to allow the alleged infringer to reconstitute the whole, or a substantial part, of the database.[232] In this case, given the size of the BHB database, there was 'no possibility that, through the cumulative effect of its acts, William Hill might reconstitute and make available to the public the whole or a substantial part of the contents of the BHB database'.[233]

Term of Protection

As noted above, the term of protection provided for the database right in Art 10 is 15 years and Art 10(3) further provides that any substantial change in a database will itself qualify for protection. A final point in the *William Hill* case is the extent of the term of protection in relation to dynamic databases. Very few databases remain static, but are regularly updated in an incremental fashion: what effect does this have on the term of protection? Does each amendment effectively create a new database, so that a new term of protection is initiated? If so, that may have the effect of extending the protection for dynamic databases in perpetuity – an ironic result given that the original philosophy behind the database right is to provide a weaker protection for those databases that do not qualify for full copyright protection. This had been referred as a question by the Court of Appeal, but remains unresolved by the ECJ decision. Given that the ECJ's decision had the effect of depriving BHB of the benefit of the database right, it did not feel it necessary to answer this question. The matter had been discussed in the Advocate General's opinion, who concluded that, having brought a database up to date, the whole database must be the object of new investment. The consequence was that a new term of protection must commence with each update – that is, Art 10(3) of the Directive did indeed provided for a 'rolling' *sui generis* right. Although the logic behind this argument cannot be denied, how easily it sits with the ECJ's generally restrictive interpretation to other provisions of the Directive is difficult to assess. Overall, the four cases decided at the end of 2004 had the effect of apparently curbing what had been seen as the wider excesses of the Directive, which had the potential to harm the public domain of information and ideas.[234] Although they might not have been welcomed by certain database owners, they probably represented a more realistic approach to the position of the database right in the general hierarchy of intellectual property rights.

The Meaning of 'Extraction'

The ECJ considered the scope of 'extraction' in C-304/07 *Directmedia Publishing GmbH v Albert-Ludwigs-Universitat Freiburg*.[235] The case concerned a project at the University in Freiburg that involved the creation of a database of 1,100 poetry titles intended to represent the most important poems in Germany from the period 1730–1900. The list, which was selected from around 20,000 titles in a variety of German anthologies, had taken two-and-a-half years to compile and received funding of €34,900 from the University. Directmedia marketed a CD of '1,000 poems everyone should have', of which 856 were from the University list. Directmedia admitted using the database, but denied simply copying, asserting that it had performed a critical examination of the contents in order to

---

231 Ibid, [78].
232 Ibid, [86] and [87].
233 Ibid, [91].
234 J Lipton, 'Databases as intellectual property: New legal approaches' [2003] EIPR 139, 144.
235 [2008] ECR I–7565; see also Anne Christopher and Kate Freeman, 'Directmedia Publishing GmbH v Albert-Ludwigs-Universitat Freiburg' (2009) 31 EIPR 151.

decide on the selection. In addition, the CD contained full text, whereas the University list contained only author, date of publication, opening line, and details of citations in anthologies. The University's claim for copyright infringement was rejected by the German courts, but, in relation to the database right, questions were referred about whether extraction required physical copying, or whether it was sufficient to consult, assess, and then select some material. Unlike the spin-off cases, it was clear that the substantial investment in creating the database qualified it for the protection of the database right. Having considered the Directive and its Recitals, the ECJ concluded that 'extraction' should not be narrowly construed and limited to technical criteria; neither did addition of other material preclude a finding that parts of the first database had been extracted. It was also held that the intention of Directmedia was irrelevant; it made no difference that the new product would not be in competition with the original one.

The ECJ returned to the scope of 'extraction' in C-545/07 *Apis-Hristovich EOOD v Lakorda AD*, a case from Bulgaria involving a database of legal materials.[236] The Court reiterated that the objective of transfer (that is, whether a competing product was intended) was immaterial, and that the Directive covered bother temporary and permanent transfer of data within the concept of extraction. In this case, the database in question consisted of official legal data that were publicly accessible, but the ECJ held that as long as the criteria regarding investment, etc, were met, this did not preclude it from being protected by the database right.

Copyright in Databases

As mentioned above, the Directive makes provision in Art 3 for copyright protection of databases that is entirely independent of the *sui generis* database right. Article 3(1) has been implemented in the UK by amendment to the **CPDA 1988**, s 3(1), which now includes databases as literary works, distinct from tables and compilation. A new s 3A provides that for a database to qualify for copyright protection, it must be original, meaning that the database constitutes the author's own intellectual creation by virtue of the selection or arrangement of the contents of the database. These provisions were considered recently in further litigation about the compilation of football fixtures and the resulting databases. In *Football Dataco Ltd v Brittens Pools Ltd*,[237] the fixtures that formed the subject matter of the database were compiled, taking into account a number of complex and interrelating factors – namely, that all teams in a league had to play every other team twice (once at home and once away), that no club played at home (or away) for three consecutive matches, that no club had four home (or away) matches in any five, that, as far as possible, at all times each club should have played an equal number of home and away matches, and that, as far as possible, all clubs should have an equal number of home and away midweek matches. In addition, there might be further geographical and date considerations and requests to take into account. The fixtures could not be determined purely mechanically, because some of these rules might clash, and so a judgment had to be made as to which rule should prevail in any particular instance. The effect was that the claimant's main effort was in creating the fixtures and that the further process of compiling a database of the fixture lists was trivial. Floyd J, following the *Fixtures Marketing* cases discussed above, thus had no difficulty in finding that the database did not qualify for the database right.

In considering the Art 3 protection, however, he considered that the Directive was 'seeking to harmonise copyright protection of systematically arranged individually accessible collections of independent works ...'.[238] He distinguished the process of selection and arrangement from the gathering of data, and found that the former could be taken into account in the Art 3 right. He took

---

236 [2009] ECR I–1627; see also 'ECJ advises on protection of databases' (2009) 251 EU Focus 21.
237 [2010] EWHC 841 (Ch); see also Mark Rodgers, 'Football fixture lists and the Database Directive: *Football Dataco Ltd v Brittens Pools Ltd*' (2010) 32 EIPR 593; Colin Sawdy, 'High Court decision revisits protection of databases in the United Kingdom: *Football Dataco Ltd v Brittens Pools Ltd*' (2010) 21 Ent LR 221.
238 [2010] EWHC 841 (Ch), [67].

note of the Recitals to the Directive and also found assistance from the German case of *Pharma Intranet Information AG v IMS Health GmbH & Co OHG*.[239] On the evidence, the selection was not purely deterministic and could reasonably be considered the author's own intellectual creation. Floyd J therefore found the database contents to be within Art 3, but, in so doing, he ruled out any other copyright that might feasibly be held, such as a table or compilation. It remains to be seen whether this standard for copyright subsistence in a database will be upheld in future cases.

Database Protection outside Europe

At present, the creation and harmonisation of database rights in the EU is specific to that jurisdiction and, despite attempts in the US Congress, similar modifications have not yet been adopted elsewhere. Following *Feist*, Lavenue noted that it was paradoxical that even though the USA might be the world leader in the database market, database content was not provided with specific intellectual property protection.[240] Nevertheless, cases in the USA have continued to support the *Feist* reasoning.[241] In addition, although there have been a number of attempts to legislate in the USA including, for example, attempts to pass the Collections of Information Antipiracy Act and the Consumer and Investor Access to Information Act at the end of the 1990s, and, later, the Database and Collections of Information Misappropriation Act in 2003,[242] no legislation has been enacted. There are powerful lobby groups on both sides of the debate and academic opinion over the need for, and suggested form of, a database right is divided. Thus Thakur concludes that 'a robust global model with an international *sui generis* regime is, undoubtedly, a necessity so as to bring the United States database industry also under the protective umbrella for an effective stimulation of databases in the global community',[243] whereas Greenbaum warns that 'the United States should not be pressured by the European Union to follow in its unproven protectionist policies'.[244]

A completely different approach was first taken in Australia where, notwithstanding the apparent impact of *Feist* in the common law world, it appeared that the 'sweat of the brow' test had certainly not been rejected. In *Desktop Marketing Systems Pty Ltd v Telstra Corp Ltd*,[245] the Federal Court of Australia allowed copyright protection to a database on the basis of 'industrious collection'. The database in question was a purely factual compilation being, as in *Feist*, a public telephone directory produced by Telstra. After an extensive review of relevant case law and a consideration of a number of issues related to originality, the decision was that the overriding concern was whether the work originated with the creator, even if the amount of effort in arranging and compiling the information might be rather minimal. The case referred to the differing situation in the UK as a result of the **Database Directive**, but concluded that any parallel action was for the legislature in Australia rather than the courts. After *Desktop*, it appeared that very little effort was needed for databases to be protected by copyright as compilations in Australia. The principle on which it was based appeared to be 'simple, certain and close to immutable',[246] and were followed in a number of cases. Recently however, the situation has apparently undergone a transformation following the High Court of

239 [2005] ECC 12, discussed ibid, [89]–[90].
240 LM Lavenue, 'Database rights and technical data rights: The expansion of intellectual property for the protection of databases' (1997) 38 Santa Clara L Rev 1.
241 See, eg, *Assessment Technologies of WI, LLC v Wiredata Inc* 350 F 3d 640 (7th Cir 2003); JM Blanke, 'Case note' (2004) 20 CHTLJ 755.
242 See, eg, J Gibson, 'Re-reifying data' (2004) 80 Notre Dame L Rev 163; JA Loy, 'Database and Collections of Information Misappropriation Act of 2003: Unconstitutionally expanding copyright law?' 7 NYUJ Legis & Pub Pol'y 449.
243 Thakur, op cit, 130.
244 DS Greenbaum, 'The database debate: In support of an inequitable solution' (2003) 13 Alb LJ Sci & Tech 431, 501; see also J Edwards, 'Has the dreaded data doomsday arrived? Past, present, and future effects of the European Union's database directive on database and information availability in the European Union' (2004) 39 Ga L Rev 215.
245 [2002] FCAFC 112, available online at www.austlii.edu.au/au/cases/cth/FCAFC/2002/112.html; see also SE Strasser, 'Industrious effort is enough' [2002] EIPR 599.
246 Mark Davison, 'Nine Network Australia Pty Ltd v IceTV Pty Ltd and Telstra Corp Ltd v Phone Directories Co Pty Ltd: Copyright protection for compilations – Australia does a U-turn' (2010) 32 EIPR 457, 458.

Australia's decision in *Nine Network Australia Pty Ltd v IceTV Pty Ltd*.[247] A detailed analysis of what is a complex case is beyond the scope of this chapter, but, in brief, it questioned the assessment of originality in *Desktop* and appeared to abandon the 'sweat of the brow' standard, although without making clear what standard should replace it. Generally, though, the earlier decision was subjected to considerable criticism, it being suggested that the reasoning in *Desktop Marketing* with respect to compilations might be 'out of line with the understanding of copyright law over many years', and that the emphasis in that case on 'labour and expense' per se should be treated with caution.[248]

The *Ice* decision was subsequently applied in *Telstra Corp Ltd v Phone Directories Co Pty Ltd*, which again considered the subsistence of copyright in telephone directories.[249] Following the decision in *Ice*, these were no longer found to be protected by copyright on the basis that the 'sweat of the brow' test had now been abandoned. Both cases again compared the Australian situation with that in Europe under the **Database Directive**. However, as pointed out by Davison,[250] who advocates caution in respect of introducing a *sui generis* right in Australia, the court failed to mention that other jurisdictions that reject the 'sweat of the brow' test – notably the USA – have nevertheless not provided a standalone right. This discussion shows that there is a considerable polarisation between Europe and other jurisdictions in the intellectual property protection accorded to databases. Although the *sui generis* database right was introduced to promote investment in, and development of, the market, there is no real evidence of the actual effect that the existence of the right has had on the market in Europe; neither do those jurisdictions without such a right appear to be at any major disadvantage.

Concluding Remarks

The discussion in this chapter has demonstrated that the unique nature of computer software, and the particular products and inventions that it makes possible, have created a considerable challenge for intellectual property law. Despite the individual protagonists who champion copyright, patents, or *sui generis* rights, it is apparent that, in appropriate situations, all of these mechanisms have been, and are being, used to foster and protect exploitation of computer software and products relying on it. Globalisation is a significant feature of the software market and this has forced different jurisdictions, even in the absence of suitable international treaties, to take account of the legal and regulatory activity in other jurisdictions to an unprecedented degree. It should perhaps be no surprise that the needs and requirements of a worldwide market may operate as a more potent force for international harmonisation than intergovernmental cooperation.

---

247 [2009] HCA 14. available online at www.austlii.edu.au/au/cases/cth/HCA/2009/14.html; see also Davison, op cit.
248 Ibid, [188].
249 [2010] FCA 44, available online at www.austlii.edu.au/au/cases/cth/FCA/2010/44.html
250 Op cit.

Chapter 11

Software Licences, Free and Open Source Licensing (F/OSS), and 'Software as a Service' (SaaS)

Chapter Contents

Introduction

Types of Contract

There are a wide range of contracts that can relate to computer hardware and software, including: contracts for the sale or lease of hardware, or of a hardware and software package; contracts licensing software; contracts for the maintenance of hardware or software (or support contracts); distribution agreements between manufacturers and distributors of software or hardware; and bureau services contracts, under which one party that has computer hardware and software supplies computer services or facilities to a party that does not have its own hardware or software. Detailed discussion of each of these would (and does) merit a separate book.[1] Thus, this chapter and the first half of the next are concerned primarily with the key issues that may arise in relation to contracts concerned with computer software.

See Chapter 12

The reason for this narrow choice of topic is simple: hardware clearly constitutes goods, and contracts dealing with goods are familiar from other contexts; it is software that poses the significantly different questions. Although the term 'software' can be used to mean anything that is not hardware, it will be used here to mean computer programs, unless otherwise indicated. This is the type of software that raises significant issues for information technology (IT) law.

Bespoke and Standard Software

Discussion of contracts dealing with software requires a distinction to be made between different basic types of software. At one end of the spectrum is 'bespoke' software – that is, software written by a supplier for a particular user, often for a user-specific task.[2] At the other end is mass-produced software, which is simply bought 'off the shelf' by many users. Somewhere in between will be modified standard software, for which the basic program will be the same in each case, but will then be modified to some extent to meet the needs of the individual user.[3] This division may be relevant, for example, in considering whether a contract for the supply of software should be regarded as a contract for the sale of goods or the supply of services (or something else).[4]

The Software Licence

When computers first began to be sold, the software was merely something that came with them; it simply was not seen as something to be separately exploited. The focus was on the hardware. It was in the early 1970s that serious consideration began to be given to software as a resource to be protected and exploited, and the practice grew up of using licences to do so. The licence would set out what the acquirer could, and could not, do with the software. Despite initial uncertainty, it became clear that licensing does, indeed, provide an appropriate approach to the exploitation of software. With the recognition that copyright can exist in software,[5] the licence has become the vehicle by which the acquirer is given rights to use the software. In so doing, it provides the means by which those who develop software can recoup the large costs of that development, make a profit, and encourage further development. There are difficulties in licensing software when the developer does not deal directly with the end-user and, with the trend away from bespoke to off-the-shelf software, this has become a common situation.

---

1 See, eg, Richard Morgan and Kit Burden, *Morgan and Burden on Computer Contracts*, 8th edn, 2009, London: Sweet & Maxwell.
2 See, eg, *St Albans City and District Council v International Computers Ltd* [1997] FSR 251.
3 See, eg, *Watford Electronics Ltd v Sanderson Cfl Ltd* [2002] FSR 19.
4 See further Ken Moon, 'The nature of computer programs: Tangible? Goods? Personal property? Intellectual property?' (2009) 31(8) EIPR 396.
5 See CDPA 1988, ss 1 and 3.

If the end-user does not deal with the developer, how is his or her use to be licensed? The answer is that there may be a chain of contracts. The end-user may be a sublicensee of a distributor who obtained a licence from the developer – the distributor's licence, including the right to create sublicenses. However, the mass production of standard software has posed its own legal difficulties. How are licences to be 'mass produced' when someone can acquire software simply by walking into a shop, selecting software from a display, and paying for it at a till? The attempt to create licences in this type of case, by means of what has been called the 'shrink-wrap' licence, will be returned to below.

Goods or Services or Something Else?

One problem that is of particular conceptual and practical significance is the legal nature of software. As discussed in the previous chapter, the nature of computer programs has raised issues in

relation to the choice of intellectual property protection. At one level, a program is basically information and hence the use of copyright to protect the intellectual property rights. But does this prevent software also being regarded as 'goods'? Or should the supply of software be regarded as a service? On a practical level, these questions arise in the context of the applicability of legislation such as the **Sale of Goods Act 1979 (SoGA 1979)**, the **Supply of Goods and Services Act 1982**, and the **Commercial Agents (Council Directive) Regulations 1993**.[6] The issue of classification will be returned to in the next chapter, which addresses the question of liability for defective software.

Scope of the Chapter

Two chapters in a book on IT law cannot deal in depth with all aspects of contract law; instead, the discussion here will focus on some aspects of contract law that are particularly relevant in the context of software transactions. As the title implies, this chapter deals with the licensing of software and related issues; the next deals with the issues around the suitability/quality of the software.

Terms

When software is in question, some of the most significant terms will be those licensing its use. (Licence terms will be considered below.) First, we should briefly consider sources of contractual terms, although pre-contractual statements becoming terms will be looked at below in relation to the quality/functionality of the software.

If the relevant party signed a contractual document, its contents will provide contractual terms, whether he or she has any knowledge of them or not.[7] If such a document is not signed, then, in the absence of actual knowledge of its contents, its effectiveness to import terms into the contract will depend upon whether there has been reasonably sufficient notice of it.[8] This is an objective test, requiring sufficient notice for the reasonable person, rather than the particular individual concerned.[9] Even if clauses have not been appropriately introduced into a particular transaction, they may be

---

6 SI 1993/3053.

7 *L'Estrange v F Graucob Ltd* [1934] 2 KB 394. There are limited exceptions, including fraud, misrepresentation (*Curtis v Chemical Cleaning and Dyeing Co* [1951] 1 KB 805) and non est factum (*Lloyds Bank Plc v Waterhouse* [1993] 2 FLR 97, in which the fundamental basis of the signed contract was completely different from what the party intended).

8 *Parker v South Eastern Rly Co Ltd* (1877) 2 CPD 416. See, generally, Laurence Koffman and Elizabeth Macdonald, *The Law of Contract*, 7th edn, 2010, Oxford: Oxford University Press, pp 165–172.

9 *Thompson v LM & S Rly* [1930] 1 KB 41.

imported if there has previously been a consistent course of dealings between the parties involving those terms.[10] There is a considerable degree of artificiality in the way in which clauses can become terms of a contract. It means that written contractual terms – particularly standard terms – may be seen as having very little to do with the agreement of the parties in any subjective sense.

Contract terms may be implied,[11] as well as express. They may be implied by statute, such as the terms implied by ss 13–15 of the **SoGA 1979**. Otherwise, at common law, they may be implied in fact, in law, or by custom. Terms are implied in fact on the basis of the parties' intention, but within very narrow confines. A range of tests have been applied, including whether it is necessary to imply the term to give the contract 'business efficacy',[12] and also the 'officious bystander' test – that is, whether the term was so obvious that, had an officious bystander approached the contracting parties and suggested it, they would have said that of course the term in question was included.[13]

See Chapter
← 12

In *BP Refinery (Westernport) Pty Ltd v Shire of Hasting*,[14] Lord Simon of Glaisdal stated that it was 'not . . . necessary to review exhaustively the authorities on the implication of a term in a contract', but that the following conditions ('which may overlap') must be satisfied:

(1) it must be reasonable and equitable;
(2) it must be necessary to give business efficacy to the contract, so that no term will be implied if the contract is effective without it;
(3) it must be so obvious that 'it goes without saying';
(4) it must be capable of clear expression;
(5) it must not contradict any express term of the contract.[15]

However, in *Attorney General of Belize v Belize Telecom Ltd*, Lord Hoffman ruled that such tests were, in fact, simply variations on a single theme and that the fundamental question was what 'the instrument, read as a whole against the relevant background, would reasonably be understood to mean'.[16] In his view, Lord Simon's list was to be regarded:

. . . not as series of independent tests which must each be surmounted, but rather as a collection of different ways in which judges have tried to express the central idea that the proposed implied term must spell out what the contract actually means, or in which they have explained why they did not think that it did so.[17]

The implication of terms in law is not based on the intention of the parties, but upon necessity and the type of contract[18] – that is, the term must be one that it is 'necessary' to imply into the type of contract in question. Intention is relevant only to the extent that a term will not be implied in the face of a contrary term.[19]

The final issue to be addressed here is the question of the interpretation, or construction, of the contract. Obviously, once the terms have been established, the interpretation of the contract has

---

10 See, eg, *Circle Freight International v Medeast Gulf Exports* [1988] 2 Lloyd's Rep 427; see, generally, Koffman and MacDonald, op cit, paras 7.26–7.43.
11 See, generally, Koffman and Macdonald, ibid, paras 7.23–7.47.
12 *The Moorcock* (1889) LR 14 PD 64.
13 *Shirlaw v Southern Foundries Ltd* [1939] 2 KB 206, 227, per Mackinnon LJ.
14 *BP Refinery (Westernport) Pty Ltd v Shire of Hastings* (1977) 180 CLR 266 (PC).
15 Ibid, 282–3.
16 *Attorney General of Belize & ors v Belize Telecom Ltd* [2009] UKPC 10, [21]. See further KFK Low and KCF Loi, 'The many "tests" for terms implied in fact: Welcome clarity' (2009) 125(Oct) LQR 561.
17 Ibid, [27].
18 *Liverpool CC v Irwin* [1976] 2 All ER 39.
19 *Johnstone v Bloomsbury HA* [1991] 2 All ER 293, in which the Court of Appeal indicated that an express contrary term might be treated as an exclusion clause falling within UCTA 1977 in appropriate circumstances.

to be ascertained. The objective when construing or interpreting a contract is that of determining the parties' intention, objectively ascertained. Traditionally, there has been an overwhelming emphasis upon the written words used and a restrictive approach to what further evidence of the parties' intention could be considered. However, in *Investors Compensation Scheme Ltd v West Bromwich Building Society*,[20] the House of Lords took the view that a 'fundamental change . . . has overtaken this branch of the law', the result of which has largely been to discard the previous 'intellectual baggage of interpretation' and to give such documents the meaning obtained from 'the common sense principles by which any serious utterance would be interpreted in ordinary life'.[21]

In this case, Lord Hoffmann provided a summary of principles that are now frequently referred to by the courts.[22] These principles require the interpretation to take account of what the document would mean to a reasonable person with all of the requisite background knowledge. Other than information about the parties' previous negotiations and declarations of subjective intent, this knowledge is taken to included everything that was available to the parties at the time of contracting and anything that might affect the manner in which the reasonable man would understand the document. Lord Hoffman went on to explain that the background information was important, because it allowed the reasonable man to resolve any ambiguities or even, referring to *Mannai Investments Co Ltd v Eagle Star Life Ass Co Ltd*,[23] to decide that the wrong words or syntax had been used. Although it should not easily be assumed that the meaning of the formal documents departed from the 'natural and ordinary meaning' of the words, this should be a permissible conclusion in cases in which the background information showed that the words did not, in fact, convey the intention of the parties.

Copyright Ownership

When software is acquired under a commission, the copyright interest in it is unlikely to be acquired as well; rather there will be a right to use it under the terms of a licence. However, there will be some cases in which the acquirer also acquires the copyright. This might happen in relation to software that the acquirer commissioned the developer to devise for him or her. In such cases, it is advantageous to both parties to own the copyright. Chappatte[24] notes, in particular, that the end-user acquires substantial benefits from copyright ownership including the avoidance of all restrictions on use, the possibility of gaining royalties for subsequent reuse, and (what is often the most important benefit vis-à-vis competitors) obtaining control over the software. He contrasts this with the disadvantages for the software house, which relate not only to the loss of the above rights, but also include the consequent administrative burdens of maintaining a register of proprietary interests together with the problem of ensuring that its software designers do not inadvertently use software developed for one user in a project for another customer. Given the nature of the software development process, this last issue is a very real problem and many of the copyright infringement cases discussed earlier are based on related scenarios.

 See Chapter 10 →

As Lord Hoffman has pointed out, terms will be implied only when no express provision has been made. This is usually the end of the matter, since 'if the parties had intended something to happen, the instrument would have said so'.[25] So, in cases in which acquirers seek to obtain the copyright in the software, it is crucial that they do so by means of express contract terms, for while the courts have the power to imply an assignment of copyright, they are often disinclined to use it.

20 *Investors Compensation Scheme Ltd v West Bromwich Building Society* [1998] 1 All ER 98.
21 Ibid, 114.
22 Ibid.
23 [1997] 3 All ER 352.
24 Philip Chappatte, 'Specific problems in the licensing of software' (1995) 11 CL &P 16.
25 *Attorney General of Belize*, above, [17].

Disputes are most likely to arise in relation to commissioned works and there have been occasions on which the courts have found it necessary to imply a term to give effect to the parties' apparent intentions concerning copyright. In such cases, the law will imply either an equitable copyright assignment or a licence, depending on the particular circumstances. In the absence of an express term, a licence rather than an assignment was implied in *Robin Ray v Classic FM*.[26] In arriving at this decision, Lightman J considered in detail the relevant law on implied terms and set out a list of nine propositions summarising the situations in which a contractor was entitled to retain copyright. These were subsequently described as 'masterful' by Jacob LJ in *Griggs Group Ltd v Evans*.[27] In brief, Lightman J concluded that if the contract makes provision for entitlement, that will be given effect, but in the absence of any contractual terms to the contrary, whether express or implied, the contractor retains copyright. There is, however, no entitlement to copyright merely because the work has been commissioned. Any terms that are implied must do no more than is necessary in the circumstances and must not conflict with any express terms. Specifically in relation to copyright, this means that a licence will usually be implied rather than an assignment, as this will be the least term that will achieve what the parties are deemed to have intended at the date of the agreement. Nevertheless, an assignment can be implied if the surrounding circumstances demonstrate that the client needs actually to own the copyright.[28]

The nature of software development – in which programmers will frequently seek to reuse source code that they have created for previous projects – means, however, that the UK courts are unwilling to imply terms assigning copyright from developer to acquirer. This is, first, because the likely need to be able to reuse source code without infringing the assigned copyright would mean that it was unlikely that a developer would intend to make such an assignment, and that if it did intend to do so, it would be a sufficiently unusual business step as to merit clear express terms in the contract. Second, when implying a term into a contract, the courts will usually examine whether the document, considered in the light of the background to it, could reasonably be understood to have meant to have achieved an assignment. In as much as the software would still be usable by the acquirer without an assignment of the copyright and the impact on the developer of implying such a term would be significant, it is hard to see a court reaching that conclusion.[29]

A rare victory for an acquirer came in *Cyprotex Discovery Ltd v University of Sheffield*,[30] in which a highly convoluted set of facts arising from a seriously defective research contract led both the High Court and Court of Appeal to explore means of reaching a conclusion that supported what they saw as the underlying factual basis and commercial purpose of the contract. The facts clearly showed that an employee of Cyprotex had created the software code that was the subject of the dispute and that, in the absence of any agreement to the contrary, Cyprotex owned the copyright. However, the University of Sheffield was the focal point of the research collaboration, carried the responsibility for the research being financed, and had agreed to license the software to the other parties to the research contract. If Cyprotex were to retain the copyright, there would be no such obligation to license. In these circumstances, both courts found for the University: the High Court on what the judge admitted was a 'strained interpretation' of the contract that aimed to avoid making 'commercial nonsense of the Research Agreement';[31] and the Court of Appeal on an argument (rejected by the lower court) based on a side agreement between the parties that the Court held meant that Cyprotex's employee was actually an agent of the University.[32] The judge at first instance

26 [1998] FSR 622.
27 [2005] EWCA (Civ) 11, [14].
28 See also discussion in Peter Groves, 'Copyright in commissioned work: Court of Appeal put the boot in' (2005) 16(3) Ent L Rev 56; Rebecca Baines, 'Copyright in commissioned works: A cause for uncertainty' [2005] EIPR 122.
29 See *Meridian International Services Ltd v Richardson* [2008] EWCA Civ 609; *Infection Control Enterprises Ltd v Virrage Industries Ltd* [2009] EWHC 2602.
30 *Cyprotex Discovery Ltd v University of Sheffield* [2003] EWHC 760 (TCC); [2004] EWCA Civ 380.
31 [2003] EWHC 760 (TCC), [135]
32 [2004] EWCA Civ 380, [71]

additionally noted that if the 'strained interpretation' were wrong, then because there was a clear intention that Sheffield should own the copyright in the program, it would be appropriate to imply a term assigning the copyright to Sheffield.[33]

However, the best that an acquirer can usually hope for in such circumstances is likely to be a licence sufficient to make the arrangement between acquirer and developer commercially workable. Thus, in *Clearsprings Management Ltd v Businesslinx Ltd*,[34] Clearsprings and Businesslinx, a small software development company, entered into a software development contract under which Businesslinx was to provide the necessary software to Clearsprings to enable it to operate a web-based database system. The contract was silent on the ownership of the software to be developed. Shortly after the contract had started, Clearsprings sent an email stating that it wanted to have the copyright so that it could, if it wanted to, sell it to third parties – at which point a dispute arose between the two companies as to the ownership.

Both parties accepted that Businesslinx was the first owner of the copyright. However, Clearsprings asserted that it was an implied term of the contract between it and the Businesslinx that Clearsprings would own by assignment, or at least have an exclusive licence under, all existing and future copyrights in the software. Failing that, Clearsprings maintained that there should be implied terms to the effect that it had a licence to use the software, and that this was to be perpetual, irrevocable, exclusive, and royalty-free. The implied licence would allow it to repair, maintain, and upgrade the software to meet its business requirements, and to distribute and sublicense software to third parties on its own terms. Businesslinx, on the other hand, argued that to imply an assignment of copyright or an exclusive licence to Clearsprings would prevent Businesslinx from making use of generic code incorporated in the software. It stated it had told Clearsprings that it would be using its pre-existing code in developing the new software, and that it was common practice amongst software developers to reuse quantities of code written for one client in one application when writing a similar or related application for another client.

In his judgment, Christopher Floyd QC noted that, although it was not established that Businesslinx had expressly told Clearsprings that it would use pre-existing software in developing the new software, it was an accepted practice that pre-existing code would be used to create bespoke software. Absent specific instruction from Clearsprings that the software had to be entirely bespoke, it was thus to be expected that Businesslinx would import pre-existing code into the code for Clearsprings and use it in other projects, and seek to continue to develop it. In such circumstances, there was little to support Clearsprings' claim for an exclusive licence.[35] All that was necessary to give business efficacy to the contract was an implied licence for Clearsprings to use the software for the purposes of its business and an implied restriction on Businesslinx's use of information about Clearsprings' business practices.[36] If there were insufficient grounds to grant an exclusive implied licence, then there were clearly insufficient grounds for granting an assignment of copyright.[37]

In sum, Clearsprings was thus entitled to an implied non-exclusive, personal copyright licence, which would be perpetual, irrevocable, and royalty-free, and would permit Clearsprings to repair, maintain, and upgrade the system in accordance with its business requirements. However, it would not entitle it to sublicense the software.[38]

---

33 [2003] EWHC 760 (TCC), [136]

34 *Clearsprings Management Ltd v Businesslinx Ltd* [2005] EWHC 1487.

35 Ibid, [39]–[48].

36 Ibid, [48].

37 Ibid, [49].

38 See also *Wrenn v Landamore* [2007] EWHC 1833 (Ch), [2008] EWCA Civ 496, in which the acquirer was held to be entitled to an implied exclusive licence and an entitlement to access the source code.

The Licence

Licence Terms

The software licence will deal with such matters as:

- to whom the licence is granted;
- the equipment on which, and location at which, it may be used;
- the use to which the software can be put[39] (for example, sublicensing is usually forbidden);
- whether the source code or object code is supplied (normally, the acquirer only receives the object code);
- whether the licence is exclusive or non-exclusive (normally, it will be non-exclusive, unless it is being granted to a distributor who is to exploit the software through sublicensing it);
- whether the licensee can transfer the licence;[40]
- the duration of the licence, which may be for a fixed or indefinite period (it will normally state that it is to terminate on the occurrence of certain breaches by the licensee or on the licensee's insolvency);[41]
- confidentiality (the licence may state that the 'software' is confidential information that should not be disclosed, if the licensor is attempting to gain the protection afforded to such information);
- exemption clauses (the licensor will insert an exemption clause in an attempt to exclude or restrict any liability that he or she might incur to the licensee).

The effectiveness of exemption clauses must be considered in the light of the **Unfair Contract Terms Act 1977 (UCTA 1977)**, which is considered in the next chapter. In addition, the **Unfair Terms in Consumer Contracts Regulations 1999**[42] will subject to a test of 'fairness' many non-individually negotiated terms in contracts between sellers or suppliers and consumers. Here, some further consideration should be given to the importance of the source code and the recognition of its significance by the courts.

See Chapter 12

Source Code

See Chapter 10

The difference between source code and object code has already been discussed, but, in this context, some further consideration should be given to the difference between them, the significance of these differences to the licensee, and the courts' recognition of the importance of source code under certain circumstances. Most off-the-shelf software programs are received by the consumer in their machine-language format. This means that the user can run the program directly, but cannot easily read or modify it.

As noted in the last chapter, the object code is rarely intelligible to human beings. The source code is used to write the program and, as a result, it is needed if any bugs are to be corrected or improvements made. Obviously, the licensee of the program would prefer to have a licence that extends not only to the object code, but also to the source code, but the licensor will want to maintain control of the source code to prevent the program information from becoming known. The most likely form of arrangement through which the licensee might achieve access to the source code in limited circumstances is an escrow arrangement.

---

39 Defining the use rendered 'lawful' by the licence may be particularly important in the light of the CDPA 1988, s 50C, which bases its limited right to, eg, copy, adapt, or correct errors in software on what is necessary for the software's 'lawful' use.
40 The copyright holder may wish to prevent a licence from being transferred to a rival.
41 Such termination has serious potential consequences for a licensee whose business is organised around the use of the software. The purchaser of such a business may require a check to see that the relevant software licences have not been infringed.
42 SI 1999/2083.

A simple escrow agreement consists of a three-way contractual arrangement entered into by the licensor, the licensee, and an independent third party – the escrow agent. Under the arrangement, the licensor agrees to deposit the source code of the software with the escrow agent, and the parties agree the conditions under which the source code will be released by the escrow agent to the licensee to enable ongoing maintenance. Common reasons for such release will include the licensor going into liquidation, cancelling further development of the software, being acquired by a competitor of the licensee, or failing to maintain and update the software under its contractual maintenance obligations.

A source code escrow agreement will usually include terms that:

- identify the subject of the escrow – usually the source code of a particular program – and such documentation, software tools or libraries, and hardware as is required for the licensee to maintain the software;
- require that the source code in escrow be updated within a short period of time after new releases and updates;
- specify the conditions that will trigger release of the source code to the licensee and those that will not, such as removal of support for a product that is to be succeeded by an equivalent upgrade or replacement product from the licensor;
- specify the rights of the licensee with regard to the use of the released source code, such as permitting general maintenance or error correction; and
- identify the fees payable to, and responsibilities of, the escrow agent, which may include verification of source code's authenticity.

Software escrow is clearly not suited to all types of software licence agreement. A large company such as Microsoft, with significant market share in particular applications, is unlikely to agree to such an arrangement, even if its many off-the-shelf licensees desire it to do so.[43] It is most likely to be used in the commercial bespoke software sector, in which the interest of the licensor in attracting and keeping clients justifies the costs and risks of escrow. This will be particularly true for small software developers who want to persuade companies to take on their software in mission-critical business areas, or who are seeking to attract large client licensees without having to risk making their source code immediately available.

While, as noted above, the English courts have been loath to assign copyright in source code to acquirers of commissioned software, they have nonetheless recognised the importance of access to source code by licensees under particular circumstances. As a result, they have shown some willingness to interpret the contract, or to imply terms, in such a way as to allow the acquirer to use the source code in circumstances in which it is necessary to make the contract commercially viable.[44]

In *Saphena Computing Ltd v Allied Collection Agencies*,[45] the availability and use of source codes for error correction was considered. The case was concerned with an attempt to provide an 'online' computer system for a debt collecting agency. The plaintiff supplier experienced difficulties in trying to make the software function as required. The time that it spent in attempting to deal with the problems eventually led the defendant acquirer to agree to a termination of the contract. It then called in a third party to deal with the problems. The particular point that needs to be considered here is the question of whether the defendant was entitled to possession of the source code, and in order to remedy the defects in the software. Havery QC (the Official Receiver) considered the question in

---

43 For example, Microsoft announced in June 2009 that it was no longer going to support its popular Money personal finance software, and that support for the software would end in January 2011.
44 But see *Mars UK v Teknowledge Ltd* [2000] FSR 138.
45 *Saphena Computing Ltd v Allied Collection Agencies* [1995] FSR 616.

general terms under the original supply agreement, and in the more specific situation of the agreement to terminate an incomplete supply contract. He noted that the source code remained the property of the plaintiff, but that unlike more tangible products, a purchaser was not in a position either to repair or improve the program. It could not, he decided, have been the intention of the parties that, when the business relationship ended, the software should remain in a state that was not entirely fit for purpose. On this basis, although he concluded there was no right to the source code, he was prepared to imply a term to give business efficacy to the termination agreement and allow copying of the source code to the extent necessary to ensure fitness for the intended purpose. Once the source program has been made available to the acquirer, s 50C(2) of the **Copyright, Designs and Patents Act 1988 (CDPA 1988)** will now be relevant to the question of whether it can be copied in order to correct errors and will be discussed further below.

There are indications of willingness to go somewhat further to make the contract workable in *Psychometric Services v Merant*,[46] in which what was in question was the ordering of the supply of the source code to the acquirer. The case was again concerned with a problem caused by uncompleted software. The acquirer was arguing that the supplier was in breach and that it wanted to have the software completed by someone else. Laddie J only had to consider whether, as a matter of interim relief, to order the supply of the source code to the acquirer. (The dire financial situation of the acquirer if the program was not swiftly made to function pointed to such relief.) However, what is of interest are the indications of his willingness to interpret the contract so as to find an entitlement to the source code by the acquirer. He found an express term that 'strongly supports PSL's claim to the source code',[47] and he had already pointed out that, in any event, had everything happened as it should have done under the contract, the 'loyalty period' of maintenance by the supplier needed to last for only two years (and might even have been shorter in some circumstances). At the end of that period, if the acquirer was not entitled to the source code, 'none of the inevitable bugs would be able to be fixed. No development [would] be possible'.[48] Laddie J made the point that the suppliers did not 'dissent strongly' from the proposition and that, if it was correct, 'the agreement made no commercial sense at all'.[49] There is an impetus to interpret contract terms in a way that makes good commercial sense[50] and against a construction that achieves an unreasonable result. The 'more unreasonable the result the more unlikely it is that the parties can have intended it, and if they do intend it the more necessary it is that they [should] make that intention abundantly clear'.[51]

The EC Software Directive

Basic Use of Software

It is generally said that using software will be in breach of copyright unless the user has a licence. This is because its use almost inevitably requires it to be copied onto hardware and, in the absence of a licence, such copying has generally been said to entail a breach of copyright.[52] However, what must be considered is the effect on this of Art 5(1) of the **Software Directive**.[53] This might be seen as providing the acquirer with a right to make the copy required for the basic use of software.

---

46 *Psychometric Services v Merant* [2002] FSR 8.
47 Ibid, [37].
48 Ibid, [36].
49 Ibid.
50 *Antaios Cia Naviera SA v Salen Rederierna AB* [1985] AC 191, 221.
51 *L Schuler AG v Wickman Machine Tool Sales Ltd* [1974] AC 235, 251.
52 See CDPA 1988, s 17(1), (2), and (6).
53 Directive 2009/24/EC of the European Parliament and of the Council of 23 April 2009 on the legal protection of computer programs (Codified version) [2009] OJ l111/16.

Article 5(1) states:

> In the absence of specific contractual provisions, the acts referred to in Article 4(a) and (b) shall not require authorisation by the rightholder where they are necessary for the use of the computer program by the lawful acquirer in accordance with its intended purpose, including for error correction.

The 'acts' referred to in Art 4(a) and (b) are, inter alia, the 'permanent or temporary reproduction of computer programs', and 'the translation, adaptation, arrangement and any other alteration of a computer program and the reproduction thereof'. This means that the Directive might be seen as providing the right to make the copy of software that its basic use requires. However, any such right would be limited and it would seem that the copyright owner could prevent any such right from being acquired by including an express contrary term.

Article 5(1) has been implemented in what is now s 50C of the **CDPA 1988**, which states:

(1) It is not an infringement of copyright for the lawful user of a copy of a computer program to copy or adapt it, provided that the copying or adapting-

    (a) is necessary for his lawful use; and

    (b) is not prohibited under any term or condition of an agreement under which his use is lawful.

(2) It may, in particular be necessary for the lawful use of a computer program to copy or adapt it for the purpose of correcting errors in it . . . [54]

This section seems generally restrictive of any notion of a right to make basic use of software. There is an important difference between the Directive's references to 'lawful acquirer' and use of the software in accordance with its 'intended purpose', and the statutory references to 'lawful user' and 'lawful use'. It would seem that someone might well be argued to be a 'lawful acquirer' although he or she lacks the rights to make him or her a 'lawful user'; the same point can be made in relation to 'lawful use' and 'intended purpose' ('lawful user' is defined in s 50A(2)). Prima facie, the person who purchases software in a shop should be regarded as a 'lawful acquirer', but, on any natural meaning of the words, it seems doubtful that he or she can be registered as a 'lawful user' unless he or she has an effective licence. However, whatever the natural meaning of the words, because the provision is intended to give effect to a provision of a Directive, it should be construed in a way so as to achieve that implementation. 'Lawful user' may thus be understood here as 'lawful acquirer'.

Back-up Copies

Making back-up copies of software is commonly regarded as sound practice. A disk can be affected, and the program corrupted, by a number of factors, such as a faulty disk drive, heat, or an electro-magnetic field. Some copyright holders even put instructions in the manual that, before the software is put to any other use, it should be copied and a copy put in a safe place, to be used in the event of the other becoming corrupted. However, some copyright holders do not want any copies of this type made, perhaps for security reasons. Consideration should now be given to s 50A of the 1988 Act, which states that it is not an infringement of copyright for a 'lawful user' of a copy of a computer program to make any back-up copy of it 'which it is necessary for him to have for the

---

54 It should be noted that s 50C would require a contrary contract term. If the Directive is construed so that there is no right under Art 5(1) where there is a contrary agreement, it does not seem to require any such agreement to be contractual.

purposes of his lawful use' (s 50A(I)). This right to make a necessary back-up copy cannot be removed by any contrary agreement. Section 50A(3) states that, where an act is permitted by the section, 'it is irrelevant whether or not there exists any term or condition in an agreement which purports to prohibit or restrict the act'. Any such term is void under s 296A. Section 50A is based on Art 5(2). Both are of limited scope. The right to make a back-up copy, irrespective of contrary agreement, is limited to cases in which it is 'necessary' to make such a copy. If 'necessary' is strictly construed, this would be of very limited application. In most cases, a back-up copy will be highly desirable, but not strictly necessary, in the sense of 'essential to' the actual use of the program. However, 'necessary' may be understood in its context. In a commercial context, it might be taken to mean 'necessary' for the commercial use of the software. It might then be found that having a readily accessible back-up copy would often be necessary for its commercial use, the business user effectively being unable to use it if it could become unavailable to him or her for a time, through corruption of the disk, for example. This last approach was envisaged by Singleton. She suggested that, where licensors did not want to allow users to make back-up copies for reasons of security, for example, then compliance with this section could be achieved by providing a 24-hour duplication service (or alternatively depositing a copy in a bank or other secure place) to deal with those occasions on which the program had been deleted or corrupted. The availability and use of this service could be reflected in the terms of the licence and it would remove the 'necessity' for the user to make a back-up copy.[55]

Error Correction

Error correction will normally require the use of the source code, rather than merely the object code. It will not normally be undertaken by the acquirer of software. In particular, a maintenance agreement will often be made in relation to software, coming into effect once acceptance has occurred and encompassing error correction.[56] The question may arise as to whether the error in question amounts to a breach of the supply contract, and that will depend upon the express and implied terms of that contract.

However, the point on which to focus here is whether the acquirer can correct errors in the software. Article 5 of the Directive includes 'error correction' within the acts that are not in breach of copyright when they are necessary for the intended purpose of a program.[57] Similarly, s 50C of the **CPDA 1988** states that, subject to contrary agreement, the copying or adapting that is necessary for the lawful use of a program is not a breach of copyright. Section 50C(2) makes it clear that 'it may, in particular, be necessary for the lawful use of a computer program to copy or adapt it for the purpose of correcting errors in it'. Some of the difficulties in interpreting these provisions were outlined above. It should be noted that, whatever the extent of the 'right' conferred by the Directive, it is not the acquirer's 'right' to have errors corrected; he or she can merely correct them without being in breach of copyright. In addition, it would seem that there is no obligation, in these provisions, on the seller to supply the source code, which is generally needed for error correction. The contractual obligation is normally only to supply the object code, but it may provide for the supply of the source code. The Directive and the legislation would not seem to make the source code, as such, available to any greater extent to the acquirer.

---

55 Susan Singleton, 'Computer software agreements and the implementation of the EC Directive' (1993) 9 CL & P 50.
56 There will be difficulties for the acquirer of software if access to the source code for necessary error correction is denied because the copyright holder becomes insolvent or otherwise ceases to function. To deal with these situations, source code 'escrow' (see above) can be used. There may, however, be difficulties with this under insolvency law.
57 It has been argued to the contrary that, on its wording, Art 5(1) does not only encompass the error correction that is necessary for the intended purpose of the program, but rather treats error correction as an intended purpose: M Sherwood-Edwards, 'Seven degrees of separation: The Software Directive and UK implementation' (1993) 9(55) CL & P 169.

'Shrink-wrap' Licences[58]

Software may be acquired via the web, directly from the copyright holder. In such a situation, there is obviously no difficulty in creating a contractual licence for the acquirer of the software – all that is required is that the licence terms appear appropriately on the website for them to be incorporated.[59] However, the more common situation is for the end-user to acquire the software from a supplier who is not the copyright holder. This raises the issue of the creation of the licence, which has been termed the 'shrink-wrap' licence problem.

The problem of the effectiveness of the shrink-wrap licence can be epitomised by the purchase of software 'off the shelf' from a shop. The purchaser will take his or her newly acquired software home, open the box, and discover that it is contained in an envelope, on which it is stated that opening the envelope constitutes acceptance of the copyright holder's licence terms. (These are also included in the box.) Alternatively, on starting to use the software, the acquirer may discover an on-screen message stating that the software cannot be used unless there is an agreement to licence terms by 'clicking' on a button (if the acquirer is online, which may generate a message to the copyright holder). This is referred to as 'click wrap'. Whatever form it takes, the statement on-screen or on the box may also include that if the purchaser does not want to accept the licence terms, the software may be returned to the shop from which it was purchased for a full refund.[60]

There are numerous variations on the fact situation indicated above. The packaging arrangements may vary, but all raise the same type of issues. It may also be that the software is not acquired from a shop, but by mail or telephone order. The software may also be downloaded from the web, from a supplier's website, and a form of 'click wrap' will then be in question. Again, many of the same issues arise as under the above fact situation. Primary consideration will be given to the purchase in a shop, with comments on other situations in which that is required. The basic question in each situation is whether the shrink-wrap licence is effective, and there are two basic possibilities to consider in relation to this:[61] it might be argued that it is part of the contract made between the supplier, S, and the acquirer, A, for the acquisition of the software (that is, the supply in the shop); alternatively, it might be considered part of a contract formed between A and the copyright holder, C, when the envelope is opened.

Acquisition Contract

In considering the acquisition of software from a shop, the first point to consider is with whom the acquirer, A, contracts. Prima facie, at that stage, there is simply a contract between the shop, S, and A. The transaction certainly looks like a simple sale of the software by S to A. On this basis, two issues need to be addressed: first, the timing of the introduction of the licence terms; and, second, the fact that the copyright holder, C, is a third party to the acquisition contract.

---

58 See, generally, Clive Gringras, 'The validity of shrink-wrap licences' (1996) 4(2) Int JLIT 77; Diane Rowland and Andrew Campbell, 'Supply of software: Copyright and contract issues' (2002) 10(1) Int JLIT 23; Phillip Johnson, 'All wrapped up? A review of the enforceability of "shrink-wrap" and "click-wrap" licences in the United Kingdom and the United States', (2003) 25(2) EIPR 98.
59 Such licences are often termed 'click-wrap' licences. As has been the case with 'shrink-wrap' licences, these have not been the subject of particular scrutiny by the courts in England and Wales. Their effectiveness has been more widely explored in the USA, where such 'agreements are generally enforceable provided that the user has the opportunity to review the contractual terms prior to clicking': Nancy S Kim, 'The software licensing dilemma' [2008] BYU L Rev 1103, 1125, citing *Davidson & Assoc v Jung* 422 F 3d 630, 638–39 (8th Cir 2005), *Forrest v Verizon Commc'n, Inc* 805 A 2d 1007, 1010 (DC 2002), and *Caspi v Microsoft Network, LLC* 732 A 2d 528, 532 (NJ Super Ct App Div 1999) as positive rulings; *Specht v Netscape Commc'n, Corp* 306 F 3d 17, 28–30 (2nd Cir 2002) and *Comb v Paypal, Inc* 218 F Supp 2d 1165, 1172–3 (ND Cal 2002) as negative rulings.
60 There may be difficulties in finding that the supplier is under an obligation to the acquirer to take back the software and return the price paid, particularly where the software packaging has been opened.
61 A third possibility, combining elements of the two considered, was arrived at in the Scottish court in *Beta Computers (Europe) Ltd v Adobe Systems (Europe) Ltd* [1996] FSR 367.

The first point to be made is simply that new terms cannot be introduced into a contract once it has been made.[62] If the licence terms are not introduced into the transaction until after the contract in the shop has been made, they cannot be part of the contract between A and S.

Contract formation is normally analysed in terms of offer and acceptance. An offer expresses a willingness to be contractually bound by certain terms,[63] if the other party accepts them. An acceptance occurs when the other party agrees to the same terms.[64] In a shop, the offer is normally made by the customer when the goods are taken to the till, and it is accepted by the assistant.[65] If the existence of licence terms does not become apparent until after the box has been opened, and that does not take place before offer and acceptance have occurred, obviously, they have been introduced after the contract was made and cannot be part of it. This was recognised in the Scottish case of *Beta Computers (Europe) Ltd v Adobe Systems (Europe) Ltd*.[66] The same point can also be made in relation to the mail order or telephone order of software. In those cases, the contract will normally be made when the acquirer's order (the offer) is accepted by dispatch of the goods (in the case of mail order) or by express acceptance on the telephone, in the case of a telephone order. If not even the existence of the licence was indicated prior to A's opening of the box, it cannot form part of the contract terms, and a similar point can be made in relation to web-based order and delivery.

The situation also has to be considered in which the licence terms are referred to on the outside of the box[67] (or on the website, when that is from where the software is acquired). Clauses may be incorporated into contracts from unsigned documents on the basis of reasonably sufficient notice.[68] It should also be noted that incorporation by reference is possible – that is, the document providing notice does not have to contain the terms, but can merely refer to where they can be found.[69] The test is objective[70] and whether incorporation by notice occurs is basically[71] a question of fact in each case,[72] dependent upon such matters as the legibility and prominence of the relevant writing. One factor that has been seen as relevant to the test generally is whether the place in which the notice is to be found is the type of place in which the reasonable person would expect to find a contractual term. One reason why the clause on the deckchair ticket in *Chapelton v Barry UDC*[73] did not provide reasonably sufficient notice of an exemption clause was that the ticket was seen as something that the reasonable person would view merely as a method of proving that the deckchair hire charge had been paid, rather than as a document containing contract terms. One question is whether people normally expect to find contract terms referred to on the back of a box containing software. The size and position of any such notice on the box would also be relevant, and it would,

---

62 *Olley v Marlborough Court Hotel* [1949] 1 KB 532; *Thornton v Shoe Lane Parking* [1971] 2 QB 163.

63 See, eg, *Gibson v Manchester CC* [1979] 1 WLR 294.

64 *Jones v Daniel* [1894] 2 Ch 332.

65 *Pharmaceutical Society of Great Britain v Boots Cash Chemists* [1953] 1 QB 401.

66 [1996] FSR 367; see below, pp 409–410.

67 This fact seems to have been emphasised by the US court in *ProCD, Inc v Zeidenberg* 86 F 3d 1447 (7th Cir 1996).

68 *Parker v South Eastern Rly Co* (1877) 2 CPD 416. The 'red hand rule' has been added to this, so that the more unreasonable or unusual a clause, the greater the degree of notice required to provide reasonably sufficient notice: *Thornton v Shoe Lane Parking* [1971] 1 QB 163; *Interfoto Picture Library v Stiletto Visual Programmes* [1988] 1 All ER 348. The name of the rule stems from a famous dictum of Denning LJ, as he then was, in *Spurling v Bradshaw* [1956] 1 WLR 461, 461: 'The more unreasonable a clause is, the greater the notice which must be given of it. Some clauses which I have seen would need to be printed in red ink on the face of the document with a red hand pointing to [them] before the notice could be held to be sufficient.' On incorporation more generally, see Koffman and MacDonald, op cit, pp 166–172.

69 *Thompson v LM & S Rly* [1930] 1 KB 41. It would seem that a copy of the terms should be accessible before a contract.

70 In *Thompson*, ibid, it was indicated that it was irrelevant that the passenger in question was illiterate. The reasonable person was to be presumed to be able to read English. The situation would be otherwise where the party seeking to incorporate the terms knew, or should, as a reasonable person, have known that the other party, or the group to which he or she belongs, was in some way less able to read or understand the notice: *Richardson, Spence & Co v Rowntree* [1894] AC 217; *Geier v Kujawa, Weston and Warne Bros (Transport)* [1970] 1 Lloyd's Rep 364.

71 But note the 'red hand rule' (above).

72 *Hood v Anchor Line* [1918] AC 837, 834.

73 *Chapelton v Barry UDC* [1940] 1 KB 532.

for example, be ineffective if the shop were to have stuck a price tag, or some other label, over it.[74] It should be easier for such incorporation to take place as acquirers, in general, begin to assume that the acquisition of software will involve licence terms.[75]

However, if the licence is incorporated into the contract between S and A, the fact that C is a third party to that agreement must now be considered. Traditionally, the response in English law would have been that incorporation of the licence into the contract between A and S could not assist C. Traditionally, the doctrine of privity of contract would not have allowed a third party, C, to enforce contract terms, even if they were for the third party's benefit. However, privity has now been considerably modified by the **Contracts (Rights of Third Parties) Act 1999**. Basically, a third party may now enforce a term of the contract if either:

(a) 'the contract expressly provides that he may'; or
(b) 'the term purports to confer a benefit on him' and it does not appear that the parties did not intend the term to be enforceable by the third party.[76]

The overall effect of this would seem to be that if the licence terms are appropriately drafted (and they are drafted by C), then A will indirectly acquire a licence to use the software (through a chain from C, via S, to A) and C will have a right to enforce the licence terms, which can be regarded as providing him or her with a benefit. (The benefit of the protection of an exemption clause is expressly recognised as falling within the 1999 Act.)[77] An analogy might be made with the Scottish case of *Beta v Adobe*,[78] in which, under Scottish law, the court did not have to contend with the privity rule and a third party could gain the benefit of a contract under the doctrine of *ius quaesitum tertio*.

Opening the Envelope

The second possibility to consider is that of a second contract, separate from the acquisition contract, made when A opens the packet or clicks on the button on screen. The argument would be that the offer is made by C and A accepts by performing the stated act of opening the envelope. Acceptance of an offer normally requires communication and communication may occur in the click wrap situation if the acquirer is online, but it is possible to have acceptance by conduct.[79] However, that conduct would have to be unequivocal and another explanation of the opening of the envelope may be possible. It could be argued that A may not be responding to C's offer of a licence, but, rather, that he or she is exercising a right already acquired. The contention would be that, at the time that the software was acquired from S, A also acquired certain basic rights to use it. Such rights might stem from the legislation implementing the **Software Directive**, from a common law licence, or from terms implied into the contract between S and A.

As was indicated above, Art 5(1) of the **Software Directive** provides the lawful acquirer of software with a right to, inter alia, copy it where such copying is necessary for its use in accordance with its 'intended purpose'. The reference to 'lawful acquirer' might well be seen as encompassing the person who buys software in a shop and as providing him or her with a right, which would explain the opening of the software packet as something other than an acceptance of the licence. However, as has already been indicated, s 50C of the **CDPA 1988**, the provision intended as an implementation of Art 5(1), does not refer to the 'lawful acquirer' of software, but rather to its

---

74 *Sugar v LM & S Rly* [1941] 1 All ER 172.
75 *Alexander v Rly Executive* [1951] 2 KB 882, 886.
76 Contracts (Rights of Third Parties) Act 1999, s 1.
77 Ibid, s 1(6).
78 [1996] FSR 371.
79 *Brogden v Metropolitan Rly Co* (1877) 2 App Cas 666.

'lawful user', and also refers to 'lawful use' rather than 'intended purpose'. It seems doubtful whether, without using an implied term (considered below) or some such device, the acquirer of the software in the shop can be seen as a 'lawful user' unless the licence is effective. Certainly, that would seem to be the case in any natural construction of 'lawful user', but the point should be made that something other than a natural construction of the section may be required if it is to be seen as a proper implementation of the Directive. In addition, as it stands, any natural interpretation of the reference to 'lawful user' in s 50C is open to the criticism of circularity.[80]

Another possible explanation for the opening of the envelope is that the common law provides a limited licence for the acquirer of software so that the acquisition is not rendered pointless. An analogy with patent law might lead to such a conclusion.[81]

The point must be made, however, that it is, in any event, now unclear to what extent this analogy is still possible in the face of Art 5(1) of the **Software Directive**. That Article provides for the basic use of software in the absence of contractual provision. Certainly, it would seem that a non-contractual[82] implied licence should not provide a means to reduce an acquirer's rights below the level provided for by Art 5, and the impetus for non-contractual rights to be implied may not survive the Directive at all.

The final possibility to be considered here is that the opening of the software envelope was based not on acceptance of the licence, but on a right to use the software derived from an implied term in the contract under which the software was acquired (that is, the contract made in the shop with S, in our primary example). Certainly, in *Saphena Computing Ltd v Allied Collection Agencies Ltd*,[83] in which software was supplied to the defendants for the purposes of their business as a debt-collecting agency, the court regarded it as 'perfectly clear' that there had to be an implied term 'that the defendants should have a copyright licence to enable them to use the software for that purpose'.[84] Courts may well be reluctant to find that a supply of software is quite pointless because the acquirer has no right to use the software. They may be willing to imply a term in law giving a basic right to use the software on the basis that such a term is necessary in that type[85] of contract. Of course, there are difficulties with the idea of an implied term conferring rights to do what would otherwise be a breach of copyright if the contract is not between the acquirer and the copyright holder. A chain of implied terms might be suggested, although such a chain would be vulnerable to the insertion of an express contrary term in the first contractual link between the copyright holder and the person to whom he or she supplies.[86]

Obviously, there are considerable hurdles in the way of finding that there were two effective contracts – the supply contract and the licence. It should also be noted that the two-contract analysis was considered, and rejected, by the Scottish court in *Beta v Adobe*,[87] because of the difficulties that might ensue. If the situation was construed as one that could give rise to two distinct contracts, with S, the supplier, not being a party to any second licence or contract, Lord Penrose was concerned that A, the acquirer, might not be able to recover the purchase price of the software, or might refuse to pay it, if he or she did not wish to accept the licence terms. Any statement on the packaging that A can recover the purchase price if the licence is unacceptable will not be contractually enforceable

---

80 'Lawful user' is defined in s 50A(2). For criticism of the phrase, see Sherwood-Edwards, op cit.

81 Graham P Smith, 'Shrinkwrap licensing in the Scottish courts' (1996) 4(2) Int JLIT 131, 140–1.

82 But note that s 50C, 'implementing Article 5(1)', merely refers to contrary agreement, without specifying that it must be contractual.

83 *Saphena Computing Ltd v Allied Collection Agencies Ltd* [1995] FSR 617.

84 Ibid, 637, Havery QC (Off Ref).

85 The argument here would seem to apply whether the transaction is a sale of the disk or merely a hiring of it (as may sometimes be argued to be the case). In either situation, its acquisition is completely undermined if it cannot be used.

86 Even a term that would otherwise be implied in law will not be implied in the face of an express contrary term, although sometimes the express contrary term might be rendered ineffective and the implication therefore allowed, under UCTA 1977: *Johnstone v Bloomsbury HA* [1991] 2 All ER 293; see also UCTA 1977, s 3; Elizabeth Macdonald, 'Exclusion clauses: The ambit of s 13(1) of the Unfair Contract Terms Act 1977' (1992) 12 LS 277.

87 *Beta v Adobe* [1996] FSR 371.

by A against S, unless it has been properly incorporated into the contract between A and S. However, A might be able to claim that S's supply was in breach of contract.[88] It might be argued that the supply of software that, without further agreement with C, could not be used without infringing C's copyright would be in breach of the term implied by s 12 of the **SoGA 1979**[89] that the seller has a right to sell the goods. In *Niblett Ltd v Confectioner's Materials Co Ltd*,[90] a breach of that implied term was found when the sellers supplied tins of condensed milk were labelled in such a way as to infringe a third party's trade mark.

The problem considered by Lord Penrose, outlined above, obviously arises if the view is taken that A cannot use the software without accepting the licence terms. However, Lord Penrose's other concern with the two contract analysis was in relation to the possibility that C's attempt to create a licence with A would be ineffective, but A would nevertheless be able to use the software. He was concerned that S might be liable to C, through a breach of the contract under which C supplied the software to S, and, more significantly, that the position of C, as the copyright owner, would be undermined.

Pragmatism

The desire of the Scottish court in *Beta v Adobe* not to undermine the position of the holder of the copyright was noted above, together with Lord Penrose's view that it was generally in the interests of both the industry and the general management of transactions that effect should be given to the provisions of a licence. There may thus be an impetus to find shrink-wrap licences to be effective because that result is viewed as being of practical benefit.[91]

Something of this approach is also to be found in the US case of *ProCD Inc v Mathew Zeidenberg*.[92] In that case, unlike the earlier *Step Saver* case,[93] the licence was held to be effective against a background of the court's view of the benefits of such a conclusion. In *ProCD v Zeidenberg*, ProCD used different licence terms to differentiate between consumer and commercial purchases of its database. The consumer was charged US$150 for the purchase, which was much less than the commercial buyer, but was also authorised to do much less with the database than the commercial buyer. The court took that the view that it was beneficial to both consumers and commercial buyers that ProCD should take such an approach, which was obviously dependent on the effectiveness of the licence terms.

Since the *ProCD* case, despite considerable US academic debate over the validity of shrink-wrap licences and the rationales for finding them enforceable (or not), it appears that courts have generally been inclined to find them to be enforceable.[94] A move to create a statutory means of ensuring the validity of shrink-wrap licences in the USA was made with the Uniform Computer Information Transactions Act of 1999 (UCITA).[95] This was a draft state contract law designed to standardise the law, and to provide the default rules for licensing software and all other forms of digital information, as the US **Uniform Commercial Code** does for the sale of goods.[96] Despite strong support from major industry players, UCITA was seen as too heavily weighted in favour of large software

---

88   A restitutionary claim might also be made, but it would prove problematic to argue that a total failure of consideration had occurred when A had, technically, received title to the disk: see the approach taken in *Rowland v Divall* [1923] 2 KB 500.

89   If the contract is not one for the sale of goods, then it can be argued that an analogous term has been breached: see Chapter 12.

90   *Niblett Ltd v Confectioner's Materials Co Ltd* [1921] 3 KB 387.

91   *Beta v Adobe* [1996] FSR 371, 379.

92   *ProCD Inc v Mathew Zeidenberg* 86 F 3d 1447 (7th Cir 1996); but see Smith, op cit, 140–1.

93   *Step-saver Data Systems Inc v Wyse Technology and Software Link Inc* 939 F 2d 91 (3rd Cir 1991).

94   Robert W Gomulkiewicz, 'The Federal Circuit's licensing law jurisprudence: Its nature and influence' (2009) 84 Wash L Rev 199, citing Mark Lemley, Peter S Menell, and Robert P Merges, *Software and Internet Law*, 3rd edn, 2006, New York: Aspen Law & Business, p 337: 'Since ProCD, a majority of courts have enforced shrinkwrap licenses.'

95   Uniform Computer Information Transactions Act (UCITA), available online at www.law.upenn.edu/bll/archives/ulc/ucita/ucita200.pdf

96   In fact, UCITA was originally envisioned as a new §2B of the Uniform Commercial Code.

vendors[97] and was only passed into law by two states, Virginia and Maryland. Four states – West Virginia, North Carolina, Vermont, and Iowa – were sufficiently concerned about the impact of UCITA on consumers' rights that they adopted laws ('bomb shelters') that made UCITA-based contracts unenforceable in those states. In 2003, UCITA was effectively abandoned by its sponsor, the US National Conference of Commissioners on Uniform State Laws.[98]

More recently, in May 2009, the American Law Institute (ALI) approved a set of Principles of the Law of Software Contracts, which are designed to be legal principles to guide courts in deciding disputes involving transactions in software and to guide the drafting of software contracts.[99] These contain provisions dealing with what the Principles term 'standard form licenses' – that is, licences covering standard transfers of a small number of copies, or right of access to small number of users. The term is designed to cover end-user licence agreements (EULAs), and would apply to all kinds of software licences, including open source, shareware, and freeware. Section 2.02(b) covers the formation of standard-form transfers of generally available software, and states that a contract will be formed and the transferee is bound if a reasonable transferor would believe the transferee to be bound. Section 2.02(b) then sets out what is termed a 'safe harbor', which will ensure enforcement of a licence. This includes that:

- the standard-form licence is available prior to the transfer of the software;
- the licensee has reasonable access to the standard-form licence prior to the payment (or completion of the transaction if no payment is received);
- for electronic transactions, the licensee must signify agreement at the end of, or next to, the electronic standard-form licence;
- for standard-form licences printed on, or attached to a package, or separately wrapped from the software, the licensee must fail to return the unopened packaged software for a full refund within a reasonable period of time; and
- the licensee must be able to store and reproduce a copy of the standard-form licence, if it is only available electronically.

Section 2.02(e) places the burden of proving that these requirements have been met on the licensor. In addition to the terms of the 'safe harbor', the principles require that the standard-form licence terms must be 'reasonably comprehensible', such that a 'person of average intelligence and education can understand the language with ordinary effort', and that a standard-form licence will still be subject to public policy, unconscionability, and other invalidating defence. Standard-form licences may also not require advance agreement from the licensee to contract modifications (section 2.03).

The ALI principles are designed to be 'soft law' – that is, to be used as guidance and not as a template for state laws. However, due to their source, they are likely to be influential in US courts as demonstrating good practice in software contracting.

In the UK, there has been a dearth of commentary on shrink-wrap (and clickwrap) licences in academic and practitioner circles, and no further judicial discussion, since *Beta v Adobe*, in the courts. This may be because:

- consumers have adjusted to the concept of shrink-wrap licences (if they were aware of them and their content in the first place);

---

97 See, eg, David A Szwak, 'Uniform Computer Information Transactions Act (UCITA): The consumer's perspective' (2002) 63 Louis L Rev 27.

98 See Gomulkiewicz, op cit, 208–13.

99 The ALI began working on the Principles of the Law of Software Contracts in 2004. The official text of this project was published by the ALI in 2010 as *Principles of the Law of Software Contracts: Official Text*. See further Robert A Hillman and Maureen A O'Rourke, 'Principles of the law of software contracts' (2010) 53(9) J Commun ACM 26–8.

- software producers (or their distributors) have been willing to negotiate settlement of disputes with consumers outside the courts;
- consumers are more aware of the abilities and limitations of the software that they are purchasing due to the availability of online information; or
- the net cost of bringing a case claiming the invalidity of all or part of a shrink-wrap licence is prohibitive compared to the cost of much consumer software.

Whatever the reasons, initiatives such as the ALI Principles of the Law of Software Contracts suggest that the time may be ripe for reconsideration of the issue of shrink-wrap licences in the UK – if only to ensure that US-centric legal interpretations of such licences are parsed for compatibility with UK contract law, intellectual property law, and conflict-of-laws obligations.[100]

Free and Open Source Software Licensing (F/OSS)[101]

As was noted at the beginning of this chapter, when computers entered the commercial market-place in the 1950s, software was not considered as an item to be sold separately. As Campbell-Kelly and Garcia-Swartz note in their longitudinal analysis of IBM's changing policy towards supply of software, companies such as IBM initially bundled basic software with their hardware, and actively collaborated with their customers in developing software specific to their customers' needs. During this period, there were essentially no independent software producers, so if IBM wanted to sell (or lease) its computers, it either had to produce the software itself, or rely on its customers to generate it using the basic software utilities that IBM provided. In order to facilitate this, IBM provided the source code for all its programs to its end-users – the source code was 'open'.[102] Gradually, for IBM, that model began to change during the 1960s, as it moved away from collaborative software production and began to produce its own bundled programs; however, the source code remained open, because customers still needed to customise software according to their needs.

However, by the 1970s, IBM, faced with pressure from competitors in the computer market alleging that its bundling practices were anti-competitive, began to unbundle its software and market it separately from the hardware. While the source code still remained open to customers, IBM was now beginning to use licences and copyright to restrict third-party access.[103] This process was facilitated by the US **Copyright Act of 1976**, which explicitly provided copyright protection to computer programs. Finally, in the early 1980s, IBM moved to an 'object code only' policy, whereby customers were not supplied with the source code. This was driven in part by the threat of competitors' hardware being used to run competing programs derived from analysis of IBM source code. There was also the fact that, as the computing marketplace became more competitive, the cost of hardware was declining and IBM was beginning to generate a significant proportion of its revenue from software. Maintaining that revenue appeared to require the closing of the company's source code.[104]

100 See further Michael L Rustad and Maria Vittoria Onufrio, *The Exportability of the Principles of Software: Lost in Translation?*, 2009, Stetson University College of Law Research Paper No 2009-03/Suffolk University Law School Research Paper No 09-45; available online at http://ssrn.com/abstract=1466875
101 See further van R Wendel de Joode, JA de Bruijn, and MJG van Eeten, *Protecting the Virtual Commons: Self-organizing Open Source and Free Software Communities and Innovative Intellectual Property Regimes*, 2003, The Hague: TMC Asser Press; Rod Dixon, *Open Source Software Law*, 2003, Norwood MA: Artech House; Lawrence Rosen, *Open Source Licensing: Software Freedom and Intellectual Property Law*, 2004, London: Prentice Hall; Mikko Välimäki, *The Rise of Open Source Licensing: A Challenge to the Use of Intellectual Property in the Software Industry*, 2005, Helsinki: Turre, available online at http://lib.tkk.fi/Diss/2005/isbn9529187793/isbn9529187793.pdf
102 Martin Campbell-Kelly and Daniel D Garcia-Swartz. 'Pragmatism, not ideology: Historical perspectives on IBM's adoption of open-source software'. (2009) 21 (3) Inform Econ Pol 229, 233.
103 Ibid, 235–7.
104 Ibid, 237–9. Interestingly, Campbell-Kelly and Garcia-Swartz go on to describe how, since the late 1990s, in some areas of its operations, IBM has begun to embrace open sources again – notably the open source operating system Linux.

Free Software

IBM's journey from open source to closed source was largely mirrored across the computer industry, led by the software development houses. However, this change was not always well received. Initially, for example, the software industry sought to retain access to IBM's source code, claiming the need for access to maintain effective interoperability of their programs with those of IBM (while this may seem illogical, it is worth bearing in mind just how dominant a player IBM was in the computer marketplace at the time).[105] Equally annoyed, however, were a large number of 'hackers'[106] based at companies and universities, who were used to being able to access the source code of the computers that their institution operated, and to making such modifications, upgrades, and code fixes as they felt necessary. It is from this group that the concept of 'free software' arose.

The essential concept underlying free software is that users should have the 'freedom to run, copy, distribute, study, change and improve'[107] software. It does not mean that software should not be capable of being paid for: '"Free software" is a matter of liberty, not price. To understand the concept, you should think of "free" as in "free speech," not as in "free beer."'[108] The leading light in the free software movement was (and is) a computer programmer called Richard Stallman. According to Stallman, while he was working at the Massachusetts Institute of Technology (MIT) Artificial Intelligence Laboratory (AI Lab) in the late 1970s and early 1980s, two incidents occurred that made him question the direction that the software industry was taking. The first was the deliberate use of 'timebomb' coding[109] by a fellow programmer to control the ability of end-users to use particular software; the second was the denial of source code to a program used to run the AI Labs Xerox® laser printer under a non-disclosure agreement.[110] Both of these developments, Stallman felt, meant that commercial imperatives were destroying the cooperative environment in which programmers had worked, to the detriment of both programmers and the effective development of software.[111] Shortly afterwards, in 1982, the AI Lab itself moved from its existing open mainframe computer operating system to a proprietary system. This left Stallman with a dilemma: he could stay and work within a software development system in which he did not believe, or he would have to strike out in a different direction.[112]

In 1984, Stallman left employment at MIT and began work on a project to develop a new operating system called GNU, designed to be compatible with, but eventually replace, the proprietary Unix operating system. This project involved the development not only of the base operating system or 'kernel', but also of a range of programs including command processors, assemblers, compilers, interpreters, debuggers, text editors, and mailers.[113] Stallman intended that GNU would remain open, and 'free' – that is, that users would have the freedom to:

- run the program, for any purpose;
- modify the program to suit their needs, meaning access to the source code;

---

105 Ibid, 238.
106 'Hacker' has not always had the primarily pejorative meaning that is usually placed on it today. In the early days of computing, the term appears to have been used mainly to denote skilful or quick programmers. However, its precise etymology remains disputed: see Guy L Steele and Eric S Raymond (eds), *The New Hacker's Dictionary*, 3rd edn, 1996, Cambridge, MA: MIT Press.
107 Free Software Foundation, 'The Free Software Definition', online at www.fsf.org/licensing/essays/free-sw.html
108 Ibid.
109 A software timebomb is a software routine that causes the program in which it is embedded to stop functioning, or to function in a restricted fashion, after a predetermined time. Such timebombs were often used by software companies as a means of 'renting' their software for particular periods. Modern licences have largely superseded such mechanisms, although 'trialware' – software obtained on a trial basis by end-users – may contain such routines. 'Timebombs' and 'logic bombs' have been increasingly associated with computer misuse – see Chapter 4 – which may also have led to their decline in popularity in legitimate circumstances.
110 See Sam Williams, *Free as in Freedom: Richard Stallman's Crusade for Free Software*, 2002, Sebastopol, CA: O'Reilly Media, ch 1, available online at http://oreilly.com/openbook/freedom/ch01.html
111 See Richard M Stallman, 'The GNU operating system and the free software movement', in Chris DiBona, Sam Ockman, and Mark Stone, *Open Sources: Voices from the Open Source Revolution*, 1999, Sebastopol, CA: O'Reilly Media, available online at http://oreilly.com/catalog/opensources/book/stallman.html
112 Ibid.
113 Ibid.

- redistribute copies, either gratis or for a fee; and
- distribute modified versions of the program, so that the community could benefit from their improvements.[114]

The problem with granting these freedoms to other users was that they came with no obligation for those users to offer the same terms to others. Thus a software company could incorporate 'free' software source code into its proprietary products and then sell the result only as object code, under a proprietary licence, including non-disclosure agreements. Even if some element of control was kept over the 'free' source code, for example, requiring the 'free' source code to be provided to users by the software company, there was also the issue of circumstances in which a company had made non-trivial modifications to that code, or incorporated it into larger, more complex programs – in principle, it would be able to withhold those improvements to the original 'free' code from other programmers.[115]

Stallman's innovative solution was hinted at in his article 'The GNU Manifesto' in 1985,[116] in which he wrote that:

> GNU is not in the public domain. Everyone will be permitted to modify and redistribute GNU, but no distributor will be allowed to restrict its further redistribution. That is to say, proprietary modifications will not be allowed. I want to make sure that all versions of GNU remain free.

What Stallman proposed was to use a copyright licensing strategy to ensure that his freedoms applied not only to the original source code provided, but also to any source code created using that original source code, such as where the original source code was incorporated into a larger piece of source code, or where the original source code was improved or extended. In other words, by accepting Stallman's licence, a programmer would be agreeing to distribute his or her new, improved, or expanded source code under the same or an equivalent licence. This would mean him or her giving up certain rights that would otherwise be exclusively reserved to him or her by copyright as the copyright holder. Such licences have become known as 'copyleft' licences, because the copyright holder 'leaves' what would otherwise be exclusive rights available to others. It is important to remember, when discussing 'free' software licences (and open source software licences), that they are still copyright licences and that to grant such a licence requires a person or organisation to have the right under copyright law to do so, for example, as a creator, employer, or assignee. The first copyleft software licence that Stallman created was the Emacs General Public Licence (GPL);[117] this was to form the basis of the widely used GNU GPL. In 1985, Stallman set up the Free Software Foundation (FSF), a non-profit organisation that today sponsors the GNU project, holds copyright on a large proportion of the GNU operating system and other free software, and publishes a range of free software licences, including the GNU GPL, the GNU Lesser General Public Licence (GNU LGPL), the GNU Affero General Public Licence (GNU AGPL), and the GNU Free Document Licence (GNU FDL).

Stallman was not alone in seeking to make software source code widely available, although others were not as concerned that their source code remain outside what Gomulkiewicz[118] terms the 'binary use' software model (that is, software that is only distributed in object/binary code, such as Microsoft Office). A team of programmers at the University of California at Berkeley also tackled the issue of 'freeing' the Unix operating system. Unlike Stallman, they did not start from scratch, but rather evaluated the existing software and replaced any source code elements that were not authored

114 See, GNU, 'The Free Software Definition', available online at www.gnu.org/philosophy/free-sw.html
115 Ibid.
116 Richard M Stallman, 'The GNU Manifesto' (1985) 10(3) *Dr Dobb's Journal of Software Tools* 30, available (annotated) online at http://manybooks.net/titles/stallmanother05gnumanifesto.html
117 Robert W Gomulkiewicz, 'General Public License 3.0: Hacking the Free Software Movement's Constitution' (2005) 42(4) Hous L Rev 1015, 1024; see the Emacs General Public License, online at www.free-soft.org/gpl_history/emacs_gpl.html
118 Ibid, 1021.

by members of the project. These 'free' source code programs were released from 1989 onwards under the Berkeley Software Distribution (BSD) Licence.[119] This licence, and others modelled on it, like the MIT Licence[120] and Apache licence,[121] simply aimed to encourage reuse of the source code provided, and contained no copyleft requirement with regard to circumstances in which the original source code was incorporated into a larger piece of source code, or in which the original source code was improved or extended. Because of this degree of latitude permitted to end-users as to reuse, even in proprietary products, these licences became known as 'permissive' licences.

A Permissive Licence: The Modified BSD Licence

It has been estimated that variations on the BSD 'permissive' licence[122] are used for roughly 6 per cent of open source software projects, placing it fourth on the list of most popular free licences behind the GPL and associated LGPL, which are used by around 64 per cent of open source software projects.[123] The BSD licence, in its 'modified' form below, permits a licensee to:

● use, copy and distribute the unmodified source or binary forms of the licensed program; and
● use, copy and distribute modified source or binary forms of the licensed program.

It requires only that the licensee ensure that:

● all distributed copies are accompanied by the licence; and
● the names of the previous contributors are not used to promote any modified versions without their written consent.

The 'permissive' non-copyleft nature of the BSD licence means that source code licensed under it can be used in both 'open source' and 'closed source' software: for example, Microsoft Windows has used BSD-derived code in its implementation of TCP/IP. Would-be licensors wishing simply to see their source code used as widely as possible, and who do not require either a financial return or that licensees make improved and extended versions of the code, or other code in which the licensed code is included, available upon public distribution of the object code, are likely to use this licence.

The modified BSD License template[124]
Copyright (c) <YEAR>, <OWNER>

All rights reserved.

Redistribution and use in source and binary forms, with or without modification, are permitted provided that the following conditions are met:

---

119 Paul B de Laat, 'Copyright or copyleft? An analysis of property regimes for software development' (2005) 34(10) Research Policy 1511, 1519; Marshall Kirk McKusick, 'Twenty years of Berkeley Unix: From AT&T-owned to freely redistributable', in Chris DiBona, Sam Ockman, and Mark Stone (eds), *Open Sources: Voices From the Open Source Revolution*, 1999, Sebastopol, CA: O'Reilly, pp 31–46.
120 The MIT License, online at www.opensource.org/licenses/mit-license.html
121 Apache License, Version 2.0, online at www.opensource.org/licenses/apache2.0.php
122 The BSD licence has gone through three iterations: the original BSD licence, which contained a clause on advertising (four clauses); the 'modified' version with the advertising clause removed (three clauses); and the 'simplified' version, which removes the 'no-endorsement' clause (two clauses) – see below.
123 See statistics provided at Black Duck Software, 'Top 20 Most Commonly Used Licenses in Open Source Projects', available online at www.blackducksoftware.com/oss/licensesøp20
124 The BSD License (modified), online at www.opensource.org/licenses/bsd-license.php

Redistributions of source code must retain the above copyright notice, this list of conditions and the following disclaimer.

Redistributions in binary form must reproduce the above copyright notice, this list of conditions and the following disclaimer in the documentation and/or other materials provided with the distribution.

Neither the name of the <ORGANIZATION> nor the names of its contributors may be used to endorse or promote products derived from this software without specific prior written permission.

THIS SOFTWARE IS PROVIDED BY THE COPYRIGHT HOLDERS AND CONTRIBUTORS "AS IS" AND ANY EXPRESS OR IMPLIED WARRANTIES, INCLUDING, BUT NOT LIMITED TO, THE IMPLIED WARRANTIES OF MERCHANTABILITY AND FITNESS FOR A PARTICULAR PURPOSE ARE DISCLAIMED. IN NO EVENT SHALL THE COPYRIGHT HOLDER OR CONTRIBUTORS BE LIABLE FOR ANY DIRECT, INDIRECT, INCIDENTAL, SPECIAL, EXEMPLARY, OR CONSEQUENTIAL DAMAGES (INCLUDING, BUT NOT LIMITED TO, PROCUREMENT OF SUBSTITUTE GOODS OR SERVICES; LOSS OF USE, DATA, OR PROFITS; OR BUSINESS INTERRUPTION) HOWEVER CAUSED AND ON ANY THEORY OF LIABILITY, WHETHER IN CONTRACT, STRICT LIABILITY, OR TORT (INCLUDING NEGLIGENCE OR OTHERWISE) ARISING IN ANY WAY OUT OF THE USE OF THIS SOFTWARE, EVEN IF ADVISED OF THE POSSIBILITY OF SUCH DAMAGE.

A key problem with 'permissive' licences is the issue of 'freeriding'. This is where 'the product of open source contributors' efforts is monetized by a party that did not contribute to the project ...'.[125] While this is not a problem wholly restricted to 'permissive' licences, it is sometimes cited as a reason why such licences are not more widely used.[126] However, it is worth noting that the range of motivations for developing free and open source software (F/OSS), for both individual developers and companies, are complex and certainly much wider in scope than simple direct financial gain. For developers, issues such as talent signalling, reputation gain, learning, and altruism are perceived as motivations. For companies, broad external input, improved software quality, and (as with IBM, above) wider consumer choice for particular hardware all play a part.[127]

An Inheritable Licence: The GPL/GPL v.3

The GNU GPL, like the BSD licence, has been through several iterations. The original version was drafted in 1989 by Richard Stallman, to provide a unified licence for all GNU 'free' software.[128] The second version was released in 1991[129] with relatively minor changes, bar what Stallman refers to as the 'liberty or death' clause, designed to limit the impact of software patents on GNU licensed source code.[130] The current version was released in 2007 after considerable amendment.[131] The last two versions will be considered here.

---

125 See Oded Nov and George Kuk, 'Open source content contributors' response to free-riding: The effect of personality and context' (2008) 24(6) Comp Hum Behav 2848.
126 For example, Brian Fitzgerald and Nic Suzor, 'Legal issues for the use of free and open source software in government' (2005) 29(2) Mel U L Rev 412, 413.
127 See Nov, op cit; Andrea Bonaccorsi and Cristina Rossi, 'Comparing motivations of individual programmers and firms to take part in the open source movement: From community to business' (2006) 18(4) Knowledge, Technology & Policy 40.
128 Free Software Foundation Europe (FSFE), 'Transcript of Richard Stallman at the 2nd International GPLv3 Conference, 21 April 2006', available online at http://fsfe.org/projects/gplv3/fisl-rms-transcript.en.html
129 The GNU General Public License, Version 2 (GPLv2), online at www.opensource.org/licenses/gpl-2.0.php
130 FSFE, op cit; see section 7 of GPLv2, ibid.
131 The GNU General Public License, Version 3 (GPLv3), online at www.opensource.org/licenses/gpl-3.0.html

The second version of the GPL (GPL v.2) permits a licensee to:

- copy and distribute unmodified copies of the licensed program;[132]
- modify a copy or copies of the licensed program or any portion of it, and copy and distribute such modifications;[133]
- copy and distribute the program or a work based on it, in object code or executable form.[134]

These permissions are subject to the licensee providing:

- on both modified and unmodified copies of the program, an appropriate copyright notice and disclaimer of warranty, all of the notices that refer to the GPL and to the absence of any warranty, and a copy of the GPL v.2;[135]
- where the program has been modified, a modification notice, including the date of modification.[136]

He or she must also ensure that:

- any work containing the source code licensed under the GPL v.2 that is distributed or published by the licensor is licensed as a whole under the GPL v.2;[137]
- where any work is distributed in object code or as an executable program, the complete corresponding machine-readable source code is also supplied, or is made available to third parties by reasonable alternative means.[138]

Licensees breaching GPL v.2 lose their rights under it, but this does not void the rights of those who have received properly licensed copies of the GPL v.2 licensed source code, and who have themselves not breached the GPL v.2.[139] Modification or distribution of GPL v.2 licensed source code is taken to indicate acceptance by a licensor of the GPL v.2 terms.[140] Where legal conditions, including patent restrictions, are imposed on, or agreed by, a distributor/licensee of a GPL v.2 licensed program, this will breach the terms of the GPL v.2 and, in such circumstances, the licensee may not distribute the GPL v.2 program.[141] The GPL v.2 also includes an express exclusion of any warranty of merchantability or fitness for purpose, as far as any applicable law permits.[142] It should be noted that the requirement on a licensee to make any modified source code available applies only if the licensee distributes, or otherwise makes available, the software to the public. If the software is modified for use solely by the licensee, then there is no obligation to make the source code publicly available.

The latest version of the GPL, version 3 (GPL v.3), is drafted in a more legalistic form, is more precise (and less US law-specific) in its definitions,[143] and is considerably longer than its two predecessors.[144] It attempts to address issues that have arisen from the GPL v.2, as well as issues that have developed out of changes in the technological environment. At its core, however, the GPL v.3 retains the key elements of the GPL v.2. It permits a licensee to:

---

132 GPL v.2, section 1.
133 Ibid, section 2.
134 Ibid, section 3.
135 Ibid, sections 1 and 2.
136 Ibid, section 2(a).
137 Ibid, section 2(b).
138 Ibid, section 3(a) and (b).
139 Ibid, sections 4 and 6.
140 Ibid, section 5.
141 Ibid, section 7.
142 Ibid, sections 11 and12.
143 GPL v.3, section 0.
144 See further John Tsai, 'For better or worse: Introducing the GNU General Public License Version 3' (2008) 23(1) Berk Tech LJ 547.

- run the unmodified program, and to make, run, and propagate 'covered works' (that is, 'the unmodified Program or a work based on the Program') that are not 'conveyed' (which refers to 'any kind of propagation that enables other parties to make or receive copies') — in-house modifications and modifications made by third parties at the direction of the licensee, which are not made available outside that arrangement, fall within this category;[145]
- copy and distribute unmodified copies of the licensed program (that is, convey verbatim copies);[146]
- modify a copy or copies of the licensed program or any portion of it, and copy and distribute such modifications (that is, convey modified source versions);[147]
- copy and distribute the program or a work based on it, in object code or executable form (that is, convey non-source forms).[148]

These permissions are subject to the licensee providing:

- on both modified and unmodified copies of the program, an appropriate copyright notice and disclaimer of warranty, all of the notices that refer to the GPL and to the absence of any warranty, and a copy of the GPL v.3,[149] including any other 'additional permissions' (that is, terms additional to the GPL v.3 that make exceptions from one or more of its conditions) allowed under section 7 of the GPL v.3;[150]
- where the program has been modified, a modification notice, including the date of modification.[151]

The licensee must also ensure that:

- any work containing the source code licensed under the GPL v.3 that is distributed or published by the licensor is licensed as a whole under the GPL v.3,[152] including any other 'additional permissions' (that is, terms additional to the GPL v.3 that make exceptions from one or more of its conditions) allowed under section 7 of the GPL v.3;
- where any work is distributed in object code or as an executable program, the complete corresponding machine-readable source code is also supplied or is made available to third parties by reasonable alternative means.[153]

The GPL v.3 also retains:

- termination for breach of the licence, but softens the position under GPL v.2 by permitting a licensee to avoid termination by remedying a breach within 30 days of reasonable notice of violation of the GPL v.3 by a relevant copyright holder;[154]
- the position that a licensor is deemed to have accepted the licence by virtue of modifying or propagating (but not receiving or running) a covered work;[155]
- automatic licensing of downstream recipients, whereby each new recipient automatically receives a licence from the original licensors to run, modify, and propagate that work, subject

---

145 GPL v.3, section 2.
146 Ibid, section 4.
147 Ibid, section 5.
148 Ibid, section 6.
149 Ibid, sections 4 and 5.
150 See the exhaustive list ibid, section 7(a)–(f).
151 Ibid, section 5(a).
152 Ibid, section 5(c).
153 Ibid, section 6(a)–(e).
154 Ibid, section 8.
155 Ibid, section 9.

to the GPL v.3,[156] and that this remains even if a conveyor or licensor upstream of them has had their licence terminated for breach;[157]

- the requirement that a licensor cannot limit the freedoms of others by accepting conditions that contradict the GPL v.3 (in such circumstances, the licensor may not convey the covered work);[158]
- a disclaimer of any warranties and exclusion of liability to the extent permitted by applicable laws.[159]

Significant policy changes from the GPL v.2 can be seen in a number of key areas. First, the GPL v.3 tackles the issue of software patents much more directly. It is clear that, the copyright provisions of the GPL notwithstanding, the use of software patents could hinder the four freedoms that the GPL aims to protect (see above). The GPL v.2 appeared to suggest that use of source code under the GPL v.2 licence created an implied licence of any software patent in added source code for downstream users.[160] The GPL v.3, on the other hand, contains a dedicated section on patents.[161] This requires that:

- anyone conveying software under the GPL v.3, whether newly written or a modified source version, in which they have a patent claim must provide every recipient with any patent licences necessary for them to exercise the rights granted via the GPL v.3 – that is, if a company combines any GPL v.3 licensed software into software for which it has a patent, it must grant all downstream users a licence in relation to that patent;
- if a distributor conveys a covered work, knowingly relying on his or her own licence of a patent held by a third party that could be used to prevent downstream users from exercising the rights granted via the GPL v.3, via infringement proceeding threats from the third party, then the distributor must ensure that downstream parties are also granted appropriate licence rights;
- where a third party is indirectly granted a patent licence that grants rights to source code in a GPL v.3 covered work, then those rights must be granted to all other GPL v.3 licensees of the covered work.

Second, and somewhat controversially, the GPL v.3 addresses the issue of digital rights management (DRM), by requiring that no covered work can be deemed to be part of an 'effective technical measure' under Art 11 of the World Intellectual Property Organization (WIPO) **Copyright Treaty**. Article 11 requires treaty signatories to 'provide adequate legal protection and effective legal remedies against the circumvention of effective technological measures' that are used by authors, performers, and producers of phonograms to restrict acts with respect to their copyrighted works that are not authorised by the rights holders, or permitted by law. When a GPL v.3 licensee enables other parties to make or receive copies of a covered work, he or she must waive any legal right that he or she has to prevent the circumvention of technological measures, in as far as that circumvention occurs as a result of downstream parties exercising GPL v.3 rights with regard to the covered work, and disclaim any restrictions on the operation or modification of the covered work that would allow the licensee or third parties to enforce prohibitions on the circumvention of technological measures.[162] In effect, this means that any DRM system released under the GPL v.3 (or containing GPL v.3 software) could be circumvented by a program without constituting a violation

---

156 Ibid, section 10.
157 Ibid, section 8.
158 Ibid, section 12.
159 Ibid, sections 15 and 16.
160 See GPL v.2, Preamble: 'We wish to avoid the danger that redistributors of a free program will individually obtain patent licenses, in effect making the program proprietary. To prevent this, we have made it clear that any patent must be licensed for everyone's free use or not licensed at all.'
161 GPL v.3, section 11.
162 Ibid, section 3. For application of Article 11 to proprietary software see Chapter 9.

of laws implementing Art 11 of the WIPO **Copyright Treaty**. These would include the US **Digital Millennium Copyright Act of 1998 (DMCA 1998)**,[163] and EU Member State legislation implementing the EU **Copyright Directive**,[164] including s 264 of the **CDPA 1988**.

Third, the GPL v.3 tackles the issue of 'tivoisation'. This concept, popularised by Richard Stallman, refers to the use of GPL v.2 software by the popular model of digital video recorder (DVR), the TiVo, which allows users to capture television programming to internal hard disk storage for viewing later. The TiVo uses a GNU/Linux-based operating system that, because Linux is licensed under the GPL v.2, requires the TiVo's manufacturers to make the source code of its program available. The manufacturer has duly made the source code available online, or by post.[165] However, if a TiVo user downloads the software and modifies it, and then attempts to upload it to his or her TiVo, he or she will discover that the machine has been set up to reject such modified code. It does this by performing digital signature checks in hardware that require the modified software to contain codes known only to the manufacturer. This was perceived by the FSF as contrary to the spirit, if not to the letter, of the GPL v.2, and the GPL v.3 was thus drafted to attempt to prevent future efforts at 'tivoisation'. The GPL v.3 does not prevent a vendor licensee from using software containing GPL v.3 licensed code on hardware that has been designed so that an executable requires a specific key signature in order for it to operate, but the licensee must provide the necessary signature key, or other necessary elements, so that the hardware will accept and run any modified executables.[166]

Like the DRM provisions, the 'anti-tivoisation' measures are controversial in as much as they appear to move the GPL into a more political sphere than simply the protection of the four freedoms. Critics have suggested that sections aimed at promoting the FSF's opposition to DRM and to hardware-based code lockdowns have no place in a software licence.[167] It is worth remembering, however, that the GPL v.3 is one of a range of licences available for F/OSS projects, and that the impact of both the DRM and 'anti-tivoisation' sections in the GPL v.3 can thus be avoided by not using GPL v.3 licensed source code, such as by 'forking' existing GPL v.2 code.[168] Many existing F/OSS projects may not wish to move from GPL v.2 to GPL v.3, or may not feel able to do so – for example, Linus Torvalds, who directs the development of the Linux kernel, has indicated that there are no plans to adopt the GPL v.3.[169]

Finally, the GPL v.3 attempts to bring some clarity to the issue of licence incompatibility. There are a wide range of F/OSS licences currently available,[170] and they are often incompatible in some regard – that is, they contain requirements that mean that code licensed under them cannot be used with code licensed under a different licence. This incompatibility causes problems for programmers attempting to create software using source code under different licences and potentially 'balkanises' F/OSS-licensed code. While a number of solutions have been suggested to the problem and a

---

163 Digital Millennium Copyright Act of 1998 (DCMA 1998), s 103 of which adds a new Ch 12 to Title 17 USC. USC §1201 implements the obligation to provide adequate and effective protection against circumvention of technological measures used by copyright owners to protect their works.

164 Directive 2001/29/EC of the European Parliament and of the Council of 22 May 2001 on the harmonisation of certain aspects of copyright and related rights in the information society, OJ 2001 L167/10.

165 TiVo, GNU/Linux Source Code, online at www.tivo.com/linux/

166 GPL v.3, section 6.

167 For example, Douglas Ferguson, 'Recent development, syntax errors: Why Version 3 of the GNU General Public License needs debugging' (2006) 7(2) NC JL & Tech 397.

168 Software forking is when developers take a copy of the source code of a program and start independent development on it, creating a new piece of software, based on, but different from, the existing piece. This is easily done with F/OSS, because no permissions are required to take and modify the source code. If future Linux kernel developments were licensed under the GPL3, then TiVo could take code created under the GPL2 (in which there is no 'anti-tivoisation' clause) and develop their own line of GPL2 source code, without needing to use GPL3 licensed source code. However, this would restrict both the range of source code and programmer base available to TiVo in the future.

169 'The Linux kernel is under the GPL version 2. Not anything else. Some individual files are licenceable [sic] under v3, but not the kernel in general. And quite frankly, I don't see that changing': Linus Torvalds, 25 January 2006, online at http://lkml.org/lkml/2006/1/25/273

170 The Open Source Initiative (see below) recognises approximately seventy F/OSS licences.

number of organisations provide services to help to avoid problems caused by licence incompatibilities (for example, Koders.com by Black Duck Software is a source code search engine that permits developers to limit their code search to specific licences[171]), this is a continuing issue. The GPL v.2 did not permit any modification of its terms, which led to incompatibility with other F/OSS licences and also potential problems in countries other than the USA where the wording of warranty disclaimers and limitation of liability clauses differed from those of the USA. The GPL v.3 allows for limited modifications to reduce these problems, including, for material added to a covered work:

- disclaiming warranty or limiting liability differently from the terms of sections 15 and 16 of the GPL v.3;
- requiring preservation of specified reasonable legal notices or author attributions in that material or in the appropriate legal notices displayed by works containing it;
- prohibiting misrepresentation of the origin of that material, or requiring that modified versions of such material be marked in reasonable ways as different from the original version;
- limiting the use for publicity purposes of names of licensors or authors of the material;
- declining to grant rights under trade mark law for use of some trade names, trade marks, or service marks;
- requiring indemnification of licensors and authors of that material by anyone who conveys the material (or modified versions of it), with contractual assumptions of liability to the recipient for any liability that these contractual assumptions directly impose on those licensors and authors.[172]

The net result of these permitted modifications is that the GPL v.3 is compatible with a wider range of other F/OSS licences, including the Apache licence, MIT licence, and later versions of the BSD licence. What this means in practice is that where a licensee wishes to combine code licensed under another open-source licence, with GPL v.3-licensed code, the licensee can now usually license the entire work, as a whole, under the GPL v.3 licence without breaching the other licences. There remains the problem that GPL v.2 is, by itself, not compatible with GPL v.3 – that is, there is no legal way to combine code under GPL v.2 with code under GPL v.3 in a single program. This was a recognised issue with GPL v.2 and has been addressed by the FSF in two ways:

- the use of contributor agreements assigning copyright to the FSF, thus allowing the FSF to relicense as copyright owner;
- encouraging GPL v.2 licensors to license under a specific version or 'any later version', thus allowing existing source code licensed under GPL v.2 or 'any later version' to be relicensed under GPL v.3 without direct contributor approval.[173]

Dual Licensing

It is important to remember that the holder of a copyright in the source code of a computer program can, like any other copyright holder, license his or her exclusive rights in his or her work to different licensees under different licence terms. It is possible, therefore, for the copyright holder of the source code in a computer program to make it available for licensing under a proprietary fee-based licence option, as well as an open source licence option, such as one of the versions of the GPL (GPLx). In such cases, a licensee choosing the GPLx licence option would be required to release the full source code with any distribution of object code/executable that contained the GPLx licensed code. In contrast, a licensee choosing the proprietary fee-based licence option would

171 Cited in DM German and AE Hassan, 'License integration patterns: Addressing license mismatches in component-based development', Paper read at 31st International Conference on Software Engineering, 2009, 16–24 May, Vancouver.
172 GPL v.3, section 7(a)–(f).
173 Tsai, op cit, 579.

be able to distribute the object code/executable alone, and would have no obligation to release his or her source code.[174]

Open Source Software

There has been a tendency over time, particularly in the popular media, to refer to all software released under licences such as the modified BSD licence and the GPLx family of licences, as 'open source software'. This catch-all phrase tends to disguise the fact that there are several distinct schools of thought on the nature of software development. The split between the permissive ethos of those who created the BSD licence and the activist ethos of the Stallman/FSF is one example of this. The other key split is between the 'free software' purists (such as Stallman/FSF), and the 'open source software' school, who feel that the politicised nature of the FSF's approach hinders the uptake of 'open' programming in the business environment. Indeed, it appears to have been this concern that led to the adoption of the phrase 'open source software' as a more commercially friendly alternative to 'free software'. Stallman himself has noted the differences between 'open source' and 'free software' rooted in their different premises – namely, that whereas:

> . . . open source is a development methodology; free software is a social movement. The latter focuses on the social problem of nonfree software and the ethical imperative of free software. The open source movement, on the other hand, emphasises the ability to improve the software creating a better, more effective solution to a practical problem than nonfree software.[175]

This divergence of opinion helps to explain some of the opposition to the FSF's introduction of the GPL v.3, which was seen by a significant number of those in the open source community as dealing with issues that were outwith the remit of a software licence.

The Open Source Initiative (OSI)

The Open Source Initiative (OSI) was established in 1998 as a California public benefit corporation.[176] Its establishment came about as a result of the decision of Netscape Communications to release the source code of its popular Netscape Web browser as free software in January 1998. This, it is claimed, was inspired by the publication of the classic paper about the impact of 'free software' development (the phrase was changed by its author to 'open source software' in later iterations) *The Cathedral and the Bazaar*[177] in 1997. Its aim was 'to dump the moralizing and confrontational attitude that had been associated with "free software" in the past and sell the idea strictly on the same pragmatic, business-case grounds that had motivated Netscape'.[178]

In many respects, the FSF and OSI appear to have similar goals. However, the OSI is not ideologically opposed to closed-source software and, broadly speaking, is disinclined to involve itself in the campaigning that the FSF has adopted against both DRM technology and 'tivoisation'. It has significant interaction with traditional software companies, such as IBM, Hewlett Packard, and Sun, as well as with smaller companies working within an open source business model, such as Red Hat and Mandrake.

---

174 See Mikko Välimäki, 'Dual licensing in open source software industry' (2003) 8(1) Systèmes d'Information et Management 63, available online at www.valimaki.com/org/dual_licensing.pdf; Robert W Gomulkiewicz, 'Entrepreneurial open source software hackers: MySQL and its dual licensing' (2004) 9(1) CLRTJ 203.

175 Richard M Stallman, 'Why open source misses the point of free software' (2007; 2010), available online at www.gnu.org/philosophy/open-source-misses-the-point.html

176 In October 2009, the OSI's corporate status was suspended by the state of California, apparently on the grounds of failure to file required material with the state authorities. It was reinstated in February 2010.

177 Eric S Raymond, *The Cathedral and the Bazaar: Musings on Linux and Open Source by an Accidental Revolutionary*, 1999, Sebastopol, CA: O'Reilly Media.

178 Open Source Initiative, 'History of the OSI', online at www.opensource.org/history

The two key roles that the OSI has played in the F/OSS community take the form of the creation and maintenance of the Open Source Definition (OSD), and its (self-appointed) community role as the body that reviews and approves licences as OSD-conformant.[179]

The Open Source Definition

The OSI OSD was based on an existing set of free software principles known as the Debian Free Software Guidelines.[180] It was adopted in revised form by the OSI in February 1998, and has remained largely unchanged since 2004, when the OSI added clause 10 to address issues surrounding click-wrap licensing. In principle, any software licence creator who wishes his or her licence to be recognised as an 'open source' licence by the 'open source community' will have to ensure that it meets the requirements of the OSD, and passes the OSI's approval process.

The Open Source Definition[181]

Introduction
Open source doesn't just mean access to the source code. The distribution terms of open-source software must comply with the following criteria:

1.   Free Redistribution
The license shall not restrict any party from selling or giving away the software as a component of an aggregate software distribution containing programs from several different sources. The license shall not require a royalty or other fee for such sale.

2.   Source Code
The program must include source code, and must allow distribution in source code as well as compiled form. Where some form of a product is not distributed with source code, there must be a well-publicized means of obtaining the source code for no more than a reasonable reproduction cost preferably, downloading via the Internet without charge. The source code must be the preferred form in which a programmer would modify the program. Deliberately obfuscated source code is not allowed. Intermediate forms such as the output of a preprocessor or translator are not allowed.

3.   Derived Works
The license must allow modifications and derived works, and must allow them to be distributed under the same terms as the license of the original software.

4.   Integrity of The Author's Source Code
The license may restrict source-code from being distributed in modified form only if the license allows the distribution of "patch files" with the source code for the purpose of modifying the program at build time. The license must explicitly permit distribution of software built from modified source code. The license may require derived works to carry a different name or version number from the original software.

---

179 Open Source Initiative, 'The Licence Review Process', online at www.opensource.org/approval
180 Debian is a free operating system based on the Linux kernel and tools from the GNU project. It was one of the early free software projects, beginning in 1993. The Debian Free Software Guidelines form part of the 'Debian Social Contract', online at www.debian.org/social_contract.html
181 Open Source Initiative, 'The Open Source Definition', online at www.opensource.org/docs/osd

5. No Discrimination Against Persons or Groups

The license must not discriminate against any person or group of persons.

6. No Discrimination Against Fields of Endeavor

The license must not restrict anyone from making use of the program in a specific field of endeavor. For example, it may not restrict the program from being used in a business, or from being used for genetic research.

7. Distribution of License

The rights attached to the program must apply to all to whom the program is redistributed without the need for execution of an additional license by those parties.

8. License Must Not Be Specific to a Product

The rights attached to the program must not depend on the program's being part of a particular software distribution. If the program is extracted from that distribution and used or distributed within the terms of the program's license, all parties to whom the program is redistributed should have the same rights as those that are granted in conjunction with the original software distribution.

9. License Must Not Restrict Other Software

The license must not place restrictions on other software that is distributed along with the licensed software. For example, the license must not insist that all other programs distributed on the same medium must be open-source software.

10. License Must Be Technology-Neutral

No provision of the license may be predicated on any individual technology or style of interface.

The OSD is broad enough to cover an array of licences, including both the modified BSD and the GLPx family of licences. While it does not mandate the type of copyleft/reciprocity conditions (also known as 'viral', 'infectious', or 'hereditary' conditions) found in the GLPx licences, neither does it prohibit them.[182] In December 2009, there were 72 licences approved by the OSI as 'open source'. The 'proliferation' of F/OSS licences has brought concerns that there are too many licences available and that incompatibilities between different licences will cause confusion. The OSI has suggested that it will seek to reduce the number of licences on its list of approved licences, but has made little headway beyond labelling some of the OSD-compliant licences as 'redundant' or 'superseded'.[183]

Open Source Developments

While 'community' pressure is clearly a significant factor in both individual and organisational compliance with the terms of a F/OSS licence,[184] the acid test for F/OSS licences is, of course, whether they can be relied upon to achieve the licensor's goals when subjected to judicial scrutiny. At the present time, there is no case law relating to F/OSS licences in England and Wales (or Scotland). There have been several successful cases brought for infringement of the GPL in

---

182 However, recent F/OSS developments – notably the recognition of the GPL3 as an OSI approved licence – have caused some controversy, as both the GPL3 measures against DRM/TPM and 'tivoisation' are arguably discriminatory under clause 6. Controversy has also surrounded Microsoft's application for OSI approval for its Public (Ms-PL) and Reciprocal (Ms-RL) licences (both granted).

183 See further Robert W Gomulkiewicz, 'Open source license proliferation: Helpful diversity or hopeless confusion' (2009) 30 Wash U JL & Pol'y 261.

184 Richard Kemp, 'Current developments in open source software' (2009) 25(6) CLSR 569, 580–1.

Germany,[185] a case in France in which the court appears (as part of a broader contract discussion) to view the GPL positively,[186] and a number of cases addressing aspects of F/OSS licences in the USA.

As with other jurisdictions, the majority of US cases brought alleging infringement of F/OSS licences have settled out of court. The Software Freedom Law Center (SFLC)[187] has brought numerous cases, primarily on behalf of the principal developers of BusyBox, a software application that works with the Linux kernel and which is often used with embedded devices such as wireless connectivity devices. Busybox is licensed under the GPL v.2. To date, virtually all of these cases have settled out of court.[188] Until recently, therefore, US courts have only tended to consider the legality of the GPL and other F/OSS licences tangentially, indicating a willingness to consider the GPL and similar licences to be valid, but not actually providing a clear decision on the matter.[189] In *Wallace v IBM*,[190] the plaintiff alleged that the GPL v.2 violated US anti-trust law in that 'IBM, Red Hat, and Novell have conspired among themselves and with others (including the Free Software Foundation) to eliminate competition in the operating system market by making Linux available at an unbeatable price'.[191] The court was unpersuaded by this argument, noting that:

> ... the GPL keeps price low forever and precludes the reduction of output that is essential to monopoly ... antitrust laws forbid conspiracies 'in restraint of trade', ... the GPL does not restrain trade ... Nor does it help to call the GPL 'price fixing'. Although it sets a price of zero, agreements to set maximum prices usually assist consumers and therefore are evaluated under the Rule of Reason ... The GPL and open-source software have nothing to fear from the antitrust laws.[192]

However, the most important US case concerning F/OSS licences to date did not concern the GPL, but instead a rather more obscure F/OSS licence known as the Artistic License version 1.0 (ALv1).[193] The ALv1, which has now been superseded by the ALv2, permits licensees to copy, modify, and distribute the software provided that they place certain notices in those works as attribution to its original author and, where necessary, identify that they have changed the software, to preserve the original author's reputation.[194] In *Jacobsen v Katzer*,[195] the case was brought by a model railway hobbyist, who managed and contributed code to an open source project, the Java Model Railroad Interface Project (JMRI). The JMRI developed software that controlled model trains and which was

---

185 For example, *Welte v Deutschland GmbH* Landgericht München I (LG) (Munich District Court) 9 May 2004, No 21 06123/04; *Welte v D-Link Germany GmbH*, Landgericht Frankfurt Am Main (LG) (Frankfurt Am Main District Court) 6 September 2006, No 2-6 0224/06; *Welte v Skype*, Landgericht München I (LG) (Munich District Court) July 2007, No 7 05245/07. Harald Welte founded gpl-violations.org in 2004 to raise awareness about past and present violations of the GPL. He has been responsible for over a hundred settlements of GPL infringements, including several successful legal actions.

186 *SA Edu4 v Associations AFPA*, 04/24298 (Cour D'Appel de Paris, 16 September 2009).

187 The Software Freedom Law Center, online at www.softwarefreedom.org/

188 Cases have been filed against, then settled with: Monsoon Multimedia; Xterasys Corporation; High-Gain Antennas, LLC; Verizon Communications, Inc; Bell Microproducts, Inc; Super Micro Computer, Inc; Extreme Networks, Inc. In December 2009, the SFLC filed further cases against 14 consumer electronics companies, including Best Buy, Samsung, Westinghouse, and JVC.

189 See, eg, *Progress Software Corp v MySQL AB* 195 F Supp 2d 328 (D Mass 2002), in which the federal court in Massachusetts assumed that the GPL was enforceable (case settled before trial); *Computer Associates International v Quest Software Inc* 333 F Supp 2d 688 (ND Ill 2004), in which the federal court in the Northern District of Illinois analysed the Bison licence (a licence similar to the GPL) and assumed that it was enforceable.

190 *Wallace v IBM* 467 F 3d 1104 (7th Cir 2006).

191 Ibid, 1106.

192 Ibid, 1107–8.

193 Artistic License version 1.0 (ALv1), online at www.opensource.org/licenses/artistic-license-1.0.php

194 See Lawrence Rosen, 'Bad facts make good law: The *Jacobsen* Case and open source' (2009) 1(1) IFOSS L Rev 27, available online at www.ifosslr.org/ifosslr/article/view/5

195 See further Erich M Fabricius, '*Jacobsen v Katzer*: Failure of the Artistic License and repercussions for open source' (2008) 9 NC JL & Tech 65, discussing the lower court decision; Robert W Gomulkiewicz, 'Conditions and covenants in license contracts: Tales from a test of the Artistic License' (2009) 17(3) Tex Intell Prop LJ 335, discussing the Circuit Court of Appeal decision.

distributed under the ALv1. A company run by the defendant had taken software created by the JMRI and included it in its proprietary software. It did not, however, comply with the attribution requirements of the ALv1. Amongst other things, it did not include with the modified and distributed software:

- the author' names;
- the JMRI copyright notices;
- references to the terms of the Artistic License;
- an identification of SourceForge,[196] or JMRI, as the original source of the definition files; and
- a description of how the files or computer code had been changed from the original source code.

Jacobsen thus sought a preliminary injunction against Katzer for infringement of his copyright, because of Katzer's failure to observe the terms of the ALv1. However, the district court refused the preliminary injunction, holding that a non-exclusive licence such as the ALv1 provided a waiver of the licensor's right to sue for infringement while the licensee's use of the work remained within the scope of the licence – thus Katzer did not commit copyright infringement by copying and redistributing the JMRI software source code files. The court further held that the licence provisions requiring attribution did not constitute a restriction on the scope of the licence. Thus, Katzer's failure to include the information required by the ALv1 did not mean that Katzer was doing something that the licence did not permit (that is, acting outside the scope of the licence); rather it was a breach of the terms of the licence. The court was thus minded to treat the notice requirements in the Artistic License as being a contractual covenant, which in turn led it to treat the issue as one of contractual breach, rather than copyright infringement. As damages were the traditional remedy for breach of contract, the court refused the preliminary injunction.[197]

On appeal to the Federal Circuit Court of Appeals,[198] the Court reassessed the issue of copyright infringement/contractual breach and considered in particular whether the terms of the Artistic License were conditions of, or merely covenants to, the copyright licence. The district court's analysis had clearly treated the ALv1 licence limitations as covenants rather than conditions, and this interpretation was firmly rejected by the Court of Appeals. The licence stated that the document created conditions; further, these conditions were vital to ensure compliance with the requirement to retain the reference to the original source, and maintain knowledge of subsequent uses and the collaborative effort involved. The explicit restrictions placed on the right to modify and distribute the work were both 'clear and necessary' to accomplish the objectives of the open source licensing collaboration.[199] The Court underlined the right of copyright holders to control the modification and distribution of copyright material; this was not only a question of economic benefits and monetary payments.

> Copyright holders who engage in open source licensing have the right to control the modification and distribution of copyrighted material . . . Copyright licenses are designed to support the right to exclude; money damages alone do not support or enforce that right. The choice to exact consideration in the form of compliance with the open source requirements of disclosure and explanation of changes, rather than as a dollar-denominated fee, is entitled to no less legal recognition. Indeed, because a calculation of damages is inherently speculative, these types of license restrictions might well be rendered meaningless absent the ability to enforce through injunctive relief.[200]

---

196 SourceForge is a web-based source code repository that offers free access to hosting and tools for F/OSS developers, online at http://sourceforge.net/about
197 *Jacobsen v Katzer*, WL 2358628, 6–7 (ND Cal, 17 August 2007).
198 *Jacobsen v Katzer* 535 F 3d 1373 (Fed Cir 2008).
199 Ibid, 1381.
200 Ibid, 1381–2.

Having clearly identified the ALv1 conditions as being copyright licence conditions, the Court of Appeals then remanded the case back to the district court for reconsideration of the appropriateness of injunctive relief. This was again refused by the district court,[201] on the grounds that Jacobsen had not provided adequate admissible evidence to show that he was likely to succeed on the merits, that he was likely to suffer irreparable harm in the absence of preliminary relief, that the balance of equities tipped in his favour, and that an injunction would be in the public interest.[202] The case eventually settled in Jacobsen's favour, with a permanent injunction against Katzer reproducing the software and the settlement agreement requiring a payment of US$100,000 to the open source movement.[203]

The Jacobsen case thus represents a positive result for the F/OSS community, in as much as it is a recognition (at least in California) both that breach of a F/OSS licence term can be copyright infringement and that the most appropriate remedy in such circumstances is likely to be injunctive relief: either negative, in terms of removing the licensee's ability to distribute an infringing work; or positive, in terms of forcing the licensee to release source code, or properly attribute the authors. Some issues remain: for example, the Court of Appeals clearly looked carefully at the licence terms when determining whether they were to be deemed licence conditions or contractual covenants, and the unclear terminology in some F/OSS licences may pose future problems in their interpretation. The GPL v.2, however, explicitly uses conditions, not covenants: it permits redistribution 'provided that' the user meets a list of 'conditions'.

As far as UK law is concerned, commentators both prior to[204] and after[205] the US Court of Appeals ruling in the Jacobsen case seem agreed that a F/OSS licence would be enforceable in the UK courts, although there is some uncertainty as to whether the UK courts would treat such a licence as either a 'bare licence' or a fully contractual licence. As with the Jacobsen case, the importance of such distinctions may lie not so much in the determination of whether the bare or contractual licence has been breached, as in what remedy is available. Henley suggests that if a situation such as that in Jacobsen were to arise in England and Wales, it would be likely that no contract would be found and that the Artistic License would be treated as a bare licence. Nonetheless, if it were deemed to be a contract, Henley envisages a similar approach to that in Jacobsen depending on whether the breach involved a condition or a less critical term. In either case, use of the software in breach of the licence could still constitute copyright infringement for which an interim injunction might be available.[206]

A concern for those using F/OSS licences, should they be deemed to be contractual licences rather than bare licences, is that this classification would potentially open licensors to actions by licensees (and the licence itself to deeper judicial scrutiny and broader contractual interpretation).[207]

Software as a Service (SaaS)

The future development of software licensing, and the concomitant legal perspectives on issues such as whether software is a good or a service, whether access may be granted to object and/or

---

201 Jacobsen v Katzer 609 F Supp 2d 925 (ND Cal 2009).

202 Per Winter v Natural Resources Defense Council, Inc 129 S Ct 365 (2008).

203 Jacobsen v Katzer 2010 WL 2985829 (ND Cal 2010); see Suzanne K Nusbaum, 'Copyright cases' (2010) 66 Bus Law 205, 207.

204 For example, Andrés Guadamuz Gonzalez, 'Viral contracts or unenforceable documents? Contractual validity of copyleft licenses' (2004) 26(8) EIPR 331.

205 For example, Mark Henley, 'Jacobsen v Katzer and Kamind Associates: An English legal perspective' (2009) 1(1) IFOSS L Rev 41, available online at www.ifosslr.org/ifosslr/article/view/4

206 Ibid, 43–4; see also Kemp, op cit, 578.

207 Henley, op cit, 44.

source code, and whether users should be permitted to make back-up copies or to decompile for error correction, are likely to depend on business and end-user decisions about the most efficient and cost-effective ways for them to access and utilise software.

Presently, for many home end-users, the primary way in which they utilise software is by purchasing a software package and a licence to install that software on one or more machines that they own. In the corporate environment, purchased software may be installed across individual machines within a company, or programs may be run on a company server that can be accessed by individual workstations. In both home and corporate circumstances, the licence for such software is usually either:

- a 'perpetual' licence that is paid once and does not need to be renewed annually – normally valid for the software version supplied at the time of purchase, with full version upgrades (as opposed to minor upgrades and bug fixes) likely to require an additional payment;
- a 'subscription' licence valid for a set period of time, at the end of which, if the licence is not renewed, the software ceases to work – typically including any upgrades provided by the vendor during the lifetime of the licence.[208]

Additionally, the licence is usually restricted in terms of the number of iterations of the software that can be run simultaneously. Home computing licences often restrict installation to one machine, although the use of portable computers has led some vendors to permit multiple installations. In a corporate environment, there are a variety of licensing/pricing options available, the most popular being:[209]

- *per seat* – the company pays a licence fee per machine on which the software is installed, or per server via which it can be accessed by workstations (use being restricted to specific machines);
- *floating user/concurrent user* – the company pays a licence fee based on the number of people able to access the software simultaneously;
- *named user* – the licence fee is paid in relation to a specific user rather than a specific machine;
- *per metric* – the licence fee is dependent upon metrics, such as actual usage, or financial targets, etc;
- *per central processing unit* (CPU) – the licence permits an unlimited number of end-users to use the software running on a single CPU (usually applied to server-based software).

All of these options require both home and corporate software users to install the software on their own machines, and to maintain and where necessary upgrade the software. Corporate users will often incur significant hardware and technical support costs in ensuring that software is properly licensed, such as that the company is not under or over-licensed, and that systems are effectively maintained, such as that server/network maintenance, hardware compatibility checks, and instal-lation of software patches are carried out. Home users also often struggle with installation and upgrading of even basic software packages.

Application Service Provision (ASP), Cloud Computing, and SaaS

As noted in the previous section, the traditional model for software use has been for an individual or company to purchase a software package, along with a software licence appropriate to its

---

208 Jiadao Li, Wolfgang Ziegler, Oliver Wäldrich, and Daniel Mallman, *Towards SLA Based Software License Management in Grid Computing*, CoreGRID Technical Report Number TR-0136, 2008, available online at www.coregrid.net/mambo/images/stories/ TechnicalReports/tr-0136.pdf, pp 3–4, Software companies will often choose to offer their products under both types of licence.
209 Acresso Software, *2008 Key Trends in Software Pricing and Licensing*, available online at www.softsummit.com/library/ reports/2008KeyTrendsSurvey.pdf

intended use. This places the burden of maintaining both the necessary hardware and software, as well as ensuring compliance with often quite complex licence conditions, upon the users. Even where licensees are willing to comply with the licences, it may be difficult and costly, particularly in the corporate environment, for them to gauge accurately the extent of their compliance (or for the licensor to enforce licensee compliance).

These issues have led to a number of possible solutions being offered that aim to reduce both the technical overheads imposed on users and the complexities of existing licensing practices. This section will briefly outline three key developments with relevance to software licensing that have seen significant media coverage over the past decade – application service provision (ASP), cloud computing, and Software as a Service (SaaS) – and their interrelationship.[210] All three terms relate to ways of removing the need to install software on a user's machine by hosting it at a service provider, with the user then able to utilise the software remotely via a network.

As a term, ASP has the longest history; it appears to have diminished in use partly because of technological changes, but also because new providers have sought to distinguish their services from previous (and sometimes failed) examples. An early, 'general business' ASP provider would:

- host standard software packages that would otherwise be based on a customer's machines or servers – but the software packages were usually not specifically designed for this method of delivery and thus the ASP vendor would often be reselling or renting legacy applications;
- provide access to the software via a network, such as a dedicated line, virtual private network, or the internet, through which a customer's users could then log on to the ASP's application server to run the software;
- manage the licensing process, regardless of whether the rights to the software were owned by the vendor or a third party, which might entail taking over the licences previously granted to the customer by a third-party software company;
- manage and maintain a standardised version of the software, including upgrades and bug fixes; and
- provide the service on a subscription basis, such as on a per use basis or on a monthly/annual fee basis.

Such general business ASP providers often faced difficulties in pricing their services, handling licensing issues, and dealing with customer demands for integration of different software and services, and for customer support. They also struggled to supply services that demanded high bandwidth in a technological environment in which access to such bandwidth, even amongst corporate customers, was limited.[211] As a result, many fell victim to the dot.com crash.

However, the principle of 'software as a service' has endured, particularly in the form of enterprise[212] and vertical market[213] ASP vendors. As technology has improved and businesses have increasingly seen outsourcing of non-core operations as a high priority, more opportunities have opened up for provision of such services. Contemporary SaaS providers tend to provide their own software solutions rather than third-party applications, and both the software itself and the hardware supporting it tend to be optimised for network (usually internet) delivery. Applications are usually designed as 'multi-tenant', allowing multiple customers to share the same application,

---

210 As with many other areas of developing information technology, the area of 'outsourced' software provision is replete with jargon. Some of the jargon is created by vendors and interest groups, and some by the media. Terms are often used by different parties to mean different things and theoretically distinct terms are often used interchangeably. There is no agreed version of any of the terms.

211 Sushil K Sharma and Jatinder ND Gupta, 'Application service providers: Issues and challenges' (2002) 15(3) Logistics Information Management 160, 164–7.

212 Enterprise ASP vendors (eg, Oracle) supply high-end software applications, such as enterprise resource planning (ERP), customer relationship management (CRM), and supply chain management (SCM) software.

213 Vertical market ASP vendors (eg, Portera Systems) supply software applications to a particular industry or industries.

running on the same operating system, on the same hardware, with the same data storage mechanism, but segregating each customer's data. The fact that the application is maintained by the SaaS provider on its own server(s) means that upgrading and optional enhancements can be rapidly made available to the entire user base of a customer. The concept of SaaS is rapidly developing in the consumer and small-to-medium-sized enterprise (SME) marketplace, with developments such as Gmail and Google Apps. When a user uses Google Apps, the 'data and the applications themselves are served from Google's highly secure, scalable, and reliable data centers'.[214] This means that a user can access and use his or her data from anywhere that he or she can access the internet.

The concept of 'cloud computing' takes matters one step further. It describes a situation in which a range of services, including some types of SaaS, can be provided via the internet (which is often represented by a cloud in diagrams and flowcharts), from:

> . . . massively scalable datacentres running hundreds of thousands of CPUs as a single computer engine, using virtualisation technology. That approach means workloads are distributed across multiple machines — which can also be located in multiple datacentres — and capacity can be allocated or scaled back according to a customer's needs.[215]

In essence, when a user accesses an application 'in the cloud', they are connecting not only to a single remote server, but potentially to any of a number of machines, which may be located in one or more data centres, in more than one country. If a corporate customer has a fluctuating number of users, or fluctuating patterns of usage, a cloud computing system is capable of adjusting the computer capacity available to the customer at any point. A SaaS vendor using a cloud computing model supplies the hardware infrastructure and the software product, and interacts with the user through a front-end portal. It may own its own data centres, but equally may obtain some or all of its data centre capacity from a range of third parties.

Licences or Service Level Agreements?

In most circumstances in which a customer is using a SaaS service, he or she will be doing so without ever receiving a copy of the software, which remains entirely under the control of the vendor. He or she will purchase access to the software on a subscription basis, and expect the vendor to ensure that the software is available during the term of subscription, is maintained and updated, and, in the case of some software, is customised to his or her requirements. The role of the traditional software licence in this environment is thus largely redundant; what replaces the licence is usually a service level agreement (SLA) between the vendor and the customer,[216] to be considered in the next chapter.

See Chapter 12 →

SaaS, F/OSS, and the Affero GPL

The increasing popularity of the SaaS model, whereby the user does not receive a copy of a software program for installation locally, but accesses the functionality of the software over the internet, causes some problems for the F/OSS model described above. In particular, the copyleft provisions of the GPL v.2 only come into play where there is distribution of a work containing the licensed code.

---

214 Google Apps, online at www.google.com/apps/
215 Cath Everett, 'Five cloud computing myths exploded' (2009) ZDNet.co.uk, 2 February, available online at http://resources.zdnet.co.uk/articles/0,1000001991,39605991-1,00.htm
216 See Helen Eliadis and Adrian Rand, *Setting Expectations in SaaS: The Importance of the Service Level Agreement to SaaS Providers and Consumers*, 2007, Washington, DC: Software & Information Industry Association; Li et al, op cit.

GPL v.2

Preamble

. . . if you *distribute* copies of such a program, whether gratis or for a fee, you must give the recipients all the rights that you have. You must make sure that they, too, receive or can get the source code. And you must show them these terms so they know their rights.

. . .

Terms and Conditions for Copying, Modification and Distribution

. . .

2. . . .

b)   You must cause any work that you *distribute* or publish, which in whole or in part contains or is derived from the Program or any part thereof, to be licensed as a whole at no charge to all third parties under the terms of this License.

The GPL v.2 thus does not take account of the server-based/web services business model. It is therefore possible for an SaaS vendor (for example, Google) to take code covered by the GPL v.2, make a modified version of that software, and provide public access to it via its service, and yet not be obliged to release the modified source code.[217]

This is seen by many in the free software movement both as 'freeriding' and contrary to the free software ethos, because SaaS vendors could use F/OSS code, but contribute little, or nothing, back to the F/OSS community. As a result, an attempt was made during the early drafting of the GPL v.3 to close this apparent loophole by adding a clause covering use of GPL licensed code in networked services. This, however, sparked considerable opposition, not least from companies such as Google, which provide several SaaS offerings incorporating GPL code. The furore caused the FSF to rethink its position and instead simply to clarify the relationship of the GPL v.3 licence with regard to SaaS:

GPL v.3

Preamble

. . . if you distribute copies of such a program, whether gratis or for a fee, you must pass on to the recipients the same freedoms that you received. You must make sure that they, too, receive or can get the source code. And you must show them these terms so they know their rights.

. . .

Terms and Conditions

0. Definitions.

. . .

To 'convey' a work means any kind of propagation that enables other parties to make or receive copies. Mere interaction with a user through a computer network, with no transfer of a copy, is not conveying.

---

217 See Kemp, op cit, 579; Mikko Välimäki, 'GNU General Public License and the distribution of derivative works' (2005) 1 JILT, available online at www2.warwick.ac.uk/fac/soc/law/elj/jilt/2005_1/valimaki/

While the FSF accepted that placing a direct clause in the GPL v.3 might damage the licence's chances of significant uptake, it has provided software developers with another alternative. This takes the form of the Affero GPL v.3 (AGPLv3).[218] This licence, which is OSI-approved, is broadly similar to the GPL v.3, with the addition of a clause explicitly requiring that where a program licensed under the AGPLv3 is modified by a licensee and made available to users who interact with it remotely through a computer network, the source code of the modified program must be made available to users from a network server at no charge.

Both the AGPLv3 and the GPL v.3 also contain clauses that make the two licences compatible.

AGPLv3

Terms and Conditions

13. Remote Network Interaction; Use with the GNU General Public License.
Notwithstanding any other provision of this License, if you modify the Program, your modified version must prominently offer all users interacting with it remotely through a computer network (if your version supports such interaction) an opportunity to receive the Corresponding Source of your version by providing access to the Corresponding Source from a network server at no charge, through some standard or customary means of facilitating copying of software. This Corresponding Source shall include the Corresponding Source for any work covered by version 3 of the GNU General Public License that is incorporated pursuant to the following paragraph.

Notwithstanding any other provision of this License, you have permission to link or combine any covered work with a work licensed under version 3 of the GNU General Public License into a single combined work, and to convey the resulting work. The terms of this License will continue to apply to the part which is the covered work, but the work with which it is combined will remain governed by version 3 of the GNU General Public License.

GPL3

Terms and Conditions

13. Use with the GNU Affero General Public License.
Notwithstanding any other provision of this License, you have permission to link or combine any covered work with a work licensed under version 3 of the GNU Affero General Public License into a single combined work, and to convey the resulting work. The terms of this License will continue to apply to the part which is the covered work, but the special requirements of the GNU Affero General Public License, section 13, concerning interaction through a network will apply to the combination as such.

Conclusions

The field of computer software licensing is one that constantly gains in complexity. While new technological developments add to the ways in which licensors seek to exploit their software, and consumers demand new ways to access, share, and use software, many of the pre-existing methods will survive for the foreseeable future. While increased bandwidth may encourage consumers to

---

218 GNU Affero GPL v.3, online at www.opensource.org/licenses/agpl-v3.html

download even large programs, such as Microsoft's Windows 7 and Office 2007, via the internet, much software is still bought on tangible media such as CDs and DVDs, so knowledge of shrink-wrap and browse-wrap licences (and their legal uncertainties) is still important. While the uptake of SaaS is on the increase, there are many reasons why potential users still shy away from adopting SaaS solutions across the board: lack of confidence in SaaS suppliers performance, lack of adequate SaaS services to meet particular user needs, limited customisation, privacy, and business confidentiality concerns, to name but a few. As such, the 'in-house' or 'on-premise' model of software use, in which customers purchase mass-market software packages or commission bespoke software solutions for their own private use, is likely to remain a dominant model.

The diverse motivations of both software licensors and licensees, exemplified in, but not exclusive to, the development of F/OSS licensing, also complicate matters for those seeking to advise parties on the legal implications of particular forms of software licensing. Increasing recent litigation around F/OSS licences, combined with licensing conditions targeting particular business methods, such as DRM, 'tivoisation', and SaaS, suggest interesting times ahead as lawyers and lawmakers seek to establish workable mechanisms for protecting reasonable licensor requirements, preventing unfair terms being placed on licensees, and maintaining a viable environment for future software development.

To date, the history of software licensing displays a considerable degree of pragmatism, not to say utilitarianism, on the part of legislators and the courts. Whether evaluating the ownership of intellectual property rights in commissioned software, the validity of shrink-wrap and browse-wrap licences, or the form and purpose of F/OSS licences, the courts appear to have trodden a careful path with regard to the rights and responsibilities of the parties, keeping a weather eye towards any undue impact on the future development of software.

Chapter 12

Defective Software

Chapter Contents

Introduction

This chapter is concerned with liability for defective software, and will address the issue first by reference to liability under contract law and then in terms of tortious liability.

Contractual liability may occur in relation to the acquisition of software by itself (a program) or of a system (software and hardware). Whether supplied by itself or as part of a system, it is, in general, the software that raises questions unique to the area of information technology (IT) law, and that will be focused on here. The complexity of modern software raises questions about how to assess the obligations undertaken in a contract for its supply and thus to determine whether there has been a breach, and the chapter opens by considering the debate about the 'perfectibility' of software and examining the question of the relationship of bugs to breaches. It will then look more fully at the contractual obligations, whether arising from express or implied terms, before considering the impact of exemption clauses. In considering implied terms, this chapter addresses the question of whether one of the statutory regimes implying terms into certain types of contract can apply to a contract for the supply of software, such as that of the **Sale of Goods Act 1979 (SoGA 1979)** or the **Supply of Goods and Services Act 1982 (SGSA 1982)**.

The ways in which companies and consumers acquire and use software alter as computer technology develops and end-user expectations change. This can be seen with the development of the modern Software as a Service (SaaS) provision model, in which end-users do not receive, install or run the software that they use on their own computer systems, but instead access it remotely, via a SaaS provider's servers. As the nature of software provision undergoes change, the software contracting process has to adapt in tandem. In the SaaS environment, it appears that greater emphasis will be placed on different elements of a software contract, such as the availability and reliability of the service provision, etc. Thus, for some forms of software provision, current software contracts may evolve into more flexible arrangements based on service level agreements (SLAs).

See Chapter ◄ 11

As computer control becomes increasingly ubiquitous, failure of systems containing software will often have an impact on many people who are not parties to the contract to supply that software.[1] They may suffer economic loss or physical injury.[2] Such failures may have large-scale consequences, such as was seen with failure of the computer-aided despatch system of the London Ambulance Service in October and November 1992. The report of the Inquiry into the incident demonstrates a number of the difficult issues that may arise when attempting to apportion liability in an incident such as this.[3] While such failures are accidental, due either to software programming deficiencies and errors, or unforeseen combinations of circumstances with which the software cannot cope, an increasing number of problems are arising from deliberate exploitation of defective software.

Attacks by cybercriminals upon commercial and home machines are often predicated upon the use of one or more known 'exploits' – software defects that have either not been addressed by the vendor of the software, or for which updates or patches provided by the vendor have not been applied by users of significant numbers of machines. In an era in which malicious software can be distributed worldwide in a matter of hours, and large groups of compromised machines or 'botnets' can be used to launch coordinated and concerted denial-of-service (DoS) attacks upon commercial and government systems, the risks posed make the imposition of liability for defective software increasingly likely. A key question will be upon whom that liability is imposed.[4]

---

1 For an ever-growing list of examples, see the ACM Committee on Computers and Public Policy, The Risks Digest: Forum on Risks to the Public in Computers and Related Systems, available online at www.risks.org
2 See, eg, Diane Rowland, 'Liability for defective software' [1991] Cambrian LR 78; Ian Lloyd, 'Liability for defective software' (1991) 32 Reliab Eng Syst Safe 193; DW Lannetti, 'Toward a revised definition of "product" under the Restatement (Third) of Torts: Products liability' (2000) 35 Tort & Ins LJ 845.
3 South West Thames RHA, *Report of the Inquiry into the London Ambulance Service*, 1993, London: Communications Directorate; see also Moira Simpson, '999! My computer's stopped breathing!' (1994) 10(2) CLSR 76.
4 See, eg, Michael L Rustad and Thomas H Koenig, 'The tort of negligent enablement of cybercrime' (2005) 20 Berkeley Tech LJ 1553.

Can Software Be 'Perfect'?

An elemental problem when assessing contractual or tortious liability for defective software is establishing a baseline for what would constitute 'acceptable' software in a given circumstance. The first problem in tackling such an assessment is that the market for software spans from mass-produced software, through modular and customisable software, to acquirer-specified and commissioned bespoke software. Constructing an overarching test of acceptability for such a broad spectrum of products, in which the outcome of software defects or 'bugs' could be relatively minor inconvenience caused to many users or significant financial loss caused to a specific user (and a multitude of variables in between), is likely to be unachievable. Attempting to derive a set of legal principles to fit all circumstances will thus be prone to placing too much burden on software suppliers in some circumstances, and providing too little protection to acquirers in others. This was amply demonstrated in the outcry surrounding the proposed US legislative standard known as the Uniform Computer Information Transactions Act (UCITA),[5] which sought to produce such a 'one-size-fits all' approach for computer software contracting. While many of the elements of UCITA might have been acceptable in a business-to-business (B2B) bespoke contract, in which the parties were of similar bargaining power, their application in the market for mass-produced software both for individuals and smaller business organisations would have signally altered the relationship between suppliers and acquirers in favour of the major software companies.[6]

See Chapter
11 →

The extent to which defects can be eliminated from software is another controversial subject. On the one hand, a large proportion of the software industry, and many commentators, argue that eliminating defects is effectively impossible because:

- modern software packages are simply too complex, involving millions of lines of source code, often written by teams of programmers, and frequently constructed using pre-existing code to reduce development time and cost;[7]
- software packages have to interact with computer operating systems and other software, as well as a range of hardware produced by different manufacturers, and the variations in environment that result from this make it impossible to ensure that a software package will work correctly in all circumstances;[8] and
- it is simply commercially infeasible for software vendors to attempt to eliminate all software defects prior to delivery – defect risk assessment and beta testing are thus seen as the most effective means of avoiding potential liability, rather than seeking to produce perfect software.[9]

In the words of the drafters of the UCITA:

> Merchantability does not require a perfect program, but only . . . the average standards applicable in commerce for programs having the particular type of use. The presence of some defects may be consistent with merchantability standards . . . While perfection is an aspiration, it is not a requirement of an implied warranty for goods, computer programs or any other property. Indeed, a perfect program may not be possible at all.

---

5 Uniform Computer Information Transactions Act (UCITA), available online at www.law.upenn.edu/bll/archives/ulc/ucita/ucita200.pdf
6 See, eg, Nim Razook, 'The politics and promise of UCITA' (2003) 36(4) Creighton L Rev 667; Louise Longdin, 'Liability for defects in bespoke software' (2000) 8(1) Int JLIT 1.
7 See, eg, Longdin, op cit, 9.
8 See, eg, Seldon J Childers, 'Don't stop the music: No strict products liability for embedded software' (2008) 19(1) U Fla JL & Pub Pol'y 125, 153.
9 See, eg, Longdin, op cit, 11.

> In the late 1990's, a popular operating system program for small computers used by both
> consumers and commercial licensees contained over ten million lines of code or instructions.
> In a computer, these instructions interact with each other and with code and operations of
> other programs . . . Most computer programs not only have many lines of code, but must utilize
> and interact with code in third-party programs, further multiplying the possible interactions. It
> is often literally impossible or commercially unreasonable to guarantee that software of any
> complexity contains no errors that might cause unexpected behavior or intermittent malfunc-
> tions, so-called 'bugs.' The presence of minor errors is fully within common expectations.[10]

On the other hand, critics argue that while eliminating all software defects may be impossible, software companies could do significantly more to reduce software defects. Software defects may not be
wholly preventable, they argue, but mass-market software suppliers are willing to ship software with
known defects and often do not react expeditiously to remedy serious defects (for example, security
flaws) when these become known to them.[11] Focusing on the argument that software cannot be
'perfect', when considering contractual or tortious liability for defective software, is thus to miss the
point that software developers are capable of producing software with *fewer* key defects. However, they
have little incentive to invest in doing so, because, at present, they are able to avoid many of the financial consequences, which are instead passed on to their customers and often, indirectly, to the wider
public.[12] It is suggested that the fact that legislatures and the courts have not been inclined to place
greater responsibility for defective software upon software companies[13] helps to create a situation in
which there is no economic advantage for software companies that seek to improve their production
standards. Thus, in the mass-market environment, in which there is commercial advantage to be
gained by regularly producing new versions of software and providing new software features, there
is little incentive to increase production costs and slow development by seeking to prevent or to
eliminate defects if there is little or no economic penalty for failing to do so. This has led for calls for
greater legal liability for defects, particularly in areas in which the software is mission-critical or in
which significant harm is caused as a result of security breaches facilitated by software defects.[14]

Bugs and Breaches

One of the fundamental issues in relation to system supply contracts is that of the relationship of
bugs to breaches – that is, when a bug (or bugs) will constitute a breach. That point will be
addressed below and is the focus of this section. First, however, the point should briefly be made
that it may be necessary to distinguish between a 'bug' and something that the acquirer perceives
as a problem with the software, but which is the absence of a function that the supplier did not set
out to provide, because it was never specified by the acquirer. The point was recognised in *Cooperative
Group v International Computers Ltd*:[15]

> 197 . . . A bug is, when reduced to its essentials, a respect in which software does not perform
> as expected. In considering what was expected one has to have regard to what was specified as

---

10 National Conference of Commissioners on Uniform State Laws, Uniform Computer Information Transactions Act (2002),
    Comment on s 403 UCITA, available online at www.law.upenn.edu/bll/archives/ulc/ucita/2002final.htm
11 See, eg, David Rice, *Geekonomics: The Real Cost of Insecure Software*, 2008, London: Addison Wesley.
12 Frances E Zollers, Andrew McMullin, Sandra N Hurd, and Peter Shears, 'No more soft landings for software: Liability for defects
    in an industry that has come of age' (2005) 21(4) CHTLJ 745.
13 And indeed have sometimes expressly reduced the impact of any potential liability, eg, the US Year 2000 Computer Date Change
    Act 2000, cited in Kevin R Pinkney, 'Putting blame where blame is due: Software manufacturer and customer liability for
    security-related software failure' (2003) 13(1) Alb LJ Sci & Tech 43.
14 For example, Pinkney, op cit; Rustad, op cit; Rice, op cit; Zollers et al, op cit; Michael D Scott, 'Tort liability for vendors of
    insecure software: Has the time finally come?' (2008) 67(2) Md L Rev 425.
15 *Cooperative Group v International Computers Ltd* [2003] EWHC1 (TCC).

the functionality to be provided. Vagueness of wording of the relevant specification is the first area in which different assessors may reach different conclusions as to whether a supposed bug really is a bug or not. A conclusion that what it is said the software should do was not covered by the specification as written could lead to the view either that what was complained of was not a bug at all, or that it was really a request for the software to be modified to provide a different functionality, in other words, a change.

However, as has been indicated, the primary focus here is on identifying when a bug will be a breach. The starting point is the comment of Steyn J in *Eurodynamic Systems plc v General Automation Ltd*[16] that:

> . . . The expert evidence convincingly showed that it is regarded as acceptable practice to supply computer programmes (including system software) that contain errors and bugs.

> . . . Not every bug or error in a computer programme can therefore be categorised as a breach of contract . . .

This makes the point that not every error or bug will be a breach, but does not tell us *when* a bug will be a breach. It raises the issue of the extent to which industry practice should help in determining when a breach will occur.[17] These issues were examined in the cases of *Saphena Computing v Allied Collection Agencies*,[18] *St Alban's City and Distinct Council v International Computers Ltd*,[19] and *SAM Business Systems v Hedley & Co*.[20] In *Saphena*, the supplier had contracted to supply an 'online' computer system for a debt collection agency. However, it was unable to make the software function as required. Due to the delays, the parties agreed to terminate the contractual arrangements by mutual consent. The acquirer then sought to use a third party to correct the problems with the system. As a result, Saphena brought proceedings for, amongst other things, breach of contract by the acquirer for non-payment for the software. One of the issues considered by the court was whether Saphena's failure to correct the bugs meant that it was itself in breach.

Expert testimony was adduced by Saphena as to the software development process: this suggested that it was commonly understood that the supply of bespoke software would involve 'a process of feedback and reassessment' between buyer and seller, with the buyer running 'acceptance tests' to ensure that the program worked as the buyer intended and feeding information back to the supplier. For a variety of reasons, it was often the case that software was not initially as required, and that modification and retesting until a satisfactory solution was achieved was the norm. Staughton LJ noted that this testimony was largely uncontested and that it appeared to be a normal expectation that delivery of bespoke software was not a single transaction, but involved a period of testing and modification. As such, he decided that Saphena had both the right and the duty under the contract to test and modify the software, subject to a reasonable time limit.

It was decided that the termination agreement between the parties included an agreement that the supplier was not liable for any defects unremedied at the point of termination. In the absence of such an agreement, there would appear to have been two possible outcomes:

- where the acquirer has not made plain, and not made part of the contract, something that he or she wanted the software to do, then failing to provide that function cannot be a breach of contract by the supplier;

---

16 *Eurodynamic Systems plc v General Automation Ltd* (1988) unreported, 6 September.
17 See, for a broader discussion of this issue, Elizabeth Macdonald, 'Bugs and breaches' (2005) 13(1) Int JLIT 118; Dominic Callaghan and Carol O'Sullivan, 'Who should bear the cost of software bugs?' (2005) 21(1) CLSR 56.
18 *Saphena Computing v Allied Collection Agencies* [1995] FSR 616.
19 *St Alban's City and District Council v International Computers Ltd* [1996] 4 All ER 481.
20 *SAM Business Systems v Hedley & Co* [2003] 1 All ER (Comm) 465.

- where the software is not performing the functions specified in the contract, the court will look to the stage of the contract that had been reached prior to the termination of an agreement, to determine whether the bugs, at that point in the development process, would lead to the conclusion that the supplier was in breach.

The *St Albans* case also involved the use of software in a developmental stage. In this case, ICL contracted to provide St Albans Council with software to implement the collection of the Community Charge. However, during this developmental stage, the software was required to be used to determine the number of charge payers, a requirement imposed on the Council by legislation. The Council's invitation to tender, which ICL had accepted, stated that the system supplied should enable the Council to comply with a number of known and, at that time, unknown legislative measures. The software proved unable to determine the number of charge payers accurately, overstating the number of charge payers in the council's area, resulting in the Council losing significant sums of money. ICL sought to avoid liability by arguing, following *Saphena*, that there could be no breach because the software was still in development.

Nourse LJ was unpersuaded by this line of argument, noting that even if the parties knew that the software was still in the process of development when supplied, if the performance of specific functions was clearly required by the contract, at a particular stage of development, then the developer could not avoid the obligation to provide these. ICL had agreed to express contractual terms that required the system to make an accurate return of the number of charge payers by a particular date and had failed to achieve this.

Thus, while *Saphena* saw judicial acceptance that software might still contain bugs during its developmental phase and that this phase might continue for a 'reasonable' time without constituting an actionable breach, *St Albans* makes it clear that, even during a development stage, a supplier cannot use this as a reason for failing to meet an express contractual requirement of particular performance at a particular time.

In *SAM Business Systems*, the supplier was providing a standard software package for use by the acquirer in its stockbroking business. The software consisted of a ready-made package of software modules made by SAM for stockbrokers and others, which, while not an 'off-the-shelf' package, was sold as a developed package with some customisable elements. While the package worked well for other clients of the supplier, it proved unsuitable for Hedley & Co. The supplier sought to rely on dicta in *Saphena*, arguing that while the package had 'admitted bugs', these should be expected in a software package. The judge rejected that contention, noting that, in *Saphena*, 'the court was dealing with an undeveloped system which was sold with bugs "warts and all" ', and that even in *St Albans*, in which a bespoke system was being developed, the court had held that the supplier had to supply software capable of meeting the requirements expected of it at the time of supply.

He noted that this case, however, concerned a software package that was being sold on the basis that it was being used successfully elsewhere. In such circumstances, it did not seem unreasonable to expect that a system should have no bugs at all, and if it did, that these should be treated as defects. The question then would be whether the plaintiffs suffered consequential loss as a result of the defects: if the defects were quickly addressed without extra cost to the buyer, then there would be less likelihood of consequential loss.

In essence, the contrasts between *St Albans*, *Saphena*, and the *SAM Business Systems* case make the point that whether a bug is a breach will depend upon what the parties contracted for, and whether a system is 'in development' or 'tried and tested'; even if a system is 'in development', it may have to satisfy certain requirements at certain stages of that process. However, that then raises the issue of establishing for what the parties *did* contract – a point that will be considered below, when the terms of the contract are considered further. Here, a few preliminary points can be made. First, in relation to the point made in *SAM Business Systems* about 'tried and tested systems' and bugs: should the situation really be regarded as one in which the system should not have any bugs in it and, if there are any bugs, should they be regarded' as breaches? In *Morgan and Stedman on Computer Contracts*, a point is made of the incidence of bugs in even 'the most widely used software':

> . . . even the best designed and tested programs are liable to cough at totally unexpected data. Indeed some of the most best known and most widely used software is known to be subject to a large number of bugs, albeit few which have a material impact on the overall operation of the software. . . . It may be said that there is no such thing as an absolutely perfect program . . . Having said this, it is obvious that there are . . . eminently usable programs and appallingly unusable ones.[21]

It would seem that if the difficulty of eliminating bugs were to be taken into account, it would be unlikely that any software or system supplier entering into B2B contracts would be found by a court to have guaranteed a total absence of bugs from its software, in the absence of the most explicit statement, even if the system has been said to be 'tried and tested'. This may be borne out to some extent by the lack of recent reported case law on the point, not to mention being reinforced in the business-to-consumer (B2C) environment by the average home computer user's increasing familiarity with internet-delivered 'high-priority updates', 'service packs', and 'security patches'.[22]

However, having referred to 'general knowledge', some consideration should be given to the courts' use of 'expert evidence' regarding, for example, 'acceptable practice'[23] or what 'necessarily' has to occur in the development of software.[24] In the absence of an (unlikely) guarantee of an absence of bugs, what will often be in question in determining whether there has been a breach will be the meeting of some general standard by the software (although there may also be express terms dealing with specific areas of the functionality of the program, such as speed). That general standard is likely to be 'reasonable fitness for the buyer's particular purpose', whether that is arrived at under s 14(3) of the **SoGA 1979**, expressly, or by implication at common law. In any event, any 'general standard' is likely to have some dependence upon what is reasonable in the relevant circumstances, whether those circumstances are the 'buyer's particular purpose' or otherwise. It is understandable that, in attempting to set such a general objective level of performance, the courts should turn to the views of experts and industry practice. The concern must be, however, that low standards can thereby propagate themselves and enjoy the protection of a finding that following them will not produce a breach of contract. In the words of Minasi:

> . . . 90 percent of bugs consumers report to software vendors are already known to the vendors. . . . fully 15 percent – one in seven – of software firms surveyed about software quality said that they regularly shipped out software that they'd never even tested.
>
> Try to imagine even the possibility of this in other industries.[25]

Contracting for Software

When discussing the application of the law of contract to the acquisition of software, it is worth noting that only a very limited number of cases dealing specifically with software have reached the High Court or higher courts. As will be seen below, these cases have dealt almost (if not entirely) exclusively with

---

21 Richard Morgan and Kit Burden, *Morgan and Burden on Computer Contracts*, 8th edn, 2009, London: Sweet & Maxwell, pp 8–9.
22 Since March 2007, the author's own PC, running Windows XP, has had no fewer than 650 such 'updates' for Microsoft products alone.
23 *Eurodynamic Systems*, above.
24 *Saphena Computing*, above.
25 Mark Minasi, *The Software Conspiracy*, 2000, New York: McGraw Hill, p 6.

circumstances involving either bespoke software or software customised to a purchaser's requirements. Additionally, they have involved B2B contracts between parties that were in a position to enter into detailed contractual negotiations (even if they, in fact, did not do so), if not on equal terms, then at least in circumstances in which they were in a position to draw upon expert technical and legal advice (even if they, in fact, did not). This has a number of consequences for those seeking to determine the likely outcome of contractual disputes for defect software. First, the software-specific case law in UK contract law answers few of the key legal (or policy) questions pertaining to liability for defects in mass-market software. Second, in circumstances involving software of any kind, the lack of case law means that while commentators can, of course, point to precedents involving other types of good and service, the unique nature and role of software may cause these to appear of dubious relevance, even to the lay reader. Finally, the speed of technological change means that commonly held understandings key to existing precedents (for example, that software is usually provided to a purchaser in a tangible medium, or that there might be a 'bright line' between a 'developmental' and 'tried and tested' software package) may simply no longer hold true (wireless networks are an unconvincing tangible medium, while an operating system that requires three 'service packs' in six years, and then additional security patches, seems difficult to characterise as 'tried and tested'). This section should be read with those caveats in mind.

Pre-contractual Statements: Terms and Misrepresentations

In most circumstances in which software is purchased, there may be discussions between the supplier and the acquirer as to the needs of the acquirer and whether the software will fulfil them. Such discussions are most likely in relation to bespoke or modified standard software. If, after the acquisition, the acquirer is unhappy with the software, disputes may arise as to what was said about it and the legal effect of any such statements. The acquirer may claim that the supplier is liable, on the basis that the pre-contractual statements became terms, or that they were misrepresentations. Such claims have occurred in relation to the acquisition of software and computer systems: for example, *Micron Computer Systems Ltd v Wang*[26] and *Mackenzie Patten & Co v British Olivetti Ltd*.[27] These two possible bases of liability should be considered.

Pre-contractual Statements Becoming Terms

The question of whether a pre-contractual statement has become a term usually centres on whether the statement was a mere representation or a warranty.[28] The basic test for whether a pre-contractual statement became a term of the contract is the intention of the parties[29] and that intention is objectively ascertained.[30] 'Intention' is not always easy to ascertain. However, certain indicators of the parties' intention have been focused on by the courts, such as where it is clear to both parties that the statement in question is key to the decision to contract.[31]

In the context of software contracts, the indicators that are most likely to be relevant are reliance and the relative expertise of the parties: for example, where one party relies on the statements of the other party and that other party possesses the greater expertise. Case law suggests that, in such circumstances, the courts regard the expertise of one party as relevant to the question of whether a statement has become a term.[32] This is illustrated by *Mackenzie Patten & Co v British Olivetti Ltd*.[33] In that

---

26 *Micron Computer Systems Ltd v Wang* (1990) unreported, 9 May.

27 *Mackenzie Patten & Co v British Olivetti Ltd* (1984) unreported, 11 January.

28 'Warranty' can be used in more than one sense. In this context, it is used simply to mean a term.

29 For example, *Heilbut, Symons & Co v Buckleton* [1913] AC 30.

30 For example, *Thake v Maurice* [1986] 1 All ER 497.

31 For example, *Bannerman v White* (1861) 10 CBNS 844.

32 See, eg, *Oscar Chess Ltd v Williams* [1957] 1 All ER 325 (party making the representation clearly had no particular knowledge or expertise); *Dick Bentley Productions Ltd v Harold Smith (Motors) Ltd* [1965] 2 All ER 65 (party making the representation had, or should have had, the particular knowledge or expertise).

33 *Mackenzie Patten*, above.

case, a solicitors' practice purchased hardware and software. The purchasers had no expertise or knowledge of computers, and relied on the seller's statements as to its suitability for their needs and as to the functions that it could perform. It proved unsuitable and could not perform one of the functions that the solicitors had wanted. The solicitors sued, claiming both breach of a term and misrepresentation. They succeeded on the basis that the seller's statements had become terms of the contract. The judge emphasised the purchasers' lack of expertise and reliance on that of the seller.[34] The remedy, as is usually the case for breach of contract, was damages.

Pre-contractual Statements as Misrepresentations

A misrepresentation requires a statement of existing or past fact by the misrepresentor to the misrepresentee that induces the misrepresentee to contract with the misrepresentor. In other words, what is needed is a pre-contractual statement of fact by one party to the other on which that other party relies in deciding to contract.[35] As already noted, reliance may well be present where there is an imbalance of knowledge or expertise, as there often will be in the acquisition of software. The point that needs to be considered here, because of its particular relevance to the situation in which advice is being given on the suitability of software, is the division between statements of opinion and statements of fact.

For a misrepresentation to be found, there must be a statement of fact; statements of opinion or intention will not suffice.[36] However, the courts have been willing to find statements of fact where, at first sight, there appears to be merely a statement of opinion or intention, such as where what is stated to be one party's intention or opinion is not in fact that party's intention or opinion – there is thus a misrepresentation that the party has that intention[37] or holds that opinion. The courts have also been willing to find statements of fact where what is apparently merely a statement of opinion is made by an expert or the person who is in the best position to assess the situation.[38] This type of argument might prove relevant in relation to a software contract. In that context, it is likely to be the statement of an expert that is in question and the implied statement of fact there would seem to be that the expert has properly used his or her expertise in forming his or her opinion.[39]

A misrepresentation makes a contract voidable and so the contract can be rescinded, provided that one of the bars to rescission is not operative.[40] Damages can also be claimed for misrepresentation. If the case is one in which the misrepresentation involves fraud, the tort action for deceit can be used. Alternatively, damages may be available because the situation is covered by the tort action for negligent misstatement,[41] or because it falls within the ambit of s 2(1) of the **Misrepresentation Act 1967**:

> Where a person has entered into a contract after a misrepresentation has been made to him by another party thereto and as a result thereof he has suffered loss, then, if the person making the misrepresentation would be liable to damages in respect thereof had the misrepresentation been made fraudulently, that person shall be so liable notwithstanding that the misrepresentation was not made fraudulently, unless he proves that he had reasonable ground to believe and did believe up to the time the contract was made the facts represented were true.

---

34 The alternative claim, based on misrepresentation, was not addressed by the judge once he had found for the purchasers on the basis of a breach.
35 For example, *Smith v Chadwick* (1884) 9 App Cas 187.
36 For example, *Bissett v Wilkinson* [1927] AC 177
37 For example, *Edgington v Fitzmaurice* (1885) 29 Ch D 459.
38 For example, *Brown v Raphael* [1958] 1 Ch 636.
39 For example, *Esso Petroleum Co Ltd v Mardon* [1976] QB 801.
40 See further Laurence Koffman and Elizabeth Macdonald, *The Law of Contract*, 7th edn, 2010, Oxford: Oxford University Press, paras 13.68–13.83.
41 *Hedley Byrne and Co Ltd v Heller & Partners Ltd* [1964] AC 465.

All of the actions for damages, including that under s 2(1),[42] will result in damages being calculated on the tortious, rather than the contractual, basis: they will put the injured party in the position in which he or she would have been had the misrepresentation not occurred – that is, their pre-contractual position.[43]

The action under s 2(1) will normally be the most favourable of the actions for damages. Obviously, the common law action for negligent misstatement merely requires the injured party to prove negligence, rather than the fraud that has to be established for the action for deceit, although the action for negligent misstatement will also require proof of a duty of care. However, the action under s 2(1) is generally the easiest for the injured party to use. Under s 2(1), it is for the person who made the misrepresentation to prove that he or she reasonably believed in the truth of what was being asserted – that is, it is for the misrepresentor to disprove negligence under this action, reversing the burden of proof from that applicable under the action for negligent misstatement[44] – and, of course, no duty of care is required.

Entire Agreement Clauses[45]

'Entire' or 'whole agreement' clauses are widely used boilerplate clauses, which aim to determine the scope of the contract and to ensure that there are no terms additional to those contained in a specified contractual document or documents. In addition, they may well also aim to ensure that there is no potential for liability for misrepresentation in relation to any pre-contractual statements that have not become part of the terms stated in such documents. For example:

> The parties agree that these terms and conditions . . . represent the entire agreement between the parties . . . and that no statement or representations made by either party have been relied upon by the other in agreeing to enter into the Contract.[46]

In the context of a software or system contract – particularly one dealing with software or a system that is to be developed or adapted for the acquirer, in which the identification of the obligations undertaken, or representations made, by the supplier is particularly important – such clauses are likely to be incorporated and may play a key role. While there have been some indications of a willingness to question whether these clauses produce the effect that they set out to achieve,[47] the trend has been to place emphasis upon the certainty achieved by such clauses and to see them as effective.[48]

Case law suggests that, in the context of whether a pre-contractual statement becomes a term, a very mechanical approach is being taken by the courts. The entire agreement clause is often taken at face value without even any question of conflicting terms being raised. The certainty produced by this approach is emphasised.[49]

Thus the approach in relation to misrepresentations is somewhat different, with 'evidential estoppel' being used to prevent any successful claim that, in addition to those specified, there was a (mis)representation on which a party relied. Such an approach does have more potential for examination of the circumstances and a conclusion that there was a (mis)representation despite the clause. This is because of the requirements for an evidential estoppel. In this context, they can be identified as that the:

---

42 *Royscott Trust Ltd v Rogerson* [1991] 3 All ER 294.
43 See *Robinson v Harman* (1880) 5 App Cas 25, 35, per Parke B.
44 See *Howard Marine & Dredging Co Ltd v A Ogden & Sons (Excavations) Ltd* [1978] QB 574.
45 See further, Gerard McMeel, 'Construction of contracts and the role of "entire agreement" clauses' (2008) 3(1) CMLJ 58.
46 *Watford Electronics Ltd v Sanderson CFL Ltd* [2001] EWCA Civ 317.
47 See further Macdonald, op cit.
48 *Inntrepreneur v East Crown* [2000] 2 Lloyd's Rep 61, per Lightman J.
49 *Watford Electronics*, above, per Chadwick LJ, citing *EA Grimstead & Son Ltd v McGarrigan* (1999) unreported, 27 October.

- statements (that is, as to non-reliance on the (mis)representation) in the clause were clear and unequivocal;
- representee had intended that the representor would act upon those statements (as to non-reliance); and
- representor had believed those statements (as to non-reliance) to be true and had acted upon them.[50]

The difficulties that may arise in fulfilling those requirements are plain when it is emphasised that the 'statements' as to non-reliance that are in question will usually be in a standard-form contract produced by the representor. They are being used to claim that the representee has so asserted his or her non-reliance that he or she is estopped from proving that he or she relied on the representation. Those requirements for an evidential estoppel may present difficulties, not least because it may be difficult for party A, who has made representations on which A intended that B should rely, to satisfy the court that he or she entered into the contract in the belief that a statement by B that B had not relied upon those representations was true.[51]

Given the potential impact of entire agreement clauses, it is unsurprising that the courts have considered, at least in relation to B2B contracts, the impact of legislation on such clauses. There is some debate over the application of the **Unfair Contract Terms Act 1977 (UCTA 1977)** to an 'entire agreement' clause, but it appears, following *SAM Business Systems*, that the 1977 Act would apply, with the court adopting the traditional approach of weighing up the 'reasonableness' factors set out in that Act together with all of the circumstances of the case.[52]

Equally, it appears that any contractual clause that has the effect of preventing a party from pursuing a claim for misrepresentation could be treated as an exclusion clause falling within s 3 of the **Misrepresentation Act 1967** (below) and subject to the reasonableness test as set out in of the **UCTA 1977**:[53]

If a contract contains a term that would exclude or restrict—

(a)   any liability to that a party to a contract may be subject by reason of any misrepresentation made by him before the contract was made; or
(b)   any remedy available to another party to the contract by reason of such a misrepresentation,

that term shall be of no effect except in so far as it satisfies the requirement of reasonableness as stated in section 11(1) of the Unfair Contract Terms Act 1977; and it is for those claiming that the term satisfies that requirement to show that it does.

However, it is possible to argue that because of the requirements for an evidential estoppel, there is less scope, and less need for the application of s 3 of the **Misrepresentation Act 1967** to a clause setting out to generate such an estoppel in relation to any (mis)representations.[54]

With regard to B2C contracts, the **Unfair Terms in Consumer Contracts Regulations 1999**[55] (see below) should be considered. They relate only to non-individually negotiated terms in

---

50   See *Grimstead v McGarrigan*, above; *Lowe v Lombank* [1960] 1 All ER 611.
51   McMeel, op cit, 73.
52   *SAM Business Systems*, above. It should be noted that a key determination of 'reasonableness' in this case was the fact that the supplier provided the customer with a money-back guarantee if the customer rejected the goods within a short acceptance period. This was regarded as a fair balance for the exclusion of liability, given the enormous potential liabilities: see Katie Landeryou, 'Interpretation of software contracts: *SAM Business Systems Limited v Hedley and Company*' (2003) 19(4) CLSR 311.
53   See *Peart Stevenson Associates Ltd v Holland* [2008] EWHC 1868 (QB), citing obiter statements of Bridge LJ and Scarman LJ in *Cremdean Properties Ltd v Nash* (1977) 241 EG 837.
54   See ibid, citing obiter statements of Chadwick LJ in *EA Grimstead & Son Ltd*, above, and *Watford Electronics Ltd*, above.
55   SI 1999/2083.

contracts between consumers and sellers or suppliers, but, in that consumer context, they are not restricted to a particular type of term, such as exemption clauses. In other words, entire agreement clauses are covered by the Regulations without any need to try to categorise them as exemption clauses. Many such terms will fall within the Regulations' 'grey list' of terms that 'may be unfair' (Sch 2, para 1(n)) and in the first Office of Fair Trading (OFT) bulletin on the operation of the Regulations, entire agreement clauses were identified as amongst the unfair terms most commonly encountered by the OFT.[56]

System/Software Specifications

Contracts to develop software, or a computer system, for a particular business often create the most difficult problems in relation to the contents of the contract. A large part of the contract is likely simply to be the supplier's standard terms, encompassing, for example, its entire agreement clauses and standard exemption clauses.

Here, we are concerned with the terms that will be more particular to the individual contract: the specification of the software/system. A particular difficulty with development contracts is identifying exactly what the acquiring party requires. As part of the contracting process, the parties should draw up a detailed functional specification, which then becomes part of the contract. This should state, in detail, what the proposed software will do. The importance of this was indicated above in the discussion of when bugs will amount to breaches, as, ultimately, that will depend upon what the contract terms required. However, it may not be easy to draw up such specification – the software developer is an expert in software and what can be done with it, but he or she is not an expert in the acquirer's business, whatever that may be, and it is obvious that problems may arise from this information gap. The acquirer may end up with a system that does not do some of what he or she needed it to do because those needs have not been explained to the software developer. In *Micron Computer Systems Ltd v Wang (UK) Ltd*,[57] the purchaser of a system had expected the system to perform what he termed 'transaction logging'; it did not do so. It was found that this did not mean that the system was in breach of a term that it should be 'reasonably fit' for the buyer's particular purpose. The buyer had never made known to the seller that 'transaction logging' was required. As was indicated above, when the software, or system, does not do what the acquirer expected, the question prior to whether a bug is a breach is whether there is a bug at all – that is, whether those expectations of the acquirer were reflected in the contract specification.

When development of software, or a system, is in question, what is required at any particular stage of the development may need to be considered. The relationship between the stage of development and the bugs remaining will need to be considered if the question of breach arises whilst the software/system is still 'in development'. The point was made above, in *Saphena Computing*,[58] that no breach was found at the stage of development at which the parties agreed to terminate their contract. However, as we have seen, in *St Albans*, in dismissing submissions that the suppliers had not breached, which were based on the line taken by Staughton LJ in *Saphena*, Nourse LJ said:

> Parties who respectively agree to supply and acquire a system recognising that it is still in the course of development cannot be taken, merely by virtue of that recognition, to intend that the supplier shall be at liberty to supply software which cannot perform the function expected of it at the stage of development at which it is supplied.[59]

---

56 Office of Fair Trading (OFT), *Unfair Standard Terms*, OFT Bulletin No 1, May 1996, London: HMSO, p 19, para 1.18, cited in Ruth Atkins, 'Computer contracts: Capturing requirements and apportioning responsibilities' (2003) 17(2) IRLCT 219.
57 *Micron Computer*, above; see also *Anglo Group Plc v Winther Browne & Co Ltd* [2000] 72 Con LR 118, discussed in Atkins, op cit, 223–4.
58 *Saphena*, above.
59 *St Albans*, above, 487.

Further, because, at the time when a contract is made, it may be difficult for the parties to define accurately the software required, particularly when a development contract is in question, contracts may well need to be modified before their performance is completed. This was recognised in *Saphena* in which Havery QC regarded the contract as envisaging the modification of the content of the term that the goods should be 'reasonably fit' for the acquirer's particular purpose. He said:

> ... it was an implied term of each contract for the supply of software that the software would be reasonably fit for any purpose which had been communicated to the plaintiff's before the contract was made and for any purpose subsequently communicated, provided in the latter case that the plaintiffs accepted the defendant's instructions to make the relevant modifications. The making of the modifications constitutes or implies acceptance of the instructions ...[60]

The *BSkyB v EDS* Litigation

A recent case that considered in detail several of the issues outlined in this section and elsewhere in the chapter – notably negligent and fraudulent misrepresentation, entire agreement clauses, and exclusion clauses – is that of *BSkyB Ltd and Sky Subscribers Services Ltd v HP Enterprise Services UK Ltd (formerly Electronic Data Systems Ltd) and Electronic Data systems LLC (formerly Electronic Data Systems Corp)*,[61] more commonly referred to as *BSkyB v EDS*.

This case concerned the failed provision by EDS of a new customer relationship management (CRM) system for use in BSkyB's call centres. During the tender process in March 2000, EDS made various representations with regard to its skills in regard to providing such a service, its ability to deliver the project within a tight time frame (nine months to the first-stage 'go live' and 18 months to completion) and the cost (£48 million). This led to EDS's subsidiary EDSL signing a letter of intent with BSkyB in August 2000, followed by a prime contract between BSkyB's subsidiary, SSSL, and EDSL in November 2000.[62]

It rapidly became apparent that EDS was not going to be able to deliver within the time frame, or for the contracted cost.[63] In 2001, the parties sought to renegotiate the contract, the outcome of that was a replanning of delivery, and a Letter of Agreement to supersede the prime contract. Matters still did not improve and, in 2002, BSkyB took over EDS's role under a memorandum of understanding. Legal proceedings began in 2004 and, by the time the case came to court, BSkyB was claiming damages of £709 million, which included the cost of completing the CRM system, loss of profits through failure to retain customers (reduction of 'customer churn'), and loss of savings due to inability to reduce the volume of customer calls to its call centres.

It seems clear that BSkyB could make out a plausible prima facie case against EDS for breach of contract. It alleged that EDS was in breach under both the prime contract,[64] and the letter of agreement[65] for its failure to:

- provide the skilled, experienced, and qualified personnel that the project required;
- deliver what was specified in the prime contract/letter of agreement; and
- exercise reasonable skill and care or conform to good industry practice.

---

60 *Saphena*, above, 644.
61 *BSkyB Ltd and Sky Subscribers Services Ltd v HP Enterprise Services UK Ltd (formerly Electronic Data Systems Ltd) and Electronic Data Systems LLC (formerly Electronic Data Systems Corp)* [2010] EWHC 86 (TCC). See Matthew Lawson and Piers Elliott, 'Reach for the sky' (2010) 154(7) Solicitors Journal 16; Matthew Lawson and Piers Elliott, 'The sky's the limit' (2010) 160(7405) NLJ 257; Duncan McCall and George Woods, 'BSkyB v EDS' (2010) 20(6) Computers & Law 6.
62 For simplicity, the parties will hereafter be referred to throughout as 'BSkyB' and 'EDS'.
63 In fact, the system was not fully functional until 2006, and was estimated to have cost BSkyB £268 million.
64 BSkyB, above, [1223].
65 Ibid, [1257]–[1258].

In his extensive ruling, Mr Justice Ramsay largely concurred with those allegations.[66]

However, bringing an action on those grounds alone was likely to be problematic, because the prime contract contained a limitation clause capping EDS's liability under the contract at an aggregrate £30 million. This meant, first, that BSkyB would not be able to recoup anywhere close to its estimated losses, and second, that the possible cost of litigation might pose too great a financial risk compared to the potential gains. BSkyB thus made additional alternative claims with the aim of avoiding the effect of the limitation clause:

- a claim that there had been intentional misrepresentation and negligent misrepresentation, at common law and under the **Misrepresentation Act 1967**, the latter claim to be covered by the contractual liability cap, but the former tortious claim not (intentional misrepresentation – deceit – would also allow both foreseeable and unforeseeable damages to be recoverable);[67]
- a claim against EDS's subsidiary by BSkyB for intentional and negligent misrepresentation (because BSkyB was not a party to the prime contract, thus avoiding the liability cap); and
- a claim against EDS by BSkyB and its subsidiary for intentional and negligent misrepresentation (because EDS was not a party to the prime contract, thus avoiding the liability cap).

Mr Justice Ramsey held that the last two claims could not be sustained, given the way in which the parties had structured their contractual relationship, referencing prior case law[68] to the effect that '[a]n alternative liability in tort will not be admitted if its effect would be to permit the plaintiff to circumvent or escape a contractual exclusion or limitation of liability for the act or omission that would constitute the tort'.[69] This left the issue of intentional misrepresentation. In order to demonstrate this, BkyB had to show that:

- EDS made a representation;
- the representation was false;
- EDS knew it to be untrue or was reckless as to whether it was true;
- EDS intended that the claimant should act in reliance on the representation; and
- BSkyB relied on the representation to its detriment.[70]

BSkyB alleged that EDS had made intentional misrepresentations in five key areas: the resources, time, and cost that would be required for a successful implementation, the use of proven technology, and EDS's development and use of suitable methodologies for the project. It was eventually held that intentional misrepresentation was made out only with regard to the time required. In large part, this was due to the high standard of proof required to succeed with claims of deceit. As Mr Justice Ramsay noted:

> The court . . . has to determine who made each representation; whether that person was authorised to speak on behalf of the corporation; whether that person had the required state of mind and, if not, whether some other person who directed the representation to be made had the required state of mind. If the person who made the statement or directed it to be made did not have a dishonest state of mind, then the claim for deceit fails.[71]

66 Ibid, [1256] and [1345]–[1346].
67 *Royscot Trust Ltd v Rogerson* [1991] 2 QB 297; BSkyB, [549].
68 *Pacific Associates v Baxter* [1990] 1 QB 993; *Henderson v Merrett* [1995] 2 AC 145; *JP Morgan Chase Bank and ors v Springwell Navigation Corp* [2008] EWHC 1186 (Comm).
69 BSkyB, above, [540]–[543].
70 Ibid, [305].
71 Ibid, [323], citing *Lennards Carrying Co Ltd v Asiatic Petroleum Co Ltd* [1915] AC 705; *El Ajou v Dollar Holdings Plc (No 1)* [1994] 2 All ER 685; *Man Nutzfahrzeuge AG & ors v Freightliner Ltd* [2005] EWHC 2347 (Comm); *Armstrong v Strain* [1952] 1 KB 232.

A key element in the judge's determination that intentional misrepresentation took place related to the testimony of EDS's head of CRM practice, Joe Galloway, who was the lead salesman during the tender process. Mr Galloway's veracity as a witness was severely undermined by the plaintiffs' counsel being able to demonstrate that he had deliberately and repeatedly given perjured evidence during the proceedings. After an extensive analysis of this credibility,[72] the judge noted that '[w]hilst, of course, this does not prove that Joe Galloway made dishonest representations, it is a significant factor which I have to take into account in assessing whether he was dishonest in his dealings with Sky'.[73] This left EDS with an uphill – and ultimately losing – battle to disprove BkyB's allegations of deceit.

In addition to the finding of breaches of contract and fraudulent misstatement, the judge also found that EDS's statements in negotiations with BSkyB, prior to the letter of agreement, amounted to negligent representations that it had developed an achievable plan to complete the project, which had been the product of proper analysis and replanning. The fact that this was not the case, but EDS had intended BSkyB to rely upon it and BSkyB did rely upon it, in entering into the letter of agreement rather than seeking alternative arrangements, resulted in liability for negligent misstatement and under s 2(1) of the **Misrepresentation Act 1967**.

In terms of avoiding liability, EDS had already effectively limited its liability for BSkyB's claims for contractual breach, negligent misrepresentation, or under s 2(1) of the **Misrepresentation Act 1967** to an aggregate £30 million.[74] It also successfully argued that, except for the claims based on deceit, its clause 'neither party shall have any liability to the other party in respect of (i) any consequential or indirect loss or (ii) loss of profits, revenue, business, goodwill and/or anticipated savings' should be read as two separate parts, and not simply as one part referring to indirect losses, thus allowing it to exclude losses that were neither consequential or indirect, such as BSkyB's claim for lost profits and business benefits in respect of failure to achieve reduced call-handling costs, which had been expected as a result of the reduction of the number of staff required to handle customer calls under the new system. However, EDS also attempted to argue that its entire agreement clause excluded liability for negligent misrepresentations. The clause stated:

> . . . this Agreement and the Schedules shall together represent the entire understanding and constitute the whole agreement between the parties in relation to its subject matter and supersede any previous discussions, correspondence, representations or agreement between the parties with respect thereto notwithstanding the existence of any provision of any such prior agreement that any rights or provisions of such prior agreement shall survive its termination. The term 'this Agreement' shall be construed accordingly. This clause does not exclude liability of either party for fraudulent mis-representation.

EDS's argument was based on the premise that the final sentence, referring to the non-exclusion of fraudulent mis-representation, had the strong implication that non-fraudulent misrepresentation was intended to be excluded. This was rejected. Mr Justice Ramsey held that:

> Those words do not, in my judgment, amount to an agreement that representations are withdrawn, overridden or of no legal effect so far as any liability for misrepresentation may be concerned. The provision is concerned with the terms of the Agreement. It provides that the Agreement represents the entire understanding and constitutes the whole agreement. It is in that context that the Agreement supersedes any previous representations. That is, representations are superseded and do not become terms of the Agreement unless they are included in

---

72 BSkyB, [174]–[196].

73 Some legal commentators have suggested that the outcome of the case may carry less precedental weight because of the unusual fact circumstances.

74 BSkyB, [412]–[418].

the Agreement. If it had intended to withdraw representations for all purposes then the language would, in my judgment, have had to go further.[75]

In other words, while it was open to the parties to agree to exclude expressly all non-fraudulent misrepresentations, should they wish to do so, by means of a 'contractual renunciation of the right to rely on anything said or done in the course of the negotiations as giving rise to a ground of complaint, or indeed for any other purpose',[76] such a broad exclusion could not be simply implied from the wording of EDS's entire agreement clause.

Finally, EDS claimed that the letter of agreement that superseded the prime contract, and impliedly settled not only all known and unknown claims that BSkyB had, or might have had, against EDS for any breach of the prime contract, but also any complaints that could be advanced on the basis of breach of contract:

> The terms set out in this letter have been agreed between us, subject to the approval of our respective managements, in full and final settlement of:
>
> (a)   all known claims which SSSL may have against EDS or which EDS may have against SSSL and/or British Sky Broadcasting Group Plc for any breach of the Prime Contract as of the date of both parties signing this letter; and
>
> (b)   all unknown claims which SSSL may have against EDS or which EDS may have against SSSL and/or British Sky Broadcasting Group Plc for any breach of the Prime Contract during the period up to and including 17 June 2001.

This would effectively mean that the tortious claims for deceit and/or negligent misrepresentation would also fall, because the matters relied upon as founding such claims would, if proved, constitute a breach of the warranties and obligations contained in the prime contract.[77] This argument, too, was rejected. Making reference to the principles in *BP Refinery (Westernport) Pty Ltd v Shire of Hastings*,[78] as regards circumstances in which a court will imply terms – notably, the need to give business efficacy to the contract, or that the terms implied must be so obvious that 'it goes without saying' – Mr Justice Ramsey stated that:

See Chapter 11

> The purpose of the settlement was to wipe the slate clean in respect of claims for breach of the Prime Contract. If the parties wished to, they could have incorporated words to include wider claims such as claims which could be advanced by way of breach of contract. They did not do so. It is not for the court to rewrite their bargain . . . If the court re-wrote an exclusion of contractual claims to exclude all claims which could be framed in that way, that would be to change the bargain which the parties had made. There is nothing necessary or obvious in such a term.[79]

The result of the case, at the time of writing, is that EDS has paid £200 million to BSkyB by way of an interim award, although EDS has indicated that it will appeal the judgment. While the case itself does not appear to have changed significantly, or even updated, the law as it stood,[80] it is likely that software suppliers will be reassessing their contractual provisions with regard to non-reliance clauses and waivers of non-contractual remedies. There may also be a move towards greater clarity

75   Ibid, [382].
76   As was the case in *Man Nutzfahrzeuge AG & ors v Freightliner Ltd & ors* [2005] EWHC 2347.
77   BSkyB, [421]–[423].
78   (1978) 52 ALJR 20.
79   BSkyB, [435]–[438].
80   Consider, eg, in the area of IT law, the prior case of *South West Water v ICL* [1999] BLR 420 (misrepresentations about the availability of a subcontractor).

in the planning of large-scale projects – and perhaps even a greater degree of realism on the part of both suppliers and purchasers about achievable timetabling and costs.

There will certainly be notice taken of the time and cost of proceedings. The trial commenced in October 2007. The hearing took place over 110 days across almost a whole court year. It involved over 500,000 documents and 70 witnesses, and the court bundle comprised some 400 files. When the hearing concluded in July 2008, the 468-page judgment took a further 18 months to emerge. This is likely to have implications for the desire of companies to find themselves engaging in such litigation. It may also be the beginning of the end for the long-standing view that, because IT projects are inherently risky, a failure to meet represented timings and costs even by significant margins can still fall within acceptable business practice.

Terms: Is Software a Good or a Service (or both)?

A contractual claim concerning defective software is likely to require judicial consideration of whether terms should be implied into the contract under one of the statutory regimes. The **SoGA 1979**, for example, implies terms that goods must correspond with their description (s 13) and sample (s 15), and that they should be of satisfactory quality (s. 14(2)) and reasonably fit for the buyer's particular purpose (s 14(3)). Sections 8–10 of the **Supply of Goods and Services Act 1982 (SGSA 1982)** imply similar terms into contracts for the hire of goods, and s 13 implies a term into a contract for services that the services will be carried out with reasonable care and skill. Obviously, if applicable, such terms could be very helpful to someone seeking damages for defects in a program, but, before the content and application of those terms is considered, there is a major issue to be addressed – that is, the classification of contracts for the supply of software. Can a contract for the supply of software constitute a contract for the sale of goods? Even if software can be described as 'goods', would a contract for its supply be better classified as a contract for services? Once that is resolved, consideration can be given to the content of these types of terms.

However, two initial points should be made. First, even if a software contract is not seen to fit within one of the statutory regimes, software may well be found to be subject to the same type of implied terms at common law – particularly the requirement of reasonable fitness for the acquirer's particular purpose. Second, it would seem that a contract for the supply of a system involving both hardware and software will be categorised as one for the supply of goods (unless the services element dominates the particular contract).[81] These two points mean that the content of the implied terms should be considered even if software itself cannot be categorised as goods.

The central question addressed below is whether software can be 'goods', but some initial points should be made to clarify the discussion. Programs are still commonly supplied on a disk or other such medium, and the focus will be on that method of supply. Unless otherwise indicated, references to 'software' will be to programs on disks. It will be made clear when what is being looked at is the treatment of any program that has been downloaded via a network.

Goods: Definition and Arguments

The starting point for considering whether software can be goods should be the statutory definition of 'goods'. Section 61 of the **SoGA 1979** states: ' "Goods" includes all personal chattels other than things in action and money . . .' One argument is that a computer program cannot be goods, because it is, in nature, information and not a 'personal chattel'. Another is that it is intellectual property and so is covered by the exclusion from the definition of 'things in action'. These two arguments should be considered and then further arguments will be addressed.

---

81 *Toby Constructions Products Pty Ltd v Computa Bar (Sales) Pty Ltd* [1983] NSWLR 48; *St Albans*, above.

Software as Information

It is clear that software consists of information in the form of the particularly arrangement of source code. Following the line of reasoning in *Oxford v Moss*[82] (in which confidential information was held not to be 'property' within the meaning of s 4 of the **Theft Act 1968**), it seems plausible that, despite its having clear value, which is recognised in law via the medium of intellectual property rights, software should therefore not be considered as goods in the context of sale of goods.[83] However, when a program is embodied on a computer disk or other such medium, the argument that it is simply information can be challenged from two perspectives: the physical; and the functional.

(a)   *Physical/tangible* There has been relatively little discussion of the physical or tangible nature of software in the UK case law compared, in particular, to the USA.[84] The physical argument – that the program has physical form on the disk or other such medium – was recognised indirectly in Sir Iain Glidewell's obiter comments in the *St Albans* case.[85] It was also employed in the criminal case of *R v Whiteley*,[86] in which the question was whether the alteration and deletion of computer files by a 'hacker' could constitute criminal damage within s 1(1) of the **Criminal Damage Act 1971**. The court held that deletion or alteration of computer data imposed a physical change in the nature of the disks (the rearrangement of magnetic particles), and this change could be considered 'damage' for the purpose of the Act. This reasoning suggests that software could be considered to have a physical manifestation in the media in which it is stored.

However, neither case provides convincing support for the idea that software itself has a physical or tangible form, and the concept is further undermined by the ability to acquire software across a network, such as the internet, with no obvious storage mechanism. The *coup de grâce* must surely be delivered to such notions by the wireless network, in which not only the software, but also the very transfer mechanism by which it is acquired is intangible.

(b)   *Functional.* The second point to be raised against the argument that software cannot be goods because it is information, is that based on its functional aspect. It should be asked whether a program, embodied on a disk and ready to be fed into a computer, is merely information. Is it distinguishable from the exam paper in *Oxford v Moss*,[87] which was referred to by Scott? If a program is likened to a literary work, which is the categorisation applied to it to provide it with the protection of copyright, then it is most like an instruction manual or 'how to' book, which was the analogy made by Sir Iain Glidewell in *St Albans*. Certainly, software is not like a novel! However, a program differs from even an instruction manual. It does not simply tell the individual what to do; the software interacts directly, with the hardware. In *St Albans*, at first instance, Scott Baker J was of the opinion that software 'is not simply abstract information like information passed by word of mouth. Entering software alters the contents of the hardware'.[88] This may not be an entirely accurate view of the effect of software on hardware, but the general idea is clear enough: software is not mere information; rather it has a direct effect on hardware. Another point can also be made, following on from this. If there is a defect in software, there may well not be a point at which an individual has an opportunity to exercise judgment, assess what is occurring, and intervene to prevent some unexpected, and unwanted, result. Software may be information, but it is not simply information.

---

82 *Oxford v Moss* [1978] 68 Cr App R 183.
83 See further Andrew Scott, 'Software as goods: *Nullum simile est idem*' (1987) 4 CL & P 133.
84 Ken Moon, 'The nature of computer programs: Tangible? Goods? Personal property? Intellectual property?' (2009) 31(8) EIPR 396, 398–400.
85 *St Albans*, above.
86 *R v Whiteley* (1991) 93 Cr App R 25, per Lord Lane LCJ; see also *Cox v Riley* [1986] CLR 460. The type of situation that was considered in *Whiteley* was taken outside the scope of the Criminal Damage Act 1971 by the Computer Misuse Act 1990. See further discussion in Chapter 4.
87 *Oxford v Moss* (1978) 68 Cr App R 183.
88 *St Albans v ICL* [1995] FSR 686, 699.

An analogy can be made here with the US case of *Winter v G P Puttnam & Sons* decided in the Court of Appeals for the Ninth Circuit.[89] In that case, the question arose as to the applicability of product liability laws to a book on collecting and cooking mushrooms. It was held that the information contained in the book was not a product. What is of interest here is that, in coming to that conclusion, the Court contrasted the situation before it with one involving software. It was indicated that software would be a product. The software was seen as something more than only information.[90] It could thus be contended that the functional aspect of software strengthens the case for the 'goods' categorisation to cover both a disk and the program embodied on it. On the other hand, as commentators have pointed out, despite wide coverage at the time, *Winter* has had little influence in the USA, probably due to its unusual fact circumstances, the paucity of argument in the judgment surrounding the suggestion that software was more than only information, and the disinclination of either the Ninth Circuit or any other US court to pursue and expand upon that line of reasoning.[91]

Software as Intellectual Property

As we have seen, the definition of 'goods' in the 1979 Act excludes 'things in action', and it might be argued that programs are covered by this exclusion and therefore are not goods. However, the program is not itself copyright; it is protected by copyright. This was recognised by Steyn J in *Eurodynamics Systems v General Automation Ltd*:[92] 'Although the ideas and concepts involved in software remained [the defendants'] intellectual property, the reality of the transaction is that there has been the transfer of a product.'

When there is a contract for the supply of a program, it is not simply an assignment of intellectual property rights. In fact, as has been indicated, in most cases, there will not be an assignment of the copyright in a program, although licences are normally granted. Properly identified, the problem is whether, when intellectual property rights are in question, they dominate the transaction to prevent the disk, with the program embodied in it, from being regarded as goods. Copyright restrictions are not seen as preventing a book, video tape, or CD from being goods, but such items do not have a functional use in the way that software does, and that difference in use is not only noteworthy in itself, but also makes a considerable difference to the impact of intellectual property rights. Intellectual property rights impact upon the enjoyment of books and videos to a very much more limited extent than upon the enjoyment of software.[93] A book can be read or a video watched without any need for the purchaser to obtain a licence to avoid being in breach of copyright. In contrast, the use of software will entail copying it onto hardware, which, in the absence of a licence, would prima facie be in breach of copyright,[94] although the impact of the EC **Software Directive** on this must now be borne in mind.[95] In other words, the basic purpose for which a book or video is purchased can be fulfilled without any need for the purchaser to consider intellectual property rights; the same is not true of software. Indeed, the view has been taken that software cannot be likened to books or other such goods, but must be regarded as *sui generis*.[96]

See Chapter 11 →

---

89 *Winter v G P Puttnam & Sons* 938 F 2d 1033 (9th Cir 1991). See further Michael R Maule, 'Applying strict products liability to computer software' (1992) 27(4) Tulsa LJ 735, 737; Lori A Weber, 'Bad bytes: The application of strict products liability to computer software' (1992) 66(2) St John's L Rev 469, 470; Patrick T Miyaki, 'Computer software defects: Should computer software manufacturers be held strictly liable for computer software defects?' (1992) 8(1) CHTLJ 121.

90 In fact, this type of distinction has been made in relation to US product liability laws in a way that might be used to argue that a program supplied as a written source code could constitute goods: see *Saloomey v Jeppesen* 707 F 2d 671 (1983).

91 Childers, op cit, 143.

92 *Eurodynamics Systems v General Automation Ltd* (1988) unreported, 6 September.

93 See *Beta Computers (Europe) Ltd v Adobe Systems (Europe) Ltd* [1996] FSR 387.

94 CDPA 1988, s 17(1).

95 That is, EC Directive 91/250/EC on the legal protection of computer programs.

96 *Beta Computers*, above, 396, per Lord Penrose.

However, the argument that software cannot be goods because of the intellectual property rights involved was considered by the US Court of Appeals for the Third Circuit in *Advent Systems Ltd v Unisys Corp*.[97] The Court had to determine the applicability of Art 2 of the **Uniform Commercial Code** to a contract under which Advent agreed to supply hardware and 'license software' to Unisys.[98] Weiss L, delivering the opinion of the Court, said that 'a computer program may be copyrightable as intellectual property does not alter the fact that once in the form of a floppy disk or other medium, the program is tangible, movable and available in the marketplace'.[99] The Court emphasised the physical embodiment of the program in a disk or other such medium in concluding that it was goods, and not merely intellectual property, and fell within Art 2. This same approach could be taken to indicate that a program embodied on a disk would be goods under the **SoGA 1979**. However, there is a further argument, based on the significance of the intellectual property rights in software, as to whether a contract for the provision of software is capable of being a contract for the sale of goods.

Section 2(1) of the **SoGA 1979** states that a contract for sale of goods is 'a contract by which the seller transfers or agrees to transfer the property in goods to the buyer for a money consideration called the price'. The 'property in goods' is not the physical object, but, basically, the ownership of the goods. The person to whom a disk is supplied will take it subject to the restrictions of copyright and a licence will normally be involved. The question is whether those restrictions are sufficient to prevent that person acquiring the 'property' in the goods. Certainly, copyright restrictions are not seen as preventing there from being a sale of a book, video tape, or CD, but, as has been indicated, such restrictions impact rather differently on books from their effect on software. However, if a disk with a program on it were to be classified as 'goods', it may be doubted whether this type of argument would prevail.

Of course, if there is clearly no transfer of the ownership, even of the disk or other such medium (which may well occur where non-standard software is in question), but a mere supply under an agreement that the disk will be returned when the program licence terminates, then the contract will not fall within the 1979 Act. However, it should be remembered that similar terms to those implied by the **SoGA 1979** are implied into contracts for the hire of goods by the **SGSA 1982**.

Pragmatism vs Appropriateness

In the *St Albans* case, both Scott Baker J and Sir Iain Glidewell indicated that a program supplied on a disk or other such medium, but without any hardware, should be treated as 'goods'. Scott Baker J's reasoning was basically pragmatic. He took the view that, otherwise, no statutory regime would apply and the recipient would be unprotected in the absence of express terms. This type of pragmatic argument had been positively received by early commentators.[100]

However, even though there are undoubted attractions in finding software to be included in a well-established legal category, it must be considered whether that is appropriate. The law may say that, henceforth, elephants are to be called 'mice', but the law cannot say that elephants *are* mice. Is software too unlike other things that are categorised as 'goods' for the label to be appropriate? The goods to which software is most akin are books, music CDs, and video tapes, but one of the factors used to indicate that software is not only information, its functional aspect, also makes it very different from those types of good. Additionally, despite the comment of Scott Baker J in the *St Albans* case,[101] it should be noted that programs are not always transferred using a disk or some other such medium. Could a program transferred across a network constitute goods? That seems unlikely,[102]

---

97 *Advent Systems Ltd v Unisys Corp* 925 F 2d 670 (1991); cf *Conopco Inc v McCreadie* 826 F Supp 855 (1991). The argument was not considered, as such, in *Beta Computers*, but some support for it may be found in the approach taken there.
98 Article 2 applies to goods and intellectual property is outside the Uniform Commercial Code: see, generally, Andrew Rodau, 'Computer software: Does Article 2 of the Uniform Commercial Code apply?' (1986) Emory LJ 853.
99 *Advent*, above, 145.
100 Brian Napier, 'The future of information technology law' (1992) 51(1) CLJ 46.
101 *St Albans*, above, 699.
102 Such a categorisation would seem contrary to an approach that emphasises the importance of the embodiment of the program in a disk or other such medium.

but, if it cannot, then a problem with the pragmatic argument arises. The 'goods' categorisation might provide an existing legal framework for consideration of some transactions involving computer programs, but certainly not all. Would categorising as goods a program embodied, and transferred, on a disk or other such medium inappropriately divorce its legal categorisation from that of programs transferred without the use of such a medium?[103] In *Beta Computers (Europe) Ltd v Adobe Systems (Europe) Ltd*, a Scottish case that dealt with the question of the effectiveness of a 'shrink wrap' licence, Lord Penrose, obiter, considered the contention that software should be regarded as goods. He said:

See Chapter 11 →

> This reasoning [that software is goods] appears to me to be unattractive, at least, in the context with which this case is concerned. It appears to emphasise the role of the physical medium and to relate the transaction in the medium to sale or hire of goods. It would have the somewhat odd result that the dominant characteristic of the complex product, in terms of value or the significant interests of the parties, would be subordinated to the medium by which it was transmitted to the user in analysing the true nature and effect of the contract.[104]

Common Law Considerations

It is worth noting Scott Baker J's concerns, in the *St Albans* case, that if the supply of software is not a supply of goods, it will be 'something to which no statutory rules apply, thus leaving the recipient unprotected in the absence of express agreement'.[105] The **SoGA 1979** is largely based on the **Sale of Goods Act 1893** of the same name. Legislation covering other contracts dealing with goods occurred much later (for example, the **SGSA 1982**). However, prior to the existence of wider legislation, the common law often proved capable of implying the same, or similar, terms into contracts dealing with goods that did not fall within the **Sale of Goods Acts**.[106] Similarly, it would not be impossible for the court to find that the common law implied terms that programs should be of 'satisfactory quality' and 'reasonably fit' for the purchaser's 'particular purpose', even if, in all cases or some cases, software is not categorised as goods. When the Court of Appeal considered the *St Albans* case, Sir Iain Glidewell thought that, in the absence of an express term requiring the program to be fit for its purpose, one could have been implied at common law.[107]

As will be seen, when consideration is given to the terms implied by s 14 of the **SoGA 1979**, those terms requiring the goods to be of 'satisfactory quality' and 'reasonable fitness' for the buyer's 'particular purpose' are flexible in their content, and similar terms dealing with the functioning of the program may be appropriate, generally, in contracts for the supply of programs. It is worthwhile considering the terms implied by the **SoGA 1979** not only because software may be categorised as goods in some cases, but also because, even if that is not seen as appropriate in any case, the common law may imply the same or similar terms. In any event, they should be addressed, because it would seem that a system involving both hardware and software will be treated as goods.[108]

Services

Even if software can be goods and ownership of the disk passes, it may still be argued that it is inappropriate that its supply should be categorised as a sale of goods. It may be argued that the transaction should be regarded as a contract for work and materials (or, more broadly, for 'services'),

---

103 And of some cases in which such a medium was used, but not delivered to the recipient of the program, as in *St Albans*, above.
104 *Beta Computers*, above, 376.
105 *St Albans*, above. There was an express term that the computer system would be reasonably fit for the buyer's purpose in the *St Albans* case.
106 For example, *Dodd v Wilson* [1946] 2 All ER 691.
107 *St Albans*, above, 494. The implication envisaged would appear to have been one made 'in fact', but such an implied term might be found more generally 'in law'.
108 *Toby Constructions*, above; *St Albans*, above.

rather than for goods. Of course, there may well be found to be a contract for services if no goods are in question. However, what is of particular note here is the distinction between a contract for services, which also involves goods, and one that is simply for the sale of goods. The line between such contracts for services and contracts for the sale of goods has been one that the courts have attempted to draw in many different contexts, and it has never proved an easy categorisation to make.[109] Nevertheless, it may be a very important distinction. If a contract for the supply of software is one for the sale of goods, then, subject to the possibility of their inapplicability, or of the effectiveness of an exemption clause, the software will have to comply with the statutory implied terms as to description (s 13 of the **SoGA 1979**), satisfactory quality (s 14(2)), and reasonable fitness for the buyer's particular purpose (s. 14(3)). Whilst the terms implied by s 14 set standards by reference to the 'reasonable person' (s 14(2)) or require 'reasonable fitness' (s 14(3)), they are all nevertheless strict. The seller cannot escape liability for his or her breach by proving that the problem with the goods was not due to any fault on his or her part.[110] In contrast, if what is in question is the provision of a service, then the relevant implied term stems from s 13 of the **SGSA 1982**, which merely requires that, where the supplier of a service acts in the course of a business, he or she should do so with due care. The strict terms, requiring goods to be, inter alia, of satisfactory quality would apply only to goods supplied incidentally to the service.[111]

Two basic approaches to distinguishing contracts for the sale of goods and contracts for the supply of services can be found. These can be seen in the cases of *Lee v Griffin*[112] and *Robinson v Graves*.[113] *Lee v Griffin* was concerned with a contract made by a dentist to supply a set of false teeth, made to fit the individual patient. On appeal, that was concluded to be a contract for the sale of goods, on the basis that if the services produced goods, the ownership of which the supplier transferred to the other party, there was a contract for the sale of goods, save only where the transfer of ownership of any goods could be regarded as relatively insignificant, as in the example of the solicitor drawing up the deed. In *Robinson v Graves*, a contract was made with an artist for a portrait of a particular individual and the Court of Appeal looked to the dominant element in the contract – the end product or the skill and expertise of the person providing the services – and concluded that it was a contract for the services of the artist, rather than one for the sale of goods.

In the context of contracts concerned with software and the statutory regimes, the impact of a contract being for services rather than goods can be illustrated. If there is a contract to write a bespoke program, which is categorised as a contract for services, then the strict liability would seem only to apply to the fabric of the disk.[114] The content of the program would be the outcome of the services and the relevant statutorily implied term would simply be that requiring the services to be performed with due care. In other words, the strict liability terms would not apply to the product of the services; they would apply only to goods transferred to the other party incidentally to those services. A more complex problem might arise where the contract is for the supply and installation into the purchaser's system of an 'off the shelf' program. If such a contract were characterised as being one for services, because of the work involved in the installation, then it would seem that any aspect of the program adapted by that installation would only be covered by the requirement that the work should be carried out with due care. However, if the 'off the shelf' software were to be characterised as goods, then any defect in the program that was not caused by the

---

109 See, eg, Robert A Samek, 'Contracts for work and materials' (1962) 36 ALJ 66.
110 *Kendall v Lillico* [1969] 2 AC 31; *Frost v Aylesbury Dairy Co* [1905] 1 KB 685.
111 In *Dodd v Wilson*, above, the contract was for the services of a vet. He was strictly liable when a vaccine with which he inoculated a cow was not reasonably fit for its purpose. Of course, had the problem been with, eg, the way in which the injection was given, he would only have been liable in the absence of due care.
112 *Lee v Griffin* (1861) 1 B & S 272. See also, eg, *J Marcel (Furriers) Ltd v Tapper* [1953] 1 WLR 49.
113 *Robinson v Graves* [1935] 1 KB 579.
114 But see the assumption in *Saphena*, above, 652, per Staughton LJ, that it made no difference to the applicability of the strict liability terms as to quality whether the contract was characterised as being for goods or services.

installation would seem to be subject to the strict requirements of the statutorily implied terms as to fitness for purpose and satisfactory quality.

The Supply of Software

Obviously, the acquisition of bespoke software provides the strongest case for arguing that a contract for the supply of software must be regarded as one for services rather than goods. However, even then, the categorisation should not be assumed in every case. Two particular examples can be suggested in which a contract for bespoke software might nevertheless be characterised as one for goods. The first example relates to the case in which, although the software is being written because it was requested by one particular company, the suppliers realise that there will be a market to supply it to other companies and intend to do so.[115] It might be argued that the intent to 'mass supply' the software subsequently could affect the characterisation of a contract to supply what was, at that stage, bespoke software, making it appropriate to characterise it as being for goods, rather than services. The other example concerns the 'turnkey contract'. Even where goods are to be manufactured by a seller, it is possible for that seller to contract simply in relation to a result (the goods), rather than the manufacture and delivery of the goods. The former case may be argued to be one for the sale of goods rather than the supply of services and this argument would seem to apply to the so-called turnkey contract – that is, the type of contract in which a complete system is installed and then simply handed over to the party to whom it is being supplied. In such contracts, the way in which the supplier arrives at the completed product seems to be irrelevant to the other party. It is a contract purely concerned with results and a 'goods' rather than 'services' categorisation may be appropriate, even where what is in question is bespoke software.

After considering bespoke software, modified standard (or modified 'off the shelf') software should be looked at. The approach taken in *Robinson v Graves*[116] could provide a strong argument in favour of the services classification where some modified standard software is in question, depending upon the extent and novelty of the modification.

At the other end of the spectrum from bespoke software is standard, or 'off the shelf', software. There seems to be little scope for an argument that, even if such software is goods, a contract for its supply must nevertheless be characterised as one for services.[117] In *Toby Constructions Products Ltd v Computer Bar Sales Pty Ltd*, in which the contract was for the supply of a computer system composed of hardware and 'off the shelf' software, Rogers J concluded that he was dealing with a contract for goods and dismissed the argument that it was services that were in question. He said:

> Whilst representing the fruits of much research work, [the software] was in current jargon, off the shelf, in a sense, mass produced. There can be no comparison with a one-off painting. Rather is the comparison with a mass-produced print of a painting.[118]

Another Fine Intangible Mess . . .

When one considers the state of play today in relation to software and its uncertain place in the existing statutory framework governing contracts, it is perhaps hard to comprehend how UK law has so signally failed to address the issue. On the part of the courts, it is at least partially attributable to the fact that the judiciary can only address the issues placed before them and that, on the whole, questions going to the nature of software do not seem to have arisen very often. That having been said, when such issues have arisen, as in *Eurodynamics*, *St Albans*, and *Beta*, the courts seem disinclined to address them directly.

---

115 This was the fact situation in *Saphena Computing*, which led to a dispute as to the ownership of copyright.
116 See p 455 above.
117 But see *James Ashley v London Borough of Sutton* [1995] Tr LRep 350.
118 *Toby Constructions*, above, 51.

There appears to have been a similar reluctance to address the issue by the legislature. It is interesting to speculate why that might be so. In New Zealand, the perceived solution has been to amend the definition of 'goods' in the **Sale of Goods Act 1908** to include 'software', howsoever it is delivered.[119] This has been criticised as 'statutory fantasy',[120] on the grounds that there are no other 'goods' that can be 'converted to electromagnetic signals which are then transmitted from one geographical location to another to emerge as goods again at the other end'.[121] Thus the New Zealand law achieves the aim of providing a clear statutory regime for software, but only at the cost of doing some violence to the traditional meaning of the word 'goods'. In the USA, where the issue seems equally unresolved, a proposed legislative standard in the form of the Uniform Computer Information Transactions Act (UCITA),[122] designed to standardise the law and provide the default rules for licensing and contracting of software and all other forms of digital information, as the US **Uniform Commercial Code** does for the sale of goods, failed to find much support.[123] Drawing upon those examples, one might surmise that Parliament has been unwilling to involve itself in an issue in which there:

- has been relatively little concerted pressure from either the software industry or other interested parties for a 'root and branch' reformulation of the ad hoc contract paradigm for software;
- is the possibility of simply increasing the current uncertainty or complexity in contract law, without necessarily reaching a satisfactory solution, because of the need to address different types of software contract (off-the-shelf, bespoke, customisable) being sold to different types of acquirer (general public, small-to-medium-sized enterprises [SMEs], corporations, etc) through different media (tangible medium, network) in a marketplace that is constantly evolving ('open source software', SaaS, etc).

Whatever the reason, what appears to have developed is, as Moon notes, an environment in which a highly important sector of the economy is governed by laws that are currently failing to 'understand intangibles in general and to evolve to properly recognise them without the use of anachronistic legal fictions which pretend that they are tangibles in situations which have diminishing applicability in modern (electronic) commerce'.[124]

Implied Terms: Fitness for Purpose etc.

Sections 13–15 of the **SoGA 1979** imply terms into contracts for the sale of goods. They may prove very useful to the purchaser of defective software if such software is categorised as goods. However, as has been suggested, even if software by itself is not so characterised, a system involving both hardware and software may well be still be labelled as such,[125] and in any event, even in relation to software, the courts may imply similar terms at common law.[126] The value of examining these terms does not solely lie in the possibility that software will be construed as goods.

The possibility of excluding or restricting liability for breaches of the terms implied by ss 13–15 is restricted by s 6 of the **UCTA 1977**. The status of the implied terms should also be

---

119 New Zealand Sale of Goods Amendment Act 2003.
120 Moon, op cit, 402.
121 Ibid.
122 UCITA.
123 Although the American Law Institute's recently released Principles of the Law of Software Contracts (see Chapter 11) covers much of the same ground. However, the Principles are designed to be persuasive rather than to provide a model basis for legislation.
124 Moon, op cit, 407.
125 *Toby Constructions*, above; *St Albans*, above.
126 *St Albans*, above.

noted. They are conditions, and breach of a condition normally gives the injured party the right to reject the goods, as well as to claim damages, no matter how trivial the breach. However, the effect of a breach of these conditions was modified by s 4 of the **Sale and Supply of Goods Act 1994 (SSGA 1994)**. Section 15A of the **SoGA 1979** now states that (subject to contrary intention in the contract), if the buyer does not 'deal as consumer',[127] then he or she has no right to reject the goods for a breach that is so trivial that it would be unreasonable to do so.

However, there are now additional remedies to consider in relation to breach of the terms implied by ss 13–15. The **Sale and Supply of Goods to Consumers Regulations 2002**[128] have inserted ss 48A–48F into the **SoGA 1979** providing a consumer (that is, any natural person who is acting for purposes outside his or her trade, business, or profession) with additional remedies in relation to goods that do not conform to the contract at the time of delivery. Goods do not so conform if there is a breach of an express term or a breach of a term implied by ss 13, 14, or 15. The additional remedies are repair, replacement, reduction of purchase price, or rescission of the contract. Replacement and repair take precedence.

The original rights to reject the goods and terminate the contract will remain, but if the consumer has asked for repair or replacement under the new scheme, he or she will have to give the seller a reasonable time in which to comply before exercising the original right to reject (s 48D).

Sale by Description (s 13 SoGA 1979)

Section 13(1) of the **SoGA 1979** states:

> Where there is a contract for the sale of goods by description, there is an implied term that the goods will correspond with their description.

Two basic questions arise under the section: when is a sale 'by description' and what constitutes 'a description' for the purposes of s 13?

'By Description'

Obvious examples will immediately spring to mind of situations in which there will clearly be a sale 'by description'. It would seem inevitable that there will be a sale by description when the contract is for unascertained goods. In relation to specific goods, the obvious example of a sale by description is where the buyer has not seen the goods before the contract is made.[129] However, it is clear that sale by description is not restricted to such cases. There may be a sale by description in which goods are seen, and even selected, by the buyer. Section 13(3) states:

> A sale of goods is not prevented from being a sale by description by reason only that, being exposed for sale or hire, they are selected by the buyer.

This means that goods displayed in a shop and selected from the shelf by the buyer may still be sold by description. However, the emphasis here is on 'may'. The question still arises as to when the goods involved in such sales, or other types of sales, are sold by description. In *Grant v Australian Knitting Mills*,[130] Lord Wright said: '. . . a thing is sold by description though it is specific, so long as it is sold not merely as the specific thing but as the thing corresponding to a description.'[131] In

---

127   This phrase is taken from the Unfair Contract Terms Act 1977, in which it is defined in s 12 (s 61(5A) of the Sale of Goods Act 1979).
128   SI 2002/3045, implementing EC Directive 1999/44/EC.
129   *Varley v Whipp* [1900] 1 QB 513.
130   [1936] AC 85.
131   Ibid, 100.

other words, the question is whether the parties were merely contracting about the thing in front of them (for example), or that thing was something corresponding to a description on which the buyer is relying.[132] In the latter case, the sale is 'by description'.[133] As we shall see, there is only very limited scope for a descriptive term to be the appropriate type of description to fall within s 13.

What Constitutes a 'Description'?

At first sight, it might seem obvious what is being referred to when s 13 says that goods must correspond with their 'description'. However, not everything that would be regarded as a description of the goods in everyday terms will constitute a 'description' for the purposes of s 13. In fact, modern case law takes a very restrictive view of which descriptions fall within s 13. The starting point is that only descriptions that are also terms of the contract in their own right can constitute 'descriptions' for the purposes of s 13. In other words, s 13 does not alter the balance between terms and representations.[134] However, not even all descriptive terms constitute 'descriptions' for the purposes of s 13.

In the past, a very wide approach was taken in relation to which descriptive terms were capable of falling within s 13.[135] The more modern, and narrower, approach to s 13 is that only descriptive terms that state what is 'essential' about the goods, in the eyes of the parties, fall within s 13 – and it is clear that 'essential' has to be understood restrictively.[136] That being the case, it would seem that such descriptive terms would be conditions in their own right. This might be seen as making s 13 irrelevant and unnecessary. However, the impact of s 6 of the **UCTA 1977** must be borne in mind. That section provides significant protection against the exclusion or restriction of liability for breach of the statutorily implied terms. Certainly, those who deal as consumers acquire greater protection against a clause exempting liability for breach of one of the terms implied by the **SoGA 1979** than for breach of a simple express term of the contract. (see pp 470–471).

In the context of software, questions relevant to s 13 of the 1979 Act might arise in relation to the statement that, for example, what was being supplied was a 'word-processing program suitable for office use'. Provided that the entire statement is part of the contract terms, the question of the scope of s 13 might become relevant. For example, s 13 might cover a statement that:

- what was being supplied was a 'word-processing program', in which case there would be a clear breach if what was supplied was not a word-processing program, but a spreadsheet program – but if what has been supplied is a program that would be an efficient word processor, but for the defects in it, there seems less likely to be a breach as a merely defective program is still likely to be regarded as a word-processing program by the 'men in the marketplace';
- the word-processing program is for 'office use'. Words indicating the quality of the goods may be part of the 'description' for the purposes of s 13, but that will not usually be the case; they will usually merely be of relevance to the terms implied by s 14(2) and (3), or in their own right, as express conditions, warranties, or innominate terms. However, the basic test must be applied in each case. What is important is the perceptions of the parties. It must be asked whether such a descriptive term 'identified' the goods in the relevant sense. If the statement that the program was for 'office use' was found to fall within s 13, then the 'men in the marketplace' test should be applied to the particular complaint – for example, that the program could not handle the integration of different documents well enough.

---

132 See also Beale v Taylor [1967] 1 WLR 1193.
133 [1991] 1 QB 564, per Nourse LJ.
134 Harlingdon & Leinster Enterprises, above; T & J Harrison v Knowles and Foster [1918] 1 KB 608; See further below, in relation to what purpose is served by s 13 in the light of this.
135 Re Moore & Co and Landauer & Co [1921] 2 KB 519.
136 Ashington Piggeries v Christopher Hill [1972] AC 441.

Satisfactory Quality (s 14 SoGA 1979)

Section 14 of the **SoGA 1979** implies a term that the goods are of satisfactory quality. The basic test in s 14(2A) is what the reasonable person would regard as satisfactory. Of course, the reasonable person does not make the assessment in a vacuum, but against a background of 'any description of the goods, the price (if relevant) and all other relevant circumstances' and the assessment is also assisted by the list in s 14(2B) of 'aspects of the quality of goods'. Before the test of satisfactory quality is addressed, the background factors to the implication of the term will be considered (for example, the term is implied where the contract was made 'in the course of a business'), as well as the situations identified in s 14(2C), in that there will not be a breach of the term requiring goods to be of satisfactory quality.

Sale 'in the Course of a Business'

For the term requiring goods to be of satisfactory quality to be implied by s 14(2), the seller must contract 'in the course of a business'. The same applies to the term implied by s 14(3). Section 61(1) tells us that 'business' includes 'a profession and the activities of any government department or local or public authority', but there is no further definition of 'business' or the phrase 'in the course of a business'. In *Stevenson v Rogers*, Potter LJ noted that the phrase was there to 'distinguish between a sale made in the course of a seller's business and a purely private sale of goods outside the confines of the business (if any) carried on by the seller', thus as long as a sale is even incidental to the seller's business and not a 'purely private sale', it should be considered 'in the course of a business' for the purposes of s 14(2).[137]

'Goods Supplied under the Contract'

This seems to mean 'goods delivered in purported pursuance of the contract', so that if the problem is something added to the goods contracted for, the seller cannot avoid liability simply by saying that there is nothing wrong with the contract goods themselves.[138] In the context of software, this type of argument might be raised if a computer virus was inadvertently supplied with the medium on which a program was supplied.

Exceptions

Section 14(2C) contains exceptions. If it applies, the buyer will not be able to claim that there has been a breach of the implied term. We are here concerned with the exceptions in s 14(2C)(a) and (b).[139] Subsection (a) refers to the situation in which a matter that would otherwise have made the goods of unsatisfactory quality does not do so because it was drawn to the buyer's attention before the contract was made; subs (b) deals with the situation in which a matter that would have made the goods of unsatisfactory quality does not do so because, before contracting, the buyer examined the goods and that examination should have revealed the matter in question. Because the reference is to 'that' examination, the exception should only relate to matters that should have been revealed by the examination actually made, however cursory, and not a 'reasonable examination'. There is no obligation on the buyer to make any examination at all. In fact, odd as it may seem, given the presence of the exception in s 14(2C)(b), it may be argued that it is better for the buyer not to examine the goods.[140]

When software is in question, even a very detailed examination will not bring every 'bug' in the program to light and it should be emphasised that the exception should only relate to matters that should have been discovered by the examination actually made by the buyer. In addition, the

---

137 [1999] 1 All ER 613, 623; see Elizabeth MacDonald, ' "In the course of a business": A fresh examination' [1999] 3 Web JCLI, available online at http://webjcli.ncl.ac.uk/1999/issue3/macdonald3.html
138 *Wilson v Rickett, Cockerell & Co Ltd* [1954] 1 QB 598, 607, *per* Denning LJ.
139 Section 14(2C)(c) refers to the situation in which a sale is by sample: see below.
140 Unless the sale is by sample: see s 14(2C)(c).

point can be made that, for the exception in s 14(2C)(b) to apply, the buyer's examination will have to have been of 'the goods'. If software is purchased, it will often not have been the 'the goods' sold that were examined, but another copy used for demonstration purposes. However, even if the exception will not technically apply, any difficulty revealed by an examination of another copy might affect what the reasonable person would regard as satisfactory – that is, it might affect the application of the basic test of satisfactory quality (see s 14(2A)).[141] In addition, the exception in s 14(2C)(a) is not restricted to matters drawn to the buyer's attention using 'the goods' sold to the buyer. Some limitation of the software sold to the buyer might be drawn to the buyer's attention by using another copy of that software.

There may be some difficulty with the exceptions where some matter that, but for the exceptions, would make the goods of unsatisfactory quality becomes known to the buyer prior to the contract of sale, but it is reasonably believed to be unimportant and rectifiable, and subsequently proves to be neither.[142] This sort of situation might arise in relation to software that is required to be interoperable with other software, but is believed to require only minor modification before this can happen, but the degree of necessary interoperability is, in fact, not attainable.

What Constitutes Satisfactory Quality?

As we have seen, the basic test of satisfactory quality is set out in s 14(2A). It refers to the standard that 'a reasonable person would regard as satisfactory, taking account of any description, the price (if relevant) and all other relevant circumstances'. The reference to the standard of a reasonable person makes the test very flexible and able to encompass the vastly different types of good to which the Act applies. The disadvantage of flexibility is that it makes it difficult to apply the term. There is some further assistance in the identification of certain 'aspects of the quality of goods' in s 14(2B). Where the buyer deals as consumer, subss (2D)–(2F) give additional significance to any 'public statements' on the 'specific characteristics of the goods' by the 'seller, the producer, or his representative'.[143]

When considering whether goods are of the standard that a reasonable person would regard as satisfactory, it should be a matter of balancing the problems with the goods against the standard suggested by such matters as description and price. In relation to software, a program might be of unsatisfactory quality if it was so difficult to use that doing anything with it would take the average consumer an inordinate length of time. That would particularly be the case if the program was marketed as one that was easy to use by the average consumer. In the light of the above discussion, it may seem odd that the reference to price in s 14(2A) is qualified by the phrase 'if relevant'. The immediate reaction to this may well be that the price must always be relevant. However, it is a factor over which care must be taken. It would not be relevant to set the standard for goods generally that were sold in, for example, the 'January sales' if the goods were not presented as 'seconds', or in any way 'shop soiled' or 'defective'.[144] In addition, the price factor may need to be treated with some care in relation to novel software. When a novel program is first put on the market, it will be expensive, but it will have problems that have not yet come to light. Later versions will resolve the problems. It would seem that, despite the expense of a novel program when it is first put on the market, the reasonable person could nevertheless regard it as being of a satisfactory standard even though there were some problems with it.[145] Obviously, whether it is of satisfactory quality would be a matter of the number and extent of the problems.

---

141 The case would be inappropriate to be a sale by sample: see s 15, below.
142 See, eg, R & B Customs Brokers v United Dominion Trust [1988] 1 All ER 847, 856, per Neill LJ.
143 Those subsections were added by the Sale and Supply of Goods to Consumers Regulations 2002, SI 2002/3045, implementing EC Directive 1999/44/EC.
144 Price would also seem to be less directly significant if the purchase were in some sense a 'risk': see *Harlingdon & Leinster Enterprises*, above.
145 But see *St Albans*, above.

Another point to be considered here is the use of 'expert evidence' of 'acceptable practice' in the industry to assist in establishing 'satisfactory quality'. In considering, above, when a bug is a breach, generally, it was noted that the courts referred to such evidence (see p 440), but also that potential difficulties might arise from doing so, in terms of industry acceptance of a low standard. In *Micron Computer Systems Ltd v Wang*,[146] against the background of the industry norm, it was decided that the time taken by the system to 'back up' did not make it unmerchantable, and neither did the failure of the hard disk after one year. That was regarded as normal and to be expected.

After looking at the basic test of satisfactory quality, some consideration should also be given to the 'aspects' of quality identified in s 14(2B). Depending on the circumstances, they may be relevant to the reasonable person's assessment of what constitutes a satisfactory standard for the type of goods in question. 'Purpose' may be regarded as referring to the mere functioning of the goods. In the context of a car, it may now be seen as merely referring to whether the car will get from A to B, without any requirement of a degree of style, comfort, and reliability. Questions of style, comfort, and reliability can now fall under other aspects of quality identified in s 14(2B), or could simply be encompassed within the general test of what a reasonable person would regard as satisfactory. In relation to software, different versions of the same program may be supplied for home and office use. Provided that it was clear at the time of purchase that what was being bought was the version intended for home use, it would seem that the 'kind' of goods would not be ones that were commonly supplied for office use. Under those circumstances, the aspect of quality identified by s 14(2B)(a) would not indicate that the software was of unsatisfactory quality if it were not reasonably fit for office use, provided that it were reasonably fit for home use.

Finally, before leaving consideration of this implied term, some thought can be given to the issues raised by the reaction of the judge in *SAM Business Systems v Hedley & Co*[147] to the contention that the software was not in breach of contract because it was being used elsewhere. Judge Peter Bowsher QC said:

> The 'use at other sites' is a continuing theme. I am no more impressed by it than if I were told by a garage that there were 1000 other cars of the same type as the one I had bought where there was no complaint of the defect that I was complaining of so why should I be complaining of a defect? We have all heard of Monday cars, so maybe this was a Monday software programme.[148]

This raises two issues. The first is that some further thought should be given here to the appropriate borderline between the scope of the implied term as to satisfactory quality and that addressed in the next section, as to reasonable fitness for the buyer's particular purpose. An argument that software is working well elsewhere may well be relevant to determine if it meets the general standard that is required by satisfactory quality, if the problem stems from something particular to the particular acquirer, such as integration with an existing unusual system. It should be emphasised that when fitness for purpose is referred to in this context as an 'aspect of quality', it is fitness for the purposes for which goods of the kind in question are 'commonly supplied'. Purposes that are beyond those for which the software is commonly supplied can only be relevant in so far as they have been expressly or impliedly made known to the supplier and are covered by the implied term dealing with fitness for the buyer's particular purpose.

The second point to be made here relates to the judge's reference to 'Monday cars' and the way in which defects in software occur. There might be a problem in relation to a particular copy of software. There might be some problem with the disk, for example, which was introduced during the manufacturing process and which might only affect that disk or a batch of disks. That sort of

---

146 (1990) unreported, 9 May.
147 [2003] 1All ER (Comm) 465; see further Macdonald, op cit.
148 Ibid, [104].

problem is likely to lead to software that is obviously defective and may well simply not run. However, in relation to software, the problem is more likely to be part of the program. This will impact upon every copy of the program and there is no scope for 'Monday software' in relation to this type of problem.

Fitness for the Buyer's Particular Purpose

The implied term dealing with fitness for the buyer's purpose is now contained in s 14(3) of the **SoGA 1979**. Its requirement that the goods should be of 'satisfactory quality' sets a general standard for the goods. It is not a standard that relates to the buyer's intended use of the goods. In contrast, the term implied by s 14(3) may result in the seller guaranteeing that the goods are reasonably fit for the buyer's purpose. Of course, the seller should not be required to provide goods fit for some unusual and unknown purpose of the buyer, and the term is restricted to the situation in which the particular purpose has been expressly or impliedly made known to the seller and the buyer has reasonably relied on the skill or judgment of the seller. In addition, the term only requires *reasonable* fitness for the buyer's particular purpose and the standard thereby set for the goods will depend upon how broadly or narrowly the particular purpose has been made known to the seller. These points will be considered further below in looking at the specific elements of s 14(3).

The reference to 'particular' does not mean that the purpose must be very narrow; it merely means 'specified'. A particular purpose may be very general,[149] but, whether it is wide or narrow, it must be expressly or impliedly made known to the seller.

In some cases, it will be easy to establish that the particular purpose has been impliedly made known.[150] It will usually be clear what a buyer's general purpose is in buying software. A word-processing program will usually be purchased to word-process. However, if the buyer's purpose is a more specialised one, and if s 14(3) is to apply, that specialised purpose will have to be brought to the seller's attention expressly if the buyer is to gain the protection of the implied term. In *Micron Computer Systems Ltd v Wang*,[151] the buyer failed to make it known to the seller that it wanted a system that would perform 'transaction logging'. The failure of the system to do this, therefore, did not mean that it was not reasonably fit for the buyer's particular purpose.

In more general terms, the test has been put in terms of whether the buyer's actual purpose was 'reasonably foreseeable'.[152] For example, if a buyer only asks for a particular type of program, the applicability of s 14(3) to the question of compatibility depends upon whether it is reasonably foreseeable that the buyer's actual purpose is to use the software as part of a system so that he or she needs compatible software.

The situation should also be different where the goods are of a type that is known to have to be particularised to the user in relation to the relevant aspect of his or her use.[153]

It should be emphasised that, for the term to be implied, not only must the buyer rely upon the seller to provide goods that are reasonably fit for the buyer's particular purpose, but it must also be reasonable for the buyer so to rely. Reliance can be partial, provided that it relates to the aspect of the goods' fitness that is relevant to the buyer's claim.[154] Reliance may not exist, or may not be reasonable, if the buyer has the greater expertise or is in a much better position to make an assessment of the goods' suitability.[155]

In the context of the requirements of reasonable reliance and that the particular purpose of the buyer should be expressly or impliedly made known to the seller, some thought can be given to the

---

149   *Kendall*, above, 114, per Lord Pearce.
150   *Preist v Last* [1903] 2 KB 148.
151   *Micron Computer*, above.
152   *Ashington Piggeries*, above.
153   *Manchester Liners Ltd v Rea Ltd* [1922] 2 AC 74.
154   *Cammell Laird & Co Ltd v Manganese Bronze and Brass Co Ltd* [1934] AC 402.
155   For example, *Tehran Europe v ST Belton* [1968] 2 QB 545.

suggestions for implied terms in system supply contracts in *Anglo Group v Winther Brown*.[156] In that case, HH Judge Tomlin suggested that, in relation to a contract for the supply of a standard computer system, there should, inter alia, be implied terms that:

(a) the purchaser communicates clearly any special needs to the supplier;

(b) the purchaser takes reasonable steps to ensure the supplier understands those needs;

(c) the supplier communicates to the purchaser whether or not those precise needs can be met and if so how they can be met. If they cannot be met precisely the appropriate options should be set out by the supplier.

It can be seen that most of this is, in a sense, indirectly 'required' by the implied term under consideration here, in that any 'special needs' will have to be made known to the seller if they are to be encompassed within the requirement of 'reasonable fitness for the buyer's particular purpose'. If they are so 'special' that they need to be explained to be understood, then, without such explanation, they may not have been sufficiently made known and, in any event, reliance on the skill or judgment of the seller may well not be reasonable. In addition, once sufficient communication has been made to ensure that the implied term as to reasonable fitness encompasses the buyer's special needs, it is in the interests of the supplier to make plain any limits on what can he or she can achieve, or he or she will be liable if the software is not 'reasonably fit for the buyer's particular purpose'. This well-known and established implied term would seem to render unnecessary those set out above, which were contended for in *Anglo Group v Winther Brown*. In addition, the point can also be made that the judge there would seem to have been referring to implied terms that would operate during the negotiation of the contract – in other words, a situation in which there would normally be no contract and no basis to create contractual obligations to state 'special needs', etc. There is in contrast no difficulty in generating a need to state any such 'special needs' to ensure their inclusion in the scope of what will be an implied term of the contract once made. There is a further point to be made here in relation to the fact that, as was indicated above (see p 450), at the time when a contract is made, it may be difficult for the parties to define accurately the software required, particularly when a development contract is in question, and software development contracts may well need to be modified before their performance is completed. This was reflected in the view taken by Havery QC of the evolving nature of the coverage of the term that the software would be reasonably fit for the acquirer's purposes. In *Saphena Computing*, he said:

> . . . it was an implied term of each contract for the supply of software that the software would be reasonably fit for any purpose which had been communicated to the plaintiff's before the contract was made and for any purpose subsequently communicated, provided in the latter case that the plaintiffs accepted the defendant's instructions to make the relevant modifications. The making of the modifications constitutes or implies acceptance of the instructions.[157]

Obviously, what is normally envisaged under s 14(3) is that the goods should be reasonably fit for the buyer's purposes that were made known before, or at the time of, contracting. Contract obligations cannot change once the contract is made unless the contract is modified. Havery QC's version of the 'fitness for purpose' implied term, with its in-built expectation of variation, would seem to be a common law version of the normal statutory implied term.

However, even if the particular purpose has been expressly or impliedly made known to the seller and the buyer reasonably relied on the seller, the question still has to be asked whether the

---

156 1 March 2000; see further Macdonald, op cit.
157 *Saphena Computing*, above, 644.

implied term has been breached. Where the particular purpose that is made known is a general purpose, the fact that the goods are not fit for the buyer's more specific, actual, purpose only means that they are not fit for part of the buyer's particular purpose. Being unfit for only part of the particular purpose does not necessarily mean that they are not *reasonably* fit for the particular purpose *as a whole*.: the 'width of the [particular] purpose is compensated, from the seller's point of view, by the dilution of his responsibility'.[158] More generally, 'reasonable fitness for the buyer's particular purpose' will depend upon the seriousness of the problem with the goods and the proportion of the 'particular purpose' that is affected.[159] In addition, the point can be made that the implied term may be breached by an accumulation of smaller difficulties. In *Saphena*, Havery QC (Off Ref) said:

> ... its main problems were those which are evidence of a lack of tuning – principally slow operation and poor design of input and output procedures ... it is clear to me that on the evidence [these defects] represent a shortfall of the system below the standard required of fitness for its purpose.[160]

Sale by Sample (s 15 SoGA 1979)

Section 15 of the **SoGA 1979** provides for implied conditions where the sale is by sample. Like s 13, and unlike s 14(2) and (3), there is no requirement that the sale should be 'in the course of a business', although other sales are unlikely to be 'by sample'. Section 15 seems unlikely to have much application in relation to the sale of software. Software will seldom be bought under circumstances that mean that there is provision of a sample from a larger bulk of goods. If a disk is supplied with a 'cut-down' version of a program on it to encourage the purchase of the full program, in everyday terms, that may well be described as 'a sample', but it would seem that it should not be regarded as part of the 'bulk' (that is, the full program); it is a copy of part of it. The term would be apposite if there were a purchase of multiple disk copies of a particular program and one of the copies had been tested before the purchase.

Relevance of the Implied Terms

The implied terms considered above deal with the situation in which there is a sale of goods. It has already been pointed out that similar terms are implied if the goods are not sold, but hired out,[161] and that a contract involving the provision of software and hardware together would seem to be accepted as one under which goods are supplied.[162] The question does remain as to the classification of software (that is, whether it can it be goods). However, the statutory terms will have a broad compass in any event in system supply contracts, and it was also suggested above that these or similar terms may well be implied into software contracts by analogy at common law,[163] even if software is not regarded as goods, but as something *sui generis*.

Acceptance Tests

In looking at the performance required under the contract and the liability of the supplier for breach, consideration must be given to the contractual role of acceptance tests. Acceptance tests are central to a contract for the development or significant customisation of software (or a system). They should be set out in the contract and would usually involve a set of tests designed to see how the software will work across the range of functions required of it. Successful completion of the acceptance tests will normally trigger payment, but what else will it do? It should be remembered

---

158 *Ashington Piggeries*, above, 497, per Lord Wilberforce.
159 *Kendall*, above.
160 *Saphena Computing*, above, 644.
161 SGSA 1982, ss 8–10.
162 *Toby Constructions*, above; *St Albans*, above.
163 See *St Albans*, above.

that such testing may well not bring all bugs to light. As was stated above: 'Testing reveals the presence of bugs; it cannot confirm their absence.' There are a number of points to consider here.

First, acceptance has an established meaning in sale of goods contracts. In relation to such contracts, under s 35 of the **SoGA 1979**, acceptance can occur in three ways:

- when the buyer intimates to the seller that he or she accepts them;
- when the goods have been delivered to the buyer and the buyer performs an act inconsistent with the ownership of the seller; or
- when the buyer retains the goods beyond a reasonable time without intimating to the seller that he or she rejects them.

The effect of 'acceptance' within s 35 is that the buyer can no longer reject the goods. Even if a breach of condition subsequently comes to light, the buyer's remedy lies in damages. If the contract is one for the sale of goods, then the buyer's acknowledgement of successful completion of 'acceptance tests' could be seen as intimation of 'acceptance' in this technical sense. However, it is a technical sense, and even if the contract is seen as one for the sale of goods, it may well not be being used in this way. Essentially what is in issue is the interpretation of the contract: what impact did the parties (objectively) intend the acceptance tests to have? This can be considered further.

At the extreme, the supplier may want successful acceptance testing to mark the point at which any problems with the software system cease to be dealt with under the supply contract (or the supply part of a single contract) and are dealt with under the maintenance contract (or maintenance part). So, in *Morgan and Burden on Computer Contracts*, we find an example of a clause seeking to finish the supplier's liability under the supply contract:

> The licensee's acceptance of delivery of the software shall be conclusive evidence that the licensee has examined the software and found it to be complete, in accordance with the description in the specification, in good order and condition, fit for any purpose for which it may be required and in every way satisfactory . . .[164]

However, as we have seen, no matter how extensive the acceptance testing, there are likely still to be bugs that will only subsequently reveal themselves. So what will the effect of such a clause be? Without the clause, some of those bugs would certainly be breaches for which the supplier would be liable. It seems unlikely that the court will accept such a clause at face value as effectively defining the contractual obligations: rather, it would seem that such a clause would normally be treated as an exemption clause and so subject to the **UCTA 1977** and ineffective unless it satisfies the requirement of reasonableness.[165] In addition, in *SAM Business Systems Ltd v Hedley & Co*, the point was made that even if an exemption clause is effective, it will not mean that it can make the remedying of bugs that constitute breaches something for which the acquirer should have to pay under a maintenance contract.[166]

A less extreme approach by the supplier may be a more positive recognition of the likelihood of bugs being discovered after acceptance testing. There would be a basic ousting or rejection of a damages claim, but accompanied by a 'warranty' that any bugs that meant that the software did not comply with the contract would be rectified by the supplier. Obviously, any such 'warranty' would be stated to run for a limited period. Again, **UCTA 1977** would be relevant, but with the supplier in an improved position, because of its 'warranty' when the application of the requirement of reasonableness arises.

---

164 Morgan and Burden, op cit, 58.
165 Under UCTA 1977, ss 3 and 6; see p 464.
166 *SAM Business Systems*, above.

Damages[167]

A software 'bug' can cause considerable losses to a business when its impact is felt. The potential scope of the losses that a bug can cause are graphically illustrated by what occurred when one affected AT&T's long-distance telephone network. Within ten minutes, 50 per cent of calls were failing to get through and a day's telephone traffic was lost before software 'patches' could be installed to avoid the bug. The direct cost of the day's lost traffic to AT&T was between US$60 million and US$75 million, and, obviously, losses would also have been made by AT&T's customers. Additionally, there were long-term effects on AT&T through loss of confidence. As a company, its advertising had concentrated on its reliability to justify its pricing being higher than that of its competitors.[168]

Of course, the potential for losses caused by defective software will vary from business to business and the extent to which the business is dependent on the software, as well as the specific defect. It will also depend on the type of contract. The point has already been made as to the difficulties involved in drafting and performing a software development contract, for example (see p 445 above). However, the damages recovered under contract law for any loss, no matter how large or small, depend upon the same basic rules. The basic principle on which an award of contractual damages is made is that damages should place the injured party in the position in which he or she would have been had the contract been properly performed[169] – that is, the position in which he or she would have been had there been no breach. This means that, when a contract is breached, the injured party can recover for the profits that he or she would have made had the contract been performed. In other words, in contract, the injured party can recover his or her expectation loss. It is, of course, possible for an injured party merely to claim expenditure wasted because of the breach.[170] That party will not, however, be able to evade the basic principle by so doing. He or she will not recover any expenditure that the party in breach can establish would have been lost even if the contract had been performed.[171] Claiming for wasted expenditure does not allow the injured party to recover more than he or she would have obtained had the contract been performed – that is, an award of damages does not relieve the injured party from the consequences of having made a bad bargain.

There are certain limitations on awards of damages made under the above basic principle. For example, the injured party will not recover for a loss that is too remote. This means that he or she will not recover for a loss that, at the time the contract was made, was not within the reasonable contemplation of the parties as liable to result from the breach.[172]

An award of damages may also be circumscribed by the duty to mitigate. This so-called duty means that the injured party will not be able to recover for any loss that he or she could have avoided by behaving reasonably after the breach.[173] In *Salvage Association v CAP Financial Services Ltd*,[174] the question arose as to the damages recoverable when a system development contract had been terminated by SA because of CAP's inability to successfully complete the system. The injured party, SA, was able to recover all of the money that it had expended on the CAP system, because the court felt that SA's decision to abandon its use entirely was reasonable.[175] Had it been found that the reasonable course was not to abandon the CAP system entirely, but to contract with another company for its completion,

---

167 See, generally, Koffman and Macdonald, op cit, ch 21.
168 See Dai Davies, 'Anatomy of a disaster' (1990) 6 CSLR 27.
169 *Robinson v Harman* (1880) 5 App Cas 25, 35, per Parke B.
170 *Anglia TV v Reed* [1971] 3 All ER 690.
171 *CCC Films (London) Ltd v Impact Quadrant Films Ltd* [1984] 3 All ER 298; *C & P Haulage v Middleton* [1983] 3 All ER 94.
172 *Hadley v Baxendale* (1854) 9 Ex 341; *Koufos v Czarnikow Ltd* [1969] 1 AC 350; *Parsons (H) (Livestock) v Uttley Ingham & Co Ltd* [1978] 1 All ER 525.
173 *British Westinghouse Electric and Manufacturing Co Ltd v Underground Electric Rlys Co of London* [1912] AC 673, 689, per Lord Haldane.
174 *Salvage Association v CAP Financial Services Ltd* [1995] FSR 654.
175 Ibid, 680.

then the duty to mitigate would mean that SA's recovery would not have encompassed any expenditure on the CAP system, which would not have been wasted had that system been salvaged.[176]

In addition, the 'duty to mitigate' means that the cost of steps taken to deal with the breach by the acquirer will not be recoverable unless the actions were a reasonable response to the breach. In *SAM Business Systems Ltd v Hedley & Co*,[177] the supplier of a system that did not function effectively argued that the acquirer had acted unreasonably in seeking the advice of a consultant on a replacement system. Its contention was based on the fact that no such consultation had taken place before acquisition of the supplier's system. Had the supplier succeeded, the consultant's fees would not have been recoverable in damages, but the judge did not accept its view. He took the line that it was 'perfectly reasonable if a firm finds itself in a mess to go to a consultant for help in getting out of the mess whether or not they employed a consultant to take the course that got them into the mess'.[178]

Exemption Clauses

Exemption clauses are basically clauses that exclude or restrict, or appear to exclude or restrict, liability for breach of contract or other liability arising through tort, bailment, or statute.[179] They may be aimed at totally excluding liability ('exclusion clauses') or merely restricting or limiting it ('limitation clauses') by, for example, limiting the sum recoverable in damages.

To be effective in relation to contractual liability, an exemption clause must have been incorporated into the contract, it must be appropriately worded to cover the breach that occurred, and it must not be rendered ineffective by legislation – basically, either **UCTA 1977** or the **Unfair Terms in Consumer Contracts Regulations 1999**.[180] The question of incorporation of clauses into contracts has already been looked at (see p 407), but brief consideration should be given to the construction of the contract (that is, interpreting it, or, more specifically, asking if the clause is appropriately worded to cover the breach) and the legislation must be considered.

Construction

Traditionally, a strict approach is taken to the interpretation of exemption clauses and the *contra proferentem* rule is applied, which means that, if there is any ambiguity in the clause, it will be construed in the way that is least favourable to the party seeking to rely upon it.[181] One particular aspect of the *contra proferentem* rule occurs in relation to liability for negligence (for example, a negligent breach or negligence in tort).[182] If a clause expressly refers to liability for negligence obviously, it will cover that liability.[183] The difficulties arise where there is no express reference to negligence as such, but a widely worded general clause is used, which it is argued encompasses liability for negligence (for example, a clause referring to 'any liability'). In these circumstances, the courts have taken an approach that means that the clause is more likely to be construed as covering liability for negligence if there is no other liability for it to cover,[184] and less likely to be construed as covering negligence if there is other strict liability for it to cover.[185] The idea would seem to be that

---

176 Obviously, in those circumstances, the cost of salvaging the system would have been recoverable – this is the other side of the duty to mitigate.
177 *SAM Business Systems Ltd v Hedley & Co* [2003] 1 All ER (Comm) 465.
178 Ibid, [155].
179 See Koffman and Macdonald, op cit, chs 9 and 10.
180 SI 1999/2083.
181 *Investors Compensation Scheme Ltd v West Bromwich Building Soc* [1998] 1 All ER 98, 114.
182 *Canada Steamship Lines Ltd v R* [1952] AC 192 (PC), 208, per Lord Morton.
183 For example, *Spriggs v Sotheby Parke Bernet & Co* [1986] 1 Lloyd's Rep 487.
184 For example, *Alderslade v Hendon Laundry Ltd* [1945] 1 KB 189.
185 *White v John Warwick & Co Ltd* [1953] 2 All ER 1021.

it is unlikely that the injured party would have accepted a clause covering the other party's liability in the event of negligence and, if there is other liability, the clause can be assigned a purpose without the need for it to be understood as covering negligence.

Unfair Contract Terms Act 1977

Scope of the Act

Despite its name, **UCTA 1977** does not deal with 'unfair terms' as such. For the most part, the Act applies to clauses that 'exclude or restrict liability'.[186] It can, basically, be said that the Act applies to 'exemption clauses'. Of course, it does not apply to all exemption clauses and the scope of the Act should be considered. It should, however, first be noted that it considerably overlaps with the **Unfair Terms in Consumer Contracts Regulations 1999**, which are considered below, and the Law Commissions are considering the substitution of a single unified and simplified piece of legislation.[187]

As has been indicated, the scope of the Act should now be addressed and, basically, it applies to 'business liability' (s 1). However, certain contracts are excluded from its operation in whole, or in part (Sch 1). The important exclusion to consider here is that to be found in Sch 1, para 1(c), which removes from the scope of ss 2–4 of the Act contracts in so far as they relate to the creation, transfer, or termination of intellectual property rights. The scope of this ouster from the operation of the Act was considered in *The Salvage Association v CAP Financial Services Ltd*,[188] which suggested a restrictive approach to the para 1(c) exclusion.

There are also provisions dealing with the application of the Act in relation to contracts with an international element (see ss 26 and 27). If the exemption clauses in question are capable of falling within the 1977 Act, it must be decided which, if any, of the 'active sections' is relevant. These are the sections that state that something is to happen to a certain exemption clause – that is, either that it is automatically ineffective or that it is effective only if it 'satisfies the requirement of reasonableness'. There are also 'definition sections', which assist in determining the scope of the 'active sections', and these will be looked at once the 'active sections' have been considered.

The Active Sections

Section 2 deals with liability arising from negligence.[189] Section 2(1) renders automatically ineffective clauses that 'exclude or restrict liability' for negligently caused death or personal injury. Such terms are 'blacklisted' – that is, their reasonableness or otherwise is irrelevant. Section 2(2) deals with clauses excluding or restricting any other sort of negligently caused loss or damage and renders them ineffective except in so far as they satisfy the 'requirement of reasonableness'. The section deals not only with contractual clauses, but also covers, for example, non-contractual disclaimers, which may be used to try to exclude or restrict such liability in tort.

Section 3 deals with the situation in which one party 'deals as consumer' or on the other party's 'written standard terms of business'. Contracts may come within both of the situations covered. Someone who deals as consumer may well contract on the other party's written standard terms of business. The meaning of 'deals as consumer' is dealt with by s 12 and is considered below

---

186　There is provision, most notably in ss 3(2)(b) and 13, to prevent it from being evaded by the redrafting of clauses to avoid its scope by avoiding the use of clauses in the form of exclusions or restrictions of liability.

187　See further, Elizabeth Macdonald, 'Unifying unfair terms legislation' (2004) 67 MLR 69.

188　*The Salvage Association v CAP Financial Services Ltd* [1995] FSR 654.

189　Section 1(1) makes it clear that this covers the situation in which there is a breach of the duty to take reasonable care or exercise reasonable skill arising under the contract or in tort or under the Occupiers' Liability Act 1957.

(see p 471). There is no statutory definition of 'written standard terms of business': whether a party has a set of 'written standard terms' should depend upon the pattern and degree of usage of the relevant terms.[190] If the relevant party clearly has 'written standard terms of business', the question may arise as to whether the alterations of them in the instant case are such that the contract cannot be regarded as having been made on that party's written standard terms of business. Determining that should be a matter of the extent of alteration of the original terms, and also of which terms are altered (some terms in a set of standard terms being intended to be particularised to individual contracts).[191] One further point to be made is that what is required by s 3 is not merely that written standard terms of business be used, but also that they should be the written standard terms of the relevant party. Should terms used throughout a particular trade and commonly used by the party in question be regarded as that party's 'written standard terms of business' for the purposes of s 3?[192]

Once it is determined that the contract in question falls within s 3, it should be noted that the scope of the section extends beyond terms that, in form, 'exclude or restrict liability'. Such terms are covered by s 3(2)(a) and are rendered ineffective unless they 'satisfy the requirement of reasonableness'. However, s 3(2)(b) extends the scope of the section beyond terms in the form of exclusions or restrictions of liability. It is one of the provisions of the Act that prevents its easy evasion by drafting that avoids those forms. Section 3(2)(b)(i), for example, extends the reasonableness test to terms under which the party who contracts on his or her own written standard terms of business, or who contracts with someone who deals as consumer, claims to render a performance substantially different from that which was reasonably expected of him or her.

Section 6 covers exemption clauses dealing with the terms implied into contracts for the sale or hire purchase of goods. There are analogous provisions in s 7 dealing with other contracts under which possession or ownership of goods passes. Section 6(1)(a) renders automatically ineffective any term excluding or restricting liability in relation to the terms implied by s 12 of the **SoGA 1979**. Section 6(2)(a) does the same in relation to the exclusion or restriction of liability for breach of the terms implied by ss 13–15 of the 1979 Act, provided that the buyer 'deals as consumer'. These are the other terms 'blacklisted' by the 1977 Act. However, if the buyer does not 'deal as consumer', liability for breach of the terms implied by ss 13–15 of the **SoGA 1979** can be excluded or restricted by a clause that satisfies the requirement of reasonableness.[193] Section 6 also contains analogous provisions dealing with exemptions of the terms implied into hire purchase contracts.[194] Obviously, the question of whether the buyer 'deals as consumer' is very important in the context of s 6 (see below).

Unlike most of the other active sections, s 4 does not refer to terms that 'exclude or restrict liability'. It deals with terms under which someone who 'deals as consumer' has to indemnify the other party in relation to that other party's liability for negligence or breach of contract. Such clauses are ineffective unless they satisfy the requirement of reasonableness. Section 5 of **UCTA 1977** is of very limited application. It was enacted to deal with a very specific problem – that of manufacturers or distributors of goods attempting to remove their liability for goods that proved defective 'in consumer use' due to the negligence of the manufacturers or distributors. The relevant clause would be found in a 'guarantee', which also stated that the consumer had certain rights. This section does not apply between parties to a contract under which, or in pursuance of which, possession or ownership of goods passes (s 5(3)). It does not cover clauses in contracts between sellers and buyers of goods.

190 *Flammar Interocean Ltd v Denmac Ltd* [1990] 1 Lloyd's Rep 434; *Chester Grosvenor Hotel Co Ltd v Alfred McAlpine Management Ltd* (1992) 56 Build LR 115; *The Salvage Association v CAP Financial Services Ltd* [1995] FSR 654; *St Albans City and DC v ICL* [1995] FSR 686.
191 *St Albans*, above.
192 For consideration of this case, see *British Fermentation Products Ltd v Compair Reavell Ltd* [1999] 2 All ER (Comm) 389.
193 Section 6(3).
194 On the terms implied by the SGA 1979, ss 13–15, see below.

Section 10 deals with one of the ways in which the other sections of the Act might have been avoided. It prevents a term from being used in a second contract to achieve the exclusion or restriction of liability that the Act would prevent in a first contract.

Definitions: 'Deals as Consumer'

This phrase is dealt with by s 12. It is vital to the question of whether someone deals as consumer to determine whether he or she contracts 'in the course of a business', which was addressed in R & B Customs Brokers v United Dominion Trust.[195] The plaintiff company was in business as a freight forwarding agent. It purchased a car, on credit terms, for the use of its two directors and sole shareholders. The car proved to be defective and did not comply with the terms implied by s 14(3) of the **SoGA 1979**, but there was an exemption clause. The question arose as to whether the buyer dealt as consumer within s 12 of **UCTA 1977** and that hinged upon whether it had contracted 'in the course of a business'. The Court of Appeal took the line that, basically, that depended upon whether the contract was integral to the business or, if merely incidental to it, regularly occurring. The contract was not integral to the buyer's business – its business was acting as freight forwarding agents, not buying and selling cars – and it was only the second or third such transaction undertaken, so it was incidental to the business and had not occurred regularly.[196]

Definitions: The 'Requirement of Reasonableness'

The requirement of reasonableness is a key feature of the Act, with the effectiveness of exemption clauses often depending on whether they can satisfy the test. Section 11(5) of **UCTA 1977** places the burden of proving 'reasonableness' on the person seeking to use the clause. The assessment of reasonableness does not occur in the light of the actual breach that occurred, but on the basis of what was known, or should reasonably have been contemplated, at the time of contracting.[197] There will be a greater possibility of a clause being effective if it is of narrow application and it would seem advisable to draft several clauses to cover different aspects of liability, rather than one wide one. In that way, at least some of the exemptions may be effective.[198]

Before considering the factors relevant to the 'requirement of reasonableness', the courts' approach to appeals in relation to the application of this test should be noted. In *George Mitchell Ltd v Finney Lock Seeds Ltd*,[199] Lord Bridge took the view that there could be legitimate differences of opinion on the reasonableness test and that:

> . . . when asked to review such a decision on appeal, the appellate court should treat the original decision with the utmost respect and refrain from interference with it unless satisfied that it proceeded upon some erroneous principle or was plainly and obviously wrong.[200]

Decisions on the 'reasonableness' of a clause in one case are therefore of limited precedent value.[201]

Consideration should now be given to the working of the test and it should be noted that Sch 2 contains guidelines as to its operation.[202] These guidelines are a non-exhaustive list of relevant

---

195 [1988] 1 All ER 847.
196 See Koffman and Macdonald, op cit, paras 10.62–10.69.
197 Section 11(1); see *Stewart Gill Ltd v Horatio Myer & Co Ltd* [1992] 2 All ER 257.
198 *Rees Hough Ltd v Redland Reinforced Plastics Ltd* [1985] 2 Con LR 109.
199 *George Mitchell Ltd v Finney Lock Seeds Ltd* [1983] 2 AC 803.
200 Ibid, 816.
201 But see Lord Griffiths' comments on future cases in *Smith v Bush* [1990] 1 AC 831.
202 By s 11(2), these guidelines are relevant to the reasonableness test when applied under ss 6 or 7. However, they are the type of factors that are likely to be relevant, simply on the facts in many cases, and will then be looked at on that basis (eg, *Phillips Products Ltd v Hyland* [1987] 2 All ER 620, 628).

factors and that, in itself, is indicative of the functioning of the test, which, basically, involves a weighing of the relevant factors in each case. These were outlined in the House of Lords' decision in Smith v Bush, as follows.

- Were the parties of equal bargaining power?
- Could advice have been sourced from elsewhere at reasonable cost and in reasonable time?
- Was the task being contracted for a particularly risky one?
- Was insurance available at reasonable cost and would a prudent professional have sought to insure against the risk?[203]

There will obviously be a variety of factors to be considered in each case and their importance will have to be assessed in the context of the particular case. The parties' relative bargaining powers may be relevant, as may the question of whether the party against whom the clause is being used knew its contents or had ample opportunity to ascertain them.[204]

However, although the application of the test is a weighing process and any factor is merely one indicator, some factors may be more significant than others. The existence, or otherwise, of an alternative to the particular contract has been important in some cases.[205] It may be easier for a party to establish that his or her exemption clause is reasonable if it can also be established that he or she also offered an alternative, higher priced contract that did not contain the exemption clause.[206] However, the court will consider not merely the existence of an alternative, but also its reality. In Smith v Bush, cost was the factor making the alternative unrealistic, but insufficiently drawing an alternative to the attention of the other party might also adversely affect the court's view of it.

However, it may be that the most generally significant factor is that of insurance. As we have seen, insurance was considered in Smith v Bush, and particular reference is made to it in s 11(4), in the context of determining the reasonableness of limitation clauses. The basic questions will be as to which party was in the best position to insure, and at what cost.[207] Section 11(4) of the **UCTA 1977** states:

> (4)   Where by reference to a contract term or notice a person seeks to restrict liability to a specified sum of money, and the question arises (under this or any other Act) whether the term or notice satisfies the requirement of reasonableness, regard shall be had in particular (but without prejudice to subsection (2) above in the case of contract terms) to—
>
> (a)   the resources which he could expect to be available to him for the purpose of meeting the liability should it arise; and
> (b)   how far it was open to him to cover himself by insurance.

A difficult or dangerous task with a high risk of failure involved may indicate the reasonableness of an exemption clause. In the context of system or software supply contracts, what is involved will not normally be a dangerous task, but we have seen that it may be difficult to supply software without bugs. That is particularly so when the development of a system is in question, but may also be so when standard software is to be modified to meet the acquirer's requirements, and even when what is in issue is the supply of standard software, there may be difficulty in discerning the 'fit' between the software and the needs of the 'acquirer'. The significance of the 'risk' factor in consid-

---

203 Smith v Bush, above, per Lord Griffith.
204 For example, Singer Co (UK) Ltd v Tees and Hartlepool Port Authority [1988] 2 Lloyd's Rep 164; Stag Line Ltd v Tyne Ship Repair Group Ltd (The Zinnia) [1984] 2 Lloyd's Rep 211.
205 RW Green Ltd v Cade Bros Farms [1978] 1 Lloyd's Rep 602; Woodman v Photrade Processing Ltd (1981) unreported.
206 Woodman, ibid.
207 See, eg, Photo Production Ltd v Securicor Ltd [1980] AC 827.

ering the reasonableness of exemption clauses in software/system supply contracts can be seen in *Watford Electronics Ltd v Sanderson CFL Ltd*[208] and *SAM Business Systems Ltd v Hedley & Co Ltd*, as can the need to look at, and weigh, all of the relevant factors, such as the bargaining position of the parties, their awareness of the risk allocation, its relationship to the price, the extent of the clause, and the remedies left to the acquirer.[209]

In *Watford Electronics*, the parties had entered into a contract for the supply of a computer system. Watford was itself a supplier of computer products, principally by mail order, and with particular expertise in the supply of personal computers. Sanderson supplied equipment, together with software licences, to Watford Electronics for approximately £104,000, subject to its standard terms and conditions of supply. The relevant term stated:

> Neither the Company nor the Customer shall be liable to the other for any claims for indirect or consequential losses whether arising from negligence or otherwise. In no event shall the Company's liability under the Contract exceed the price paid by the Customer to the Company for the Equipment connected with any claim.

During negotiations, Watford had successfully negotiated for a price reduction and some modification of the terms – notably, an addendum to the exemption clause, which provided that:

> Sanderson CFL Limited commit to their best endeavours in allocating appropriate resources to the project to minimise any losses that may arise from the contract.

The computer system supplied did not perform effectively and, after several years of problems, was replaced with a system from another supplier. In bringing action, Watford claimed damages in excess of £5 million on the basis of misrepresentation, breach of implied contractual warranties (that is, satisfactory quality, and using skill and care in supplying services), and common law negligence. At first instance, the court held that the **UCTA 1977** applied to the contract, and that the limit of liability clause was unreasonable in its entirety under the Act and could not be relied upon by the defendant to exclude or restrict its liability to the claimant, or to impose a limit on that liability.[210]

On appeal, Chadwick LJ noted the requirement to have regard to the factors in Sch 2 of the **UCTA 1977**, and suggested, given that the facts that the parties were of equal bargaining strength, the inclusion of the term would clearly affect Sanderson's decision as to the price at which it was prepared to sell its product and Watford must have known this, Watford knew of the term and should have understood what effect it was intended to have, and the product was, to some extent, modified to meet the special needs of the customer, it was not unreasonable to conclude that the term excluding indirect loss was a fair and reasonable one to include in the contract, despite some countervailing factors.[211] Additionally, although Chadwick LJ concluded that s 11(4) of the 1977 Act did not apply to the term excluding indirect loss, he felt that its criteria of examination of the parties' resources and ability to insure were still relevant to an assessment of overall reasonableness.[212] His key criteria for assessing reasonableness in regard to the instant case specifically identified the nature of software as an issue, noting that it was necessary to recognise that:

- the software was customised and thus carried a higher risk to the supplier in case of unsatisfactory performance;

---

208 *Watford Electronics Ltd v Sanderson CFL Ltd* [2001] EWCA Civ 317.
209 *SAM Business Systems Ltd v Hedley & Co Ltd* [2003] 1 All ER (Comm) 465.
210 *Watford Electronics Ltd v Sanderson CFL Ltd* [2000] 2 All ER (Comm) 984 (TCC).
211 Ibid, [52].
212 Ibid, [53].

- the parties would or should have been aware of that risk;
- while Sanderson was in the better position to assess the risk that the product would fail to perform, Watford was in the better position to assess the amount of any potential loss; and
- such loss would be capable of being insured against, and that both parties should have been aware that the decision as to who would bear that cost would inevitably have an effect on the supplier's decision on its pricing and the purchaser's willingness to buy.[213]

As a result of these issues, it was reasonable for the contract to determine on which party the loss would fall.[214]

In the *SAM Business Systems* case,[215] the claimant, SAM, supplied software under a licence agreement and maintenance agreement to the defendant stockbrokers, Hedley's, for use in their business. Both agreements incorporated SAM's standard terms and conditions. The licence agreement contained the following terms:

> 3.2 . . . there are no warranties, either expressed or implied, by this agreement. These include, but are not limited to, implied warranties of merchantability or fitness for a particular purpose, and all such warranties are expressly disclaimed to the extent permissible by law.

> 3.3 . . . SAM will not be responsible for any direct, incidental or consequential damages such as, but not limited to, loss of profits resulting from the use of the software, even if SAM have been advised of the possibility of such damage . . . any liability to which SAM might otherwise become subject shall, in aggregate, be limited to the licence fee paid.

The agreement also contained details of a process for acceptance testing that permitted Hedley's to reject the software if it failed to meet required acceptance criteria and a clause that stated that, should this be the case, then the:

> 2.11 . . . client shall have the right at its entire discretion to rescind this agreement and to be repaid all sums which have previously been paid to SAM in respect of the licence under this agreement. This shall be the sole and exclusive remedy available to the client in the event of the application software not being accepted.

The software proved to be unsuitable, but Hedley's failed to utilise the acceptance testing/rejection mechanism in the agreement. At trial, the judge found that the software was defective, that SAM had misrepresented its capabilities, and that, following *St Albans v ICL*, there was breach of implied terms, including that the software would be reasonably fit for its intended purpose and of satisfactory quality. This left SAM relying upon its limitations and exclusions to avoid the resulting liabilities.

In analysing the reasonableness of the exclusion and limitation clauses, the judge paid attention not only to the 'reasonableness' factors in **UCTA 1977**, but also to the following.

- The parties were of generally equal bargaining power in terms of their size and resources.
- Hedley's were in a weaker negotiating position in that instance (they required a Millennium-compliant system at short notice), but they had put themselves in that position.
- Hedley's ability to obtain similar services elsewhere without such limitations and exclusions were limited, because it appeared to be standard practice for SAM's competitors to exclude

---

213 Ibid, [54].
214 Ibid, [55].
215 *SAM Business Systems*, above.

warranties of merchantability or fitness for purpose – but Hedley's had neither asked any questions about the terms, nor attempted to negotiate changes.[216]

The judge also took note of the particular business environment and factors in play in the particular fact situation.[217]

However, despite this, the judge noted that, were it not for the 'money-back guarantee' in clause 2.11, he would still have found the exclusion of liability clauses as 'quite unreasonable'.[218] Thus while *Watford v Sanderson* could be seen as indicating a generally non-interventionist approach in commercial contracts between parties of basically equal bargaining power, *SAM v Hedley* notes the need to consider all of the factors in each case and previous case law can be reflected on in that light. Obviously, in both of the above cases, the risk involved in the supply of software is plainly recognised.[219]

Unfair Terms in Consumer Contracts Regulations 1999

The **Unfair Terms in Consumer Contracts Regulations 1999** implement the EC **Directive on Unfair Terms in Consumer Contracts**.[220] They do not simply apply to exemption clauses; rather, they apply a fairness test to non-individually negotiated terms in contracts between consumers and sellers or suppliers, with certain 'core' terms being exempted from the test, provided that they are in plain, intelligible language.

The definition of 'consumer' is in reg 3. It is restricted to 'natural persons', which means that a company cannot be a consumer for the purposes of the Regulations. This differs from the category of those who 'deal as consumers' under **UCTA 1977** and, in general, a mechanistic approach to the categorisation under the Regulations seems likely, with businesses simply being excluded from its protection without any consideration of how central the contract in question is to the operation of the business.[221]

The fairness test is applied to terms that have not been individually negotiated. Most such terms will be contained in standard-form contracts, but the category does not seem to be solely limited to such terms. Regulation 5(2) states that:

> . . . a term shall always be regarded as not having been individually negotiated where it has been drafted in advance and the consumer has not been able to influence the substance of the term.

The exclusion of certain 'core' terms from the fairness test is covered by reg 6(2). It would seem to cover terms defining the main subject matter of the contract or stating the price and its exact scope is problematic,[222] but in *Director General of Fair Trading v First National Bank*,[223] the House of Lords made it clear that a restrictive approach should be taken to its coverage. It should cover only terms 'falling squarely within it'.[224] Further, it should be emphasised that it is restricted to cases in which the 'core' terms are in 'plain, intelligible language'. In any event, it would seem that the 'core' terms should always be taken into account in assessing the fairness of other terms.[225]

---

216 Ibid, [69]–[71].
217 Ibid, [72].
218 Ibid, [73].
219 Elizabeth Macdonald, '*Watford v Sanderson*: The requirement of reasonableness in system supply contracts and more generally' (2001) 4 Web JCLI, available online at http://webjcli.ncl.ac.uk/2001/issue4/macdonald4.html
220 [1993] OJ L 95/29 – made under Art 100A on the basis that it is concerned with the establishment of an internal market.
221 Contrast the approach to 'deals as consumer' under the 1977 Act: see p 471 above.
222 Macdonald (1994) op cit.
223 [2002] 1 All ER 97.
224 Ibid, [12], per Lord Bingham.
225 See Recital 19 of the Directive.

Regulation 5(1) states that a term shall be regarded as unfair if:

... contrary to the requirement of good faith it causes a significant imbalance in the parties' rights and obligations arising under the contract to the detriment of the consumer.

Like 'reasonableness' under the 1977 Act, this is assessed against the background of the circumstances at the time of contracting.[226] Looking for a significant imbalance in the parties' rights and obligations would seem to require a weighing of the rights and obligations of the two parties. Some consideration was given to the meaning of good faith in *Director General of Fair Trading v First National Bank*.[227] In that case, Lord Bingham saw it as a matter of 'fair and open dealing', with the supplier ensuring that all contract terms were comprehensible and that potentially disadvantageous terms were clearly signposted to the consumer, and not taking advantage of information asymmetries or other factors likely to unfairly disadvantage the consumer.[228] Further assistance in determining which terms will be unfair can be found in Sch 2 to the Regulations, which contains a non-exhaustive list of terms that 'may be regarded as unfair'.

The consumer can use the Regulations in the same way as someone can use **UCTA 1977** against an exemption clause. An unfair term will not bind the consumer[229] and the consumer can rely on this when in dispute with a seller or supplier. However, the Regulations also provide for a different form of attack on unfair terms. The Director General of Fair Trading has the power to, inter alia, obtain injunctions to prevent the use of unfair terms more generally[230] and, under the 1999 Regulations, that power has been extended to certain qualifying bodies listed in Sch 1, such as the Consumers' Association.

Liability and Tort

Introduction

Unlike some of the other areas of law considered in this book, liability for defective software has no dedicated statutes to examine and no case law of significance to assist in predicting how existing legal principles might be applied to such situations. Some cases founded in contract have now come before the UK courts, but, as will have been noted above, are a long way from answering some of the fundamental questions posed by such circumstances. At time of writing, there have still been no cases based in tort, although there has been much speculation as to how tortious principles should be applied. What follows is, therefore, an attempt to review briefly and distil a number of the arguments that have been discussed into a coherent framework, and to suggest how the law might move forward in this area. The case law cited has been chosen in an attempt to provide suitable analogies with other situations; many of these are favourites of other commentators, but, where they make a useful point, no excuse should be needed for a re-examination. It must be remembered, though, that such cases can only be useful by way of analogy and some will perform this task rather better than others.

In the event of a system containing defective software failing, it has long been argued (but never tested in practice) that there may be liability in negligence and also, for cases of physical injury or damage, under the **Consumer Protection Act 1987 (CPA 1987)**.

---

226 Regulation 6(1).
227 [2002] 1 All ER 97.
228 [17]; see also [36], per Lord Steyn.
229 Regulation 8(1).
230 Regulation 12.

The Consumer Protection Act 1987

The **CPA 1987** was passed to implement the EC **Product Liability Directive**.[231] Article 1 of the Directive provides, quite simply, that 'The producer shall be liable for damage caused by a defect in his product'. 'Product' is then further defined in Art 2 to include 'all movables . . . even though incorporated into another movable or into an immovable'. This can be compared with the relevant section of the **CPA 1987**,[232] which provides that '"product" means any goods or electricity and . . . includes a product which is composed in another product, whether by virtue of being a component part or raw material or otherwise'. In theory, the effect of product liability legislation, for those situations in which it applies, is to eliminate the necessity to show negligence and, instead, replace it with the requirement to demonstrate a causal link between the defect in the product and the damage caused. This is often referred to as a type of strict liability on the grounds that the culpability of the producer in relation to the defect is not a relevant factor.

Is Software a Product?

Can computer software fall within this definition of 'product'? This question has stimulated much debate. Rusch points out that:

> . . . for anyone who has struggled with software that does not function as expected or causes unanticipated difficulties, the idea of a products liability regime applying to software is attractive. Not only that, given that software controls the functioning of many types of goods, malfunctioning software may create unreasonable risks of harm.[233]

Some of the arguments are, essentially, a reflection of the tangibility/intangibility debate already discussed in relation to software as goods and will not be repeated here,[234] but other arguments are inextricably linked with the concept of product and the underlying premises on which the Act and Directive are based.[235] The realisation that there might be problems with the categorisation of computer software had dawned prior to implementation of the Directive:

> Special problems arise with those industries dealing with products concerned with information such as books, records, tapes and computer software . . . It does not appear that the Directive is intended to extend liability in such situations. On the other hand, it is important that liability is extended to the manufacturer of a machine which contains defective software and is thereby unsafe . . . the line between those cases may however not be easy to draw, particularly in the field of new technology where the distinction between hardware and software is becoming increasingly blurred.[236]

This suggests that, even though software can be regarded as pure information in some respects, the development of technology, together with the way in which it might be used to control systems and apparatus, may conspire to make an apparently logical boundary indistinct. However, it appeared that, by the time of implementation, this issue had officially disappeared and the advice following implementation was that, in the event of a defect in software leading to physical damage,

---

231 Council Directive 85/374/EEC of 25 July 1985 on the approximation of the laws, regulations and administrative provisions of the Member States concerning liability for defective products, [1985] OJ L 210/29.
232 CPA 1987, s 2(1).
233 Linda J Rusch, 'Products liability trapped by history: Our choice of rules rules our choices' (2003) 76 Temp L Rev 739, 777.
234 See pp 450–454. above.
235 See Jacob Hirschbaeck, 'Is software a product?' (1989) 5 CL & P 154; Lloyd, op cit; Rowland, op cit.
236 Department of Trade and Industry (DTI), *Implementation of the EC Directive on Product Liability*, 1985, London: HMSO, para 47.

liability would rest with the producer of the complete system,[237] implicitly rejecting the notion of software as a product in its own right.

Predictably, this did not silence the academic debate and there is still a considerable divergence of views on the answer to the question. These differing approaches can be found not only in specialist works, but also in standard texts on the law of tort – for example: 'It is unclear whether books and computer software, which may endanger persons if they contain inaccuracies, fall within the definition of "products".'[238] Debate has focused on:

- the 'software as pure information' theory, which is usually held to be fatal to a classification of software as a product;
- the pragmatic approach, which considers the end result of the defect rather than its location; and
- the goods/services distinction.

If the first of these is to be argued successfully, it is important that all of the attributes of computer software are fully taken into account. In order to make the problem accessible, a number of writers have used quite simple analogies with, for example, recipe books.[239] This analogy considers both recipes and software to be simply sets of instructions – thus, the argument goes, if there is liability for mistakes in recipes, then there should be the possibility of liability for mistakes in computer programs, albeit that discovering mistakes in computer programs is going to be a rather less simple matter than finding a mistake in a recipe.[240] Despite the apparent ease of spotting a mistake (or a defect?) in a recipe, there was no liability for breach of warranty in the US case of *Cardozo v True*,[241] in which a recipe book failed to point out that a particular ingredient in a recipe was poisonous unless cooked properly. Arguably, a novice in either cookery or programming may have equal difficulty in detecting the defect in the relevant medium. A more useful distinction might be between choosing to rely on information and being compelled to so rely.[242]

Although the fact of inputting inaccurate data may result in a malfunction, which, in turn, produces certain adverse consequences, this is a gross simplification of both the nature and the function of computer control in most systems. The potential defects that are likely to give rise to the severest problems are errors in coding or logic that cause the mode of operation of the computer-controlled system to depart from its specification. This may not be traceable to any particular human error, as such, but instead may be due to a 'design error' in the software. This is, arguably, the point at which software begins to diverge from 'pure information'; although capable of reduction to written format, the program is designed to be a working entity and is 'engineered' in the true sense of the word, just as much as a more conventional control system might be. This suggests that the more accurate view is to consider a defect in the software as a design fault. Approaching the issue from this angle can be argued to constitue a pragmatic approach – the argument is that the precise coding error should not be the focus of liability; rather the failure of the system to operate as specified, for whatever reason.

The final issue raised is that of the goods/services debate[243] – the extent to which the categorisation of the contract to supply software can be described in terms of a contract for goods, or a contract for services, and the impact that this categorisation might have on the boundaries of the definition of product.

---

237 DTI, *Guide to the Consumer Protection Act 1987*, 1987, London: HMSO, para 11.
238 Keith M Stanton, *The Modern Law of Tort*, 1994, London: Sweet & Maxwell, p 222.
239 David Howarth, *Textbook on Tort*, 1995, London: Butterworths, p 412.
240 Ibid.
241 342 So 2d 1053 (Fla App 1977).
242 Rowland, op cit.
243 See the discussion above at pp 450–456.

It has been argued that it would be rational for the law to treat mass-market software or 'off the shelf' software as a good/product, and thus to impose strict liability upon suppliers, because the supplier has made the choice to go to mass market, and can both control the risk of defect by defining the parameters of the program and spreading the cost of failure across multiple transactions. Additionally, the mass-market buyer is likely to have limited knowledge of the computer program, to have had no input into the design and implementation of the product, and to have only limited opportunity to test and seek corrections to faulty programs. Thus it is reasonable to use strict liability as a means of equalising the cost of faulty software between suppliers and buyers of mass-market software.

Conversely, with bespoke software, the supplier has a limited market, perhaps of only one buyer, and it is harder, or impossible, for the supplier to spread the cost of a software failure, focusing the risk of failure. The bespoke software buyer is also likely to have had input to the design of the software, and much greater opportunity to test and obtain corrections to a faulty program over a longer term.[244] In this case, it would seem appropriate to allow supplier and buyer to allocate the risk of their transaction by contract.[245]

Evidence of the European Commission's view of the intention of the Directive, if not necessarily of the logic of classifying software as a product, was illustrated in the answer to the following question asked in the European Parliament: 'Does the EEC Directive on product liability also cover . . . computer software?'[246] The answer to this was unequivocal on the basis that, because the term 'product' was defined as all movables even though incorporated into another movable or into an immovable, the Directive also applied to software.

Is There a Defect?

If, indeed, computer software can be construed as a product, how is a defect in that software to be identified? This may raise practical, as well as legal, problems. In fact, the relevant issue may be not so much a question as to whether the sought after goal exists, but rather whether it is possible to demonstrate how far the search is from the target. The degree of complexity of most computer programs, creating manifold combinations and permutations, means that most computer software is impossible to test exhaustively for all foreseeable conditions. Comprehensive testing is therefore out of the question. Many faults will be discovered by routine testing, but identifying defects that will compromise safety are more likely to be discovered by the testing of boundary conditions than by testing normal operating conditions. It is usual to assume that, in any piece of software, some residual 'bugs' will remain, but not all of these will give rise to 'defects' – only those that could lead to damage.

'Defect' was defined in Art 6 of the Directive as follows:

1   A product is defective when it does not provide the safety that a person is entitled to expect, taking all circumstances into account, including:

   (a)   the presentation of the product;
   (b)   the use to which it could reasonably be expected that the product would be put;
   (c)   the time when the product was put into circulation.

2   A product shall not be considered defective for the sole reason that a better product is subsequently put into circulation.

---

244 Simon Whittaker, 'European product liability and intellectual products' (1989) 105 LQR 125, 135.
245 See the approach of the some US courts, eg, *Hou-Tex Inc v Landmark Graphic* 26 SW 3d 103, 107 (Tex-App, Houston 14th Dist 2000), in which the court accepted that the particular software at issue was a product on the grounds that it was 'a highly technical tool used to create a graphic representation from technical data'; however, the court noted that it was making no general assertion that all computer programs could be defined as products. See further Michael L Rustad and Thomas H Koenig, 'Cybertorts and legal lag: An empirical analysis' (2003) 13 S Cal Interdisc LJ 77, 135.
246 Written Question 706/88, [1989] OJ C 114/42.

This was implemented in s 3(1) of the **CPA 1987**, which provides that 'there is a defect in a product . . . if the safety of the product is not such as persons generally are entitled to expect; and for those purposes "safety" in relation to a product, shall include safety with respect to products comprised in that product'.

How, then, can this be assessed in systems containing software? It has been suggested both that 'in those more complex situations where modern tort liability also operates, eg cases of foreseeable misuse or complex design systems where the standard is neither agreed nor obvious, the "expectations test" is misleading and inadequate',[247] and also that '[t]he "consumer expectations" test for legal defectiveness . . . has had limited appeal as an operational rule for complex design defect cases. Primarily this is because the consumer simply does not have adequate information to know what to expect'.[248] A comparison can be made with the situation for 'conventional' products, in which the general safety record may have a particular relevance in ascertaining whether the product was defective. This is unlikely to be the case for systems involving computer software, in which failure-free operation in the past is not necessarily an indication of failure-free operation in the future, especially for products that are likely to be used in different situations and conditions. In such circumstances, a fault could remain hidden for some time until triggered by a particular combination of inputs that may not have occurred before. In addition, the operative time at which a diagnosis of defectiveness needs to be made is the moment of supply. It is possible that the software may have been updated, modified, or otherwise upgraded, making it difficult to assess the defectiveness of either the original version or successive iterations, but, in the absence of such changes, software does not 'wear out' in the same way as hardware.

Causation

The final factor that has to be established is that the defect caused the damage. This may be difficult to prove, depending on the nature and type of software involved. It goes without saying that any physical damage will always be inflicted by hardware, and so a causal link has to be established between the apparently defective software instructions, their effect on the hardware, and the consequence to the victim. Such observations perhaps highlight the difference between software and pure information: once computer software has commenced giving instructions to the system under its control, it may activate an inevitable sequence of events that becomes difficult to interrupt.

It may be difficult to establish causation if there has also been some human input or intervention. In so-called fly-by-wire aircraft, such as the Airbus A320 (now superseded by the A330 and A340), the pilot flies the plane not directly, but by means of a joystick connected to the appropriate mechanisms via a computer.[249] The presence of the computer allows for intelligent control of the aircraft, which should be able to compensate for both malfunctions and pilot error. The role of the pilot (or, indeed, the operator/controller of other computerised systems) often only becomes crucial in the event of failure of the normal operating system. What is the situation if defective software causes such a malfunction and the pilot is unable to land the plane safely? What was the cause of the accident? Clearly, each case will hinge on its particular circumstances, but there are a number of general observations that can be made. There will be appropriate procedures that should be carried out in the event of a failure and, if the pilot fails to carry these out, there may be a break in the chain of causation and the accident may be put down to 'pilot error'. However, the danger with human intervention being confined to abnormal cases can mean that there is very little

---

247 Jane Stapleton, *Product Liability*, 1994, London: Butterworths, p 235.
248 P Nicholas, 'State of the art evidence: From logical construct to judicial retrenchment' (1991) 20 AALR 285.
249 In fact, the A320 has five on-board computers, some of which are back-ups designed to switch into use if a fault is detected in the operational computer.

opportunity to practise and become proficient in such skills.[250] In addition, it is entirely possible that a situation could arise in which the computer would 'not allow' the pilot to take corrective action or, alternatively, in which the back-up system of control provided was inadequate to land the plane safely, especially in adverse weather conditions, even for an expert pilot. Although the root cause of the mishap might be the defective software, at least some of these elements would qualify as a *novus actus interveniens* sufficient to break the chain of causation.[251]

In the mid-1980s, defects in the software controlling the Therac-25 radiotherapy machine[252] resulted in substantial overdoses of radiation being administered to several patients, with resulting injury, illness, and death in some cases. Conceptually, this appears to be an example of a situation in which it is easier to accept the link between the defective software and the damage. Suppose, instead, that the software error had resulted in an underdose of radiation, with the result that patients died not from the effects of the radiation, but from the cancer for which they were supposedly being treated. In this scenario, the damage would be the result of the original disease – that is, it would not be caused by the radiotherapy machine, which could not, therefore, be classed as 'legally defective'.

The Development Risks Defence

Notwithstanding the label of 'strict liability' applied to the products liability regime introduced by the EC Directive and the **CPA 1987**, it is possible for producers to escape liability if they can avail themselves of the so-called 'development risks' defence contained in Art 7(e) of the Directive, 'that the state of scientific and technical knowledge at the time when he put the product into circulation was not such as to enable the existence of the defect to be discovered'. This is a controversial defence and the Member States were given the choice as to whether to include it in their implementing legislation. The UK included the defence in s 4(1)(e) of the 1987 Act:

> . . . that the state of scientific and technical knowledge at the relevant time was not such that a producer of products of the same description as the product in question might be expected to have discovered the defect if it had existed in his products while they were under his control.

The emphasis of the UK defence refers to a comparison with other producers – that is, a negligence-type test – whereas the Directive implies an obligation to consider the available knowledge in the world at large.[253] Thus, in relation to the UK defence, Reed suggests that, given the practice in the industry, 'it is arguable that a software producer who failed to discover a quite serious defect in his software would nevertheless be able to take advantage of the defence, so long as the defect is not in an area of the program that would be tested as a matter of course by others in the industry'.[254]

A number of commentators have discussed the various possible combinations envisaged by the defence.[255] The two outer extremes are those in which the defect is either unknown and undiscoverable, or known and discoverable. In the former, there will be no liability, whereas there will always be liability in the latter case. In between these two extremes are the situations in which the defect is either known but undiscoverable, or, conversely, unknown but discoverable. The latter is,

---

250 Apparently, human error is involved in about 60 per cent of all aircraft accidents. Although this does not necessarily indicate 'pilot error', it does show that human factors are also a relevant consideration: see, eg, N Storey, *Safety-critical Computer Systems*, 1996, Harlow: Addison-Wesley.

251 Consider the facts in *Airbus Industrie v Patel and ors* [1998] 2 All ER 257 (HL) – the case itself concerns jurisdictional issues.

252 See further Nancy G Leveson, *Safeware: System Safety and Computers*, 1995, Reading, MA: Addison-Wesley, Appendix A.

253 Christopher Newdick, 'Risk, uncertainty and "knowledge" in the development risks defence' (1991) 20 AALR 309.

254 Chris Reed and Alison Welterveden, 'Liability', in C Reed and J Angel (eds), *Computer Law*, 5th edn, 2003, Oxford: Oxford University Press, ch 3, p 115.

255 See, eg, Newdick, op cit; Christopher Hodges, *Product Liability: European Laws and Practice*, 1993, London: Sweet & Maxwell.

arguably, the usual position, and one in which it is incumbent on the producer to utilise the current state of knowledge to uncover the defect. The former is more difficult to rationalise, but is, perhaps, the one that best describes the position with respect to potential defects in software. It is never possible to provide assurance that any software is free from error and such errors are capable of becoming defects if they compromise the safety of the system. Techniques used to develop software for use in safety-critical systems take this fact into account by starting from the premise that such software is bound to contain errors. The use of the definite article in the wording of the defence seems to indicate that it refers to a specific defect. Such a concept is difficult to apply to software development and, based on this, the use of the defence appears problematic. On the other hand, if we start from the presumption of the presence of a defect, it may be that the situation is accurately represented by the phrase 'known but undiscoverable'. It has been suggested that where the danger is known, but science has not developed a means of eliminating the danger, then it would be open to the manufacturer to argue that the product is not defective, instead of pleading a defence of development risks.[256] In relation to defective software, though, the view has also been expressed that 'the argument that a software producer could not be expected to discover his own mistakes is not a compelling one'.[257] Since software is developed by human ingenuity, any faults should be regarded as introduced, rather than inherent. Neither is it clear how all of these factors affect, or are affected by, the question of resource allocation for research. Stapleton points out that the full pre-circulation screening test for some defects, including bugs in complex software, would be 'astronomically expensive', but suggests also that '[t]o give the defence substance then it must protect in cases of defects which could only be discovered, if at all, by extraordinary means'.[258] It is plain that testing cannot be carried on forever, but when should a producer stop testing? Does this, necessarily, entail a comparison with the behaviour of the 'reasonable' producer?

It is also important to note that the issue of when knowledge becomes available is crucial – the defence is unavailable after the date at which the existence of the defect could have been discovered. This may be especially pertinent for non-research-based industries (this market is becoming increasingly relevant as increasing numbers of domestic appliances contain software), for which it is likely that there will be a lapse in time before the requisite information concerning the defect is available to the producer.

It is difficult to assess how important the availability of a development risks defence might be to the software industry. A number of other EU Member States have chosen not to include the defence and producers exporting to those countries will need to take responsibility for their own development risks, even though this is unnecessary in relation to the domestic market. In addition, there is no similar defence in contract where liability is imposed when a defect would not be able to be detected even by the 'utmost skill and judgment on the part of the seller'.[259]

Negligence

Whether or not the **CPA 1987** can ever be said to apply to systems containing software, there will always be some situations involving defects in software in which the regime is inappropriate, either because of the nature of the software at issue or because of the nature of the damage. In such cases, potential liability will be determined by the principles of negligence. Even then, there have been suggestions that negligence will not be capable of founding liability. It was suggested in *Ministry of Housing and Local Government v Sharp*, a case concerning an inaccurate land certificate, that, due to the

---

256 Euan McKendrick, 'Product liability and the development risks defence' [1990] Law for Business 252; cf Newdick's view that the defence cannot be available once the possibility of a defect has been foreseen, op cit.
257 Lloyd, op cit.
258 Stapleton, op cit.
259 *Kendall*, above, 84, per Lord Reid.

likelihood of computerisation of the Land Registry, the Registrar's absolute statutory duty of care should be held to exist independently of negligence, since computers might produce an inaccurate certificate without negligence on the part of anyone.[260] It might be supposed that the average person (and even the average judge!) now has a greater general understanding of computing, at least to the extent of realising that computers can only be as accurate as the person who wrote the program, input the data, or interpreted the output made them. Nonetheless, there is still some truth in Tapper's assertion that '[i]t is common experience that computer systems do malfunction without any negligence on anyone's part, Just because they are so complicated, and exhaustive testing in all possible situations in which they might be used is impossible'. The challenge is to distinguish the failures that are due to negligence from those that are not.

Where the loss generated as a result of a defect in software is purely economic, then, if there is no remedy available in contract, the only possibility will be to consider liability for negligent misstatement, the operative principles for which were set out in *Hedley Byrne v Heller*.[261] In order to limit the class of potential claimants, a special relationship is required between the parties, plus evidence of reliance on the statement. This test for liability could be appropriate when the loss is a consequence of relying on the output of the software – unless the act of reliance on the output can itself be construed as negligent. Such an approach might be suitable when considering the potential liability for artificial intelligence and expert systems, because it can be argued that diagnostic expert systems are tools to 'aid' professionals in making their diagnoses. They should not be relied on absolutely, because they are no substitute for intelligent thought, but merely a useful pointer to a particular course of action. This could also be the case where the output is accurate, but insufficient by itself. It has also been suggested that, given the problems with the intangible nature of software, the tort of negligent misstatement might have more general application in relation to computer software, in which the program instructions are 'relied upon' by the computer to attain the relevant result.

In the case of bespoke software, which, being categorised as the provision of services, is unlikely to fall within the ambit of product liability legislation, it will be necessary to show that the system was designed negligently.

> . . . claims relating to the inadequate design of products can be made in negligence. There may well be practical reasons why such claims were in the past less often made than were claims for manufacturing errors but the propriety of such claims in negligence is without doubt. Many past negligence cases rested on a plaintiff's complaint that her predicament was made worse by the negligence of the defendant in relation to the design . . . The highly publicised Thalidomide litigation of the late 1960s and early 1970s was a classic example in the UK of a negligent design and R&D allegation, yet it was never challenged as being outside the realm of *Donoghue v Stevenson* negligence liability. A number of other UK design cases can be found typically focusing on the inadequacy of R&D or failure to warn [cites cases]. Moreover in recent years UK appellate courts have clearly confirmed manufacturer liability in negligence for the design condition of products. Although the issues raised on appeal in *Lambert v Lewis* did not focus on the trial judge's finding of liability against the manufacturer of a towing hitch on the basis of negligent design both the Court of Appeal and the House of Lords expressly accepted that finding.[262]

How is the negligence of a designer of software systems to be judged? By what criteria should the achievements and failures of software engineers be assessed? It is clear that the individuals in question possess, or should possess, special expertise, and one area of law that has developed to examine the achievements of those professing a particular expertise is that of professional negligence. There

---

260 *Ministry of Housing and Local Government v Sharp* [1970] 2 QB 223, 275, *per* Salmon LJ.
261 *Hedley Byrne v Heller* [1964] AC 465.
262 Stapleton, op cit, 251.

have, as yet, been no cases that have had to consider the role of software engineer as designer or the status of software engineer as a 'professional'. Could such a person be construed as coming within this latter category? Jackson and Powell refer to the four attributes that are deemed to be necessary characteristics of professions – namely, the nature of the work, the moral aspect, collective organisation, and status.[263] Thus the nature of the work is expected, or presumed, to be of high intellectual content, requiring particular study and qualifications; professionals are expected to have some moral commitment to the community at large; they are expected to be governed by an organisation that sets the standards for, and regulates the conduct of, its members; and there should be evidence that they are accorded a particular status by the community. How far do these factors pertain to software engineers?

The extent to which software engineering may be regarded as a profession is debatable,[264] but, where the work undertaken is of a safety-critical nature, the relevant factors are becoming increasingly pertinent. Many transport systems, particularly air and rail, rely on computer control, as do major hazard installations such as nuclear reactors and chemical plants. Failure of such systems is likely to result in disaster such that it seems inconceivable that persons designing the software for those applications would not be cognisant of their duty to the public at large. The 'profession' in the UK is governed by two professional organisations, the Institution of Electrical Engineers (IEE) and the British Computer Society (BCS), which together have considered the entry qualifications and continuing professional development necessary for those engaged in such work. Both organisations create standards and codes of conduct to which their members are expected to adhere.[265]

In any case, where the software engineer has contracted to design specialist bespoke software, the **SGSA 1982** will imply a term that 'reasonable care and skill' will be used in the performance of the contract. It is submitted that such a term will, in any case, require a similar level of competence as that appropriate to the professional in negligence. Nonetheless, in negligence, there will not necessarily be a duty of care towards all those who might be affected by the failure of the software. It is clear that there is a very different range of foreseeable claimants in relation to defects in the design of a radiotherapy machine as compared with a fly-by-wire aircraft, for example. There are policy considerations that may pull in either direction and the dividing line may not be easy to draw. There may be such potential for damage that it may be considered unjust to hold the designer liable, but, equally, both contractor and client may have their own particular knowledge and expertise about the system such that an apportionment of liability may be more appropriate.

There will again be the necessity to show causation. Returning to the example of the radiotherapy machines,[266] although an arguable case of negligence might be made out in relation to the overdose, because of the problems with proving causation, a claim of negligence might, again, be difficult to substantiate where the software fault resulted in an underdose. If a design standard was mandated for the design of the equipment and was not adhered to in either case, it is difficult to support the conclusion that the designer in the one instance is less culpable than the other. Two cases involving ambulance services may shed some light on how the courts might approach causation and duty of care in such circumstances. In *R v Poplar Coroner, ex p Thomas*[267] and *Kent v London Ambulance Service*,[268] questions of causation and duty of care were raised in regard to patients who

263 John Powell, Roger Stewart, and The Hon Mr Justice Jackson, *Jackson & Powell on Professional Liability*, 6th edn with 3rd Supp, 2009, London: Sweet & Maxwell.
264 See, eg, Diane Rowland, 'Negligence, professional competence and computer systems' [1999] 2 JILT, available online at www2.warwick.ac.uk/fac/soc/law/elj/jilt/1999_2/rowland/; Rustad and Koenig, op cit, 137, note that 'as the field of information technology matures, it is likely that software developers, web site designers and Internet security specialists will begin to professionalise by developing industry standards of care'.
265 See, eg, the BCS Code of Conduct, available online at www.bcs.org/server.php?show=nav.6030 and Code of Good Practice, available online at www.bcs.org/upload/pdf/cop.pdf
266 See p 481 above.
267 *R v Poplar Coroner, ex p Thomas* [1993] 2 WLR 547.
268 *Kent v London Ambulance Service* [1999] Lloyd's Rep Med 58.

were already seriously ill, but whose conditions might have been improved if the ambulance called for them had not been delayed. In the former case (in which causation, but not duty of care, was at issue), Dillon LJ pointed out with regard to causation that any number of events might have intervened to cause the ambulance to arrive late – not least the fact that the patient was so ill that it was simply not possible to travel the necessary distance in time.[269] Simon Brown LJ noted, however, that courts were often able to find there to have been several different causes of a given eventuality, and it was not implausible in the case before them to find the death to have been caused at least in part by the late arrival of the ambulance.[270] In the latter case, Kennedy LJ outlined the difficulties faced by the ambulance service in carrying out its task. However, he went on to note:

> . . . that if the ambulance service undertakes to attend, the person who has been promised that assistance, and those acting on his or her behalf normally abandon the search for other possible means of transport to the hospital . . . I . . . recognise that if a duty of care does exist it must make allowance for those factors to which I have just referred but I consider . . . that a court might well find not only sufficient proximity but also that it is just, fair and reasonable that a duty of care should be imposed.[271]

Although neither of these cases involved software failures, they may nevertheless provide important pointers as to whether a duty of care might be adjudged to arise in safety-critical cases. Kennedy LJ implied, albeit indirectly, that the reliance on the emergency services was a factor. In cases in which software controls a safety-critical function, there is clearly no option but to rely on the correct operation of that software, which is the responsibility of those who created it. Also in *Kent*, Schiemann LJ was inclined to find sufficient proximity between the parties to give rise to a duty of care merely from the fact that the degree of foreseeability of harm was high,[272] a condition that will inevitably be satisfied in relation to safety-critical systems. However, although a relevant factor, it is clear from a number of other cases that the mere foreseeability of harm may not, of itself, give rise to a duty of care. As pointed out by Lord Bridge: 'It is never sufficient to ask simply whether A owes B a duty of care. It is always necessary to determine the scope of the duty by reference to the kind of damage from which A must take care to save B.'[273] Nonetheless, in safety-critical cases, the likelihood of severe harm cannot be ignored and must surely be an essential factor in the equation.

Assuming that there are no problems in respect of causation, the standard of care required of a professional is that of the ordinarily competent member of that profession, as set out by McNair J in *Bolam v Friern HMC*:

> When you get situations which involve the use of some special skill or competence, then the test as to whether there has been negligence or not, is not the test of the man on the top of the Clapham Omnibus, because he has not got that special skill. The test is the standard of the ordinary skilled man exercising and professing that special skill. A man need not possess the highest expert skill; it is well established law that it is sufficient if he exercises the ordinary skill of an ordinary competent man exercising that particular art.[274]

This basic test, then, has been refined in relation to different professions taking note of the fact that professions can be divided into two groups: those who cannot guarantee the results of their labour;

---

269 *Poplar Coroner*, above, 552.
270 Ibid, 554.
271 *Kent*, above, 63.
272 Ibid, 64.
273 *Caparo Industries plc v Dickman and ors* [1990] 2 AC 605, 627; see also Rowland (1999), op cit.
274 [1957] 1 WLR 582, 586.

and those who could be said to impliedly warrant to produce a particular result.[275] Engineers are likely to fall into the latter category, as noted by Lord Scarman in *IBA v EMI and BICC*: 'In the absence of any terms (express or implied) negating the obligation, one who contracts to design an article for a purpose made known to him undertakes that the design is reasonably fit for the purpose.'[276] This can be construed as requiring a higher standard than the basic *Bolam* test.[277]

A number of facets of the standard of care required of the emerging profession of the software engineer have been identified,[278] but, of these, some are of particular concern to this discipline. The first is: on whom does the duty fall to identify the system as safety-related? Whereas it might be thought that the procurer would be in the best position to make this assessment, it cannot necessarily be assumed that the procurer is aware that safety-critical applications require design and implementation procedures that are any different from those used for 'normal' computer systems. This may be especially pertinent for systems for which the safety connection is not immediately obvious.[279] However, neither can it be assumed that the software engineer is likely to be in a better position to make this assessment.

A common measure of the standard of care is provided by adherence to relevant standards and codes of practice,[280] and there is no reason why this should be any different for the software engineer. This can include compliance not only with externally approved standards, but also with generally accepted practice in the industry. As pointed out by Viscount Simonds, 'it would be unfortunate if an employer who has adopted a practice, system or set-up ... which has been widely used without complaint could not rely on it as at least a prima facie defence to an action of negligence'.[281] However, the fact of general acceptance of a particular practice does not automatically mean that the practice is a good one or that it should not be modified and reviewed in the light of technical developments.[282]

An important consideration for a technologically advanced industry such as the software industry is the legitimate concern that innovation should not be stifled by legal rules. Designs for systems that are 'at the cutting edge of technology' may not have been tried and tested in the same way as a more pedestrian project, and the industry owes its success to its ability to create and market new methods of control or new systems and products. Nonetheless, where there are safety implications in a design, the law has not shied away from requiring the highest consideration of the safety factors, as evidenced in the case of *IBA v EMI and BICC* concerning the collapse of the Emley Moor television transmitter in 1969.[283]

The power of software arises principally from the relative ease with which highly complex systems can be created and changed. There is a consequent temptation to undertake development without adherence to appropriate engineering principles and to quite readily undertake a 'venture into the unknown referred to in *IBA v EMI and BICC*'; after all, software can be changed easily and it is tempting to think that any faults can be corrected easily. However, unless software is designed very carefully a seemingly simple change can have an unexpected side effect that may not become apparent for some considerable time afterwards, so that any departure from strict quality assurance procedures during development almost certainly becomes another 'venture into the unknown'. In

275 Diane Rowland and Jem J Rowland, 'Competence and legal liability in the development of software for safety-related applications' (1993) 2 Computers and Artificial Intelligence 229.
276 (1980) 14 BLR 1.
277 *Greaves & Co v Baynham Meikle* [1974] 1 WLR 1261, 1269, aff'd [1975] 1WLR 1095.
278 See further Rowland and Rowland, op cit; John Cooke, 'Architects and engineers: Practising in the public interest' (1991) 14 UNSWLJ 73.
279 Elisabeth Geake, 'Did ambulance chiefs specify safety software?' (1992) 136 New Scientist 5.
280 *Bevan Investments v Blackhall and Struthers (No 2)* [1973] 2 NZLR 45.
281 *Cavanagh v Ulster Weaving Ltd* [1960] AC 145, 158.
282 Rowland and Rowland, op cit, 238.
283 (1980) 14 BLR 1. For a more detailed consideration of this case, see, eg, KM Stanton and AM Dugdale, 'Design responsibility in civil engineering work' (1981) 131 NLJ 583.

the case of software the 'dimensions' of such ventures are not readily assessed, so that departure from established methods can be particularly risky.

Finally, what is the standard that can be expected if the client requests (and pays for) the services of an acknowledged expert? Is the expertise of such a person to be judged by reference to the standards of the 'ordinarily competent practitioner'? It seems reasonable to suggest that the standard of such individuals should, instead, be assessed by reference to a more limited class of those with specialist knowledge. This might create problems where the class is small, such that the general or accepted standard is difficult to determine, but it has been confirmed that even a small number of specialists can constitute a reasonable body of opinion; the question is one of quality, not quantity.[284] In any event, if the specialist is in possession of actual knowledge that might not be possessed by the general body of that profession, then he or she is under a duty to make use of that actual knowledge.[285]

Thus, although there may be a number of possible causes of action that could be pursued in the event of defective software that resulted in damage, there is considerable uncertainty about the scope and boundaries of liability, and also about those on whom liability might fall. Modern technology relies extensively on software and it is perhaps surprising that there has been little activity in the courts as yet. Neither does this seem to be due to the excellence of the software: Hatton pointed out over a decade ago that '[a]n explosion in the volume of software would not be a cause for concern if software quality was improving at the same rate proportionately. Unfortunately the plain truth is that software is simply not getting much better'.[286] It is, perhaps, surprising therefore that, since then, the judiciary has not been called upon to decide some of the issues raised in this chapter.

---

284 *De Freitas v O'Brien* [1995] 6 Med LR 108, 115, per Otton LJ.
285 See, eg, *Wimpey Construction v Poole* [1984] 2 Lloyd's Rep 499.
286 Les Hatton, 'Software failures, follies and fallacies' (1997) 43(2) IEE Rev 49, 49.

Bibliography

Anon, 'Computer programs as goods under the UCC' (1979) 77 Mich L Rev 1149

Abel, SM, 'Trademark issues in cyberspace: The brave new frontier' (1999) 5 MTTLR 91

Abid, JG, 'Software patents on both sides of the Atlantic' (2005) 23 J Marshall J Computer & Info L 815

Acohido, B, 'DIY cybercrime kits power growth in net phishing attacks' (2010) *USA Today*, 18 January, available online at www.usatoday.com/money/industries/technology/2010-01-17-Internet-scams-phishing_N.htm

Ahlert, C, 'Technologies of control: How code controls communication', in C Hardy and C Möller (eds), *Spreading the Word on the Internet*, 2003, Vienna: OSCE

Akdeniz, Y, 'Governing racist content on the internet: National and international responses' (2007) 56 UNB LJ 103

——, *Internet Child Pornography and the Law: National and International Responses*, 2008, London: Ashgate

——, 'Section 3 of the Computer Misuse Act 1990: An antidote for computer viruses!' [1996] 3 Web JCLI, available online at http://webjcli.ncl.ac.uk/1996/issue3/akdeniz3.html

—— and Walker, C, 'UK government policy on encryption: Trust is the key' (1998) 3 Journal of Civil Liberties 110

—— and Walker, C, 'Whisper who dares: Encryption, privacy rights and the new world disorder', in Y Akdeniz, C Walker, and D Wall (eds), *The Internet, Law and Society*, 2000, London: Longman

Akehurst, M, 'Jurisdiction in international law' (1972–73) 46 British Yearbook of International Law 145

Albert, MR, 'E-buyer beware: Why online auction fraud should be regulated' (2002) 39 Am Bus LJ 575

Aldesco, AI, 'The demise of anonymity: A constitutional challenge to the Convention on Cybercrime' (2002) 23 Loy LA Ent L Rev 81

Aldhouse, FGB, 'Data protection, privacy and the media' (1999) 4 Comm L 8

——, 'UK data protection: Where are we in 1991?' (1991) 5 LCT Yearbook 180

Al Ibrahim, M, Ababneh, A, and Tahat, H, 'The postal acceptance rule in the digital age' (2007) 2 JICLT 47

Allgrove, B, and Ganley, P, 'Search engines, data aggregators and UK copyright law: a proposal' [2007] EIPR 227

All Party Internet Group (APIG), *Revision of the Computer Misuse Act: Report of an Inquiry by the All Party Internet Group*, 2004, London: HMSO

All Party Parliamentary Communications Group, *Can We Keep Our Hands off the Net? Report of an Inquiry by the All Party Parliamentary Communications Group*, 2009, available online at www.apcomms.org.uk/uploads/apComms_Final_Report.pdf

Alongi, EA, 'Has the US canned spam?' (2004) 46 Ariz L Rev 263

American Bar Association (ABA), 'Achieving legal and business order in cyberspace: A report on global jurisdiction issues created by the internet' (2000) 55 Business Lawyer 1801, available online at www.kentlaw.edu/cyberlaw/docs/drafts/draft.rtf

American Bar Association (ABA) Joint Working Group on Electronic Contracting Practices, 'Browse-wrap agreements: Validity of implied assent in electronic form agreements' (2003) 59 Business Lawyer 279.

American Civil Liberties Union (ACLU), 'Letter to the Senate Foreign Relations Committee on the Council of Europe Convention on Cybercrime' (2004) 16 June, available online at www.aclu.org/technology-and-liberty/aclu-letter-senate-foreign-relations-committee-council-europe-convention-cybercrime

——, 'Memo on the Council of Europe Convention on Cybercrime' (2004) 16 June, available online at www.aclu.org/technology-and-liberty/aclu-memo-council-europe-convention-cybercrime

Anderson, N, 'Thomas verdict: Willful infringement, $1.92 million penalty' (2009) *arstechnica.com*, 18 June, available online at http://arstechnica.com/tech-policy/news/2009/06/jammie-thomas-retrial-verdict.ars

Andrews, JA, 'Reversing copyright misuse: Enforcing contractual prohibitions on software reverse engineering' (2004) 41 Hous L Rev 975

Arasaratnam, N, 'Brave new (online) world' (2000) 23 UNSWLJ 205

Arden J, 'Electronic commerce' (1999) 149 NLJ 1685

Argy, P, 'Internet content regulation: An Australian Computer Society perspective' (2000) 23 UNSWLJ 265

Armon, O, 'Is this as good as it gets? An appraisal of the Uniform Domain Name Dispute Resolution Policy' (2003) 20(12) Computer & Internet Lawyer 1

Arnold, R, 'Infringement of copyright in computer software by non-textual copying: First decision at trial by an English court' [1993] EIPR 250

Arnold-Moore, T, 'Legal pitfalls in cyberspace: Defamation on computer networks' (1994) 5 JLIS 165

Arthur, C, 'Microsoft offers $250,000 bounty on Conficker worm author's head' (2009) *GuardianOnline*, 13 February, available online at www.guardian.co.uk/media/2009/feb/13/microsoft-offers-250k-bounty-conficker-worm

Asarch, CG, 'Is turnabout fair play? Copyright law and the fair use of computer software loaded into RAM' (1996) 95 Mich L Rev 654

Ashford, W, 'BBC botnet experiment broke law, says lawyer' (2009) *Computer Weekly*, 13 March, available online at www.computerweekly.com/Articles/2009/03/13/235257/bbc-botnet-experiment-broke-law-says-lawyer.htm

Atiyah, PS, Adams, JN, and MacQueen, H (eds), *The Sale of Goods*, 10th edn, 2000, Harlow: Longman

Atkins, R, 'Computer contracts: Capturing requirements and apportioning responsibilities' (2003) 17(2) IRLCT 219.

Attorney General of Australia, *Electronic Commerce: Building the Legal Framework – Report of the Electronic Commerce Expert Group to the Attorney-General*, 1998, Canberra: Government of Australia

Attridge, DJM 'Challenging claims! Patenting computer programs in Europe and the USA' [2001] IPQ 22

Auburn, F, 'Usenet news and the law' (1995) 1 Web JCLI, available online at http://webjcli.ncl.ac.uk/articles1/auburn1.html

Audal, J, Lu, Q, and Roman, P, 'Computer crimes' (2008) 45 Am Crim L Rev 233

Audit Commission, *Computer Fraud Survey*, 1985, London: HMSO

——, *Your Business @ Risk*, 2001, London: HMSO

Australian Law Reform Commission, *Choice of Law*, 1992, Report No 58, Canberra: Australian Government

Ayres, I, and Braithwaite, J, *Responsive Regulation: Transcending the Deregulation Debate*, 1992, Oxford: Oxford University Press

Bainbridge, D, 'Computer programs and copyright: More exceptions to infringement' (1993) 56 MLR 591

——, *Introduction to Computer Law*, 2000, London: Longman

Baines, R, 'Copyright in commissioned works: A cause for uncertainty' [2005] EIPR 122

Bakir Munir, A, 'Unsolicited commercial e-mail: Implementing the EU Directive' (2004) 10 CTLR 105

Baldwin, R, 'Regulation: After "command and control"', in K Hawkins (ed), *The Human Face of Law*, 1997, Oxford: Clarendon

—— and Cave, M, *Understanding Regulation: Theory, Strategy and Practice*, 1999, Oxford: Oxford University Press

—— and McCrudden, C, *Regulation and Public Law*, 1987, London: Weidenfeld & Nicholson

——, Cave, M, and Lodge, M (eds), *The Oxford Handbook of Regulation*, 2010, Oxford: Oxford University Press

——, Scott, C, and Hood, C (eds), *A Reader on Regulation*, 1998, Oxford: Oxford University Press

Band, J, 'Copyright owners v the Google Print Library Project' (2006) 17 Ent L Rev 21

Banzhaf, J, 'Copyright protection for computer software' (1964) 64 Colum L Rev 1274

Barlow, JP, 'Selling wine without bottles: The economy of mind on the global net', in P Bernt Hugenholtz (ed), *The Future of Copyright in a Digital Environment*, 1996, The Hague: Kluwer

Battle, M, Bailie, MW, Hagan, E, and Eltringham, S, *Prosecuting Computer Crimes*, 2007, Washington, DC: Office of Legal Education, available online at www.justice.gov/criminal/cybercrime/ccmanual/ccmanual.pdf

Bauer, FL, *Decrypted Secrets: Methods and Maxims of Cryptology*, 4th edn, 2006, Berlin: Springer

BBC News, 'Deal signed on.com domain future' (2006) 4 December, available online at http://news.bbc.co.uk/2/hi/technology/6199394.stm

——, 'Google censors itself for China' (2006) 25 January, available online at http://news.bbc.co.uk/1/hi/technology/4645596.stm

——, 'Google releases censorship tools' (2010) 21 September, available online at www.bbc.co.uk/news/technology-11380677

——, 'Web censorship: Correspondent reports' (2006) 29 May, available online at http://news.bbc.co.uk/2/hi/technology/5024874.stm

Beale, H (ed), *Chitty on Contracts*, 29th edn, 2004, London: Sweet & Maxwell

Beale, I, 'Computer eavesdropping: Fact or fantasy' (1986) 1 CLSR 16

Bennett, C, 'Convergence revisited', in PE Agre and M Rotenberg (eds), *Technology and Privacy: The New Landscape*, 1998, Cambridge, MA: MIT Press

Bently, L, and Burrell, R, 'Copyright and the information society in Europe: A matter of timing as well as content' (1997) 34 CMLR 1197

—— and Sherman, B, *Intellectual Property Law*, 3rd edn, 2009, Oxford: Oxford University Press

Berg, T, 'The changing face of cybercrime' (2007) 86 Mich BJ 18

Berkovic, N, 'Rudd retreats on web filter legislation' (2010) *The Australian*, 19 April

Bernal, P, 'Collaborative consent: Harnessing the strengths of the internet for consent in the online environment' (2010) 24 Int Rev LCT 287

Berners-Lee, T, 'Links and law: Myths', 1997, available online at www.w3.org/DesignIssues/LinkMyths.html

——, 'Realising the full potential of the Web', Presentation at W3C meeting, London, 3 December 1997, available online at www.w3.org/1998/02/Potential.html

Bernstein, MH, *Regulating Business by Independent Commission*, 1955, Princeton, NJ: Princeton University Press

Bettinger, T (ed), *Domain Name Law and Practice*, 2005, Oxford: Oxford University Press

Bettink, WW, and Wentholt, F, 'Kazaa victory leaves permissibility of file-sharing software undecided' (2004) Houthoff Buruma Newsletter, March

Bhatt, H, 'RIPA 2000: A human rights examination' (2006) 10(3) Int J Hum Right 285

Black, JM, 'Decentring regulation: Understanding the role of regulation and self regulation in a "post-regulatory" world' (2001) 54 CLP 103

Blanks Hindman, E, 'Protection childhood: Rights, social goals and the First Amendment in the context of the Child Online Protection Act (2010) 15 Comm L Pol'y 1

Blanke, JM, 'Assessment technologies of WI, LLC vWIREdata Inc: Seventh Circuit decision reinforces the non-copyrightability of facts in a database' (2004) 20 CHTLJ 755

——, 'Case note' (2004) 20 CHTLJ 755

Blume, P, 'Transborder data flow: Is there a solution in sight?' (2000) 8 IJLIT 65

Bohm, N, 'The Phorm "Webwise" system: A legal analysis' (2008) 23 April, available online at www.fipr.org/080423phormlegal.pdf

Bonaccorsi, A, and Rossi, C, 'Comparing motivations of individual programmers and firms to take part in the open source movement: From community to business' (2006) 18(4) Knowledge, Technology & Policy 40

Booton, D, and Mole, P, 'The action freezes? The Draft Directive on the Patentability of Computer-related Inventions' [2002] IPQ 289

Bott, F, Coleman, A, Eaton J, and Rowland, D, *Professional Issues in Software Engineering*, 3rd edn, 2000, London: Taylor & Francis

Boyd-Farell, R, 'Legal analysis of the implications of MGM v Grokster for BitTorrent' (2006) 11 Intell Prop L Bull 77, 78

Bracha, O, 'Standing copyright law on its head? The googlization of everything and the many faces of property' (2007) 85 Tex L Rev 1799

Braithwaite, N, 'The internet and bulletin board defamations' (1995) 145 NLJ 1216

—— and Carolina, R, 'Multimedia defamation' (1994) 12 Int Media Law 19

Branigan, T, 'China relaxes internet censorship for Olympics' (2008) *The Guardian*, 1 August, available online at www.guardian.co.uk/world/2008/aug/01/china.olympics

Bremer, C, 'Download pirates face being banned from the internet under Sarkozy law' (2008) *The Times*, 19 June, p 39

Bremer, K, *Strafbare Internet-Inhalte in International Hinsicht: Ist der Nationalstaat wirklich überholt?*, 2001, Frankfurt am Main: Peter Lang Verlag, available online at http://ub-dok.uni-trier.de/diss/diss60/20000927/20000927.pdf

Brenner, SW, Carrier, B, and Henninger, J, 'The Trojan horse defense in cybercrime cases' (2004) 21 CHTLJ 1

Brooks, G, 'Implications of Ezsia's Case for subject access: Proportionality may apply to searches of data' (2008) 8 PDP 5(3)

Brownsword, R, 'Code, control, and choice: Why east is east and west is west' (2005) 25 Legal Studies 1

Brunnstein, K, and Fischer-Huebner, S, 'How far can the criminal law help to control IT misuse?' (1995) 9 LC & T Yearbook 111

Burdon, M, Lane, W, and von Nessen, P, 'The mandatory notification of data breaches: Issues arising for Australian and EU legal developments' (2010) 26 CSLR 115

Burk, DL, 'Jurisdiction in a world without borders' (1997) 1 Va JLT, available online at www.vjolt.net/vol1/issue/vol1_art3.html

——, 'Proprietary rights in hypertext linkages' (1998) 2 JILT, available online at www2.warwick.ac.uk/fac/soc/law/elj/jilt/1998_2/burk/

Burkeman, O, 'Forty years of the internet: How the world changed forever' (2009) *The Guardian*, 23 October, available online at www.guardian.co.uk/technology/2009/oct/23/internet-40-history-arpanet

Burton, PF, 'Regulation and control of the internet: Is it feasible? Is it necessary?' (1995) 21 J Inf Sci 413

Calandrillo, SP, and Davison, EM, 'The dangers of the Digital Millennium Copyright Act: Much ado about nothing?' (2008) 50 Wm & Mary L Rev 349

Calcutt, D, *Review of Press Regulation*, Cmnd 2135, 1993, London: HMSO

——, et al, *Privacy and Related Matters* ('Calcutt Report'), Cmnd 1102, 1990, London: HMSO

Calkins, MM, Nikitov, A, and Richardson, V, 'Mineshafts on Treasure Island: A relief map of the eBay fraud landscape' (2007) 8 U Pitt J Tech L & Pol'y 1

Callaghan, D, and O'Sullivan, C, 'Who should bear the cost of software bugs?' (2005) 21(1) CLSR 56

Calleja, R, 'The E-Bill and the E-Directive' [2000] CL Feb/Mar 27

Campbell, KJ, 'Copyright on the internet: The view from Shetland' [1997] EIPR 255

Campbell-Kelly, M, 'Not all bad: An historical perspective on software patents' 11 Mich Telecomm & Tech L Rev 191

—— and Garcia-Swartz. DD, 'Pragmatism, not ideology: Historical perspectives on IBM's adoption of open-source software'. (2009) 21 (3) Inform Econ Pol 229

Capeller, W, 'Not such a neat net: Some comments on virtual criminality' (2001) 10 Social and Legal Studies 230

Caral, JMA, 'Lessons from ICANN: Is self-regulation of the internet fundamentally flawed?' (2004) 12 Int'l JL & Info Tech 1

Carey, P, *Data Protection: A Practical Guide to UK and EU Law*, 2009, Oxford: Oxford University Press

Carter-Ruck, P, and Starte, H, *Carter-Ruck on Libel and Slander*, 5th edn, 1997, London: Butterworths

Castor, SD, 'Internet Child Protection Registry Acts: Protection children, parents and . . . pornographers? Allowing states to balance the First Amendment with parents' rights to privacy and sovereignty in the home' (2009) 59 Cath U L Rev 231

Cerina, P, 'The originality requirement in the protection of databases in Europe and the United States' (1993) 24 IIC 579

Cesare, K, 'Prosecuting computer virus authors: The need for an adequate and immediate international solution' (2001) 14 Transnat'l Law 135

Chalton, S, 'E-commerce and the European arrest warrant' (2003) 8(4) Communications Law 329

——, 'Interpretation in the UK of EC Directive 96/9 on the Legal Protection of Databases' (2000) 5 Comm L 79

Chalton, SNL, and Gaskill, SJ (eds), *Encyclopedia of Data Protection 1988–2005*, 2006, London: Sweet & Maxwell

Chancellor of the Exchequer, *Gowers Review of Intellectual Property*, 2006, London: HMSO, available online at www.hm-treasury.gov.uk/gowers_review_index.htm

Chandrani, R, 'RIP e-commerce' (2000) 11 C & L 30

Chapman, M, 'Can a computer be deceived? Dishonesty offences and electronic transfer of funds' (2000) 64 J Crim L 89

Chappatte, P, 'Specific problems in the licensing of software' (1995) 11 CL &P 16

Charlesworth, A, 'Addiction and hacking' (1993a) 143 NLJ 540

——, 'Between flesh and sand: Rethinking the Computer Misuse Act 1990' (1995) 9 LC & T Yearbook 31

——, 'Clash of the data titans? US and EU data privacy regulation' (2000) 6 EPL 253

——, 'Information privacy law in the European Union: E pluribus unum or ex uno plures' (2003) 54 Hastings LJ 931

——, 'Legislating against computer misuse: The trials and tribulations of the UK Computer Misuse Act 1990' (1993b) J L & IS 80

——, 'Munitions, wiretaps and MP3s: The changing interface between privacy and encryption policy in the information society', in K De Leeuw and JA Bergstra (eds), *The History of Information Security*, 2007 Amsterdam: Elsevier

——, 'The future of UK data protection regulation' (2006) 11(1) Inform Secur Tech Rep 46

Chaudri, A, 'Internet domain names and the interaction with intellectual property' (2008) 24(4) CLSR 360

Chen, P, 'Pornography, protection, prevarication: The politics of internet censorship' (2000) 23 UNSWLJ 221

Chevlin, D, 'Schemes and scams: Auction fraud and the culpability of host auction web sites' (2005) 18 Loy Consumer L Rev 223

Childers, SJ, 'Don't stop the music: No strict products liability for embedded software' (2008) 19(1) U Fla JL & Pub Pol'y 125

Chissick, M, and Kelman, A, *Electronic Commerce: Law and Practice*, 2nd edn, 2000, London: Sweet & Maxwell

Chisum, DS, 'The patentability of computer algorithms' (1986) 47 Pitt UL Rev 959

Chong, S, 'Internet meta-tags and trade mark issues' [1998] EIPR 275

Christian, C, 'Down and out in cyberspace' (1993) 90 Law Soc Gazette 2

Christopher, A, and Freeman, K, '*Directmedia Publishing GmbH v Albert-Ludwigs-Universitat Freiburg*' (2009) 31 EIPR 151

Clark, CG, 'The Truth in Domain Names Act of 2003 and a preventative measure to combat typosquatting' (2004) 89 Cornell L Rev 1476

Clarkson, CMV, and Hill, J, *Jaffey on the Conflict of Laws*, 1997, London: Butterworths

Clay, A, '*Nova Productions Ltd v Mazooma Games Ltd*: Game over for Nova' (2007) 18 Ent L Rev 187.

Clayton, R, 'The Phorm "Webwise" system' (2008) 18 May, available online at www.cl.cam.ac.uk/~rnc1/080518-phorm.pdf

Clough, B, and Mungo, P, *Approaching Zero: Data Crime and the Computer Underworld*, 1993, London: Faber & Faber

Clough, J, 'Now you see it, now you don't: Digital images and the meaning of possession' (2008) 19 Crim LF 205

CNN, 'Women buy pills online for "home abortions"', 11 July 2008, available online at http://edition.cnn.com/2008/HEALTH/07/11/abortion.pills/index.html?eref=edition_europe

Cobley, C, 'Child pornography on the internet' (1997) 2 Comm L 30

Cohen, J, 'The patenting of computer software' [1999] EIPR 607

Collins, L (ed), *Dicey, Morris & Collins on The Conflict of Laws*, 14th edn, 2006, London: Sweet & Maxwell

ComScore, 'Global search market draws more than 100 billion searches per month', Press release, 31 August 2009, available online at www.comscore.com/Press_Events/Press_Releases/2009/8/Global_Search_Market_Draws_More_than_100_Billion_Searches_per_Month

Conley, JM, and Bryan, RM, 'Computer crime legislation in the US' (1999) 8 ICTL 35

Connolly, JP, and Cameron, S, 'Fair dealing in webbed links of Shetland yarn' [1998] JILT, available online at www2.warwick.ac.uk/fac/soc/law/elj/jilt/1998_2/connolly/

Cooke, J, 'Architects and engineers: Practising in the public interest' (1991) 14 NSW ULJ 73

Coote, B, 'Correspondence with description in the law of sale of goods' (1976) ALJ 154

Corbett, S, 'What if object code had been excluded from protection as a literary work in copyright law? A New Zealand perspective' (2008) Mich St L Rev 173

Corker, J, Nugent, S, and Porter, J, 'Regulating internet content: A co-regulatory approach' (2000) 23 UNSWLJ 198

Cornish, WR, 'Computer program copyright and the Berne Convention' [1990] EIPR 129

——, 'Computer program copyright and the Berne Convention', in M Lehmann and CF Tapper (eds), *Handbook of European Software Law*, 1993, Oxford: Clarendon

——, *Intellectual Property*, 4th edn, 1999, London: Sweet & Maxwell

——, 'Interoperable systems and copyright' [1989] EIPR 391

—— and Llewellyn, D, *Intellectual Property*, 5th edn, 2003, London: Sweet & Maxwell

—— and ——, *Intellectual Property*, 6th edn, 2007, London: Sweet and Maxwell

Coroneos, P, 'Internet content policy and regulation in Australia', in B Fitzgerald, F Gao, D O'Brien, and S Xiaoxiang Shi (eds), *Copyright Law, Digital Content and the Internet in the Asia-Pacific*, 2008, Sydney: Sydney University Press

Cortés Diéguez, JP, 'An analysis of the UDRP experience: Is it time for reform?' (2008) 24(4) CLSR 349

Costantino, M, 'Fairly used: Why Google's Book Project should prevail under the fair use defense' 17 Fordham Intell Prop Media & Ent LJ 235

Cowley, D, 'Criminal damage: Computer disc' (1992) 56 JCL 37

Crook, JR, 'Senate approves UK Extradition Treaty and other bilateral and multilateral treaties, attaches reservations and understandings' (2007) 101 Am J Int'l Law 199

Cumbley, R, and Church, P, 'What is personal data? The House of Lords identifies the issues – *Common Services Agency v Scottish Information Commissioner*' [2008] UKHL 47, [2008] 24 CLSR 565

Czarnota, B, and Hart, RJ, *Legal Protection of Computer Programs in Europe: A Guide to the EC Directive*, 1991, London: Butterworths

Dahm, AL, 'Database protection v deep linking' (2004) 82 Tex L Rev 1053

Daintith, TC, 'The techniques of government', in J Jowell and D Oliver (eds), *The Changing Constitution*, 3rd edn, 1994, Oxford: Oxford University Press

Daly, M, 'Life after *Grokster*: Analysis of US and European approaches to file-sharing' [2007] EIPR 319

Daniels, DWT, 'Learned Hand never played Nintendo: A better way to think about non-literal, non-visual software copyright cases' (1994) 61 Chicago UL Rev 613

Data Protection Registrar, *Eighth Report of the Data Protection Registrar*, 1992, London: HMSO,

——, *Tenth Report of the Data Protection Registrar*, 1994, London: HMSO

——, *Eleventh Report of the Data Protection Registrar*, 1995, London: HMSO

——, *Fourteenth Report of the Data Protection Registrar*, 1998, London: HMSO

Davidson, DM, 'Common law, uncommon software' (1986) 47 Pitt UL Rev 1037

Davies, D, 'Anatomy of a disaster' (1990) 6 CSLR 27

Davies, G, and Trigg, G, 'Being data retentive: A knee jerk reaction' (2006) 11(1) Communications Law 18

Davies, L, 'A model for internet regulation', 1998a, available online at www.scl.org

——, 'Contract formation on the internet: Shattering a few myths', in L Edwards and C Waelde (eds), *Law & the Internet*, 1997, Oxford: Hart

Davies, S, 'Computer program claims' [1998b] EIPR 429

Davis, BJ, 'Untangling the "publisher" versus "information content provider" paradox of section 230: Toward a rational application of the Communications Decency Act in defamation suits against internet service providers' (2002) 32 N M L Rev 75

Davison, MJ, '*Nine Network Australia Pty Ltd v IceTV Pty Ltd* and *Telstra Corp Ltd v Phone Directories Co Pty Ltd*: Copyright protection for compilations – Australia does a U-turn' (2010) 32 EIPR 457

—— and Bernt Hugenholtz, P, 'Football fixtures, horseraces and spinoffs: The ECJ domesticates the database right' [2005] EIPR 113

Deazley, R, *On the Origins of the Right to Copy*, 2005, Oxford: Hart Publishing

Debusseré, F, 'Court finds peer-to-peer music file-sharing illegal' (2005) 18 Stibbe ICT Law Newsletter, available online at www.stibbe.be/assets/publications/newsletters/stibbe_ict_law_newsletter_no_18.pdf

Debusseré, F, 'International jurisdiction over e-consumer contracts in the European Union: *Quid novi sub sole?*' (2002) 10 Int JLIT 344

——, 'The EU E-Privacy Directive: A monstrous attempt to starve the cookie monster?' (2005) 13 IJLIT 70

Decker, C, 'Cyber Crime 2.0: An argument to update the United States Criminal Code to reflect the changing nature of cyber crime' (2008) 81 S Cal L Rev 959

Deene, J, 'Originality in software law: Belgian doctrine and jurisprudence remain divided' (2007) 2 JIPLP 692

Deibert, R, Palfray, J, Rohozinski, R, and Zittrain, J (eds), *Access Denied*, 2008, Cambridge, MA: MIT Press

Delacourt, JT, 'The international impact of internet regulation' (1997) 38 Harv Int LJ 207

De Laat, PB, 'Copyright or copyleft? An analysis of property regimes for software development' (2005) 34(10) Research Policy 1511

Department for Business, Enterprise and Regulatory Reform (BERR), *Consultation Document on the Electronic Commerce Directive: The Liability of Hyperlinkers, Location Tool Services and Content Aggregators*, December 2006, London: HMSO, available online at www.berr.gov.uk/files/file35905.pdf

——, *Implementation of the Directive on Privacy and Electronic Communications*, March 2003, London: HMSO, available online at www.berr.gov.uk/files/file15097.pdf

——, *UK Strategic Export Control Lists*, 2009, London: HMSO

Department for Business, Innovation and Skills (BIS), *A Guide for Business to the Electronic Commerce (EC Directive) Regulations 2002 (SI 2002/2013)*, 2002, London: HMSO

——, *Digital Economy Bill: Online Infringement of Copyright – Detail Regarding Clauses 4–16*, 2010, London: HMSO

Department for Culture, Media and Sport, *Draft Gambling Bill: Regulatory Impact Assessment*, 2003, London: HMSO

——/Department for Business, Innovation and Skills (BIS), *Digital Britain*, Cm 7650, 2009, London: HMSO

Department of National Heritage, *Review of Press Regulation*, Cm 2135, 1993, London: HMSO

Department of Trade and Industry (DTI), *A Guide for Business to the Electronic Commerce (EC Directive) Regulations 2002 (SI 2002/2013)*, London: HMSO

——, *Building Confidence in Electronic Commerce: A Consultation Document*, URN 99/642, 1999, London: HMSO

——, *DTI Consultation Document on the Electronic Commerce Directive: The Liability of Hyperlinkers, Location Tool Services and Content Aggregators*, June 2005, London: HMSO, available online at www.berr.gov.uk/files/file13986.pdf

——, *Guide to the Consumer Protection Act 1987*, 1987, London: HMSO

——, *Implementation of the EC Directive on Product Liability*, 1985, London: HMSO

——, *Licensing of Trusted Third Parties for the Provision of Encryption Services: Public Consultation Paper on Detailed Proposals for Legislation*, 1997, London: HMSO

——, *Notes for Business: Lawful Business Practice Regulations Information*, URN 06/1481, London: HMSO

——, *Paper on Regulatory Intent concerning Use of Encryption on Public Networks*, 1996, London: HMSO

Derclaye, E, 'Databases *sui generis* right: Should we adopt the spin-off theory?' [2004] EIPR 402

Determann, L, 'Case update: German Compuserve director acquitted on appeal' (1999) 23 Hastings Int'l & Comp L Rev 109

Deturbide, M, 'Liability of internet service providers for defamation in the US and Britain: Same competing interests, different responses' (2000) 3 JILT, available online at www2.warwick.ac.uk/fac/soc/law/elj/jilt/2000_3/deturbide/

DeutscheWelle, 'German spies caught reading journalist's e-mails' (2008) DeutscheWelle, 21 April

Deveci, HA, 'Databases: Is *sui generis* a stronger bet than copyright?' (2004a) 12 Int'l JL & Info Tech 178

——, 'Hyperlinks oscillating at the crossroads' (2004b) 10 CTLR 82

Dines, S, 'Actual interpretation yields actual dissemination: An analysis of the make available theory argued in peer-to-peer file sharing lawsuits and why courts ought to reject it' (2009) 32 Hastings Comm & Ent LJ 157

Diver, L, 'Would the current ambiguities with the legal protection of software be solved by the creation of a *sui generis* property right for computer software?' (2008) 3 JIPLP 125

Dixon, R, *Open Source Software Law*, 2003, Norwood MA: Artech House

Dockins, M, 'Internet links: The good, the bad, the tortuous and a two-part test' (2005) 36 U Tol L Rev 367

Dommering, EJ, and Hugenholtz, PB (eds), *Protecting Works of Fact: Copyright, Freedom of Expression and Information Law*, 1991, The Hague: Kluwer

Donohue, LK, *The Cost of Counterterrorism: Power, Politics, and Liberty*, 2008, Cambridge: Cambridge University Press

Dooley, S, 'Defamation on the internet' (1995) 1 CTLR 191

Dorsett, R, *Risks Digest: Forum on Risks to the Public in Computers and Related Systems* (1990) 9(72) ACM Committee on Computers and Public Policy

Douma, E, 'The Uniform Computer Information Transactions Act and the issue of preemption of contractual provisions prohibiting reverse engineering, dissassembly or decompilation' (2001) 11 Alb LJ Sci & Tech 249

Downing, RW, 'Shoring up the weakest link: What lawmakers around the world need to consider in developing comprehensive laws to combat cybercrime' (2005) 43 Colum J Transnat'l Law 705

Downing, S, and Harrington, J, 'The postal rule in electronic commerce: A reconsideration' (2000) 5(2) Comm L 43

Drake, CD, and Wright, FB, *Law of Health and Safety at Work: The New Approach*, 1983, London: Sweet and Maxwell

Drexl, J, 'What is protected in a computer program? Copyright protection in the US and Europe' (1994) 15 IIC

Dumbill, EA, 'Computer Misuse Act 1990: Recent developments' (1992) 8 CLSR 105

Dunn, SA, 'Defining the scope of copyright protection for computer software' (1986) 38 Stan L Rev 497

Dutson, S, 'The internet, the conflict of laws, international litigation and intellectual property: The implications of the international scope of the internet on intellectual property infringements' [1997] JBL 495

Edstrom, J, and Nillson, H, 'The Pirate Bay: Predictable and yet . . .' [2009] EIPR 483

Edwards, J, 'Has the dreaded data doomsday arrived? Past, present, and future effects of the European Union's Database Directive on database and information availability in the European Union' (2004a) 39 Ga L Rev 215

Edwards, L, 'Canning the spam: Is there a case for legal control of junk electronic mail?', in L Edwards and C Waelde (eds), *Law and the Internet: A Framework for Electronic Commerce*, 2000, Oxford: Hart

——, 'Dawn of the death of distributed denial of service: How to kill zombies' (2006) 24 Cardozo Arts & Ent LJ 23

——, 'Stuck in "neutral"? Google, AdWords and the E-Commerce Directive Immunities' (2009–10) 20(5) Society for Computers and Law, available online at www.scl.org/site.aspx?i=ed14010

——, 'The fall and rise of intermediary liability online', in L Edwards and C Waelde (eds), *Law and the Internet*, 3rd edn, 2009, Oxford: Hart Publishing

——, 'The Scotsman, the Greek, the Mauritian company and the internet: Where on earth do things happen in cyberspace?' (2004b) 8 Edin LR 99

Electronic Frontiers Australia (EFA), 'Internet censorship: Law and policy around the world' (2002) 28 March, available online at www.efa.org.au/Issues/Censor/cens3.html

Electronic Privacy Information Centre (EPIC), *Surfer Beware III: Privacy Policies without Privacy Protection*, 1999, available online at www.epic.org/reports/surfer-beware3.html

Eliadis, H, and Rand, A, *Setting Expectations in SaaS: The Importance of the Service Level Agreement to SaaS Providers and Consumers*, 2007, Washington, DC: Software & Information Industry Association

Elliott, C, and Gravatt, B, 'Domain name disputes in a cross-border context' [1999] EIPR 417

Endeshaw, A, 'Computer misuse law in Singapore' (1999) 8 ICTL 5

Englund, SR, 'Idea, process or protected expression? Determining the scope of copyright protection of the structure of computer programs' (1990) 88 Mich L Rev 866

E-Policy News, 'Privacy & data protection: Safe Harbor agreement approved by EU Member States' (2000) June, available online at http://ec.europa.eu/archives/ISPO/ecommerce/epolicy/2000-06.html

Ess, P, 'Bundesgerichtshof clarifies software patentability prerequisites: First step towards legal certainty in Europe?' (2010) 5 JIPIL 827

Etzioni, A, 'The capture theory of regulations: Revisited' (2009) 46(4) Society 319

European Commission, *Application of a Methodology Designed to Assess the Adequacy of the Level of Protection of Individuals with regard to Processing Personal Data*, 1998a, Luxembourg: OOPEC

——, *Consumer: EU Crackdown on Websites Selling Consumer Electronic Goods*, IP/09/1292, 9 September 2009, Brussels: European Commission

——, *Creative Content in A European Digital Single Market: Challenges for the Future*, A Reflection Document of DG INFSO and DG MARKT, 22 October 2009, available online at http://ec.europa.eu/avpolicy/docs/other_actions/col_2009/reflection_paper.pdf

——, 'European Parliament sends software patent packing' (2005) *European Research Headlines*, 20 July, available online at http://ec.europa.eu/research/headlines/news/article_05_07_20_en.html

——, *First Report on the Application of Directive 2000/31/EC of the European Parliament and of the Council of 8 June 2000 on Certain Legal Aspects of Information Society Services, in Particular Electronic Commerce, in the Internal Market*, 2003, Brussels: European Commission COM(2003)702 final

——, *Illegal and Harmful Content on the Internet*, COM (1996) 487, 1996, Brussels: EC Commission

——, *Preparation of a Methodology for Evaluating the Adequacy of the Level of Protection of Individuals with regard to the Processing of Personal Data*, 1998b, Luxembourg: OOPEC

——, *Report on the Operation of Directive 1999/93/EC on a Community Framework for Electronic Signatures*, COM(2006)120final, 2006, Brussels: European Commission

——, *Report to the Trade Barriers Regulation Committee: Examination Procedure concerning an Obstacle to Trade, within the Meaning of Council Regulation (EC) No 3286/94, consisting of Measures Adopted by the United States of America Affecting Trade in Remote Gambling Services* 10 June 2009, Brussels: EC

——, 'The European Commission refers UK to Court over privacy and personal data protection', Press release, 30 September 2010, available online at http://ec.europa.eu/unitedkingdom/press/press_releases/2010/pr1097_en.htm

Everett, C, 'Five cloud computing myths exploded' (2009) ZDNet.co.uk, 2 February, available online at http://resources.zdnet.co.uk/articles/0,1000001991,39605991-1,00.htm

Ewing, M, 'The perfect storm: The Safe Harbor and the Directive on Data Protection' (2002) 24 Hous J Int'l L 315

Fabricius, EM, '*Jacobsen v Katzer*: Failure of the Artistic License and repercussions for open source' (2008) 9 NC JL & Tech 65

Fafinski, S, 'Access denied: Computer misuse in an era of technological change' (2006) 70 JCL 424

——, 'Computer misuse: The implications of the Police and Justice Act 2006' (2008) 72 JCL 53

Fawcett, JJ, and Torremans, P, *Intellectual Property and Private International Law*, 1998, Oxford: Oxford University Press

Federal Trade Commission (FTC), 'FTC approves final settlement order with Dave & Busters; FTC rejects COPPA Safe Harbor application' (2010) 6 August, available online at www.ftc.gov/opa/2010/06/davecoppa.shtm

——, *Privacy Online: A Report to Congress*, 1998, available online at www.ftc.gov/reports/privacy3/toc.htm

——, *Privacy Online: Fair Information Practices in the Electronic Marketplace*, 2000, available online at www.ftc.gov/reports/privacy2000/privacy2000.pdf

——, *Self-Regulation and Privacy Online*, 1999, available online at www.ftc.gov/reports/privacy3/toc.htm

Feldman, D, 'Secrecy, dignity or autonomy? Views of privacy as a civil liberty' (1994) 10 CL & P 41

Fellas, J, 'The patentability of software-related inventions in the US' [1999] EIPR 330

Feng, Z, 'China to introduce new legislation to deal with ISP liability for copyright infringement' (2004) 5 World Internet Law Report 19

Ferguson, D, 'Recent development, syntax errors: Why Version 3 of the GNU General Public License needs debugging' (2006) 7(2) NC JL & Tech 397

Ferguson, G, and Wadham, J, 'Privacy and surveillance: A review of the Regulation of the Investigatory Powers Act 2000' (2003) Special edn EHRLR 101

Fisch Nigri, D, 'Computer crime: Why should we still care?' (1993) 9 CLSR 274

Fischman Afori, O, 'Implied license: An emerging new standard in copyright law' (2009) 25 CHTLJ 275

Fitzgerald, B, and Suzor, N, 'Legal issues for the use of free and open source software in government' (2005) 29(2) Mel U L Rev 412

Fitzpatrick, S, 'Copyright imbalance: US and Australian responses to the WIPO Digital Copyright Treaty' [2000] EIPR 214

Flanagan, A, 'The law and computer crime: Reading the script of reform' (2005) 13 IJLIT 98

Fletcher, H, 'China blocks iTunes over all-star Tibet album free download' (2008) *TimesOnline*, 22 August, available online at http://technology.timesonline.co.uk/tol/news/tech_and_web/article4579783.ece

Foged, T, 'US v EU anti-circumvention legislation: Preserving the public's privileges in the digital age' [2002] EIPR 525

Fong, K, 'Non-literal copying infringes copyright in software: *Data Access Corporation v Powerflex Services Pty Ltd*' [1997] EIPR 256

Ford, R, 'Smokers and tramps join 8,000 council surveillance targets' (2010) *Timesonline*, 25 May, available online at www.timesonline.co.uk/tol/news/politics/article7134529.ece

Foss, M and Bygrave, LA 'International consumer purchases through the internet: Jurisdictional issues pursuant to European Law' (2000) 8 Int JLIT 99

Foundation for Information Policy Research (FIPR), *Consultation Response on the Data Sharing Review*, 2008, available online at www.fipr.org/080215datasharing.pdf

Freed, RN, 'Information technology: The birth, life and death of computer law, Part 3' (1992) 8 CL & Security Rep 19

——, 'Legal interests' relation to software programs' (1986) 3 CL & P 141

——, 'The protection of computer software in the USA' (1982) C & L 6

——, 'The birth, life and death of computer law' (1990–91) 7 CL & Security Rep 107

Free Software Foundation Europe (FSFE), 'Transcript of Richard Stallman at the 2nd International GPLv3 Conference, 21 April 2006', available online at http://fsfe.org/projects/gplv3/fisl-rms-transcript.en.html

Froomkin, AM, 'Semi-private international rule-making', in C Marsden (ed), *Regulating the Global Society*, 2000, London: Routledge

Fuller, LL, 'Consideration and form' (1941) 41 Col LR 799

Gabrilovich, E, and Gontmakher, A, 'The homograph attack' (2002) 45(2) Commun ACM 128

Gall, G, 'European Patent Office Guidelines 1985 on the Protection of Inventions Relating to Computer Programs' (1985) 2 CL & P 2

Gamble, A, 'Google's Book Search Project: Searching for fair use or infringement' 9 Tul J Tech & Intell Prop 365

Ganley, P, 'Digital copyright and the new creative dynamics' (2004) 12 IJLIT 282

Garnett, R, 'Are foreign interest infringers beyond the reach of the law?' (2000) 23 NSW ULJ 105

Garrie, DB, 'The legal status of software' (2005) 23 J Marshall J Computer & Info Law 711

—— and Wong, R, 'The future of consumer web data: A European/US perspective' (2007) 15 Int Rev LTC 129

Garrigues, CC, 'Databases: A subject matter for copyright or for a neighboring rights regime?' [1997] EIPR 3

Gavison, R, 'Privacy and the limits of law' (1980) 89 Yale LJ 421

Geake, E, 'Did ambulance chiefs specify safety software?' (1992) 136 New Scientist 5

Geiger, C, 'Legal or illegal? That is the question! Private copying and downloading on the internet' (2008) 39 IIC 597

Gellman, R, 'Disintermediation and the internet' (1996) 13 Gov Inform Q 1

——, 'Does privacy law work?', in PE Agre and M Rotenberg (eds), *Technology and Privacy: The New Landscape*, 1998, Cambridge, MA: MIT Press

Georgosouli, A, 'The nature of the FSA policy of rule use: A critical overview' (2008) 28(1) Legal Studies 119

German, DM, and Hassan, AE, 'License integration patterns: Addressing license mismatches in component-based development', Paper read at 31st International Conference on Software Engineering, 2009, 16–24 May, Vancouver

Gertz, R, 'Mr Collie Goes to London: The House of Lords decision in *Common Services Agency vs. The Scottish Information Commissioner*' (2009) 3(1) Studies in Ethics, Law, and Technology 4, available online at www.bepress.com/selt/vol3/iss1/art4

Gibbons, T, 'Computer-generated pornography' (1995) 9 LC & T Yearbook 83

——, 'Defamation reconsidered' (1996) 16 OJLS 587

Gibson, J, 'Re-reifying data' (2004) 80 Notre Dame L Rev 163

Giles, LE, *Electronic Commerce and Private International Law*, 2008, Aldershot: Ashgate

Gillespie, A, 'Children, chatrooms and the law' [2001] Crim LR 435

——, 'Sentences for offences involving child pornography' [2003] Crim LR 81

——, 'The Sexual Offences Act 2003: Tinkering with "child pornography" ' [2004] Crim LR 361

Ginsburg, J, 'Creation and commercial value: Copyright protection of works of information' (1990) 90 Col L Rev 1865

——, 'Four reasons and a paradox: The manifest superiority of copyright over *sui generis* protection of computer software' (1994) 94 Colum L Rev 2559

——, 'Putting cars on the information superhighway: Authors, exploiters and copyright in cyberspace' (1995) 95 Colum L Rev 1466

Giuliano, M, and Lagarde, P, *Report on the Convention on Law Applicable to Contractual Obligations* ('Guiliano–Lagarde Report'), 1980, OJ C-282/1, Brussels: European Commission

Glad, BJ, 'Determining what constitutes creation or development of content under the Communications Decency Act' (2004) 34 Sw U L Rev 258

Glatt, C, 'Comparative issues in contract formation' (1998) 6 Int JLIT 34

Gobla, KA, 'The infeasibility of Federal internet regulation' (1997) 102 Dickinson L Rev 93

—— and Akdeniz, Y, 'The regulation of pornography and child pornography on the internet' [1997] 1 JILT, available online at http://elj.warwick.ac.uk/jilt/Internet/97_1akdz

Goldstein, P, 'The EC Software Directive: A view from the USA', in M Lehmann and CF Tapper (eds), *Handbook of European Software Law: Pt I*, 1993, Oxford: Clarendon

Gomulkiewicz, RW, 'Conditions and covenants in license contracts: Tales from a test of the Artistic License' (2009) 17(3) Tex Intell Prop LJ 335

——, 'Entrepreneurial open source software hackers: MySQL and its dual licensing' (2004) 9(1) CLRTJ 203

——, 'General Public License 3.0: Hacking the Free Software Movement's Constitution' (2005) 42(4) Hous L Rev 1015

——, 'Open source license proliferation: Helpful diversity or hopeless confusion' (2009) 30 Wash U JL & Pol'y 261

——, 'The Federal Circuit's licensing law jurisprudence: Its nature and influence' (2009) 84 Wash L Rev 199

Goodin, D, 'eBay scammer gets four years in slammer' (2009) *The Register*, 28 April, available online at www.theregister.co.uk/2009/04/28/ebay_scammer_sentenced/

Goodman, MD, and Brenner, SW, 'The emerging consensus on criminal conduct in cyberspace' (2002) UCLA J L & Tech 139

Goodwin, W, 'The law must be changed to redefine criminal activities' (2002) *Computer Weekly*, 14 March, available online at www.computerweekly.com/Articles/2002/03/14/185735/the-law-must-be-changed-to-redefine-criminal-activities.htm

Goold, B, '*Liberty and others v The United Kingdom*: A new chance for another missed opportunity' [2009] Public Law 5

Gordon, SE, 'The very idea? Why copyright is an inappropriate way to protect computer programs' [1998] EIPR 10

Grabosky, P, 'Virtual criminality: Old wine in new bottles?' (2001) 10 Social and Legal Studies 243

—— and Smith, RG, *Crime in the Digital Age*, 1998, Annandale, NSW: Transaction Publishers

Graydon, SM, 'Phishing and pharming: The new evolution of identity theft' (2006) 60 Consumer Fin LQR 335

Greenbaum, DS, 'The database debate: In support of an inequitable solution' (2003) 13 Alb LJ Sci & Tech 431

Greenleaf, G, 'Law in cyberspace' (1996) 70 Aust LJ 33

Gringras, C, 'The validity of shrink-wrap licences' (1996) 4(2) IJLIT 77

Groemminger, BK, 'Personal privacy on the internet: Should it be a cyberspace entitlement?' (2003) 36 Ind L Rev 827

Grosche, A, 'Software patents: Boon or bane for Europe' (2006) 14 IJLIT 257

Groves, P, 'Copyright in commissioned work: Court of Appeal put the boot in' (2005) 16(3) Ent L Rev 56

Guadamuz González, A, 'Attack of the killer acronyms: The future of information technology law' (2004) 18(3) IRLCT 411

——, 'The licence/contract dichotomy in open licenses: A comparative analysis' (2009) 30 U La Verne L Rev 296

——, 'The software patent debate' (2006) 1 JIPLP 196

——, 'Viral contracts or unenforceable documents? Contractual validity of copyleft licenses' (2004) 26(8) EIPR 331

Guest, AG (ed), *Benjamin's Sale of Goods*, 4th edn, 1992, London: Sweet & Maxwell

Gulamhusein, A, 'Gary McKinnon case is acid test of coalition government's integrity' (2010) *Law Society Gazette*, 7 June, available online at www.lawgazette.co.uk/opinion/gary-mckinnon-case-acid-test-coalition-government-s-integrity

Gunningham, NA, and Grabosky, P, *Smart Regulation: Designing Environmental Policy*, 1998, Oxford: Oxford University Press

—— and Rees, J, 'Industry self-regulation: An institutional perspective' (1997) 19 Law & Pol 363

Haaf, J, 'The EC Directive on the Legal Protection of Computer Programs: Decompilation and security for confidential programming techniques' (1992) 30 Col J Transnat L 401

Halbert, D, 'Discourses of danger and the computer hacker' (1997) 13 The Information Society 361

Handa, S, and Buchan, J, 'Copyright as it applies to the protection of computer programs in Canada' (1995) 26 IIC 48

Handsley, E, and Biggins, B, 'The sheriff rides into town: A day of rejoicing for innocent westerners' (2000) 23 UNSWLJ 257

Hardcastle, R, *Law and the Human Body: Property Rights, Ownership and Control*, 2007, Oxford: Hart Publishing

Harding, C, 'The Anti-cartel Enforcement Industry: Criminological Perspectives on Cartel Criminalisation' in Caron Beaton-Wells and Ariel Ezrachi(eds) *Criminalising Cartels: Critical Studies of an International Regulatory Movement* (2011), Oxford: Hart Publishing

Harding, L, 'Oceans apart: Overview of the US legal framework' (2010) 21(2) Computers and Law 27

Hargittai, E, 'The social, political, economic, and cultural dimensions of search engines: An introduction' (2007) 12 Journal of Computer-Mediated Communication 769

Harrington, D, 'The engineers have it! Patenting computer programs in the USA' (1996) 1 Comm L 232

Hart, M, 'The Copyright in the Information Society Directive: An overview' [2002] EIPR 58

Harvey, BW, and Meisel, F, *Auctions Law and Practice*, 3rd edn, 2006, Oxford: Oxford University Press

Haslam, E, 'Contracting by electronic means' (1996) 146 NLJ 549

Hatton, L, 'Software failures, follies and fallacies' (1997) IEE Rev 49

Hawkins, K, *Law as Last Resort: Prosecution Decision-making in a Regulatory Agency*, 2002, Oxford: Oxford University Press

Hayes, DL, 'What's left of look and feel? A current analysis' (1993) 10 CL 1

Heitman, K, 'Vapours and mirrors' (2000) 23 UNSWLJ 246

Held, T, and Schulz, W, *Regulated Self-regulation as a Form of Modern Government*, 2004, Eastleigh: University of Luton Press

Helmer, S, and Davies, I, 'File-sharing and downloading: Goldmine or minefield?' (2009) 4 JIPL 51

Henley, M, '*Jacobsen v Katzer and Kamind Associates*: An English legal perspective' (2009) 1(1) IFOSS L Rev 41, available online at www.ifosslr.org/ifosslr/article/view/4

Henslee, W, 'Money for nothing and music for free? Why the RIAA should continue to sue illegal file-sharers' (2009) 9 J Marshall Rev Intell Prop L 1

Hetcher, SA, 'The de facto Federal Privacy Commission' (2000) 19 John Marshall J of Comp & Info Law 109

——, 'The half-fairness of Google's plan to make the world's collection of books searchable' 13 Mich Telecomm & Tech L Rev 1

Heyer, C, 'Parliamentary oversight of intelligence: The German approach', in S Yui-Sang Tsang (ed), *Intelligence and Human Rights in the Era of Global Terrorism*, 2007, Westport CN: Praeger

Hidalgo, PG, 'Copyright protection of computer software in the European Community: Current protection and the effect of the adopted Directive' (1993) 27 Int Lawyer 113

Hill, S, 'Driving a Trojan horse and cart through the Computer Misuse Act' (2003) 14(5) C&L 31

Hillman, RA, and O'Rourke, MA, 'Principles of the law of software contracts' (2010) 53(9) J Commun ACM 26

Hirsch, A, 'Computer hacker Gary McKinnon to be extradited to US' (2009) *The Guardian*, 26 November, available online at www.guardian.co.uk/world/2009/nov/26/computer-hacker-gary-mckinnon-extradition

——, 'Superdatabase tracking all calls and emails legitimate, says DPP' (2009) *The Guardian*, 9 January, available online at www.guardian.co.uk/uk/2009/jan/09/dpp-keir-starmer-superdatabase

Hirschbaeck, J, 'Is software a product?' (1989) 5 CL & P 154

Hirst, M, 'Computers and the English law of evidence' (1992) 1(3) LC&AI 365

Hodges, C, *Product Liability: European Laws and Practice*, 1993, London: Sweet & Maxwell

Hoey, A, 'Analysis of the Police and Criminal Evidence Act s 69: Computer-generated evidence' (1996) 1 Web JCLI, available online at http://webjcli.ncl.ac.uk/1996/issue1/hoey1.html

Holwerda, T, 'Judge: Norwegian ISP does not have to block the Pirate Bay' (2009) *Osnews*, 7 November, available online at www.osnews.com/story/22456

Home Affairs Committee, *Computer Pornography*, HC No 126, 1993–94, London: HMSO

——, *Eighth Report: The National DNA Database* (2010) HC 222-I, Session 2009–10, available online at www.publications.parliament.uk/pa/cm200910/cmselect/cmhaff/222/22202.htm

Home Office, *Acquisition and Disclosure of Communications Data: Code of Practice*, 2007, London: HMSO

——, *Computers: Safeguards for Privacy*, Cmnd 6354, 1975, London: HMSO

——, *Covert Surveillance: Code of Practice*, 2002, London: HMSO

——, *Data Protection: The Government's Proposals*, Cm 3725, 1997, London: HMSO

——, *Fraud Law Reform: Consultation on Proposals for Legislation*, 2004, London: HMSO

——, *Crime in England and Wales 2007/8*, Statistical Bulletin 07/08, 2008, London: HMSO, available online at www.homeoffice.gov.uk/rds/crimeew0809.html

——, *Crime in England and Wales 2008/9*, Statistical Bulletin 11/09, 2009, London: HMSO, available online at www.homeoffice.gov.uk/rds/crimeew0809.html

——, *Interception of Communications: Code of Practice*, 2002, London: HMSO

——, *Interception of Communications in the United Kingdom: A Consultation Paper*, Cmnd 4368, 1999, London: HMSO

——, *Investigation of Protected Electronic Information: Code of Practice*, 2007, London: HMSO

——, *On the Possession of Extreme Pornographic Material*, Consultation Paper, 2005, London: HMSO

——, *Privy Council Review of Intercept as Evidence*, Cmnd 7324, 2008, London: HMSO

——, *Regulation of Investigatory Powers Act 2000: Consolidating Orders and Codes of Practice – A Consultation Paper*, Consultation Paper, 2009, London: HMSO

——, *Regulation of Investigatory Powers Act 2000: Consolidating Orders and Codes of Practice – Summary of Responses to the 2009 Consultation Paper*, 2009, London: HMSO

——, 'Regulation of Investigatory Powers Bill published today', Press release 022/2000, 10 February 2000, London: HMSO

——, *Report of the Committee of Privy Councillors Appointed to Inquire into the Interception of Communications* (the 'Birkett Report'), Cmnd 283, 1957, London: HMSO

——, 'Targeted online advertising', FOI Release 9187, 29 April 2009, available online at www.homeoffice.gov.uk/about-us/freedom-of-information/released-information/foi-archive-crime/9187_targeted_online_advertising

——, *The Interception of Communications in Great Britain*, Cmnd 7873, 1980, London: HMSO

——, *The Interception of Communications in the United Kingdom*, Cmnd 9438, 1985, London: HMSO

Hood, CC, *The Tools of Government*, 1983, London: Macmillan

Hoofnagle, CJ, *Privacy Self Regulation: A Decade of Disappointment – A Report for the Electronic Privacy Information Center*, 2005, available online at http://epic.org/reports/decadedisappoint.html

Hoon Lim, P, and Longdin, L, 'Fresh lessons for first movers in software copyright disputes: A cross-jurisdictional convergence' (2009) 40 IIC 374

Hörnle, J, 'Country of origin regulation in cross-border media: One step beyond the freedom to provide services?' (2005) 54 ICLQ 89

——, 'Germany: Denial of service attack – Case review' (2006) 8 EBL 11

——, 'The UK perspective on the country of origin rule in the E-Commerce Directive: A rule of administrative law applicable to private law disputes?' (2004) 12 IntJLIT 333

Hornung, G, and Schnabel, C, 'Data protection in Germany II: Recent decisions on online-searching of computers, automatic number plate recognition and data retention' (2009) 25(2) CLSR 115

Horsfield-Bradbury, J, 'Making available as distribution: File sharing and the Copyright Act' (2008) 22 Harv JL & Tech 273

House of Commons Culture, Media and Sport Committee, *Press Standards, Privacy and Libel: Second Report of Session 2009–10*, 2010, London: HMSO

House of Lords/House of Commons Joint Committee on the Draft Gambling Bill, *Draft Gambling Bill*, 2004, London: HMSO

House of Lords Science and Technology Committee, *Fifth Report of Session 2006–07: Personal Internet Security*, 2007, London: HMSO

Howarth, D, *Textbook on Tort*, 1995, London: Butterworths

Huet, J, and Ginsburg, JC, 'Computer programs in Europe: A comparative analysis of the 1991 EC Software Directive' (1992) 30 Col J Transnat L 327

Hugenholtz, PB, 'Caching and copyright: The right of temporary copying' [2000] EIPR 482

——, 'Program schedules, event data and telephone subscriber listings under the Database Directive' (2003) Eleventh Annual Conference on International IP Law and Policy, Fordham University School of Law, 14–25 April, New York

Human Rights Watch, *World Report 2010*, 2010, available online at www.hrw.org/world-report-2010

Hunter, D, 'Mind your language: Copyright in computer languages in Australia' [1998] EIPR 98

——, 'Reverse engineering computer software: Australia parts company with the world' (1993) 9 CL & P 122

Hurt, C, 'Regulating public morals and private markets: Online securities trading, internet gambling and the speculation paradox' (2005) 86 BUL Rev 371

Husack, D, 'The criminal law as last resort' [2004] OJLS 207

Information Commissioner's Office (ICO), 'Binding Corporate Rules', available online at www. ico.gov.uk/for_organisations/data_protection/overseas/binding_corporate_rules.aspx

——, 'ICO seizes covert database of construction industry workers' (2009) Press release, 9 March, available online at www.ico.gov.uk/upload/documents/pressreleases/2009/tca_ release_060309.pdf

——, *Personal Information Online: Code of Practice*, 2010, available online at www.ico.gov.uk/upload/ documents/library/data_protection/detailed_specialist_guides/personal_information_ online_cop.pdf

Inman, JA, and Inman, RR, 'Responsibility as an issue in internet communication: Reading flames as defamation' (1996) 1 J Tech L & P 5

Interception of Communications Commissioner (ICC), *Report of the Interception of Communications Commissioner for 2007*, 2008, London: HMSO

——, *Report of the Interception of Communications Commissioner for 2008*, 2009, London: HMSO

International Telecommunication Union (ITU), *ITU Survey on Anti-spam Legislation Worldwide*, 2005, CYB/06, available online at www.itu.int/osg/spu/spam/legislation/Background_Paper_ ITU_Bueti_Survey.pdf

Internet Crime Complaint Center, *Internet Crime Report*, 2009, available online at www.ic3.gov/ media/annualreport/2009_IC3Report.pdf

Internet Watch Foundation (IWF), 'About the Internet Watch Foundation (IWF)', available online at www.iwf.org.uk/public/page.103.htm

——, 'Government, Parliamentarians, and UKCCIS', available online at www.iwf.org.uk/ government/page.6.htm

Jackson, M, 'Computer crime laws: Are they really needed? The Australian experience' (1995) 9 LC & T Yearbook 47

Jackson, R, and Powell, J, *Jackson and Powell on Professional Negligence*, 4th edn, 1997, London: Sweet & Maxwell

Jaffe, LL, 'The independent agency: A new scapegoat' (1956) 65 Yale LJ 1068

Jagessar, U, and Sedgwick, V, 'When is personal data not "personal data"? The impact of *Durant v FSA*' [2005] 21 CLSR 505

James, NJ, 'Handing over the keys: Contingency, power and resistance in the context of section 3LA of the Australian Crimes Act 1914' (2004) 23 U Queensland LJ 10

Jarvie, N, 'Control of cybercrime: Is an end to our privacy in the internet a price worth paying? Part 2' (2003) 9 CTLR 110

Jawahitha, S, 'Negligent liability and e-consumers in Malaysia' (2004) 10 CTLR 200

Jay, R, *Data Protection Law and Practice*, 3rd edn, 2007, London: Sweet & Maxwell

—— and Hamilton, A, *Data Protection: Law and Practice*, 2nd edn, 2003, London: Sweet & Maxwell

Jenkins Jr, HW, 'Google and the search for the future' (2010) *Wall Street Journal*, 14 August, available online at http://online.wsj.com/article/SB1000142405274870490110457542329409952 7212.html

Johnson, DR, and Post, D, 'Law and borders: The rise of law in cyberspace' (1996) 48 Stan L Rev 1367

Johnson, M, and Rogers, KM, 'The Fraud Act 2006: The e-crime prosecutor's champion or the creator of a new inchoate offence?' (2007) 21 Int Rev LCT 295

Johnson, P, 'All wrapped up? A review of the enforceability of "shrink-wrap" and "click-wrap" licences in the United Kingdom and the United States' (2003) 25(2) EIPR 98

Jones, R, 'UK Data Retention Regulations' (2008) 24(2) CLSR 147

Jones, S, 'Computer terrorist or mad boffin?' (1996) 146 NLJ 46

Jordan, T, and Taylor, P, 'A sociology of hackers' (1998) 46 Sociological Review 758

Junger, PD, 'You can't patent software: Patenting software is wrong' 58 Case W Res L Rev 333

Kabay, ME, 'Understanding studies and surveys of computer crime', in S Bosworth, ME Kabay, and E Whyne (eds), *Computer Security Handbook*, 5th edn, 2009, New York: Wiley

Kagan, RA, 'Regulatory enforcement', in DH Rosenbloom and RD Schwartz (eds), *Handbook of Regulation and Administrative Law*, 1994, New York: Dekker

Kahn, D, *The Codebreakers: The Comprehensive History of Secret Communication from Ancient Times to the Internet*, 1996, New York: Scribner

Kalathil, S, and Boas, TC, 'The internet and state control in authoritarian regimes: China, Cuba and the counterrevolution' (2001) *Carnegie Endowment Working Papers, Global Policy Program No 21*, available online at www.carnegieendowment.org/files/21KalathilBoas.pdf

Kane, B, and Delange, BT, 'A tale of two internets: Web 2.0 slices, dices, and is privacy resistant' (2009) 45 Idaho L Rev 317

Karjala, DS, 'Copyright protection of computer software in the United States and Japan, Part I' [1991] EIPR 195

——, 'Copyright protection of computer software in the United States and Japan: Part 2' [1991] EIPR 231

——, 'Distinguishing patent and copyright subject matter' (2003) 35 Conn L Rev 439

——, 'Recent US and international developments in software protection, Part 2' [1994] EIPR 58

Katyal, NK, 'Criminal law in cyberspace' (2001) 149 U Pa L Rev 1003

Kelleher, D, 'International computer crime' (1997) 147 NLJ 445

Kemp, R, 'Current developments in open source software' (2009) 25(6) CLSR 569

Kergévant, C, 'Are copyright and *droit d'auteur* viable in the light of information technology?' (1996) 10 Int Rev LCT 55

Keyser, M, 'The Council of Europe Convention on Cybercrime' (2003) 12 J Transnat'l L & Pol'y 287

Kim, NS, 'The software licensing dilemma' [2008] BYU L Rev 1103

Kirby, M, 'Privacy in cyberspace' (1998) 21 NSW ULJ 323

Kirk, J, 'Irish ISP: We won't block the Pirate Bay' (2009) PC World, 24 February, available online at www.pcworld.com/article/160114/irish_isp_we_wont_block_the_pirate_bay.html

Klang, M, 'A critical look at the regulation of computer viruses' (2003) 11 IJLIT 162

Klein, S, 'Search engines and copyright: An analysis of the Belgian *Copiepresse* decision in consideration of British and German copyright law' (2008) 39 IIC 451

Kociubinski, B, 'Copyright and the evolving law of internet search' (2006) BU J Sci & Tech L 372

Koempel, F, 'Digital Economy Bill' (2010) 16 CTLR 39

Koffman, L, and Macdonald, E, *The Law of Contract*, 6th edn, 2007, Oxford: Oxford University Press

Kohl, U, *Jurisdiction and the Internet: Regulatory Competence over Online Activity*, 2007, Cambridge: Cambridge University Press

———, 'Legal reasoning and legal change in the age of the internet: Why the ground rules are still valid' (1999) 7 Int JLIT 123

Kolb, R, 'The exercise of criminal jurisdiction over international terrorists', in A Bianchi (ed), *Enforcing International Law Norms Against Terrorism*, 2004, Oxford: Hart

Kong, L, 'Data protection and transborder data flow in the European and global context' (2010) 21 EJIL 441

Koo, D, 'Patent and copyright protection of computer programs' [2002] IPQ 172

Kosta, E, and Valcke, P, 'Retaining the Data Retention Directive' (2006) 22(5) CLSR 370

Krieger, TW, 'Internet domain names and trademarks: Strategies for protecting brand names in cyberspace' (1998) 32(1) Suffolk UL Rev 47

Krocker, ER, 'The Computer Directive and the balance of rights' [1997] EIPR 247

Kumaralingam, A, '*Caldwell* recklessness is dead, long live *mens rea*'s fecklessness cases' (2004) 67 MLR 491

Kuner, C, *European Data Protection Law: Corporate Compliance and Regulation*, 2nd edn, 2007, Oxford: Oxford University Press

Kwiatkowski, FJ, 'Hacking and the criminal law revisited' (1987) 4 CL & P 15

Kwong, DL, 'The copyright–contract intersection: *Softman Products Co v Adobe Systems Inc & Bowers v Baystate Technologies Inc*' (2003) 18 Berkeley Tech LJ 349

Laakkonen, A, and Whaite, R, 'The EPO leads the way, but where to?' [2001] EIPR 244

Labour Party, *Communicating Britain's Future: Labour Party Policy on the Superhighway*, 1995, London: Labour Party

Laddie, H, Prescott, P, Vitoria, M, Speck, A, and Lane, L, *The Modern Law of Copyright and Designs: Vol 1*, 2000, London: Butterworths

Lai, S, 'Database protection in the United Kingdom: The new deal and its effect on software protection' [1998] EIPR 32

———, *The Copyright Protection of Computer Software in the United Kingdom*, 2000, Oxford: Hart Publishing

Laidlaw, EB, 'Private power, public interest: An examination of search engine accountability' (2009) 17 IJLIT 113

Lake, WT, 'Seeking compatibility or avoiding development costs? A reply on software copyright in the EC' [1989] EIPR 431

LaMotta, L, 'The most expensive web addresses' (2007) *Forbes.com*, 29 June, available online at www.forbes.com/2007/06/28/google-news-corp-ent-tech-cx_ll_0629webaddresses.html

Landeryou, K, 'Interpretation of software contracts: *SAM Business Systems Limited v Hedley and Company*' (2003) 19(4) CLSR 311

Lannetti, DW, 'Toward a revised definition of "product" under the Restatement (Third) of Torts: Products Liability' (2000) 35 Tort & Ins LJ 845

Larkin, E, 'Google's shareholders vote against anti-censorship proposal' (2007) PC World, 10 May, available online at www.pcworld.com/article/131745/google_shareholders_vote_against_anticensorship_proposal.html

Larusson, HK, 'Uncertainty in the scope of copyright: The case of illegal file-sharing in the UK' [2009] EIPR 124

Lavenue, LM, 'Database rights and technical data rights: The expansion of intellectual property for the protection of databases' (1997) 38 Santa Clara L Rev 1

Law Commission, *Defamation and the Internet: A Preliminary Investigation, Scoping Study 2*, December 2002, London: HMSO, available online at www.lawcom.gov.uk/docs/defamation2.pdf

———, *Electronic Commerce: Formal Requirements in Commercial Transactions*, 2001, London: HMSO

——, *Fraud*, Law Com No 276, Cm 5560, 2002a, London: HMSO

——, *Legislating the Criminal Code: Fraud and Deception*, Consultation Paper No 155, 1999, London: HMSO

——, *Offences of Dishonesty: Money Transfer*, Law Com No 243, 1996, London: HMSO

——, *Reforming the Present Law: Hacking*, Working Paper No 110, 1988, London: HMSO

——, *Report on Computer Misuse*, Cm 819, 1989, London: HMSO

——, *Report on Formalities for Contracts for Sale of Land*, Law Com No 164, 1987, London: HMSO

——, *Report on Liability for Defective Products*, Law Com No 82, 1977, London: HMSO (Scottish Law Commission Report No 45)

——, *The Parol Evidence Rule*, Law Com No 154, Cmnd 9700, 1986, London: HMSO

——, *Unfair Terms in Contracts*, Consultation Paper No 166, 2002b, London: HMSO (Scottish Law Commission Discussion Paper No 119)

Lawson, M, and Elliott, P, 'Reach for the sky' (2010) 154(7) Solicitors Journal 16

—— and ——, 'The sky's the limit' (2010) 160(7405) NLJ 257

Leathers, DR, 'Giving bite to the EU–US data privacy safe harbor: Model solutions for effective enforcement' (2009) 41 Case W Res J Int'l L 193

Lee, JCJ, 'The ongoing design duty in *Universal Music Australia Pty Ltd v Sharman License Holdings Ltd*: Casting the scope of copyright infringement even wider' (2007) 15 IJLIT 275

Leigh, LH, 'Some observations on the Police and Justice Act 2006' (2007) 171 JPN 28

Leitner, J, 'A legal and cultural comparison of file-sharing disputes in Japan and the Republic of Korea and implications for future cyber-regulation (2008) 2 Colum J Asian L 1

Lemley, MA, and Reese, RA 'Reducing digital copyright infringement without restricting innovation' (2004) 56 Stan L Rev 1345

——, Menell, PS, and Merges, RP, *Software and Internet Law*, 3rd edn, 2006, New York: Aspen Law & Business

Lenno, MJ, 'US patent rights in financial services software' (1994) 10 CL & P 17

Lessig, L, *Code: And Other Laws of Cyberspace*, 1999a, New York: Basic Books

——, 'The law of the horse: What cyberlaw might teach' (1999b) 113 Harv L Rev 501

Leveson, NG, *Safeware: System Safety and Computers*, 1995, Reading, MA: Addison-Wesley

Levine, ME, and Forrence, JL, 'Regulatory capture, public interest, and the public agenda: Toward a synthesis' (1990) 6(Special Issue) JL Econ & Org 167

Li, J, Ziegler, W, Wäldrich, O, and Mallman, D, *Towards SLA Based Software License Management in Grid Computing*, CoreGRID Technical Report Number TR-0136, 2008, available online at www.coregrid.net/mambo/images/stories/TechnicalReports/tr-0136.pdf

Likhovski, M, 'Fighting the patent wars' [2001] EIPR 267

Lindsay, D, *International Domain Name Law*, 2007, Oxford: Hart Publishing

LinkLaters, 'France: The Hadopi Law and France's controversial fight against piracy' (1009) *LinkLaters.com*, 16 October, available online at www.linklaters.com/Publications/Publication1403Newsletter/20091016/Pages/FranceTheHadopiLaw.aspx

Lipstein, K, 'Intellectual property: Jurisdiction or choice of law' (2002) 61(2) CLJ 294

Lipton, J, 'Databases as intellectual property: New legal approaches' [2003] EIPR 139

Lloyd, I, *Information Technology Law*, 4th edn, 2004, Oxford: Oxford University Press

——, *Legal Aspects of the Information Society*, 2000, London: Butterworths

——, 'Legal barriers to electronic contracts: Formal requirements and digital signatures', in L Edwards and C Waelde (eds), *Law and the Internet*, 1997, Oxford: Hart

——, 'Liability for defective software' (1991) 32 Reliab Eng Syst Safe 193

——, 'Patenting software: Humpty Dumpty rules' [1995] SLT 163

——, 'The Interception of Communications Act 1985' (1986) 49(1) MLR 86.

—— and Simpson, M, *Law on the Electronic Frontier: Hume Papers on Public Policy*, 1994, Edinburgh: Edinburgh University Press

Lombois, C, *Droit Penal International*, 2nd edn, 1979, Paris: Daloz

Longdin, L, 'Liability for defects in bespoke software' (2000) 8(1) Int JLIT 1

Leong, SHS, 'Pre-action discovery against a network service provider and unmasking the John Does of alleged online copyright infringements in Singapore' [2009] EIPR 185

Lord Chancellor's Department, *Infringement of Privacy*, Consultation Paper, 1993, London: Scottish Office

Loring, TB, 'An analysis of the informational privacy protection afforded by the European Union and the United States' (2002) 37 Tex Int'l LJ 421

Low, KFK, and Loi, KCF, 'The many "tests" for terms implied in fact: Welcome clarity' (2009) 125(Oct) LQR 561

Lowe, AV (ed), *Extraterritorial Jurisdiction: An Annotated Collection of Legal Materials*, 1983, Cambridge: Grotius Publications

Lowrie, AD, 'Developments in US case law' (1997) 28 IIC 868

Loy, JA, 'Database and Collections of Information Misappropriation Act of 2003: Unconstitutionally expanding copyright law?' 7 NYUJ Legis & Pub Pol'y 449

Ludbrook, T, 'Defamation and the internet: Where are we now and where are we going? Part I' (2004) 15 Ent LR 173

——, 'Defamation and the internet: Where are we now and where are we going? Part II' (2004) 15 Ent LR 203

Lunney, GS, '*Lotus v Borland*: Copyright and computer programs' [1996] Tul L Rev 239

Macdonald, E, 'Bugs and breaches' (2005) 13 Int JLIT 118

——, 'Exclusion clauses: The ambit of s 13(1) of the Unfair Contract Terms Act 1977' (1992) 12 LS 277

——, '"In the course of a business": A fresh examination' (1999a) 3 Web JCLI, available online at http://webjcli.ncl.ac.uk/1999/issue3/macdonald3.html

——, 'Unifying unfair terms legislation' (2004) 67 MLR 69

——, '*Watford v Sanderson*: The requirement of reasonableness in system supply contracts and more generally' (2001) 4 Web JCLI, available online at http://webjcli.ncl.ac.uk/2001/issue4/macdonald4.html

—— and Poyton, D, 'E-commerce: Recognizing the context', in I Davies (ed), *Issues in Interaction of Commercial Law*, 2005, Ashgate: Aldershot

MacEwan, N, 'The Computer Misuse Act 1990: Lessons from its past and predictions for its future' [2008] Crim L Rev 955

Mackaay, E, 'The economics of emergent property rights on the internet', in P Bernt Hugenholtz (ed), *The Future of Copyright in a Digital Environment*, 1996, The Hague: Kluwer

Macmillan, F, and Blakeney, M, 'The internet and communication carriers' liability' [1998] EIPR 52

MacQueen, HL, 'Copyright in cyberspace: *Shetland Times v Wills*' [1998] JBL 297

Magnus, U, and Mankowski, P (eds), *Brussels I Regulation*, 2007, Brussels: Sellier European Law Publishers

Mahalingham Carr, I, and Williams, KS, 'A step too far in controlling computers? The Singapore Computer Misuse (Amendment) Act 1998' (2000) 8 Int JLIT 48

Makkai, T, and Braithwaite, J, 'In and out of the revolving door: Making sense of regulatory capture' (1992) 12(1) JPP 61

Maltby, J, 'Juggling comity and self-government: The enforcement of foreign libel judgments in US courts' (1994) 94 Colum L Rev 1978

Maltz, T, 'Customary law and power in internet communities' (1996) 2 J Computermediated Comm, available online at www.ascusc.org/jcmc/vol2/issue1/custom.html

Manchester, C, 'Computer pornography' [1995] Crim LR 546

Mandelson, Lord, 'Keynote address', Cabinet Conference, 26–28 October 2009, available online at www.cabinetforum.org/conference/archive/l._keynote_address_-_rt_hon_lord_mandelson/

——, 'The future of the creative industries' (2009) 29 October, available online at www.bis.gov.
    uk/News/Speeches/creative-industries
Mann, FA, 'The doctrine of jurisdiction in international law' (1964) 111 Recueil des Cours 1
——, 'The doctrine of international jurisdiction revisited after twenty years' (1984) 186 Recueil
    des Cours 9
Mann, S, 'Oceans apart: Data transfers between the EEA and USA' (2010) 21(2) Computers and
    Law 22,
Manner, M, 'A BitTorrent P2P network shut down and its operation deemed illegal in Finland'
    (2009) 20 Ent LR 21
——, Siniketo, T, and Polland, U, 'The Pirate Bay ruling: When the fun and games end' (2009)
    20 Ent LR 197
Marchini, R, 'Navitaire v easyJet: What now for look and feel?' (2005) 15(6) Computers and
    Law 31
Mares, F, 'The Regulation of Investigatory Powers Act 2000: Overview of the case of R v Clifford
    Stanford (CA (Crim Div) 1 February 2006) and the offence of unlawfully intercepting
    telecommunications on a private system (section 1(2) offence)' (2006) 22(3) CLSR 254
Marston, G, 'The parol evidence rule: The Law Commission speaks' [1986] CLJ 192
Mashima, R, 'Examination of the interrelationship among the software industry structure, Keiretsu
    and Japanese intellectual property protection for software' (1999) 33 Int LJ 119
Mason, S, 'Electronic signatures explained' (2002) Jan/Feb Internet Newsletter for Lawyers,
    available online at www.venables.co.uk/n0201signatures.htm
——, 'Lawyers and electronic signatures' (2005) July/Aug Internet Newsletter for Lawyers,
    available online at www.venables.co.uk/n0507signatures.htm
Massey, R, 'Outsourcing: New standard contractual clauses for the transfer of personal data outside
    the EU' [2010] 16 CTLR 88
Maule, MR, 'Applying strict products liability to computer software' (1992) 27(4) Tulsa LJ 735
Maurashat, A, and Watt, R, 'Clean feed: Australia's internet filtering proposal' (2009) 12 Internet
    Law Bulletin; [2009] UNSWLRS 60
Mayer-Schönberger, V, 'Generational development of data protection in Europe', in PE Agre and
    Marc Rotenberg (eds), Technology and Privacy: The New Landscape, 1998, Cambridge, MA: MIT Press
McCall, D, and Woods, G, 'BSkyB v EDS' (2010) 20(6) Computers & Law 6
McCarthy, JT, McCarthy on Trademarks and Unfair Competition, 4th edn, 1998–2009 (looseleaf), Eagan,
    MN: West Publishing
McCarthy, K, Sex.Com: One Domain, Two Men, Twelve Years and the Brutal Battle for the Jewel in the Internet's Crown,
    2007, London: Quercus Publishing
McCullagh, D, 'Bush pushes for cybercrime treaty' (2003) cnet News, 18 November, available online
    at http://news.cnet.com/Bush-pushes-for-cybercrime-treaty/2100-1028_3-5108854.
    html?tag=mncol;txt
McGlynn, C, and Rackley, E, 'Criminalising extreme pornography: A lost opportunity' [2009]
    Crim L Rev 245
McGuire, JF, 'When speech is heard around the world: Internet content regulation in the United
    States and Germany' (1999) 74 NYUL Rev 750
McKendrick, E, 'Product liability and the development risks defence' [1990] Law for Business 252
McKusick, MK, 'Twenty years of Berkeley Unix: From AT&T-owned to freely redistributable', in
    Chris DiBona, Sam Ockman, and Mark Stone (eds), Open Sources: Voices From the Open Source
    Revolution, 1999, Sebastopol, CA: O'Reilly
McMeel, G, 'Construction of contracts and the role of "entire agreement" clauses' (2008) 3(1)
    CMLJ 58
McNealy, JE, 'Angling for phishers: Legislative responses to deceptive e-mail' (2008) 13 Comm L
    & Pol'y 275

Mel, HX, and Baker, DM, *Cryptography Decrypted*, 5th edn, 2002, Indianapolis, IN: Addison-Wesley Professional

Melley, B, 'California eBay scam artist sent to federal prison' (2004) *USA Today*, 27 May, available online at www.usatoday.com/tech/news/2004-05-27-ebay-art-fraud_x.htm

Menell, PS, 'An analysis of the scope of copyright protection for application programs' (1989) 41 Stan L Rev 1045

Mertzel, NJ, 'Copying 0.03% of software code base was not *de minimis*' (2008) 3 JIPLP 547

Meyer-Rochow, R, 'The application of passing off as a remedy against domain name piracy' [1998] EIPR 405

Miles, S, and Stoker, E, '*Nova Productions Ltd v Mazooma Games Ltd*' (2006) 17 Ent L Rev 181

Millé, A, 'Copyright in the cyberspace era' [1997] EIPR 570

Miller, AR, 'Copyright protection for computer programs, databases and computer-generated works: Is anything new since CONTU?' (1993) 106 Harv L Rev 977

——, *The Assault on Privacy: Computers, Databanks and Dossiers*, 1971, Ann Arbor, MI: Michigan University Press

Minasi, M, *The Software Conspiracy*, 2000, New York: McGraw-Hill

Mitchell, TA, 'Copyright, Congress and constitutionality: How the Digital Millennium Copyright Act goes too far' (2004) 79 Notre Dame L Rev 2115

Mitnick, B, *The Political Economy of Regulation*, 1980, New York: Columbia University Press

Mitrou, L, 'Communications data retention: A Pandora's Box for rights and liberties?', in A Acquisti and S Gritzalis (eds), *Digital Privacy: Theory, Technologies, and Practices*, 2007, Abingdon: CRC Press

Miyaki, PT, 'Computer software defects: Should computer software manufacturers be held strictly liable for computer software defects?' (1992) 8(1) CHTLJ 121

Mo, J, '*Cinepoly Records Co Ltd v Hong Kong Broadband Network Ltd*' [2009] EIPR 48

Moerel, L, 'The country-of-origin principle in the E-Commerce Directive: The expected one-stop shop' (2001) 7 CTLR 184

Moon, K, 'The nature of computer programs: Tangible? Goods? Personal property? Intellectual property?' (2009) 31(8) EIPR 396

Moran, M, 'Understanding the regulatory state' (2002) 32 B J Pol Sci 391

Morgan, R, and Burden, R, *Morgan and Burden on Computer Contracts*, 6th edn, 2001, London, Sweet & Maxwell

—— and ——, *Morgan and Burden on Computer Contracts*, 8th edn, 2009, London: Sweet & Maxwell

Moringiello, JM, and Reynolds, WL, 'Survey of the law of cyberspace: Electronic contracting cases 2006–2007' (2007) 63 Business Lawyer 219

—— and ——, 'Survey of the law of cyberspace: Electronic contracting cases 2007–2008' (2008) 64 Business Lawyer 199

Morris Jr, JB, and Wong, CM, 'Revisiting user control: The emergence and success of a First Amendment theory for the internet age' (2009) 8 First Amend L Rev 109

Morton, J, 'opinion.com' [1997] EIPR 496

Mossoff, A, 'Spam: Oy, what a nuisance' (2004) 19 Berkeley Tech LJ 625

Moutsatsos, SS, and Cummings, JCR, '*Apple v Microsoft*: Has the pendulum swung too far?' (1993) 9 CL & P 162

Mueller, ML, *Ruling the Root: Internet Governance and the Taming of Cyberspace*, 2002, Cambridge, MA: MIT Press

Müller, BC, 'Case comment' (2003) 8 Comm L 375

Murdoch, J, *Law of Estate Agency and Auctions*, 4th edn, 2003, London: Estates Gazette

Murray, A, *The Regulation of Cyberspace: Control in the Online Environment*, 2007, Abingdon: Glasshouse

——, 'Volume litigation: More harmful than helpful?' (2010) 20 Computers and Law 46

—— and Scott, C, 'Controlling the new media: Hybrid responses to new forms of power' (2002) 65(4) MLR 491

Na, N, 'Testing the boundaries of copyright protection: The Google Books Library Project and the fair use doctrine' 16 Cornell JL & Pub Pol'y 417

Napier, B, 'The future of information technology law' (1992) 51(1) CLJ 46

Narodick, BI, 'Smothered by judicial love: How *Jacobsen v Katzer* could bring open source software development to a standstill' (2010) 16 BU J Sci & Tech L 264

National Geographic, 'Internet's 40th "birthday" marked' (2009) 31 August, available online at http://news.nationalgeographic.com/news/2009/08/090831-internet-40th-video-ap.html

National Institute of Justice, *Computer Crime: Criminal Justice Resource Manual 2*, 1989, Washington, DC: US Department of Justice

National Fraud Strategic Authority, *The National Fraud Strategy: A New Approach to Combating Fraud*, 2009, London: HMSO, available from www.attorneygeneral.gov.uk/nfa/GuidetoInformation/Documents/National%20Fraud%20Strategy

Nehf, JP, 'Borderless trade and the consumer interest: Protecting the consumer in the age of e-commerce' (1999) 38 Col J Transnat Law 457

Newdick, C, 'Risk, uncertainty and "knowledge" in the development risks defence' (1991) 20 AALR 309

Newell, A, 'The models are broken, the models are broken' (1986) 47 Pitt UL Rev 1023

Newman, J, 'The patentability of computer-related inventions in Europe' [1997] EIPR 701

Newton, J, 'Software patents in the UK' (1996) 1 Comm L 202

Nicholas, P, 'State of the art evidence: From logical construct to judicial retrenchment' (1991) 20 AALR 2850

Nicholl, CC, 'Can computers make contracts?' [1998] JBL 35

Niemann, J-M, 'Online auctions: Germany – Online auctions under German contract' (2001) 17(2) CLSR 114

Nimmer, D, 'A riff on fair use in the Digital Millennium Copyright Act' (2000) 148 U Pa L Rev 673

Nolan, J, 'The China dilemma: Internet censorship and corporate responsibility' (2009) 4 Asian J Comp Law Article 3

Nov, O, and Kuk, G, 'Open source content contributors' response to free-riding: The effect of personality and context' (2008) 24(6) Comp Hum Behav 2848

Nusbaum, SK, 'Copyright cases' (2010) 66 Bus Law 205

Oates, J, 'Tsunami hacker convicted' (2005) *The Register*, 6 October, available online at www.theregister.co.uk/2005/10/06/tsunami_hacker_convicted/

Oberding, JM, and Norderhaug, T, 'A separate jurisdiction for cyberspace?' (1996) 2 Computer-mediated Comm

Office of Fair Trading (OFT), *Unfair Contract Terms Guidance*, OFT 311, 2008, London: HMSO

——, *Unfair Standard Terms*, OFT Bulletin No 1, May 1996, London: HMSO

——/Department of Trade and Industry (DTI), *A Guide for Businesses on Distance Selling*, OFT698, 2006, London: HMSO

Office of Surveillance Commissioners, *Annual Report of the Chief Surveillance Commissioner to the Prime Minister and to Scottish Ministers for 2008–2009*, 2009, HC 704 SG/2009/94, London: HMSO

Office of the Attorney General, *Fraud Review: Final Report*, 2006, London: HMSO, available online at www.northeastfraudforum.co.uk/government-fraud-review

——, *Guidance on the Use of the Common Law Offence of Conspiracy to Defraud*, 2007, London: HMSO, available online at www.attorneygeneral.gov.uk/Publications/Documents/conspiracy%20to%20defraud%20final.pdf

Office of the Prime Minister, *Communications Interception Standing Inquiry: The Interception of Communications in Great Britain*, Cmnd 8191, 1981, London: HMSO

Ogilvie, JWL, 'Defining computer program parts under Learned Hand's abstractions tests in software copyright infringement cases' (1992) 91 Mich L Rev 526

Ogus, A, *Regulation: Legal Form and Economic Theory*, 1994, Oxford: Oxford University Press
——, 'Rethinking self-regulation' (1995) 15 OJLS 97
Oliver, J, 'Kazaa on trial in Australia' (2005) 15(6) Computers and Law 36
Olson, KK, 'Transforming fair use online: The Ninth Circuit's productive-use analysis of visual search engines' (2009) 14 Comm L & Pol'y 153
Okano, A, 'Digitized book search engines and copyright concerns' 3 Shidler JL Com & Tech 13
Orange, A, 'Developments in the domain name system: For better or for worse' [1999] 3 JILT, available online at www2.warwick.ac.uk/fac/soc/law/elj/jilt/1999_3/orange/
O'Regan, KM, 'Downloading personhood: A Hegelian theory of copyright law' (2009) 7 Can J L & Tech 1
Øren, JST, 'Electronic agents and the notion of establishment' (2001) 9 Int JLIT 249
——, 'International jurisdiction over consumer contracts in e-Europe' (2003) 52 ICLQ 665
Organisation for Economic Co-operation and Development (OECD), *A Borderless World: Realising the Potential of Global Electronic Commerce—Conference Conclusions*, 1998, SG/EC(98)14 final, available online at www.oecd.org/officialdocuments/publicdisplaydocumentpdf/?cote=SG/EC(98)14/FINAL&docLanguage=En
——, *Guidelines on the Protection of Privacy and Transborder Flows of Personal Data*, available online at www.oecd.org/document/18/0,3343,en_2649_34255_1815186_1_1_1_1,00.html
Organisation for Economic Co-operation and Development (OECD) Spam Taskforce, *Anti-spam Regulation*, 2005, DSTI/CP/ICCP/SPAM(2005)10/FINAL, available online at www.oecd.org/dataoecd/29/12/35670414.pdf
Organisation for Economic Co-operation and Development (OECD) Working Party on Information Security and Privacy, *Ministerial Declaration on the Protection of Privacy on Global Networks*, DSTI/ICCP/REG(98)10/FINAL, 1998, Ottowa, ON: OECD, available online at www.oecd.org/dataoecd/39/13/1840065.pdf
Ormerod, DC, 'Interception of communications: Meaning of "control" of the operation or the use of a private telecommunications system' [2006] Crim LR 1069
——, 'The Fraud Act 2006: Criminalising lying' [2007] Crim L Rev 193
—— and McKay, S, 'Telephone intercepts and their admissibility' [2004] Crim LR 15
Osborne, D, 'Domain names, registration and dispute resolution and recent UK cases' [1997] EIPR 644
Ottolia, A, 'Preserving users' rights in DRM: Dealing with juridical particularism in the information society' (2004) 35 IIC 491
Out-law.com, 'Google image search results do not infringe copyright, says German court' (2010) Out-law.com, 30 April, available online at www.out-law.com/page-10980
——, 'Google is not liable for defamatory snippets in search results, rules High Court' (2009) Out-law.com, 17 July, available online at www.out-law.com/page-10181
——, 'Government denies wi-fi operators copyright exemption' (2010) Out-law.com, 1 March, available online at www.out-law.com/page-10798
——, 'House of Lords ends Durant's data protection saga' (2005) Out-law.com, 30 November, available online at www.out-law.com/page-6405
——, 'Kazaa is legal, says Dutch Supreme Court' (2004) Outlaw.com, 5 January, available online at www.out-law.com/page-4169
——, 'Peer proposes copyright exemption for search engines' (2010) Out-law.com, 12 January, available online at www.out-law.com/page-10658
——, 'Rescuecom drops AdWords suit' (2010) Out-law.com, 8 March, available online at www.out-law.com/page-10818
——, 'The legislative farce of the Digital Economy Bill' (2010) Out-law.com, 7 April, available online at http://out-law.com/page-10900

Owen, R, 'Comedian Sabina Guzzanti "insulted Pope" in "poofter devils" gag' (2008) *TimesOnline*, 21 September, available online at www.timesonline.co.uk/tol/news/world/europe/article4732048.ece

Oxman, BH, 'Jurisdiction of states', in R Bernhardt (ed), *Encyclopaedia of Public International Law, Vol 10*, 1987, Amsterdam: North Holland Publishing Co

Page, AC, 'Self-regulation: The constitutional dimension' (1986) 49 MLR 141

Page, J, 'YouTube is cut off over cartoons' (2008) *The Times*, 25 February, p 30.

Palekar, NS, 'Privacy protection: When is "adequate" actually adequate?' (2008) 18 Duke J Comp & Int'l L 549

Palfrey, T, 'Policing the transmission of pornographic material' (1996) 5 ICTL 197

——, 'Pornography and the possible criminal liability of internet service providers under the Obscene Publication(s) and Protection of Children Act' (1997) 6 ICTL 187

Pangiotidou, E, 'The patentability of computer programs according to the Commission's new proposals for a directive and to the EPO Boards of Appeal decisions' (2003) 9 CTLR 126

Pastukhov, O, 'Internationalised domain names: The window of opportunity for cybersquatters' (2006) 4 IPQ 421

Pattenden, R, 'Privilege against self-incrimination' (2009) 13(1) IJEP 69

Pereira, G, 'Internet regulation to start on Monday' (1996) *Straits Times*, 13 July

Perkins, A, 'Encryption use: Law and anarchy on the digital frontier' (2005) 41 Hous L Rev 1625

Perri 6, *The Future of Privacy Volume 1: Private Life and Public Policy*, 1998, London Demos

Perrow, M, 'Click's botnet experiment' (2009) BBC News, 13 March, available online at www.bbc.co.uk/blogs/theeditors/2009/03/click_botnet_experiment.html

Petley, J, 'Web control' (2009) 38 Index on Censorship 78

Pinkney, KR, 'Putting blame where blame is due: Software manufacturer and customer liability for security-related software failure' (2003) 13(1) Alb LJ Sci & Tech 43

Poullet, Y, 'Data protection between property and liberties', in HWK Kaspersen and A Oskamp (eds), *Amongst Friends in Computers and Law*, 1990, The Hague: Kluwer

——, 'Data protection legislation: What is at stake for our society and our democracy?' (2009) 25 CLSR 211,

——, et al, *Preparation of a Methodology for Evaluating the Adequacy of the Level of Protection of Individuals with Regard to the Processing of Personal Data*, 1998, Luxembourg: OOPEC

Powell, AR, 'Creators, consumers and distributors: Understanding the moral structure of digital copyright' (2009) 5 ISJLP 383

Powell, J, Stewart, R, and Jackson, J, *Jackson & Powell on Professional Liability*, 6th edn with 3rd supp, 2009, London: Sweet & Maxwell

Press, T, 'Patent protection for computer-related inventions', in C Reed (ed), *Computer Law*, 3rd edn, 1996, London: Blackstone

Prestin, D, 'Where to draw the line between reverse engineering and infringement: *Sony Computer Entertainment Inc v Connectix Corp*' (2002) 3 Minn Intell Prop Rec 137

Price, SA, 'Understanding contemporary cryptography and its wider impact upon the general law' (1999) 13 Int Rev LC & T 95

Proskine, EA, 'Google's technicolor dreamcoat: A copyright analysis of the Google Book Search Library Project' 21 Berkeley Tech LJ 213

Prosperetti, E, 'The Peppermint "Jam": Peer to peer goes to court in Italy' (2007) 18 Ent LR 280

Prosser, A, 'Self-regulation, co-regulation and the Audio-visual Media Services Directive' (2008) 31(1) J Consum Pol 99

Puathasnanon, S, 'Cyberspace and personal jurisdiction: The problem of using internet contacts to establish minimum contacts' (1998) 31 Loy LA L Rev 691

Pun, KH, 'Five years since the Software Regulations: China's recent developments in software copyright' (1997) 28 IIC 347

Quadrature du Net, La, 'HADOPI 2 validated: A defeat for the rule of law' (2009) *Laquadature.net*, 24 October, available online at www.laquadrature.net/en/hadopi-2-validated-a-defeat-for-the-rule-of-law

Raab, C, 'The governance of data protection', in J Kooiman (ed), *Modern Governance*, 1993, London: Sage

——, et al, *Application of a Methodology Designed to Assess the Adequacy of the Level of Protection of Individuals with Regard to Processing Personal Data*, 1998, Luxembourg: OOPEC

Ramberg, C, *Internet Marketplaces: The Law of Auctions and Exchanges Online*, 2002, Oxford: Oxford University Press

Randall, KC, 'Universal jurisdiction under international law' (1988) 66 Texas L Rev 785

Raskind, LJ, 'The uncertain case for special legislation protecting computer software' (1986) 47 Pitt UL Rev 1131

Raymond, ES, *The Cathedral and the Bazaar: Musings on Linux and Open Source by an Accidental Revolutionary*, 1999, Sebastopol, CA: O'Reilly Media

Razook, N, 'The politics and promise of UCITA' (2003) 36(4) Creighton L Rev 667

Reed, C, 'Controlling World Wide Web links: Property rights, access rights and unfair competition' (1998) 6 Indiana J Global LS 167

——, *Digital Information Law: Electronic Documents and Requirements of Form*, 1996, London: Centre for Commercial Law Studies, Queen Mary and Westfield College, University of London

——, 'Reverse engineering computer programs without infringing copyright' [1991] EIPR 47

——, 'Taking sides on technology neutrality' (2007) 4:3 SCRIPTed 263, available online at www. law.ed.ac.uk/ahrc/script-ed/vol4-3/reed.asp

——, 'What is a signature?' 2000 (3) JILT, available online at www2.warwick.ac.uk/fac/soc/law/elj/jilt/2000_3/reed/

—— and Slatter, G, 'E-commerce' in C Reed and J Angel (eds), *Computer Law*, 5th edn, 2003, Oxford: Oxford University Press

—— and Welterveden, A, 'Liability', in C Reed and J Angel (eds), *Computer Law*, 5th edn, 2003, Oxford: Oxford University Press

Reed, KM, 'From the Great Firewall of China to the Berlin Firewall: The cost of content regulation on internet commerce' (2000) 13 Transnational Lawyer 451

Reid, AS, and Ryder, N, 'For whose eyes only? A critique of the United Kingdom's Regulation of Investigatory Powers Act 2000' (2001) 10(2) ICTL 179

Reporters without Borders, 'A "journey to the heart of internet censorship" on eve of party congress' (2007), 10 October, available online at http://en.rsf.org/china-a-journey-to-the-heart-of-internet-10-10-2007,23924.html

——, 'Publication of second annual report on cyberspace: "The internet under surveillance – Obstacles to the free flow of information online"' (2003) 19 June, available online at http://en.rsf.org/publication-of-second-annual-19-06-2003,07280.html

——, 'Singapore' (2007) 1 February, available online at http://en.rsf.org/singapore-singapore-01-02-2007,20796.html

Reydams, L, *Universal Jurisdiction: International and Municipal Legal Perspectives*, 2003, Oxford: Oxford University Press

Rice, D, *Geekonomics: The Real Cost of Insecure Software*, 2008, London: Addison Wesley.

Richards, NM, and Solove, DJ, 'Privacy's other path: Recovering the law of confidentiality' (2007) 96 Geo LJ 123

Rinck, GM, 'The maturing US law on copyright protection for computer programs: *Computer Associates v Altai* and other recent case developments' [1992] EIPR 351

Roberts, AJ, 'Evidence: privilege against self-incrimination: Key to encrypted material' [2009] Crim L Rev 191

Robertson, S, 'The legislative farce of the Digital Economy Bill' (2010) Out-law.com, 4 April, available online at http://out-law.com/page-10900

Robins, MD, 'Electronic trespass: An old theory in a new context' (1998) 15 Computer Law 1.

Rodau, A, 'Computer software: Does Article 2 of the Uniform Commercial Code apply?' (1986) Emory LJ 853

Rodgers, M, 'Football fixture lists and the Database Directive: Football Dataco Ltd v Brittens Pools Ltd' (2010) 32 EIPR 593

Rodway, S, and Church, P, 'Wanting it all: Unreasonable subject access requests' (2008) 19(2) Comp & L 24

Rogers, MK, 'A social learning theory and moral disengagement analysis of criminal computer behavior: An exploratory study' (2001) Unpublished PhD Thesis, Winnipeg, MB: University of Manitoba

——, Seigfried, K, and Tidkea, K, 'Self-reported computer criminal behavior: A psychological analysis' (2006) 3S Digital Investigation S 116

Rogerson, P, 'Habitual residence: The new domicile?' (2000) 49 ICLQ 86

Romman, KH, 'The Google Book Search Library Project: A market analysis approach to fair use' 43 Hous L Rev 807

Room, S, 'Regulators need to build bridges, not burn them' (2009) The Lawyer, 30 November.

Roosendaal, A, and Van Esch, S, 'Commercial websites: Consumer protection and power shifts' (2007) 6(1) JITLP 13

Rosen, L, 'Bad facts make good law: The Jacobsen case and open source' (2009) 1(1) IFOSS L Rev 27, available online at www.ifosslr.org/ifosslr/article/view/5

——, Open Source Licensing: Software Freedom and Intellectual Property Law, 2004, London: Prentice Hall

Roversi, A, Hate on the Net, Extremist Sites, Neo-fascism On-line, Electronic Jihad, 2008, Farnham: Ashgate

Rowbottom, J, 'Obscenity laws and the internet: Targeting the supply and demand' [2006] Crim L Rev 97

Rowe, H, Data Protection Act 1998: A Practical Guide, 2000, Croydon: Tolley

Rowland, D, 'Cyberspace: A contemporary utopia?' [1998] JILT, Pt 3, available online at www2.warwick.ac.uk/fac/soc/law/elj/jilt/1998_3/rowland/

——, 'Data retention and the war against terrorism: A considered and proportionate response?' [2004] JILT 3, available online at www2.warwick.ac.uk/fac/soc/law/elj/jilt/2004_3/rowland/

——, 'Free expression and defamation', in M Klang and A Murray (eds), Human Rights in the Digital Age, 2005, London: Glasshouse Press

——, 'Liability for defective software' [1991] Cambrian LR 78

——, 'Negligence, professional competence and computer systems' [1999] 2 JILT, available online at www2.warwick.ac.uk/fac/soc/law/elj/jilt/1999_2/rowland/

——, 'Privacy, freedom of expression and CyberSLAPPs: Fostering anonymity on the internet?' (2003) 17 Int Rev LCT 303

——, 'The EC Database Directive: An original solution to an unoriginal problem?' [1997] Web JCLI, available online at http://webjcli.ncl.ac.uk/1997/issue5/rowland5.html

——, 'Virtual worlds, real rights?', in Marco Odello and Sofia Cavandoli (eds), Emerging Areas of Human Rights in the 21st Century: The Role of the Universal Declaration of Human Rights, 2010, London: Routledge

—— and Campbell, A, 'Content and access agreements: An analysis of some of the legal issues arising out of linking and framing' (2002) 16 Int Rev LCT 171

—— and ——, 'Supply of software: Copyright and contract issues' (2002) 10(1) IJLIT 23

—— and Rowland, JJ, 'Competence and legal liability in the development of software for safety-related applications' (1993) 2 Computers and Artificial Intelligence 229

Royal Commission on Criminal Procedure, Report of the Royal Commission on Criminal Procedure, Cmnd 8092-I, 1981, London: HMSO

Rusch, LJ, 'Products liability trapped by history: Our choice of rules rules our choices.' (2003) 76 Temp L Rev 739

Rustad, ML, and Koenig, TH, 'Cybertorts and legal lag: An empirical analysis' (2003) 13 S Cal Interdisc LJ 77

—— and ——, 'The tort of negligent enablement of cybercrime' (2005) 20 Berkeley Tech LJ 1553

—— and Onufrio, MV, *The Exportability of the Principles of Software: Lost in Translation?*, 2009, Stetson University College of Law Research Paper No 2009-03/Suffolk University Law School Research Paper No 09-45; available online at http://ssrn.com/abstract=1466875

Sabbagh, D, 'Digital Economy Act likely to increase households targeted for piracy' (2010) *GuardianOnline*, 12 April, available online at www.guardian.co.uk/media/2010/apr/12/digital-economy-bill-households-piracy

Sableman, M, 'Link law: The emerging law of internet hypertext links' (1999) 15 CL & P 557

——, 'Link law revisited: Internet linking law at five years' (2001) 16 Berkeley Technology LJ 1273

Samek, RA, 'Contracts for work and materials' (1962) 36 ALJ 66

Samuelson, P, 'Intellectual property and the digital economy: Why the anti-circumvention regulations need to be revised' (1999) 14 Berkeley Tech LJ 519

——, 'Unbundling fair uses' (2009) 77 Fordham L Rev 2537

—— and Sheffner, B, 'Unconstitutionally excessive statutory damage awards in copyright cases' (2009) 158 U Pa L Rev PENNumbra 53

—— and Wheatland, T, 'Statutory damages in copyright law: A remedy in need of reform' (2009) 51 Wm & Mary L Rev 439

——, Davis, R, Kapor, MD, and Reichman, JH, 'A manifesto concerning the legal protection of computer programs' (1994) 94 Colum L Rev 2308

Savirimuthu, A, and Savirimuthu, J, 'Identity theft and systems theory: The Fraud Act 2006 in perspective' (2007) 4(4) SCRIPTed, available online at www.law.ed.ac.uk/ahrc/script-ed/vol4-4/savirimuthu.asp

Savirithmu, J, 'Legal reflections on the Google Print Library Project' (2006) 1 JIPL&P 801

Sawdy, C, 'High Court decision revisits protection of databases in the United Kingdom: *Football Dataco Ltd v Brittens Pools Ltd*' (2010) 21 Ent LR 221

Saxby, S, 'A jurisprudence for information technology law' (1994) 2(1) IntJLIT 1

—— (ed), *Encyclopedia of Information Technology Law*, 1990, London: Sweet & Maxwell

Schifreen, R, 'The internet: Where did IT all go wrong?' (2008) 5(2) ScriptEd, available online at www.law.ed.ac.uk/ahrc/script-ed/vol5-2/schifreen.asp

Schley, GM, 'The Digital Millennium Copyright Act and the First Amendment: How far should courts go to protect intellectual property rights?' (2004), 3 J High Tech L 115

Schønning, P, 'Internet and the applicable copyright law: A Scandinavian perspective' [1999] EIPR 45

Schriver, RR, 'You cheated, you lied: The Safe Harbor agreement and its enforcement by the Federal Trade Commission' (2002) 70 Fordham L Rev 2777

Schulz, T, 'Carving up the internet: Jurisdiction, legal orders, and the private/public international law interface' (2008) 19 Eur J Intl L 799

Schwartz, B, *The Paradox of Choice: Why More is Less*, 2003, New York: Ecco

Schwarz, PM, 'Property, privacy and personal data' (2004) 117 Harv L Rev 2055

Scott, A, 'Software as goods: *Nullum simile est idem*' (1987) 4 CL & P 133

Scott, MD, 'Tort liability for vendors of insecure software: Has the time finally come?' (2008) 67(2) Md L Rev 425

Scottish Law Commission, *Report on Computer Crime*, Cmnd 174, 1987, London: HMSO

Seaman, A, 'E-commerce, jurisdiction and choice of law' [1999–2000] CL Dec/Jan 29

Secretary of State for the Home Department, *Computers: Safeguards for Privacy*, Cmnd 6354, 1975, London: HMSO

——, *Report of the Committee on Data Protection*, Cmnd 7341, 1978, London: HMSO

——, *Report of the Committee on Privacy*, Cmnd 5012, 1972, London: HMSO

Selis, P, Ramasastry, A, and Sato, A, 'Bidder beware: Towards a fraud-free marketplace – Best practices for the online auction industry', available online at www.atg.wa.gov/InternetSafety/OnlineAuctions.aspx

Send, D, 'Regulation of the interactive digital media industry in Singapore', in B Fitzgerald, F Gao, D O'Brien, and S Xiaoxiang Shi (eds), *Copyright Law, Digital Content and the Internet in the Asia-Pacific*, 2008, Sydney: Sydney University Press

Sha, W, and Yu, D, 'Internet content provider licences in the People's Republic of China internet industry: A practical perspective', in B Fitzgerald, F Gao, D O'Brien, and S Xiaoxiang Shi (eds), *Copyright Law, Digital Content and the Internet in the Asia-Pacific*, 2008, Sydney: Sydney University Press

Sharma, SK, and Gupta, JND, 'Application service providers: Issues and challenges' (2002) 15(3) Logistics Information Management 160

Sherwood-Edwards, M, 'Seven degrees of separation: The Software Directive and UK implementation' (1993) 9 CL & P 169

Shiels, M, 'Trojan virus steals banking info' (2008) BBC News, 21 October, available online at http://news.bbc.co.uk/1/hi/technology/7701227.stm

Shillito, R, 'Making bones of sticks and stones law' (1994) 91(38) Law Soc Gazette, 19 October

Sieber, U, *Legal Aspects of Computer-Related Crime in the Information Society: Report for the European Commission of the Outcome of the COMCRIME Study*, 1998, available online at www.edc.uoc.gr/~panas/PATRA/sieber.pdf

Simpson, M, '999! My computer's stopped breathing!' (1994) 10(2) CLSR 76

Sinclair, D, 'Self-regulation versus command and control? Beyond false dichotomies' (1997) 19(4) Law & Policy 529

Singleton, S, 'Computer software agreements and the implementation of the EC Directive' (1993) 9 CL & P 50

Slyck News, 'US court loses case in Estonia over KaZaA' (2002) *Slyck News*, 21 December, available online at www.slyck.com/story306_US_Court_Loses_Case_in_Estonia_Over_KaZaA

Smith, GJH, *Internet Law and Regulation*, 4th edn, 2007, London: Sweet & Maxwell

——, 'When is a computer not a computer?' (1994) 10(2) CLSR 84

Smith, G (ed), *Internet Law and Regulation*, 4th edn, 2007, London: Sweet and Maxwell

——, 'Shrinkwrap licensing in the Scottish courts' (1990) 4 Int JLIT 131

Smith, JC, *Law of Theft*, 8th edn, 1997, London: Butterworths

Smith-Ekstrand, V, 'Drawing swords after Feist: Efforts to legislate the database pirate' (2002) 7 Comm L & Pol'y 317

Sommer, P, 'Computer misuse prosecutions' (2006) 16(5) Computers and Law 24

Son, S, 'Can black dot (shrinkwrap) licenses override federal reverse engineering rights? The relationship between copyright, contract and antitrust laws' (2004) 6 Tul J Tech & Intell Prop 63

Sookman, BB, 'Technological protection measures (TPMs) and copyright protection: The case for TPMs' (2005) 11 CTLR 143

South West Thames RHA, *Report of the Inquiry into the London Ambulance Service*, 1993, London: Communications Directorate

Spar, DL, *Ruling the Waves: Cycles of Discovery, Chaos, and Wealth from the Compass to the Internet*, 2001, London: Harcourt

Spencer, JR, 'Telephone-tap evidence and administrative detention in the UK', in M Wade and A Maljevic (eds), *A War on Terror? The European Stance on a New Threat: Changing Laws and Human Rights Implications*, 2009, Guildford: Springer

——, 'The drafting of criminal legislation: Need it be so impenetrable?' (2008) 67 CLJ 585

——, 'The Sexual Offences Act 2003: (2) Child and family offences' [2003] Crim LR 347

Spindler, G, 'Internet-auctions versus consumer protection: The case of the Distant Selling Directive' (2005) 6(3) GLJ, available online at www.germanlawjournal.com/article. php?id=585

Sprinkel, SC, 'Global internet regulation: The residual effects of the "iloveyou" computer virus and the Draft Convention on Cyber-Crime' (2002) 25 Suffolk Transnat'l L Rev 491

St Oren, J, 'Jurisdiction over consumer contracts in e-Europe' (2003) 52 ICLQ 665

Stallman, RM, 'The GNU Manifesto' (1985) 10(3) *Dr Dobb's Journal of Software Tools* 30, available (annotated) online at http://manybooks.net/titles/stallmanother05gnumanifesto.html

——, 'The GNU operating system and the free software movement', in Chris DiBona, Sam Ockman, and Mark Stone, *Open Sources: Voices from the Open Source Revolution*, 1999, Sebastopol, CA: O'Reilly Media, available online at http://oreilly.com/catalog/opensources/book/ stallman.html

——, 'Why open source misses the point of free software' (2007; 2010), available online at www.gnu.org/philosophy/open-source-misses-the-point.html

Stallworthy, M, 'Data protection: Regulation in a deregulatory state' [1990] Statute L Rev 130

Stangret, LA, 'The legalities of linking on the worldwide web' (1997) 2 Comm L 202

Stanton, KM, *The Modern Law of Tort*, 1994, London: Sweet & Maxwell

—— and Dugdale, AM, 'Design responsibility in civil engineering work' (1981) 131 NLJ 583

Stapleton, J, *Product Liability*, 1994, London: Butterworths

Starmer, M, 'Video game company hunts down individual gamers in clampdown on illicit peer to peer file sharing' (2009) Ent L Rev 20

Steele, GL, and Raymond, ES (eds), *The New Hacker's Dictionary*, 3rd edn, 1996, Cambridge, MA: MIT Press

Stein, AR, 'The unexceptional problem of jurisdiction in cyberspace' (1998) 32 The International Lawyer 1167

Sterling, JAL, 'Philosophical and legal challenges in the context of copyright and digital technology' (2000) 31 IIC 508

Stern, RH, 'An ill-conceived analysis of reverse engineering of software as copyright infringement: *Sega Enterprises v Accolade*' [1992] EIPR 107

——, 'Is the centre beginning to hold in US copyright law?' [1993] 2 EIPR 39

——, 'Reverse engineering of software as copyright infringement: An update – *Sega Enterprises v Accolade*' [1993] EIPR 34

——, 'The bundle of rights suited to the new technology' (1986) 47 Pitt UL Rev 1229

Sterne, RG, Sokohl, RE, and Axenfield, RR, 'The shifting sands of section 101 and section 112 requirements for computer program-related inventions' [1994] Int Lawyer 29

Stewart, B, 'The economics of data privacy: Should we place a dollar value on personal autonomy and dignity?' (2004) 26th International Conference on Privacy and Personal Data Protection, Worclaw, 14–16 September

Steyn, Lord J, 'Contract law: Fulfilling the reasonable expectations of honest men' (1997) 113 LQR 433

Stols, D, '*Brein v KPN Telecom* and the Dutch Civil Code: ISPs under pressure' (2007) 18 Ent LR 147

Storey, N, *Safety-critical Computer Systems*, 1996, Harlow: Addison-Wesley

Strasser, SE, 'Industrious effort is enough' [2002] EIPR 599

Strowel, A (ed), *Peer-to-peer File Sharing and Secondary Liability in Copyright Law*, 2009, Cheltenham: Edward Elgar

Stylianou, K, 'ELSA Copyright Survey: What does the young generation believe about copyright?' [2009] IPQ 391

Sullivan, GR, 'Fraud: The latest Law Commission proposals' (2003) J Crim L 139

Sullivan, JD, and De Leeuw, MB, 'Spam after CAN-SPAM: How inconsistent thinking has made a hash out of unsolicited commercial e-mail policy' (2004) 20 CHTLJ 887

Susman, AM, 'International electronic trading: Some legal issues' [2000] CL Feb/Mar 29

Suter, TA, Kopp, SW, and Hardesty, DM, 'The effect of consumers' ethical beliefs on copying behaviour' (2006) 29 J Consum Policy 190

Svantesson, DJB, 'Borders on, or border around: The future of the internet' (2006) 16 ALBLJST 343

——, 'Geo-location technologies and other means of placing borders on the 'borderless' internet' (2004) 23 John Marshall J Comp & Info Law 101

Sweney, M, 'Lord Mandelson sets date for blocking filesharers' internet connections' (2009) GuardianOnline, 28 October, available online at www.guardian.co.uk/technology/2009/oct/28/mandelson-date-blocking-filesharers-connections

Swire, PP, 'Of elephants, mice, and privacy: International choice of law and the internet' (1998) 32 International Lawyer 991

—— and Litan, RE, None of Your Business: World Data Flows, Electronic Commerce and the European Privacy Directive, 1998, Washington DC: Brookings Institution

Swope, R, 'Peer-to-peer file sharing and copyright infringement: Danger ahead for individuals sharing files on the internet' (2004) 44 Santa Clara L Rev 861

Synodinou, T-E, 'The lawful user and a balancing of interests in European copyright law' (2010) 41 IIC 819

Symantec Internet Security, Threat Report Vol XIV: Trends for 2008, 2009, available online at www.symantec.com/business/theme.jsp?themeid=threatreport

Szwak, DA, 'Uniform Computer Information Transactions Act (UCITA): The consumer's perspective' (2002) 63 Louis L Rev 27

Tapper, CF, 'Computer crime: Scotch mist?' [1987] Crim LR 4

——, 'United Kingdom', in M Lehmann and CF Tapper (eds), Handbook of European Software Law, Pt II, 1993, Oxford: Clarendon

Taylor, G, 'The Council of Europe Cybercrime Convention: A civil liberties perspective' (2002), available online at www.crime-research.org/library/CoE_Cybercrime.html

Taylor, NW, 'R (on the application of McKinnon) v DPP' [2010] Crim L Rev 422

Telegraph, The, 'Gary McKinnon: Timeline of the computer hacker's case' (2009) The Telegraph, 31 July, available online at www.telegraph.co.uk/news/worldnews/northamerica/usa/5945693/Gary-McKinnon-timeline-of-the-computer-hackers-case.html

Terry, NP, 'State of the art evidence: From logical construct to judicial retrenchment' (1991) 20 Anglo-Am L Rev 285

Teter, TS, 'Merger and the machines: An analysis of the pro-compatibility trend in computer software copyright cases' (1993) 45 Stan L Rev 1061

Thakur, N, 'Database protection in the European Union and the United States: The European Database Directive as an optimum global model' [2001] IPQ 100

Thomas, R, and Martin, J, 'The underground economy: Priceless' (2006), available online at www.team-cymru.org/ReadingRoom/Articles/

Thurrott, P, 'April Fools: World preps for Conficker attack' (2010) Paul Thurrott's Supersite for Windows, 6 October, available online at www.winsupersite.com/article/windows-server/april-fools-world-preps-for-conficker-attack

Tiberi, L, and Zamboni, M, 'Liability of internet service providers' (2003) 9 CTLR 49

Times, The, 'Reassuring as far as it goes' (1981) The Times, 4 March

——, 'Tabs on the tappers' (1985) The Times, 6 March

——, 'Whitelaw pledge on Bill to control telephone tapping' (1984) The Times, 20 March

Timofeeva, YA, 'Worldwide prescriptive jurisdiction in internet content controversies: A comparative analysis' (2005) 20 Conn J Int'l L 199

Tomkins, A, 'Now you hear me, now you don't' (1994) 57(6) MLR 941

Touloumis, T, 'Buccaneers and bucks from the internet: Pirate Bay and the entertainment industry' (2009) 19 Seton Hall J Sports and Ent L 253

Trager, R, and Turner, S, 'The internet down under: Can free speech be protected in a democracy without a Bill of Rights?' (2000) 23 U Ark Little Rock L Rev 123

Travis, A, *Bound and Gagged: A Secret History of Obscenity in Britain*, 2000, London: Profile

Trudel, P, 'Jurisdiction over the internet: A Canadian perspective' (1998) 32 The International Lawyer 1027

Tsai, J, 'For better or worse: Introducing the GNU General Public License Version 3' (2008) 23(1) Berk Tech LJ 547

Tucker, RL, 'Information superhighway robbers: The tortious misuse of links, frames, metatags and domain names' (1999) 4 Va JLT 8

Turner, C, 'Google Library Project settlement agreement' (2009) 20 Ent LR 183

Turner, M, 'European national news' (2010) 26 CLSR 237

—— and Callaghan, D, 'You can look but don't touch! The impact of the *Google v Copiepresse* decision on the future of the internet' [2008] EIPR 34

——, Traynor, M, and Smith, H, 'E-Commerce Directive: UK implementation – Electronic Commerce (EC Directive) Regulations 2002: Worth the wait?' (2002) 18(6) CLSR 396

Tyree, AL, 'Electronic signatures' (2008), available online at http://austlii.edu.au/~alan/electronic-signatures.html

United Nations Commission on International Trade Law (UNCITRAL), *Promoting Confidence in Electronic Commerce: Legal Issues on International Use of Electronic Authentication and Signature Methods*, 2009, Vienna: United Nations, available online at www.uncitral.org/pdf/english/texts/electcom/08-55698_Ebook.pdf

——, *UNCITRAL Model Law on Electronic Signatures with Guide to Enactment*, 2001, Vienna: United Nations, available online at www.uncitral.org/pdf/english/texts/electcom/ml-elecsig-e.pdf

Urban, JM, and Quilter, L, *Efficient Process or 'Chilling Effects'? Takedown Notices under Section 512 of the Digital Millennium Copyright Act: Summary Report*, 2005, Berkeley, CA: University of Southern California/ University of California, available online at http://mylaw.usc.edu/documents/512Rep-ExecSum_out.pdf

Välimäki, M, 'Dual licensing in open source software industry' (2003) 8(1) Systèmes d'Information et Management 63, available online at www.valimaki.com/org/dual_licensing.pdf

——, 'GNU General Public License and the distribution of derivative works' (2005) 1 JILT, available online at www2.warwick.ac.uk/fac/soc/law/elj/jilt/2005_1/valimaki/

——, *The Rise of Open Source Licensing: A Challenge to the Use of Intellectual Property in the Software Industry*, 2005, Helsinki: Turre, available online at http://lib.tkk.fi/Diss/2005/isbn9529187793/isbn9529187793.pdf

Van Eechoud, MMM, *Choice of Law in Copyright and Related Rights: Alternative to the Lex Protectionis*, 2003, The Hague: Kluwer Law International

Van Overstraten, T, and Szafran, E, 'Data protection on the internet: Technical considerations and European legal framework' (2001) 5 CTLR 56

Van Someren, N, 'RIPA Part III: The intricacies of decryption' (2007) 4(3–4) Digital Investigation 113

Varas, CT, 'Sealing the cracks: A proposal to update the anti-cybersquatting regime to combat advertising-based cybersquatting' (2008) 3(4) JIPLP 246

Vass, S, 'Lessons from Robertson's victory', 2004, *Sunday Herald*, 12 September.

Vassilaki, IE, 'Anmerkung' (2001) 4 Computer und Recht 262

Velasco, J, 'The copyrightability of non-literal elements of computer programs' (1994) 94 Col L Rev 242

Vernooij, NW, 'Rome I: An update on the law applicable to contractual obligations in Europe' (2009) 15 Colum J Eur L 71

Vilasau, M, 'Traffic data retention v data protection: The New European Framework' (2007) 13(2) CTLR 52

Vincent, D, *The Culture of Secrecy: Britain, 1832–1998*, 1998, Oxford: Oxford University Press

Vincents, OB, 'Interception of internet communications and the right to privacy: An evaluation of some provisions of the Regulation of Investigatory Powers Act against the jurisprudence of the European Court of Human Rights' [2007] EHRLR 637

——, 'Secondary liability for copyright infringement in the BitTorrent platform: Placing the blame where it belongs' [2008] EIPR 4

Von Helfeld, A, 'Protection of inventions comprising computer programs by the European and German Patent Offices: A confrontation' (1986) 3 CL & P 182

Voon, T, 'Online pornography in Australia: Lessons from the First Amendment' (2001) 24 UNSWLJ 141

Wacks, R, *Privacy and Press Freedom*, 1995, London: Blackstone

Waelde, C, and MacQueen, H, 'From entertainment to education' [2004] IPQ 259

Walden, I, 'Communication service providers: Forensic source and investigatory tool' (2006) 11(1) Inform Secur Tech Rep 10

Walker, C, 'Data retention in the UK: Pragmatic and proportionate, or a step too far?' (2009) 25(4) CLSR 325

——, 'Email interception and RIPA: The Court of Appeal rules on the "right to control" defence' (2006) 11(1) Communications Law 22

Ward, M, 'Campaigners hit by decryption law' (2007) *BBC News*, 20 November, available online at http://news.bbc.co.uk/1/hi/technology/7102180.stm

Warren, S, and Brandeis, L, 'The right to privacy' (1890) 4 Harv L Rev 193

Wasik, M, *Crime and the Computer*, 1990, Oxford: Clarendon

——, Introduction (1995) 9 LC & T Yearbook ix

——, 'Misuse of information technology: What should the role of the criminal law be?' (1991) 5 LC & T Yearbook 158

—— and Piperaki, A, 'Computer crime: The Scottish Law Commission proposals' (1987) 3 LC & T Yearbook 109

Waters, P, and Leonard, PG, 'The lessons of recent EC and US developments for protection of computer software under Australian law' [1991] EIPR 125

Watkins, T, and Rau, A, 'Intellectual property in artificial neural networks: In particular under the EPC' (1996) 27 IIC 447

Watnick, V, 'The electronic formation of contracts and the common law "mailbox rule"' (2004) 56 Baylor L Rev 175

Watson, C, Scourfield, T, and Fairbairn, S, 'Why the *SABAM v Tiscali* questions matter' (2010) 21 Computers and Law 22

Weber, LA, 'Bad bytes: The application of strict products liability to computer software' (1992) 66(2) St John's L Rev 469

Wei, W, 'ISP indirect copyright liability: Conflicts of rights on the internet' (2009) 15 CTLR 181

Wendel de Joode, R, de Bruijn, JA, and van Eeten, MJG, *Protecting the Virtual Commons: Self-organizing Open Source and Free Software Communities and Innovative Intellectual Property Regimes*, 2003, The Hague: TMC Asser Press

Westin, AF, *Privacy and Freedom*, 1967, London: Bodley Head

White House, 'Data Privacy Accord with EU (Safe Harbor)', Press release, 31 May 2000, available online at http://clinton4.nara.gov/WH/New/Europe-0005/factsheets/data-privacy-accord-with-eu.html

Whitley, EA, and Hosein, I, 'Policy discourse and data retention: The technology politics of surveillance in the United Kingdom' (2005) 29(11) Telecommunications Policy 857

Whittaker, S, 'European product liability and intellectual products' (1989) 105 LQR 125

Wiebe, A, 'European copyright protection of software from a German perspective' (1993) 9 CL & P 79

Wiese, H, 'The justification of the information society in the digital age' [2002] EIPR 387

Wilkins, JS, 'Protecting computer programs as compilations under *Computer Associates v Altai*' (1994) 104 Yale LJ 435

Williams, AWS, 'European Commission: Proposed Directive for Patents for Software-related Inventions' [2004] EIPR 368

Williams, S, *Free as in Freedom: Richard Stallman's Crusade for Free Software*, 2002, Sebastopol, CA: O'Reilly Media

Williams, V, *Surveillance and Intelligence Law Handbook*, 2005, Oxford: Oxford University Press

Wilson, C, 'Internationalised domain names: Problems and opportunities' (2004) 10(7) CTLR 174

Winn, PA, 'The guilty eye: Unauthorized access, trespass and privacy' (2007) 62 Bus Law 1395

Wistam, H, and Andersson, T, 'The Pirate Bay trial' (2009) 15 CTLR 129

Withey, C, 'The Fraud Act 2006: Some early observations and comparisons with the former law' (2007) 71 J Crim L 220

Wolf, C, 'New directions in enforcement and policy at the FTC and the impact on businesses' (2010) 1005 PLI/Pat 421

Working Group on Data Retention, 'Position on the processing of traffic data for "security purposes"' (2009) 21 March, available online at www.statewatch.org/news/2009/mar/eu-dat-ret-wg-e-security-position-paper.pdf

World Economic Forum, 'Is the internet at risk?' (2009) weforum.org, 31 January, available online at www.weforum.org/en/knowledge/Events/2009/AnnualMeeting/index.htm

——, 'The future of India's cyberculture' (2008) weforum.org, 16 November, available online at www.weforum.org/en/knowledge/Events/2008/index.htm

World Intellectual Property Organization (WIPO), *The Impact of the Internet on Intellectual Property Law*, 2002, Geneva: WIPO, available online at www.wipo.int/copyright/en/ecommerce/ip_survey/chap3.html

Wu, T, 'When code isn't law' (2003) 89 Va L Rev 679

Younger, K, et al, *Report of the Committee on Privacy* ('Younger Report'), Cmnd 5012, 1972, London: HMSO

Yum, KH, 'The interaction between American and foreign libel law: US courts refuse to enforce English libel judgments' (2000) 49 ICLQ 132

Zadra-Symes, LJ, '*Computer Associates v Altai*: The retreat from *Whelan v Jaslow*' [1992] EIPR 327

Zeman, E, 'Google caves to Pentagon wishes' (2008) *Information Week*, 7 March

Zimmerman, D, 'Global limits on 'look and feel': Defining the scope of software copyright protection by international agreement' (1996) 34 Col J Transnat L 503

Zittrain, JL, *Jurisdiction*, 2005, New York: Foundation Press

——, 'Privacy 2.0' (2008) U Chi Legal F 65.

——, and Edelman, B, *Localized Google Search Result Exclusions: Statement of Issues and Call for Data*, 2002, Cambridge, MA: Berkman Center for Internet & Society, Harvard Law School, available online at http://cyber.law.harvard.edu/filtering/google/

Zollers, FE, McMullin, A, Hurd, SN, and Shears, P, 'No more soft landings for software: Liability for defects in an industry that has come of age' (2005) 21(4) CHTLJ 745

Zumbansen, P, 'Contracting in the internet: German contracting law and internet auctions' (2001) 2(7) NJW, available online at www.germanlawjournal.com/article.php?id=65

Zynda, T, '*Ticketmaster Corp v Tickets.com Inc*: Preserving minimum requirements of contract on the internet' (2004) 19 Berkeley Tech LJ 495

Index